Plate B "Blessed State," by F. K. Musgrave. (Copyright © 1989 K. Musgrave and B. Mandelbrot.)

Plate D "Luxo Jr.," by J. Lasseter, W. Reeves, E. Ostby, and S. Leffler. (Copyright © 1986 Pixar.)

SECOND EDITION IN C

Computer Graphics

PRINCIPLES AND PRACTICE

SECOND EDITION IN C

Computer Graphics

PRINCIPLES AND PRACTICE

James D. Foley
Georgia Institute of Technology

Andries van Dam
Brown University

Steven K. Feiner
Columbia University

John F. Hughes
Brown University

ADDISON-WESLEY PUBLISHING COMPANY
Reading, Massachusetts • Menlo Park, California • New York
Don Mills, Ontario • Wokingham, England • Amsterdam • Bonn
Sydney • Singapore • Tokyo • Madrid • San Juan • Milan • Paris

Sponsoring Editor: Peter S. Gordon
Production Supervisor: Bette J. Aaronson
Production Supervisor for the C edition: Juliet Silveri
Copy Editor: Lyn Dupré
Text Designer: Herb Caswell
Technical Art Consultant: Joseph K. Vetere
Illustrators: C&C Associates
Cover Designer: Marshall Henrichs
Manufacturing Manager: Roy Logan

This book is in the **Addison-Wesley Systems Programming Series**
Consulting editors: IBM Editorial Board

Library of Congress Cataloging-in-Publication Data

Computer graphics: principles and practice / James D. Foley . . . [et
al.]. — 2nd ed. in C.
    p. cm.
  Includes bibliographical references and index.
  ISBN 0-201-84840-6
  1. Computer graphics. I. Foley, James D., 1942–
T385.C5735 1996
006.6'6—dc20

    95-13631
    CIP

Reprinted with corrections, July 1997.

Reprinted with corrections November 1992, November 1993, and July 1995.

Text printed on recycled and acid-free paper.

ISBN 0201848406

12 1314151617 DOC 02 01 00 99

12th Printing November 1999

To Marylou, Heather, Jenn, my parents, and my teachers

Jim

To Debbie, my father, my mother in memoriam, and
my children Elisa, Lori, and Katrin

Andy

To Jenni, my parents, and my teachers

Steve

To my family, my teacher Rob Kirby, and
my father in memoriam

John

And to all of our students.

THE SYSTEMS PROGRAMMING SERIES

Foreword

The field of systems programming primarily grew out of the efforts of many programmers and managers whose creative energy went into producing practical, utilitarian systems programs needed by the rapidly growing computer industry. Programming was practiced as an art where each programmer invented his own solutions to problems with little guidance beyond that provided by his immediate associates. In 1968, the late Ascher Opler, then at IBM, recognized that it was necessary to bring programming knowledge together in a form that would be accessible to all systems programmers. Surveying the state of the art, he decided that enough useful material existed to justify a significant codification effort. On his recommendation, IBM decided to sponsor The Systems Programming Series as a long term project to collect, organize, and publish those principles and techniques that would have lasting value throughout the industry. Since 1968 eighteen titles have been published in the Series, of which six are currently in print.

The Series consists of an open-ended collection of text-reference books. The contents of each book represent the individual author's view of the subject area and do not necessarily reflect the views of the IBM Corporation. Each is organized for course use but is detailed enough for reference.

Representative topic areas already published, or that are contemplated to be covered by the Series, include: database systems, communication systems, graphics systems, expert systems, and programming process management. Other topic areas will be included as the systems programming discipline evolves and develops.

The Editorial Board

Preface

Interactive graphics is a field whose time has come. Until recently it was an esoteric specialty involving expensive display hardware, substantial computer resources, and idiosyncratic software. In the last few years, however, it has benefited from the steady and sometimes even spectacular reduction in the hardware price/performance ratio (e.g., personal computers for home or office with their standard graphics terminals), and from the development of high-level, device-independent graphics packages that help make graphics programming rational and straightforward. Interactive graphics is now finally ready to fulfill its promise to provide us with pictorial communication and thus to become a major facilitator of man/machine interaction. (From preface, *Fundamentals of Interactive Computer Graphics*, James Foley and Andries van Dam, 1982)

This assertion that computer graphics had finally arrived was made before the revolution in computer culture sparked by Apple's Macintosh and the IBM PC and its clones. Now even preschool children are comfortable with interactive-graphics techniques, such as the desktop metaphor for window manipulation and menu and icon selection with a mouse. Graphics-based user interfaces have made productive users of neophytes, and the desk without its graphics computer is increasingly rare.

At the same time that interactive graphics has become common in user interfaces and visualization of data and objects, the rendering of 3D objects has become dramatically more realistic, as evidenced by the ubiquitous computer-generated commercials and movie special effects. Techniques that were experimental in the early eighties are now standard practice, and more remarkable "photorealistic" effects are around the corner. The simpler kinds of pseudorealism, which took hours of computer time per image in the early eighties, now are done routinely at animation rates (ten or more frames/second) on personal computers. Thus "real-time" vector displays in 1981 showed moving wire-frame objects made of tens of thousands of vectors without hidden-edge removal; in 1990 real-time raster displays can show not only the same kinds of line drawings but also moving objects composed of as many as one hundred thousand triangles rendered with Gouraud or Phong shading and specular highlights and with full hidden-surface removal. The highest-performance systems provide real-time texture mapping, antialiasing, atmospheric attenuation for fog and haze, and other advanced effects.

Graphics software standards have also advanced significantly since our first edition. The SIGGRAPH Core '79 package, on which the first edition's SGP package was based, has all but disappeared, along with direct-view storage tube and refresh vector displays. The much more powerful PHIGS package, supporting storage and editing of structure hierarchy, has become an official ANSI and ISO standard, and it is widely available for real-time geometric graphics in scientific and engineering applications, along with PHIGS+, which supports lighting, shading, curves, and surfaces. Official graphics standards complement lower-level, more efficient de facto standards, such as Apple's QuickDraw, X Window System's Xlib 2D integer raster graphics package, and Silicon Graphics' GL 3D library. Also widely available are implementations of Pixar's RenderMan interface for photorealistic rendering and PostScript interpreters for hardcopy page and screen image description. Better graphics software has been used to make dramatic improvements in the "look and feel"of user interfaces, and we may expect increasing use of 3D effects, both for aesthetic reasons and for providing new metaphors for organizing and presenting, and navigating through information.

Perhaps the most important new movement in graphics is the increasing concern for modeling objects, not just for creating their pictures. Furthermore, interest is growing in describing the time-varying geometry and behavior of 3D objects. Thus graphics is increasingly concerned with simulation, animation, and a "back to physics" movement in both modeling and rendering in order to create objects that look and behave as realistically as possible.

As the tools and capabilities available become more and more sophisticated and complex, we need to be able to apply them effectively. Rendering is no longer the bottleneck. Therefore researchers are beginning to apply artificial-intelligence techniques to assist in the design of object models, in motion planning, and in the layout of effective 2D and 3D graphical presentations.

Today the frontiers of graphics are moving very rapidly, and a text that sets out to be a standard reference work must periodically be updated and expanded. This book is almost a total rewrite of the *Fundamentals of Interactive Computer Graphics,* and although this second edition contains nearly double the original 623 pages, we remain painfully aware of how much material we have been forced to omit.

Major differences from the first edition include the following:

- The vector-graphics orientation is replaced by a raster orientation.

- The simple 2D floating-point graphics package (SGP) is replaced by two packages— SRGP and SPHIGS—that reflect the two major schools of interactive graphics programming. SRGP combines features of the QuickDraw and Xlib 2D integer raster graphics packages. SPHIGS, based on PHIGS, provides the fundamental features of a 3D floating-point package with hierarchical display lists. We explain how to do applications programming in each of these packages and show how to implement the basic clipping, scan-conversion, viewing, and display list traversal algorithms that underlie these systems.

- User-interface issues are discussed at considerable length, both for 2D desktop metaphors and for 3D interaction devices.

- Coverage of modeling is expanded to include NURB (nonuniform rational B-spline) curves and surfaces, a chapter on solid modeling, and a chapter on advanced modeling techniques, such as physically based modeling, procedural models, fractals, L-grammar systems, and particle systems.

- Increased coverage of rendering includes a detailed treatment of antialiasing and greatly expanded chapters on visible-surface determination, illumination, and shading, including physically based illumination models, ray tracing, and radiosity.

- Material is added on advanced raster graphics architectures and algorithms, including clipping and scan-conversion of complex primitives and simple image-processing operations, such as compositing.
- A brief introduction to animation is added.

This text can be used by those without prior background in graphics and only some background in Pascal programming, basic data structures and algorithms, computer architecture, and simple linear algebra. An appendix reviews the necessary mathematical foundations. The book covers enough material for a full-year course, but is partitioned into groups to make selective coverage possible. The reader, therefore, can progress through a carefully designed sequence of units, starting with simple, generally applicable fundamentals and ending with more complex and specialized subjects.

Basic Group.   Chapter 1 provides a historical perspective and some fundamental issues in hardware, software, and applications. Chapters 2 and 3 describe, respectively, the use and the implementation of SRGP, a simple 2D integer graphics package. Chapter 4 introduces graphics hardware, including some hints about how to use hardware in implementing the operations described in the preceding chapters. The next two chapters, 5 and 6, introduce the ideas of transformations in the plane and 3-space, representations by matrices, the use of homogeneous coordinates to unify linear and affine transformations, and the description of 3D views, including the transformations from arbitrary view volumes to canonical view volumes. Finally, Chapter 7 introduces SPHIGS, a 3D floating-point hierarchical graphics package that is a simplified version of the PHIGS standard, and describes its use in some basic modeling operations. Chapter 7 also discusses the advantages and disadvantages of the hierarchy available in PHIGS and the structure of applications that use this graphics package.

User Interface Group.   Chapters 8-10 describe the current technology of interaction devices and then address the higher-level issues in user-interface design. Various popular user-interface paradigms are described and critiqued. In the final chapter user-interface software, such as window managers, interaction technique-libraries, and user-interface management systems, is addressed.

Model Definition Group.   The first two modeling chapters, 11 and 12, describe the current technologies used in geometric modeling: the representation of curves and surfaces by parametric functions, especially cubic splines, and the representation of solids by various techniques, including boundary representations and CSG models. Chapter 13 introduces the human color-vision system, various color-description systems, and conversion from one to another. This chapter also briefly addresses rules for the effective use of color.

Image Synthesis Group.   Chapter 14, the first in a four-chapter sequence, describes the quest for realism from the earliest vector drawings to state-of-the-art shaded graphics. The artifacts caused by aliasing are of crucial concern in raster graphics, and this chapter discusses their causes and cures in considerable detail by introducing the Fourier transform and convolution. Chapter 15 describes a variety of strategies for visible-surface determination in enough detail to allow the reader to implement some of the most important ones. Illumination and shading algorithms are covered in detail in Chapter 16. The early part of this chapter discusses algorithms most commonly found in current hardware, while the remainder treats texture, shadows, transparency, reflections, physically based illumination models, ray tracing, and radiosity methods. The last chapter in this group, Chapter 17, describes both image manipulations, such as scaling, shearing, and rotating pixmaps, and image storage techniques, including various image-compression schemes.

Advanced Techniques Group. The last four chapters give an overview of the current state of the art (a moving target, of course). Chapter 18 describes advanced graphics hardware used in high-end commercial and research machines; this chapter was contributed by Steven Molnar and Henry Fuchs, authorities on high-performance graphics architectures. Chapter 19 describes the complex raster algorithms used for such tasks as scan-converting arbitary conics, generating antialiased text, and implementing page-description languages, such as PostScript. The final two chapters survey some of the most important techniques in the fields of high-level modeling and computer animation.

The first two groups cover only elementary material and thus can be used for a basic course at the undergraduate level. A follow-on course can then use the more advanced chapters. Alternatively, instructors can assemble customized courses by picking chapters out of the various groups.

For example, a course designed to introduce students to primarily 2D graphics would include Chapters 1 and 2, simple scan conversion and clipping from Chapter 3, a technology overview with emphasis on raster architectures and interaction devices from Chapter 4, homogeneous mathematics from Chapter 5, and 3D viewing only from a "how to use it" point of view from Sections 6.1 to 6.3. The User Interface Group, Chapters 8-10, would be followed by selected introductory sections and simple algorithms from the Image Synthesis Group, Chapters 14, 15, and 16.

A one-course general overview of graphics would include Chapters 1 and 2, basic algorithms from Chapter 3, raster architectures and interaction devices from Chapter 4, Chapter 5, and most of Chapters 6 and 7 on viewing and SPHIGS. The second half of the course would include sections on modeling from Chapters 11 and 13, on image synthesis from Chapters 14, 15, and 16, and on advanced modeling from Chapter 20 to give breadth of coverage in these slightly more advanced areas.

A course emphasizing 3D modeling and rendering would start with Chapter 3 sections on scan converting, clipping of lines and polygons, and introducing antialiasing. The course would then progress to Chapters 5 and 6 on the basic mathematics of transformations and viewing, Chapter 13 on color, and then cover the key Chapters 14, 15, and 16 in the Image Synthesis Group. Coverage would be rounded off by selections in surface and solid modeling, Chapter 20 on advanced modeling, and Chapter 21 on animation from the Advanced Techniques Group.

Graphics Packages. The SRGP and SPHIGS graphics packages, designed by David Sklar, coauthor of the two chapters on these packages, are available from the publisher for the IBM PC (ISBN 0-201-54700-7), the Macintosh (ISBN 0-201-54701-5), and UNIX workstations running X11, as are many of the algorithms for scan conversion, clipping, and viewing (see page 1175).

Acknowledgments. This book could not have been produced without the dedicated work and the indulgence of many friends and colleagues. We acknowledge here our debt to those who have contributed significantly to one or more chapters; many others have helped by commenting on individual chapters, and we are grateful to them as well. We regret any inadvertent omissions. Katrina Avery and Lyn Dupré did a superb job of editing. Additional valuable editing on multiple versions of multiple chapters was provided by Debbie van Dam, Melissa Gold, and Clare Campbell. We are especially grateful to our production supervisor, Bette Aaronson, our art director, Joe Vetere, and our editor, Keith Wollman, not only for their great help in producing the book, but also for their patience and good humor under admittedly adverse circumstances—if we ever made a promised deadline during these frantic five years, we can't remember it!

Computer graphics has become too complex for even a team of four main authors and three guest authors to be expert in all areas. We relied on colleagues and students to amplify our knowledge, catch our mistakes and provide constructive criticism of form and content. We take full responsibility for any remaining sins of omission and commission. Detailed technical readings on one or more chapters were provided by John Airey, Kurt Akeley, Tom Banchoff, Brian Barsky, David Bates, Cliff Beshers, Gary Bishop, Peter Bono, Marvin Bunker, Bill Buxton, Edward Chang, Norman Chin, Michael F. Cohen, William Cowan, John Dennis, Tom Dewald, Scott Draves, Steve Drucker, Tom Duff, Richard Economy, David Ellsworth, Nick England, Jerry Farrell, Robin Forrest, Alain Fournier, Alan Freiden, Christina Gibbs, Melissa Gold, Mark Green, Cathleen Greenberg, Margaret Hagen, Griff Hamlin, Pat Hanrahan, John Heidema, Rob Jacob, Abid Kamran, Mike Kappel, Henry Kaufman, Karen Kendler, David Kurlander, David Laidlaw, Keith Lantz, Hsien-Che Lee, Aaron Marcus, Nelson Max, Deborah Mayhew, Barbara Meier, Gary Meyer, Jim Michener, Jakob Nielsen, Mark Nodine, Randy Pausch, Ari Requicha, David Rosenthal, David Salesin, Hanan Samet, James Sanford, James Sargent, Robin Schaufler, Robert Scheifler, John Schnizlein, Michael Shantzis, Ben Shneiderman, Ken Shoemake, Judith Schrier, John Sibert, Dave Simons, Jonathan Steinhart, Maureen Stone, Paul Strauss, Seth Tager, Peter Tanner, Brice Tebbs, Ben Trumbore, Yi Tso, Greg Turk, Jeff Vroom, Colin Ware, Gary Watkins, Chuck Weger, Kevin Weiler, Turner Whitted, George Wolberg, and Larry Wolff.

Several colleagues, including Jack Bresenham, Brian Barsky, Jerry Van Aken, Dilip Da Silva (who suggested the uniform midpoint treatment of Chapter 3) and Don Hatfield, not only read chapters closely but also provided detailed suggestions on algorithms.

Welcome word-processing relief was provided by Katrina Avery, Barbara Britten, Clare Campbell, Tina Cantor, Joyce Cavatoni, Louisa Hogan, Jenni Rodda, and Debbie van Dam. Drawings for Chapters 1–3 were ably created by Dan Robbins, Scott Snibbe, Tina Cantor, and Clare Campbell. Figure and image sequences created for this book were provided by Beth Cobb, David Kurlander, Allen Paeth, and George Wolberg (with assistance from Peter Karp). Plates II.21–37, showing a progression of rendering techniques, were designed and rendered at Pixar by Thomas Williams and H.B. Siegel, under the direction of M.W. Mantle, using Pixar's PhotoRealistic RenderMan software. Thanks to Industrial Light &

Magic for the use of their laser scanner to create Plates II.24–37, and to Norman Chin for computing vertex normals for Color Plates II.30–32. L. Lu and Carles Castellsagué wrote programs to make figures.

Jeff Vogel implemented the algorithms of Chapter 3, and he and Atul Butte verified the code in Chapters 2 and 7. David Sklar wrote the Mac and X11 implementations of SRGP and SPHIGS with help from Ron Balsys, Scott Boyajian, Atul Butte, Alex Contovounesios, and Scott Draves. Randy Pausch and his students ported the packages to the PC environment.

We have installed an automated electronic mail server to allow our readers to obtain machine-readable copies of many of the algorithms, suggest exercises, report errors in the text and in SRGP/SPHIGS, and obtain errata lists for the text and software. Send email to "graphtext @ cs.brown.edu" with a Subject line of "Help" to receive the current list of available services. (See page 1175 for information on how to order SRGP and SPHIGS.)

Preface to the C Edition

This is the C-language version of a book originally written with examples in Pascal. It includes all changes through the ninth printing of the Pascal second edition, as well as minor modifications to several algorithms, and all its Pascal code has been rewritten in ANSI C. The interfaces to the SRGP and SPHIGS graphics packages are now defined in C, rather than Pascal, and correspond to the new C implementations of these packages. (See page 1175 for information on obtaining the software.)

We wish to thank Norman Chin for converting the Pascal code of the second edition to C, proofreading it, and formatting it using the typographic conventions of the original. Thanks to Matt Ayers for careful proofing of Chapters 2, 3, and 7, and for useful suggestions about conversion problems.

Washington, D.C.   J.D.F.
Providence, R.I.   A.v.D.
New York, N.Y.   S.K.F.
Providence, R.I.   J.F.H.

Contents

CHAPTER 4
GRAPHICS HARDWARE   145

CHAPTER 5
GEOMETRICAL TRANSFORMATIONS   201

CHAPTER 6
VIEWING IN 3D   229

CHAPTER 11
REPRESENTING CURVES AND SURFACES   471

CHAPTER 12
SOLID MODELING   533

CHAPTER 13
ACHROMATIC AND COLORED LIGHT   563

CHAPTER 14
THE QUEST FOR VISUAL REALISM   605

CHAPTER 20
ADVANCED MODELING TECHNIQUES   1011

CHAPTER 21
ANIMATION   1057

APPENDIX: MATHEMATICS FOR COMPUTER GRAPHICS   1083

BIBLIOGRAPHY   1113

INDEX   1153

1
Introduction

Computer graphics started with the display of data on hardcopy plotters and cathode ray tube (CRT) screens soon after the introduction of computers themselves. It has grown to include the creation, storage, and manipulation of models and images of objects. These models come from a diverse and expanding set of fields, and include physical, mathematical, engineering, architectural, and even conceptual (abstract) structures, natural phenomena, and so on. Computer graphics today is largely *interactive:* The user controls the contents, structure, and appearance of objects and of their displayed images by using input devices, such as a keyboard, mouse, or touch-sensitive panel on the screen. Because of the close relationship between the input devices and the display, the handling of such devices is included in the study of computer graphics.

Until the early 1980s, computer graphics was a small, specialized field, largely because the hardware was expensive and graphics-based application programs that were easy to use and cost-effective were few. Then, personal computers with built-in raster graphics displays—such as the Xerox Star and, later, the mass-produced, even less expensive Apple Macintosh and the IBM PC and its clones—popularized the use of *bitmap graphics* for user-computer interaction. A *bitmap* is a ones and zeros representation of the rectangular array of points (*pixels* or *pels*, short for "picture elements") on the screen. Once bitmap graphics became affordable, an explosion of easy-to-use and inexpensive graphics-based applications soon followed. Graphics-based user interfaces allowed millions of new users to control simple, low-cost application programs, such as spreadsheets, word processors, and drawing programs.

The concept of a "desktop" now became a popular metaphor for organizing screen space. By means of a *window manager*, the user could create, position, and resize

1

rectangular screen areas, called *windows,* that acted as virtual graphics terminals, each running an application. This allowed users to switch among multiple activities just by pointing at the desired window, typically with the mouse. Like pieces of paper on a messy desk, windows could overlap arbitrarily. Also part of this desktop metaphor were displays of icons that represented not just data files and application programs, but also common office objects, such as file cabinets, mailboxes, printers, and trashcans, that performed the computer-operation equivalents of their real-life counterparts. *Direct manipulation* of objects via "pointing and clicking" replaced much of the typing of the arcane commands used in earlier operating systems and computer applications. Thus, users could select icons to activate the corresponding programs or objects, or select buttons on pull-down or pop-up screen menus to make choices. Today, almost all interactive application programs, even those for manipulating text (e.g., word processors) or numerical data (e.g., spreadsheet programs), use graphics extensively in the user interface and for visualizing and manipulating the application-specific objects. Graphical interaction via raster displays (displays using bitmaps) has replaced most textual interaction with alphanumeric terminals.

Even people who do not use computers in their daily work encounter computer graphics in television commercials and as cinematic special effects. Computer graphics is no longer a rarity. It is an integral part of all computer user interfaces, and is indispensable for visualizing two-dimensional (2D), three-dimensional (3D), and higher-dimensional objects: Areas as diverse as education, science, engineering, medicine, commerce, the military, advertising, and entertainment all rely on computer graphics. Learning how to program and use computers now includes learning how to use simple 2D graphics as a matter of routine.

1.1 IMAGE PROCESSING AS PICTURE ANALYSIS

Computer graphics concerns the pictorial *synthesis* of real or imaginary objects from their computer-based models, whereas the related field of *image processing* (also called *picture processing*) treats the converse process: the *analysis* of scenes, or the *reconstruction* of models of 2D or 3D objects from their pictures. Picture analysis is important in many arenas: aerial surveillance photographs, slow-scan television images of the moon or of planets gathered from space probes, television images taken from an industrial robot's "eye," chromosome scans, X-ray images, computerized axial tomography (CAT) scans, and fingerprint analysis all exploit image-processing technology (see Color Plate I.1). Image processing has the subareas *image enhancement, pattern detection and recognition,* and *scene analysis and computer vision.* Image enhancement deals with improving image quality by eliminating noise (extraneous or missing pixel data) or by enhancing contrast. Pattern detection and recognition deal with detecting and clarifying standard patterns and finding deviations (distortions) from these patterns. A particularly important example is optical character recognition (OCR) technology, which allows for the economical bulk input of pages of typeset, typewritten, or even handprinted characters. Scene analysis and computer vision allow scientists to recognize and reconstruct a 3D model of a scene from several 2D images. An example is an industrial robot sensing the relative sizes, shapes, positions, and colors of parts on a conveyor belt.

Although both computer graphics and image processing deal with computer processing of pictures, they have until recently been quite separate disciplines. Now that they both use raster displays, however, the overlap between the two is growing, as is particularly evident in two areas. First, in interactive image processing, human input via menus and other graphical interaction techniques helps to control various subprocesses while transformations of continuous-tone images are shown on the screen in real time. For example, scanned-in photographs are electronically touched up, cropped, and combined with others (even with synthetically generated images) before publication. Second, simple image-processing operations are often used in computer graphics to help synthesize the image of a model. Certain ways of transforming and combining synthetic images depend largely on image-processing operations.

1.2   THE ADVANTAGES OF INTERACTIVE GRAPHICS

Graphics provides one of the most natural means of communicating with a computer, since our highly developed 2D and 3D pattern-recognition abilities allow us to perceive and process pictorial data rapidly and efficiently. In many design, implementation, and construction processes today, the information pictures can give is virtually indispensable. Scientific visualization became an important field in the late 1980s, when scientists and engineers realized that they could not interpret the prodigious quantities of data produced in supercomputer runs without summarizing the data and highlighting trends and phenomena in various kinds of graphical representations.

Creating and reproducing pictures, however, presented technical problems that stood in the way of their widespread use. Thus, the ancient Chinese proverb "a picture is worth ten thousand words" became a cliché in our society only after the advent of inexpensive and simple technology for producing pictures—first the printing press, then photography.

Interactive computer graphics is the most important means of producing pictures since the invention of photography and television; it has the added advantage that, with the computer, we can make pictures not only of concrete, "real-world' objects but also of abstract, synthetic objects, such as mathematical surfaces in 4D (see Color Plates I.3 and I.4), and of data that have no inherent geometry, such as survey results. Furthermore, we are not confined to static images. Although static pictures are a good means of communicating information, dynamically varying pictures are frequently even better—to coin a phrase, a moving picture is worth ten thousand static ones. This is especially true for time-varying phenomena, both real (e.g., the deflection of an aircraft wing in supersonic flight, or the development of a human face from childhood through old age) and abstract (e.g., growth trends, such as nuclear energy use in the United States or population movement from cities to suburbs and back to the cities). Thus, a movie can show changes over time more graphically than can a sequence of slides. Similarly, a sequence of frames displayed on a screen at more than 15 frames per second can convey smooth motion or changing form better than can a jerky sequence, with several seconds between individual frames. The use of dynamics is especially effective when the user can control the animation by adjusting the speed, the portion of the total scene in view, the amount of detail shown, the geometric relationship of the objects in the scene to one another, and so on. Much of interactive graphics technology therefore contains hardware and software for user-controlled motion dynamics and update dynamics.

With *motion dynamics*, objects can be moved and tumbled with respect to a stationary observer. The objects can also remain stationary and the viewer can move around them, pan to select the portion in view, and zoom in or cut for more or less detail, as though looking through the viewfinder of a rapidly moving video camera. In many cases, both the objects and the camera are moving. A typical example is the flight simulator (Color Plates I.5a and I.5b), which combines a mechanical platform supporting a mock cockpit with display screens for windows. Computers control platform motion, gauges, and the simulated world of both stationary and moving objects through which the pilot navigates. These multimillion-dollar systems train pilots by letting the pilots maneuver a simulated craft over a simulated 3D landscape and around simulated vehicles. Much simpler flight simulators are among the most popular games on personal computers and workstations. Amusement parks also offer ''motion-simulator'' rides through simulated terrestrial and extraterrestrial landscapes. Video arcades offer graphics-based dexterity games (see Color Plate I.6) and racecar-driving simulators, video games exploiting interactive motion dynamics: The player can change speed and direction with the ''gas pedal'' and ''steering wheel,'' as trees, buildings, and other cars go whizzing by (see Color Plate I.7). Similarly, motion dynamics lets the user fly around and through buildings, molecules, and 3D or 4D mathematical space. In another type of motion dynamics, the ''camera'' is held fixed, and the objects in the scene are moved relative to it. For example, a complex mechanical linkage, such as the linkage on a steam engine, can be animated by moving or rotating all the pieces appropriately.

Update dynamics is the actual change of the shape, color, or other properties of the objects being viewed. For instance, a system can display the deformations of an airplane structure in flight or the state changes in a block diagram of a nuclear reactor in response to the operator's manipulation of graphical representations of the many control mechanisms. The smoother the change, the more realistic and meaningful the result. Dynamic interactive graphics offers a large number of user-controllable modes with which to encode and communicate information: the 2D or 3D shape of objects in a picture, their gray scale or color, and the time variations of these properties. With the recent development of digital signal processing (DSP) and audio synthesis chips, audio feedback can now be provided to augment the graphical feedback and to make the simulated environment even more realistic.

Interactive computer graphics thus permits extensive, high-bandwidth user–computer interaction. This significantly enhances our ability to understand data, to perceive trends, and to visualize real or imaginary objects—indeed, to create ''virtual worlds'' that we can explore from arbitrary points of view (see Color Plates I.15 and I.16). By making communication more efficient, graphics makes possible higher-quality and more precise results or products, greater productivity, and lower analysis and design costs.

1.3 REPRESENTATIVE USES OF COMPUTER GRAPHICS

Computer graphics is used today in many different areas of industry, business, government, education, entertainment, and, most recently, the home. The list of applications is enormous and is growing rapidly as computers with graphics capabilities become commodity products. Let's look at a representative sample of these areas.

■   *User interfaces.* As we mentioned, most applications that run on personal computers and workstations, and even those that run on terminals attached to time-shared computers and network compute servers, have user interfaces that rely on desktop window systems to manage multiple simultaneous activities, and on point-and-click facilities to allow users to select menu items, icons, and objects on the screen; typing is necessary only to input text to be stored and manipulated. Word-processing, spreadsheet, and desktop-publishing programs are typical applications that take advantage of such user-interface techniques. The authors of this book used such programs to create both the text and the figures; then, the publisher and their contractors produced the book using similar typesetting and drawing software.

■   *(Interactive) plotting in business, science, and technology.* The next most common use of graphics today is probably to create 2D and 3D graphs of mathematical, physical, and economic functions; histograms, bar and pie charts; task-scheduling charts; inventory and production charts; and the like. All these are used to present meaningfully and concisely the trends and patterns gleaned from data, so as to clarify complex phenomena and to facilitate informed decision making.

■   *Office automation and electronic publishing.* The use of graphics for the creation and dissemination of information has increased enormously since the advent of desktop publishing on personal computers. Many organizations whose publications used to be printed by outside specialists can now produce printed materials inhouse. Office automation and electronic publishing can produce both traditional printed (hardcopy) documents and electronic (softcopy) documents that contain text, tables, graphs, and other forms of drawn or scanned-in graphics. Hypermedia systems that allow browsing of networks of interlinked multimedia documents are proliferating (see Color Plate I.2).

■   *Computer-aided drafting and design.* In computer-aided design (CAD), interactive graphics is used to design components and systems of mechanical, electrical, electromechanical, and electronic devices, including structures such as buildings, automobile bodies, airplane and ship hulls, very large-scale-integrated (VLSI) chips, optical systems, and telephone and computer networks. Sometimes, the user merely wants to produce the precise drawings of components and assemblies, as for online drafting or architectural blueprints. Color Plate I.8 shows an example of such a 3D design program, intended for nonprofessionals: a "customize your own patio deck" program used in lumber yards. More frequently, however, the emphasis is on interacting with a computer-based model of the component or system being designed in order to test, for example, its structural, electrical, or thermal properties. Often, the model is interpreted by a simulator that feeds back the behavior of the system to the user for further interactive design and test cycles. After objects have been designed, utility programs can *postprocess* the design database to make parts lists, to process "bills of materials," to define numerical control tapes for cutting or drilling parts, and so on.

■   *Simulation and animation for scientific visualization and entertainment.* Computer-produced animated movies and displays of the time-varying behavior of real and simulated objects are becoming increasingly popular for scientific and engineering visualization (see Color Plate I.10). We can use them to study abstract mathematical entities as well as mathematical models of such phenomena as fluid flow, relativity, nuclear and chemical reactions, physiological system and organ function, and deformation of mechanical structures under various kinds of loads. Another advanced-technology area is interactive cartooning. The simpler kinds of systems for producing ''flat'' cartoons are becoming cost-effective in creating routine ''in-between'' frames that interpolate between two explicitly specified ''key frames.'' Cartoon characters will increasingly be modeled in the computer as 3D shape descriptions whose movements are controlled by computer commands, rather than by the figures being drawn manually by cartoonists (see Color Plates D and F). Television commercials featuring flying logos and more exotic visual trickery have become common, as have elegant special effects in movies (see Color Plates I.12, I.13, II.18, and G). Sophisticated mechanisms are available to model the objects and to represent light and shadows.

■   *Art and commerce*. Overlapping the previous category is the use of computer graphics in art and advertising; here, computer graphics is used to produce pictures that express a message and attract attention (see Color Plates I.9, I.11, and H). Personal computers and Teletext and Videotex terminals in public places such as museums, transportation terminals, supermarkets, and hotels, as well as in private homes, offer much simpler but still informative pictures that let users orient themselves, make choices, or even ''teleshop'' and conduct other business transactions. Finally, slide production for commercial, scientific, or educational presentations is another cost-effective use of graphics, given the steeply rising labor costs of the traditional means of creating such material.

■   *Process control*. Whereas flight simulators or arcade games let users interact with a simulation of a real or artificial world, many other applications enable people to interact with some aspect of the real world itself. Status displays in refineries, power plants, and computer networks show data values from sensors attached to critical system components, so that operators can respond to problematic conditions. For example, military commanders view field data—number and position of vehicles, weapons launched, troop movements, casualties—on *command and control* displays to revise their tactics as needed; flight controllers at airports see computer-generated identification and status information for the aircraft blips on their radar scopes, and can thus control traffic more quickly and accurately than they could with the unannotated radar data alone; spacecraft controllers monitor telemetry data and take corrective action as needed.

■   *Cartography*. Computer graphics is used to produce both accurate and schematic representations of geographical and other natural phenomena from measurement data. Examples include geographic maps, relief maps, exploration maps for drilling and mining, oceanographic charts, weather maps, contour maps, and population-density maps.

1.4 CLASSIFICATION OF APPLICATIONS

The diverse uses of computer graphics listed in the previous section differ in a variety of ways, and a number of classifications may be used to categorize them. The first classification is by *type (dimensionality) of the object* to be represented and the *kind of picture* to be produced. The range of possible combinations is indicated in Table 1.1.

Some of the objects represented graphically are clearly abstract, some are real; similarly, the pictures can be purely symbolic (a simple 2D graph) or realistic (a rendition of a still life). The same object can, of course, be represented in a variety of ways. For example, an electronic printed circuit board populated with integrated circuits can be portrayed by many different 2D symbolic representations or by 3D synthetic photographs of the board.

The second classification is by the *type of interaction*, which determines the user's degree of control over the object and its image. The range here includes *offline plotting*, with a predefined database produced by other application programs or digitized from physical models; *interactive plotting*, in which the user controls iterations of ''supply some parameters, plot, alter parameters, replot''; *predefining* or *calculating the object and flying around it* in real time under user control, as in real-time animation systems used for scientific visualization and flight simulators; and *interactive designing*, in which the user starts with a blank screen, defines new objects (typically by assembling them from predefined components), and then moves around to get a desired view.

The third classification is by the *role of the picture*, or the degree to which the picture is an end in itself or is merely a means to an end. In cartography, drafting, raster painting, animation, and artwork, for example, the drawing is the end product; in many CAD applications, however, the drawing is merely a representation of the geometric properties of the object being designed or analyzed. Here the drawing or construction phase is an important but small part of a larger process, the goal of which is to create and postprocess a common database using an integrated suite of application programs.

A good example of graphics in CAD is the creation of a VLSI chip. The engineer makes a preliminary chip design using a CAD package. Once all the gates are laid out, she then subjects the chip to hours of simulated use. From the first run, for instance, she learns that the chip works only at clock speeds above 80 nanoseconds (ns). Since the target clock speed of the machine is 50 ns, the engineer calls up the initial layout and redesigns a portion of the logic to reduce its number of stages. On the second simulation run, she learns that the chip will not work at speeds below 60 ns. Once again, she calls up the drawing and redesigns a portion of the chip. Once the chip passes all the simulation tests, she invokes a postprocessor to create a database of information for the manufacturer about design and materials specifications, such as conductor path routing and assembly drawings. In this

TABLE 1.1 CLASSIFICATION OF COMPUTER GRAPHICS BY OBJECT AND PICTURE

Type of object	Pictorial representation	Example
2D	Line drawing	Fig. 2.1
	Gray scale image	Fig. 1.1
	Color image	Color Plate I.2
3D	Line drawing (or *wireframe*)	Color Plates II.21–II.23
	Line drawing, with various effects	Color Plates II.24–II.27
	Shaded, color image with various effects	Color Plates II.28–II.39

example, the representation of the chip's geometry produces output beyond the picture itself. In fact, the geometry shown on the screen may contain *less* detail than the underlying database.

A final categorization arises from the logical and temporal *relationship between objects and their pictures*. The user may deal, for example, with only one picture at a time (typical in plotting), with a time-varying sequence of related pictures (as in motion or update dynamics), or with a structured collection of objects (as in many CAD applications that contain hierarchies of assembly and subassembly drawings).

1.5   DEVELOPMENT OF HARDWARE AND SOFTWARE FOR COMPUTER GRAPHICS

This book concentrates on fundamental principles and techniques that were derived in the past and are still applicable today—and generally will be applicable in the future. In this section, we take a brief look at the historical development of computer graphics, to place today's systems in context. Fuller treatments of the interesting evolution of this field are presented in [PRIN71], [MACH78], [CHAS81], and [CACM84]. It is easier to chronicle the evolution of hardware than to document that of software, since hardware evolution has had a greater influence on how the field developed. Thus, we begin with hardware.

Crude plotting on hardcopy devices such as teletypes and line printers dates from the early days of computing. The Whirlwind Computer developed in 1950 at the Massachusetts Institute of Technology (MIT) had computer-driven CRT displays for output, both for operator use and for cameras producing hardcopy. The SAGE air-defense system developed in the middle 1950s was the first to use *command and control* CRT display consoles on which operators identified targets with light pens (hand-held pointing devices that sense light emitted by objects on the screen). The beginnings of modern interactive graphics, however, are found in Ivan Sutherland's seminal doctoral work on the Sketchpad drawing system [SUTH63]. He introduced data structures for storing symbol hierarchies built up via easy replication of standard components, a technique akin to the use of plastic templates for drawing circuit symbols. He also developed interaction techniques that used the keyboard and light pen for making choices, pointing, and drawing, and formulated many other fundamental ideas and techniques still in use today. Indeed, many of the features introduced in Sketchpad are found in the PHIGS graphics package discussed in Chapter 7.

At the same time, it was becoming clear to computer, automobile, and aerospace manufacturers that CAD and computer-aided manufacturing (CAM) activities had enormous potential for automating drafting and other drawing-intensive activities. The General Motors DAC system [JACK64] for automobile design, and the Itek Digitek system [CHAS81] for lens design, were pioneering efforts that showed the utility of graphical interaction in the iterative design cycles common in engineering. By the mid-sixties, a number of research projects and commercial products had appeared.

Since at that time computer input/output (I/O) was done primarily in batch mode using punched cards, hopes were high for a breakthrough in interactive user–computer communication. Interactive graphics, as "the window on the computer," was to be an integral part of vastly accelerated interactive design cycles. The results were not nearly so dramatic, however, since interactive graphics remained beyond the resources of all but the most technology-intensive organizations. Among the reasons for this were these:

- The high *cost* of the graphics hardware, when produced without benefit of economies of scale—at a time when automobiles cost a few thousand dollars, computers cost several millions of dollars, and the first commercial computer displays cost more than a hundred thousand dollars

- The need for large-scale, expensive *computing resources* to support massive design databases, interactive picture manipulation, and the typically large suite of postprocessing programs whose input came from the graphics-design phase

- The *difficulty of writing large, interactive programs* for the new time-sharing environment at a time when both graphics and interaction were new to predominantly batch-oriented FORTRAN programmers

- *One-of-a-kind, nonportable software*, typically written for a particular manufacturer's display device and produced without the benefit of modern software-engineering principles for building modular, structured systems; when software is nonportable, moving to new display devices necessitates expensive and time-consuming rewriting of working programs.

It was the advent of graphics-based personal computers, such as the Apple Macintosh and the IBM PC, that finally drove down the costs of both hardware and software so dramatically that millions of graphics computers were sold as "appliances" for office and home; when the field started in the early sixties, its practitioners never dreamed that personal computers featuring graphical interaction would become so common so soon.

1.5.1 Output Technology

The display devices developed in the mid-sixties and in common use until the mid-eighties are called *vector*, *stroke*, *line drawing*, or *calligraphic displays*. The term *vector* is used as a synonym for *line* here; a *stroke* is a short line, and *characters* are made of sequences of such strokes. We shall look briefly at vector-system architecture, because many modern raster graphics systems use similar techniques. A typical vector system consists of a display processor connected as an I/O peripheral to the central processing unit (CPU), a display buffer memory, and a CRT. The buffer stores the computer-produced *display list* or *display program*; it contains point- and line-plotting commands with (x, y) or (x, y, z) endpoint coordinates, as well as character-plotting commands. Figure 1.1 shows a typical vector architecture; the display list in memory is shown as a symbolic representation of the output commands and their (x, y) or character values.

The commands for plotting points, lines, and characters are interpreted by the display processor. It sends digital and point coordinates to a *vector generator* that converts the digital coordinate values to analog voltages for beam-deflection circuits that displace an electron beam writing on the CRT's phosphor coating (the details are given in Chapter 4). The essence of a vector system is that the beam is deflected from endpoint to endpoint, as dictated by the arbitrary order of the display commands; this technique is called *random scan*. (Laser shows also use random-scan deflection of the laser beam.) Since the light output of the phosphor decays in tens or at most hundreds of microseconds, the display

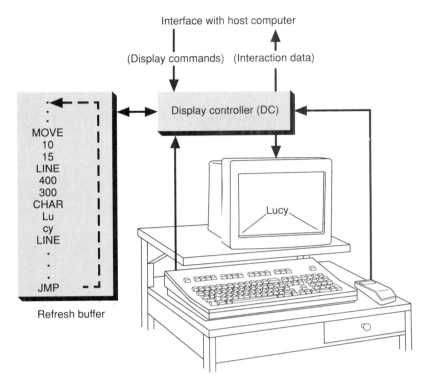

Interface with host computer

(Display commands)   (Interaction data)

Display controller (DC)

MOVE
10
15
LINE
400
300
CHAR
Lu
cy
LINE
·
·
·
JMP

Refresh buffer

Lucy

Fig. 1.1 Architecture of a vector display.

processor must cycle through the display list to *refresh* the phosphor at least 30 times per second (30 Hz) to avoid flicker; hence, the buffer holding the display list is usually called a *refresh buffer*. Note that, in Fig. 1.1, the jump instruction loops back to the top of the display list to provide the cyclic refresh.

In the sixties, buffer memory and processors fast enough to refresh at (at least) 30 Hz were expensive, and only a few thousand lines could be shown without noticeable flicker. Then, in the late sixties, the direct-view storage tube (DVST) obviated both the buffer and the refresh process, and eliminated all flicker. This was the vital step in making interactive graphics affordable. A DVST stores an image by writing that image once with a relatively slow-moving electron beam on a storage mesh in which the phosphor is embedded. The small, self-sufficient DVST terminal was an order of magnitude less expensive than was the typical refresh system; further, it was ideal for a low-speed (300- to1200-baud) telephone interface to time-sharing systems. DVST terminals introduced many users and programmers to interactive graphics.

Another major hardware advance of the late sixties was attaching the display to a minicomputer; with this configuration, the central time-sharing computer was relieved of the heavy demands of refreshed display devices, especially user-interaction handling, and updating the image on the screen. The minicomputer typically ran application programs as well, and could in turn be connected to the larger central mainframe to run large analysis programs. Both minicomputer and DVST configurations led to installations of thousands of graphics systems. Also at this time, the hardware of the display processor itself was becoming more sophisticated, taking over many routine but time-consuming jobs from the graphics software. Foremost among such devices was the invention in 1968 of refresh display hardware for geometric transformations that could scale, rotate, and translate points and lines on the screen in real time, could perform 2D and 3D clipping, and could produce parallel and perspective projections (see Chapter 6).

The development in the early seventies of inexpensive raster graphics, based on television technology, contributed more to the growth of the field than did any other technology. *Raster displays* store the display *primitives* (such as lines, characters, and solidly shaded or patterned areas) in a refresh buffer in terms of their component pixels, as shown in Fig. 1.2. In some raster displays, there is a hardware display controller that receives and interprets sequences of output commands similar to those of the vector displays (as shown in the figure); in simpler, more common systems, such as those in personal computers, the display controller exists only as a software component of the graphics library package, and the refresh buffer is just a piece of the CPU's memory that can be read out by the image display subsystem (often called the video controller) that produces the actual image on the screen.

The complete image on a raster display is formed from the *raster*, which is a set of horizontal *raster lines,* each a row of individual pixels; the raster is thus stored as a matrix of pixels representing the entire screen area. The entire image is scanned out sequentially by

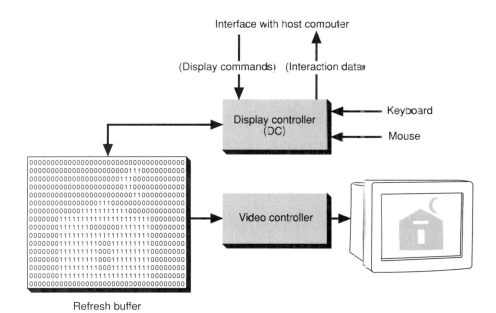

Fig. 1.2 Architecture of a raster display.

the video controller, one raster line at a time, from top to bottom and then back to the top (as shown in Fig. 1.3). At each pixel, the beam's intensity is set to reflect the pixel's intensity; in color systems, three beams are controlled—one each for the red, green, and blue primary colors—as specified by the three color components of each pixel's value (see Chapters 4 and 13). Figure 1.4 shows the difference between random and raster scan for displaying a simple 2D line drawing of a house (part a). In part (b), the vector arcs are notated with arrowheads showing the random deflection of the beam. Dotted lines denote deflection of the beam, which is not turned on ("blanked"), so that no vector is drawn. Part (c) shows the unfilled house rendered by rectangles, polygons, and arcs, whereas part (d) shows a filled version. Note the jagged appearance of the lines and arcs in the raster scan images of parts (c) and (d); we shall discuss that visual artifact shortly.

In the early days of raster graphics, refreshing was done at television rates of 30 Hz; today, a 60-Hz or higher refresh rate is used to avoid flickering of the image. Whereas in a vector system the refresh buffer stored op-codes and endpoint coordinate values, in a raster system the entire image of, say, 1024 lines of 1024 pixels each, must be stored explicitly. The term *bitmap* is still in common use to describe both the refresh buffer and the array of pixel values that map one for one to pixels on the screen. Bitmap graphics has the advantage over vector graphics that the actual display of the image is handled by inexpensive scan-out logic: The regular, repetitive raster scan is far easier and less expensive to implement than is the random scan of vector systems, whose vector generators must be highly accurate to provide linearity and repeatability of the beam's deflection.

The availability of inexpensive solid-state random-access memory (RAM) for bitmaps in the early seventies was the breakthrough needed to make raster graphics the dominant hardware technology. Bilevel (also called monochrome) CRTs draw images in black and white or black and green; some plasma panels use orange and black. Bilevel bitmaps contain a single bit per pixel, and the entire bitmap for a screen with a resolution of 1024 by 1024 pixels is only 2^{20} bits, or about 128,000 bytes. Low-end color systems have 8 bits per pixel, allowing 256 colors simultaneously; more expensive systems have 24 bits per pixel,

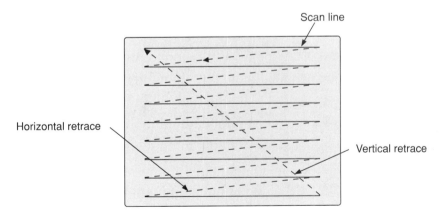

Fig. 1.3 Raster scan.

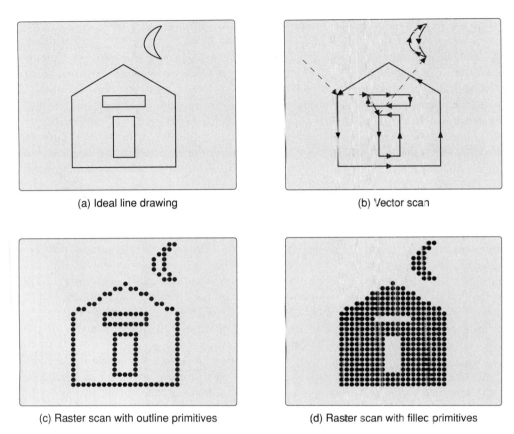

(a) Ideal line drawing   (b) Vector scan

(c) Raster scan with outline primitives   (d) Raster scan with fillec primitives

Fig. 1.4 Random scan versus raster scan. We symbolize the screen as a rounded rectangle filled with a light gray shade that denotes the white background; the image is drawn in black on this background.

allowing a choice of any of 16 million colors; and refresh buffers with 32 bits per pixel, and screen resolution of 1280 by 1024 pixels are available even on personal computers. Of the 32 bits, 24 bits are devoted to representing color, and 8 to control purposes, as discussed in Chapter 4. Beyond that, buffers with 96 bits (or more) per pixel[1] are available at 1280 by 1024 resolution on the high-end systems discussed in Chapter 18. A typical 1280 by 1024 color system with 24 bits per pixel requires 3.75 MB of RAM—inexpensive by today's standards. The term *bitmap*, strictly speaking, applies only to 1-bit-per-pixel bilevel systems; for multiple-bit-per-pixel systems, we use the more general term *pixmap* (short for pixel map). Since *pixmap* in common parlance refers both to the contents of the refresh

---

[1]Of these 96 bits, typically 64 bits are used for two 32-bit color-and-control buffers to allow *double-buffering* of two images: while one image is being refreshed, the second one is being updated. The remaining 32-bit buffer is used to implement a hardware technique called z-buffering, used to do visible-surface determination for creating realistic 3D images (see Chapters 14 and 15).

buffer and to the buffer memory itself, we use the term *frame buffer* when we mean the actual buffer memory.

The major advantages of raster graphics over vector graphics include lower cost and the ability to display areas filled with solid colors or patterns, an especially rich means of communicating information that is essential for realistic images of 3D objects. Furthermore, the refresh process is independent of the complexity (number of polygons, etc.) of the image, since the hardware is fast enough that each pixel in the buffer can be read out on each refresh cycle. Most people do not perceive flicker on screens refreshed above 70 Hz. In contrast, vector displays flicker when the number of primitives in the buffer becomes too large; typically a maximum of a few hundred thousand short vectors may be displayed flicker-free.

The major disadvantage of raster systems compared to vector systems arises from the discrete nature of the pixel representation. First, primitives such as lines and polygons are specified in terms of their endpoints (vertices) and must be *scan-converted* into their component pixels in the frame buffer. The term derives from the notion that the programmer specifies endpoint or vertex coordinates in random-scan mode, and this information must be reduced by the system to pixels for raster-scan–mode display. Scan conversion is commonly done with software in personal computers and low-end workstations, where the microprocessor CPU is responsible for all graphics. For higher performance, scan conversion can be done by special-purpose hardware, including *raster image processor* (RIP) chips used as coprocessors or accelerators.

Because each primitive must be scan-converted, real-time dynamics is far more computationally demanding on raster systems than on vector systems. First, transforming 1000 lines on a vector system can mean transforming 2000 endpoints in the worst case. In the next refresh cycle, the vector-generator hardware automatically redraws the transformed lines in their new positions. In a raster system, however, not only must the endpoints be transformed (using hardware transformation units identical to those used by vector systems), but also each transformed primitive must then be scan-converted using its new endpoints, which define its new size and position. None of the contents of the frame buffer can be salvaged. When the CPU is responsible for both endpoint transformation and scan conversion, only a small number of primitives can be transformed in real time. Transformation and scan-conversion hardware is thus needed for dynamics in raster systems; as a result of steady progress in VLSI, that has become feasible even in low-end systems.

The second drawback of raster systems arises from the nature of the raster itself. Whereas a vector system can draw a continuous, smooth line (and even some smooth curves) from essentially any point on the CRT face to any other, the raster system can display mathematically smooth lines, polygons. and boundaries of curved primitives such as circles and ellipses only by approximating them with pixels on the raster grid. This can cause the familiar problem of "jaggies" or "staircasing," as shown in Fig. 1.4 (c) and (d). This visual artifact is a manifestation of a sampling error called *aliasing* in signal-processing theory; such artifacts occur when a function of a continuous variable that contains sharp changes in intensity is approximated with discrete samples. Both theory and practice in modern computer graphics are concerned with techniques for *antialiasing* on gray-scale or color systems. These techniques specify gradations in intensity of neighboring pixels at edges of primitives, rather than setting pixels to maximum or zero intensity only; see Chapters 3, 14, and 19 for further discussion of this important topic.

1.5.2   Input Technology

Input technology has also improved greatly over the years. The clumsy, fragile light pen of vector systems has been replaced by the ubiquitous mouse (first developed by office-automation pioneer Doug Engelbart in the mid-sixties [ENGE68]), the data tablet, and the transparent, touch-sensitive panel mounted on the screen. Even fancier input devices that supply not just (x, y) locations on the screen, but also 3D and even higher-dimensional input values (degrees of freedom), are becoming common, as discussed in Chapter 8. Audio communication also has exciting potential, since it allows hands-free input and natural output of simple instructions, feedback, and so on. With the standard input devices, the user can specify operations or picture components by typing or drawing new information or by pointing to existing information on the screen. These interactions require no knowledge of programming and only a little keyboard use: The user makes choices simply by selecting menu buttons or icons, answers questions by checking options or typing a few characters in a form, places copies of predefined symbols on the screen, draws by indicating consecutive endpoints to be connected by straight lines or interpolated by smooth curves, paints by moving the cursor over the screen, and fills closed areas bounded by polygons or paint contours with shades of gray, colors, or various patterns.

1.5.3   Software Portability and Graphics Standards

Steady advances in hardware technology have thus made possible the evolution of graphics displays from one-of-a-kind special output devices to the standard human interface to the computer. We may well wonder whether software has kept pace. For example, to what extent have early difficulties with overly complex, cumbersome, and expensive graphics systems and application software been resolved? Many of these difficulties arose from the primitive graphics software that was available, and in general there has been a long, slow process of maturation in such software. We have moved from low-level, *device-dependent* packages supplied by manufacturers for their particular display devices to higher-level, *device-independent* packages. These packages can drive a wide variety of display devices, from laser printers and plotters to film recorders and high-performance real-time displays. The main purpose of using a device-independent package in conjunction with a high-level programming language is to promote *application-program portability*. This portability is provided in much the same way as a high-level, machine-independent language (such as FORTRAN, Pascal, or C) provides portability: by isolating the programmer from most machine peculiarities and providing language features readily implemented on a broad range of processors. "Programmer portability" is also enhanced in that programmers can now move from system to system, or even from installation to installation, and find familiar software.

  A general awareness of the need for standards in such device-independent graphics packages arose in the mid-seventies and culminated in a specification for a *3D Core*

Graphics System (the Core, for short) produced by an ACM SIGGRAPH[2] Committee in 1977 [GSPC77] and refined in 1979 [GSPC79]. The first three authors of this book were actively involved in the design and documentation of the 1977 Core.

The Core specification fulfilled its intended role as a baseline specification. Not only did it have many implementations, but also it was used as input to official (governmental) standards projects within both ANSI (the American National Standards Institute) and ISO (the International Standards Organization). The first graphics specification to be officially standardized was GKS (the Graphical Kernel System [ANSI85b]), an elaborated, cleaned-up version of the Core that, unlike the Core, was restricted to 2D. In 1988, GKS-3D [INTE88], a 3D extension of GKS, became an official standard, as did a much more sophisticated but even more complex graphics system called PHIGS (Programmer's Hierarchical Interactive Graphics System [ANSI88]). GKS supports the grouping of logically related primitives—such as lines, polygons, and character strings—and their attributes into collections called *segments*; these segments may not be nested. PHIGS, as its name implies, does support nested hierarchical groupings of 3D primitives, called *structures*. In PHIGS, all primitives, including invocations of substructures, are subject to geometric transformations (scaling, rotation, and translation) to accomplish dynamic movement. PHIGS also supports a retained database of structures that the programmer may edit selectively; PHIGS automatically updates the screen whenever the database has been altered. PHIGS has been extended with a set of features for modern, pseudorealistic rendering[3] of objects on raster displays; this extension is called PHIGS+ [PHIG88]. PHIGS implementations are large packages, due to the many features and to the complexity of the specification. PHIGS and especially PHIGS+ implementations run best when there is hardware support for their transformation, clipping, and rendering features.

This book discusses graphics software standards at some length. We first study SRGP (the Simple Raster Graphics Package), which borrows features from Apple's popular QuickDraw integer raster graphics package [ROSE85] and MIT's X Window System [SCHE88a] for output and from GKS and PHIGS for input. Having looked at simple applications in this low-level raster graphics package, we then study the scan-conversion and clipping algorithms such packages use to generate images of primitives in the frame buffer. Then, after building a mathematical foundation for 2D and 3D geometric transformations and for parallel and perspective viewing in 3D, we study a far more powerful package called SPHIGS (Simple PHIGS). SPHIGS is a subset of PHIGS that operates on primitives defined in a floating-point, abstract, 3D world-coordinate system

---

[2]SIGGRAPH is the Special Interest Group on Graphics, one of the professional groups within ACM, the Association for Computing Machinery. ACM is one of the two major professional societies for computer professionals; the IEEE Computer Society is the other. SIGGRAPH publishes a research journal and sponsors an annual conference that features presentations of research papers in the field and an equipment exhibition. The Computer Society also publishes a research journal in graphics.

[3]A pseudorealistic rendering is one that simulates the simple laws of optics describing how light is reflected by objects. Photorealistic rendering uses better approximations to the way objects reflect and refract light; these approximations require more computation but produce images that are more nearly photographic in quality (see Color Plate E).

independent of any type of display technology, and that supports some simple PHIGS+
features. We have oriented our discussion to PHIGS and PHIGS+ because we believe they
will have much more influence on interactive 3D graphics than will GKS-3D, especially
given the increasing availability of hardware that supports real-time transformations and
rendering of pseudorealistic images.

1.6 CONCEPTUAL FRAMEWORK FOR INTERACTIVE GRAPHICS

1.6.1 Overview

The high-level conceptual framework shown in Fig. 1.5 can be used to describe almost any
interactive graphics system. At the hardware level (not shown explicitly in the diagram), a
computer receives input from interaction devices, and outputs images to a display device.
The software has three components. The first is the *application program*; it creates, stores
into, and retrieves from the second component, the *application model*, which represents the
data or objects to be pictured on the screen. The application program also handles user
input. It produces views by sending to the third component, the *graphics system*, a series of
graphics output commands that contain both a detailed geometric description of *what* is to
be viewed and the attributes describing *how* the objects should appear. The graphics system
is responsible for actually producing the picture from the detailed descriptions and for
passing the user's input to the application program for processing.

The graphics system is thus an intermediary between the application program and the
display hardware that effects an *output transformation* from objects in the application model
to a view of the model. Symmetrically, it effects an *input transformation* from user actions
to inputs to the application program that will cause the application to make changes in the
model and/or picture. The fundamental task of the designer of an interactive graphics
application program is to specify what classes of data items or objects are to be generated
and represented pictorially, and how the user and the application program are to interact in
order to create and modify the model and its visual representation. Most of the
programmer's task concerns creating and editing the model and handling user interaction,
not actually creating views, since that is handled by the graphics system.

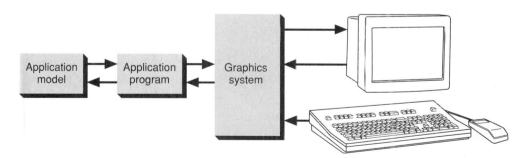

Fig. 1.5 Conceptual framework for interactive graphics.

1.6.2 Application Modeling

The application model captures all the data, objects, and relationships among them that are relevant to the display and interaction part of the application program and to any nongraphical postprocessing modules. Examples of such postprocessing modules are analyses of the transient behavior of a circuit or of the stresses in an aircraft wing, simulation of a population model or a weather system, and pricing computations for a building. In the class of applications typified by "painting" programs such as MacPaint and PCPaint, the intent of the program is to produce an image by letting the user set or modify individual pixels. Here an explicit application model is not needed—the picture is both means and end, and the displayed bitmap or pixmap serves in effect as the application model.

More typically, however, there is an identifiable application model representing application objects through some combination of data and procedural description that is independent of a particular display device. Procedural descriptions are used, for example, to define fractals, as described in Section 20.3. A data model can be as rudimentary as an array of data points or as complex as a linked list representing a network data structure or a relational database storing a set of relations. We often speak of storing the *application model* in the *application database;* the terms are used interchangeably here. Models typically store descriptions of *primitives* (points, lines and polygons in 2D or 3D, and polyhedra and free-form surfaces in 3D) that define the shape of components of the object, object *attributes* such as line style, color, or surface texture; and *connectivity* relationships and positioning data that describe how the components fit together.

The objects stored in the model can differ greatly in the amount of intrinsic geometry needed to specify them. At the geometry-is-everything end of the spectrum, an industrial robot of the type discussed in Chapter 7 is described almost completely in terms of the geometry of its component polyhedra, each of which is a collection of 3D polygonal facets connected at common edges defined in terms of common vertices and enclosing a volume. A spreadsheet has much less intrinsic geometry. The spatial relationships between adjacent cells are stored, but the exact size or placement of each cell on the "paper" is not stored; instead, these values are determined dynamically by the spreadsheet program as a function of the contents of cells. At the geometry-free end of the spectrum, a demographic model storing statistics, such as income and age of individuals in some population, has no intrinsic geometry. These statistics can then be operated on by a procedure to derive some *geometrical interpretation*, such as a 2D graph, scatter diagram, or histogram.

Another class of applications without intrinsic geometry deals with the directed-graph networks used in various fields such as engineering and project management. These networks may be represented internally by adjacency matrices describing how nodes are connected, plus some property data for nodes and edges, and the application must then derive a layout in a predefined format in order to create a view of the graph. This representation might be created once and subsequently edited, as for a VLSI circuit layout computed over many hours. The model would then contain both a nongeometric and an almost purely geometric description of the circuit. Alternatively, if a layout for a particular application is simple and fast enough to derive, such as a project-scheduling chart with labeled boxes and arrows, it can be created on the fly each time the data on which it is based change.

Geometric data in the application model often are accompanied by nongeometric textual or numeric property information useful to a postprocessing program or the interactive user. Examples of such data in CAD applications include manufacturing data; "price and supplier" data; thermal, mechanical, electrical, or electronic properties; and mechanical or electrical tolerances.

1.6.3 Describing to the Graphics System What Is to Be Viewed

The application program creates the application model either a priori as a result of prior computation, as in an engineering or scientific simulation on a supercomputer, or as part of an interactive session at the display device during which the user guides the construction process step by step to choose components and geometric and nongeometric property data. The user can ask the application program at any time to show a view of the model it has created so far. (The word *view* is used intentionally here, both in the sense of a visual rendering of some geometric properties of the objects being modeled and in the technical database sense of a 2D presentation of some properties of some subset of the model.)

Models are application-specific and are created independently of any particular display system. Therefore, the application program must convert a description of the portion of the model to be viewed from the internal representation of the geometry (whether explicitly stored in the model or derived on the fly) to whatever procedure calls or commands the graphics system uses to create an image. This conversion process has two phases. First, the application program traverses the application database that stores the model in order to extract the portions to be viewed, using some selection or query criteria. Then, the extracted geometry is put in a format that can be sent to the graphics system. The selection criteria can be geometric in nature (e.g., the portion of the model to be viewed has been shifted via the graphics equivalent of a pan or zoom camera operation), or they can be similar to traditional database query criteria (e.g., create a view of all the activities after March 15, 1989 in the scheduling chart for producing this book).

The data extracted during the database traversal must either be geometric in nature or must be converted to geometric data; the data can be described to the graphics system in terms of both primitives that the system can display directly and attributes that control the primitives' appearance. Display primitives typically match those stored in geometric models: lines, rectangles, polygons, circles, ellipses, and text in 2D, and polygons, polyhedra, and text in 3D. Advanced graphics systems such as PHIGS+ support additional primitives, including curves and surfaces defined by polynomials of higher degrees.

If the model stores geometric primitives not directly supported by the graphics package, the application program must reduce them to those that are accepted by the system. For example, if spheres and free-form surfaces are not supported, the application must approximate such surfaces by *tiling* or *tessellating* them with meshes of polygons that the graphics system can handle. Appearance attributes supported by the graphics package also tend to correspond to the ones stored in the model, such as color, line style, and line width. In addition to primitives and attributes, advanced graphics packages such as PHIGS support facilities for specifying geometric transformations for scaling, rotating, and positioning components, for specifying how components are to be viewed in 3D, and for grouping logically related primitives, attributes, and transformations so that they can be invoked by a single reference to a named structure.

The graphics system typically consists of a set of output subroutines corresponding to the various primitives, attributes, and other elements. These are collected in a *graphics-subroutine library* or *package* that can be called from high-level languages such as C, Pascal, or LISP. The application program specifies geometric primitives and attributes to these subroutines, and the subroutines then drive the specific display device and cause it to display the image. Much as conventional I/O systems create logical I/O units to shield the application programmer from the messy details of hardware and device drivers, graphics systems create a *logical display device*. Thus, the graphics programmer can ignore such details as which part of image generation is done in the display hardware and which is done by the graphics package, or what the coordinate system of the display is. This abstraction of the display device pertains both to the output of images and to interaction via logical input devices. For example, the mouse, data tablet, touch panel, 2D joystick, or trackball can all be treated as the *locator* logical input device that returns an (x, y) screen location. The application program can ask the graphics system either to *sample* the input devices or to wait at a specified point until an *event* is generated when the user activates a device being waited on. With input values obtained from sampling or waiting for an event, the application program can handle user interactions that alter the model or the display or that change its operating mode.

1.6.4 Interaction Handling

The typical application-program schema for interaction handling is the *event-driven loop*. It is easily visualized as a finite-state machine with a central wait state and transitions to other states that are caused by user-input events. Processing a command may entail nested event loops of the same format that have their own states and input transitions. An application program may also sample input devices such as the locator by asking for their values at any time; the program then uses the returned value as input to a processing procedure that also changes the state of the application program, the image, or the database. The event-driven loop is characterized by the following pseudocode schema:

```
generate initial display, derived from application model as appropriate
while (!quit ) {      /* User has not selected the "quit" option */
    enable selection of commands objects
    /* Program pauses indefinitely in "wait state" until user acts */
    wait for user selection
    switch (selection) {
        process selection to complete command or process completed command,
            updating model and screen as needed
    }
}
```

Let's examine the application's reaction to input in more detail. The application program typically responds to user interactions in one of two modes. First, the user action may require only that the screen be updated—for example, by highlighting of a selected object or by making available a new menu of choices. The application then needs only to update its internal state and to call the graphics package to update the screen; it does not need not to update the database. If, however, the user action calls for a change in the model—for example, by adding or deleting a component—the application must update the model and then call the graphics package to update the screen from the model. Either the entire model is retraversed to regenerate the image from scratch, or, with more sophisticated incremental-update algorithms, the screen is updated selectively. It is important to understand that no significant change can take place in the objects on the screen without a corresponding change in the model. The screen is indeed the window on the computer in that the user, in general, is manipulating not an image but the model that is literally and figuratively behind the image. Only in painting and image-enhancement applications are the model and the image identical. Therefore, it is the application's job to interpret user input. The graphics system has no responsibility for building or modifying the model, either initially or in response to user interaction; its only job is to create images from geometric descriptions and to pass along the user's input data.

The event-loop model, although fundamental to current practice in computer graphics, is limited in that the user–computer dialogue is a *sequential*, ping-pong model of alternating user actions and computer reactions. In the future, we may expect to see more of *parallel* conversations, in which simultaneous input and output using multiple communications channels—for example, both graphics and voice—take place. Formalisms, not to mention programming-language constructs, for such free-form conversations are not yet well developed; we shall not discuss them further here.

1.7 SUMMARY

Graphical interfaces have replaced textual interfaces as the standard means for user–computer interaction. Graphics has also become a key technology for communicating ideas, data, and trends in most areas of commerce, science, engineering, and education. With graphics, we can create artificial realities, each a computer-based "exploratorium" for examining objects and phenomena in a natural and intuitive way that exploits our highly developed skills in visual-pattern recognition.

Until the late eighties, the bulk of computer-graphics applications dealt with 2D objects; 3D applications were relatively rare, both because 3D software is intrinsically far more complex than is 2D software and because a great deal of computing power is required to render pseudorealistic images. Therefore, until recently, real-time user interaction with 3D models and pseudorealistic images was feasible on only very expensive high-performance workstations with dedicated, special-purpose graphics hardware. The spectacular progress of VLSI semiconductor technology that was responsible for the advent of inexpensive microprocessors and memory led in the early 1980s to the creation of 2D, bitmap-graphics–based personal computers. That same technology has made it possible, less than a decade later, to create subsystems of only a few chips that do real-time 3D animation with color-shaded images of complex objects, typically described by thousands of polygons. These subsystems can be added as 3D accelerators to workstations or even to personal computers using commodity microprocessors. It is clear that an explosive growth of 3D applications will parallel the current growth in 2D applications. Furthermore, topics such as photorealistic rendering that were considered exotic in the 1982 edition of this book are now part of the state of the art and are available routinely in graphics software and increasingly in graphics hardware.

Much of the task of creating effective graphic communication, whether 2D or 3D, lies in modeling the objects whose images we want to produce. The graphics system acts as the intermediary between the application model and the output device. The application program is responsible for creating and updating the model based on user interaction; the graphics system does the best-understood, most routine part of the job when it creates views of objects and passes user events to the application. It is important to note that, although this separation between modeling and graphics was accepted practice at the time this book was written, our chapters on modeling (Chapters 11, 12, and 20) and animation (Chapter 21), as well as the growing literature on various types of physically based modeling, show that graphics is evolving to include a great deal more than rendering and interaction handling. Images and animations are no longer merely illustrations in science and engineering—they have become part of the content of science and engineering and are influencing how scientists and engineers conduct their daily work.

EXERCISES

1.1 List the interactive graphics programs you use on a routine basis in your "knowledge work": writing, calculating, graphing, programming, debugging, and so on. Which of these programs would work almost as well on an alphanumerics-only terminal?

1.2 The phrase "look and feel" has been applied extensively to the user interface of graphics programs. Itemize the major components—such as icons, windows, scroll bars, and menus—of the look of the graphics interface of your favorite word-processing or window-manager program. List the kinds of graphics capabilities these "widgets" require. What opportunities do you see for applying color and 3D depictions to the look? For example, how might a "cluttered office" be a more powerful spatial metaphor for organizing and accessing information than is a "messy desktop?"

1.3 In a similar vein to that of Exercise 1.2, what opportunities do you see for dynamic icons to augment or even to replace the static icons of current desktop metaphors?

1.4 Break down your favorite graphics application into its major modules, using the conceptual model of Figure 1.5 as a guide. How much of the application actually deals with graphics per se? How much deals with data-structure creation and maintainance? How much deals with calculations, such as simulation?

1.5 The terms *simulation* and *animation* are often used together and even interchangeably in computer graphics. This is natural when the behavioral (or structural) changes over time of some physical or abstract system are being visualized. Construct some examples of systems that could benefit from such visualizations. Specify what form the simulations would take and how they would be executed.

1.6 As a variation on Exercise 1.5, create a high-level design of a graphical "exploratorium" for a nontrivial topic in science, mathematics, or engineering. Discuss how the interaction sequences would work and what facilities the user should have for experimentation.

1.7 Consider an image containing a set of 10,000 1-inch unconnected vectors. Contrast the storage required for a vector display list with that for a 1-bit raster image for a 1024-by-1024 bilevel display to store this image. Assume that it takes a 8-bit "op-code" to specify "vector-draw," and four 10-bit coordinates (i.e., 6 bytes) to store a vector in the vector display list. How do these numbers vary as a function of the number and size of the vectors, the number of bits per pixel, and the resolution of the raster display? What conclusion can you draw about the relative sizes of refresh memory required?

1.8 Without peeking at Chapter 3, construct a straightforward algorithm for scan converting a line in the first quadrant.

1.9 Aliasing is a serious problem in that it produces unpleasant or even misleading visual artifacts. Discuss situations in which these artifacts matter, and those in which they do not. Discuss various ways to minimize the effects of jaggies, and explain what the "costs" of those remedies might be.

2

Programming in the Simple Raster Graphics Package (SRGP)

**Andries van Dam
and David F. Sklar**

In Chapter 1, we saw that vector and raster displays are two substantially different hardware technologies for creating images on the screen. Raster displays are now the dominant hardware technology, because they support several features that are essential to the majority of modern applications. First, raster displays can fill areas with a uniform color or a repeated pattern in two or more colors; vector displays can, at best, only simulate filled areas with closely spaced sequences of parallel vectors. Second, raster displays store images in a way that allows manipulation at a fine level: individual pixels can be read or written, and arbitrary portions of the image can be copied or moved.

The first graphics package we discuss, SRGP (Simple Raster Graphics Package), is a device-independent graphics package that exploits raster capabilities. SRGP's repertoire of primitives (lines, rectangles, circles and ellipses, and text strings) is similar to that of the popular Macintosh QuickDraw raster package and that of the Xlib package of the X Window System. Its interaction-handling features, on the other hand, are a subset of those of SPHIGS, the higher-level graphics package for displaying 3D primitives (covered in Chapter 7). SPHIGS (Simple PHIGS) is a simplified dialect of the standard PHIGS graphics package (Programmer's Hierarchical Interactive Graphics System) designed for both raster and vector hardware. Although SRGP and SPHIGS were written specifically for this text, they are also very much in the spirit of mainstream graphics packages, and most of what you will learn here is immediately applicable to commercial packages. In this book, we introduce both packages; for a more complete description, you should consult the reference manuals distributed with the software packages.

We start our discussion of SRGP by examining the operations that applications perform in order to draw on the screen: the specification of primitives and of the attributes that affect their image. (Since graphics printers display information essentially as raster displays do, we need not concern ourselves with them until we look more closely at hardware in Chapter 4.) Next we learn how to make applications interactive using SRGP's input procedures. Then we cover the utility of pixel manipulation, available only in raster displays. We conclude by discussing some limitations of integer raster graphics packages such as SRGP.

Although our discussion of SRGP assumes that it controls the entire screen, the package has been designed to run in window environments (see Chapter 10), in which case it controls the interior of a window as though it were a virtual screen. The application programmer therefore does not need to be concerned about the details of running under control of a window manager.

2.1 DRAWING WITH SRGP

2.1.1 Specification of Graphics Primitives

Drawing in integer raster graphics packages such as SRGP is like plotting graphs on graph paper with a very fine grid. The grid varies from 80 to 120 points per inch on conventional displays to 300 or more on high-resolution displays. The higher the resolution, the better the appearance of fine detail. Figure 2.1 shows a display screen (or the surface of a printer's paper or film) ruled in SRGP's integer Cartesian coordinate system. Note that pixels in SRGP lie at the intersection of grid lines.

The origin (0, 0) is at the bottom left of the screen; positive x increases toward the right and positive y increases toward the top. The pixel at the upper-right corner is (width-1, height-1), where width and height are the device-dependent dimensions of the screen.

On graph paper, we can draw a continuous line between two points located anywhere on the paper; on raster displays, however, we can draw lines only between grid points, and the line must be approximated by intensifying the grid-point pixels lying on it or nearest to it. Similarly, solid figures such as filled polygons or circles are created by intensifying the pixels in their interiors and on their boundaries. Since specifying each pixel of a line or closed figure would be far too onerous, graphics packages let the programmer specify primitives such as lines and polygons via their vertices; the package then fills in the details using scan-conversion algorithms, discussed in Chapter 3.

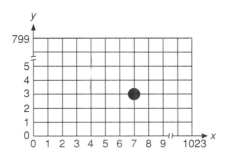

Fig. 2.1 Cartesian coordinate system of a screen 1024 pixels wide by 800 pixels high. Pixel (7, 3) is shown.

SRGP supports a basic collection of primitives: lines, polygons, circles and ellipses, and text.[1] To specify a primitive, the application sends the coordinates defining the primitive's shape to the appropriate SRGP primitive-generator procedure. It is legal for a specified point to lie outside the screen's bounded rectangular area; of course, only those portions of a primitive that lie inside the screen bounds will be visible.

Lines and polylines. The following SRGP procedure draws a line from $(x1, y1)$ to $(x2, y2)$:

> **void** SRGP_lineCoord (**int** $x1$, **int** $y1$, **int** $x2$, **int** $y2$);

Thus, to plot a line from $(0, 0)$ to $(100, 300)$, we simply call

> SRGP_lineCoord (0, 0, 100, 300);

Because it is often more natural to think in terms of endpoints rather than of individual x and y coordinates, SRGP provides an alternate line-drawing procedure:

> **void** SRGP_line (point $pt1$, point $pt2$);

Here "point" is a defined type, a record of two integers holding the point's x and y values:

> **typedef struct** {
>   **int** x, y;
> } point;

A sequence of lines connecting successive vertices is called a *polyline*. Although polylines can be created by repeated calls to the line-drawing procedures, SRGP includes them as a special case. There are two polyline procedures, analogous to the coordinate and point forms of the line-drawing procedures. These take arrays as parameters:

> **void** SRGP_polyLineCoord (**int** *vertexCount*, **int** **xArray*, **int** **yArray*);
> **void** SRGP_polyLine (**int** *vertexCount*, point **vertices*);

where "*xArray*," "*yArray*," and "*vertices*" are pointers to user-declared arrays—arrays of integers, integers, and points, respectively.

The first parameter in both of these polyline calls tells SRGP how many vertices to expect. In the first call, the second and third parameters are integer arrays of paired x and y values, and the polyline is drawn from vertex ($xArray$[0], $yArray$[0]), to vertex ($xArray$[1], $yArray$[1]), to vertex ($xArray$[2], $yArray$[2]), and so on. This form is convenient, for instance, when plotting data on a standard set of axes, where $xArray$ is a predetermined set

---

[1] Specialized procedures that draw a single pixel or an array of pixels are described in the SRGP reference manual.

[2] We use C with the following typesetting conventions. C keywords and built-in types are in boldface and user-defined types are in normal face. Symbolic constants are in uppercase type, and variables are italicized. Comments are in braces, and pseudocode is italicized. For brevity, declarations of constants and variables are omitted when obvious.

of values of the independent variable and *yArray* is the set of data being computed or input by the user. As an example, let us plot the output of an economic analysis program that computes month-by-month trade figures and stores them in the 12-entry integer data array *balanceOfTrade*. We will start our plot at (200, 200). To be able to see the differences between successive points, we will graph them 10 pixels apart on the *x* axis. Thus, we will create an integer array, *months*, to represent the 12 months, and will set the entries to the desired *x* values, 200, 210, . . ., 310. Similarly, we must increment each value in the data array by 200 to put the 12 *y* coordinates in the right place. Then, the graph in Fig. 2.2 is plotted with the following code:

```
/* Plot the axes */
SRGP_lineCoord (175, 200, 320, 200);
SRGP_lineCoord (200, 140, 200, 280);

/* Plot the data */
SRGP_polyLineCoord (12, months, balanceOfTrade);
```

We can use the second polyline form to draw shapes by specifying pairs of *x* and *y* values together as points, passing an array of such points to SRGP. We create the bowtie in Fig. 2.3 by calling

```
SRGP_polyLine (7, bowtieArray);
```

The table in Fig. 2.3 shows how *bowtieArray* was defined.

Markers and polymarkers. It is often convenient to place *markers* (e.g., dots, asterisks, or circles) at the data points on graphs. SRGP therefore offers companions to the line and polyline procedures. The following procedures will create a marker symbol centered at (*x*, *y*):

```
void SRGP_markerCoord (int x, int y);
void SRGP_marker (point pt);
```

The marker's style and size can be changed as well, as explained in Section 2.1.2. To create

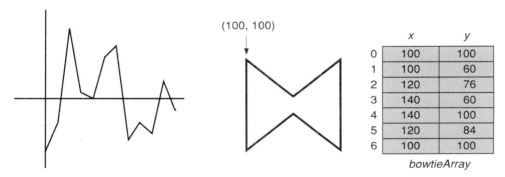

Fig. 2.2 Graphing a data array.   **Fig. 2.3** Drawing a polyline.

a sequence of identical markers at a set of points, we call either of

> **void** SRGP_polyMarkerCoord (**int** *vertexCount*, **int** *xArray*, **int** *yArray*);
> **void** SRGP_polyMarker (**int** *vertexCount*, point *vertices*);

Thus, the following additional call will add markers to the graph of Fig. 2.2 to produce Fig. 2.4.

> SRGP_polyMarkerCoord (12, *months*, *balanceOfTrade*);

Polygons and rectangles.   To draw an outline polygon, we can either specify a polyline that closes on itself by making the first and last vertices identical (as we did to draw the bowtie in Fig. 2.3), or we can use the following specialized SRGP call:

> **void** SRGP_polygon (**int** *vertexCount*, point *vertices*);

This call automatically closes the figure by drawing a line from the last vertex to the first. To draw the bowtie in Fig. 2.3 as a polygon, we use the following call, where *bowtieArray* is now an array of only six points:

> SRGP_polygon (6, *bowtieArray*);

Any rectangle can be specified as a polygon having four vertices, but an upright rectangle (one whose edges are parallel to the screen's edges) can also be specified with the SRGP "rectangle" primitive using only two vertices (the lower-left and the upper-right corners).

> **void** SRGP_rectangleCoord (**int** *leftX*, **int** *bottomY*, **int** *rightX*, **int** *topY*);
> **void** SRGP_rectanglePt (point *bottomLeft*, point *topRight*);
> **void** SRGP_rectangle (rectangle *rect*);

The "rectangle" record stores the bottom-left and top-right corners:

> **typedef struct** {
>   point *bottomLeft*, *topRight*;
> } rectangle;

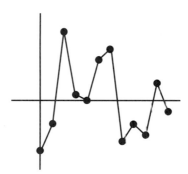

Fig. 2.4 Graphing the data array using markers.

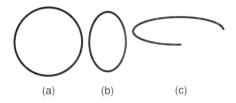

(a)   (b)   (c)

Fig. 2.5 Ellipse arcs.

Thus the following call draws an upright rectangle 101 pixels wide and 151 pixels high:

SRGP_rectangleCoord (50, 25, 150, 175);

SRGP provides the following utilities for creating rectangles and points from coordinate data.

point SRGP_defPoint (**int** x, **int** y);
rectangle SRGP_defRectangle (**int** *leftX*, **int** *bottomY*, **int** *rightX*, **int** *topY*);

Our example rectangle could thus have been drawn by

rect = SRGP_defRectangle (50, 25, 150, 175);
SRGP_rectangle (*rect*);

Circles and ellipses.   Figure 2.5 shows circular and elliptical arcs drawn by SRGP. Since circles are a special case of ellipses, we use the term *ellipse arc* for all these forms, whether circular or elliptical, closed or partial arcs. SRGP can draw only standard ellipses, those whose major and minor axes are parallel to the coordinate axes.

Although there are many mathematically equivalent methods for specifying ellipse arcs, it is convenient for the programmer to specify arcs via the upright rectangles in which they are inscribed (see Fig. 2.6); these upright rectangles are called *bounding boxes* or *extents*.

The width and height of the extent determine the shape of the ellipse. Whether or not the arc is closed depends on a pair of angles that specify where the arc starts and ends. For convenience, each angle is measured in *rectangular degrees* that run counterclockwise, with 0° corresponding to the positive portion of the x axis, 90° to the positive portion of the y

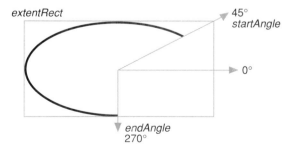

Fig. 2.6 Specifying ellipse arcs.

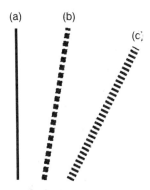

Fig. 2.7 Lines of various widths and styles.

axis, and 45° to the "diagonal" extending from the origin to the top-right corner of the rectangle. Clearly, only if the extent is a square are rectangular degrees equivalent to circular degrees.

The general ellipse procedure is

> **void** SRGP_ellipseArc (rectangle *extentRect*, **double** *startAngle*, **double** *endAngle*);

2.1.2 Attributes

Line style and line width. The appearance of a primitive can be controlled by specification of its *attributes*.[3] The SRGP attributes that apply to lines, polylines, polygons, rectangles, and ellipse arcs are *line style*, *line width*, *color*, and *pen style*.

Attributes are set *modally*; that is, they are global state variables that retain their values until they are changed explicitly. Primitives are drawn with the attributes in effect at the time the primitives are specified; therefore, changing an attribute's value in no way affects previously created primitives—it affects only those that are specified after the change in attribute value. Modal attributes are convenient because they spare programmers from having to specify a long parameter list of attributes for each primitive, since there may be dozens of different attributes in a production system.

Line style and line width are set by calls to

> **void** SRGP_setLineStyle (CONTINUOUS / DASHED / DOTTED/... lineStyle);[4]
> **void** SRGP_setLineWidth (**int** *width*);

The width of a line is measured in screen units—that is, in pixels. Each attribute has a default: line style is CONTINUOUS, and width is 1. Figure 2.7 shows lines in a variety of widths and styles; the code that generated the figure is shown in Fig. 2.8.

---

[3] The descriptions here of SRGP's attributes often lack fine detail, particularly on interactions between different attributes. The detail is omitted because the exact effect of an attribute is a function of its implementation, and, for performance reasons, different implementations are used on different systems; for these details, consult the implementation-specific reference manuals

[4] Here and in the following text, we use a shorthand notation. In SRGP, these symbolic constants are actually values of an enumerated data type "lineStyle."

```
SRGP_setLineWidth (5);
SRGP_lineCoord (55, 5, 55, 295);        /* Line a */

SRGP_setLineStyle (DASHED);
SRGP_setLineWidth (10);
SRGP_lineCoord (105, 5, 155, 295);      /* Line b */

SRGP_setLineWidth (15);
SRGP_setLineStyle (DOTTED);
SRGP_lineCoord (155, 5, 285, 255)       /* Line c */
```

Fig. 2.8 Code used to generate Fig. 2.7.

We can think of the line style as a bit mask used to write pixels selectively as the primitive is scan-converted by SRGP. A zero in the mask indicates that this pixel should not be written and thus preserves the original value of this pixel in the frame buffer. One can think of this pixel of the line as transparent, in that it lets the pixel "underneath" show through. CONTINUOUS thus corresponds to the string of all 1s, and DASHED to the string 1111001111001111 . . ., the dash being twice as long as the transparent interdash segments.

Each attribute has a default; for example, the default for line style is CONTINUOUS, that for line width is 1, and so on. In the early code examples, we did not set the line style for the first line we drew; thus, we made use of the line-style default. In practice, however, making assumptions about the current state of attributes is not safe, and in the code examples that follow we set attributes explicitly in each procedure, so as to make the procedures modular and thus to facilitate debugging and maintenance. In Section 2.1.4, we see that it is even safer for the programmer to save and restore attributes explicitly for each procedure.

Attributes that can be set for the marker primitive are

void SRGP_setMarkerSize (**int** *markerSize*);
void SRGP_setMarkerStyle (MARKER_CIRCLE / MARKER_SQUARE/... markerStyle);

Marker size specifies the length in pixels of the sides of the square extent of each marker. The complete set of marker styles is presented in the reference manual; the circle style is the default shown in Fig. 2.4.

Color.   Each of the attributes presented so far affects only some of the SRGP primitives, but the integer-valued color attribute affects all primitives. Obviously, the color attribute's meaning is heavily dependent on the underlying hardware; the two color values found on every system are 0 and 1. On bilevel systems, these colors' appearances are easy to predict—color-1 pixels are black and color-0 pixels are white for black-on-white devices, green is 1 and black is 0 for green-on-black devices, and so on.

The integer color attribute does not specify a color directly; rather, it is an index into SRGP's *color table*, each entry of which defines a color or gray-scale value in a manner that the SRGP programmer does not need to know about. There are 2^d entries in the color table, where d is the *depth* (number of bits stored for each pixel) of the frame buffer. On bilevel implementations, the color table is hardwired; on most color implementations, however,

SRGP allows the application to modify the table. Some of the many uses for the indirectness provided by color tables are explored in Chapters 4 17, and 21.

There are two methods that applications can use to specify colors. An application for which machine independence is important should use the integers 0 and 1 directly; it will then run on all bilevel and color displays. If the application assumes color support or is written for a particular display device, then it can use the implementation-dependent *color names* supported by SRGP. These names are symbolic constants that show where certain standard colors have been placed within the default color table for that display device. For instance, a black-on-white implementation provides the two color names COLOR_BLACK (1) and COLOR_WHITE (0); we use these two values in the sample code fragments in this chapter. Note that color names are not useful to applications that modify the color table.

We select a color by calling

void SRGP_setColor (**int** *colorIndex*);

2.1.3   Filled Primitives and Their Attributes

Primitives that enclose areas (the so-called *area-defining* primitives) can be drawn in two ways: *outlined* or *filled*. The procedures described in the previous section generate the former style: closed outlines with unfilled interiors. SRGP's filled versions of area-defining primitives draw the interior pixels with no outline. Figure 2.9 shows SRGP's repertoire of filled primitives, including the filled ellipse arc, or *pie slice*.

Note that SRGP does not draw a contrasting outline, such as a 1-pixel-thick solid boundary, around the interior; applications wanting such an outline must draw it explicitly. There is also a subtle issue of whether pixels on the border of an area-defining primitive should actually be drawn or whether only pixels that lie strictly in the interior should. This problem is discussed in detail in Sections 3.5 and 3.6.

To generate a filled polygon, we use SRGP_fillPolygon or SRGP_fillPolygonCoord, with the same parameter lists used in the unfilled versions of these calls. We define the other area-filling primitives in the same way, by prefixing "fill" to their names. Since polygons

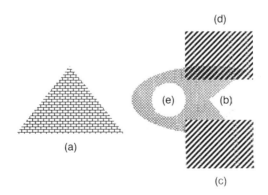

Fig. 2.9 Filled primitives. (a–c) Bitmap pattern opaque. (d) Bitmap pattern transparent. (e) Solid.

may be concave or even self-intersecting, we need a rule for specifying what regions are interior and thus should be filled, and what regions are exterior. SRGP polygons follow the *odd-parity* rule. To determine whether a region lies inside or outside a given polygon, choose as a test point any point inside the particular region. Next, choose a ray that starts at the test point and extends infinitely in any direction, and that does not pass through any vertices. If this ray intersects the polygon outline an odd number of times, the region is considered to be interior (see Fig. 2.10).

SRGP does not actually perform this test for each pixel while drawing; rather, it uses the optimized polygon scan-conversion techniques described in Chapter 3, in which the odd-parity rule is efficiently applied to an entire row of adjacent pixels that lie either inside or outside. Also, the odd-parity ray-intersection test is used in a process called *pick correlation* to determine the object a user is selecting with the cursor, as described in Chapter 7.

Fill style and fill pattern for areas.   The fill-style attribute can be used to control the appearance of a filled primitive's interior in four different ways, using

> **void** SRGP_setFillStyle (
> SOLID / BITMAP_PATTERN_OPAQUE / BITMAP_PATTERN_TRANSPARENT /
> PIXMAP_PATTERN drawStyle);

The first option, SOLID, produces a primitive uniformly filled with the current value of the color attribute (Fig. 2.9e, with color set to COLOR_WHITE). The second two options, BITMAP_PATTERN_OPAQUE and BITMAP_PATTERN_TRANSPARENT, fill primitives with a regular, nonsolid pattern, the former rewriting all pixels underneath in either the current color, or another color (Fig. 2.9c), the latter rewriting some pixels underneath the primitive in the current color, but letting others show through (Fig. 2.9d). The last option, PIXMAP_PATTERN, writes patterns containing an arbitrary number of colors, always in opaque mode.

Bitmap fill patterns are bitmap arrays of 1s and 0s chosen from a table of available

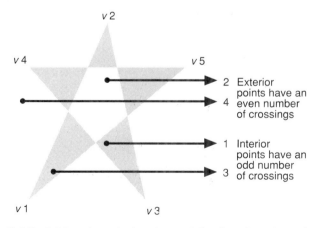

Fig. 2.10 Odd-parity rule for determining interior of a polygon.

patterns by specifying

  void SRGP_ setFillBitmapPattern (**int** *patternIndex*):

Each entry in the pattern table stores a unique pattern; the ones provided with SRGP, shown in the reference manual, include gray-scale tones (ranging from nearly black to nearly white) and various regular and random patterns. In transparent mode, these patterns are generated as follows. Consider any pattern in the pattern table as a small bitmap—say, 8 by 8—to be repeated as needed (*tiled*) to fill the primitive. On a bilevel system, the current color (in effect, the *foreground* color) is written where there are 1s in the pattern; where there are 0s—the "holes"—the corresponding pixels of the original image are not written, and thus "show through" the partially transparent primitive written on top. Thus, the bitmap pattern acts as a "memory write-enable mask" for patterns in transparent mode, much as the line-style bit mask did for lines and outline primitives.

  In the more commonly used BITMAP_PATTERN_OPAQUE mode, the 1s are written in the current color, but the 0s are written in another color, the *background color,* previously set by

  void SRGP_ setBackgroundColor (**int** *colorIndex*);

On bilevel displays, each bitmap pattern in OPAQUE mode can generate only two distinctive fill patterns. For example, a bitmap pattern of mostly 1s can be used on a black-and-white display to generate a dark-gray fill pattern if the current color is set to black (and the background to white), and a light-gray fill pattern if the current color is set to white (and the background to black). On a color display, any combination of a foreground and a background color may be used for a variety of two-tone effects. A typical application on a bilevel display always sets the background color whenever it sets the foreground color, since opaque bitmap patterns are not visible if the two are equal; an application could create a SetColor procedure to set the background color automatically to contrast with the foreground whenever the foreground color is set explicitly.

  Figure 2.9 was created by the code fragment shown in Fig. 2.11. The advantage of

```
SRGP_ setFillStyle (BITMAP_PATTERN_OPAQUE);
SRGP_ setFillBitmapPattern (BRICK_BIT_PATTERN);            /* Brick pattern */
SRGP_ fillPolygon (3, triangleCoords);                     /* a */

SRGP_ setFillBitmapPattern (MEDIUM_GRAY_BIT_PATTERN);      /* 50 percent gray */
SRGP_ fillEllipseArc (ellipseArcRect, 60.0, 290.0);        /* b */

SRGP_ setFillBitmapPattern (DIAGONAL_BIT_PATTERN);
SRGP_ fillRectangle (opaqueFilledRect);                    /* c */

SRGP_ setFillStyle (BITMAP_PATTERN_TRANSPARENT);
SRGP_ fillRectangle (transparentFilledRect);              /* d */

SRGP_ setFillStyle (SOLID);
SRGP_ setColor (COLOR_WHITE);
SRGP_ fillEllipse (circleRect);                           /* e */
```

Fig. 2.11 Code used to generate Fig. 2.9.

having two-tone bitmap patterns is that the colors are not specified explicitly, but rather are determined by the color attributes in effect, and thus can be generated in any color combination. The disadvantage, and the reason that SRGP also supports pixmap patterns, is that only two colors can be generated. Often, we would like to fill an area of a display with multiple colors, in an explicitly specified pattern. In the same way that a bitmap pattern is a small bitmap used to tile the primitive, a small pixmap can be used to tile the primitive, where the pixmap is a pattern array of color-table indices. Since each pixel is explicitly set in the pixmap, there is no concept of holes, and therefore there is no distinction between transparent and opaque filling modes. To fill an area with a color pattern, we select a fill style of PIXMAP_PATTERN and use the corresponding pixmap pattern-selection procedure:

> **void** SRGP_ setFillPixmapPattern (**int** *patternIndex*);

Since both bitmap and pixmap patterns generate pixels with color values that are indices into the current color table, the appearance of filled primitives changes if the programmer modifies the color-table entries. The SRGP reference manual discusses how to change or add to both the bitmap and pixmap pattern tables. Also, although SRGP provides default entries in the bitmap pattern table, it does not give a default pixmap pattern table, since there is an indefinite number of color pixmap patterns that might be useful.

Pen pattern for outlines.   The advantages of patterning are not restricted to the use of this technique in area-defining primitives; patterning can also be used to affect the appearance of lines and outline primitives, via the *pen-style* attribute. Using the line-width, line-style, and pen-style attributes, it is possible, for example, to create a 5-pixel-thick, dot-dashed ellipse whose thick dashes are patterned. Examples of solid and dashed thick lines with various patterns in transparent and opaque mode and their interactions with previously drawn primitives are shown in Fig. 2.12; the code that generated the image is in Fig. 2.13. The use of a pen pattern for extremely narrow lines (1 or 2 pixels wide) is not recommended, because the pattern is not discernible in such cases.

The interaction between line style and pen style is simple: 0s in the line-style mask

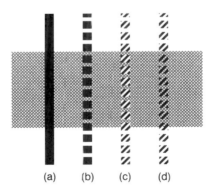

(a)   (b)   (c)   (d)

Fig. 2.12 Interaction between pen style and line style. (a) Continuous solid. (b) Dashed solid. (c) Dashed bitmap pattern opaque. (d) Dashed bitmap pattern transparent.

```
/* We show only the drawing of the lines, not the background rectangle. */
/* We draw the lines in order from left to right */

SRGP_setLineWidth (15);     /* Thick lines show the interaction better. */

SRGP_setLineStyle (CONTINUOUS);
SRGP_setPenStyle (SOLID);
SRGP_line (pta1, pta2);      /* a: Solid, continuous */

SRGP_setLineStyle (DASHED);
SRGP_line (ptb1, ptb2);      /* b: Solid, dashed */

SRGP_setPenBitmapPattern (DIAGONAL_BIT_PATTERN);
SRGP_setPenStyle (BITMAP_PATTERN_OPAQUE);
SRGP_line (ptc1, ptc2);      /* c: Dashed, bitmap pattern opaque */

SRGP_setPenStyle (BITMAP_PATTERN_TRANSPARENT);
SRGP_line (ptd1, ptd2);      /* d: Dashed, bitmap pattern transparent */
```

Fig. 2.13 Code used to generate Fig. 2.12.

fully protect the pixels on which they fall, so the pen style influences only those pixels for which the line-style mask is 1.

Pen style is selected with the same four options and the same patterns as fill style. The same bitmap and pixmap pattern tables are also used, but separate indices are maintained so that resetting a pen style's pattern index will not affect the fill style's pattern index.

```
void SRGP_setPenStyle (SOLID / BITMAP_PATTERN_OPAQUE/... drawStyle);
void SRGP_setPenBitmapPattern (int patternIndex);
void SRGP_setPenPixmapPattern (int patternIndex);
```

Application screen background. We have defined "background color" as the color of the 0 bits in bitmap patterns used in opaque mode, but the term *background* is used in another, unrelated way. Typically, the user expects the screen to display primitives on some uniform *application screen background pattern* that covers an opaque window or the entire screen. The application screen background pattern is often solid color 0, since SRGP initializes the screen to that color upon initialization. However, the background pattern is sometimes nonsolid, or solid of some other color; in these cases, the application is responsible for setting up the application screen background by drawing a full-screen rectangle of the desired pattern, before drawing any other primitives.

A common technique to "erase" primitives is to redraw them in the application screen background pattern, rather than redrawing the entire image each time a primitive is deleted. However, this "quick and dirty" updating technique yields a damaged image when the erased primitive overlaps with other primitives. For example, assume that the screen background pattern in Fig. 2.9 is solid white and that we erase the rectangle marked (c) by redrawing it using solid COLOR_WHITE. This would leave a white gap in the filled ellipse arc (b) underneath. "Damage repair" involves going back to the application database and respecifying primitives (see Exercise 2.9).

2.1.4   Saving and Restoring Attributes

As you can see, SRGP supports a variety of attributes for its various primitives. Individual attributes can be saved for later restoration; this feature is especially useful in designing application procedures that perform their functions without side effects—that is, without affecting the global attribute state. For each attribute-setting SRGP procedure, there is a corresponding inquiry procedure that can be used to determine the current value; for example,

> lineStyle SRGP_inquireLineStyle (**void**);

For convenience, SRGP allows the inquiry and restoration of the entire set of attributes—called the *attribute group*—via

> **void** SRGP_inquireAttributes (*attributeGroup* *group*);
> **void** SRGP_setAttributes (*attributeGroup* *group*);

In the current implementation of SRGP, unlike in previous versions, the application program can access the internal fields of the attributeGroup structure. Directly modifying these fields, however, is a bit tricky and the programmer does so at her own risk.

2.1.5   Text

Specifying and implementing text drawing is always complex in a graphics package, because of the large number of options and attributes text can have. Among these are the style or *font* of the characters (Times Roman, Helvetica, Clarinda, etc.), their appearance ("Roman," **bold**, *italic*, underlined, etc.), their size (typically measured in *points*[5]) and widths, the intercharacter spacing, the spacing between consecutive lines, the angle at which characters are drawn (horizontal, vertical, or at a specified angle), and so on.

The most rudimentary facility, typically found in simple hardware and software, is fixed-width, monospace character spacing, in which all characters occupy the same width, and the spacing between them is constant. At the other end of the spectrum, proportional spacing varies both the width of characters and the spacing between them to make the text as legible and aesthetically pleasing as possible. Books, magazines, and newspapers all use proportional spacing, as do most raster graphics displays and laser printers. SRGP provides in-between functionality: Text is horizontally aligned, character widths vary, but space between characters is constant. With this simple form of proportional spacing, the application can annotate graphics diagrams, interact with the user via textual menus and fill-in forms, and even implement simple word processors. Text-intensive applications, however, such as desktop-publishing programs for high-quality documents, need special-ized packages that offer more control over text specification and attributes than does SRGP. PostScript [ADOB87] offers many such advanced features and has become an industry standard for describing text and other primitives with a large variety of options and attributes.

---

[5]A point is a unit commonly used in the publishing industry; it is equal to approximately $\frac{1}{72}$ inch.

Text is generated by a call to

void SRGP_ text (point *origin*, **char** *∗text*);

The location of a text primitive is controlled by specification of its *origin*, also known as its *anchor point*. The *x* coordinate of the origin marks the left edge of the first character, and the y coordinate specifies where the baseline of the string should appear. (The *baseline* is the hypothetical line on which characters rest, as shown in the textual menu button of Fig. 2.14. Some characters, such as "y" and "q," have a tail, called the *descender*, that goes below the baseline.)

A text primitive's appearance is determined by only two attributes, the current color and the font, which is an index into an implementation-dependent table of fonts in various sizes and styles:

void SRGP_ setFont (**int** *fontIndex*);

Each character in a font is defined as a rectangular bitmap, and SRGP draws a character by filling a rectangle using the character's bitmap as a pattern, in bitmap-pattern-transparent mode. The 1s in the bitmap define the character's interior, and the 0s specify the surrounding space and gaps such as the hole in "o." (Some more sophisticated packages define characters in pixmaps, allowing a character's interior to be patterned.)

Formatting text.   Because SRGP implementations offer a restricted repertoire of fonts and sizes, and because implementations on different hardware rarely offer equivalent repertoires, an application has limited control over the height and width of text strings. Since text-extent information is needed in order to produce well-balanced compositions (for instance, to center a text string within a rectangular frame), SRGP provides the following procedure for querying the extent of a given string using the current value of the font attribute:

void SRGP_ inquireTextExtent (
      char *∗text*, **int** *∗width*, **int** *∗height*, **int** *∗descent*);

Although SRGP does not support bitmap opaque mode for writing characters, such a mode can be simulated easily. As an example, the procedure in Fig. 2.15 shows how extent

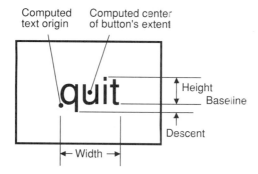

Fig. 2.14 Dimensions of text centered within a rectangular button and points computed from these dimensions for centering purposes.

```
void MakeQuitButton (rectangle buttonRect)
{
    point centerOfButton, textOrigin;
    int width, height, descent;

    SRGP_setFillStyle (SOLID);
    SRGP_setColor (COLOR_WHITE);
    SRGP_fillRectangle (buttonRect);
    SRGP_setColor (COLOR_BLACK);
    SRGP_setLineWidth (2);
    SRGP_Rectangle (buttonRect);

    SRGP_inquireTextExtent ("quit", &width, &height, &descent);

    centerOfButton.x = (buttonRect.bottomLeft.x + buttonRect.topRight.x) / 2;
    centerOfButton.y = (buttonRect.bottomLeft.y + buttonRect.topRight.y) / 2;

    textOrigin.x = centerOfButton.x - (width / 2);
    textOrigin.y = centerOfButton.y - (height / 2);

    SRGP_text (textOrigin,"quit");
}   /* MakeQuitButton */
```

Fig. 2.15 Code used to create Fig. 2.14.

information and text-specific attributes can be used to produce black text, in the current font, centered within a white enclosing rectangle, as shown in Fig. 2.14. The procedure first creates the background button rectangle of the specified size, with a separate border, and then centers the text within it. Exercise 2.10 is a variation on this theme.

2.2 BASIC INTERACTION HANDLING

Now that we know how to draw basic shapes and text, the next step is to learn how to write interactive programs that communicate effectively with the user, using input devices such as the keyboard and the mouse. First, we look at general guidelines for making effective and pleasant-to-use interactive programs; then, we discuss the fundamental notion of logical (abstract) input devices. Finally, we look at SRGP's mechanisms for dealing with various aspects of interaction handling.

2.2.1 Human Factors

The designer of an interactive program must deal with many matters that do not arise in a noninteractive, batch program. These are the so-called *human factors* of a program, such as its interaction style (often called ''look and feel'') and its ease of learning and of use, and they are as important as its functional completeness and correctness. Techniques for user–computer interaction that exhibit good human factors are studied in more detail in Chapters 8 and 9. The guidelines discussed there include these:

- Provide *simple and consistent* interaction sequences.
- *Do not overload the user* with too many different options and styles.
- *Show the available options clearly* at every stage of the interaction.
- *Give appropriate feedback* to the user.
- Allow the users to *recover gracefully* from mistakes.

We attempt to follow these guidelines for good human factors in our sample programs. For example, we typically use menus to allow the user to indicate the next function he wants to execute by picking a text button in a menu of such buttons with a mouse. Also common are *palettes* (iconic menus) of basic geometric primitives, application-specific symbols, or fill patterns. Menus and palettes satisfy our first three guidelines in that their entries prompt the user with the list of available options and provide a single, consistent way of choosing among these options. Unavailable options may be either deleted temporarily or "grayed out" by being drawn in a low-intensity gray-scale pattern rather than a solid color (see Exercise 2.15).

Feedback occurs at every step of a menu operation to satisfy the fourth guideline: The application program will *highlight* the menu choice or object selection—for example, display it in inverse video or framed in a rectangle—to draw attention to it. The package itself may also provide an *echo* that gives an immediate response to the manipulation of an input device. For example, characters appear immediately at the position of the cursor as keyboard input is typed; as the mouse is moved on the table or desktop, a cursor echoes the corresponding location on the screen. Graphics packages offer a variety of cursor shapes that can be used by the application program to reflect the state of the program. In many display systems, the cursor shape can be varied dynamically as a function of the cursor's position on the screen. In many word-processing programs, for example, the cursor is shown as an arrow in menu areas and as a blinking vertical bar in text areas.

Graceful error recovery, our fifth guideline, is usually provided through *cancel* and *undo/redo* features. These require the application program to maintain a record of operations (see Chapter 9).

2.2.2 Logical Input Devices

Device types in SRGP. A major goal in designing graphics packages is device-independence, which enhances portability of applications. SRGP achieves this goal for graphics output by providing primitives specified in terms of an abstract integer coordinate system, thus shielding the application from the need to set the individual pixels in the frame buffer. To provide a level of abstraction for graphics input, SRGP supports a set of *logical input devices* that shield the application from the details of the physical input devices available. The two logical devices supported by SRGP are

- *Locator,* a device for specifying screen coordinates and the state of one or more associated buttons
- *Keyboard,* a device for specifying character string input

SRGP maps the logical devices onto the physical devices available (e.g., the locator could map to a mouse, joystick, tablet, or touch-sensitive screen). This mapping of logical to physical is familiar from conventional procedural languages and operating systems, where I/O devices such as terminals, disks, and tape drives are abstracted to logical data files to achieve both device-independence and simplicity of application programming.

Device handling in other packages.   SRGP's input model is essentially a subset of the GKS and PHIGS input models. SRGP implementations support only one logical locator and one keyboard device, whereas GKS and PHIGS allow multiple devices of each type. Those packages also support additional device types: the *stroke* device (returning a polyline of cursor positions entered with the physical locator), the *choice* device (abstracting a function-key pad and returning a key identifier), the *valuator* (abstracting a slider or control dial and returning a floating-point number), and the *pick* device (abstracting a pointing device, such as a mouse or data tablet, with an associated button to signify a selection, and returning the identification of the logical entity picked). Other packages, such as QuickDraw and the X Window System, handle input devices in a more device-dependent way that gives the programmer finer control over an individual device's operation, at the cost of greater application-program complexity.

Chapter 8 presents the history of logical devices and elaborates further on their properties. Here, we briefly summarize modes of interacting with logical devices in general, and then examine SRGP's interaction procedures in more detail.

2.2.3   Sampling Versus Event-Driven Processing

There are two fundamental techniques for receiving information created by user interactions. In *sampling* (also called *polling*), the application program queries a logical input device's current value (called the *measure* of the device) and continues execution. The sampling is performed regardless of whether the device's measure has changed since the last sampling; indeed, only by continuous sampling of the device will changes in the device's state be known to the application. This mode is costly for interactive applications, because they would spend most of their CPU cycles in tight sampling loops waiting for measure changes.

An alternative to the CPU-intensive polling loop is the use of *interrupt-driven* interaction; in this technique, the application enables one or more devices for input and then continues normal execution until interrupted by some input *event* (a change in a device's state caused by user action); control then passes asynchronously to an interrupt procedure, which responds to the event. For each input device, an *event trigger* is defined; the event trigger is the user action that causes an event to occur. Typically, the trigger is a button push, such as a press of the mouse button (''mouse down'') or a press of a keyboard key.

To free applications programmers from the tricky and difficult aspects of asynchronous transfer of control, many graphics packages, including GKS, PHIGS, and SRGP, offer *event-driven* interaction as a synchronous simulation of interrupt-driven interaction. In this technique, an application enables devices and then continues execution. In the background, the package monitors the devices and stores information about each event in an *event queue* (Fig. 2.16). The application, at its convenience, checks the event queue and processes the

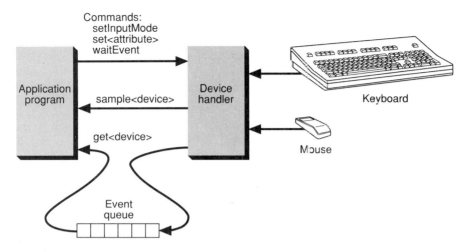

Fig. 2.16 Sampling versus event-handling using the event queue.

events in temporal order. In effect, the application specifies when it would like to be "interrupted."

When an application checks the event queue, it specifies whether it would like to enter a wait state. If the queue contains one or more event reports, the head event (representing the event that occurred earliest) is removed, and its information is made available to the application. If the queue is empty and a wait state is not desired, the application is informed that no event is available and it is free to continue execution. If the queue is empty and a wait state is desired, the application pauses until the next event occurs or until an application-specified maximum-wait-time interval passes. In effect, event mode replaces polling of the input devices with the much more efficient waiting on the event queue.

In summary, in sampling mode, the device is polled and an event measure is collected, regardless of any user activity. In event mode, the application either gets an event report from a prior user action or waits until a user action (or timeout) occurs. It is this "respond only when the user acts" behavior of event mode that is the essential difference between sampled and event-driven input. Event-driven programming may seem more complex than sampling, but you are already familiar with a similar technique used with the scanf function in a C program: C enables the keyboard, and the application waits in the scanf until the user has completed entering a line of text. You can access individual key-press events in C using the getc function.

Simple event-driven programs in SRGP or similar packages follow the reactive "ping-pong" interaction introduced in Section 1.6.4 and pseudocoded in Fig. 2.17; it can be nicely modeled as a finite-state automaton. More complex styles of interaction, allowing simultaneous program and user activity, are discussed in Chapters 8 through 10.

Event-driven applications typically spend most of their time in a wait state, since interaction is dominated by "think time" during which the user decides what to do next; even in fast-paced game applications, the number of events a user can generate in a second

```
initialize, including generating the initial image;
activate interactive device(s) in event mode;
while (user has not requested quit) {      /* main event loop */
    wait for user-triggered event on any of several devices;
    switch (device that caused event) {
        case DEVICE_1: collect DEVICE_1 event measure data, process, respond;
        case DEVICE_2: collect DEVICE_2 event measure data, process, respond;
        . . .

    }
}
```

Fig. 2.17 Event-driven interaction scheme.

is a fraction of what the application could handle. Since SRGP typically implements event mode using true (hardware) interrupts, the wait state effectively uses no CPU time. On a multitasking system, the advantage is obvious: The event-mode application requires CPU time only for short bursts of activity immediately following user action, thereby freeing the CPU for other tasks.

One other point, about correct use of event mode, should be mentioned. Although the queueing mechanism does allow program and user to operate asynchronously, the user should not be allowed to get too far ahead of the program, because each event should result in an echo as well as some feedback from the application program. It is true that experienced users have learned to use "typeahead" to type in parameters such as file names or even operating-system commands while the system is processing earlier requests, especially if at least a character-by-character echo is provided immediately. In contrast, "mouseahead" for graphical commands is generally not as useful (and is much more dangerous), because the user usually needs to see the screen updated to reflect the application model's current state before the next graphical interaction.

2.2.4 Sample Mode

Activating, deactivating, and setting the mode of a device.   The following procedure is used to activate or deactivate a device; it takes a device and a mode as parameters:

void SRGP_setInputMode (
        LOCATOR / KEYBOARD inputDevice, INACTIVE / SAMPLE / EVENT inputMode);

Thus, to set the locator to sample mode, we call

    SRGP_setInputMode (LOCATOR, SAMPLE):

Initially, both devices are inactive. Placing a device in a mode in no way affects the other input device—both may be active simultaneously and even then need not be in the same mode.

The locator's measure.   The locator is a logical abstraction of a mouse or data tablet, returning the cursor position as a screen (x, y) coordinate pair, the number of the button which most recently experienced a transition, and the state of the buttons as a *chord* array (since multiple buttons can be pressed simultaneously). The second field lets the application know which button caused the trigger for that event.

```
typedef struct {
    point position;
    int buttonOfMostRecentTransition;
    enum {UP, DOWN} buttonChord[MAX_BUTTON_COUNT];      /* Typically 1 to 3 */
} locatorMeasure;
```

Having activated the locator in sample mode with the SRGP_setInputMode procedure, we can ask its current measure using

void SRGP_sampleLocator (locatorMeasure *measure);

Let us examine the prototype sampling application shown in Fig. 2.18: a simple "painting" loop involving only button 1 on the locator. Such painting entails leaving a trail of paint where the user has dragged the locator while holding down this button; the locator is sampled in a loop as the user moves it. First, we must detect when the user starts painting by sampling the button until it is depressed; then, we place the paint (a filled rectangle in our simple example) at each sample point until the user releases the button.

The results of this sequence are crude: the paint rectangles are arbitrarily close together or far apart, with their density completely dependent on how far the locator was moved between consecutive samples. The sampling rate is determined essentially by the speed at which the CPU runs the operating system, the package, and the application.

Sample mode is available for both logical devices; however, the keyboard device is almost always operated in event mode, so techniques for sampling it are not addressed here.

2.2.5   Event Mode

Using event mode for initiation of sampling loop.   Although the two sampling loops of the painting example (one to detect the button-down transition, the other to paint until

```
set up color/pattern attributes, and brush size in halfBrushHeight and halfBrushWidth;
SRGP_setInputMode (LOCATOR, SAMPLE);

/* First, sample until the button goes down. */
do {
    SRGP_sampleLocator (&locMeasure);
} while (locMeasure.buttonChord[0] == UP);

/* Perform the painting loop: */
/* Continuously place brush and then sample, until button is released. */
do {
    rect = SRGP_defRectangle (locMeasure.position.x - halfBrushWidth,
                              locMeasure.position.y - halfBrushHeight,
                              locMeasure.position.x + halfBrushWidth,
                              locMeasure.position.y + halfBrushHeight);
    SRGP_fillRectangle (rect);
    SRGP_sampleLocator (&locMeasure);
} while (locMeasure.buttonChord[0] == DOWN);
```

Fig. 2.18 Sampling loop for painting.

the button-up transition) certainly do the job, they put an unnecessary load on the CPU. Although this may not be a serious concern in a personal computer, it is not advisable in a system running multiple tasks, let alone doing time-sharing. Although it is certainly necessary to sample the locator repetitively for the painting loop itself (because we need to know the position of the locator at all times while the button is down), we do not need to use a sampling loop to wait for the button-down event that initiates the painting interaction. Event mode can be used when there is no need for measure information while waiting for an event.

SRGP_waitEvent.   At any time after SRGP_setInputMode has activated a device in event mode, the program may inspect the event queue by entering the wait state with

> inputDevice SRGP_ waitEvent (**int** *maxWaitTime*);

The procedure returns immediately if the queue is not empty; otherwise, the first parameter specifies the maximum amount of time (measured in ⅟₆₀ second) for which the procedure should wait for an event if the queue is empty. A negative *maxWaitTime* (specified by the symbolic constant INDEFINITE) causes the procedure to wait indefinitely, whereas a value of zero causes it to return immediately, regardless of the state of the queue.

The identity of the device that issued the head event is returned in the *device* parameter. The special value NO_DEVICE is returned if no event was available within the specified time limit—that is, if the device timed out. The device type can then be tested to determine how the head event's measure should be retrieved (described later in this section).

The keyboard device.   The trigger event for the keyboard device depends on the *processing mode* in which the keyboard device has been placed. EDIT mode is used when the application receives strings (e.g., file names, commands) from the user, who types and edits the string and then presses the Return key to trigger the event. In RAW mode, used for interactions in which the keyboard must be monitored closely, every key press triggers an event. The application uses the following procedure to set the processing mode.

> **void** SRGP_ setKeyboardProcessingMode (EDIT / RAW keyboardMode);

In EDIT mode, the user can type entire strings, correcting them with the backspace key as necessary, and then use the Return (or Enter) key as trigger. This mode is used when the user is to type in an entire string, such as a file name or a figure label. All control keys except backspace and Return are ignored, and the measure is the string as it appears at the time of the trigger. In RAW mode, on the other hand, each character typed, including control characters, is a trigger and is returned individually as the measure. This mode is used when individual keyboard characters act as commands—for example, for moving the cursor, for simple editing operations, or for video-game actions. RAW mode provides no echo, whereas EDIT mode echoes the string on the screen and displays a *text cursor* (such as an underscore or block character) where the next character to be typed will appear. Each backspace causes the text cursor to back up and to erase one character.

When SRGP_waitEvent returns the device code KEYBOARD, the application obtains the measure associated with the event by calling

> void SRGP_ getKeyboard (**char** *measure. **int** measureSize);

When the keyboard device is active in RAW mode, its measure is always exactly one character in length. In this case, the first character of the measure string returns the RAW measure.

The program shown in Fig. 2.19 demonstrates the use of EDIT mode. It receives a list of file names from the user, deleting each file so entered. When the user enters a null string (by pressing Return without typing any other characters), the interaction ends. During the interaction, the program waits indefinitely for the user to enter the next string.

Although this code explicitly specifies where the text prompt is to appear, it does not specify where the user's input string is typed (and corrected with the backspace). The location of this keyboard echo is specified by the programmer, as discussed in Section 2.2.7.

The locator device. The trigger event for the locator device is a press or release of a mouse button. When SRGP_waitEvent returns the device code LOCATOR, the application obtains the measure associated with the event by calling

> void SRGP_ getLocator (locatorMeasure *measure);

Typically, the *position* field of the measure is used to determine in which area of the screen the user designated the point. For example, if the locator cursor is in a rectangular region where a menu button is displayed, the event should be interpreted as a request for some action; if it is in the main drawing area, the point might be inside a previously drawn object to indicate it should be selected, or in an "empty" region to indicate where a new object should be placed.

The pseudocode shown in Fig. 2.20 (similar to that shown previously for the keyboard) implements another use of the locator, letting the user specify points at which markers are to be placed. The user exits the marker-placing loop by pressing the locator button while the cursor points to a screen button, a rectangle containing the text ' quit.''

In this example, only the user's pressing of locator button 1 is significant; releases of the button are ignored. Note that the button must be released before the next button-press event can take place—the event is triggered by a transition, not by a button state. Furthermore, to ensure that events coming from the other buttons do not disturb this

```
SRGP_ setInputMode (KEYBOARD, EVENT);      /* Assume only the keyboard is active. */
SRGP_ setKeyboardProcessingMode (EDIT);
pt = SRGP_ defPoint (100, 100);
SRGP_ text (pt, "Specify one or more files to be deleted; to exit, press Return. ');

/* main event loop */
do {
    device = SRGP_ waitEvent (INDEFINITE);
    SRGP_ getKeyboard (measure, measureSize).
    if (*measure != NULL)
        DeleteFile (measure);                      /* DeleteFile does confirmation, etc. */
} while (*measure != NULL);
```

Fig. 2.19 EDIT-mode keyboard interaction.

```
const int QUIT_BUTTON = 0, QUIT_MASK = 0x1;

create the on-screen Quit button;
SRGP_setLocatorButtonMask (QUIT_MASK);
SRGP_setInputMode (LOCATOR, EVENT);        /* Assume only locator is active. */

/* main event loop */
terminate = FALSE;
while (!terminate) {
    device = SRGP_waitEvent (INDEFINITE);
    SRGP_getLocator (&measure);
    if (measure.buttonChord[QUIT_BUTTON] == DOWN) {
        if (PickedQuitButton (measure.position))
            terminate = TRUE;
        else
            SRGP_marker (measure.position);
    }
}
```

Fig. 2.20 Locator interaction.

interaction, the application tells SRGP which buttons are to trigger a locator event by calling

void SRGP_setLocatorButtonMask (**int** *activeButtons*);

The default locator-button mask is set to one, but no matter what the mask is, all buttons always have a measure. On implementations that support fewer than three buttons, references to any nonexistent buttons are simply ignored by SRGP, and these buttons' measures always contain UP.

The function PickedQuitButton compares the measure position against the bounds of the quit button rectangle and returns a Boolean value signifying whether or not the user picked the quit button. This process is a simple example of *pick correlation*, as discussed in in the next section.

Waiting for multiple events.   The code fragments in Figs. 2.19 and 2.20 did not illustrate event mode's greatest advantage: the ability to wait for more than one device at the same time. SRGP queues events of enabled devices in chronological order and lets the application program take the first one off the queue when SRGP_waitEvent is called. Unlike hardware interrupts, which are processed in order of priorities, events are thus processed strictly in temporal order. The application examines the returned device code to determine which device caused the event.

The procedure shown in Fig. 2.21 allows the user to place any number of small circle markers anywhere within a rectangular drawing area. The user places a marker by pointing to the desired position and pressing button 1; she requests that the interaction be terminated by either pressing button 3 or typing "q" or "Q."

2.2.6 Pick Correlation for Interaction Handling

A graphics application customarily divides the screen area into regions dedicated to specific purposes. When the user presses the locator button, the application must determine exactly

```
const int PLACE_BUTTON = 0, PLACE_MASK = 0x1,
         QUIT_BUTTON = 2, QUIT_MASK = 0x4;

generate initial screen layout;
SRGP_setInputMode (KEYBOARD, EVENT);
SRGP_setKeyboardProcessingMode (RAW);
SRGP_setInputMode (LOCATOR, EVENT);
SRGP_setLocatorButtonMask (PLACE_MASK | QUIT_MASK);      /* Ignore middle button. */

/* Main event loop */
terminate = FALSE;
while (!terminate) {
    device = SRGP_waitEvent (INDEFINITE);
    switch (device) {
        case KEYBOARD:
            SRGP_getKeyboard (keyMeasure, keyMeasureSize);
            terminate = (keyMeasure[0] == 'q') || (keyMeasure[0] == 'Q');
            break;
        case LOCATOR:
            SRGP_getLocator (&locMeasure);
            switch (locMeasure.buttonOfMostRecentTransition) {
                case PLACE_BUTTON:
                    if ((locMeasure.buttonChord[PLACE_BUTTON] == DOWN)
                        && InDrawingArea (locMeasure.position))
                        SRGP_marker (locMeasure.position);
                    break;
                case QUIT_BUTTON:
                    terminate = TRUE;
                    break;
            }   /* button switch */
    }   /* device switch */
}   /* while */
```

Fig. 2.21 Use of several devices simultaneously.

what screen button, icon, or other object was selected, if any, so that it can respond appropriately. This determination, called *pick correlation*, is a fundamental part of interactive graphics.

An application program using SRGP performs pick correlation by determining in which region the cursor is located, and then which object within that region, if any, the user is selecting. Points in an empty subregion might be ignored (if the point is between menu buttons in a menu, for example) or might specify the desired position for a new object (if the point lies in the main drawing area). Since a great many regions on the screen are upright rectangles, almost all the work for pick correlation can be done by a simple, frequently used Boolean function that checks whether a given point lies in a given rectangle. The GEOM package distributed with SRGP includes this function (GEOM_ptInRect) as well as other utilities for coordinate arithmetic. (For more information on pick correlation, see Section 7.12.)

Let us look at a classic example of pick correlation. Consider a painting application with a *menu bar* across the top of the screen. This menu bar contains the names of pull-down menus, called menu *headers*. When the user picks a header (by placing the cursor on top of the header's text string and pressing a locator button), the corresponding *menu body* is displayed on the screen below the header and the header is highlighted. After the user selects an entry on the menu (by releasing the locator button),[6] the menu body disappears and the header is unhighlighted. The rest of the screen contains the main drawing area in which the user can place and pick objects. The application, in creating each object, has assigned it a unique identifier (ID) that is returned by the pick-correlation procedure for further processing of the object.

When a point is obtained from the locator via a button-down event, the high-level interaction-handling schema shown in Fig. 2.22 is executed; it is essentially a dispatching procedure that uses pick correlation within the menu bar or the main drawing area to divide the work among menu- and object-picking procedures. First, if the cursor was in the menu bar, a subsidiary correlation procedure determines whether the user selected a menu header. If so, a procedure (detailed in Section 2.3.1) is called to perform the menu interaction; it returns an index specifying which item within the menu's body (if any) was chosen. The menu ID and item index together uniquely identify the action that should be taken in response. If the cursor was not in the menu bar but rather in the main drawing area, another subsidiary correlation procedure is called to determine what object was picked, if any. If an object was picked, a processing procedure is called to respond appropriately.

The procedure CorrelateMenuBar performs a finer correlation by calling GEOM_point-InRect once for each menu header in the menu bar; it accesses a database storing the rectangular screen extent of each header. The procedure CorrelateDrawingArea must do more sophisticated correlation because, typically, objects in the drawing area may overlap and are not necessarily rectangular.

2.2.7   Setting Device Measure and Attributes

Each input device has its own set of attributes, and the application can set these attributes to custom-tailor the feedback the device presents to the user. (The button mask presented earlier is also an attribute; it differs from those presented here in that it does not affect feedback.) Like output-primitive attributes, input-device attributes are set modally by specific procedures. Attributes can be set at any time, whether or not the device is active.

In addition, each input device's measure, normally determined by the user's actions, can also be set by the application. Unlike input-device attributes, an input device's measure is reset to a default value when the device is deactivated; thus, upon reactivation, devices initially have predictable values, a convenience to the programmer and to the user. This automatic resetting can be overridden by explicitly setting a device's measure while it is inactive.

Locator echo attributes.   Several types of echo are useful for the locator. The

---

[6]This sequence, corresponding to the Macintosh menu-interaction style, is only one of many different ways the user interface could be designed.

```
void HighLevelInteractionHandler (locatorMeasure measureOfLocator)
{
    if (GEOM_pointInRect (measureOfLocator.position, menuBarExtent)) {
        /* Find out which menu's header, if any, the user selected. */
        /* Then, pull down that menu's body. */
        menuID = CorrelateMenuBar (measureOfLocator.position);
        if (menuID > 0) {
            chosenItemIndex = PerformPulldownMenuInteraction (menuID);
            if (chosenItemIndex > 0)
                PerformActionChosenFromMenu (menuID, chosenItemIndex);

        }
    } else {        /* The user picked within the drawing area; find out what and respond. */
        objectID = CorrelateDrawingArea (measureOfLocator.position);
        if (objectID > 0)
            ProcessObject (objectID);

    }
}   /* HighLevelInteractionHandler */
```

Fig. 2.22 High-level interaction scheme for menu handling.

programmer can control both echo type and cursor shape with

void SRGP_setLocatorEchoType (
    NO_ECHO / CURSOR / RUBBER_LINE / RUBBER_RECT echoType);

The default is CURSOR, and SRGP implementations supply a cursor table from which an application selects a desired cursor shape (see the reference manual). A common use of the ability to specify the cursor shape dynamically is to provide feedback by changing the cursor shape according to the region in which the cursor lies. RUBBER_LINE and RUBBER_RECT echo are commonly used to specify a line or box. With these set, SRGP automatically draws a continuously updated line or rectangle as the user moves the locator. The line or rectangle is defined by two points, the anchor point (another locator attribute) and the current locator position. Figure 2.23 illustrates the use of these two modes for user specification of a line and a rectangle.

In Fig. 2.23(a), the echo is a cross-hair cursor, and the user is about to press the locator button. The application initiates a rubber echo, anchored at the current locator position, in response to the button press. In parts (b) and (c), the user's movement of the locator device is echoed by the rubber primitive. The locator position in part (c) is returned to the application when the user releases the button, and the application responds by drawing a line or rectangle primitive and restoring normal cursor echo (see part d).

The anchor point for rubber echo is set with

void SRGP_setLocatorEchoRubberAnchor (point position);

An application typically uses the *position* field of the measure obtained from the most recent locator-button–press event as the anchor position, since that button press typically initiates the rubber-echo sequence.

Locator measure control.   The *position* portion of the locator measure is automatically

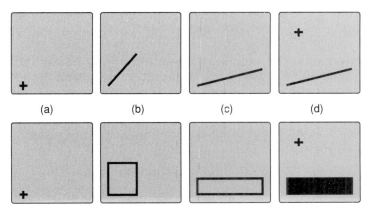

Fig. 2.23 Rubber-echo scenarios.

reset to the center of the screen whenever the locator is deactivated. Unless the programmer explicitly resets it, the measure (and feedback position, if the echo is active) is initialized to that same position when the device is reactivated. At any time, whether the device is active or inactive, the programmer can reset the locator's measure (the *position* portion, not the fields concerning the buttons) using

>   **void** SRGP_setLocatorMeasure (point *position*);

Resetting the measure while the locator is inactive has no immediate effect on the screen, but resetting it while the locator is active changes the echo (if any) accordingly. Thus, if the program wants the cursor to appear initially at a position other than the center when the locator is activated, a call to SRGP_setLocatorMeasure with that initial position must precede the call to SRGP_setInputMode. This technique is commonly used to achieve continuity of cursor position: The last measure before the locator was deactivated is stored, and the cursor is returned to that position when it is reactivated.

Keyboard attributes and measure control. Unlike the locator, whose echo is positioned to reflect movements of a physical device, there is no obvious screen position for a keyboard device's echo. The position is thus an attribute (with an implementation-specific default value) of the keyboard device that can be set via

>   **void** SRGP_setKeyboardEchoOrigin (point *origin*);

The default measure for the keyboard is automatically reset to the null string when the keyboard is deactivated. Setting the measure explicitly to a nonnull initial value just before activating the keyboard is a convenient way to present a default input string (displayed by SRGP as soon as echoing begins) that the user can accept as is or modify before pressing the Return key, thereby minimizing typing. The keyboard's measure is set via

>   **void** SRGP_setKeyboardMeasure (**char** *measure*);

2.3 RASTER GRAPHICS FEATURES

By now, we have introduced most of the features of SRGP. This section discusses the remaining facilities that take particular advantage of raster hardware, especially the ability to save and restore pieces of the screen as they are overlaid by other images, such as windows or temporary menus. Such image manipulations are done under control of window- and menu-manager application programs. We also introduce offscreen bitmaps (called *canvases*) for storing windows and menus, and we discuss the use of clipping rectangles.

2.3.1 Canvases

The best way to make complex icons or menus appear and disappear quickly is to create them once in memory and then to copy them onto the screen as needed. Raster graphics packages do this by generating the primitives in invisible, offscreen bitmaps or pixmaps of the requisite size, called *canvases* in SRGP, and then copying the canvases to and from display memory. This technique is, in effect, a type of buffering. Moving blocks of pixels back and forth is faster, in general, than is regenerating the information, given the existence of the fast SRGP_copyPixel operation that we shall discuss soon.

An SRGP *canvas* is a data structure that stores an image as a 2D array of pixels. It also stores some control information concerning the size and attributes of the image. Each canvas represents its image in its own Cartesian coordinate system, which is identical to that of the screen shown in Fig. 2.1; in fact, the screen is itself a canvas, special solely in that it is the only canvas that is displayed. To make an image stored in an off-screen canvas visible, the application must copy it onto the screen canvas. Beforehand, the portion of the screen image where the new image—for example, a menu—will appear can be saved by copying the pixels in that region to an offscreen canvas. When the menu selection has taken place, the screen image is restored by copying back these pixels.

At any given time, there is one *currently active* canvas: the canvas into which new primitives are drawn and to which new attribute settings apply. This canvas may be the screen canvas (the default we have been using) or an offscreen canvas. The coordinates passed to the primitive procedures are expressed in terms of the local coordinate space of the currently active canvas. Each canvas also has its own complete set of SRGP attributes, which affect all drawing on that canvas and are set to the standard default values when the canvas is created. Calls to attribute-setting procedures modify only the attributes in the currently active canvas. It is convenient to think of a canvas as a virtual screen of program-specified dimensions, having its own associated pixmap, coordinate system, and attribute group. These properties of the canvas are sometimes called the *state* or *context* of the canvas.

When SRGP is initialized, the *screen canvas* is automatically created and made active. All our programs thus far have generated primitives into only that canvas. It is the only canvas visible on the screen, and its ID is SCREEN_CANVAS, an SRGP constant. A new offscreen canvas is created by calling the following procedure, which returns the ID allocated for the new canvas:

canvasID SRGP_createCanvas (**int** *width*, **int** *height*);

Like the screen, the new canvas's local coordinate system origin (0, 0) is at the bottom-left corner and the top-right corner is at (*width*–1, *height*–1). A 1 by 1 canvas is therefore defined by width and height of 1, and its bottom-left and top-right corners are both (0, 0)! This is consistent with our treatment of pixels as being at grid intersections: The single pixel in a 1 by 1 canvas is at (0, 0).

A newly created canvas is automatically made active and its pixels are initialized to color 0 (as is also done for the screen canvas before any primitives are displayed). Once a canvas is created, its size cannot be changed. Also, the programmer cannot control the number of bits per pixel in a canvas, since SRGP uses as many bits per pixel as the hardware allows. The attributes of a canvas are kept as part of its ''local'' state information; thus, the program does not need to save the currently active canvas's attributes explicitly before creating a new active canvas.

The application selects a previously created canvas to be the currently active canvas via

> **void** SRGP_useCanvas (canvasID *id*);

A canvas being activated in no way implies that that canvas is made visible; an image in an offscreen canvas must be copied onto the screen canvas (using the SGRP_copyPixel procedure described shortly) in order to be seen.

Canvases are deleted by the following procedure, which may not be used to delete the screen canvas or the currently active canvas.

> **void** SRGP_deleteCanvas (canvasID *id*);

The following procedures allow inquiry of the size of a canvas; one returns the rectangle which defines the canvas coordinate system (the bottom-left point always being (0, 0)), and the other returns the width and height as separate quantities.

> rectangle SRGP_inquireCanvasExtent (canvasID *id*);
> **void** SRGP_inquireCanvasSize (canvasID *id*, **int** *∗width*, **int** *∗height*);

Let us examine the way canvases can be used for the implementation of Perform-PulldownMenuInteraction, the procedure called by the high-level interaction handler presented in Fig. 2.22 and Section 2.2.6. The procedure is implemented by the pseudocode of Fig. 2.24, and its sequence of actions is illustrated in Fig. 2.25. Each menu has a unique

```
int PerformPulldownMenuInteraction (int menuID);
/* The saving/copying of rectangular regions of canvases is described in Section 2.3.3. */
{
     highlight the menu header in the menu bar;
     menuBodyScreenExtent = screen-area rectangle at which menu body should appear;
     save the current pixels of the menuBodyScreenExtent in a temporary canvas;
          /* See Fig. 2.25a. */
     copy menu body image from body canvas to menuBodyScreenExtent;
          /* See Fig. 2.25b and C code in Fig. 2.28. */
     wait for button-up signaling the user made a selection, then get locator measure;
     copy saved image from temporary canvas back to menuBodyScreenExtent;
          /* See Fig. 2.25c */
     if (GEOM_pointInRect (measureOfLocator.position, menuBodyScreenExtent))
          calculate and return index of chosen item, using y coord of measure position;
     else
          return 0;
}    /* PerformPulldownMenuInteraction */
```

Fig. 2.24 Pseudocode for PerformPulldownMenuInteraction.

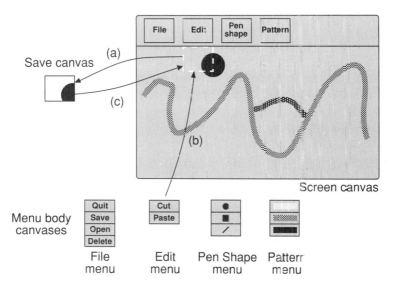

Fig. 2.25 Saving and restoring area covered by menu body.

ID (returned by the CorrelateMenuBar function) that can be used to locate a database record containing the following information about the appearance of the menu body:

- The ID of the canvas storing the menu's body
- The rectangular area (called *menuBodyScreenExtent* in the pseudocode), specified in screen-canvas coordinates, in which the menu's body should appear when the user pulls down the menu by clicking in its header

2.3.2　Clipping Rectangles

Often, it is desirable to restrict the effect of graphics primitives to a subregion of the active canvas, to protect other portions of the canvas. To facilitate this, SRGP maintains a *clip rectangle* attribute. All primitives are clipped to the boundaries of this rectangle; that is, primitives (or portions of primitives) lying outside the clip rectangle are not drawn. Like any attribute, the clip rectangle can be changed at any time, and its most recent setting is stored with the canvas's attribute group. The default clipping rectangle (what we have used so far) is the full canvas; it can be changed to be smaller than the canvas, but it cannot extend beyond the canvas boundaries. The relevant set and inquiry calls for the clip rectangle are

> **void** SRGP_setClipRectangle (rectangle *clipRect*);
> rectangle SRGP_inquireClipRectangle (**void**);

A painting application like that presented in Section 2.2.4 would use the clip rectangle to restrict the placement of paint to the drawing region of the screen, ensuring that the surrounding menu areas are not damaged. Although SRGP offers only a single upright rectangle clipping boundary, some more sophisticated software such as POSTSCRIPT offers multiple, arbitrarily shaped clipping regions.

2.3.3   The SRGP_copyPixel Operation

The powerful SRGP_copyPixel command is a typical raster command that is often called bitBlt (bit block transfer) or pixBlt (pixel Blt) when implemented directly in hardware; it first became available in microcode on the pioneering ALTO bitmap workstation at Xerox Palo Alto Research Center in the early 1970s [INGA81]. This command is used to copy an array of pixels from a rectangular region of a canvas, the *source* region, to a *destination* region in the currently active canvas (see Fig. 2.26). The SRGP facility provides only restricted functionality in that the destination rectangle must be of the same size as the source. In more powerful versions, the source can be copied to a destination region of a different size, being automatically scaled to fit (see Chapter 19). Also, additional features may be available, such as *masks* to selectively shield desired source or destination pixels from copying (see Chapter 19), and *halftone patterns* that can be used to "screen" (i.e., shade) the destination region.

SRGP_copyPixel can copy between any two canvases and is specified as follows:

void SRGP_copyPixel (
        canvasID *sourceCanvas*, rectangle *sourceRect*, point *destCorner*);

The *sourceRect* specifies the source region in an arbitrary canvas, and *destCorner* specifies the bottom-left corner of the destination rectangle inside the currently active canvas, each in their own coordinate systems. The copy operation is subject to the same clip rectangle that prevents primitives from generating pixels into protected regions of a canvas. Thus, the region into which pixels are ultimately copied is the intersection of the extent of the destination canvas, the destination region, and the clip rectangle, shown as the striped region in Fig. 2.27.

To show the use of copyPixel in handling pull-down menus, let us implement the fourth statement of pseudocode—"copy menu body image"—from the PerformPulldownMenu-Interaction function (Fig. 2.24). In the third statement of the pseudocode, we saved in an offscreen canvas the screen region where the menu body is to go; now, we wish to copy the menu body to the screen.

The Pascal code is shown in Fig. 2.28. We must be sure to distinguish between the two rectangles that are of identical size but that are expressed in different coordinate systems.

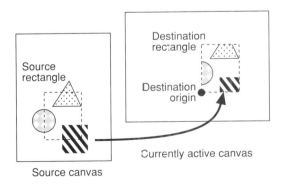

Fig. 2.26 SRGP_copyPixel.

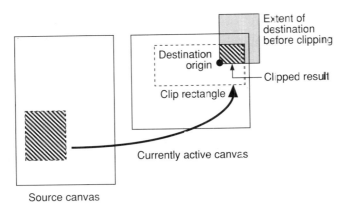

Fig. 2.27 Clipping during copyPixel.

The first rectangle, which we call *menuBodyExtent* in the code, is simply the extent of the menu body's canvas in its own coordinate system. This extent is used as the source rectangle in the SRGP_copyPixel operation that puts the menu on the screen. The *menuBodyScreenExtent* is a rectangle of the same size that specifies in screen coordinates the position in which the menu body should appear; that extent's bottom-left corner is horizontally aligned with the left side of the menu header, and its top-right corner abuts the bottom of the menu bar. (Figure 2.25 symbolizes the Edit menu's screen extent as a dotted outline, and its body extent as a solid outline.) The *menuBodyScreenExtent*'s bottom-left point is used to specify the destination for the SRGP_copyPixel that copies the menu body. It is also the source rectangle for the initial save of the screen area to be overlaid by the menu body and the destination of the final restore.

```
/* This code fragment copies a menu-body image onto screen, */
/* at the screen position stored in the body's record. */

/* Save the ID of the currently active canvas. */
saveCanvasID = SRGP_inquireActiveCanvas();

/* Save the screen canvas' clip-rectangle attribute value. */
SRGP_useCanvas (SCREEN_CANVAS);
saveClipRectangle = SRGP_inquireClipRectangle ();

/* Temporarily set screen clip rectangle to allow writing to all of the screen. */
SRGP_setClipRectangle (SCREEN_EXTENT);

/* Copy menu body from its canvas to its proper area below the header in the menu bar. */
SRGP_copyPixel (menuCanvasID, menuBodyExtent, menuBodyScreenExtent.bottomLeft);

/* Restore screen attributes and active canvas. */
SRGP_setClipRectangle (saveClipRectangle);
SRGP_useCanvas (saveCanvasID);
```

Fig. 2.28 Code for copying the menu body to the screen.

Notice that the application's state is saved and restored to eliminate side effects. We set the screen clip rectangle to SCREEN_EXTENT before copying; alternatively, we could set it to the exact *menuBodyScreenExtent*.

2.3.4   Write Mode or RasterOp

SRGP_copyPixel can do more than just move an array of pixels from a source region to a destination. It can also execute a logical (bitwise) operation between each corresponding pair of pixels in the source and destination regions, then place the result in the destination region. This operation can be symbolized as

$$D \leftarrow S \text{ op } D$$

where **op**, frequently called the *RasterOp* or *write mode*, consists in general of the 16 Boolean operators. Only the most common of these—**replace, or, xor,** and **and**—are supported by SRGP; these are shown for a 1-bit-per-pixel image in Fig. 2.29.

Write mode affects not only SRGP_copyPixel, but also any new primitives written onto a canvas. As each pixel (either of a source rectangle of a SRGP_copyPixel or of a primitive) is stored in its memory location, either it is written in destructive **replace** mode or its value is logically combined with the previously stored value of the pixel. (This bitwise combination of source and destination values is similar to the way a CPU's hardware performs arithmetic or logical operations on the contents of a memory location during a read–modify–write memory cycle.) Although **replace** is by far the most common mode, **xor** is quite useful for generating dynamic objects, such as cursors and rubberband echoes, as we discuss shortly.

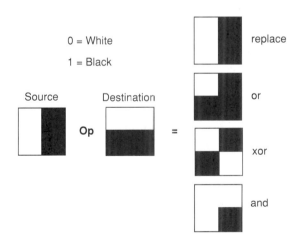

Fig. 2.29 Write modes for combining source and destination pixels.

We set the write-mode attribute with:

void SRGP_setWriteMode (
        WRITE_REPLACE / WRITE_XOR / WRITE_OR / WRITE_AND writeMode);

Since all primitives are generated according to the current write mode, the SRGP programmer must be sure to set this mode explicitly and not to rely on the default setting of WRITE_REPLACE.

To see how RasterOp works, we look at how the package actually stores and manipulates pixels; this is the only place where hardware and implementation considerations intrude on the abstract view of raster graphics that we have maintained so far.

RasterOps are performed on the pixel values, which are indices into the color table, not on the hardware color specifications stored as entries in the color table. Thus, for a bilevel, 1-bit-per-pixel system, the RasterOp is done on two indices of 1 bit each. For an 8-bit-per-pixel color system, the RasterOp is done as a bitwise logical operation on two 8-bit indices.

Although the interpretation of the four basic operations on 1-bit-per-pixel monochrome images shown in Fig. 2.29 is natural enough, the results of all but **replace** mode are not nearly so natural for n-bit-per-pixel images ($n > 1$), since a bitwise logical operation on the source and destination indices yields a third index whose color value may be wholly unrelated to the source and destination colors.

The **replace** mode involves writing over what is already on the screen (or canvas). This destructive write operation is the normal mode for drawing primitives, and is customarily used to move and pop windows. It can also be used to "erase" old primitives by drawing over them in the application screen background pattern.

The **or** mode on bilevel displays makes a nondestructive addition to what is already on the canvas. With color 0 as white background and color 1 as black foreground, **or**ing a gray fill pattern onto a white background changes the underlying bits to show the gray pattern. But **or**ing the gray pattern over a black area has no effect on the screen. Thus, **or**ing a light-gray paint swath over a polygon filled with a brick pattern merely fills in the bricks with the brush pattern; it does not erase the black edges of the bricks, as **replace** mode would. Painting is often done in **or** mode for this reason (see Exercise 2.7).

The **xor** mode on bilevel displays can be used to invert a destination region. For example, to highlight a button selected by the user, we set **xor** mode and generate a filled rectangle primitive with color 1, thereby toggling all pixels of the button: 0 **xor** 1 = 1, 1 **xor** 1 = 0. To restore the button's original status, we simply stay in **xor** mode and draw the rectangle a second time, thereby toggling the bits back to their original state. This technique is also used internally by SRGP to provide the locator's rubber-line and rubber-rectangle echo modes (see Exercise 2.4).

On many bilevel graphics displays, the **xor** technique is used by the underlying hardware (or in some cases software) to display the locator's cursor image in a nondestructive manner. There are some disadvantages to this simple technique; when the cursor is on top of a background with a fine pattern that is almost 50 percent black and 50 percent white, it is possible for the cursor to be only barely noticeable. Therefore, many bilevel displays and most color displays use **replace** mode for the cursor echo; this technique complicates the echo hardware or software (see Exercise 2.5).

The **and** mode can be used, for example, to reset pixels selectively in the destination region to color 0.

2.4 LIMITATIONS OF SRGP

Although SRGP is a powerful package supporting a large class of applications, inherent limitations make it less than optimal for some applications. Most obviously, SRGP provides no support for applications displaying 3D geometry. There are also more subtle limitations that affect even many 2D applications:

- The machine-dependent integer coordinate system of SRGP is too inflexible for those applications that require the greater precision, range, and convenience of floating-point.

- SRGP stores an image in a canvas in a semantics-free manner as a matrix of unconnected pixel values rather than as a collection of graphics objects (primitives), and thus does not support object-level operations, such as "delete," "move," "change color." Because SRGP keeps no record of the actions that produced the current screen image, it also cannot refresh a screen if the image is damaged by other software, nor can it re–scan-convert the primitives to produce an image for display on a device with a different resolution.

2.4.1 Application Coordinate Systems

In the previous chapter, we introduced the notion that, for most applications, drawings are only a means to an end, and that the primary role of the application database is to support such processes as analysis, simulation, verification, and manufacturing. The database must therefore store geometric information using the range and precision required by these processes, independent of the coordinate system and resolution of the display device. For example, a VLSI CAD/CAM program may need to represent circuits that are 1 to 2 centimeters (cm) long at a precision of half a micron, whereas an astronomy program may need a range of 1 to 10^9 light-years with a precision of a million miles. For maximum flexibility and range, many applications use floating-point *world coordinates* for storing geometry in their database.

Such an application could do the mapping from world to device coordinates itself; however, considering the complexity of this mapping (which we shall discuss in Chapter 6), it is convenient to use a graphics package that accepts primitives specified in world coordinates and maps them to the display device in a machine-independent manner. The recent availability of inexpensive floating-point chips offering roughly the performance of integer arithmetic has significantly reduced the time penalty associated with the use of floating-point—the flexibility makes it well worth its cost to the applications that need it.

For 2D graphics, the most common software that provides floating-point coordinates is Adobe's PostScript (see Chapter 19), used both as the standard page-description language for driving hardcopy printers and (in an extension called Display PostScript) as the graphics package for windowing systems on some workstations. For 3D floating-point graphics, PHIGS and PHIGS+ are now widely available, and various 3D extensions to PostScript are appearing.

2.4.2 Storage of Primitives for Respecification

Consider what happens when an application using SRGP needs to redraw a picture at a different size, or at the same size on a display device with a different resolution (such as a higher-resolution printer). Because SRGP has no record of the primitives it has drawn, the application must respecify the entire set of primitives to SRGP after scaling the coordinates.

If SRGP were enhanced to retain a record of all specified primitives, the application could let SRGP regenerate them from its own storage. SRGP could then support another commonly needed operation, refreshing the screen. On some graphics systems, the application's screen image can be damaged by messages from other users or applications; unless the screen canvas can be refreshed from a redundantly stored copy in an offscreen canvas, respecification of the primitives is the only way to repair the damage.

The most important advantage of having the package store primitives is the support of editing operations that are the essence of drawing or construction applications, a class of programs that is quite different from the painting applications illustrated in this chapter's examples. A *painting program* allows the user to paint arbitrary swaths using a brush of varying size, shape, color, and pattern. More complete painting programs also allow placement of such predefined shapes as rectangles, polygons, and circles. Any part of the canvas can be subsequently edited at a pixel level; portions of an object can be covered with paint, or arbitrary rectangular regions of the canvas can be copied or moved elsewhere. The user cannot point to a previously drawn shape or to a painted swath and then delete or move it as a coherent, indivisible object. This limitation exists because a painting program allows an object, once placed on the canvas, to be mutilated and fragmented, losing its identity as a coherent object. For example, what would it mean for the user to point to a fragment of an object that had been split into pieces that were independently positioned in various areas of the screen? Would the user be referring to the fragment itself, or to the entire original object? In essence, the ability to affect individual pixels makes pick correlation—and therefore object picking and editing—impossible.

A *drawing program*, conversely, allows the user to pick and edit any object at any time. These applications, also called *layout editors* or *graphical illustrators*, allow a user to position standard shapes (also called *symbols, templates,* or *objects*) and then to edit the layout by deleting, moving, rotating, and scaling these shapes. Similar interactive programs that allow users to assemble complex 3D objects from simpler ones are called *geometric editors* or *construction programs*.

Scaling, screen refreshing, and object-level editing all require the storage and respecification of primitives by the application or by the graphics package. If the application stores the primitives, it can perform the respecification; however, these operations are more complex than they may seem at first glance. For example, a primitive can be deleted trivially by erasing the screen and respecifying all the primitives (except, of course, the deleted one); however, a more efficient method is to erase the primitive's image by drawing

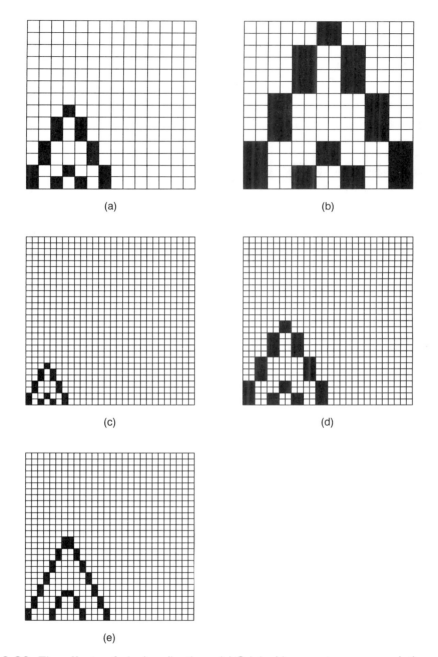

Fig. 2.30 The effects of pixel replication. (a) Original image at screen resolution. (b) Zoomed (2×) image at screen resolution. (c) Original image printed on device with twice the screen's resolution. (d) Zoomed image on same device as (c), using pixel replication to maintain image size. (e) Original image printed on same device as (c), using re–scan-conversion to maintain image size.

the application screen background on top of it and then to respecify any primitives that may have been damaged. Because these operations are both complex and frequently needed, there is good reason for moving their functionality into the graphics package itself.

An object-level, geometric graphics package, such as GKS or PHIGS, lets the application define objects using a 2D or 3D floating-point coordinate system. The package stores objects internally, allows the application to edit the stored objects, and updates the screen whenever necessary due to an editing operation. The package also performs pick correlation, producing an object ID when given a screen coordinate. Because these packages manipulate objects, they cannot permit pixel-level manipulations (copyPixel and write mode)—this is the price of preserving object coherence. Thus, neither a raster graphics package without primitive storage nor a geometric graphics package with primitive storage satisfies all needs. Chapter 7 discusses the pros and cons of the retention of primitives in the graphics package.

Image scaling via pixel replication.   If neither the application nor the package has a record of the primitives (as is typical of most painting programs), scaling cannot be done by respecifying the primitives with scaled endpoint coordinates. All that can be done is to scale the contents of the canvas using read-pixel and write-pixel operations. The simple, fast way to scale up a bitmap/pixmap image (to make it larger) is via *pixel replication*, as shown in Fig. 2.30(a,b); here, each pixel is replaced by an N by N block of pixels, thus enlarging the image by a scale factor of N.

With pixel replication, the image becomes larger, but it also becomes coarser, since no new information is provided beyond that contained in the original pixel-level representation (compare Fig. 2.30a to Fig. 2.30b). Moreover, pixel replication can increase an image's size by only an integer factor. We must use a second technique—area sampling and filtering (discussed in Chapters 3, 14, 17, and 19)—to scale up or down properly. Filtering works best on pixmaps with depth > 1.

The problem of image scaling arises frequently, particularly when an image created by a painting program is to be printed. Let us consider sending a canvas to a printer that provides twice the resolution of the screen. Each pixel is now one-half its original size; thus, we can show the original image with the same number of pixels at half the size (Fig. 2.30c), or we can use pixel replication to produce an image of the original size without taking advantage of the finer resolution of the printer (Fig. 2.30d). Either way, something is lost, size or quality, and the only scaling method that does not sacrifice quality is respecification (Fig. 2.30e).

2.5   SUMMARY

In this chapter, we have discussed a simple but powerful raster graphics package, SRGP. It lets the application program draw 2D primitives subject to various attributes that affect the appearance of those primitives. Drawing can be performed directly onto the screen canvas or onto an offscreen canvas of any desired size. Drawing can be restricted to a rectangular region of a canvas via the clip rectangle attribute. Besides the standard 2D shapes, SRGP also supports intra- and intercanvas copying of rectangular regions. Copying and drawing can be affected by the write-mode attribute, allowing a destination pixel's current value to play a role in the determination of its new value.

SRGP also introduces the notion of logical input devices, which are high-level abstractions of physical input devices. The SRGP keyboard device abstracts the physical keyboard, and the locator device abstracts such devices as the mouse, the data tablet, and the joystick. Logical devices may operate either in sampled (polled) mode or in event mode. In event mode, a user action triggers the placing of an event report on the event queue, which the application may examine at its own convenience. In sample mode, the application continuously examines the device's measure for important changes.

Because SRGP scan converts primitives to their component pixels and does not store their original geometry, the only editing SRGP permits is the alteration of individual pixels, by drawing new primitives or by using the copyPixel operation on blocks of pixels. Object manipulations such as moving, deleting, or resizing must be done by the application program itself, which must respecify the updated image to SRGP.

Other systems offer a different set of features for graphics. For example, the PostScript language offers floating-point primitives and attributes, including far more general curved shapes and clipping facilities. PHIGS is a subroutine package that offers manipulation of hierarchically modeled objects, defined in a 3D floating-point world-coordinate system. These objects are stored in an editable database; the package automatically regenerates the image from this stored representation after any editing operation.

SRGP is a subroutine package, and many developers are finding that an interpreted language such as Adobe's PostScript provides maximal power and flexibility. Also, opinions differ on which should become standard—subroutine packages (integer or floating-point, with or without retention of primitives) or display languages such as PostScript that do not retain primitives. Each has its appropriate application domain, and we expect each to persist for some time.

In the next chapter, we see how SRGP does its drawing via scan conversion and clipping. In the following chapters, after an overview of hardware, we discuss the mathematics of transformations and 3D viewing in preparation for learning about PHIGS.

EXERCISES

2.1 SRGP runs in window environments, but does not allow the application to take advantage of multiple windows: The screen canvas is mapped to a single window on the screen, and no other canvases are visible. What changes would you make to the SRGP design and application-programmer interface to allow an application to take advantage of a window system?

2.2 An SRGP application can be fully machine-independent only if it uses solely the two colors 0 and 1. Develop a strategy for enhancing SRGP so that SRGP simulates color when necessary, allowing an application to be designed to take advantage of color but still to operate in a useful way on a bilevel display. Discuss the problems and conflicts that any such strategy creates.

2.3 Implement an animation sequence in which several trivial objects move and resize. First, generate each frame by erasing the screen and then specifying the objects in their new positions. Then, try *double-buffering*; use an offscreen canvas as a buffer into which each frame is drawn before being copied to the screen canvas. Compare the two methods' results. Also, consider the use of SRGP_copyPixel. Under what restricted circumstances is it useful for animation?

2.4 Implement a rubber-echo interaction, without using the built-in locator echo. Watch for artifacts, especially upon initiation and termination of the interaction feedback.

2.5 Implement nondestructive cursor tracking without using SRGP's built-in cursor echo. Use a bitmap or pixmap pattern to store a cursor's image, with 0s in the pattern representing transparency. Implement an **xor** cursor on a bilevel display, and a replace-mode cursor on a bilevel or color display. To test the tracking, you should perform a sampling loop with the SRGP locator device and move the cursor over a nonempty screen background.

2.6 Consider implementing the following feature in a painting application: The user can paint an **xor** swath that inverts the colors under the brush. It might seem that this is easily implemented by setting the write mode and then executing the code of Fig. 2.18. What complications arise? Propose solutions.

2.7 Some painting applications provide a "spray-painting" mode, in which passing the brush over an area affects an apparently random minority of the pixels in the area. Each time the brush passes over an area, different pixels are touched, so the more an area is touched by the brush, the "denser" the paint becomes. Implement a spray-painting interaction for a bilevel display. (Beware: The most obvious algorithms produce streaks or fail to provide increasing density. You will have to create a library of sparse bitmaps or patterns; see the reference manual for information on making custom patterns.)

2.8 Implement transparent-background text for bilevel displays, without using SRGP's built-in text primitive. Use an offscreen canvas to store the bitmap shape for each character, but support no more than six characters—this is not a lesson in font design! (Hint: You may have to use two different algorithms to support both colors 0 and 1.)

2.9 A drawing program can update the screen after a deletion operation by filling the deleted object's shape with the application screen background pattern. This of course may damage other objects on the screen. Why is it not sufficient to repair the damage by simply respecifying all objects whose rectangular extents intersect the extent of the deleted object? Discuss solutions to the problem of optimizing damage repair.

2.10 Implement a procedure that draws text centered within an opaque rectangle with a thin border. Allow the caller to specify the colors for the text, background, and border; the screen position at which the center of the "button" should be placed; a pair of min/max dimensions for both width and height; and the font and the text string itself. If the string cannot fit on one line within the button at its maximum length, break the string at appropriate places (e.g., spaces) to make multiline text for the button.

2.11 Implement an onscreen valuator logical input device that allows the user to specify a temperature by using the mouse to vary the length of a simulated column of mercury. The device's attributes should include the range of the measure, the initial measure, the desired granularity of the measure (e.g., accuracy to 2 F degrees), and the desired length and position of the thermometer's screen image. To test your device, use an interaction that simulates an indefinite waitEvent where the only active device is the valuator.

2.12 Imagine customizing an SRGP implementation by adding an onscreen valuator device (like that described in Exercise 2.11) to the input model and supporting it for both event and sample modes. What kinds of problems might arise if the implementation is installed on a workstation having only one physical locator device? Propose solutions.

2.13 Implement a "rounded-rectangle" primitive—a rectangle whose corners are rounded, each corner being an ellipse arc of 90 rectangular degrees. Allow the application to have control of the radii of the ellipse arc. Support both outlined and filled versions.

PROGRAMMING PROJECTS

2.14 Implement the pull-down menu package whose high-level design is presented in code fragments in Sections 2.2.6, 2.3.1, and 2.3.3. Have the package initialize the menu bar and menu bodies by reading strings from an input file. Allow the program to deactivate a menu to make the header disappear, and to activate a menu (with its horizontal position on the menu bar as a parameter) to make that menu appear.

2.15 Enhance your menu package from Exercise 2.14 by implementing disabling of selected menu items. Disabled items in a menu body should appear "grayed out"; since SRGP does not support the drawing of text using a pen style, on a bilevel display you must paint over solid text using a write mode in order to achieve this effect.

2.16 Enhance your menu package from Exercise 2.14 by highlighting the item to which the locator currently points while the user is choosing an item from the menu body.

2.17 Implement a layout application that allows the user to place objects in a square subregion of the screen. Ellipses, rectangles, and equilateral triangles should be supported. The user will click on a screen button to select an object type or to initiate an action (redraw screen, save scene to file, restore scene from file, or quit).

2.18 Add object editing to your layout application from Exercise 2.17. The user must be able to delete, move, and resize or rescale objects. Use this simple pick-correlation method: scan the objects in the application database and choose the first object whose rectangular extent encloses the locator position. (Show that this naive method has a disturbing side effect: It is possible for a visible object to be unpickable!) Be sure to give the user feedback by highlighting the currently selected object.

2.19 Add an extra half dimension to your layout application from Exercise 2.17 by implementing overlap priority. The user must be able to push/pop an object (force its priority to be the very lowest/highest). Enhance pick correlation to use overlap priority to resolve conflicts. How does the push/pop functionality, along with the use of priority by the pick correlator, allow the user to override the inaccuracy of naive pick correlation?

2.20 Optimize the screen-update algorithm of your layout application from Exercise 2.17 using the results of Exercise 2.9, so that a minimum number of objects is respecified in response to an edit operation.

2.21 Enhance your layout application from Exercise 2.17 so that the keyboard and locator are enabled simultaneously, to provide keyboard abbreviations for common operations. For example, pressing the "d" key could delete the currently selected object.

2.22 Design and implement analytical techniques for pick correlation for the three types of objects supported by your layout application from Exercise 2.17. Your new techniques should provide full accuracy; the user should no longer have to use pop/push to pick a visible low-priority object.

3
Basic Raster Graphics Algorithms for Drawing 2D Primitives

A raster graphics package approximates mathematical ("ideal") primitives, described in terms of vertices on a Cartesian grid, by sets of pixels of the appropriate intensity of gray or color. These pixels are stored as a bitmap or pixmap in CPU memory or in a frame buffer. In the previous chapter, we studied the features of SRGP, a typical raster graphics package, from an *application programmer's* point of view. The purpose of this chapter is to look at SRGP from a *package implementor's* point of view—that is, in terms of the fundamental algorithms for scan converting primitives to pixels, subject to their attributes, and for clipping them against an upright clip rectangle. Examples of scan-converted and clipped primitives are shown in Fig. 3.1.

More advanced algorithms that handle features not supported in SRGP are used in more sophisticated and complex packages; such algorithms are treated in Chapter 19. The algorithms in this chapter are discussed in terms of the 2D integer Cartesian grid, but most of the scan-conversion algorithms can be extended to floating point, and the clipping algorithms can be extended both to floating point and to 3D. The final section introduces the concept of antialiasing—that is, minimizing jaggies by making use of a system's ability to vary a pixel's intensity.

3.1 OVERVIEW

3.1.1 Implications of Display-System Architecture

The fundamental conceptual model of Section 1.7 presents a graphics package as the system that mediates between the application program (and its application data structure/model) and the display hardware. The package gives the application program a device-

(a)   (b)

Fig. 3.1 Clipping SRGP primitives to a rectangular clip region. (a) Primitives and clipping rectangle. (b) Clipped results.

independent interface to the hardware, as shown in Fig. 3.2, where SRGP's procedures are partitioned into those forming an output pipeline and those forming an input pipeline.

In the *output pipeline*, the application program takes descriptions of objects in terms of primitives and attributes stored in or derived from an application model or data structure, and specifies them to the graphics package, which in turn clips and scan converts them to the pixels seen on the screen. The package's primitive-generation procedures specify *what* is to be generated, the attribute procedures specify *how* primitives are to be generated, the SRGP_copyPixel procedure specifies *how* images are to be modified, and the canvas-control procedures specify *where* the images are to be generated. In the *input pipeline*, a user interaction at the display end is converted to measure values returned by the package's sampling or event-driven input procedures to the application program; it typically uses those

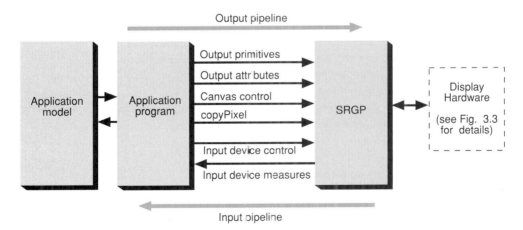

Fig. 3.2 SRGP as intermediary between the application program and the graphics system, providing output and input pipelines.

values to modify the model or the image on the screen. Procedures relating to input include those to initialize and control input devices and those to obtain the latter's measures during interaction. We do not cover either SRGP's canvas management or its input handling in this book, since these topics have little to do with raster graphics and are primarily data-structure and low-level systems-software issues, respectively.

An SRGP implementation must communicate with a potentially wide variety of display devices. Some display systems are attached as peripherals with their own internal frame buffers and display controllers. These display controllers are processors specialized to interpret and execute drawing commands that generate pixels into the frame buffer. Other, simpler systems are refreshed directly from the memory used by the CPU. Output-only subsets of the package may drive raster hardcopy devices. These various types of hardware architectures are discussed in more detail in Chapters 4 and 18. In any display-system architecture, the CPU must be able to read and write individual pixels in the frame buffer. It is also convenient to be able to move rectangular blocks of pixels to and from the frame buffer to implement the copyPixel (bitBlt) type of operation. This facility is used not for generating primitives directly but to make portions of offscreen bitmaps or pixmaps visible and to save and restore pieces of the screen for window management, menu handling, scrolling, and so on.

Whereas all implementations for systems that refresh from CPU memory are essentially identical because all the work is done in software, implementations for display controller and hardcopy systems vary considerably, depending on what the respective hardware devices can do by themselves and what remains for the software to do. Naturally, in any architecture, software scan conversion must be used to generate both primitives and attributes not directly supported in hardware. Let's look briefly at the range of architectures and implementations.

Displays with frame buffers and display controllers.   SRGP has the least amount of work to do if it drives a display controller that does its own scan conversion and handles all of SRGP's primitives and attributes directly. In this case, SRGP needs only to convert its internal representation of primitives, attributes, and write modes to the formats accepted by the display peripheral that actually draws the primitives (Fig. 3.3 a).

The display-controller architecture is most powerful when memory mapping allows the CPU to access the frame buffer directly and the display controller to access the CPU's memory. The CPU can then read and write individual pixels and copyPixel blocks of pixels with normal CPU instructions, and the display controller can scan convert into offscreen canvases and also use its copyPixel instruction to move pixels between the two memories or within its own frame buffer. When the CPU and the display controller can run asynchronously, there must be synchronization to avoid memory conflicts. Often, the display controller is controlled by the CPU as a coprocessor. If the display peripheral's display controller can only scan convert into its own frame buffer and cannot write pixels into CPU memory, we need a way to generate primitives in an offscreen canvas. The package then uses the display controller for scan conversion into the screen canvas but must do its own software scan conversion for offscreen canvases. The package can, of course, copyPixel images scan converted by the hardware from the frame buffer to offscreen canvases.

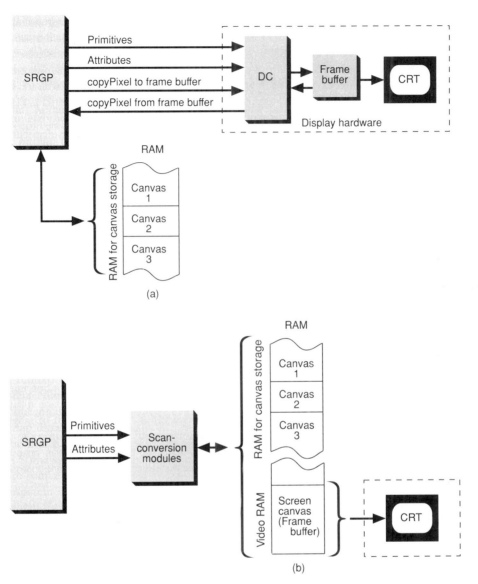

Fig. 3.3 SRGP driving two types of display systems. (a) Display peripheral with display controller and frame buffer. (b) No display controller, memory-shared frame buffer.

Displays with frame buffers only.   For displays without a display controller, SRGP does its own scan conversion into both offscreen canvases and the frame buffer. A typical organization for such an SRGP implementation that drives a shared-memory frame buffer is shown in Fig. 3.3 (b). Note that we show only the parts of memory that constitute the frame buffer and store the canvases managed by SRGP; the rest of the memory is occupied by all the usual software and data, including, of course, SRGP itself.

Hardcopy devices. As explained in Chapter 4, hardcopy devices range in their capabilities along the same spectrum as display systems. The simplest devices accept only one scan line at a time and rely on the software to provide that scan line exactly when it is to be imaged on film or on paper. For such simple hardware, SRGP must generate a complete bitmap or pixmap and scan it out one line at a time to the output device. Slightly smarter devices can accept an entire frame (page) at a time. Yet more powerful equipment has built-in scan-conversion hardware, often called raster image processors (RIPs). At the high end of the scale, PostScript printers have internal ''engines'' that read PostScript programs describing pages in a device-independent fashion; they interpret such programs to produce the primitives and attributes that are then scan converted. The fundamental clipping and scan-conversion algorithms are essentially independent of the raster device's output technology; therefore, we need not address hardcopy devices further in this chapter.

3.1.2   The Output Pipeline in Software

Here we examine the output pipeline driving simple frame-buffer displays only in order to address the problems of software clipping and scan conversion. The various algorithms introduced are discussed at a general, machine-independent level, so they apply to both software and hardware (or microcode) implementations.

As each output primitive is encountered by SRGP, the package *scan converts* the primitive: Pixels are written in the current canvas according to their applicable attributes and current write mode. The primitive is also *clipped* to the clip rectangle; that is, pixels belonging to the primitive that are outside the clip region are not displayed. There are several ways of doing clipping. The obvious technique is to clip a primitive prior to scan conversion by computing its analytical intersections with the clip-rectangle boundaries; these intersection points are then used to define new vertices for the clipped version of the primitive. The advantage of clipping before scan converting is, of course, that the scan converter must deal with only the clipped version of the primitive, not with the original (possibly much larger) one. This technique is used most often for clipping lines, rectangles, and polygons, for which clipping algorithms are fairly simple and efficient.

The simplest, brute-force clipping technique, called *scissoring*, is to scan convert the entire primitive but to write only the visible pixels in the clip-rectangle region of the canvas. In principle, this is done by checking each pixel's coordinates against the (x, y) bounds of the rectangle before writing that pixel. In practice, there are shortcuts that obviate having to check adjacent pixels on a scan line, as we shall see later. This type of clipping is thus accomplished on the fly; if the bounds check can be done quickly (e.g., by a tight inner loop running completely in microcode or in an instruction cache), this approach may actually be faster than first clipping the primitive and then scan converting the resulting, clipped portions. It also generalizes to arbitrary clip regions.

A third technique is to generate the entire collection of primitives into a temporary canvas and then to copyPixel only the contents of the clip rectangle to the destination canvas. This approach is wasteful of both space and time, but is easy to implement and is often used for text. Data structures for minimizing this overhead are discussed in Chapter 19.

Raster displays invoke clipping and scan-conversion algorithms each time an image is created or modified. Hence, these algorithms not only must create visually satisfactory images, but also must execute as rapidly as possible. As discussed in detail in later sections, scan-conversion algorithms use *incremental methods* to minimize the number of calculations (especially multiplies and divides) performed during each iteration; further, these calculations employ integer rather than floating-point arithmetic. As shown in Chapter 18, speed can be increased even further by using multiple parallel processors to scan convert simultaneously entire output primitives or pieces of them.

3.2 SCAN CONVERTING LINES

A scan-conversion algorithm for lines computes the coordinates of the pixels that lie on or near an ideal, infinitely thin straight line imposed on a 2D raster grid. In principle, we would like the sequence of pixels to lie as close to the ideal line as possible and to be as straight as possible. Consider a 1-pixel-thick approximation to an ideal line; what properties should it have? For lines with slopes between −1 and 1 inclusive, exactly 1 pixel should be illuminated in each column; for lines with slopes outside this range, exactly 1 pixel should be illuminated in each row. All lines should be drawn with constant brightness, independent of length and orientation, and as rapidly as possible. There should also be provisions for drawing lines that are more than 1 pixel wide, centered on the ideal line, that are affected by line-style and pen-style attributes, and that create other effects needed for high-quality illustrations. For example, the shape of the endpoint regions should be under programmer control to allow beveled, rounded, and mitered corners. We would even like to be able to minimize the jaggies due to the discrete approximation of the ideal line by using antialiasing techniques exploiting the ability to set the intensity of individual pixels on n-bits-per-pixel displays.

For now, we consider only "optimal," 1-pixel-thick lines that have exactly 1 bilevel pixel in each column (or row for steep lines). Later in the chapter, we consider thick primitives and deal with styles.

To visualize the geometry, we recall that SRGP represents a pixel as a circular dot centered at that pixel's (x, y) location on the integer grid. This representation is a convenient approximation to the more or less circular cross-section of the CRT's electron beam, but the exact spacing between the beam spots on an actual display can vary greatly among systems. In some systems, adjacent spots overlap; in others, there may be space between adjacent vertical pixels; in most systems, the spacing is tighter in the horizontal than in the vertical direction. Another variation in coordinate-system representation arises in systems, such as the Macintosh, that treat pixels as being centered in the rectangular box between adjacent grid lines instead of on the grid lines themselves. In this scheme, rectangles are defined to be all pixels interior to the mathematical rectangle defined by two corner points. This definition allows zero-width (null) canvases: The rectangle from (x, y) to (x, y) contains no pixels, unlike the SRGP canvas, which has a single pixel at that point. For now, we continue to represent pixels as disjoint circles centered on a uniform grid, although we shall make some minor changes when we discuss antialiasing.

Figure 3.4 shows a highly magnified view of a 1-pixel-thick line and of the ideal line that it approximates. The intensified pixels are shown as filled circles and the nonintensified

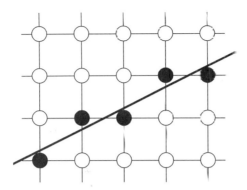

Fig. 3.4 A scan-converted line showing intensified pixels as black circles.

pixels are shown as unfilled circles. On an actual screen, the diameter of the roughly circular pixel is larger than the interpixel spacing, so our symbolic representation exaggerates the discreteness of the pixels.

Since SRGP primitives are defined on an integer grid, the endpoints of a line have integer coordinates. In fact, if we first clip the line to the clip rectangle, a line intersecting a clip edge may actually have an endpoint with a noninteger coordinate value. The same is true when we use a floating-point raster graphics package. (We discuss these noninteger intersections in Section 3.2.3.) Assume that our line has slope $|m| \leq 1$; lines at other slopes can be handled by suitable changes in the development that follows. Also, the most common lines—those that are horizontal, are vertical, or have a slope of ± 1—can be handled as trivial special cases because these lines pass through only pixel centers (see Exercise 3.1).

3.2.1 The Basic Incremental Algorithm

The simplest strategy for scan conversion of lines is to compute the slope m as $\Delta y/\Delta x$, to increment x by 1 starting with the leftmost point, to calculate $y_i = mx_i + B$ for each x_i, and to intensify the pixel at $(x_i, \text{Round}(y_i))$, where $\text{Round}(y_i) = \text{Floor}(0.5 + y_i)$. This computation selects the closest pixel—that is, the pixel whose distance to the true line is smallest.[1] This brute-force strategy is inefficient, however, because each iteration requires a floating-point (or binary fraction) multiply, addition, and invocation of Floor. We can eliminate the multiplication by noting that

$$y_{i+1} = mx_{i+1} + B = m(x_i + \Delta x) + B = y_i + m\Delta x,$$

and, if $\Delta x = 1$, then $y_{i+1} = y_i + m$.

Thus, a unit change in x changes y by m, which is the slope of the line. For all points (x_i, y_i) on the line, we know that, if $x_{i+1} = x_i + 1$, then $y_{i+1} = y_i + m$; that is, the values of x and y are defined in terms of their previous values (see Fig. 3.5). This is what defines an

---

[1] In Chapter 19, we discuss various measures of closeness for lines and general curves (also called *error measures*).

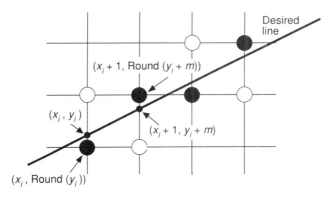

Fig. 3.5 Incremental calculation of (x_i, y_i).

incremental algorithm: At each step, we make incremental calculations based on the preceding step.

We initialize the incremental calculation with (x_0, y_0), the integer coordinates of an endpoint. Note that this incremental technique avoids the need to deal with the y intercept, B, explicitly. If $|m| > 1$, a step in x creates a step in y that is greater than 1. Thus, we must reverse the roles of x and y by assigning a unit step to y and incrementing x by $\Delta x = \Delta y/m = 1/m$. Line, the procedure in Fig. 3.6, implements this technique. The start point must be the left endpoint. Also, it is limited to the case $-1 \leq m \leq 1$, but other slopes may be accommodated by symmetry. The checking for the special cases of horizontal, vertical, or diagonal lines is omitted.

WritePixel, used by Line, is a low-level procedure provided by the device-level software; it places a value into a canvas for a pixel whose coordinates are given as the first two arguments.[2] We assume here that we scan convert only in replace mode; for SRGP's other write modes, we must use a low-level ReadPixel procedure to read the pixel at the destination location, logically combine that pixel with the source pixel, and then write the result into the destination pixel with WritePixel.

This algorithm is often referred to as a *digital differential analyzer (DDA)* algorithm. The DDA is a mechanical device that solves differential equations by numerical methods: It traces out successive (x, y) values by simultaneously incrementing x and y by small steps proportional to the first derivative of x and y. In our case, the x increment is 1, and the y increment is $dy/dx = m$. Since real variables have limited precision, summing an inexact m repetitively introduces cumulative error buildup and eventually a drift away from a true Round(y_i); for most (short) lines, this will not present a problem.

3.2.2 Midpoint Line Algorithm

The drawbacks of procedure Line are that rounding y to an integer takes time, and that the variables y and m must be real or fractional binary because the slope is a fraction. Bresenham developed a classic algorithm [BRES65] that is attractive because it uses only

---

[2]If such a low-level procedure is not available, the SRGP_pointCoord procedure may be used, as described in the SRGP reference manual.

```
void Line (                          /* Assumes -1 ≤ m ≤ 1, x0 < x1 */
        int x0, int y0,              /* Left endpoint */
        int x1, int y1,              /* Right endpoint */
        int value)                   /* Value to place in line's pixels */
{
        int x;                       /* x runs from x0 to x1 in unit increments. */

        double dy = y1 - y0;
        double dx = x1 - x0;
        double m = dy / dx;
        double y = y0;
        for (x = x0; x <= x1; x++) {
            WritePixel (x, Round (y), value);   /* Set pixel to value */
            y += m;                             /* Step y by slope m */
        }
}   /* Line */
```

Fig. 3.6   The incremental line scan-conversion algorithm.

integer arithmetic, thus avoiding the Round function, and allows the calculation for (x_{i+1}, y_{i+1}) to be performed incrementally—that is, by using the calculation already done at (x_i, y_i). A floating-point version of this algorithm can be applied to lines with arbitrary real-valued endpoint coordinates. Furthermore, Bresenham's incremental technique may be applied to the integer computation of circles as well, although it does not generalize easily to arbitrary conics. We therefore use a slightly different formulation, the *midpoint technique*, first published by Pitteway [PITT67] and adapted by Van Aken [VANA84] and other researchers. For lines and integer circles, the midpoint formulation, as Van Aken shows [VANA85], reduces to the Bresenham formulation and therefore generates the same pixels. Bresenham showed that his line and integer circle algorithms provide the best-fit approximations to true lines and circles by minimizing the error (distance) to the true primitive [BRES77]. Kappel discusses the effects of various error criteria in [KAPP85].

We assume that the line's slope is between 0 and 1. Other slopes can be handled by suitable reflections about the principal axes. We call the lower-left endpoint (x_0, y_0) and the upper-right endpoint (x_1, y_1).

Consider the line in Fig. 3.7, where the previously selected pixel appears as a black circle and the two pixels from which to choose at the next stage are shown as unfilled circles. Assume that we have just selected the pixel P at (x_P, y_P) and now must choose between the pixel one increment to the right (called the east pixel, E) or the pixel one increment to the right and one increment up (called the northeast pixel, NE). Let Q be the intersection point of the line being scan-converted with the grid line $x = x_P + 1$. In Bresenham's formulation, the difference between the vertical distances from E and NE to Q is computed, and the sign of the difference is used to select the pixel whose distance from Q is smaller as the best approximation to the line. In the midpoint formulation, we observe on which side of the line the midpoint M lies. It is easy to see that, if the midpoint lies above the line, pixel E is closer to the line; if the midpoint lies below the line, pixel NE is closer to the line. The line may pass between E and NE, or both pixels may lie on one side, but in any

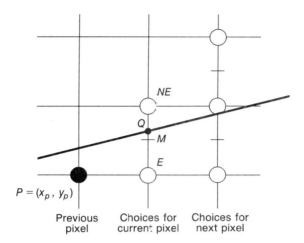

Fig. 3.7 The pixel grid for the midpoint line algorithm, showing the midpoint M, and the E and NE pixels to choose between.

case, the midpoint test chooses the closest pixel. Also, the error—that is, the vertical distance between the chosen pixel and the actual line—is always $\leq 1/2$.

The algorithm chooses NE as the next pixel for the line shown in Fig. 3.7. Now all we need is a way to calculate on which side of the line the midpoint lies. Let's represent the line by an implicit function[3] with coefficients a, b, and c: $F(x, y) = ax + by + c = 0$. (The b coefficient of y is unrelated to the y intercept B in the slope-intercept form.) If $dy = y_1 - y_0$, and $dx = x_1 - x_0$, the slope-intercept form can be written as

$$y = \frac{dy}{dx}x + B \; ;$$

therefore,

$$F(x, y) = dy \cdot x - dx \cdot y + B \cdot dx = 0.$$

Here $a = dy$, $b = -dx$, and $c = B \cdot dx$ in the implicit form.[4]

It can easily be verified that $F(x, y)$ is zero on the line, positive for points below the line, and negative for points above the line. To apply the midpoint criterion, we need only to compute $F(M) = F(x_p + 1, y_p + \frac{1}{2})$ and to test its sign. Because our decision is based on the value of the function at $(x_p + 1, y_p + \frac{1}{2})$, we define a *decision variable* $d = F(x_p + 1, y_p + \frac{1}{2})$. By definition, $d = a(x_p + 1) + b(y_p + \frac{1}{2}) + c$. If $d > 0$, we choose pixel NE; if $d < 0$, we choose E; and if $d = 0$, we can choose either, so we pick E.

Next, we ask what happens to the location of M and therefore to the value of d for the next grid line; both depend, of course, on whether we chose E or NE. If E is chosen, M is

---

[3] This functional form extends nicely to the implicit formulation of both circles and ellipses.

[4] It is important for the proper functioning of the midpoint algorithm to choose a to be positive; we meet this criterion if dy is positive, since $y_1 > y_0$.

incremented by one step in the x direction. Then,

$$d_{new} = F(x_P + 2, y_P + \tfrac{1}{2}) = a(x_P + 2) + b(y_P + \tfrac{1}{2}) + c,$$

but

$$d_{old} = a(x_P + 1) + b(y_P + \tfrac{1}{2}) + c.$$

Subtracting d_{old} from d_{new} to get the incremental difference, we write $d_{new} = d_{old} + a$.

We call the increment to add after E is chosen Δ_E; $\Delta_E = a = dy$. In other words, we can derive the value of the decision variable at the next step incrementally from the value at the current step without having to compute $F(M)$ directly, by merely adding Δ_E.

If NE is chosen, M is incremented by one step each in both the x and y directions. Then,

$$d_{new} = F(x_P + 2, y_P + \tfrac{3}{2}) = a(x_P + 2) + b(y_P + \tfrac{3}{2}) + c.$$

Subtracting d_{old} from d_{new} to get the incremental difference, we write

$$d_{new} = d_{old} + a + b.$$

We call the increment to add to d after NE is chosen Δ_{NE}; $\Delta_{NE} = a + b = dy - dx$.

Let's summarize the incremental midpoint technique. At each step, the algorithm chooses between 2 pixels based on the sign of the decision variable calculated in the previous iteration; then, it updates the decision variable by adding either Δ_E or Δ_{NE} to the old value, depending on the choice of pixel.

Since the first pixel is simply the first endpoint (x_0, y_0), we can directly calculate the initial value of d for choosing between E and NE. The first midpoint is at $(x_0 + 1, y_0 + \tfrac{1}{2})$, and

$$F(x_0 + 1, y_0 + \tfrac{1}{2}) = a(x_0 + 1) + b(y_0 + \tfrac{1}{2}) + c$$

$$= ax_0 + by_0 + c + a + b/2$$

$$= F(x_0, y_0) + a + b/2.$$

But (x_0, y_0) is a point on the line and $F(x_0, y_0)$ is therefore 0; hence, d_{star} is just $a + b/2 = dy - dx/2$. Using d_{start}, we choose the second pixel, and so on. To eliminate the fraction in d_{start}, we redefine our original F by multiplying it by 2; $F(x, y) = 2(ax + by + c)$. This multiplies each constant and the decision variable by 2, but does not affect the sign of the decision variable, which is all that matters for the midpoint test.

The arithmetic needed to evaluate d_{new} for any step is simple addition. No time-consuming multiplication is involved. Further, the inner loop is quite simple, as seen in the midpoint algorithm of Fig. 3.8. The first statement in the loop, the test of d, determines the choice of pixel, but we actually increment x and y to that pixel location after updating the decision variable (for compatibility with the circle and ellipse algorithms). Note that this version of the algorithm works for only those lines with slope between 0 and 1; generalizing the algorithm is left as Exercise 3.2. In [SPRO82], Sproull gives an elegant derivation of Bresenham's formulation of this algorithm as a series of program transformations from the original brute-force algorithm. No equivalent of that derivation for circles or ellipses has yet appeared, but the midpoint technique does generalize, as we shall see.

```
void MidpointLine (int x0, int y0, int x1, int y1, int value)
{
    int dx = x1 − x0;
    int dy = y1 − y0;
    int d = 2 * dy − dx;             /* Initial value of d */
    int incrE = 2 * dy;             /* Increment used for move to E */
    int incrNE = 2 * (dy − dx);     /* Increment used for move to NE */
    int x = x0;
    int y = y0;
    WritePixel (x, y, value);       /* The start pixel */

    while (x < x1) {
        if (d <= 0) {               /* Choose E */
            d += incrE;
            x++;
        } else {                    /* Choose NE */
            d += incrNE;
            x++;
            y++;
        }
        WritePixel (x, y, value);   /* The selected pixel closest to the line */
    } /* while */

} /* MidpointLine */
```

Fig. 3.8 The midpoint line scan-conversion algorithm.

For a line from point (5, 8) to point (9, 11), the successive values of d are 2, 0, 6, and 4, resulting in the selection of NE, E, NE, and then NE, respectively, as shown in Fig. 3.9. The line appears abnormally jagged because of the enlarged scale of the drawing and the artificially large interpixel spacing used to make the geometry of the algorithm clear. For the same reason, the drawings in the following sections also make the primitives appear blockier than they look on an actual screen.

3.2.3 Additional Issues

Endpoint order. Among the complications to consider is that we must ensure that a line from P_0 to P_1 contains the same set of pixels as the line from P_1 to P_0, so that the appearance of the line is independent of the order of specification of the endpoints. The only place where the choice of pixel is dependent on the direction of the line is where the line passes exactly through the midpoint and the decision variable is zero; going left to right, we chose to pick E for this case. By symmetry, while going from right to left, we would also expect to choose W for $d = 0$, but that would choose a pixel one unit up in y relative to the one chosen for the left-to-right scan. We therefore need to choose SW when $d = 0$ for right-to-left scanning. Similar adjustments need to be made for lines at other slopes.

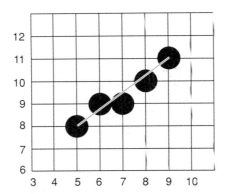

Fig. 3.9 The midpoint line from point (5, 8) to point (9, 11).

The alternative solution of switching a given line's endpoints as needed so that scan conversion always proceeds in the same direction does not work when we use line styles. The line style always "anchors" the specified write mask at the start point, which would be the bottom-left point, independent of line direction. That does not necessarily produce the desired visual effect. In particular, for a dot-dash line pattern of, say 111100, we would like to have the pattern start at whichever start point is specified, not automatically at the bottom-left point. Also, if the algorithm always put endpoints in a canonical order, the pattern might go left to right for one segment and right to left for the adjoining segment, as a function of the second line's slope; this would create an unexpected discontinuity at the shared vertex, where the pattern should follow seamlessly from one line segment to the next.

Starting at the edge of a clip rectangle. Another issue is that we must modify our algorithm to accept a line that has been analytically clipped by one of the algorithms in Section 3.12. Fig. 3.10(a) shows a line being clipped at the left edge, $x = x_{min}$, of the clip rectangle. The intersection point of the line with the edge has an integer x coordinate but a real y coordinate. The pixel at the left edge, $(x_{min}, \text{Round}(mx_{min} + B))$, is the same pixel that would be drawn at this x value for the unclipped line by the incremental algorithm.[5] Given this initial pixel value, we must next initialize the decision variable at the midpoint between the E and NE positions in the next column over. It is important to realize that this strategy produces the correct sequence of pixels, while clipping the line at the x_{min} boundary and then scan converting the clipped line from $(x_{min}, \text{Round}(mx_{min} + B))$ to (x_1, y_1) using the integer midpoint line algorithm would not—that clipped line has a different slope!

The situation is more complicated if the line intersects a horizontal rather than a vertical edge, as shown in Fig. 3.10 (b). For the type of shallow line shown, there will be multiple pixels lying on the scan line $y = y_{min}$ that correspond to the bottom edge of the clip region. We want to count each of these as inside the clip region, but simply computing the analytical intersection of the line with the $y = y_{min}$ scan line and then rounding the x value of the intersection point would produce pixel A, not the leftmost point of the span of pixels shown, pixel B. From the figure, it is clear that the leftmost pixel of the span, B, is the one

---

[5]When $mx_{min} + B$ lies exactly halfway between horizontal grid lines, we actually must round down. This is a consequence of choosing pixel E when $d = 0$.

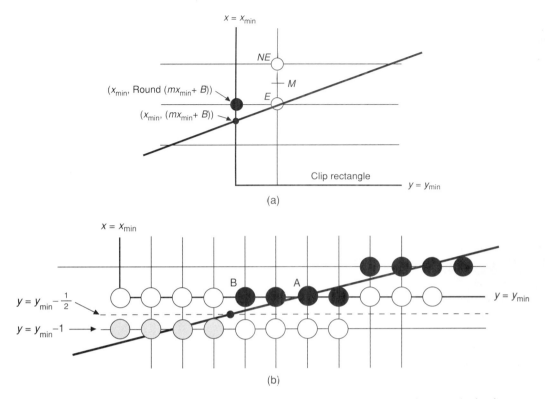

Fig. 3.10 Starting the line at a clip boundary. (a) Intersection with a vertical edge. (b) Intersection with a horizontal edge (gray pixels are on the line but are outside the clip rectangle).

that lies just above and to the right of the place on the grid where the line first crosses above the midpoint $y = y_{min} - \frac{1}{2}$. Therefore, we simply find the intersection of the line with the horizontal line $y = y_{min} - \frac{1}{2}$, and round up the x value; the first pixel, B, is then the one at $(\text{Round}(x_{y_{min}-\frac{1}{2}}), y_{min})$.

Finally, the incremental midpoint algorithm works even if endpoints are specified in a floating-point raster graphics package; the only difference is that the increments are now reals, and the arithmetic is done with reals.

Varying the intensity of a line as a function of slope.   Consider the two scan converted lines in Fig. 3.11. Line B, the diagonal line, has a slope of 1 and hence is $\sqrt{2}$ times as long as A, the horizontal line. Yet the same number of pixels (10) is drawn to represent each line. If the intensity of each pixel is I, then the intensity per unit length of line A is I, whereas for line B it is only $I/\sqrt{2}$; this discrepancy is easily detected by the viewer. On a bilevel display, there is no cure for this problem, but on an n-bits-per-pixel system we can compensate by setting the intensity to be a function of the line's slope. Antialiasing, discussed in Section 3.17, achieves an even better result by treating the line as a thin rectangle and computing

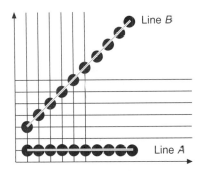

Fig. 3.11 Varying intensity of raster lines as a function of slope.

appropriate intensities for the multiple pixels in each column that lie in or near the rectangle.

Treating the line as a rectangle is also a way to create thick lines. In Section 3.9, we show how to modify the basic scan-conversion algorithms to deal with thick primitives and with primitives whose appearance is affected by line-style and pen-style attributes. Chapter 19 treats several other enhancements of the fundamental algorithms, such as handling endpoint shapes and creating joins between lines with multiple-pixel width.

Outline primitives composed of lines.   Knowing how to scan convert lines, how do we scan convert primitives made from lines? Polylines can be scan-converted one line segment at a time. Scan converting rectangles and polygons as area-defining primitives could be done a line segment at a time but that would result in some pixels being drawn that lie outside a primitive's area—see Sections 3.5 and 3.6 for special algorithms to handle this problem. Care must be taken to draw shared vertices of polylines only once, since drawing a vertex twice causes it to change color or to be set to background when writing in **xor** mode to a screen, or to be written at double intensity on a film recorder. In fact, other pixels may be shared by two line segments that lie close together or cross as well. See Section 19.7 and Exercise 3.8 for a discussion of this, and of the difference between a polyline and a sequence of connected line segments.

3.3   SCAN CONVERTING CIRCLES

Although SRGP does not offer a circle primitive, the implementation will benefit from treating the circular ellipse arc as a special case because of its eight-fold symmetry, both for clipping and for scan conversion. The equation of a circle centered at the origin is $x^2 + y^2 = R^2$. Circles not centered at the origin may be translated to the origin by integer amounts and then scan converted, with pixels written with the appropriate offset. There are several easy but inefficient ways to scan convert a circle. Solving for y in the implicit circle equation, we get the explicit $y = f(x)$ as

$$y = \pm\sqrt{R^2 - x^2}.$$

To draw a quarter circle (the other quarters are drawn by symmetry), we can increment x from 0 to R in unit steps, solving for $+y$ at each step. This approach works, but it is inefficient because of the multiply and square-root operations. Furthermore, the circle will have large gaps for values of x close to R, because the slope of the circle becomes infinite there (see Fig. 3.12). A similarly inefficient method, which does, however, avoid the large gaps, is to plot $(R \cos\theta, R \sin\theta)$ by stepping θ from $0°$ to $90°$.

3.3.1 Eight-Way Symmetry

We can improve the drawing process of the previous section by taking greater advantage of the symmetry in a circle. Consider first a circle centered at the origin. If the point (x, y) is on the circle, then we can trivially compute seven other points on the circle, as shown in Fig. 3.13. Therefore, we need to compute only one $45°$ segment to determine the circle completely. For a circle centered at the origin, the eight symmetrical points can be displayed with procedure CirclePoints (the procedure is easily generalized to the case of circles with arbitrary origins):

```
void CirclePoints (int x, int y, int value)
{
    WritePixel (x, y, value);
    WritePixel (y, x, value);
    WritePixel (y, −x, value);
    WritePixel (x, −y, value);
    WritePixel (−x, −y, value);
    WritePixel (−y, −x, value);
    WritePixel (−y, x, value);
    WritePixel (−x, y, value);
}   /* CirclePoints */
```

We do not want to call CirclePoints when $x = y$, because each of four pixels would be set twice; the code is easily modified to handle that boundary condition.

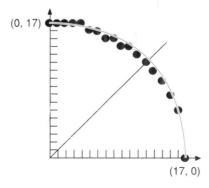

Fig. 3.12 A quarter circle generated with unit steps in x, and with y calculated and then rounded. Unique values of y for eacn x produce gaps.

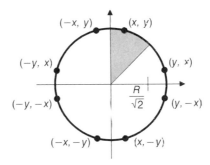

Fig. 3.13 Eight symmetrical points on a circle.

3.3.2 Midpoint Circle Algorithm

Bresenham [BRES77] developed an incremental circle generator that is more efficient than the methods we have discussed. Conceived for use with pen plotters, the algorithm generates all points on a circle centered at the origin by incrementing all the way around the circle. We derive a similar algorithm, again using the midpoint criterion, which, for the case of integer center point and radius, generates the same, optimal set of pixels. Furthermore, the resulting code is essentially the same as that specified in patent 4,371,933 [BRES83].

We consider only 45° of a circle, the second octant from $x = 0$ to $x = y = R/\sqrt{2}$, and use the CirclePoints procedure to display points on the entire circle. As with the midpoint line algorithm, the strategy is to select which of 2 pixels is closer to the circle by evaluating a function at the midpoint between the 2 pixels. In the second octant, if pixel P at (x_P, y_P) has been previously chosen as closest to the circle, the choice of the next pixel is between pixel E and SE (see Fig. 3.14).

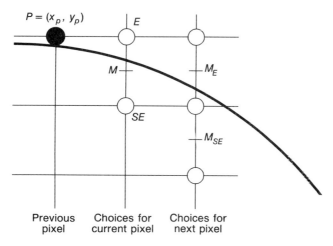

Fig. 3.14 The pixel grid for the midpoint circle algorithm showing M and the pixels E and SE to choose between.

Let $F(x, y) = x^2 + y^2 - R^2$; this function is 0 on the circle, positive outside the circle, and negative inside the circle. It can be shown that if the midpoint between the pixels E and SE is outside the circle, then pixel SE is closer to the circle. On the other hand, if the midpoint is inside the circle, pixel E is closer to the circle.

As for lines, we choose on the basis of the decision variable d, which is the value of the function at the midpoint,

$$d_{old} = F(x_P + 1, y_P - \tfrac{1}{2}) = (x_P + 1)^2 + (y_P - \tfrac{1}{2})^2 - R^2.$$

If $d_{old} < 0$, E is chosen, and the next midpoint will be one increment over in x. Then,

$$d_{new} = F(x_P + 2, y_P - \tfrac{1}{2}) = (x_P + 2)^2 + (y_P - \tfrac{1}{2})^2 - R^2,$$

and $d_{new} = d_{old} + (2x_P + 3)$; therefore, the increment $\Delta_E = 2x_P + 3$.

If $d_{old} \geq 0$, SE is chosen,[6] and the next midpoint will be one increment over in x and one increment down in y. Then

$$d_{new} = F(x_P + 2, y_P - \tfrac{3}{2}) = (x_P + 2)^2 + (y_P - \tfrac{3}{2})^2 - R^2.$$

Since $d_{new} = d_{old} + (2x_P - 2y_P + 5)$, the increment $\Delta_{SE} = 2x_P - 2y_P + 5$.

Recall that, in the linear case, Δ_E and Δ_{NE} were constants; in the quadratic case, however, Δ_E and Δ_{SE} vary at each step and are functions of the particular values of x_P and y_P at the pixel chosen in the previous iteration. Because these functions are expressed in terms of (x_P, y_P), we call P the *point of evaluation*. The Δ functions can be evaluated directly at each step by plugging in the values of x and y for the pixel chosen in the previous iteration. This direct evaluation is not expensive computationally, since the functions are only linear.

In summary, we do the same two steps at each iteration of the algorithm as we did for the line: (1) choose the pixel based on the sign of the variable d computed during the previous iteration, and (2) update the decision variable d with the Δ that corresponds to the choice of pixel. The only difference from the line algorithm is that, in updating d, we evaluate a linear function of the point of evaluation.

All that remains now is to compute the initial condition. By limiting the algorithm to integer radii in the second octant, we know that the starting pixel lies on the circle at $(0, R)$. The next midpoint lies at $(1, R - \tfrac{1}{2})$, therefore, and $F(1, R - \tfrac{1}{2}) = 1 + (R^2 - R + \tfrac{1}{4}) - R^2 = \tfrac{5}{4} - R$. Now we can implement the algorithm directly, as in Fig. 3.15. Notice how similar in structure this algorithm is to the line algorithm.

The problem with this version is that we are forced to do real arithmetic because of the fractional initialization of d. Although the procedure can be easily modified to handle circles that are not located on integer centers or do not have integer radii, we would like a more efficient, purely integer version. We thus do a simple program transformation to eliminate fractions.

First, we define a new decision variable, h, by $h = d - \tfrac{1}{4}$, and we substitute $h + \tfrac{1}{4}$ for d in the code. Now, the intialization is $h = 1 - R$, and the comparison $d < 0$ becomes $h < -\tfrac{1}{4}$.

---

[6]Choosing SE when $d = 0$ differs from our choice in the line algorithm and is arbitrary. The reader may wish to simulate the algorithm by hand to see that, for $R = 17$, 1 pixel is changed by this choice.

```
void MidpointCircle (int radius, int value)
/* Assumes center of circle is at origin */
{
    int x = 0;
    int y = radius;
    double d = 5.0 / 4.0 − radius;
    CirclePoints (x, y, value);

    while (y > x) {
        if (d < 0)              /* Select E */
            d += 2.0 * x + 3.0;
        else {                  /* Select SE */
            d += 2.0 * (x − y) + 5.0;
            y−−;
        }
        x++;
        CirclePoints (x, y, value);
    }  /* while */
}  /* MidpointCircle */
```

Fig. 3.15 The midpoint circle scan-conversion algorithm.

However, since h starts out with an integer value and is incremented by integer values (Δ_E and Δ_{SE}), we can change the comparison to just $h < 0$. We now have an integer algorithm in terms of h; for consistency with the line algorithm, we will substitute d for h throughout. The final, fully integer algorithm is shown in Fig. 3.16.

Figure 3.17 shows the second octant of a circle of radius 17 generated with the algorithm, and the first octant generated by symmetry (compare the results to Fig. 3.12).

Second-order differences. We can improve the performance of the midpoint circle algorithm by using the incremental computation technique even more extensively. We noted that the Δ functions are linear equations, and we computed them directly. Any polynomial can be computed incrementally, however, as we did with the decision variables for both the line and the circle. In effect, we are calculating *first-* and *second-order partial differences*, a useful technique that we encounter again in Chapters 11 and 19. The strategy is to evaluate the function directly at two adjacent points, to calculate the difference (which, for polynomials, is always a polynomial of lower degree), and to apply that difference in each iteration.

If we choose E in the current iteration, the point of evaluation moves from (x_P, y_P) to $(x_P + 1, y_P)$. As we saw, the first-order difference is $\Delta_{E_{old}}$ at $(x_P, y_P) = 2x_P + 3$. Therefore,

$$\Delta_{E_{new}} \text{ at } (x_P + 1, y_P) = 2(x_P + 1) + 3,$$

and the second-order difference is $\Delta_{E_{new}} - \Delta_{E_{old}} = 2$.

```
void MidpointCircle (int radius, int value)
/* Assumes center of circle is at origin. Integer arithmetic only */
{
    int x = 0;
    int y = radius;
    int d = 1 - radius;
    CirclePoints (x, y, value);

    while (y > x) {
        if (d < 0)             /* Select E */
            d += 2 * x + 3;
        else {                 /* Select SE */
            d += 2 * (x - y) + 5;
            y--;
        }
        x++;
        CirclePoints (x, y, value);
    }  /* while */
}  /* MidpointCircle */
```

Fig. 3.16 The integer midpoint circle scan-conversion algorithm.

Similarly, $\Delta_{SE_{old}}$ at $(x_P, y_P) = 2x_P - 2y_P + 5$. Therefore,

$$\Delta_{SE_{new}} \text{ at } (x_P + 1, y_P) = 2(x_P + 1) - 2y_P + 5,$$

and the second-order difference is $\Delta_{SE_{new}} - \Delta_{SE_{old}} = 2$.

If we choose SE in the current iteration, the point of evaluation moves from (x_P, y_P) to $(x_P + 1, y_P - 1)$. Therefore,

$$\Delta_{E_{new}} \text{ at } (x_P + 1, y_P - 1) = 2(x_P + 1) + 3,$$

and the second-order difference is $\Delta_{E_{new}} - \Delta_{E_{old}} = 2$. Also,

$$\Delta_{SE_{new}} \text{ at } (x_P + 1, y_P - 1) = 2(x_P + 1) - 2(y_P - 1) + 5,$$

and the second-order difference is $\Delta_{SE_{new}} - \Delta_{SE_{old}} = 4$.

The revised algorithm then consists of the following steps: (1) choose the pixel based on the sign of the variable d computed during the previous iteration; (2) update the decision variable d with either Δ_E or Δ_{SE}, using the value of the corresponding Δ computed during the previous iteration; (3) update the Δs to take into account the move to the new pixel, using the constant differences computed previously; and (4) do the move. Δ_E and Δ_{SE} are initialized using the start pixel $(0, R)$. The revised procedure using this technique is shown in Fig. 3.18.

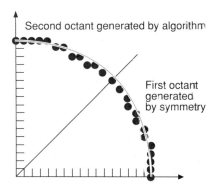

Fig. 3.17 Second octant of circle generated with midpoint algorithm, and first octant generated by symmetry.

```
void MidpointCircle (int radius, int value)
/* This procedure uses second-order partial differences to compute increments */
/* in the decision variable. Assumes center of circle is at origin */
{
    int x = 0;
    int y = radius;
    int d = 1 − radius;
    int deltaE = 3;
    int deltaSE = −2 * radius + 5;
    CirclePoints (x, y, value);

    while (y > x) {
        if (d < 0) {                /* Select E */
            d += deltaE;
            deltaE += 2;
            deltaSE += 2;
        } else {
            d += deltaSE;           /* Select SE */
            deltaE += 2;
            deltaSE += 4;
            y−−;
        }
        x++;
        CirclePoints (x, y, value);
    } /* while */
} /* MidpointCircle */
```

Fig. 3.18 Midpoint circle scan-conversion algorithm using second-order differences.

3.4 SCAN CONVERTING ELLIPSES

Consider the standard ellipse of Fig. 3.19, centered at $(0, 0)$. It is described by the equation

$$F(x, y) = b^2x^2 + a^2y^2 - a^2b^2 = 0,$$

where $2a$ is the length of the major axis along the x axis, and $2b$ is the length of the minor axis along the y axis. The midpoint technique discussed for lines and circles can also be applied to the more general conics. In this chapter, we consider the standard ellipse that is supported by SRGP; in Chapter 19, we deal with ellipses at any angle. Again, to simplify the algorithm, we draw only the arc of the ellipse that lies in the first quadrant, since the other three quadrants can be drawn by symmetry. Note also that standard ellipses centered at integer points other than the origin can be drawn using a simple translation. The algorithm presented here is based on Da Silva's algorithm, which combines the techniques used by Pitteway [PITT67], Van Aken [VANA84] and Kappel [KAPP85] with the use of partial differences [DASI89].

 We first divide the quadrant into two regions; the boundary between the two regions is the point at which the curve has a slope of -1 (see Fig. 3.20).

 Determining this point is more complex than it was for circles, however. The vector that is perpendicular to the tangent to the curve at point P is called the *gradient*, defined as

$$\text{grad } F(x, y) = \partial F/\partial x \, \mathbf{i} + \partial F/\partial y \, \mathbf{j} = 2b^2x \, \mathbf{i} + 2a^2y \, \mathbf{j}.$$

The boundary between the two regions is the point at which the slope of the curve is -1, and that point occurs when the gradient vector has a slope of 1—that is, when the $\mathbf{i}$ and $\mathbf{j}$ components of the gradient are of equal magnitude. The $\mathbf{j}$ component of the gradient is larger than the $\mathbf{i}$ component in region 1, and vice versa in region 2. Thus, if at the next midpoint, $a^2(y_P - \frac{1}{2}) \le b^2(x_P + 1)$, we switch from region 1 to region 2.

 As with any midpoint algorithm, we evaluate the function at the midpoint between two pixels and use the sign to determine whether the midpoint lies inside or outside the ellipse and, hence, which pixel lies closer to the ellipse. Therefore, in region 1, if the current pixel is located at (x_P, y_P), then the decision variable for region 1, d_1, is $F(x, y)$ evaluated at $(x_P + 1, y_P - \frac{1}{2})$, the midpoint between E and SE. We now repeat the process we used for deriving the

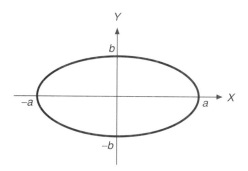

Fig. 3.19 Standard ellipse centered at the origin.

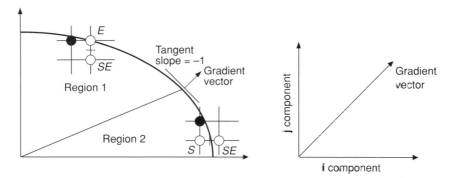

Fig. 3.20 Two regions of the ellipse defined by the 45° tangent.

two Δs for the circle. For a move to E, the next midpoint is one increment over in x. Then,

$$d_{old} = F(x_P + 1, y_P - \tfrac{1}{2}) = b^2(x_P + 1)^2 + a^2(y_P - \tfrac{1}{2})^2 - a^2b^2,$$

$$d_{new} = F(x_P + 2, y_P - \tfrac{1}{2}) = b^2(x_P + 2)^2 + a^2(y_P - \tfrac{1}{2})^2 - a^2b^2.$$

Since $d_{new} = d_{old} + b^2(2x_P + 3)$, the increment $\Delta_E = b^2(2x_P + 3)$.

For a move to SE, the next midpoint is one increment over in x and one increment down in y. Then,

$$d_{new} = F(x_P + 2, y_P - \tfrac{3}{2}) = b^2(x_P + 2)^2 + a^2(y_P - \tfrac{3}{2})^2 - a^2b^2.$$

Since $d_{new} = d_{old} + b^2(2x_P + 3) + a^2(-2y_P + 2)$, the increment $\Delta_{SE} = b^2(2x_P + 3) + a^2(-2y_P + 2)$.

In region 2, if the current pixel is at (x_P, y_P), the decision variable d_2 is $F(x_P + \tfrac{1}{2}, y_P - 1)$, the midpoint between S and SE. Computations similar to those given for region 1 may be done for region 2.

We must also compute the initial condition. Assuming integer values a and b, the ellipse starts at $(0, b)$, and the first midpoint to be calculated is at $(1, b - \tfrac{1}{2})$. Then,

$$F(1, b - \tfrac{1}{2}) = b^2 + a^2(b - \tfrac{1}{2})^2 - a^2b^2 = b^2 + a^2(-b + \tfrac{1}{4}).$$

At every iteration in region 1, we must not only test the decision variable d_1 and update the Δ functions, but also see whether we should switch regions by evaluating the gradient at the midpoint between E and SE. When the midpoint crosses over into region 2, we change our choice of the 2 pixels to compare from E and SE to SE and S. At the same time, we have to initialize the decision variable d_2 for region 2 to the midpoint between SE and S. That is, if the last pixel chosen in region 1 is located at (x_P, y_P), then the decision variable d_2 is initialized at $(x_P + \tfrac{1}{2}, y_P - 1)$. We stop drawing pixels in region 2 when the y value of the pixel is equal to 0.

As with the circle algorithm, we can either calculate the Δ functions directly in each iteration of the loop or compute them with differences. Da Silva shows that computation of second-order partials done for the Δs can, in fact, be used for the gradient as well [DASI89]. He also treats general ellipses that have been rotated and the many tricky boundary conditions for very thin ellipses. The pseudocode algorithm of Fig. 3.21 uses the simpler direct evaluation rather than the more efficient formulation using second-order differences; it also skips various tests (see Exercise 3.9). In the case of integer a and b, we can eliminate the fractions via program transformations and use only integer arithmetic.

```
void MidpointEllipse (int a, int b, int value)
/* Assumes center of ellipse is at the origin. Note that overflow may occur */
/* for 16-bit integers because of the squares. */
{
    double d2;

    int x = 0;
    int y = b;
    double d1 = b² − (a²b) + (0.25 a²),
    EllipsePoints (x, y, value);              /* The 4-way symmetrical WritePixel */

    /* Test gradient if still in region 1 */
    while ( a²(y − 0.5) > b²(x + 1) ) {       /* Region 1 */
        if (d1 < 0)                           /* Select E */
            d1 += b²(2x + 3);
        else {                                /* Select SE */
            d1 += b²(2x + 3) + a²(−2y + 2);
            y−−;
        }
        x++;
        EllipsePoints (x, y, value);
    }  /* Region 1 */

    d2 = b²(x + 0.5)² + a²(y − 1)² − a²b²;
    while (y > 0) {                           /* Region 2 */
        if (d2 < 0) {                         /* Select SE */
            d2 += b²(2x + 2) + c²(−2y + 3);
            x++;
        } else
            d2 += a²(−2y + 3);               /* Select S */
        y−−;
        EllipsePoints (x, y, value);
    }  /* Region 2 */
}  /* MidpointEllipse */
```

Fig. 3.21 Pseudocode for midpoint ellipse scan-conversion algorithm.

Now that we have seen how to scan convert lines 1 pixel thick as well as unfilled primitives, we turn our attention to modifications of these algorithms that fill area-defining primitives with a solid color or a pattern, or that draw unfilled primitives with a combination of the line-width and pen-style attributes.

3.5   FILLING RECTANGLES

The task of filling primitives can be broken into two parts: the decision of which pixels to fill (this depends on the shape of the primitive, as modified by clipping), and the easier decision of with what value to fill them. We first discuss filling unclipped primitives with a solid color; we deal with pattern filling in Section 3.8. In general, determining which pixels to fill consists of taking successive scan lines that intersect the primitive and filling in *spans* of adjacent pixels that lie inside the primitive from left to right.

To fill a rectangle with a solid color, we set each pixel lying on a scan line running from the left edge to the right edge to the same pixel value; i.e., fill each span from x_{min} to x_{max}. Spans exploit a primitive's *spatial coherence*: the fact that primitives often do not change from pixel to pixel within a span or from scan line to scan line. We exploit coherence in general by looking for only those pixels at which changes occur. For a solidly shaded primitive, all pixels on a span are set to the same value, which provides *span coherence*. The solidly shaded rectangle also exhibits strong *scan-line coherence* in that consecutive scan lines that intersect the rectangle are identical; later, we also use *edge coherence* for the edges of general polygons. We take advantage of various types of coherence not only for scan converting 2D primitives, but also for rendering 3D primitives, as discussed in Section 15.2.

Being able to treat multiple pixels in a span identically is especially important because we should write the frame buffer one word at a time to minimize the number of time-consuming memory accesses. For a bilevel display, we thus write 16 or 32 pixels at a time; if spans are not word-aligned, the algorithm must do suitable masking of words containing fewer than the full set of pixels. The need for writing memory efficiently is entirely similar for implementing copyPixel, as briefly discussed in Section 3.16. In our code, we concentrate on defining spans and ignore the issue of writing memory efficiently; see Chapters 4 and 19 and Exercise 3.13.

Rectangle scan conversion is thus simply a nested **for** loop:

```
for (y from ymin to ymax of the rectangle)      /* By scan line */
    for (x from xmin to xmax )                   /* By pixel in span */
        WritePixel (x, y, value);
```

An interesting problem arises in this straightforward solution, similar to the problem of scan converting a polyline with line segments that share pixels. Consider two rectangles that share a common edge. If we scan convert each rectangle in turn, we will write the pixels on the shared edge twice, which is undesirable, as noted earlier. This problem is a manifestation of a larger problem of area-defining primitives, that of defining which pixels belong to a primitive and which pixels do not. Clearly, those pixels that lie in the mathematical interior of an area-defining primitive belong to that primitive. But what about those pixels on the boundary? If we were looking at a single rectangle (or just thinking about the problem in a mathematical way), a straightforward answer would be to include the pixels on the boundary, but since we want to avoid the problem of scan converting shared edges twice, we must define some rule that assigns boundary pixels uniquely.

A simple rule is to say that a boundary pixel—that is, a pixel lying on an edge—is not considered part of the primitive if the halfplane defined by that edge and containing the primitive lies below or to the left of the edge. Thus, pixels on left and bottom edges will be drawn, but pixels that lie on top and right edges will not be drawn. A shared vertical edge therefore "belongs" to the rightmost of the two sharing rectangles. In effect, spans within a rectangle represent an interval that is closed on the left end and open on the right end.

A number of points must be made about this rule. First, it applies to arbitrary polygons as well as to rectangles. Second, the bottom-left vertex of a rectangle still would be drawn twice—we need another rule to deal with that special case, as discussed in the next section. Third, we may apply the rule also to unfilled rectangles and polygons. Fourth, the rule causes each span to be missing its rightmost pixel, and each rectangle to be missing its topmost row. These problems illustrate that there is no "perfect" solution to the problem of not writing pixels on (potentially) shared edges twice, but implementors generally consider that it is better (visually less distracting) to have missing pixels at the right and top edge than it is to have pixels that disappear or are set to unexpected colors in **xor** mode.

3.6 FILLING POLYGONS

The general polygon scan-conversion algorithm described next handles both convex and concave polygons, even those that are self-intersecting or have interior holes. It operates by computing spans that lie between left and right edges of the polygon. The span extrema are calculated by an incremental algorithm that computes a scan line/edge intersection from the intersection with the previous scan line. Figure 3.22, which illustrates the basic polygon scan-conversion process, shows a polygon and one scan line passing through it. The intersections of scan line 8 with edges FA and CD lie on integer coordinates, whereas those for EF and DE do not; the intersections are marked in the figure by vertical tick marks labeled a through d.

We must determine which pixels on each scan line are within the polygon, and we must set the corresponding pixels (in this case, spans from $x = 2$ through 4 and 9 through 13) to

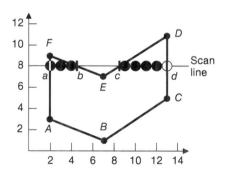

Fig. 3.22 Polygon and scan line 8.

their appropriate values. By repeating this process for each scan line that intersects the polygon, we scan convert the entire polygon, as shown for another polygon in Fig. 3.23.

Figure 3.23(a) shows the pixels defining the extrema of spans in black and the interior pixels on the span in gray. A straightforward way of deriving the extrema is to use the midpoint line scan-conversion algorithm on each edge and to keep a table of span extrema for each scan line, updating an entry if a new pixel is produced for an edge that extends the span. Note that this strategy produces some extrema pixels that lie outside the polygon; they were chosen by the scan-conversion algorithm because they lie closest to an edge, without regard to the side of the edge on which they lie—the line algorithm has no notions of interior and exterior. We do not want to draw such pixels on the outside of a shared edge, however, because they would intrude into the regions of neighboring polygons, and this would look odd if these polygons had different colors. It is obviously preferable to draw only those pixels that are strictly interior to the region, even when an exterior pixel would be closer to the edge. We must therefore adjust the scan-conversion algorithm accordingly; compare Fig. 3.23 (a) with Fig. 3.23 (b), and note that a number of pixels outside the ideal primitive are not drawn in part (b).

With this technique, a polygon does not intrude (even by a single pixel) into the regions defined by other primitives. We can apply the same technique to unfilled polygons for consistency or can choose to scan convert rectangles and polygons a line segment at a time, in which case unfilled and filled polygons do not contain the same boundary pixels!

As with the original midpoint algorithm, we use an incremental algorithm to calculate the span extrema on one scan line from those at the previous scan line without having to compute the intersections of a scan line with each polygon edge analytically. In scan line 8 of Fig. 3.22, for instance, there are two spans of pixels within the polygon. The spans can be filled in by a three-step process:

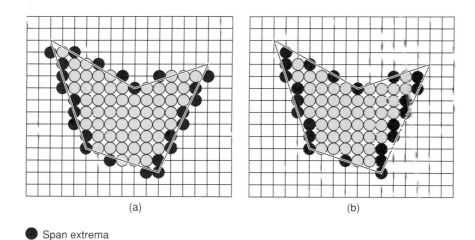

(a)   (b)

● Span extrema
○ Other pixels in the span

Fig. 3.23 Spans for a polygon. Extrema shown in black, interior pixels in gray. (a) Extrema computed by midpoint algorithm. (b) Extrema interior to polygon.

1. Find the intersections of the scan line with all edges of the polygon.

2. Sort the intersections by increasing x coordinate.

3. Fill in all pixels between pairs of intersections that lie interior to the polygon, using the odd-parity rule to determine that a point is inside a region: Parity is initially even, and each intersection encountered thus inverts the parity bit—draw when parity is odd, do not draw when it is even.

The first two steps of the process, finding intersections and sorting them, are treated in the next section. Let's look now at the span-filling strategy. In Fig. 3.22, the sorted list of x coordinates is (2, 4.5, 8.5, 13). Step 3 requires four elaborations:

3.1 Given an intersection with an arbitrary, fractional x value, how do we determine which pixel on either side of that intersection is interior?

3.2 How do we deal with the special case of intersections at integer pixel coordinates?

3.3 How do we deal with the special case in 3.2 for shared vertices?

3.4 How do we deal with the special case in 3.2 in which the vertices define a horizontal edge?

To handle case 3.1, we say that, if we are approaching a fractional intersection to the right and are inside the polygon, we round down the x coordinate of the intersection to define the interior pixel; if we are outside the polygon, we round up to be inside. We handle case 3.2 by applying the criterion we used to avoid conflicts at shared edges of rectangles: If the leftmost pixel in a span has integer x coordinate, we define it to be interior; if the rightmost pixel has integer x coordinate, we define it to be exterior. For case 3.3, we count the y_{min} vertex of an edge in the parity calculation but not the y_{max} vertex; therefore, a y_{max} vertex is drawn only if it is the y_{min} vertex for the adjacent edge. Vertex A in Fig. 3.22, for example, is counted once in the parity calculation because it is the y_{min} vertex for edge FA but the y_{max} vertex for edge AB. Thus, both edges and spans are treated as intervals that are closed at their minimum value and open at their maximum value. Clearly, the opposite rule would work as well, but this rule seems more natural since it treats the minimum endpoint as an entering point, and the maximum as a leaving point. When we treat case 3.4, horizontal edges, the desired effect is that, as with rectangles, bottom edges are drawn but top edges are not. As we show in the next section, this happens automatically if we do not count the edges' vertices, since they are neither y_{min} nor y_{max} vertices.

Let's apply these rules to scan line 8 in Fig. 3.22, which hits no vertices. We fill in pixels from point a, pixel (2, 8), to the first pixel to the left of point b, pixel (4, 8), and from the first pixel to the right of point c, pixel (9, 8), to 1 pixel to the left of point d, pixel (12, 8). For scan line 3, vertex A counts once because it is the y_{min} vertex of edge FA but the y_{max} vertex of edge AB; this causes odd parity, so we draw the span from there to 1 pixel to the left of the intersection with edge CB, where the parity is set to even and the span is terminated. Scan line 1 hits only vertex B; edges AB and BC both have their y_{min} vertices at B, which is therefore counted twice and leaves the parity even. This vertex acts as a null span—enter at the vertex, draw the pixel, exit at the vertex. Although such local minima draw a single pixel, no pixel is drawn at a local maximum, such as the intersection of scan line 9 with the vertex F, shared by edges FA and EF. Both vertices are y_{max} vertices and therefore do not affect the parity, which stays even.

3.6.1 Horizontal Edges

We deal properly with horizontal edges by not counting their vertices, as we can see by examining various cases in Fig. 3.24. Consider bottom edge AB. Vertex A is a y_{min} vertex for edge JA, and AB does not contribute. Therefore, the parity is odd and the span AB is drawn. Vertical edge BC has its y_{min} at B, but again AB does not contribute. The parity becomes even and the span is terminated. At vertex J, edge IJ has a y_{min} vertex but edge JA does not, so the parity becomes odd and the span is drawn to edge BC. The span that starts at edge IJ and hits C sees no change at C because C is a y_{max} vertex for BC, so the span continues along bottom edge CD; at D, however, edge DE has a y_{min} vertex, so the parity is reset to even and the span ends. At I, edge IJ has its y_{max} vertex and edge HI also does not contribute, so parity stays even and the top edge IH is not drawn. At H, however, edge GH has a y_{min} vertex, the parity becomes odd, and the span is drawn from H to the pixel to the left of the intersection with edge EF. Finally, there is no y_{min} vertex at G, nor is there one at F, so top edge FG is not drawn.

The algorithm above deals with shared vertices in a polygon, with edges shared by two adjacent polygons, and with horizontal edges. It allows self-intersecting polygons. As noted, it does not work perfectly in that it omits pixels. Worse, it cannot totally avoid writing shared pixels multiple times without keeping a history: Consider edges shared by more than two polygons or a y_{min} vertex shared by two otherwise disjoint triangles (see Exercise 3.14).

3.6.2 Slivers

There is another problem with our scan-conversion algorithm that is not resolved as satisfactorily as is that of horizontal edges: polygons with edges that lie sufficiently close together create a *sliver*—a polygonal area so thin that its interior does not contain a distinct span for each scan line. Consider, for example, the triangle from $(0, 0)$ to $(3, 12)$ to $(5, 12)$ to $(0, 0)$, shown in Fig. 3.25. Because of the rule that only pixels that lie interior or on a left

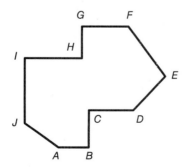

Fig. 3.24 Horizontal edges in a polygon.

or bottom edge are drawn, there will be many scan lines with only a single pixel or no pixels. The problem of having "missing" pixels is yet another example of the *aliasing* problem; that is, of representing a continuous signal with a discrete approximation. If we had multiple bits per pixel, we could use antialiasing techniques, as introduced for lines in Section 3.17 and for polygons in Section 19.3. Antialiasing would involve softening our rule "draw only pixels that lie interior or on a left or bottom edge" to allow boundary pixels and even exterior pixels to take on intensity values that vary as a function of distance between a pixel's center and the primitive; multiple primitives can then contribute to a pixel's value.

3.6.3   Edge Coherence and the Scan-Line Algorithm

Step 1 in our procedure—calculating intersections—must be done cleverly lest it be slow. In particular, we must avoid the brute-force technique of testing each polygon edge for intersection with each new scan line. Very often, only a few of the edges are of interest for a given scan line. Furthermore, we note that many edges intersected by scan line i are also intersected by scan line $i + 1$. This *edge coherence* occurs along an edge for as many scan lines as intersect the edge. As we move from one scan line to the next, we can compute the new x intersection of the edge on the basis of the old x intersection, just as we computed the next pixel from the current pixel in midpoint line scan conversion, by using

$$x_{i+1} = x_i + 1/m,$$

where m is the slope of the edge. In the midpoint algorithm for scan converting lines, we avoided fractional arithmetic by computing an integer decision variable and checking only its sign to choose the pixel closest to the mathematical line; here, we would like to use integer arithmetic to do the required rounding for computing the closest interior pixel.

Consider lines with a slope greater than $+1$ that are left edges; right edges and other slopes are handled by similar, though somewhat trickier, arguments, and vertical edges are special cases. (Horizontal edges are handled implicitly by the span rules, as we saw.) At the (x_{min}, y_{min}) endpoint, we need to draw a pixel. As y is incremented, the x coordinate of the point on the ideal line will increase by $1/m$, where $m = (y_{max} - y_{min})/(x_{max} - x_{min})$ is the

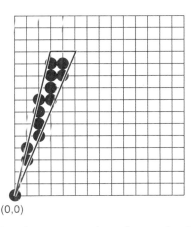

(0,0)

Fig. 3.25 Scan converting slivers of polygons.

slope of the line. This increase will result in x having an integer and a fractional part, which can be expressed as a fraction with a denominator of $y_{max} - y_{min}$. As we iterate this process, the fractional part will overflow and the integer part will have to be incremented. For example, if the slope is $\frac{5}{2}$, and x_{min} is 3, then the sequence of x values will be 3, $3\frac{2}{5}$, $3\frac{4}{5}$, $3\frac{6}{5} = 4\frac{1}{5}$, and so on. When the fractional part of x is zero, we can draw the pixel (x, y) that lies on the line, but when the fractional part of x is nonzero, we need to round up in order to get a pixel that lies strictly inside the line. When the fractional part of x becomes greater than 1, we increment x and subtract 1 from the fractional part; we must also move 1 pixel to the right. If we increment to lie exactly on a pixel, we draw that pixel but must decrement the fraction by 1 to have it be less than 1.

We can avoid the use of fractions by keeping track only of the numerator of the fraction and observing that the fractional part is greater than 1 when the numerator is greater than the denominator. We implement this technique in the algorithm of Fig. 3.26, using the variable *increment* to keep track of successive additions of the numerator until it "overflows" past the denominator, when the numerator is decremented by the denominator and x is incremented.

We now develop a *scan-line algorithm* that takes advantage of this edge coherence and, for each scan line, keeps track of the set of edges it intersects and the intersection points in a data structure called the *active-edge table* (AET). The edges in the AET are sorted on their x intersection values so that we can fill the spans defined by pairs of (suitably rounded) intersection values—that is, the span extrema. As we move to the next scan line at $y + 1$, the AET is updated. First, edges currently in the AET but not intersected by this next scan line (i.e., those whose $y_{max} = y$) are deleted. Second, any new edges intersected by this next scan line (i.e., those edges whose $y_{min} = y + 1$) are added to the AET. Finally, new x intersections are calculated, using the preceding incremental edge algorithm for edges that were in the AET but are not yet completed.

```
void LeftEdgeScan (int xmin, int ymin, int xmax, int ymax, int value)
{
    int y;

    int x = xmin;
    int numerator = xmax − xmin;
    int denominator = ymax − ymin;
    int increment = denominator;

    for (y = ymin; y <= ymax; y++) {
        WritePixel (x, y, value);
        increment += numerator;
        if (increment > denominator) {
            /* Overflow, so round up to next pixel and decrement the increment. */
            x++;
            increment −= denominator;
        }
    }
}   /* LeftEdgeScan */
```

Figure 3.26 Scan converting left edge of a polygon.

To make the addition of edges to the AET efficient, we initially create a global *edge table* (ET) containing all edges sorted by their smaller y coordinate. The ET is typically built by using a bucket sort with as many buckets as there are scan lines. Within each bucket, edges are kept in order of increasing x coordinate of the lower endpoint. Each entry in the ET contains the y_{max} coordinate of the edge, the x coordinate of the bottom endpoint (x_{min}), and the x increment used in stepping from one scan line to the next, $1/m$. Figure 3.27 shows how the six edges from the polygon of Fig. 3.22 would be sorted, and Fig. 3.28 shows the AET at scan lines 9 and 10 for that polygon. (In an actual implementation, we would probably add a flag indicating left or right edge.)

Once the ET has been formed, the processing steps for the scan-line algorithm are as follows:

1. Set y to the smallest y coordinate that has an entry in the ET; i.e., y for the first nonempty bucket

2. Initialize the AET to be empty

3. Repeat until the AET and ET are empty:

    3.1 Move from ET bucket y to the AET those edges whose $y_{min} = y$ (entering edges).

    3.2 Remove from the AET those entries for which $y = y_{max}$ (edges not involved in the next scan line), then sort the AET on x (made easier because ET is presorted).

    3.3 Fill in desired pixel values on scan line y by using pairs of x coordinates from the AET

    3.4 Increment y by 1 (to the coordinate of the next scan line)

    3.5 For each nonvertical edge remaining in the AET, update x for the new y

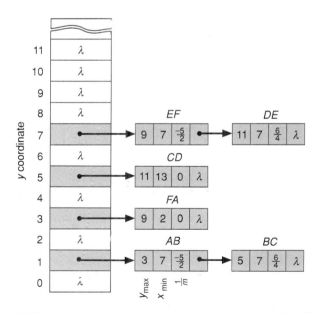

Fig. 3.27 Bucket-sorted edge table for polygon of Fig. 3.22.

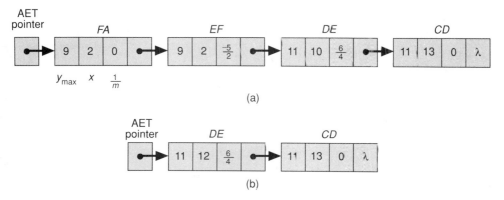

Fig. 3.28 Active-edge table for polygon of Fig. 3.22. (a) Scan line 9. (b) Scan line 10. (Note *DE*'s x coordinate in (b) has been rounded up for that left edge.)

This algorithm uses both edge coherence to calculate x intersections and scan-line coherence (along with sorting) to calculate spans. Since the sorting works on a small number of edges and since the resorting of step 3.1 is applied to a mostly or completely sorted list, either insertion sort or a simple bubble sort that is $O(N)$ in this case may be used. In Chapters 15 and 16, we see how to extend this algorithm to handle multiple polygons during visible-surface determination, including the case of handling polygons that are transparent; in Chapter 17, we see how to blend polygons that overlap at a pixel.

For purposes of scan conversion, triangles and trapezoids can be treated as special cases of polygons, since they have only two edges for any scan line (given that horizontal edges are not scan-converted explicitly). Indeed, since an arbitrary polygon can be decomposed into a mesh of triangles sharing vertices and edges (see Exercise 3.17), we could scan convert general polygons by first decomposing them into triangle meshes, and then scan converting the component triangles. Such triangulation is a classic problem in computational geometry [PREP85] and is easy to do for convex polygons; doing it efficiently for nonconvex polygons is difficult.

Note that the calculation of spans is cumulative. That is, when the current iteration of the scan-conversion algorithm in Step 3.5 generates multiple pixels falling on the same scan line, the span extrema must be updated appropriately. (Dealing with span calculations for edges that cross and for slivers takes a bit of special casing.) We can either compute all spans in one pass, then fill the spans in a second pass, or compute a span and fill it when completed. Another benefit of using spans is that clipping can be done at the same time as span arithmetic: The spans may be individually clipped at the left and right coordinates of the clip rectangle. Note that, in Section 15.10.3 we use a slightly different version of span arithmetic to combine 3D solid objects that are rendered using "raytracing."

3.7 FILLING ELLIPSE ARCS

The same general strategy of calculating spans for each scan line can be used for circles and ellipses as well. We accumulate span extrema for each iteration of the algorithm, rounding each extremum to ensure that the pixel is inside the region. As with scan converting the

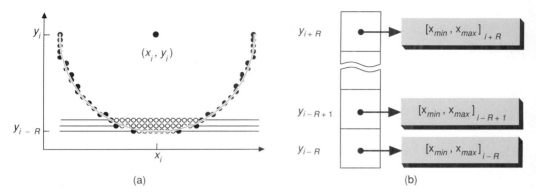

Fig. 3.29 Filling a circle with spans. (a) Three spans. (b) Span table. Each span is stored with its extrema.

unfilled primitive, we can take advantage of symmetry to scan convert only one arc, being careful of region changes, especially for ellipses. Each iteration generates either a new pixel on the same scan line, thereby potentially adjusting the span extrema, or a pixel on the next scan line, starting the next span (see Fig. 3.29). To determine whether a pixel P lies inside the region, we simply check the sign of the function $F(P)$ and choose the next pixel over if the sign is positive. Clearly, we do not want to evaluate the function directly, any more than we wanted to evaluate the function $F(M)$ at the midpoint directly; we can derive the value of the function from that of the decision variable.

Since we know that a scan line crosses the boundary only twice, we do not need any equivalent of an edge table, and we maintain only a current span. As we did for polygons, we can either make a list of such spans for each scan line intersecting the primitive and then fill them after they have all been computed, or we can fill each one as it is completed—for example, as soon as the y value is incremented.

The special case of filled wedges should be mentioned. The first problem is to calculate the intersection of the rays that define the starting and ending angles with the boundary, and to use those to set the starting and ending values of the decision variable. For circles we can do this calculation by converting from rectangular degrees to circular degrees, then using $(\text{Round}(R \cos\theta), \text{Round}(R \sin\theta))$ in the midpoint formula. The perimeter of the region to scan convert, then, consists of the two rays and the boundary arc between them. Depending on the angles, a scan line may start or end on either a ray or the boundary arc, and the corresponding incremental algorithms, modified to select only interior pixels, must be applied (see Exercise 3.19).

3.8   PATTERN FILLING

In the previous sections, we filled the interiors of SRGP's area-defining primitives with a solid color by passing the color in the *value* field of the WritePixel procedure. Here, we consider filling with a pattern, which we do by adding extra control to the part of the scan-conversion algorithm that actually writes each pixel. For pixmap patterns, this control causes the color value to be picked up from the appropriate position in the pixmap pattern, as shown next. To write bitmap patterns transparently, we do a WritePixel with foreground color at a pixel for a 1 in the pattern, and we inhibit the WritePixel for a 0, as with line style. If, on the other hand, the bitmap pattern is applied in opaque mode, the 1s and 0s select foreground and background color, respectively.

The main issue for filling with patterns is the relation of the area of the pattern to that of the primitive. In other words, we need to decide where the pattern is "anchored" so that we know which pixel in the pattern corresponds to the current pixel of the primitive.

The first technique is to anchor the pattern at a vertex of a polygon by placing the leftmost pixel in the pattern's first row there. This choice allows the pattern to move when the primitive is moved, a visual effect that would be expected for patterns with a strong geometric organization, such as the cross-hatches often used in drafting applications. But there is no distinguished point on a polygon that is obviously right for such a relative anchor, and no distinguished points at all on smoothly varying primitives such as circles and ellipses. Therefore, the programmer must specify the anchor point as a point on or within the primitive. In some systems, the anchor point may even be applied to a group of primitives.

The second technique, used in SRGP, is to consider the entire screen as being tiled with the pattern and to think of the primitive as consisting of an outline or filled area of transparent bits that let the pattern show through. The standard position for such an absolute anchor is the screen origin. The pixels of the primitive are then treated as 1s that are **and**ed with the pattern. A side effect of this technique is that the pattern does not "stick to" the primitive if the primitive is moved slightly. Instead, the primitive moves as though it were a cutout on a fixed, patterned background, and thus its appearance may change as it is moved; for regular patterns without a strong geometric orientation, users may not even be aware of this effect. In addition to being computationally efficient, absolute anchoring allows primitives to overlap and abut seamlessly.

To apply the pattern to the primitive, we index it with the current pixel's (x, y) coordinates. Since patterns are defined as small M by N bitmaps or pixmaps, we use modular arithmetic to make the pattern repeat. The $pattern[0, 0]$ pixel is considered coincident with the screen origin,[7] and we can write, for example, a bitmap pattern in transparent mode with the statement

if $(pattern[x \% M][y \% N])$
    WritePixel $(x, y, value)$;

If we are filling an entire span in **replace** write mode, we can copy a whole row of the pattern at once, assuming a low-level version of a copyPixel facility is available to write multiple pixels. Let's say, for example, that the pattern is an 8 by 8 matrix. It thus repeats for every span of 8 pixels. If the leftmost point of a span is byte-aligned—that is, if the x value of the first pixel mod 8 is 0—then the entire first row of the pattern can be written out with a copyPixel of a 1 by 8 array; this procedure is repeated as many times as is necessary to fill the span. If either end of the span is not byte-aligned, the pixels not in the span must be masked out. Implementors spend much time making special cases of raster algorithms particularly efficient; for example, they test up-front to eliminate inner loops, and they write

---

[7]In window systems, the pattern is often anchored at the origin of the window coordinate system.

hand-tuned assembly-language code for inner loops that takes advantage of special hardware features such as instruction caches or particularly efficient loop instructions. This type of optimization is discussed in Chapter 19.

3.8.1 Pattern Filling Without Repeated Scan Conversion

So far, we have discussed filling in the context of scan conversion. Another technique is to scan convert a primitive first into a rectangular work area, and then to write each pixel from that bitmap to the appropriate place in the canvas. This so-called *rectangle write* to the canvas is simply a nested **for** loop in which a 1 writes the current color and a 0 writes nothing (for transparency) or writes the background color (for opacity). This two-step process is twice as much work as filling during scan conversion, and therefore is not worthwhile for primitives that are encountered and scan-converted only once. It pays off, however, for primitives that would otherwise be scan-converted repeatedly. This is the case for characters in a given font and size, which can be scan-converted ahead of time from their outlines. For characters defined only as bitmap fonts, or for other objects, such as icons and application symbols, that are painted or scanned in as bitmap images, scan conversion is not used in any case, and the rectangle write of their bitmaps is the only applicable technique. The advantage of a pre–scan-converted bitmap lies in the fact that it is clearly faster to write each pixel in a rectangular region, without having to do any clipping or span arithmetic, than to scan convert the primitive each time from scratch while doing such clipping.[8]

But since we have to write a rectangular bitmap into the canvas, why not just copyPixel the bitmap directly, rather than writing 1 pixel at a time? For bilevel displays, writing current color 1, copyPixel works fine: For transparent mode, we use **or** write mode; for opaque mode, we use **replace** write mode. For multilevel displays, we cannot write the bitmap directly with a single bit per pixel, but must convert each bit to a full *n*-bit color value that is then written.

Some systems have a more powerful copyPixel that can make copying subject to one or more source-read or destination-write masks. We can make good use of such a facility for transparent mode (used for characters in SRGP) if we can specify the bitmap as a destination-write mask and the source as an array of constant (current) color. Then, pixels are written in the current color only where the bitmap write mask has 1s; the bitmap write mask acts as an arbitrary clip region. In a sense, the explicit nested **for** loop for implementing the rectangle write on *n*-bits-per-pixel systems simulates this more powerful "copyPixel with write mask" facility.

Now consider another variation. We wish to draw a filled letter, or some other shape, not with a solid interior but with a patterned one. For example, we would like to create a thick letter "P" with a 50 percent gray stipple pattern (graying out the character), or a house icon with a two-tone brick-and-mortar pattern. How can we write such an object in opaque mode without having to scan convert it each time? The problem is that "holes" interior to the region where there are 0s in the bitmap should be written in background color, whereas holes outside the region (such as the cavity in the "P") must still be written

---

[8]There are added complications in the case of antialiasing, as discussed in Chapter 19.

transparently so as not to affect the image underneath. In other words, we want 0s in the shape's interior to signify background color, and 0s in its exterior, including any cavities, to belong to a write mask used to protect pixels outside the shape. If we scan convert on the fly, the problem that the 0s mean different things in different regions of the bitmap does not arise, because we never look at pixels outside the shape's boundary.

We use a four-step process to avoid repeated scan conversion, as shown in the mountain scene of Fig. 3.30. Using the outline of our icon (b), the first step is to create a "solid" bitmap to be used as a write mask/clipping region, with pixels interior to the object set to 1s, and those exterior set to 0s; this is depicted in (c), where white represents background pixels (0s) and black represents 1s. This scan conversion is done only once. As the second step, any time a patterned copy of the object is needed, we write the solid bitmap

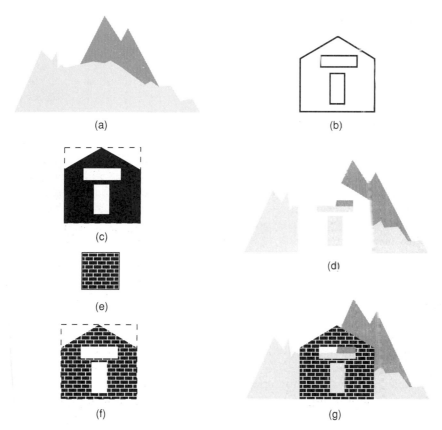

(a)   (b)

(c)

(d)

(e)

(f)   (g)

Fig. 3.30 Writing a patterned object in opaque mode with two transparent writes. (a) Mountain scene. (b) Outline of house icon. (c) Bitmap for solid version of house icon. (d) Clearing the scene by writing background. (e) Brick pattern. (f) Brick pattern applied to house icon. (g) Writing the screen transparently with patterned house icon.

transparently in background color to the canvas. This clears to background color a region of the shape of the object, as shown in (d), where the house-shaped region is set to white background within the existing mountain image. The third step is to create a patterned version of the object's solid bitmap by doing a copyPixel of a pattern rectangle (e) to the solid bitmap, using **and** mode. This turns some pixels internal to the object's shape from 1s to 0s (f), and can be seen as clipping out a piece of the arbitrarily large pattern in the shape of the object. Finally, we again write this new bitmap transparently to the same place in the canvas, but this time in the current, foreground color, as shown in (g). As in the first write to the canvas, all pixels outside the object's region are 0s, to protect pixels outside the region, whereas 0s inside the region do not affect the previously written (white) background; only where there are 1s is the (black) foreground written. To write the house with a solid red-brick pattern with gray mortar, we would write the solid bitmap in gray and the patterned bitmap in red; the pattern would have 1s everywhere except for small bands of 0s representing the mortar. In effect, we have reduced the rectangular write procedure that had to write two colors subject to a write mask to two write procedures that write transparently or copyPixel with a write mask.

3.9 THICK PRIMITIVES

Conceptually, we produce thick primitives by tracing the scan-converted single-pixel outline primitive. We place the center of a brush of a specified cross-section (or another distinguished point, such as the upper-left corner of a rectangular brush) at each pixel chosen by the scan-conversion algorithm. A single-pixel-wide line can be conceived as being drawn with a brush the size of a single pixel. However, this simple description masks a number of tricky questions. First, what shape is the brush? Typical implementations use circular and rectangular brushes. Second, what is the orientation of a noncircular brush? Does the rectangular pen always stay upright, so that the brush has constant width, or does it turn as the primitive turns, so that the vertical axis of the brush is aligned with the tangent to the primitive? What do the ends of a thick line look like, both ideally and on the integer grid? What happens at the vertex of a thick polygon? How do line style and pen style interact? We shall answer the simpler questions in this section, and the others in Chapter 19.

There are four basic methods for drawing thick primitives, illustrated in Figs. 3.31 through 3.36. We show the ideal primitives for these lines in black-on-white outline; the pixels generated to define the 1-pixel-thick scan-converted primitive in black; and the pixels added to form the thick primitive in gray. The reduced-scale versions show what the thick primitive actually looks like at still rather low resolution, with all pixels set to black. The first method is a crude approximation that uses more than 1 pixel for each column (or row) during scan conversion. The second traces the pen's cross-section along the single-pixel outline of the primitive. The third draws two copies of a primitive a thickness t apart and fills in the spans between these inner and outer boundaries. The fourth approximates all primitives by polylines and then uses a thick line for each polyline segment.

Let's look briefly at each of these methods and consider its advantages and disadvantages. All the methods produce effects that are satisfactory for many, if not most, purposes, at least for viewing on the screen. For printing, the higher resolution should be used to good advantage, especially since the speed of an algorithm for printing is not as critical as for online primitive generation. We can then use more complex algorithms to produce better-looking results. A package may even use different techniques for different primitives. For example, QuickDraw traces an upright rectangular pen for lines, but fills spans between confocal ellipse boundaries.

3.9.1 Replicating Pixels

A quick extension to the scan-conversion inner loop to write multiple pixels at each computed pixel works reasonably well for lines; here, pixels are duplicated in columns for lines with $-1 <$ slope < 1 and in rows for all other lines. The effect, however, is that the line ends are always vertical or horizontal, which is not pleasing for rather thick lines, as Fig. 3.31 shows.

The pixel-replication algorithm also produces noticeable gaps in places where line segments meet at an angle, and misses pixels where there is a shift from horizontal to vertical replication as a function of the slope. This latter anomaly shows up as abnormal thinness in ellipse arcs at the boundaries between octants, as in Fig. 3.32.

Furthermore, lines that are horizontal and vertical have a different thickness from lines at an angle, where the *thickness* of the primitive is defined as the distance between the primitive's boundaries perpendicular to its tangent. Thus, if the thickness parameter is t, a horizontal or vertical line has thickness t, whereas one drawn at 45° has an average thickness of $t/\sqrt{2}$. This is another result of having fewer pixels in the line at an angle, as first noted in Section 3.2.3; it decreases the brightness contrast with horizontal and vertical lines of the same thickness. Still another problem with pixel replication is the generic problem of even-numbered widths: We cannot center the duplicated column or row about the selected pixel, so we must choose a side of the primitive to have an "extra" pixel. Altogether, pixel replication is an efficient but crude approximation that works best for primitives that are not very thick.

3.9.2 The Moving Pen

Choosing a rectangular pen whose center or corner travels along the single-pixel outline of the primitive works reasonably well for lines; it produces the line shown in Fig. 3.33. Notice that this line is similar to that produced by pixel replication but is thicker at the endpoints. As with pixel replication, because the pen stays vertically aligned, the perceived thickness of the primitive varies as a function of the primitive's angle, but in the opposite

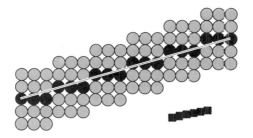

Fig. 3.31 Thick line drawn by column replication.

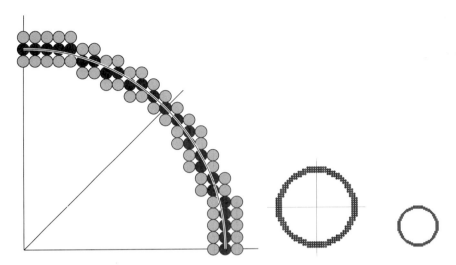

Fig. 3.32 Thick circle drawn by column replication.

way: The width is thinnest for horizontal segments and thickest for segments with slope of ±1. An ellipse arc, for example, varies in thickness along its entire trajectory, being of the specified thickness when the tangent is nearly horizontal or vertical, and thickened by a factor of $\sqrt{2}$ around ±45° (see Fig. 3.34). This problem would be eliminated if the square turned to follow the path, but it is much better to use a circular cross-section so that the thickness is angle-independent.

Now let's look at how to implement the moving-pen algorithm for the simple case of an upright rectangular or circular cross-section. The easiest solution is to copyPixel the required solid or patterned cross-section (also called *footprint*) so that its center or corner is at the chosen pixel; for a circular footprint and a pattern drawn in opaque mode, we must in addition mask off the bits outside the circular region, which is not an easy task unless our low-level copyPixel has a write mask for the destination region. The brute-force copyPixel solution writes pixels more than once, since the pen's footprints overlap at adjacent pixels. A better technique that also handles the circular-cross-section problem is to use the spans of the footprint to compute spans for successive footprints at adjacent pixels. As in filling

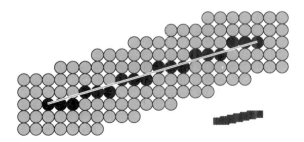

Fig. 3.33 Thick line drawn by tracing a rectangular pen.

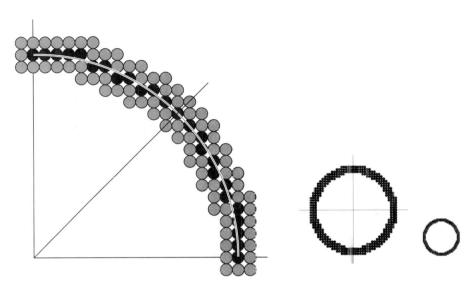

Fig. 3.34 Thick circle drawn by tracing a rectangular pen.

area-defining primitives, such combining of spans on a raster line is merely a union or merge of line segments, entailing keeping track of the minimum and maximum x of the accumulated span for each raster line. Figure 3.35 shows a sequence of two positions of the rectangular footprint and a portion of the temporary data structure that stores span extremes for each scan line. Each scan-line bucket may contain a list of spans when a thick polygon or ellipse arc is intersected more than once on a scan line, much like the active-edge table for polygons.

3.9.3 Filling Areas Between Boundaries

The third method for displaying a thick primitive is to construct the primitive's inner and outer boundary at a distance $t/2$ on either side of the ideal (single-pixel) primitive trajectory. Alternatively, for area-defining primitives, we can leave the original boundary as the outer boundary, then draw the inner boundary inward. This filling technique has the advantage of handling both odd and even thicknesses, and of not increasing the extent of a primitive when the primitive is thickened. The disadvantage of this technique, however, is that an area-defining primitive effectively "shrinks" a bit, and that its "center line," the original 1-pixel outline, appears to shift.

A thick line is drawn as a rectangle with thickness t and length of the original line. Thus, the rectangle's thickness is independent of the line's angle, and the rectangle's edges are perpendicular to the line. In general, the rectangle is rotated and its vertices do not lie on the integer grid; thus, they must be rounded to the nearest pixel, and the resulting rectangle must then be scan-converted as a polygon.

To create thick circles, we scan convert two circles, the outer one of radius $R + t/2$, the inner one of radius $R - t/2$, and fill in the single or double spans between them, as shown in Fig. 3.36.

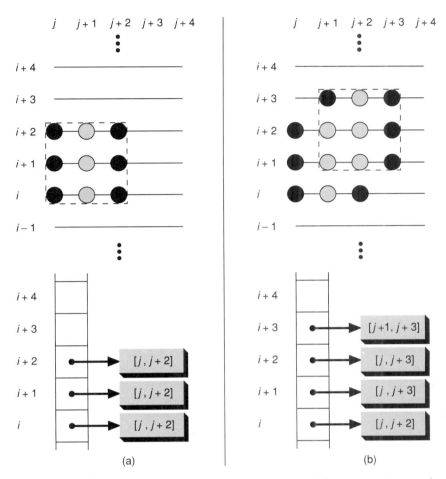

Fig. 3.35 Recording spans of the rectangular pen: (a) footprint at $x = j + 1$; (b) $x = j + 2$.

For ellipses, the situation is not nearly so simple. It is a classic result in differential geometry that the curves formed by moving a distance $t/2$ perpendicular to an ellipse are not confocal ellipses, but are described by eighth-order equations [SALM96].[9] These functions are computationally expensive to scan convert; therefore, as usual, we approximate. We scan convert two confocal ellipses, the inner with semidiameters $a - t/2$ and $b - t/2$, the outer with semidiameters $a + t/2$ and $b + t/2$. Again, we calculate spans and fill them in, either after all span arithmetic is done, or on the fly. The standard problems of thin ellipses (treated in Chapter 19) pertain. Also, the problem of generating the inner boundary, noted here for ellipses, also can occur for other primitives supported in raster graphics packages.

---

[9]The eighth-order curves so generated may have self-intersections or cusps, as may be seen by constructing the normal lines by hand.

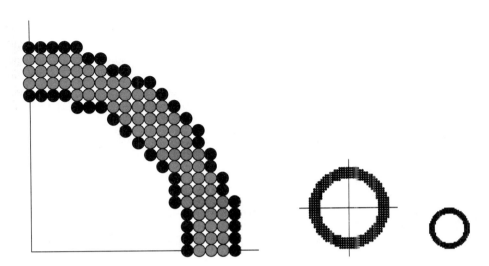

Fig. 3.36 Thick circle drawn by filling between concentric circles.

3.9.4 Approximation by Thick Polylines

We can do piecewise-linear approximation of any primitive by computing points on the boundary (with floating-point coordinates), then connecting these points with line segments to form a polyline. The advantage of this approach is that the algorithms for both line clipping and line scan conversion (for thin primitives), and for polygon clipping and polygon scan conversion (for thick primitives), are efficient. Naturally, the segments must be quite short in places where the primitive changes direction rapidly. Ellipse arcs can be represented as ratios of parametric polynomials, which lend themselves readily to such piecewise-linear approximation (see Chapter 11). The individual line segments are then drawn as rectangles with the specified thickness. To make the thick approximation look nice, however, we must solve the problem of making thick lines join smoothly, as discussed in Chapter 19.

3.10 LINE STYLE AND PEN STYLE

SRGP's line-style atribute can affect any outline primitive. In general, we must use conditional logic to test whether or not to write a pixel, writing only for 1s. We store the pattern write mask as a string of 16 **booleans** (e.g., a 16-bit **integer**); it should therefore repeat every 16 pixels. We modify the unconditional WritePixel statement in the line scan-conversion algorithm to handle this; for example,

> **if** ($bitstring[i \% 16]$)
>   WritePixel ($x, y, value$);

where the index i is a new variable incremented in the inner loop for this purpose. There is a drawback to this technique, however. Since each bit in the mask corresponds to an iteration of the loop, and not to a unit distance along the line, the length of dashes varies with the angle of the line; a dash at an angle is longer than is a horizontal or vertical dash. For engineering drawings, this variation is unacceptable, and the dashes must be calculated and scan-converted as individual line segments of length invariant with angle. Thick lines are created as sequences of alternating solid and transparent rectangles whose vertices are calculated exactly as a function of the line style selected. The rectangles are then scan-converted individually; for horizontal and vertical lines, the program may be able to copyPixel the rectangle.

Line style and pen style interact in thick outline primitives. The line style is used to calculate the rectangle for each dash, and each rectangle is filled with the selected pen pattern (Fig. 3.37).

3.11   CLIPPING IN A RASTER WORLD

As we noted in the introduction to this chapter, it is essential that both clipping and scan conversion be done as rapidly as possible, in order to provide the user with quick updates resulting from changes to the application model. Clipping can be done analytically, on the fly during scan conversion, or as part of a copyPixel with the desired clip rectangle from a canvas storing unclipped primitives to the destination canvas. This third technique would be useful in situations where a large canvas can be generated ahead of time, and the user can then examine pieces of it for a significant period of time by panning the clip rectangle, without updating the contents of the canvas.

Combining clipping and scan conversion, sometimes called *scissoring*, is easy to do for filled or thick primitives as part of span arithmetic: Only the extrema need to be clipped, and no interior pixels need be examined. Scissoring shows yet another advantage of span coherence. Also, if an outline primitive is not much larger than the clip rectangle, not many pixels, relatively speaking, will fall outside the clip region. For such a case, it may well be faster to generate each pixel and to clip it (i.e., to write it conditionally) than to do analytical clipping beforehand. In particular, although the bounds test is in the inner loop, the expensive memory write is avoided for exterior pixels, and both the incremental computation and the testing may run entirely in a fast memory, such as a CPU instruction cache or a display controller's microcode memory.

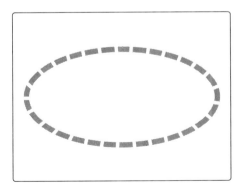

Fig. 3.37 Combining pen pattern and line style.

Other tricks may be useful. For example, one may "home in" on the intersection of a line with a clip edge by doing the standard midpoint scan-conversion algorithm on every ith pixel and testing the chosen pixel against the rectangle bounds until the first pixel that lies inside the region is encountered. Then the algorithm has to back up, find the first pixel inside, and to do the normal scan conversion thereafter. The last interior pixel could be similarly determined, or each pixel could be tested as part of the scan-conversion loop and scan conversion stopped the first time the test failed. Testing every eighth pixel works well, since it is a good compromise between having too many tests and too many pixels to back up (see Exercise 3.26).

For graphics packages that operate in floating point, it is best to clip analytically in the floating-point coordinate system and then to scan convert the clipped primitives, being careful to initialize decision variables correctly, as we did for lines in Section 3.2.3. For integer graphics packages such as SRGP, there is a choice between preclipping and then scan converting or doing clipping during scan conversion. Since it is relatively easy to do analytical clipping for lines and polygons, clipping of those primitives is often done before scan conversion, while it is faster to clip other primitives during scan conversion. Also, it is quite common for a floating-point graphics package to do analytical clipping in its coordinate system and then to call lower-level scan-conversion software that actually generates the clipped primitives; this integer graphics software could then do an additional raster clip to rectangular (or even arbitrary) window boundaries. Because analytic clipping of primitives is both useful for integer graphics packages and essential for 2D and 3D floating-point graphics packages, we discuss the basic analytical clipping algorithms in this chapter.

3.12 CLIPPING LINES

This section treats analytical clipping of lines against rectangles;[10] algorithms for clipping other primitives are handled in subsequent sections. Although there are specialized algorithms for rectangle and polygon clipping, it is important to note that SRGP primitives built out of lines (i.e., polylines, unfilled rectangles, and polygons) can be clipped by repeated application of the line clipper. Furthermore, circles and ellipses may be piecewise-linearly approximated with a sequence of very short lines, so that boundaries can be treated as a single polyline or polygon for both clipping and scan conversion. Conics are represented in some systems as ratios of parametric polynomials (see Chapter 11), a representation that also lends itself readily to an incremental, piecewise linear approximation suitable for a line-clipping algorithm. Clipping a rectangle against a rectangle results in at most a single rectangle. Clipping a convex polygon against a rectangle results in at most a single convex polygon, but clipping a concave polygon may produce more than one concave polygon. Clipping a circle or ellipse against a rectangle results in as many as four arcs.

Lines intersecting a rectangular clip region (or any convex polygon) are always clipped to a single line segment; lines lying on the clip rectangle's border are considered inside and hence are displayed. Figure 3.38 shows several examples of clipped lines.

---

[10]This chapter does not cover clipping primitives to multiple rectangles (as when windows overlap in a windowing system) or to nonrectangular regions; the latter topic is discussed briefly in Section 19.7.

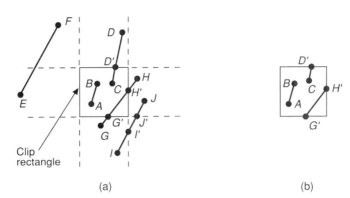

Fig. 3.38 Cases for clipping lines.

3.12.1 Clipping Endpoints

Before we discuss clipping lines, let's look at the simpler problem of clipping individual points. If the x coordinate boundaries of the clip rectangle are at x_{min} and x_{max}, and the y coordinate boundaries are at y_{min} and y_{max}, then four inequalities must be satisfied for a point at (x, y) to be inside the clip rectangle:

$$x_{min} \le x \le x_{max}, \; y_{min} \le y \le y_{max}.$$

If any of the four inequalities does not hold, the point is outside the clip rectangle.

3.12.2 Clipping Lines by Solving Simultaneous Equations

To clip a line, we need to consider only its endpoints, not its infinitely many interior points. If both endpoints of a line lie inside the clip rectangle (e.g., AB in Fig. 3.38), the entire line lies inside the clip rectangle and can be *trivially accepted*. If one endpoint lies inside and one outside (e.g., CD in the figure), the line intersects the clip rectangle and we must compute the intersection point. If both endpoints are outside the clip rectangle, the line may (or may not) intersect with the clip rectangle (EF, GH, and IJ in the figure), and we need to perform further calculations to determine whether there are any intersections, and if there are, where they occur.

The brute-force approach to clipping a line that cannot be trivially accepted is to intersect that line with each of the four clip-rectangle edges to see whether any intersection points lie on those edges; if so, the line cuts the clip rectangle and is partially inside. For each line and clip-rectangle edge, we therefore take the two mathematically infinite lines that contain them and intersect them. Next, we test whether this intersection point is "interior"—that is, whether it lies within both the clip rectangle edge and the line; if so, there is an intersection with the clip rectangle. In Fig. 3.38, intersection points G' and H' are interior, but I' and J' are not.

When we use this approach, we must solve two simultaneous equations using multiplication and division for each <edge, line> pair. Although the slope-intercept formula for lines learned in analytic geometry could be used, it describes infinite lines, whereas in graphics and clipping we deal with finite lines (called *line segments* in mathematics). In addition, the slope-intercept formula does not deal with vertical lines—a serious problem, given our upright clip rectangle. A parametric formulation for line segments solves both problems:

$$x = x_0 + t(x_1 - x_0), \ y = y_0 + t(y_1 - y_0).$$

These equations describe (x, y) on the directed line segment from (x_0, y_0) to (x_1, y_1) for the parameter t in the range $[0, 1]$, as simple substitution for t confirms. Two sets of simultaneous equations of this parametric form can be solved for parameters t_{edge} for the edge and t_{line} for the line segment. The values of t_{edge} and t_{line} can then be checked to see whether both lie in $[0, 1]$; if they do, the intersection point lies within both segments and is a true clip-rectangle intersection. Furthermore, the special case of a line parallel to a clip-rectangle edge must also be tested before the simultaneous equations can be solved. Altogether, the brute-force approach involves considerable calculation and testing; it is thus inefficient.

3.12.3   The Cohen–Sutherland Line-Clipping Algorithm

The more efficient Cohen–Sutherland algorithm performs initial tests on a line to determine whether intersection calculations can be avoided. First, endpoint pairs are checked for trivial acceptance. If the line cannot be trivially accepted, *region checks* are done. For instance, two simple comparisons on x show that both endpoints of line *EF* in Fig. 3.38 have an x coordinate less than x_{min} and thus lie in the region to the left of the clip rectangle (i.e., in the outside halfplane defined by the left edge); therefore, line segment *EF* can be *trivially rejected* and needs to be neither clipped nor displayed. Similarly, we can trivially reject lines with both endpoints in regions to the right of x_{max}, below y_{min}, and above y_{max}.

   If the line segment can be neither trivially accepted nor rejected, it is divided into two segments at a clip edge, so that one segment can be trivially rejected. Thus, a segment is iteratively clipped by testing for trivial acceptance or rejection, and is then subdivided if neither test is successful, until what remains is completely inside the clip rectangle or can be trivially rejected. The algorithm is particularly efficient for two common cases. In the first case of a large clip rectangle enclosing all or most of the display area, most primitives can be trivially accepted. In the second case of a small clip rectangle, almost all primitives can be trivially rejected. This latter case arises in a standard method of doing pick correlation in which a small rectangle surrounding the cursor, called the *pick window*, is used to clip primitives to determine which primitives lie within a small (rectangular) neighborhood of the cursor's *pick point* (see Section 7.12.2).

   To perform trivial accept and reject tests, we extend the edges of the clip rectangle to divide the plane of the clip rectangle into nine regions (see Fig. 3.39). Each region is assigned a 4-bit code, determined by where the region lies with respect to the outside halfplanes of the clip-rectangle edges. Each bit in the outcode is set to either 1 (true) or 0 (false); the 4 bits in the code correspond to the following conditions:

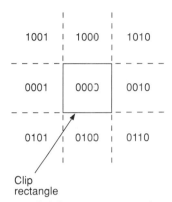

Fig. 3.39 Region outcodes.

First bit	outside halfplane of top edge, above top edge	$y > y_{max}$
Second bit	outside halfplane of bottom edge, below bottom edge	$y < y_{min}$
Third bit	outside halfplane of right edge, to the right of right edge	$x > x_{max}$
Fourth bit	outside halfplane of left edge, to the left of left edge	$x < x_{min}$

Since the region lying above and to the left of the clip rectangle, for example, lies in the outside halfplane of the top and left edges, it is assigned a code of 1001. A particularly efficient way to calculate the outcode derives from the observation that bit 1 is the sign bit of $(y_{max} - y)$; bit 2 is that of $(y - y_{min})$; bit 3 is that of $(x_{max} - x)$; and bit 4 is that of $(x - x_{min})$. Each endpoint of the line segment is then assigned the code of the region in which it lies. We can now use these endpoint codes to determine whether the line segment lies completely inside the clip rectangle or in the outside halfplane of an edge. If both 4-bit codes of the endpoints are zero, then the line lies completely inside the clip rectangle. However, if both endpoints lie in the outside halfplane of a particular edge, as for *EF* in Fig. 3.38, the codes for both endpoints each have the bit set showing that the point lies in the outside halfplane of that edge. For *EF*, the outcodes are 0001 and 1001, respectively, showing with the fourth bit that the line segment lies in the outside halfplane of the left edge. Therefore, if the logical **and** of the codes of the endpoints is not zero, the line can be trivially rejected.

If a line cannot be trivially accepted or rejected, we must subdivide it into two segments such that one or both segments can be discarded. We accomplish this subdivision by using an edge that the line crosses to cut the line into two segments: The section lying in the outside halfplane of the edge is thrown away. We can choose any order in which to test edges, but we must, of course, use the same order each time in the algorithm; we shall use the top-to-bottom, right-to-left order of the outcode. A key property of the outcode is that bits that are set in a nonzero outcode correspond to edges crossed: If one endpoint lies in the outside halfplane of an edge and the line segment fails the trivial-rejection tests, then the other point must lie on the inside halfplane of that edge and the line segment must cross it. Thus, the algorithm always chooses a point that lies outside and then uses an outcode bit that is set to determine a clip edge; the edge chosen is the first in the top-to-bottom, right-to-left order—that is, it is the leftmost bit that is set in the outcode.

The algorithm works as follows. We compute the outcodes of both endpoints and check for trivial acceptance and rejection. If neither test is succesful, we find an endpoint that lies outside (at least one will), and then test the outcode to find the edge that is crossed and to determine the corresponding intersection point. We can then clip off the line segment from the outside endpoint to the intersection point by replacing the outside endpoint with the intersection point, and compute the outcode of this new endpoint to prepare for the next iteration.

For example, consider the line segment *AD* in Fig. 3.40. Point *A* has outcode 0000 and point *D* has outcode 1001. The line can be neither trivially accepted or rejected. Therefore, the algorithm chooses *D* as the outside point, whose outcode shows that the line crosses the top edge and the left edge. By our testing order, we first use the top edge to clip *AD* to *AB*, and we compute *B*'s outcode as 0000. In the next iteration, we apply the trivial acceptance/rejection tests to *AB*, and it is trivially accepted and displayed.

Line *EI* requires multiple iterations. The first endpoint, *E*, has an outcode of 0100, so the algorithm chooses it as the outside point and tests the outcode to find that the first edge against which the line is cut is the bottom edge, where *EI* is clipped to *FI*. In the second iteration, *FI* cannot be trivially accepted or rejected. The outcode of the first endpoint, *F*, is 0000, so the algorithm chooses the outside point *I* that has outcode 1010. The first edge clipped against is therefore the top edge, yielding *FH*. *H*'s outcode is determined to be 0010, so the third iteration results in a clip against the right edge to *FG*. This is trivially accepted in the fourth and final iteration and displayed. A different sequence of clips would have resulted if we had picked *I* as the initial point: On the basis of its outcode, we would have clipped against the top edge first, then the right edge, and finally the bottom edge.

In the code of Fig. 3.41, we use constant integers and bitwise arithmetic to represent the outcodes, because this representation is more natural than an array with an entry for each outcode. We use an internal procedure to calculate the outcode for modularity; to improve performance, we would, of course, put this code in line.

We can improve the efficiency of the algorithm slightly by not recalculating slopes (see Exercise 3.28). Even with this improvement, however, the algorithm is not the most efficient one. Because testing and clipping are done in a fixed order, the algorithm will sometimes perform needless clipping. Such clipping occurs when the intersection with a rectangle edge is an "external intersection"; that is, when it does not lie on the clip-rectangle boundary (e.g., point *H* on line *EI* in Fig. 3.40). The Nicholl, Lee, and

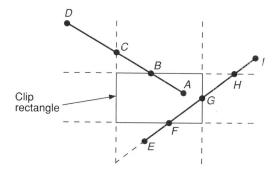

Fig. 3.40 Illustration of Cohen–Sutherland line clipping.

```
typedef unsigned int outcode;
enum {TOP = 0x1, BOTTOM = 0x2, RIGHT = 0x4, LEFT = 0x8};

void CohenSutherlandLineClipAndDraw (
    double x0, double y0, double x1, double y1, double xmin, double xmax,
    double ymin, double ymax, int value)
/* Cohen-Sutherland clipping algorithm for line P0 = (x0, y0) to P1 = (x1, y1) and */
/* clip rectangle with diagonal from (xmin, ymin) to (xmax, ymax) */
{
    /* Outcodes for P0, P1, and whatever point lies outside the clip rectangle */
    outcode outcode0, outcode1, outcodeOut;
    boolean accept = FALSE, done = FALSE;
    outcode0 = CompOutCode (x0, y0, xmin, xmax, ymin, ymax);
    outcode1 = CompOutCode (x1, y1, xmin, xmax, ymin, ymax);
    do {
        if (!(outcode0 | outcode1)) {              /* Trivial accept and exit */
            accept = TRUE; done = TRUE;
        } else if (outcode0 & outcode1)            /* Logical and is true, so trivial reject and exit */
            done = TRUE;
        else {
            /* Failed both tests, so calculate the line segment to clip: */
            /* from an outside point to an intersection with clip edge. */
            double x, y;
            /* At least one endpoint is outside the clip rectangle; pick it. */
            outcodeOut = outcode0 ? outcode0 : outcode1;
            /* Now find intersection point; */
            /* use formulas y = y0 + slope * (x − x0), x = x0 + (1/slope) * (y − y0). */
            if (outcodeOut & TOP) {                 /* Divide line at top of clip rect */
                x = x0 + (x1 − x0) * (ymax − y0) / (y1 − y0);
                y = ymax;
            } else if (outcodeOut & BOTTOM) {       /* Divide line at bottom edge of clip rect */
                x = x0 + (x1 − x0) * (ymin − y0) / (y1 − y0);
                y = ymin;
            } else if (outcodeOut & RIGHT) {        /* Divide line at right edge of clip rect */
                y = y0 + (y1 − y0) * (xmax − x0) / (x1 − x0);
                x = xmax;
            } else {                                /* Divide line at left edge of clip rect */
                y = y0 + (y1 − y0) * (xmin − x0) / (x1 − x0);
                x = xmin;
            }
            /* Now we move outside point to intersection point to clip, */
            /* and get ready for next pass. */
            if (outcodeOut == outcode0) {
                x0 = x; y0 = y; outcode0 = CompOutCode (x0, y0, xmin, xmax, ymin, ymax);
            } else {
                x1 = x; y1 = y; outcode1 = CompOutCode (x1, y1, xmin, xmax, ymin, ymax);
            }
        } /* Subdivide */
    } while (done == FALSE);
```

Fig. 3.41 *(Cont.)*.

```
        if (accept)
            MidpointLineReal (x0, y0, x1, y1, value);     /* Version for double coordinates */
}   /* CohenSutherlandLineClipAndDraw */

outcode CompOutCode (
        double x, double y, double xmin, double xmax, double ymin, double ymax);
{
    outcode code = 0;
    if (y > ymax)
        code |= TOP;
    else if (y < ymin)
        code |= BOTTOM;
    if (x > xmax)
        code |= RIGHT;
    else if (x < xmin)
        code |= LEFT;
    return code;
}   /* CompOutCode */
```

Fig. 3.41 Cohen–Sutherland line-clipping algorithm.

Nicholl [NICH87] algorithm, by contrast, avoids calculating external intersections by subdividing the plane into many more regions; it is discussed in Chapter 19. An advantage of the much simpler Cohen–Sutherland algorithm is that its extension to a 3D orthographic view volume is straightforward, as seen in Section 6.5.3

3.12.4   A Parametric Line-Clipping Algorithm

The Cohen–Sutherland algorithm is probably still the most commonly used line-clipping algorithm because it has been around longest and has been published widely. In 1978, Cyrus and Beck published an algorithm that takes a fundamentally different and generally more efficient approach to line clipping [CYRU78]. The Cyrus–Beck technique can be used to clip a 2D line against a rectangle or an arbitrary convex polygon in the plane, or a 3D line against an arbitrary convex polyhedron in 3D space. Liang and Barsky later independently developed a more efficient parametric line-clipping algorithm that is especially fast in the special cases of upright 2D and 3D clip regions [LIAN84]. In addition to taking advantage of these simple clip boundaries, they introduced more efficient trivial rejection tests that work for general clip regions. Here we follow the original Cyrus–Beck development to introduce parametric clipping. Since we are concerned only with upright clip rectangles, however, we reduce the Cyrus–Beck formulation to the more efficient Liang–Barsky case at the end of the development.

Recall that the Cohen–Sutherland algorithm, for lines that cannot be trivially accepted or rejected, calculates the (x, y) intersection of a line segment with a clip edge by substituting the known value of x or y for the vertical or horizontal clip edge, respectively. The parametric line algorithm, however, finds the value of the parameter t in the parametric representation of the line segment for the point at which that segment intersects the infinite line on which the clip edge lies. Because all clip edges are in general intersected by the line, four values of t are calculated. A series of simple comparisons is used to determine which (if any) of the four values of t correspond to actual intersections. Only then are the (x, y) values for one or two actual intersections calculated. In general, this approach saves time over the Cohen–Sutherland intersection-calculation algorithm because it avoids the repetitive looping needed to clip to multiple clip-rectangle edges. Also, calculations in 1D parameter space are simpler than those in 3D coordinate space. Liang and Barsky improve on Cyrus–Beck by examining each t-value as it is generated, to reject some line segments before all four t-values have been computed.

The Cyrus–Beck algorithm is based on the following formulation of the intersection between two lines. Figure 3.42 shows a single edge E_i of the clip rectangle and that edge's outward normal N_i (i.e., outward to the clip rectangle[11]), as well as the line segment from P_0 to P_1 that must be clipped to the edge. Either the edge or the line segment may have to be extended to find the intersection point.

As before, this line is represented parametrically as

$$P(t) = P_0 + (P_1 - P_0)t,$$

where $t = 0$ at P_0 and $t = 1$ at P_1. Now, pick an arbitrary point P_{E_i} on edge E_i and consider the three vectors $P(t) - P_{E_i}$ from P_{E_i} to three designated points on the line from P_0 to P_1: the intersection point to be determined, an endpoint of the line on the inside halfplane of the edge, and an endpoint on the line in the outside halfplane of the edge. We can distinguish in which region a point lies by looking at the value of the dot product $N_i \cdot [P(t) - P_{E_i}]$. This value is negative for a point in the inside halfplane, zero for a point on the line containing the edge, and positive for a point that lies in the outside halfplane. The definitions of inside and outside halfplanes of an edge correspond to a counterclockwise enumeration of the edges of the clip region, a convention we shall use throughout this book. Now we can solve for the value of t at the intersection of $P_0 P_1$ with the edge:

$$N_i \cdot [P(t) - P_{E_i}] = 0.$$

First, substitute for $P(t)$:

$$N_i \cdot [P_0 + (P_1 - P_0)t - P_{E_i}] = 0.$$

Next, group terms and distribute the dot product:

$$N_i \cdot [P_0 - P_{E_i}] + N_i \cdot [P_1 - P_0]t = 0.$$

Let $D = (P_1 - P_0)$ be the vector from P_0 to P_1, and solve for t:

$$t = \frac{N_i \cdot [P_0 - P_{E_i}]}{-N_i \cdot D}. \tag{3.1}$$

Note that this gives a valid value of t only if the denominator of the expression is nonzero.

---

[11]Cyrus and Beck use inward normals, but we prefer to use outward normals for consistency with plane normals in 3D, which are outward. Our formulation therefore differs only in the testing of a sign.

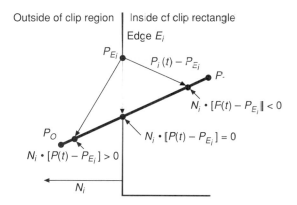

Fig. 3.42 Dot products for three points outside, inside, and on the boundary of the clip region.

For this to be true, the algorithm checks that

$N_i \neq 0$ (that is, the normal should not be 0; this could occur only as a mistake),

$D \neq 0$ (that is, $P_1 \neq P_0$),

$N_i \cdot D \neq 0$ (that is, the edge E_i and the line from P_0 to P_1 are not parallel. If they were parallel, there can be no single intersection for this edge, so the algorithm moves on to the next case.).

Equation (3.1) can be used to find the intersections between $P_0 P_1$ and each edge of the clip rectangle. We do this calculation by determining the normal and an arbitrary P_{Ei}—say, an endpoint of the edge—for each clip edge, then using these values for all line segments. Given the four values of t for a line segment, the next step is to determine which (if any) of the values correspond to internal intersections of the line segment with edges of the clip rectangle. As a first step, any value of t outside the interval [0, 1] can be discarded, since it lies outside $P_0 P_1$. Next, we need to determine whether the intersection lies on the clip boundary.

We could try simply sorting the remaining values of t, choosing the intermediate values of t for intersection points, as suggested in Fig. 3.43 for the case of line 1. But how do we distinguish this case from that of line 2, in which no portion of the line segment lies in the clip rectangle and the intermediate values of t correspond to points not on the clip boundary? Also, which of the four intersections of line 3 are the ones on the clip boundary?

The intersections in Fig. 3.43 are characterized as "potentially entering" (PE) or "potentially leaving" (PL) the clip rectangle, as follows: If moving from P_0 to P_1 causes us to cross a particular edge to enter the edge's inside halfplane, the intersection is PE; if it causes us to leave the edge's inside halfplane, it is PL. Notice that, with this distinction, two interior intersection points of a line intersecting the clip rectangle have opposing labels.

Formally, intersections can be classified as PE or PL on the basis of the angle between $P_0 P_1$ and N_i: If the angle is less than 90°, the intersection is PL; if it is greater than 90°, it is PE. This information is contained in the sign of the dot product of N_i and $P_0 P_1$:

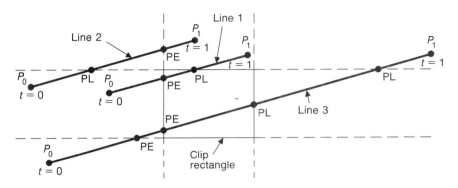

Fig. 3.43 Lines lying diagonal to the clip rectangle.

$$N_i \cdot D < 0 \Rightarrow \text{PE (angle greater than 90),}$$
$$N_i \cdot D > 0 \Rightarrow \text{PL (angle less than 90).}$$

Notice that $N_i \cdot D$ is merely the denominator of Eq. (3.1), which means that, in the process of calculating t, the intersection can be trivially categorized.

With this categorization, line 3 in Fig. 3.43 suggests the final step in the process. We must choose a (PE, PL) pair that defines the clipped line. The portion of the infinite line through $P_0 P_1$ that is within the clipping region is bounded by the PE intersection with the largest t value, which we call t_E, and the PL intersection with the smallest t value, t_L. The intersecting line segment is then defined by the range (t_E, t_L). But because we are interested in intersecting $P_0 P_1$, not the infinite line, the definition of the range must be further modified so that $t = 0$ is a lower bound for t_E and $t = 1$ is an upper bound for t_L. What if $t_E > t_L$? This is exactly the case for line 2. It means that no portion of $P_0 P_1$ is within the clip rectangle, and the entire line is rejected. Values of t_E and t_L that correspond to actual intersections are used to calculate the corresponding x and y coordinates.

The completed algorithm for upright clip rectangles is pseudocoded in Fig. 3.44. Table 3.1 shows for each edge the values of N_i, a canonical point on the edge, P_{E_i}, the vector $P_0 - P_{E_i}$ and the parameter t. Interestingly enough, because one coordinate of each normal is 0, we do not need to pin down the corresponding coordinate of P_{E_i} (denoted by an indeterminate x or y). Indeed, because the clip edges are horizontal and vertical, many simplifications apply that have natural interpretations. Thus we see from the table that the numerator, the dot product $N_i \cdot (P_0 - P_{E_i})$ determining whether the endpoint P_0 lies inside or outside a specified edge, reduces to the directed horizontal or vertical distance from the point to the edge. This is exactly the same quantity computed for the corresponding component of the Cohen-Sutherland outcode. The denominator dot product $N_i \cdot D$, which determines whether the intersection is potentially entering or leaving, reduces to $\pm dx$ or dy: if dx is positive, the line moves from left to right and is PE for the left edge, PL for the right edge, and so on. Finally, the parameter t, the ratio of numerator and denominator, reduces to the distance to an edge divided by dx or dy, exactly the constant of proportionality we could calculate directly from the parametric line formulation. Note that it is important to preserve the signs of the numerator and denominator instead of cancelling minus signs, because the numerator and denominator as signed distances carry information that is used in the algorithm.

precalculate N_i and select a P_{E_i} for each edge;

```
for (each line segment to be clipped) {
    if (P₁ == P₀)
        line is degenerate so clip as a point;
    else {
        tₑ = 0; tₗ = 1;
        for (each candidate intersection with a clip edge) {
            if (Nᵢ • D != 0) {      /* Ignore edges parallel to line for now */
                calculate t;
                use sign of Nᵢ • D to categorize as PE or PL:
                if (PE) tₑ = max (tₑ, t);
                if (PL) tₗ = min (tₗ, t);
            }
        }
        if (tₑ > tₗ)
            return NULL;
        else
            return P(tₑ) and P(tₗ) as true clip intersections;
    }
}
```

Fig. 3.44 Pseudocode for Cyrus–Beck parametric line clipping algorithm.

The complete version of the code, adapted from [LIAN84] is shown in Fig. 3.45. The procedure calls an internal function, CLIPt(), that uses the sign of the denominator to determine whether the line segment-edge intersection is potentially entering (PE) or leaving (PL), computes the parameter value of the intersection and checks to see if trivial rejection can be done because the new value of t_E or t_L would cross the old value of t_L or t_E, respectively. It also signals trivial rejection if the line is parallel to the edge and on the

TABLE 3.1 CALCULATIONS FOR PARAMETRIC LINE CLIPPING ALGORITHM*

Clip edge$_i$	Normal N_i	P_{Ei}	$P_0 - P_{Ei}$	$t = \dfrac{N_i \cdot (P_1 - P_{Ei})}{-N_i \cdot D}$
left: $x = x_{min}$	$(-1, 0)$	(x_{min}, y)	$(x_0 - x_{min}, y_0 - y)$	$\dfrac{-(x_0 - x_{min})}{(x_1 - x_0)}$
right: $x = x_{max}$	$(1, 0)$	(x_{max}, y)	$(x_0 - x_{max}, y_0 - y)$	$\dfrac{(x_0 - x_{max})}{-(x_1 - x_0)}$
bottom: $y = y_{min}$	$(0, -1)$	(x, y_{min})	$(x_0 - x, y_0 - y_{min})$	$\dfrac{-(y_0 - y_{min})}{(y_1 - y_0)}$
top: $y = y_{max}$	$(0, 1)$	(x, y_{max})	$(x_0 - x, y_0 - y_{max})$	$\dfrac{(y_0 - y_{max})}{-(y_1 - y_0)}$

*The exact coordinates of the point P_{E_i} on each edge are irrelevant to the computation, so they have been denoted by variables x and y. For a point on the right edge, $x=x_{min}$ as indicated in the first row, third entry.

void Clip2D (**double** *x0, **double** *y0, **double** *x1, **double** *y1, boolean *visible)
/* Clip 2D line segment with endpoints (x0, y0) and (x1, y1), against upright */
/* clip rectangle with corners at (xmin, ymin) and (xmax, ymax); these are */
/* globals or could be passed as parameters also. The flag visible is set TRUE. */
/* if a clipped segment is returned in endpoint parameters. If the line */
/* is rejected, the endpoints are not changed and visible is set to FALSE. */
{
    double dx = *x1 − *x0;
    double dy = *y1 − *y0;
    /* Output is generated only if line is inside all four edges. */
    *visible = FALSE;
    /* First test for degenerate line and clip the point; ClipPoint returns */
    /* TRUE if the point lies inside the clip rectangle. */
    if (dx == 0 && dy == 0 && ClipPoint (*x0, *y0))
        *visible = TRUE;
    else {
        double tE = 0.0;
        double tL = 1.0;
        if (CLIPt (dx, xmin − *x0, &tE, &tL))   /* Inside wrt left edge */
            if (CLIPt (−dx, *x0 − xmax, &tE, &tL))   /* Inside wrt right edge */
                if (CLIPt (dy, ymin − *y0, &tE, &tL))   /* Inside wrt bottom edge */
                    if (CLIPt (−dy, *y0 − ymax, &tE, &tL)) { /* Inside wrt top edge */
                    *visible = TRUE;
                    /* Compute PL intersection, if tL has moved */
                    if (tL < 1) {
                        *x1 = *x0 + tL * dx;
                        *y1 = *y0 + tL * dy;
                    }
                    /* Compute PE intersection, if tE has moved */
                    if (tE > 0) {
                        *x0 += tE * dx;
                        *y0 += tE * dy;
                    }
                }
    }
} /* Clip2D */

boolean CLIPt (**double** denom, **double** num, **double** *tE, **double** *tL)
/* This function computes a new value of tE or tL for an interior intersection */
/* of a line segment and an edge. Parameter denom is −(N_i • D), which reduces to */
/* ± Δx, Δy for upright rectangles (as shown in Table 3.1); its sign */
/* determines whether the intersection is PE or PL. Parameter num is $N_i \bullet (P_0 - P_{E_i})$ */
/* for a particular edge/line combination, which reduces to directed horizontal */
/* and vertical distances from P_0 to an edge; its sign determines visibility */
/* of P_0 and is used to trivially reject horizontal or vertical lines. If the */
/* line segment can be trivially rejected, FALSE is returned; if it cannot be, */
/* TRUE is returned and the value of tE or tL is adjusted, if needed, for the */
/* portion of the segment that is inside the edge. */

Fig. 3.45 (Cont.).

```
{
      double t;

      if (denom > 0) {              /* PE intersection */
            t = num / denom;        /* Value of t at the intersection */
            if (t > tL)             /* tE and tL crossover */
                  return FALSE;     /* so prepare to reject line */
            else if (t > tE)        /* A new tE has been found */
                  tE = t;
      } else if (denom < 0) {       /* PL intersection */
            t = num / denom;        /* Value of t at the intersection */
            if (t < tE)             /* tE and tL crossover */
                  return FALSE;     /* so prepare to reject line */
            else                    /* A new tL has been found */
                  tL = t;
      } else if (num > 0)           /* Line on outside of edge */
            return FALSE;
      return TRUE;
}     /* CLIPt */
```

Fig. 3.45 Code for Liang–Barsky parametric line-clipping algorithm.

outside; i.e., would be invisible. The main procedure then does the actual clipping by moving the endpoints to the most recent values of t_E and t_L computed, but only if there is a line segment inside all four edges. This condition is tested for by a four-deep nested **if** that checks the flags returned by the function signifying whether or not the line segment was rejected.

In summary, the Cohen–Sutherland algorithm is efficient when outcode testing can be done cheaply (for example, by doing bitwise operations in assembly language) and trivial acceptance or rejection is applicable to the majority of line segments. Parametric line clipping wins when many line segments need to be clipped, since the actual calculation of the coordinates of the intersection points is postponed until needed, and testing can be done on parameter values. This parameter calculation is done even for endpoints that would have been trivially accepted in the Cohen–Sutherland strategy, however. The Liang–Barsky algorithm is more efficient than the Cyrus–Beck version because of additional trivial rejection testing that can avoid calculation of all four parameter values for lines that do not intersect the clip rectangle. For lines that cannot be trivially rejected by Cohen–Sutherland because they do not lie in an invisible halfplane, the rejection tests of Liang–Barsky are clearly preferable to the repeated clipping required by Cohen–Sutherland. The Nicholl et al. algorithm of Section 19.1.1 is generally preferable to either Cohen–Sutherland or Liang–Barsky but does not generalize to 3D, as does parametric clipping. Speed-ups to Cohen–Sutherland are discussed in [DUVA90]. Exercise 3.29 concerns instruction counting for the two algorithms covered here, as a means of contrasting their efficiency under various conditions.

3.13   CLIPPING CIRCLES AND ELLIPSES

To clip a circle against a rectangle, we can first do a trivial accept/reject test by intersecting the circle's extent (a square of the size of the circle's diameter) with the clip rectangle, using the algorithm in the next section for polygon clipping. If the circle intersects the rectangle, we divide it into quadrants and do the trivial accept/reject test for each. These tests may lead in turn to tests for octants. We can then compute the intersection of the circle and the edge analytically by solving their equations simultaneously, and then scan convert the resulting arcs using the appropriately initialized algorithm with the calculated (and suitably rounded) starting and ending points. If scan conversion is fast, or if the circle is not too large, it is probably more efficient to scissor on a pixel-by-pixel basis, testing each boundary pixel against the rectangle bounds before it is written. An extent check would certainly be useful in any case. If the circle is filled, spans of adjacent interior pixels on each scan line can be filled without bounds checking by clipping each span and then filling its interior pixels, as discussed in Section 3.7.

To clip ellipses, we use extent testing at least down to the quadrant level, as with circles. We can then either compute the intersections of ellipse and rectangle analytically and use those (suitably rounded) endpoints in the appropriately initialized scan-conversion algorithm given in the next section, or clip as we scan convert.

3.14   CLIPPING POLYGONS

An algorithm that clips a polygon must deal with many different cases, as shown in Fig. 3.46. The case in part (a) is particularly noteworthy in that the concave polygon is clipped into two separate polygons. All in all, the task of clipping seems rather complex. Each edge of the polygon must be tested against each edge of the clip rectangle; new edges must be added, and existing edges must be discarded, retained, or divided. Multiple polygons may result from clipping a single polygon. We need an organized way to deal with all these cases.

3.14.1   The Sutherland–Hodgman Polygon-Clipping Algorithm

Sutherland and Hodgman's polygon-clipping algorithm [SUTH74b] uses a divide-and-conquer strategy: It solves a series of simple and identical problems that, when combined, solve the overall problem. The simple problem is to clip a polygon against a single infinite clip edge. Four clip edges, each defining one boundary of the clip rectangle (see Fig. 3.47), successively clip a polygon against a clip rectangle.

Note the difference between this strategy for a polygon and the Cohen–Sutherland algorithm for clipping a line: The polygon clipper clips against four edges in succession, whereas the line clipper tests the outcode to see which edge is crossed, and clips only when

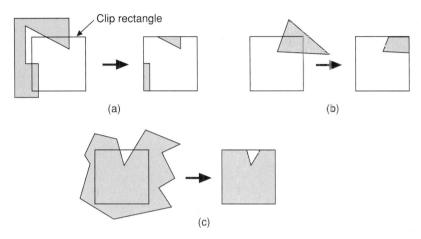

Fig. 3.46 Examples of polygon clipping. (a) Multiple components. (b) Simple convex case. (c) Concave case with many exterior edges.

necessary. The actual Sutherland–Hodgman algorithm is in fact more general: A polygon (convex or concave) can be clipped against any convex clipping polygon; in 3D, polygons can be clipped against convex polyhedral volumes defined by planes. The algorithm accepts a series of polygon vertices $v_1, v_2, \ldots, v_n$. In 2D, the vertices define polygon edges from v_i to v_{i+1} and from v_n to v_1. The algorithm clips against a single, infinite clip edge and outputs another series of vertices defining the clipped polygon. In a second pass, the partially clipped polygon is then clipped against the second clip edge, and so on.

The algorithm moves around the polygon from v_n to v_1 and then on back to v_n, at each step examining the relationship between successive vertices and the clip edge. At each step,

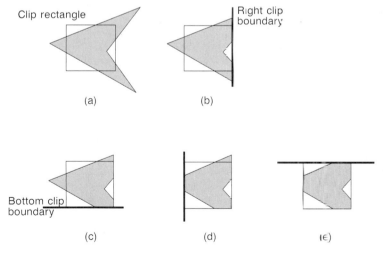

Fig. 3.47 Polygon clipping, edge by edge. (a) Before clipping. (b) Clip on right. (c) Clip on bottom. (d) Clip on left. (e) Clip on top; polygon is fully clipped.

zero, one, or two vertices are added to the output list of vertices that defines the clipped polygon. Four possible cases must be analyzed, as shown in Fig. 3.48.

Let's consider the polygon edge from vertex s to vertex p in Fig. 3.48. Assume that start point s has been dealt with in the previous iteration. In case 1, when the polygon edge is completely inside the clip boundary, vertex p is added to the output list. In case 2, the intersection point i is output as a vertex because the edge intersects the boundary. In case 3, both vertices are outside the boundary, so there is no output. In case 4, the intersection point i and p are both added to the output list.

Function SutherlandHodgmanPolygonClip( ) in Fig. 3.49 accepts an array *inVertex-Array* of vertices and creates another array *outVertexArray* of vertices. To keep the code simple, we show no error checking on array bounds, and we use the function Output( ) to place a vertex into *outVertexArray*. The function Intersect( ) calculates the intersection of the polygon edge from vertex s to vertex p with *clip Boundary*, which is defined by two vertices on the clip polygon's boundary. The function Inside( ) returns **true** if the vertex is on the inside of the clip boundary, where "inside" is defined as "to the left of the clip boundary when one looks from the first vertex to the second vertex of the clip boundary." This sense corresponds to a counterclockwise enumeration of edges. To calculate whether a point lies outside a clip boundary, we can test the sign of the dot product of the normal to the clip boundary and the polygon edge, as described in Section 3.12.4. (For the simple case of an upright clip rectangle, we need only test the sign of the horizontal or vertical distance to its boundary.)

Sutherland and Hodgman show how to structure the algorithm so that it is reentrant [SUTH74b]. As soon as a vertex is output, the clipper calls itself with that vertex. Clipping is performed against the next clip boundary, so that no intermediate storage is necessary for the partially clipped polygon: In essence, the polygon is passed through a "pipeline" of clippers. Each step can be implemented as special-purpose hardware with no intervening buffer space. This property (and its generality) makes the algorithm suitable for today's hardware implementations. In the algorithm as it stands, however, new edges may be introduced on the border of the clip rectangle. Consider Fig. 3.46 (a)—a new edge is introduced by connecting the left top of the triangle and the left top of the rectangle. A

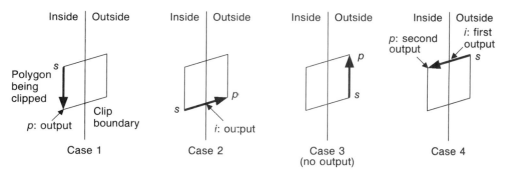

Fig. 3.48 Four cases of polygon clipping.

postprocessing phase can eliminate these edges, as discussed in Chapter 19. A polygon-clipping algorithm based on the parametric-line representation for clipping to upright rectangular clip regions is discussed, along with the Weiler algorithm for clipping polygons to polygons, in Section 19.1.

3.15 GENERATING CHARACTERS

3.15.1   Defining and Clipping Characters

There are two basic techniques for defining characters. The most general but most computationally expensive way is to define each character as a curved or polygonal outline and to scan convert it as needed. We first discuss the other, simpler way, in which each character in a given font is specified as a small rectangular bitmap. Generating a character then entails simply using a copyPixel to copy the character's image from an offscreen canvas, called a *font cache*, into the frame buffer at the desired position.

The font cache may actually be in the frame buffer, as follows. In most graphics systems in which the display is refreshed from a private frame buffer that memory is larger than is strictly required for storing the displayed image. For example, the pixels for a rectangular screen may be stored in a square memory, leaving a rectangular strip of "invisible" screen memory. Alternatively, there may be enough memory for two screens, one of which is being refreshed and one of which is being drawn in, to double-buffer the image. The font cache for the currently displayed font(s) is frequently stored in such invisible screen memory because the display controller's copyPixel works fastest within local image memory. A related use for such invisible memory is for saving screen areas temporarily obscured by popped-up images, such as windows, menus, and forms.

The bitmaps for the font cache are usually created by scanning in enlarged pictures of characters from typesetting fonts in various sizes; a typeface designer can then use a paint program to touch up individual pixels in each character's bitmap as necessary. Alternatively, the type designer may use a paint program to create, from scratch, fonts that are especially designed for screens and low-resolution printers. Since small bitmaps do not scale well, more than one bitmap must be defined for a given character in a given font just to provide various standard sizes. Furthermore, each type face requires its own set of bitmaps. Therefore, a distinct font cache is needed for each font loaded by the application.

Bitmap characters are clipped automatically by SRGP as part of its implementation of copyPixel. Each character is clipped to the destination rectangle on a pixel-by-pixel basis, a technique that lets us clip a character at any row or column of its bitmap. For systems with slow copyPixel operations, a much faster, although cruder, method is to clip the character or even the entire string on an all-or-nothing basis by doing a trivial accept of the character or string extent. Only if the extent is trivially accepted is the copyPixel applied to the character or string. For systems with a fast copyPixel, it is still useful to do trivial accept/reject testing of the string extent as a precursor to clipping individual characters during the copyPixel operation.

SRGP's simple bitmap font-cache technique stores the characters side by side in a canvas that is quite wide but is only as tall as the tallest character; Fig. 3.50 shows a portion

```
typedef point vertex;                    /* point holds double x, y */
typedef vertex edge[2];
typedef vertex vertexArray[MAX];         /* MAX is a declared constant */

static void Output (vertex, int *, vertexArray);
static boolean Inside (vertex, edge);
static vertex Intersect (vertex, vertex, edge);

void SutherlandHodgmanPolygonClip (
        vertexArray inVertexArray,       /* Input vertex array */
        vertexArray outVertexArray,      /* Output vertex array */
        int inLength,                    /* No. of entries in inVertexArray */
        int *outLength,                  /* No. of entries in outVertexArray */
        edge clipBoundary)               /* Edge of clip polygon */
{
    vertex s, p,                         /* Start, end pt. of current polygon edge */
    i;                                   /* Intersection pt. with a clip boundary */
    int j;                               /* Vertex loop counter */

    *outLength = 0;    /* Start with the last vertex in inVertexArray */
    s = inVertexArray[inLength − 1];
    for (j = 0; j < inLength; j++) {
        p = inVertexArray[j];   /* Now s and p correspond to the vertices in Fig. 3.48 */
        if (Inside (p, clipBoundary)) {          /* Cases 1 and 4 */
            if (Inside (s, clipBoundary))        /* Case 1 */
                Output (p, outLength, outVertexArray);
            else {                               /* Case 4 */
                i = Intersect (s, p, clipBoundary);
                Output (i, outLength, outVertexArray);
                Output (p, outLength, outVertexArray);
            }
        } else                                   /* Cases 2 and 3 */
            if (Inside (s, clipBoundary)) {      /* Case 2 */
                i = Intersect (s, p, clipBoundary);
                Output (i, outLength, outVertexArray);
            }                                    /* No action for case 3 */
        s = p;                                   /* Advance to next pair of vertices */
    }  /* for */
}  /* SutherlandHodgmanPolygonClip */

/* Adds newVertex to outVertexArray and then updates outLength */
static void Output (vertex newVertex, int *outLength, vertexArray outVertexArray)
{
...
}
/* Checks whether the vertex lies inside the clip edge or not */
static boolean Inside (vertex testVertex, edge clipBoundary)
```

Fig. 3.49 *(Cont.)*.

```
{
...
}
```

/∗ Clips polygon edge (*first, second*) against *clipBoundary*, outputs the new point ∗/
static vertex Intersect (vertex *first*, vertex *second*, edge *clipBoundary*)
```
{
...
}
```

Fig. 3.49 Sutherland–Hodgman polygon-clipping algorithm.

of the cache, along with discrete instances of the same characters at low resolution. Each
loaded font is described by a struct (declared in Fig. 3.51) containing a reference to the
canvas that stores the characters' images, along with information on the height of the
characters and the amount of space to be placed between adjacent characters in a text string.
(Some packages store the space between characters as part of a character's width, to allow
variable intercharacter spacing.)

As described in Section 2.1.5, descender height and total height are constants for a
given font—the former is the number of rows of pixels at the bottom of the font cache used
only by descenders, and the latter is simply the height of the font-cache canvas. The width
of a character, on the other hand, is not considered a constant; thus, a character can occupy
the space that suits it, rather than being forced into a fixed-width character box. SRGP puts
a fixed amount of space between characters when it draws a text string, the amount being
specified as part of each font's descriptor. A word-processing application can display lines
of text by using SRGP to display individual words of text, and can right-justify lines by
using variable spacing between words and after punctuation to fill out lines so that their
rightmost characters are aligned at the right margin. This involves using the text-extent
inquiry facilities to determine where the right edge of each word is, in order to calculate the
start of the next word. Needless to say, SRGP's text-handling facilities are really too crude
for sophisticated word processing, let alone for typesetting programs, since such applications require far finer control over the spacing of individual letters to deal with such effects
as sub- and superscripting, kerning, and printing text that is not horizontally aligned.

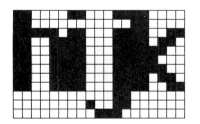

Fig. 3.50 Portion of an example of a font cache.

```
typedef struct {
      int leftX, width;                    /* Horizontal location, width of image in font cache */
} charLocation;

typedef struct {
      canvasID cache;
      int descenderHeight, totalHeight;    /* Height is a constant; width varies */
      int interCharacterSpacing;           /* Measured in pixels */
      charLocation locationTable[128];     /* Explained in the text */
} fontCacheDescriptor;
```

Fig. 3.51 Type declarations for the font cache.

3.15.2 Implementation of a Text Output Primitive

In the code of Fig. 3.52, we show how SRGP text is implemented internally: Each character in the given string is placed individually, and the space between characters is dictated by the appropriate field in the font descriptor. Note that complexities such as dealing with mixed fonts in a string must be handled by the application program.

```
void SRGP_characterText (
      point origin,                        /* Where to place the character in the current canvas */
      char *stringToPrint,
      fontCacheDescriptor fontInfo)
{
    int i;

    /* Origin specified by the application is for baseline and does not include descender. */
    origin.y -= fontInfo.descenderHeight;

    for (i = 0; i < strlen (stringToPrint); i++) {
        rectangle fontCacheRectangle;
        char charToPrint = stringToPrint[i];
        /* Find the rectangular region within the cache wherein the character lies */
        charLocation *fip = &fontInfo.locationTable[charToPrint];

        fontCacheRectangle.bottomLeft = SRGP_defPoint (fip->leftX, 0);
        fontCacheRectangle.topRight = SRGP_defPoint (fip->leftX + fip->width - 1,
                                                    fontInfo.totalHeight - 1);

        SRGP_copyPixel (fontInfo.cache, fontCacheRectangle, origin);
        /* Update the origin to move past the new character plus intercharacter spacing */
        origin.x += fip->width + interCharacterSpacing;
    }
} /* SRGP_characterText */
```

Fig. 3.52 Implementation of character placement for SRGP's text primitive.

We mentioned that the bitmap technique requires a distinct font cache for each combination of font, size, and face for each different resolution of display or output device supported. A single font in eight different point sizes and four faces (normal, bold, italic, bold italic) thus requires 32 font caches! Figure 3.53(a) shows a common way of allowing a single font cache to support multiple face variations: The italic face is approximated by splitting the font's image into regions with horizontal "cuts," then offsetting the regions while performing a sequence of calls to SRGP_copyPixel.

This crude approximation does not make pleasing characters; for example, the dot over the "*i*" is noncircular. More of a problem for the online user, the method distorts the intercharacter spacing and makes picking much more difficult. A similar trick to achieve boldface is to copy the image twice in **or** mode with a slight horizontal offset (Fig. 3.53b). These techniques are not particularly satisfactory, in that they can produce illegible characters, especially when combined with subscripting.

A better way to solve the storage problem is to store characters in an abstract, device-independent form using polygonal or curved outlines of their shapes defined with floating-point parameters, and then to transform them appropriately. Polynomial functions called *splines* (see Chapter 11) provide smooth curves with continuous first and higher derivatives and are commonly used to encode text outlines. Although each character definition takes up more space than its representation in a font cache, multiple sizes may be derived from a single stored representation by suitable scaling; also, italics may be quickly approximated by shearing the outline. Another major advantage of storing characters in a completely device-independent form is that the outlines may be arbitrarily translated, rotated, scaled, and clipped (or used as clipping regions themselves).

The storage economy of splined characters is not quite so great as this description suggests. For instance, not all point sizes for a character may be obtained by scaling a single abstract shape, because the shape for an aesthetically pleasing font is typically a function of point size; therefore, each shape suffices for only a limited range of point sizes. Moreover, scan conversion of splined text requires far more processing than the simple copyPixel implementation, because the device-independent form must be converted to pixel coordinates on the basis of the current size, face, and transformation attributes. Thus, the font-cache technique is still the most common for personal computers and even is used for many workstations. A strategy that offers the best of both methods is to store the fonts in outline form but to convert the ones being used in a given application to their bitmap equivalents—for example, to build a font cache on the fly. We discuss processing of splined text in more detail in Section 19.4.

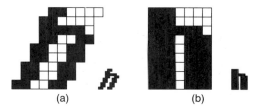

(a)   (b)

Fig. 3.53 Tricks for creating different faces for a font. (a) Italic. (b) Bold.

3.16   SRGP_copyPixel

If only WritePixel and ReadPixel low-level procedures are available, the SRGP_copyPixel procedure can be implemented as a doubly nested **for** loop for each pixel. For simplicity, assume first that we are working with a bilevel display and do not need to deal with the low-level considerations of writing bits that are not word-aligned; in Section 19.6, we cover some of these more realistic issues that take hardware-memory organization into account. In the inner loop of our simple SRGP_copyPixel, we do a ReadPixel of the source and destination pixels, logically combine them according to the SRGP write mode, and then WritePixel the result. Treating **replace** mode, the most common write mode, as a special case allows a simpler inner loop that does only a ReadPixel/WritePixel of the source into the destination, without having to do a logical operation. The clip rectangle is used during address calculation to restrict the region into which destination pixels are written.

3.17   ANTIALIASING

3.17.1   Increasing Resolution

The primitives drawn so far have a common problem: They have jagged edges. This undesirable effect, known as *the jaggies* or *staircasing*, is the result of an all-or-nothing approach to scan conversion in which each pixel either is replaced with the primitive's color or is left unchanged. Jaggies are an instance of a phenomenon known as *aliasing*. The application of techniques that reduce or eliminate aliasing is referred to as *antialiasing*, and primitives or images produced using these techniques are said to be *antialiased*. In Chapter 14, we discuss basic ideas from signal processing that explain how aliasing got its name, why it occurs, and how to reduce or eliminate it when creating pictures. Here, we content ourselves with a more intuitive explanation of why SRGP's primitives exhibit aliasing, and describe how to modify the line scan-conversion algorithm developed in this chapter to generate antialiased lines.

Consider using the midpoint algorithm to draw a 1-pixel-thick black line, with slope between 0 and 1, on a white background. In each column through which the line passes, the algorithm sets the color of the pixel that is closest to the line. Each time the line moves between columns in which the pixels closest to the line are not in the same row, there is a sharp jag in the line drawn into the canvas, as is clear in Fig. 3.54(a). The same is true for other scan-converted primitives that can assign only one of two intensity values to pixels.

Suppose we now use a display device with twice the horizontal and vertical resolution. As shown in Fig. 3.54 (b), the line passes through twice as many columns and therefore has twice as many jags, but each jag is half as large in x and in y. Although the resulting picture looks better, the improvement comes at the price of quadrupling the memory cost, memory bandwidth, and scan-conversion time. Increasing resolution is an expensive solution that only diminishes the problem of jaggies—it does not eliminate the problem. In the following sections, we look at antialiasing techniques that are less costly, yet result in significantly better images.

3.17.2   Unweighted Area Sampling

The first approach to improving picture quality can be developed by recognizing that, although an ideal primitive such as the line has zero width, the primitive we are drawing has

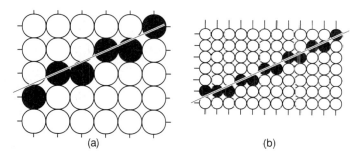

Fig. 3.54 (a) Standard midpoint line on a bilevel display. (b) Same line on a display that has twice the linear resolution.

nonzero width. A scan-converted primitive occupies a finite area on the screen—even the thinnest horizontal or vertical line on a display surface is 1 pixel thick and lines at other angles have width that varies over the primitive. Thus, we think of any line as a rectangle of a desired thickness covering a portion of the grid, as shown in Fig. 3.55. It follows that a line should not set the intensity of only a single pixel in a column to black, but rather should contribute some amount of intensity to each pixel in the columns whose area it intersects. (Such varying intensity can be shown on only those displays with multiple bits per pixel, of course.) Then, for 1-pixel-thick lines, only horizontal and vertical lines would affect exactly 1 pixel in their column or row. For lines at other angles, more than 1 pixel would now be set in a column or row, each to an appropriate intensity.

But what is the geometry of a pixel? How large is it? How much intensity should a line contribute to each pixel it intersects? It is computationally simple to assume that the pixels form an array of nonoverlapping square tiles covering the screen, centered on grid points. When we refer to a primitive overlapping all or a portion of a pixel, we mean that it covers (part of) the tile; to emphasize this we sometimes refer to the square as the *area represented by the pixel*.) We also assume that a line contributes to each pixel's intensity an amount

Figure 3.55 Line of nonzero width from point (1,1) to point (10,4).

proportional to the percentage of the pixel's tile it covers. A fully covered pixel on a black and white display will be colored black, whereas a partially covered pixel will be colored a gray whose intensity depends on the line's coverage of the pixel. This technique, as applied to the line shown in Fig. 3.55, is shown in Fig. 3.56.

For a black line on a white background, pixel (2, 1) is about 70 percent black, whereas pixel (2, 2) is about 25 percent black. Pixels not intersected by the line, such as (2, 3), are completely white. Setting a pixel's intensity in proportion to the amount of its area covered by the primitive softens the harsh, on−off characteristic of the edge of the primitive and yields a more gradual transition between full on and full off. This blurring makes a line look better at a distance, despite the fact that it spreads the on–off transition over multiple pixels in a column or row. A rough approximation to the area overlap can be found by dividing the pixel into a finer grid of rectangular subpixels, then counting the number of subpixels inside the line—for example, below the line's top edge or above its bottom edge (see Exercise 3.32).

We call the technique of setting intensity proportional to the amount of area covered *unweighted area sampling*. This technique produces noticeably better results than does setting pixels to full intensity or zero intensity, but there is an even more effective strategy called *weighted area sampling*. To explain the difference between the two forms of area sampling, we note that unweighted area sampling has the following three properties. First, the intensity of a pixel intersected by a line edge decreases as the distance between the pixel center and the edge increases: The farther away a primitive is, the less influence it has on a pixel's intensity. This relation obviously holds because the intensity decreases as the area of overlap decreases, and that area decreases as the line's edge moves away from the pixel's center and toward the boundary of the pixel. When the line covers the pixel completely, the overlap area and therefore the intensity are at a maximum; when the primitive edge is just tangent to the boundary, the area and therefore the intensity are zero.

A second property of unweighted area sampling is that a primitive cannot influence the intensity at a pixel at all if the primitive does not intersect the pixel—that is, if it does not intersect the square tile represented by the pixel. A third property of unweighted area

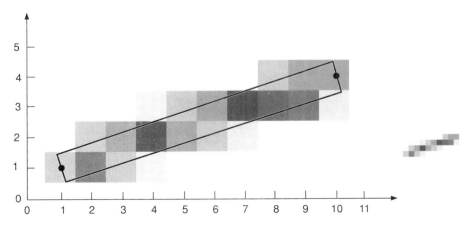

Fig. 3.56 Intensity proportional to area covered.

sampling is that equal areas contribute equal intensity, regardless of the distance between the pixel's center and the area; only the total amount of overlapped area matters. Thus, a small area in the corner of the pixel contributes just as much as does an equal-sized area near the pixel's center.

3.17.3 Weighted Area Sampling

In weighted area sampling, we keep unweighted area sampling's first and second properties (intensity decreases with decreased area overlap, and primitives contribute only if they overlap the area represented by the pixel), but we alter the third property. We let equal areas contribute unequally: A small area closer to the pixel center has greater influence than does one at a greater distance. A theoretical basis for this change is given in Chapter 14, where we discuss weighted area sampling in the context of filtering theory.

To retain the second property, we must make the following change in the geometry of the pixel. In unweighted area sampling, if an edge of a primitive is quite close to the boundary of the square tile we have used to represent a pixel until now, but does not actually intersect this boundary, it will not contribute to the pixel's intensity. In our new approach, the pixel represents a circular area larger than the square tile; the primitive *will* intersect this larger area; hence, it will contribute to the intensity of the pixel.

To explain the origin of the adjectives *unweighted* and *weighted*, we define a *weighting function* that determines the influence on the intensity of a pixel of a given small area *dA* of a primitive, as a function of *dA*'s distance from the center of the pixel. This function is constant for unweighted area sampling, and decreases with increasing distance for weighted area sampling. Think of the weighting function as a function, $W(x, y)$, on the plane, whose height above the (x, y) plane gives the weight for the area *dA* at (x, y). For unweighted area sampling with the pixels represented as square tiles, the graph of W is a box, as shown in Fig. 3.57.

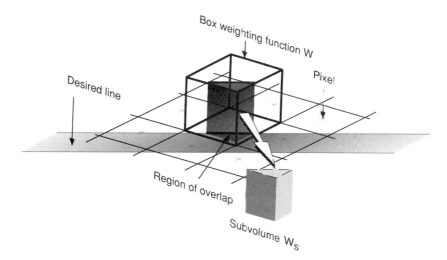

Fig. 3.57 Box filter for square pixe

The figure shows square pixels, with centers indicated by crosses at the intersections of grid lines; the weighting function is shown as a box whose base is that of the current pixel. The intensity contributed by the area of the pixel covered by the primitive is the total of intensity contributions from all small areas in the region of overlap between the primitive and the pixel. The intensity contributed by each small area is proportional to the area multiplied by the weight. Therefore, the total intensity is the integral of the weighting function over the area of overlap. The volume represented by this integral, W_S, is always a fraction between 0 and 1, and the pixel's intensity I is $I_{max} \cdot W_S$. In Fig. 3.57, W_S is a wedge of the box. The weighting function is also called a *filter function*, and the box is also called a *box filter*. For unweighted area sampling, the height of the box is normalized to 1, so that the box's volume is 1, which causes a thick line covering the entire pixel to have an intensity $I = I_{max} \cdot 1 = I_{max}$.

Now let us construct a weighting function for weighted area sampling; it must give less weight to small areas farther away from the pixel center than it does to those closer. Let's pick a weighting function that is the simplest decreasing function of distance; for example, we choose a function that has a maximum at the center of the pixel and decreases linearly with increasing distance from the center. Because of rotational symmetry, the graph of this function forms a circular cone. The circular base of the cone (often called the *support* of the filter) should have a radius larger than you might expect; the filtering theory of Chapter 14 shows that a good choice for the radius is the unit distance of the integer grid. Thus, a primitive fairly far from a pixel's center can still influence that pixel's intensity; also, the supports associated with neighboring pixels overlap, and therefore a single small piece of a primitive may actually contribute to several different pixels (see Fig. 3.58). This overlap also ensures that there are no areas of the grid not covered by some pixel, which would be the case if the circular pixels had a radius of only one-half of a grid unit.[12]

As with the box filter, the sum of all intensity contributions for the cone filter is the volume under the cone and above the intersection of the cone's base and the primitive; this volume W_S is a vertical section of the cone, as shown in Fig. 3.58. As with the box filter, the height of the cone is first normalized so that the volume under the entire cone is 1; this allows a pixel whose support is completely covered by a primitive to be displayed at maximum intensity. Although contributions from areas of the primitive far from the pixel's center but still intersecting the support are rather small, a pixel whose center is sufficiently close to a line receives some intensity contribution from that line. Conversely, a pixel that, in the square-geometry model, was entirely covered by a line of unit thickness[13] is not quite as bright as it used to be. The net effect of weighted area sampling is to decrease the contrast between adjacent pixels, in order to provide smoother transitions. In particular, with weighted area sampling, a horizontal or vertical line of unit thickness has more than 1 pixel

---

[12]As noted in Section 3.2.1, pixels displayed on a CRT are roughly circular in cross-section, and adjacent pixels typically overlap; the model of overlapping circles used in weighted area sampling, however, is not directly related to this fact and holds even for display technologies, such as the plasma panel, in which the physical pixels are actually nonoverlapping square tiles.

[13]We now say a ''a line of unit thickness'' rather than ''a line 1 pixel thick'' to make it clear that the unit of line width is still that of the SRGP grid, whereas the pixel's support has grown to have a two-unit diameter.

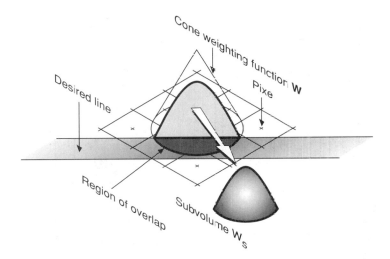

Fig. 3.58 Cone filter for circular pixel with diameter of two grid units.

intensified in each column or row, which would not be the case for unweighted area sampling.

The conical filter has two useful properties: rotational symmetry and linear decrease of the function with radial distance. We prefer rotational symmetry because it not only makes area calculations independent of the angle of the line, but also is theoretically optimal, as shown in Chapter 14. We also show there, however, that the cone's linear slope (and its radius) are only an approximation to the optimal filter function, although the cone filter is still better than the box filter. Optimal filters are computationally most expensive, box filters least, and therefore cone filters are a very reasonable compromise between cost and quality. The dramatic difference between an unfiltered and filtered line drawing is shown in Fig. 3.59. Notice how the problems of indistinct lines and moiré patterns are greatly ameliorated by filtering. Now we need to integrate the cone filter into our scan-conversion algorithms.

3.17.4 Gupta–Sproull Antialiased Lines

The Gupta–Sproull scan-conversion algorithm for lines [GUPT81a] described in this section precomputes the subvolume of a normalized filter function defined by lines at various directed distances from the pixel center, and stores them in a table. We use a pixel area with radius equal to a grid unit—that is, to the distance between adjacent pixel centers—so that a line of unit thickness with slope less than 1 typically intersects three supports in a column, minimally two and maximally five, as shown in Fig. 3.60. For a radius of 1, each circle partially covers the circles of its neighboring pixels.

Figure 3.61 shows the geometry of the overlap between line and pixel that is used for table lookup of a function Filter (D, t). Here D is the (angle-independent) distance between pixel and line centers, t is a constant for lines of a given thickness, and function Filter() is dependent on the shape of the filter function. Gupta and Sproull's paper gives the table for a cone filter for a 4-bit display; it contains fractional values of Filter (D, t) for equal

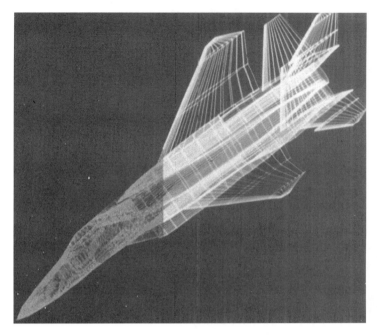

Fig. 3.59 Filtered line drawing. The left half is unfiltered; the right half is filtered. (Courtesy of Branko Gerovac, Digital Equipment Corporation.)

increments of D ranging from 0 to 1.5 and for $t = 1$. The function, by definition, is 0 outside the support, for $D \geq 1 + \frac{1}{2} = \frac{24}{16}$ in this case. The precision of the distance is only 1 in 16, because it need not be greater than that of the intensity—4 bits, in this case.

Now we are ready to modify the midpoint line scan-conversion algorithm. As before, we use the decision variable d to choose between E and NE pixels, but must then set the intensity of the chosen pixel and its two vertical neighbors, on the basis of the distances from these pixels to the line. Figure 3.61 shows the relevant geometry; we can calculate the

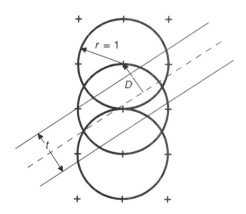

Fig. 3.60 One-unit-thick line intersects 3-pixel supports.

true, perpendicular distance D from the vertical distance v, using simple trigonometry.

Using similar triangles and knowing that the slope of the line is dy/dx, we can see from the diagram that

$$D = v \cos\phi = \frac{vdx}{\sqrt{dx^2 + dy^2}} \qquad (3.2)$$

The vertical distance v between a point on the line and the chosen pixel with the same x coordinate is just the difference between their y coordinates. It is important to note that this distance is a signed value. That is, if the line passes below the chosen pixel, v is negative; if it passes above the chosen pixel, v is positive. We should therefore pass the absolute value of the distance to the filter function. The chosen pixel is also the middle of the 3 pixels that must be intensified. The pixel above the chosen one is a vertical distance $1 - v$ from the line, whereas the pixel below is a vertical distance $1 + v$ from the line. You may want to verify that these distances are valid regardless of the relative position of the line and the pixels, because the distance v is a signed quantity.

Rather than computing v directly, our strategy is to use the incremental computation of $d = F(M) = F(x_P + 1, y_P + \frac{1}{2})$. In general, if we know the x coordinate of a point on the line, we can compute that point's y coordinate using the relation developed in Section 3.2.2, $F(x, y) = 2(ax + by + c) = 0$:

$$y = (ax + c)/-b.$$

For pixel E, $x = x_P + 1$, and $y = y_P$, and $v = y - y_P$; thus

$$v = ((a(x_P + 1) + c)/-b) - y_P.$$

Now multiplying both sides by $-b$ and collecting terms,

$$-bv = a(x_P + 1) + by_P + c = F(x_P + 1, y_P)/2.$$

But $b = -dx$. Therefore, $vdx = F(x_P + 1, y_P)/2$. Note that vdx is the numerator of Eq. (3.2) for D, and that the denominator is a constant that can be precomputed. Therefore, we

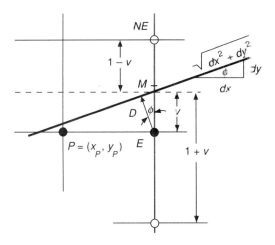

Fig. 3.61 Calculating distances to line in midpoint algorithm.

would like to compute vdx incrementally from the prior computation of $d = F(M)$, and avoid division by 2 to preserve integer arithmetic. Thus, for the pixel E,

$$2vdx = F(x_P + 1, y_P) = 2a(x_P + 1) + 2by_P + 2c$$
$$= 2a(x_P + 1) + 2b(y_P + \tfrac{1}{2}) - 2b/2 + 2c$$
$$= d + dx.$$

Thus

$$D = \frac{d + dx}{2\sqrt{x^2 + y^2}}$$

and the constant denominator is $1/(2\sqrt{x^2 + y^2})$. The corresponding numerators for the pixels at $y_P + 1$ and $y_P - 1$ are then easily obtained as $2(1 - v)dx = 2dx - 2vdx$, and $2(1 + v)dx = 2dx + 2vdx$, respectively.

Similarly, for pixel NE,

$$2vdx = F(x_P + 1, y_P + 1) = 2a(x_P + 1) + 2b(y_P + \tfrac{1}{2}) + 2b/2 + 2c,$$
$$= d - dx,$$

and the corresponding numerators for the pixels at $y_P + 2$ and y_P are again $2(1 - v)dx = 2dx - 2vdx$ and $2(1 + v)dx = 2dx + 2vdx$, respectively.

We have put a dot in front of the statements added to the midpoint algorithm of Section 3.2.2 to create the revised midpoint algorithm shown in Fig. 3.62. The WritePixel of E or NE has been replaced by a call to IntensifyPixel for the chosen pixel and its vertical neighbors; IntensifyPixel does the table lookup that converts the absolute value of the distance to weighted area overlap, a fraction of maximum intensity. In an actual implementation, this simple code, of course, would be inline.

The Gupta–Sproull algorithm provides an efficient incremental method for antialiasing lines, although fractional arithmetic is used in this version. The extension to antialiasing endpoints by using a separate look-up table is covered in Section 19.3.5. Since the lookup works for the intersection with the edge of the line, it can also be used for the edge of an arbitrary polygon. The disadvantage is that a single look-up table applies to lines of a given thickness only. Section 19.3.1 discusses more general techniques that consider any line as two parallel edges an arbitrary distance apart. We also can antialias characters either by filtering them (see Section 19.4) or, more crudely, by taking their scanned-in bitmaps and manually softening pixels at edges.

3.18   SUMMARY

In this chapter, we have taken our first look at the fundamental clipping and scan-conversion algorithms that are the meat and potatoes of raster graphics packages. We have covered only the basics here; many elaborations and special cases must be considered for robust implementations. Chapter 19 discusses some of these, as well as such topics as general regions and region filling. Other algorithms that operate on bitmaps or pixmaps are discussed in Chapter 17, and a fuller treatment of the theory and practice of antialiasing is found in Chapters 14 and 19.

static void IntensifyPixel (**int**, **int**, **double**)

void AntiAliasedLineMidpoint (**int** x0, **int** y0, **int** x1, **int** y1)
/* This algorithm uses Gupta-Sproull's table of intensity as a function of area */
/* coverage for a circular support in the IntensifyPixel function. Note that */
/* overflow may occur in the computation of the denominator for 16-bit integers, */
/* because of the squares. */
{
    int dx = x1 − x0;
    int dy = y1 − y0;
    int d = 2 * dy − dx;   /* Initial value d_{start} as before */
    int incrE = 2 * dy;   /* Increment used for move to E */
    int incrNE = 2 * (dy − dx);   /* Increment used for move to NE */
  • **int** two_v_dx = 0;   /* Numerator; = 0 for start pixel */
  • **double** invDenom = 1.0 /
      (2.0 * sqrt (dx * dx + dy * dy)); /* Precomputed inverse denominator */
  • **double** two_dx_invDenom =   /* Precomputed constant */
      2.0 * dx * invDenom;
    int x = x0;
    int y = y0;
  • IntensifyPixel (x, y, 0);   /* Start pixel */
  • IntensifyPixel (x, y + 1, two_dx_invDenom); /* Neighbor */
  • IntensifyPixel (x, y − 1, two_dx_invDenom); /* Neighbor */
    while (x < x1) {
      if (d < 0) {   /* Choose E */
  •   two_v_dx = d + dx;
        d += incrE;
        x++;
      } **else** {   /* Choose NE */
  •   two_v_dx = d − dx;
        d += incrNE;
        x++;
        y++;
      }
      /* Now set chosen pixel and its neighbors */
  •   IntensifyPixel (x, y, two_v_dx * invDenom);
  •   IntensifyPixel (x, y + 1, two_v_dx_invDenom − two_v_dx * invDenom);
  •   IntensifyPixel (x, y − 1, two_v_dx_invDenom − two_v_dx * invDenom);
    }
} /* AntiAliasedLineMidpoint */

void IntensifyPixel (**int** x, **int** y, **double** distance)
{
    double intensity = Filter (Round (fabs (distance)));
    /* Table lookup done on an integer index; thickness 1 */
    WritePixel (x, y, intensity);
} /* IntensifyPixel */

Fig. 3.62 Gupta–Sproull algorithm for antialiased scan conversion of lines.

The most important idea of this chapter is that, since speed is essential in interactive raster graphics, incremental scan-conversion algorithms using only integer operations in their inner loops are usually the best. The basic algorithms can be extended to handle thickness, as well as patterns for boundaries or for filling areas. Whereas the basic algorithms that convert single-pixel-wide primitives try to minimize the error between chosen pixels on the Cartesian grid and the ideal primitive defined on the plane, the algorithms for thick primitives can trade off quality and "correctness" for speed. Although much of 2D raster graphics today still operates, even on color displays, with single-bit-per-pixel primitives, we expect that techniques for real-time antialiasing will soon become prevalent.

EXERCISES

3.1 Implement the special-case code for scan converting horizontal and vertical lines, and lines with slopes of ± 1.

3.2 Modify the midpoint algorithm for scan converting lines (Fig. 3.8) to handle lines at any angle.

3.3 Show why the point-to-line error is always $\leq \frac{1}{2}$ for the midpoint line scan-conversion algorithm.

3.4 Modify the midpoint algorithm for scan converting lines of Exercise 3.2 to handle endpoint order and intersections with clip edges, as discussed in Section 3.2.3.

3.5 Modify the midpoint algorithm for scan converting lines (Exercise 3.2) to write pixels with varying intensity as a function of line slope.

3.6 Modify the midpoint algorithm for scan converting lines (Exercise 3.2) to deal with endpoints that do not have integer coordinates—this is easiest if you use floating point throughout your algorithm. As a more difficult exercise, handle lines of *rational* endpoints using only integers.

3.7 Determine whether the midpoint algorithm for scan converting lines (Exercise 3.2) can take advantage of symmetry by using the decision variable d to draw simultaneously from both ends of the line toward the center. Does your algorithm consistently accommodate the case of equal error on an arbitrary choice that arises when dx and dy have a largest common factor c and dx/c is even and dy/c is odd ($0 < dy < dx$), as in the line between (0, 0) and (24, 9)? Does it deal with the subset case in which dx is an integer multiple of $2dy$, such as for the line between (0, 0) and (16, 4)? (Contributed by J. Bresenham.)

3.8 Show how polylines may share more than vertex pixels. Develop an algorithm that avoids writing pixels twice. Hint: Consider scan conversion and writing to the canvas in **xor** mode as separate phases.

3.9 Expand the pseudocode for midpoint ellipse scan conversion of Fig. 3.21 to code that tests properly for various conditions that may arise.

3.10 Apply the technique of forward differencing shown for circles in Section 3.3.2 to develop the second-order forward differences for scan converting standard ellipses. Write the code that implements this technique.

3.11 Develop an alternative to the midpoint circle scan-conversion algorithm of Section 3.3.2 based on a piecewise-linear approximation of the circle with a polyline.

3.12 Develop an algorithm for scan converting unfilled rounded rectangles with a specified radius for the quarter-circle corners.

3.13 Write a scan-conversion procedure for solidly filled upright rectangles at arbitrary screen positions that writes a bilevel frame buffer efficiently, an entire word of pixels at a time.

3.14 Construct examples of pixels that are "missing" or written multiple times, using the rules of Section 3.6. Try to develop alternative, possibly more complex, rules that do not draw shared pixels on shared edges twice, yet do not cause pixels to be missing. Are these rules worth the added overhead?

3.15 Implement the pseudocode of Section 3.6 for polygon scan conversion, taking into account in the span bookkeeping of potential sliver polygons.

3.16 Develop scan-conversion algorithms for triangles and trapezoids that take advantage of the simple nature of these shapes. Such algorithms are common in hardware.

3.17 Investigate triangulation algorithms for decomposing an arbitrary, possibly concave or self-intersecting, polygon into a mesh of triangles whose vertices are shared. Does it help to restrict the polygon to being, at worst, concave without self-intersections or interior holes? (See also [PREP85].)

3.18 Extend the midpoint algorithm for scan converting circles (Fig. 3.15) to handle filled circles and circular wedges (for pie charts), using span tables.

3.19 Extend the midpoint algorithm for scan converting ellipses (Fig. 3.21) to handle filled elliptical wedges, using span tables.

3.20 Implement both absolute and relative anchor algorithms for polygon pattern filling, discussed in Section 3.9, and contrast them in terms of visual effect and computational efficiency.

3.21 Apply the technique of Fig. 3.30 for writing characters filled with patterns in opaque mode. Show how having a copyPixel with a write mask may be used to good advantage for this class of problems.

3.22 Implement a technique for drawing various symbols such as cursor icons represented by small bitmaps so that they can be seen regardless of the background on which they are written. Hint: Define a mask for each symbol that "encloses" the symbol—that is, that covers more pixels than the symbol—and that draws masks and symbols in separate passes.

3.23 Implement thick-line algorithms using the techniques listed in Section 3.9. Contrast their efficiency and the quality of the results they produced.

3.24 Extend the midpoint algorithm for scan converting circles (Fig. 3.16) to handle thick circles.

3.25 Implement a thick-line algorithm that accommodates line style as well as pen style and pattern.

3.26 Implement scissoring as part of scan converting lines and unfilled polygons, using the fast-scan-plus-backtracking technique of checking every ith pixel. Apply the technique to filled and thick lines and to filled polygons. For these primitives, contrast the efficiency of this type of on-the-fly clipping with that of analytical clipping.

3.27 Implement scissoring as part of scan converting unfilled and filled circles and ellipses. For these primitives, contrast the feasibility and efficiency of this type of on-the-fly clipping with that of analytical clipping.

3.28 Modify the Cohen–Sutherland line-clipping algorithm of Fig. 3.41 to avoid recalculation of slopes during successive passes.

3.29 Contrast the efficiency of the Sutherland–Cohen and Cyrus–Beck algorithms for several typical and atypical cases, using instruction counting. Are horizontal and vertical lines handled optimally?

3.30 Consider a convex polygon with n vertices being clipped against a clip rectangle. What is the maximum number of vertices in the resulting clipped polygon? What is the minimum number? Consider the same problem for a concave polygon. How many polygons might result? If a single polygon results, what is the largest number of vertices it might have?

3.31 Explain why the Sutherland–Hodgman polygon-clipping algorithm works for only convex clipping regions.

3.32 Devise a strategy for subdividing a pixel and counting the number of subpixels covered (at least to a significant degree) by a line, as part of a line-drawing algorithm using unweighted area sampling.

3.33 Create tables with various decreasing functions of the distance between pixel center and line center. Use them in the antialiased line algorithm of Fig. 3.62. Contrast the results produced with those produced by a box-filtered line.

3.34 Generalize the antialiasing techniques for lines to polygons. How might you handle nonpolygonal boundaries of curved primitives and characters?

4
Graphics Hardware

In this chapter, we describe how the important hardware elements of a computer graphics display system work. Section 4.1 covers hardcopy technologies: printers, pen plotters, electrostatic plotters, laser printers, ink-jet plotters, thermal-transfer plotters, and film recorders. The basic technological concepts behind each type of device are described briefly, and a concluding section compares the various devices. Section 4.2, on display technologies, discusses monochrome and color shadow-mask CRTs, the direct-view storage tube (DVST), liquid-crystal displays (LCDs), plasma panels, electroluminescent displays, and several more specialized technologies. Again, a concluding section discusses the pros and cons of the various display technologies.

Raster display systems, which can use any of the display technologies discussed here, are discussed in Section 4.3. A simple, straightforward raster system is first introduced, and is then enhanced with respect to graphics functionality and integration of raster- and general-purpose processors into the system address space. Section 4.4 describes the role of the look-up table and video controller in image display, color control, animation, and image mixing. The almost-obsolete vector (also called *random, calligraphic, stroke*) display system is discussed briefly in Section 4.5, followed in Section 4.6 by user interaction devices such as tablets, mice, touch panels, and so on. Again, operational concepts rather than technological details are stressed. Section 4.7 briefly treats image-input devices, such as film scanners, by means of which an existing image can by input to a computer.

Figure 4.1 shows the relation of these hardware devices to one another. The key element is the integrated CPU and display processor known as a *graphics workstation*, typically consisting of a CPU capable of executing at least several million instructions per second (MIPS), a large disk, and a display with resolution of at least 1000 by 800. The

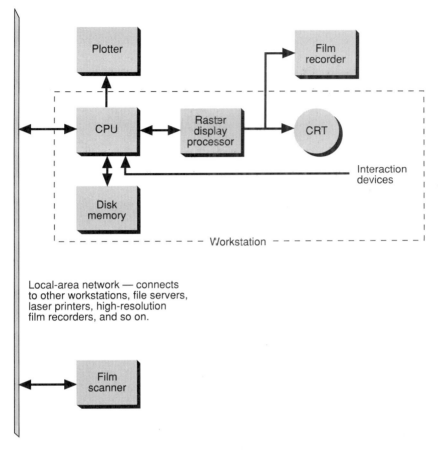

Fig. 4.1 Components of a typical interactive graphics system.

local-area network connects multiple workstations for file sharing, electronic mail, and access to shared peripherals such as high-quality film plotters, large disks, gateways to other networks, and higher-performance computers.

4.1 HARDCOPY TECHNOLOGIES

In this section, we discuss various hardcopy technologies, then summarize their character-istics. Several important terms must be defined first.

The image quality achievable with display devices depends on both the addressability and the dot size of the device. *Dot size* (also called *spot size*) is the diameter of a single dot on the device's output. *Addressability* is the number of individual (not necessarily distinguishable) dots per inch that can be created; it may differ in the horizontal and vertical directions. Addressability in x is just the reciprocal of the distance between the centers of dots at addresses (x, y) and $(x + 1, y)$; addressability in y is defined similarly. *Interdot distance* is the reciprocal of addressability.

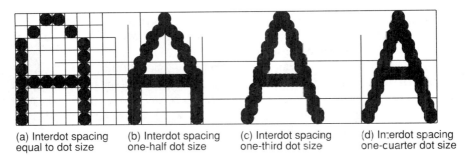

(a) Interdot spacing   (b) Interdot spacing   (c) Interdot spacing   (d) Interdot spacing
equal to dot size   one-half dot size   one-third dot size   one-cuarter dot size

Fig. 4.2 The effects of various ratios of the dot size to the interdot distance.

It is usually desirable that dot size be somewhat greater than the interdot distance, so that smooth shapes can be created. Figure 4.2 illustrates this reasoning. Tradeoffs arise here, however: dot size several times the interdot distance allows very smooth shapes to be printed, whereas a smaller dot size allows finer detail.

Resolution, which is related to dot size and can be no greater than addressability, is the number of distinguishable lines per inch that a device can create. Resolution is defined as the closest spacing at which adjacent black and white lines can be distinguished by observers (this again implies that horizontal and vertical resolution may differ). If 40 black lines interleaved with 40 white lines can be distinguished across one inch, the resolution is 80 lines per inch (also referred to as 40 line-pairs per inch).

Resolution also depends on the cross-sectional intensity distribution of a spot. A spot with sharply delineated edges yields higher resolution than does one with edges that trail off, as shown in Fig. 4.3.

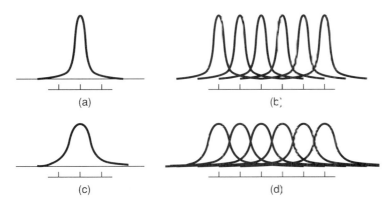

(a)   (b)

(c)   (d)

Fig. 4.3 The effect of cross-sectional spot intensity on resolution. (a) A spot with well-defined edges. (b) Several such overlapping spots. (c) A wider spot, with less height, since the energy is spread out over a larger area; its edges are not well defined, as are those in (a). (d) Several of these spots overlapping. The distinction between the peaks in (b) is much clearer in (d). The actual image intensity is the sum of each spot's intensity.

Many of the devices to be discussed can create only a few colors at any one point. Additional colors can be obtained with dither patterns, described in Chapter 13, at the cost of decreased spatial resolution of the resulting image.

Dot-matrix printers use a print head of from 7 to 24 *pins* (thin, stiff pieces of wire), each of which can be individually *fired*, to strike a ribbon against the paper. The print head moves across the paper one step at a time, the paper is advanced one line, and the print head makes another pass across the paper. Hence, these printers are raster output devices, requiring scan conversion of vector images prior to printing.

The addressability of a dot-matrix printer does not need to be limited by the physical distance between pins on the print head. There can be two columns of pins, offset vertically by one-half the interpin spacing, as seen in Fig. 4.4. Alternatively, two passes over the paper can be used to achieve the same effect, by advancing the paper by one-half the interpin spacing between the first and second passes.

Colored ribbons can be used to produce color hardcopy. Two approaches are possible. The first is using multiple print heads, each head with a different color ribbon. Alternatively and more commonly, a single print head is used with a multicolored ribbon.

More colors than are actually on the ribbon can be created by overstriking two different colors at the same dot on the paper. The color on top may be somewhat stronger than that underneath. Up to eight colors can be created at any one dot by overstriking with three colors—typically cyan, magenta, and yellow. However, the black resulting from striking all three is quite muddy, so a true black is often added to the ribbon.

Just as there are random and raster displays, so too there are random and raster plotters. *Pen plotters* move a pen over a piece of paper in random, vector-drawing style. In drawing a line, the pen is positioned at the start of the line, lowered to the paper, moved in a straight path to the endpoint of the line, raised, and moved to the start of the next line. There are two basic varieties of pen plotters. The *flatbed plotter* moves the pen in x and y on a sheet of paper spread out on a table and held down by electrostatic charge, by vacuum, or simply by being stretched tightly (Fig. 4.5). A carriage moves longitudinally over the table. On the carriage is a pen mount moving latitudinally along the carriage; the pen can be raised and lowered. Flatbed plotters are available in sizes from 12 by 18 inches to 6 by 10 feet and

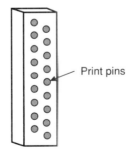

Fig. 4.4 A dot-matrix print head with two columns of print pins, offset vertically by half the interpin spacing to increase resolution.

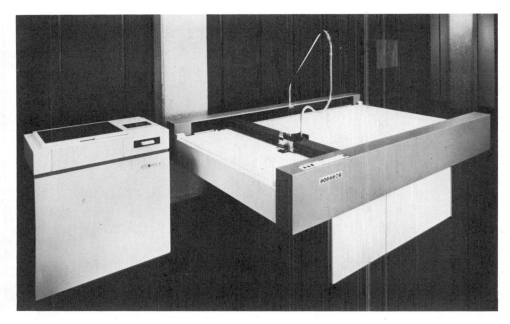

Fig. 4.5 A flatbed plotter. (Courtesy of CalComp–California Computer Products, Inc.)

larger. In some cases, the "pen" is a light source for exposing photographic negatives or a knife blade for scribing, and often pens of multiple colors or widths are used.

In contrast, *drum plotters* move the paper along one axis and the pen along the other axis. Typically, the paper is stretched tightly across a drum, as shown in Fig. 4.6. Pins on the drum engage prepunched holes in the paper to prevent slipping. The drum can rotate both forward and backward. By contrast, many *desk-top plotters* move the paper back and forth between pinch rollers, while the pen moves across the paper (Fig. 4.7).

Pen plotters include a microprocessor that accepts commands such as "draw line," "move," "draw circle," "draw text," "set line style," and "select pen." (The microprocessor sometimes also optimizes pen movements to minimize the distance the pen moves while up; Anderson [ANDE83] has developed an efficient algorithm for doing this.) The microprocessor decomposes the output primitives into incremental pen movements in any of the eight principal directions. A feedback system of position sensors and servomotors implements the motion commands, and an electromagnet raises and lowers the pen. Plotting speed depends on the acceleration and velocity with which the pen can be moved. In turn, pen acceleration is partially a function of the mass of the plot head; many multipen plotters keep all but the active pens at the side of the plotter to minimize this mass.

In contrast to the pen plotter, the *electrostatic plotter* places a negative charge on those parts of white paper that are to be black, then flows positively charged black toner over the paper (Fig. 4.8). The toner particles adhere to the paper where the charge has been deposited. The charge is placed on the paper, which in current systems can be up to 72

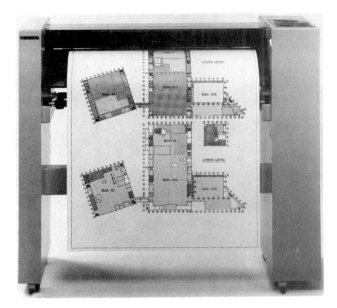

Fig. 4.6 A drum plotter. (Courtesy of Hewlett-Packard Company.)

inches wide, one row at a time. The paper moves at speeds up to 3 inches per second under a fine comb of electric contacts spaced horizontally 100 to 400 to the inch. Each contact is either on (to impart a negative charge) or off (to impart no charge). Each dot on an electrostatic plot is either black or white; gray levels must be created with dither patterns.

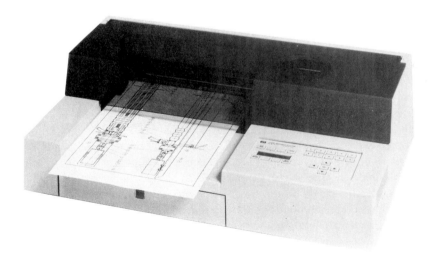

Fig. 4.7 A desk-top plotter. (Courtesy of Hewlett-Packard Company.)

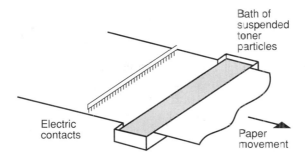

Fig. 4.8 Organization of an electrostatic plotter.

Electrostatic plotters may include a scan-conversion capability, or scan conversion can be done by the CPU. In the latter case, because the density of information on a 400 by 400 dot-per-square inch electrostatic plotter is quite high (see Exercise 4.1), correspondingly high transfer rates are needed.

Some color electrostatic plotters make multiple passes over the paper, rewinding to the start of the plot after each pass. On the first pass, black calibration marks are placed near the edge of the paper. Subsequent passes complete the plot with black, cyan, magenta, and yellow toners, using the calibration marks to maintain alignment. Others use multiple heads to deposit all the colors in a single pass.

Electrostatic plotters are often faster than pen plotters, and can also double as high-quality printers. On the other hand, pen plotters create images with higher contrast than those made by electrostatic plotters, since the latter deposit a toner even in areas where the paper is not negatively charged.

Laser printers scan a laser beam across a positively charged rotating drum coated with selenium. The areas hit by the laser beam lose their charge, and the positive charge remains only where the copy is to be black. A negatively charged powdered toner adheres to the positive areas of the drum and is then transferred to blank paper to form the copy. In color xerography, this process is repeated three times, once for each primary color. Figure 4.9 is a partial schematic of a monochrome laser printer.

Just as with the electrostatic plotter, the positive charge is either present or not present at any one spot on the drum, and there is either black or not black at the corresponding spot

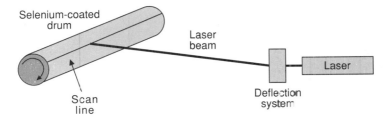

Fig. 4.9 Organization of a laser printer (the toner-application mechanism and the paper feeder are not shown).

on the copy. Hence, the laser printer is a two-level monochrome device or an eight-color color device.

Laser printers have a microprocessor to do scan conversion and to control the printer. An increasing number of laser printers accept the Postscript document and image description language as a defacto standard [ADOB85a]. Postscript provides a procedural description of an image to be printed, and can also be used to store image descriptions (Chapter 19). Most laser printers work with 8.5- by 11-inch or 8.5- by 14-inch paper, but considerably wider (30-inch) laser printers are available for engineering drawing and map-making applications.

Ink-jet printers spray cyan, magenta, yellow, and sometimes black ink onto paper. In most cases, the ink jets are mounted on a head in a printerlike mechanism. The print head moves across the page to draw one scan line, returns while the paper advances by one inter–scan-line spacing, and draws the next scan line. Slight irregularities in interline spacing can arise if the paper transport moves a bit too much or too little. Another approach is to wrap the paper around a drum; the drum then rotates rapidly while the print head slowly moves along the drum. Figure 4.10 shows this arrangement. In both cases, all the colors are deposited simultaneously, unlike the multipass laser and electrostatic plotters and printers. Most ink-jet printers are limited to on–off (i.e., bilevel) control of each pixel: a few have a variable dot-size capability.

Some ink-jet printers accept video input as well as digital, which makes them attractive for creating hardcopy images of raster display screens. Note that the resolution of a resulting image is limited by the resolution of the video input—typically between 640 by 480 and 1280 by 1024. Ink-jet printers tend to require more maintenance than do many of the other types.

Thermal-transfer printers, another raster hardcopy device, are reminiscent of electrostatic plotters. Finely spaced (typically 200-per-inch) heating nibs transfer pigments from colored wax paper to plain paper. The wax paper and plain paper are drawn together over the strip of heating nibs, which are selectively heated to cause the pigment transfer. For color printing (the most common use of this technology), the wax paper is on a roll of alternating cyan, magenta, yellow, and black strips, each of a length equal to the paper size. Because the nibs heat and cool very rapidly, a single color hardcopy image can be created in less than 1 minute. Some thermal-transfer printers accept a video signal and digital bitmap input, making them convenient for creating hardcopy of video images.

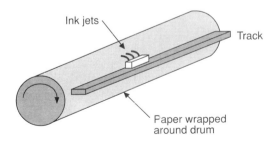

Ink jets

Track

Paper wrapped around drum

Fig. 4.10 A rotary ink-jet plotter.

Thermal sublimation dye transfer printers work similarly to the thermal transfer printers, except the heating and dye transfer process permit 256 intensities each of cyan, magenta, and yellow to be transferred, creating high-quality full-color images with a spatial resolution of 200 dots per inch. The process is slower than wax transfer, but the quality is near-photographic.

A *camera* that photographs an image displayed on a cathode-ray (television) tube can be considered another hardcopy device. This is the most common hardcopy technology we discuss that yields a large number of colors at a single resolution point; film can capture many different colors.

There are two basic techniques for color film recorders. In one, the camera records the color image directly from a color CRT. Image resolution is limited because of the shadow mask of the color monitor (see Section 4.2.2) and the need to use a raster scan with the color monitor. In the other approach, a black-and-white CRT is photographed through color filters, and the different color components of the image are displayed in sequence (Fig 4.11). This technique yields very high-quality raster or vector images. Colors are mixed by double-exposing parts of the image through two or more filters, usually with different CRT intensities.

Input to film recorders can be a raster video signal, a bitmap, or vector-style instructions. Either the video signal can drive a color CRT directly, or the red, green, and blue components of the signal can be electronically separated for time-sequential display through filters. In either case, the video signal must stay constant during the entire recording cycle, which can be up to 1 minute if relatively slow (low-sensitivity) film is being used. High-speed, high-resolution bitmap or vector systems are expensive, because the drive electronics and CRT itself must be designed and calibrated carefully. As speed and resolution decrease, costs are reduced dramatically.

The recently developed *Cycolor* technique embeds in paper millions of microcapsules filled with one of three colored dyes—cyan, magenta, or yellow. The capsules harden selectively when exposed to light of a specific color. For instance, when exposed to green

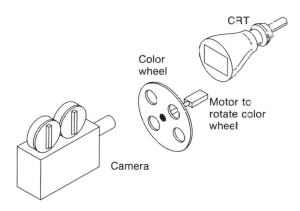

Fig. 4.11 A film recorder for making color photographs using colored filters.

TABLE 4.1 A COMPARISON OF SEVERAL MONOCHROME HARDCOPY TECHNOLOGIES*

	Pen plotter	Dot matrix	Electro-static	Laser	Ink jet	Thermal	Photo
intensity levels per dot	2	2	2	2	2–many	2	many
addressability, points per inch	1000+	to 250	to 400	to 1500	to 200	to 200	to 800
dot size, thousandths of inch	6–15	10–18	8	5	8–20	7–10	6–20
relative cost range	L–M	VL–L	M	M–H	L–M	L–M	L–H
relative cost per image	L	VL	M	M	L	M	H
image quality	L–M	L–M	M	H	M	M	H
speed	L	M	H–H	M–H	M	M	L

*VL = very low, L = low, M = medium, H = high.

light, chemicals in the magenta-filled capsule cause that capsule to harden. The paper is passed through pressure rollers and pressed against a sheet of plain paper. The unhardened capsules (cyan and yellow, in this example) break, but the hardened capsule (magenta) does not. The cyan and yellow colors mix and are transferred to the plain paper, creating a high-quality green image. Unlike most other technologies, this one requires only a single pass.

Table 4.1 summarizes the differences among black-and-white hardcopy devices; Table 4.2 covers most of the color hardcopy devices. Considerable detail on the technology of hardcopy devices can be found in [DURB88]. The current pace of technological innovation is, of course, so great that the relative advantages and disadvantages of some of these devices will surely change. Also, some of the technologies are available in a wide range of prices and performances. Film recorders and pen plotters, for instance, can cost from about $1000 to $100,000.

Note that, of all the color devices, only the film recorder, Cycolor, and some ink-jet printers can capture a wide range of colors. All the other technologies use essentially a binary on–off control for the three or four colors they can record directly. Note also that color control is tricky: there is no guarantee that the eight colors on one device will look anything like the eight colors on the display or on another hardcopy device (Chapter 13).

Wide laser printers are becoming available: they will slowly preempt electrostatic plotters, which have a lower contrast ratio between black and white and are more difficult to maintain.

TABLE 4.2 A COMPARISON OF SEVERAL COLOR HARDCOPY TECHNOLOGIES*

	Pen plotter	Dot matrix	Electro-static	Laser	Ink jet	Thermal	Photo
color levels per dot	to 16	8	8	8	8–many	8–many	many
addressability, points per inch	1000+	to 250	to 400	to 1500	to 200	to 200	to 800
dot size, thousandths of inch	15–6	18–10	8	5	20–8	10–7	20–6
relative cost range	L–M	VL	M–H	M–H	L–M	M	M–H
relative cost per image	L	VL	M	M	L	M	H
image quality	L–M	L	M	H	M	M–H	M–H
speed	L	L–M	M	M	M	L–M	L

*VL = very low, L = low, M = medium, H = high.

4.2 DISPLAY TECHNOLOGIES

Interactive computer graphics demands display devices whose images can be changed quickly. Nonpermanent image displays allow an image to be changed, making possible dynamic movement of portions of an image. The CRT is by far the most common display device and will remain so for many years. However, solid-state technologies are being developed that may, in the long term, substantially reduce the dominance of the CRT.

The *monochromatic CRTs* used for graphics displays are essentially the same as those used in black-and-white home television sets. Figure 4.12 shows a highly stylized cross-sectional view of a CRT. The electron gun emits a stream of electrons that is accelerated toward the phosphor-coated screen by a high positive voltage applied near the face of the tube. On the way to the screen, the electrons are forced into a narrow beam by the focusing mechanism and are directed toward a particular point on the screen by the magnetic field produced by the deflection coils. When the electrons hit the screen, the phosphor emits visible light. Because the phosphor's light output decays exponentially with time, the entire picture must be *refreshed* (redrawn) many times per second, so that the viewer sees what appears to be a constant, unflickering picture.

The refresh rate for raster-scan displays is usually at least 60 frames per second, and is independent of picture complexity. The refresh rate for vector systems depends directly on picture complexity (number of lines, points, and characters): The greater the complexity, the longer the time taken by a single refresh cycle and the lower the refresh rate.

The stream of electrons from the heated cathode is accelerated toward the phosphor by a high voltage, typically 15,000 to 20,000 volts, which determines the velocity achieved by the electrons before they hit the phosphor. The control-grid voltage determines how many electrons are actually in the electron beam. The more negative the control-grid voltage is, the fewer the electrons that pass through the grid. This phenomenon allows the spot's

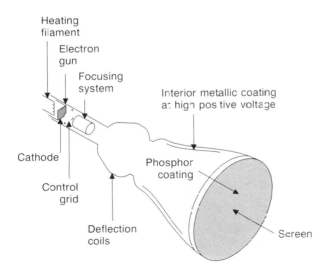

Fig. 4.12 Cross-section of a CRT (not to scale).

intensity to be controlled, because the light output of the phosphor decreases as the number of electrons in the beam decreases.

The focusing system concentrates the electron beam so that the beam converges to a small point when it hits the phosphor coating. It is not enough for the electrons in the beam to move parallel to one another. They would diverge because of electron repulsion, so the focusing system must make them converge to counteract the divergence. With the exception of this tendency to diverge, focusing an electron beam is analogous to focusing a light beam. An optical lens and an electron lens both have a focal distance, which in the case of the CRT is set such that the beam is focused on the screen. The cross-sectional electron density of the beam is Gaussian (that is, normal), and the intensity of the light spot created on the phosphor has the same distribution, as was shown in Fig. 4.3. The spot thus has no distinct edges, and hence spot size is usually specified as the diameter at which the intensity is 50 percent of that at the center of the spot. The typical spot size in a high-resolution monochrome CRT is 0.005 inches.

Figure 4.13 illustrates both the focusing system of and a difficulty with CRTs. The beam is shown in two positions. In one case, the beam converges at the point at which it strikes the screen. In the second case, however, the convergence point is behind the screen, and the resulting image is therefore somewhat blurred. Why has this happened? The faceplates of most CRTs are nearly flat, and hence have a radius of curvature far greater than the distance from the lens to the screen. Thus, not all points on the screen are equidistant from the lens, and if the beam is in focus when it is directed at the center of the screen, it is not in focus anywhere else on the screen. The further the beam is deflected from the center, the more defocused it is. In high-precision displays, the system solves this problem by focusing the lens dynamically as a function of the beam's position; making CRTs with sharply curved faceplates is not a good solution.

When the electron beam strikes the phosphor-coated screen of the CRT, the individual electrons are moving with kinetic energy proportional to the acceleration voltage. Some of this energy is dissipated as heat, but the rest is transferred to the electrons of the phosphor

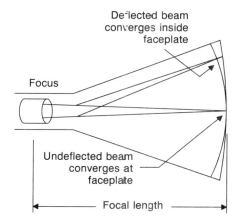

Fig. 4.13 Focusing of the electron beam. The focal length varies as a function of the deflection angle.

atoms, making them jump to higher quantum-energy levels. In returning to their previous quantum levels, these excited electrons give up their extra energy in the form of light, at frequencies (i.e., colors) predicted by quantum theory. Any given phosphor has several different quantum levels to which electrons can be excited, each corresponding to a color associated with the return to an unexcited state. Further, electrons on some levels are less stable and return to the unexcited state more rapidly than others. A phosphor's *fluorescence* is the light emitted as these very unstable electrons lose their excess energy while the phosphor is being struck by electrons. *Phosphorescence* is the light given off by the return of the relatively more stable excited electrons to their unexcited state once the electron beam excitation is removed. With typical phosphors, most of the light emitted is phosphorescence, since the excitation and hence the fluorescence usually last just a fraction of a microsecond. A phosphor's *persistence* is defined as the time from the removal of excitation to the moment when phosphorescence has decayed to 10 percent of the initial light output. The range of persistence of different phosphors can reach many seconds, but for most phosphors used in graphics equipment it is usually 10 to 60 microseconds. This light output decays exponentially with time. Characteristics of phosphors are detailed in [SHER79].

The *refresh rate* of a CRT is the number of times per second the image is redrawn; it is typically 60 per second for raster displays. As the refresh rate decreases, *flicker* develops because the eye can no longer integrate the individual light impulses coming from a pixel. The refresh rate above which a picture stops flickering and fuses into a steady image is called the *critical fusion frequency*, or *CFF*. The process of fusion is familiar to all of us; it occurs whenever we watch television or motion pictures. A flicker-free picture appears constant or steady to the viewer, even though, in fact, any given point is "off" much longer than it is "on."

One determinant of the CFF is the phosphor's persistence: The longer the persistence, the lower the CFF. The relation between fusion frequency and persistence is nonlinear: Doubling persistence does not halve the CFF. As persistence increases into the several-second range, the fusion frequency becomes quite small. At the other extreme, even a phosphor with absolutely no persistence at all can be used, since all the eye really requires is to see some light for a short period of time, repeated at a frequency above the CFF.

Persistence is not the only factor affecting CFF. CFF also increases with image intensity and with ambient room lighting, and varies with different wavelengths of emitted light. Finally, it depends on the observer. Fusion is, after all, a physiological phenomenon, and differences among viewers of up to 20 Hz in CFF have been reported [ROGO83]. Cited fusion frequencies are thus usually averages for a large number of observers. Eliminating flicker for 99 percent of viewers of very high-intensity images (especially prevalent with black-on-white raster displays) requires refresh rates of 80 to 90 Hz.

The *horizontal scan rate* is the number of scan lines per second that the circuitry driving a CRT is able to display. The rate is approximately the product of the refresh rate and the number of scan lines. For a given scan rate, an increase in the refresh rate means a decrease in the number of scan lines.

The *resolution* of a monochromatic CRT is defined just as is resolution for hardcopy devices. Resolution is usually measured with a *shrinking raster*: A known number of equally spaced parallel lines that alternate between black and white are displayed, and the interline spacing is uniformly decreased until the lines just begin to merge together into a uniform field of gray. This merging happens at about the point where the interline spacing is equal to the diameter at which the spot intensity is 60 percent of the intensity at the center of the spot. The resolution is the distance between the two outermost lines, divided by the number of lines in the raster. There is a clear dependence between spot size and achievable resolution: The larger the spot size, the lower the achievable resolution.

In the shrinking-raster process, the interline spacing is decreased not by modifying the contents of a raster bitmap, but by changing the gain (amount of amplification) of the vertical or horizontal deflection amplifiers, depending on whether the vertical or horizontal resolution is being measured. These amplifiers control how large an area on the screen is covered by the bitmap image. Thus, CRT resolution is (properly) not a function of the bitmap resolution, but may be either higher or lower than that of the bitmap.

Resolution is not a constant. As the number of electrons in the beam increases, resolution tends to decrease, because a bright line is wider than a dim line. This effect is a result of *bloom*, the tendency of a phosphor's excitation to spread somewhat beyond the area being bombarded, and also occurs because the spot size of an intense electron beam is bigger than that of a weak beam. Vertical resolution on a raster monitor is determined primarily by spot size; if the vertical resolution is n lines per inch, the spot size needs to be about $1/n$ inches. Horizontal resolution (in which the line-pairs are vertical) is determined by both spot size and the speed with which the electron beam can be turned on and off as it moves horizontally across the screen. This rate is related to the bandwidth of the display, as discussed in the next paragraph. Research on defining the resolution of a display precisely and on our ability to perceive images is ongoing. The *modulation transfer function*, used extensively in this research, relates a device's input signal to its output signal [SNYD85].

The bandwidth of a monitor has to do with the speed with which the electron gun can be turned on or off. To achieve a horizontal resolution of n pixels per scan line, it must be possible to turn the electron gun on at least $n/2$ times and off another $n/2$ times in one scan line, in order to create alternating on and off lines. Consider a raster scan of 1000 lines by 1000 pixels, displayed at a 60-Hz refresh rate. One pixel is drawn in about 11 nanoseconds [WHIT84], so the period of an on–off cycle is about 22 nanoseconds, which corresponds to a frequency of 45 MHz. This frequency is the minimum bandwidth needed to achieve 1000 lines (500 line-pairs) of resolution, but is not the actual bandwidth because we have ignored the effect of spot size. The nonzero spot size must be compensated for with a higher bandwidth which causes the beam to turn on and off more quickly, giving the pixels sharper edges than they would have otherwise. It is not unusual for the actual bandwidth of a 1000 by 1000 monitor to be 100 MHz. The actual relationships among resolution, bandwidth, and spot size are complex, and only recently has progress been made in quantifying them [INFA85].

Color television sets and color raster displays use some form of *shadow-mask CRT*. Here, the inside of the tube's viewing surface is covered with closely spaced groups of red, green, and blue phosphor dots. The dot groups are so small that light emanating from the individual dots is perceived by the viewer as a mixture of the three colors. Thus, a wide range of colors can be produced by each group, depending on how strongly each individual phosphor dot is excited. A *shadow mask*, which is a thin metal plate perforated with many small holes and mounted close to the viewing surface, is carefully aligned so that each of the three electron beams (one each for red, green, and blue) can hit only one type of phosphor dot. The dots thus can be excited selectively.

Figure 4.14 shows one of the most common types of shadow-mask CRT, a *delta–delta* CRT. The phosphor dots are arranged in a triangular *triad* pattern, as are the three electron guns. The guns are deflected together, and are aimed (converged) at the same point on the viewing surface. The shadow mask has one small hole for each triad. The holes are precisely aligned with respect to both the triads and the electron guns, so that each dot in the triad is exposed to electrons from only one gun. High-precision delta–delta CRTs are particularly difficult to keep in alignment. An alternative arrangement, the *precision in-line delta CRT* shown in Fig. 4.15, is easier to converge and is gaining in popularity for high-precision (1000-scan-lines) monitors. In this case, the three beams simultaneously expose three in-line phosphor dots. However, the in-line arrangement does slightly reduce image sharpness at the edges of the tube. Still in the research laboratory but likely to become commercially viable is the *flat-panel color CRT*, in which the electron beams move parallel to the viewing surface, and are then turned 90° to strike the surface.

The need for the shadow mask and triads imposes a limit on the resolution of color CRTs not present with monochrome CRTs. In very high-resolution tubes, the triads are placed on about 0.21-millimeter centers; those in home television tubes are on about 0.60-millimeter centers (this distance is also called the *pitch* of the tube). Because a finely focused beam cannot be guaranteed to hit exactly in the center of a shadow-mask hole, the beam diameter (the diameter at which the intensity is 50 percent of the maximum) must be about $\frac{7}{4}$ times the pitch. Thus, on a mask with a pitch of 0.25-millimeter (0.01 inches),

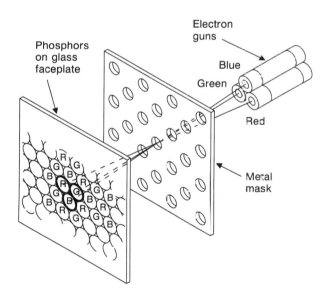

Fig. 4.14 Delta-delta shadow-mask CRT. The three guns and phosphor dots are arranged in a triangular (delta) pattern. The shadow mask allows electrons from each gun to hit only the corresponding phosphor dots.

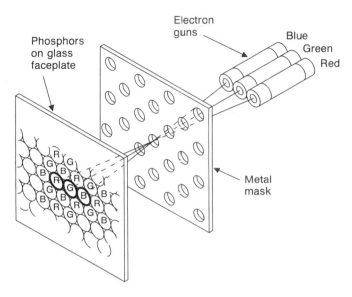

Fig. 4.15 A precision in-line CRT: the three electron guns are in a line.

the beam is about 0.018 inches across, and the resolution can be no more than about $\frac{1}{0.018}$ = 55 lines per inch. On a 0.25-millimeter pitch, 19-inch (diagonal measure) monitor, which is about 15.5 inches wide by 11.6 inches high [CONR85], the resolution achievable is thus only 15.5 × 55 = 850 by 11.6 × 55 = 638. This value compares with a typical addressability of 1280 by 1024, or 1024 by 800. As illustrated in Fig. 4.2, a resolution somewhat less than the addressability is useful.

The pitch of the shadow mask is clearly an important limit on the resolution of shadow-mask CRTs. As pitch decreases, resolution can increase (assuming bandwidth and dot size are appropriate). The smaller the pitch is, however, the more difficult the tube is to manufacture. A small-pitch shadow mask is more fragile, making it more difficult to mount. It is also more likely to warp from heating by the electron beam. The *flat-tension-mask* tube has a flat faceplate, with the mask stretched tightly to maintain its position; a pitch of 0.15 millimeter is achievable with this technology.

The shadow mask also limits CRT brightness. Typically, only 20 percent of the electrons in the beam hit the phosphors—the rest hit the mask. Thus, fewer electrons make light than in a monochrome CRT. The number of electrons in the beam (the *beam current*) can be increased, but a higher current makes focusing more difficult and also generates more heat on the shadow mask, further exacerbating mask warping. Because the flat tension mask is more resistant to heating distortions, it allows a higher beam current and hence a brighter image.

Most high-quality shadow-mask CRTs have diagonals of 15 to 21 inches, with slightly curved faceplates that create optical distortions for the viewer. Several types of flat-face CRTs are becoming available, including a 29-inch–diagonal tube with a pitch of 0.31 millimeter. Of course, the price is high, but it will come down as demand develops.

The *direct-view storage tube* (DVST) is similar to the standard CRT, except that it does not need to be refreshed because the image is stored as a distribution of charges on the inside surface of the screen. Because no refresh is needed, the DVST can display complex images without the high scan rate and bandwidth required by a conventional CRT. The major disadvantage of the DVST is that modifying any part of an image requires redrawing the entire modified image to establish a new charge distribution in the DVST. This redraw can be unacceptably slow (many seconds for a complex image).

The ubiquitous Tektronix 4010 display terminal, based on the DVST, was the first low-cost, widely available interactive graphics terminal. It was the Model T of computer graphics, and was so pervasive that its instruction set became a defacto standard. Even today, many display systems include a Tektronix-compatibility feature, so that buyers can continue to run their (often large) libraries of older software developed for the 4010. Now, however, DVSTs have been superseded by raster displays and have essentially disappeared from the graphics scene.

A *liquid-crystal display* (LCD) is made up of six layers, as shown in Fig. 4.16. The front layer is a vertical polarizer plate. Next is a layer with thin grid wires electrodeposited on the surface adjoining the crystals. Next is a thin (about 0.0005-inch) liquid-crystal layer, then a layer with horizontal grid wires on the surface next to the crystals, then a horizontal polarizer, and finally a reflector.

The liquid-crystal material is made up of long crystalline molecules. The individual molecules normally are arranged in a spiral fashion such that the direction of polarization of polarized light passing through is rotated 90°. Light entering through the front layer is polarized vertically. As the light passes through the liquid crystal, the polarization is rotated 90° to horizontal, so the light now passes through the rear horizontal polarizer, is reflected, and returns through the two polarizers and crystal.

When the crystals are in an electric field, they all line up in the the same direction, and thus have no polarizing effect. Hence, crystals in the electric field do not change the polarization of the transmitted light, so the light remains vertically polarized and does not pass through the rear polarizer: The light is absorbed, so the viewer sees a dark spot on the display.

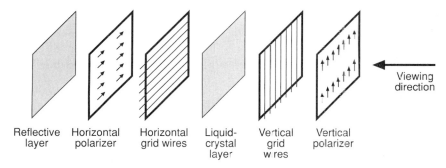

|Reflective
layer|Horizontal
polarizer|Horizontal
grid wires|Liquid-
crystal
layer|Vertical
grid
wires|Vertical
polarizer|

Viewing direction

Fig. 4.16 The layers of a liquid-crystal display (LCD), all of which are sandwiched together to form a thin panel.

A dark spot at point (x_1, y_1) is created via *matrix addressing*. The point is selected by applying a negative voltage $-V$ to the horizontal grid wire x_1 and a positive voltage $+V$ to the vertical grid wire y_1: Neither $-V$ nor $+V$ is large enough to cause the crystals to line up, but their difference is large enough to do so. Now the crystals at (x_1, y_1) no longer rotate the direction of polarization of the transmitted light, so it remains vertically polarized and does not pass through the rear polarizer: The light is absorbed, so the viewer sees a dark spot on the display.

To display dots at (x_1, y_1) and (x_2, y_2), we cannot simply apply the positive voltage to x_1 and x_2 and the negative voltage to y_1 and y_2: that would cause dots to appear at (x_1, y_1), (x_1, y_2), (x_2, y_1), and (x_2, y_2), because all these points will be affected by the voltage. Rather, the points must be selected in succession, one after the other, and this selection process must be repeated, to refresh the activation of each point. Of course, if $y_1 = y_2$, then both points on the row can be selected at the same time.

The display is refreshed one row at a time, in raster-scan fashion. Those points in a row that are ''on'' (i.e., dark in the case of a black-on-white LCD display) are selected only about $1/N$ of the time, where N is the number of rows. Fortunately, once the crystals are lined up, they stay that way for several hundred milliseconds, even when the voltage is withdrawn (the crystals' equivalent of phosphors' persistence). But even so, the crystal is not switched on all the time.

Active matrix panels are LCD panels that have a transistor at each (x, y) grid point. The transistors are used to cause the crystals to change their state quickly, and also to control the degree to which the state has been changed. These two properties allow LCDs to be used in miniature television sets with continuous-tone images. The crystals can also be dyed to provide color. Most important, the transistor can serve as a memory for the state of a cell and can hold the cell in that state until it is changed. That is, the memory provided by the transistor enables a cell to remain on all the time and hence to be brighter than it would be if it had to be refreshed periodically. Color LCD panels with resolutions up to 800 by 1000 on a 14-inch diagonal panel have been built.

Advantages of LCDs are low cost, low weight, small size, and low power consumption. In the past, the major disadvantage was that LCDs were passive, reflecting only incident light and creating no light of their own (although this could be corrected with backlighting): Any glare washed out the image. In recent years, use of active panels has removed this concern.

Nonactive LCD technology has been adapted to color displays, and is sold commercially as the Tektronix liquid-crystal shutter (LCS). The LCS, placed in front of a standard black-and-white CRT, consists of three layers. The back layer, closest to the CRT, is a vertical polarizer, to polarize light emitted from the CRT. The layer also has a thin coating of a transparent conducting material. The next layer is the liquid crystal, and the third (front) layer is a color polarizer that transmits vertically polarized light as red and horizontally polarized light as green. This front layer also has a thin coating of the transparent conductor. If the crystals are in their normal state, they rotate the polarization plane by 90°, so the light is horizontally polarized as it approaches the color polarizer of the third layer, and is seen as green. If the appropriate voltage is applied to the conductive coatings on the front and back layers, then the crystals line up and do not affect the vertical polarization, so the light is seen as red.

The crystals are switched back and forth between their two states at a rate of 60 Hz. At the same time and in synchrony, images to be seen as red and green are alternated on the monochrome display. Mixtures of red and green are created by intensifying the same spot during the red and green phases, potentially with different intensities.

The LCS is an alternative to the shadow-mask CRT, but has limited color resolution. It is possible, however, that this technology can be extended to work with three colors. If it can be, the shadow mask will no longer be a limiting factor in achieving higher-resolution full-color displays. Spot size and bandwidth will be the major determinants, as with monochrome CRTs. Eliminating the shadow mask also will increase ruggedness. Because LCD displays are small and light, they can be used in head-mounted displays such as that discussed in Section 8.1.6.

The *plasma panel* is an array of tiny neon bulbs. Each bulb can be put into an "on" (intensified) state or an "off" state, and remains in the state until explicitly changed to the other. This memory property means that plasma panels need not be refreshed. Plasma panels typically have 50 to 125 cells per inch, with a 10- to 15-inch diagonal, but 40- by 40-inch panels with 50 cells per inch are sold commercially, and even larger and denser panels can be custom-made.

The neon bulbs are not discrete units, but rather are part of a single integrated panel made of three layers of glass, as seen in Fig. 4.17. The inside surface of the front layer has thin vertical strips of an electrical conductor; the center layer has a number of holes (the bulbs), and the inside surface of the rear layer has thin horizontal strips of an electrical conductor. Matrix addressing is used to turn bulbs on and off. To turn on a bulb, the system adjusts the voltages on the corresponding lines such that their difference is large enough to pull electrons from the neon molecules, thus firing the bulb and making it glow. Once the glow starts, a lower voltage is applied to sustain it. To turn off a bulb, the system momentarily decreases the voltages on the appropriate lines to less than the sustaining

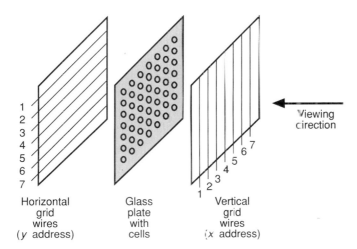

Fig. 4.17 The layers of a plasma display, all of which are sandwiched together to form a thin panel.

voltage. Bulbs can be turned on or off in about 15 microseconds. In some panel designs, the individual cells are replaced with an open cavity, because the neon glow is contained in a localized area. In this case, the front and back glass layers are separated by spacers. Some plasma panels can also display multiple gray levels.

The plasma panel has the advantages of being flat, transparent, and rugged, and of not needing a bitmap refresh buffer. It can be used with a rear-projection system to mix photographic slides as static background for computer-generated dynamic graphics, but has found most use in military applications, where small size and ruggedness are important. However, its cost, although continually decreasing, is still relatively high for its limited resolution. Color has been demonstrated in the laboratory, but is not commercially available.

Electroluminescent (EL) displays consist of the same gridlike structure as used in LCD and plasma displays. Between the front and back panels is a thin (typically 500-nanometers) layer of an electroluminescent material, such as zinc sulfide doped with manganese, that emits light when in a high electric field (about 10^6 volts per centimeter). A point on the panel is illuminated via the matrix-addressing scheme, several hundred volts being placed across the horizontal and vertical selection lines. Color electroluminescent displays are also available.

These displays are bright and can be switched on and off quickly, and transistors at each pixel can be used to store the image. Typical panel sizes are 6 by 8 inches up to 12 by 16 inches, with 70 addressable dots per inch. These displays' major disadvantage is that their power consumption is higher than that of the LCD panel. However, their brightness has led to their use in some portable computers.

Electrophoretic displays use positively charged colored particles suspended in a solution of a contrasting color, sealed between two parallel, closely spaced plates that have matrix-addressing selection lines. A negative voltage on the front selection line and a positive voltage on the rear selection line pulls the colored particles toward the front plate, where they are seen instead of the colored liquid. Reversing the voltages pulls the particles toward the rear plate, so the colored liquid is seen. The display has a memory: The particles stay where they have been placed until moved explicitly.

Most large-screen displays use some form of *projection CRT,* in which the light from a small (several-inch-diameter) but very bright monchrome CRT is magnified and projected from a curved mirror. Color systems use three projectors with red, green, and blue filters. A shadow-mask CRT does not create enough light to be projected onto a large (2-meter-diagonal) screen.

The *GE light-valve projection system* is used for very large screens, where the light output from the projection CRT would not be sufficient. A light valve is just what its name implies: A mechanism for controlling how much light passes through a valve. The light source can have much higher intensity than a CRT. In the most common approach, an electron gun traces an image on a thin oil film on a piece of glass. The electron charge causes the film to vary in thickness: A negatively charged area of the film is "stretched out," as the electrons repel one another, causing the film to become thinner. Light from the high-intensity source is directed at the glass, and is refracted in different directions because of the variation in the thickness of the oil film. Optics involving Schlieren bars and lenses project light that is refracted in certain directions on the screen, while other light is not

TABLE 4.3 COMPARISON OF DISPLAY TECHNOLOGIES

	CRT	Electro-luminescent	Liquid crystal	Plasma panel
power consumption	fair	fair–good	excellent	fair
screen size	excellent	good	fair	excellent
depth	poor	excellent	excellent	good
weight	poor	excellent	excellent	excellent
ruggedness	fair–good	good–excellent	excellent	excellent
brightness	excellent	excellent	fair–good	excellent
addressability	good–excellent	good	fair–good	good
contrast	good–excellent	good	fair	good
intensity levels per dot	excellent	fair	fair	fair
viewing angle	excellent	good	poor	good–excellent
color capability	excellent	good	good	fair
relative cost range	low	medium–high	low	high

projected. Color is possible with these systems, through use of either three projectors or a more sophisticated set of optics with a single projector. More details are given in [SHER79]. Other similar light-valve systems use LCDs to modulate the light beam.

Table 4.3 summarizes the characteristics of the four major display technologies. The pace of technological innovation is such, however, that some of the relationships may change over the next few years. Also, note that the liquid-crystal comparisons are for passive addressing; with active matrix addressing; gray levels and colors are achievable. More detailed information on these display technologies is given in [APT85; BALD85; CONR85; PERR85; SHER79; and TANN85].

4.3 RASTER-SCAN DISPLAY SYSTEMS

The basic concepts of raster graphics systems were presented in Chapter 1, and Chapter 2 provided further insight into the types of operations possible with a raster display. In this section, we discuss the various elements of a raster display, stressing two fundamental ways in which various raster systems differ one from another.

First, most raster displays have some specialized hardware to assist in scan converting output primitives into the pixmap, and to perform the raster operations of moving, copying, and modifying pixels or blocks of pixels. We call this hardware a *graphics display processor*. The fundamental difference among display systems is how much the display processor does versus how much must be done by the graphics subroutine package executing on the general-purpose CPU that drives the raster display. Note that the graphics display processor is also sometimes called a *graphics controller* (emphasizing its similarity to the control units for other peripheral devices) or a *display coprocessor*. The second key differentiator in raster systems is the relationship between the pixmap and the address space of the general-purpose computer's memory, whether the pixmap is part of the general-purpose computer's memory or is separate.

In Section 4.3.1, we introduce a simple raster display consisting of a CPU containing the pixmap as part of its memory, and a video controller driving a CRT. There is no display processor, so the CPU does both the application and graphics work. In Section 4.3.2, a graphics processor with a separate pixmap is introduced, and a wide range of graphics-processor functionalities is discussed in Section 4.3.3. Section 4.3.4 discusses ways in which the pixmap can be integrated back into the CPU's address space, given the existence of a graphics processor.

4.3.1 Simple Raster Display System

The simplest and most common raster display system organization is shown in Fig. 4.18. The relation between memory and the CPU is exactly the same as in a nongraphics computer system. However, a portion of the memory also serves as the pixmap. The video controller displays the image defined in the frame buffer, accessing the memory through a separate access port as often as the raster-scan rate dictates. In many systems, a fixed portion of memory is permanently allocated to the frame buffer, whereas some systems have several interchangeable memory areas (sometimes called *pages* in the personal-computer world). Yet other systems can designate (via a register) any part of memory for the frame buffer. In this case, the system may be organized as shown in Fig. 4.19, or the entire system memory may be dual-ported.

The application program and graphics subroutine package share the system memory and are executed by the CPU. The graphics package includes scan-conversion procedures, so that when the application program calls, say, SRGP_lineCoord ($x1$, $y1$, $x2$, $y2$), the graphics package can set the appropriate pixels in the frame buffer (details on scan-conversion procedures were given in Chapter 3). Because the frame buffer is in the address space of the CPU, the graphics package can easily access it to set pixels and to implement the PixBlt instructions described in Chapter 2.

The video controller cycles through the frame buffer, one scan line at a time, typically 60 times per second. Memory reference addresses are generated in synchrony with the raster scan, and the contents of the memory are used to control the CRT beam's intensity or

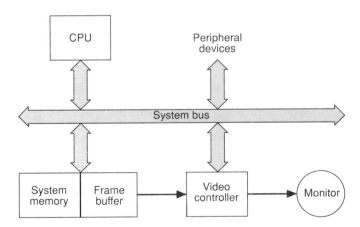

Fig. 4.18 A common raster display system architecture. A dedicated portion of the system memory is dual-ported, so that it can be accessed directly by the video controller, without the system bus being tied up.

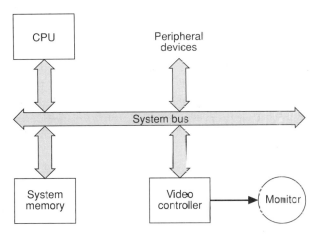

Fig. 4.19 A simple raster display system architecture. Because the frame buffer may be stored anywhere in system memory, the video controller accesses the memory via the system bus.

color. The video controller is organized as shown in Fig. 4.20. The raster-scan generator produces deflection signals that generate the raster scan; it also controls the X and Y address registers, which in turn define the memory location to be accessed next.

Assume that the frame buffer is addressed in x from 0 to x_{max} and in y from 0 to y_{max}; then, at the start of a refresh cycle, the X address register is set to zero and the Y register is set to y_{max} (the top scan line). As the first scan line is generated, the X address is incremented up through x_{max}. Each pixel value is fetched and is used to control the intensity of the CRT beam. After the first scan line, the X address is reset to zero and the Y address is decremented by one. The process continues until the last scan line ($y = 0$) is generated.

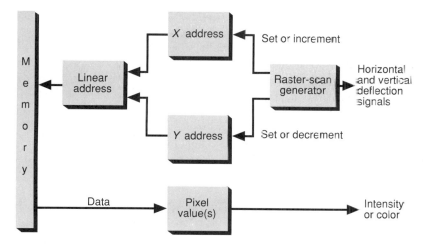

Fig. 4.20 Logical organization of the video controller.

In this simplistic situation, one memory access is made to the frame buffer for each pixel to be displayed. For a medium-resolution display of 640 pixels by 480 lines refreshed 60 times per second, a simple way to estimate the time available for displaying a single 1-bit pixel is to calculate $1/(480 \times 640 \times 60) = 54$ nanoseconds. This calculation ignores the fact that pixels are not being displayed during horizontal and vertical retrace (see Exercise 4.10). But typical RAM memory chips have cycle times around 200 nanoseconds: They cannot support one access each 54 nanoseconds! Thus, the video controller must fetch multiple pixel values in one memory cycle. In the case at hand, the controller might fetch 16 bits in one memory cycle, thereby taking care of 16 pixels $\times$ 54 ns/pixel = 864 nanoseconds of refresh time. The 16 bits are loaded into a register on the video controller, then are shifted out to control the CRT beam intensity, one each 54 nanoseconds. In the 864 nanoseconds this takes, there is time for about four memory cycles: one for the video controller and three for the CPU. This sharing may force the CPU to wait for memory accesses, potentially reducing the speed of the CPU by 25 percent. Of course, cache memory on the CPU chip can be used to ameliorate this problem.

It may not be possible to fetch 16 pixels in one memory cycle. Consider the situation when the pixmap is implemented with five 64-KB–memory chips, with each chip able to deliver 1 bit per cycle (this is called a 64-KB by 1 chip organization), for a total of 5 bits in the 200-nanoseconds cycle time. This is an average of 40 nanoseconds per bit (i.e., per pixel), which is not much faster than the 54 nanoseconds/pixel scan rate and leaves hardly any time for accesses to the memory by the CPU (except during the approximately 7-microsecond inter–scan-line retrace time and 1250-microsecond interframe vertical retrace time). With five 32-KB by 2 chips, however, 10 pixels are delivered in 200 nanoseconds, leaving slightly over half the time available for the CPU. With a 1600 by 1200 display, the pixel time is $1/(1600 \times 1200 \times 60) = 8.7$ nanoseconds. With a 200-nanoseconds memory cycle time, $200/8.7 = 23$ pixels must be fetched each cycle. A 1600 $\times$ 1200 display needs 1.92 MB of memory, which can be provided by eight 256-KB chips. Again, 256-KB by 1 chips can provide only 8 pixels per cycle: on the other hand, 32-KB by 8 chips can deliver 64 pixels, freeing two-thirds of the memory cycles for the CPU.

Access to memory by the CPU and video controller is clearly a problem: Table 4.4 shows that problem's magnitude. The solution is RAM architectures that accommodate the needs of raster displays. Chapter 18 discusses these architectures.

We have thus far assumed monochrome, 1-bit-per-pixel bitmaps. This assumption is fine for some applications, but is grossly unsatisfactory for others. Additional control over the intensity of each pixel is obtained by storing multiple bits for each pixel: 2 bits yield four intensities, and so on. The bits can be used to control not only intensity, but also color. How many bits per pixel are needed for a stored image to be perceived as having continuous shades of gray? Five or 6 bits are often enough, but 8 or more bits can be necessary. Thus, for color displays, a somewhat simplified argument suggests that three times as many bits are needed: 8 bits for each of the three additive primary colors red, blue, and green (see Chapter 13).

Systems with 24 bits per pixel are still relatively expensive, however, despite the decreasing cost of solid-state RAM. Furthermore, many color applications do not require 2^{24} different colors in a single picture (which typically has only 2^{18} to 2^{20} pixels). On the other hand, there is often need for both a small number of colors in a given picture or

TABLE 4.4 PERCENTAGE OF TIME AN IMAGE IS BEING TRACED
DURING WHICH THE PROCESSOR CAN ACCESS THE MEMORY
CONTAINING THE BITMAP*

Visible area pixels × lines	Chip size	Number of chips	Pixels per access	ns between accesses by video controller	Percent of time for processor accesses
512 × 512	256K × 1	1	1	64	0
512 × 512	128K × 2	1	2	127	0
512 × 512	64K × 4	1	4	254	20
512 × 512	32K × 8	1	8	507	60
512 × 512	16K × 16	1	16	1017	80
1024 × 1024	256K × 1	4	4	64	0
1024 × 1024	128K × 2	4	8	127	0
1024 × 1024	64K × 4	4	16	254	20
1024 × 1024	32K × 8	4	32	407	60
1024 × 1024	16K × 16	4	64	1017	80
1024 × 1024	1M × 1	1	1	16	0
1024 × 1024	64K × 16	1	16	254	21
1024 × 1024	32K × 32	1	32	509	61

*A 200-nanosecond memory cycle time and 60-Hz display rate are assumed throughout. The pixel time for a 512 × 512 display is assumed to be 64 nanoseconds; that for 1024 × 1024, 16 nanoseconds. These times are liberal, since they do not include the horizontal and vertical retrace times; the pixel times are actually about 45 and 11.5 nanoseconds, respectively.

application and the ability to change colors from picture to picture or from application to application. Also, in many image-analysis and image-enhancement applications, it is desirable to change the visual appearance of an image without changing the underlying data defining the image, in order, say, to display all pixels with values below some threshold as black, to expand an intensity range, or to create a pseudocolor display of a monochromatic image.

For these various reasons, the video controller of raster displays often includes a *video look-up table* (also called a *look-up table* or *LUT*). The look-up table has as many entries as there are pixel values. A pixel's value is used not to control the beam directly, but rather as an index into the look-up table. The table entry's value is used to control the intensity or color of the CRT. A pixel value of 67 would thus cause the contents of table entry 67 to be accessed and used to control the CRT beam. This look-up operation is done for each pixel on each display cycle, so the table must be accessible quickly, and the CPU must be able to load the look-up table on program command.

In Fig. 4.21, the look-up table is interposed between the frame buffer and the CRT display. The frame buffer has 8 bits per pixel, and the look-up table therefore has 256 entries.

The simple raster display system organizations of Figs. 4.18 and 4.19 are used in many inexpensive personal computers. Such a system is inexpensive to build, but has a number of disadvantages. First, scan conversion in software is slow. For instance, the (x, y) address of each pixel on a line must be calculated, then must be translated into a memory address consisting of a byte and bit-within-byte pair. Although each of the individual steps is simple, each is repeated many times. Software-based scan conversion slows down the

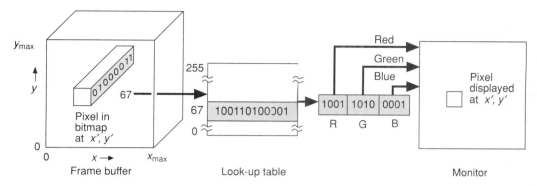

Fig. 4.21 Organization of a video look-up table. A pixel with value 67 (binary 01000011) is displayed on the screen with the red electron gun at $\frac{9}{15}$ of maximum, green at $\frac{10}{15}$, and blue at $\frac{1}{15}$. This look-up table is shown with 12 bits per entry. Up to 24 bits are common.

overall pace of user interaction with the application, potentially creating user dissatisfaction.

The second disadvantage of this architecture is that as the addressability or the refresh rate of the display increases, the number of memory accesses made by the video controller also increases, thus decreasing the number of memory cycles available to the CPU. The CPU is thus slowed down, especially with the architecture in Fig. 4.19. With the dual-porting of part of the system memory shown in Fig. 4.18, the slowdown occurs only when the CPU is accessing the frame buffer, usually for scan conversion or raster operations. These two disadvantages must be weighed against the ease with which the CPU can access the frame buffer and against the architectural simplicity of the system.

4.3.2 Raster Display System with Peripheral Display Processor

The raster display system with a peripheral display processor is a common architecture (see Fig. 4.22) that avoids the disadvantages of the simple raster display by introducing a separate graphics processor to perform graphics functions such as scan conversion and raster operations, and a separate frame buffer for image refresh. We now have two processors: the general-purpose CPU and the special-purpose display processor. We also have three memory areas: the system memory, the display-processor memory, and the frame buffer. The system memory holds data plus those programs that execute on the CPU: the application program, graphics package, and operating system. Similarly, the display-processor memory holds data plus the programs that perform scan conversion and raster operations. The frame buffer contains the displayable image created by the scan-conversion and raster operations.

In simple cases, the display processor can consist of specialized logic to perform the mapping from 2D (x, y) coordinates to a linear memory address. In this case, the scan-conversion and raster operations are still performed by the CPU, so the display-processor memory is not needed; only the frame buffer is present. Most peripheral display processors also perform scan conversion. In this section, we present a prototype system. Its

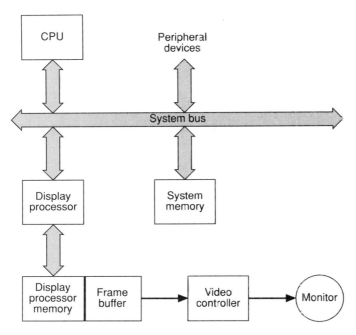

Fig. 4.22 Raster system architecture with a peripheral display processor.

features are a (sometimes simplified) composite of many typical commercially available systems, such as the plug-in graphics cards used with IBM's PC, XT, AT, PS, and compatible computers.

The frame buffer is 1024 by 1024 by 8 bits per pixel, and there is a 256-entry look-up table of 12 bits, 4 each for red, green, and blue. The origin is at lower left, but only the first 768 rows of the pixmap (y in the range of 0 to 767) are displayed. The display has six status registers, which are set by various instructions and affect the execution of other instructions. These are the CP (made up of the X and Y position registers), FILL, INDEX, WMODE, MASK, and PATTERN registers. Their operation is explained next.

The instructions for the simple raster display are as follows:

Move (x, y) The X and Y registers that define the current position (CP) are set to x and y. Because the pixmap is 1024 by 1024, x and y must be between 0 and 1023.

MoveR (dx, dy) The values dx and dy are added to the X and Y registers, thus defining a new CP. The dx and dy values must be between -1024 and $+1023$, and are represented in 2's-complement notation. The addition may cause overflow and hence a wraparound of the X and Y register values.

Line (x, y) A line is drawn from CP to (x, y), and this position becomes the new CP.

LineR (dx, dy) A line is drawn from CP to CP + (dx, dy), and this position becomes the new CP.

Point (x, y) The pixel at (x, y) is set, and this position becomes the new CP.

PointR (dx, dy) The pixel at CP + (dx, dy) is set, and this position becomes the new CP.

Rect (x, y) A rectangle is drawn between the CP and (x, y). The CP is unaffected.

RectR (dx, dy) A rectangle is drawn between the CP and CP + (dx, dy). The parameter dx can be thought of as the rectangle width, and dy as the height. The CP is unaffected.

Text $(n, address)$ The n characters at memory location $address$ are displayed, starting at the CP. Characters are defined on a 7- by 9-pixel grid, with 2 extra pixels of vertical and horizontal spacing to separate characters and lines. The CP is updated to the lower-left corner of the area in which character $n + 1$ would be displayed.

Circle $(radius)$ A circle is drawn centered at the CP. The CP is unaffected.

Arc $(radius, startAngle, endAngle)$ An arc of a circle centered at the CP is drawn. Angles are in tenths of a degree, measured positively counterclockwise from the x axis. The CP is unaffected.

CircleSector $(radius, startAngle, endAngle)$ A "pie slice" is drawn consisting of a closed area with lines going from the CP to the endpoints of the arc. The CP is unaffected.

Polygon $(n, address)$ At $address$ is stored a vertex list $(x_1, y_1, x_2, y_2, x_3, y_3, \ldots, x_n, y_n)$. A polygon is drawn starting at (x_1, y_1), through all the vertexes up to (x_n, y_n), and then back to (x_1, y_1). The CP is unaffected.

AreaFill $(flag)$ The $flag$ is used to set the FILL flag in the raster display. When the flag is set to ON (by a nonzero value of $flag$), all the areas created by the commands Rect, RectR, Circle, CircleSector, Polygon are filled in as they are created, using the pattern defined with the Pattern command.

PixelValue $(index)$ The pixel value $index$ is loaded into the INDEX register. Its value is loaded into the pixmap when any of the output primitives in the preceding list are scan-converted.

Pattern $(row1, row2, \ldots, row16)$ The 16 2-byte arguments define the pattern used to fill areas created by Rect, RectR, Circle, CircleSector, and Polygon. The pattern is a 16 by 16 array of bits, stored in the PATTERN register. When a filled area is being created and the FILL register is ON, then, if a bit in the PATTERN register is a 1, the pixel value in the INDEX register is loaded into the pixmap; otherwise, the pixmap is unaffected. A solid fill is created if all the bits of the PATTERN register are ON.

WBlockR $(dx, dy, address)$ The 8-bit pixel values stored starting at $address$ in main memory are written into the rectangular region of the pixmap from CP to CP + (dx, dy). Writing begins at the upper-left corner of the region and proceeds row by row, top to bottom.

RBlockR $(dx, dy, address)$ A rectangular region of the pixmap, from CP to CP + (dx, dy), is read into the main memory area beginning at $address$. Reading begins at the upper-left corner of the region and proceeds row by row, top to bottom.

RasterOp $(dx, dy, xdest, ydest)$ A rectangular region of the frame buffer, from CP to CP + (dx, dy), is combined with the region of the same size with lower-left corner at $(xdest, ydest)$, overwriting that region. The combination is controlled by the WMODE register.

WMode $(mode)$ The value of $mode$ is loaded into the WMODE register. This register controls how pixels in the frame buffer are combined with any pixel value being written into the frame buffer. There are four $mode$ values: **replace**, **xor**, **and**, and **or**. The modes behave as described in Chapter 2. Note that, for simplicity, the preceding command descriptions have been written as though **replace** were the only write-mode value. In **xor** mode, new values written into the frame buffer are combined with the current value using a bit-by-bit exclusive-or operation.

Mask (*mask*) The 8-bit *mask* value is loaded into the MASK register. This register controls which bits of the frame buffer are modified during writing to the frame buffer: 1 allows modification of the corresponding bit; 0 inhibits modification.

LuT (*index, red, green, blue*) Entry *index* in the look-up table is loaded with the given color specification. The low-order 4 bits of each color component are loaded into the table.

Table 4.5 summarizes these commands. Notice that the MASK and WMODE registers affect *all* commands that write into the frame buffer.

The commands and immediate data are transferred to the display processor via a first-in, first-out (FIFO) buffer (i.e., a queue) in a dedicated portion of the CPU address space. The graphics package places commands into the queue, and the display accesses the instructions and executes them. Pointers to the start and end of the buffer are also in specific memory locations, accessible to both the CPU and display. The pointer to the start of the buffer is modified by the display processor each time a byte is removed; the pointer to the end of the buffer is modified by the CPU each time a byte is added. Appropriate testing is done to ensure that an empty buffer is not read and that a full buffer is not written. Direct memory access is used to fetch the addressed data for the instructions.

A queue is more attractive for command passing than is a single instruction register or location accessed by the display. First, the variable length of the instructions favors the queue concept. Second, the CPU can get ahead of the display, and queue up a number of display commands. When the CPU has finished issuing display commands, it can proceed to do other work while the display empties out the queue.

Programming examples. Programming the display is similar to using the SRGP package of Chapter 2, so only a few examples will be given here. A "Z" means that a hexadecimal value is being specified; an "A" means that the address of the following parenthetical list is used.

A white line on a completely black background is created as follows:

LuT	5, 0, 0, 0	Look-up–table entry 5 is black
LuT	6, Z'F', Z'F', Z'F'	Look-up–table entry 6 is white
WMode	replace	
AreaFill	true	Turn on the FILL flag
Pattern	32Z'FF'	32 bytes of all 1s, for solid pattern
Mask	Z'FF'	Enable writing to all planes
PixelValue	5	Scan convert using pixel value of 5
Move	0, 0	
Rect	1023, 767	Visible part of frame buffer now black
PixelValue	6	Scan convert using pixel value of 6
Move	100, 100	
LineR	500, 400	Draw the line

TABLE 4.5 SUMMARY OF THE RASTER DISPLAY COMMANDS*

Command mnemonic	Arguments and lengths	How CP is affected	Registers that affect command
Move	x(2), y(2)	CP := (x, y)	—
MoveR	dx(2), dy(2)	CP := CP + (dx, dy)	CP
Line	x(2), y(2)	CP := (x, y)	CP, INDEX, WMODE, MASK
LineR	dx(2), dy(2)	CP := CP + (dx, dy)	CP, INDEX, WMODE, MASK
Point	x(2), y(2)	CP := (x, y)	CP, INDEX, WMODE, MASK
PointR	dx(2), dy(2)	CP := CP + (dx, dy)	CP, INDEX, WMODE, MASK
Rect	x(2), y(2)	—	CP, INDEX, WMODE, MASK, FILL, PATTERN
RectR	dx(2), dy(2)	—	CP, INDEX, WMODE, MASK, FILL, PATTERN
Text	n(1), address(4)	CP := next char pos'n	CP, INDEX, WMODE, MASK
Circle	radius(2)	—	CP, INDEX, WMODE, MASK, FILL, PATTERN
Arc	radius(2), startAngle(2), endAngle(2)	—	CP, INDEX, WMODE, MASK
CircleSector	radius(2), startAngle(2), endAngle(2)	—	CP, INDEX, WMODE, MASK, FILL, PATTERN
Polygon	n(1), address(4)	—	CP, INDEX, WMODE, MASK, FILL, PATTERN
AreaFill	flag(1)	—	—
PixelValue	index(1)	—	—
Pattern	address(4)	—	—
WBlockR	dx(2), dy(2), address(4)	—	CP, INDEX, WMODE, MASK
RBlockR	dx(2), dy(2), address(4)	—	CP, INDEX, WMODE, MASK
RasterOp	dx(2), dy(2), xdest(2), dest(2)	—	CP, INDEX, WMODE, MASK
Mask	mask(1)	—	—
WMode	mode(1)	—	—
LuT	index(1), red(1), green(1), blue(1)	—	—

*The number in parentheses after each argument is the latter's length in bytes. Also indicated are the effect of the command on the CP, and which registers affect how the command operates.

A red circle overlapping a blue triangle, all on a black background, are created with:

LuT	5, 0, 0, 0	Look-up–table entry 5 is black
LuT	7, Z'F', 0, 0	Look-up–table entry 7 is red
LuT	8, 0, 0, Z'F'	Look-up–table entry 8 is blue
WMode	replace	
AreaFill	Z'FF'	On
Pattern	32Z'FF'	32 bytes of all 1s, for solid pattern
Mask	Z'FF'	Enable writing to all planes
PixelValue	5	Get ready for black rectangle
Move	0, 0	
Rect	1023, 767	Visible part of frame buffer now black
PixelValue	8	Next do blue triangle as a three-vertex polygon
Polygon	3, A(200, 200, 800, 200, 500, 700)	
PixelValue	7	Put red circle on top of triangle
Move	511, 383	Put CP at center of display
Circle	100	Radius-100 circle at CP

4.3.3   Additional Display-Processor Functionality

Our simple display processor performs only some of the graphics-related operations that might be implemented. The temptation faced by the system designer is to offload the main CPU more and more by adding functionality to the display processor, such as by using a local memory to store lists of display instructions, by doing clipping and the window-to-viewport transformation, and perhaps by providing pick-correlation logic and automatic feedback when a segment is picked. Ultimately, the display processor becomes another general-purpose CPU doing general interactive graphics work, and the designer is again tempted to provide special-function hardware to offload the display processor.

This *wheel of reincarnation* was identified by Myer and Sutherland in 1968 [MYER68]. These authors' point was that there is a tradeoff between special-purpose and general-purpose functionality. Special-purpose hardware usually does the job faster than does a general-purpose processor. On the other hand, special-purpose hardware is more expensive and cannot be used for other purposes. This tradeoff is an enduring theme in graphics system design.

If clipping (Chapter 3) is added to the display processor, then output primitives can be specified to the processor in coordinates other than device coordinates. This specification can be done in floating-point coordinates, although some display processors operate on only integers (this is changing rapidly as inexpensive floating-point chips become available). If only integers are used, the coordinates used by the application program must be integer, or the graphics package must map floating-point coordinates into integer coordinates. For this mapping to be possible, the application program must give the graphics package a rectangle guaranteed to enclose the coordinates of all output primitives specified to the package. The rectangle must then be mapped into the maximum integer range, so that everything within the rectangle is in the integer coordinate range.

If the subroutine package is 3D, then the display processor can perform the far more complex 3D geometric transformations and clipping described in Chapters 5 and 6. Also, if the package includes 3D surface primitives, such as polygonal areas, the display processor can also perform the visible surface-determination and rendering steps discussed in Chapters 15 and 16. Chapter 18 discusses some of the fundamental approaches to organizing general- and special-purpose VLSI chips to perform these steps quickly. Many commercially available displays provide these features.

Another function that is often added to the display processor is *local segment storage*, also called *display list storage*. Display instructions, grouped into named segments and having unclipped integer coordinates, are stored in the display-processor memory, permitting the display processor to operate more autonomously from the CPU.

What exactly can a display processor do with these stored segments? It can transform and redraw them, as in zooming or scrolling. Local dragging of segments into new positions can be provided. Local picking can be implemented by having the display processor compare the cursor position to all the graphics primitives (more efficient ways of doing this are discussed in Chapter 7). Regeneration, required to fill in the holes created when a segment is erased, can also be done from segment storage. Segments can be created, deleted, edited, and made visible or invisible.

Segments can also be copied or referenced, both reducing the amount of information that must be sent from the CPU to the display processor and economizing on storage in the display processor itself. For instance, the display instructions to create a VLSI chip pad configuration to be used many times in a drawing can be sent to the display processor just once and can be stored as a segment. Each occurrence of the pad is then sent as a display instruction referencing the segment. It is possible to build up a complex hierarchical data structure using this capability, and many commercial display processors with local segment memory can copy or reference other segments. When the segments are displayed, a reference to another segment must be preceded by saving the display processor's current state, just as a subroutine call is preceded by saving the CPU's current state. References can be nested, giving rise to a *structured display file* or *hierarchical display list,* as in PHIGS [ANSI88], which is discussed further in Chapter 7. In the GKS graphics package [ENDE87; HOPG86], which uses a linear, unnested display list, an existing segment can be copied into a segment that is being created.

The segment data structures need not be in the display-processor memory (Fig. 4.22): They can be built directly by the graphics package in system memory and accessed by the display processor. This option, of course, requires that the display processor be able to read from system memory, which implies that the display processor must be directly on the system bus—RS-232 and Ethernet-speed connections are not viable.

If all the information being displayed is represented in a segment data structure, then the display processor can also implement window-manager operations such as move, open, close, resize, scroll, push, and pop. When a window is panned, the segments are retraversed with a new viewing transformation in effect. At some point, the wheel of reincarnation will again come into play, but we must also keep in mind the startlingly low cost of special-purpose VLSI chips: By the time this book becomes outdated, window manager chips are likely to cost only a few dollars each. Indeed, the pace of technological innovation is such that the graphics functionality found in display processors will continue its dramatic increase in scope and decrease in cost.

Although this raster display system architecture with its graphics display and separate frame buffer has many advantages over the simple raster display system of Section 4.3.1, it also has some disadvantages. If the display processor is accessed by the CPU as a peripheral on a direct-memory-access port or on an RS-232 interface, then there is considerable operating-system overhead each time an instruction is passed to it (this is not an issue for a display processor whose instruction register is memory-mapped into the CPU's address space, since then it is easy for the graphics package to set up the registers directly).

There is also a marked partitioning of the memories, as was shown in Fig. 4.22. Building the display list in the display-list memory is slow because of the need to issue a display-processor instruction to add or delete elements. The display list may have to be duplicated in the main processor's memory, because it cannot always be read back. An environment in which the display list is built directly in main memory by the graphics subroutine package can thus be more flexible, faster, and easier to program.

The raster-operation command is a particular difficulty. Conceptually, it should have four potential source–destination pairs: system memory to system memory, system memory to frame buffer, frame buffer to system memory, and frame buffer to frame buffer (here, the frame buffer and display processor memory of Fig. 4.22 are considered identical, since they are in the same address space). In display-processor systems, however, the different source–destination pairs are handled in different ways, and the system-memory-to-system-memory case may not exist. This lack of symmetry complicates the programmer's task and reduces flexibility. For example, if the offscreen portion of the pixmap becomes filled with menus, fonts, and so on, then it is difficult to use main memory as an overflow area. Furthermore, because the use of pixmaps is so pervasive, failure to support raster operations on pixmaps stored in main memory is not really viable.

Another problem is that the output of scan-conversion algorithms *must* go to the frame buffer. This requirement precludes *double-buffering*: scan converting a new image into system memory, then copying it into the pixmap to replace the image currently stored there. In addition, certain window-manager strategies and animation techniques require partially or completely obscured windows to be kept current in offscreen canvases, again requiring scan conversion into system memory (Chapters 10 and 19).

The display processor defined earlier in this section, like many real display processors, moves raster images between the system memory and frame buffer via I/O transfers on the system bus. Unfortunately, this movement can be too slow for real-time operations, such as animation, dragging, and popping up windows and menus: The time taken in the operating system to initiate the transfers and the transfer rate on the bus get in the way. This problem can be partially relieved by increasing the display processor's memory to hold more offscreen pixmaps, but then that memory is not available for other purposes—and there is almost never enough memory anyway!

4.3.4   Raster Display System with Integrated Display Processor

We can ameliorate many of the shortcomings of the peripheral display processor discussed in the previous section by making the frame buffer part of the system memory, thus creating the *single-address-space* (SAS) display system architecture shown in Fig. 4.23. Here the display processor, the CPU, and the video controller are all on the system bus and can thus all access system memory. The origin and, in some cases, the size of the frame buffer are held in registers, making double-buffering a simple matter of reloading the register: The

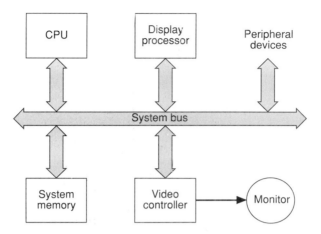

Fig. 4.23 A single-address-space (SAS) raster display system architecture with an integral display processor. The display processor may have a private memory for algorithms and working storage.

results of scan conversion can go either into the frame buffer for immediate display, or elsewhere in system memory for later display. Similarly, the source and destination for raster operations performed by the display processor can be anywhere in system memory (now the only memory of interest to us). This arrangement is also attractive because the CPU can directly manipulate pixels in the frame buffer simply by reading or writing the appropriate bits.

SAS architecture has, however, a number of shortcomings. Contention for access to the system memory is the most serious. We can solve this problem at least partially by dedicating a special portion of system memory to be the frame buffer and by providing a second access port to the frame buffer from the video controller, as shown in Fig. 4.24. Another solution is to use a CPU chip containing instruction- or data-cache memories, thus reducing the CPU's dependence on frequent and rapid access to the system memory. Of course, these and other solutions can be integrated in various ingenious ways, as discussed in more detail in Chapter 18. In the limit, the hardware PixBlt may work on only the frame buffer. What the application programmer sees as a single PixBlt instruction may be treated as several different cases, with software simulation if the source and destination are not supported by the hardware. Some processors are actually fast enough to do this, especially if they have an instruction-cache memory in which the tight inner loop of the software simulation can remain.

As suggested earlier, nontraditional memory-chip organizations for frame buffers also can help to avoid the memory-contention problem. One approach is to turn on all the pixels on a scan line in one access time, thus reducing the number of memory cycles needed to scan convert into memory, especially for filled areas. The video RAM (VRAM) organization, developed by Texas Instruments, can read out all the pixels on a scan line in one cycle, thus reducing the number of memory cycles needed to refresh the display. Again, Chapter 18 gives more detail on these issues.

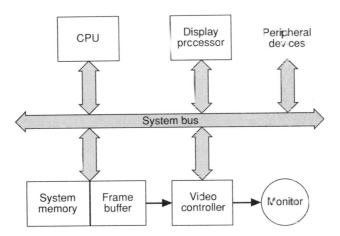

Fig. 4.24 A more common single-address-space raster display system architecture with an integral display processor (compare to Fig. 4.23). The display processor may have a private memory for algorithms and working storage. A dedicated portion of the system memory is dual-ported so that it can be accessed directly by the video controller, without the system bus being tied up.

Another design complication arises if the CPU has a virtual address space, as do the commonly used Motorola 680x0 and Intel 80x86 families, and various reduced-instruction-set-computer (RISC) processors. In this case memory addresses generated by the display processor must go through the same dynamic address translation as other memory addresses. In addition, many CPU architectures distinguish between a kernel operating system virtual address space and an application program virtual address space. It is often desirable for the frame buffer (canvas 0 in SRGP terminology) to be in the kernel space, so that the operating system's display device driver can access it directly. However, the canvases allocated by the application program must be in the application space. Therefore display instructions which access the frame buffer must distinguish between the kernel and application address spaces. If the kernel is to be accessed, then the display instruction must be invoked by a time-consuming operating system service call rather than by a simple subroutine call.

Despite these potential complications, more and more raster display systems do in fact have a single-address-space architecture, typically of the type in Fig. 4.24. The flexibility of allowing both the CPU and display processor to access any part of memory in a uniform and homogeneous way is very compelling, and does simplify programming.

4.4 THE VIDEO CONTROLLER

The most important task for the video controller is the constant refresh of the display. There are two fundamental types of refresh: *interlaced* and *noninterlaced*. The former is used in broadcast television and in raster displays designed to drive regular televisions. The refresh cycle is broken into two fields, each lasting $\frac{1}{60}$ second; thus, a full refresh lasts $\frac{1}{30}$ second. All odd-numbered scan lines are displayed in the first field, and all even-numbered ones are displayed in the second. The purpose of the interlaced scan is to place some new information in all areas of the screen at a 60-Hz rate, since a 30-Hz refresh rate tends to cause flicker. The net effect of interlacing is to produce a picture whose effective refresh rate is closer to 60 than to 30 Hz. This technique works as long as adjacent scan lines do in fact display similar information; an image consisting of horizontal lines on alternating scan lines would flicker badly. Most video controllers refresh at 60 or more Hz and use a noninterlaced scan.

The output from the video controller has one of three forms: RGB, monochrome, or NTSC. For RGB (red, green, blue), separate cables carry the red, green, and blue signals to control the three electron guns of a shadow-mask CRT, and another cable carries the synchronization to signal the start of vertical and horizontal retrace. There are standards for the voltages, wave shapes, and synchronization timings of RGB signals. For 480–scan-line monochrome signals, RS-170 is the standard; for color, RS-170A; for higher-resolution monochrome signals, RS-343. Frequently, the synchronization timings are included on the same cable as the green signal, in which case the signals are called *composite video*. Monochrome signals use the same standards but have only intensity and synchronization cables, or merely a single cable carrying composite intensity and synchronization.

NTSC (National Television System Committee) video is the signal format used in North American commercial television. Color, intensity, and synchronization information is combined into a signal with a bandwidth of about 5 MHz, broadcast as 525 scan lines, in two fields of 262.5 lines each. Just 480 lines are visible; the rest occur during the vertical retrace periods at the end of each field. A monochrome television set uses the intensity and synchronization information; a color television set also uses the color information to control the three color guns. The bandwidth limit allows many different television channels to broadcast over the frequency range allocated to television. Unfortunately, this bandwidth limits picture quality to an effective resolution of about 350 by 350. Nevertheless, NTSC is the standard for videotape-recording equipment. Matters may improve, however, with increasing interest in 1000-line high-definition television (HDTV) for videotaping and satellite broadcasting. European and Soviet television broadcast and videotape standards are two 625–scan-line, 50-Hz standards, SECAM and PAL.

Some video controllers superimpose a programmable cursor, stored in a 16 by 16 or 32 by 32 pixmap, on top of the frame buffer. This avoids the need to PixBlt the cursor shape into the frame buffer each refresh cycle, slightly reducing CPU overhead. Similarly, some video controllers superimpose multiple small, fixed-size pixmaps (called *sprites*) on top of the frame buffer. This feature is used often in video games.

4.4.1 Animation with the Lookup Table

Raster images can be animated in several ways. To show a rotating object, we can scan convert into the pixmap successive views of the object from slightly different locations, one after the other. This scan conversion must be done at least 10 (preferably 15 to 20) times per second to give a reasonably smooth effect, and hence a new image must be created in no more than 100 milliseconds. However, if scan-converting the object takes much of this 100 milliseconds—say 75 milliseconds—then the complete object can be displayed for only 25 milliseconds before it must be erased and redrawn—a distracting effect. Double-buffering is used to avoid this problem. The frame buffer is divided into two images, each with half of the bits per pixel of the overall frame buffer. If we call the two halves of the pixmap *image0* and *image1*, we can describe the animation as follows:

Load look-up table to display all pixel value as background color;
Scan convert object into image0;
Load look-up table to display only image0;
do {
    Scan convert object into image1;
    Load look-up table to display only image1;
    Rotate object data structure description;
    Scan convert object into image0;
    Load look-up table to display only image0;
    Rotate object data structure description;
} **while** (*not terminated*);

Of course, if rotating and scan converting the object takes more than 100 milliseconds, the animation is quite jerky, but the transition from one image to the next appears to be instantaneous, as loading the look-up table typically takes less than 1 millisecond.

Another form of look-up–table animation displays a short, repetitive sequence of images [SHOU79]. Suppose we want to display a bouncing ball. Figure 4.25 shows how the frame buffer is loaded; the numbers indicate the pixel values placed in each region of the frame buffer. Figure 4.26 shows how to load the look-up table at each step to display all but one of the balls at background color 0. By cycling the contents of the look-up table, we can achieve motion effects. Not only can balls be bounced, but the effect of moving lights on movie marquees can be simulated, as can the motion of fluids through pipes and the rotation of wheels. This is discussed further in Section 21.1.4.

For more complicated cyclic animation, such as rotating a complex wire-frame object, it may be impossible to keep the separate images from overlapping in the frame buffer. In that case, some of the displayed images will have "holes" in them. A few such holes are not especially distracting, especially if realism is not essential. As more holes appear, however, the animation loses its effectiveness and double-buffering becomes more attractive.

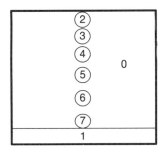

Fig. 4.25 Contents of the frame buffer for a bouncing-ball animation.

Entry number	Colors loaded in table at each step in animation										
	1	2	3	4	5	6	7	8	9	10	11
0	white	white	white	white	white	white	white	white	white	white	white
1	black	black	black	black	black	black	black	black	black	black	black
2	red										red
3		red								red	
4			red						red		
5				red				red			
6					red		red				
7						red					

Fig. 4.26 Look-up table to bounce a red ball on a black surface against a white background. Unspecified entries are all white.

4.4.2 Bitmap Transformations and Windowing

With some video controllers, the pixmap is decoupled from the view surface; that is, the direct, fixed correspondence between positions in the frame buffer and positions on the display is removed. An *image transformation* then defines the correspondence. The image transformation transforms from the frame buffer to the view surface. The transformation can, in general, include a translation, scaling, rotation, and an additional clipping operation.

Figure 4.27 shows the type of transformation found on some raster displays. Part of the frame buffer, defined by a rectangular clip region, is enlarged to fill the entire view surface. The ratio between the size of the window and the view surface must be an integer (3, in the figure). Pixels in the frame buffer outside the window are not used, and none of the pixel values are modified; the transformations are applied by the video controller at the refresh rate.

The image transformation can be changed many times per second so as to give the real-time–dynamics effect of scrolling over or zooming into an image. Also, a sequence of arbitrary images can be shown rapidly by loading each image into a different area of the frame buffer. The image transformation is changed periodically to display a full-screen view first of one area, then of the next, and so on.

The scaling needed to enlarge an image is trivially accomplished by repeating pixel values from within the window as the image is displayed. For a scale factor of 2, each pixel

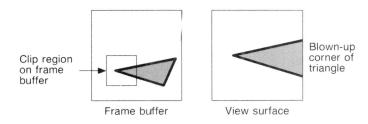

Frame buffer   View surface

Fig. 4.27 Portion of the frame buffer enlarged on the view surface.

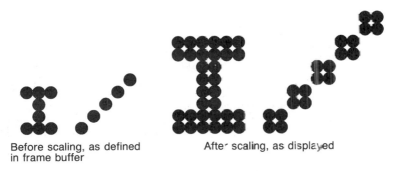

Before scaling, as defined   After scaling, as displayed
in frame buffer

Fig. 4.28 Effect of scaling up a pixmap by a factor of 2.

value is used four times, twice on each of two successive scan lines. Figure 4.28 shows the effect of scaling up a letter and adjoining line by a factor of 2. Unless the image's storage has higher resolution than does its display, scaling up does not reveal more detail: the image is enlarged but has a more jagged appearance. Thus, this animation effect sacrifices spatial resolution but maintains a full range of colors, whereas the double-buffering described in the previous section maintains spatial resolution but decreases the number of colors available in any one image.

In a more general application of image transformations, the scaled image covers only the part of the view surface defined by a viewport, as in Fig. 4.29. Now we must define to the system what is to appear on the view surface outside of the viewport. One possibility is to display some constant color or intensity; another, shown in the figure, is to display the frame buffer itself. The hardware implementation for the latter option is simple. Registers containing the viewport boundary coordinates are compared to the X, Y registers defining the raster scan's current position. If the beam is in the viewport, pixels are fetched from within the window area of the frame buffer and are replicated as required. Otherwise, pixels are fetched from the position in the frame buffer with the same (x, y) coordinates as the beam.

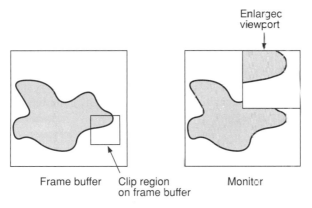

Enlarged
viewport

Frame buffer   Clip region   Monitor
                on frame buffer

Fig. 4.29 A portion of the frame buffer, specified by the clip region on the frame buffer, scaled up by a factor of 2 and overlaid on the unscaled frame buffer.

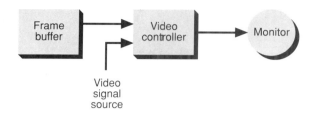

Fig. 4.30 A video controller mixing images from frame buffer and video-signal source.

There are VLSI chips that implement many of these image display functions. These various transformations are special cases of general window-manager operations that might be desired. Window-manager chips are available for use in the video controller [SHIR86]. Each window has a separate pixmap in the system memory, and a data structure in the memory defines window sizes and origins. As a scan line is displayed, the chip knows which window is visible and hence knows from which pixmap to fetch pixels. These and other more advanced hardware issues are discussed in Chapter 18.

4.4.3   Video Mixing

Another useful video-controller function is video mixing. Two images, one defined in the frame buffer and the other defined by a video signal coming from a television camera, recorder, or other source, can be merged to form a composite image. Examples of this merging are seen regularly on television news, sports, and weather shows. Figure 4.30 shows the generic system organization.

There are two types of mixing. In one, a graphics image is set into a video image. The chart or graph displayed over the shoulder of a newscaster is typical of this style. The mixing is accomplished with hardware that treats a designated pixel value in the frame buffer as a flag to indicate that the video signal should be shown instead of the signal from the frame buffer. Normally, the designated pixel value corresponds to the background color of the frame-buffer image, although interesting effects can be achieved by using some other pixel value instead.

The second type of mixing places the video image on top of the frame-buffer image, as when a weather reporter stands in front of a full-screen weather map. The reporter is actually standing in front of a backdrop, whose color (typically blue) is used to control the mixing: Whenever the incoming video is blue, the frame buffer is shown; otherwise, the video image is shown. This technique works well as long as the reporter is not wearing a blue tie or shirt!

4.5   RANDOM-SCAN DISPLAY PROCESSOR

Figure 4.31 shows a typical random (vector) display system. It is generically similar to the display-processor–based raster system architecture discussed in Section 4.3.2. There is of course no pixmap for refreshing the display, and the display processor has no local memory

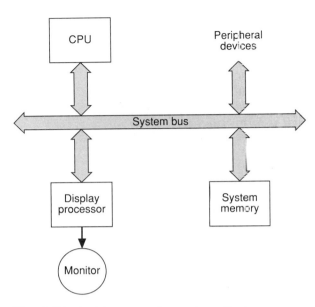

Fig. 4.31 Architecture of a random display system.

for scan-conversion algorithms, since that functionality is typically implemented using programmed logic arrays or microcode.

The random-scan graphics-display processor is often called a *display processing unit* (DPU), or a *graphics controller*. The DPU has an instruction set and instruction address register, and goes through the classic instruction fetch, decode, execute cycle found in any computer. Because there is no pixmap, the display processor must execute its program 30 to 60 times per second in order to provide a flicker-free display. The program executed by the DPU is in main memory, which is shared by the general CPU and the DPU.

The application program and graphics subroutine package also reside in main memory and execute on the general CPU. The graphics package creates a display program of DPU instructions and tells the DPU where to start the program. The DPU then asynchronously executes the display program until it is told to stop by the graphics package. A JUMP instruction at the end of the display program transfers control back to its start, so that the display continues to be refreshed without CPU intervention.

Figure 4.32 shows a set of instructions and mnemonics for a simple random-scan DPU. The processor has X and Y registers and an instruction counter. The instructions are defined for a 16-bit word length. The R/A (relative/absolute) modifier on the LD instructions indicates whether the following coordinate is to be treated as an 11-bit relative coordinate or a 10-bit absolute coordinate. In the former case, the 11 bits are added to either the X or the Y register; in the latter, the 10 bits replace the register contents. (Eleven bits are needed for relative moves for a 2's-complement representation of values in the range −1024 to +1023.)

The same R/A interpretation is used for the JUMP instruction, except the instruction counter is modified, thereby effecting a change in the flow of control. The SM, SP, and SL instructions afford compact representation of contour lines, scatter plots, and the like.

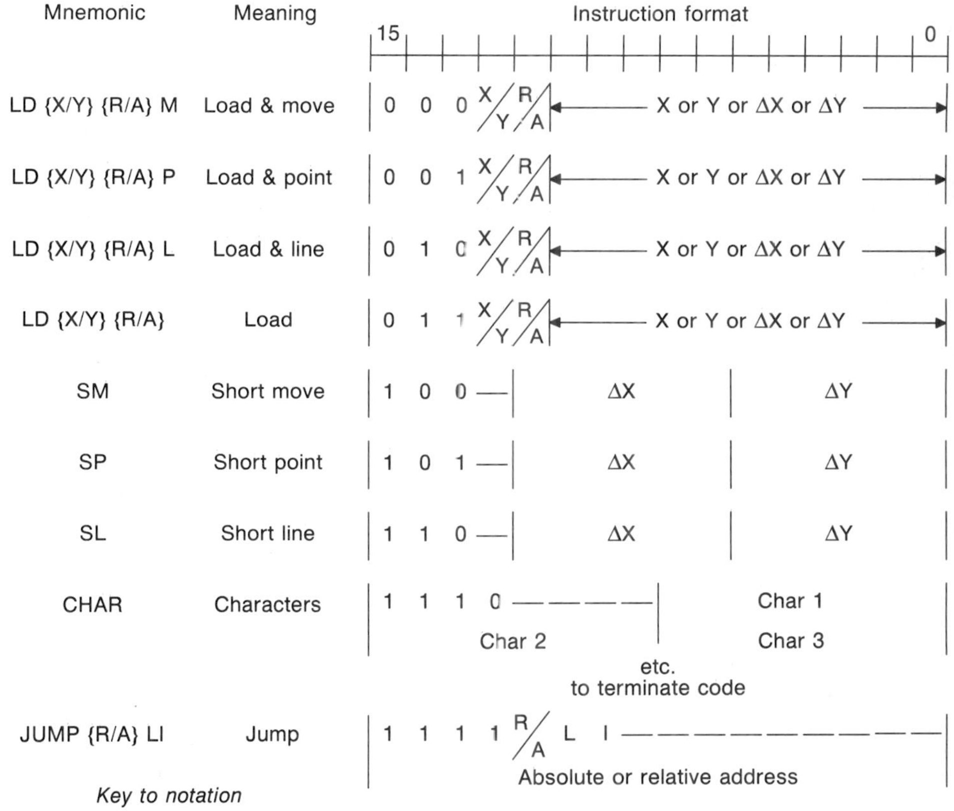

Mnemonic	Meaning	Instruction format
		15 ─────────────────────── 0
LD {X/Y} {R/A} M	Load & move	`0 0 0` X/Y R/A ◄─── X or Y or ΔX or ΔY ───►
LD {X/Y} {R/A} P	Load & point	`0 0 1` X/Y R/A ◄─── X or Y or ΔX or ΔY ───►
LD {X/Y} {R/A} L	Load & line	`0 1 0` X/Y R/A ◄─── X or Y or ΔX or ΔY ───►
LD {X/Y} {R/A}	Load	`0 1 1` X/Y R/A ◄─── X or Y or ΔX or ΔY ───►
SM	Short move	`1 0 0 —` ΔX | ΔY
SP	Short point	`1 0 1 —` ΔX | ΔY
SL	Short line	`1 1 0 —` ΔX | ΔY
CHAR	Characters	`1 1 1 0 — — — —` Char 1 | Char 2 | Char 3 (etc. to terminate code)
JUMP {R/A} LI	Jump	`1 1 1 1` R/A L I — — — — — — — — Absolute or relative address

Key to notation

X/Y: 0 ⇒ Load X, 1 ⇒ Load Y
R/A: 0 ⇒ 11 bits of ΔX or ΔY, 1 ⇒ 10 bits of X or Y
{ }: Choose one of, for use in mnemonic code
L: Frame lock bit, 1 ⇒ delay jump until next clock tick
I: Interrupt bit, 1 ⇒ interrupt CPU

Fig. 4.32 Instruction set for the random-scan display system.

Figure 4.33 is a simple DPU program, written in assembler style, that uses many of these instructions. Notice how the square and diamond are drawn: The first move instruction is absolute, but the rest are relative, so as to facilitate dragging the objects around the screen. If relative instructions were not used, then dragging would require modifying the coordinates of all the instructions used to display the object. The final instruction jumps back to the start of the DPU program. Because the frame lock bit is set, as indicated by the L modifier, execution of the jump is delayed until the next tick of a 30-Hz clock in order to allow the DPU to refresh at 30 Hz but to prevent more frequent refreshing of small programs, which could burn the phosphor.

Notice that, with this instruction set, only one load command (mnemonic LD) is needed to draw or move either horizontally or vertically, because the other coordinate is held constant; oblique movements, however, require two load commands. The two loads can be in either x-then-y or y-then-x order, with the second of the two always specifying a

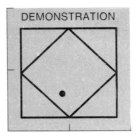

SQUARE:	LDXA	100	Get ready for square
	LDYAM	100	Move to (100, 100)
	LDXRL	800	Line to (900, 100)
	LDYRL	700	Line to (900, 800)
	LDXRL	−800	Line to (100, 800)
	LDYRL	−700	Line to (100, 100), the starting point
POINT:	LDXA	300	for square
	LDYAP	450	Point at (300, 450)
DIAMOND:	LDXA	100	
	LDYAM	450	Move to (100, 450)
	LDXR	400	
	LDYRL	−350	Line to (500, 100)
	LDXR	400	
	LDYRL	350	Line to (900, 450)
	LDYR	350	
	LDXRL	−400	Line to (500, 800)
	LDXR	−400	
	LDYRL	−350	Line to (100, 450), the starting point
TEXT:	LDXA	200	for diamond
	LDYAM	900	Move to (200, 900) for text
	CHAR	'DEMONSTRATION *t*'	*t* is terminate code
	JUMPRL	SQUARE	Regenerate picture, frame lock

Fig. 4.33 Program for the random-scan display processor.

move, draw-point, or draw-line operation. For the character command (mnemonic CHAR), a character string follows, ended by a nondisplayable termination code.

There are two main differences between these DPU instructions and the instruction set for a general-purpose computer. With the exception of the JUMP command, all the instructions here are rather special-purpose. A register can be loaded and added to, but the result cannot be stored; the register controls only the position of the CRT beam. The second difference, again excluding JUMP, is that all data are immediate; that is, they are part of the instruction. LDXA 100 means "load the data value 100 into the X register," not "load the contents of address 100 into the X register," as in a computer instruction. This restriction is removed in some of the more advanced DPUs described in Chapter 18.

There are only a few differences between the instruction sets for typical random and raster display processors. The random processor lacks area-filling, bit-manipulation, and look-up table commands. But because of the instruction counter, the random processor does have transfer of control commands. Random displays can work at higher resolutions than can raster displays and can draw smooth lines lacking the jagged edges found on raster displays. The fastest random displays can draw about 100,000 short vectors in a refresh cycle, allowing real-time animation of extremely complex shapes.

4.6 INPUT DEVICES FOR OPERATOR INTERACTION

In this section, we describe the workings of the most common input devices. We present a brief and high-level discussion of how the types of devices available work. In Chapter 8, we discuss the advantages and disadvantages of the various devices, and also describe some more advanced devices.

Our presentation is organized around the concept of *logical devices*, introduced in Chapter 2 as part of SRGP and discussed further in Chapters 7 and 8. There are five basic logical devices: the *locator*, to indicate a position or orientation; the *pick*, to select a displayed entity; the *valuator*, to input a single real number; the *keyboard*, to input a character string; and the *choice*, to select from a set of possible actions or choices. The logical-device concept defines equivalence classes of devices on the basis of the type of information the devices provide to the application program.

4.6.1 Locator Devices

Tablet. A *tablet* (or *data tablet*) is a flat surface, ranging in size from about 6 by 6 inches up to 48 by 72 inches or more, which can detect the position of a movable stylus or puck held in the user's hand. Figure 4.34 shows a small tablet with both a stylus and puck (hereafter, we generally refer only to a stylus, although the discussion is relevant to either). Most tablets use an electrical sensing mechanism to determine the position of the stylus. In one such arrangement, a grid of wires on $\frac{1}{4}$- to $\frac{1}{2}$-inch centers is embedded in the tablet surface. Electromagnetic signals generated by electrical pulses applied in sequence to the wires in the grid induce an electrical signal in a wire coil in the stylus. The strength of the

Fig. 4.34 A data tablet with both a stylus and a puck. The stylus has a pressure-sensitive switch in the tip, which closes when the stylus is pressed. The puck has several pushbuttons for command entry, and a cross-hair cursor for accuracy in digitizing drawings that are placed on the tablet. (Courtesy of Summagraphics Corporation.)

signal induced by each pulse is used to determine the position of the stylus. The signal strength is also used to determine roughly how far the stylus or cursor is from the tablet ("far," "near," (i.e., within about $\frac{1}{2}$ inch of the tablet), or "touching"). When the answer is "near" or "touching," a cursor is usually shown on the display to provide visual feedback to the user. A signal is sent to the computer when the stylus tip is pressed against the tablet, or when any button on the puck (pucks have up to 16 buttons) is pressed.

The tablet's (x, y) position, button status, and nearness state (if the nearness state is "far," then no (x, y) position is available) is normally obtained 30 to 60 times per second. Some tablets can generate an interrupt when any of the following events occur:

- t units of time have passed (thus, the tablet serves as a clock to trigger the updating of the cursor position).

- The puck or stylus has moved more than some distance d. This distance-interval sampling is useful in digitizing drawings in order to avoid recording an excessive number of points.

- The nearness state has changed (some tablets do not report a change from "near" to "far").

- The tip switch or a puck button has been pressed or released. It is important to have available both *button-down* and *button-up* events from the tablet and other such devices. For instance, a button-down event might cause a displayed object to start growing larger, and the button-up event then might stop the size change.

- The cursor enters a specified rectangular area of the tablet surface.

Relevant parameters of tablets and other locator devices are their resolution (number of distinguishable points per inch), linearity, repeatability, and size or range. These parameters are particularly crucial for digitizing maps and drawings; they are of less concern when the device is used only to position a screen cursor, because the user has the feedback of the screen cursor position to guide his hand movements, and because the resolution of a typical display is much less than that of even inexpensive tablets.

Other tablet technologies use sound (sonic) coupling and resistive coupling. The *sonic tablet* uses sound waves to couple the stylus to microphones positioned on the periphery of the digitizing area. Sound bursts are created by an electrical spark at the tip of the stylus. The delay between when the spark occurs and when its sound arrives at each microphone is proportional to the distance from the stylus to each microphone (see Fig. 4.35). The sonic tablet is advantageous for digitizing drawings bound in thick books, where a normal tablet stylus does not get close enough to the tablet to record an accurate position. Also, it does not require a dedicated working area, as the other tablets do. Sonic coupling is also useful in 3D positioning devices, as discussed in Chapter 8.

One type of *resistive tablet* uses a battery-powered stylus that emits high-frequency radio signals. The tablet, which is just a piece of glass, is coated with a thin layer of conducting material in which an electrical potential is induced by the radio signals. The strength of the signals at the edges of the tablet is inversely proportional to the distance to the stylus and can thus be used to calculate the stylus position. Another similar tablet uses a resistive polymer mesh stretched across the faceplate of a CRT [SUNF86]. The stylus

Microphone

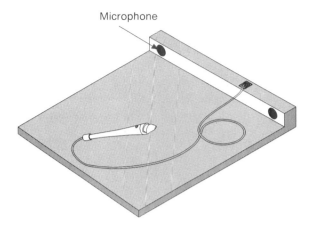

Fig. 4.35 A 2D sound tablet. Sound waves emitted from the stylus are received by the two microphones at the rear of the tablet.

applies an electrical potential to the mesh, and the stylus's position is determined from the voltage drop across the mesh.

Most tablet styluses have to be connected to the tablet controller by a wire. The stylus of the resistive tablet can be battery-powered, as shown in Fig. 4.36. Such a stylus is attractive because there is no cord to get in the way. On the other hand, walking away with it in your pocket is easy to do!

Several types of tablets are transparent, and thus can be back-lit for digitizing X-ray films and photographic negatives, and can also be mounted directly over a CRT. The resistive tablet is especially well suited for this, as it can be curved to the shape of the CRT.

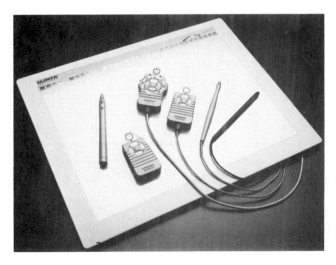

Fig. 4.36 The Penmouse tablet with its cordless three-button, battery-powered stylus and puck. (Courtesy of Kurta Corporation.)

Mouse. A mouse is a small hand-held device whose relative motion across a surface can be measured. Mice differ in the number of buttons and in how relative motion is detected. Other important differences between various types of mice are discussed in Section 8.1.7. The motion of the roller in the base of a *mechanical mouse* is converted to digital values that are used to determine the direction and magnitude of movement. The *optical mouse* is used on a special pad having a grid of alternating light and dark lines. A light-emitting diode (LED) on the bottom of the mouse directs a beam of light down onto the pad, from which it is reflected and sensed by detectors on the bottom of the mouse. As the mouse is moved, the reflected light beam is broken each time a dark line is crossed. The number of pulses so generated, which is equal to the number of lines crossed, are used to report mouse movements to the computer.

Because mice are relative devices, they can be picked up, moved, and then put down again without any change in reported position. (A series of such movements is often called "stroking" the mouse.) The relative nature of the mouse means that the computer must maintain a "current mouse position," which is incremented or decremented by mouse movements.

Trackball. The *trackball*, one of which is shown in Fig. 4.37, is often described as an upside-down mechanical mouse. The motion of the trackball, which rotates freely within its housing, is sensed by potentiometers or shaft encoders. The user typically rotates the trackball by drawing the palm of her hand across the ball. Various switches are usually mounted within finger reach of the trackball itself and are used in ways analogous to the use of mouse and tablet-puck buttons.

Joystick. The *joystick* (Fig. 4.38) can be moved left or right, forward or backward; again, potentiometers sense the movements. Springs are often used to return the joystick to its home center position. Some joysticks, including the one pictured, have a third degree of freedom: the stick can be twisted clockwise and counterclockwise. The *isometric joystick*,

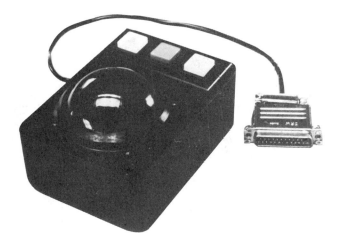

Fig. 4.37 Trackball with several nearby switches. (Courtesy of Measurement Systems, Inc.)

Fig. 4.38 A joystick with a third degree of freedom. The joystick can be twisted clockwise and counterclockwise. (Courtesy of Measurement Systems, Inc.)

shown in Fig. 4.39, is rigid: strain gauges on the shaft measure slight deflections caused by force applied to the shaft.

It is difficult to use a joystick to control the absolute position of a screen cursor directly, because a slight movement of the (usually) short shaft is amplified five or ten times in the movement of the cursor. This makes the screen cursor's movements quite jerky and does not allow quick and accurate fine positioning. Thus, the joystick is often used to control the velocity of the cursor movement rather than the absolute cursor position. This means that the current position of the screen cursor is changed at rates determined by the joystick.

The *joyswitch*, a variant of the joystick, is found in some home and arcade computer games. The stick can be moved in any of eight directions: up, down, left, right, and the four

Fig. 4.39 An isometric joystick. (Courtesy of Measurement Systems, Inc.)

diagonal directions. Small switches sense in which of the eight directions the stick is being pushed.

Touch panel. Mice, trackballs, and joysticks all take up work-surface area. The *touch panel* allows the user to point at the screen directly with a finger to move the cursor around on the screen. Several different technologies are used for touch panels. Low-resolution panels (from 10 to 50 resolvable positions in each direction) use a series of infrared LEDs and light sensors (photodiodes or phototransistors) to form a grid of invisible light beams over the display area. Touching the screen breaks one or two vertical and horizontal light beams, thereby indicating the finger's position. If two parallel beams are broken, the finger is presumed to be centered between them; if one is broken, the finger is presumed to be on the beam.

A capacitively coupled touch panel can provide about 100 resolvable positions in each direction. When the user touches the conductively coated glass panel, electronic circuits detect the touch position from the impedance change across the conductive coating [INTE85].

One high-resolution panel (about 500 resolvable positions in each direction) uses sonar-style ranging. Bursts of high-frequency sound waves traveling alternately horizontally and vertically are introduced at the edge of a glass plate. The touch of a finger on the glass causes part of the wave to be reflected back to its source. The distance to the finger can be calculated from the interval between emission of the wave burst and its arrival back at the source. Another high-resolution panel uses two slightly separated layers of transparent material, one coated with a thin layer of conducting material and the other with resistive material. Fingertip pressure forces the layers to touch, and the voltage drop across the resistive substrate is measured and is used to calculate the coordinates of the touched position. Low-resolution variations of this method use bars of conducting material or thin wires embedded in the transparent material. Touch-panel technologies have been used to make small positioning pads for keyboards.

The most significant touch-panel parameters are resolution, the amount of pressure required for activation (not an issue for the light-beam panel), and transparency (again, not an issue for the light-beam panel). An important issue with some of the technologies is parallax: If the panel is $\frac{1}{2}$ inch away from the display, then users touch the position on the panel that is aligned with their eyes and the desired point on the display, not at the position on the panel directly perpendicular to the desired point on the display.

Users are accustomed to some type of tactile feedback, but touch panels of course offer none. It is thus especially important that other forms of immediate feedback be provided, such as an audible tone or highlighting of the designated target or position.

Light pen. *Light pens* were developed early in the history of interactive computer graphics. The pen is misnamed; it *detects* light pulses, rather than emitting light as its name implies. The event caused when the light pen sees a light pulse on a raster display can be used to save the video controller's X and Y registers and interrupt the computer. By reading the saved values, the graphics package can determine the coordinates of the pixel seen by the light pen. The light pen cannot report the coordinates of a point that is completely black, so special techniques are needed to use the light pen to indicate an arbitrary position: one is to display, for a single frame time, a dark blue field in place of the regular image.

The light pen, when used with a vector display, acts as a pick rather than a positioning device. When the light pen senses light, the DPU is stopped and the CPU is interrupted. The CPU then reads the DPU's instruction address register, the contents of which can be used to determine which output primitive was being drawn when the interrupt occurred. As with the raster display, a special technique, called *light-pen tracking*, is needed to indicate positions within a single vector with the light pen [FOLE82].

The light pen is an aging technology with limited use. Unless properly adjusted, light pens sometimes detect false targets, such as fluorescent lights or other nearby graphics primitives (e.g., adjacent characters), and fail to detect intended targets. When used over several hours, a light pen can be tiring for inexperienced users, because it must be picked up, pointed, and set down for each use.

4.6.2 Keyboard Devices

The *alphanumeric keyboard* is the prototypical text input device. Several different technologies are used to detect a key depression, including mechanical contact closure, change in capacitance, and magnetic coupling. The important functional characteristic of a keyboard device is that it creates a code (ASCII, EBCDIC, etc.) uniquely corresponding to a pressed key. It is sometimes desirable to allow *chording* (pressing several keys at once) on an alphanumeric keyboard, to give experienced users rapid access to many different commands. This is in general not possible with the standard *coded keyboard*, which returns an ASCII code per keystroke and returns nothing if two keys are pressed simultaneously (unless the additional keys were shift, control, or other special keys). In contrast, an *unencoded keyboard* returns the identity of all keys that are pressed simultaneously, thereby allowing chording.

4.6.3 Valuator Devices

Most valuator devices that provide scalar values are based on potentiometers, like the volume and tone controls of a stereo set. Valuators are usually rotary potentiometers (dials), typically mounted in a group of eight or ten, as in Fig. 4.40. Simple rotary potentiometers

Fig. 4.40 A bank of eight rotary potentiometers. The readouts on the light-emitting diodes (LED) above each dial can be used to label each dial, or to give the current setting. (Courtesy of Evans and Sutherland Computer Corporation.)

Fig. 4.41 Function keys with light-emitting diode (LED) labels, integrated with a keyboard unit. (Courtesy of Evans and Sutherland Computer Corporation.)

can be rotated through about 330°; this may not be enough to provide both adequate range and resolution. Continuous-turn potentiometers can be rotated freely in either direction, and hence are unbounded in range. Linear potentiometers, which are of necessity bounded devices, are used infrequently in graphics systems.

4.6.4 Choice Devices

Function keys are the most common choice device. They are sometimes built as a separate unit, but more often are integrated with a keyboard. Other choice devices are the *buttons* found on many tablet pucks and on the mouse. Choice devices are generally used to enter commands or menu options a graphics program. Dedicated-purpose systems can use function keys with permanent key-cap labels. So that labels can be changeable or "soft," function keys can include a small LCD or LED display next to each button or in the key caps themselves, as shown in Fig. 4.41. Yet another alternative is to place buttons on the bezel of the display, so that button labels can be shown on the display itself, right next to the physical button.

4.7   IMAGE SCANNERS

Although data tablets can be used to digitize existing line drawings manually, this is a slow and tedious process, unsuitable for more than a few simple drawings—and it does not work at all for half-tone images. Image scanners provide an efficient solution. A television camera used in conjunction with a digital frame grabber is an inexpensive way to obtain moderate-resolution (1000 by 1000, with multiple intensity levels) raster images of black-and-white or color photographs. Slow-scan charge-coupled–device (CCD) television cameras can create a 2000 by 2000 image in about 30 seconds. An even lower-cost approach uses a scan head, consisting of a grid of light-sensing cells, mounted on the print head of a printer; it scans images at a resolution of about 80 units per inch. These resolutions are not acceptable for high-quality publication work, however. In such cases, a *photo scanner* is used. The photograph is mounted on a rotating drum. A finely collimated light beam is directed at the photo, and the amount of light reflected is measured by a photocell. For a negative, transmitted light is measured by a photocell inside the drum,

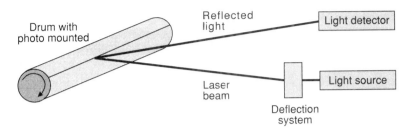

Fig. 4.42 A photo scanner. The light source is deflected along the drum axis, and the amount of reflected light is measured.

which is transparent. As the drum rotates, the light source slowly moves from one end to the other, thus doing a raster scan of the entire photograph (Fig. 4.42). For colored photographs, multiple passes are made, using filters in front of the photocell to separate out various colors. The highest-resolution scanners use laser light sources, and have resolutions greater then 2000 units per inch.

Another class of scanner uses a long thin strip of CCDs, called a *CCD array*. A drawing is digitized by passing it under the CCD array, incrementing the drawing's movement by whatever resolution is required. Thus, a single pass, taking 1 or 2 minutes, is sufficient to digitize a large drawing. Resolution of the CCD array is 200 to 1000 units per inch, which is less than that of the photo scanner. Such a scanner is shown in Fig. 4.43.

Line drawings can easily be scanned using any of the approaches we have described. The difficult part is distilling some meaning from the collection of pixels that results. *Vectorizing* is the process of extracting lines, characters, and other geometric primitives

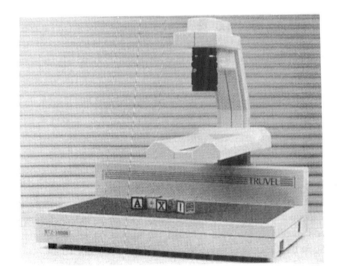

Fig. 4.43 A liquid-crystal display (LCD) scanner. The lens and linear LCD array in the scanning head (top) move left to right to scan a photo or object. (Photographs provided by Truvel Corporation.)

from a raster image. This task requires appropriate algorithms, not scanning hardware, and is essentially an image-processing problem involving several steps. First, thresholding and edge enhancement are used to clean up the raster image—to eliminate smudges and smears and to fill in gaps. Feature-extraction algorithms are then used to combine adjacent "on" pixels into geometric primitives such as straight lines. At a second level of complexity, pattern-recognition algorithms are used to combine the simple primitives into arcs, letters, symbols, and so on. User interaction may be necessary to resolve ambiguities caused by breaks in lines, dark smudges, and multiple lines intersecting near one another.

A more difficult problem is organizing a collection of geometric primitives into meaningful data structures. A disorganized collection of lines is not particularly useful as input to a CAD or topographic (mapping) application program. The higher-level geometric constructs represented in the drawings need to be recognized. Thus, the lines defining the outline of a county should be organized into a polygon primitive, and the small "+" representing the center of an arc should be grouped with the arc itself. There are partial solutions to these problems. Commercial systems depend on user intervention when the going gets tough, although algorithms are improving continually.

EXERCISES

4.1 For an electrostatic plotter with 18-inch-wide paper, a resolution of 200 units to the inch in each direction, and a paper speed of 3 inches per second, how many bits per second must be provided to allow the paper to move at full speed?

4.2 If long-persistence phosphors decrease the fusion frequency, why not use them routinely?

4.3 Write a program to display test patterns on a raster display. Three different patterns should be provided: (1) horizontal lines 1 pixel wide, separated by 0, 1, 2, or 3 pixels; (2) vertical lines 1 pixel wide, separated by 0, 1, 2, or 3 pixels; and (3) a grid of 1-pixel dots on a grid spaced at 5-pixel intervals. Each pattern should be displayable in white, red, green, or blue, as well as alternating color bars. How does what you observe when the patterns are displayed relate to the discussion of raster resolution?

4.4 Prepare a report on technologies for large-screen displays.

4.5 How long would it take to load a 512 by 512 by 1 bitmap, assuming that the pixels are packed 8 to a byte and that bytes can be transferred and unpacked at the rate of 100,000 bytes per second? How long would it take to load a 1024 by 1280 by 1 bitmap?

4.6 Design the logic of a hardware unit to convert from 2D raster addresses to byte plus bit-within-byte addresses. The inputs to the unit are as follows: (1) (x, y), a raster address; (2) *base*, the address of the memory byte that has raster address $(0, 0)$ in bit 0; and (3) x_{max}, the maximum raster x address (0 is the minimum). The outputs from the unit are as follows: (1) *byte*, the address of the byte that contains (x, y) in one of its bits; and (2) *bit*, the bit within *byte* which contains (x, y). What simplifications are possible if $x_{max} + 1$ is a power of 2?

4.7 Program a raster copy operation that goes from a bitmap into a virtual-memory area that is scattered across several pages. The hardware raster copy on your display works only in physical address space, so you must set up a scatter-write situation, with multiple moves invoked, one for each logical page contained in the destination.

4.8 Design an efficient instruction-set encoding for the simple raster display instruction set of Section 4.3.2. By "efficient" is meant "minimizing the number of bits used per instruction."

4.9 Using the instruction set for the simple raster display of Section 4.3.2, write program segments to do the following.

   a. Double-buffer a moving object. You need not actually write the code that moves and draws the object; just indicate its placement in the overall code sequence.

   b. Draw a pie chart, given as input a list of data values. Use different colors for each slice of the pie, choosing colors you believe will look good together.

   c. Animate the left-to-right movement of circles arranged in a horizontal row. Each circle is five units in radius and the circles are placed on 15-unit centers. Use the animation technique discussed in Section 4.4.1. At each step in the animation, every fourth circle should be visible.

   d. Write a program that uses RasterOp to drag a 25 by 25 icon around on the screen, using an offscreen area of the bitmap to store both the icon and the part of the bitmap currently obscured by the icon.

4.10 In a raster scan of n lines with m pixels per line displayed at r cycles per second, there is a certain amount of time during which no image is being traced: the horizontal retrace time t_h, which occurs once per scan line, and the vertical retrace time t_v, which occurs once per frame.

   a. Derive equations for the percentage of time that no image is being traced, remembering that different equations are needed for the interlaced and noninterlaced cases, because the two fields per frame of an interlaced scan each require a vertical retrace time.

   b. Evaluate the equation for the following values, taken from [WHIT84]:

Visible area pixels × lines	Refresh rate, Hz	Interlace	Vertical retrace time, microseconds	Horizontal retrace time, microseconds
640 × 485	30	yes	1271	11
1280 × 1024	30	yes	1250	7
640 × 485	60	no	1250	7
1280 × 1024	60	no	600	4

   c. What is the meaning of the percentages you have calculated?

4.11 Develop a design strategy for a video controller that can display a 960 by x image on a 480 by $x/2$ display, where x is the horizontal resolution. (This is the type of device needed to drive a video recorder from a high-resolution display system.)

4.12 A raster display has 4 bits per pixel and a look-up table with 12 bits per entry (4 bits each for red, green, and blue). Think of the four planes of the pixmap as being partitioned to hold two images: image 1 in the two high-order planes, image 0 in the two low-order planes. The color assignments for each of the 2-bit pixel values in each image are 00 = red, 01 = green, 10 = blue, and 11 = white.

   a. Show how to load the look-up table so that just image 1 is displayed.

   b. Show how to load the look-up table so that just image 0 is displayed.
Note that these are the look-up tables needed for the two phases of double-buffering, as discussed in Section 4.4.1.

4.13 Given a 16-entry by 12-bit-per-entry look-up table with two 2-bit images, show how it should be loaded to produce the lap-dissolve given by the expression $image1 * t + image0 * (1 - t)$ for values of $t = 0.0, 0.25$, and 0.5. The look-up table color assignments are the same as in Exercise 4.12. (See Chapter 17.)

4.14 In Section 4.4.1, two animation methods are discussed. What are the advantages and disadvantages of each?

4.15 Redesign the simple DPU instruction set of Fig. 4.32 for a 16-bit word, assuming that all opcodes are equal in length.

4.16 Consider means for picking (as with a light pen) a line on a raster display when all that can be detected is a single pixel.

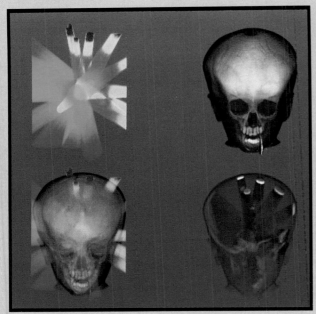

Plate I.1 Radiation therapy planning simulation. Volume rendering is used to display the interaction of radiation beams and a child's head. (Image by R. Drebin, Silicon Graphics. Copyright © 1988 Pixar. CT scans provided by F. Zonneveld, N.V. Philips.)

Plate I.2 Local map automatically generated by the IGD hypermedia system, showing the currently visited node in the center, possible source nodes in the left column and possible destination nodes in the right column. (Courtesy of S. Feiner, S. Nagy, and A. van Dam, Brown University Computer Graphics Group.)

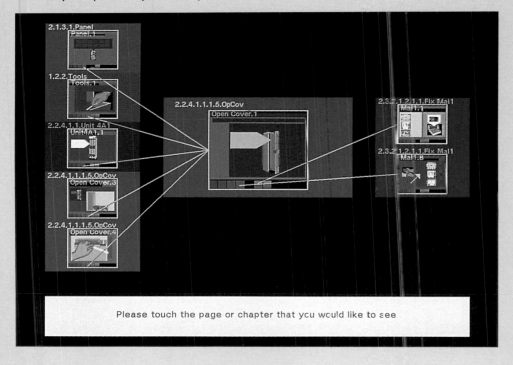

Plate I.3 One stage in the process of smoothly turning a sphere inside out. The sphere is sliced to show interior structure. (Copyright © 1989 John Hughes, Brown University Computer Graphics Group.)

Plate I.4 Animated sequences of stereographic projections of the sphere and hypersphere as they are rotated in 3- and 4-space, respectively. For further information, see [KOCA87]. (Image by D. Laidlaw and H. Kocak.)

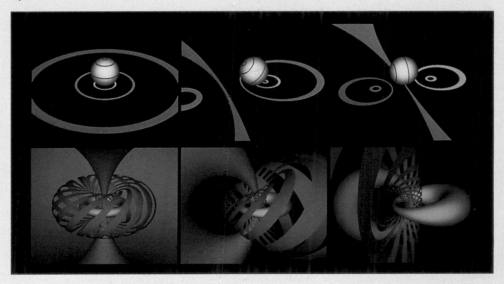

Plate I.5 (a) The cockpit of an F5 flight simulator; the pilot's view is projected onto a dome surrounding the cockpit. (b) The view from the cockpit of a flight simulator. The fighter jet is modeled geometrically, whereas the terrain is photo-textured. (Courtesy of R. Economy, General Electric Company.)

(a)

(b)

Plate I.6 A video game in which the player must pack 3D shapes together in a small space. The deep perspective and wireframe drawing of the piece aid in this task. (Courtesy of Larry Lee, California Dreams.)

▼

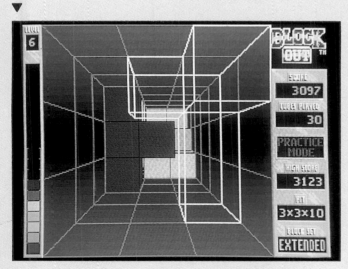

Plate I.7 *Hard Drivin'* arcade video game. (Courtesy of Atari Games Corporation, copyright © 1988 Atari Games Corporation.)

Plate I.8 Home improvement design center from Innovis. (Courtesy of Innovis Interactive Technologies, Tacoma, WA.)

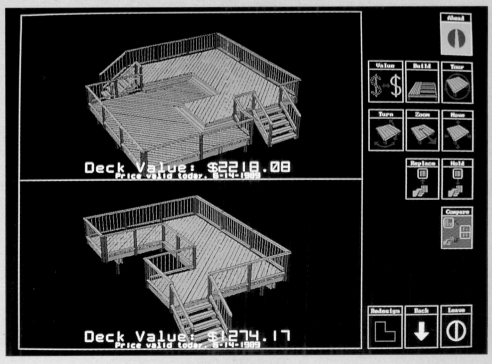

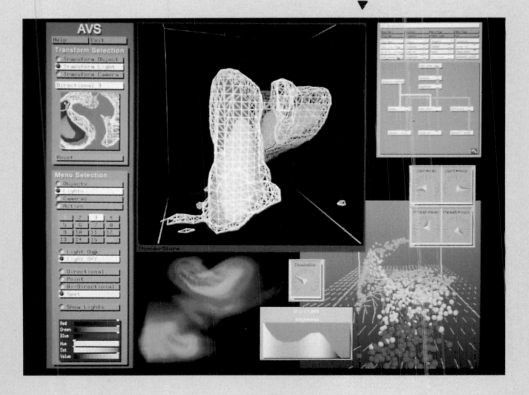

Plate I.11 (a) Chevrolet Astro Van, product launch material. (Copyright © 1985 Digital Productions.) (b) Castle interior. (Copyright © 1985 Digital Productions. Both images courtesy of G. Demos.)

(a)

(b)

Plate I.12 *The Abyss* — Pseudopod sequence. (Copyright © 1989 Twentieth Century Fox. All rights reserved. Courtesy of Industrial Light & Magic, Computer Graphics Division.)

Plate I.13 Command ship from *The Last Starfighter*. The texture-mapped ship has 450,000 polygons. (Copyright © 1984 Digital Productions. Courtesy of G. Demos.)

Plate I.14 A spaceball six-degree of freedom positioning device. (Courtesy of Spatial Systems, Inc.)

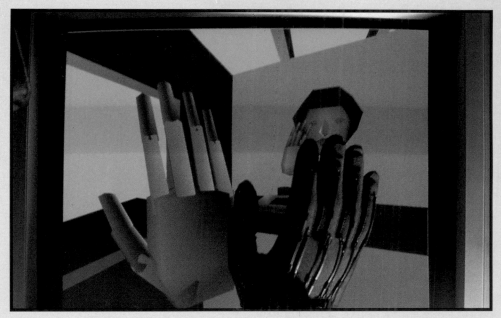

Plate I.15 A DataGlove (right) and computer image of the glove. The DataGlove measures finger movements and hand orientation and position. The computer image of the hand tracks the changes. (Courtesy of Jaron Lanier, VPL.)

Plate I.16 A user wearing a head-mounted stereo display, DataGloves, and microphone for issuing commands. These devices are used to create a virtual reality for the user, by changing the stereo display presentation as the head is moved, with the DataGloves used to manipulate computer-generated objects. (Courtesy of Michael McGreevy and Scott Fisher, NASA Ames Research Center, Moffett Field, CA.)

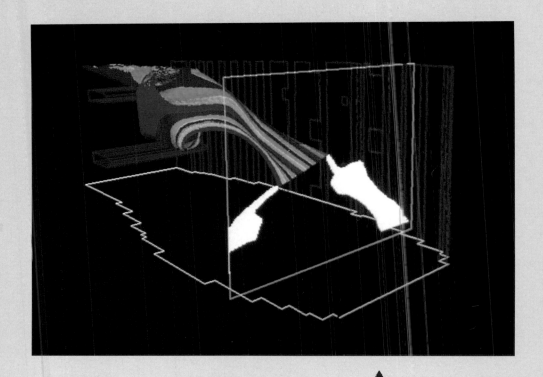

▲

Plate I.17 Krueger's Videotouch system, in which a user's hand movements are used to manipulate an object. The hands' outlines are displayed along with the objects to provide natural feedback. (Courtesy of Myron Krueger, Artificial Reality Corp.)

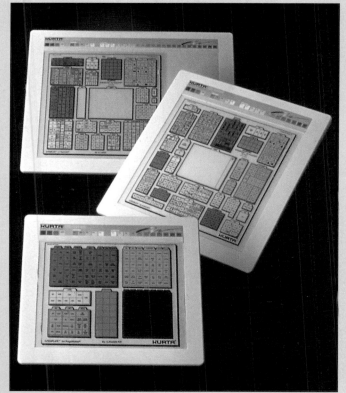

Plate I.18 Tablet-based menus. Color is used to group related menu items. (Courtesy of Kurta Corporation.)

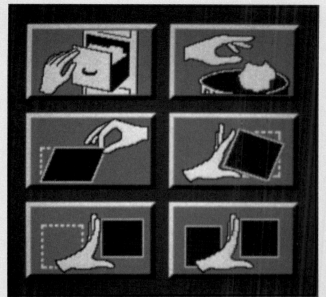

Plate I.19 A menu using a hand to show operations. The second and third rows use before and after representations of the object operated upon to indicate the meaning. From left to right, top to bottom, the commands are: File, Delete, Shear, Rotate, Move, and Copy. (Courtesy of Peter Tierney, © 1988 Cybermation, Inc.)

Plate I.20 A menu of operations on text. From left to right, top to bottom, the meanings are: select font, set height, set width (using before and after representation), slant (using before and after representation), set letter spacing, set line spacing. (Courtesy of Peter Tierney, © 1988 Cybermation, Inc.)

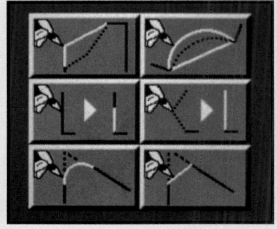

Plate I.21 A menu of operations on geometric objects, all showing before and after representations. From left to right, top to bottom, the meanings are: move point, change radius of an arc (or change a line to an arc), add vertex (one segment becomes two), remove vertex (two line segments become one), fillet corner, and chamfer corner. (Courtesy of Peter Tierney, © 1988 Cybermation, Inc.)

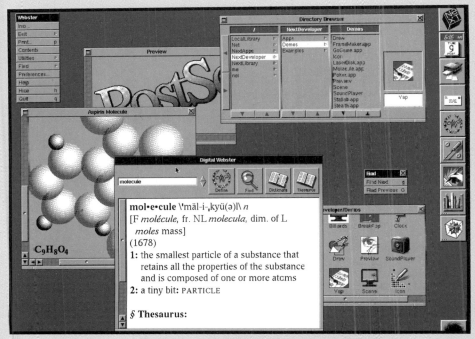

Plate I.22 The NeXT user interface. (Courtesy of NeXT, Inc. © 1989 NeXT, Inc.)

Plate I.23 Editable graphical history in Chimera. (a) Editor window shows picture created by Chimera's user. (b) History window shows sequence of before-after panel pairs created by Chimera. (Courtesy of David Kurlander and Steven Feiner, Columbia University.)

(a)

(b)

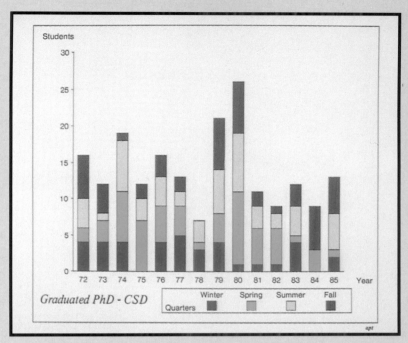

Plate I.24 A stacked bar chart created automatically by A Presentation Tool (APT) in response to a request to plot the number of graduating students per quarter from 1972 to 1985. APT generated this presentation as being more effective than many others it considered. (Courtesy of Jock Mackinlay.)

Plate I.25 Picture of a radio generated by IBIS to satisfy input communicative goals to show location of function dial and its change of state. IBIS determines the objects to include, rendering style, viewing and lighting specs, and picture composition. (Courtesy of Dorée Duncan Seligmann and Steven Feiner, Columbia University.)

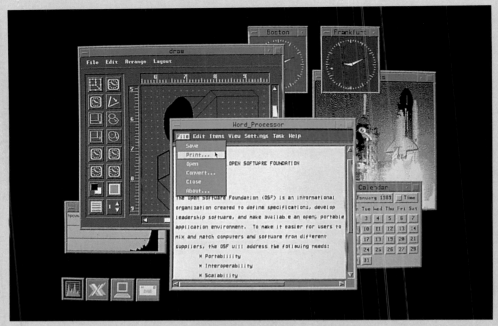

Plate I.26 The OSF/Motif user interface. In this image, different shades of blue are used to distinguish visual elements. (Courtesy of Open Software Foundation.)

Plate I.27 The OSF/Motif user interface. The color slider bars are used to define colors for use in windows. Notice the use of shading on the edges of buttons, menus, and so forth, to create a 3D effect. (Courtesy of Open Software Foundation.)

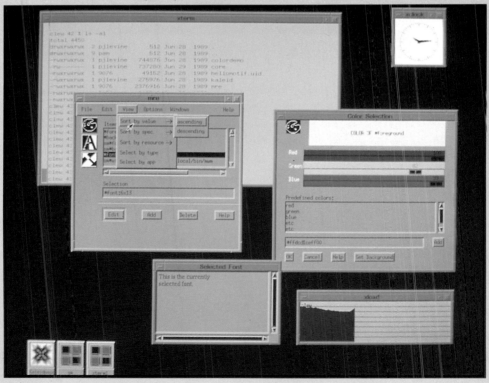

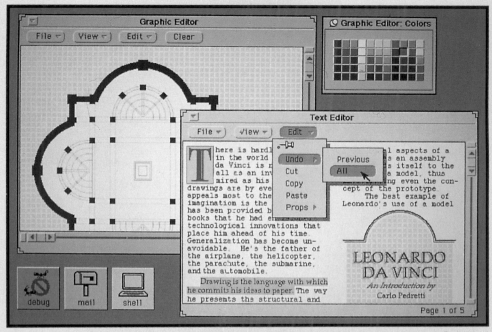

Plate I.28 The OPEN LOOK user interface. Yellow is used to highlight selected text. Subdued shades are used for the background and window borders. (Courtesy of Sun Microsystems.)

Plate I.29 The OPEN LOOK user interface. (Courtesy of Sun Microsystems.)

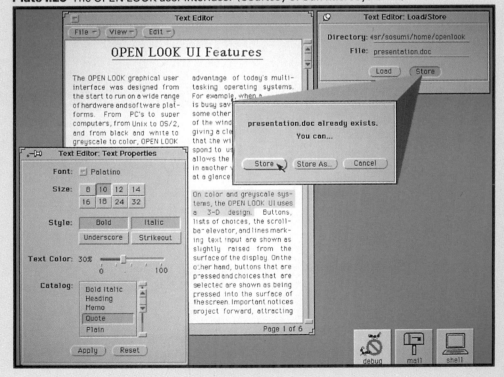

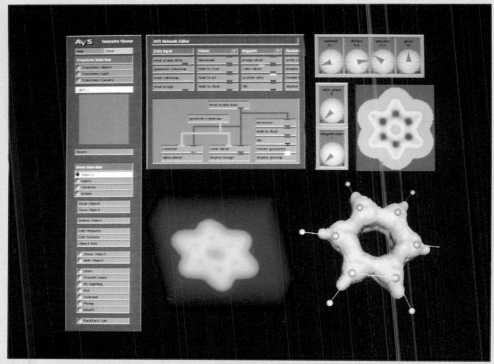

Plate I.30 The Application Visualization System (AVS) interface. The data flow diagram (middle center) is constructed interactively by the user from the menu of processing elements (top center). In this example, inputs from the the control dials (to the right) control the display of XYZ. (Courtesy of Stardent, Inc.)

Plate I.31 Objects modeled with NURBS, using the Alpha_1 modeling system. (Courtesy of University of Utah.)

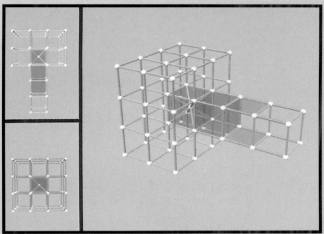

Plate I.32 Three views of a 3D nonmanifold representation with blue faces, yellow edges, and white vertices. In model shown, two solid cubes share a common face, rightmost cube has two dangling faces connected to a cubic wireframe, and leftmost cube has interior and exterior finite–element-method mesh wireframes. (Courtesy of K. Weiler, D. McLachlan, H. Thorvaldsdóttir; created using Dóre, © 1989 Ardent Computer Corporation.)

PANTONE® MC	PANTONE® MC	PANTONE® C	PANTONE® C	PANTONE® MC	PANTONE® MC	PANTONE® C	PANTONE® C
PANTONE® MC	PANTONE® MC	PANTONE® C	PANTONE® C	PANTONE® MC	PANTONE® MC	PANTONE® C	PANTONE® C
PANTONE®	PANTONE®	PANTONE®	PANTONE®	PANTONE®	PANTONE®	PANTONE®	PANTONE®

Plate I.33 A portion of a PANTONE® Color Specifier 747XR page. Color names (obscured in this reproduction) are shown along with the color samples. The color names are keyed to mixtures of standard inks that will reproduce the color. (Courtesy of Pantone, Inc. PANTONE® is Pantone, Inc.'s check-standard trademark for color reproduction and color reproduction materials. Process color reproduction may not match PANTONE®-identified solid color standards. Refer to current PANTONE® Color Publications for the accurate color.)

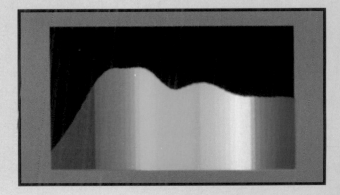

Plate I.34 The colors of the spectrum, from violet on the left to red on the right. The height of the curve is the spectral power distribution of illuminant C. (Courtesy of Barbara Meier, Brown University.)

5

Geometrical
Transformations

This chapter introduces the basic 2D and 3D geometrical transformations used in computer graphics. The translation, scaling, and rotation transformations discussed here are essential to many graphics applications and will be referred to extensively in succeeding chapters.

The transformations are used directly by application programs and within many graphics subroutine packages. A city-planning application program would use translation to place symbols for buildings and trees at appropriate positions, rotation to orient the symbols, and scaling to size the symbols. In general, many applications use the geometric transformations to change the position, orientation, and size of objects (also called *symbols* or *templates*) in a drawing. In Chapter 6, 3D rotation, translation, and scaling will be used as part of the process of creating 2D renditions of 3D objects. In Chapter 7, we see how a contemporary graphics package uses transformations as part of its implementation and also makes them available to application programs.

5.1 2D TRANSFORMATIONS

We can *translate* points in the (x, y) plane to new positions by adding translation amounts to the coordinates of the points. For each point $P(x, y)$ to be moved by d_x units parallel to the x axis and by d_y units parallel to the y axis to the new point $P'(x', y')$, we can write

$$x' = x + d_x, \qquad y' = y + d_y. \tag{5.1}$$

If we define the column vectors

$$P = \begin{bmatrix} x \\ y \end{bmatrix}, \; P' = \begin{bmatrix} x' \\ y' \end{bmatrix}, \; T = \begin{bmatrix} d_x \\ d_y \end{bmatrix}, \tag{5.2}$$

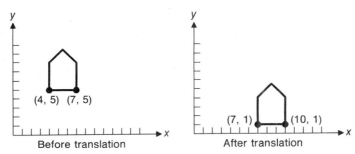

Fig. 5.1 Translation of a house.

then (5.1) can be expressed more concisely as

$$P' = P + T. \tag{5.3}$$

We could translate an object by applying Eq. (5.1) to every point of the object. Because each line in an object is made up of an infinite number of points, however, this process would take an infinitely long time. Fortunately, we can translate all the points on a line by translating only the line's endpoints and by drawing a new line between the translated endpoints; this is also true of scaling (stretching) and rotation. Figure 5.1 shows the effect of translating the outline of a house by $(3, -4)$.

Points can be *scaled* (stretched) by s_x along the x axis and by s_y along the y axis into new points by the multiplications

$$x' = s_x \cdot x, \qquad y' = s_y \cdot y. \tag{5.4}$$

In matrix form, this is

$$\begin{bmatrix} x' \\ y' \end{bmatrix} = \begin{bmatrix} s_x & 0 \\ 0 & s_y \end{bmatrix} \cdot \begin{bmatrix} x \\ y \end{bmatrix} \text{ or } P' = S \cdot P, \tag{5.5}$$

where S is the matrix in Eq. (5.5).

In Fig. 5.2, the house is scaled by $\frac{1}{2}$ in x and $\frac{1}{4}$ in y. Notice that the scaling is about the origin: The house is smaller *and* is closer to the origin. If the scale factors were greater than 1, the house would be both larger and further from the origin. Techniques for scaling about some point other than the origin are discussed in Section 5.2. The proportions of the house have also changed: a *differential* scaling, in which $s_x \neq s_y$, has been used. With a *uniform* scaling, in which $s_x = s_y$, the proportions are unaffected.

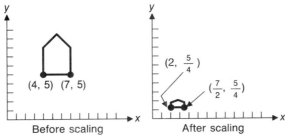

Fig. 5.2 Scaling of a house. The scaling is nonuniform, and the house changes position.

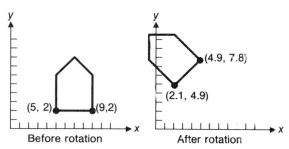

Fig. 5.3 Rotation of a house. The house also changes position.

Points can be *rotated* through an angle θ about the origin. A rotation is defined mathematically by

$$x' = x \cdot \cos\theta - y \cdot \sin\theta, \quad y' = x \cdot \sin\theta + y \cdot \cos\theta. \qquad (5.6)$$

In matrix form, we have

$$\begin{bmatrix} x' \\ y' \end{bmatrix} = \begin{bmatrix} \cos\theta & -\sin\theta \\ \sin\theta & \cos\theta \end{bmatrix} \cdot \begin{bmatrix} x \\ y \end{bmatrix} \text{ or } P' = R \cdot P, \qquad (5.7)$$

where R is the rotation matrix in Eq. (5.7). Figure 5.3 shows the rotation of the house by 45°. As with scaling, rotation is about the origin; rotation about an arbitrary point is discussed in Section 5.2.

Positive angles are measured *counterclockwise* from x toward y. For negative (clockwise) angles, the identities $\cos(-\theta) = \cos\theta$ and $\sin(-\theta) = -\sin\theta$ can be used to modify Eqs. (5.6) and (5.7).

Equation (5.6) is easily derived from Fig. 5.4, in which a rotation by θ transforms $P(x, y)$ into $P'(x', y')$. Because the rotation is about the origin, the distances from the origin to P and to P', labeled r in the figure, are equal. By simple trigonometry, we find that

$$x = r \cdot \cos\phi, \quad y = r \cdot \sin\phi \qquad (5.8)$$

and

$$\begin{aligned} x' &= r \cdot \cos(\theta + \phi) = r \cdot \cos\phi \cdot \cos\theta - r \cdot \sin\phi \cdot \sin\theta, \\ y' &= r \cdot \sin(\theta + \phi) = r \cdot \cos\phi \cdot \sin\theta + r \cdot \sin\phi \cdot \cos\theta. \end{aligned} \qquad (5.9)$$

Substituting Eq. (5.8) into Eq. (5.9) yields Eq. (5.6).

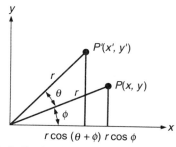

Fig. 5.4 Derivation of the rotation equation.

5.2 HOMOGENEOUS COORDINATES AND MATRIX REPRESENTATION OF 2D TRANSFORMATIONS

The matrix representations for translation, scaling, and rotation are, respectively,

$$P' = T + P, \tag{5.3}$$
$$P' = S \cdot P, \tag{5.5}$$
$$P' = R \cdot P. \tag{5.7}$$

Unfortunately, translation is treated differently (as an addition) from scaling and rotation (as multiplications). We would like to be able to treat all three transformations in a consistent way, so that they can be combined easily.

If points are expressed in *homogeneous coordinates*, all three transformations can be treated as multiplications. Homogeneous coordinates were first developed in geometry [MAXW46; MAXW51] and have been applied subsequently in graphics [ROBE65; BLIN77b; BLIN78a]. Numerous graphics subroutine packages and display processors work with homogeneous coordinates and transformations.

In homogeneous coordinates, we add a third coordinate to a point. Instead of being represented by a pair of numbers (x, y), each point is represented by a triple (x, y, W). At the same time, we say that two sets of homogeneous coordinates (x, y, W) and (x', y', W') represent the same point if and only if one is a multiple of the other. Thus, (2, 3, 6) and (4, 6, 12) are the same points represented by different coordinate triples. That is, each point has many different homogeneous coordinate representations. Also, at least one of the homogeneous coordinates must be nonzero: (0, 0, 0) is not allowed. If the W coordinate is nonzero, we can divide through by it: (x, y, W) represents the same point as $(x/W, y/W, 1)$. When W is nonzero, we normally do this division, and the numbers x/W and y/W are called the Cartesian coordinates of the homogeneous point. The points with $W = 0$ are called points at infinity, and will not appear very often in our discussions.

Triples of coordinates typically represent points in 3-space, but here we are using them to represent points in 2-space. The connection is this: If we take all the triples representing the same point—that is, all triples of the form (tx, ty, tW), with $t \neq 0$—we get a line in 3-space. Thus, each homogeneous *point* represents a *line* in 3-space. If we *homogenize* the point (divide by W), we get a point of the form $(x, y, 1)$. Thus, the homogenized points form the plane defined by the equation $W = 1$ in (x, y, W)-space. Figure 5.5 shows this

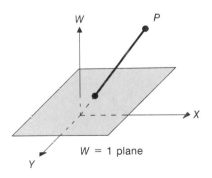

Fig. 5.5 The *XYW* homogeneous coordinate space, with the $W = 1$ plane and point $P(X, Y, W)$ projected onto tne $W = 1$ plane.

relationship. Points at infinity are not represented on this plane.

Because points are now three-element column vectors, transformation matrices, which multiply a point vector to produce another point vector, must be 3 × 3. In the 3 × 3 matrix form for homogeneous coordinates, the translation equations Eq. (5.1) are

$$\begin{bmatrix} x' \\ y' \\ 1 \end{bmatrix} = \begin{bmatrix} 1 & 0 & d_x \\ 0 & 1 & d_y \\ 0 & 0 & 1 \end{bmatrix} \cdot \begin{bmatrix} x \\ y \\ 1 \end{bmatrix}. \tag{5.10}$$

We caution the reader that some graphics textbooks, including [FOLE82], use a convention of premultiplying matrices by row vectors, rather than postmultiplying by column vectors. Matrices must be transposed to go from one convention to the other, just as the row and column vectors are transposed:

$$(P \cdot M)^T = M^T \cdot P^T.$$

Equation (5.10) can be expressed differently as

$$P' = T(d_x, d_y) \cdot P, \tag{5.11}$$

where

$$T(d_x, d_y) = \begin{bmatrix} 1 & 0 & d_x \\ 0 & 1 & d_y \\ 0 & 0 & 1 \end{bmatrix}. \tag{5.12}$$

What happens if a point P is translated by $T(d_{x1}, d_{y1})$ to P' and then translated by $T(d_{x2}, d_{y2})$ to P''? The result we expect intuitively is a net translation $T(d_{x1} + d_{x2}, d_{y1} + d_{y2})$. To confirm this intuition, we start with the givens:

$$P' = T(d_{x1}, d_{y1}) \cdot P, \tag{5.13}$$
$$P'' = T(d_{x2}, d_{y2}) \cdot P'. \tag{5.14}$$

Now, substituting Eq. (5.13) into Eq. (5.14), we obtain

$$P'' = T(d_{x2}, d_{y2}) \cdot (T(d_{x1}, d_{y1}) \cdot P) = (T(d_{x2}, d_{y2}) \cdot T(d_{x1}, d_{y1})) \cdot P. \tag{5.15}$$

The matrix product $T(d_{x2}, d_{y2}) \cdot T(d_{x1}, d_{y1})$ is

$$\begin{bmatrix} 1 & 0 & d_{x2} \\ 0 & 1 & d_{y2} \\ 0 & 0 & 1 \end{bmatrix} \cdot \begin{bmatrix} 1 & 0 & d_{x1} \\ 0 & 1 & d_{y1} \\ 0 & 0 & 1 \end{bmatrix} = \begin{bmatrix} 1 & 0 & d_{x1} + d_{x2} \\ 0 & 1 & d_{y1} + d_{y2} \\ 0 & 0 & 1 \end{bmatrix}. \tag{5.16}$$

The net translation is indeed $T(d_{x1} + d_{x2}, d_{y1} + d_{y2})$. The matrix product is variously referred to as the *compounding, catenation, concatenation,* or *composition* of $T(d_{x1}, d_{y1})$ and $T(d_{x2}, d_{y2})$. Here, we shall normally use the term *composition*.

Similarly, the scaling equations Eq. (5.4) are represented in matrix form as

$$\begin{bmatrix} x' \\ y' \\ 1 \end{bmatrix} = \begin{bmatrix} s_x & 0 & 0 \\ 0 & s_y & 0 \\ 0 & 0 & 1 \end{bmatrix} \cdot \begin{bmatrix} x \\ y \\ 1 \end{bmatrix}. \tag{5.17}$$

Defining

$$S(s_x, s_y) = \begin{bmatrix} s_x & 0 & 0 \\ 0 & s_y & 0 \\ 0 & 0 & 1 \end{bmatrix},$$ (5.18)

we have

$$P' = S(s_x, s_y) \cdot P.$$ (5.19)

Just as successive translations are additive, we expect that successive scalings should be multiplicative. Given

$$P' = S(s_{x1}, s_{y1}) \cdot P,$$ (5.20)
$$P'' = S(s_{x2}, s_{y2}) \cdot P',$$ (5.21)

then, substituting Eq. (5.20) into Eq. (5.21), we get

$$P'' = S(s_{x2}, s_{y2}) \cdot (S(s_{x1}, s_{y1}) \cdot P) = (S(s_{x2}, s_{y2}) \cdot S(s_{x1}, s_{y1})) \cdot P.$$ (5.22)

The matrix product $S(s_{x2}, s_{y2}) \cdot S(s_{x1}, s_{y1})$ is

$$\begin{bmatrix} s_{x2} & 0 & 0 \\ 0 & s_{y2} & 0 \\ 0 & 0 & 1 \end{bmatrix} \cdot \begin{bmatrix} s_{x1} & 0 & 0 \\ 0 & s_{y1} & 0 \\ 0 & 0 & 1 \end{bmatrix} = \begin{bmatrix} s_{x1} \cdot s_{x2} & 0 & 0 \\ 0 & s_{y1} \cdot s_{y2} & 0 \\ 0 & 0 & 1 \end{bmatrix}.$$ (5.23)

Thus, the scalings are indeed multiplicative.

Finally, the rotation equations Eq. (5.6) can be represented as

$$\begin{bmatrix} x' \\ y' \\ 1 \end{bmatrix} = \begin{bmatrix} \cos\theta & -\sin\theta & 0 \\ \sin\theta & \cos\theta & 0 \\ 0 & 0 & 1 \end{bmatrix} \cdot \begin{bmatrix} x \\ y \\ 1 \end{bmatrix}.$$ (5.24)

Letting

$$R(\theta) = \begin{bmatrix} \cos\theta & -\sin\theta & 0 \\ \sin\theta & \cos\theta & 0 \\ 0 & 0 & 1 \end{bmatrix},$$ (5.25)

we have

$$P' = R(\theta) \cdot P.$$ (5.26)

Showing that two successive rotations are additive is left as Exercise 5.2.

In the upper-left 2×2 submatrix of Eq. (5.25), consider each of the two rows as vectors. The vectors can be shown to have three properties:

1. Each is a unit vector

2. Each is perpendicular to the other (their dot product is zero)

3. The first and second vectors will be rotated by $R(\theta)$ to lie on the positive x and y axes, respectively (in the presence of conditions 1 and 2, this is equivalent to the submatrix having a determinant of 1).

The first two properties are also true of the columns of the 2 × 2 submatrix. The two directions are those into which vectors along the positive x and y axes are rotated. These properties suggest two useful ways to go about deriving a rotation matrix when we know the effect desired from the rotation. A matrix having these properties is called *special orthogonal*.

A transformation matrix of the form

$$\begin{bmatrix} r_{11} & r_{12} & t_x \\ r_{21} & r_{22} & t_y \\ 0 & 0 & 1 \end{bmatrix},$$

(5.27)

where the upper 2 × 2 submatrix is orthogonal, preserves angles and lengths. That is, a unit square remains a unit square, and becomes neither a rhombus with unit sides, nor a square with nonunit sides. Such transformations are also called *rigid-body* transformations, because the body or object being transformed is not distorted in any way. An arbitrary sequence of rotation and translation matrices creates a matrix of this form.

What can be said about the product of an arbitrary sequence of rotation, translation, and scale matrices? They are called *affine* transformations, and have the property of preserving parallelism of lines, but not lengths and angles. Figure 5.6 shows the results of applying a −45° rotation and then a nonuniform scaling to the unit cube. It is clear that neither angles nor lengths have been preserved by this sequence, but parallel lines have remained parallel. Further rotation, scale, and translation operations will not cause the parallel lines to cease being parallel. $R(\theta)$, $S(s_x, s_y)$, and $T(d_x, d_y)$ are also affine.

Another type of primitive transformation, *shear transformations*, are also affine. Two-dimensional shear transformations are of two kinds: a shear along the x axis and a shear along the y axis. Figure 5.7 shows the effect of shearing the unit cube along each axis. The operation is represented by the matrix

$$SH_x = \begin{bmatrix} 1 & a & 0 \\ 0 & 1 & 0 \\ 0 & 0 & 1 \end{bmatrix}.$$

(5.28)

The term a in the shear matrix is the proportionality constant. Notice that the product $SH_x [x \ \ y \ \ 1]^T$ is $[x + ay \ \ y \ \ 1]^T$, clearly demonstrating the proportional change in x as a function of y.

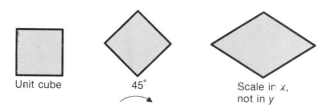

Unit cube   45°   Scale in x, not in y

Fig. 5.6 A unit cube is rotated by −45° and is nonuniformly scaled. The result is an affine transformation of the unit cube, in which parallelism of lines is maintained, but neither angles nor lengths are maintained.

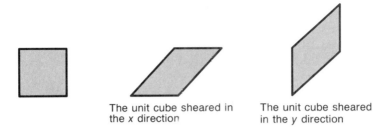

The unit cube sheared in   The unit cube sheared
the x direction   in the y direction

Fig. 5.7 The primitive-shear operations applied to the unit cube. In each case, the lengths of the oblique lines are now greater than 1.

Similarly, the matrix

$$SH_y = \begin{bmatrix} 1 & 0 & 0 \\ b & 1 & 0 \\ 0 & 0 & 1 \end{bmatrix} \tag{5.29}$$

shears along the y axis.

5.3 COMPOSITION OF 2D TRANSFORMATIONS

The idea of composition was introduced in the preceding section. Here, we use composition to combine the fundamental R, S, and T matrices to produce desired general results. The basic purpose of composing transformations is to gain efficiency by applying a single composed transformation to a point, rather than applying a series of transformations, one after the other.

Consider the rotation of an object about some arbitrary point P_1. Because we know how to rotate only about the origin, we convert our original (difficult) problem into three separate (easy) problems. Thus, to rotate about P_1, we need a sequence of three fundamental transformations:

1. Translate such that P_1 is at the origin
2. Rotate
3. Translate such that the point at the origin returns to P_1.

This sequence is illustrated in Fig. 5.8, in which our house is rotated about $P_1(x_1, y_1)$. The first translation is by $(-x_1, -y_1)$, whereas the later translation is by the inverse (x_1, y_1). The result is rather different from that of applying just the rotation.

The net transformation is

$$T(x_1, y_1) \cdot R(\theta) \cdot T(-x_1, -y_1) = \begin{bmatrix} 1 & 0 & x_1 \\ 0 & 1 & y_1 \\ 0 & 0 & 1 \end{bmatrix} \cdot \begin{bmatrix} \cos\theta & -\sin\theta & 0 \\ \sin\theta & \cos\theta & 0 \\ 0 & 0 & 1 \end{bmatrix} \cdot \begin{bmatrix} 1 & 0 & -x_1 \\ 0 & 1 & -y_1 \\ 0 & 0 & 1 \end{bmatrix}$$

$$= \begin{bmatrix} \cos\theta & -\sin\theta & x_1(1 - \cos\theta) + y_1\sin\theta \\ \sin\theta & \cos\theta & y_1(1 - \cos\theta) - x_1\sin\theta \\ 0 & 0 & 1 \end{bmatrix}. \tag{5.30}$$

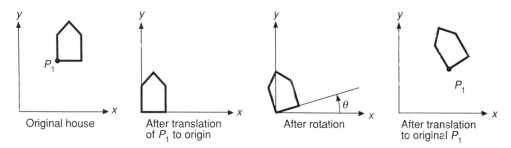

Fig. 5.8 Rotation of a house about the point P_1 by an angle θ.

A similar approach is used to scale an object about an arbitrary point P_1. First, translate such that P_1 goes to the origin, then scale, then translate back to P_1. In this case, the net transformation is

$$T(x_1, y_1) \cdot S(s_x, s_y) \cdot T(-x_1, -y_1) = \begin{bmatrix} 1 & 0 & x_1 \\ 0 & 1 & y_1 \\ 0 & 0 & 1 \end{bmatrix} \cdot \begin{bmatrix} s_x & 0 & 0 \\ 0 & s_y & 0 \\ 0 & 0 & 1 \end{bmatrix} \cdot \begin{bmatrix} 1 & 0 & -x_1 \\ 0 & 1 & -y_1 \\ 0 & 0 & 1 \end{bmatrix}$$

$$= \begin{bmatrix} s_x & 0 & x_1(1 - s_x) \\ 0 & s_y & y_1(1 - s_y) \\ 0 & 0 & 1 \end{bmatrix}. \tag{5.31}$$

Suppose we wish to scale, rotate, and position the house shown in Fig. 5.9 with P_1 as the center for the rotation and scaling. The sequence is to translate P_1 to the origin, to perform the scaling and rotation, and then to translate from the origin to the new position P_2 where the house is to be placed. A data structure that records this transformation might contain the scale factor(s), rotation angle, and translation amounts, and the order in which the transformations were applied, or it might simply record the composite transformation matrix:

$$T(x_2, y_2) \cdot R(\theta) \cdot S(s_x, s_y) \cdot T(-x_1, -y_1). \tag{5.32}$$

If M_1 and M_2 each represent a fundamental translation, scaling, or rotation, when is $M_1 \cdot M_2 = M_2 \cdot M_1$? That is, when do M_1 and M_2 commute? In general, of course, matrix multiplication is *not* commutative. However, it is easy to show that, in the following special cases, commutativity holds:

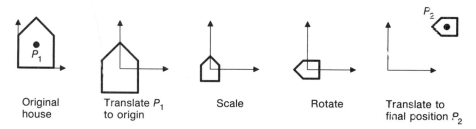

| Original house | Translate P_1 to origin | Scale | Rotate | Translate to final position P_2 |

Fig. 5.9 Rotation of a house about the point P_1, and placement such that what was at P_1 is at P_2.

$\boldsymbol{M_1}$	$\boldsymbol{M_2}$
Translate	Translate
Scale	Scale
Rotate	Rotate
Scale (with $s_x = s_y$)	Rotate

In these cases, we need not be concerned about the *order* of matrix manipulation.

5.4   THE WINDOW-TO-VIEWPORT TRANSFORMATION

Some graphics packages allow the programmer to specify output primitive coordinates in a floating-point *world-coordinate* system, using whatever units are meaningful to the application program: angstroms, microns, meters, miles, light-years, and so on. The term *world* is used because the application program is representing a world that is being interactively created or displayed to the user.

Given that output primitives are specified in world coordinates, the graphics subroutine package must be told how to map world coordinates onto screen coordinates (we use the specific term *screen coordinates* to relate this discussion specifically to SRGP, but that hardcopy output devices might be used, in which case the term *device coordinates* would be more appropriate). We could do this mapping by having the application programmer provide the graphics package with a transformation matrix to effect the mapping. Another way is to have the application programmer specify a rectangular region in world coordinates, called the *world-coordinate window*, and a corresponding rectangular region in screen coordinates, called the *viewport*, into which the world-coordinate window is to be mapped. The transformation that maps the window into the viewport is applied to all of the output primitives in world coordinates, thus mapping them into screen coordinates. Figure 5.10 shows this concept. As seen in this figure, if the window and viewport do not have the same height-to-width ratio, a *non*uniform scaling occurs. If the application program changes the window or viewport, then new output primitives drawn onto the screen will be affected by the change. Existing output primitives are not affected by such a change.

The modifier *world-coordinate* is used with *window* to emphasize that we are not discussing a *window-manager window*, which is a different and more recent concept, and

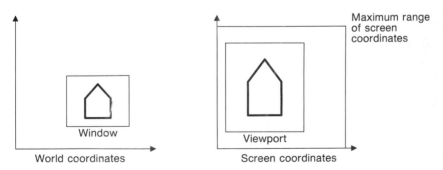

Fig. 5.10 The window in world coordinates and the viewport in screen coordinates determine the mapping that is applied to all the output primitives in world coordinates.

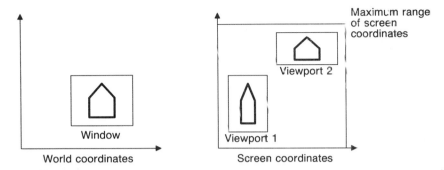

Fig. 5.11 The effect of drawing output primitives with two viewports. Output primitives specifying the house were first drawn with viewport 1, the viewport was changed to viewport 2, and then the application program again called the graphics package to draw the output primitives.

which unfortunately has the same name. Whenever there is no ambiguity as to which type of window is meant, we will drop the modifier.

If SRGP were to provide world-coordinate output primitives, the viewport would be on the current canvas, which defaults to canvas 0, the screen. The application program would be able to change the window or the viewport at any time, in which case subsequently specified output primitives would be subjected to a new transformation. If the change included a different viewport, then the new output primitves would be located on the canvas in positions different from those of the old ones, as shown in Fig. 5.11.

A window manager might map SRGP's canvas 0 into less than a full-screen window, in which case not all of the canvas or even of the viewport would necessarily be visible. In Chapter 10, we further discuss the relationships among world-coordinate windows, viewports, and window-manager windows.

Given a window and viewport, what is the transformation matrix that maps the window from world coordinates into the viewport in screen coordinates? This matrix can be developed as a three-step transformation composition, as suggested in Fig. 5.12. The

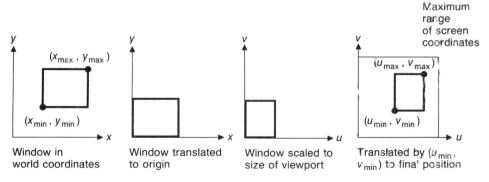

Fig. 5.12 The steps in transforming a world-coordinate window into a viewport.

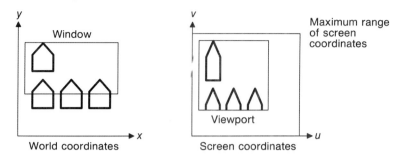

Fig. 5.13 Output primitives in world coordinates are clipped against the window. Those that remain are displayed in the viewport.

window, specified by its lower-left and upper-right corners, is first translated to the origin of world coordinates. Next, the size of the window is scaled to be equal to the size of the viewport. Finally, a translation is used to position the viewport. The overall matrix M_{wv} is:

$$M_{wv} = T(u_{min}, v_{min}) \cdot S\left(\frac{u_{max} - u_{min}}{x_{max} - x_{min}}, \frac{v_{max} - v_{min}}{y_{max} - y_{min}}\right) \cdot T(-x_{min}, -y_{min})$$

$$= \begin{bmatrix} 1 & 0 & u_{min} \\ 0 & 1 & v_{min} \\ 0 & 0 & 1 \end{bmatrix} \cdot \begin{bmatrix} \dfrac{u_{max} - u_{min}}{x_{max} - x_{min}} & 0 & 0 \\ 0 & \dfrac{v_{max} - v_{min}}{y_{max} - y_{min}} & 0 \\ 0 & 0 & 1 \end{bmatrix} \cdot \begin{bmatrix} 1 & 0 & -x_{min} \\ 0 & 1 & -y_{min} \\ 0 & 0 & 1 \end{bmatrix}$$

$$= \begin{bmatrix} \dfrac{u_{max} - u_{min}}{x_{max} - x_{min}} & 0 & -x_{min} \cdot \dfrac{u_{max} - u_{min}}{x_{max} - x_{min}} + u_{min} \\ 0 & \dfrac{v_{max} - v_{min}}{y_{max} - y_{min}} & -y_{min} \cdot \dfrac{v_{max} - v_{min}}{y_{max} - y_{min}} + v_{min} \\ 0 & 0 & 1 \end{bmatrix}. \quad (5.33)$$

Multiplying $P = M_{wv} [x \quad y \quad 1]^T$ gives the expected result:

$$P = \left[(x - x_{min}) \cdot \frac{u_{max} - u_{min}}{x_{max} - x_{min}} + u_{min} \quad (y - y_{min}) \cdot \frac{v_{max} - v_{min}}{y_{max} - y_{min}} + v_{min} \quad 1\right]. \quad (5.34)$$

Many graphics packages combine the window–viewport transformation with clipping of output primitives against the window. The concept of clipping was introduced in Chapter 3; Fig. 5.13 illustrates clipping in the context of windows and viewports.

5.5 EFFICIENCY

The most general composition of R, S, and T operations produces a matrix of the form

$$M = \begin{bmatrix} r_{11} & r_{12} & t_x \\ r_{21} & r_{22} & t_y \\ 0 & 0 & 1 \end{bmatrix}. \quad (5.35)$$

The upper 2×2 submatrix is a composite rotation and scale matrix, whereas t_x and t_y are composite translations. Calculating $M \cdot P$ as a vector multiplied by a 3×3 matrix takes nine multiplies and six adds. The fixed structure of the last row of Eq. (5.35), however, simplifies the actual operations to

$$x' = x \cdot r_{11} + y \cdot r_{12} + t_x \qquad (5.36)$$
$$y' = x \cdot r_{21} + y \cdot r_{22} + t_y,$$

reducing the process to four multiplies and four adds—a significant speedup, especially since the operation can be applied to hundreds or even thousands of points per picture. Thus, although 3×3 matrices are convenient and useful for composing 2D transformations, we can use the final matrix most efficiently in a program by exploiting its special structure. Some hardware matrix multipliers have parallel adders and multipliers, thereby diminishing or removing this concern.

Another area where efficiency is important is creating successive views of an object, such as a molecule or airplane, rotated a few degrees between each successive view. If each view can be created and displayed quickly enough (30 to 100 milliseconds each), then the object will appear to be rotating dynamically. To achieve this speed, we must transform each individual point and line of the object as quickly as possible. The rotation equations (Eq. (5.6)) require four multiplies and two adds. We can decrease the operation count by recognizing that, because θ is small (just a few degrees), $\cos\theta$ is very close to 1. In this approximation, Eq. (5.6) becomes

$$x' = x - y \sin\theta, \qquad y' = x \sin\theta + y, \qquad (5.37)$$

which requires just two multiplies and two adds. The savings of two multiplies can be significant on computers lacking hardware multipliers.

Equation (5.37), however, is only an approximation to the correct values of x' and y': a small error is built in. Each time the formulae are applied to the new values of x and y, the error gets a bit larger. If we repeat the formulae indefinitely, the error will overwhelm the correct values, and the rotating image will begin to look like a collection of randomly drawn lines.

A better approximation is to use x' instead of x in the second equation:

$$x' = x - y \sin\theta,$$
$$y' = x' \sin\theta + y = (x - y \sin\theta)\sin\theta + y = x \sin\theta + y(1 - \sin^2\theta) \qquad (5.38)$$

This is a better approximation than is Eq. (5.37) because the determinant of the corresponding 2×2 matrix is 1, which means that the areas transformed by Eq. (5.38) are unchanged. Note that cumulative errors can also arise when using the correct rotation equations repeatedly (see Exercise 5.19).

5.6 MATRIX REPRESENTATION OF 3D TRANSFORMATIONS

Just as 2D transformations can be represented by 3×3 matrices using homogeneous coordinates, so 3D transformations can be represented by 4×4 matrices, providing we use homogeneous coordinate representations of points in 3-space as well. Thus, instead of representing a point as (x, y, z), we represent it as (x, y, z, W), where two of these quadruples represent the same point if one is a nonzero multiple of the other; the quadruple $(0, 0, 0, 0)$ is not allowed. As in 2D, a standard representation of a point (x, y, z, W) with $W \neq 0$ is given by $(x/W, y/W, z/W, 1)$. Transforming the point to this form is called *homogenizing*, as before. Also, points whose W coordinate is zero are called points at infinity. There is a geometrical interpretation as well. Each point in 3-space is being represented by a line through the origin in 4-space, and the homogenized representations of these points form a 3D subspace of 4-space which is defined by the single equation $W = 1$.

The 3D coordinate system used in this text is *right-handed*, as shown in Fig. 5.14. By convention, positive rotations in a right-handed system are such that, when looking from a positive axis toward the origin, a 90° *counterclockwise* rotation will transform one positive axis into the other. This table follows from this convention:

If axis of rotation is	Direction of positive rotation is
x	y to z
y	z to x
z	z to y

These positive directions are also depicted in Fig. 5.14. The reader is warned that not all graphics texts follow this convention.

We use a right-handed system here because it is the standard mathematical convention, even though it is convenient in 3D graphics to think of a left-handed system superimposed on the face of a display (see Fig. 5.15), since a left-handed system gives the natural interpretation that larger z values are further from the viewer. Notice that, in a left-handed system, positive rotations are *clockwise* when looking from a positive axis toward the origin. This definition of positive rotations allows the same rotation matrices given in this section to be used for either right- or left-hand coordinate systems. Conversion from right to left and left to right is discussed in Section 5.8.

Translation in 3D is a simple extension from that in 2D:

$$T(d_x, d_y, d_z) = \begin{bmatrix} 1 & 0 & 0 & d_x \\ 0 & 1 & 0 & d_y \\ 0 & 0 & 1 & d_z \\ 0 & 0 & 0 & 1 \end{bmatrix}. \tag{5.39}$$

That is, $T(d_x, d_y, d_z) \cdot [x \quad y \quad z \quad 1]^T = [x + d_x \quad y + d_y \quad z + d_z \quad 1]^T$.

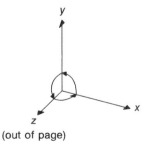

Fig. 5.14 The right-handed coordinate system.

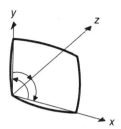

Fig. 5.15 The left-handed coordinate system, with a superimposed display screen.

Scaling is similarly extended:

$$S(s_x, s_y, s_z) = \begin{bmatrix} s_x & 0 & 0 & 0 \\ 0 & s_y & 0 & 0 \\ 0 & 0 & s_z & 0 \\ 0 & 0 & 0 & 1 \end{bmatrix}. \tag{5.40}$$

Checking, we see that $S(s_x, s_y, s_z) \cdot [x \quad y \quad z \quad 1]^T = [s_x \cdot x \quad s_y \cdot y \quad s_z \cdot z \quad 1]^T$.
The 2D rotation of Eq. (5.26) is just a 3D rotation about the z axis, which is

$$R_z(\theta) = \begin{bmatrix} \cos\theta & -\sin\theta & 0 & 0 \\ \sin\theta & \cos\theta & 0 & 0 \\ 0 & 0 & 1 & 0 \\ 0 & 0 & 0 & 1 \end{bmatrix}. \tag{5.41}$$

This is easily verified: A 90° rotation of $[1 \, 0 \, 0 \, 1]^T$, which is the unit vector along the x axis, should produce the unit vector $[0 \, 1 \, 0 \, 1]^T$ along the y axis. Evaluating the product

$$\begin{bmatrix} 0 & -1 & 0 & 0 \\ 1 & 0 & 0 & 0 \\ 0 & 0 & 1 & 0 \\ 0 & 0 & 0 & 1 \end{bmatrix} \cdot \begin{bmatrix} 1 \\ 0 \\ 0 \\ 1 \end{bmatrix} \tag{5.42}$$

gives the predicted result of $[0 \, 1 \, 0 \, 1]^T$.
The x-axis rotation matrix is

$$R_x(\theta) = \begin{bmatrix} 1 & 0 & 0 & 0 \\ 0 & \cos\theta & -\sin\theta & 0 \\ 0 & \sin\theta & \cos\theta & 0 \\ 0 & 0 & 0 & 1 \end{bmatrix}. \tag{5.43}$$

The y-axis rotation matrix is

$$R_y(\theta) = \begin{bmatrix} \cos\theta & 0 & \sin\theta & 0 \\ 0 & 1 & 0 & 0 \\ -\sin\theta & 0 & \cos\theta & 0 \\ 0 & 0 & 0 & 1 \end{bmatrix}. \tag{5.44}$$

The columns (and the rows) of the upper-left 3×3 submatrix of $R_z(\theta)$, $R_x(\theta)$, and $R_y(\theta)$ are mutually perpendicular unit vectors and the submatrix has a determinant of 1, which means the three matrices are special orthogonal, as discussed in Section 5.2. Also, the upper-left 3×3 submatrix formed by an arbitrary sequence of rotations is special orthogonal. Recall that orthogonal transformations preserve distances and angles.

All these transformation matrices have inverses. The inverse for T is obtained by negating d_x, d_y, and d_z; for S, by replacing s_x, s_y, and s_z by their reciprocals; that for each of the three rotation matrices is obtained by negating the angle of rotation.

The inverse of any orthogonal matrix B is just B's transpose: $B^{-1} = B^T$. In fact, taking the transpose does not need to involve even exchanging elements in the array that stores the matrix—it is necessary only to exchange row and column indexes when accessing the array. Notice that this method of finding an inverse is consistent with the result of negating θ to find the inverse of R_x, R_y, and R_z.

Any number of rotation, scaling, and translation matrices can be multiplied together. The result always has the form

$$M = \begin{bmatrix} r_{11} & r_{12} & r_{13} & t_x \\ r_{21} & r_{22} & r_{23} & t_y \\ r_{31} & r_{32} & r_{33} & t_z \\ 0 & 0 & 0 & 1 \end{bmatrix}. \tag{5.45}$$

As in the 2D case, the 3×3 upper-left submatrix R gives the aggregate rotation and scaling, whereas T gives the subsequent aggregate translation. Some computational efficiency is achieved by performing the transformation explicitly as

$$\begin{bmatrix} x' \\ y' \\ z' \end{bmatrix} = R \cdot \begin{bmatrix} x \\ y \\ z \end{bmatrix} + T, \tag{5.46}$$

where R and T are submatrices from Eq. (5.45).

Corresponding to the two-dimensional shear matrices in Section 5.2 are three 3D shear matrices. The (x, y) shear is

$$SH_{xy}(sh_x, sh_y) = \begin{bmatrix} 1 & 0 & sh_x & 0 \\ 0 & 1 & sh_y & 0 \\ 0 & 0 & 1 & 0 \\ 0 & 0 & 0 & 1 \end{bmatrix}. \tag{5.47}$$

Applying SH_{xy} to the point $[x \quad y \quad z \quad 1]^T$, we have $[x + sh_x \cdot z \quad y + sh_y \cdot z \quad z \quad 1]^T$. Shears along the x and y axes have a similar form.

So far, we have focused on transforming individual points. We transform lines, these being defined by two points, by transforming the endpoints. Planes, if they are defined by three points, may be handled the same way, but usually they are defined by a plane equation, and the coefficients of this plane equation must be transformed differently. We may also need to transform the plane normal. Let a plane be represented as the column vector of plane-equation coefficients $N = [A \quad B \quad C \quad D]^T$. Then a plane is defined by all points P such that $N \cdot P = 0$, where $\cdot$ is the vector dot product and $P = [x \quad y \quad z \quad 1]^T$. This dot product gives rise to the familiar plane equation $A x + B y + C z + D = 0$, which can also be expressed as the product of the row vector of plane-equation coefficients times the column vector P: $N^T \cdot P = 0$. Now suppose we transform all points P on the plane by some matrix M. To maintain $N^T \cdot P = 0$ for the transformed points, we would like to transform N by some (to be determined) matrix Q, giving rise to the equation $(Q \cdot N)^T \cdot M \cdot P = 0$. This expression can in turn be rewritten as $N^T \cdot Q^T \cdot M \cdot P = 0$, using the identity $(Q \cdot N)^T = N^T \cdot Q^T$. The equation will hold if $Q^T \cdot M$ is a multiple of the identity matrix. If the multiplier is 1, this leads to $Q^T = M^{-1}$, or $Q = (M^{-1})^T$. This means that the column vector N' of coefficients for a plane transformed by M is given by

$$N' = (M^{-1})^T \cdot N.$$

The matrix $(M^{-1})^T$ need not in general exist, because the determinant of M might be zero. This would happen if M includes a projection (we might want to investigate the effect of a perspective projection on a plane). It is possible to use, instead of $(M^{-1})^T$, the matrix of cofactors of M used in finding the inverse of M using Cramer's rule. See the Appendix for more details.

If just the normal of the plane is to be transformed (for example, to perform the shading calculations discussed in Chapter 16) and if M consists of only the composition of translation, rotation, and uniform scaling matrices, then the mathematics is even simpler. The N' of Eq. (5.48) can be simplified to $[A'\ B'\ C'\ 0]^T$. (With a zero W component, a homogeneous point represents a point at infinity, which can be thought of as a direction.)

5.7   COMPOSITION OF 3D TRANSFORMATIONS

In this section, we discuss how to compose 3D transformation matrices, using an example that will be useful in Section 6.4. The objective is to transform the directed line segments P_1P_2 and P_1P_3 in Fig. 5.16 from their starting position in part (a) to their ending position in part (b). Thus, point P_1 is to be translated to the origin, P_1P_2 is to lie on the positive z axis, and P_1P_3 is to lie in the positive y axis half of the (y, z) plane. The lengths of the lines are to be unaffected by the transformation.

Two ways to achieve the desired transformation are presented. The first approach is to compose the primitive transformations T, R_x, R_y, and R_z. This approach, although somewhat tedious, is easy to illustrate, and understanding it will help us to build an understanding of transformations. The second approach, using the properties of orthogonal matrices described in the previous section, is explained more briefly but is more abstract.

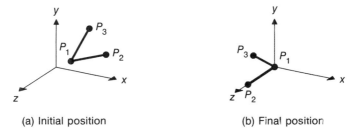

(a) Initial position   (b) Final position

Fig. 5.16 Transforming P_1, P_2, and P_3 from their initial (a) to their final (b) position.

To work with the primitive transformations, we again break a difficult problem into simpler subproblems. In this case, the desired transformation can be done in four steps:

1. Translate P_1 to the origin
2. Rotate about the y axis such that P_1P_2 lies in the (y, z) plane
3. Rotate about the x axis such that P_1P_2 lies on the z axis
4. Rotate about the z axis such that P_1P_3 lies in the (y, z) plane.

Step 1: Translate P_1 to the origin. The translation is

$$T(-x_1, -y_1, -z_1) = \begin{bmatrix} 1 & 0 & 0 & -x_1 \\ 0 & 1 & 0 & -y_1 \\ 0 & 0 & 1 & -z_1 \\ 0 & 0 & 0 & 1 \end{bmatrix}. \tag{5.49}$$

Applying T to P_1, P_2, and P_3 gives

$$P'_1 = T(-x_1, -y_1, -z_1) \cdot P_1 = \begin{bmatrix} 0 \\ 0 \\ 0 \\ 1 \end{bmatrix}, \tag{5.50}$$

$$P'_2 = T(-x_1, -y_1, -z_1) \cdot P_2 = \begin{bmatrix} x_2 - x_1 \\ y_2 - y_1 \\ z_2 - z_1 \\ 1 \end{bmatrix}, \tag{5.51}$$

$$P'_3 = T(-x_1, -y_1, -z_1) \cdot P_3 = \begin{bmatrix} x_3 - x_1 \\ y_3 - y_1 \\ z_3 - z_1 \\ 1 \end{bmatrix}, \tag{5.52}$$

Step 2: Rotate about the y axis. Figure 5.17 shows P_1P_2 after step 1, along with the projection of P_1P_2 onto the (x, z) plane. The angle of rotation is $-(90 - \theta) = \theta - 90$. Then

$$\cos(\theta - 90) = \sin\theta = \frac{z'_2}{D_1} = \frac{z_2 - z_1}{D_1},$$

$$\sin(\theta - 90) = -\cos\theta = -\frac{x'_2}{D_1} = -\frac{x_2 - x_1}{D_1}, \tag{5.53}$$

where

$$D_1 = \sqrt{(z'_2)^2 + (x'_2)^2} = \sqrt{(z_2 - z_1)^2 + (x_2 - x_1)^2}. \tag{5.54}$$

When these values are substituted into Eq. (5.44), we get

$$P''_2 = R_y(\theta - 90) \cdot P'_2 = [0 \quad y_2 - y_1 \quad D_1 \quad 1]^T. \tag{5.55}$$

As expected, the x component of P''_2 is zero, and the z component is the length D_1.

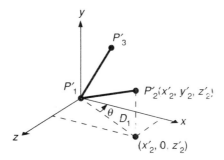

Fig. 5.17 Rotation about the y axis: The projection of $P_1'P_2'$, which has length D_1, is rotated into the z axis. The angle θ shows the positive direction of rotation about the y axis: The actual angle used is $-(90 - \theta)$.

Step 3: Rotate about the x axis. Figure 5.18 shows P_1P_2 after step 2. The angle of rotation is ϕ, for which

$$\cos\phi = \frac{z_2''}{D_2}, \quad \sin\phi = \frac{y_2''}{D_2}, \tag{5.56}$$

where $D_2 = |P_1''P_2''|$, the length of the line $P_1''P_2''$. But the length of line $P_1''P_2''$ is the same as the length of line P_1P_2, because rotation and translation transformations preserve length, so

$$D_2 = |P_1''P_2''| = |P_1P_2| = \sqrt{(x_2 - x_1)^2 + (y_2 - y_1)^2 + (z_2 - z_1)^2}. \tag{5.57}$$

The result of the rotation in step 3 is

$$P_2''' = R_x(\phi) \cdot P_2'' = R_x(\phi) \cdot R_y(\theta - 90) \cdot P_2'$$
$$= R_x(\phi) \cdot R_y(\theta - 90) \cdot T \cdot P_2 = [0 \quad 0 \quad |P_1P_2| \quad 1]^T. \tag{5.58}$$

That is, P_1P_2 now coincides with the positive z axis.

Step 4: Rotate about the z axis. Figure 5.19 shows P_1P_2 and P_1P_3 after step 3, with P_2''' on the z axis and P_3''' at the position

$$P_3''' = [x_3''' \quad y_3''' \quad z_3''' \quad 1]^T = R_x(\phi) \cdot R_y(\theta - 90) \cdot T(-x_1, -y_1, -z_1) \cdot P_3. \tag{5.59}$$

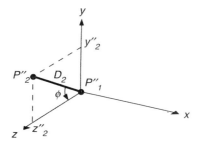

Fig. 5.18 Rotation about the x axis: $P_1''P_2''$ is rotated into the z axis by the positive angle ϕ. D_2 is the length of the line segment. The line segment $P_1''P_3''$ is not shown, because it is not used to determine the angles of rotation. Both lines are rotated by $R_x(\phi)$.

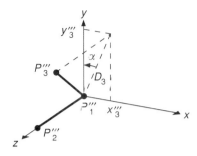

Fig. 5.19 Rotation about the z axis: The projection of $P_1'P_3'$, whose length is D_3, is rotated by the positive angle α into the y axis, bringing the line itself into the (y, z) plane. D_3 is the length of the projection.

The rotation is through the positive angle α, with

$$\cos\alpha = y_3'''/D_3, \quad \sin\alpha = x_3'''/D_3, \quad D_3 = \sqrt{x_3'''^2 + y_3'''^2}. \tag{5.60}$$

Step 4 achieves the result shown in Fig. 5.16(b).

The composite matrix

$$R_z(\alpha) \cdot R_x(\phi) \cdot R_y(\theta - 90) \cdot T(-x_1, -y_1, -z_1) = R \cdot T \tag{5.61}$$

is the required transformation, with $R = R_z(\alpha) \cdot R_x(\phi) \cdot R_y(\theta - 90)$. We leave it to the reader to apply this transformation to P_1, P_2, and P_3 to verify that P_1 is transformed to the origin, P_2 is transformed to the positive z axis, and P_3 is transformed to the positive y half of the (y, z) plane.

The second way to obtain the matrix R is to use the properties of orthogonal matrices discussed in Section 5.2. Recall that the unit row vectors of R rotate into the principal axes. Replacing the second subscripts of Eq. (5.45) with x, y, and z for notational convenience

$$R = \begin{bmatrix} r_{1x} & r_{2x} & r_{3x} \\ r_{1y} & r_{2y} & r_{3y} \\ r_{1z} & r_{2z} & r_{3z} \end{bmatrix}. \tag{5.62}$$

Because R_z is the unit vector along P_1P_2 that will rotate into the positive z axis,

$$R_z = [r_{1z} \quad r_{2z} \quad r_{3z}]^T = \frac{P_1P_2}{|P_1P_2|}. \tag{5.63}$$

In addition, the R_x unit vector is perpendicular to the plane of P_1, P_2, and P_3 and will rotate into the positive x axis, so that R_x must be the normalized cross-product of two vectors in the plane:

$$R_x = [r_{1x} \quad r_{2x} \quad r_{3x}]^T = \frac{P_1P_3 \times P_1P_2}{|P_1P_3 \times P_1P_2|}. \tag{5.64}$$

Finally,

$$R_y = [r_{1y} \quad r_{2y} \quad r_{3y}]^T = R_z \times R_x \tag{5.65}$$

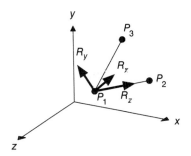

Fig. 5.20 The unit vectors R_x, R_y, and R_z, which are transformed into the principal axes.

will rotate into the positive y axis. The composite matrix is given by

$$\begin{bmatrix} r_{1x} & r_{2x} & r_{3x} & 0 \\ r_{1y} & r_{2y} & r_{3y} & 0 \\ r_{1z} & r_{2z} & r_{3z} & 0 \\ 0 & 0 & 0 & 1 \end{bmatrix} \cdot T(-x_1, -y_1, -z_1) = R \cdot T, \tag{5.66}$$

where R and T are as in Eq. (5.61). Figure 5.20 shows the individual vectors R_x, R_y, and R_z.

Let's consider another example. Figure 5.21 shows an airplane defined in the x_p, y_p, z_p coordinate system and centered at the origin. We want to transform the airplane so that it heads in the direction given by the vector DOF (direction of flight), is centered at P, and is not banked, as shown in Fig. 5.22. The transformation to do this consists of a rotation to head the airplane in the proper direction, followed by a translation from the origin to P. To find the rotation matrix, we just determine in what direction each of the x_p, y_p, and z_p axes is heading in Fig. 5.22, make sure the directions are normalized, and use them as column vectors in a rotation matrix.

The z_p axis must be transformed to the DOF direction, and the x_p axis must be transformed into a horizontal vector perpendicular to DOF—that is, in the direction of $y \times DOF$, the cross-product of y and DOF. The y_p direction is given by $z_p \times x_p = DOF \times (y \times$

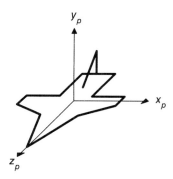

Fig. 5.21 An airplane in the (x_p, y_p, z_p) coordinate system.

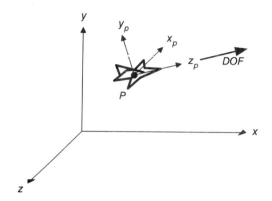

Fig. 5.22 The airplane of Figure 5.21 positioned at point P, and headed in direction *DOF*.

DOF), the cross-product of z_p and x_p; hence, the three columns of the rotation matrix are the normalized vectors $|y \times DOF|$, $|DOF \times (y \times DOF)|$, and $|DOF|$:

$$
R = \begin{bmatrix} |y \times DOF| & |DOF \times (y \times DOF)| & |DOF| & 0 \\ & & & 0 \\ & & & 0 \\ 0 & 0 & 0 & 1 \end{bmatrix}. \tag{5.67}
$$

The situation if *DOF* is in the direction of the y axis is degenerate, because there is an infinite set of possible vectors for the horizontal vector. This degeneracy is reflected in the algebra, because the cross-products $y \times DOF$ and $DOF \times (y \times DOF)$ are zero. In this special case, R is not a rotation matrix.

5.8   TRANSFORMATIONS AS A CHANGE IN COORDINATE SYSTEM

We have been discussing transforming a set of points belonging to an object into another set of points, when both sets are in the same coordinate system. With this approach, the coordinate system stays unaltered and the object is transformed with respect to the origin of the coordinate system. An alternative but equivalent way of thinking about a transformation is as a change of coordinate systems. This view is useful when multiple objects, each defined in its own local coordinate system, are combined, and we wish to express these objects' coordinates in a single, global coordinate system. This will be the case in Chapter 7.

Let us define $M_{i \leftarrow j}$ as the transformation that converts the representation of a point in coordinate system j into its representation in coordinate system i.

We define $P^{(i)}$ as the representation of a point in coordinate system i, $P^{(j)}$ as the representation of the point in system j, and $P^{(k)}$ as the representation of the point in coordinate system k; then,

$$
P^{(i)} = M_{i \leftarrow j} \cdot P^{(j)} \text{ and } P^{(j)} = M_{j \leftarrow k} \cdot P^{(k)}. \tag{5.68}
$$

Substituting, we obtain

$$P^{(i)} = M_{i \leftarrow j} \cdot P^{(j)} = M_{i \leftarrow j} \cdot M_{j \leftarrow k} \cdot P^{(k)} = M_{i \leftarrow k} \cdot P^{(k)}, \qquad (5.69)$$

so

$$M_{i \leftarrow k} = M_{i \leftarrow j} \cdot M_{j \leftarrow k}. \qquad (5.70)$$

Figure 5.23 shows four different coordinate systems. We see by inspection that the transformation from coordinate system 2 to 1 is $M_{1 \leftarrow 2} = T(4, 2)$ (finding this transformation by inspection is not always simple—see the Appendix). Similarly, $M_{2 \leftarrow 3} = T(2, 3) \cdot S(0.5, 0.5)$ and $M_{3 \leftarrow 4} = T(6.7, 1.8) \cdot R(-45°)$. Then $M_{1 \leftarrow 3} = M_{1 \leftarrow 2} \cdot M_{2 \leftarrow 3} = T(4, 2) \cdot T(2, 3) \cdot S(0.5, 0.5)$. The figure also shows a point that is $P^{(1)} = (10, 8)$, $P^{(2)} = (6, 6)$, $P^{(3)} = (8, 6)$, and $P^{(4)} = (4, 2)$ in coordinate systems 1 through 4, respectively. It is easy to verify that $P^{(i)} = M_{i \leftarrow j} \cdot P^{(j)}$ for $1 \leq i, j \leq 4$.

We also notice that $M_{i \leftarrow j} = M_{j \leftarrow i}^{-1}$. Thus, $M_{2 \leftarrow 1} = M_{1 \leftarrow 2}^{-1} = T(-4, -2)$. Because $M_{1 \leftarrow 3} = M_{1 \leftarrow 2} \cdot M_{2 \leftarrow 3}$, $M_{1 \leftarrow 3}^{-1} = M_{2 \leftarrow 3}^{-1} \cdot M_{1 \leftarrow 2}^{-1} = M_{3 \leftarrow 2} \cdot M_{2 \leftarrow 1}$.

In Section 5.6, we discussed left- and right-handed coordinate systems. The matrix that converts from points represented in one to points represented in the other is its own inverse, and is

$$M_{R \leftarrow L} = M_{L \leftarrow R} = \begin{bmatrix} 1 & 0 & 0 & 0 \\ 0 & 1 & 0 & 0 \\ 0 & 0 & -1 & 0 \\ 0 & 0 & 0 & 1 \end{bmatrix}. \qquad (5.71)$$

The approach used in previous sections—defining all objects in the world-coordinate system, then transforming them to the desired place—implies the somewhat unrealistic notion that all objects are initially defined on top of one another in the same world-coordinate system. It is more natural to think of each object as being defined in its own coordinate system and then being scaled, rotated, and translated by redefinition of its coordinates in the new world-coordinate system. In this second point of view, one thinks naturally of separate pieces of paper, each with an object on it, being shrunk or stretched, rotated or placed on the world-coordinate plane. One can also, of course, imagine that the

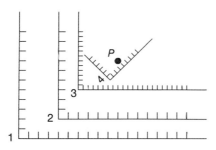

Fig. 5.23 The point P and coordinate systems 1, 2, 3, and 4.

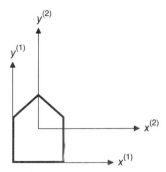

Fig. 5.24 The house and two coordinate systems. Coordinates of points on the house can be represented in either coordinate system.

plane is being shrunk or stretched, tilted, or slid relative to each piece of paper. Mathematically, all these views are identical.

Consider the simple case of translating the set of points that define the house shown in Fig. 5.8 to the origin. This transformation is $T(-x_1, -y_1)$. Labeling the two coordinate systems as in Fig. 5.24, we see that the transformation that maps coordinate system 1 into 2—that is, $M_{2 \leftarrow 1}$—is $T(x_1, y_1)$, which is just $T(-x_1, -y_1)^{-1}$. Indeed, the general rule is that the transformation that transforms a set of points in a single coordinate system is just the inverse of the corresponding transformation to change the coordinate system in which a point is represented. This relation can be seen in Fig. 5.25, which is derived directly from Fig. 5.9. The transformation for the points represented in a single coordinate system is just

$$T(x_2, y_2) \cdot R(\theta) \cdot S(s_x, s_y) \cdot T(-x_1, -y_1). \tag{5.32}$$

In Fig. 5.25, the coordinate-system transformation is just

$$\begin{aligned} M_{5 \leftarrow 1} &= M_{5 \leftarrow 4} \, M_{4 \leftarrow 3} \, M_{3 \leftarrow 2} \, M_{2 \leftarrow 1} \\ &= (T(x_2, y_2) \cdot R(\theta) \cdot S(s_x, s_y) \cdot T(-x_1, -y_1))^{-1} \\ &= T(x_1, y_1) \cdot S(s_x^{-1}, s_y^{-1}) \cdot R(-\theta) \cdot T(-x_2, -y_2), \end{aligned} \tag{5.72}$$

so that

$$P^{(5)} = M_{5 \leftarrow 1} P^{(1)} = T(x_1, y_1) \cdot S(s_x^{-1}, s_y^{-1}) \cdot R(-\theta) \cdot T(-x_2, -y_2) \cdot P^{(1)}. \tag{5.73}$$

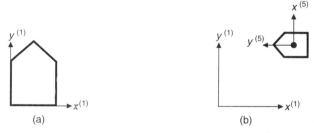

(a)   (b)

Fig. 5.25 The original house (a) in its coordinate system and the transformed house (b) in its coordinate system with respect to the original coordinate system.

An important question related to changing coordinate systems is changing transformations. Suppose $Q^{(j)}$ is a transformation in coordinate system j. It might, for example, be one of the composite transformations derived in previous sections. Suppose we wanted to find the transformation $Q^{(i)}$ in coordinate system i that could be applied to points $P^{(i)}$ in system i and produce exactly the same results as though $Q^{(j)}$ were applied to the corresponding points $P^{(j)}$ in system j. This equality is represented by $Q^{(i)} \cdot P^{(i)} = M_{i \leftarrow j} \cdot Q^{(j)} \cdot P^{(j)}$. Substituting $P^{(i)} = M_{i \leftarrow j} \cdot P^{(j)}$, this expression becomes $Q^{(i)} \cdot M_{i \leftarrow j} \cdot P^{(j)} = M_{i \leftarrow j} \cdot Q^{(j)} \cdot P^{(j)}$. Simplifying, we have $Q^{(i)} = M_{i \leftarrow j} \cdot Q^{(j)} \cdot M_{i \leftarrow j}^{-1}$.

The change-of-coordinate-system point of view is useful when additional information for subobjects is specified in the latters' own local coordinate systems. For example, if the front wheel of the tricycle in Fig. 5.26 is made to rotate about its z_{wh} coordinate, all wheels must be rotated appropriately, and we need to know how the tricycle as a whole moves in the world-coordinate system. This problem is complex because several successive changes of coordinate systems occur. First, the tricycle and front-wheel coordinate systems have initial positions in the world-coordinate system. As the bike moves forward, the front wheel rotates about the z axis of the wheel-coordinate system, and simultaneously the wheel- and tricycle-coordinate systems move relative to the world-coordinate system. The wheel- and tricycle-coordinate systems are related to the world-coordinate system by time-varying translations in x and z plus a rotation about y. The tricycle- and wheel-coordinate systems are related to each other by a time-varying rotation about y as the handlebars are turned. (The tricycle-coordinate system is fixed to the frame, not to the handlebars.)

To make the problem a bit easier, we assume that the wheel and tricycle axes are parallel to the world-coordinate axes and that the wheel moves in a straight line parallel to the world-coordinate x axis. As the wheel rotates by an angle α, a point P on the wheel rotates through the distance αr, where r is the radius of the wheel. Since the wheel is on the ground, the tricycle moves forward αr units. Therefore, the rim point P on the wheel moves and rotates with respect to the initial wheel-coordinate system with a net effect of translation by αr and rotation by α. Its new coordinates P' in the original wheel-coordinate system are thus

$$P'^{(wh)} = T(\alpha r, 0, 0) \cdot R_z(\alpha) \cdot P^{(wh)}, \tag{5.74}$$

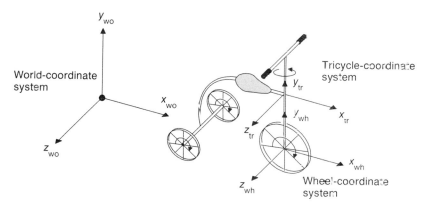

Fig. 5.26 A stylized tricycle with three coordinate systems.

and its coordinates in the new (translated) wheel-coordinate system are given by just the rotation

$$P'^{(\text{wh}')} = R_z(\alpha) \cdot P^{(\text{wh})}. \tag{5.75}$$

To find the points $P^{(\text{wo})}$ and $P'^{(\text{wo})}$ in the world-coordinate system, we transform from the wheel to the world-coordinate system:

$$P^{(\text{wo})} = M_{\text{wo}\leftarrow\text{wh}} \cdot P^{(\text{wh})} = M_{\text{wo}\leftarrow\text{tr}} \cdot M_{\text{tr}\leftarrow\text{wh}} \cdot P^{(\text{wh})}. \tag{5.76}$$

$M_{\text{wo}\leftarrow\text{tr}}$ and $M_{\text{tr}\leftarrow\text{wh}}$ are translations given by the initial positions of the tricycle and wheel. $P'^{(\text{wo})}$ is computed with Eqs. (5.74) and (5.76):

$$P'^{(\text{wo})} = M_{\text{wo}\leftarrow\text{wh}} \cdot P'^{(\text{wh})} = M_{\text{wo}\leftarrow\text{wh}} \cdot T(\alpha r, 0, 0) \cdot R_z(\alpha) \cdot P^{(\text{wh})}. \tag{5.77}$$

Alternatively, we recognize that $M_{\text{wo}\leftarrow\text{wh}}$ has been changed to $M_{\text{wo}\leftarrow\text{wh}'}$ by the translation of the wheel-coordinate system, and get the same result as Eq. (5.77), but in a different way:

$$P'^{(\text{wo})} = M_{\text{wo}\leftarrow\text{wh}'} \cdot P'^{(\text{wh}')} = (M_{\text{wo}\leftarrow\text{wh}} \cdot M_{\text{wh}\leftarrow\text{wh}'}) \cdot (R_z(\alpha) \cdot P^{\text{wh}}). \tag{5.78}$$

In general, then, we derive the new $M_{\text{wo}\leftarrow\text{wh}'}$ and $M_{\text{tr}'\leftarrow\text{wh}'}$ from their previous values by applying the appropriate transformations from the equations of motion of the tricycle parts. We then apply these updated transformations to updated points in local coordinate systems and derive the equivalent points in world-coordinate systems. We leave to the reader the problem of turning the tricycle's front wheel to change direction and of computing rotation angles for the rear wheels, using the wheels' radius and the tricycle's trajectory.

EXERCISES

5.1 Prove that we can transform a line by transforming its endpoints and then constructing a new line between the transformed endpoints.

5.2 Prove that two successive 2D rotations are additive: $R(\theta_1) \cdot R(\theta_2) = R(\theta_1 + \theta_2)$.

5.3 Prove that 2D rotation and scaling commute if $s_x = s_y$ or if $\theta = n\pi$ for integral n, and that otherwise they do not.

5.4 Find an expression relating the accumulated error in Eq. (5.37) to θ and the number of incremental rotations performed. Do the same for Eq. (5.38).

5.5 Write a program for your favorite computer to perform 2D incremental rotation. How much time is needed per endpoint? Compare this value to the time needed per endpoint for absolute 2D rotation.

5.6 A drawing consisting of N endpoints is to be rotated dynamically about a single axis. Multiplication on your computer takes time t_m; addition takes time t_a. Write expressions for the time needed to rotate the N points by using Eqs. (5.37), (5.38), and (5.7). Ignore control steps. Now evaluate the expressions with N as a variable, using the actual instruction times for your computer.

5.7 Apply the transformations developed in Section 5.7 to the points P_1, P_2, and P_3 to verify that these points transform as intended.

5.8 Rework Section 5.7, assuming that $|P_1P_2| = 1$, $|P_1P_3| = 1$ and that direction cosines of P_1P_2 and P_1P_3 are given (direction cosines of a line are the cosines of the angles between the line and the x, y, and z axes). For a line from the origin to (x, y, z), the direction cosines are $(x/d, y/d, z/d)$, where d is the length of the line.

5.9 Another reason that homogeneous coordinates are attractive is that 3D points at infinity in Cartesian coordinates can be represented explicitly in homogeneous coordinates. How can this be done?

5.10 Show that Eqs. (5.61) and (5.66) are equivalent.

5.11 Given a unit cube with one corner at $(0, 0, 0)$ and the opposite corner at $(1, 1, 1)$, derive the transformations necessary to rotate the cube by θ degrees about the main diagonal (from $(0, 0, 0)$ to $(1, 1, 1)$) in the counterclockwise direction when looking along the diagonal toward the origin.

5.12 Suppose that the base of the window is rotated at an angle θ from the x axis, as in the Core System [GSPC79]. What is the window-to-viewport mapping? Verify your answer by applying the transformation to each corner of the window, to see that these corners are transformed to the appropriate corners of the viewport.

5.13 Consider a line from the origin of a right-handed coordinate system to the point $P(x, y, z)$. Find the transformation matrices needed to rotate the line into the positive z axis in three different ways, and show by algebraic manipulation that, in each case, the P does go to the z axis. For each method, calculate the sines and cosines of the angles of rotation.

  a. Rotate about the x axis into the (x, y) plane, then rotate about the y axis into the z axis.
  b. Rotate about the y axis into the (y, z) plane, then rotate about the x axis into the z axis.
  c. Rotate about the z axis into the (x, z) plane, then rotate about the y axis into the z axis.

5.14 An object is to be scaled by a factor S in the direction whose direction cosines are (α, β, γ). Derive the transformation matrix.

5.15 Find the 4×4 transformation matrix that rotates by an angle θ about an arbitrary direction given by the direction vector $U = (u_x, u_y, u_z)$. Do this by composing the transformation matrix that rotates U into the z axis (call this M) with a rotation by $R_z(\theta)$, then composing this result with M^{-1}. The result should be

$$
\begin{bmatrix}
u_x^2 + \cos\theta(1 - u_x^2) & u_x u_y(1 - \cos\theta) - u_z\sin\theta & u_z u_x(1 - \cos\theta) + u_y\sin\theta & 0 \\
u_x u_y(1 - \cos\theta) + u_z\sin\theta & u_y^2 + \cos\theta(1 - u_y^2) & u_y u_z(1 - \cos\theta) - u_x\sin\theta & 0 \\
u_z u_x(1 - \cos\theta) - u_y\sin\theta & u_y u_z(1 - \cos\theta) + u_x\sin\theta & u_z^2 + \cos\theta(1 - u_z^2) & 0 \\
0 & 0 & 0 & 1
\end{bmatrix} .(5.79)
$$

Verify that, if U is a principal axis, the matrix reduces to R_x, R_y, or R_z. See [FAUX79] for a derivation based on vector operations. Note that negating both U and θ leave the result unchanged. Explain why this is true.

5.16 Prove the properties of $R(\theta)$ described at the end of Section 5.2.

5.17 Extend the incremental rotation discussed in Section 5.4 to 3D, forming a composite operation for rotation about an arbitrary axis.

5.18 Suppose the lowest rate at which an object can be rotated without being annoyingly slow is $360°$ over 30 seconds. Suppose also that, to be smooth, the rotation must be in steps of at most $4°$. Use the results from Exercise 5.6 to determine how many points can be rotated using absolute rotation, and using incremental rotation.

5.19 Suppose that you are creating an interface to rotate an object by applying many incremental rotations, using "Spin X," "Spin Y" and "Spin Z" buttons. Each time one of these buttons is pressed, the current rotation matrix is replaced by its product with a matrix that rotates slightly around the specified axis. Although this idea is mathematically correct, in practice cumulative floating-point roundoff errors will result that will cause points to be transformed incorrectly. Show that by applying the Gram-Schmidt process to the columns of the matrix (see Section A.3.6) you can convert the new matrix back to an orthonormal matrix. Also explain why, if it is already orthonormal, applying this process will not change it.

6

Viewing
in 3D

The 3D viewing process is inherently more complex than is the 2D viewing process. In 2D, we simply specify a window on the 2D world and a viewport on the 2D view surface. Conceptually, objects in the world are clipped against the window and are then transformed into the viewport for display. The extra complexity of 3D viewing is caused in part by the added dimension and in part by the fact that display devices are only 2D.

The solution to the mismatch between 3D objects and 2D displays is accomplished by introducing *projections*, which transform 3D objects onto a 2D projection plane. Much of this chapter is devoted to projections: what they are, their mathematics, and how they are used in a current graphics subroutine package, PHIGS [ANSI88]. Their use is also discussed further in Chapter 7.

In 3D viewing, we specify a *view volume* in the world, a projection onto a projection plane, and a viewport on the view surface. Conceptually, objects in the 3D world are clipped against the 3D view volume and are then projected. The contents of the projection of the view volume onto the projection plane, called the *window*, are then transformed (mapped) into the viewport for display. Figure 6.1 shows this conceptual model of the 3D viewing process, which is the model presented to the users of numerous 3D graphics subroutine packages. Just as with 2D viewing, a variety of strategies can be used to implement the viewing process. The strategies need not be identical to the conceptual model, so long as the results are those defined by the model. A typical implementation strategy for wire-frame line drawings is described in Section 6.5. For graphics systems that perform visible-surface determination and shading, a somewhat different pipeline, discussed in Chapter 16, is used.

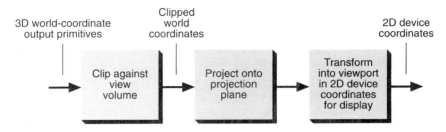

Fig. 6.1 Conceptual model of the 3D viewing process.

6.1 PROJECTIONS

In general, projections transform points in a coordinate system of dimension n into points in a coordinate system of dimension less than n. In fact, computer graphics has long been used for studying n-dimensional objects by projecting them into 2D for viewing [NOLL67]. Here, we shall limit ourselves to the projection from 3D to 2D. The projection of a 3D object is defined by straight projection rays (called *projectors*) emanating from a *center of projection*, passing through each point of the object, and intersecting a *projection plane* to form the projection. Figure 6.2 shows two different projections of the same line. Fortunately, the projection of a line is itself a line, so only line endpoints need actually to be projected.

The class of projections we deal with here is known as *planar geometric projections* because the projection is onto a plane rather than some curved surface and uses straight rather than curved projectors. Many cartographic projections are either nonplanar or nongeometric. Similarly, the Omnimax film format requires a nongeometric projection [MAX82].

Planar geometric projections, hereafter referred to simply as *projections,* can be divided into two basic classes: *perspective* and *parallel*. The distinction is in the relation of the center of projection to the projection plane. If the distance from the one to the other is finite, then the projection is perspective: if the distance is infinite, the projection is parallel.

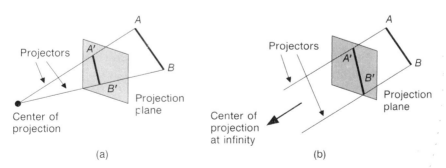

Fig. 6.2 (a) Line *AB* and its perspective projection *A'B'*. (b) Line *AB* and its parallel projection *A'B'*. Projectors *AA'* and *BB'* are parallel.

Figure 6.2 illustrates these two cases. The parallel projection is so named because, with the center of projection infinitely distant, the projectors are parallel. When defining a perspective projection, we explicitly specify its *center of projection*; for a parallel projection, we give its *direction of projection*. The center of projection, being a point, has homogeneous coordinates of the form $(x, y, z, 1)$. Since the direction of projection is a vector (i.e., a difference between points), it can be computed by subtracting two points $d = (x, y, z, 1) - (x', y', z', 1) = (a, b, c, 0)$. Thus, *directions* and *points at infinity* correspond in a natural way. A perspective projection whose center is a point at infinity becomes a parallel projection.

The visual effect of a perspective projection is similar to that of photographic systems and of the human visual system, and is known as *perspective foreshortening*: The size of the perspective projection of an object varies inversely with the distance of that object from the center of projection. Thus, although the perspective projection of objects tend to look realistic, it is not particularly useful for recording the exact shape and measurements of the objects; distances cannot be taken from the projection, angles are preserved only on those faces of the object parallel to the projection plane, and parallel lines do not in general project as parallel lines.

The parallel projection is a less realistic view because perspective foreshortening is lacking, although there can be different constant foreshortenings along each axis. The projection can be used for exact measurements and parallel lines do remain parallel. As with the perspective projection, angles are preserved only on faces of the object parallel to the projection plane.

The different types of perspective and parallel projections are discussed and illustrated at length in the comprehensive paper by Carlbom and Paciorek [CARL78]. In the following two subsections, we summarize the basic definitions and characteristics of the more commonly used projections; we then move on in Section 6.2 to understand how the projections are actually specified to PHIGS.

6.1.1 Perspective Projections

The perspective projections of any set of parallel lines that are not parallel to the projection plane converge to a *vanishing point*. In 3D, the parallel lines meet only at infinity, so the vanishing point can be thought of as the projection of a point at infinity. There is of course an infinity of vanishing points, one for each of the infinity of directions in which a line can be oriented.

If the set of lines is parallel to one of the three principal axes, the vanishing point is called an *axis vanishing point*. There are at most three such points, corresponding to the number of principal axes cut by the projection plane. For example, if the projection plane cuts only the z axis (and is therefore normal to it), only the z axis has a principal vanishing point, because lines parallel to either the y or x axes are also parallel to the projection plane and have no vanishing point.

Perspective projections are categorized by their number of principal vanishing points and therefore by the number of axes the projection plane cuts. Figure 6.3 shows two different one-point perspective projections of a cube. It is clear that they are one-point

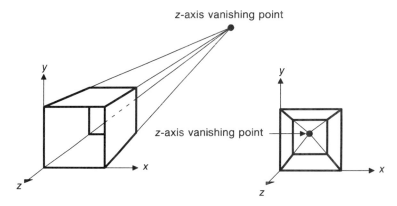

Fig. 6.3 One-point perspective projections of a cube onto a plane cutting the z axis, showing vanishing point of lines perpendicular to projection plane.

projections because lines parallel to the x and y axes do not converge; only lines parallel to the z axis do so. Figure 6.4 shows the construction of a one-point perspective with some of the projectors and with the projection plane cutting only the z axis.

Figure 6.5 shows the construction of a two-point perspective. Notice that lines parallel to the y axis do not converge in the projection. Two-point perspective is commonly used in architectural, engineering, industrial design, and in advertising drawings. Three-point perspectives are used less frequently, since they add little realism beyond that afforded by the two-point perspective.

6.1.2 Parallel Projections

Parallel projections are categorized into two types, depending on the relation between the direction of projection and the normal to the projection plane. In *orthographic* parallel

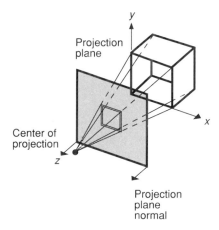

Fig. 6.4 Construction of one-point perspective projection of cube onto plane cutting the z axis. Projection-plane normal is parallel to z axis. (Adapted from [CARL78], Association for Computing Machinery, Inc.; used by permission.)

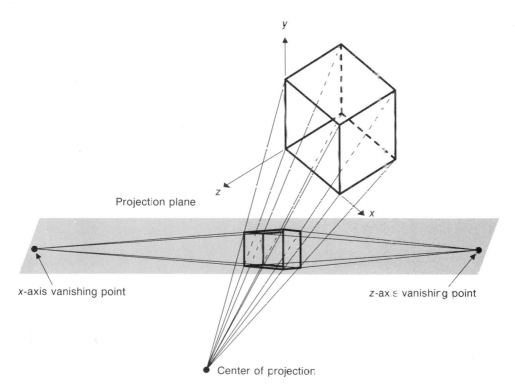

Fig. 6.5 Two-point perspective projection of a cube. The projection plane cuts the x and z axes.

projections, these directions are the same (or the reverse of each other), so the direction of projection is normal to the projection plane. For the *oblique* parallel projection, they are not.

The most common types of orthographic projections are the *front-elevation*, *top-elevation* (also called *plan-elevation*), and *side-elevation* projections. In all these, the projection plane is perpendicular to a principal axis, which is therefore the direction of projection. Figure 6.6 shows the construction of these three projections; they are often used in engineering drawings to depict machine parts, assemblies, and buildings, because distances and angles can be measured from them. Since each depicts only one face of an object, however, the 3D nature of the projected object can be difficult to deduce, even if several projections of the same object are studied simultaneously.

Axonometric orthographic projections use projection planes that are not normal to a principal axis and therefore show several faces of an object at once. They resemble the perspective projection in this way, but differ in that the foreshortening is uniform rather than being related to the distance from the center of projection. Parallelism of lines is preserved but angles are not, while distances can be measured along each principal axis (in general, with different scale factors).

The *isometric projection* is a commonly used axonometric projection. The projection-plane normal (and therefore the direction of projection) makes equal angles with each principal axis. If the projection-plane normal is (d_x, d_y, d_z), then we require that $|d_x| = |d_y|$

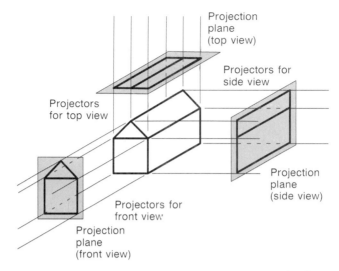

Fig. 6.6 Construction of three orthographic projections.

$= |d_z|$ or $\pm d_x = \pm d_y = \pm d_z$. There are just eight directions (one in each octant) that satisfy this condition. Figure 6.7 shows the construction of an isometric projection along one such direction, $(1, -1, -1)$.

The isometric projection has the useful property that all three principal axes are equally foreshortened, allowing measurements along the axes to be made to the same scale (hence the name: *iso* for equal, *metric* for measure). In addition, the principal axes project so as to make equal angles one with another, as shown in Fig. 6.8.

Oblique projections, the second class of parallel projections, differ from orthographic projections in that the projection-plane normal and the direction of projection differ.

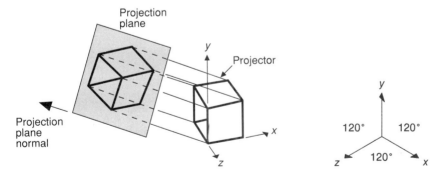

Fig. 6.7 Construction of an isometric projection of a unit cube. (Adapted from [CARL78], Association for Computing Machinery, Inc.; used by permission.)

Fig. 6.8 Isometric projection of unit vectors, with direction of projection (1, 1, 1).

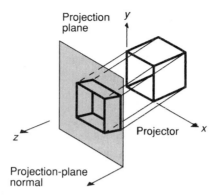

Fig. 6.9 Construction of oblique projection. (Adapted from [CARL 78], Association for Computing Machinery, Inc.; used by permission.)

Oblique projections combine properties of the front, top, and side orthographic projections with those of the axonometric projection: the projection plane is normal to a principal axis, so the projection of the face of the object parallel to this plane allows measurement of angles and distances. Other faces of the object project also, allowing distances along principal axes, but not angles, to be measured. Oblique projections are widely, although not exclusively, used in this text because of these properties and because they are easy to draw. Figure 6.9 shows the construction of an oblique projection. Notice that the projection-plane normal and the direction of projection are not the same.

Two frequently used oblique projections are the *cavalier* and the *cabinet*. For the cavalier projection, the direction of projection makes a 45° angle with the projection plane. As a result, the projection of a line perpendicular to the projection plane has the same length as the line itself; that is, there is no foreshortening. Figure 6.10 shows several cavalier projections of the unit cube onto the (x, y) plane; the receding lines are the projections of the cube edges that are perpendicular to the (x, y) plane, and they form an angle α to the horizontal. This angle is typically 30° or 45°.

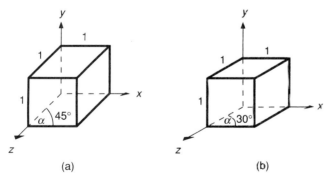

Fig. 6.10 Cavalier projection of the unit cube onto the $z = 0$ plane. All edges project at unit length. In (a), the direction of projection is $(\sqrt{2}/2, \sqrt{2}/2, -1)$; in (b), it is $(\sqrt{3}/2, 1/2, -1)$.

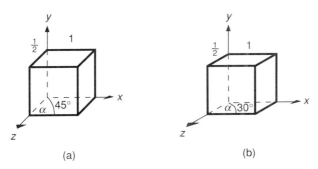

Fig. 6.11 Cabinet projection of the unit cube onto the $z = 0$ plane. Edges parallel to the x and y axes project at unit length. In (a), the direction of projection is $(\sqrt{2}/4, \sqrt{2}/4, -1)$; in (b), it is $(\sqrt{3}/4, 1/4, -1)$.

Cabinet projections, such as those in Fig. 6.11, have a direction of projection that makes an angle of $\arctan(2) = 63.4°$ with the projection plane, so lines perpendicular to the projection plane project at one-half their actual length. Cabinet projections are a bit more realistic than cavalier ones are, since the foreshortening by one-half is more in keeping with our other visual experiences.

Figure 6.12 helps to explain the angles made by projectors with the projection plane for cabinet and cavalier projections. The (x, y) plane is the projection plane and the point P' is the projection of $(0, 0, 1)$ onto the projection plane. The angle α and length l are the same as are used in Figs. 6.10 and 6.11, and we can control them by varying the direction of projection (l is the length at which the z-axis unit vector projects onto the (x, y) plane; α is the angle the projection makes with the x axis). Designating the direction of projection as $(dx, dy, -1)$, we see from Fig. 6.12 that $dx = l\cos\alpha$ and $dy = l\sin\alpha$. Given a desired l and α, the direction of projection is $(l\cos\alpha, l\sin\alpha, -1)$.

Figure 6.13 shows the logical relationships among the various types of projections. The common thread uniting them all is that they involve a projection plane and either a center of projection for the perspective projection, or a direction of projection for the parallel projection. We can unify the parallel and perspective cases further by thinking of the center of projection as defined by the direction to the center of projection from some reference

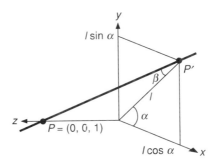

Fig. 6.12 Oblique parallel projection of $P = (0, 0, 1)$ onto $P' = (l\cos\alpha, l\sin\beta, 0)$. The direction of projection is $P' - P = (l\cos\alpha, l\sin\beta, -1)$.

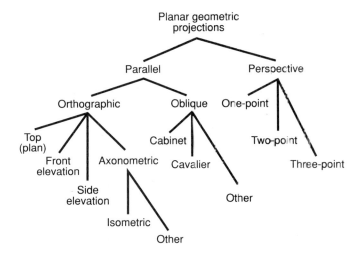

Fig. 6.13 The subclasses of planar geometric projections. *Plan view* is another term for a top view. *Front* and *side* are often used without the term *elevation*.

point, plus the distance to the reference point. When this distance increases to infinity, the projection becomes a parallel projection. Hence, we can also say that the common thread uniting these projections is that they involve a projection plane, a direction to the center of projection, and a distance to the center of projection.

In the next section, we consider how to integrate these various types of projections into the 3D viewing process.

6.2 SPECIFYING AN ARBITRARY 3D VIEW

As suggested by Fig. 6.1, 3D viewing involves not just a projection but also a view volume against which the 3D world is clipped. The projection and view volume together provide all the information needed to clip and project into 2D space. Then, the 2D transformation into physical device coordinates is straightforward. We now build on the planar-geometric-projection concepts introduced in the preceding section to show how to specify a view volume. The viewing approach and terminology presented here is that used in PHIGS.

The projection plane, henceforth called the *view plane* to be consistent with the graphics literature, is defined by a point on the plane called the *view reference point* (VRP) and a normal to the plane called the *view-plane normal* (VPN).[1] The view plane may be anywhere with respect to the world objects to be projected: it may be in front of, cut through, or be behind the objects.

Given the view plane, a window on the view plane is needed. The window's role is similar to that of a 2D window: its contents are mapped into the viewport, and any part of

---

[1] PHIGS has an additional variable, the view-plane distance (VPD): the view plane can be a distance VPD from the VRP. VPD is positive in the direction of VPN. See Exercise 6.22.

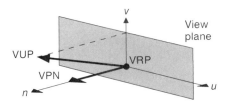

Fig. 6.14 The view plane is defined by VPN and VRP; the *v* axis is defined by the projection of VUP along VPN onto the view plane. The *u* axis forms the right-handed viewing reference-coordinate system with VPN and *v*.

the 3D world that projects onto the view plane outside of the window is not displayed. We shall see that the window also plays an important role in defining the view volume.

To define a window on the view plane, we need some means of specifying minimum and maximum window coordinates along two orthogonal axes. These axes are part of the 3D *viewing-reference coordinate* (VRC) system. The origin of the VRC system is the VRP. One axis of the VRC is VPN; this axis is called the *n* axis. A second axis of the VRC is found from the *view up vector* (VUP), which determines the *v*-axis direction on the view plane. The *v* axis is defined such that the projection of VUP parallel to VPN onto the view plane is coincident with the *v* axis. The *u*-axis direction is defined such that *u*, *v*, and *n* form a right-handed coordinate system, as in Fig. 6.14. The VRP and the two direction vectors VPN and VUP are specified in the right-handed world-coordinate system. (Some graphics packages use the *y* axis as VUP, but this is too restrictive and fails if VPN is parallel to the *y* axis, in which case VUP would be undefined.)

With the VRC system defined, the window's minimum and maximum *u* and *v* values can be defined, as in Fig. 6.15. This figure illustrates that the window need not be symmetrical about the view reference point, and explicitly shows the center of the window, CW.

The center of projection and direction of projection (DOP) are defined by a *projection reference point* (PRP) plus an indicator of the projection type. If the projection type is perspective, then PRP is the center of projection. If the projection type is parallel, then the DOP is from the PRP to CW. The CW is in general *not* the VRP, which need not even be within the window bounds.

The PRP is specified in the VRC system, not in the world-coordinate system; thus, the position of the PRP relative to the VRP does not change as VUP or VRP are moved. The

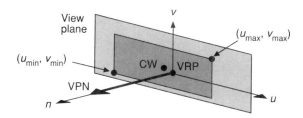

Fig. 6.15 The view reference-coordinate system (VRC) is a right-handed system made up of the *u*, *v*, and *n* axes. The *n* axis is always the VPN. CW is the center of the window.

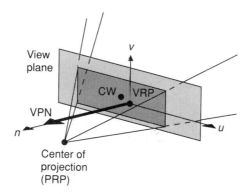

Fig. 6.16 The semi-infinite pyramid view volume for perspective projection. CW is the center of the window.

advantage of this is that the programmer can specify the direction of projection required, for example, by a cavalier projection, and then change VPN and VUP (hence changing VRC), without having to recalculate the PRP needed to maintain the desired projection. On the other hand, moving the PRP about to get different views of an object may be more difficult.

The *view volume* bounds that portion of the world that is to be clipped out and projected onto the view plane. For a perspective projection, the view volume is the semi-infinite pyramid with apex at the PRP and edges passing through the corners of the window. Figure 6.16 shows a perspective-projection view volume. Positions behind the center of projection are not included in the view volume and thus are not projected. In reality, of course, our eyes see an irregularly shaped conelike view volume. However, a pyramidal view volume is mathematically more tractable, and is consistent with the concept of a rectangular viewport.

For parallel projections, the view volume is an infinite parallelepiped with sides parallel to the direction of projection, which is the direction from the PRP to the center of the window. Figures 6.17 and 6.18 show parallel-projection view volumes and their

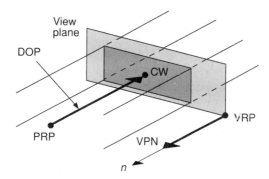

Fig. 6.17 Infinite parallelepiped view volume of parallel orthographic projection. The VPN and direction of projection (DOP) are parallel. DOP is the vector from PRP to CW, and is parallel to the VPN.

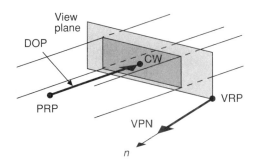

Fig. 6.18 Infinite parallelepiped view volume of oblique orthographic projection. The direction of projection (DOP) is not parallel to the VPN.

relation to the view plane, window, and PRP. For orthographic parallel projections, but not for oblique parallel projections, the sides of the view volume are normal to the view plane.

At times, we might want the view volume to be finite, in order to limit the number of output primitives projected onto the view plane. Figures 6.19, 6.20, and 6.21 show how the view volume is made finite with a *front clipping plane* and *back clipping plane*.These planes, sometimes called the *hither* and *yon* planes, are parallel to the view plane; their normal is the VPN. The planes are specified by the signed quantities *front distance* (F) and *back distance* (B) relative to the view reference point and along the VPN, with positive distances in the direction of the VPN. For the view volume to be positive, the front distance must be algebraically greater than the back distance.

Limiting the view volume in this way can be useful in order to eliminate extraneous objects and to allow the user to concentrate on a particular portion of the world. Dynamic modification of either the front or rear distances can give the viewer a good sense of the spatial relationships between different parts of the object as these parts appear and disappear from view (see Chapter 14). For perspective projections, there is an additional motivation. An object very distant from the center of projection projects onto the view surface as a

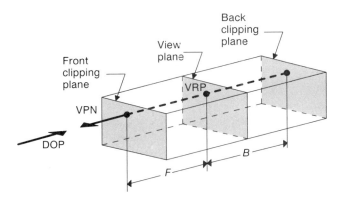

Fig. 6.19 Truncated view volume for an orthographic parallel projection. DOP is the direction of projection.

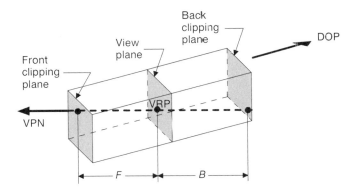

Fig. 6.20 Truncated view volume for oblique parallel projection showing VPN oblique to direction of projection (DOP); VPN is also normal to the front and back clipping planes.

"blob" of no distinguishable form. In displaying such an object on a plotter, the pen can wear through the paper; on a vector display, the CRT phosphor can be burned by the electron beam; and on a film recorder, the high concentration of light causes a fuzzy white area to appear. Also, an object very near the center of projection may extend across the window like so many disconnected pick-up sticks, with no discernible structure. Specifying the view volume appropriately can eliminate such problems.

How are the contents of the view volume mapped onto the display surface? First, consider the unit cube extending from 0 to 1 in each of the three dimensions of *normalized projection coordinates* (NPC). The view volume is transformed into the rectangular solid of NPC, which extends from x_{min} to x_{max} along the x axis, from y_{min} to y_{max} along the y axis, and from z_{min} to z_{max} along the z axis. The front clipping plane becomes the z_{max} plane and the back clipping plane becomes the z_{min} plane. Similarly, the u_{min} side of the view volume becomes the x_{min} plane and the u_{max} side becomes the x_{max} plane. Finally, the v_{min} side of the view volume becomes the y_{min} plane and the v_{max} side becomes the y_{max} plane. This rectangular solid portion of NPC, called a *3D viewport*, is within the unit cube.

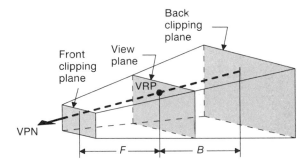

Fig. 6.21 Truncated view volume for perspective projection.

The $z = 1$ face of this unit cube, in turn, is mapped into the largest square that can be inscribed on the display. To create a wire-frame display of the contents of the 3D viewport (which are the contents of the view volume), the z-component of each output primitive is simply discarded, and the output primitive is displayed. We will see in Chapter 15 that hidden surface removal simply uses the z-component to determine which output primitives are closest to the viewer and hence are visible.

PHIGS uses two 4×4 matrices, the view orientation matrix and the view mapping matrix, to represent the complete set of viewing specifications. The VRP, VPN, and VUP are combined to form the *view orientation matrix*, which transforms positions represented in world coordinates into positions represented in VRC. This is the transformation that takes the u, v, and n axes into the x, y, and z axes, respectively.

The view volume specifications, given by PRP, u_{min}, u_{max}, v_{min}, v_{max}, F, and B, along with the 3D viewport specification, given by x_{min}, x_{max}, y_{min}, y_{max}, z_{min}, z_{max}, are combined to form the *view mapping matrix*, which transforms points in VRC to points in normalized projection coordinates. The subroutine calls that form the view orientation matrix and view mapping matrix are discussed in Section 7.3.4.

In the next section, we see how to obtain various views using the concepts introduced in this section. In Section 6.4 the basic mathematics of planar geometric projections is introduced, whereas in Section 6.5 the mathematics and algorithms needed for the entire viewing operation are developed.

6.3 EXAMPLES OF 3D VIEWING

In this section, we consider how the basic viewing concepts introduced in the previous section can be applied to create a variety of projections, such as those shown in Figs. 6.22 and 6.23. Because the house shown in these figures is used throughout this section, it will be helpful to remember its dimensions and position, which are indicated in Fig. 6.24. For each view discussed, we give a table showing the VRP, VPN, VUP, PRP, window, and

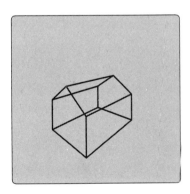

Fig. 6.22 Two-point perspective projection of a house.

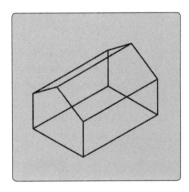

Fig. 6.23 Isometric projection of a house.

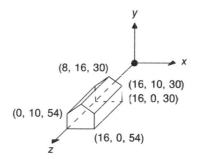

Fig. 6.24 The house extends from 30 to 54 in z, from 0 to 16 in x, and from 0 to 16 in y.

projection type (perspective or parallel). The 3D viewport default, which is the unit cube in NPC, is assumed throughout this section. The notation (WC) or (VRC) is added to the table as a reminder of the coordinate system in which the viewing parameter is given. The form of the table is illustrated here for the default viewing specification used by PHIGS. The defaults are shown in Fig. 6.25(a). The view volume corresponding to these defaults is

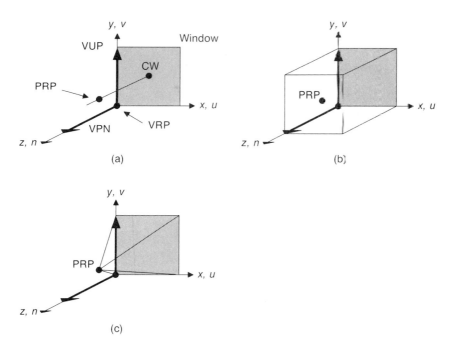

Fig. 6.25 (a) The default viewing specification: VRP is at the origin, VUP is the y axis, and VPN is the z axis. This makes the VRC system of u, v, and n coincide with the x, y, z world-coordinate system. The window extends from 0 to 1 along u and v, and PRP is at (0.5, 0.5, 1.0). (b) Default parallel projection view volume. (c) View volume if default projection were perspective.

shown in Fig. 6.25(b). If the type of projection is perspective rather than parallel, then the view volume is the pyramid shown in Fig. 6.25(c).

Viewing parameter	Value	Comments
VRP(WC)	(0, 0, 0)	origin
VPN(WC)	(0, 0, 1)	z axis
VUP(WC)	(0, 1, 0)	y axis
PRP(VRC)	(0.5, 0.5, 1.0)	
window (VRC)	(0, 1, 0, 1)	
projection type	parallel	

Readers wanting to review how all these parameters interrelate are encouraged to construct a house, the world coordinate system, and the VRC system with Tinker Toys, as pictured in Fig. 6.26. The idea is to position the VRC system in world coordinates as in the viewing example and to imagine projectors from points on the house intersecting the view plane. In our experience, this is a useful way to understand (and teach) 3D viewing concepts.

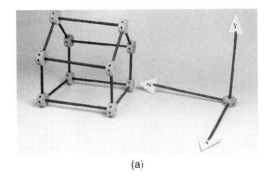

(a)

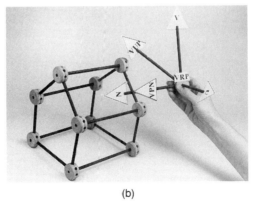

(b)

Fig. 6.26 Stick models useful for understanding 3D viewing. (a) House and world-coordinate system. (b) House and VRC system.

6.3.1 Perspective Projections

To obtain the front one-point perspective view of the house shown in Fig. 6.27 (this and all similar figures were made with the SPHIGS program, discussed in Chapter 7), we position the center of projection (which can be thought of as the position of the viewer) at $x = 8$, $y = 6$, and $z = 84$. The x value is selected to be at the horizontal center of the house and the y value to correspond to the approximate eye level of a viewer standing on the (x, z) plane; the z value is arbitrary. In this case, z is removed 30 units from the front of the house ($z = 54$ plane). The window has been made quite large, to guarantee that the house fits within the view volume. All other viewing parameters have their default values, so the overall set of viewing parameters is as follows:

VRP(WC)	(0, 0, 0)
VPN(WC)	(0, 0, 1)
VUP(WC)	(0, 1, 0)
PRP(VRC)	(8, 6, 84)
window(VRC)	(−50, 50, −50, 50)
projection type	perspective

Although the image in Fig. 6.27 is indeed a perspective projection of the house, it is very small and is not centered on the view surface. We would prefer a more centered projection of the house that more nearly spans the entire view surface, as in Fig. 6.28. We can produce this effect more easily if the view plane and the front plane of the house coincide. Now, because the front of the house extends from 0 to 16 in both x and y, a window extending from −1 to 17 in x and y produces reasonable results.

We place the view plane on the front face of the house by placing the VRP anywhere in the $z = 54$ plane; (0, 0, 54), the lower-left front corner of the house, is fine. For the center of projection to be the same as in Fig. 6.27, the PRP, which is in the VRC system, needs to be at (8, 6, 30). Figure 6.29 shows this new arrangement of the VRC, VRP, and PRP,

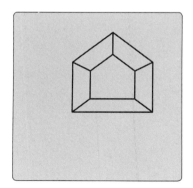

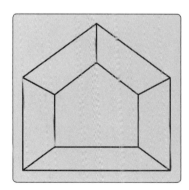

Fig. 6.27 One-point perspective projection of the house.

Fig. 6.28 Centered perspective projection of a house.

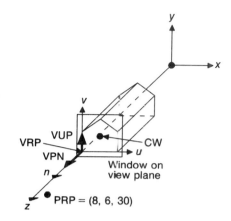

Fig. 6.29 The viewing situation for Fig. 6.28.

which corresponds to the following set of viewing parameters:

VRP(WC)	(0, 0, 54)
VPN(WC)	(0, 0, 1)
VUP(WC)	(0, 1, 0)
PRP(VRC)	(8, 6, 30)
window(VRC)	(−1, 17, −1, 17)
projection type	perspective

This same result can be obtained in many other ways. For instance, with the VRP at (8, 6, 54), as in Fig. 6.30, the center of projection, given by the PRP, becomes (0, 0, 30). The window must also be changed, because its definition is based on the VRC system, the origin of which is the VRP. The appropriate window extends from −9 to 9 in u and from −7 to 11 in v. With respect to the house, this is the same window as that used in the previous

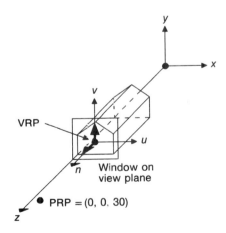

Fig. 6.30 An alternative viewing situation for Fig. 6.28.

example, but it is now specified in a different VRC system. Because the view-up direction is the y axis, the u axis and x axis are parallel, as are the v and y axes. In summary, the following viewing parameters, shown in Fig. 6.30, also produce Fig. 6.28:

VRP(WC)	(8, 6, 54)
VPN(WC)	(0, 0, 1)
VUP(WC)	(0, 1, 0)
PRP(VRC)	(0, 0, 30)
window(VRC)	(−9, 9, −7, 11)
projection type	perspective

Next, let us try to obtain the two-point perspective projection shown in Fig. 6.22. The center of projection is analogous to the position of a camera that takes snapshots of world-coordinate objects. With this analogy in mind, the center of projection in Fig. 6.22 seems to be somewhat above and to the right of the house, as viewed from the positive z axis. The exact center of projection is (36, 25, 74). Now, if the corner of the house at (16, 0, 54) is chosen as the VRP, then this center of projection is at (20, 25, 20) relative to it. With the view plane coincident with the front of the house (the $z = 54$ plane), a window ranging from −20 to 20 in u and from −5 to 35 in v is certainly large enough to contain the projection. Hence, we can specify the view of Fig. 6.31 with the viewing parameters:

VRP(WC)	(16, 0, 54)
VPN(WC)	(0, 0, 1)
VUP(WC)	(0, 1, 0)
PRP(VRC)	(20, 25, 20)
window(VRC)	(−20, 20, −5, 35)
projection type	perspective

This view is similar to, but clearly is not the same as, that in Fig. 6.22. For one thing, Fig. 6.22 is a two-point perspective projection, whereas Fig. 6.31 is a one-point perspective. It is apparent that simply moving the center of projection is not sufficient to produce Fig. 6.22. In fact, we need to reorient the view plane such that it cuts both the x and

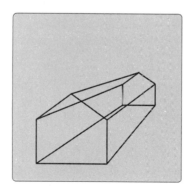

Fig. 6.31 Perspective projection of a house from (36, 25, 74) with VPN parallel to the z axis.

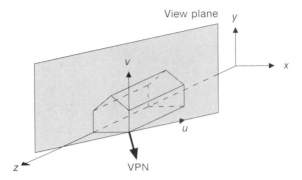

Fig. 6.32 The view plane and VRC system corresponding to Fig. 6.22.

z axes, by setting VPN to (1, 0, 1). Thus, the viewing parameters for Fig. 6.22 are as follows:

VRP(WC)	(16, 0, 54)
VPN(WC)	(1, 0, 1)
VUP(WC)	(0, 1, 0)
PRP(VRC)	$(0, 25, 20\sqrt{2})$
window(VRC)	(−20, 20, −5, 35)
projection type	perspective

Figure 6.32 shows the view plane established with this *VPN*. The $20\sqrt{2}$ n component of the *PRP* is used so that the center of projection is a distance $20\sqrt{2}$ away from the VRP in the (x, y) plane, as shown in Fig. 6.33.

There are two ways to choose a window that completely surrounds the projection, as does the window in Fig. 6.22. One can estimate the size of the projection of the house onto the view plane using a sketch, such as Fig. 6.33, to calculate the intersections of projectors

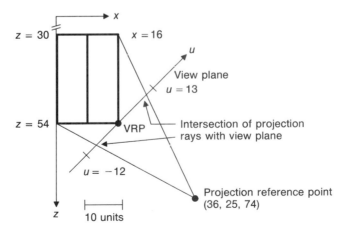

Fig. 6.33 Top (plan) view of a house for determining an appropriate window size.

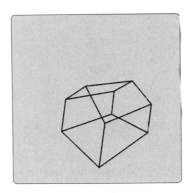

Fig. 6.34 Projection of house produced by rotating VUP.

with the view plane. A better alternative, however, is to allow the window bounds to be variables in a program that are determined interactively via a valuator or locator device.

Figure 6.34 is obtained from the same projection as is Fig. 6.22, but the window has a different orientation. In all previous examples, the v axis of the VRC system was parallel to the y axis of the world-coordinate system; thus, the window (two of whose sides are parallel to the v axis) was nicely aligned with the vertical sides of the house. Figure 6.34 has exactly the same viewing parameters as does Fig. 6.22, except that VUP has been rotated away from the y axis by about $10°$.

Another way to specify viewing parameters for perspective projections is suggested in Fig. 6.35. This figure is modeled after the way a photographer might think about positioning a camera. Six parameters are needed: the center of projection, which is the camera position; the center of attention, which is a point at which the camera is aimed (the VPN is the vector from the center of attention to the center of projection); VUP, the up vector; D, the distance from the center of projection to the projection plane; W, the width of the window on the projection plane, and H, the height of the window on the projection plane. The center of attention need not be on the view plane. In this model, the VPN is

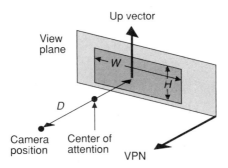

Fig. 6.35 Another way to specify a view, with a camera position (the center of projection), center of attention, up vector, distance from the center of projection to the projection plane, and the height and width of the window on the projection plane. VPN is parallel to the direction from the center of attention to the camera position.

always pointed directly at the center of projection, and the view volume is symmetrical about its center line. The positions are all given in world coordinates—there is no concept of viewing coordinates. Exercise 6.24 asks you to convert from these six viewing parameters into the viewing model given here.

6.3.3 Parallel Projections

We create a front parallel projection of the house (Fig. 6.36) by making the direction of projection parallel to the z axis. Recall that the direction of projection is determined by the PRP and by the center of the window. With the default VRC system and a window of $(-1, 17, -1, 17)$, the center of the window is $(8, 8, 0)$. A PRP of $(8, 8, 100)$ provides a direction of projection parallel to the z axis. Figure 6.37 shows the viewing situation that creates Fig. 6.36. The viewing parameters are as follows:

VRP(WC)	(0, 0, 0)
VPN(WC)	(0, 0, 1)
VUP(WC)	(0, 1, 0)
PRP(VRC)	(8, 8, 100)
window(VRC)	(−1, 17, −1, 17)
projection type	parallel

To create the side view (Fig. 6.38), we require the viewing situation of Fig. 6.39, with the (y, z) plane (or any plane parallel to it) as the view plane. This situation corresponds to the following viewing parameters:

VRP(WC)	(0, 0, 54)	
VPN(WC)	(1, 0, 0)	x axis
VUP(WC)	(0, 1, 0)	y axis
PRP(VRC)	(12, 8, 16)	
window(VRC)	(−1, 25, −5, 21)	
projection type	parallel	

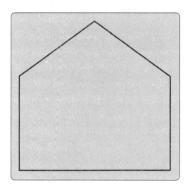

Fig. 6.36 Front parallel projection of the house.

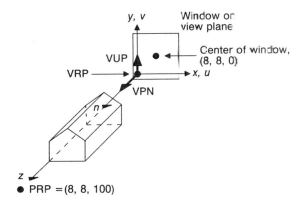

Fig. 6.37 Viewing situation that creates Fig. 6.36, a front view of the house. The PRP could be any point with $x = 8$ and $y = 8$.

The center of the window is at $(12, 8, 0)$ in VRC; hence, the PRP has these same u and v coordinates.

We create a top view of the house by using the (x, z) plane as the view plane and VPN as the y axis. The default view-up direction of $+y$ must be changed; we use the negative x axis. With VRP again specified as a corner of the house, we have the viewing situation in Fig. 6.40, defined by the following viewing parameters:

VRP(WC)	$(16, 0, 54)$	
VPN(WC)	$(0, 1, 0)$	y axis
VUP(WC)	$(-1, 0, 0)$	negative x axis
PRP(VRC)	$(12, 8, 30)$	
window(VRC)	$(-1, 25, -5, 21)$	
projection type	parallel	

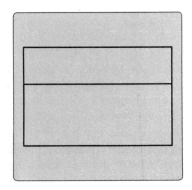

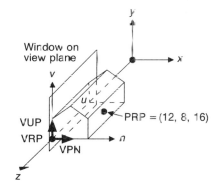

Fig. 6.38 Parallel projection from the side of the house.

Fig. 6.39 The viewing situation for Fig. 6.38.

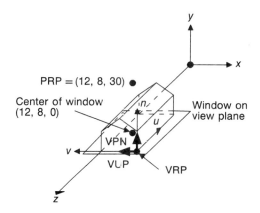

Fig. 6.40 The viewing situation for a top view of the house.

Figure 6.23 is an isometric (parallel orthographic) projection in the direction $(-1, -1, -1)$, one of the eight possible directions for an isometric (see Section 6.1.2). The following viewing parameters create such an isometric projection:

VRP(WC)	$(8, 8, 42)$
VPN(WC)	$(1, 1, 1)$
VUP(WC)	$(0, 1, 0)$
PRP(VRC)	$(0, 0, 10)$
window(VRC)	$(-20, 20, -20, 20)$
projection type	parallel

A cavalier projection with angle α (see Fig. 6.10) is specified with

VRP(WC)	$(8, 8, 54)$	middle front of house
VPN(WC)	$(0, 0, 1)$	z axis
VUP(WC)	$(0, 1, 0)$	y axis
PRP(VRC)	$(\cos\alpha, \sin\alpha, 1)$	
window(VRC)	$(-15, 15, -15, 15)$	
projection type	parallel	

The window is symmetrical about VRP, which implies that VRP, the origin of the VRC system, is the window's center. Placing PRP as specified means that the direction of projection, which is the vector from PRP to the window center, is $(0, 0, 0) -$ PRP $= -$ PRP, or its negative PRP. From Section 6.1.2, we know that the cavalier projection's direction of projection is that given in the preceding table: $-$ PRP $= -(\cos\alpha, \sin\alpha, 1)$. Now notice what happens if a cavalier projection onto a plane of constant x instead of constant z is desired: only VRP, VPN, and VUP need to be changed to establish a new VRC system. The PRP, window, and projection type can remain fixed.

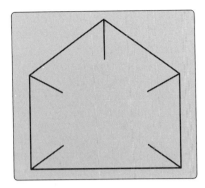

Fig. 6.41 Perspective projection of the house with back clipping plane at $z = 31$.

6.3.4 Finite View Volumes

In all the examples so far, the view volume has been assumed to be infinite. The front and back clipping planes, described Section 6.2, help to determine a *finite view volume*. These planes, both of which are parallel to the view plane, are at distances F and B respectively from the view reference point, measured from VRP along VPN. To avoid a negative view volume, we must ensure that F is algebraically greater than B.

A front perspective view of the house with the rear wall clipped away (Fig. 6.41) results from the following viewing specification, in which F and B have been added. If a distance is given, then clipping against the corresponding plane is assumed; otherwise, it is not. The viewing specification is as follows:

VRP(WC)	(0, 0, 54)	lower-left front of house
VPN(WC)	(0, 0, 1)	z axis
VUP(WC)	(0, 1, 0)	y axis
PRP(VRC)	(8, 6, 30)	
window(VRC)	(−1, 17, −1, 17)	
projection type	perspective	
F(VRC)	+1	one unit in front of house, at $z = 54 + 1 = 55$
B(VRC)	−23	one unit from back of house, at $z = 54 - 23 = 31$

The viewing situation for this case is the same as that in Fig. 6.29, except for the addition of the clipping planes.

If the front and back clipping planes are moved dynamically, the 3D structure of the object being viewed can often be discerned more readily than it can with a static view.

6.4 THE MATHEMATICS OF PLANAR GEOMETRIC PROJECTIONS

In this section, we introduce the basic mathematics of planar geometric projections. For simplicity, we start by assuming that, in the perspective projection, the projection plane is normal to the z axis at $z = d$, and that, in the parallel projection, the projection plane is the $z = 0$ plane. Each of the projections can be defined by a 4×4 matrix. This is convenient, because the projection matrix can be composed with transformation matrices, allowing two operations (transform, then project) to be represented as a single matrix. In the next section, we discuss arbitrary projection planes.

In this section, we derive 4×4 matrices for several projections, beginning with a projection plane at a distance d from the origin and a point P to be projected onto it. To calculate $P_p = (x_p, y_p, z_p)$, the perspective projection of (x, y, z) onto the projection plane at $z = d$, we use the similar triangles in Fig. 6.42 to write the ratios

$$\frac{x_p}{d} = \frac{x}{z}; \qquad \frac{y_p}{d} = \frac{y}{z}. \tag{6.1}$$

Multiplying each side by d yields

$$x_p = \frac{d \cdot x}{z} = \frac{x}{z/d}, \qquad y_p = \frac{d \cdot y}{z} = \frac{y}{z/d}. \tag{6.2}$$

The distance d is just a scale factor applied to x_p and y_p. The division by z causes the perspective projection of more distant objects to be smaller than that of closer objects. All values of z are allowable except $z = 0$. Points can be behind the center of projection on the negative z axis or between the center of projection and the projection plane.

The transformation of Eq. (6.2) can be expressed as a 4×4 matrix:

$$M_{\text{per}} = \begin{bmatrix} 1 & 0 & 0 & 0 \\ 0 & 1 & 0 & 0 \\ 0 & 0 & 1 & 0 \\ 0 & 0 & 1/d & 0 \end{bmatrix}. \tag{6.3}$$

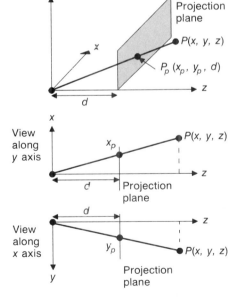

Fig. 6.42 Perspective projection.

Multiplying the point $P = [x \; y \; z \; 1]^T$ by the matrix M_{per} yields the general homogeneous point $[X \; Y \; Z \; W]^T$:

$$\begin{bmatrix} X \\ Y \\ Z \\ W \end{bmatrix} = M_{per} \cdot P = \begin{bmatrix} 1 & 0 & 0 & 0 \\ 0 & 1 & 0 & 0 \\ 0 & 0 & 1 & 0 \\ 0 & 0 & 1/d & 0 \end{bmatrix} \cdot \begin{bmatrix} x \\ y \\ z \\ 1 \end{bmatrix} \qquad (6.4)$$

or

$$[X \; Y \; Z \; W]^T = \left[x \; y \; z \; \frac{z}{d} \right]^T. \qquad (6.5)$$

Now, dividing by W (which is z/d) and dropping the fourth coordinate to come back to 3D, we have

$$\left(\frac{X}{W}, \frac{Y}{W}, \frac{Z}{W} \right) = (x_p, y_p, z_p) = \left(\frac{x}{z/d}, \frac{y}{z/d}, d \right); \qquad (6.6)$$

these equations are the correct results of Eq. (6.1), plus the transformed z coordinate of d, which is the position of the projection plane along the z axis.

An alternative formulation for the perspective projection places the projection plane at $z = 0$ and the center of projection at $z = -d$, as in Fig. 6.43. Similarity of the triangles now gives

$$\frac{x_p}{d} = \frac{x}{z + d}, \qquad \frac{y_p}{d} = \frac{y}{z + d}. \qquad (6.7)$$

Multiplying by d, we get

$$x_p = \frac{d \cdot x}{z + d} = \frac{x}{(z/d) + 1}, \qquad y_p = \frac{d \cdot y}{z + d} = \frac{y}{(z/d) + 1}. \qquad (6.8)$$

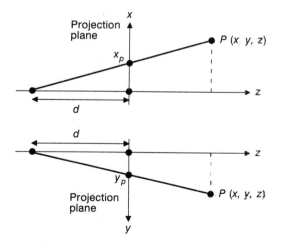

Fig. 6.43 Alternative perspective projection.

The matrix is

$$M'_{per} = \begin{bmatrix} 1 & 0 & 0 & 0 \\ 0 & 1 & 0 & 0 \\ 0 & 0 & 0 & 0 \\ 0 & 0 & 1/d & 1 \end{bmatrix}. \tag{6.9}$$

This formulation allows d, the distance to the center of projection, to tend to infinity.

The orthographic projection onto a projection plane at $z = 0$ is straightforward. The direction of projection is the same as the projection-plane normal—the z axis, in this case. Thus, point P projects as

$$x_p = x, \quad y_p = y, \quad z_p = 0. \tag{6.10}$$

This projection is expressed by the matrix

$$M_{ort} = \begin{bmatrix} 1 & 0 & 0 & 0 \\ 0 & 1 & 0 & 0 \\ 0 & 0 & 0 & 0 \\ 0 & 0 & 0 & 1 \end{bmatrix}. \tag{6.11}$$

Notice that as d in Eq. (6.9) tends to infinity, Eq. (6.9) becomes Eq. (6.11).

M_{per} applies only in the special case in which the center of projection is at the origin; M_{ort} applies only when the direction of projection is parallel to the z axis. A more robust formulation, based on a concept developed in [WEIN87], not only removes these restrictions but also integrates parallel and perspective projections into a single formulation. In Fig. 6.44, the projection of the general point $P = (x, y, z)$ onto the projection plane is $P_p = (x_p, y_p, z_p)$. The projection plane is perpendicular to the z axis at a distance z_p from the origin, and the center of projection (COP) is a distance Q from the point $(0, 0, z_p)$. The direction from $(0, 0, z_p)$ to COP is given by the normalized direction vector (d_x, d_y, d_z). P_p is

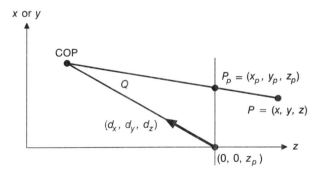

Fig. 6.44 The intersection of the line from COP to $P = (x, y, z)$ with the projection plane at $z = z_p$ is the projection of the point P. The COP is distance Q from the point $(0, 0, z_p)$, in direction (d_x, d_y, d_z).

on the line between COP and P, which can be specified parametrically as

$$\text{COP} + t(P - \text{COP}), \qquad 0 \le t \le 1. \tag{6.12}$$

Rewriting Eq. (6.12) as separate equations for the arbitrary point $P' = (x', y', z')$ on the line, with COP $= (0, 0, z_p) + Q(d_x, d_y, d_z)$, yields

$$x' = Q \, d_x + (x - Q \, d_x)t, \tag{6.13}$$
$$y' = Q \, d_y + (y - Q \, d_y)t, \tag{6.14}$$
$$z' = (z_p + Q \, d_z) + (z - (z_p + Q \, d_z))t. \tag{6.15}$$

We find the projection P_p of the point P, at the intersection of the line between COP and P with the projection plane, by substituting $z' = z_p$ into Eq. (6.15) and solving for t:

$$t = \frac{z_p - (z_p + Q \, d_z)}{z - (z_p + Q \, d_z)}. \tag{6.16}$$

Substituting this value of t into Eq. (6.13) and Eq. (5.14) to find $x' = x_p$ and $y' = y_p$ yields

$$x_p = \frac{x - z\dfrac{d_x}{d_z} + z_p\dfrac{d_x}{d_z}}{\dfrac{z_p - z}{Q \, d_z} + 1}, \tag{6.17}$$

$$y_p = \frac{y - z\dfrac{d_y}{d_z} + z_p\dfrac{d_y}{d_z}}{\dfrac{z_p - z}{Q \, d_z} + 1}. \tag{6.18}$$

Multiplying the identity $z_p = z_p$ on the right-hand side by a fraction whose numerator and denominator are both

$$\frac{z_p - z}{Q \, d_z} + 1 \tag{6.19}$$

maintains the identity and gives z_p the same denominator as x_p and y_p:

$$z_p = z_p\frac{\dfrac{z_p - z}{Q \, d_z} + 1}{\dfrac{z_p - z}{Q \, d_z} + 1} = \frac{-z\dfrac{z_p}{Q \, d_z} + \dfrac{z_p^2 + z_p Q \, d_z}{Q \, d_z}}{\dfrac{z_p - z}{Q \, d_z} + 1}. \tag{6.20}$$

Now Eqs. (6.17), (6.18), and (6.20) can be rewritten as a 4×4 matrix M_{general} arranged so that the last row of M_{general} multiplied by $[x \quad y \quad z \quad 1]^T$ produces their common denominator, which is the homogeneous coordinate W and is hence the divisor of X, Y, and Z:

$$
M_{general} = \begin{bmatrix}
1 & 0 & -\dfrac{d_x}{d_z} & z_p\dfrac{d_x}{d_z} \\[2mm]
0 & 1 & -\dfrac{d_y}{d_z} & z_p\dfrac{d_y}{d_z} \\[2mm]
0 & 0 & -\dfrac{z_p}{Q\,d_z} & \dfrac{z_p^2}{Q\,d_z} + z_p \\[2mm]
0 & 0 & -\dfrac{1}{Q\,d_z} & \dfrac{z_p}{Q\,d_z} + 1
\end{bmatrix}.
\tag{6.21}
$$

$M_{general}$ specializes to all three of the previously derived projection matrixes M_{per}, M'_{per}, and M_{ort}, given the following values:

	z_p	Q	$[d_x \quad d_y \quad d_z]$
M_{ort}	0	∞	$[0 \quad 0 \quad -1]$
M_{per}	d	d	$[0 \quad 0 \quad -1]$
M'_{per}	0	d	$[0 \quad 0 \quad -1]$

When $Q \neq \infty$, $M_{general}$ defines a one-point perspective projection. The vanishing point of a perspective projection is calculated by multiplying the point at infinity on the z axis, represented in homogeneous coordinates as $[0 \quad 0 \quad 1 \quad 0]^T$, by $M_{general}$. Taking this product and dividing by W gives

$$
x = Q\,d_x, \quad y = Q\,d_y, \quad z = z_p.
$$

Given a desired vanishing point (x, y) and a known distance Q to the center of projection, these equations uniquely define $[d_x \quad d_y \quad d_z]$, because $\sqrt{d_x^2 + d_y^2 + d_z^2} = 1$.

Similarly, it is easy to show that, for cavalier and cabinet projections onto the (x, y) plane, with α the angle shown in Figs. 6.10 and 6.11,

	z_p	Q	$[d_x \qquad\quad d_y \qquad d_z]$
Cavalier	0	∞	$[\cos\alpha \quad \sin\alpha \quad -1]$
Cabinet	0	∞	$\left[\dfrac{\cos\alpha}{2} \quad \dfrac{\sin\alpha}{2} \quad -1\right]$

In this section, we have seen how to formulate M_{per}, M'_{per}, and M_{ort}, all of which are special cases of the more general $M_{general}$. In all these cases, however, the projection plane is perpendicular to the z axis. In the next section, we remove this restriction and consider the clipping implied by finite view volumes.

6.5   IMPLEMENTING PLANAR GEOMETRIC PROJECTIONS

Given a view volume and a projection, let us consider how the *viewing operation* of clipping and projecting is actually applied. As suggested by the conceptual model for viewing (Fig. 6.1), we could clip lines against the view volume by calculating their intersections with each of the six planes that define the view volume. Lines remaining after clipping would be projected onto the view plane, by solution of simultaneous equations for the intersection of the projectors with the view plane. The coordinates would then be transformed from 3D world coordinates to 2D device coordinates. However, the large number of calculations required for this process, repeated for many lines, involves considerable computing. Happily, there is a more efficient procedure, based on the divide-and-conquer strategy of breaking down a difficult problem into a series of simpler ones.

Certain view volumes are easier to clip against than is the general one (clipping algorithms are discussed in Section 6.5.3). For instance, it is simple to calculate the intersections of a line with each of the planes of a parallel-projection view volume defined by the six planes

$$x = -1, \quad x = 1, \quad y = -1, \quad y = 1, \quad z = 0, \quad z = -1. \tag{6.22}$$

This is also true of the perspective-projection view volume defined by the planes

$$x = z, \quad x = -z, \quad y = z, \quad y = -z, \quad z = -z_{min}, \quad z = -1. \tag{6.23}$$

These *canonical view volumes* are shown in Fig. 6.45.

Our strategy is to find the *normalizing transformations* N_{par} and N_{per} that transform an arbitrary parallel- or perspective-projection view volume into the parallel and perspective canonical view volumes, respectively. Then clipping is performed, followed by projection into 2D, via the matrices in Section 6.4. This strategy risks investing effort in transforming points that are subsequently discarded by the clip operation, but at least the clipping is easy to do.

Figure 6.46 shows the sequence of processes involved here. We can reduce it to a transform–clip–transform sequence by composing steps 3 and 4 into a single transformation matrix. With perspective projections, a division is also needed to map from homogeneous coordinates back to 3D coordinates. This division is done following the second transformation of the combined sequence. An alternative strategy, clipping in homogeneous coordinates, is discussed in Section 6.5.4.

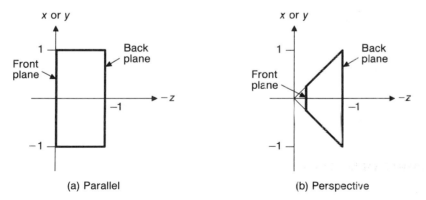

(a) Parallel   (b) Perspective

Fig. 6.45 The two canonical view volumes, for the (a) parallel and (b) perspective projections. Note that $-z$ is to the right.

3D world-
coordinate
output
primitives

2D device
coordinates

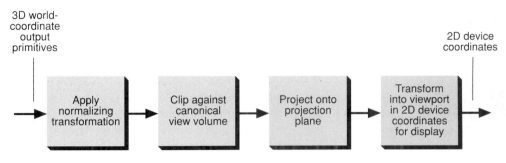

Fig. 6.46 Implementation of 3D viewing.

Readers familiar with PHIGS will notice that the canonical view volumes of Eqs. (6.22) and (6.23) are different than the *default view volumes* of PHIGS: the unit cube from 0 to 1 in x, y, and z for parallel projection, and the pyramid with apex at $(0.5, 0.5, 1.0)$ and sides passing through the unit square from 0 to 1 in x and y on the $z = 0$ plane for perspective projection. The canonical view volumes are defined to simplify the clipping equations and to provide the consistency between parallel and perspective projections discussed in Section 6.5.4. On the other hand, the PHIGS default view volumes are defined to make 2D viewing be a special case of 3D viewing. Exercise 6.26 concerns the PHIGS defaults.

In the next two sections, we derive the normalizing transformations for perspective and parallel projections, which are used as the first step in the transform–clip–transform sequence.

6.5.1 Parallel Projection

In this section, we derive the normalizing transformation N_{par} for parallel projections in order to transform world-coordinate positions such that the view volume is transformed into the canonical view volume defined by Eq. (6.22). The transformed coordinates are clipped against this canonical view volume, and the clipped results are projected onto the $z = 0$ plane, then are transformed into the viewport for display.

Transformation N_{par} is derived for the most general case, the oblique (rather than orthographic) parallel projection. N_{par} thus includes a shear transformation that causes the direction of projection in viewing coordinates to be parallel to z, even though in (u, v, n) coordinates it is not parallel to VPN. By including this shear, we can do the projection onto the $z = 0$ plane simply by setting $z = 0$. If the parallel projection is orthographic, the shear component of the normalization transformation becomes the identity.

The series of transformations that make up N_{par} is as follows:

1. Translate the VRP to the origin

2. Rotate VRC such that the n axis (VPN) becomes the z axis, the u axis becomes the x axis, and the v axis becomes the y axis

3. Shear such that the direction of projection becomes parallel to the z axis

4. Translate and scale into the parallel-projection canonical view volume of Eq. (6.22).

In PHIGS, steps 1 and 2 define the *view-orientation matrix*, and steps 3 and 4 define the *view-mapping matrix*.

Figure 6.47 shows this sequence of transformations as applied to a parallel-projection view volume and to an outline of a house; Fig. 6.48 shows the parallel projection that results.

Step 1 is just the translation $T(-\text{VRP})$. For step 2. we use the properties of orthonormal matrices discussed in Section 5.5 and illustrated in the derivation of Eqs. (5.66) and (5.67). The row vectors of the rotation matrix to perform step 2 are the unit vectors that are rotated by R into the x, y, and z axes. VPN is rotated into the z axis, so

$$R_z = \frac{\text{VPN}}{\|\text{VPN}\|}. \tag{6.24}.$$

The u axis, which is perpendicular to VUP and to VPN and is hence the cross-product of the unit vector along VUP and R_z (which is in the same direction as VPN), is rotated into the x axis, so

$$R_x = \frac{\text{VUP} \times R_z}{\|\text{VUP} \times R_z\|}. \tag{6.25}$$

Similarly, the v axis, which is perpendicular to R_z and R_x, is rotated into the y axis, so

$$R_y = R_z \times R_x. \tag{6.26}$$

Hence, the rotation in step 2 is given by the matrix

$$R = \begin{bmatrix} r_{1x} & r_{2x} & r_{3x} & 0 \\ r_{1y} & r_{2y} & r_{3y} & 0 \\ r_{1z} & r_{2z} & r_{3z} & 0 \\ 0 & 0 & 0 & 1 \end{bmatrix}, \tag{6.27}$$

where r_{1x} is the first element of R_x, and so on.

The third step is to shear the view volume along the z axis such that all of its planes are normal to one of the coordinate system axes. We do this step by determining the shear to be applied to the direction of projection (DOP) to make DOP coincident with the z axis. Recall that DOP is the vector from PRP to the center of the window (CW), and that PRP is specified in the VRC system. The first two transformation steps have brought VRC into correspondence with the world-coordinate system, so the PRP is now itself in world coordinates. Hence, DOP is $CW - PRP$. Given

$$\text{DOP} = \begin{bmatrix} dop_x \\ dop_y \\ dop_z \\ 0 \end{bmatrix}, \quad \text{CW} = \begin{bmatrix} \dfrac{u_{\max} + u_{\min}}{2} \\ \dfrac{v_{\max} + v_{\min}}{2} \\ 0 \\ 1 \end{bmatrix}, \quad \text{PRP} = \begin{bmatrix} prp_u \\ prp_v \\ prp_n \\ 1 \end{bmatrix}, \tag{6.28}$$

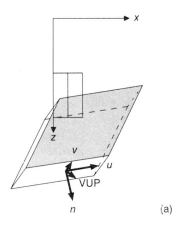

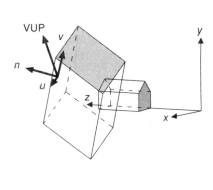

(a)

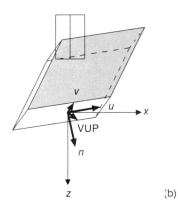

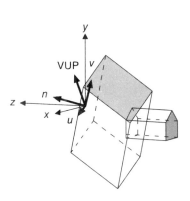

(b)

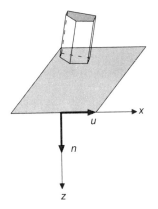

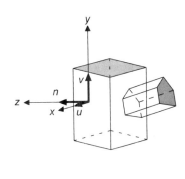

(c)

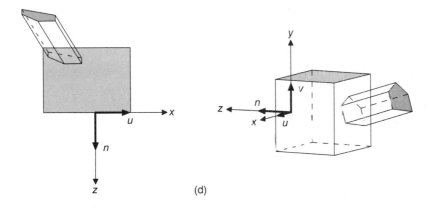

(d)

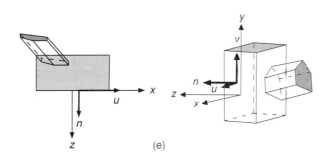

(e)

Fig. 6.47 Results at various stages in the parallel-projection viewing pipeline. A top and off-axis parallel projection are shown in each case. (a) The original viewing situation. (b) The VRP has been translated to the origin. (c) The (u, v, n) coordinate system has been rotated to be aligned with the (x, y, z) system. (d) The view volume has been sheared such that the direction of projection (DOP) is parallel to the z axis. (e) The view volume has been translated and scaled into the canonical parallel-projection view volume. The viewing parameters are VRP = (0.325, 0.8, 4.15), VPN = (.227, .267, 1.0), VUP = (.293, 1.0, .227), PRP = (0.6, 0.0, −1.0), Window = (−1.425, 1.0, −1.0, 1.0), $F = 0.0$, $B = −1.75$. (Figures made with program written by Mr. L. Lu, The George Washington University.)

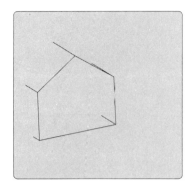

Fig. 6.48 Final parallel projection of the clipped house.

then

$$DOP = CW - PRP$$

$$= \left[\frac{u_{\max} + u_{\min}}{2} \quad \frac{v_{\max} + v_{\min}}{2} \quad 0 \quad 1 \right]^{T} - [prp_u \quad prp_v \quad prp_n \quad 1].^{T} \qquad (6.29)$$

Figure 6.49 shows the DOP so specified and the desired transformed DOP'.

The shear can be accomplished with the (x, y) shear matrix from Section 5.6 Eq. (5.47). With coefficients shx_{par} and shy_{par}, the matrix is

$$SH_{par} = SH_{xy}(shx_{par}, shy_{par}) = \begin{bmatrix} 1 & 0 & shx_{par} & 0 \\ 0 & 1 & shy_{par} & 0 \\ 0 & 0 & 1 & 0 \\ 0 & 0 & 0 & 1 \end{bmatrix}. \qquad (6.30)$$

As described in Section 5.6, SH_{xy} leaves z unaffected, while adding to x and y the terms $z \cdot shx_{par}$ and $z \cdot shy_{par}$. We want to find shx_{par} and shy_{par} such that

$$DOP' = [0 \quad 0 \quad dop_z \quad 0]^{T} = SH_{par} \cdot DOP. \qquad (6.31)$$

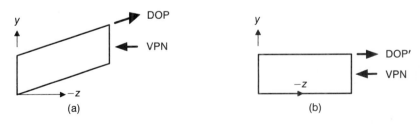

Fig. 6.49 Illustration of shearing using side view of view volume as example. The parallelogram in (a) is sheared into the rectangle in (b); VPN is unchanged because it is parallel to the z axis.

Performing the multiplication of Eq. (6.31) followed by algebraic manipulation shows that the equality occurs if

$$shx_{par} = -\frac{dop_x}{dop_z}, \quad shy_{par} = -\frac{dop_y}{dop_z}. \tag{6.32}$$

Notice that, for an orthographic projection, $dop_x = dop_y = 0$, so $shx_{par} = shy_{par} = 0$, and the shear matrix reduces to the identity.

Figure 6.50 shows the view volume after these three transformation steps have been applied. The bounds of the volume are

$$u_{min} \le x \le u_{max}, \quad v_{min} \le y \le v_{max}, \quad B \le z \le F; \tag{6.33}$$

here F and B are the distances from VRP along the VPN to the front and back clipping planes, respectively.

The fourth and last step in the process is transforming the sheared view volume into the canonical view volume. We accomplish this step by translating the front center of the view volume of Eq. (6.33) to the origin, then scaling to the $2 \times 2 \times 1$ size of the final canonical view volume of Eq. (6.22). The transformations are

$$T_{par} = T\left(-\frac{u_{max} + u_{min}}{2}, -\frac{v_{max} + v_{min}}{2}, -F\right). \tag{6.34}$$

$$S_{par} = S\left(\frac{2}{u_{max} - u_{min}}, \frac{2}{v_{max} - v_{min}}, \frac{1}{F - B}\right). \tag{6.35}$$

If F and B have not been specified (because front- and back-plane clipping are off), then any values that satisfy $B \le F$ may be used. Values of 0 and 1 are satisfactory.

In summary, we have:

$$N_{par} = S_{par} \cdot T_{par} \cdot SH_{par} \cdot R \cdot T(-VRP). \tag{6.36}$$

N_{par} transforms an arbitrary parallel-projection view volume into the parallel-projection canonical view volume, and hence permits output primitives to be clipped against the parallel-projection canonical view volume.

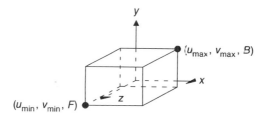

Fig. 6.50 View volume after transformation steps 1 to 3.

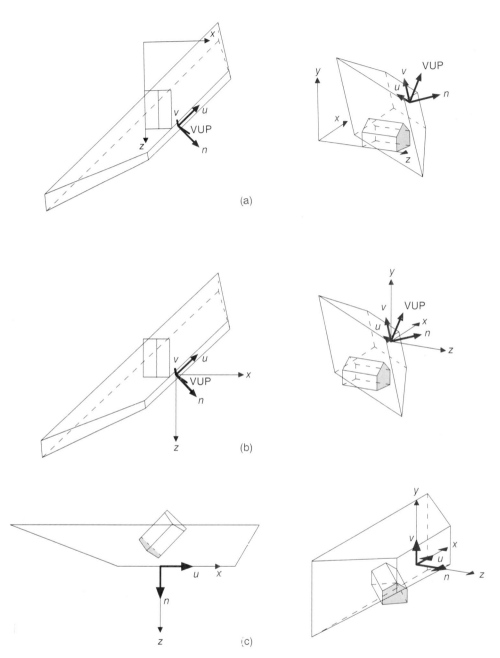

Fig. 6.51 Results at various stages in the perspective-projection viewing pipeline. A top and off-axis parallel projection are shown in each case. (a) The original viewing situation. (b) The VRP has been translated to the origin. (c) The (u, v, n) coordinate system has been rotated to be aligned with the (x, y, z) system. (d) The center of projection (COP) has been translated to the origin. (e) The view volume has been sheared, so the direction of projection (DOP) is parallel to the z axis. (f) The view volume

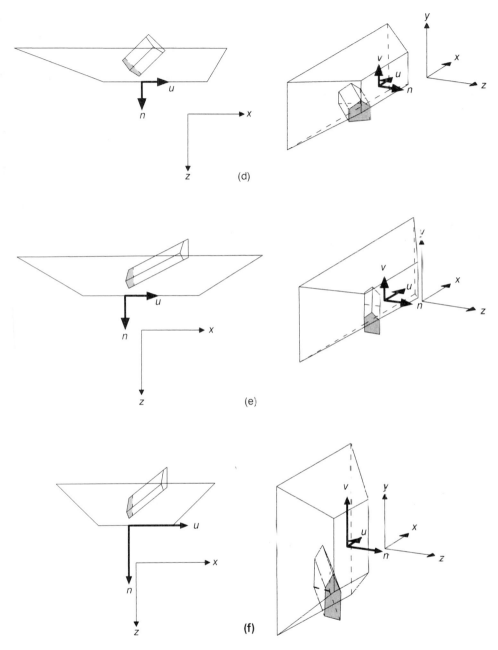

(d)

(e)

(f)

has been scaled into the canonical perspective-projection view volume. The viewing parameters are VRP = (1.0, 1.275, 2.6), VPN = (1.0, 0.253, 1.0), VUP = (0.414, 1.0, 0.253), PRP = (1.6, 0.0, 1.075), Window = (−1.325, 2.25, −0.575, 0.575), $F = 0$, $B = -1.2$. (Figures made with program written by Mr. L. Lu, The George Washington University.)

6.5.2 Perspective Projection

We now develop the normalizing transformation N_{per} for perspective projections. N_{per} transforms world-coordinate positions such that the view volume becomes the perspective-projection canonical view volume, the truncated pyramid with apex at the origin defined by Eq. (6.23). After N_{per} is applied, clipping is done against this canonical volume and the results are projected onto the view plane using M_{per} (derived in Section 6.4).

The series of transformations making up N_{per} is as follows:

1. Translate VRP to the origin
2. Rotate VRC such that the n axis (VPN) becomes the z axis, the u axis becomes the x axis, and the v axis becomes the y axis
3. Translate such that the center of projection (COP), given by the PRP, is at the origin
4. Shear such that the center line of the view volume becomes the z axis
5. Scale such that the view volume becomes the canonical perspective view volume, the truncated right pyramid defined by the six planes of Eq. (6.23).

Figure 6.51 shows this sequence of transformations being applied to a perspective-projection view volume and to a house. Figure 6.52 shows the resulting perspective projection.

Steps 1 and 2 are the same as those for the parallel projection: $R \cdot T(-\text{VRP})$. Step 3 is a translation of the center of projection (COP) to the origin, as required for the canonical perspective view volume. COP is specified relative to VRP in VRC by the PRP = (prp_u, prp_v, prp_n). Viewing-reference coordinates have been transformed into world coordinates by steps 1 and 2, so the specification for COP in VRC is now also in world coordinates. Hence, the translation for step 3 is just $T(-\text{PRP})$.

To compute the shear for step 4, we examine Fig. 6.53, which shows a side view of the view volume after transformation steps 1 to 3. Notice that the center line of the view volume, which goes through the origin and the center of the window, is not the same as the $-z$ axis. The purpose of the shear is to transform the center line into the $-z$ axis. The center line of the view volume goes from PRP (which is now at the origin) to CW, the center

Fig. 6.52 Final perspective projection of the clipped house.

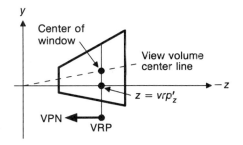

Fig. 6.53 Cross-section of view volume after transformation steps 1 to 3.

of the window. It is hence the same as the direction of projection for the parallel projection, that is, CW − PRP. Therefore the shear matrix is SH_{par}, the same as that for the parallel projection! Another way to think of this is that the translation by −PRP in step 3, which took the center of projection to the origin, also translated CW by −PRP, so, after step 3, the center line of the view volume goes through the origin and CW − PRP.

After the shear is applied, the window (and hence the view volume) is centered on the z axis. The bounds of the window on the projection plane are

$$-\frac{u_{max} - u_{min}}{2} \le x \le \frac{u_{max} - u_{min}}{2}, \tag{6.37}$$

$$-\frac{v_{max} - v_{min}}{2} \le y \le \frac{v_{max} - v_{min}}{2}.$$

The VRP, which before step 3 was at the origin, has now been translated by step 3 and sheared by step 4. Defining VRP′ as VRP after the transformations of steps 3 and 4,

$$\text{VRP}' = SH_{par} \cdot T(-\text{PRP}) \cdot [0 \ 0 \ 0 \ 1]^T. \tag{6.38}$$

The z component of VRP′, designated as vrp_z', is equal to $-prp_n$, because the (x, y) shear SH_{par} does not affect z coordinates.

The final step is a scaling along all three axes to create the canonical view volume defined by Eq. (6.23), and shown in Fig. 6.54. Thus, scaling is best thought of as being done in two substeps. In the first substep, we scale differentially in x and y, to give the sloped planes bounding the view-volume unit slope. We accomplish this substep by scaling the window so its half-height and half-width are both $-vrp_z'$. The appropriate x and y scale factors are $-2 \cdot vrp_z'/(u_{max} - u_{min})$ and $-2 \cdot vrp_z'/(v_{max} - v_{min})$, respectively. In the second substep, we scale uniformly along all three axes (to maintain the unit slopes) such that the back clipping plane at $z = vrp_z' + B$ becomes the $z = -1$ plane. The scale factor for this substep is $-1/(vrp_z' + B)$. The scale factor has a negative sign so that the scale factor will be positive, since $vrp_z' + B$ is itself negative.

Bringing these two substeps together, we get the perspective scale transformation:

$$S_{per} = S\left(\frac{2 \, vrp_z'}{(u_{max} - u_{min})(vrp_z' + B)}, \frac{2 \, vrp_z'}{(v_{max} - v_{min})(vrp_z' + B)}, \frac{-1}{vrp_z' + B}\right). \tag{6.39}$$

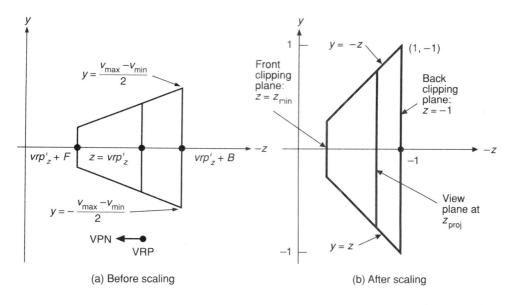

(a) Before scaling   (b) After scaling

Fig. 6.54 Cross-section of view volume before and after final scaling steps. In this example, F and B have opposite signs, so the front and back planes are on opposite sides of VRP.

Applying the scale to z changes the positions of the projection plane and clipping planes to the new positions:

$$z_{proj} = -\frac{vrp_z'}{vrp_z' + B}, \quad z_{min} = -\frac{vrp_z' + F}{vrp_z' + B}, \quad z_{max} = -\frac{vrp_z' + B}{vrp_z' + B} = -1. \quad (6.40)$$

In summary, the normalizing viewing transformation that takes the perspective-projection view volume into the perspective-projection canonical view volume is

$$N_{per} = S_{per} \cdot SH_{par} \cdot T(-\text{PRP}) \cdot R \cdot T(-\text{VRP}). \quad (6.41)$$

Similarly, recall the normalizing viewing transformation that takes the parallel-projection view volume into the parallel-projection canonical view volume:

$$N_{par} = S_{par} \cdot T_{par} \cdot SH_{par} \cdot R \cdot T(-\text{VRP}). \quad (6.36)$$

These transformations occur in homogeneous space. Under what conditions can we now come back to 3D to clip? So long as we know that $W > 0$. This condition is easy to understand. A negative W implies that, when we divide by W, the signs of Z and z will be opposite. Points with negative Z will have positive z and might be displayed even though they should have been clipped.

When can we be sure that we will have $W > 0$? Rotations, translations, scales, and shears (as defined in Chapter 5) applied to points, lines, and planes will keep $W > 0$; in fact, they will keep $W = 1$. Hence, neither N_{per} nor N_{par} affects the homogeneous coordinate of transformed points, so division by W will not normally be necessary to map back into

3D, and clipping against the appropriate canonical view volume can be performed. After clipping against the perspective-projection canonical view volume, the perspective-projection matrix M_{per}, which involves division, must be applied.

It is possible to get $W < 0$ if output primitives include curves and surfaces that are represented as functions in homogeneous coordinates and are displayed as connected straight-line segments. If, for instance, the sign of the function for W changes from one point on the curve to the next while the sign of X does not change, then X/W will have different signs at the two points on the curve. The rational B-splines discussed in Chapter 11 are an example of such behavior. Negative W can also result from using some transformations other than those discussed in Chapter 5, such as with "fake" shadows [BLIN88].

In the next section, several algorithms for clipping in 3D are discussed. Then, in Section 6.5.4, we discuss how to clip when we cannot ensure that $W > 0$.

6.5.3   Clipping Against a Canonical View Volume in 3D

The canonical view volumes are the unit cube for parallel projections and the truncated right regular pyramid for perspective projections. Both the Cohen–Sutherland and Cyrus–Beck clipping algorithms discussed in Chapter 3 readily extend to 3D.

The extension of the 2D Cohen–Sutherland algorithm for the canonical parallel view volume uses an outcode of 6 bits; a bit is true (1) when the appropriate condition is satisfied:

bit 1—point is above view volume	$y > 1$
bit 2—point is below view volume	$y < -1$
bit 3—point is right of view volume	$x > 1$
bit 4—point is left of view volume	$x < -1$
bit 5—point is behind view volume	$z < -1$
bit 6—point is in front of view volume	$z > 0$

As in 2D, a line is trivially accepted if both endpoints have a code of all zeros, and is trivially rejected if the bit-by-bit logical **and** of the codes is not all zeros. Otherwise, the process of line subdivision begins. Up to six intersections may have to be calculated, one for each side of the view volume.

The intersection calculations use the parametric representation of a line from $P_0(x_0, y_0, z_0)$ to $P_1(x_1, y_1, z_1)$:

$$x = x_0 + t(x_1 - x_0), \tag{6.42}$$

$$y = y_0 + t(y_1 - y_0), \tag{6.43}$$

$$z = z_0 + t(z_1 - z_0) \quad 0 \le t \le 1. \tag{6.44}$$

As t varies from 0 to 1, the three equations give the coordinates of all points on the line, from P_0 to P_1.

To calculate the intersection of a line with the $y = 1$ plane of the view volume, we replace the variable y of Eq. (6.43) with 1 and solve for t to find $t = (1 - y_0)/(y_1 - y_0)$. If t is outside the 0 to 1 interval, the intersection is on the infinite line through points P_0 and P_1 but is not on the portion of the line between P_0 and P_1 and hence is not of interest. If t is in

[0, 1], then its value is substituted into the equations for x and z to find the intersection's coordinates:

$$x = x_0 + \frac{(1 - y_0)(x_1 - x_0)}{y_1 - y_0}, \quad z = z_0 + \frac{(1 - y_0)(z_1 - z_0)}{y_1 - y_0}. \tag{6.45}$$

The algorithm uses outcodes to make the t in [0, 1] test unnecessary.

The outcode bits for clipping against the canonical perspective view volume are as follows:

bit 1—point is above view volume $y > -z$
bit 2—point is below view volume $y < z$
bit 3—point is right of view volume $x > -z$
bit 4—point is left of view volume $x < z$
bit 5—point is behind view volume $z < -1$
bit 6—point is in front of view volume $z > z_{min}$

Calculating the intersections of lines with the sloping planes is simple. On the $y = z$ plane, for which Eq. (6.43) must be equal to Eq. (6.44), $y_0 + t(y_1 - y_0) = z_0 + t(z_1 - z_0)$. Then,

$$t = \frac{z_0 - y_0}{(y_1 - y_0) - (z_1 - z_0)}. \tag{6.46}$$

Substituting t into Eqs. (6.42) and (6.43) for x and y gives

$$x = x_0 + \frac{(x_1 - x_0)(z_0 - y_0)}{(y_1 - y_0) - (z_1 - z_0)}, \quad y = y_0 + \frac{(y_1 - y_0)(z_0 - y_0)}{(y_1 - y_0) - (z_1 - z_0)}. \tag{6.47}$$

We know that $z = y$. The reason for choosing this canonical view volume is now clear: The unit slopes of the planes make the intersection computations simpler than would arbitrary slopes.

The Cyrus–Beck clipping algorithm was formulated for clipping a line against a general convex 3D polyhedron, and specialized to the 3D viewing pyramid [CYRU78]. Liang and Barsky later independently developed a more efficient and more specialized version for upright 2D and 3D clip regions [LIAN84]. In 2D, at most four values of t are computed, one for each of the four window edges; in 3D, at most six values. The values are kept or discarded on the basis of exactly the same criteria as those for 2D until exactly two values of t remain (the values will be in the interval [0, 1]). For any value of t that is neither 0 nor 1, Eqs. (6.42), (6.43), and (6.44) are used to compute the values of x, y, and z. In the case of the parallel-projection canonical view volume, we do the extension to 3D by working with the code given in Section 3.12.4. In the case of the perspective-projection canonical view volume, new values of N_i, P_{Ei}, $P_0 - P_{Ei}$, and t need to be found for the six planes; they are given in Table 6.1. The actual code developed by Liang and Barsky but modified to be consistent with our variable names and to use outward rather than inward normals is given in Fig. 6.55. The correspondence between the numerator and denominator of the fractions in the last column of Table 6.1 and the terms in the code can be seen by inspection. The sign of $-N_i \cdot D$, which is the denominator of t, is used by procedure CLIPt in Fig. 6.55 to determine whether the intersection is potentially entering or potentially leaving. Hence, in

TABLE 6.1 KEY VARIABLES AND EQUATIONS FOR CYRUS–BECK 3D CLIPPING AGAINST THE CANONICAL PERSPECTIVE PROJECTION VIEW VOLUME*

Clip edge	Outward normal N_i	Point on edge, P_{Ei}	$P_0 - P_{Ei}$	$t = \dfrac{N_i \cdot (P_0 - P_{Ei})}{-N_i \cdot D}$	
right: $x = -z$	$(1, 0, 1)$	$(x, y, -x)$	$(x_0 - x, y_0 - y, z_0 + x)$	$\dfrac{(x_0 - x) + (z_0 + x)}{-(dx + dz)}$	$= \dfrac{x_0 + z_0}{-dx - dz}$
left: $x = z$	$(-1, 0, 1)$	(x, y, x)	$(x_0 - x, y_0 - y, z_0 - x)$	$\dfrac{-(x_0 - x) + (z_0 - x)}{dx - dz}$	$= \dfrac{-x_0 + z_0}{dx - dz}$
bottom: $y = z$	$(0, -1, 1)$	(x, y, y)	$(x_0 - x, y_0 - y, z_0 - y)$	$\dfrac{-(y_0 - y) + (z_0 - y)}{dy - dz}$	$= \dfrac{-y_0 + z_0}{dy - dz}$
top: $y = -z$	$(0, 1, 1)$	$(x, y, -y)$	$(x_0 - x, y_0 - y, z_0 + y)$	$\dfrac{(y_0 - y) + (z_0 + y)}{-dy - dz}$	$= \dfrac{y_0 + z_0}{-dy - dz}$
front: $z = z_{min}$	$(0, 0, 1)$	(x, y, z_{min})	$(x_0 - x, y_0 - y, z_0 - z_{min})$	$\dfrac{(z_0 - z_{min})}{-dz}$	$= \dfrac{z_0 - z_{min}}{-dz}$
back: $z = -1$	$(0, 0, -1)$	$(x, y, -1)$	$(x_0 - x, y_0 - y, z_0 + 1)$	$\dfrac{-(z_0 + 1)}{dz}$	$-\dfrac{-z_0 - 1}{dz}$

*The variable D, which is $P_1 - P_0$, is represented as (dx, dy, dz). The exact coordinates of the point P_{Ei} on each edge are irrelevant to the computation, so they have been denoted by variables x, y, and z. For a point on the right edge, $z = -x$, as indicated in the first row, third entry.

```
void Clip3D (double *x0, double *y0, double *z0, double *x1, double *y1, double *z1,
    double *zmin, boolean *accept)
{
    double tmin = 0.0, tmax = 1.0;
    double dx = *x1 − *x0, dz = *z1 − *z0;
    *accept = FALSE;          /* Assume initially that none of the line is visible */
    if (CLIPt (−dx − dz, *x0 + *z0, &tmin, &tmax))               /* Right side */
        if (CLIPt (dx − dz, −*x0 + *z0, &tmin, &tmax)) {         /* Left side */
            /* If get this far, part of line is in −z ≤ x ≤ z */
            double dy = *y1 − *y0;
            if (CLIPt (dy − dz, −*y0 + *z0, &tmin, &tmax))       /* Bottom */
                if (CLIPt (−dy − dz, *y0 + *z0, &tmin, &tmax))   /* Top */
                    /* If get this far, part of line is in −z ≤ x ≤ z, −z ≤ y ≤ z */
                    if (CLIPt (−dz, *z0 − *zmin, &tmin, &tmax))  /* Front */
                        if (CLIPt (dz, −*z0 − 1, &tmin, &tmax)) { /* Back */
                            /* If get here, part of line is visible in −z ≤ x ≤ z, */
                            /* −z ≤ y ≤ z, −1 ≤ z ≤ zmin */
                            *accept = TRUE;                       /* Part of line is visible */
                            /* If endpoint 1 (t = 1) is not in the region, compute intersection */
                            if (tmax < 1.0) {                     /* Eqs. 6.37 to 6.39 */
                                *x1= *x0 + tmax * dx;
                                *y1= *y0 + tmax * dy;
                                *z1= *z0 + tmax * dz;
                            }
                            /* If endpoint 0 (t = 0) is not in the region, compute intersection */
                            if (tmin > 0.0) {                     /* Eqs. 6.37 to 6.39 */
                                *x0 += tmin * dx;
                                *y0 += tmin * dy;
                                *z0 += tmin * dz;
                            }
                        }   /* Calculating intersection */
        }
}   /* Clip3D */
```

Fig. 6.55 The Liang–Barsky 2D clipping algorithm, extended to the 3D canonical perspective-projection view volume. The code is from [LIAN84]. The function CLIPt is in Chapter 3, Fig. 3.45.

the algebraic simplifications done in the table, the sign of the denominator of t is always maintained.

The Sutherland–Hodgman polygon-clipping algorithm can be readily adapted to 3D. We use six clipping planes rather than four, by making six calls to S_H_CLIP (Chapter 3) instead of four.

Once the clipping is done, the surviving output primitives are projected onto the projection plane with either M_{ort} or M_{per}, and are transformed for display into the physical-device-coordinate viewport.

6.5.4   Clipping in Homogeneous Coordinates

There are two reasons to clip in homogeneous coordinates. The first has to do with efficiency: It is possible to transform the perspective-projection canonical view volume into the parallel-projection canonical view volume, so a single clip procedure, optimized for the parallel-projection canonical view volume, can always be used. However, the clipping must be done in homogeneous coordinates to ensure correct results. A single clip procedure is typically provided in hardware implementations of the viewing operation (Chapter 18). The second reason is that points that can occur as a result of unusual homogeneous transformations and from use of rational parametric splines (Chapter 11) can have negative W and can be clipped properly in homogeneous coordinates but not in 3D.

With regard to clipping, it can be shown that the transformation from the perspective-projection canonical view volume to the parallel-projection canonical view volume is

$$M = \begin{bmatrix} 1 & 0 & 0 & 0 \\ 0 & 1 & 0 & 0 \\ 0 & 0 & \dfrac{1}{1 + z_{min}} & \dfrac{-z_{min}}{1 + z_{min}} \\ 0 & 0 & -1 & 0 \end{bmatrix}, \qquad z_{min} \neq -1. \qquad (6.48)$$

Recall from Eq. (6.40) that $z_{min} = -(vrp_z' + F)/(vrp_z' + B)$, and from Eq. (6.33) that VRP′ $= SH_{par} \cdot T(-PRP) \cdot [0\ 0\ 0\ 1]^T$. Figure 6.56 shows the results of applying M to the perspective-projection canonical view volume.

The matrix M is integrated with the perspective-projection normalizing transformation N_{per}:

$$N_{per}' = M \cdot N_{per} = M \cdot S_{per} \cdot SH_{par} \cdot T(-PRP) \cdot R \cdot T(-VRP). \qquad (6.49)$$

By using N_{per}' instead of N_{per} for perspective projections, and by continuing to use N_{par} for parallel projections, we can clip against the parallel-projection canonical view volume rather than against the perspective-projection canonical view volume.

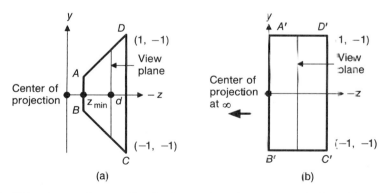

Fig 6.56 Side views of normalized perspective view volume before (a) and after (b) application of matrix M.

The 3D parallel-projection view volume is defined by $-1 \le x \le 1, -1 \le y \le 1, -1 \le z \le 0$. We find the corresponding inequalities in homogeneous coordinates by replacing x by X/W, y by Y/W, and z by Z/W, which results in

$$-1 \le X/W \le 1, \quad -1 \le Y/W \le 1, \quad -1 \le Z/W \le 0. \tag{6.50}$$

The corresponding plane equations are

$$X = -W, X = W, Y = -W, Y = W, Z = -W, Z = 0. \tag{6.51}$$

To understand how to use these limits and planes, we must consider separately the cases of $W > 0$ and $W < 0$. In the first case, we can multiply the inequalities of Eq. (6.50) by W without changing the sense of the inequalities. In the second case, the multiplication changes the sense. This result can be expressed as

$$W > 0: \quad -W \le X \le W, \quad -W \le Y \le W, \quad -W \le Z \le 0, \tag{6.52}$$

$$W < 0: \quad -W \ge X \ge W, \quad -W \ge Y \ge W, \quad -W \ge Z \ge 0. \tag{6.53}$$

In the case at hand—that of clipping ordinary lines and points—only the region given by Eq. (6.52) needs to be used, because prior to application of M, all visible points have $W > 0$ (normally $W = 1$).

As we shall see in Chapter 11, however, it is sometimes desirable to represent points directly in homogeneous coordinates with arbitrary W coordinates. Hence, we might have a $W < 0$, meaning that clipping must be done against the regions given by Eqs. (6.52) and (6.53). Figure 6.57 shows these as region A and region B, and also shows why both regions must be used.

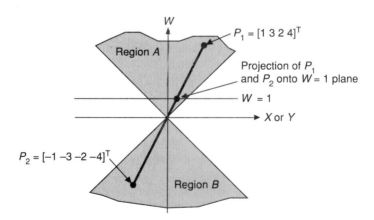

Fig. 6.57 The points P_1 and P_2 both map into the same point on the $W = 1$ plane, as do all other points on the line through the origin and the two points. Clipping in homogeneous coordinates against just region A will incorrectly reject P_2.

The point $P_1 = [1 \quad 3 \quad 2 \quad 4]^T$ in region A transforms into the 3D point $(\frac{1}{4}, \frac{3}{4}, \frac{2}{4})$, which is in the canonical view volume $-1 \le x \le 1, -1 \le y \le 1, -1 \le z \le 0$. The point $P_2 = -P_1 = [-1 \quad -3 \quad -2 \quad -4]^T$, which is *not* in region A but *is* in region B, transforms into the same 3D point as P_1; namely, $(\frac{1}{4}, \frac{3}{4}, \frac{2}{4})$. If clipping were only to region A, then P_2 would be discarded incorrectly. This possibility arises because the homogeneous coordinate points P_1 and P_2 differ by a constant multiplier (-1), and we know that such homogeneous points correspond to the same 3D point (on the $W = 1$ plane of homogeneous space).

There are two solutions to this problem of points in region B. One is to clip all points twice, once against each region. But doing two clips is expensive. A better solution is to negate points, such as P_2, with negative W, and then to clip them. Similarly, we can clip properly a line whose endpoints are both in region B of Fig. 6.57 by multiplying both endpoints by -1, to place the points in region A.

Another problem arises with lines such as P_1P_2, shown in Fig. 6.58, whose endpoints have opposite values of W. The projection of the line onto the $W = 1$ plane is two segments, one of which goes to $+\infty$, the other to $-\infty$. The solution now is to clip twice, once against each region, with the possibility that each clip will return a visible line segment. A simple way to do this is to clip the line against region A, to negate both endpoints of the line, and to clip again against region A. This approach preserves one of the original purposes of clipping in homogeneous coordinates: using a single clip region. Interested readers are referred to [BLIN78a] for further discussion.

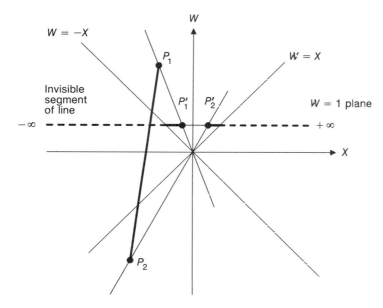

Fig. 6.58 The line P_1P_2 projects onto two line segments, one from $P_2{'}$ to $+\infty$, the other from $P_1{'}$ to $-\infty$ (shown as solid thick lines where they are in the clip region, and as dashed thick lines where they are outside the clip region). The line must be clipped twice, once against each region.

Given Eq. (6.51), the Cohen–Sutherland or Cyrus–Beck algorithm can be used for the actual clipping. ([LIAN84] gives code for the Cyrus–Beck approach; see also Exercise 6.25.) The only difference is that the clipping is in 4D, as opposed to 3D.

6.5.5 Mapping into a Viewport

Output primitives are clipped in the normalized projection coordinate system, which is also called the 3D screen coordinate system. We will assume for this discussion that the canonical parallel projection view volume has been used for clipping (the perspective projection M transforms the perspective projection view volume into the parallel projection view volume if this assumption is incorrect). Hence the coordinates of all output primitives that remain are in the view volume $-1 \le x \le 1, -1 \le y \le 1, -1 \le z \le 0$.

The PHIGS programmer specifies a 3D viewport into which the contents of this view volume are mapped. The 3D viewport is contained in the unit cube $0 \le x \le 1, 0 \le y \le 1, 0 \le z \le 1$. The $z = 1$ front face of the unit cube is mapped into the largest square that can be inscribed on the display screen. We assume that the lower left corner of the square is at $(0, 0)$. For example, on a display device with a horizontal resolution of 1024 and a vertical resolution of 800, the square is the region $0 \le x \le 799, 0 \le y \le 799$. Points in the unit cube are displayed by discarding their z coordinate. Hence the point $(0.5, 0.75, 0.46)$ would be displayed at the device coordinates $(400, 599)$. In the case of visible-surface determination (Chapter 15), the z coordinate of each output primitive is used to determine which primitives are visible and which are obscured by other primitives with larger z.

Given a 3D viewport within the unit cube with coordinates $x_{v.min}$, $x_{v.max}$, and so forth, the mapping from the canonical parallel projection view volume into the 3D viewport can be thought of as a three-step process. In the first step, the canonical parallel projection view volume is translated so its corner, $(-1, -1, -1)$, becomes the origin. This is effected by the translation $T(1, 1, 1)$. Next, the translated view volume is scaled into the size of the 3D viewport, with the scale

$$S\left(\frac{x_{v.max} - x_{v.min}}{2}, \frac{y_{v.max} - y_{v.min}}{2}, \frac{z_{v.max} - z_{v.min}}{1}\right).$$

Finally, the properly scaled view volume is translated to the lower-left corner of the viewport by the translation $T(x_{v.min}, y_{v.min}, z_{z.min})$. Hence the composite canonical view volume to 3D viewport transformation is

$$M_{VV3DV} = T(x_{v.min}, y_{v.min}, z_{v.min}) \cdot S\left(\frac{x_{v.max} - x_{v.min}}{2}, \frac{y_{v.max} - y_{v.min}}{2}, \frac{z_{v.max} - z_{v.min}}{1}\right) \cdot T(1, 1, 1) \tag{6.54}$$

Note that this is similar to, but not the same as, the window to viewport transformation M_{WV} developed in Section 5.4.

6.5.6 Implementation Summary

There are two generally used implementations of the overall viewing transformation. The first, depicted in Fig. 6.46 and discussed in Sections 6.5.1 through 6.5.3, is appropriate when output primitives are defined in 3D and the transformations applied to the output primitives never create a negative W. Its steps are as follows:

1. Extend 3D coordinates to homogeneous coordinates

2. Apply normalizing transformation N_{par} or N_{per}

3. Divide by W to map back to 3D (in some cases, it is known that $W = 1$, so the division is not needed)

4. Clip in 3D against the parallel-projection or perspective-projection canonical view volume, whichever is appropriate

5. Extend 3D coordinates to homogeneous coordinates

6. Perform parallel projection using M_{ort}, Eq. (6.11), or perform perspective projection, using M_{per}, Eq. (6.3) with $d = -1$ (because the canonical view volume lies along the $-z$ axis)

7. Translate and scale into device coordinates using Eq. (6.54)

8. Divide by W to map from homogeneous to 2D coordinates; the division effects the perspective projection.

Steps 6 and 7 are performed by a single matrix multiplication, and correspond to stages 3 and 4 in Fig. 6.46.

The second way to implement the viewing operation is required whenever output primitives are defined in homogeneous coordinates and might have $W < 0$, when the transformations applied to the output primitives might create a negative W, or when a single clip algorithm is implemented. As discussed in Section 6.5.4, its steps are as follows:

1. Extend 3D coordinates to homogeneous coordinates

2. Apply normalizing transformation N_{par} or N_{per}' (which includes M, Eq. (6.48))

3. If $W > 0$, clip in homogeneous coordinates against the volume defined by Eq. 6.52; else, clip in homogeneous coordinates against the two view volumes defined by Eqs. (6.52) and (6.53)

4. Translate and scale into device coordinates using Eq. (6.54)

5. Divide by W to map from homogeneous coordinates to 2D coordinates; the division effects the perspective projection.

6.6 COORDINATE SYSTEMS

Several different coordinate systems have been used in Chapters 5 and 6. In this section, we summarize all the systems, and also discuss their relationships to one another. Synonyms used in various references and graphics subroutine packages are also given. Figure 6.59 shows the progression of coordinate systems, using the terms generally used in this text; in any particular graphics subroutine package, only some of the coordinate systems are actually used. We have chosen names for the various coordinate systems to reflect common usage; some of the names therefore are not logically consistent with one another. Note that the term *space* is sometimes used as a synonym for *system*.

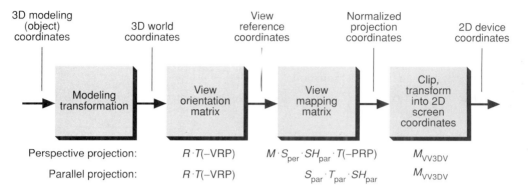

Fig. 6.59 Coordinate systems and how they relate to one another. The matrices underneath each stage effect the transformation applied at that stage for the perspective and parallel projections.

Starting with the coordinate system that is furthest removed from the actual display device, on the left of Fig. 6.59, individual objects are defined in an *object-coordinate system*. PHIGS calls this the *modeling-coordinate system*; the term *local coordinate system* is also commonly used. As we shall discuss further in Chapter 7, there is often a hierarchy of modeling coordinate systems.

Objects are transformed into the *world-coordinate system*, the system in which a scene or complete object is represented in the computer, by the *modeling transformation*. This system is sometimes called the *problem-coordinate system* or *application-coordinate system*.

The *view-reference coordinate system* is used by PHIGS as a coordinate system to define a view volume. It is also called the (u, v, n) system, or the (u, v, VPN) system. The Core system [GSPC79] used a similar, but unnamed, left-handed system. The left-handed system is used so that, with the eye or camera at the origin looking toward $+z$, increasing values of z are farther away from the eye, x is to the right, and y is up.

Other packages, such as Pixar's RenderMan [PIXA88], place constraints on the view-reference coordinate system, requiring that the origin be at the center of projection and that the view plane normal be the z axis. We call this the *eye-coordinate system*; Renderman and some other systems use the term *camera-coordinate system*. Referring back to Section 6.5, the first three steps of the perspective-projection normalizing transformation convert from the world-coordinate system into the eye-coordinate system. The eye-coordinate system is sometimes left-handed.

From eye coordinates, we next go to the *normalized-projection coordinate system*, or *3D screen coordinates*, the coordinate system of the parallel-projection canonical view volume (and of the perspective-projection canonical view volume after the perspective transformation). The Core system calls this system *3D normalized device coordinates*. Sometimes, the system is called *3D logical device coordinates*. The term *normalized* generally means that all the coordinate values are in either the interval [0, 1] or [−1, 1], whereas the term *logical* generally means that coordinate values are in some other prespecified range, such as [0, 1023], which is typically defined to correspond to some widely available device's coordinate system. In some cases, this system is not normalized.

Projecting from 3D into 2D creates what we call the *2D device coordinate system*, also called the *normalized device-coordinate system*, the *image-coordinate system* by [SUTH74], or the *screen-coordinate system* by RenderMan. Other terms used include *screen coordinates*, *device coordinates*, *2D device coordinates*, *physical device coordinates* (in contrast to the logical device coordinates mentioned previously). RenderMan calls the physical form of the space *raster coordinates*.

Unfortunately, there is no single standard usage for many of these terms. For example, the term *screen-coordinate system* is used by different authors to refer to the last three systems discussed, covering both 2D and 3D coordinates, and both logical and physical coordinates.

EXERCISES

6.1 Write a program that accepts a viewing specification, calculates either N_{par} or N_{per}, and displays the house.

6.2 Program 3D clipping algorithms for parallel and perspective projections.

6.3 Show that, for a parallel projection with $F = -\infty$ and $B = +\infty$, the result of clipping in 3D and then projecting to 2D is the same as the result of projecting to 2D and then clipping in 2D.

6.4 Show that, if all objects are in front of the center of projection and if $F = -\infty$ and $B = +\infty$, then the result of clipping in 3D against the perspective-projection canonical view volume followed by perspective projection is the same as first doing a perspective projection into 2D and then clipping in 2D.

6.5 Verify that S_{per} (Section 6.5.2) transforms the view volume of Fig. 6.54(a) into that of Fig. 6.54(b).

6.6 Write the code for 3D clipping against the unit cube. Generalize the code to clip against any rectangular solid with faces normal to the principal axes. Is the generalized code more or less efficient than that for the unit-cube case?

6.7 Write the code for 3D clipping against the perspective-projection canonical view volume. Now generalize to the view volume defined by

$$-a \cdot z_v \leq x_v \leq b \cdot z_v, \quad -c \cdot z_v \leq y_v \leq d \cdot z_v, \quad z_{min} \leq z_v \leq z_{max}.$$

This is the general form of the view volume after steps 1 to 4 of the perspective normalizing transformation. Which case is more efficient?

6.8 Write the code for 3D clipping against a general six-faced polyhedral view volume whose faces are defined by

$$A_i x + B_i y + C_i z + D_i = 0, \ 1 \leq i \leq 6.$$

Compare the computational effort needed with that required for each of the following:
  a. Clipping against either of the canonical view volumes
  b. Applying N_{par} and then clipping against the unit cube.

6.9 Consider a line in 3D going from the world-coordinate points P_1 (6, 10, 3) to P_2 (−3, −5, 2) and a semi-infinite viewing pyramid in the region $-z \leq x \leq z$, $-z \leq y \leq z$, which is bounded by the planes $z = +x$, $z = -x$, $z = +y$, $z = -y$. The projection plane is at $z = 1$.

    a. Clip the line in 3D (using parametric line equations), then project it onto the projection plane. What are the clipped endpoints on the plane?

    b. Project the line onto the plane, then clip the lines using 2D computations. What are the clipped endpoints on the plane?

(Hint: If your answers to (a) and (b) are not identical, try again!)

6.10 Show what happens when an object "behind" the center of projection is projected by M_{per} and then clipped. Your answer should demonstrate why, in general, one cannot project and then clip.

6.11 Consider the 2D viewing operation, with a rotated window. Devise a normalized transformation to transform the window into the unit square. The window is specified by u_{min}, v_{min}, u_{max}, v_{max} in the VRC coordinate system, as in Fig. 6.60. Show that this transformation is the same as that for the general 3D N_{par}, when the projection plane is the (x, y) plane and VUP has an x component of $-\sin\theta$ and a y component of $\cos\theta$ (i.e., the parallel projection of VUP onto the view plane is the v axis).

6.12 The matrix M_{per} in Section 6.4 defines a one-point perspective projection. What is the form of the 4×4 matrix that defines a two-point perspective? What is the form of the matrix that defines a three-point perspective? (Hint: Try multiplying M_{per} by various rotation matrices.)

6.13 What is the effect of applying M_{per} to points whose z coordinate is less than zero?

6.14 Devise a clipping algorithm for a cone-shaped (having a circular cross-section) view volume. The cone's apex is at the origin, its axis is the positive z axis, and it has a 90° interior angle. Consider using a spherical coordinate system.

6.15 Design and implement a set of utility subroutines to generate a 4×4 transformation matrix from an arbitrary sequence of R, S, and T primitive transformations.

6.16 Draw a decision tree to be used when determining the type of a projection used in creating an image. Apply this decision tree to the figures in this chapter that are projections from 3D.

6.17 Evaluate the speed tradeoffs of performing 3D clipping by using the Cohen–Sutherland algorithm versus using the 3D Cyrus–Beck algorithm. First, write an assembly-language version of the program. Count operations executed for each fundamentally different case treated by the algorithms, and weight the cases equally. (For example, in the Cohen–Sutherland algorithm, trivial accept, trivial reject, and calculating 1, 2, 3, or 4 interesections are the fundamentally different cases.) Ignore the time taken by subroutine calls (assume that in-line code is used). Differentiate instructions by the number of cycles they require.

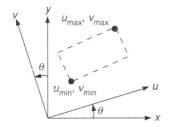

Fig. 6.60 A rotated window.

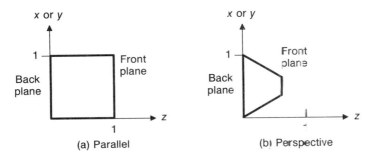

Fig. 6.61 The default view volumes used by PHIGS. The view volumes are slightly different from those used in this chapter, as given in Fig. 6.45.

6.18 In Exercise 6.17, we made the assumption that all cases were equally likely. Is this a good assumption? Explain your answer. Apply either of the algorithms to a variety of real objects, using various view volumes, to get a sense of how the mix of cases varies in a realistic setting.

6.19 The canonical view volume for the parallel projection was taken to be the $2 \times 2 \times 1$ rectangular parallelepiped. Suppose the unit cube in the positive octant, with one corner at the origin, is used instead.
    a. Find the normalization N_{par}' for this view volume.
    b. Find the corresponding homogeneous-coordinate view volume.

6.20 Give the viewing parameters for top, front, and side views of the house with the VRP in the middle of the window. Must the PRP be different for each of the views? Why or why not?

6.21 Verify that Eq. (6.48) does indeed transform the canonical perspective view volume of Fig. 6.56(a) into the canonical parallel view volume of Fig. 6.56(b).

6.22 In PHIGS, the viewing specification allows the view plane to be at a distance VPD from the VRP. Redevelop the canonical viewing transformations N_{par} and N_{per} to include VPD. Set VPD = 0 to make sure that your results specialize to those in the text.

6.23 Reformulate the derivations of N_{per} and N_{par} to incorporate the matrix $M_{general}$.

6.24 Show how to convert from the six viewing parameters of Fig. 6.35 into the viewing parameters discussed in this chapter. Write and test a utility subroutine to effect the conversion.

6.25 For the homogeneous clip planes $X = -W$, $X = W$, $Y = -W$, $Y = W$, $Z = 0$, $Z = -W$, complete a table like Table 6.1 for using the Cyrus–Beck clipping approach for the W > 0 region given by $W > 0$, $-W \le X \le W$, $-W \le Y \le W$, $-W \le Z \le 0$.

6.26 PHIGS uses the default view volumes shown in Fig. 6.61. These are slightly different from the canonical view volumes used in this chapter, as shown in Fig. 6.45. Modify the N_{par} and N_{per} transformations to map into the PHIGS default.

6.27 Stereo pairs are two views of the same scene made from slightly different projection reference points, but with the same view reference point. Let d be the stereo separation; that is, the distance between the two reference points. If we think of the reference points as our eyes, then d is the distance between our eyes. Let P be the point midway between our eyes. Given P, d, VRP, VPN, and VUP, derive expressions for the two projection reference points.

7
Object Hierarchy and Simple PHIGS (SPHIGS)

**Andries van Dam
and David Sklar**

A graphics package is an intermediary between an application program and the graphics hardware. The output primitives and interaction devices that a graphics package supports can range from rudimentary to extremely rich. In Chapter 2, we described the fairly simple and low-level SRGP package, and we noted some of its limitations. In this chapter, we describe a package based on a considerably richer but more complex standard graphics package, PHIGS (Programmer's Hierarchical Interactive Graphics System[1]). A *standard graphics package* such as PHIGS or GKS (Graphical Kernel System) implements a specification designated as standard by an official national or international standards body; GKS and PHIGS have been so designated by ANSI (American National Standards Institute) and ISO (International Standards Organization). The main purpose of such standards is to promote portability of application programs and of programmers. Nonofficial standards are also developed, promoted, and licensed by individual companies or by consortia of companies and universities; Adobe's PostScript and MIT's X Window System are two of the current industry standards.

The package described here is called SPHIGS (for Simple PHIGS; pronounced "ess-figs") because it is essentially a subset of PHIGS. It preserves most of PHIGS's capabilities and power, but simplifies or modifies various features to suit straightforward applications. SPHIGS also includes several enhancements adapted from PHIGS+ extensions. Our aim in designing SPHIGS has been to introduce concepts in the simplest possible

---

[1] The term "PHIGS" in this chapter also includes a set of extensions to PHIGS, called PHIGS+, that supports advanced geometric primitives such as polyhedra, curves, and surfaces, as well as rendering techniques that use lighting, shading, and depth-cueing, discussed in Chapters 14–16.

285

way, not to provide a package that is strictly upward-compatible with PHIGS. However, an SPHIGS application can easily be adapted to run with PHIGS. Footnotes present some of the important differences between SPHIGS and PHIGS; in general, an SPHIGS feature is also present in PHIGS unless otherwise noted.

There are three major differences between SPHIGS and integer raster packages, such as SRGP or the Xlib package of the X Window System. First, to suit engineering and scientific applications, SPHIGS uses a 3D, floating-point coordinate system, and implements the 3D viewing pipeline discussed in Chapter 6.

The second, farther-reaching difference is that SPHIGS maintains a database of structures. A *structure* is a logical grouping of primitives, attributes, and other information. The programmer can modify structures in the database with a few editing commands; SPHIGS ensures that the screen's image is an accurate representation of the contents of the stored database. Structures contain not only specifications of primitives and attributes, but also invocations of subordinate structures. They thus exhibit some of the properties of procedures in programming languages. In particular, just as procedure hierarchy is induced by procedures invoking subprocedures, structure hierarchy is induced by structures invoking substructures. Such hierarchical composition is especially powerful when one can control the geometry (position, orientation, size) and appearance (color, style, thickness, etc.) of any invocation of a substructure.

The third difference is that SPHIGS operates in an abstract, 3D world-coordinate system, not in 2D screen space, and therefore does not support direct pixel manipulation. Because of these differences, SPHIGS and SRGP address different sets of needs and applications; as we pointed out in Chapter 2, each has its place—no single graphics package meets all needs.

Because of its ability to support structure hierarchy, SPHIGS is well suited to applications based on models with component–subcomponent hierarchy; indeed, the SPHIGS structure hierarchy can be viewed as a special-purpose modeling hierarchy. We therefore look at modeling in general in Section 7.1, before discussing the specifics of geometric modeling with SPHIGS. Sections 7.2 through 7.9 show how to create, display, and edit the SPHIGS structure database. Section 7.10 discusses interaction, particularly pick correlation. The remainder of the chapter presents PHIGS features not found in SPHIGS, discusses implementation issues, and closes with evaluations of SPHIGS and of alternative methods for encoding hierarchy.

7.1 GEOMETRIC MODELING

7.1.1 What Is a Model?

You have encountered many examples of models in courses in the physical and social sciences. For example, you are probably familiar with the Bohr model of the atom, in which spheres representing electrons orbit a spherical nucleus containing neutron and proton spheres. Other examples are the exponential unconstrained growth model in biology, and macro- or microeconometric models that purport to describe some aspect of an economy. A model is a representation of some (not necessarily all) features of a concrete or abstract entity. The purpose of a model of an entity is to allow people to visualize and understand the structure or behavior of the entity, and to provide a convenient vehicle for "experimentation" with and prediction of the effects of inputs or changes to the model. Quantitative models common in physical and social sciences and engineering are usually expressed as systems of equations, and the modeler will experiment by varying the values of independent variables, coefficients, and exponents. Often, models simplify the actual structure or behavior of the modeled entity to make the model easier to visualize or, for those models represented by systems of equations, to make the model computationally tractable.

We restrict ourselves in this book to the discussion of computer-based models—in particular, to those that lend themselves to graphic interpretation. Graphics can be used to create and edit the model, to obtain values for its parameters, and to visualize its behavior and structure. The model and the graphical means for creating and visualizing it are distinct; models such as population models need not have any inherent graphical aspects. Among common types of models for which computer graphics is used are these:

- *Organizational models* are hierarchies representing institutional bureaucracies and taxonomies, such as library classification schemes and biological taxonomies. These models have various directed-graph representations, such as the organization chart.

- *Quantitative models* are equations describing econometric, financial, sociological, demographic, climatic, chemical, physical, and mathematical systems. These are often depicted by graphs or statistical plots.

- *Geometric models* are collections of components with well-defined geometry and, often, interconnections between components, including engineering and architectural structures, molecules and other chemical structures, geographic structures, and vehicles. These models are usually depicted by block diagrams or by pseudorealistic "synthetic photographs."

Computer-assisted modeling allows pharmaceutical drug designers to model the chemical behavior of new compounds that may be effective against particular diseases, aeronautical engineers to predict wing deformation during supersonic flight, pilots to learn to fly, nuclear-reactor experts to predict the effects of various plant malfunctions and to develop the appropriate remedies, and automobile designers to test the integrity of the passenger compartment during crashes. In these and many other instances, it is far easier, cheaper, and safer to experiment with a model than with a real entity. In fact, in many situations, such as training of space-shuttle pilots and studies of nuclear-reactor safety, modeling and simulation are the only feasible method for learning about the system. For these reasons, computer modeling is replacing more traditional techniques, such as wind-tunnel tests. Engineers and scientists now can perform many of their experiments with digital wind tunnels, microscopes, telescopes, and so on. Such numerically based simulation and animation of models is rapidly becoming a new paradigm in science, taking its place beside the traditional branches of theory and physical experimentation. Needless to say, the modeling and simulation are only as good as the model and its inputs—the caution "garbage in, garbage out" pertains especially to modeling.

Models need not necessarily contain intrinsically geometric data; abstractions such as organizational models are not spatially oriented. Nonetheless, most such models can be represented geometrically; for example, an organizational model may be represented by an organization chart, or the results of a clinical drug evaluation may be represented by a histogram. Even when a model represents an intrinsically geometric object, no fixed graphical representation in the model or view of that model is dictated. For example, we can choose whether to represent a robot as a collection of polyhedra or of curved surfaces, and we can specify how the robot is to be "photographed"—from which viewpoint, with which type of geometric projection, and with what degree of realism. Also, we may choose to show either the structure or the behavior of a model pictorially; for instance, we may want to see both a VLSI circuit's physical layout on the chip and its electrical and logical behaviors as functions of inputs and time.

7.1.2 Geometric Models

Geometric or graphical models describe components with inherent geometrical properties and thus lend themselves naturally to graphical representation. Among the ingredients a geometric model may represent are the following:

- Spatial layout and shape of components (i.e., the *geometry* of the entity), and other attributes affecting the appearance of components, such as color

- Connectivity of components (i.e., the structure or *topology* of the entity); note that connectivity information may be specified abstractly (say, in an adjacency matrix for networks or in a tree structure for a hierarchy), or may have its own intrinsic geometry (the dimensions of channels in an integrated circuit)

- Application-specific data values and properties associated with components, such as electrical characteristics or descriptive text.

Associated with the model may be processing algorithms, such as linear-circuit analysis for discrete circuit models, finite-element analysis for mechanical structures, and energy minimization for molecular models.

There is a tradeoff between what is stored explicitly in the model and what must be computed prior to analysis or display—a classical space–time tradeoff. For example, a model of a computer network could store the connecting lines explicitly or could recompute them from a connectivity matrix with a simple graph-layout algorithm each time a new view is requested. Enough information must be kept with the model to allow analysis and display, but the exact format and the choices of encoding techniques depend on the application and on space-time tradeoffs.

7.1.3 Hierarchy in Geometric Models

Geometric models often have a hierarchical structure induced by a bottom-up construction process: Components are used as building blocks to create higher-level entities, which in turn serve as building blocks for yet higher-level entities, and so on. Like large programming systems, hierarchies are seldom constructed strictly bottom-up or top-down; what matters is the final hierarchy, not the exact construction process. Object hierarchies are common because few entities are monolithic (indivisible); once we decompose an entity into a collection of parts, we have created at least a two-level hierarchy. In the uncommon

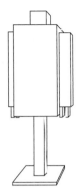

Fig. 7.1 Perspective view of simplified android robot.

case that each object is included only once in a higher-level object, the hierarchy can be symbolized as a tree, with objects as nodes and inclusion relations between objects as edges. In the more common case of objects included multiple times, the hierarchy is symbolized by a *directed acyclic graph* (DAG). As a simple example of object hierarchy, Fig. 7.1 shows a perspective view of a rudimentary "android" robot; Fig. 7.2(a) shows the robot's structure as a DAG. Note that we can duplicate the multiply included objects to convert the DAG to a tree (Fig. 7.2b). By convention, the arrows are left off as redundant because the ordering relationship between nodes is indicated by the nodes' relative positions in the tree—if node A is above node B, then A includes B.

The robot is composed of an upper body swiveling on a base. The upper body is composed of a head that rotates relative to a trunk; the trunk also has attached to it two identical arms that may rotate independently through a horizontal axis "at the shoulder." The arm is composed of a fixed part, "the hand," and a thumb that slides parallel to the hand to form a primitive gripper. Thus, the thumb object is invoked once in the arm, and the arm object is invoked twice in the upper body. We discuss the creation of this robot throughout this chapter; its shape is also presented in three orthographic projections in windows 2–4 of the screen shown in Fig. 7.7(b).

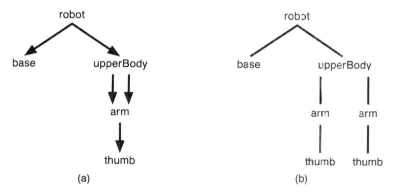

Fig. 7.2 Hierarchy of robot components. (a) Directed acyclic graph (DAG). (b) Tree.

Although an object in a hierarchy is composed of geometric primitives as well as inclusions of lower-level subobjects, the DAG and the tree representing the robot's hierarchy show only references to subobjects. This is analogous to the procedure-hierarchy diagram commonly used to show the calling structure of a program in a high-level procedural language. It is important to note that it is up to the designer to decide exactly how a composite object is hierarchically constructed. For example, the robot could have been modeled as a two-level hierarchy, with a root object consisting of a base, a head and a trunk as geometric primitives (parallelepipeds, say), and two references to an "atomic" arm object composed of geometric primitives only.

Many systems, such as computer networks or chemical plants, can be represented by network diagrams, in which objects are not only included multiple times, but are also interconnected arbitrarily. Such networks are also modeled as graphs, possibly even containing cycles, but they can still exhibit properties of object-inclusion hierarchy when subnetworks occur multiple times.

To simplify the task of building complex objects (and their models), we commonly use application-specific atomic components as the basic building blocks. In 2D, these components are often drawn by using plastic or computer-drawn templates of standard symbolic shapes (also called symbols or stencils). In drawing programs, these shapes, in turn, are composed of geometric primitives, such as lines, rectangles, polygons, ellipse arcs, and so on. In 3D, shapes such as cylinders, parallelepipeds, spheres, pyramids, and surfaces of revolution are used as basic building blocks. These 3D shapes may be defined in terms of lower-level geometric primitives, such as 3D polygons; in this case, smoothly curved surfaces must be approximated by polygonal ones, with attendant loss of resolution. Alternatively, in advanced modeling systems that deal directly with free-form surfaces or volumes, shapes such as parametric polynomial surfaces, and solids such as cylinders, spheres, and cones, are themselves geometric primitives and are defined analytically, without loss of resolution—see Chapters 11 and 12. We use the term *object* in this chapter for those 2D or 3D components that are defined in their own modeling coordinate systems in terms of geometric primitives and lower-level objects, and that usually have not only geometrical data but also associated application data. An object is thus a (composite) shape and all its data.

A hierarchy, then, is created for a variety of purposes:

▪ To construct complex objects in a modular fashion, typically by repetitive invocations of building blocks that vary in geometric and appearance attributes

▪ To increase storage economy, since it suffices to store only references to objects that are used repeatedly, rather than the complete object definition each time

▪ To allow easy update propagation, because a change in the definition of one building-block object is automatically propagated to all higher-level objects that use that object (since they now refer to an updated version); the analogy between object and procedure hierarchy is useful here, in that a change to the body of a procedure is also reflected in all invocations of that procedure.

The application can use a variety of techniques to encode hierarchical models. For example, a network or relational database can be used to store information on objects and on relationships between objects. Alternatively, a more efficient, customized linked-list structure can be maintained by the application program, with records for objects and pointers for relationships. In some models, connections between objects are objects in their own right; they must also be represented with data records in the model. Yet another alternative is to use an object-oriented database [ZDON90]. Object-oriented programming environments such as SmallTalk [GOLD83], MacApp [SCHM86] and ET++ [WEIN88] are increasingly being used to store modeling information for the geometric objects in graphics application programs.

Interconnections.   In most networks, objects are placed in specified locations (either interactively by the user or automatically by the application program) and then are interconnected. Interconnections may be abstract and thus of arbitrary shape (e.g., in hierarchy or network diagrams, such as organization charts or project-scheduling charts), or they may have significant geometry of their own (e.g., a VLSI chip). If connections are abstract, we can use various standard conventions for laying out hierarchical or network diagrams, and we can employ attributes such as line style, line width, or color to denote various types of relationships (e.g., "dotted-line responsibility" in an organization chart). Connections whose shape matters, such as the channels connecting transistors and other components of a VLSI circuit, are essentially objects in their own right. Both abstract and nonabstract connections are often *constrained* to have horizontal or vertical orientations (sometimes called the *Manhattan* layout scheme) to simplify visualization and physical construction.

Parameter passing in object hierarchy.   Objects invoked as building blocks must be positioned in exactly the right place in their parent objects, and, in order to fit, often must be resized and reoriented as well. Homogeneous coordinate matrices were used to transform primitives in Chapter 5 and to normalize the view volume in Chapter 6, and it should come as no surprise that, in a hierarchical model, one frequently applies scaling, rotation, and translation matrices to subobjects. Sutherland first used this capability for graphical modeling in Sketchpad [SUTH63], coining the terms *master* for the definition of an object and *instance* for a geometrically transformed invocation. As discussed in Section 4.3.3, graphics systems using hierarchical display lists (also called structured display files) implement master–instance hierarchy in hardware, using subroutine jumps and high-speed floating-point arithmetic units for transformations.   Because we want to distinguish geometric transformations used in normalizing the view volume from those used in building object hierarchy, we often speak of the latter as *modeling transformations*. Mathematically, of course, there is no difference between modeling and normalizing transformations.

Once again, in analogy with procedure hierarchy, we sometimes speak of a parent object "calling" a child object in a hierarchy, and passing it "geometric parameters" corresponding to its scale, orientation, and position in the parent's coordinate system. As we see shortly, graphics packages that support object hierarchy, such as SPHIGS, can store, compose, and apply transformation matrices to vertices of primitives, as well as to vertices of instantiated child objects. Furthermore, attributes affecting appearance can also be passed to instantiated objects. In Section 7.5.3, however, we shall see that the SPHIGS parameter-passing mechanism is not as general as is that of a procedural language.

7.1.4 Relationship between Model, Application Program, and Graphics System

So far, we have looked at models in general, and geometric models with hierarchy and modeling transformations in particular. Before looking at SPHIGS, let us briefly review the conceptual model of graphics first shown in Fig. 1.5 and elaborated in Fig. 3.2, to show the interrelationship between the model, the application program, and the graphics system. In the diagram in Fig. 7.3, application programs are divided into five subsystems, labeled (a) through (e):

a. Build, modify, and maintain the model by adding, deleting, and replacing information in it

b. Traverse (scan) the model to extract information for display

c. Traverse the model to extract information used in the analysis of the model's behavior/performance

d. Display both information (e.g., rendering of a geometric model, output of an analysis) and user-interface "tools" (e.g., menus, dialog boxes)

e. Perform miscellaneous application tasks not directly involving the model or display (e.g., housekeeping).

The term *subsystem* does not imply major modules of code—a few calls or a short procedure may be sufficient to implement a given subsystem. Furthermore, a subsystem may be distributed throughout the application program, rather than being gathered in a separate program module. Thus, Fig. 7.3 simply shows logical components, not necessarily program structure components; moreover, while it does differentiate the procedures that

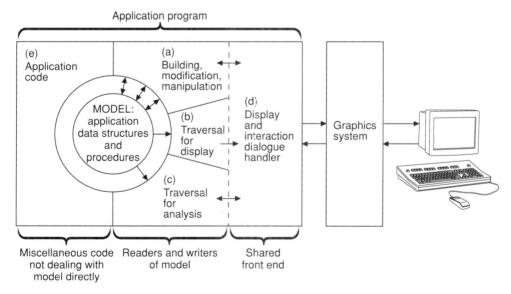

Fig. 7.3 The application model and its readers and writers.

build, modify, analyze, or display the model, it is not always clear whether to call a particular module part of the model or part of the model-maintenance code. It could be argued, for example, that a circuit-analysis module is really part of the model's definition because it describes how the circuit behaves. For a programmer using a traditional procedural language such as Pascal or C, Fig. 7.3 works best if one thinks of the model as primarily containing data. People familiar with object-oriented programming languages will find the mixture of data and procedures a natural one.

In many application programs, especially industrial ones, an ''80/20'' rule holds: the major portion of the program (80 percent) deals with modeling of entities, and only a minor portion (20 percent) deals with making pictures of them. In other words, in many applications such as CAD, pictorial representation of models is a means to an end, the end being analysis, physical construction, numerically controlled machining, or some other type of postprocessing. Naturally, there are also many applications for which ''the picture is the thing''—for example, painting, drafting, film and video production, and animation of scenes for flight simulators. Of these, all but painting also require a model from which the images are rendered. In short, most graphics involves significant modeling (and simulation) and there is considerable support for the saying, ''graphics *is* modeling''; Chapters 11, 12, and 20 are devoted to that important subject.

7.2 CHARACTERISTICS OF RETAINED-MODE GRAPHICS PACKAGES

In discussing the roles of the application program, the application model, and the graphics package, we glossed over exactly what capabilities the graphics package has and what happens when the model is modified. As noted in Chapter 2, SRGP operates in *immediate mode* and keeps no record of the primitives and attributes passed to it. Thus, deletions of and changes to application objects necessitate the removal of information on the screen and therefore either selective modification or complete regeneration of the screen; either of these requires the application to respecify primitives from its model. PHIGS, on the other hand, operates in *retained mode*: It keeps a record of all primitives and other related information to allow subsequent editing and automatic updating of the display, thereby offloading the application program.

7.2.1 Central Structure Storage and its Advantages

PHIGS stores information in a special-purpose database called the *central structure storage* (CSS). A *structure* in PHIGS is a sequence of *elements*—primitives, appearance attributes, transformation matrices, and 'invocations of subordinate structures—whose purpose is to define a coherent geometric object. Thus, PHIGS effectively stores a special-purpose modeling hierarchy, complete with modeling transformations and other attributes passed as ''parameters'' to subordinate structures. Notice the similarities between the CSS modeling hierarchy and a hardware hierarchical display list that stores a master–instance hierarchy. In effect, PHIGS may be viewed as the specification of a device-independent hierarchical display-list package; a given implementation is, of course, optimized for a particular display device, but the application programmer need not be concerned with that. Whereas many

PHIGS implementations are purely software, there is increasing use of hardware to implement part or all of the package.

As does a display list, the CSS duplicates geometric information stored in the application's more general-purpose model/database to facilitate rapid *display traversal*—that is, the traversal used to compute a new view of the model. The primary advantage of the CSS, therefore, is rapid automatic screen regeneration whenever the application updates the CSS. This feature alone may be worth the duplication of geometric data in the application database and the CSS, especially when the PHIGS implementation uses a separate processor as a "traversal engine" to offload display traversal from the CPU running the application (see Chapter 18). Small edits, such as changing a transformation matrix, are also done efficiently in PHIGS.

A second advantage of the CSS is automatic pick correlation: The package determines the identity and place within the hierarchy of the primitive picked by the user (see Sections 7.10.2 and 7.12.2). The pick-correlation facility exemplifies a common technique of moving frequently needed functionality into the underlying graphics package.

A third advantage of the CSS is that its editing facilities, in combination with the features of hierarchical modeling, make it easy to create various dynamic effects—for example, motion dynamics—in which time-varying transformations are used to scale, rotate, and position subobjects within parent objects. For example, we can model our simple robot so that each joint is represented by a rotation applied to a substructure (e.g., the arm is a rotated subordinate of the upper body), and dynamically rotate the arm by editing a single rotation matrix.

7.2.2   Limitations of Retained-Mode Packages

Although the CSS (as a special-purpose entity built primarily for display and fast incremental updating) facilitates certain common modeling operations, it is neither necessary nor sufficient for all modeling purposes. It is not necessary because an application can do its own screen regeneration when the model is changed, can do its own pick correlation (albeit with considerable work), and can implement its own object hierarchy via procedures defining objects and accepting transformations and other parameters. The CSS is generally not sufficient because, in most applications, a separately built and updated application data structure is still necessary to record all appropriate data for each application object. Thus, there is duplication of all geometric data, and the two representations must be synchronized properly. For all these reasons, some graphics packages support floating-point coordinates and generalized 2D and 3D viewing facilities without any type of structure storage. The rationale for such immediate-mode packages is that maintaining the CSS is often not worth the overhead, since the application typically maintains an application model sufficient for regenerating the screen image.

For applications in which there is significant structural change between successive images, using a retained-mode package does not pay. For example, in a "digital–wind-tunnel" analysis of an airplane wing, where the surface is represented by a mesh of triangles, most of the vertices shift slightly in position as the wing is subjected to aerodynamic forces. Editing a structure database for such a case makes no sense, since most of the data are replaced for each new image. Indeed, editing the PHIGS structure database is not advised unless the number of elements to be edited is small relative to the size of the networks being displayed. The editing tools provided by PHIGS are rudimentary; for example, it is easy to change a modeling transformation, but to change a vertex of a polygon requires deleting the polygon and respecifying the changed version. Typically, implementations are likely to be optimized for display traversal, since that is the most common operation, rather than for massive editing. Furthermore, the application model must be updated in any case, and it is easier and faster to update just one database than to update two of them.

Because of these limitations, some implementations of PHIGS offer an immediate-mode output facility, although for technical reasons that facility is not part of the official PHIGS specification.

7.3 DEFINING AND DISPLAYING STRUCTURES

The previous section has discussed general properties of PHIGS and SPHIGS. With this section, we begin describing the SPHIGS package in detail; unless otherwise noted, the discussion is generally also applicable to PHIGS. The manipulations permitted on SPHIGS structures include the following:

- Opening (to initiate editing) and closing (to conclude editing)

- Deleting

- Inserting *structure elements* (the three primary types of structure elements are primitives, attributes, including those that specify modeling transformations, and elements that invoke substructures). An element is a data record that is created and inserted into the currently open structure whenever an *element-generator* procedure is called and that stores that procedure's parameters.

- Deleting structure elements

- *Posting* for display (by analogy to posting a snapshot on a bulletin board), subject to a *viewing operation* that specifies how to map the floating-point coordinates to the screen's coordinate system.

7.3.1 Opening and Closing Structures

To create a structure—for example, the collection of primitives and attributes forming the arm component of the robot in Fig. 7.2—we bracket calls to the element-generator procedures with calls to

```
void SPH_openStructure (int structureID);
void SPH_closeStructure (void);
```

These procedures do for structures essentially what the standard open- and close-file commands do for disk files. Unlike disk files, however, only one structure may be open at any time, and all elements specified while it is open are stored in it. Once closed, structures may be reopened for editing (see Section 7.9).

We note two additional properties of structures. First, primitives and attributes can be specified only as elements of a structure (much as all statements in a C program must be specified in some procedure or function). There are no rules about how many elements may be stored in a structure; a structure can be empty, or can contain an arbitrarily large number of elements, limited only by memory space. Of course, the elements forming a structure should be, in general, a logically cohesive set defining a single object.

Second, structure IDs are integers. Since they are normally used only by the application program, not by the interactive user, they do not need to have the more general form of character strings, although the application programmer is free to define symbolic constants for structure IDs. Integer IDs also allow a convenient mapping between objects in the application data structure and the objects' corresponding structure IDs.

7.3.2 Specifying Output Primitives and Their Attributes

The procedures that generate output-primitive elements look like their SRGP counterparts, but there are important differences. First, points are specified with three double-precision coordinates (x, y, and z). Moreover, these procedures place elements in the currently open structure in the CSS rather than directly altering the screen image—displaying structures is a separate operation described in Section 7.3.3. In this chapter, the term *primitive* is used as shorthand for three related entities: an element-generation procedure, such as SPH_poly-Line; the structure element generated by that procedure (for example, the polyLine element); and the displayed image created when a primitive element is executed during display traversal of central structure storage. SPHIGS *executes* a primitive element by transforming the primitive's coordinates by modeling transformations and a viewing operation, including clipping it to the view volume, and then *rasterizing* it (i.e., converting it to pixels). Attributes are more specialized than in SRGP, in that each type of primitive has its own attributes. Thus, attributes such as color and line style are in effect "typed," so that the programmer can, for example, reset the current color for lines while preserving the current colors for polyhedra and text.

Primitives. SPHIGS has fewer output primitives than SRGP does, because the 3D "solid" equivalents of some of SRGP's primitives (e.g., an ellipsoid) are computationally expensive to implement, especially with respect to transformations, clipping, and scan conversion.

Most of the SPHIGS primitives are identical to their SRGP counterparts in their specification methods (except that the points are 3D):

> **void** SPH_polyLine (**int** *vertexCount*, point *∗vertices*);
> **void** SPH_polyMarker (**int** *vertexCount*, point *∗vertices*);
> **void** SPH_fillArea (**int** *vertexCount*, point *∗vertices*);   /∗ Like SRGP_polygon ∗/
> **void** SPH_text (point *origin*, **char** *∗str*);   /∗ Not fully 3D; see Section 7.7.2 ∗/

Note that SPHIGS does not verify that fill areas (or facets, described next) are planar, and the results are undefined if they are not.

Now, consider the definition of a simple house, shown in Fig. 7.4. We can describe this house to SPHIGS by specifying each face (also called a *facet*) as a fill area, at the cost of unnecessary duplication in the specification and storage (in CSS) of each shared vertex. This duplication also slows down display generation, since the viewing-operation calculation would be performed on a single vertex more than once. It is far more efficient in storage

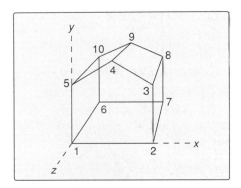

Fig. 7.4 A simple house defined as a set of vertices and facets.

and processing time to specify the facets using indirect references to the shared vertices. We thus think of a polyhedron as a collection of facets, each facet being a list of vertex indices and each index being a "pointer" into a list of vertices. We can describe a polyhedron's specification using the following notation:

Polyhedron = {VertexList, FacetList}
VertexList = {V1, V2, V3, V4, V5, V6, V7, V8, V9, V10}
$V1 = (x_1, y_1, z_1)$, $V2 = (x_2, y_2, z_2)$ . . .
FacetList = {front = {1, 2, 3, 4, 5}, right = {2, 7, 8, 3}, . . . bottom = {. . .} ;

SPHIGS offers this efficient form of specification with its *polyhedron primitive*. In SPHIGS terminology, a polyhedron is a collection of facets that may or may not enclose a volume. In a closed polyhedron such as our house, vertices are typically shared by at least three facets, so the efficiency of the indirect method of specification is especially high. The appearance of a polyhedron is affected by the same attributes that apply to fill areas.

The list of facets is presented to the polyhedron element generator in the form of a single array of integers (SPHIGS type "vertexIndex*") storing a concatenated set of facet descriptions. Each facet description is a sequence of $(V+1)$ integers, where V is the number of vertices in the facet. The first V integers are indices into the vertex list; the last integer is (-1) and acts as a sentinel ending the facet specification. Thus, we would specify the facets of the house (via the fourth parameter of the procedure, described next) by sending the array: 1, 2, 3, 4, 5, −1, 2, 7, 8, 3, −1, ...

void SPH_polyhedron (**int** *vertexCount*, **int** *facetCount*, point **vertices*, vertexIndex **facets*);

Note that the SPHIGS rendering algorithms require that a facet's two sides be distinguishable (external versus internal). Thus, the vertices must be specified in counterclockwise (right-hand rule) order, as one examines the external side of the facet.[2]

---

[2] SPHIGS requires that one side of each facet be deemed "external," even if the polyhedron's facets do not form a closed object. Furthermore, the "internal" side of a polyhedron facet is never visible.

As a simple example, the following C code creates a structure consisting of a single polyhedron modeling the house of Fig. 7.4:

```
SPH_openStructure (HOUSE_STRUCT);
    SPH_polyhedron (10, 7, houseVertexList, houseFacetDescription);
SPH_closeStructure();
```

In essence, SPHIGS supports polygonal geometry only. More advanced 3D modeling primitives are covered later —polynomially defined smooth curves and surfaces in Chapter 11, and solid primitives in Chapter 12.

Attributes.   The procedures listed in Fig. 7.5 generate attribute elements. During display traversal, the execution of an attribute element changes the attribute's value in a modal fashion: The new value stays in effect until it is changed explicitly. Attributes are bound to primitives during display traversal, as discussed in the next section and in Section 7.7.

The attributes of fill areas are different from those in SRGP. Both fill-area and polyhedron primitives have interiors and edges whose attributes are specified separately. The interior has only the color attribute, whereas the edge has style, width, and color attributes. Moreover, the visibility of edges can be turned off via the edge-flag attribute, which is useful for various rendering modes, as discussed in Section 7.8.

Line/edge width and marker size are specified in a *nongeometric* manner: They are not defined using world-coordinate–system units and therefore are not subject to geometric transformations. Thus, modeling transformations and the viewing operation may change a line's apparent length, but not its width. Similarly, the length of dashes in a noncontinuous line style is independent of the transformations applied to the line. However, unlike in SRGP, pixels are not used as the units of measurement, because their sizes are device-dependent. Rather, a nominal width/size has been preset for each device, so that a

polyLine:
    void SPH_setLineStyle (CONTINUOUS / DASHED / DOTTED / DOT_DASHED lineStyle);
    void SPH_setLineWidthScaleFactor (**double** *scaleFactor*);
    void SPH_setLineColor (**int** *colorIndex*);

fill area and polyhedron:
    void SPH_setInteriorColor (**int** *colorIndex*);
    void SPH_setEdgeFlag (EDGE_VISIBLE / EDGE_INVISIBLE flag);
    void SPH_setEdgeStyle (CONTINUOUS / DASHED / DOTTED / DOT_DASHED lineStyle);
    void SPH_setEdgeWidthScaleFactor (**double** *scaleFactor*);
    void SPH_setEdgeColor (**int** *colorIndex*);

polyMarker:
    void SPH_setMarkerStyle (MARKER_CIRCLE / MARKER_SQUARE/... markerStyle);
    void SPH_setMarkerSizeScaleFactor (**double** *scaleFactor*);
    void SPH_setMarkerColor (**int** *colorIndex*);

text:
    void SPH_setTextFont (**int** *fontIndex*);
    void SPH_setTextColor (**int** *colorIndex*);

Fig. 7.5 Procedures generating attribute elements.

unit of width/size will have roughly the same appearance on any output device; the SPHIGS application specifies a (noninteger) multiple of that nominal width/size.

SPHIGS does not support patterns, for three reasons. First, SPHIGS reserves patterns to simulate color shading on bilevel systems. Second, smooth shading of patterned areas on a color system is much too computationally intensive for most display systems. Third, the type of geometric pattern called "hatching" in PHIGS is also too time-consuming, even for display systems with real-time transformation hardware.

7.3.3   Posting Structures for Display Traversal

SPHIGS records a newly created structure in the CSS, but does not display it until the application *posts* the structure subject to a particular viewing specification.[3] SPHIGS then performs a *display traversal* of the structure's elements in the CSS, executing each element in order from the first to the last. Executing a primitive element contributes to the screen image (if a portion of the primitive is in view). Executing an attribute element (both geometric transformations and appearance attributes) changes the collection of attributes stored in a state vector (the *attribute-traversal state*) that is applied to subsequent primitives as they are encountered, in modal fashion. Thus, attributes are applied to primitives in display-traversal order.

The following procedure adds a structure to the list of posted structures maintained internally by SPHIGS:

>   **void** SPH_postRoot (**int** *structureID*, **int** *viewIndex*);

The term *root* indicates that, in posting a structure S that invokes substructures, we are actually posting the hierarchical DAG, called the *structure network*, whose root is S. Even if a posted structure does not invoke substructures, it is called a root; all posted structures are roots.

The *viewIndex* parameter chooses an entry in the table of *views* (discussed in the next section); this entry specifies how the coordinates of the structure's primitives are to be mapped to the screen's integer coordinate space.

We can erase an object's image from the screen by deleting structures (or elements) from the CSS (see Section 7.9) or by using the less drastic SPH_unpostRoot procedure that removes the root from the list of posted roots, without deleting it from the CSS:

>   **void** SPH_unpostRoot (**int** *structureID*, **int** *viewIndex*);

7.3.4   Viewing

The synthetic camera.   It is helpful to think of a 3D graphics package as a synthetic camera that takes "snapshots" of a 3D world inhabited by geometrically defined objects. Creating a structure is equivalent to positioning an object in a photography studio; posting a structure is analogous to activating an instant camera previously set up to point at the scene, and then having the snapshot of the scene posted on a bulletin board. As we see shortly,

---

[3]This way of specifying structure display is the most significant difference between PHIGS and SPHIGS. In PHIGS's more general mechanism, the view specification is a structure element; this allows the view to be changed during display traversal and to be edited like any other element. Many current PHIGS implementations also support the simpler SPHIGS-style posting mechanism.

each time anything changes in the scene, our synthetic camera automatically produces a new, updated image that is posted in place of the old one. To create animation, we show multiple static images in rapid succession, as a movie camera does.

Continuing the metaphor, let us consider how the synthetic picture is produced. First, the camera operator must position and orient the camera; then, he must decide how much of the scene should appear: For example, is the image to be a closeup of a portion of an object of interest, or a long-distance view of the entire scene? Subsequently, the photographer must decide how large a print to make for posting on the bulletin board: Is it to be a wallet-sized print or a poster? Finally, the place on the bulletin board where the photograph is to be posted must be determined. In SPHIGS, these criteria are represented in a *view* that includes a specification of a viewing operation; this operation's *viewport* specifies the size of the photograph and its position on the bulletin board. Not all objects in the structure database need be photographed with the same "camera setting." Indeed, multiple views may be specified for the bulletin board, as we shall see shortly.

The viewport. As discussed in the previous chapter, the viewport specifies a parallelepiped in the NPC system to which the contents of the view volume defined in VRC is mapped. Since the NPC system is mapped to the physical device's integer-coordinate system in a fixed manner, the viewport also specifies where the image is to appear on the screen. The 3D NPC system is mapped to the 2D screen coordinate system in this manner: The NPC unit cube having one corner at $(0, 0, 0)$ and the opposing corner at $(1, 1, 1)$ is mapped to the largest square that can be inscribed on the screen, with the z coordinate simply ignored. For example, on a display device having a resolution of 1024 horizontally and 800 vertically, a point $(0.5, 0.75, z)_{NPC}$ is mapped to $(512, 599)_{DC}$. For portability, an application should not use NPC space lying outside the unit cube; often, however, the benefits of taking full advantage of a nonsquare screen shape are worth the portability cost.

The view table. SPHIGS maintains a table of views that has an implementation-dependent number of entries. Each view consists of a specification of the view volume and viewport, called the *view representation*, and a list (initially empty) of the roots posted to it. Entry 0 in the table defines a *default view* having the volume described in Fig. 6.25 (b), with the front and back planes at $z = 0$ and $z = -\infty$, respectively. The viewport for this default view is the NPC unit cube.

The view representations for all entries in the table (except view 0) may be edited by the application via

> **void** SPH_setViewRepresentation (
>   **int** *viewIndex*, matrix_4x4 *voMatrix*, matrix_4x4 *vmMatrix*,
>   **double** *NPCviewport_minX*, **double** *NPCviewport_maxX*,
>   **double** *NPCviewport_minY*, **double** *NPCviewport_maxY*,
>   **double** *NPCviewport_minZ*, **double** *NPCviewport_maxZ*);

The two 4×4 homogeneous-coordinate matrices are the view-orientation and view-mapping matrices described in Chapter 6. They are produced by the procedures shown in Fig. 7.6.

/* To set up UVN viewing reference coordinate system */
matrix_4x4 SPH_evaluateViewOrientationMatrix (
        point *viewRefPoint*,
        vector_3D *viewPlaneNormal*, vector_3D *viewUpVector*,
        matrix_4x4 *voMatrix*);

/* To set up view volume and to describe how it is to be mapped to NPC space */
matrix_4x4 SPH_evaluateViewMappingMatrix (
        /* First, we specify the view-volume in VRC */
        double *umin*, **double** *umax*, **double** *vmin*, **double** *vmax*   /* View-plane boundaries */
        PARALLEL / PERSPECTIVE projectionType,
        point *projectionReferencePoint*;   /* In VRC */
        double *frontPlaneDistance*, **double** *backPlaneDistance*,   /* Clipping planes */
        /* Then, we specify the NPC viewport. */
        double *NPCvp_minX*, **double** *NPCvp_maxX*,
        double *NPCvp_minY*, **double** *NPCvp_maxY*,
        double *NPCvp_minZ*, **double** *NPCvp_maxZ*,
        matrix_4x4 *vmMatrix*);

Fig. 7.6 Utilities for calculating viewing-transformation matrices.

Multiple views.   The view index specified during posting refers to a specific NPC viewport describing where on the screen (bulletin board) the image of the structure (photograph) is to appear. Just as one can tack several photographic prints on a board, an application can divide the screen into a number of viewports.

The use of multiple views is powerful in many ways. We can display several different structures simultaneously in individual areas of the screen by posting them with different views. In Fig. 7.7(a), we present a schematic representation of the view table, showing only the pointers to the lists of structure networks posted to each view. We can see that there is one view showing a street scene; also, there are three separate views of a robot. The robot

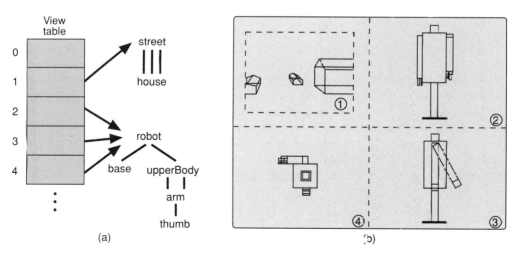

(a)   (b)

Fig. 7.7 Multiple views sharing screen space. (a) Schematic diagram of view table. Each view entry points to a list of the roots posted to that view. (b) Resulting image. Dashed viewport extents and circled numbers show the viewports and their associated view indices.

structure was posted three times, each time with a different view index. Figure 7.7(b) shows the resulting screen image. The multiple views of the robot vary not only in their viewport specifications, but also in their view-volume specifications.

The preceding scenario implies that each view has at most one posted structure; in fact, however, any number of roots can be posted to a single view. Thus, we can display different root structures in a single unified picture by posting them together to a view. In this case, our metaphorical camera would take a single composite snapshot of a scene that contains many different objects.

Another property of viewports is that, unlike real snapshots and window-manager windows, they are transparent.[4] In practice, many applications *tile* the viewports to avoid overlapping; however, we can also use overlapping to advantage. For example, we can "compose" two distinct images created by different viewing transformations or showing objects defined in different units of measurement; thus, in building a close-up diagram of an engine part, we could inset a small picture showing the entire engine (for context) overlapping the large close-up picture. (To avoid confusion, we would do this by selecting an area of the closeup that is just background.)

To regenerate the screen, SPHIGS displays the posted networks by traversing the roots posted to each view in the view table, in increasing order of view index, starting with view 0; thus, the images of objects posted to view N have *display priority* over the images of objects posted to a view with an index less than N, and therefore potentially overlap them. This ordering is significant, of course, only when viewports actually overlap.[5]

Note that an application can manufacture many independent WC spaces and can use any units of measurement desired. In Fig. 7.7, for example, the street structure is defined in a WC space in which each increment on an axis represents 10 yards, whereas the robot is defined in a wholly independent WC space measured in centimeters. Although each root structure is modeled in its own WC space, there is only one NPC space per display device, shared by all posted structures, since that space is an abstraction of the display device.

7.3.5   Graphics Applications Sharing a Screen via Window Management

When the first standard graphics packages were being designed in the early 1970s, only a single graphics application ran at a given time, and it used the entire screen. The design of PHIGS began in the late 1970s, when this mode of operation was still dominant and before window managers were generally available. Thus, the unit cube of the NPC space was traditionally mapped to the screen in its entirety.

Modern graphics workstations with multitasking operating systems allow multiple graphics applications to run simultaneously, sharing the workstation's resources, the screen, and the set of input devices, under control of a window manager. In this environment, each application is assigned to its own window, which acts as a "virtual

---

[4] Some versions of PHIGS offer opaque viewports as an alternative to tiling; the term *shielding* is typically used to refer to this nonstandard feature.

[5] This trivial view-priority system is less sophisticated than that of PHIGS, which allows explicit view priorities to be assigned by the application.

screen.'' The user can resize and move these windows by calling on the functionality of the
window manager. The primary advantage is that each application can act as though it
controls an entire screen; it does not need to know that its screen is only a portion of the
actual display device's screen. An SPHIGS application therefore need not be modified for a
window-manager environment; the package and the window manager cooperate to map
NPC space to an assigned window rather than to the entire screen.[6] Figure 7.8 shows two
SPHIGS applications and a terminal-emulator program running concurrently on a graphics
workstation. Because SPHIGS maps the NPC space to the largest square that fits within the
window-manager window, some portion of any nonsquare window is unavailable to the
SPHIGS application, as illustrated by the SPHIGS window showing the table and chair
scene.

---

[6] It is sometimes desirable to display only a portion of NPC space in a window-manager window.
PHIGS supports the specification of an NPC *workstation window*, which is used to clip the image
produced by display traversal; the clipped portion is then mapped to a *workstation viewport* of the
same aspect ratio, specified in physical device coordinates. This workstation transformation can also
be used to map a rectangular portion of NPC space to the physical display, allowing use of a
nonsquare screen region.

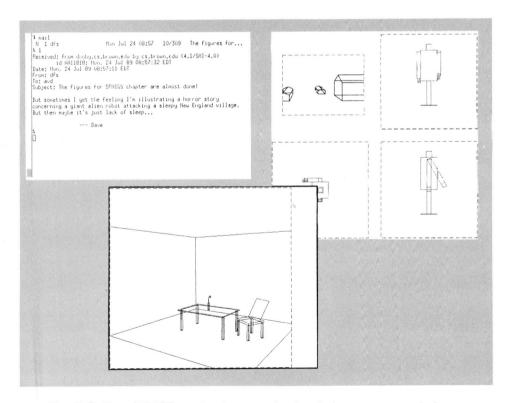

Fig. 7.8 Two SPHIGS applications running in window-manager windows.

7.4   MODELING TRANSFORMATIONS

Section 7.3.2 contained a Pascal code fragment that created a simple structure modeling a house. For simplicity's sake, we placed one of the house's corners at the origin, aligned the house's sides with the principal axes, and gave it dimensions that were whole units. We shall say that an object defined at the origin and (largely) aligned with the principal axes is *standardized*; not only is it easier to define (determine the vertex coordinates of) a standardized object than it is to define one arbitrarily positioned in space, but also it is easier to manipulate the geometry of a standardized object in order to resize, reorient, or reposition it.

Let us say we want our house to appear at a different location, not near the origin. We could certainly recompute the house's vertices ourselves, and create the house structure using the same Pascal code shown in Section 7.3.2 (changing only the vertex coordinates). Instead, however, let us examine the powerful technique of transforming a standardized building-block object in order to change its dimensions or placement.

As we saw in Chapter 5, we can transform a primitive such as a polygon by multiplying each vertex, represented as a column vector $[x, y, z, 1]^T$, by a 4 × 4 homogeneous-coordinate transformation matrix. The following utility functions create such matrices:

>   matrix_4x4 SPH_scale (**double** *scaleX*, **double** *scaleY*, **double** *scaleZ*, matrix_4x4 *result*);
>   matrix_4x4 SPH_rotateX (**double** *angle*, matrix_4x4 *result*);
>   matrix_4x4 SPH_rotateY (**double** *angle*, matrix_4x4 *result*);
>   matrix_4x4 SPH_rotateZ (**double** *angle*, matrix_4x4 *result*);
>   matrix_4x4 SPH_translate (**double** *deltaX*, **double** *deltaY*, **double** *deltaZ*, matrix_4x4 *result*);

A different scale factor may be specified for each of the axes, so an object can be "stretched" or "shrunk" nonuniformly. For rotation, the angle parameter, expressed in degrees, represents counterclockwise motion about the designated principal axis, from the point of view of someone looking along the axis from $+\infty$ toward the origin.

The matrices can be used to create a transformation element to be placed in a structure. The following procedure is the element generator:

>   **void** SPH_setLocalTransformation (
>   matrix_4x4 *matrix*, REPLACE / PRECONCATENATE / POSTCONCATENATE mode);

The use of the prefix "local" here refers to how SPHIGS displays a structure. As SPHIGS traverses a structure, it stores a *local matrix* as a piece of state information applicable to only the structure being traversed. The local matrix is by default initialized to the identity matrix. Whenever a setLocalTransformation element is encountered, the local matrix is modified in some way: It either is replaced or is changed by a multiplication operation, as specified by the *mode* parameter. Whenever a primitive is encountered during traversal, each of its vertices is transformed by the local matrix and then is subjected to the viewing transformation for display. (As we shall see later, hierarchy complicates this rule.)

The following code creates a structure containing our house at an arbitrary location, and posts that structure for display using the default view. The house maintains its original standardized size and orientation.

```
SPH_openStructure (HOUSE_STRUCT);
    SPH_setLocalTransformation (SPH_translate (...), REPLACE);
    SPH_polyhedron (...);      /* Vertices here are standardized as before */
SPH_closeStructure ();
SPH_postRoot (HOUSE_STRUCT, 0);
```

Simple transformations like this one are uncommon. We typically wish not only to translate the object, but also to affect its size and orientation. When multiple transformations of primitives are desired, the application "builds" the local matrix by successively concatenating (i.e., composing) individual transformation matrices in the exact order in which they are to be applied. In general, standardized building-block objects are scaled, then rotated, and finally translated to their desired location; as we saw in Chapter 5, this order avoids unwanted translations or shearing.

The following code creates and posts a house structure that is moved away from the origin and is rotated to a position where we see its side instead of its front:

```
SPH_openStructure (MOVED_HOUSE_STRUCT);
    SPH_setLocalTransformation (SPH_rotateY (...), REPLACE);
    SPH_setLocalTransformation (SPH_translate (...), PRECONCATENATE);
    SPH_polyhedron (...);      /* Vertices here are standardized as before */
SPH_closeStructure ();
SPH_postRoot (MOVED_HOUSE_STRUCT, 0);
```

The use of the PRECONCATENATE mode for the translation matrix ensures that premultiplication is used to compose the translation matrix with the rotation matrix, and thus that the translation's effect "follows" the rotation's. Premultiplication is thus a far more common mode than is postmultiplication, since it corresponds to the order of the individual transformation elements. Since SPHIGS performs scaling and rotation relative to the principal axes, the programmer must generate the matrices needed to map an arbitrary axis to one of the principal axes, as discussed in Chapter 5.

The composition of the transformation elements is performed by SPHIGS at *traversal time*; thus, each time the display is regenerated, the composition must be performed. An alternative method for specifying a contiguous sequence of transformations increases the efficiency of the display-traversal process: Instead of making a structure element for each one, we compose them ourselves at *specification time* and generate a single transformation element. The following function does matrix multiplication at specification time:

```
matrix_4x4 SPH_composeMatrix (matrix_4x4 mat1, matrix_4x4 mat2, matrix_4x4 result);
```

The two setLocalTransformation elements in the preceding code can thus be replaced by

```
SPH_setLocalTransformation (
    SPH_composeMatrix (SPH_translate (...), SPH_rotateY (...), result), REPLACE);
```

The disadvantage of this method is that it is no longer possible to make a dynamic change to the size, orientation, or position of a primitive by selectively "editing" the desired member of the sequence of setLocalTransformation elements; rather, the entire composite must be recomputed and respecified. The rule of thumb for efficiency is thus to use composition at specification time unless the individual transformations are to be updated selectively, in which case they should be specified individually.

Let us create the street structure that contains three copies of our simple house, as first seen in Fig. 7.7. A perspective view of the "house" on the left, the "mansion" on the right, and the "cottage" in the middle is shown in Fig. 7.9(a). We have added dashed lines parallel to the x axis and tick marks for the x axis to indicate the relative positions of the houses, and have used a display mode of SPHIGS that shows the wireframe edges of polyhedra with hidden edges removed (see Section 7.8). The leftmost house in the figure is an untransformed instance of our standardized house, and the other two copies differ in size, orientation, and position.

The brute-force way to create this street structure is to specify the standardized house polyhedron three times, preceded by the desired transformation elements, as shown in the schematic representation of the structure of Fig. 7.9(b). We show a block of consecutive transformation elements as a single unit; the first element uses REPLACE mode and all others use PRECONCATENATION mode, with the multiplication symbol ($\cdot$) separating them to indicate composition. The code generating the structure is shown in Fig. 7.10.

We can eliminate the redundant specifications of the standardized house polyhedron by defining a Pascal procedure to perform the call generating the house polyhedron, as shown in the pseudocode of Fig. 7.11. Because the house is defined by a single polyhedron call, the efficiency of this technique is not obvious in this example; however, if our house were

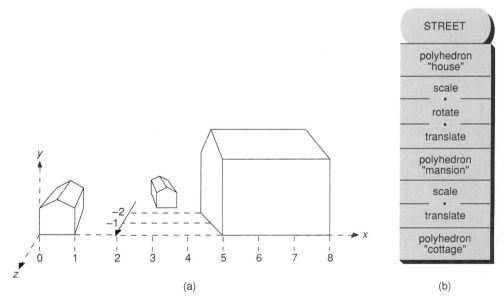

(a)   (b)

Fig. 7.9 Modeling a street with three houses. (a) Perspective view. (b) Structure.

```
SPH_openStructure (STREET_STRUCT);
    SPH_polyhedron (...);      /* Define first house, in its standardized form */

    /* Mansion is house scaled by 2 in x, 3 in y, 1 in z, rotated 90° about y, */
    /* then translated; note that its left side is subsequently front-facing */
    /* and lies in the (x, y) plane. */
    SPH_setLocalTransformation (SPH_scale (2.0, 3.0, 1.0, result), REPLACE);
    SPH_setLocalTransformation (SPH_rotateY (90.0, result), PRECONCATENATE);
    SPH_setLocalTransformation (SPH_translate (8.0, 0.0, 0.0, result), PRECONCATENATE);
    SPH_polyhedron (...);

    /* Cottage is house uniformly scaled by 0.75, unrotated, set back in z and over in x */
    SPH_setLocalTransformation (SPH_scale (0.75, 0.75, 0.75, result), REPLACE);
    SPH_setLocalTransformation (SPH_translate (3.5, 0.0, -2.5, result), PRECONCATENATE);
    SPH_polyhedron (...);
SPH_closeStructure ();
SPH_postRoot (STREET_STRUCT, 0);
```

Fig. 7.10 Code used to generate Fig. 7.9.

more complex and required a series of attribute and primitive specifications, this method clearly would require less C code. Moreover, the technique provides another benefit of modularization: We can change the house's shape or style by editing the House procedure without having to edit the code that creates the street.

We call a procedure such as House that generates a sequence of elements defining a standardized building block, and that is made to be used repetitively with arbitrary geometrical transformations, a *template procedure*. The template procedure is a convenience for the programmer and also represents good programming practice. Note, however, that although the House procedure adds a level of procedure hierarchy to the C program, no structure hierarchy is created—the model of the street is still "flat." Indeed, the structure network produced by the code of Fig. 7.11 is indistinguishable from that produced by the code of Fig. 7.10. There is no "savings" in terms of the number of elements produced for the structure.

```
void House (void)
{
    SPH_polyhedron (...);
}

/* Mainline */
SPH_openStructure (STREET_STRUCT);
    House ();                    /* First House */
    set local transformation matrix;
    House ();                    /* Mansion */
    set local transformation matrix;
    House ();                    /* Cottage */
SPH_closeStructure ();
SPH_postRoot (STREET_STRUCT, 0);
```

Fig. 7.11 Use of a template procedure to model the street.

One change we could make to our template procedure is to have it accept a transformation matrix as a parameter, which it would then use to specify a setLocalTransformation element.[7] Although in some cases passing transformation parameters would be convenient, this method lacks the generality inherent in our original method of being able to specify an arbitrary number of transformations before calling the template.

7.5   HIERARCHICAL STRUCTURE NETWORKS

7.5.1   Two-Level Hierarchy

So far, we have dealt with three types of structure elements: output primitives, appearance attributes, and transformations. Next, we show how the power of SPHIGS derives in large part from structure hierarchy, implemented via an element that "calls" a substructure when executed during traversal. Structure hierarchy should not be confused with the template-procedure hierarchy of the previous section. Template-procedure hierarchy is resolved at specification time, when the CSS is being edited, and produces in-line elements, not substructure invocations. By contrast, structure hierarchy induced by invocation of substructures is resolved when the CSS is traversed for display—the execution of an invocation element acts as a subroutine call. In Section 7.15, we take another look at the relative advantages and disadvantages of template-procedure hierarchy and structure hierarchy.

The *structure-execution element* that invokes a substructure is created by

void SPH_executeStructure (**int** *structureID*);

Let us replace the template procedure of the previous section by a procedure that builds a house structure in the CSS (see Fig. 7.12). This procedure is called exactly once by the mainline procedure, and the HOUSE_STRUCT is never posted; rather, its display results from its being invoked as a subobject of the street structure. Note that the only differences in the STREET_STRUCT specification are the addition of the call to the procedure that builds the house structure and the replacement of each template procedure call by the generation of an execute-structure element. Although the displayed image is the same as that of Fig. 7.9(a), the structure network is different, as shown in Fig. 7.13, in which the execute-structure element is depicted as an arrow.

Posting STREET_STRUCT tells SPHIGS to update the screen by traversing the STREET_STRUCT structure network; the traversal is in the form of a depth-first tree walk, just as a procedure/subroutine hierarchy is executed. In the preceding example, the traverser initializes the street structure's local matrix to the identity matrix, and then performs the first invocation of the house substructure, applying the street structure's local matrix to each of the house's vertices as though the house polyhedron were a primitive element in the street structure itself. When it returns from the first invocation, it sets the local matrix to a desired composite transformation, and then performs the second invocation, applying the

---

[7]Newman defines *display procedures* as template procedures that take scaling, rotation, and translation parameters [NEWM71].

```
void BuildStandardizedHouse (void)
{
    SPH_openStructure (HOUSE_STRUCT);
        SPH_polyhedron (...);
    SPH_closeStructure ();
}

/* Mainline */
BuildStandardizedHouse ();
SPH_openStructure (STREET_STRUCT);
    SPH_executeStructure (HOUSE_STRUCT);        /* First house */
    set local transformation matrix;
    SPH_executeStructure (HOUSE_STRUCT);        /* Mansion */
    set local transformation matrix;
    SPH_executeStructure (HOUSE_STRUCT);        /* Cottage */
SPH_closeStructure ();
SPH_postRoot (STREET_STRUCT, 0);
```

Fig. 7.12 Use of a subordinate structure to model the street

new composite matrix to the vertices of the house to create the second instantiation of the house. When it returns, the local matrix is again changed; the new composite is applied to the house's vertices to produce the third house instance.

We think of a structure as an independent object, with its primitives defined in its own floating-point modeling-coordinate system (MCS); this way of thinking facilitates the building of low-level standardized building blocks. As we noted in Section 5.8, a transformation maps the vertices in one coordinate system into another; here, SPHIGS uses the local matrix of structure S to transform the primitives of substructures into S's own MCS.

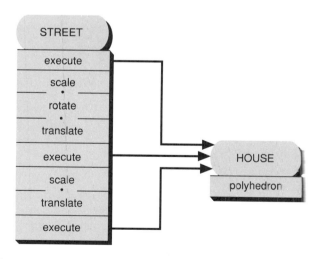

Fig. 7.13 Structure network showing invocation of subordinate structure.

7.5.2   Simple Three-Level Hierarchy

As a simple example of three-level hierarchy, we extend the house in our street example. The new house is composed of the original standardized house (renamed SIMPLE_HOUSE_STRUCT) and a chimney suitably scaled and translated to lie in the right place on top of the house. We could revise the house structure by adding the chimney's facets directly to the original polyhedron, or by adding a second polyhedron to the structure, but we choose here to induce three-level hierarchy by decomposing the house into two subobjects. An advantage of this modularization is that we can define the chimney in a standardized manner (at the origin, of unit size) in its own MCS (as shown in Fig. 7.14a),

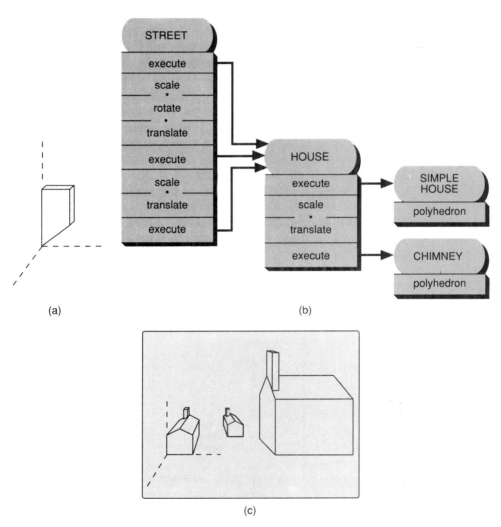

Fig. 7.14 Three-level hierarchy for street. (a) Standardized chimney. (b) Structure network. (c) Resulting image.

and then use scaling and translation to place it on the roof in the house's MCS. If we had to define the chimney to fit exactly on the roof and to map into the house's MCS without scaling, we would have to do messy calculations to compute the vertices explicitly. With modularity, however, we simply define the standardized chimney such that its bottom facet has the same slope as the roof itself; with that condition met, uniform scaling and arbitrary translation can be applied.

The revised house structure is built via

```
SPH_openStructure (HOUSE_STRUCT);
    SPH_executeStructure (SIMPLE_HOUSE_STRUCT);
    set local matrix to scale/translate standardized chimney onto roof of simple house;
    SPH_executeStructure (CHIMNEY_STRUCT);
SPH_closeStructure ();
```

What happens when this two-level house object is instantiated by the street structure with a transformation to yield the three-level hierarchy shown in Fig. 7.14(b)? Since SPHIGS transforms a parent by transforming the latter's component elements and substructures, we are assured that the two component primitives (the simple house and the chimney) are transformed together as a single unified object (Fig. 7.14c). The key point is that the street-structure specification did not need to be changed at all. Thus, the designer of the street structure does not need to be concerned with the internal details of how the house is constructed or subsequently edited—it is a black box.

7.5.3   Bottom-Up Construction of the Robot

Let us now look at a more interesting example, our simple robot, which combines the key ideas of modeling using structure hierarchy and of repeated editing of transformations to achieve motion dynamics. A complex object or system hierarchy is usually conceptualized and informally described top-down. For example, a computer-science department building is composed of floors, which are composed of offices and laboratories which are composed of furniture and equipment, and so on. Recall that our simple android robot is composed of an upper body and a pedestal base; the upper body is composed of a trunk, a head, and two identical arms, each of which is composed of a fixed hand and a "sliding" (translating) thumb as gripper.

Even though we design top-down, we often implement bottom-up, defining building blocks for use in the definitions of higher-level building blocks, and so on, to create the hierarchy of building blocks. Thus, in constructing the robot, we define the thumb building block for the robot's arm, then the arm itself, and then join two instances of the arm building block onto the upper body, and so on, as shown in the symbolic parts hierarchy of Fig. 7.2 and in the more detailed structure network diagram of the upper body in Fig. 7.15.

Let us look at the bottom-up construction process in more detail to see what geometry and transformations are involved. It makes sense to design the arm and thumb in the same units of measurement, so that they fit together easily. We define the thumb structure in a standardized position in its own MCS in which it "hangs" along the y axis (Fig.7.16a). The arm structure is defined with the same unit of measurement as that used for the thumb;

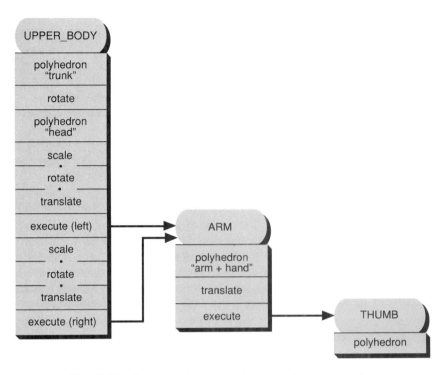

Fig. 7.15 Structure hierarchy for robot's upper body.

it consists of the arm+hand polyhedron (standardized, hanging down along the y axis, as shown in Fig. 7.16b) and a translated invocation of the thumb structure. The translation element preceding the invocation of the thumb is responsible for moving the thumb from its standardized position at the origin to its proper place on the wrist of the arm (c).

The arm-invoking-thumb network is a two-level hierarchy similar to the street–house example. By editing the translation element in the arm structure, we can "slide" the thumb along the wrist of the arm (Fig. 7.16d).[8]

Next, we build the upper body. Since we want to be able to rotate the head, we first specify the trunk polyhedron, then a rotation, and next the head polyhedron (Fig. 7.16e). Our next step is to have the upper-body structure invoke the arm structure twice. What transformations should precede these invocations? If our sole concern is positioning (i.e., translating) each arm correctly in the upper-body MCS, we may produce a picture like Fig. 7.16(f), where the arm and upper body were clearly designed at different scales. This is easy to fix: We can add a scale transformation preceding the translation (Fig. 7.16g). However, a scale and a translation is not enough if we want arms that can swing on the axis

---

[8] The observant reader may have wondered how the thumb actually slides in this model, since it is not really attached in any way to the arm hand. In fact, none of the components of our robot model is attached to another via objects representing joints. Modeling of joints and the constraints that determine their modes of operation are beyond the scope of this book.

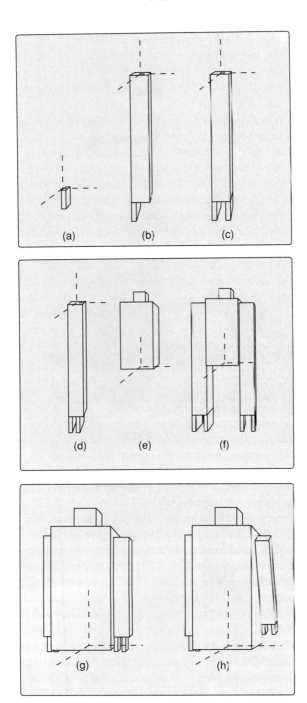

Fig. 7.16 Constructing the robot's upper body. (a) Thumb. (b) Fixed arm plus hand. (c) Completed arm. (d) Completed arm with translated thumb. (e) Trunk and head. (f) Upper body with outsized arms. (g) Corrected arms. (h) Left arm rotated.

connecting the two shoulders (for movement much like that of the arm of a marching soldier); for this, we place a rotation element in the structure, preceding the translation. We have completed our definition of the upper-body structure; assembling the full robot is Exercise 7.1. Fig. 7.16(h) shows the upper body as it looks when the left arm's rotation element is nonzero.

Because each arm invocation is preceded by an independent sequence of transformations, the motion of each arm can be controlled independently. One arm can be hanging down while the other arm swings, as in Fig. 7.16(h). Indeed, the difference in the transformations is what distinguishes the left and right arms. Notice, however, that the movable thumb is not only on the same side of, but also is the same distance from, the fixed hand on both left and right arms, because it is part of the arm's internal definition. (In fact, if the application simply changes the translation element in the arm structure, all the thumbs on all the robot instances suddenly move!) Thus we must rotate one of the arms 180° about the y axis in order to make the arms symmetric. A structure invoking the arm can control the arm's size, orientation, and position only *as a whole*, and cannot alter the arm's internal construction in any way. As we said earlier, a substructure is essentially a black box; the invoker needs to know what geometry is defined by the substructure, but it does not need to know how the substructure was created, and indeed cannot affect any of the substructure's internals. In Section 7.14.2, we discuss why it is impossible to control the two thumbs independently with a single arm structure invoked twice, and we show how to solve this problem by creating multiple arm structures that are identical in form but have potentially differing internal transformations.

In summary, in specifying any structure, we deal with only what primitives and lower-level substructures are included in it, what modeling transformations should be used to position its component parts, and what attributes should be used to affect their appearance. We need not, and cannot, deal with the internals of lower-level structures. Furthermore, we design components without concern for how they will be used by invoking structures, since transformations can be used to obtain desired size, orientation, and position. In practice, it is helpful to standardize a component in its local MCS, so that it is easy to scale and rotate about principal axes.

Two additional points must be mentioned. First, a programmer does not need to design purely top-down and to implement purely bottom-up; by analogy to the programming technique of using "stubs and drivers," dummy substructures can be used in the structure hierarchy. A dummy can be an empty structure; in fact, SPHIGS allows a structure to execute a substructure that has not (yet) been created, in which case SPHIGS automatically creates the referenced substructure and initializes it to be empty. In some cases, it is desirable for the dummy to be a simple object (say, a parallelepiped) of approximately the same size as the more complex version that is specified later. This technique permits top-down debugging of complex structure hierarchies before all components are defined fully. Second, we have not yet compared structure hierarchy to template-procedure hierarchy. For now, we say that structure hierarchy works well if we need to instantiate multiple copies of a building block and to control (to a limited extent) the appearance and placement of each copy but not its internal definition. We discuss the tradeoffs between template procedure and structure hierarchy more fully in Section 7.15.

7.5.4 Interactive Modeling Programs

Interactive 3D construction and modeling programs facilitate the construction of object hierarchies through the bottom-up assembly process just described. Most such programs offer a palette of icons representing the program's fundamental set of building blocks. If the drawing program is application-specific, so are the building blocks; otherwise, they are such common atoms as polylines, polygons, cubes, parallelepipeds, cylinders, and spheres. The user can select an icon in order to instantiate the associated building block, and can then specify transformations to be applied to the building-block instance. Such specification is typically done via input devices, such as the mouse or control dials, that let the user experiment with the instance's size, orientation, and position until it "looks right." Since it is difficult to judge spatial relationships in 2D projections of 3D scenes, more sophisticated interaction techniques use 3D grids, often with "gravity fields" surrounding intersection points, numerical scales, sliders of various types, numerical feedback on the position of vertices, and so on (see Section 8.2.6). Some construction programs allow the user to combine instances of fundamental graphical building blocks to create a higher-level building block, which is then added to the building-block palette, to be used in building even higher-level objects.

7.6 MATRIX COMPOSITION IN DISPLAY TRAVERSAL

So far, we have discussed how a programmer constructs a model, using top-down design and (more or less) bottom-up implementation. Regardless of how the model was constructed, SPHIGS displays the model by performing a top-down, depth-first search of the DAG rooted at the posted structure. During traversal, SPHIGS processes all the geometry specified by multiple levels of transformation and invocation. To see what is involved, we observe that, during top-down traversal, when a root structure A invokes structure B, which in turn invokes structure C, this is is tantamount to saying that B was constructed bottom-up by transformation of primitives defined in C's MCS to B's MCS, and that A was then similarly constructed by transformation of B's primitives (including any defined via invocation of C) to A's MCS. The net effect was that C's primitives were transformed twice, first from MCS_C to MCS_B and then from MCS_B to MCS_A.

Using the notation developed in Section 5.8, let $M_{B \leftarrow C}$ denote the value of the local matrix for structure B that, at the time of invocation of C, maps vertices in MCS_C to their properly transformed positions in MCS_B. Thus, to map a vertex from MCS_C to MCS_B, we write $V^{(B)} = M_{B \leftarrow C} \cdot V^{(C)}$ (where $V^{(H)}$ indicates the vector representing a vertex whose coordinates are expressed in coordinate-system H), and similarly, $V^{(A)} = M_{A \leftarrow B} \cdot V^{(B)}$. Thus, to mimic the bottom-up construction process, the traverser must successively apply the transformations that map the vertices from C to B and then from B to A:

$$V^{(A)} = M_{A \leftarrow B} \cdot V^{(B)} = M_{A \leftarrow B} \cdot (M_{B \leftarrow C} \cdot V^{(C)}) \tag{7.1}$$

By matrix associativity, $V^{(A)} = (M_{A \leftarrow B} \cdot M_{B \leftarrow C}) \cdot V^{(C)}$. Therefore, the traverser simply composes the two local matrices and applies the resulting matrix to each of C's vertices.

Using tree notation, let the root be at level 1 and the successive children be at levels 2, 3, 4, ... Then, by induction, for any structure at level j ($j > 4$), we can transform a vertex $V^{(j)}$ in that structure's MCS into the vertex $V^{(1)}$ in the root coordinate system via

$$V^{(1)} = (M_{1\leftarrow 2} \cdot M_{2\leftarrow 3} \ldots M_{(j-1)\leftarrow j}) \cdot V^{(j)} \tag{7.2}$$

Since SPHIGS allows primitives to be transformed within the local MCS with the local matrix, a vertex $V^{(j)}$ is obtained by applying the local matrix to the coordinate values of the primitive:

$$V^{(j)} = M^{(j)} \cdot V^{(\text{prim})} \tag{7.3}$$

We use $M^{(j)}$ to denote the local matrix while the structure is being traversed to show that the matrix is being used to transform primitives into the structure's own level-j MCS. If the structure subsequently invokes a subordinate, the matrix's use changes; it is then used to transform the invoked structure at level $j + 1$ into the level-j MCS, and we denote it with $M_{j\leftarrow(j+1)}$. This does not imply that the matrix's value changes—only its use does.

Combining Eqs. (7.2) and (7.3) using associativity, we get

$$V^{(1)} = (M_{1\leftarrow 2} \cdot M_{2\leftarrow 3} \ldots \cdot M_{(j-1)\leftarrow j} \cdot M^{(j)}) \cdot V^{(\text{prim})} \tag{7.4}$$

Thus, to transform a primitive at level j in the hierarchy to the MCS of the root (which is the world-coordinate space), all we need to do is to apply the composition of the current values of the local matrix for each structure from the root down to the structure in which the primitive is defined. This composite of local matrices—the term in parentheses in Eq. (7.4)—is called the *composite modeling transformation matrix* (CMTM). When the state of a traversal is such that a level-j structure's elements are being executed, the CMTM is the composition of j matrices. Only the last of those matrices ($M^{(j)}$) may be changed by the structure, because a structure may modify only its local matrix.[9] Thus, while the structure is active, the first $j - 1$ matrices in the CMTM list are constant. The composite of these $j - 1$ matrices is the *global matrix* (GM)—the term in parentheses in Eq. (7.2)—for the level-j structure being executed. It is convenient for SPHIGS to maintain the GM during the traversal of a structure; when a setLocalTransformation element modifies the local matrix (LM), SPHIGS can easily compute the new CMTM by postconcatenating the new local matrix to the GM.

We can now summarize the traversal algorithm, to be elaborated in Section 7.12.1. SPHIGS does a depth-first traversal, saving the CMTM, GM, and LM just before any structure invocation; it then initializes the substructure's GM and CMTM to the inherited CMTM, and its LM to the identity matrix. The CMTM is applied to vertices and is updated by changes to the LM. Finally, when the traverser returns, it restores the CMTM, GM, and LM of the parent structure and continues. Because of the saving and restoring of the matrices, parents affect their children but not vice versa.

---

[9]We present the global matrix as a derived entity that cannot be modified by a structure. In true PHIGS, a structure can modify the GM active during its execution, but this power is still "localized" in the sense that it in no way affects the local matrices of its ancestors.

Let us watch as SPHIGS traverses the three-level upper-body–arm–thumb hierarchy of Fig. 7.15. We have posted the UPPER_BODY structure as a root. Figure 7.17(a) shows a sequence of snapshots of the traversal state; a snapshot has been created for each point marked with a number in the structure network diagram of Fig. 7.17(b).

The traversal state is maintained via a stack, shown in Fig. 7.17(a) growing downward, with the currently active structure in a solid rectangle and its ancestors in dashed ones. The values of the three state matrices for the currently active structure are shown to the right of the stack diagram. Arcs show the scope of a transformation: The GM arc illustrates that a structure's ancestors contribute to the GM, and the CMTM arc shows that the CMTM is the product of the GM and LM. Recall that in each group of transformations, the first is in REPLACE mode and the rest are PRECONCATENATED. Thus the first "rotate" in the structure applies only to the head since it will be REPLACEd by the first "scale" that applies to the left arm.

At point 1 in Fig. 7.17(b), the traverser is about to execute the first element in the root. Because a root has no ancestors, its GM is identity; the LM is also identity, as is the case whenever a structure's execution begins. At point 2, the LM is set to the composite of the (Scale, Rotate, Translate) transformation triplet. Therefore, the CMTM is updated to the product of the identity GM and the SRT composite, and is then ready for use in transforming the arm subobject to the upper body MCS to become the left arm via $(SRT)_{ub \leftarrow la}$. Next, at point 3, the traverser is about to execute the first element of the arm structure. The GM for the arm execution is, as one would expect for a level-2 instantiation, its parent's LM at the point of invocation.

At point 4, the arm LM is set to position the thumb within the arm $(T_{arm \leftarrow th})$, and the CMTM is updated to the product of the GM and LM. This level-2 CMTM becomes the GM for the level-3 instantiation of the thumb (point 5). Since the LM of the thumb is identity, the CMTM of the thumb has the desired effect of transforming thumb coordinates first to arm coordinates, then to upper-body coordinates. At point 6, the traverser has returned from the thumb and arm invocations, back to the upper body. The matrices for the upper-body structure are as they were before the invocation, since its subordinates cannot change its local matrix. At point 7, the LM of the upper body is replaced with a new composite for the right arm. When we have descended into the thumb structure for the right arm (point 8), the CMTM is almost identical to that at point 5; the only difference is the level-2 matrix that moves the arm into position on the upper body.

To animate a composite object such as the robot, we need only to think about how each child structure is to be affected in its parent, and to define the appropriate transformation elements for each component that can be edited dynamically later. Thus, to make the robot spin about its axis, raise its arm, and open its hand, we change the rotation matrix in the robot structure to affect the upper body, the rotation matrix in the upper-body structure to affect the arm, and the translation matrix in the arm structure to affect the thumb. The transformations are done independently at each level of the hierarchy, but the net effect is cumulative. The difficult part of specifying an animation is working backward from a desired result, such as "the robot moves to the northwest corner of the room and picks up a block from the table," to derive the sequence of transformations yielding that result. Chapter 21 briefly discusses the issues involved in such "inverse kinematics" problems.

(1) $\boxed{\text{UpperBody}}$ $\left.\begin{array}{l}\text{GM = identity}\\ \text{LM = identity}\end{array}\right)$ CMTM = identity

(2) $\boxed{\text{UpperBody}}$ $\left.\begin{array}{l}\text{GM = identity}\\ \text{LM = (SRT)}_{ub \leftarrow la}\end{array}\right)$ CMTM = (SRT)$_{ub \leftarrow la}$

(3) $\begin{array}{c}\overline{\text{UpperBody}}\\ \boxed{\text{Arm}}\end{array}$ $\left.\begin{array}{l}\text{GM = (SRT)}_{ub \leftarrow la}\\ \text{LM = identity}\end{array}\right)$ CMTM = (SRT)$_{ub \leftarrow la}$

(4) $\begin{array}{c}\overline{\text{UpperBody}}\\ \boxed{\text{Arm}}\end{array}$ $\left.\begin{array}{l}\text{GM = (SRT)}_{ub \leftarrow la}\\ \text{LM = }T_{arm \leftarrow th}\end{array}\right)$ CMTM = (SRT)$_{ub \leftarrow la} \cdot T_{arm \leftarrow th}$

(5) $\begin{array}{c}\overline{\text{UpperBody}}\\ \overline{\text{Arm}}\\ \boxed{\text{Thumb}}\end{array}$ $\left.\begin{array}{l}\text{GM = (SRT)}_{ub \leftarrow la} \cdot T_{arm \leftarrow th}\\ \text{LM = identity}\end{array}\right)$ CMTM = (SRT)$_{ub \leftarrow la} \cdot T_{arm \leftarrow th}$

(6) $\boxed{\text{UpperBody}}$ $\left.\begin{array}{l}\text{GM = identity}\\ \text{LM = (SRT)}_{ub \leftarrow la}\end{array}\right)$ CMTM = (SRT)$_{ub \leftarrow la}$

(7) $\boxed{\text{UpperBody}}$ $\left.\begin{array}{l}\text{GM = identity}\\ \text{LM = (SRT)}_{ub \leftarrow ra}\end{array}\right)$ CMTM = (SRT)$_{ub \leftarrow ra}$

(8) $\begin{array}{c}\overline{\text{UpperBody}}\\ \overline{\text{Arm}}\\ \boxed{\text{Thumb}}\end{array}$ $\left.\begin{array}{l}\text{GM = (SRT)}_{ub \leftarrow ra} \cdot T_{arm \leftarrow th}\\ \text{LM = identity}\end{array}\right)$ CMTM = (SRT)$_{ub \leftarrow ra} \cdot T_{arm \leftarrow th}$

(a)

Fig. 7.17 Traversal of a three-level hierarchy. (a) Snapshots of traversal-state stack. (b) Annotated structure network.

7.7 APPEARANCE-ATTRIBUTE HANDLING IN HIERARCHY

7.7.1 Inheritance Rules

The attribute-traversal state is set by attribute elements during traversal, and, as in SRGP, is applied modally to all primitives encountered. We saw how parents affect their children via geometric transformations. What rules pertain to appearance attributes? In our street example, the houses all have the default color. To give an object a particular color (e.g., to make a house brown), we can specify that color as an initial element in the object structure itself, but that makes the object's color intrinsic and not changeable during traversal. We

Fig. 7.17 *(Cont'd.)*

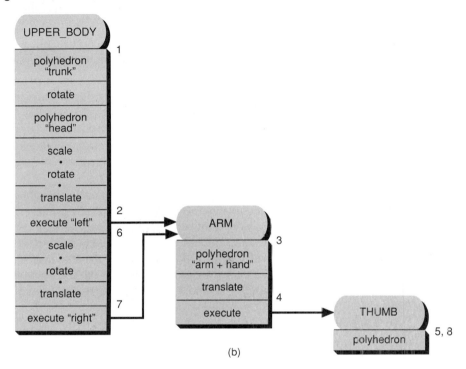

(b)

would prefer to "pass the color as a parameter," so that the child can inherit it the way a child inherits the CMTM as its GM.

Indeed, in SPHIGS, each substructure inherits the traversal state as the latter exists at the time of the invocation of the substructure, and can then modify that state at will without affecting its ancestors. In other words, attributes and transformations are bound dynamically at traversal time, rather than statically at specification time. This dynamic binding is one of the major features of SPHIGS, making it easy to customize instances of a substructure.

What substructures do with the inherited state depends on the type of data involved. We saw that, for geometric transformations, the substructure inherits the GM but cannot override its inheritance, since it can affect only its own local matrix. Attributes are simpler in that the substructure inherits the parent's attributes as the initial values of its local attribute state, but can change its local state subsequently. There is no need to distinguish between global and local attributes, since there is no notion of composing attributes. Note that this mechanism has the same problem we discovered with transformation inheritance— just as our robot's two arm instances cannot have differing thumb transformations, its two arm instances cannot have the same color for the fixed part but differing colors for the thumb.

In the structure network of Fig. 7.18(a), the street structure sets the colors for the house substructure. The resulting image is shown in Fig. 7.18(b), and the code generating the network is shown in Fig. 7.19.

An attribute can be reset within a substructure to override the inherited value. The following code fragment specifies a revised house structure whose chimney is always red.

```
SPH_openStructure (HOUSE_STRUCT);
    SPH_executeStructure (SIMPLE_HOUSE_STRUCT);
    SPH_setInteriorColor (COLOR_RED);
    set up transformation;
    SPH_executeStructure (CHIMNEY_STRUCT);
SPH_closeStructure ();
```

Let us use this new house structure in conjunction with the street structure generated by the code in Fig. 7.19. Figure 7.20 shows the structure network and the resulting image. The traverser starts at STREET_STRUCT; the interior- and edge-color attributes have their default values. The edge color is set to white, a value it retains throughout display traversal of this network. The first setInteriorColor causes yellow to be inherited by the first instance of HOUSE_STRUCT, which in turn passes yellow to SIMPLE_HOUSE_STRUCT, whose polyhedron is shown in that color. When the traverser returns from SIMPLE_HOUSE_STRUCT to

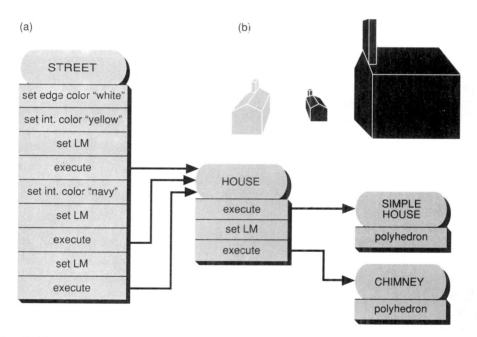

Fig. 7.18 Use of attribute inheritance to model street with colored houses. (a) Structure network. (b) Resulting image. (Interior colors are simulated by patterns.)

```
SPH_openStructure (STREET_STRUCT);
    SPH_setEdgeColor (COLOR_WHITE);

    SPH_setInteriorColor (COLOR_YELLOW);
    set up transformation;
    SPH_executeStructure (HOUSE_STRUCT);

    SPH_setInteriorColor (COLOR_NAVY);
    set up transformation;
    SPH_executeStructure (HOUSE_STRUCT);

    set up transformation;
    SPH_executeStructure (HOUSE_STRUCT);
SPH_closeStructure ();
```

Fig. 7.19 Code used to generate Fig. 7.18.

HOUSE_STRUCT, the interior-color attribute is immediately changed to red by the next element. The invocation of CHIMNEY_STRUCT therefore results in a red chimney with white edges. None of these operations affect the attribute group for STREET_STRUCT, of course; when the traverser returns from HOUSE_STRUCT, STREET_STRUCT's interior-color attribute is restored to yellow. The interior-color attribute is then changed to navy to prepare for drawing two navy houses.

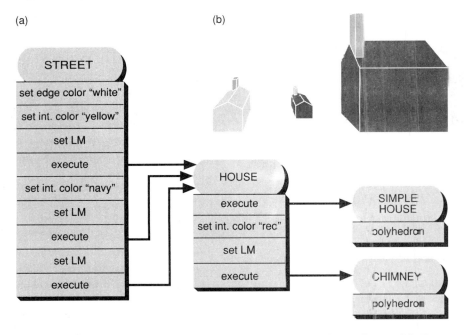

Fig. 7.20 Subordinate structure overriding an inherited attribute. (a) Structure network. (b) Resulting view.

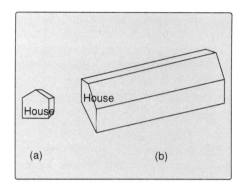

Fig. 7.21 The nongeometric nature of text in SPHIGS. (a) Before transformation. (b) After transformation.

7.7.2   SPHIGS Attributes and Text Unaffected By Transformations

In true PHIGS implementations, text can be subjected to transformations like any other primitive. Thus, the text characters on the sides of a truck, displayed in perspective, are rotated and shown with appropriate perspective foreshortening, as though the letters were made out of individual polylines or fill areas. Similarly, dashes in dashed lines should be subject to geometric transformations and perspective foreshortening. However, just as attributes in SPHIGS are nongeometric for performance reasons, so is text. As in SRGP, the font of the text determines the text's screen size, and a text string cannot even be rotated—the image of a text string is always upright in the plane of the screen, and is never compressed or expanded. Thus, rotation and scaling affect text's origin, but not its size and orientation (Fig. 7.21). SPHIGS primitive text is thus useful primarily for labeling.

7.8   SCREEN UPDATING AND RENDERING MODES

SPHIGS constantly updates the screen image to match the current status of the CSS and view table. The following actions all can make an arbitrary amount of the screen image obsolete:

■   An entry in the view table is changed

■   A structure is closed (after having been opened and edited)

■   A structure is deleted

■   A structure is posted or unposted.

Whenever SPHIGS is called to perform one of these actions, it must regenerate the screen image to display the current state of all posted networks. How SPHIGS chooses to generate the image is a function of the rendering mode the application has selected. These modes present a choice between quality and speed of regeneration: The higher the quality, the longer it takes to render the image. The rendering mode is set by

procedure SPH_setRenderingMode (*mode* : WIREFRAME / FLAT / LIT_FLAT / GOURAUD);

We summarize the four SPHIGS rendering modes here; they are discussed much more fully in Chapters 14 through 16.

Wireframe rendering mode.   WIREFRAME mode is the fastest but least realistic form of display. Objects are drawn as though made of wire, with only their edges showing. The visible (within the view volume) portions of all edges of all objects are shown in their entirety, with no hidden-edge removal. Primitives are drawn in temporal order—that is, in the order in which the traverser encounters them in the posted structure networks in the database; this order is affected by the display-priority determined by the view index, as mentioned in Section 7.3.4.

All edge attributes affect screen appearance in their designated way in this mode; in fact, when the edge flag is set to EDGE_INVISIBLE, fill areas and polyhedra are entirely invisible in this mode.

Shaded rendering modes.   In its other three rendering modes, SPHIGS displays fill areas and polyhedra in a more realistic fashion by drawing fill areas and facets as filled polygons. The addition of shaded areas to the rendering process increases the complexity significantly, because spatial ordering becomes important—portions of objects that are hidden (because they are obscured by portions of "closer" objects) must not be displayed. Methods for determining visible surfaces (also known as hidden-surface removal) are discussed in Chapter 15.

For the three shaded rendering modes, SPHIGS "shades" the interior pixels of visible portions of the facets; the quality of the rendering varies with the mode. For FLAT shading, the mode used often in this chapter's figures, all facets of a polyhedron are rendered in the current interior color, without being influenced by any light sources in the scene. Visible portions of edges are shown (if the edge flag is EDGE_VISIBLE) as they would appear in WIREFRAME mode. If the interior color is set to match the screen background, only the edges show—this use of FLAT rendering, which produced Figs. 7.9(a) and 7.14(c), simulates wireframe with hidden-edge removal.

The two highest-quality rendering modes produce images illuminated by a light source;[10] illumination and shading models are discussed in Chapter 16. These images are nonuniformly "shaded;" the colors of the pixels are based on, but are not exactly, the value of the interior-color attribute. In LIT_FLAT mode, all the pixels on a particular facet have the same color, determined by the angle at which the light hits the facet. Because each facet is of a uniform color, the image has a "faceted" look, and the contrast between adjacent faces at their shared edge is noticeable. GOURAUD mode colors the pixels to provide a smooth shaded appearance that eliminates the faceted look.

In FLAT mode, the edge-flag attribute should be set to EDGE_VISIBLE, because, without visible edges, the viewer can determine only the silhouette boundary of the object. In the two highest-quality modes, however, edge visibility is usually turned off, since the shading helps the user to determine the shape of the object.

---

[10] The PHIGS + extension provides many facilities for controlling rendering, including specification of the placement and colors of multiple light sources, of the material properties of objects characterizing their interaction with light, and so on; see Chapters 14 through 16.

7.9   STRUCTURE NETWORK EDITING FOR DYNAMIC EFFECTS

As with any database, we must be able not only to create and query (in order to display) the SPHIGS structure database, but also to edit it in a convenient way. An application edits a structure via the procedures described in this section; if the application also maintains an application model, it must ensure that the two representations are edited in tandem. *Motion dynamics* requires modification of viewing or modeling transformations; *update dynamics* requires changes in or replacement of structures. The programmer may choose to edit a structure's internal element list if the changes are relatively minor; otherwise, for major editing, it is common to delete and then to respecify the structure in its entirety.

In the remainder of this section, we present methods for intrastructure editing; see the SPHIGS reference manual for information on editing operations that affect entire structures (e.g., deletion, emptying), and for more detailed descriptions of the procedures presented here.

7.9.1   Accessing Elements with Indices and Labels

The rudimentary editing facilities of both SPHIGS and PHIGS resemble those of old-fashioned line-oriented program editors that use line numbers. The elements in a structure are indexed from 1 to N; whenever an element is inserted or deleted, the index associated with each higher-indexed element in the same structure is incremented or decremented. The unique *current element* is that element whose index is stored in the *element-pointer* state variable. When a structure is opened with the SPH_openStructure call, the element pointer is set to N (pointing to the last element) or to 0 for an empty structure. The pointer is incremented when a new element is inserted after the current element, and is decremented when the current element is deleted. The pointer may also be set explicitly by the programmer using absolute and relative positioning commands:

```
void SPH_setElementPointer (int index);
void SPH_offsetElementPointer (int delta);      /* + for forward, – for backward */
```

Because the index of an element changes when a preceding element is added or deleted in its parent structure, using element indices to position the element pointer is liable to error. Thus, SPHIGS allows an application to place "landmark" elements, called *labels*, within a structure. A label element is given an integer identifier when it is generated:

```
void SPH_label (int id);
```

The application can move the element pointer via

```
void SPH_moveElementPointerToLabel (int id);
```

The pointer is then moved forward in search of the specified label. If the end of the structure is reached before the label is found, the search terminates unsuccessfully. Thus, it is advisable to move the pointer to the very front of the structure (index 0) before searching for a label.

7.9.2 Intrastructure Editing Operations

The most common editing action is insertion of new elements into a structure. Whenever an element-generating procedure is called, the new element is placed immediately after the current element, and the element pointer is incremented to point to the new element.[11]

Another form of insertion entails copying all the elements of a given structure into the open structure (immediately after the current element):

> **void** SPH_copyStructure (**int** *structureID*);

Elements are deleted by the following procedures:

> **void** SPH_deleteElement (**void**);
> **void** SPH_deleteElementsInRange (**int** *firstIndex*, **int** *secondIndex*);
> **void** SPH_deleteElementsBetweenLabels (**int** *firstLabel*, **int** *secondLabel*);

In all cases, after the deletion is made, the element pointer is moved to the element immediately preceding the ones deleted, and all survivors are renumbered. The first procedure deletes the current element. The second procedure deletes the elements lying between and including the two specified elements. The third procedure is similar, but does not delete the two label elements.

Note that these editing facilities all affect an entire element or a set of elements; there are no provisions for selective editing of data fields within an element. Thus, for example, when a single vertex needs to be updated the programmer must respecify the entire polyhedron.

An editing example.   Let us look at a modification of our simple street example. Our street now consists of only the first house and the cottage, the former being fixed and the latter being movable. We create a label in front of the cottage, so we can subsequently edit the transformation in order to move the cottage.

To move the cottage, we reopen the street structure, move the pointer to the label, and then offset to the transformation element, replace the transformation element, and close the structure. The screen is automatically updated after the structure is closed, to show the cottage in its new position. This code is shown in Fig. 7.22(a), and its sequence of operations is illustrated in (b).

7.9.3 Instance Blocks for Editing Convenience

The previous editing example suggests that we place a label in front of each element we wish to edit, but creating so many labels is clearly too laborious. There are several techniques for avoiding this tedium. The first is to bracket an editable group of elements with two labels, and to use the labels in deleting or replacing the entire group. Another common technique is to group the set of elements in a fixed format and to introduce the group with a single label.

---

[11]We show the use of insert ''mode'' in our editing examples; however, SPHIGS also supports a ''replace'' editing mode in which new elements write over extant ones. See the reference manual for details.

SPH_openStructure (STREET_STRUCT);
    /* When a structure is opened, the element pointer is initially at its very end. We */
    /* must first move the pointer to the beginning, so we can search for labels. */
    SPH_setElementPointer (0);
    SPH_moveElementPointerToLabel (COTTAGE_TRANSLATION_LABEL);
    SPH_offsetElementPointer (1);   /* Pointer now points at transform element. */
    SPH_deleteElement ();   /* We replace here via a delete/insert combination */
    SPH_setLocalTransformation (*newCottageTranslationMatrix*, PRECONCATENATE);
SPH_closeStructure ();

(a)

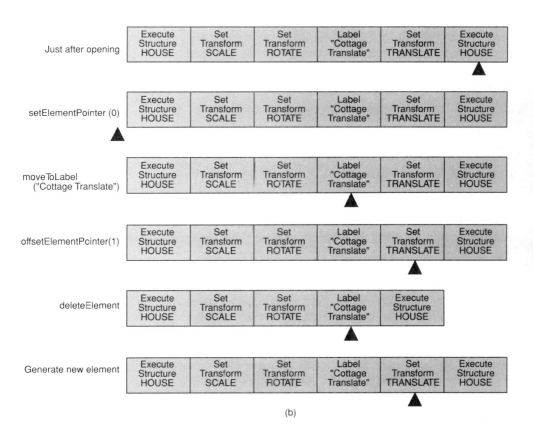

(b)

Fig. 7.22 Editing operations. (a) Code performing editing. (b) Snapshot sequence of structure during editing. The black triangle shows the element pointer's position. (Syntax of calls abbreviated for illustrative purposes.)

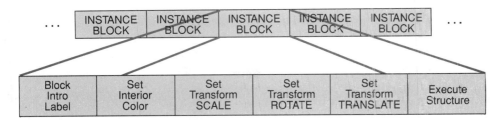

Fig. 7.23 Sample instance-block format.

To edit any member of the group, one moves the element pointer to the label, then offsets the pointer from that label into the group itself. Because the group's format is fixed, the offset is an easily determined small integer.

A special case of this technique is to design a standard way of instantiating substructures by preceding the structure-execution element with a common list of attribute-setting elements. A typical format of such a sequence of elements, called an *instance block,* is shown in Fig. 7.23; first comes the label uniquely identifying the entire block, then an interior-color setting, then the three basic transformations, and finally the invocation of the symbol structure.

We can create a set of symbolic constants to provide the offsets:

```
const int INTERIOR_COLOR_OFFSET = 1;
const int SCALE_OFFSET = 2;
const int ROTATION_OFFSET = 3;
const int TRANSLATION_OFFSET = 4;
```

Using the fixed format for the block guarantees that a particular attribute is modified in the same way for any instance. To change the rotation transformation of a particular instance, we use the following code:

```
SPH_openStructure (ID of structure to be edited);
    SPH_setElementPointer (0);
    SPH_moveElementPointerToLabel (the desired instance-block label);
    SPH_offsetElementPointer (ROTATION_OFFSET).
    SPH_deleteElement ();
    SPH_setLocalTransformation (newMatrix. mode);
SPH_closeStructure ();
```

Another nice feature of instance blocks is that the label introducing each block is easy to define: If the application keeps an internal database identifying all instances of objects, as is common, the label can be set to the unique number that the application itself uses to identify the instance internally.

7.9.4 Controlling Automatic Regeneration of the Screen Image

SPHIGS constantly updates the screen image to reflect the current status of its structure storage database and its view table. On occasion, however, we want to inhibit this regeneration, either to increase efficiency or to avoid presenting the user with a continuously changing image that is confusing and that shows irrelevant intermediate stages of editing.

As we have seen, SPHIGS itself suppresses regeneration during the editing of a structure; no matter how many changes are made, an image is regenerated only when the structure is closed. This "batching" of updates is done for efficiency, since any deletion or transformation of a primitive can cause an arbitrary amount of damage to the screen image—damage that requires either selective damage repair or brute-force retraversal of all posted networks in one or more views. It is clearly faster for SPHIGS to calculate the cumulative effect of a number of consecutive edits just once, before regeneration.

A similar situation arises when several consecutive changes are made to different structures—for instance, when a structure and its substructures are deleted via consecutive calls to deleteStructure. To avoid this problem, an application can suppress automatic regeneration before making a series of changes, and allow it again afterward:

> **void** SPH_setImplicitRegenerationMode (ALLOWED / SUPPRESSED value);

Even while implicit regeneration is suppressed, the application may explicitly demand a screen regeneration by calling

> **void** SPH_regenerateScreen (**void**);

7.10   INTERACTION

Both SRGP's and SPHIGS's interaction modules are based on the PHIGS specification, and thus they have the same facilities for setting device modes and attributes, and for obtaining measures. The SPHIGS keyboard device is identical to that of SRGP, except that the echo origin is specified in NPC space with the z coordinate ignored. The SPHIGS locator device's measure has an additional field for the z coordinate, but is otherwise unchanged. SPHIGS also adds two new interaction facilities. The first is *pick correlation*, augmenting the locator functionality to provide identification of an object picked by the user. The second is the *choice* device, described in the reference manual, which supports menus. Section 10.1 provides a critical review of the PHIGS interaction devices in general.

7.10.1   Locator

The SPHIGS locator returns the cursor position in NPC coordinates, with $z_{NPC} = 0$.[12] It also returns the index of the highest-priority view whose viewport encloses the cursor.

```
typedef struct {
    point position;        /* [x, y, 0]NPC screen position */
    int viewIndex;         /* Index of view whose viewport encloses the cursor */
    int buttonOfMostRecentTransition;
    enum {UP, DOWN} buttonChord[MAX_BUTTON_COUNT];
} locatorMeasure;
```

---

[12] In PHIGS, the locator returns points in the 3D world-coordinate system. Many implementations, however, cannot return a meaningful z value; only high-performance workstations that support control dials and multiple real-time views can offer a comfortable user interface for pointing in 3D (see Chapter 8).

When two viewports overlap and the cursor position lies in the intersection of their bounds, the viewport having the highest index (in the view table) is returned in the second field. Thus, the view index is used to establish view priority for input as well as for output. The view-index field is useful for a variety of reasons. Consider an application that allows the user to specify bounds of a viewport interactively, much as one can move or resize a window manager's windows. In response to a prompt to resize, the user can pick any location within the viewport. The application program can then use the *viewIndex* field to determine which view was picked, rather than doing a point-in-rectangle test on viewport boundaries. The view index is also used in applications with some output-only views; such applications can examine the returned view index to determine whether the correlation procedure even needs to be called.

7.10.2 Pick Correlation

Because the SPHIGS programmer thinks in terms of modeled objects rather than of the pixels composing their images, it is useful for the application to be able to determine the identity of an object whose image a user has picked. The primary use of the locator, therefore, is to provide an NPC point for input to the pick-correlation procedure discussed in this section. As we saw with SRGP, pick correlation in a flat-earth world is a straightforward matter of detecting *hits*—primitives whose images lie close enough to the locator position to be considered chosen by the user. If there is more than one hit, due to overlapping primitives near the cursor, we disambiguate by choosing the one most recently drawn, since that is the one that lies "on top." Thus, a 2D pick correlator examines the primitives in inverse temporal order, and picks the first hit. Picking objects in a 3D, hierarchical world is a great deal more complex, for the reasons described next; fortunately, SPHIGS relieves an application of this task.

Picking in a hierarchy.   Consider the complexity introduced by hierarchy. First, what information should be returned by the pick-correlation utility to identify the picked object? A structure ID is not enough, because it does not distinguish between multiple instances of a structure. Only the full *path*—a description of the complete ancestry from root to picked primitive—provides unique identification.

Second, when a particular primitive is picked, which level of the hierarchy did the user mean? For example, if the cursor is placed near one of our robot's thumbs, does the user mean to select the thumb, the arm, the upper body, or the entire robot? At times, the actual primitive is intended, at times the leaf structure is intended, and any other level is possibly intended, up to the very root! Some applications resolve this problem by providing a feedback mechanism allowing the user to step through the levels from primitive to root, in order to specify exactly which level is desired (see Exercise 7.13).

Comparison criterion.   How is proximity to an object defined when the comparison should really be done in 3D? Since the locator device effectively yields a 2D NPC value, there is no basis for comparing the z coordinates of primitives to the locator position. Thus, SPHIGS can compare the cursor position only to the screen images of the primitives, not to the WC locations of the primitives. If a primitive is a hit, it is deemed a *candidate* for correlation. In wireframe mode, SPHIGS picks the very first candidate encountered during traversal; the reason for this strategy is that there is no obvious depth information in a wireframe image, so the user does not expect pick correlation to take relative depth into account. (A side effect of the strategy is that it optimizes pick correlation.) In shaded rendering modes, SPHIGS picks the candidate whose *hit point* (the NPC point, on the primitive's normalized (3D NPC) surface, to which the user pointed directly) is closest to the viewpoint—the one "in front," as discussed in Section 7.12.2.

Pick-correlation utility. To perform pick correlation, the application program calls a SPHIGS pick-correlation utility[13] with an NPC point and a view index, typically returned by a previous interaction with the locator:

> **void** SPH_pickCorrelate (
>   point *position*, **int** *viewIndex*, pickInformation **pickInfo*);

The returned information identifies the primitive picked and its ancestry via a *pick path*, as described by Pascal data types in Fig. 7.24.

When no primitive is close enough to the cursor position, the value of *pickLevel* returned is 0 and the *path* field is undefined. When *pickLevel* is greater than 0, it specifies the length of the path from the root to the picked primitive—that is, the primitive's depth within the network. In this latter case, entries [1] through [*pickLevel*] of the *path* array return the identification of the structure elements involved in the path leading from root to picked primitive. At the deepest level (entry [*pickLevel*]), the element identified is the primitive that was picked; at all other levels (entries [*pickLevel*–1] through [1]), the elements are all structure executions. Each entry in *path* identifies one element with a record that gives the structure ID of the structure containing the element, the index of the element

---

[13]Full PHIGS has the Pick logical input device that returns the same measure as the SPH_pickCorrelate procedure.

```
typedef struct {
    int structureID;
    int elementIndex;
    /* Enumerated type: polyline, polyhedron, execute-structure, etc. */
    elementTypeCode elementType;
    int pickID;
} pickPathItem;

typedef pickPathItem pickPath[MAX_HIERARCHY_LEVEL];

typedef struct {
    int pickLevel;
    pickPath path;
} pickInformation;
```

Fig. 7.24 Pick-path storage types.

in that structure, a code presenting the type of the element, and the pick ID of the element (discussed next).

Figure 7.25 uses the structure network of Fig. 7.15 for the robot's upper body, and shows the pick information returned by several picks within the structure's displayed image.

How does the pick path uniquely identify each instance of a structure that is invoked arbitrarily many times within the hierarchy? For example, how do we distinguish a pick on the robot's left thumb from a pick on its right thumb? The pick paths for the two thumbs are identical except at the root level, as demonstrated by points *a* and *e* in Fig. 7.25.

The *pick identifier* can provide pick correlation at a finer resolution than does a structure ID. Although the element index can be used to identify individual elements, it is subject to change when the structure is edited. Therefore, using the pick ID is easier, because the pick ID is not affected by editing of other elements. It has a default value of 0 and is modally set within a structure. One generates a pick-ID element via

void SPH_setPickIdentifier (**int** *id*);

The pick-ID element is ignored during display traversal. Also, a pick ID has no notion of inheritance: it is initially 0 when SPHIGS begins the traversal of any structure, whether it is a root or a substructure. Because of these two aspects, pick IDs do not behave like attributes. Multiple primitives within a structure may have unique IDs or share the same one; this permits arbitrarily fine resolution of pick correlation within a structure, as needed by the application. Although labels and pick IDs are thus different mechanisms, the former used for editing and the latter for pick correlation, they are often used in conjunction. In particular, when structures are organized using the instance-block technique described in Section 7.9.2, a pick-ID element is also part of the block, and the pick ID itself is typically set to the same integer value as that of the block label.

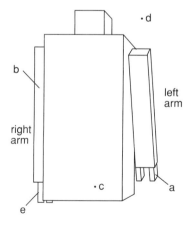

Refer to the structure network shown in Fig. 7.15.

(a) level = 3
        path[1] : struct UPPER _BODY, element 7
        path[2] : struct ARM, element 3
        path[3] : struct THUMB, element 1

(b) level = 2
        path[1] : struct UPPER_BODY, element 11
        path[2] : struct ARM, element 1

(c) level = 1
        path[1] : struct UPPER_BODY, element 1

(d) level = 0

(e) level = 3
        path[1] : struct UPPER_BODY, element 11
        path[2] : struct ARM, element 3
        path[3] : struct THUMB, element 1

Fig. 7.25 Example of pick correlation.

7.11   ADDITIONAL OUTPUT FEATURES

7.11.1   Attribute Bundles

Standard PHIGS provides a mechanism for setting attribute values indirectly. An application can, during its initialization sequence, store a collection of attribute values in an *attribute bundle*. Each type of primitive has its own type of bundle, and a PHIGS package provides storage for many bundles, each bundle identified by an integer ID. For example, we could store a "favorite" polyline attribute set in bundle 1. Subsequently, while editing a structure, we would prepare for the specification of a polyline primitive by inserting an element that, when executed during traversal, specifies that polyline attributes are to be taken from bundle 1 (rather than from the explicitly specified traversal attribute state).

Attribute bundles are often used as a "shorthand" to simplify the task of specifying attributes. Consider an application in which a large number of unrelated primitives must appear with identical attributes. Because the primitives are not related, the inheritance mechanism does not help. Indeed, without attribute bundles, the application would have to specify the desired attribute set redundantly, at various places throughout the structure networks.

Implementors of PHIGS packages sometimes initialize the attribute bundles in order to provide workstation-dependent preselected attribute sets that take advantage of the workstation's best features. The application programmer can choose to accept the bundles' initial values, as "suggestions" from the implementor, or to modify them with the bundle-editing commands. Changing definitions of bundles in the bundle table without changing structure networks is a simple mechanism for dynamically changing the appearance of objects.

7.11.2   Name Sets for Highlighting and Invisibility

SPHIGS supports two traditional feedback techniques that applications commonly use in conjunction with the SPHIGS picking facility: highlighting objects and making objects invisible. The former technique is typically used to provide feedback when the user picks an object; the latter declutters the screen by showing only desired detail. By default, all primitives that are part of a posted network are visible and unhighlighted. A set of primitives may be given an integer *name*, to identify the primitives for subsequent toggling of their visibility or highlighting status.

Because a group of unrelated primitives can share a name, and because a single primitive can have any number of names, the name feature can allow a complex object to be organized in several ways orthogonal to the structure hierarchy induced by structure invocation. For instance, an office-building model represented as a set of floor substructures could also be represented as a union of several systems: the plumbing network, the electrical wiring, and so on. Simply by giving all pipe primitives a common name (PLUMBING), we ensure that, even though the pipe primitives may be scattered among the actual structure hierarchy, we can nevertheless refer to them as a single unit.

When we want, say, to make the plumbing subsystem invisible, we add the name PLUMBING to the global *invisibility filter;* the screen is immediately updated to remove images of pipe objects. Similarly, by setting the invisibility filter to the names of all the subsystems except the electrical subsystem, we can display the electrical subsystem in isolation. The highlighting filter works similarly. Both filters are initially empty, and are affected only by explicit calls that add or remove names.[14] Note that changing a filter, like changing a viewing specification, triggers screen regeneration; indeed, these operations change the rendered view of the CSS much as queries in traditional database programs are used to show different "views" of data.

The method used to bind names to primitives dynamically is very similar to the way attributes are assigned to primitives. SPHIGS maintains, as part of display traversal state, a *traversal name set* of zero or more names. A root inherits an empty name set. A child inherits the parent's name set when it is invoked, as it does attributes in general; thus, multiple instances of a building-block object can either share names or be named individually. The SPHIGS reference manual describes structure elements that, when executed during traversal, add names or remove names from this name set.

7.11.3   Picture Interchange and Metafiles

Although PHIGS and other standard graphics packages are system- and device-independent to promote portability, a given implementation of such packages in a particular environment is likely to be highly optimized in a nonportable way for performance reasons. The internal representation of the CSS, for example, may contain machine-specific information for structures and elements. To provide a medium of exchange among different implementations of PHIGS, the graphics standards committee has defined an archive file format. This portion of the standard is a machine- and environment-independent form of the contents of the CSS, without any viewing information. The PHIGS archive file thus is a portable snapshot of the structure database at a given time and permits PHIGS implementations to share geometric models.

PHIGS implementations may also support the writing of a metafile, which can contain a snapshot of what the application is currently presenting on the display surface. When these metafiles conform to the ANSI and ISO Computer Graphics Metafile (CGM) standard [ARNO88], the pictures contained in them can be transferred to such application environments as desktop publishing and interactive graphics art enhancement workstations. A CGM file is also a machine- and device-independent form of the CSS, but, unlike archive files, viewing information is also used in the creation of the picture represented in the CGM.

The CGM is typically created by having a PHIGS output device driver traverse the CSS to produce code for the CGM "virtual device," much as an ordinary device driver produces display code for a real display system. Other systems then can read the metafile into their CSS via an input device driver that converts from the prescribed metafile format to whatever is used by the particular implementation. Because the metafile is a 2D view of a 3D scene, any application obtaining the picture information via a CGM will have only the 2D view to work with: the original 3D geometry will be lost. If the 3D model is to be exchanged in a standard format, archive files must be used.

---

[14] The PHIGS detectability filter allows the application to specify primitives that cannot be picked. Moreover, PHIGS' filter scheme is more powerful, having separate inclusion and exclusion filters.

Other types of metafiles might be useful for debugging and backup purposes. An audit trail metafile is an historical transcript file containing a list of all calls to the graphics package procedures (and the values sent to them as parameters) in temporal order. It would, therefore, need to be run from start to finish, in order to recreate the CSS at the end of the session. Another type of transcript file records user actions: Running the application program with that transcript file reproduces the original sequence of PHIGS calls and thus the same CSS/image. No standards exist nor are standards planned for such transcript files, and neither a CGM nor a PHIGS archive file contains any historical information.

7.12   IMPLEMENTATION ISSUES

Much of the internal functionality of SPHIGS involves the maintenance (editing) and use (traversal) of the view table and the CSS. We do not discuss maintenance here, since it is essentially a conventional data-structures problem and not graphics-specific. Rather, this section focuses on the mechanics of displaying structures and of doing pick correlation.

The display traverser is invoked whenever the screen image must be updated. When implicit regeneration is allowed, the following operations prompt traversal: closing a structure, posting and unposting, changing a viewing transformation, changing rendering mode, and changing a filter. To generate the contents of a view, each structure posted to the view is traversed.

To display a posted structure network, SPHIGS visits the component structures' elements using a recursive descent, depth-first traversal, and performs the appropriate action for each element, based on the element's type. This display process that maps a model to an image on screen (or hardcopy) is referred to as display traversal in the context of PHIGS, but more generally as *rendering;* its implementation in software and/or hardware is referred to as the *rendering pipeline*.

Pick-correlation traversal is very similar to display traversal. The primitives encountered during traversal are compared to the locator position to find candidates. Traversal can be halted at the first candidate when wireframe rendering is being used; otherwise, a complete traversal is performed and the candidate closest to the viewpoint in z is chosen.

7.12.1   Rendering

The conceptual *rendering pipeline* that implements display traversal is illustrated in Fig. 7.26. Its first stage is the actual depth-first traversal of the CSS itself. (Alternatively, if an immediate-mode graphics package is used, the application may traverse the application model or generate primitives and attributes procedurally.) Each primitive encountered during traversal is passed through the remainder of the pipeline: First, the modeling transformations (described in Chapter 5) are applied to map the primitive from modeling coordinates to world coordinates. Then, the viewing operation is applied to transform and clip the primitive to the canonical view volume, and then to map it to the NPC parallelepiped (described in Chapter 6). Since these processes are independent of the display device and deal with vertex geometry in floating-point coordinates, this portion of

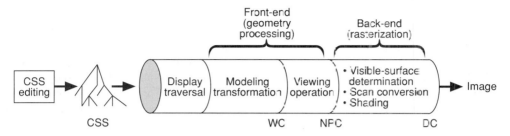

Fig. 7.26 The SPHIGS rendering pipeline.

the pipeline immediately following traversal is often referred to as the geometry-processing subsystem.

The back end of the pipeline takes transformed, clipped primitives and produces pixels; we will refer to this pixel processing as *rasterization*. This process is, of course, straightforward for wireframe mode: The NPC coordinates are easily mapped (via scaling and translating, with z ignored) to integer device coordinates, and then the underlying raster graphics package's line-drawing function is invoked to do the actual scan conversion. Shaded rendering, however, is quite complex, and is composed of three subprocesses: *visible-surface determination* (determining which portions of a primitive are actually visible from the synthetic camera's point of view), *scan conversion* (determining the pixels covered by a primitive's image), and *shading* (determining which color to assign to each covered pixel). The exact order in which these subprocesses are performed varies as a function of the rendering mode and implementation method. Detailed descriptions of the rasterization subprocesses are contained in Chapters 14 through 16.

Traversal. Since all stages of the rendering pipeline but the first one are covered in other chapters, we need to discuss only the traversal stage here. In a simple implementation, SPHIGS regenerates the screen by erasing it and then retraversing all posted roots (a list of which is stored with each view). Optimizing regeneration in order to traverse as little of the CSS as possible is quite difficult, because the effect of a trivial operation is potentially enormous. For example, it is difficult to determine how much of the screen must be regenerated due to the editing of a structure: It is possible that the structure is never invoked and thus has no effect on the screen, but it is also possible that it is a commonly invoked building block appearing in most of the views. Even when the implementation can determine that only a single view has been affected by an operation, refreshing that view may damage the images of objects in overlapping viewports of higher priority. Doing damage repair efficiently is, in general, a complicated task requiring considerable bookkeeping.

In implementations on high-performance workstations, where the image can be traversed and regenerated in a fraction of a second, the bookkeeping space and time overhead needed to regenerate the screen selectively is probably not worthwhile, and therefore complete regeneration is used most frequently. In either the complete or selective regeneration schemes, the double-buffering technique described later in this section can be used to prevent annoying visual discontinuities on the screen during display traversal.

The traversal of a structure can be done in hardware or software; here, we show a procedural-language implementation, the pseudocode for which is given in Fig. 7.27. The procedure inherits a *traversal state*, which it then maintains as its local state for the duration of its activation. The attribute values (including the name set) and three transformation matrices (GM, LM, and their product, CMTM) form the traversal state, and the attributes and the CMTM are passed down from parent activation to child activation. (The activation of the procedure for a root structure inherits an identity GM and an attribute record filled with default values). The procedure visits each element in the structure and performs an operation based on the element's type, as indicated in Fig. 7.27.

Optimization via extent checking.   The traversal strategy we have presented traverses a network's contents unconditionally; during traversal, all structure invocations are executed, and no part of the DAG is skipped. Frequently, however, not all of a network's objects are visible, since modeling and viewing tranformations in effect when the traversal is performed can cause large parts of a network to lie outside of the viewing volume.

What information do we need to trivially reject a subordinate structure during traversal? Say we have come to an element "Execute structure S" and can quickly compute the bounds of this instance, S_i, in NPC space. We could then ask the question, "Does S_i lie completely outside of the NPC viewport?" If it does, we skip over the structure-execution element and refrain from descending into structure S. Since structure S may be the root of

```
void TraverseStructureForDisplay (structID, attributeState, GM)
{
    LM = identity matrix;
    CMTM = GM;

    for (each element in structure structID) {
        switch (element type) {
            case attribute or name-set modification:
                update attributeState;
                break;
            case LM setting:
                replace or update LM;
                update CMTM by postconcatenating LM to GM;
                break;
            case primitive:
                pass primitive through rest of rendering pipeline;
                break;
            case execute structure:      /* A recursive call */
                TraverseStructureForDisplay
                    (ID of structure to be executed, attributeState, CMTM);
                break;
            default:                      /* ignore labels and pickIDs */
                break;
        }
    }
}   /* TraverseStructureForDisplay */
```

Fig. 7.27 Pseudocode for display traversal.

an arbitrarily complex subnetwork, avoiding its traversal can reap potentially enormous time savings. In fact, this method allows us to trivially reject an entire network by comparing the root structure's NPC bounds with that of the viewport.

To implement this optimization, we need a simple method for computing the bounds of an arbitrarily complex object, and an efficient way of comparing these bounds to the NPC viewport. The representation that fits both these criteria is the *NPC extent*, defined as the smallest bounding box that completely encloses the NPC version of the object and is aligned with the principal axes. If we can show that the extent of an instance does not intersect with the viewport, we have proved that the instance is completely invisible. The extent is ideal because a viewport is itself an aligned box, and because it is very cheap to calculate the intersection of two aligned boxes (see Exercise 7.5). Trivial rejection is not the only optimization gained by the use of the NPC extent. We can also trivially accept—that is, discover instances that lie completely within the view volume and thus do not need to be clipped. The extent technique for trivial-accept/trivial-reject testing of substructures was first used in hardware in the BUGS system [VAND74] and is described also in [CLAR76].

Because instances are not explicitly stored in the CSS, we must calculate an instance's NPC extent from its structure's MC extent, which we store in the CSS. To perform extent checking during traversal, we thus first transform the MC extent to NPC, to determine the instance's NPC extent. Because a transformed extent box is not necessarily upright in NPC, we must determine the NPC extent of the transformed MC extent; that NPC extent is what we compare against the viewport.

To calculate the extent of a structure S, we must calculate the union of the extents of its primitives and descendants. We can calculate the extent of a polyhedron or fill area by traversing its MC vertex list, transformed by the local matrix, to determine minimum and maximum values of x, y, and z. These six numbers determine the extent: the box with one corner at $(x_{min}, y_{min}, z_{min})$ and the opposite corner at $(x_{max}, y_{max}, z_{max})$.

There is one other issue involved in maintaining extent information. When should the MC extent of a structure be calculated? It is not enough to do it whenever the structure is edited; a structure's MC extent is affected not only by its contents but also by the contents of any of its descendants. Thus, after each editing operation, an arbitrary number of structure extents must be recalculated. Moreover, recalculation requires traversal of an arbitrarily large subset of the CSS. We can optimize extent calculation by doing it not after each edit but during normal display traversal. This technique has the advantage of updating the extents of only those structures that are actually visible (part of a posted network), and it ensures that no structure's extent is calculated more than once in response to an arbitrarily large batch of editing operations. [SKLA90] presents this optimization technique in greater detail.

Animation and double-buffering. Software implementations of SPHIGS are well suited for rapidly producing animation prototypes, but are poorly suited for presenting high-quality real-time animations, because rendering is inherently time-consuming and the extent-checking optimization technique does not work well when a great deal of editing is performed between "frames." Animation prototypes are usually rendered in WIREFRAME mode, with automatic regeneration disabled, using a cyclical algorithm: The application edits the structure database to describe the next scene, explicitly requests regeneration, then edits to describe the next scene, and so on. If the scene is not very complicated, WIREFRAME mode can be fast enough to present an almost–real-time animation of a modest number of primitives with just software. With some hardware assistance, higher-quality shading modes can perform in real-time.

One side effect of some simple implementations is that, between the "frames" of the animation, viewers see the screen being erased and can (more or less) see the objects being drawn as the traverser performs regeneration. An SPHIGS implementation can reduce this visual artifact by double buffering: using an offscreen canvas/bitmap to store the next frame while that frame is being drawn; then, when the regeneration is complete, the contents of that canvas can be copied onto the screen. When this technique is used on a system with a very fast copyPixel operation, the switch between frames is not noticeable, but there are still discontinuities in the motion of the objects in the scene. In fact, the *animation rate* (i.e., the number of frames per second) may decrease due to the increased overhead of the copyPixel, but the decrease in visual artifacts in many cases justifies the cost. Hardware double-buffering, as described in Section 4.4.1, is much better, since it avoids the copyPixel time.

7.12.2   Pick Correlation

In pick correlation, SPHIGS traverses those networks posted to the viewport in which the specified NPC point lies. The traversal is nearly identical to that performed during display; the modeling-transformation matrices are maintained, and much of the rendering pipeline is performed. Moreover, the pick ID, ignored during display traversal, is maintained as part of the local traversal state in the recursive traversal procedure. (The attribute group does not need to be maintained because during hit detection SPHIGS does not take into account attributes such as line thickness.)

Let us first examine pick correlation for wireframe rendering, where traversal is halted at the very first hit. Because traversal is recursive, the pick path is easily determined the moment the first hit is found: Each activation of the traversal procedure is responsible for one level of information in the pick path. Each primitive is transformed to NPC before being compared to the locator position for hit detection. (Hit-detection techniques are described later in this section.) When a hit is discovered by an activation of the procedure, it returns, and the recursion is unwound. Before returning, each activation stores its pick information into one level of a global pick-information array. (See Exercise 7.9.)

In shaded rendering modes, the order in which primitives are encountered during traversal has no bearing on whether they appear in front of or in back of other primitives whose images map to the same part of the screen. Therefore, the SPHIGS pick-correlation algorithm cannot simply choose the first hit detected. Rather, it must traverse all posted structure networks, maintaining a list of candidate hits. When traversal is completed, the candidates are compared to determine the candidate whose NPC hit point is closest to the viewpoint—that is, the one whose z coordinate is algebraically largest. To calculate a candidate's z coordinate at the hit point, we can plug the x and y coordinates of the locator measure into the appropriate equations for each primitive: the (parametric) line equation for edges, and the plane equation for facets (see Exercises 7.7 and 7.8). Another approach using a hardware visible-surface determination algorithm is described in Section 15.4. Pick-correlation traversal can, of course, be optimized in a variety of ways, including the extent-checking techniques used to optimize display traversal.

Analytical hit detection.   Two fundamental methods, analytical and clipping, are used for hit detection. For analytical hit detection, algebraic equations are used to determine whether the NPC primitive lies sufficiently close to the 2D NPC locator measure. We first convert to 2D by ignoring the z coordinate for an orthographic projection or use the perspective transform of Section 6.5.4 to create an orthographic view volume. Some examples of analytical techniques follow:

- In WIREFRAME mode, a function PtNearLineSegment is used to compute the distance in NPC from the cursor position to each edge of a facet or fill area, and to each line segment of a polyline. This same function would be used in shaded rendering modes for polyline primitives. The line equation is used for the computation (see Exercise 7.10).

- In shaded rendering modes, a function PtInPolygon is used to test for hits on fill areas and facets. One popular algorithm for determining if the NPC cursor position lies inside a polygon, based on the odd-parity rule described in Section 2.1.3, casts a ray from the locator position and determines how many times the ray intersects the polygon. The algorithm traverses the edge list, testing for intersections and special cases (e.g., intersections at vertices, edge–ray colinearity). The polygon scan-conversion algorithm described in Section 3.7 tackles a very similar problem and can be adapted for use as a PtInPolygon function (see Exercise 7.12). This algorithm handles the general case of concave and self-intersecting polygons. Optimized computational geometry algorithms are available if it can be guaranteed that polygons do not self-intersect, or that a horizontal ray intersects only two edges, or that the polygon is convex [PREP85].

- Hit detection for nongeometric text is most easily performed by comparing the locator position to the text's rectangular screen extent.

- Packages that support primitives such as ellipses and curves and surfaces require more complex pick-correlation algorithms of the sort mentioned in Chapters 11 and 19. Furthermore, the problems are similar to those encountered in ray tracing, as described in Chapter 15.

Hit detection via clipping.   Some hardware clipping devices and optimized software clipping utilities return state information, allowing an application to determine whether any part of a primitive's image lies inside a 2D integer clip rectangle, without having actually to draw the primitive. An SPHIGS implementation can use this type of clipping to test for candidacy: The clip rectangle is set to a *pick window*—a small square surrounding the cursor position—and then traversal is performed. Each primitive (transformed to integer device coordinates) is given to the clipper, which returns a Boolean "hit-detection" result (see Exercise 7.11). Alternatively, if the clipper does not return any such state information, we can draw each primitive into an offscreen bitmap using the pick-window clip rectangle; if any pixels are changed, the primitive is deemed a candidate.

7.13   OPTIMIZING DISPLAY OF HIERARCHICAL MODELS

7.13.1   Elision

We can model a building as a parts hierarchy by saying that it consists of floors, the floors consist of offices, and so on; there are no primitives in the hierarchy's nodes until we get to the level of bricks, planks, and concrete slabs that consist of polyhedra. Although this representation might be useful for construction purposes, it is not as useful for display, where we sometimes wish to see a cruder, simplified picture that eliminates confusing and unneeded details (and that is faster to render). The term *elision* refers to the decision by a display traverser to refrain from descending into a substructure.

Pruning.   In Section 7.12.1, we showed how a display traverser can avoid executing a subordinate structure by checking its NPC extent against the viewport, to determine whether the substructure lies wholly outside (i.e., is fully clipped by) the view volume. This type of elision, a typical feature of optimized display traversers, is called *pruning*.

Culling.   In addition, a traverser can examine the size of the subordinate's NPC extent, and can choose to elide the substructure if that substructure's extent is so small that, after transformation and projection, the image of the object would be compressed into a few pixels. This type of elision is called *culling*; on systems that support it, the application typically can specify a minimum extent size, below which a substructure is culled.

When a substructure is pruned, it is not drawn at all; however, that is not the best approach for culling. The object is being culled not because it is invisible from the current point of view, but because its image is too tiny for its details to be discernible. Rather than not draw it at all, most implementations draw it as an abstract form, typically a parallelipiped representing its WC extent, or simply a rectangle (the 2D projection of its NPC extent).

Level-of-detail elision.   Pruning and culling are optimization techniques, preventing traversal that is unnecessary (pruning) or that would produce an unusable image (culling). Elision can also be used to give the user control over the amount of detail presented in a view of the CSS. For example, a user examining our building model could specify a low level of detail in order to view the building as simply a set of parallelepipeds representing the individual floors, or could increase the level of detail so as to see in addition the walls that form office boundaries.

The MIDAS microprocessor architecture simulator [GURW81] was one of the earliest systems in which alternate representations of subobjects were traversed automatically by the display processor, depending on the size of the projection of the subobject on the screen. This logical-zoom facility made successively more detail appear as the user dynamically zoomed in on the processor block in the CPU architecture block diagram. Also, at increased zoom factors, one could see digits representing address, data, and control bytes moving from source to destination over system buses during the simulation of the instruction cycle.

Elision in MIDAS was implemented using a conditional-execution facility of the BUGS vector-graphics system [VAND74]: The hierarchical display list included a conditional substructure execution element that tested the screen extent of the substructure. A similar feature described in the 1988 specification of PHIGS+ in the form of a conditional-execution element, allowing pruning and culling to be performed explicitly by elements within the CSS.

7.13.2 Structure Referral

Certain implementations of PHIGS and PHIGS+ allow a nonstandard form of structure execution, called *referral*, that bypasses the expensive state saving and restoring of the ExecuteStructure mechanism. Whereas we could argue that a better, transparent approach to increasing efficiency is to optimize the implementation of the ExecuteStructure operation itself (so that the operation saves only as much state as required at any given time), it is simpler to add a RefstStructure operation and to let the programmer use it for those cases where an invoked child structure does not have any attribute-setting elements.

A second use of RefStructure is to allow a child to influence its parents' attributes. This is useful when a group of objects do not have a common parent, but do need to "inherit" the same group of attributes, including potentially an arbitrary number of modeling transformations. In this case, we can create a structure A that consists of transformation and appearance attribute settings, and then have each of the object structures refer to structure A. By editing structure A later, we indirectly affect all structures referring to A. If only appearance attributes need to be affected, PHIGS attribute bundles provide an alternative, standard mechanism for changing the appearance of diverse structures.

7.14 LIMITATIONS OF HIERARCHICAL MODELING IN PHIGS

Although this chapter has emphasized geometric modeling hierarchy, it is important to realize that hierarchy is only one of many forms of data representation. In this section, we discuss the limitations of hierarchy in general and in PHIGS in particular; in the next section, we present some alternatives to structure hierarchy.

7.14.1 Limitations of Simple Hierarchy

As mentioned in Section 1.7.2, some applications have no real structure for their data (e.g., data for scatter plots), or have at most a (partial) ordering in their data (e.g., a function represented algebraically). Many other applications are more naturally expressed as networks—that is, as general (directed) graphs (which may have hierarchial subnets). Among these are circuit and electrical-wiring diagrams, transportation and communications networks, and chemical-plant–piping diagrams. Another example of simple hierarchy's insufficiency for certain types of models is Rubik's cube, a collection of components in which the network and any hierarchy (say of layers, rows, and columns) is fundamentally altered after any transformation.

For other types of models, a single hierarchy does not suffice. For example, the pen holder on an (x, y) plotter is moved by, and therefore "belongs" to, both the horizontal and vertical arms. In short, whether the application model exhibits pure hierarchy, pure network without hierarchy, hierarchy in a network with cross-links, or multiple hierarchies, SPHIGS can be used to display it, but we may not want, or be able, to use structure hierarchy in its full generality.

7.14.2   Limitations of SPHIGS "Parameter Passing"

The black-box nature of structures is good for modularity but, as shown in our robot example, can be limiting. For example, how can we build a robot with two identical arms and have the robot use its right arm to pick up a cylinder from a table and move away with that cylinder? The pick-up operation can be performed by editing the arm structure to add an invocation of the cylinder structure, so that as the robot or arm moves subsequently, the cylinder moves along with it. But if we implement the robot by having a single arm structure invoked twice by the upper-body structure, the result of that operation would be that both the left and right arm would be holding a cylinder! Thus, we have no choice but to build two separate arm structures, with unique structure IDs, each invoked only once. Let us extend this example. If we wish to have an army of robots with independently controlled arms, we must build two unique arm structures for each robot! Obviously, here is a case where structure hierarchy is not as useful as we first thought.

The reason that structure hierarchy does not support instances of structures differing in the settings of transformations at various hierarchical levels is that structure hierarchy has neither the general parameter-passing mechanism of procedure hierarchy nor general flow-of-control constructs. Rather, it is essentially a data organization with rudimentary interactions between structures and at most limited conditional execution of structures (in PHIGS+). We have seen that a parent's transformations are inherited by all the children, and there is no provision for a particular child to be affected selectively.

By contrast, in a procedure hierarchy, a "root" procedure passes parameters that are either used directly by procedures the root calls, or passed down by those procedures to lower-level procedures. Thus, the root can pass down parameters arbitrarily deeply and selectively via intermediate procedures. Furthermore, with parameters, a procedure can control not just the data on which a lower-level procedure operates, but even the way in which the lower-level procedure operates. To change its operation, the lower-level procedure uses flow-of-control constructs to test parameters and selectively enables or disables code segments. Because of structure hierarchy's lack of general parameter-passing and flow-of-control mechanisms, our analogy between structure hierarchy and procedure hierarchy in the introduction was a superficial one.

By augmenting the attribute-binding model of PHIGS, we could specify attributes for selected object instances at arbitrary levels in a hierarchy. A system that has such a general mechanism is SCEFO [STRA88], which allows the programmer to specify an attribute that is to be applied when the traversal reaches a certain state, the state being represented by a pathname similar to the pick path returned by the PHIGS pick device. With this facility, it would be possible to control individually the colors or positions of the thumb instances in our robot, without having to create two virtually identical arm masters, by making use of the fact that the two thumb instances have unique pathnames.

Another limitation in the PHIGS parameter-passing mechanism is that it handles transformations and appearance attributes for which inheritance rules are very simple. It would not be easy to support operations more complex than geometric transformations; a more general model is needed to support set operations on solid primitives (Chapter 12), and deformation operations such as bend, taper, and twist (Chapter 20).

7.15   ALTERNATIVE FORMS OF HIERARCHICAL MODELING

We have just concluded that structure hierarchy is only one way—and not always the best way—to encode hierarchy. In this section, we discuss alternatives to structure hierarchy.

7.15.1   Procedure Hierarchy

In the spectrum from pure data hierarchy to pure procedure hierarchy, structure hierarchy is almost all the way at the data end, since it lacks general flow of control. By contrast, a template procedure (i.e., a procedure defining a template object, consisting of primitives or of calls to subordinate template procedures) can use parameters and arbitrary flow of control. Template procedures can be used in two different ways. First, they can be used with a retained-mode graphics package such as SPHIGS. Here, they are used as a means to the end of creating structure hierarchy. Second, they can be used to specify primitives and attributes to an immediate-mode graphics package. Here, they are not means to ends, but rather are ends in themselves; that is, they are the sole representation of the hierarchy used for display. In this case, display traversal is effected by procedure traversal—practical only if the CPU can provide a reasonable rate of retraversal. (In general, smooth dynamics requires at least 15 frames per second; 30 frames per second looks noticeably better.) The procedures themselves implement inheritance and maintain transformation matrices and attribute states, using techniques similar to those presented in our discussion of traversal implementation in Section 7.12. Newman's display procedures mentioned in Section 7.4 were an early example of the use of procedure hierarchy for dynamics.

Pick correlation is a bit tricky in dynamic procedure traversal, since it requires retraversing the procedure hierarchy. If the first candidate is to be chosen (i.e., if the rendering mode is wireframe), it is difficult to halt the traversal as soon as a hit is detected and to return from an arbitrary level of the procedure activation stack. If a nonwire frame rendering mode is used, there must be a way of interacting with the rendering pipeline to obtain the candidates and their z values corresponding to the cursor position. Each procedure is also complicated by the fact that it must be used both for display and for correlation traversal.

We can combine procedure and structure hierarchy by using template procedures to create structures. For example, our robot can be built using template procedures for each of the parts; each procedure creates display commands or a SPHIGS structure, depending on whether we choose immediate mode or retained structure mode, respectively. The upper-body procedure can pass parameters to the arm and thumb procedures to initialize their transformations individually and to allow the arms and thumbs to operate independently. In retained mode, each invocation of the robot template procedure thus creates a unique SPHIGS network, with unique names for all the child structures. For example, two arm structures would be created, with their own, separate invocations of thumbs. Leaf nodes such as the thumb can still be shared among multiple networks, since they can be instanced with individual transforms by their callers. To create unique structure IDs, we can assign a unique interval of integer space to each root, and can number its parts within that interval.

What are the limitations of using only procedure hierarchy? First, unless the programming environment supports dynamic code creation, it is difficult to edit or construct procedures at run time. Creating new data structures is far easier. Therefore, procedure hierarchy is typically used when the set of template objects is predefined and only the attributes need to be varied dynamically. Structures created by template procedures can, of course, be edited with all the PHIGS machinery.

Second, if the procedure hierarchy is used to create immediate-mode graphics, the CPU, involved in constantly retraversing the procedure hierarchy, is much less available for application processing. We can offload the CPU in a multiprocessor system by having another CPU dedicated to procedure traversal. Alternatively, in retained mode, structure-network traversal can be performed by a special-purpose hardware coprocessor or a separate CPU.

Third, even for minor edits, an immediate-mode procedure hierarchy must be retraversed in its entirety and all display primitives must be retransmitted to the graphics packages. For display systems connected over networks or communication lines, this requirement produces heavy communication traffic. It is far more efficient for minor edits, for both the CPU and the communications system, to store and manage a structure database in a display peripheral that can be modified incrementally and traversed rapidly.

7.15.2   Data Hierarchy

Unlike procedure hierarchy, data hierarchy is well suited to dynamic creation. Like template-procedure hierarchy, it can be used in conjunction with either immediate- or retained-mode graphics packages. If immediate mode is used, the CPU must retraverse the application model and drive the package sufficiently quickly to provide dynamic update rates. Objects are created and edited by changing the application model and retraversing it to update the screen. The application must do its own pick correlation, by retraversal. As with an immediate-mode procedure hierarchy, however, if the display subsystem is on a communications network, retransmittal of graphics commands for any update is considerably slower than is sending update commands to a structure database in the peripheral.

Like the structure-hierarchy technique, the data-hierarchy approach lacks the flexibility of the procedure-hierarchy method due to the absence of general flow-of-control mechanisms; these must be embodied via flags in the data structures. Object-oriented environments with run-time code creation and binding offer an attractive, totally general combination of data and procedure hierarchy; there is a natural match between the notion of an object–subobject hierarchy and that of a class–instance hierarchy. As processor performance improves, object-oriented environments are likely to become a dominant paradigm in dynamic computer graphics.

7.15.3   Using Database Systems

Since a general-purpose database has more power than does a special-purpose one, we should consider using standard database systems for computer graphics [WELL76; GARR80]. Unfortunately, such databases are designed to work with large volumes of data in secondary storage and to give response times measured on a human time scale. They are designed to process user-input queries or even batch transactions with times measured, at best, in milliseconds, whereas real-time graphics demands microsecond access to elements. Using a memory-resident database would work best if the database were optimized for fast traversal and had built-in graphics data types and operators. At least, it would have to be able to invoke procedures for retrieved items, passing parameters extracted from fields in the database.

Although several systems have used relational databases for graphics, the limitations on the structure of the data imposed by the relational model, as well as the slowness of standard relational databases, have restricted these systems to research environments. As object-oriented environments are useful for combining data and procedures, such an environment used in conjunction with an object-oriented database has the potential for removing the restrictions of relational databases. The slow performance of object-oriented databases, however, may make them infeasible for real-time graphics in the near term.

7.16 SUMMARY

This chapter has given a general introduction to geometric models, emphasizing hierarchical models that represent parts assemblies. Although many types of data and objects are not hierarchical, most human-made objects are at least partly so. PHIGS and our adaptation, SPHIGS, are designed to provide efficient and natural representations of geometric objects stored essentially as hierarchies of polygons and polyhedra. Because these packages store an internal database of objects, a programmer can make small changes in the database with little effort, and the package automatically produces an updated view. Thus, the application program builds and edits the database, typically in response to user input, and the package is responsible for producing specified views of the database. These views use a variety of rendering techniques to provide quality–speed tradeoffs. The package also provides locator and choice input devices, as well as pick correlation to allow the selection of objects at any level in a hierarchy. Highlighting and visibility filters can be used for selective enabling and disabling as another form of control over the appearance of objects.

Because the nature of structures and the means for searching and editing them are restricted, such a special-purpose system is best suited to motion dynamics and light update dynamics, especially if the structure database can be maintained in a display terminal optimized to be a PHIGS peripheral. If much of the structure database must be updated between successive images, or if the application database can be traversed rapidly and there is no bottleneck between the computer and the display subsystem, it is more efficient to use a graphics package in immediate mode, without retaining information.

Structure hierarchy lies between pure data and pure procedure hierarchy. It has the advantage of dynamic editing that is characteristic of data hierarchy. It also allows a simple form of parameter passing to substructures (of geometric or appearance attributes), using the attribute-traversal state mechanism. Because of the lack of general flow-of-control constructs, however, the parameter-passing mechanism is restricted, and structures cannot selectively set different attributes in different instances of a substructure. Instead, template procedures can be used to set up multiple copies of (hierarchical) structures that are identical in structure but that differ in the geometric or appearance attributes of substructures. Alternatively, they can be used to drive an immediate-mode package.

SPHIGS is oriented toward geometric models made essentially from polygons and polyhedra, especially those that exhibit hierarchy; in Chapters 11 and 12, we look at geometric models that have more complex primitives and combinations of primitives. Before turning to those more advanced modeling topics, we first consider interaction tools, techniques, and user interfaces.

EXERCISES

7.1 a. Complete the robot model of Fig. 7.16 by adding a base on which the upper body swivels and create a simple animation of its movement through a room.

   b. Create an SPHIGS application producing an animation in which a one-armed robot approaches a table on which an object lies, picks up the object, and walks off with it (see Section 7.14 for the reason for specifying a one-armed robot).

7.2 Enhance the robot animation to provide user interaction. Let there be a number of objects on the table, and allow the user to choose (using the locator) the object that the robot should pick up.

7.3 Redesign the two-armed robot model so as to allow the thumbs on each arm to be controlled individually, so that each arm can pick up objects individually.

7.4 Enhance a robot animation so that three views of the animation are shown simultaneously, including one overhead orthographic view and one "robot's eye" view that shows us what the robot itself "sees" as it moves.

7.5 Design the addition of pruning elision to the recursive display traverser of Fig. 7.27. Assume the MC extent of a structure is stored in the structure's record. You must transform an MC extent box into an NPC extent box, meeting the requirement that extent boxes be aligned with the principal axes.

7.6 Update our recursive display traverser so that it maintains the MC extent information stored for each structure. Assume that, whenever a structure S is closed after being edited, a Boolean "extentObsolete" field in S's record is set. Assume also that functions are available that, given any primitive, return the primitive's NPC extent.

7.7 Design an algorithm for calculating analytically the hit point of a candidate line, given the line's NPC endpoints and the locator measure.

7.8 Design an algorithm for calculating analytically the hit point of a candidate fill area.

7.9 Design, using pseudocode, a recursive pick-correlation traverser that supports only wireframe mode.

7.10 Implement the function PtNearLineSegment analytically for use in pick correlation. To be a candidate, the line segment's image must come within P pixel widths of the locator position.

7.11 Implement the function PtNearLineSegment using clipping. Modify the Liang–Barsky clipping algorithm (of Fig. 3.45) to optimize it, because the clipped version of the segment is not needed—only a Boolean value is to be returned.

7.12 Implement the function PtInPolygon for use in pick correlation. Treat the special cases of rays that pass through vertices or are coincident with edges. See [PREP85] and [FORR85] for discussions of the subtleties of this problem.

7.13 Design a user interface for picking that lets the user indicate the desired level of a hierarchy. Implement and test your interface with the robot model by writing an application that allows the user to highlight portions of the robot's anatomy, from individual parts to whole subsystems.

8

Input Devices,
Interaction Techniques,
and Interaction Tasks

This is the first of three chapters on designing and implementing graphical user–computer interfaces. High-quality user interfaces are in many ways the "last frontier" in providing computing to a wide variety of users, since hardware and software costs are now low enough to bring significant computing capability to our offices and homes. Just as software engineering has recently given structure to an activity that once was totally ad hoc, so too the new area of user-interface engineering is generating user-interface principles and design methodologies.

Interest in the quality of user–computer interfaces is new in the formal study of computers. The emphasis until the early 1980s was on optimizing two scarce hardware resources, computer time and memory. Program efficiency was the highest goal. With today's plummeting hardware costs and increasingly powerful graphics-oriented personal-computing environments (as discussed in Chapter 1), however, we can afford to optimize user efficiency rather than computer efficiency. Thus, although many of the ideas presented in this chapter require additional CPU cycles and memory space, the potential rewards in user productivity and satisfaction well outweigh the modest additional cost of these resources.

The quality of the user interface often determines whether users enjoy or despise a system, whether the designers of the system are praised or damned, whether a system succeeds or fails in the market. Indeed, in such critical applications as air-traffic control and nuclear-power-plant monitoring, a poor user interface can contribute to and even cause accidents of catastrophic proportions.

The desktop user-interface metaphor, with its windows, icons, and pull-down menus, all making heavy use of raster graphics, is popular because it is easy to learn and requires little typing skill. Most users of such systems are not computer programmers and have little sympathy for the old-style hard-to-learn keyboard-oriented command-language interfaces that many programmers take for granted. The designer of an interactive graphics application must be sensitive to users' desire for easy-to-learn yet powerful interfaces.

On the other hand, in the future, the level of computer sophistication of workers will increase, as more users enter the workforce already computer-literate through computer use at home and school. Developers of some educational and game software will continue to design for the computer-naive user, while developers of workplace systems will be able to assume an increased awareness of general computer concepts.

In this chapter, we discuss basic elements of user interfaces: input devices, interaction techniques, and interaction tasks. Input devices were introduced in Chapters 2 and 4: here we elaborate on their use. Interaction techniques are ways to use input devices to enter information into the computer, whereas interaction tasks classify the fundamental types of information entered with the interaction techniques. Interaction techniques are the primitive building blocks from which a user interface is crafted.

In Chapter 9, we discuss the issues involved in putting together the building blocks into a complete user-interface design. The emphasis is on a top-down design approach; first, design objectives are identified, and the design is then developed through a stepwise refinement process. The pros and cons of various dialogue styles—such as what you see is what you get (WYSIWYG), command language, and direct manipulation—are discussed, and window-manager issues that affect the user interface are also described. Design guidelines, the dos and don'ts of interface design, are described and illustrated with various positive and negative examples. Many of the topics in Chapters 8 and 9 are discussed in much greater depth elsewhere; see the texts by Baecker and Buxton [BAEC87], Hutchins, Hollan, and Norman [HUTC86], Mayhew [MAYH90], Norman [NORM88], Rubenstein and Hersh [RUBE84], and Shneiderman [SHNE87]; the reference book by Salvendy [SALV87]; and the survey by Foley, Wallace, and Chan [FOLE84].

Many of the examples used in Chapters 8 and 9 are taken from the user interface of Apple Computer's Macintosh. Although the Macintosh user interface is not perfect, it is a huge improvement over previous commonly available interfaces. Developed in the early 1980s, the Macintosh was built primarily on pioneering work at Xerox Corporation's Palo Alto Research Center (PARC) in the mid-1970s, and has been imitated and in some cases extended by systems such as Microsoft Windows, Presentation Manager, NeXT's NeXT Step, the Commodore Amiga, Digital Research's GEM, and many others. (Much of this book was written on the Macintosh, using Microsoft Word, and many of the figures were drawn on the Macintosh using Freehand.)

Chapter 10 treats user-interface software. It is one thing to design graphic user interfaces that are easy to learn and fast to use; it is quite another to implement them. Having the right software tools is of critical importance. This chapter reviews the input-handling capabilities of SRGP and SPHIGS, and then discusses more general and more powerful input-handling capabilities. The internal structures and implementation strategies of window managers, a critical element in many high-quality user interfaces, are described. Finally, the key concepts of user-interface management systems (UIMSs) are presented. UIMSs provide a means for interface designers and implementors quickly to develop, try out, and modify their interface concepts, and thus decrease the cost of the essential testing and refinement steps in user-interface development.

We focus in this chapter on input devices—those pieces of hardware by which a user enters information into a computer system. We have already discussed many such devices in Chapter 4. In this chapter, we introduce additional devices, and discuss reasons for preferring one device over another. In Section 8.1.6, we describe input devices oriented specifically toward 3D interaction. We continue to use the logical device categories of locator, keyboard, choice, valuator, and pick used by SRGP, SPHIGS, and other device-independent graphics subroutine packages.

An *interaction task* is the entry of a unit of information by the user. The four basic interaction tasks are *position*, *text*, *select*, and *quantify*. The unit of information input in a position interaction task is of course a position. Similarly, the text task yields a text string; the select task yields an object identification; and the quantify task yields a numeric value. Many different *interaction techniques* can be used for a given interaction task. For instance, a selection task can be carried out by using a mouse to select items from a menu, using a keyboard to enter the name of the selection, pressing a function key, or using a speech recognizer. Similarly, a single device can be used for different tasks: A mouse is often used for both positioning and selecting.

Interaction tasks are distinct from the logical input devices discussed in earlier chapters. Interaction tasks are defined by *what* the user accomplishes, whereas logical input devices categorize *how* that task is accomplished by the application program and the graphics package. Interaction tasks are user-centered, whereas logical input devices are a programmer and graphics-package concept.

By analogy with a natural language, single actions with input devices are similar to the individual letters of the alphabet from which words are formed. The sequence of input-device actions that makes up an interaction technique is analogous to the sequence of letters that makes up a word. A word is a unit of meaning; just as several interaction techniques can be used to carry out the same interaction task, so too words that are synonyms convey the same meaning. All the units of meaning entered by the user can be categorized as one of the four basic interaction tasks, just as words can be categorized as verb, noun, adjective, and so on. An interactive dialogue is made up of interaction-task sequences, just as a sentence is constructed from word sequences.

8.1   INTERACTION HARDWARE

Here, we introduce some interaction devices not covered in Section 4.6, elaborate on how they work, and discuss the advantages and disadvantages of various devices. The presentation is organized around the logical-device categorization of Section 4.6, and can be thought of as a more detailed continuation of that section.

The advantages and disadvantages of various interaction devices can be discussed on three levels: device, task, and dialogue (i.e., sequence of several interaction tasks). The *device level* centers on the hardware characteristics per se, and does not deal with aspects of the device's use controlled by software. At the device level, for example, we note that one mouse shape may be more comfortable to hold than another, and that a data tablet takes up more space than a joystick.

At the *task level*, we might compare interaction techniques using different devices for the same task. Thus, we might assert that experienced users can often enter commands more quickly via function keys or a keyboard than via menu selection, or that users can pick displayed objects more quickly using a mouse than they can using a joystick or cursor control keys.

At the *dialogue level*, we consider not just individual interaction tasks, but also sequences of such tasks. Hand movements between devices take time: Although the positioning task is generally faster with a mouse than with cursor-control keys, cursor-control keys may be faster than a mouse *if* the user's hands are already on the keyboard and will need to be on the keyboard for the next task in sequence after the cursor is repositioned. Dialogue-level issues are discussed in Chapter 9, where we deal with constructing complete user interfaces from the building blocks introduced in this chapter. Much confusion can be avoided when we think about devices if we keep these three levels in mind.

Important considerations at the device level, discussed in this section, are the device footprints (the *footprint* of a piece of equipment is the work area it occupies), operator fatigue, and device resolution. Other important device issues—such as cost, reliability, and maintainability—change too quickly with technological innovation to be discussed here. Also omitted are the details of connecting devices to computers; by far the most common means is the serial asynchronous RS-232 terminal interface, generally making interfacing quite simple.

8.1.1 Locator Devices

It is useful to classify locator devices according to three independent characteristics: absolute or relative, direct or indirect, and discrete or continuous.

Absolute devices, such as a data tablet or touch panel, have a frame of reference, or origin, and report positions with respect to that origin. *Relative* devices—such as mice, trackballs, and velocity-control joysticks—have no absolute origin and report only changes from their former position. A relative device can be used to specify an arbitrarily large change in position: A user can move a mouse along the desk top, lift it up and place it back at its initial starting position, and move it again. A data tablet can be programmed to behave as a relative device: The first (x, y) coordinate position read after the pen goes from "far" to "near" state (i.e., close to the tablet) is subtracted from all subsequently read coordinates to yield only the change in x and y, which is added to the previous (x, y) position. This process is continued until the pen again goes to "far" state.

Relative devices cannot be used readily for digitizing drawings, whereas absolute devices can be. The advantage of a relative device is that the application program can reposition the cursor anywhere on the screen.

With a *direct* device—such as a light pen or touch screen—the user points directly at the screen with a finger or surrogate finger; with an *indirect* device—such as a tablet, mouse, or joystick—the user moves a cursor on the screen using a device not on the screen. New forms of eye–hand coordination must be learned for the latter; the proliferation of computer games in homes and arcades, however, is creating an environment in which many casual computer users have already learned these skills. However, direct pointing can cause arm fatigue, especially among casual users.

A *continuous* device is one in which a smooth hand motion can create a smooth cursor motion. Tablets, joysticks, and mice are all continuous devices, whereas cursor-control keys are *discrete* devices. Continuous devices typically allow more natural, easier, and faster cursor movement than do discrete devices. Most continuous devices also permit easier movement in arbitrary directions than do cursor control keys.

Speed of cursor positioning with a continuous device is affected by the *control-to-display ratio*, commonly called the C/D ratio [CHAP72]; it is the ratio between hand movement (the control) and cursor movement (the display). A large ratio is good for accurate positioning, but makes rapid movements tedious; a small ratio is good for speed but not for accuracy. Fortunately, for a relative positioning device, the ratio need not be constant, but can be changed adaptively as a function of control-movement speed. Rapid movements indicate the user is making a gross hand movement, so a small ratio is used; as the speed decreases, the C/D ratio is increased. This variation of C/D ratio can be set up so that a user can use a mouse to position a cursor accurately across a 15-inch screen without repositioning her wrist! For indirect discrete devices (cursor-control keys), there is a similar technique: the distance the cursor is moved per unit time is increased as a function of the time the key has been held down.

Precise positioning is difficult with direct devices, if the arm is unsupported and extended toward the screen. Try writing your name on a blackboard in this pose, and compare the result to your normal signature. This problem can be mitigated if the screen is angled close to horizontal. Indirect devices, on the other hand, allow the heel of the hand to rest on a support, so that the fine motor control of the fingers can be used more effectively. Not all continuous indirect devices are equally satisfactory for drawing, however. Try writing your name with a joystick, a mouse, and a tablet pen stylus. Using the stylus is fastest, and the result is most pleasing.

Other interesting positioning devices include the Versatron *footmouse* [VERS84], which remains static on the floor: The user places the ball of his foot on the device, keeping his heel on the floor, and controls the footmouse with left–right and forward–backward movements. The experimental *mole* is a pivoted foot rest with integrated switches [PEAR86, PEAR88] that, like the footmouse, leaves the hands free. The Personics *headmouse* [PERS85] uses a head-mounted set of three microphones to measure the distance to a sound source, translating small rotational movements of the head into cursor movements. *Eye trackers* can determine where the eye is pointing and hence can cause a cursor to move or the object pointed at to be selected [BOLT80; BOLT84; WARE87]. These devices are often less accurate and considerably more expensive than are the more traditional devices, and thus would normally be considered for only hands-free applications. The 3D positioning devices discussed in Section 8.1.6 can also be used for 2D positioning.

8.1.2 Keyboard Devices

The well-known QWERTY keyboard has been with us for many years. It is ironic that this keyboard was originally designed to *slow down* typists, so that the typewriter hammers would not be so likely to jam. Studies have shown that the newer Dvorak keyboard [DVOR43], which places vowels and other high-frequency characters under the home positions of the fingers, is somewhat faster than is the QWERTY design [GREE87]. It has not been widely accepted. Alphabetically organized keyboards are sometimes used when many of the users are nontypists. But more and more people are being exposed to QWERTY keyboards, and several experiments have shown no advantage of alphabetic over QWERTY keyboards [HIRS70; MICH71].

The *chord keyboard* has five keys similar to piano keys, and is operated with one hand, by pressing one or more keys simultaneously to "play a chord." With five keys, 31 different chords can be played. Learning to use a chord keyboard (and other similar stenographer-style keyboards) takes longer than learning the QWERTY keyboard, but skilled users can type quite rapidly, leaving the second hand free for other tasks. This increased training time means, however, that such keyboards are not suitable substitutes for general use of the standard alphanumeric keyboard.

Other keyboard-oriented considerations, involving not hardware but software design, are arranging for a user to enter frequently used punctuation or correction characters without needing simultaneously to press the control or shift keys, and assigning dangerous actions (such as delete) to keys that are distant from other frequently used keys.

8.1.3 Valuator Devices

Some valuators are *bounded*, like the volume control on a radio—the dial can be turned only so far before a stop is reached that prevents further turning. A bounded valuator inputs an absolute quantity. A continuous-turn potentiometer, on the other hand, can be turned an *unbounded* number of times in either direction. Given an initial value, the unbounded potentiometer can be used to return absolute values; otherwise, the returned values are treated as relative values. The provision of some sort of echo enables the user to determine what relative or absolute value is currently being specified. The issue of C/D ratio, discussed in the context of positioning devices, also arises in the use of slide and rotary potentiometers to input values.

8.1.4 Choice Devices

Function keys are a common choice device. Their placement affects their usability: keys mounted on the CRT bezel are harder to use than are keys mounted in the keyboard or in a nearby separate unit. A foot switch can be used in applications in which the user's hands are engaged yet a single switch closure must be frequently made. For example, used with a headmouse (described in Section 8.1.1), a foot switch could easily provide functionality equivalent to a single-button mouse.

8.1.5 Other Devices

Here we discuss some of the less common, and in some cases experimental, 2D interaction devices. Voice recognizers, which are useful because they free the user's hands for other uses, apply a pattern-recognition approach to the waveforms created when we speak a word. The waveform is typically separated into a number of different frequency bands, and the variation over time of the magnitude of the waveform in each band forms the basis for the pattern matching. However, mistakes can occur in the pattern matching, so it is especially important that an application using a recognizer provide convenient correction capabilities.

Voice recognizers differ in whether or not they must be trained to recognize the waveforms of a particular speaker, and whether they can recognize connected speech as opposed to single words or phrases. Speaker-independent recognizers have very limited vocabularies—typically, they include only the digits and 50 to 100 words. Some discrete-word recognizers can recognize vocabularies of up to a few thousand different words after appropriate training. But if the user has a cold, the recognizer must be retrained. The user of a recognizer must pause for a fraction of a second after each word to cue the system that a word end has occurred; the pause is typically 100 to 200 milliseconds, and can be longer if the set of possible words is large. The more difficult task of recognizing connected speech from a limited vocabulary can also be performed by commercial hardware, but at a higher cost. The larger the vocabulary, however, the more artificial-intelligence techniques are needed to use the context and meaning of a sequence of sentences to remove ambiguity. A few systems with vocabularies of 20,000 or more words can recognize sentences such as "Write Mrs. Wright a letter right now!"

Voice synthesizers create waveforms that approximate, with varying degrees of realism, spoken words [KAPL85]. The simplest synthesizers use *phonemes*, the basic sound units that form words. This approach creates an artificial-sounding, inflection-free voice. More sophisticated phoneme-based systems add inflections. Other systems actually play back digitized speech patterns. They sound realistic, but require thousands of bytes of memory to store the digitized speech.

Now that several personal computers, including the Macintosh and NeXT, have standard sound synthesizers that can create both voice and music, speech feedback from computers is becoming quite common. Speech is best used to augment rather than to replace visual feedback, and is most effective when used sparingly. For instance, a training application could show a student a graphic animation of some process, along with a voice narration describing what is being seen. See [SIMP85; SIMP87] for an extensive review of speech recognition and generation, including additional guidelines for the effective application of these functions in user–computer interfaces.

Sound generators can be used to generate musical tones and other effects, which can call attention to specific situations, especially if the user is unlikely to be looking at the display. For instance, "printer out of paper" or "memory nearly full" alarms might be signaled by two different tones, in addition to messages on the screen. An attempt to reorient a line that has been constrained to be parallel to another line might cause a warning beep.

The data tablet has been extended in several ways. Many years ago, Herot and Negroponte used an experimental pressure-sensitive stylus [HERO76]: High pressure and a slow drawing speed implied that the user was drawing a line with deliberation, in which case the line was recorded exactly as drawn; low pressure and fast speed implied that the line was being drawn quickly, in which case a straight line connecting the endpoints was recorded. A more recent commercially available tablet [GTCO82] senses not only stylus pressure but orientation as well. The resulting 5 degrees of freedom reported by the tablet can be used in various creative ways. For example, Bleser, Sibert, and McGee implemented the GWPaint system to simulate various artist's tools, such as an italic pen, that are sensitive to pressure and orientation [BLES88a]. Figure 8.1 shows the artistic creativity thus afforded.

Fig. 8.1 *Numeral 2*, a drawing in the spirit of Jasper Johns, by Teresa Bleser. Drawn with the GWPaint program using a GTCO pressure- and tilt-sensitive tablet. (Courtesy of T. Bleser, George Washington University.)

Green [GREE85] applied optics principles to develop a tabletlike device that gives artists even more freedom than the pressure- and tilt-sensing tablet. The user paints on the tablet with brushes, hands, or anything else that is convenient. A television camera positioned below the tablet records the shape and motion of the brush wherever it contacts the tablet, and the resulting video signal is used to load the refresh buffer of a raster display. Resolution of 500 or 1000 units is achievable, depending on the television camera used.

An experimental touch tablet, developed by Buxton and colleagues, can sense multiple finger positions simultaneously, and can also sense the area covered at each point of contact [LEE85a]. The device is essentially a type of touch panel, but is used as a tablet on the work surface, not as a touch panel mounted over the screen. The device can be used in a rich variety of ways [BUXT85]. Different finger pressures correlate with the area covered at a point of contact, and are used to signal user commands: a light pressure causes a cursor to appear and to track finger movement; increased pressure is used, like a button-push on a mouse or puck, to begin feedback such as dragging of an object; decreased pressure causes the dragging to stop.

Another way to obtain more than just position information is to suspend a touch panel in front of a display using a few metal support strips with strain gauges [HERO78, MINS84]. Pressure applied to the touch panel translates into strain measured by the gauges. It is possible also to measure the direction of push and torque as well, by orienting the metal strips in appropriate directions. The measurements can be used to cause displayed objects to be rotated, scaled, and so on.

The decreasing costs of input devices and the increasing availability of computer power are likely to lead to the continuing introduction of novel interaction devices. Douglas Engelbart invented the mouse in the 1960s, and nearly 20 years passed before it became popular [PERR89]. What the next mouse will be is not yet clear, but we hope that it will have a much shorter gestation period.

8.1.6 3D Interaction Devices

Some of the 2D interaction devices are readily extended to 3D. Joysticks can have a shaft that twists for a third dimension (see Fig. 4.38). Trackballs can be made to sense rotation about the vertical axis in addition to that about the two horizontal axes. In both cases, however, there is no direct relationship between hand movements with the device and the corresponding movement in 3-space.

The Spaceball (see Color Plate I.14) is a rigid sphere containing strain gauges. The user pushes or pulls the sphere in any direction, providing 3D translation and orientation. In this case, at least the directions of movement correspond to the user's attempts at moving the rigid sphere, although the hand does not actually move.

A number of devices, on the other hand, can record 3D hand movements. The experimental *Noll Box*, developed by Michael Noll, permits movement of a knob in a 12-inch cube volume, sensed by slider mechanisms linked to potentiometers. The Polhemus 3SPACE three-dimensional position and orientation sensor uses electromagnetic coupling between three transmitter antennas and three receiver antennas. The transmitter antenna coils, which are at right angles to one another to form a Cartesian coordinate system, are pulsed in turn. The receiver has three similarly arranged receiver antennas; each time a transmitter coil is pulsed, a current is induced in each of the receiver coils. The strength of the current depends both on the distance between the receiver and transmitter and on the relative orientation of the transmitter and receiver coils. The combination of the nine current values induced by the three successive pulses is used to calculate the 3D position and orientation of the receiver. Figure 8.2 shows this device in use for one of its common purposes: digitizing a 3D object.

The DataGlove records hand position and orientation as well as finger movements. As shown in Fig. 8.3, it is a glove covered with small, lightweight sensors. Each sensor is a short length of fiberoptic cable, with a light-emitting diode (LED) at one end and a phototransistor at the other end. The surface of the cable is roughened in the area where it is to be sensitive to bending. When the cable is flexed, some of the LED's light is lost, so less light is received by the phototransistor. In addition, a Polhemus position and orientation sensor records hand movements. Wearing the DataGlove, a user can grasp objects, move and rotate them, and then release them, thus providing very natural interaction in 3D [ZIMM87]. Color Plate I.15 illustrates this concept.

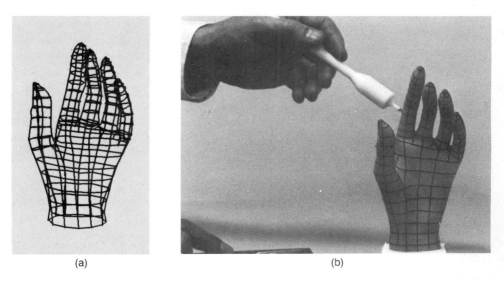

(a)   (b)

Fig. 8.2 (a) A wireframe display of the result. (b) The Polhemus 3D position sensor being used to digitize a 3D object. (3Space digitizer courtesy of Polhemus, Inc., Colchester, VT.)

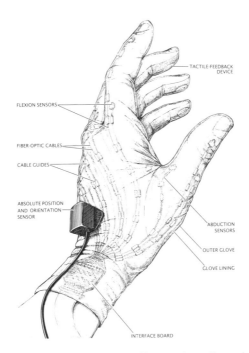

Fig. 8.3 The VPL DataGlove, showing the fiberoptic calbes that are used to sense finger movements, and the Polhemus position and orientation sensor. (From J. Foley, Interfaces for Advanced Computing, Copyright © 1987 by *SCIENTIFIC AMERICAN, Inc.* All rights reserved.)

Considerable effort has been directed toward creating what are often called *artificial realites* or *virtual realities*; these are completely computer-generated environments with realistic appearance, behavior, and interaction techniques [FOLE87]. In one version, the user wears a head-mounted stereo display to show proper left- and right-eye views, a Polhemus sensor on the head allows changes in head position and orientation to cause changes to the stereo display, a DataGlove permits 3D interaction, and a microphone is used for issuing voice commands. Color Plate I.16 shows this combination of equipment.

Several other technologies can be used to record 3D positions. The sonic-tablet technology discussed in Section 4.6.1 can be extended to 3D to create a *sonic pen*. In one approach, three orthogonal strip microphones are used. The hand-held pen sparks 20 to 40 times per second, and the time for the sound to arrive at each of the three microphones determines the radius of the three cylinders on which the pen is located. The location is thus computed as the intersection of three cylinders. A similar approach uses three or four standard microphones; here, the pen location is computed as the intersection of spheres with centers at the microphones and radii determined by the time the sound takes to arrive at each microphone.

All these systems work in relatively small volumes—8 to 27 cubic feet. Optical sensors can give even greater freedom of movement [BURT74; FUCH77a]. LEDs are mounted on the user (either at a single point, such as the fingertip, or all over the body, to measure body movements). Light sensors are mounted high in the corners of a small, semidarkened room in which the user works, and each LED is intensified in turn. The sensors can determine the plane in which the LED lies, and the location of the LED is thus at the intersection of three planes. (A fourth sensor is normally used, in case one of the sensors cannot see the LED.) Small reflectors on the fingertips and other points of interest can replace the LEDs; sensors pick up reflected light rather than the LED's emitted light.

Krueger [KRUE83] has developed a sensor for recording hand and finger movements in 2D. A television camera records hand movements; image-processing techniques of contrast-enhancement and edge detection are used to find the outline of the hand and fingers. Different finger positions can be interpreted as commands, and the user can grasp and manipulate objects, as in Color Plate I.17. This technique could be extended to 3D through use of multiple cameras.

8.1.7 Device-Level Human Factors

Not all interaction devices of the same type are equivalent from a human-factors point of view (see [BUXT86] for an elaboration of this theme). For instance, mice differ in important ways. First, the physical shapes are different, ranging from a hemisphere to an elongated, low-profile rectangle. Buttons are positioned differently. Buttons on the side or front of a mouse may cause the mouse to move a bit when the buttons are pressed; buttons on the top of a mouse do not have this effect. The mouse is moved through small distances by wrist and finger movements, with the fingers grasping the mouse toward its front. Yet the part of the mouse whose position is sensed is often toward the rear, where fine control is least possible. In fact, a small leftward movement of the mouse under the fingertips can include a bit of rotation, so that the rear of the mouse, where the position sensors are, actually moves a bit to the right!

There is great variation among keyboards in design parameters, such as keycap shape, distance between keys, pressure needed to press a key, travel distance for key depression, key bounce, auditory feedback, the feeling of contact when the key is fully depressed, and the placement and size of important keys such as "return" or "enter." Improper choice of parameters can decrease productivity and increase error rates. Making the "return" key too small invites errors, as does placing a hardware "reset" key close to other keys. These and other design parameters are discussed in [KLEM71; GREE87], and have been the subject of recent international standardization efforts.

The tip of a short joystick shaft moves through a short distance, forcing use of a small C/D ratio; if we try to compensate by using a longer joystick shaft, the user cannot rest the heel of her hand on the work surface and thus does not have a steady platform from which to make fine adjustments. Accuracy and speed therefore suffer.

The implication of these device differences is that it is not enough for a user interface designer to specify a particular device class; specific device characteristics must be defined. Unfortunately, not every user interface designer has the luxury of selecting devices; often, the choice has already been made. Then the designer can only hope that the devices are well designed, and attempt to compensate in software for any hardware deficiencies.

8.2 BASIC INTERACTION TASKS

With a basic interaction task, the user of an interactive system enters a unit of information that is meaningful in the context of the application. How large or small is such a unit? For instance, does moving a positioning device a small distance enter a unit of information? Yes, if the new position is put to some application purpose, such as repositioning an object or specifying the endpoint of a line. No, if the repositioning is just one of a sequence of repositionings as the user moves the cursor to place it on top of a menu item: here, it is the menu choice that is the unit of information.

Basic interaction tasks (BITs) are indivisible; that is, if they were decomposed into smaller units of information, the smaller units would not in themselves be meaningful to the application. BITs are discussed in this section. In the next section, we treat composite interaction tasks (CITs), which are aggregates of the basic interaction tasks described here. If one thinks of BITs as atoms, then CITs are molecules.

A complete set of BITs for interactive graphics is positioning, selecting, entering text, and entering numeric quantities. Each BIT is described in this section, and some of the many interaction techniques for each are discussed. However, there are far too many interaction techniques for us to give an exhaustive list, and we cannot anticipate the development of new techniques. Where possible, the pros and cons of each technique are discussed; remember that a specific interaction technique may be good in some situations and poor in others.

8.2.1 The Position Interaction Task

The positioning task involves specifying an (x, y) or (x, y, z) position to the application program. The customary interaction techniques for carrying out this task involve either moving a screen cursor to the desired location and then pushing a button, or typing the desired position's coordinates on either a real or a simulated keyboard. The positioning device can be direct or indirect, continuous or discrete, absolute or relative. In addition, cursor-movement commands can be typed explicitly on a keyboard, as Up, Left, and so on, or the same commands can be spoken to a voice-recognition unit. Furthermore, techniques can be used together—a mouse controlling a cursor can be used for approximate positioning, and arrow keys can be used to move the cursor a single screen unit at a time for precise postioning.

A number of general issues transcend any one interaction technique. We first discuss the general issues; we introduce specific positioning techniques as illustrations.

Coordinate systems.   An important issue in positioning is the coordinate system in which feedback is provided. If a locator device is moved to the right to drag an object, in which direction should the object move? There are at least three possibilities: the object could move along the increasing x direction in the screen-coordinate system, along the increasing x direction in world coordinates, or along the increasing x direction in the object's own coordinate system.

The first alternative, increasing screen-coordinate x direction, is the correct choice. For the latter two options, consider that the increasing x direction need not in general be along the screen coordinates' x axis. For instance, if the viewing transformation includes a 180° rotation, then the world coordinates' x axis goes in the opposite direction to the screen coordinates' x axis, so that the right-going movement of the locator would cause a left-going movement of the object. Try positioning with this type of feedback by turning your mouse 180°! Such a system would be a gross violation of the human-factors principle of stimulus-response compatibility (S-R compatibility), which states that system responses to user actions must be in the same direction or same orientation, and that the magnitude of the responses should be proportional to the actions. Similar problems can occur if a data tablet is rotated with respect to the screen.

Resolution.   The resolution required in a positioning task may vary from one part in a few hundred to one part in millions. Clearly, keyboard typein of an (x, y) pair can provide unlimited resolution: The typed digit strings can be as long as necessary. What resolution can cursor-movement techniques achieve? The resolution of tablets, mice, and so on is typically as least as great as the 500 to 2000 resolvable units of the display device. By using the window-to-viewport transformation to zoom in on part of the world, it is possible to arrange for one unit of screen resolution to correspond to an arbitrarily small unit of world-coordinate resolution.

Touch panels present other interesting resolution issues. Some panels are accurate to 1000 units. But the user's finger is about $\frac{1}{2}$-inch wide, so how can this accuracy be achieved? Using the first position the finger touches as the final position does not work. The user must be able to drag a cursor around on the screen by moving or rolling his finger while it is in contact with the touch panel. Because the finger obscures the exact position being indicated, the cursor arms can be made longer than normal, or the cursor can be offset from the actual point of contact. In an experiment, dragging an offset cursor was found to be more accurate, albeit slower, than was using the first point contacted [POTT88]. In general, the touch panel is not recommended for frequent high-resolution positioning tasks.

Grids.   An important visual aid in many positioning tasks is a grid superimposed (perhaps at low intensity) on the work area, to help in aligning positions or objects. It can also be useful to force endpoints of primitives to fall on the grid, as though each grid point were surrounded by a gravity field. Gridding helps users to generate drawings with a neat appearance. To enforce gridding, the application program simply rounds locator coordinates to the nearest grid point (in some cases, only if the point is already close to a grid point). Gridding is usually applied in world coordinates. Although grids often are regular and span the entire display, irregular grids, different grids in different areas, as well as rotated grids, are all useful in creating figures and illustrations [BIER86a; FEIN82a].

Feedback.   There are two types of positioning tasks, spatial and linguistic. In a *spatial* positioning task, the user knows where the intended position is, in spatial relation to nearby elements, as in drawing a line between two rectangles or centering an object between two others. In a *linguistic* positioning task, the user knows the numeric values of the (x, y) coordinates of the position. In the former case, the user wants feedback showing the actual position on the screen; in the latter case, the coordinates of the position are needed. If the wrong form of feedback is provided, the user must mentally convert from one form to the other. Both forms of feedback can be provided by displaying both the cursor and its numeric coordinates, as in Fig 8.4.

Direction preference.   Some positioning devices impede movement in arbitrary directions; for example, certain joysticks and joyswitches give more resistance to movements off the principal axes than they do to those on the axes. This is useful only if the positioning task itself is generally constrained to horizontal and vertical movements.

Learning time.   Learning the eye–hand coordination for indirect methods is essentially the same process as learning to steer a car. Learning time is a common concern but turns out to be a minor issue. Card and colleagues [CARD78] studied the mouse and joystick. They found that, although practice improved both error rates and speed, even the novices' performance was quite good. For instance, selection time with a mouse (move cursor to target, press button) decreased with extensive practice from 2.2 to 1.7 seconds. It is true, however, that some users find the indirect coordination very difficult, until they are explicitly taught.

One specific type of postioning task is *continuous positioning*, in which a sequence of positions is used to define a curve. The path taken by the locator is approximated by a connected series of very short lines, as shown in Fig. 8.5. So that the appearance of

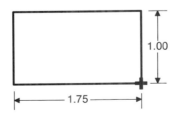

Fig. 8.4 Numeric feedback regarding size of an object being constructed. The height and width are changed as the cursor (+) is moved, so the user can adjust the object to the desired size.

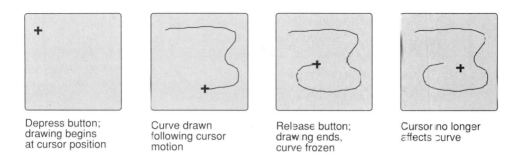

Depress button; drawing begins at cursor position	Curve drawn following cursor motion	Release button; drawing ends, curve frozen	Cursor no longer effects curve

Fig. 8.5 Continuous sketching.

smoothness is maintained, more lines may be used where the radius of curvature is small, or individual dots may be displayed on the cursor's path, or a higher-order curve can be fitted through the points (see Chapter 11).

Precise continuous positioning is easier with a stylus than with a mouse, because the stylus can be controlled precisely with finger muscles, whereas the mouse is controlled primarily with wrist muscles. Digitizing of drawings is difficult with a mouse for the same reason; in addition, the mouse lacks both an absolute frame of reference and a cross-hair. On the other hand, a mouse requires only a small table area and is less expensive than a tablet.

8.2.2 The Select Interaction Task—Variable-Sized Set of Choices

The selection task is that of choosing an element from a *choice set*. Typical choice sets are commands, attribute values, object classes, and object instances. For example, the line-style menu in a typical paint program is a set of attribute values, and the object-type (line, circle, rectangle, text, etc.) menu in such programs is a set of object classes. Some interaction techniques can be used to select from any of these four types of choice sets; others are less general. For example, pointing at a visual representation of a set element can serve to select it, no matter what the set type. On the other hand, although function keys often work quite well for selecting from a command, object class, or attribute set, it is difficult to assign a separate function key to each object instance in a drawing, since the size of the choice set is variable, often is large (larger than the number of available function keys), and changes quite rapidly as the user creates and deletes objects.

We use the terms *(relatively) fixed-sized choice set* and *varying-sized choice set*. The first term characterizes command, attribute, and object-class choice sets; the second, object-instance choice sets. The "relatively" modifier recognizes that any of these sets can change as new commands, attributes, or object classes (such as symbols in a drafting system) are defined. But the set size does not change frequently, and usually does not change much. Varying-sized choice sets, on the other hand, can become quite large, and can change frequently.

In this section, we discuss techniques that are particularly well suited to potentially large varying-sized choice sets; these include naming and pointing. In the following section, we discuss selection techniques particularly well suited to (relatively) fixed-sized choice sets. These sets tend to be small, except for the large (but relatively fixed-sized) command sets found in complex applications. The techniques discussed include typing or speaking the name, abbreviation, or other code that represents the set element; pressing a function key associated with the set element (this can be seen as identical to typing a single character on the keyboard); pointing at a visual representation (textual or graphical) of the set element in a menu; cycling through the set until the desired element is displayed; and making a distinctive motion with a continuous positioning device.

Selecting objects by naming. The user can type the choice's name. The idea is simple, but what if the user does not know the object's name, as could easily happen if hundreds of objects are being displayed, or if the user has no reason to know names? Nevertheless, this technique is useful in several situations. First, if the user is likely to know the names of various objects, as a fleet commander would know the names of the fleet's ships, then referring to them by name is reasonable, and can be faster than pointing, especially if the user might need to scroll through the display to bring the desired object into view. Second, if the display is so cluttered that picking by pointing is difficult *and* if zooming is not feasible (perhaps because the graphics hardware does not support zooming and software zoom is too slow), then naming may be a choice of last resort. If clutter is a problem, then a command to turn object names on and off would be useful.

Typing allows us to make multiple selections through wild-card or don't-care characters, if the choice set elements are named in a meaningful way. Selection by naming is most appropriate for experienced, regular users, rather than for casual, infrequent users.

If naming by typing is necessary, a useful form of feedback is to display, immediately after each keystroke, the list (or partial list, if the full list is too long) of names in the selection set matching the sequence of characters typed so far. This can help the user to remember just how the name is spelled, if he has recalled the first few characters. As soon as an unambiguous match has been typed, the correct name can be automatically highlighted on the list. Alternatively, the name can be automatically completed as soon as an unambiguous match has been typed. This technique, called *autocompletion*, is sometimes disconcerting to new users, so caution is advisable. A separate strategy for name typein is spelling correction (sometimes called *Do What I Mean*, or DWIM). If the typed name does not match one known to the system, other names that are close to the typed name can be presented to the user as alternatives. Determining closeness can be as simple as searching for single-character errors, or can include multiple-character and missing-character errors.

With a voice recognizer, the user can speak, rather than type, a name, abbreviation, or code. Voice input is a simple way to distinguish commands from data: Commands are entered by voice, the data are entered by keyboard or other means. In a keyboard environment, this eliminates the need for special characters or modes to distinguish data and commands.

Selecting objects by pointing. Any of the pointing techniques mentioned in the introduction to Section 8.2 can be used to select an object, by first pointing and then indicating (typically via a button-push) that the desired object is being pointed at. But what if the object has multiple levels of hierarchy, as did the robot of Chapter 7? If the cursor is over the robot's hand, it is not clear whether the user is pointing at the hand, the arm, or the entire robot. Commands like Select_robot and Select_arm can be used to specify the level of hierarchy. On the other hand, if the level at which the user works changes infrequently, the user will be able to work faster with a separate command, such as Set_selection_level, used to change the level of hierarchy.

A different approach is needed if the number of hierarchical levels is unknown to the system designer and is potentially large (as in a drafting system, where symbols are made up of graphics primitives and other symbols). At least two user commands are required: Up_hierarchy and Down_hierarchy. When the user selects something, the system highlights the lowest-level object seen. If this is what he desired, the user can proceed. If not, the user issues the first command: Up_hierarchy. The entire first-level object of which the detected object is a part is highlighted. If this is not what the user wants, he travels up again and still more of the picture is highlighted. If he travels too far up the hierarchy, he reverses direction with the Down_hierarchy command. In addition, a Return_to_lowest_level command can be useful in deep hierarchies, as can a hierarchy diagram in another window, showing where in the hierarchy the current selection is located. The state diagram of Fig. 8.6

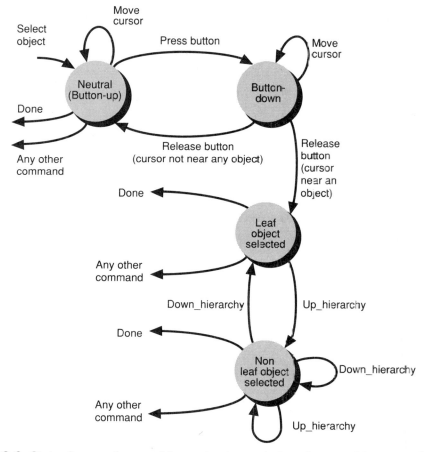

Fig. 8.6 State diagram for an object-selection technique for an arbitrary number of hierarchy levels. Up and Down are commands for moving up and down the hierarchy. In the state "Leaf object selected," the Down_hierarchy command is not available. The user selects an object by pointing at it with a cursor, and pressing and then releasing a button.

shows one approach to hierarchical selection. Alternatively, a single command, say Move_up_hierarchy, can skip back to the originally selected leaf node after the root node is reached.

Some text editors use a character–word–sentence–paragraph hierarchy. In the Xerox Star text editor, for instance, the user selects a character by positioning the screen cursor on the character and clicking the Select button on the mouse. To choose the word rather than the character, the user clicks twice in rapid succession. Further moves up the hierarchy are accomplished by additional rapid clicks.

8.2.3 The Select Interaction Task—Relatively Fixed-Sized Choice Set

Menu selection is one of the richest techniques for selecting from a relatively fixed-sized choice set. Here we discuss several key factors in menu design.

Menu order. Menu elements can be organized in many different orders, including alphabetical, logically grouped by functional purpose, most frequently used first, most important first, largest first, or most recently created/modified first. These orders can be combined in various ways. A functionally grouped menu may be ordered alphabetically within group, and the functional groups themselves ordered by frequency of use. Figure 8.7 illustrates several such possible organizations. Consistency of organization from one menu to another is useful, so a common strategy across all menus of an application is important. Several researchers have found functional order to be the most helpful, and many menu structures reflect this result.

Single-level versus hierarchical design. One of the most fundamental menu design decisions arises if the choice set is too large to display all at once. Such a menu can be subdivided into a logically structured hierarchy or presented as a linear sequence of choices

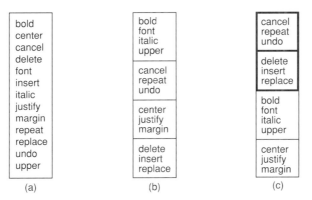

Fig. 8.7 Three menu organizations. (a) Menu using an alphabetical sequence. (b) Menu using functional grouping, with alphabetical within-group order as well as alphabetical-between-group order. (c) Menu with commands common to several different application programs placed at the top for consistency with the other application's menus; these commands have heavier borders. Menu items are some of those used in Card's menu-order experiment [CARD82].

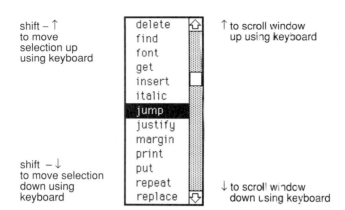

shift – ↑
to move
selection up
using keyboard

↑ to scroll window
up using keyboard

shift – ↓
to move selection
down using
keyboard

↓ to scroll window
down using keyboard

Fig. 8.8 A menu within a scrolling window. The user controls scrolling by selecting the up and down arrows or by dragging the square in the scroll bar.

to be paged or scrolled through. A scroll bar of the type used in many window managers allows all the relevant scrolling and paging commands to be presented in a concise way. A fast keyboard-oriented alternative to pointing at the scrolling commands can also be provided; for instance, the arrow keys can be used to scroll the window, and the shift key can be combined with the arrow keys to move the selection within the visible window, as shown in Fig. 8.8. In the limit, the size of the window can be reduced to a single menu item, yielding a "slot-machine" menu of the type shown in Fig. 8.9.

With a hierarchical menu, the user first selects from the choice set at the top of the hierarchy, which causes a second choice set to be available. The process is repeated until a leaf node (i.e., an element of the choice set itself) of the hierarchy tree is selected. As with hierarchical object selection, navigation mechanisms need to be provided so that the user can go back up the hierarchy if an incorrect subtree was selected. Visual feedback to give the user some sense of place within the hierarchy is also needed.

Menu hierarchies can be presented in several ways. Of course, successive levels of the hierarchy can replace one another on the display as further choices are made, but this does not give the user much sense of position within the hierarchy. The *cascading hierarchy*, as depicted in Fig. 8.10, is more attractive. Enough of each menu must be revealed that the complete highlighted selection path is visible, and some means must be used to indicate whether a menu item is a leaf node or is the name of a lower-level menu (in the figure, the right-pointing arrow fills this role). Another arrangement is to show just the name of each

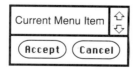

Fig. 8.9 A small menu-selection window. Only one menu item appears at a time. The scroll arrows are used to change the current menu item, which is selected when the Accept button is chosen.

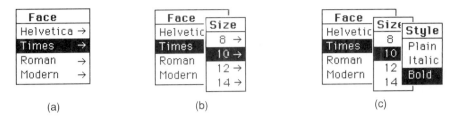

| | (a) | (b) | (c) |

Fig. 8.10 A pop-up hierarchical menu. (a) The first menu appears where the cursor is, in response to a button-down action. The cursor can be moved up and down to select the desired typeface. (b) The cursor is then moved to the right to bring up the second menu. (c) The process is repeated for the third menu.

selection made thus far in traversing down the hierarchy, plus all the selections available at the current level.

A *panel hierarchy* is another way to depict a hierarchy, as shown in Fig. 8.11; it takes up somewhat more room than the cascading hierarchy. If the hierarchy is not too large, an explicit tree showing the entire hierarchy can also be displayed.

When we design a hierarchical menu, the issue of depth versus breadth is always present. Snowberry et al. [SNOW83] found experimentally that selection time and accuracy improve when broader menus with fewer levels of selection are used. Similar results are reported by Landauer and Nachbar [LAND85] and by other researchers. However, these

Fig. 8.11 A hierarchical-selection menu. The leftmost column represents the top level; the children of the selected item in this column are shown in the next column; and so on. If there is no selected item, then the columns to the right are blank. (Courtesy of NeXT, Inc. © 1989 NeXT, Inc.)

results do not necessarily generalize to menu hierarchies that lack a natural, understandable structure.

Hierarchical menu selection almost demands an accompanying keyboard or function-key accelerator technique to speed up selection for more experienced (so-called ''power') users. This is easy if each node of the tree has a unique name, so that the user can enter the name directly, and the menu system provides a backup if the user's memory fails. If the names are unique only within each level of the hierarchy, the power user must type the complete path name to the desired leaf node.

Menu placement.   Menus can be shown on the display screen or on a second, auxiliary screen (Fig. 8.12); they can also be printed on a tablet or on function-key labels. Onscreen menus can be static and permanently visible, or can appear dynamically on request (tear-off, appearing, pop-up, pull-down, and pull-out menus).

A static menu printed on a tablet, as shown in Color Plate I.18, can easily be used in fixed-application systems. Use of a tablet or an auxiliary screen, however, requires that the user look away from the application display, and hence destroys visual continuity. The advantages are the saving of display space, which is often at a premium, and the accommodation of a large set of commands in one menu.

A pop-up menu appears on the screen when a selection is to be made, either in response to an explicit user action (typically pressing a mouse or tablet puck button), or automatically because the next dialogue step requires a menu selection. The menu normally appears at the cursor location, which is usually the user's center of visual attention, thereby

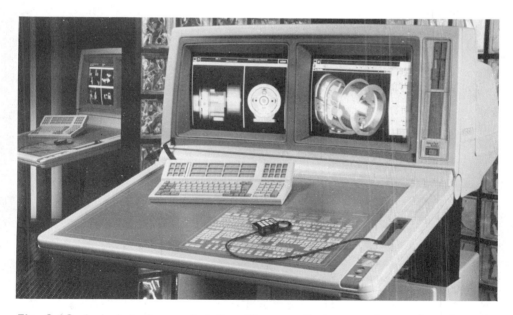

Fig. 8.12 A dual-display workstation. The two displays can be used to show the overview of a drawing on one and detail on the other, or to show the drawing on one and menus on the other. (Courtesy of Intergraph Corporation, Huntsville, Al.)

maintaining visual continuity. An attractive feature in pop-up menus is to highlight initially the most recently made selection from the choice set *if* the most recently selected item is more likely to be selected a second time than is another item, positioning the menu so the cursor is on that item. Alternatively, if the menu is ordered by frequency of use, the most frequently used command can be highlighted initially and should also be in the middle (not at the top) of the menu, to minimize cursor movements in selecting other items.

Pop-up and other appearing menus conserve precious screen space—one of the user-interface designer's most valuable commodities. Their use is facilitated by a fast RasterOp instruction, as discussed in Chapters 2 and 19.

Pop-up menus often can be context-sensitive. In several window-manager systems, if the cursor is in the window banner (the top heading of the window), commands involving window manipulation appear in the menu; if the cursor is in the window proper, commands concerning the application itself appear (which commands appear can depend on the type of object under the cursor); otherwise, commands for creating new windows appear in the menu. This context-sensitivity may initially be confusing to the novice, but is powerful once understood.

Unlike pop-up menus, pull-down and pull-out menus are anchored in a menu bar along an edge of the screen. The Apple Macintosh, Microsoft Windows, and Microsoft Presentation Manager all use pull-down menus. Macintosh menus, shown in Fig 8.13, also illustrate accelerator keys and context sensitivity. Pull-out menus, an alternative to pull-down menus, are shown in Fig. 8.14. Both types of menus have a two-level hierarchy: The menu bar is the first level, and the pull-down or pull-out menu is the second. Pull-down and pull-out menus can be activated explicitly or implicitly. In explicit activation, a button depression, once the cursor is in the menu bar, makes the second-level menu appear; the

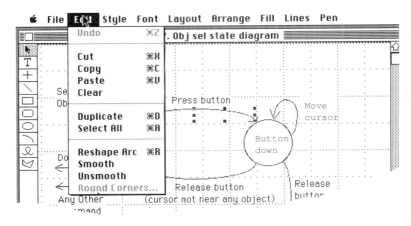

Fig. 8.13 A Macintosh pull-down menu. The last menu item is gray rather than black, indicating that it is currently not available for selection (the currently selected object, an arc, does not have corners to be rounded). The Undo command is also gray, because the previously executed command cannot be undone. Abbreviations are accelerator keys for power users. (Copyright 1988 Claris Corporation. All rights reserved.)

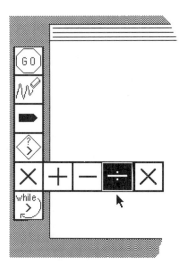

Fig. 8.14 A pull-out menu in which the leftmost, permanently displayed element shows the current selection. The newly selected menu item (reversed background) will become the current selection. This contrasts with most menu styles, in which the name of the menu is permanently displayed and the current selection is not shown after the adapted menu is dismissed. Menu is adapted from Jovanović's Process Visualization System [JOVA86]. (Courtesy of Branka Jovanović.)

cursor is moved on top of the desired selection and the button is then released. In implicit activation, moving the cursor into the heading causes the menu to appear; no button press is needed. Either selecting an entry or moving the cursor out of the menu area dismisses the menu. These menus, sometimes called "lazy" or "drop-down" menus, may also confuse new users by their seemingly mysterious appearance.

A full-screen menu can be a good or bad solution, depending on the context within which it is used. The disadvantage is that the application drawing will be obscured, removing context that might help the user to make an appropriate choice. Even this concern can be removed by using a raster display's look-up table to show the menu in a strong, bright color, over a dimmed application drawing [FEIN82a].

Visual representation. The basic decision on representation is whether menus use textual names or iconic or other graphical representations of elements of the choice set. Full discussion of this topic is deferred to the next chapter; however, note that iconic menus can be spatially organized in more flexible ways than can textual menus, because icons need not be long and thin like text strings; see Fig. 8.15. Also, inherently graphical concepts (particularly graphical attributes and geometrical primitives) are easily depicted.

Current selection. If a system has the concept of "currently selected element" of a choice set, menu selection allows this element to be highlighted. In some cases, an initial default setting is provided by the system and is used unless the user changes it. The currently selected element can be shown in various ways. The *radio-button* interaction

▶	Select
T	Text
+	Vert/Horz line
╲	Diagonal line
▢	Rectangle
▢	Rectangle with rounded corners
◯	Ellipse
◜	Quarter ellipse
ℓ	Curve
▽	Polygon

Fig. 8.15 Iconic and textual menus for the same geometric primitives. The iconic menu takes less space than does the textual menu. (Icons © 1988 Claris Corporation. All rights reserved.)

technique, patterned after the tuning buttons on car radios, is one way (Fig. 8.16). Again, some pop-up menus highlight the most recently selected item and place it under the cursor, on the assumption that the user is more likely to reselect that item than she is to select any other entry.

Size and shape of menu items. Pointing accuracy and speed are affected by the size of each individual menu item. Larger items are faster to select, as predicted by Fitts' law [FITT54; CARD83]; on the other hand, smaller items take less space and permit more menu items to be displayed in a fixed area, but induce more errors during selection. Thus, there is a conflict between using small menu items to preserve screen space versus using larger ones to decrease selection time and to reduce errors.

Pop-up *pie menus* [CALL88], shown in Fig. 8.17, appear at the cursor. As the user moves the mouse from the center of the pie toward the desired selection, the target width becomes larger, decreasing the likelihood of error. Thus, the user has explicit control over the speed-versus-error tradeoff. In addition, the distance to each menu item is the same.

Pattern recognition. In selection techniques involving pattern recognition, the user makes sequences of movements with a continuous-positioning device, such as a tablet or

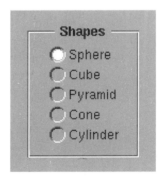

Fig. 8.16 Radio-button technique for selecting from a set of mutually exclusive alternatives. (Courtesy of NeXT, Inc. © 1989 NeXT, Inc.)

Fig. 8.17 A four-element pie menu.

mouse. The pattern recognizer automatically compares the sequence with a set of defined patterns, each of which corresponds to an element of the selection set. Figure 8.18 shows one set of sketch patterns and their related commands, taken from Wallace's SELMA queueing analyzer [IRAN71]. Proofreader's marks indicating delete, capitalize, move, and so on are attractive candidates for this approach [WOLF87].

The technique requires no typing skill and preserves tactile continuity. Furthermore, if the command involves an object, the cursor position can be used for selection. The move command used in many Macintosh applications is a good example: the cursor is positioned on top of the object to be moved and the mouse button is pressed, selecting the object under

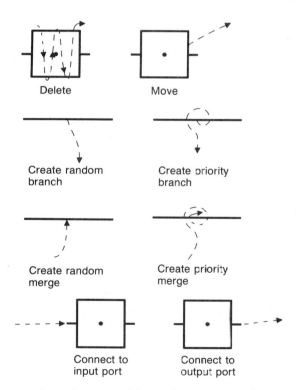

Fig. 8.18 Motions, indicated as dotted lines, that are recognized as commands. From Wallace's SELMA queuing analyzer [IRAN71].

the cursor (it is displayed in reverse video for feedback). As the user moves the mouse (still holding down the button), the object moves also. Releasing the mouse button detaches the object from the mouse. Skilled operators can work very rapidly with this technique, because hand movements between the work area and a command-entry device are eliminated. Given a data tablet and stylus, this technique can be used with at least several dozen patterns, but it is difficult for the user to learn a large number of different patterns.

Rhyne has recently combined a transparent tablet and liquid-crystal display into a prototype of a portable, lap-top computer [RHYN87]. Patterns are entered on the transparent tablet, and are recognized and interpreted as commands, numbers, and letters. The position at which information is entered is also significant. Figure 8.19 shows the device in use with a spreadsheet application.

Function keys.   Elements of the choice set can be associated with function keys. (We can think of single-keystroke inputs from a regular keyboard as function keys.) Unfortunately, there never seem to be enough keys to go around! The keys can be used in a hierarchical-selection fashion, and their meanings can be altered using chords, say by depressing the keyboard shift and control keys along with the function key itself. Learning exotic key combinations, such as "shift-option-control-L," for some commands is not easy, however, and is left as an exercise for the regular user seeking the productivity gains that typically result. Putting a "cheat-sheet" template on the keyboard to remind users of

Fig. 8.19 An IBM experimental display and transparent data tablet. A spreadsheet application is executing. The user has just circled three numbers, and has indicated that their sum is to be entered in the cell containing the sigma. A new column heading has also been printed. The system recognizes the gestures and characters, and enters appropriate commands to the spreadsheet application. (Courtesy IBM T. J. Watson Research Laboratories.)

these obscure combinations can speed up the learning process. It is even sometimes possible to define chords that make some sense, decreasing learning time. For instance, Microsoft Word on the Macintosh uses "shift-option->" to increase point size and the symmetrical "shift-option-<" to decrease point size; "shift-option-I" italicizes plain text and unitalicizes italicized text, whereas "shift-option-U" treats underlined text similarly.

One way to compensate for the lack of multiple buttons on a mouse is to use the temporal dimension to expand the possible meanings of one button—for instance, by distinguishing between a single click and two clicks made in rapid succession. If the meaning of two clicks is logically related to that of one click, this technique can be especially effective; otherwise, rote memory is needed to remember what one and two clicks mean. Examples of this technique are common: one click on a file icon selects it; two clicks opens the file. One click on the erase command enters erase mode; two clicks erase the entire screen. This technique can also be applied to each of the buttons on a multibutton mouse. Chording of mouse buttons or of keyboard keys with mouse buttons can also be used to provide the logical (but not necessarily human-factors) equivalent of more buttons. To be most useful, the organizing scheme for the chording patterns must be logical and easy to remember.

8.2.4 The Text Interaction Task

The text-string input task entails entering a character string to which the application does not ascribe any special meaning. Thus, typing a command name is *not* a text-entry task. In contrast, typing legends for a graph and typing text into a word processor *are* text input tasks. Clearly, the most common text-input technique is use of the QWERTY keyboard.

Character recognition. The user prints characters with a continuous-positioning device, usually a tablet stylus, and the computer recognizes them. This is considerably easier than recognizing scanned-in characters, because the tablet records the sequence, direction, and sometimes speed and pressure of strokes, and a pattern-recognition algorithm can match these to stored templates for each character. For instance, the capital letter "A" consists of three strokes—typically, two downward strokes and one horizontal stroke. A recognizer can be trained to identify different styles of block printing: the parameters of each character are calculated from samples drawn by the user. Character recognizers have been used with interactive graphics since the early 1960s [BROW64; TEIT64]. A simplified adaptation of Teitelman's recognizer, developed by Ledeen, is described in [NEWM73]. a commercial system is described in [WARD85; BLES86].

It is difficult to block print more than one or two characters per second (try it!), so character recognition is not appropriate for massive input of text. We write cursive letters faster than we print the same characters, but there are no simple recognition algorithms for cursive letters: the great variability among individuals' handwriting and the difficulty of segmenting words into individual letters are two of the problems.

Menu selection. A series of letters, syllables, or other basic units is displayed as a menu. The user then inputs text by choosing letters from the menu with a selection device. This technique is attractive in several situations. First, if only a short character string is to be entered and the user's hands are already on a pointing device, then menu selection may be

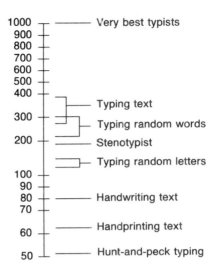

Fig. 8.20 Data-input speeds, in keystrokes per minute, of various techniques for entering text and numeric information. (Adapted from [VANC72, p. 335] and [CARD83, p. 61].)

faster than moving to the keyboard and back. Second, if the character set is large, this approach is a reasonable alternative to the keyboard.

Hierarchical menu selection can also be used with large character sets, such as are used in Chinese and Japanese. One such system uses the graphical features (strong horizontal line, strong vertical line, etc.) of the symbols for the hierarchy. A more common strategy is to enter the word in phonetic spelling, which string is then matched in a dictionary. For example, the Japanese use two alphabets, the katakana and hiragana, to type phonetically the thousands of kanji characters that their orthography borrows from the Chinese.

Evaluation of text-entry techniques.   For massive input of text, the only reasonable substitute for a skilled typist working with a keyboard is an automatic scanner. Figure 8.20 shows experimentally determined keying rates for a variety of techniques. The hunt-and-peck typist is slowed by the perceptual task of finding a key and the ensuing motor task of moving to and striking it, but the trained typist has only the motor task of striking the key, preceded sometimes by a slight hand or finger movement to reach it. Speech input, not shown on the chart, is slow but attractive for applications where the hands must be free for other purposes, such as handling paperwork.

8.2.5   The Quantify Interaction Task

The quantify interaction task involves specifying a numeric value between some minimum and maximum value. Typical interaction techniques are typing the value, setting a dial to the value, and using an up–down counter to select the value. Like the positioning task, this task may be either linguistic or spatial. When it is linguistic, the user knows the specific value to be entered; when it is spatial, the user seeks to increase or decrease a value by a certain amount, with perhaps an approximate idea of the desired end value. In the former case, the interaction technique clearly must involve numeric feedback of the value being selected (one way to do this is to have the user type the actual value); in the latter case, it is more important to give a general impression of the approximate setting of the value. This is typically accomplished with a spatially oriented feedback technique, such as display of a dial or gauge on which the current (and perhaps previous) value is shown.

One means of entering values is the potentiometer. The decision of whether to use a rotary or linear potentiometer should take into account whether the visual feedback of changing a value is rotary (e.g., a turning clock hand) or linear (e.g., a rising temperature gauge). The current position of one or a group of slide potentiometers is much more easily comprehended at a glance than are those of rotary potentiometers, even if the knobs have pointers; unfortunately, most graphics system manufacturers offer only rotary potentiometers. On the other hand, rotary potentiometers are easier to adjust. Availability of both linear and rotary potentiometers can help users to associate meanings with each device. It is important to use directions consistently: clockwise or upward movements normally increase a value.

With continuous-scale manipulation, the user points at the current-value indicator on a displayed gauge or scale, presses the selection button, drags the indicator along the scale to the desired value, and then releases the selection button. A pointer is typically used to indicate the value selected on the scale, and a numeric echo may be given. Figure 8.21 shows several such dials and their associated feedback. The range or precision of values entered in this way can be extended by using the positioning device as a relative rather than absolute device and by using a nonconstant C/D ratio, as discussed in Section 8.1.1. Then it becomes possible to increase a value by repeating a series of stroking actions: move to the right, lift mouse, move to the left, put mouse down, and so on. Thornton's number wheel [THOR79] is such a technique.

If the resolution needed is higher than the continuous-scale manipulation technique can provide, or if screen space is at a premium, an up–down counter arrangement can be used, as shown in Fig. 8.22.

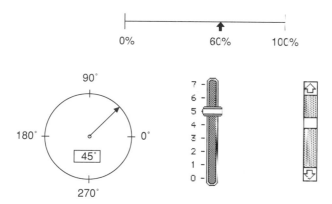

Fig. 8.21 Several dials that the user can use to input values by dragging the control pointer. Feedback is given by the pointer and, in two cases, by numeric displays. (Vertical sliders © Apple Computer, Inc.)

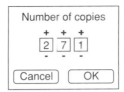

Fig. 8.22 An up–down counter for specifying a value. The user positions the cursor on ''+'' or ''–'' and holds down the selection button on the pointing device; the corresponding digit increases or decreases until the button is released.

8.2.6 3D Interaction Tasks

Two of the four interaction tasks described previously for 2D applications become more complicated in 3D: position and select. In this section, we also introduce an additional 3D interaction task: rotate (in the sense of orienting an object in 3-space). The major reason for the complication is the difficulty of perceiving 3D depth relationships of a cursor or object relative to other displayed objects. This contrasts starkly with 2D interaction, where the user can readily perceive that the cursor is above, next to, or on an object. A secondary complication arises because the commonly available interaction devices, such as mice and tablets, are only 2D devices, and we need a way to map movements of these 2D devices into 3D.

Display of stereo pairs, corresponding to left- and right-eye views, is helpful for understanding general depth relationships, but is of limited accuracy as a precise locating method. Methods for presenting stereo pairs to the eye are discussed in Chapters 14 and 18, and in [HODG85]. Other ways to show depth relationships are discussed in Chapters 14–16.

The first part of this section deals with techniques for positioning and selecting, which are closely related. The second part concerns techniques for interactive rotation.

Figure 8.23 shows a common way to position in 3D. The 2D cursor, under control of, say, a mouse, moves freely among the three views. The user can select any one of the 3D cursor's dashed lines and can drag the line, using a button-down–drag–button-up sequence. If the button-down event is close to the intersection of two dashed cursor lines, then both are selected and are moved with the mouse (gravity, discussed in Section 8.3.2, can make

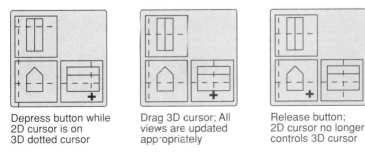

| Depress button while 2D cursor is on 3D dotted cursor | Drag 3D cursor; All views are updated appropriately | Release button; 2D cursor no longer controls 3D cursor |

Fig. 8.23 3D positioning technique using three views of the same scene (a house). The 2D cursor (+) is used to select one of the dashed 3D cursor lines.

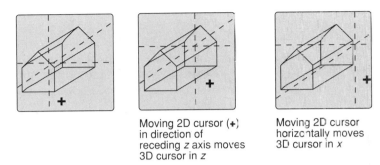

Moving 2D cursor (+)
in direction of
receding z axis moves
3D cursor in z

Moving 2D cursor
horizontally moves
3D cursor in x

Fig. 8.24 Movement of the 3D cursor is controlled by the direction in which the 2D cursor is moved.

picking the intersection especially easy). Although this method may appear restrictive in forcing the user to work in one or two dimensions at a time, it is sometimes advantageous to decompose the 3D manipulation task into simpler lower-dimensional tasks. Selecting as well as locating is facilitated with multiple views: Objects that overlap and hence are difficult to distinguish in one view may not overlap in another view.

Another possibility, developed by Nielson and Olsen [NIEL86] and depicted in Fig. 8.24, requires that all three principal axes project with nonzero length. A 3D cross-hair cursor, with cross-hairs parallel to the principal axes, is controlled by moving the mouse in the general direction of the projections of the three principal axes. Figure 8.25 shows how 2D locator movements are mapped into 3D: there are 2D zones in which mouse movements affect a specific axis. Of course, 3D movement is restricted to one axis at a time.

Both of these techniques illustrate ways to map 2D locator movements into 3D movements. We can instead use buttons to control which of the 3D coordinates are affected by the locator's 2 degrees of freedom. For example, the locator might normally control x and y; but, with the keyboard shift key depressed, it could control x and z instead (this requires that the keyboard be unencoded, as discussed in Chapter 4). Alternatively, three buttons could be used, to bind the locator selectively to an axis. Instead of mapping from a

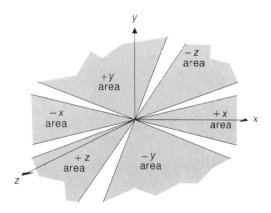

Fig. 8.25 The six regions of mouse movement, which cause the 3D cursor to move along the principal axes.

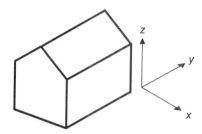

Fig. 8.26 The displayed local coordinate system of the house, which shows the three directions in which any translated object will move. To preserve stimulus-response compatibility, we can use the direction of mouse movements to determine the axes chosen, as in Fig. 8.25.

2D device into 3D, we could use a real 3D locator, such as the joysticks and trackballs discussed in Section 8.1.6

Constrained 3D movement is effective in 3D locating. Gridding and gravity can sometimes compensate for uncertainties in depth relationships and can aid exact placement. Another form of constraint is provided by those physical devices that make it easier to move along principal axes than in other directions. Some trackballs and joysticks have this property, which can also be simulated with the isometric strain-gauge and spaceball devices (Section 8.1.6).

Context-specific constraints are often more useful, however, than are these general constraints. It is possible to let the user specify that movements should be parallel to or on lines or planes other than the principal axes and planes. For example, with a method developed by Nielson and Olsen [NIEL86], the local coordinate system of the selected object defines the directions of movement as shown in Fig. 8.26. In a more general technique developed by Bier [BIER86b], the user places a coordinate system, called a *skitter*, on the surface of an object, again defining the possible directions of movement (Fig. 8.27). Another way to constrain movement to a particular plane is to give the user control over the view-plane orientation, and to limit translation to be parallel to the view plane.

One method of 3D picking—finding the output primitive that, for an (x, y) position

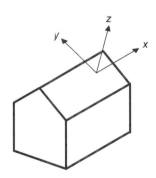

Fig. 8.27 The displayed coordinate system, placed interactively so that its (x, y) plane coincides with the plane of the roof, shows the three directions in which any translated object will move.

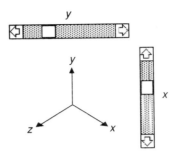

Fig. 8.28 Two slider dials for effecting rotation about the screen x and y axes.

determined by a 2D locator, has the maximum z value—was discussed in Chapter 7. Another method, which can be used with a 3D locator when wireframe views are shown—is to find the ouput primitive closest to the locator's (x, y, z) position.

As with locating and selection, the issues in 3D rotation are understanding depth relationships, mapping 2D interaction devices into 3D, and ensuring stimulus-response compatibility. An easily implemented 3D rotation technique provides slider dials or gauges that control rotation about three axes. S-R compatibility suggests that the three axes should normally be in the screen-coordinate system—x to the right, y increasing upward, z out of (or into) the screen [BRIT78]. Of course, the center of rotation either must be explicitly specified as a separate step, or must be implicit (typically the screen-coordinate origin, the origin of the object, or the center of the object). Providing rotation about the sceen's x and y axes is especially simple, as suggested in Fig. 8.28. The (x, y, z) coordinate system associated with the sliders is rotated as the sliders are moved to show the effect of the rotation. A 2D trackball can be used instead of the two sliders.

The two-axis rotation approach can be easily generalized to three axes by adding a dial for z-axis rotation, as in Fig. 8.29 (a dial is preferable to a slider for S-R compatibility).

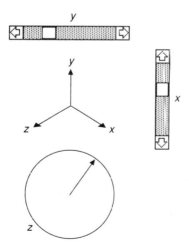

Fig. 8.29 Two slider dials for effecting rotation about the screen x and y axes, and a dial for rotation about the screen z axis. The coordinate system represents world coordinates and shows how world coordinates relate to screen coordinates.

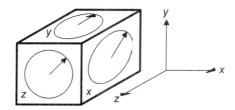

Fig. 8.30 Three dials to control rotation about three axes. The placement of the dials on the cube provides strong stimulus-response compatibility.

Even more S-R compatibility comes from the arrangement of dials on the faces of a cube shown in Fig. 8.30, which clearly suggests the axes controlled by each dial. Again, a 3D trackball could be used instead of the dials.

Mouse movements can be directly mapped onto object movements, without slider or dial intermediaries. The user can be presented a metaphor in which the two sliders of Fig. 8.28 are superimposed on top of the object being rotated, so that horizontal mouse movements are mapped into rotations about the screen-coordinate y axis, and vertical mouse movements are mapped into rotations about the screen-coordinate x axis (Fig. 8.31a). Diagonal motions have no effect. The slider dials are not really displayed; the user learns to imagine that they are present. Alternatively, the user can be told that an imaginary 2D trackball is superimposed on top of the object being rotated, so that the vertical, horizontal, or diagonal motions one would make with the trackball can be made instead with the mouse (Fig. 8.31b). Either of these methods provides two-axis rotation in 3D.

For three-axis rotations, three methods that closely resemble real-world concepts are particularly interesting. In the overlapping-sliders method [CHEN88], the user is shown two linear sliders overlapping a rotary slider, as in Fig. 8.31(c). Motions in the linear sliders control rotation about the x and y axes, while a rotary motion around the intersection of the two linear sliders controls rotation about the z axis. In a technique developed by Evans, Tanner, and Wein [EVAN81], three successive mouse positions are compared to determine whether the mouse motion is linear or rotary. Linear horizontal or vertical movements control rotation about the x and y axes, a linear diagonal movement rotates

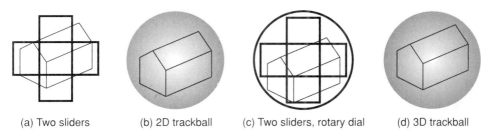

(a) Two sliders   (b) 2D trackball   (c) Two sliders, rotary dial   (d) 3D trackball

Fig. 8.31 Four methods of 3D rotation. In each case, the user makes movements with a 2D device corresponding to those that would be made if the actual devices were superimposed on the object. A 3D trackball can be twisted to give z-axis rotation, whereas a 2D trackball provides only two-axis rotation.

about both the x and y axes, and rotary movements control rotation about the z axis. While this is a relative technique and does not require that the movements be made directly over the object being rotated or in a particular area, the user can be instructed to use these motions to manipulate a 3D trackball superimposed on the object (Fig. 8.31d). In the virtual-sphere method, also developed by Chen [CHEN88], the user actually manipulates this superimposed 3D trackball in an absolute fashion as though it were real. With a mouse button down, mouse movements rotate the trackball exactly as your finger would move a real trackball. An experiment [CHEN88] comparing these latter two approaches showed no performance differences, but did yield a user preference for Chen's method.

It is often necessary to combine 3D interaction tasks. Thus, rotation requires a select task for the object to be rotated, a position task for the center of rotation, and an orient task for the actual rotation. Specifying a 3D view can be thought of as a combined positioning (where the eye is), orientation (how the eye is oriented), and scaling (field of view, or how much of the projection plane is mapped into the viewport) task. We can create such a task by combining some of the techniques we have discussed, or by designing a *fly-around* capability in which the viewer flies an imaginary airplane around a 3D world. The controls are typically pitch, roll, and yaw, plus velocity to speed up or slow down. With the fly-around concept, the user needs an overview, such as a 2D plan view, indicating the imaginary airplane's ground position and heading.

8.3 COMPOSITE INTERACTION TASKS

Composite interaction tasks (CITs) are built on top of the basic interaction tasks (BITs) described in the previous section, and are actually combinations of BITs integrated into a unit. There are three major forms of CITs: dialogue boxes, used to specify multiple units of information; construction, used to create objects requiring two or more positions; and manipulation, used to reshape existing geometric objects.

8.3.1 Dialogue Boxes

We often need to select multiple elements of a selection set. For instance, text attributes, such as italic, bold, underline, hollow, and all caps, are not mutually exclusive, and the user may want to select two or more at once. In addition, there may be several sets of relevant attributes, such as typeface and font. Some of the menu approaches useful in selecting a single element of a selection set are not satisfactory for multiple selections. For example, pull-down and pop-up menus normally disappear when a selection is made, necessitating a second activation to make a second selection.

This problem can be overcome with dialogue boxes, a form of menu that remains visible until explicitly dismissed by the user. In addition, dialogue boxes can permit selection from more than one selection set, and can also include areas for entering text and values. Selections made in a dialogue box can be corrected immediately. When all the information has been entered into the dialogue box, the box is typically dismissed explicitly with a command. Attributes and other values specified in a dialogue box can be applied immediately, allowing the user to preview the effect of a font or line-style change. An "apply" command is sometimes included in the box to cause the new values to be used

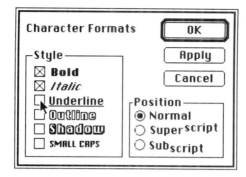

Fig. 8.32 A text-attribute dialogue box with several different attributes selected. The bold border of the "OK" button shows that the keyboard return key can be used as an alternative. The "Apply" button is used to apply new attibute values, so the user can observe their effects. "Cancel" is used to revert any changes to their previous values. Note that text attributes are described both by name and, graphically, by example. (Screen shots © 1983–1989 Microsoft Corporation. Reprinted with permission from Microsoft Corporation.)

without dismissing the box. More frequently, however, the dialogue box must be dismissed to apply the new settings. Figure 8.32 shows a dialogue box with several selected items highlighted.

8.3.2 Construction Techniques

One way to construct a line is to have the user indicate one endpoint and then the other; once the second endpoint is specified, a line is drawn between the two points. With this technique, however, the user has no easy way to try out different line positions before settling on a final one, because the line is not actually drawn until the second endpoint is given. With this style of interaction, the user must invoke a command each time an endpoint is to be repositioned.

A far superior approach is *rubberbanding*, discussed in Chapter 2. When the user pushes a button (often the tipswitch on a tablet stylus, or a mouse button), the starting position of the line is established by the cursor (usually but not necessarily controlled by a continuous-positioning device). As the cursor moves, so does the endpoint of the line; when the button is released, the endpoint is frozen. Figure 8.33 show a rubberband line-drawing sequence. The user-action sequence is shown in the state diagram in Fig. 8.34. Notice that the state "rubberband" is active *only* while a button is held down. It is in this state that cursor movements cause the current line to change. See [BUXT85] for an informative discussion of the importance of matching the state transitions in an interaction technique with the transitions afforded by the device used with the technique.

An entire genre of interaction techniques is derived from rubberband line drawing. The *rubber-rectangle* technique starts by anchoring one corner of a rectangle with a button-

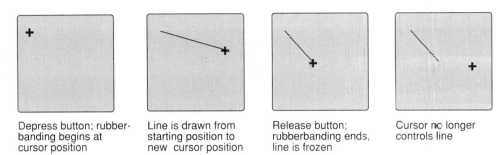

Depress button; rubber-   Line is drawn from   Release button;   Cursor no longer
banding begins at   starting position to   rubberbanding ends,   controls line
cursor position   new cursor position   line is frozen

Fig. 8.33 Rubberband line drawing.

down action, after which the opposite corner is dynamically linked to the cursor until a button-up action occurs. The state diagram for this technique differs from that for rubberband line drawing only in the dynamic feedback of a rectangle rather than a line. The *rubber-circle* technique creates a circle that is centered at the initial cursor position and that passes through the current cursor position, or that is within the square defined by opposite corners. The *rubber-ellipse* technique creates an axis-aligned ellipse inside the rectangle defined by the initial and current cursor positions. A circle results if the rectangle is square—easily done with gridding. All these techniques have in common the user-action sequence of button-down, move locator and see feedback, button-up.

One interaction technique to create a polyline (a sequence of connected lines) is an extension of rubberbanding. After entering the polyline-creation command, the user clicks on a button to anchor each rubberbanded vertex. After all the vertices have been indicated, the user indicates completion, typically by a double click on a button without moving the locator, by a click on a second mouse button, or by entry of a new command. If the new command is from a menu, the last line segment of the polyline follows the cursor to the menu, and then disappears. Figure 8.35 depicts a typical sequence of events in creating a polyline; Fig. 8.36 is the accompanying state diagram.

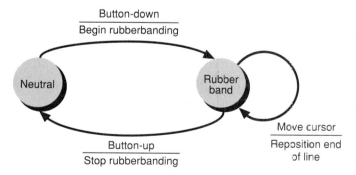

Fig. 8.34 State diagram for rubberband line drawing.

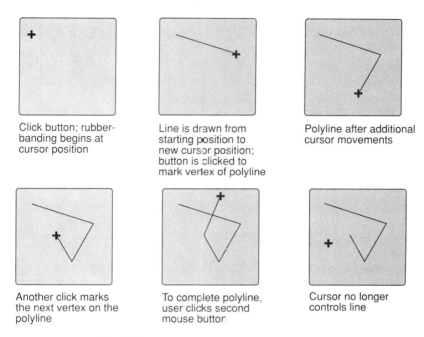

Click button; rubber-
banding begins at
cursor position

Line is drawn from
starting position to
new cursor position;
button is clicked to
mark vertex of polyline

Polyline after additional
cursor movements

Another click marks
the next vertex on the
polyline

To complete polyline,
user clicks second
mouse button

Cursor no longer
controls line

Fig. 8.35 Rubberband polyline sketching.

A polygon can be drawn similarly. In some cases, the user signals to the system that the polygon is complete by returning the cursor to the starting vertex of the polygon. In other cases, the user explicitly signals completion using a function key, and the system automatically closes the polygon. Figure 8.37 shows one way to create polygons.

Constraints of various types can be applied to the cursor positions in any of these techniques. For example, Fig. 8.38 shows a sequence of lines drawn using the same cursor

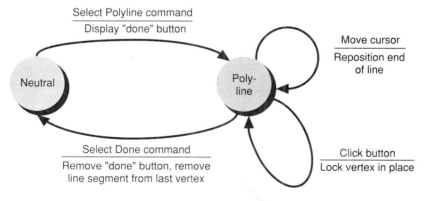

Fig. 8.36 State diagram for rubberband creation of a polyline.

   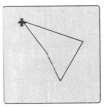

Click button; rubber-banding begins at cursor position	First edge of polygon is drawn from starting position to new cursor position, until another click on button	Second edge drawn until another click on button	Polygon is terminated when cursor is close to starting position and button is cicked

Fig. 8.37 Rubberband drawing of a polygon.

positions as in Fig. 8.33, but with a horizontal constraint in effect. A vertical line, or a line at some other orientation, can also be drawn in this manner. Polylines made entirely of horizontal and vertical lines, as in printed circuit boards, VLSI chips, and some city maps, are readily created; right angles are introduced either in response to a user command, or automatically as the cursor changes direction. The idea can be generalized to any shape, such as a circle, ellipse, or any other curve; the curve is initialized at some position, then cursor movements control how much of the curve is displayed. In general, the cursor position is used as input to a constraint function whose output is then used to display the appropriate portion of the object.

Gravity is yet another form of constraint. When constructing drawings, we frequently want a new line to begin at the endpoint of, or on, an existing line. Matching an endpoint is easy if it was created using gridding, but otherwise is difficult without a potentially time-consuming zoom. The difficulty is avoided by programming an imaginary gravity field around each existing line, so that the cursor is attracted to the line as soon as it enters the gravity field. Figure 8.39 shows a line with a gravity field that is larger at the endpoints, so that matching endpoints is especially easy.

Depress button; rubberbanding begins at cursor position	Line is drawn from starting position to *x* coordinate of new cursor position	Release button; rubberbanding ends, line frozen	Cursor no longer controls line

Fig. 8.38 Horizontally constrained rubberband line drawing.

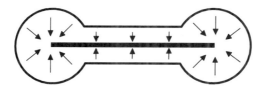

Fig. 8.39 Line surrounded by a gravity field, to aid picking points on the line: If the cursor falls within the field, it is snapped to the line.

8.3.3   Dynamic Manipulation

It is not sufficient to create lines, rectangles, and so on. In many situations, the user must be able to modify previously created geometric entities.

Dragging moves a selected symbol from one position to another under control of a cursor, as in Fig. 8.40. A button-down action typically starts the dragging (in some cases, the button-down is also used to select the symbol under the cursor to be dragged); then, a button-up freezes the symbol in place, so that further movements of the cursor have no effect on it. This button-down–drag–button-up sequence is often called *click-and-drag* interaction.

Dynamic rotation of an object can be done in a similar way, except that we must be able to identify the point or axis about which the rotation is to occur. A convenient strategy is to have the system show the current center of rotation and to allow the user to modify it as desired. Figure 8.41 shows one such scenario. Note that the same approach can be used for scaling, with the center of scaling, rather than that of rotation, being specified by the user.

The concept of *handles* is useful to provide scaling of an object, without making the user think explicitly about where the center of scaling is. Figure 8.42 shows an object with eight handles, which are displayed as small squares at the corners and on the sides of the imaginary box surrounding the object. The user selects one of the handles and drags it to scale the object. If the handle is on a corner, then the corner diagonally opposite is locked in place. If the handle is in the middle of a side, then the opposite side is locked in place.

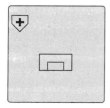
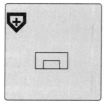

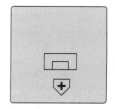

Position cursor over symbol to be moved, depress button

Symbol is highlighted to acknowledge selection

Several intermediate cursor movements

Release button; symbol locks in place

Fig. 8.40 Dragging a symbol into a new position.

Highlighted object has
been selected with
cursor

Rotate command has
been invoked, causing
center of rotation
icon to appear at
default center position
unless previously set

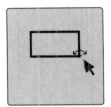

Center-of-rotation
icon is dragged into
a new position

Rectangle is now
rotated by pointing at
rectangle, depressing
button, and moving
left-right with
button down

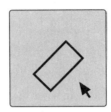

Button is released;
cursor no longer controls
rotation; icon is gone;
rectangle remains selected
for other possible
operations

Fig. 8.41 Dynamic rotation.

When this technique is integrated into a complete user interface, the handles appear only when the object is selected to be operated on. Handles are also a unique visual code to indicate that an object is selected, since other visual codings (e.g., line thickness, dashed lines, or changed intensity) might also be used as part of the drawing itself. (Blinking is another unique visual code, but tends to be distracting and annoying.)

Selecting rectangle
with cursor causes
handles to appear

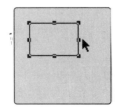

Button actions on this
handle move only
right side of rectangle

Button actions on this
handle move only
corner of rectangle

Fig. 8.42 Handles used to reshape objects.

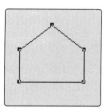

Polygon has been
selected for vertex
modification, handle
appears on each vertex

Depress-move-release
over vertex causes
vertex to move

Polygon no longer
selected; handles
have been removed

Fig. 8.43 Handles used to reposition the vertices of a polygon.

Dragging, rotating, and scaling affect an entire object. What if we wish to be able to move individual points, such as the vertices of a polygon? Vertices could be named, and the user could enter the name of a vertex and its new (x, y) coordinates. But the same point-and-drag strategy used to move an entire object is more attractive. In this case, the user points to a vertex, selects it, and drags it to a new position. The vertices adjacent to the one selected remain connected via rubberband lines. To facilitate selecting a vertex, we can establish a gravity field to snap the cursor onto a nearby vertex, we can make a vertex blink whenever the cursor is near, or we can superimpose handles over each vertex, as in Fig. 8.43. Similarly, the user can move an edge of a polygon by selecting it and dragging, with the edge maintaining its original slope. For smooth curves and surfaces, handles can also be provided to allow the user to manipulate points that control the shape, as discussed further in Chapter 11.

In the next chapter, we discuss design issues involved in combining basic and composite interaction techniques into an overall user–computer dialogue.

EXERCISES

8.1 Examine a user–computer interface with which you are familiar. List each interaction task used. Categorize each task into one of the four BITs of Section 8.2. If an interaction does not fit this classification scheme, try decomposing it further.

8.2 Implement adaptive C/D ratio cursor tracking for use with a mouse or other relative-positioning device. Experiment with different relationships between mouse velocity v and the C/D ratio r: $r = k\,v$ and $r = k\,v^2$. You must also find a suitable value for the constant k.

8.3 Conduct an experiment to compare the selection speed and accuracy of any of the following pairs of techniques:

    a. Mouse and tablet selecting from a static, onscreen menu
    b. Touch-panel and light-pen selecting from a static, onscreen menu,
    c. Wide, shallow menu and narrow, deep menu
    d. Pull-down menus that appear as soon as the cursor is in the menu bar, and pull-down menus that require a mouse-button depression.

8.4 Extend the state diagram of Fig. 8.6 to include a ''return to lowest level'' command that takes the selection back to the lowest level of the hierarchy, such that whatever was selected first is selected again.

8.5 Implement an autocompletion text-entry technique to use with an arbitrary list of words. Experiment with different word sets, such as the UNIX commands and proper names. Decide how to handle nonexistent matches, corrections typed by the user after a match has been made, and prompting for the user.

8.6 Implement cascading and panel heirarchical menus for a series of commands or for file-system subdirectories. What issues arise as you do this? Informally compare the selection speeds of each technique.

8.7 Implement pop-up menus that allow multiple selections prior to dismissal, which the user accomplishes by moving the cursor outside the menu. Alternatively, use a button click for dismissal. Which dismissal method do you prefer? Explain your answer. Ask five people who use the two techniques which dismissal method they prefer.

8.8 Implement a menu package on a color raster display that has a look-up table such that the menu is displayed in a strong, bright but partially transparent color, and all the colors underneath the menu are changed to a subdued gray.

8.9 Implement any of the 3D interaction techniques discussed in this chapter.

8.10 For each of the locating techniques discussed in Section 8.2.6, identify the line or plane into which 2D locator movements are mapped.

8.11 Draw the state diagram that controls pop-up hierarchical menus. Draw the state diagram that controls panel hierarchical menus.

9
Dialogue
Design

We have described the fundamental building blocks from which the interface to an interactive graphics system is crafted—interaction devices, techniques, and tasks. Let us now consider how to assemble these building blocks into a usable and pleasing form. *User-interface design* is still at least partly an art, not a science, and thus some of what we offer is an attitude toward the design of interactive systems, and some specific dos and don'ts that, if applied creatively, can help to focus attention on the *human factors*, also called the *ergonomics*, of an interactive system.

The key goals in user-interface design are increase in speed of learning, and in speed of use, reduction of error rate, encouragement of rapid recall of how to use the interface, and increase in attractiveness to potential users and buyers.

Speed of learning concerns how long a new user takes to achieve a given proficiency with a system. It is especially important for systems that are to be used infrequently by any one individual: Users are generally unwilling to spend hours learning a system that they will use for just minutes a week!

Speed of use concerns how long an experienced user requires to perform some specific task with a system. It is critical when a person is to use a system repeatedly for a significant amount of time.

The *error rate* measures the number of user errors per interaction. The error rate affects both speed of learning and speed of use; if it is easy to make mistakes with the system, learning takes longer and speed of use is reduced because the user must correct any mistakes. However, error rate must be a separate design objective for applications in which even one error is unacceptable—for example, air-traffic control, nuclear-power-plant control, and strategic military command and control systems. Such systems often trade off some speed of use for a lower error rate.

Rapid recall of how to use the system is another distinct design objective, since a user may be away from a system for weeks, and then return for casual or intensive use. The system should "come back" quickly to the user.

Attractiveness of the interface is a real marketplace concern. Of course, liking a system or a feature is not necessarily the same as being facile with it. In numerous experiments comparing two alternative designs, subjects state a strong preference for one design but indeed perform faster with the other.

It is sometimes said that systems cannot be both easy to learn and fast to use. Although there was certainly a time when this was often true, we have learned how to satisfy multiple design objectives. The simplest and most common approach to combining speed of use and ease of learning is to provide a "starter kit" of basic commands that are designed for the beginning user, but are only a subset of the overall command set. This starter kit is made available from menus, to facilitate ease of learning. All the commands, both starter and advanced, are available through the keyboard or function keys, to facilitate speed of use. Some advanced commands are sometimes put in the menus also, typically at lower levels of hierarchy, where they can be accessed by users who do not yet know their keyboard equivalents.

We should recognize that speed of learning is a relative term. A system with 10 commands is faster to learn than is one with 100 commands, in that users will be able to understand what each of the 10 commands does more quickly than they can what 100 do. But if the application for which the interface is designed requires rich functionality, the 10 commands may have to be used in creative and imaginative ways that are difficult to learn, whereas the 100 commands may map quite readily onto the needs of the application.

In the final analysis, meeting even one of these objectives is no mean task. There are unfortunately few absolutes in user-interface design. Appropriate choices depend on many different factors, including the design objectives, user characteristics, the environment of use, available hardware and software resources, and budgets. It is especially important that the user-interface designer's ego be submerged, so that the user's needs, not the designer's, are the driving factor. There is no room for a designer with quick, off-the-cuff answers. Good design requires careful consideration of many issues and patience in testing prototypes with real users.

9.1   THE FORM AND CONTENT OF USER–COMPUTER DIALOGUES

The concept of a *user–computer dialogue* is central to interactive system design, and there are helpful analogies between user–computer and person–person dialogues. After all, people have developed effective ways of communicating, and it makes sense to learn what we can from these years of experience. Dialogues typically involve gestures and words: In fact, people may have communicated with gestures, sounds, and images (cave pictures, Egyptian hieroglyphics) even before phonetic languages were developed. Computer graphics frees us from the limitations of purely verbal interactions with computers and enables us to use images as an additional communication modality.

Many attributes of person–person dialogues should be preserved in user–computer dialogues. People who communicate effectively share common knowledge and a common set of assumptions. So, too, there should be commonality between the user and the computer. Further, these assumptions and knowledge should be those of the user, not those of the computer-sophisticated user-interface designer. For instance, a biochemist studying the geometric structure of molecules is familiar with such concepts as atoms, bonds, dihedral angles, and residues, but does not know and should not have to know such concepts as linked lists, canvases, and event queues.

Learning to use a user interface is similar to learning to use a foreign language. Recall your own foreign-language study. Sentences came slowly, as you struggled with vocabulary and grammar. Later, as practice made the rules more familiar, you were able to concentrate on expanded vocabulary to communicate your thoughts more effectively. The new user of an interactive system must go through a similar learning process. Indeed, if new application concepts must be learned along with new grammar rules and vocabulary, the learning can be even more difficult. The designer's task, then, is to keep the user-interface rules and vocabulary simple, and to use concepts the user already knows or can learn easily.

The language of the user–computer dialogue should be efficient and complete, and should have natural sequencing rules. With an *efficient* language, the user can convey commands to the computer quickly and concisely. A *complete* language allows expression of any idea relevant to the domain of discourse. *Sequencing rules*, which define the order or syntax of the language, should have a minimum number of simple, easy-to-learn cases. Simple sequencing rules help to minimize training and allow the user to concentrate on the problem at hand; complex rules introduce discontinuities and distractions into the user's thought processes.

A user interface may be complete but inefficient; that is, expressing ideas may be difficult and time consuming. For example, a system for logic design needs to provide only a single building block, either the **nor** or the **nand**, but such a system will be laborious to use and thus inefficient. It is better to include in the system a facility for building up more complex commands from the few basic ones.

Extensibility can be exploited to make a language more efficient by defining new terms as combinations of existing terms. Extensibility is commonly provided in operating systems via scripts, cataloged procedures, or command files, and in programming languages via macros, but is less often found in graphics systems.

In person–person dialogue, one person asks a question or makes a statement, and the other responds, usually quite quickly. Even if a reply does not come immediately, the listener usually signals attentiveness via facial expressions or gestures. These are forms of *feedback*, a key component of user–computer dialogue. In both sorts of dialogue, the ultimate response may be provided either in words or with some gesture or facial expression—that is, with a graphic image.

Occasionally, too, the speaker makes a mistake. then says, "Oops, I didn't mean that," and the listener discards the last statement. Being able to undo mistakes is also important in user–computer dialogues.

In a conversation, the speaker might ask the listener for help in expressing a thought, or for further explanation. Or the speaker might announce a temporary digression to another subject, holding the current subject in abeyance. These same capabilities should also be possible in user–computer dialogues.

With this general framework, let us define the components of the user–computer interface more specifically. Two languages constitute this interface. With one, the user communicates with the computer; with the other, the computer communicates with the user. The first language is expressed via actions applied to various interaction devices, and perhaps also via spoken words. The second language is expressed graphically through lines, points, character strings, filled areas, and colors combined to form displayed images and messages, and perhaps aurally through tones or synthesized words.

Languages have two major components: the meaning of the language, and the form of the language. The *meaning* of a language is its content, or its message, whereas the *form* is how that meaning is conveyed. In person–person dialogue, the meaning "I am happy" can be conveyed with the words "I am happy," or with the words "Ich bin glücklich," or with a smile. In user–computer dialogue, the meaning "delete temp9" might be conveyed by typing the command "DELETE temp9" or by dragging an icon representing file temp9 to a trashcan icon. The form of an interface is commonly called its "look and feel."

There are two elements to meaning in interface design: the conceptual and the functional. There are also two elements to form: sequencing and binding to hardware primitives. The user-interface designer must specify each of these four elements.

The *conceptual design* is the definition of the principal application concepts that must be mastered by the user, and is hence also called the *user's model* of the application. The conceptual design typically defines *objects*, *properties* of objects, *relationships* between objects, and *operations* on objects. In a simple text editor, the objects are characters, lines, and files, a property of a file is its name, files are sequences of lines, lines are sequences of characters, operations on lines are Insert, Delete, Move, and Copy, and the operations on files are Create, Delete, Rename, Print, and Copy. The conceptual design of a user interface is sometimes described by means of a metaphor or analogy to something with which the user is already familiar, such as a typewriter, Rolodex, drafting table and instruments, desktop, or filing cabinet. Although such analogies are often helpful for initial understanding, they can become harmful if they must be stretched unrealistically to explain the more advanced capabilities provided by the computer system [HALA82].

The *functional design* specifies the detailed functionality of the interface: what information is needed for each operation on an object, what errors can occur, how the errors are handled, and what the results of each operation are. Functional design is also called *semantic design*. It defines meanings, but not the sequence of actions or the devices with which the actions are conducted.

The *sequencing design*, part of the form of an interface, defines the ordering of inputs and outputs. Sequencing design is also called *syntactic design*. For input, the sequencing comprises the rules by which indivisible units of meaning (input to the system via interaction techniques) are formed into complete sentences. Units of meaning cannot be further decomposed without loss of meaning. For example, the mouse movements and mouse button clicks needed to make a menu selection do not individually provide information to the application.

For output, the notion of sequence includes spatial and temporal factors. Therefore, output sequencing includes the 2D and 3D layout of a display, as well as any temporal variation in the form of the display. The units of meaning in the output sequence, as in the input sequence, cannot be further decomposed without loss of meaning; for example, a transistor symbol has meaning for a circuit designer, whereas the individual lines making up the symbol do not have meaning. The meanings are often conveyed graphically by symbols and drawings, and can also be conveyed by sequences of characters.

The hardware *binding design*, also called the *lexical design*, is also part of the form of an interface. The binding determines how input and output units of meaning are actually formed from hardware primitives. The input primitives are whatever input devices are available, and the output primitives are the shapes (such as lines and characters) and their attributes (such as color and font) provided by the graphics subroutine package. Thus, for input, hardware binding is the design or selection of interaction techniques, as discussed in Chapter 8. For output, hardware binding design is the combining of display primitives and attributes to form icons and other symbols.

To illustrate these ideas, let us consider a simple furniture-layout program. Its conceptual design has as objects a room and different pieces of furniture. The relation between the objects is that the room contains the furniture. The operations on the furniture objects are Create, Delete, Move, Rotate, and Select; the operations on the room object are Save and Restore. The functional design is the detailed elaboration of the meanings of these relations and operations.

The sequence design might be to select first an object and then an operation on that object. The hardware-binding component of the input language might be to use a mouse to select commands from the menu, to select furniture objects, and to provide locations. The sequence of the output design defines the screen arrangement, including its partitioning into different areas and the exact placement of menus, prompts, and error messages. The hardware-binding level of the output design includes the text font, the line thickness and color, the color of filled regions, and the way in which output primitives are combined to create the furniture symbols.

Section 9.2 discusses some of the fundamental forms a user interface can take; Section 9.3 presents a set of design guidelines that applies to all four design levels. In Section 9.4, we present issues specific to input sequencing and binding; in Section 9.5, we describe visual design rules for output sequencing and binding. Section 9.6 outlines an overall methodology for user-interface design.

9.2 USER-INTERFACE STYLES

Three common styles for user–computer interfaces are *what you see is what you get, direct manipulation,* and *iconic.* In this section, we discuss each of these related but distinct ideas, considering their applicability, their advantages and disadvantages, and their relation to one another. There is also a brief discussion of other styles of user–computer interaction: menu selection, command languages, natural-language dialogue, and question–answer dialogue. These are not emphasized, because they are not unique to graphics. (Menus are the closest, but their use certainly predates graphics. Graphics does, however, permit use of icons rather than of text as menu elements, and provides richer possibilites for text typefaces and fonts and for menu decorations.) None of these styles are mutually exclusive; successful interfaces often meld elements of several styles to meet design objectives not readily met by one style alone.

9.2.1   What You See Is What You Get

What you see is what you get, or *WYSIWYG* (pronounced wiz-ee-wig), is fundamental to interactive graphics. The representation with which the user interacts on the display in a WYSIWYG interface is essentially the same as the image ultimately created by the application. Most, but not all, interactive graphics applications have some WYSIWYG component.

Many text editors (most assuredly a graphics application) have WYSIWYG interfaces. Text that is to be printed in boldface characters is displayed in boldface characters. With a non-WYSIWYG editor, the user sees control codes in the text. For example,

In this sentence, we show @b(bold), @i(italic), and @ub(underlined bold) text.

specifies the following hardcopy output:

In this sentence, we show **bold,** *italic*, and **underlined bold** text.

A non-WYSIWYG specification of a mathematical equation might be something like

@f(@i(u)@sub(max) − @i(u)@sub(min),@i(x)@sub(max) − @i(x)@sub(min))

to create the desired result

$$\frac{u_{max} - u_{min}}{x_{max} - x_{min}}.$$

In such non-WYSIWYG systems, users must translate between their mental image of the desired results and the control codes. Confirmation that the control codes reproduce the mental image is not given until the coded input is processed.

WYSIWYG has some drawbacks. Whenever the spatial and intensity or color resolution of the screen differs from that of the hardcopy device, it is difficult to create an *exact* match between the two. Chapter 13 discusses problems that arise in accurately reproducing color. More important, some applications cannot be implemented with a pure WYSIWYG interface. Consider first text processing, the most common WYSIWYG application. Many text processors provide heading categories to define the visual characteristics of chapter, section, subsection, and other headings. Thus, "heading type" is an object property that must be visually represented. But the heading type is not part of the final hardcopy, and thus, by definition, cannot be part of the display either. There are simple solutions, such as showing heading-type codes in the left margin of the display, but they are counter to the WYSIWYG philosophy. It is for this reason that WYSIWYG is sometimes called "what you see is *all* you get." As a second example, the robot arm in Fig.

7.1 does not reveal the existence of hierarchical relationships between the robot's body, arms, and so on, and it certainly does not show these relationships. These examples are intended not as indictments of WYSIWYG but rather as reminders of its limitations.

9.2.2 Direct Manipulation

A *direct-manipulation user interface* is one in which the objects, attributes, or relations that can be operated on are represented visually; operations are invoked by actions performed on the visual representations, typically using a mouse. That is, commands are not invoked explicitly by such traditional means as menu selection or keyboarding; rather, the command is implicit in the action on the visual representation. This representation may be text, such as the name of an object or property, or a more general graphic image, such as an icon. Later in this section, we discuss the circumstances under which textual and iconic forms of visual representation are appropriate.

The Macintosh interface uses direct manipulation in part, as shown in Fig. 9.1. Disks and files are represented as icons. Dragging a file's icon from one disk to another copies the file from one disk to the other; dragging to the trashcan icon deletes the file. In the earlier Xerox Star, dragging a file to a printer icon printed the file. Shneiderman [SHNE83], who coined the phrase "direct manipulation," discusses other examples of this technique.

Direct manipulation is sometimes presented as being the best user-interface style. It is certainly quite powerful and is especially easy to learn. But the Macintosh interface can be slow for experienced users in that they are forced to use direct manipulation when another

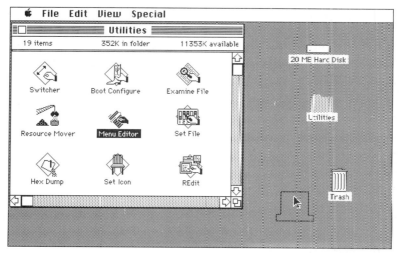

Fig. 9.1 The Macintosh screen. In the upper right is a disk icon; just below it is a directory icon, which is gray-toned to indicate that it is open. At the left is the open directory, with named icons representing the files within it. A file, represented by the icon outline around the cursor, is being dragged to the trashcan at the lower right. (Screen graphics © Apple Computer, Inc.)

style would generally be faster. Printing the file "Chapter 9" with direct manipulation requires the visual representation of the file to be found and selected, then the Print command is involved. Finding the file icon might involve scrolling through a large collection of icons. If the user knows the name of the file, typing "Print Chapter 9" is faster. Similarly, deleting all files of type "txt" requires finding and selecting each such file and dragging it to a trash can. Much faster is the UNIX-style command "rm *.txt", which uses the wild card * to find all files whose names end in ".txt."

An interface combining direct manipulation with command-language facilities can be faster to use than is one depending solely on direct manipulation. Note that direct manipulation encourages the use of longer, more descriptive names, and this tends to offset some of the speed gained from using typed commands. Some applications, such as programming, do not lend themselves to direct manipulation [HUTC86], except for simple introductory flowchart-oriented learning or for those constructs that in specialized cases can be demonstrated by example [MAUL89; MYER86].

Direct-manipulation interfaces typically incorporate other interface styles, usually commands invoked with menus or the keyboard. For instance, in most drafting programs, the user rotates an object with a command, not simply by pointing at it, grabbing a handle (as in Section 8.3.3), and rotating the handle. Indeed, it is often difficult to construct an interface in which all commands have direct-manipulation actions. This reinforces the point that a single interaction style may not be sufficient for a user interface: Mixing several styles is often better than is adhering slavishly to one style.

The form fill-in user interface is another type of direct manipulation. Here a form is filled in by pointing at a field and then typing, or by selecting from a list (a selection set) one of several possible values for the field. The limited functional domain of form fill-in and its obvious correspondence to filling in real forms makes direct manipulation a natural choice.

WYSIWYG and direct manipulation are separate and distinct concepts. For instance, the textual representation of a graphics image can be modified via direct manipulation, and the graphical image of a WYSIWYG system can be modified purely by a command-language interface. Especially when used together, however, the two concepts are powerful, easy to learn, and reasonably fast to use, as many successful user interfaces have demonstrated.

9.2.3 Iconic User Interfaces

An *icon* is a pictorial representation of an object, an action, a property, or some other concept. The user-interface designer often has the choice of using icons or words to represent such concepts. Note that the use of icons is not related to the direct-manipulation issue: Text can be directly manipulated just as well as icons can, and text can represent concepts, sometimes better than icons can.

Which is better, text or icons? As with most user-interface design questions, the answer is, "it depends." Icons have many advantages. Well-designed icons can be recognized more quickly than can words, and may also take less screen space. If carefully designed, icons can be language-independent, allowing an interface to be used in different countries.

Fig. 9.2 Icons used to represent common office objects.

Icon design has at least three separate goals, whose importance depends on the specific application at hand:

1. *Recognition*—how quickly and accurately the meaning of the icon can be recognized

2. *Remembering*—how well the icon's meaning can be remembered once learned

3. *Discrimination*—how well one icon can be distinguished from another.

See [BEWL83] for a report on experiments with several alternative icon designs; see [HEME82; MARC84] for further discussion of icon-design issues.

Icons that represent objects can be designed relatively easily; Fig. 9.2 shows a collection of such icons from various programs. Properties of objects can also be represented easily if each of their values can be given an appropriate visual representation. This certainly can be done for the properties used in interactive graphics editors, such as line thickness, texture, and font. Numeric values can be represented with a gauge or dial icon, as in Fig. 8.21.

Actions on objects (that is, commands) can also be represented by icons. There are several design strategies for doing this. First, the command icon can represent the *object* used in the real world to perform the action. Thus, scissors can be used for Cut, a brush for Paste, and a magnifying glass for Zoom. Figure 9.3 shows a collection of such command icons. These icons are potentially difficult to learn, since the user must first recognize what the icon *is*, then understand what the object represented *does*. This two-step understanding process is inherently less desirable than is the one-step process of merely recognizing what object an icon represents. To complicate matters further, suppose that the object might be used for several different actions. A brush, for example, can be used for spreading paste (to

Fig. 9.3 Command icons representing objects used to perform the corresponding command. (Copyright 1988 Claris Corporation. All rights reserved.)

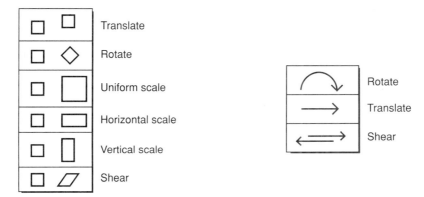

Fig. 9.4 Command icons indicating geometric transformations by showing a square before and after the commands are applied.

Fig. 9.5 Several abstract command icons for some of the actions depicted in Fig. 9.4. Not all geometric operations can be represented in this way.

paste something in place), and also for spreading paint (to color something). If both Paste and Paint could reasonably be commands in the same application, the brush icon could be ambiguous. Of course, sometimes only one interpretation will make sense for a given application.

Another design strategy for command icons is to show the command's *before and after* effects, as in Fig. 9.4 and Color Plates I.19–I.21. This works well if the representations for the object (or objects) are compact. If the command can operate on many different types of objects, however, then the specific object represented in the icon can mislead the user into thinking that the command is less general than it really is.

The NeXT user interface, implemented on a two-bit-per-pixel display, uses icons for a variety of purposes, as seen in Color Plate I.22.

A final design approach is to find a more *abstract representation* for the action. Typical examples are shown in Fig. 9.5. These representations can depend on some cultural-specific concept, such as the octagonal stop-sign silhouette, or can be more generic, such as X for Delete.

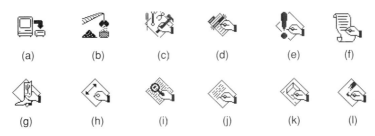

Fig. 9.6 Icons that represent Macintosh programs. What does each icon represent? In most cases, the icons suggest the type of information that is operated on or created. See Exercise 9.14 for the answers.

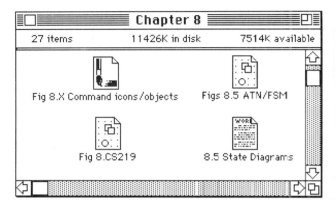

Fig. 9.7 The contents of a disk directory represented with icons and text. The icons help to distinguish one file from another. (Certain screen graphics © Apple Computer, Inc.)

Arbitrarily designed icons are not necessarily especially recognizable. Figure 9.6 shows a large number of icons used to represent Macintosh programs. We challenge you to guess what each program does! However, once learned, these icons seem to function reasonably well for remembering and discrimination.

Many visual interfaces to operating systems use icons to discriminate among files used by different application programs. All files created by an application share the same icon. If a directory or disk contains many different types of files, then the discrimination allowed by the icon shapes is useful (see Fig. 9.7). If all the files are of the same type, however, this discrimination is of no use whatsoever (see Fig. 9.8).

Icons can be poorly used. Some users dislike icons such as the trashcan, contending that such ideas are juvenile, "cute," and beneath their dignity. The designer may or may not agree with such an evaluation, but the user's opinion is usually more important than is

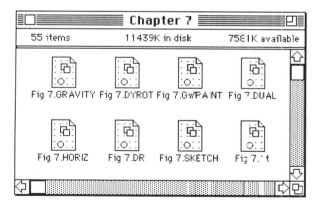

Fig. 9.8 The contents of a disk directory represented with icons and text. Since the files are all of the same type, the icons do not help to distinguish one file from another, and simply take up extra space. (Computer screen graphics © Apple Computer, Inc.)

the designer's. The user who dislikes a computer or program and thus develops a negative attitude is best taken seriously.

9.2.4   Other Dialogue Forms

The dialogue styles discussed in the previous section might be called "intrinsically graphical" in that our focus has been on graphically oriented interaction. A number of other dialogue forms are not intrinsically graphical but can be used in graphical applications. Four such forms are menus, command languages, natural-language dialogue, and question–answer dialogue. We have discussed many specific design issues concerning menus in the previous chapter. In this section, we briefly discuss more general issues involving each of these dialogue forms.

Menus are widely used in both graphical and nongraphical applications. In either case, however, the fundamental advantage of menus is that the user can work with what is called *recognition memory*, where visual images (textual or iconic menu items) are associated with already-familiar words and meanings. This contrasts with *recall memory*, where the user must recall from memory a command or concept in order to enter information into the computer. Menus reduce the memory load for users, and hence are especially attractive to novices. Menus, along with form fill-in, allow current selections to be indicated visually, further reducing the user's memory load and also allowing rapid input if the current selection is desired. On the other hand, menus limit the size of the selection set of alternatives, whereas some of the other dialogue styles do not.

Use of a *command language* is the traditional way to interact with a computer. This technique can accommodate large selection sets, is easy to extend (just add another command), and is fairly fast for experienced users who can type. Learning time is its major liability, with the need for typing skills a second factor. Errors are more likely with command languages than with menus, because of the possibility of typing and recall errors.

Natural-language dialogue is often proposed as the ultimate objective for interactive systems: If computers could understand our commands, typed or spoken in everyday English, then everyone would be able to use them. However, current voice recognizers with large vocabularies must be individually trained to recognize a particular user's voice; they also make mistakes, and must be corrected somehow. Typing long sentences is tedious. Also, because natural language does not bound the command set that an application program must handle, and also can be quite ambiguous, users of natural-language interfaces tend to make requests that cannot be fulfilled, which leads to frustration of the user and poor performance of the system.

This problem can be overcome in limited-domain (and hence limited-vocabulary) natural-language systems, in which users are familiar with the system's capabilities and hence are unlikely to make unreasonable requests. Drawing programs and operating systems are examples of such systems.

There is a fundamental flaw, however, in the argument that natural language interaction is the ultimate objective. If the argument were true, we would be satisfied to interact with one another solely by means of telephone and/or keyboard communications. It is for this reason that voice input of natural language to an interactive graphics application program is

TABLE 9.1 COMPARISON OF SEVEN USER INTERFACE STYLES

	WYSI-WYG*	Direct manipulation	Menu selection	Form fill-in	Command language	Natural language	Q/A dialogue
learning time	low	low	med	low	high	low	low
speed of use		med	med	high	high	med	low
error-proneness	low	low	low	low	high	high	low
extensibility	low	low	med	med	high	high	high
typing skill required		none	none	high	high	high**	high

*WYSIWYG has several blank fields because it is not a complete interface style, since it must be accompanied by some means of entering commands.
**Assuming keyboard input; none for voice-recognizer input.

most likely to be used in combination with other dialogue styles, to allow overlapped use of the voice and hands to speed interaction. After all, this is exactly how we work in the real world: we point at things and talk about them. This powerful concept was compellingly demonstrated a decade ago in the "Put-that-There" [BOLT80; BOLT84] program for manipulating objects. In this system, the user can move an object by pointing at it while saying "put that;" pointing elsewhere, and saying "there." A recent study of a VLSI design program using voice input of commands combined with mouse selection of objects and positions found that users worked 60 percent faster than did those who had just a mouse and keyboard [MART89].

Question–answer dialogue is computer-initiated, and the user response is constrained to a set of expected answers. Using a keyboard for input, the user can give any answer. If the set of expected answers is small, the question can include the possible answers; menu selection might even be provided instead of typing as a means for the user to respond. In the limit, question–answer dialogue becomes a sequential set of menu selections. A common failing of instances of this dialogue form is the inability to go back several steps to correct an answer. A more general problem with the sequentiality implied by this form is that of context: The user has only the context of the past and current questions to assist in interpreting the current question. With a form fill-in dialogue, by contrast, the user can see all the fields to be entered, and so can quickly tell, for instance, whether an apartment number in an address goes in the street-address field or in a separate apartment-number field.

Table 9.1 compares user-interface dialogue styles. A much more extensive discussion of the pros and cons of many of these styles can be found in [SHNE86].

9.3 IMPORTANT DESIGN CONSIDERATIONS

In this section, we describe a number of design principles to help ensure good human factors in a design: be consistent, provide feedback, minimize error possibilities, provide error recovery, accommodate multiple skill levels, and minimize memorization. Application of these principles is generally considered necessary, although by no means is sufficient, for a successful design. These and other principles are discussed more fully in [FOLE74; GAIN84; HANS71; MAYH90; RUBE84; SHNE86].

9.3.1 Be Consistent

A *consistent* system is one in which the conceptual model, functionality, sequencing, and hardware bindings are uniform and follow a few simple rules, and hence lack exceptions and special conditions. The basic purpose of consistency is to allow the user to *generalize* knowledge about one aspect of the system to other aspects. Consistency also helps to avoid the frustration induced when a system does not behave in an understandable and logical way. The best way to achieve this consistency is through a careful top-down design of the overall system.

Simple examples of consistency in the output portion of a user interface are

- The same codings are always employed. Colors always code information in the same way, just as red always means stop, and green always means go.
- System-status messages are shown at a logically (although not necessarily physically) fixed place.
- Menu items are always displayed in the same relative position within a menu, so that users can allow ''muscle memory'' to help in picking the desired item.

Examples of consistency in the input portion are

- Keyboard characters—such as carriage return, tab, line feed, and backspace—always have the same function and can be used whenever text is being input.
- Global commands—such as Help, Status, and Cancel—can be invoked at any time.
- Generic commands—such as Move, Copy, and Delete—are provided and can be applied, with predictable results, to any type of object in the system.

We should, however, remember Emerson's observation that ''A foolish consistency is the hobgoblin of little minds'' [EMER03]. Consistency can conflict with other design objectives. For instance, if dragging a file icon to the trash deletes the file, what should happen when a file icon is dragged to an electronic-mail outbox? Should the file be sent and then deleted, for consistency with dragging to the trash? Or should a copy of the file be sent? If a file is dragged to a printer icon to print the file, should the file be printed and then deleted, for consistency with dragging to the trash? Surely in these latter two cases the file should not be deleted. The *law of least astonishment,* a higher design principle, suggests that doing what the user is likely to consider normal or reasonable is more important than is maintaining pure consistency.

Figure 9.9 shows how state diagrams can help to identify inconsistency. We can see here that help is available only from the move state, not from the other states. A mixed strategy is used to let users change their minds once an action sequence has been initiated. From the move and delete states there is a Cancel command, whereas the rotate state has an Undo command. The sequence of object/operation varies: for Move and Delete, the sequence is operation then object, whereas it is the reverse for rotation. The feedback strategy is also mixed: dynamic for moving, static for rotation.

Reisner demonstrated experimentally an intuitively expected result: Given two functionally equivalent user interfaces, new users make fewer errors and learn more quickly with

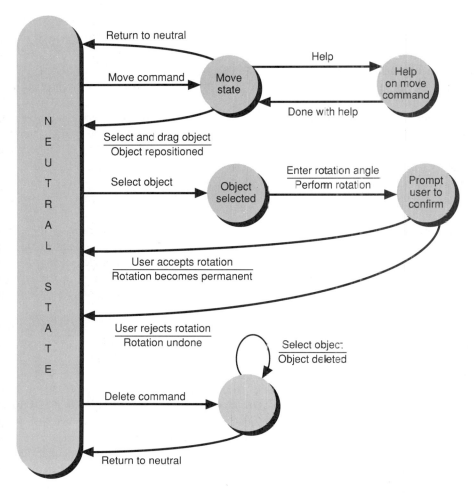

Fig. 9.9 State diagram of a user interface with an inconsistent syntax.

one that has a simpler syntactic structure [REIS82]. Thus, another useful design objective to apply is simply to minimize the number of different syntactic structures.

At the functional level, consistency requires the use of *generic commands* that apply across as broad a range as possible. For example, chairs and desks should be moved in the same way in the room-layout program discussed previously; files should be opened, deleted, and saved from within application programs with the same generic file-manipulation commands.

9.3.2   Provide Feedback

Have you ever tried conversing with a partner who neither smiles nor nods, and who responds only when forced to do so? It is a frustrating experience, because there is little or no indication that the partner understands what you are saying. Feedback is as essential in conversation with a computer as it is in human conversation. The difference is that, in normal conversation with another person, many sources of feedback (gestures, body language, facial expressions, eye contact) are usually provided without conscious action by either participant. By contrast, a workstation gives little automatic feedback (just the "power on" light and perhaps the whir of a fan), so all feedback must be planned and programmed.

Feedback can be given at three possible levels, corresponding to the functional, sequencing, and hardware-binding (semantic, syntactic, and lexical) levels of user-interface design. The designer must consciously consider each level and explicitly decide whether feedback should be present, and, if it should be, in what form. The lowest level of feedback is the hardware level. Each user action with an input device should cause immediate and obvious feedback: for instance, characters typed on a keyboard are echoed, and mouse movements are echoed by the cursor.

Feedback at the sequencing-design level occurs as each unit (word) of the input language (command, position, object, etc.) is accepted by the system. A selected object or menu command is highlighted, so the user can know that actions have been accepted (i.e., the "words" have been understood). Similar forms of feedback are prompting for the next input, lighting the function key that has just been pressed, and echoing verbal (speech) input with text output.

Another form of sequencing feedback should occur when a complete sequence has been input and is found to be well formed. This acknowledgment of receipt of a proper command is generally needed only if processing the command itself will take more than 1 or 2 seconds.

Another type of functional feedback—some indication that the computer is at least working on the problem—is necessary only if completion of the operation will take more than a few seconds. (In the absence of such feedback, users have been known to express their frustration physically on the workstation, or even on the application designer!) Such feedback can take many forms; particularly attractive is a dial or gauge to indicate the percentage complete. The user can quickly determine whether a coffee break is in order. In an experiment, Myers found a strong user preference for such indicators [MYER85].

The most useful and welcome form of functional feedback tells the user that the requested operation has been completed. This is usually done with a new or modified display that explicitly shows the results of the operation.

It is useful to distinguish between problem-domain and control-domain feedback. *Problem-domain* feedback concerns the actual objects being manipulated: their appearance, their position, their existence. *Control-domain* feedback has to do with the mechanisms for controlling the interactive system: status, current and default values, menus, and dialogue boxes.

Problem-domain feedback is needed if users can see just part of a large drawing, so that they can know which part of the world is being displayed. Figure 9.10 shows one way to do this. The approach can be even more effective with two displays—one for the overview, the other for the detail. In either case, the rectangle in the overview indicates which part of the drawing is being shown in the detailed display. Panning and zooming are generally effected by dragging and resizing the overview rectangle. Figure 9.11 shows how increasing

Overview   View
area   indicator

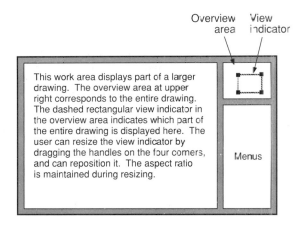

This work area displays part of a larger
drawing. The overview area at upper
right corresponds to the entire drawing.
The dashed rectangular view indicator in
the overview area indicates which part of
the entire drawing is displayed here. The
user can resize the view indicator by
dragging the handles on the four corners,
and can reposition it. The aspect ratio
is maintained during resizing.

Menus

Fig. 9.10 The view indicator is used both to give an overview and to control what is
displayed in the work area.

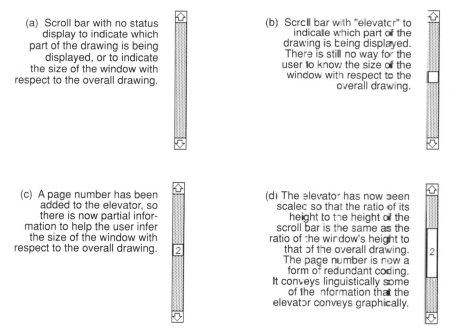

(a) Scroll bar with no status
display to indicate which
part of the drawing is being
displayed, or to indicate
the size of the window with
respect to the overall drawing.

(b) Scroll bar with "elevator" to
indicate which part of the
drawing is being displayed.
There is still no way for the
user to know the size of the
window with respect to the
overall drawing.

(c) A page number has been
added to the elevator, so
there is now partial information to help the user infer
the size of the window with
respect to the overall drawing.

(d) The elevator has now been
scaled so that the ratio of its
height to the height of the
scroll bar is the same as the
ratio of the window's height to
that of the overall drawing.
The page number is now a
form of redundant coding.
It conveys linguistically some
of the information that the
elevator conveys graphically.

Fig. 9.11 Four different levels of feedback in scroll bars, ranging from none in (a) to
redundant coding in (d).

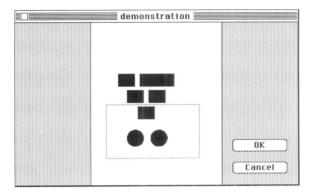

Fig. 9.12 The overview mode in MacPaint. Because the screen is very small, the overview alternates with the normal, more detailed view of the drawing. The user drags the rectangular dashed box to the desired area, and selects "OK" to see the detailed view of the enclosed area. (Copyright 1988 Claris Corporation. All rights reserved.)

amounts of feedback can be built into window scroll bars. Another approach to orienting the viewer is used in MacPaint, as shown in Fig. 9.12.

An important type of control-domain feedback is *current settings*. Current settings can be shown in a feedback area. If the menus or other tools by which settings are selected can always be displayed, then the current setting can be indicated there, as in Fig. 9.13. The pull-out menus illustrated in Fig. 8.14 also show current settings.

The positioning of feedback is important. There is a natural tendency to designate a fixed area of the screen for feedback and error messages. This can destroy *visual continuity*, however, since the user's eyes must move between the work area and the message area. Indeed, users often do not notice messages in these fixed areas. Adding audio feedback can eliminate this problem.

Placing the feedback where the user is looking, which is generally at or near the cursor, is especially attractive. Tilbrook's Newswhole system [TILB76] was one of the first to employ this idea; it uses a seated Buddha to encourage the user to be patient during computational delays, and a thumbs-down symbol to indicate a mistake.

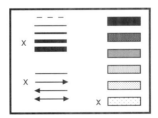

Fig. 9.13 In this menu of graphic attributes, the x indicates the current setting. The user has constant feedback if the menu can be permanently visible. If not, a more compact form of permanent feedback should be used.

9.3.3 Minimize Error Possibilities

Don't set the user up for a fall is another way to state this objective. For example,

- Do not offer menu options that will elicit an "illegal selection, command not valid now" message
- Do not let the user select Delete if there is nothing to be deleted
- Do not let the user try to change the font of the currently selected object if the object is not a text string
- Do not let the user Paste when the clipboard is empty
- Do not let the user Copy when nothing is selected to be copied
- Do not let the user select a curve-smoothing command when the currently selected object is not a curve.

In all these instances, the system should instead disable unavailable items and alert the user by changing the menu item's appearance—for instance, by making it gray instead of black.

These are all examples of *context sensitivity*: The system provides the user with only those commands that are valid in the current context or mode. When there is a context, the system should guide the user to work within that context and should make it difficult or impossible for the user to do things that are not permissible in that context.

Another aspect of this objective is to avoid *side effects*, which are results the user has not been led to expect. The classic side effect is the print command that also deletes the file being printed. Side effects arise from poor design or ineffective communication with the user regarding what a command does.

9.3.4 Provide Error Recovery

We all make mistakes. Imagine not having a backspace key on your computer keyboard! The effect on your productivity, as you became much more cautious in typing, would be devastating. There is ample experimental evidence that people are more productive if their mistakes can be readily corrected. With good error recovery, the user is free to explore unlearned system facilities without "fear of failure." This freedom encourages exploratory learning, one of the major ways in which system features are learned. We discuss four types of error recovery: Undo, Abort, Cancel, and Correct.

The most serious type of error is functional: the user has mistakenly invoked one or a series of commands and has obtained unanticipated results. An *Undo* command is needed to reverse the results of the command. There are two types of undo: single level and multilevel. The single-level undo can reverse only the most recently executed command. This Undo itself is a command, so the second of two successive Undo commands undoes the first Undo, returning the system to its state prior to the two Undo commands.

In contrast, a multilevel Undo operates on the stack of previous commands. The actual number of commands stacked up and thus able to be undone is implementation-dependent; in some cases, all commands since the session began are saved. With a multilevel undo, a *Redo* command is also needed, so that, if the user backs up too far in the command stack, the most recently undone command can be redone. Neither Undo nor Redo is entered on the stack. Several tricky issues concerning Redo are discussed in [VITT84]. For a single level, Undo and Redo are mutually exclusive: One or the other, but not both, can be available at any given time. For multilevel, Undo and Redo can be available at the same time.

Users often need help in understanding the scope of the Undo command (i.e., how much work the command will undo). They also are often confused about whether Undo applies to windowing commands, such as scrolling, as well as to application commands. If the Undo command is in a menu, the menu-item text can indicate what will be undone; instead of "undo," the entry could be "undo copy" or "undo deletion." Kurlander and Feiner have developed a graphical way to show the history of user actions and the scope of Undo, shown in Color Plate I.23 [KURL88; KURL90].

A form of undo is sometimes provided as an *explicit-accept, explicit-reject* step. After a command is carried out and its results are shown on the display, the user must accept or reject the results before doing anything else. This step adds to the number of user actions required to accomplish a task, but does force the user to think twice before confirming acceptance of dangerous actions. However, an Undo command is usually preferable because an explicit action is required only to reject the results of a command; the command is implicitly accepted when the next command (other than the Undo command) is entered. Hence, we call undo an *implicit-accept, explicit-reject* strategy.

No matter how undo is provided, its implementation requires extra programming, especially for commands that involve major changes to data structures. An easier, although less satisfactory, alternative to undo is to require the user explicitly to confirm commands for which there is no undo. This is commonly used for the file-delete command.

A user may realize that a functional-level mistake has been made while a command is still being performed. This illustrates the need for an *Abort* command to terminate prematurely a currently executing command. Like Undo, Abort must restore the system to its exact state prior to initiation of the aborted command. In fact, Abort and Undo can be thought of as essentially the same command: They both reverse the most recently specified functional-level action. A user-interface design might make both actions available with the same name.

A less dramatic type of error occurs when the user is partway through specifying information required to carry out some command, and says, "Oops, I don't really want to do this!" A poorly designed interface gives the user no choice but to proceed with the command, after which an Undo or Abort (if available) is used to recover. A well-designed interface lets the user back out of such a situation with a *Cancel* command. This is especially common with a form fill-in dialogue, where a Cancel command is often available on the form, as in Fig. 8.32. Note that Cancel can also be thought of as a specialized Undo command, with the system reverting to the state prior to the current command.

In a less serious type of error, the user may want to *correct* one of the units of information needed for a command. The dialogue style in use determines how easy to make such corrections are. Command-language input can be corrected by multiple backspaces to the item in error, followed by reentry of the corrected information and all the information that was deleted. If the system has line-editing capabilities, then the cursor can be moved back to the erroneous information without the intervening information being deleted. Form fill-in allows simple corrections as well, whereas question–answer and menu dialogues are not so forgiving. The dynamic interaction techniques discussed in Chapter 8 provide a form of error recovery: for instance, the position of an object being dragged into place is easy to change.

9.3.5 Accommodate Multiple Skill Levels

Many interactive graphics systems must be designed for a spectrum of users, ranging from the completely new and inexperienced user through the user who has worked with the system for thousands of hours. Methods of making a system usable at all skill levels are accelerators, prompts, help, extensibility, and hiding complexity.

New users normally are most comfortable with menus, forms, and other dialogue styles that provide considerable prompting, because this prompting tells them what to do and facilitates learning. More experienced users, however, place more value on speed of use, which requires use of function keys and keyboard commands. Fast interaction techniques that replace slower ones are called *accelerators*. Typical accelerators, such as one-letter commands to supplement mouse-based menu selection, have been illustrated in previous sections. The Sapphire window manager [MYER84], taking this idea even further, provides three rather than two ways to invoke some commands: pointing at different areas of the window banner and clicking different mouse buttons, a standard pop-up menu, and keyboard commands.

The Macintosh uses accelerators for some menu commands, as was shown in Fig. 8.13. Another approach is to number menu commands, so that a number can be typed from the keyboard, or a command can be selected with the cursor. Alternatively, the command name or abbreviation could be typed.

One of the fastest accelerators is the use of multiple clicks on a mouse button. For instance, the Macintosh user can select a file (represented as an icon) by clicking the mouse button with the cursor on the icon. Opening the file, the typical next step, can be done with a menu selection, an accelerator key, or an immediate second button click. The two rapid clicks are considerably faster than is either of the other two methods. From within applications, another scheme is used to open files, as illustrated in Fig. 9.14. The dialogue box permits a file name to be selected either by pointing or by typing. If the name is typed,

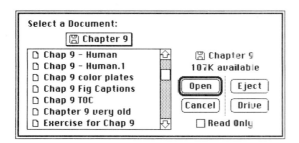

Fig. 9.14 Opening files from within a Macintosh program. The user enters the Open command, either by menu selection or with a two-key chord, causing the dialogue box to appear. The highlighted file can be opened with the ''open'' button or with the carriage-return key. The user can highlight a new file by selecting it with the cursor or by typing some or all of its name. Therefore, the user can open a file using only the keyboard, by entering the two-key chord, a partial file name, and the return key. (Computer screen graphics © Apple Computer, Inc.)

autocompletion permits the user to type only enough characters for the name to be specified unambiguously. Double clicking on a file name opens the file immediately.

Another form of accelerator is to provide command-line input as an alternative to the other styles. As users gain experience, they use the command line more and more. This transition can be aided by displaying the command-line equivalent of commands that are entered in other ways.

Unlike feedback, which acknowledges specific user actions, the purpose of *prompts* is to suggest what to do next. The more experienced the user, the less prompting is appropriate, especially if prompting is obtrusive and slows down the interaction or uses much of the screen. Many systems provide several levels of prompting controllable by the user; the inexperienced can be "led by the hand," whereas the experienced can proceed without the prompts.

Prompting can take many forms. The most direct is a displayed message that explains explicitly what to do next, such as "Specify location." A speech synthesizer can give explicit aural instructions to the user. Subtler forms of prompting are also available. On a function-key box, buttons eligible for selection can be illuminated. A prominent tracking cross or cursor can be displayed when a position must be input; a blinking underline cursor can indicate that a text string is to be input; a scale or dial can be displayed when a value is desired. Direct-manipulation graphical interfaces implicitly provide prompts: the icons that can be manipulated are the prompt.

A *help* facility allows the user to obtain additional information about system concepts, typical tasks, various commands and the methods used to invoke them, and interaction techniques. Ideally, help can be requested from any point in the interactive dialogue, always with the same mechanism. The return from help should leave the system in exactly the same state as when help was invoked, and the help should be context-sensitive. For example, if help is invoked while the system is awaiting a command, a list of commands available in this state should be shown (with menus or function keys, this may be unnecessary). The Help command followed by a command name should yield more information about the command. If help is requested while the parameters of a command are being entered, details about the parameters should be provided. A second Help command should produce more detailed information and perhaps allow more general browsing through online documentation. Sukaviriya [SUKA88] developed a system to show the user an animation of how to accomplish a task, using the current context as the basis of the animation. Some help capabilities based on hypertext systems allow the user to follow complex sets of links among various help topics.

An easy way to invoke help is to point at the entity on the screen about which help is desired. The entity could be a menu item, a status indicator (the help should explain the status and how to change it), a window banner, a scroll bar, or a previously created application object (the help should explain what the object is and what operations can be applied to it). This approach, however, can be used only for visible objects, not for more abstract concepts or for tasks that must be performed with a series of commands.

A help capability is appropriate even if prompts and menus are displayed, because it gives the user an opportunity to receive more detailed information than can be provided in a short prompt. Even experienced users forget details, particularly in a large and complex application.

Expert systems are beginning to be integrated into user interfaces to provide help that not only is context-sensitive, but also is tailored to individual user profiles. These profiles are developed automatically by the system as a new user and the system interact and learn more about each other, just as teachers learn about their students and custom-tailor their suggestions.

Making the user interface *extensible* means letting the user add additional functionality to the interface by defining new commands as combinations of existing commands. The key is to be able to save and replay sequences of user actions. A particularly appealing macro-definition capability is one in which user actions are automatically saved in a trace file. To create a macro, the user edits the trace file to identify the start and end of the macro, replace literals with parameters, and names the macro. Several commercial applications, such as Ashton-Tate's Full Impact, have such capabilities; Olsen has developed a particularly sophisticated prototype system [OLSE88].

Hiding complexity can allow new users to learn basic commands and to start doing productive work without becoming bogged down with specifying options, learning infrequently used specialized commands, or going through complicated start-up procedures. On the other hand, powerful systems of necessity have many commands, often with many variations. The solution to this quandary is to design the entire set of commands so that it has a small "starter kit" of commands. Default values (current or initial settings) that follow the law of least astonishment can often be useful to achieve this goal.

For example, a chart-making program should allow the user to request a pie chart, specify some data, and immediately see the chart. If the user is dissatisfied with some details of the chart layout, she should be able, say, to modify the radius of the pie, to change the color or texture of each pie slice, to add annotations, to change the text face or font used to display the data values, or to change the position of the data values displayed with each pie slice. But the user should not be forced to specify each of these explicitly when initially creating the chart.

Another design strategy is to make complicated and advanced commands available only via keyboard commands or function keys. This approach keeps the menus smaller and makes the system simpler and less intimidating. Alternatively, two or more sets of menus can be provided, each with successively more commands included.

Yet another way to hide complexity is to use control keys to modify the meaning of other commands. For instance, the Macintosh window manager normally activates the window that the user selects and drags to a new position. The more advanced user can reposition a window without activating it by holding down the control key (called the *command key* on the Macintosh, in appropriate deference to computer-naive users). New users simply are not told about this feature.

9.3.6 Minimize Memorization

Interface designs sometimes force unnecessary memorization. In one design-drafting system, objects are referred to by numeric rather than by alphanumeric names. To appreciate what that means, we can imagine an interactive operating system in which file names are numeric. The remembering and learning tool of mnemonic names would be unavailable, forcing rote memorization or the use of auxiliary written aids. Of course, explicit picking of displayed objects or icons further eliminates the need for memorization. It is important to invoke the user's recognition rather than recall memory whenever possible.

In one interactive graphing system, a command such as "Plot years gross net" produces a trend chart of yearly gross income and net income on a single set of axes. A reasonable way to control the style of a line is to use a command such as "Linestyle net dash" (to plot the net income with a dashed line). Unhappily, the actual command is of the form "Linestyle 3 dash." The "3" refers to the third variable named in the most recent "Plot" command—in this case, net. Since the most recent Plot command is not generally on the screen, the user must remember the order of the parameters.

Some help systems completely obscure the work area, forcing the user to memorize the context in order to interpret the help message. Then, once he understands the help information, the user must remember it while returning to the context in which the error occurred. Window managers solve this problem; help information is in one window, the application is in another.

9.4   MODES AND SYNTAX

Loosely defined, a *mode* is a state or collection of states in which just a subset of all possible user-interaction tasks can be performed. Examples of modes are these:

- A state in which only commands applicable to the currently selected object are available

- A state in which a dialogue box must be completed before another operation can be performed

- A state for making drawings in a document-preparation system in which separate programs are used to edit text, to make drawings, and to lay out the document

- A state in which available commands are determined by the current data-tablet overlay.

Thus, modes provide a context within which the system and user operate.

There are two kinds of modes: harmful ones and useful ones. A *harmful mode*, as discussed by Tesler [TESL81] and by Smith and colleagues [SMIT82], lasts for a period of time, is not associated with any particular object, is not visible to the user, and serves no meaningful role. Harmful modes confuse users; users get stuck in them and cannot get out, or users forget in which mode they are and attempt to invoke commands that are not available, potentially creating errors. Modes that decrease user productivity are harmful.

On the other hand, *useful modes* narrow the choices of what to do next, so prompts and help can be more specific and menus can be shorter and thus easier to traverse. A well-organized mode structure can reduce the burden on the user's memory and can help to organize knowledge about the interface into categories based on the mode. Useful modes increase user productivity.

Useful modes clearly indicate the current mode, provide feedback to show what commands are available, and include an easy, obvious, and fast means for exiting from the mode. Window managers provide highly visible modes, since each window represents a different mode; mode switching is effected by deactivating one window and activating another.

Users can be made aware of short-lived modes by a state of heightened muscle tension while in the mode. The "button-down–dynamic feedback–button-up" interaction techniques discussed in Chapter 8 make the user aware of the mode through the muscle tension involved in holding down the mouse button [BUXT86].

Command-language syntax has a major influence on the mode structure of a user interface. The traditional prefix syntax of Command, parameter 1, . . ., parameter n locks the user into a mode as soon as the command is specified: Only parameters can be entered, possibly in a required order. Mechanisms for error correction (Section 9.3.4) are especially important here, because otherwise the user who erroneously selects a command must continue the potentially lengthy parameter-specification process.

One of the difficulties of prefix syntax is solved by a process called *factoring* or *orthogonalization*. Commands are provided for setting each of the parameters to a current value; parameters may also have an initial (default) value. Consider, for instance, the following unfactored command syntax, where an initial capital letter indicates a command, and lowercase letters indicate parameters:

Draw_line   point point line_style line_thickness line_intensity

We can factor out the attribute specifications into either three separate commands or one overall attribute-setting command. Hence, the user would go through the sequence

Set_attributes	attribute_values	{Only if the current attribute values are inappropriate}
Draw_line	point point	

We can factor this sequence further by introducing the concept of a *current point*, which is selected by the user before she invokes the Draw_line command:

Set_attributes	attribute_values	{Only if the current attribute values are inappropriate}
Select_point	point	{Select start point}
Select_point	point	{Select end point}
Draw_line		{Draw_line has no parameters— all have been factored out}

Completely parameterless commands are not necessarily desirable. Here, for example, specifying points and then telling the system to connect them by a line eliminates the ability to do rubberband line drawing.

What about applications in which the user tends to perform the same command several times in sequence, each time on different objects? This situation suggests using a *command-mode* syntax in which the command is entered once, followed by an arbitrary number of parameter sets for the command. For instance, the syntax to delete objects could be as follows:

Delete_object	{Establish Delete_object command mode}
object	
object	
object	
⋮	
any command	{Establish new command mode}

Delete_object establishes a deletion mode so that each object selected thereafter is deleted, until any other command is selected. Note that command mode implies a prefix syntax.

If we factor out the object parameter from the command whose syntax is

Delete_object   object

we introduce the concept of a *currently selected object*, or CSO. We also need a new command, Select_object, to create a mode in which there is a CSO; this CSO can then be operated on by the Delete_object command:

Select_object	object	{Use if no object is selected, or if another CSO is desired}
Delete_object		{No parameter—the object has been factored out}

The parameter factoring has created a *postfix* syntax: The object is specified first by selection, and then the command is given. This is an especially attractive technique if the user is working with a pointing device, because we have a natural tendency to point at something before saying what to do with it; the converse order is much less natural [SUKA90].

The currently selected object is a useful concept, because the user can perform a series of operations on one object, and then move on to another. Furthermore, the Select_object command usually can be made implicit: The user simply points at the object to be selected and clicks a button. This means that factoring does not need to create extra steps.

Recall that command mode has a prefix syntax. Can its advantages be retained if a postfix syntax is preferred? The answer is yes, *if* a Repeat command, to repeat the last nonselect command, can be made available easily, say by a button-down on a multibutton mouse. If so, the user action sequence to delete several objects could be

Select_object	object	{Establish a CSO}
Delete_object		{Delete the CSO}
Select_object	object	{A new CSO}
Repeat		{Single button depression to delete}
Select_object	object	{A new CSO}
Repeat		{Single button depression to delete}
⋮		

Compare this to the action sequence that would be used with a true command mode:

Delete_object
object
object
object
⋮

Assuming that Select_object requires just a point and click, the extra steps needed to use Repeat_last_operation with an object mode, as opposed to using a command mode, are a single button-push per deletion.

Another sequencing alternative is the arbitrary *free-form syntax (no fix syntax)*, which permits intermixing of different syntaxes. Whether the user specifies an object and then an action or an action and then an object, the action is carried out on the object. For example,

Set_attributes	attribute values	
Select_object	object1	{Attributes applied to object1}
Set_attributes	attribute values	
Select_object	object2	{Attributes applied to object2}
Select_object	object3	
Set_attributes	attribute values	{Attributes applied to object3}

Note that this syntactic structure cannot assume a currently selected object; if it did, then the second Set_attributes command would immediately operate on object1, rather than on object2.

Command and currently selected-object modes can be used with a free-form syntax *if* a Do_it command is added, so the user can tell the system to carry out the current command on the currently selected object. This command does, however, add another user action, as the following sequence illustrates:

Select_object	object	{Establish a CSO}
Set_attributes	attribute values	{Establish a current command}
Do_it		{CSO receives new attributes}
Copy		{Establish a new current command}
Select_object	object	{Establish a new CSC}
Do_it		{Copy CSO; copy is now the CSO}
Do_it		{CSO copied; new copy is the CSO}

An alternative to this free-form syntax is a *mode-sensitive syntax*, which differentiates between the two sequences to make the Set_attributes command mode-sensitive:

Set_attributes	attribute values	{No CSO at this point}
Select_object	object	

and

Select_object	object	{Establish a CSO}
Set_attributes	attribute values	

Mode-sensitivity is a special case of a more general context-sensitivity, by which the effect of a command depends on the current context. In the first of the preceding sequences, where there is no CSO when Set_attributes is used, the attribute values become the global default values that are applied when new objects are created. In the second sequence, where there is a CSO, the attribute values apply to the CSO and do not change the global default values. That is, the existence or nonexistence of a CSO, which is a mode, determines the effect of the command. This technique creates a more powerful set of commands without adding any explicit new commands; however, the user must have mode feedback to know how the command will behave. Also, some users are confused by this approach, because it seems inconsistent until the rules are understood.

The general concept of factoring is important for several reasons. First, new users do not need to be concerned with factored parameters that have default values, which improves learning speed. Values for factored parameters do not need to be specified unless the current values are unacceptable, which improves speed of use. Factoring out the object from the command creates the concept of a CSO, a natural one for interactive graphics with its pointing devices. Finally, factoring reduces or eliminates the short-term modes created by prefix commands with multiple parameters. Factoring has been incorporated into a user-interface design tool so that the designer can request that specific parameters be factored; the necessary auxiliary command (Select_object) is introduced automatically [FOLE89].

There are several variations on the CSO concept. First, when an object is created, it does not need to become the CSO if there is already a CSO. Similarly, when the CSO is deleted, some other object (the most recent CSO or an object close to the CSO) can become the new CSO. In addition, a currently selected set (CSS) made of up several selected objects can be used.

9.5   VISUAL DESIGN

The visual design of a user–computer interface affects both the user's initial impression of the interface and the system's longer-term usefulness. Visual design comprises all the graphic elements of an interface, including overall screen layout, menu and form design, use of color, information codings, and placement of individual units of information with respect to one another. Good visual design strives for clarity, consistency, and attractive appearance.

9.5.1   Visual Clarity

If the meaning of an image is readily apparent to the viewer, we have *visual clarity*. An important way to achieve visual clarity is to use the visual organization of information to reinforce and emphasize the underlying logical organization. There are just a few basic visual-organization rules for accomplishing this end. Their use can have a major influence, as some of the examples will show. These rules, which have been used by graphic designers for centuries [MARC80], were codified by the Gestalt psychologist Wertheimer [WERT39] in the 1930s. They describe how a viewer organizes individual visual stimuli into larger overall forms (hence the term *Gestalt*, literally ''shape'' or ''form,'' which denotes an emphasis on the whole, rather than on the constituent parts).

The visual-organization rules concern similarity, proximity, closure, and good continuation. The rule of *similarity* states that two visual stimuli that have a common property are seen as belonging together. Likewise, the rule of *proximity* states that two visual stimuli that are close to each other are seen as belonging together. The rule of *closure* says that, if a set of stimuli almost encloses an area or could be interpreted as enclosing an area, the viewer sees the area. The *good-continuation* rule states that, given a juncture of lines, the viewer sees as continuous those lines that are smoothly connected.

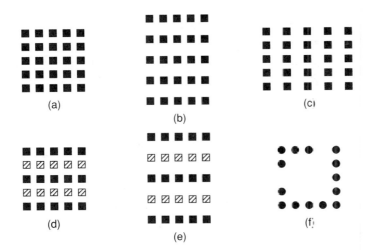

Fig. 9.15 Gestalt rules. In (a), the squares are undifferentiated. In (b), proximity induces a horizontal grouping; in (c), it induces a vertical grouping. In (d), similarity induces a horizontal grouping, which is further reinforced in (e) by a combination of proximity and similarity. In (f), closure induces a square of dots, even though two dots are missing.

Figures 9.15 and 9.16 give examples of these rules and also show how some of them can be combined to reinforce one another. Figure 9.17 shows a form before and after the visual organization rules have been applied. In part (a), everything is near to everything else, so the underlying logical groupings are unclear. Similarity (here, in the sense of being contained in a box) and proximity bind together the patterns and the choice buttons in (b). Closure completes the boxes, which are broken by the label.

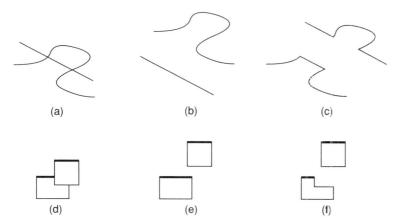

Fig. 9.16 More Gestalt rules. The two intersecting lines in (a) could be interpreted as shown in either (b) or (c). Good continuation favors (b). In a more applied context, the two overlapping windows of (d) could be interpreted as shown in either (e) or (f). Good continuation favors (e).

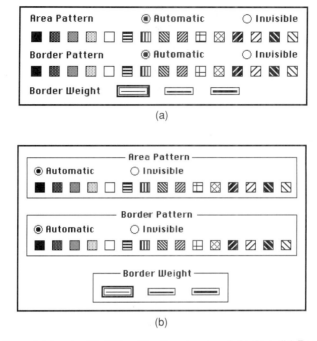

Fig. 9.17 (a) Form laid out with little attention to visual design. (b) Form created using visual grouping and closure to reinforce the logical relationships among the visual elements of the form. (Screen shots © 1983–1989 Microsoft Corporation. Reprinted with permission from Microsoft Corporation.)

The rules are applied to improve menu organization in Fig. 9.18. The leftmost organization is visually unstructured and almost conceals its logical organization. The rightmost menu uses proximity to form groups and similarity of indentation to show the two-level logical structure. In Fig. 9.19, the similarity rule has been used in two different ways (similar typographical style, similar level of indentation) to reinforce logical organization.

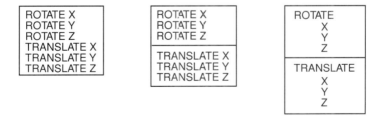

Fig. 9.18 Three designs for the same menu, showing application of visual design techniques.

A MAJOR CATEGORY
A LESS MAJOR CATEGORY
AN EVEN LESS MAJOR CATEGORY
AN EVEN LESS MAJOR CATEGORY
THE LEAST MAJOR CATEGORY
THE LEAST MAJOR CATEGORY
AN EVEN LESS MAJOR CATEGORY

(a)

A MAJOR CATEGORY

A LESS MAJOR CATEGORY

An even less major category

An even less major category

The least major category
The least major category

An even less major category

(b)

A MAJOR CATEGORY

A LESS MAJOR CATEGORY

An even less major category

An even less major category

The least major category
The least major category

An even less major category

(c)

Fig. 9.19 Three designs presenting the same information. (a) The design uses no visual reinforcement. (b) The design uses a hierarchy of typographical styles (all caps boldface, all caps, caps and lowercase, smaller font caps and lowercase) to bond together like elements by similarity. (c) The design adds indentation, another type of similarity, further to bond together like elements.

When ignored or misused, the organization rules can give false visual cues and can make the viewer infer the wrong logical organization. Figure 9.20 gives an example of false visual cues and shows how to correct them with more vertical spacing and less horizontal spacing. Figure 9.21(a) shows a similar situation.

Recall that the objective of using these principles is to achieve visual clarity by reinforcing logical relationships. Other objectives in placing information are *to minimize the eye movements* necessary as the user acquires the various units of information required for a task, and *to minimize the hand movements* required to move a cursor between the parts of the screen that must be accessed for a task. These objectives may be contradictory; the designer's task is to find the best solution.

ATE	BAT	BET
BITE	CAT	CUP
DOG	EAST	EASY
FAR	FAT	FITS
GET	GOT	GUT
HAT	HIGH	HIT

ATE	BAT	BET
BITE	CAT	CUP
DOG	EAST	EASY
FAR	FAT	FITS
GET	GOT	GUT
HAT	HIGH	HIT

(a)   (b)

Fig. 9.20 In (a), the list has a horizontal logical (alphabetical) organization, but a vertical visual organization is induced by the strong proximity relationship. In (b), the alphabetical organization is visually reinforced.

9.5.2 Visual Codings

In interface design, *coding* means creating visual distinctions among several different types of objects. Many different coding techniques are available: color, shape, size or length, typeface, orientation, intensity, texture, line width, and line style are all commonly used in computer graphics. A fundamental issue with any coding technique is to determine how many different categories a particular technique can encode. As more code values are introduced, the possibility of the viewer confusing one value with another increases. The use of a legend, indicating the meaning of each code value, can decrease the error rate.

Many experiments have been conducted to determine how many code values in different coding techniques can be used and still allow almost error-free code recognition (without a legend). For 95-percent error-free performance, 10 colors, 6 area sizes, 6 lengths, 4 intensities, 24 angles, and 15 geometric shapes are the most that can be used [VANC72]. Of course, the code values must be appropriately spaced; see [VANC72, pp. 70–71] for a list of appropriate colors.

If it is important for the viewer to distinguish among different types of information, then it is appropriate to use redundant coding: the use of two different codes to represent the same information. Part (c) of Fig. 9.19 is redundantly coded. Figure 9.22 shows a triply redundant code. Color is normally used redundantly with some other code, to accommodate color-blind users.

Before we can select a code, we must know how many code levels are needed. It is also important to understand whether the information being coded is nominative, ordinal, or ratio. *Nominative* information simply designates, or names, different types of things, such as different types of planes or ships. Nominative information has no notion of greater than or less than. *Ordinal* information is ordered and has a greater than and less than relation. But no metric is defined on ordinal information; there is no notion of varying distances

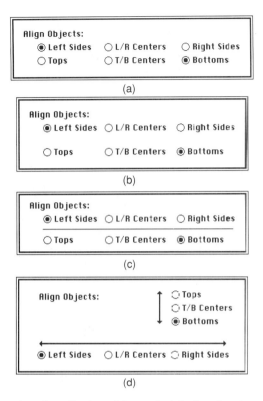

Fig. 9.21 A dialogue box for aligning objects. In (a), the visual cues group the buttons into three groups of two, rather than the proper two groups of three. In (b), the vertical spacing has been increased and the visual cues are correct. In (c), a horizontal rule instead of vertical spacing is used to achieve the same effect in less total space. In (d), the options are rearranged and arrows are used to emphasize the spatial correspondence of each button set to the associated meanings. (Copyright 1988 Claris Corporation. All rights reserved.)

between categories. *Ratio* information has such a metric; examples are temperature, height, weight, and quantity.

For a fixed number of nominative-code values, color is distinguished considerably more accurately than are shape and size, and somewhat more accurately than is intensity [CHRI75]. This suggests that color should be used for coding, but recall that 6 percent to 8

Fig. 9.22 A triply redundant code using line thickness, geometric shape, and interior fill pattern. Any one of the three codes is sufficient to distinguish between the three code values.

percent of males have at least a mild form of color blindness. As discussed in Chapter 13, this need not be a particular problem, especially if redundant coding is used.

Codes used for displaying nominative information should be devoid of any ordering, so that the viewer cannot infer an importance order in the information. Different shapes (such as the squares, circles, diamonds, etc. used for data points when several variables are plotted on the same set of axes), line styles, typefaces, and cross-hatching patterns are appropriate nominative codes. However, using many different typefaces creates a confusing image. A generally accepted guideline is that no more than two or three faces should be used in a single image. Also, differing densities of cross-hatching patterns can create an apparent ordering (Fig. 9.17).

Codes used to display ordinal information can, but need not, vary continuously, but must at least have an obvious ordering. Line styles and area-fill patterns with varying densities can be used, as can text size (many displays provide only a few text sizes, making use of this variable for ratio coding difficult). For both ratio and ordinal information, the apparent visual weight of the codes should increase as the values of the information being coded increase. In Fig. 9.19, ordinal information is being coded, and the typographical hierarchy has a visual weight that increases with the importance of the category.

Ratio information, such as size, length, or orientation, must be presented with a code that can vary continuously. Cleveland and McGill studied the use of several different continuously varying codes to display ratio information, by showing experimental subjects graphs of the same information encoded in different ways. They found the following rankings, where 1 is the most accurately recognized coding [CLEV84; CLEV85]:

1. Position along a common scale
2. Position on identical, nonaligned scales
3. Length
4. Angle between two lines, and line slope
5. Area
6. Volume, density, and color saturation
7. Color hue.

Similarly, Ware and Beatty [WARE88] found that color is effective in grouping objects, but is not effective as a ratio code.

If color were used both to group menu items and to code information in the work area (say, to distinguish layers on a VLSI chip or geographic features on a map), then the user might incorrectly conclude that the red commands in the menu could be applied to only the red elements in the work area. Similarly, a color code might, by using some bright colors and some dark colors, inadvertently imply two logical groupings, one of brighter objects, the other of darker objects. The similarity rule discussed earlier is really at the heart of coding. All like information should be coded with the same code value; all unlike information should have some other code value.

Coding of quantitative data is just a part of the more general field of displaying quantitative data. When data presentations—such as bar, pie, and trend charts—are being designed, many further considerations become important. These are beyond the scope of this text, but are important enough that you should consult key references. The lavishly illustrated books by Bertin [BERT81; BERT83] and Tufte [TUFT83] discuss how to convey quantitative data effectively. Bertin systematically analyzes the visual codes, shows how they can be used effectively, and categorizes different presentation schemes. Tufte argues for minimality in decorative accoutrements to charts and graphs, and for emphasis on the data being conveyed. He also traces the fascinating history of data presentation since 1700. Schmid provides additional guidance [SCHM84].

Mackinlay incorporated some of Bertin's ideas, along with Cleveland and McGill's results into APT, an expert system that automatically creates data presentations [MACK86]. Color Plate I.24 is an example from APT. We expect to see more developments in this promising area.

Closely related to coding are means for calling the viewer's attention to a particular piece of information, such as an error or warning message, the currently selected object, the current command, the failed piece of equipment, or the planes on a collision course. Some attention-getting techniques available are a unique color or shape, a blinking or pulsating or rotating cursor, and reverse video. A unique color was found to be more effective for attracting the viewer's attention than was a unique shape, size, or intensity [CHRI75].

Attention-getting mechanisms can be misused. A pulsating cursor (that is, a cursor whose size continuously varies between large and small) does indeed attract the user's attention. But it also tends to hold attention. When the user is looking at something else on the screen, the pulsating cursor, even though seen only peripherally, is distracting rather than helpful.

Coding of qualitative information is another important research area for user interface design. Work by Feiner and Seligmann [FEIN85; SELI89] explores the automated design of pictures that explain how to perform actions in 3D environments. Based on input about the information the pictures are supposed to communicate and who will be viewing them, a rule-based system determines the objects to include, their properties and rendering style, and the virtual camera parameters that are input to a 3D graphics system that draws the pictures. Color Plate I.25 is an example of a picture generated automatically for a maintenance and repair application.

9.5.3 Visual Consistency

Consistent application of visual-organization rules and codings, and consistent combination of visual elements into higher-level graphic objects and icons, constitute another important element of visual design. Visual consistency is, of course, part of the overall theme of consistency discussed in Section 9.3.1.

Visual elements can be thought of as letters in a graphic alphabet, to be combined into "words" whose meanings should be obvious to the viewer. For instance, dialogue boxes for Macintosh applications are constructed from a small graphic alphabet. Figures 8.16, 8.32,

Fig. 9.23 The graphic alphabet used in many Macintosh applications. The square choice boxes indicate alternatives, of which several may be selected at once. The round choice circles, called "radio buttons," indicate mutually exclusive alternatives; only one may be selected. The rounded-corner rectangles indicate actions that can be selected with the mouse. In addition, the action surrounded by the bold border can be selected with the return key on the keyboard. The rectangles indicate data fields that can be edited. (© Apple Computer, Inc.)

9.14, 9.17, and 9.21 are examples of these dialogue boxes, and Fig. 9.23 shows their graphic alphabet. Similarly, Fig. 9.24 shows the use of a small graphic alphabet to build icons, and Fig. 9.25 shows a single-element graphic alphabet.

Consistency must be maintained among as well as within single images; a consistent set of rules must be applied from one image to another. In coding, for example, it is unacceptable for the meaning of dashed lines to change from one part of an application to another. For placement consistency, keep the same information in the same relative position from one image or screen to the next, so that the user can locate information more quickly.

9.5.4 Layout Principles

Individual elements of a screen not only must be carefully designed, but also, to work together, must all be well placed in an overall context. Three basic layout rules are balance,

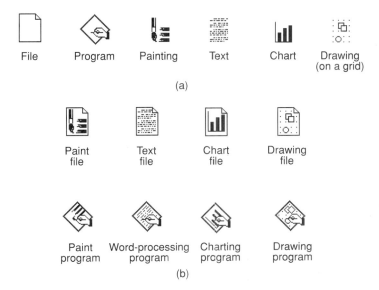

Fig. 9.24 (a) A graphics alphabet. (b) Icons formed by combining elements of the alphabet.

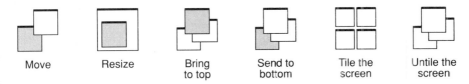

Move   Resize   Bring to top   Send to bottom   Tile the screen   Untile the screen

Fig. 9.25 Several different icons, all created from a single shape representing a window.

gridding, and proportion. Figure 9.26 shows two different designs for the same screen. Design (a) is *balanced*, nicely framing the center and drawing the eye to this area. Design (b) is unbalanced, and unnecessarily draws the eye to the right side of the area. Design (b) also has a slight irregularity in the upper right corner: the base lines of the scroll bar arrow and the pointer icon are not quite aligned. The eye is needlessly drawn to such meaningless discontinuities.

Figure 9.27 shows the benefits of using empty space between different areas, and also illustrates the concept of *gridding*; in cases (b) and (c), the sides of the three areas are all aligned on a grid, so there is a neatness, an aesthetic appeal, lacking in (a) and (d). Figure 9.28 further emphasizes the detrimental effects of not using a grid. [FEIN88] discusses an expert system that generates and uses design grids.

Proportion deals with the size of rectangular areas that are laid out on a grid. Certain ratios of the lengths of a rectangle's two sides are more aesthetically pleasing than are others, and have been used since Greco-Roman times. The ratios are those of the square, which is 1:1; of the square root, 1:1.414; of the golden rectangle, 1:1.618; and of the double square, 1:2. The double square is especially useful, because two horizontal double squares can be placed next to a vertical double square to maintain a grid. These and other design rules are discussed in [MARC80; MARC84; PARK88].

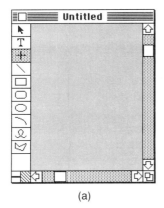

(a)

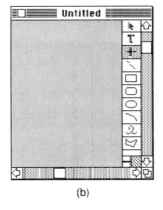

(b)

Fig. 9.26 Two alternative screen designs. Design (a) is balanced; design (b) emphasizes the right side. (Copyright 1988 Claris Corporation. All rights reserved.)

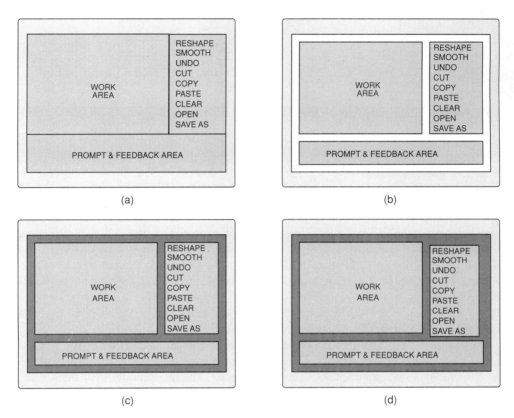

Fig. 9.27 Four screen designs. (a) A typical initial design. (b) Border area has been added. (c) The border has been strengthened to separate the three areas further. (d) The deleterious effect of not aligning elements on a grid is obvious.

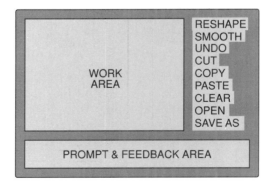

Fig. 9.28 Removing the box around the menu area creates the meaningless but attention-getting ragged-right border.

9.6 THE DESIGN METHODOLOGY

Many ideas have been presented in Chapters 8 and 9. How can a designer integrate them and work with them in a structured way? Although user-interface design is still in part an art rather than a science, we can at least suggest an organized approach to the design process. In this section, we give an overview of the key elements of such a methodology.

The first step in designing an interface is to decide what the interface is meant to accomplish. Although at first this statement may seem trite, poor requirements definitions have doomed numerous user-interface design projects at an early stage. Understanding user requirements can be accomplished in part by studying how the problem under consideration is currently solved. Another successful approach is for the designer to learn how to perform the tasks in question. The objective is to understand what prospective users currently do, and, more important, why they do it.

We do not mean to imply that the interface should exactly mimic current methods. The reason for understanding why prospective users work as they do is often to develop new and better tools. We should recognize, however, that it is sometimes better to mimic old ways to avoid massive retraining or to avoid morale problems with an existing workforce. A typical strategy is first to mimic existing methods, and also to make new methods available; over time, users can be trained in the new or augmented capabilities.

User characteristics must also be identified. What skills and knowledge do the users have? Are the users knowledgable about their work but computer-naive? Are they touch-typists? Will the users typically be eager to learn the system, or will they be reluctant? Will usage be sporadic or regular, full-time or part-time? It is important when assessing the user population to remember that what you, the system designer, would want or like is not necessarily the same as what those for whom the system is being designed might want. Your users are not necessarily created in your own image.

When the requirements have been worked out, a top-down design is next completed by working through the design levels discussed in Section 9.1: conceptual, functional, sequencing, and binding. The rationale for top-down design of user interfaces is that it is best to work out global design issues before dealing with detailed, low-level issues.

The conceptual design is developed first. Ideally, several alternative conceptual designs are developed and evaluated on the basis of how well they will allow users to carry out the tasks identified in the requirements definition. High-frequency tasks should be especially straightforward. Simplicity and generality are other criteria appropriate for the designs.

The functional design focuses on the commands and what they do. Attention must be paid to the information each command requires, to the effects of each command, to the new or modified information presented to the user when the command is invoked, and to possible error conditions. Figure 9.29 shows the focus of functional design. Notice the notations about errors being "engineered out" by subsequent lower-level design decisions. One objective of the functional design is to minimize the number of possible errors, by defining the individual commands appropriately.

The sequencing and binding designs, which together define the form of the interface, are best developed together as a whole, rather than separately. The design involves first selecting an appropriate set of dialogue styles, and then applying these styles to the specific

Function: Add_symbol_instance

Parameters: Symbol_identifier
                 Symbol_position

Description: An instance of the symbol is created and is added to the figure at the
                 desired position. The instance becomes the currently selected object
                 (CSO). The previous CSO, if any, is no longer selected.

Feedback: The instance is seen on the display and is highlighted because it is
                 selected. (If there was a CSO, it is no longer highlighted.)

Errors: 1. The Symbol_identifier is unknown (engineered out by use of a menu
                    selection to choose symbol).

                 2. The Symbol_position is outside the viewport (engineered out by
                    constraining the positioning device feedback to be within the
                    viewport).

Fig. 9.29 A typical functional specification for a command. The annotations with the
errors are added after interaction techniques are identified as part of designing the form
of the interface.

functionality. Sequences of screens, sometimes called *storyboards*, can be used to define
the visual and some of the temporal aspects of these designs. State diagrams, as discussed
in Section 9.3.1 and in Chapter 8, are also helpful in detailing user-action sequences.

The interface form can be defined by a *style guide*, a written codification of many of the
elements of user-interface form. The most common motivation for developing a style guide
is to ensure a ''look and feel'' consistency within and among applications. Some elements
of the style guide can be implemented in libraries of interaction techniques (Chapter 10);
other elements must be accommodated by the designers and programmers. Many style
guides exist, among them guides for the Macintosh [APPL87], Open Software Foundation's OSF/MOTIF [OPEN89], NASA's Transportable Application Executive [BLES88b],
and DEC's XUI [DIGI89].

The whole design process is greatly aided by interleaving design with user-interface
prototyping. A user-interface prototype is a quickly created version of some or all of
the final interface, often with very limited functionality. The emphasis is on speedy
implementation and speedy modifiability. At the start, some design questions will seem to
be unanswerable; once a prototype is available, however, the answers may become
apparent. Prototyping is often superior to using a design document, since it gives users a
more specific frame of reference, within which they can talk about their needs, likes, and
dislikes. HyperCard and Smalltalk are used extensively for rapid prototyping, as are some
of the software tools discussed in Section 10.6.

Prototyping can begin as soon as a conceptual design is worked out, and the elements
of the functional design and dialogue style can be developed concurrently. It is important to

follow the Bauhaus dictum, *form follows function*, lest the user-interface style dictate the capabilities of the overall system. As soon as even some modest elements of the interface are developed, potential users should be exposed to them, to elicit suggestions for improvements to the interface. As modifications are made and as the prototype becomes more comprehensive, users should again work with the system. This iterative cycle has come to be viewed as essential to the development of high-quality user-interface software. Further discussion of prototyping and iterative development can be found in [ALAV84; HART89].

EXERCISES

9.1 Determine how several commands in an interactive graphics application program with which you are familiar could be made into direct-manipulation operations.

9.2 Examine several interactive graphics application programs and characterize their dialogue style. List the ways in which the interfaces do and do not follow the design guidelines discussed in this chapter. Identify the design level for each point you list; for instance, consistent use of color is at the hardware-binding level.

9.3 The conceptual model for many word processors is partially based on an analogy with typewriters. List ways in which this analogy might create difficulties for a user who attempts to carry it further than is realistic.

9.4 Analyze a user interface to determine what methods, if any, are provided for error correction. Categorize the methods according to the four types discussed in Section 9.3.4.

9.5 What is the form of the state diagram representing a completely modeless interface?

9.6 Design and implement a simple graphics editor with the following functionality: create, delete, and move lines; move endpoints of lines; change the line style (dash, dotted, solid) of existing lines; set the line-style mode for lines that have not yet been created. Design this system to support two or more of the following five syntaxes, and include a command to switch from one syntax to another: object mode, command mode, object mode with Repeat_last_operation operation, free-form syntax, and free-form syntax with modes and a Do_it command.

9.7 Conduct either informal or formal controlled experiments with each of the syntaxes implemented in Exercise 9.6. Test ease of learning and speed of use. Give your users five predefined tasks to perform. Identify tasks that will be faster to perform with one syntax than with the others.

9.8 Study three different interactive graphics application programs.
   a. Identify the classes of modes and syntaxes used in each, using the definitions in Section 9.4. A single application may have several types of modes or syntaxes. If so, are there clear distinctions showing which to use when?
   b. Identify the factoring, if any, that has occurred. Are there additional possibilities for factoring? Do you think the user interface would be improved by application of the factoring?

9.9 Consider the three window organizations shown in Fig. 9.30. Count the number of mouse movements and mouse-button depressions needed to move the lower-right corner. In each case, assume that the cursor starts in the center of the window and must be returned to the center of the window. Counting mouse movements as 1.1 seconds and button depressions as 0.2 seconds, how long does each window organization take? Does this result mean that one organization is better than the others?

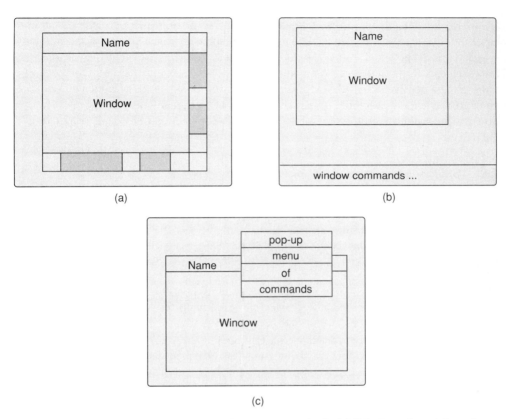

Fig. 9.30 Three means to invoke window commands. In (a) (Macintosh style), regions of the window dressing are used. To resize, the user selects and drags the lower-right corner. In (b), the commands are in the command area at the bottom of the screen. To resize, the user selects a command, and then drags the lower-right corner of the window. In (c), a pop-up menu appears at the cursor when a mouse button is pressed. To resize, the user selects the command from the pop-up menu, and drags the lower-right corner of the window.

9.10 Implement a single-level Undo command for an interactive graphics application program you have written. Decide which of several implementation strategies you will use, and justify your choice. The strategies include (1) after each command, make a complete copy of the application data structure, state variables, and so on; (2) save a record of what was changed in the application data structure; (3) save all the commands since logon, replay them to effect undo; (4) save the application data structure every 10 minutes, plus save all commands since the last such save operation; and (5) save, for each user command, the one or several commands needed to undo the user command. Would your choice differ for a multi-level Undo command?

9.11 Examine an interactive graphics application. How many commands does it have? List the "starter kit" of commands with which a new user can do a simple piece of work. How big is the starter kit with respect to the overall command set? List the ways in which defaults or other methods have been used to minimize the complexity of the starter kit. In your opinion, does the system have a good starter kit?

9.12 Explore other ways of redesigning Fig. 9.17(a) to reinforce the logical relationships of the visual elements.

9.13 Study the dialogue-box design of an application. Which methods are used to reinforce logical structure with visual structure? Can you further improve the design?

9.14 Figure 9.6 shows 12 icons that represent Macintosh programs: (a) disk copy utility, (b) resource mover, (c) icon editor, (d) menu editor, (e) alert/dialog editor, (f) edit program, (g) boot configure, (h) switcher, (i) examine file, (j) MacWrite, (k) MacDraw, and (l) MacPaint. Some of the icons indicate the associated program better than others do.

  a. Design an alternative set of icons to represent the 12 programs.
  b. Show the set of icons to 10 programmers who are not familiar with the Macintosh, and ask them to guess what each icon means. Tabulate the results.
  c. Tell 10 programmers who are not familiar with the Macintosh what each icon means. Give them 2 minutes to study the icons. Ten minutes later, show them the icons again, and ask them what the icons mean. Tabulate the results.
  d. Repeat parts (b) and (c) for the icons in the figure. What conclusions can you draw from your data?

9.15 Analyze the visual design of a graphics application. What is the visual alphabet? What visual codings are used? What visual hierarchies are established? Redesign some of the visual cues to emphasize further the underlying logical relationships.

9.16 List 10 specific examples of codings in computer graphics applications you have seen. Is the coded information nominative, ordinal, or ratio? Are the code values appropriate to the information? Are there any false codings?

9.17 Examine three different window managers. What visual code indicates which window is the "listener"—that is, the window to which keyboard input is directed? What visual code indicates which processes are active, as opposed to blocked? What other visual codings are used?

10
User
Interface
Software

The first two chapters on user interfaces, Chapters 8 and 9, concentrated on the external characteristics of user–computer interfaces. Here, we examine the software components, beyond the basic graphics packages already discussed, that are used in implementing interfaces. Figure 10.1 shows the various levels of user-interface software, and suggests the roles for each. The figure shows that the application program has access to all software levels; programmers can exploit the services provided by each level, albeit with care, because calls made to one level may affect the behavior of another level. The operating-system level is not discussed in this text, and the basics of graphics subroutine packages have already been described. Some input features of device-independent graphics subroutine packages are compared and evaluated in Section 10.1. Window-management systems, discussed in Sections 10.2 to 10.4, manage the resources of screen space and interaction devices so that several applications or multiple views of the same application can share the display. Some window-management systems have an integral graphics subroutine package that provides device-independent abstractions, whereas others simply pass graphics calls through to the underlying graphics hardware or software.

The interaction techniques discussed in Chapter 3 are useful in many applications, but require careful development to provide a pleasing look and feel. Interaction-technique toolkits, treated in Section 10.5, are built on window-management systems to give the application developer a common set of techniques. The final layer, the user-interface management system (UIMS), discussed in Section 10.6, provides additional generic user-interface support at the sequencing level of design (Section 9.1). UIMSs speed up implementation of a user interface, and facilitate making rapid changes during the interface-debugging process discussed in Section 9.6.

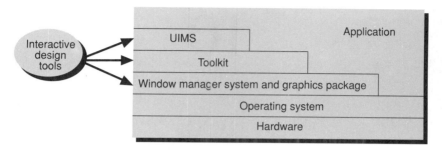

Fig. 10.1 Levels of user-interface software. The application program has access to the operating system, window-manager system and graphics package, toolkit, and user-interface management system (UIMS). The interactive design tools allow nonprogrammers to design windows, menus, dialogue boxes, and dialogue sequences.

10.1 BASIC INTERACTION-HANDLING MODELS

In this section, we elaborate on the interaction-handling capabilities of contemporary device-independent graphics subroutine packages, as introduced in Chapters 2 (SRGP) and 7 (SPHIGS). The sampling and event-driven processing in these two packages is derived from GKS [ANSI85b; ENDE86] and PHIGS [ANSI88], which share a common interaction model. Window-management systems use an event mechanism similar to, but more powerful than, the GKS/PHIGS model discussed in this section.

GKS and PHIGS have six classes of logical input devices, and there may be more than one device of each class associated with a workstation (a display and associated interaction devices). Each of the logical input devices can operate in one of three modes: sample, request, and event. Each device has an associated *measure*, which is the type of information returned by the device. The devices and their measures are as follows:

Device	Measure
locator	position in world coordinates
pick	pick path for SPHIGS, segment identification for GKS
choice	integer indicating the choice
valuator	real number
string	character string (called keyboard device in SRGP and SPHIGS)
stroke	sequence of positions in world coordinates

SRGP and SPHIGS use measures that are slightly different from these.

In *request mode*, the application program requests input from a device, and the graphics package returns control and the measure of the device only after the user has performed an action with the device. The action is called the *trigger*. The specific trigger action for each logical device class is implementation-dependent, but is typically a button-push. For instance, a mouse button triggers locator or pick devices, and the return key triggers the string device.

Request mode can be used with only one device at a time, and is intended to support the limited functionality of older graphics terminals, which are typically connected to computers via RS-232 interfaces. Interaction techniques such as keyboard accelerators cannot be used, because the application program must know in advance from which device to request input. In addition, as the measure is modified (by moving the mouse to change the locator's measure, say), the application program generally cannot provide dynamic feedback, because the application program does not regain control until the trigger action occurs. This difficulty can be eliminated by defining the trigger action as a small change in the measure.

In *sample mode*, a single device is sampled, and the measure of the device is immediately returned. We can permit the user to select one of several devices to use, by polling all eligible devices, as follows:

```
terminate = FALSE;
while (!terminate) {
    SamplePick (&status, &segmentName);
    /* status = OK means had successful pick; segmentName is identification */
    /* of picked item */
    Process pick input
    SampleString (string);
    Process string input
    /* terminate set to TRUE as part of processing string or pick */
}
```

Sampling in this way is dangerous, however. If the user makes several more inputs while the first is being processed, they will never be seen by the application program, since it stops sampling while processing the first input. Also, the sequence of user events, which is often essential to maintain, might be lost in sampling. Unlike request mode, however, sample mode is well suited for dynamic feedback from the application program, because no trigger action is required to return the device measure to the application program.

Event mode avoids the problems of sample and request modes, by allowing input to be accepted asynchronously from several different devices at once. As discussed in Section 2.3.6 of Chapter 2, the application program first enables all devices whose use is to be permitted. Once the devices are enabled, a trigger action for any of them places an event report on an input queue, in order of occurrence. As seen in Fig. 10.2, the application

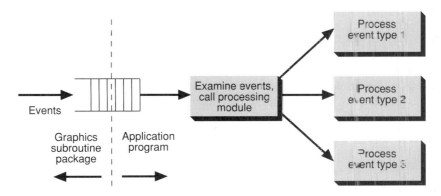

Fig. 10.2 The application program removes events from the queue and dispatches control to the appropriate procedure, which processes them.

program checks the queue to see what user actions have actually occurred, and processes the events as they are removed from the queue.

The following code fragment reimplements the previous polling example in event mode:

```
terminate = FALSE;
while (!terminate) {
    WaitEvent (timeout, &deviceClass, &deviceId);        /* Wait for user action */
    switch (deviceClass) {
        case pick: Process pick;
            break;
        case string: Process string;
            break;
    }   /* terminate set to TRUE in processing of pick or string */
}
```

Unlike request-mode input, event-mode input is asynchronous: Once a device is enabled, the application program can be executing while the user is concurrently inputting information with the enabled input devices. This is sometimes called *typeahead*, or, when done with a mouse, *mouseahead*.

The typeahead capability of the event-queue mechanism provides an opportunity to speed up interactions with the computer. Suppose a button-press (choice logical device) is used to scroll through a drawing. Each button-press scrolls, say, x inches. If the user presses the button more rapidly than the scroll can occur, events build up in the queue. The application program can look for multiple successive button events on the queue; if there are n such events, then a single scroll of nx inches can be performed, and will be much faster than n scrolls of x inches each.

Care must be taken to manage the event queue properly. If the first of two events on the queue causes the program to enable a different set of logical input devices and then to call WaitEvent, the program now may not be expecting the second event, leading to unexpected results. The call FlushDeviceEvents is provided to alleviate this problem; the application program can empty the event queue to ensure that the queue contains nothing unexpected. However, flushing the queue may leave the user wondering why the second event was never processed.

Another concern with event queues is a possible time delay between when an event occurs and when other information needed in connection with that event is obtained. Suppose we want a mouse button-down to display a diamond at the mouse position. If the buttons on the mouse can be assigned to a logical choice device and the (x, y) coordinates of the mouse to a logical locator (this contrasts with the SRGP locator, whose measure includes button status), then we can use the following approach:

```
WaitEvent (timeout, &deviceClass, &deviceId);
if (deviceClass == CHOICE && deviceId == 1) {
    SampleLocator (MOUSE, x, y);        /* Get position of diamond */
    DrawDiamond (x, y);                 /* Draw diamond at (x, y) */
}
```

At time t_1, the user makes a choice, with a choice device, to draw a diamond. The user then moves cursor to go on to another task.

At time t_2, locator is sampled and diamond is drawn. Locator has moved between t_1 and t_2.

Fig. 10.3 The effect of a time delay between an event and sampling of the cursor position associated with that event.

The problem is that, between time t_1 (when the WaitEvent procedure returns) and time t_2 (when the SampleLocator procedure obtains the (x, y) coordinates), seconds may have elapsed. In this time, the user may have moved the locator some distance, causing the unexpected result shown in Fig. 10.3. Substantial delays can easily occur on a time-shared computer if another program takes control of the processor, and on any computer that supports virtual memory when page-fault interrupts occur. Thus, although we would like the application program to be uninterruptible during the interval from t_1 to t_2, we cannot guarantee that it will be so.

In GKS and PHIGS, the risk of this time delay can be reduced and even eliminated by activating several logical devices with the same trigger. If we define the trigger to be a button-click on any of the three buttons, and associate this trigger with both the three-button choice device and the locator device, then both events will be placed on the queue (in unspecified order) at the same time. The device-dependent driver under the graphics package can do this faster than the application program can execute the preceding code segment, so the likelihood of being interrupted is less. If the operating system grants the device driver the privilege of disabling interrupts, then there will never be a time delay.

Unfortunately, some user-interface constructs are difficult to provide by means of these logical-device concepts. For instance, it is convenient to use time intervals to distinguish between two commands. Thus, we can select an icon with a single mouse button-click while the cursor is on the icon, and then open the icon with a second click within some small Δt of the first click. Making these distinctions requires that the event reports have a *timestamp* giving the time at which the event occurred. This concept is not found in GKS and PHIGS, although a timestamp could be provided readily.

10.2   WINDOW-MANAGEMENT SYSTEMS

A *window-management system* provides many of the important features of modern user-computer interfaces: applications that show results in different areas of the display, the ability to resize the screen areas in which those applications are executing, pop-up and pull-down menus, and dialogue boxes.

The window-management system is first and foremost a resource manager in much the same way that an operating system is a resource manager—only the types of resources differ. It allocates the resource of screen area to various programs that seek to use the screen, and then assists in managing these screen areas so that the programs do not interfere with one another. This aspect of window systems is further discussed in Section 10.3. The window system also allocates the resource of interaction devices to programs that require user input, and then routes the flow of input information from the devices to the event queue of the appropriate program for which the input is destined. Input handling is discussed further in Section 10.4.

Our objective with these three sections is to provide an overview of key window-management concepts: The most comprehensive treatment of the subject is [STEI89], and a historical development overview is given in [TEIT86], in a book of relevant papers [HOPG86b].

A window-management system has two important parts. The first is the *window manager*, with which the end user interacts to request that windows be created, resized, moved, opened, closed, and so on. The second is the underlying functional component, the *window system*, which actually causes windows to be created, resized, moved, opened, closed, and so on.

The window manager is built on top of the window system: The window manager uses services provided by the window system. The window manager is to its underlying window system as a command-line interpreter is to its underlying operating-system kernel. Also built on top of the window system are higher-level graphics packages and application programs. The programs built on the window system are sometimes called *client* programs, which in turn use the capabilities of the window system, itself sometimes called the *server* program. In some server–client window-management systems, such as the X Window System [SCHE88a] and NeWS [SUN87], the window manager itself appears to the window system as just another client program. In other systems, there is a closer relationship between the window manager and window system than there is between a client and server.

Some window systems, including the X Window System and NeWS, are designed to be *policy-free*, meaning that multiple window managers, each with a different look and feel, can be built on top of the window system. The window manager, not the window system, determines how windows look, and how the user interacts with windows. A policy-free window system would support all the window styles of Fig. 9.30, as well as others. Just as many different application programs can be built on top of a graphics package, many different window managers can be built on top of a policy-free window system: The window manager and graphics application program both control external appearance and behavior. For this approach to be possible, the window system must be designed to carry out a wide range of window-manager policies (see Exercise 10.10). Of course, in a specific environment, the window manager and application programs need to have a common user-interface look and feel.

If the programming interface to the window system is cleanly defined and is implemented via an interprocess communication capability, then clients of the window system can reside on computers different from that of the window system, provided the computers are connected by a high-speed network. If the window manager is itself just another client of the window system, then it too can reside on another computer. The use of interprocess communications in this way allows computation-intensive applications to reside on a powerful computer, while the user interacts with the application from a workstation. In this regard, the server–client model is just a sophisticated instance of a virtual terminal protocol; such protocols in general share this advantage.

A window-management system does not need to be built on the server–client model. For instance, the Macintosh has no well-defined separation between the window manager and window system. Such separation was not necessary for the single-active-process, single-processor design objective of the Macintosh, and would have led to additional run-time overhead.

In window systems that provide for use of interprocess communications between the window manager and window system, such as the X Window System, NeWS, and Andrew [MORR86], the interface must be designed to minimize communications delays. Several strategies can help us to meet this objective. First, asynchronous rather than synchronous communications can be used between the client and server whenever possible, so that, when the client sends a message to the server, the client does not need to wait for a reply before resuming processing and sending another message. For example, when the client program calls DrawLine, a message is sent to the server, and control returns immediately to the client.

We can sometimes realize a modest savings by minimizing the number of separate messages that must be sent between the server and client. Most network communication protocols have a minimum packet size, typically 16 to 32 bytes, and the time to send larger numbers of bytes is often proportionately less than the time needed to send the minimum packet. There is thus an advantage in batching messages, as provided in some systems with a BeginBatchOfUpdates and EndBatchOfUpdates subroutine call; all the calls made between the BeginBatch and EndBatch calls are transmitted in one message. There is also an advantage in designing single messages that replace multiple messages, such as a single message that sets multiple graphics attributes.

A third way to minimize communication is to move more functionality and generality into the server. The commands most clients send to their window system are fairly primitive: draw line, create window, copy pixmap. In the X Window System, for instance, many commands are needed to create a menu or dialogue box. A more robust and powerful strategy is to send commands to the server as programs written in a language that can be interpreted efficiently. Thus, the commands can be very general and can carry out any functionality the language can express. The cost of this generality is, of course, the time taken to execute the programs interpretively, and any additional space needed for the interpreter—a modest price with contemporary computers. The benefit can be a dramatic decrease in communications traffic. The strategy of moving more generality and functionality into the workstation is not new; exactly the same issues were discussed two decades ago when distributed graphics systems were first being built [FOLE71; FOLE76; VAND74].

This third strategy is used in the NeWS window system, which accepts as commands programs written in an extended version of the PostScript language [ADOB85a; ADOB85b]. PostScript combines traditional programming-language constructs (variables,

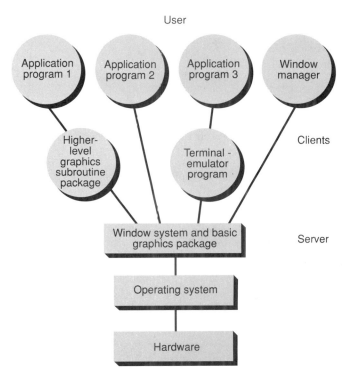

Fig. 10.4 The relationship of the window system to the operating system and application programs.

data structures, expressions, assignments, control flow, I/O) with imbedded graphics capabilities for drawing output primitives, clipping against arbitrary regions, and transforming primitives. NeWS adds extensions for processes, input, and windows. The language is further discussed in Section 19.9.

For a dialogue box to be defined in NeWS, a PostScript program defining the box is sent to the server when a program begins execution; each time the dialogue box is to appear, a short message is sent to invoke the program. This strategy avoids resending the box's definition each time. Similarly, programs to perform time-critical operations, such as rubberband drawing of lines (Chapter 8) or curves (Chapter 11), can be sent to the server, avoiding the time delays involved in each round-trip message between the server and client needed to update the rubberband line.

A graphics package is often integrated with the window system, typically a 2D nonsegmented package with capabilities similar to SRGP of Chapter 2. If the underlying hardware has 3D or segmentation capabilities, then the window-system level might pass on graphics calls to the hardware. Figure 10.4 shows how the window system and its graphics package typically relate to other system components; Fig. 10.5 shows the relationships among windows, clients, and input events. User-generated events involving windows—resizing, repositioning, pushing, popping, scrolling, and so on—are routed by the window system to the window manager; other events are routed to the appropriate application program.

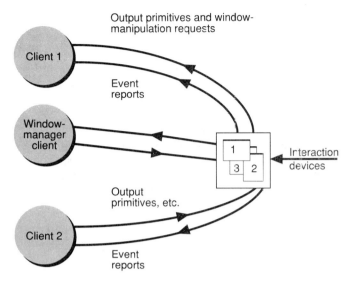

Fig. 10.5 Another view of the relationship among windows, clients, and events. Each client outputs to a window; input events are routed to the appropriate client's event queue.

10.3   OUTPUT HANDLING IN WINDOW SYSTEMS

The output resource allocated by the window system to its client programs is screen space, which must be managed so that clients do not interfere with one another's use of the screen. The strategies by which this allocation is made vary considerably from one window system to another, but fit into three broad categories. The main difference is in how parts of a window that have just been exposed (when the window is made larger, uncovered, or scrolled) are displayed. The strategies place progressively more responsibility for making this decision on the window system itself, such that the client is progressively less aware of the existence of the windows. The system may also have to manage a look-up table so as to avoid conflicts between clients.

A minimal window system takes no responsibility for drawing newly exposed portions of a window; rather, it sends a ''window-exposed'' event to the client responsible for the window. Such a window system does not save the occluded portions of windows. When the client sends output to a window, output primitives are clipped against the window system's window (which corresponds to the graphics package's viewport). If a line is drawn in a partially visible window, only the visible part of the line is drawn.

When the client responsible for the window receives the window-exposed event, the client can handle the event by establishing a clipping window on the entire portion of the world that is to be displayed in the window system's window, and then processing all the output primitives, or by using a smaller clipping window corresponding to just the newly exposed portion of the window, as shown in Fig. 10.6. Alternatively, the client can save the pixmaps of obscured windows to avoid regenerating the window's contents when the window is next uncovered. The client would simply display some or all of the saved pixmap with a PixBlt from the saved pixmap to the screen pixmap. In some cases, the window system repaints the window backgrounds and borders to provide the illusion of quick

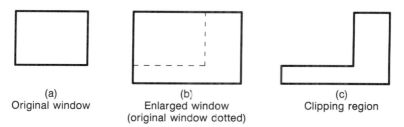

(a)   (b)   (c)
Original window   Enlarged window   Clipping region
                    (original window dotted)

Fig. 10.6 When a window (a) is enlarged to (b), the enlarged window can be updated by using the bitmap that was in the original window (a), clipping world-coordinate output primitives against the clipping region (c), and drawing those within the clip region. Note that the clip region is nonconvex, so clipping a line may result in display of more than one line segment.

response, even though the actual redraw may incur a noticable delay.

This minimal-window-system approach makes sense in systems that support diverse application data models, ranging from pixmaps through structured hierarchies to more complex relational models. The window system itself cannot have a model that is well matched for all applications. Instead, the application is given total responsibility for providing efficient storage and redrawing capabilities.

The Macintosh window system is an example of this minimalist design [APPL85]. Algorithms embedded in its Quickdraw graphics package allow clipping to arbitrary regions, such as those shown in Fig. 10.6. NeWS and X also support arbitrary-shaped windows. Some of the clipping algorithms needed to support arbitrary windows are discussed in Section 19.7.

More memory-rich window systems save the obscured parts of windows, so that the client does not need to display newly exposed portions of a window. Other window systems give the client a choice of whether or not obscured window parts are to be saved. In any case, there is a question of how much of the obscured window is saved. Typically, the maximum possible size of the window is saved, which is usually the size of the entire screen. Some window systems save a pixmap larger than the display itself, although this approach becomes more expensive as the pixmap becomes larger or deeper. Decreasing memory prices, however, are having a dramatic effect on what is cost-effective. The client must be involved in redrawing if the window is scrolled away from the part of the world that has been saved as a pixmap, or if the view must be rescaled.

A slightly different strategy is for the window manager to keep, for each window, an offscreen pixmap containing the entire window. Whenever part of a window is unobscured, the appropriate subarea of the offscreen pixmap is copied to the screen by a PixBlt. This strategy is slow for window updating, because partially obscured windows can be written into by client programs. Thus, after a client program writes into a window (which is the offscreen pixmap), the window system must copy the visible part of the window to the screen. Alternatively, the window system can directly scan convert new output primitives into both the offscreen pixmap and the visible part of the window in the onscreen pixmap, by clipping each output primitive against two clip regions: one for the visible part of the pixmap, the other for the entire offscreen pixmap. Updates to a completely unobscured window can be done faster by updating only the visible, onscreen version of the window;

the window is then copied to its offscreen pixmap only when it is about to be obscured. To avoid this whole issue, some window systems require that the window that is being written into be completely unobscured. This solution, unfortunately, also prevents multiprocessing when an active process needs to write into partially obscured windows. Several special-purpose hardware systems avoid the need to copy offscreen pixmaps to the screen pixmap. In these systems, the hardware knows where each offscreen pixmap is stored and which portion of each is to be made visible on the screen. On each refresh cycle, the video controller picks up the appropriate pixels from the offscreen pixmaps. Exposing more of a window is done not by copying pixmaps, but by giving new window-visibility information to the hardware. These hardware solutions are further discussed in Chapter 18.

A second way to implement this type of window system, developed by Pike [PIKE83] and discussed further in Section 19.8, avoids storing any information twice. Each window is partitioned into rectangular pixmaps. Invisible pixmaps are saved offscreen, whereas visible pixmaps are saved only in the onscreen refresh memory.

Yet another fundamental design strategy is to have the window system maintain a display list for each window, as in the VGTS system developed by Lantz and Nowicki [LANT84]. In essence, the window system maintains a display-list–based graphics package, such as SPHIGS, as part of the window system. Whenever a window needs to be redrawn, the display list is traversed and clipped. Fast scan-conversion hardware is desirable for this approach, so that redraw times do not become prohibitively long. Pixmap-oriented applications, such as paint programs, do not benefit from this approach, although VGTS does include a pixmap primitive.

A frequent concern is the effect of a window-resize operation on the amount of information shown in a window: what happens to the world-coordinate window when the window-manager window is resized? There are two possibilities, and the client program should be able to cause either to occur. The first possibility is that, when the user resizes the window, the world-coordinate window changes size correspondingly. The net effect is that the user sees more or less of the world, according to whether the window was made larger or smaller, but always at the same scale, as depicted in Fig. 10.7(c). The second possibility is that, when the user resizes the window, the world-coordinate window size stays fixed. Thus, as the window is enlarged, the same amount of the world is seen, but at a larger scale. In one approach, a uniform scaling is applied to the world, even if the aspect ratios of the world window and window-system window are different; this can make some part of the window-system window go unused, as in Fig. 10.7(d). Alternatively, a nonuniform scaling can be applied, distorting the contents of the world window to fit the window-system window, as in Fig. 10.7(e).

Several window systems use hierarchical windows—that is, windows that contain subwindows—as shown in Fig. 10.8. Subwindows are generally contained within their parents. Hierarchical windows can be used to implement dialogue boxes and forms of the type shown in Chapter 8. The entire dialogue box is defined as a window, and then each field, radio button, and check box is defined as a separate subwindow, and mouse button-down events are enabled for each one. When the user selects any of the subwindows, the event report contains the name of that subwindow. A typical restriction is that subwindows be contained within their parent window, so if the dialogue box is to be moved outside of the application window, the box cannot be implemented as a subwindow to the application window.

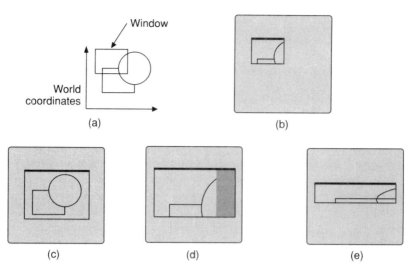

Fig. 10.7 Relationships between world-coordinate window and window-manager window. (a) A world-coordinate scene; (b) its view through a window. In (c), when the window-manager window is enlarged, more of the world is seen: the world-coordinate window is enlarged. In (d), enlarging the window-manager window creates an enlarged view of the contents of the world-coordinate window. The enlargement is done with uniform scaling, so that part of the window-manager window (gray tone) is unused. In (e), enlarging the window-manager window also creates an enlarged view of the contents of the world-coordinate window, but with nonuniform scaling so as to fill the entire window-manager window.

The design of a window-hierarchy system involves many subtleties, such as determining the effect on children of resizing a parent. Also, if a client process spawns a subprocess that then creates windows, the subprocess's windows could be considered subwindows of the spawning process's window, except that the subprocess may have its own event queue to receive input from its windows. See [ROSE83; SCHE86] for a more extensive discussion of hierarchies.

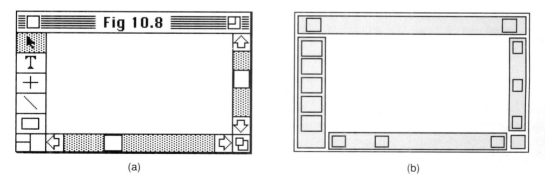

Fig. 10.8 (a) The window for a drawing program; (b) division of the window into a hierarchy of windows. In (b), a contained window is a child of the containing window.

The subroutine calls with which a typical window system must deal follow:

CreateWindow (*name*)	Create a new window; it becomes the current window
SetPosition (*xmin, ymin*)	Set position of current window
SetSize (*height, width*)	Set size of current window
SelectWindow (*name*)	Make this the current window
ShowWindow	Make the current window visible, on top of all others
HideWindow	Make the current window invisible; expose any windows the current window was hiding
SetTitle (*char_string*)	Set displayed title of current window to *char_string*
GetPosition (*xmin, xmax*)	Get position of the current window
GetSize (*height, width*)	Get size of the current window
BringToTop	Put the current window on top of all other windows
SendToBottom	Send the current window to the bottom, behind all others
DeleteWindow	Delete the current window

The other output resource allocated by a window system is look-up table entries. Imagine a window system running on an 8-bit per pixel hardware system, with two window-system clients each wanting to have a look-up table. With two clients, each could be given half the entries (128), but then the number of look-up table entries per client depends on the number of clients. A fixed upper bound on the number of clients could be established to determine the number of entries per client, but if there are in fact fewer clients, then some of the look-up table entries will be wasted. A single client at a time could be given exclusive use of the look-up table—often the client whose window contains the cursor. This solution is viable, but suffers in that the overall screen appearance can change dramatically as the table is given first to one client, then to another, and so on.

Another solution is to allocate not look-up table entries, but rather colors. If a client asks for 100 percent blue, and some entry already contains this color, the client is given the same index to use (but is not allowed to change the contents of the entry). If no entry contains 100 percent blue and there are free entries, one is allocated. Otherwise, the entry with the color closest to that requested is allocated. The danger is that the distance between the requested and actual color might be quite large; not being able to change the look-up table is also a disadvantage. Unfortunately, there is no generally satisfactory solution.

10.4 INPUT HANDLING IN WINDOW SYSTEMS

The input resource being allocated and managed by the window system for that system's clients is the set of input devices and the events the devices generate. The window system must know to which client different types of events are to be routed. The process of routing events to the proper client is sometimes called *demultiplexing*, since events destined for different clients arrive in sequential order from a single source and must then be fanned out to different clients.

The types of events are those discussed in Section 10.1, plus additional events that are specific to window systems. Some window systems generate *window-enter* and *window-leave* events, which allow a user interface to highlight the window containing the cursor without the overhead of constantly sampling the pointer device. Window systems that do not retain a record of what is displayed in each window generate *window-damage* events whenever a window needs to be redrawn. Damage occurs if the window is enlarged, uncovered, or scrolled. The window-enter and window-leave events are generated by the window system in direct response to user actions, whereas the window-damage event is a secondary event generated when a client requests that a window be changed. All these events are routed to the client's event queue. Some user actions, such as closing a window, can cause damage events to be to sent to a large number of clients. The information in the event report is similar to that discussed in Section 10.1, but is augmented with additional event types and window-specific information.

If a window hierarchy exists, child windows can be manipulated just like the parent window, and can have associated events. The window name associated with an event is that of the lowest-level window in the hierarchy that contains the cursor and for which the event was enabled. This means that different types of events can be associated with different windows. Every event placed in the event queue has as part of its record the name of the window with which it is associated. It is also possible to report an event in a subwindow not just to the subwindow, but also to all the windows that contain the subwindow. The client would do this by enabling the same event for all the windows in the hierarchical path from the outermost containing window to the lowest-level subwindow. Thus, multiple event reports, each with a different window name, will be placed in the client's event queue.

With hierarchical windows, a pop-up menu can be defined as a main window subdivided into as many subwindows as there are menu items. As the cursor moves out of the window of menu item i into the window of menu item $i + 1$, a leave-window event is placed on the event queue with the window name of menu item i, followed by an enter-window event with the window name of menu item $i + 1$. The client program processes the first event by undoing the highlight feedback on menu item i. It processes the second event similarly, creating the highlight feedback on menu item $i + 1$. If the cursor enters some region of the pop-up menu (such as a title area at the top) that is not overlaid by a subwindow, then the enter-window event includes the name of the pop-up menu window. Window hierarchies tend to be used in this way, but user response time can be degraded by the processing time needed to manage the hierarchy and its many events. A NeWS-style window system does not generate such a large number of events to be processed, because the feedback can be handled within the server.

Hierarchical windows can be used for selection of displayed objects in much the same way as SPHIGS structures can be. Of course, subwindows are not as general as structures, but they are convenient for picking rectangularly shaped, hierarchically nested regions (NeWS and X support nonrectangular windows). Other uses for hierarchical windows include causing the cursor shape to change as the cursor moves from one part of the screen to another, and allowing pick detection on the handles sometimes used for manipulating graphics objects (see Fig. 8.42).

Two basic approaches are widely used by window systems to route events to clients: real-estate–based and listener routing. Many window systems actually provide both strategies, and allow the window manager to specify which to use. Some also allow a policy provided by the window manager to be used in place of either of these two basic approaches. *Real-estate–based* routing looks at which window the cursor is in when an event occurs; all events are directed to the client that created the window and include the name of the window as part of the event report.

To do real-estate–based routing, the window system must maintain a data structure that stores the bounds of each window, as shown in Fig. 10.9. When an event occurs, the data

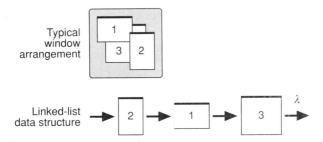

Fig. 10.9 Data structure used by the window manager to determine in which window the cursor is located, by searching for the first window on the list that brackets the cursor position.

structure is searched for the visible window containing the cursor position. If the data structure is ordered, with the most recently fully revealed window always brought to the head, then the search can terminate with the first window that contains the cursor (x, y) position. For hierarchical windows, a more complex data structure and search is needed (see Exercise 10.2).

Listener event routing, also known as *click-to-type* routing, is done when one client tells the window system to route all events of a certain type to another client (the receiving client can be, but does not need to be, the client that makes the request). For instance, the window manager can have a command that allows the user to route all keyboard input to the client that owns a particular window. The window manager implements the command by directing the window system to route keyboard events to the appropriate client program. Keyboard events are those most commonly routed explicitly, but even a mouse button-down event can be redirected.

Event distribution can cause unexpected results for users. Suppose, for instance, that the user accidentally double-clicks on a window's close (also called ''go-away'') button, although only a single click is needed to close the window. The window system routes the first click to the window manager, which closes the window. The second click is next routed to whatever was underneath the close button of the now-closed window, perhaps in turn selecting a menu command!

Message-transmission delays in a network can also wreak havoc with the user. Consider a drawing program executing in window A. To draw a rubberband line, the user generates a button-down event in window A, and then moves the cursor to wherever the line will end. This point might be outside of window A, if the line is to end in an area of the drawing that is not visible through the window. In anticipation of the cursor going out of its window, the drawing program sends the window system a request that *all* button-up events come to it, no matter where they occur. Now if the user does move the cursor outside window A, we have a *race condition*. Will the mouse-up event occur before or after the window system receives the request that all mouse-up events go to the drawing program? If the mouse-up occurs before the request is received, the event will go to whatever window the cursor is in, causing an unexpected result. If the mouse-up occurs after the request is received, all is well. The only certain way to avoid these race conditions is to require the client to tell the server that event i has been processed before the server will send event $i + 1$ to the client.

Once events come to a client, they enter an event queue of the sort shown in Figure 10.2. The client routes, or dispatches, events to various event-handling routines. The pseudocode for a typical dispatcher is

```
while (!quit) {
    WaitEvent (timeout, deviceClass, deviceId);
    switch (deviceClass) {
        case CLASS1: switch (deviceId) {
            case DEVICE1: ProcedureA (); break;
            case DEVICE2: ProcedureB (); break;
        }
        case CLASS2: switch (deviceId) {
etc.
```

As events occur and the program moves to different states, the procedures called in response to a particular event may change, further complicating the program logic.

The *dispatcher model* (also called the *notifier model*) enhances the input-handling system with a procedure that responds to the user actions, as shown in Fig. 10.10. The application program *registers* a procedure with the notifier and tells the notifier under what conditions the procedure is to be called. Procedures called by the notifier are sometimes called *callback procedures*, because they are called back by the notifier. With hierarchical windows, different callback procedures can be associated with locator events occurring in different parts of a dialogue box or in different parts of a menu. These callback procedures may modify the event before it is reported to the application, in which case they are called *filter procedures*.

The input subroutine calls with which a typical window system must deal include

EnableEvents (*eventList*)	Enable the listed set of events
WaitEvent (*timeout, eventType, windowName, eventRecord*)	Get the next event from the event queue
SetInputFocus (*window, eventList*)	Direct all input events of the type on *eventList* to *window*
CursorShape (*pixmap, x, y*)	*pixmap* defines the cursor shape; *x, y* give the position in the cursor pixmap used for reporting the cursor position

Typical types of events that can be placed on the event queue follow:

KeyPress	Keyboard key pressed
KeyRelease	Keyboard key released
ButtonPress	Locator (such as mouse) button pressed
ButtonRelease	Locator button released
Motion	Cursor has moved
LeaveNotify	Cursor has left window
EnterNotify	Cursor has entered window
WindowExpose	Window has been partially or completely exposed
ResizeRequest	Window resizing has been requested
Timer	Previously specified time or time increment has occurred

Each of these event types has a timestamp (see Section 10.1 to understand why this is needed), the name of the window where the cursor was when the event occurred, and other

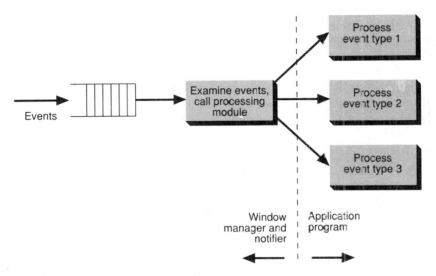

Fig. 10.10 The window manager's notifier examines the event queue and calls the procedure previously registered to process a particular event.

event-specific information, such as the new window size for a ResizeRequest.

This brief overview of window-management systems has excluded important topics, such as ensuring that the window system is sufficiently general that any and all types of window-manager policies can be provided. Also important is whether the window system is a separate process from the clients, is a subroutine library linked in with the clients, or is a part of the operating system. These and other issues are more fully discussed in [LANT87; SCHE86; SCHE88a; STEI89].

10.5 INTERACTION-TECHNIQUE TOOLKITS

The look and feel of a user–computer interface is determined largely by the collection of interaction techniques provided for it. Recall that interaction techniques implement the hardware binding portion of a user–computer interface design. Designing and implementing a good set of interaction techniques is time consuming: Interaction-technique toolkits, which are subroutine libraries of interaction techniques, are mechanisms for making a collection of techniques available for use by application programmers. This approach, which helps to ensure a consistent look and feel among application programs, is clearly a sound software-engineering practice.

Interaction-technique toolkits can be used not only by application programs, but also by the window manager, which is after all just another client program. Using the same toolkit across the board is an important and commonly used approach to providing a look and feel that unifies both multiple applications and the windowing environment itself. For instance, the menu style used to select window operations should be the same style used within applications.

As shown in Fig. 10.1, the toolkit can be implemented on top of the window-management system. In the absence of a window system, toolkits can be implemented directly on top of a graphics subroutine package; however, because elements of a toolkit include menus, dialogue boxes, scroll bars, and the like, all of which can conveniently be implemented in windows, the window system substrate is normally used. Widely used toolkits include the Andrew window-management system's toolkit [PALA88], the Macintosh toolkit [APPL85], OSF/Motif [OPEN89a] and InterViews [LINT89] for use with the X Window System, several toolkits that implement OPEN LOOK [SUN89] on both X and NeWS, Presentation Manager [MICR89], and the SunView window-management system's toolkit [SUN86]. Color Plates I.26 and I.27 show the OSF/Motif interface. Color Plates I.28 and I.29 show the OPEN LOOK interface.

In the X Window System, interaction techniques are called *widgets*, and we adopt this name for use here. A typical set of widgets includes a dialogue box, file-selection box, alert box, help box, list box, message box, radio-button bank, radio buttons, choice-button bank, choice buttons, toggle-button bank, toggle button, fixed menu, pop-up menu, text input, scroll bar, and application window. Each of these widgets is normally implemented as a window. In X, subwindows may also be used. For instance, a radio-button bank is a window containing a subwindow for each radio button. Complex dialogue boxes can have dozens of subwindows. An application window may have subwindows for scroll bars, resize buttons, and so on, as in Fig. 10.8.

Interaction-technique toolkits typically have notifiers of the type discussed in Section 10.4 to invoke callback procedures when events occur in their subwindows. The procedures are, in some cases, part of the toolkit—for instance, procedures to highlight the current menu item, to select and deselect radio buttons, and to scroll a list or file-selection box. They can also be provided by the application; for instance, there are procedures to carry out a command selected from a menu, to check the validity of each character as it is typed into a text input area, or simply to record the fact that a button has been selected. Figure 10.11

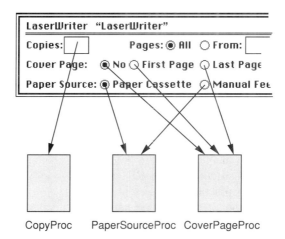

CopyProc   PaperSourceProc CoverPageProc

Fig. 10.11 Callback procedures associated with widgets in a dialogue box. CopyProc checks to ensure that each character is numeric and that the total number entered does not exceed some upper bound. PaperSourceProc manages the radio-button bank for the paper source to ensure that one and only one button is on and to maintain the current selection. CoverPageProc performs a similar function for the cover-page radio-button bank. (Screen graphics © Apple Computer, Inc.)

shows part of a dialogue box and some of the procedures that might be associated with the box.

Notice that the previous list of widgets includes both high- and low-level items, some of which are composites of others. For example, a dialogue box might contain several radio-button banks, toggle-button banks, and text-input areas. Hence, toolkits include a means of composing widgets together, typically via subroutine calls. Figure 10.12 shows just some of the code needed to specify the SunView [SUN86] dialogue box of Fig. 10.13. Some toolkits are built using object-oriented programming concepts: Each widget is an instantiation of the widget's definition, possibly with overrides of some of the methods and attributes associated with the definition. A composite consists of multiple instances.

```
print_frame =
   window_create(
      frame,   FRAME,                    {Surrounding box}
      WIN_SHOW,                          TRUE,
      FRAME_NO_CONFIRM,                  TRUE,
      FRAME_SHOW_LABEL,                  TRUE,
      FRAME_LABEL,      "Print",         {Header at top of window}
   0);                                   {Zero means end of list}

print_panel =                           {Panel inside the window}
   window_create(print_frame,           PANEL,
      WIN_ROWS,                         PRINT_WIN_ROWS,
      WIN_COLUMNS,                      PRINT_WIN_COLS,
   0);

print_uickb_name =                      {Header at top of panel}
   panel_create_item(print_panel,       PANEL_MESSAGE,
      PANEL_LABEL_STRING,               "UICKB: Untitled".
      PANEL_ITEM_X,                     ATTR_COL(PRINT_NAME_COL),
      PANEL_ITEM_Y,                     ATTR_ROW(PRINT_NAME_ROW),
   0);

print_report_choice_item =
   panel_create_item(print_panel,       PANEL_CHOICE,
      {List of mutually exclusive options}
      PANEL_ITEM_X,                     ATTR_COL(PRINT_REPORT_COL),
      PANEL_ITEM_Y,                     ATTR_ROW(PRINT_REPORT_ROW),
      PANEL_LABEL_STRING,               "Report",
      PANEL_LAYOUT,                     PANEL_VERTICAL,{Or horizontal}
      PANEL_CHOICE_STRINGS,
         "Completeness", "Consistency", "Schema", 0,
      PANEL_NOTIFY_PROC,                print_report_choice_proc,
      {Name of callback procedure}
   0);
```

Fig. 10.12 Some of the SunView code needed to specify the dialogue box of Fig. 10.13.

Fig. 10.13 Dialogue box created using the SunView window-manager system's toolkit. The code specifying this box is shown in Fig. 10.12. (Courtesy of Kevin Murray, The George Washington University.)

Creating composites by programming, no matter what the mechanism, is tedious. Interactive editors, such as those shown in Figs. 10.14 and 10.15, allow composites to be created and modified quickly, facilitating the rapid prototyping discussed in Section 9.6. Cardelli has developed a sophisticated interactive editor that allows spatial constraints between widgets to be specified [CARD88]. At run time, when the dialogue box's size can be changed by the user, the constraints are used to keep the widgets neatly spaced.

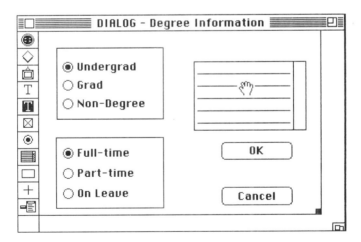

Fig. 10.14 The SmethersBarnes Prototyper dialogue-box editor for the Macintosh. A scrolling-list box is being dragged into position. The menu to the left shows the widgets that can be created; from top to bottom, they are buttons, icons, pictures, static text, text input, check boxes, radio buttons, scrolling lists, rectangles (for visual grouping, as with the radio-button banks), lines (for visual separation), pop-up menus, and scroll bars. (Courtesy of SmethersBarnes, Inc.)

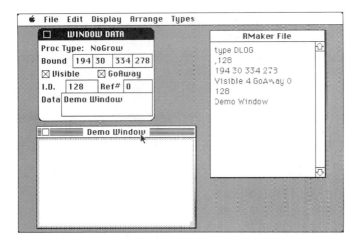

Fig. 10.15 An interactive editor for designing windows. The size, position, border style, title, and presence of the ''go away'' box can all be controlled. The editor shows the window at its actual size; the text file describing the window is at the upper right, and a dialogue box for controlling the window characteristics is at the upper left. The window's size and position can be modified by direct manipulation, in which case the values in the dialogue box are modified. The text file is written out as the permanent record of the window's design. The I.D. and Ref# form a name by which the application program can refer to the window. (Screen graphics © Apple Computer, Inc.)

The output of these editors is a representation of the composite, either as data structures that can be translated into code, or as code, or as compiled code. In any case, mechanisms are provided for linking the composite into the application program. Programming skills are not needed to use the editors, so the editors are available to user-interface designers and even to sophisticated end users. These editors are typical of the interactive design tools shown in Fig. 10.1.

Another approach to creating menus and dialogue boxes is to use a higher-level programming-language description. In Mickey [OLSE89], an extended Pascal for the Macintosh, a dialogue box is defined by a record declaration. The data type of each record item is used to determine the type of widget used in the dialogue box; enumerated types become radio-button banks, character strings become text inputs, Booleans become checkboxes, and so on. Figure 10.16 shows a dialogue box and the code that creates it. An

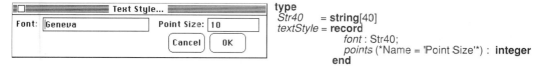

Fig. 10.16 A dialogue box created automatically by Mickey from the extended Pascal record declaration. (Courtesy of Dan Olsen, Jr., Brigham Young University.)

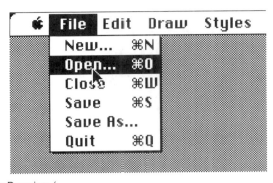

```
procedure NewDrawing (
    (* Menu = File Name = 'New...' Key = N *)
    DrawFile : OutFileDesc);              {Name of dialogue box to be shown.}
procedure OpenDrawing (
    (* Menu = File Name = 'Open...' Key = O *)
    DrawFile : InFileDesc);              {Name of dialogue box to be shown.}
procedure CloseDrawing;
    (* Menu = File Name = 'Close' Key = W *)
procedure SaveDrawing;
    (* Menu = File Name = 'Save' Key = S *)
procedure SaveDrawingAs (
    (* Menu = File Name = 'Save As...' *)
    DrawFile : OutFileDesc);              {Name of dialogue box to be shown.}
```

Fig. 10.17 A menu created automatically by Mickey from the extended Pascal record declaration. (Courtesy of Dan Olsen, Jr., Brigham Young University.)

interactive dialogue-box editor can be used to change the placement of widgets. Figure 10.17 shows a menu and the code from which it is generated.

Peridot [MYER86; MYER88] takes a radically different approach to toolkits. The interface designer creates widgets and composite widgets interactively, by example. Rather than starting with a base set of widgets, the designer works with an interactive editor to create a certain look and feel. Examples of the desired widgets are drawn, and Peridot infers relationships that allow instances of the widget to adapt to a specific situation. For instance, a menu widget infers that its size is to be proportional to the number of items in the menu choice set. To specify the behavior of a widget, such as the type of feedback to be given in response to a user action, the designer selects the type of feedback from a Peridot menu, and Peridot generalizes the example to all menu items.

10.6 USER-INTERFACE MANAGEMENT SYSTEMS

A user-interface management system (UIMS) assists in implementing at least the form of a user interface, and in some cases portions of the meaning as well. All UIMSs provide some means of defining admissible user-action sequences and may in addition support overall screen design, help and error messages, macro definition, undo, and user profiles. Some recent UIMSs also manage the data associated with the application. This is in contrast to interaction technique toolkits, which provide far less support.

UIMSs can increase programmer productivity (in one study, up to 50 percent of the code in interactive programs was user-interface code [SUTT78]), speed up the development process, and facilitate iterative refinement of a user interface as experience is gained in its use. As suggested in Fig. 10.1, the UIMS is interposed between the application program and the interaction-technique toolkit. The more powerful the UIMS, the less the need for the application program to interact directly with the operating system, window system, and toolkit.

In some UIMSs, user-interface elements are specified in a programming language that has specialized operators and data types. In others, the specification is done via interactive graphical editors, thus making the UIMS accessible to nonprogrammer interface designers.

Applications developed on top of a UIMS are typically written as a set of subroutines, often called *action routines* or *semantic action routines*. The UIMS is responsible for calling appropriate action routines in response to user inputs. In turn, the action routines influence the dialogue—for instance, by modifying what the user can do next on the basis of the outcome of a computation. Thus, the UIMS and the application share control of the dialogue—this is called the *shared-control* model. A UIMS in which the action routines have no influence over the dialogue is said to follow an *external-control* model; control resides solely in the UIMS. External control is not as powerful a model as is shared control.

UIMSs vary greatly in the specific capabilities they provide to the user–interface designer, but the one essential ingredient is a dialogue-sequence specification, to control the order in which interaction techniques are made available to the end user. For this reason, in the next section, we turn our attention to dialogue sequencing; then, in Section 10.6.2, we discuss more advanced UIMS concepts. Further background on UIMSs can be found in [HART89; MYER89; OLSE84b; OLSE87].

10.6.1   Dialogue Sequencing

Permissible sequences of user actions can be defined in a variety of ways: via transition networks (also called state diagrams), recursive transition networks, event languages, or by example, where the designer demonstrates the allowable action sequences to the system and the system "learns" what sequences are possible. Common to all these methods is the concept of a user-interface *state* and associated user actions that can be performed from that state. The notion of state has been discussed in Section 9.3.1 (state diagrams) and in Section 9.4 (modes). Each of the specification methods encodes the user-interface state in a slightly different way, each of which generalizes to the use of one or more *state variables*.

If a context-sensitive user interface is to be created, the system response to user actions must depend on the current state of the interface. System responses to user actions can include invocation of one or several action routines, changes in one or more of the state variables, and enabling, disabling, or modifying interaction techniques or menu items in preparation for the next user action. Help should also be dependent on the current state. Since the outcome of computations performed by the action routines should affect user-interface behavior, the action routines must be able to modify the state variables. Thus, state is at the heart of context-sensitivity, a concept central to contemporary user interfaces.

The simplest and least powerful, but nevertheless useful, sequence specification method is the *transition network* or *state diagram*. Transition networks have a single state variable, an integer indicating the current state. User actions cause transitions from one state to another; each transition has associated with it zero or more action routines that are called when the transition occurs. In addition, states can have associated action routines executed whenever the state is entered. This shorthand is convenient for actions that are common to all transitions entering a state.

The action routines can affect the current state of the transition network in one of two ways. First, they can place events in the event queue, which in turn drives the interaction handling. This approach implicitly modifies the state, although to ensure that the state change is immediate, the event must be put at the front of the queue, not at the back. Alternatively, the action routines can modify the state more directly by simply setting the state variable to a new value. The first approach is cleaner from a software-engineering view, whereas the second is more flexible but more error-prone.

A number of UIMSs are based on state diagrams [JACO83; JACO85; SCHU85; RUBE83; WASS85]. Some of these provide interactive transition-network editors, which makes the networks simple to specify. The first UIMS, developed by Newman and called *The Reaction Handler*, included such an editor [NEWM68]. A simple transition-network–driven UIMS is easy to implement—see Exercise 10.8.

Transition networks are especially useful for finding sequencing inconsistencies, as discussed in Section 9.3.1, and can easily be used to determine the number of steps required to complete a task sequence. Thus, they also serve as means of predicting how good a particular design will be, even before the complete interface is implemented. Consider, for example, the simple case of explicit versus implicit acceptance of results. Figure 10.18 represents a one-operand command with explicit acceptance and rejection of the results; Fig. 10.19 shows implicit acceptance and explicit rejection. In the first case, three steps are always required: enter command, enter operand, accept. In the second case, only two steps are normally needed: enter command, enter operand. Three steps are needed only when an error has been made. Minimizing steps per task is one goal in interface design, especially for experienced users, since (not surprisingly) the speed with which experienced users can input commands is nearly linearly related to the number of discrete steps (keystrokes, hand movements) required [CARD80].

Transition networks, however, have drawbacks. First, the user-interface state is typically based on a number of state variables, and having to map all possible combinations of values of these variables onto a single state is awkward and nonintuitive for the

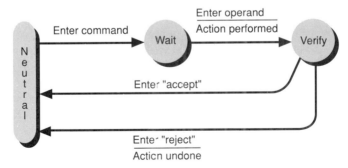

Fig. 10.18 Transition network for a dialogue with explicit acceptance and rejection of results.

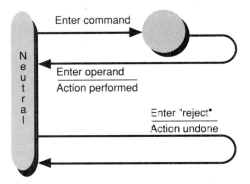

Fig. 10.19 Transition network for a dialogue with implicit acceptance and explicit rejection of results.

user-interface designer. For example, if commands are to behave in one way when there is a currently selected object (CSO) and in another way when there is no CSO, the number of states must be doubled to encode the "CSO exists–does not exist" condition. These types of context-sensitivities can expand the state space and make the transition networks difficult to create and understand. Figure 10.20, for example, shows a transition network for a simple application having the following commands:

- Select an object (establishes a CSO)
- Deselect the CSO (so there is no CSO)
- Create an object (establishes a CSO)
- Delete the CSO (so there is no CSO)
- Copy the CSO to the clipboard (requires a CSO, makes the clipboard full)
- Paste from the clipboard (requires that the clipboard be full, creates a CSO)
- Clear the clipboard (requires that the clipboard be full, empties the clipboard).

Four states are needed to encode the two possible conditions of the clipboard and the CSO. Notice also that whether or not any objects exist at all also should be encoded, since objects must exist for the command Select_object to be available in the starting state. Four more states would be needed to encode whether any objects do or do not exist.

Concurrency creates a similar state-space growth problem. Consider two user-interface elements—say, two concurrently active dialogue boxes—each with its own "state" encoding the selections currently allowable or currently made. If each dialogue-box state can be encoded in 10 states, their combination requires 100 states; for three dialogue boxes, 1000 states are needed; and so on. This exponential growth in state space is unacceptable. Jacob [JACO86] combines transition networks with object-oriented programming concepts to specify complete user interfaces while limiting the state-space explosion. Objects are self-contained entities within the interface, and each object has its own transition network to specify its behavior, which is independent of that of other objects. The UIMS portion of HUTWindows, the Helsinki University of Technology Window Manager and UIMS, uses a similar strategy [KOIV88].

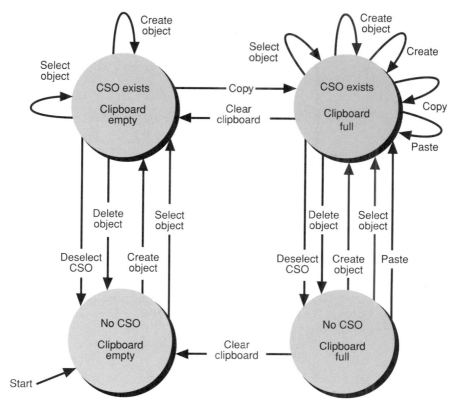

Fig. 10.20 A transition network with four states. Not all commands are available in all states. In general, action routines associated with transitions should appear on diagrams of this sort, with the names of the user actions (user commands in this case); we omit them here because the actions are obvious.

Globally available commands similarly enlarge the transition network. If help is to be globally available, each state must have an associated help state, a transition to the help state, and a reverse transition back to the originating state. This is also needed for the help to be context-sensitive. Undo must be done similarly, except that the transition from an undo state returns to a state different from the one from which it was entered. As the number of transitions relative to the number of states increases, we end up with complex "spaghetti" transition networks.

Various specialized constructs have been developed to simplify transition networks. For instance, we can alleviate the help problem by using subnetworks, in a fashion analogous to subroutines, to hide localized repetitive detail. Transition networks that can call sub-networks recursively are called *recursive transition networks*. The state variables in this case are the entire stack of saved states, plus the state of the currently active transition network. Several other powerful diagramming techniques, all derived from transition networks, are described in [WELL89].

```
<command> ::= <create> | <polyline> | <delete> | <move>  STOP
<create> ::= CREATE + <type> + <position>
<type> ::= SQUARE | TRIANGLE
<position> ::= NUMBER + NUMBER
<polyline> ::= POLYLINE + <vertex list> + END_POLY
<vertex_list> ::= <position> | <vertex_list> + <position>
<delete> ::= DELETE + OBJECT_ID
<move> ::= MOVEA + OBJECT_ID + <position>
```

Fig. 10.21 Backus–Naur form representation of the sequencing rules for a simple user interface.

Backus–Naur form (BNF) can also be used to define sequencing, and is equivalent in representational power to recursive transition networks (both are equivalent to push-down automata). BNF, illustrated in Fig. 10.21, can also be shown diagrammatically as the diagrams of Fig. 10.22. It is difficult to read BNF and to obtain a good overview of the sequencing rules, but BNF form can be processed to provide an evaluation of certain aspects of user-interface quality [BLES82, REIS82], or to generate command-language parsers [JOHN78]. Several older UIMSs were based on BNF specifications [HANA80; OLSE83; OLSE84a].

Transition networks, whether recursive or not, encode user-inteface state in a small number of state variables. *Augmented transition networks* (ATNs), a more flexible derivative of transition networks, encode user-interface state by which node of the ATN is active and by what the values of explicit state variables are. Responses can be the calling of action routines, the setting of these explicit state variables, or the changing of the node of the ATN that is active. Of course, the state variables can also be set by action routines. Figure 10.23 shows an ATN in which the Boolean state variable *cb*, set by several of the transitions, is used to affect flow of control from one state to another. The variable *cb* is **true** if the clipboard is full.

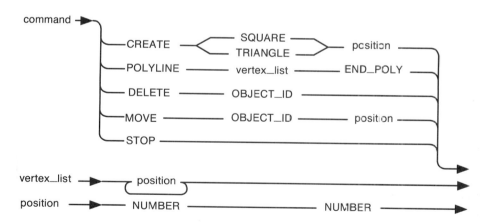

Fig. 10.22 A diagrammatic representation of the Backus–Naur form equivalent to that in Fig. 10.21.

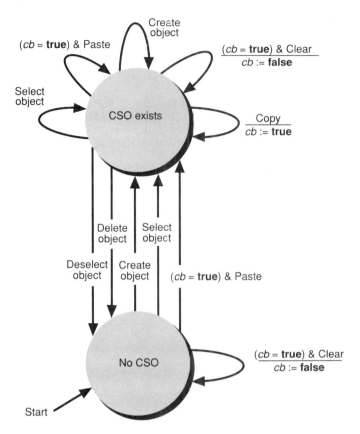

Fig. 10.23 An augmented transition network (ATN) representing the same user interface as that in Fig. 10.20. Transitions can be conditionally dependent on the value of explicit state variables (the Boolean *cb* in this case), and can also set state variables. In general, the application program can also set state variables.

Just as transition networks can be made more general with subnetworks, so too ATNs can call lower-level ATNs. ATNs that can recursively call other ATNs are called *augmented recursive transition networks* [WOOD70], and researchers have used these networks to model user interfaces [KIER85].

As transition networks become more complicated, with logical expressions on transition and subroutine calls, we are led toward more programlike specifications. After all, programming languages are the most powerful way yet developed of specifying sequencing and the multiple conditions often associated with transitions. Several *event languages* have been developed specifically for user-interface specification [CARD85; FLEC87; GARR82; GREE85a; HILL87; KASI82; SIOC89]. The user interface depicted in Figs. 10.20 and 10.23 can be described in a typical event language, as shown in Fig. 10.24. Note that event languages, unlike traditional programming languages, have no explicit flow of control. Instead, whenever an **if** condition becomes true, the associated actions are executed. Thus, the event language is a production-rule system.

```
if Event = SelectObject then
  begin
    cso := true
    perform action routine name
  end
if Event = DeselectCSO and cso = true then
  begin
    cso := false
    perform action routine name
  end
if Event = CreateObject then
  begin
    cso := true
    perform action routine name
  end
if Event = DeleteCSO and cso = true then
  begin
    cso := false
    perform action routine name
  end
if Event = CopyCSO and cso = true then
  begin
    cb := true
    perform action routine name
  end
if Event = PasteClipboard and cb = true then
  begin
    cso := true
    perform action routine name
  end
if Event = ClearClipboard and cb = true then
  begin
    cb := false
    perform action routine name
  end
```

Fig. 10.24 A typical event language, with a Pascal-like syntax.

Green [GREE87] surveys event languages and all the other sequence-specification methods we have mentioned, and shows that general event languages are more powerful than are transition networks, recursive transition networks, and grammars; he also provides algorithms for converting these forms into an event language. ATNs that have general computations associated with their arcs are also equivalent to event languages.

If event languges are so powerful, why do we bother with the various types of transition networks? Because, for simple cases, it is easier to work with diagrammatic representations. One of the goals of UIMSs is to allow nonprogrammers who specialize in user-interface design to be directly involved in creating an interface. This goal is probably best met with transition-network–oriented tools that are easier to use, although somewhat less powerful. Networks provide a useful, time-proven tool for laying out a dialogue, and they appear to help the designer to document and understand the design. The diagrammatic representations are especially compelling if user actions are performed on interaction objects such as menus, dialogue boxes, and other visible objects. Then diagrams of the type shown in Fig. 10.25 can be created interactively to define dialogue sequencing. If needed, conditions (such as the $cb =$ **true** in Fig. 10.23) can be associated with the arcs. Figure 10.26 shows one way to establish a link on such a diagram.

A quite different way to define syntax is by example. Here, the user-interface designer places the UIMS into a "learning" mode, and then steps through all acceptable sequences of actions (a tedious process in complex applications, unless the UIMS can infer general rules from the examples). The designer might start with a main menu, select an item from it, and then go through a directory to locate the submenu, dialogue box, or application-specific object to be presented to the user in response to the main menu selection. The object appears on the screen, and the designer can indicate the position, size, or other attributes that the object should have when the application is actually executed. The designer goes on to perform some operation on the displayed object and again shows what object should appear next, or how the displayed object is to respond to the operation; the designer repeats this process until all actions on all objects have been defined. This technique works for sequencing through items that have already been defined by the interface designer, but is not sufficiently general to handle arbitrary application function-ality. User-interface software tools with some degree of by-example sequencing specifica-tion include Menulay [BUXT83], TAE Plus [MILL88c] and the SmethersBarnes Prototyper [COSS89]. Peridot, mentioned earlier, builds interaction techniques, (i.e., hardware bindings) by example.

10.6.2 Advanced UIMS Concepts

UIMSs have tended to focus on sequence control and visual design. Transition networks provide a good basis for sequencing, and interactive editors are just right for visual design.

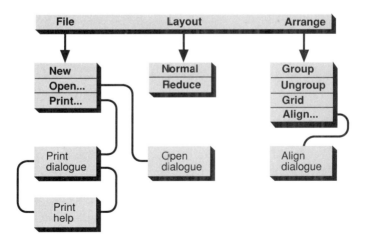

Fig. 10.25 Several menus and dialogue boxes linked together. The return paths from dialogue boxes to the main menu are not shown.

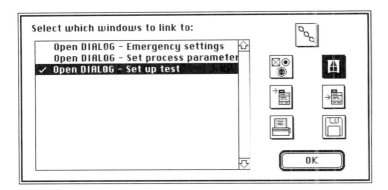

Fig. 10.26 Linking together different interaction techniques using the SmethersBarnes Prototyper. A menu item is being linked to the dialogue box "Set up test" checked in the list. The icons on the right are used to select the class of responses to be linked to the menu selection. Reading left to right underneath the "link" icon, the possibilities are enable or disable check boxes, radio buttons, and buttons in dialogue boxes; open a window or dialogue box (the class of response selected); enable or disable a menu; enable or disable a menu item; open a print dialogue box; or open a file dialogue box. (Courtesy of SmethersBarnes, Inc.)

As discussed in Chapter 9, however, a user-interface design includes conceptual, functional, sequencing, and hardware-binding levels. Much recent UIMS development has begun to address the functional and conceptual designs as well. Thus, there has come to be more focus on combining sequencing control with a higher-level model of objects and commands, and also on integrating intelligent help systems into the UIMS.

Representations at a higher level than that of transition networks are clearly needed. Consider how difficult it would be to add to the transition network of Fig. 10.20 new states to record whether any objects have yet been created. It would also be difficult to apply some of the dialogue modifications, such as CO, currently selected command, and factored attributes, discussed in Section 9.4. And the sequencing specifications provide no information about what operations can be performed on what objects, and certainly give no glimmer of what parameters are needed to perform an operation.

The first step away from a sequencing orientation and toward higher levels of abstraction was taken by COUSIN [HAYE83; HAYE84], which automatically generates menus and dialogue boxes from a specification of commands, parameters, and parameter data types. The innovation of COUSIN is in defining all the parameters needed by a command as an integral unit. COUSIN has enough information that a prefix or postfix syntax could also be generated. Green took a similar approach, adding preconditions and postconditions to specify the semantics of user commands [GREE85b]. Olsen's MIKE system [OLSE86] declares commands and parameters, also generating a user interface in a fashion similar to COUSIN. In addition, MIKE supports direct manipulation of objects to specify positions, and can cause commands to be executed when a button-down event occurs in a window or subwindow.

All these significant advances are focused on commands. If a UIMS is to mediate between the user and the application in direct-manipulation interfaces, however, it must have some knowledge of the objects to be manipulated. HIGGINS was the first UIMS to incorporate a data model [HUDS86; HUDS87; HUDS88], one that is based on objects and relations between objects. The UIMS and action routines share the data model, so that changes made to data objects can be immediately reflected in the display. *Active values* are used to propogate changes among interdependent objects and from objects to their visual representations. The George Washington University User Interface Management System (GWUIMS) uses active values and object-oriented programming concepts to achieve a similar objective [SIBE86]. GWUIMS II also uses a data model [HURL89], as does the Serpent UIMS [BASS88]. Although the details vary, all the data models make use of object-oriented programming concepts and active values, and are closely related to developments in database-management systems in the area of semantic data models [HULL87].

The User Interface Design Environment (UIDE) project [FOLE89] has developed a new user-interface specification method integrating some elements of these recent developments to include a data model, the commands that can be applied to each type of object in the data model, the parameters needed by the commands, the parameter data types, the conditions under which commands are available for use (that is, command preconditions), and the changes that occur to state variables when a command is executed (that is, command postconditions) [FOLE87; FOLE88]. To illustrate the method, we start with the sample application developed in Section 10.6.1. We add a data model, which is here a single class of objects with two subclasses, square and triangle. In addition, there are two distinguished instances of objects, the CSO and the clipboard object, both of which may or may not exist at any given time. The specification is shown in Fig. 10.27. The preconditions are the conditions on state variables that must be satisfied for a command to be invoked, whereas the postconditions are changes in state variables.

Not only is this specification sufficient to create automatically an operational interface to the application's action routines, but also it is represented such that

- Menu items can be enabled and disabled, using preconditions
- Users can be told why a command is disabled, again using preconditions
- Users can be told what to do to enable a command, by back chaining to determine what commands must be invoked to satisfy the preconditions of the command in question
- Users can be given a partial explanation of what a command does, using the postconditions
- Some user-interface design-consistency rules can be checked
- Different interaction techniques can be assigned for use in specifying commands and command parameters
- Speed of use of the interface can be predicted for various task sequences and for various interaction techniques.

Another way to define user interfaces consisting of interconnected processing modules is with data-flow diagrams. For instance, the NeXT Interface Builder, shown in Fig. 10.28,

```
class object                                    {First the data model}
    subclasses triangle, square;
    actions CreateObject, SelectObject;
    attributes position range [0..10] x [0..10]    {Attribute name and data type}
class triangle, square;
    superclass object;
    inherits   actions
    inherits   attributes
instance CSO
    of object
    actions DeselectCSO, DeleteCSO, CopyCSO
    inherits   attributes
instance CB
    of object
    actions ClearClipboard, Paste
    inherits   attributes


{Initial values for state variables}
initial Number (object) := 0; csoExists := false; cbFull := false;

{Actions on objects, with preconditions, postconditions, and parameters}
precondition Number (object) ≠ 0;
SelectObject (object);
postcondition csoExists := true;


precondition csoExists := true;
DeselectCSO (CSO);
postcondition csoExists := false;


precondition;
CreateObject (position, object);
postcondition Number (object) := Number (object) +1; csoExists := true;


precondition csoExists := true;
DeleteCSO (CSO);
postcondition Number (object) = Number (object) - 1; csoExists := false;


precondition csoExists := true;
CopyCSO (CSO);
postcondition cbFull := true;


precondition cbFull := true;
Paste (CB);
postcondition csoExists := true;


precondition cbFull := true;
ClearClipboard (CB);
postcondition cbFull := false;
```

Fig. 10.27 A high-level specification of a user interface incorporating a data model, sequencing information, and command parameters.

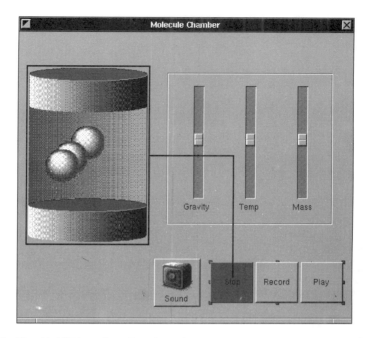

Fig. 10.28 The NeXT Interface Builder, showing a connection being made. The user has already selected the type of message to be sent from the Stop button, and has drawn the connection to the cylindrical chamber to indicate the destination of the message. (Courtesy of NeXT, Inc. © 1989 NeXT, Inc.)

allows objects to be interconnected so that output messages from one object are input to another object. Type checking is used to ensure that only compatible messages are sent and received.

Data-flow diagrams can also be used to specify the detailed behavior of some or all of a user interface, although doing so takes on considerable programming flavor and suffers the same problems of scale seen with flowcharts and transition networks. Work is this area is surveyed in [BORN86a]; a more recent project is described in [SMIT88]. A specialized system, for scientific data visualization, is shown in Color Plate I.30.

UIMSs are finding their way into regular use. Early UIMSs suffered from rigid interaction styles that did not allow custom-tailoring to suit users' needs and were overly dependent on transition networks. Commercial UIMSs are now used on a large scale, and are becoming as essential to developing interactive graphics application programs as are graphics subroutine packages, window managers, and interaction-technique toolkits.

EXERCISES

10.1 Study the user interfaces to two different window systems. Categorize each with respect to the design issues discussed in Section 9.3.

10.2 Devise the search mechanism for real-estate–based event routing with overlapping main windows, in which each main window can contain a hierarchy of spatially nested subwindows.

10.3 Survey three window-management systems to determine whether they
  a. Have hierarchical windows
  b. Implement a server–client model and, if they do, whether the implementation allows the server and client to be distributed in a network
  c. Provide real-estate or listener input event dispatching, or some combination thereof
  d. Integrate the graphics subroutine package with the window-management system, or pass graphics calls directly through to graphics hardware.

10.4 Write an interactive dialogue box or menu editor.

10.5 Implement the concepts demonstrated in MICKY [OLSE89] with a programming language and toolkit available to you.

10.6 Examine several user interfaces with which you are familiar. Identify a set of user-interface state variables used in implementing each user interface. How many of these state variables are used in the user interface to provide context-sensitive menus, help, and so on?

10.7 Document the dialogue of a user interface to a paint or drawing program. Do this (a) with state diagrams, and (b) with the specialized language introduced in Section 10.6.1. Which method did you find easier? Why? Compare your opinions with those of your classmates. Which method is easier for answering questions such as "How do I draw a circle?" "What do I do after an error message appears?"

10.8 Write a transition-network–based UIMS. Every transition in the state diagram should be represented by a state-table entry with the following information:

  ▪ Current state number
  ▪ Next state
  ▪ Event which causes the transition
  ▪ Name of procedure to call when the transition occurs.

Events should include selection of a command from a menu, typing of a command name, mouse movement, mouse button-down, and mouse button-up. You should automatically display a menu containing all possible commands (derive this list from the events in the state table), enabling only those choices available from the current state.

10.9 For each of the extensions to state diagrams discussed in Section 9.3, determine whether the modifications create a push-down automaton (is it bounded or unbounded?) or a Turing machine.

10.10 Carefully study a window-management system that includes a policy-free window system. Examine several window managers to determine whether they can be implemented with the window system. For instance, some window systems provide for borders around windows for scroll bars, a heading, and perhaps selection buttons. For the window system to be completely policy-free, you must be able to specify separately the width of the borders on the four sides of the window.

11
Representing
Curves and
Surfaces

Smooth curves and surfaces must be generated in many computer graphics applications. Many real-world objects are inherently smooth, and much of computer graphics involves modeling the real world. Computer-aided design (CAD), high-quality character fonts, data plots, and artists' sketches all contain smooth curves and surfaces. The path of a camera or object in an animation sequence (Chapter 21) is almost always smooth; similarly, a path through intensity or color space (Chapters 16 and 13) must often be smooth.

The need to represent curves and surfaces arises in two cases: in modeling existing objects (a car, a face, a mountain) and in modeling "from scratch," where no preexisting physical object is being represented. In the first case, a mathematical description of the object may be unavailable. Of course, one can use as a model the coordinates of the infinitely many points of the object, but this is not feasible for a computer with finite storage. More often, we merely approximate the object with pieces of planes, spheres, or other shapes that are easy to describe mathematically, and require that points on our model be close to corresponding points on the object.

In the second case, when there is no preexisting object to model, the user creates the object in the modeling process; hence, the object matches its representation exactly, because its only embodiment is the representation. To create the object, the user may sculpt the object interactively, describe it mathematically, or give an approximate description to be "filled in" by some program. In CAD, the computer representation is used later to generate physical realizations of the abstractly designed object.

This chapter introduces the general area of *surface modeling*. The area is quite broad, and only the three most common representations for 3D surfaces are presented here: polygon mesh surfaces, parametric surfaces, and quadric surfaces. We also discuss

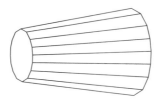

Fig. 11.1 A 3D object represented by polygons.

parametric curves, both because they are interesting in their own right and because parametric surfaces are a simple generalization of the curves.

Solid modeling, introduced in the next chapter, is the representation of volumes completely surrounded by surfaces, such as a cube, an airplane, or a building. The surface representations discussed in this chapter can be used in solid modeling to define each of the surfaces that bound the volume.

A *polygon mesh* is a set of connected polygonally bounded planar surfaces. Open boxes, cabinets, and building exteriors can be easily and naturally represented by polygon meshes, as can volumes bounded by planar surfaces. Polygon meshes can be used, although less easily, to represent objects with curved surfaces, as in Fig. 11.1; however, the representation is only approximate. Figure 11.2 shows the cross-section of a curved shape and the polygon mesh representing it. The obvious errors in the representation can be made arbitrarily small by using more and more polygons to create a better piecewise linear approximation, but this increases space requirements and the execution time of algorithms processing the representation. Furthermore, if the image is enlarged, the straight edges again become obvious. (Forrest calls this problem ''geometric aliasing'' [FORR80], by analogy to the general notion of aliasing discussed in Chapters 3 and 14.)

Parametric polynomial curves define points on a 3D curve by using three polynomials in a parameter t, one for each of x, y, and z. The coefficients of the polynomials are selected such that the curve follows the desired path. Although various degrees of polynomials can be used, we present only the most common case, cubic polynomials (that have powers of the parameter up through the third). The term *cubic curve* will often be used for such curves.

Parametric bivariate (two-variable) *polynomial surface patches* define the coordinates of points on a curved surface by using three bivariate polynomials, one for each of x, y, and z. The boundaries of the patches are parametric polynomial curves. Many fewer bivariate polynomial surface patches than polygonal patches are needed to approximate a curved

Fig. 11.2 A cross-section of a curved object and its polygonal representation.

surface to a given accuracy. The algorithms for working with bivariate polynomials, however, are more complex than are those for polygons. As with curves, polynomials of various degrees can be used, but we discuss here only the common case of polynomials that are cubic in both parameters. The surfaces are accordingly called *bicubic surfaces*.

Quadric surfaces are those defined implicitly by an equation $f(x, y, z) = 0$, where f is a quadric polynomial in x, y, and z. Quadric surfaces are a convenient representation for the familiar sphere, ellipsoid, and cylinder.

The next chapter, on solid modeling, incorporates these representations into systems to represent not just surfaces, but also bounded (solid) volumes. The surface representations described in this chapter are used, sometimes in combination with one another, to bound a 3D volume.

11.1 POLYGON MESHES

A *polygon mesh* is a collection of edges, vertices, and polygons connected such that each edge is shared by at most two polygons. An edge connects two vertices, and a polygon is a closed sequence of edges. An edge can be shared by two adjacent polygons, and a vertex is shared by at least two edges. A polygon mesh can be represented in several different ways, each with its advantages and disadvantages. The application programmer's task is to choose the most appropiate representation. Several representations can be used in a single application: one for external storage, another for internal use, and yet another with which the user interactively creates the mesh.

Two basic criteria, space and time, can be used to evaluate different representations. Typical operations on a polygon mesh are finding all the edges incident to a vertex, finding the polygons sharing an edge or a vertex, finding the vertices connected by an edge, finding the edges of a polygon, displaying the mesh, and identifying errors in representation (e.g., a missing edge, vertex, or polygon). In general, the more explicitly the relations among polygons, vertices, and edges are represented, the faster the operations are and the more space the representation requires. Woo [WOO85] has analyzed the time complexity of nine basic access operations and nine basic update operations on a polygon-mesh data structure.

In the rest of this section, several issues concerning polygon meshes are discussed: representing polygon meshes, ensuring that a given representation is correct, and calculating the coefficients of the plane of a polygon.

11.1.1 Representing Polygon Meshes

In this section, we discuss three polygon-mesh representations: explicit, pointers to a vertex list, and pointers to an edge list. In the *explicit* representation, each polygon is represented by a list of vertex coordinates:

$$P = ((x_1, y_1, z_1), (x_2, y_2, z_2), \ldots, (x_q, y_n, z_n)).$$

The vertices are stored in the order in which they would be encountered traveling around the polygon. There are edges between successive vertices in the list and between the last and first vertices. For a single polygon, this is space-efficient; for a polygon mesh, however, much space is lost because the coordinates of shared vertices are duplicated. Even worse, there is no explicit representation of shared edges and vertices. For instance, to drag a vertex and all its incident edges interactively, we must find all polygons that share the vertex. This requires comparing the coordinate triples of one polygon with those of all other polygons. The most efficient way to do this would be to sort all N coordinate triples, but this is at best an $N\log_2 N$ process, and even then there is the danger that the same vertex might, due to computational roundoff, have slightly different coordinate values in each polygon, so a correct match might never be made.

With this representation, displaying the mesh either as filled polygons or as polygon outlines necessitates transforming each vertex and clipping each edge of each polygon. If edges are being drawn, each shared edge is drawn twice; this causes problems on pen plotters, film recorders, and vector displays due to the overwriting. A problem may also be created on raster displays if the edges are drawn in opposite directions, in which case extra pixels may be intensified.

Polygons defined with *pointers to a vertex list*, the method used by SPHIGS, have each vertex in the polygon mesh stored just once, in the vertex list $V = ((x_1, y_1, z_1), \ldots, (x_n, y_n, z_n))$. A polygon is defined by a list of indices (or pointers) into the vertex list. A polygon made up of vertices 3, 5, 7, and 10 in the vertex list would thus be represented as $P = (3, 5, 7, 10)$.

This representation, an example of which is shown in Fig. 11.3, has several advantages over the explicit polygon representation. Since each vertex is stored just once, considerable space is saved. Furthermore, the coordinates of a vertex can be changed easily. On the other hand, it is still difficult to find polygons that share an edge, and shared polygon edges are still drawn twice when all polygon outlines are displayed. These two problems can be eliminated by representing edges explicitly, as in the next method.

When defining polygons by *pointers to an edge list*, we again have the vertex list V, but represent a polygon as a list of pointers not to the vertex list, but rather to an edge list, in which each edge occurs just once. In turn, each edge in the edge list points to the two vertices in the vertex list defining the edge, and also to the one or two polygons to which the edge belongs. Hence, we describe a polygon as $P = (E_1, \ldots, E_n)$, and an edge as $E = (V_1, V_2, P_1, P_2)$. When an edge belongs to only one polygon, either P_1 or P_2 is null. Figure 11.4 shows an example of this representation.

Polygon outlines are shown by displaying all edges, rather than by displaying all polygons; thus, redundant clipping, transformation, and scan conversion are avoided. Filled polygons are also displayed easily. In some situations, such as the description of a 3D honeycomblike sheet-metal structure, some edges are shared by three polygons. In such

$$V = (V_1, V_2, V_3, V_4) = ((x_1, y_1, z_1), \ldots, (x_4, y_4, z_4))$$
$$P_1 = (1, 2, 4)$$
$$P_2 = (4, 2, 3)$$

Fig. 11.3 Polygon mesh defined with indexes into a vertex list.

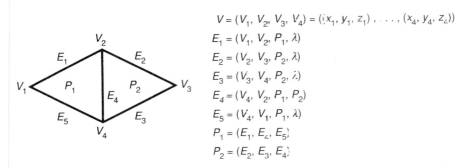

$$V = (V_1, V_2, V_3, V_4) = ((x_1, y_1, z_1), \ldots, (x_4, y_4, z_4))$$
$$E_1 = (V_1, V_2, P_1, \lambda)$$
$$E_2 = (V_2, V_3, P_2, \lambda)$$
$$E_3 = (V_3, V_4, P_2, \lambda)$$
$$E_4 = (V_4, V_2, P_1, P_2)$$
$$E_5 = (V_4, V_1, P_1, \lambda)$$
$$P_1 = (E_1, E_4, E_5)$$
$$P_2 = (E_2, E_3, E_4)$$

Fig. 11.4 Polygon mesh defined with edge lists for each polygon (λ represents null).

cases, the edge descriptions can be extended to include an arbitrary number of polygons:
$E = (V_1, V_2, P_1, P_2, \ldots, P_n)$.

In none of these three representations (i.e., explicit polygons, pointers to vertices, pointers to an edge list), is it easy to determine which edges are incident to a vertex: All edges must be inspected. Of course, information can be added explicitly to permit determining such relationships. For instance, the winged-edge representation used by Baumgart [BAUM75] expands the edge description to include pointers to the two adjoining edges of each polygon, whereas the vertex description includes a pointer to an (arbitrary) edge incident on the vertex, and thus more polygon and vertex information is available. This representation is discussed in Chapter 12.

11.1.2   Consistency of Polygon-Mesh Representations

Polygon meshes are often generated interactively, such as by operators digitizing drawings, so errors are inevitable. Thus, it is appropriate to make sure that all polygons are closed, all edges are used at least once but not more than some (application-defined) maximum, and each vertex is referenced by at least two edges. In some applications, we would also expect the mesh to be completely connected (any vertex can be reached from any other vertex by moving along edges), to be topologically planar (the binary relation on vertices defined by edges can be represented by a planar graph), or to have no holes (there exists just one boundary—a connected sequence of edges each of which is used by one polygon).

Of the three representations discussed, the explicit-edge scheme is the easiest to check for consistency, because it contains the most information. For example, to make sure that all edges are part of at least one but no more than some maximum number of polygons, the code in Fig. 11.5 can be used.

This procedure is by no means a complete consistency check. For example, an edge used twice in the same polygon goes undetected. A similar procedure can be used to make sure that each vertex is part of at least one polygon; we check whether at least two different edges of the same polygon refer to the vertex. Also, it should be an error for the two vertices of an edge to be the same, unless edges with zero length are allowed.

The relationship of "sharing an edge" between polygons is a binary equivalence relation and hence partitions a mesh into equivalence classes called *connected components*.

```
for (each edge Eⱼ in set of edges)
    use_countⱼ = 0;
for (each polygon Pᵢ in set of polygons)
    for (each edge Eⱼ of polygon P)
        use_countⱼ++;
for (each edge Eⱼ in set of edges) {
    if (use_countⱼ == 0)
        Error ();
    if (use_countⱼ > maximum)
        Error ();
}
```

Fig. 11.5 Code to ensure that all edges of explicit polygon representation are used between 1 and *maximum* times.

One usually expects a polygon mesh to have a single connected component. Algorithms for determining the connected components of a binary relation are well known [SEDG88].

More detailed testing is also possible; one can check, for instance, that each polygon referred to by an edge E_i refers in turn back to the edge E_i. This ensures that all references from polygons to edges are complete. Similarly, we can check that each edge E_i referred to by a polygon P_i also refers back to polygon P_i, which ensures that the references from edges to polygons are complete.

11.1.3   Plane Equations

When working with polygons or polygon meshes, we frequently need to know the equation of the plane in which the polygon lies. In some cases, of course, the equation is known implicitly through the interactive construction methods used to define the polygon. If it is not known, we can use the coordinates of three vertices to find the plane. Recall the plane equation

$$Ax + By + Cz + D = 0. \tag{11.1}$$

The coefficients A, B, and C define the normal to the plane, $[A \quad B \quad C]$. Given points P_1, P_2, and P_3 on the plane, that plane's normal can be computed as the vector cross-product $P_1P_2 \times P_1P_3$ (or $P_2P_3 \times P_2P_1$, etc.). If the cross-product is zero, then the three points are collinear and do not define a plane. Other vertices, if any, can be used instead. Given a nonzero cross-product, D can be found by substituting the normal $[A \quad B \quad C]$ and any one of the three points into Eq. (11.1).

If there are more than three vertices, they may be nonplanar, either for numerical reasons or because of the method by which the polygons were generated. Then another technique for finding the coefficients A, B, and C of a plane that comes close to all the vertices is better. It can be shown that A, B, and C are proportional to the signed areas of the projections of the polygon onto the (y, z), (x, z), and (x, y) planes, respectively. For example, if the polygon is parallel to the (x, y) plane, then $A = B = 0$, as expected: The projections of the polygon onto the (y, z) and (x, z) planes have zero area. This method is better because the areas of the projections are a function of the coordinates of all the vertices and so are not sensitive to the choice of a few vertices that might happen not to be coplanar with most or all of the other vertices, or that might happen to be collinear. For instance, the area (and hence coefficient) C of the polygon projected onto the (x, y) plane in Fig. 11.6 is just the area of the trapezoid A_3, minus the areas of A_1 and A_2. In general,

$$C = \frac{1}{2} \sum_{i=1}^{n} (y_i + y_{i \oplus 1})(x_{i \oplus 1} - x_i), \tag{11.2}$$

where the operator $\oplus$ is normal addition except that $n \oplus 1 = 1$. The areas for A and B are given by similar formulae, except the area for B is negated (see Exercise 11.1).

Eq. (11.2) gives the sum of the areas of all the trapezoids formed by successive edges of the polygons. If $x_{i \oplus 1} < x_i$, the area makes a negative contribution to the sum. The sign of the sum is also useful: if the vertices have been enumerated in a clockwise direction (as projected onto the plane), then the sign is positive; otherwise, it is negative.

Once we determine the plane equation by using all the vertices, we can estimate how nonplanar the polygon is by calculating the perpendicular distance from the plane to each vertex. This distance d for the vertex at (x, y, z) is

$$d = \frac{Ax + By + Cz + D}{\sqrt{A^2 + B^2 + C^2}}. \tag{11.3}$$

This distance is either positive or negative, depending on which side of the plane the point is located. If the vertex is on the plane, then $d = 0$. Of course, to determine only on which side of a plane a point is, only the sign of d matters, so division by the square root is not needed.

The plane equation is not unique; any nonzero multiplicative constant k changes the equation, but not the plane. It is often convenient to store the plane coefficients with a normalized normal; this can be done by choosing

$$k = \frac{1}{\sqrt{A^2 + B^2 + C^2}}, \tag{11.4}$$

which is the reciprocal of the length of the normal. Then, distances can be computed with Eq. (11.3) more easily, since the denominator is 1.

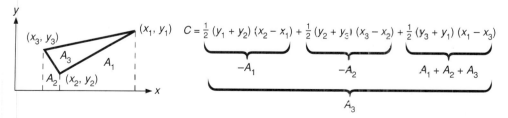

Fig. 11.6 Calculating the area C of a triangle using Eq. (11.2).

11.2 PARAMETRIC CUBIC CURVES

Polylines and polygons are first-degree, piecewise linear approximations to curves and surfaces, respectively. Unless the curves or surfaces being approximated are also piecewise linear, large numbers of endpoint coordinates must be created and stored to achieve reasonable accuracy. Interactive manipulation of the data to approximate a shape is tedious, because many points have to be positioned precisely.

In this section, a more compact and more manipulable representation of piecewise smooth curves is developed; in the following section, the mathematical development is generalized to surfaces. The general approach is to use functions that are of a higher degree than are the linear functions. The functions still generally only approximate the desired shapes, but use less storage and offer easier interactive manipulation than do linear functions.

The higher-degree approximations can be based on one of three methods. First, one can express y and z as *explicit* functions of x, so that $y = f(x)$ and $z = g(x)$. The difficulties with this are that (1) it is impossible to get multiple values of y for a single x, so curves such as circles and ellipses must be represented by multiple curve segments; (2) such a definition is not rotationally invariant (to describe a rotated version of the curve requires a great deal of work and may in general require breaking a curve segment into many others); and (3) describing curves with vertical tangents is difficult, because a slope of infinity is difficult to represent.

Second, we can choose to model curves as solutions to *implicit* equations of the form $f(x, y, z) = 0$; this is fraught with its own perils. First, the given equation may have more solutions than we want. For example, in modeling a circle, we might want to use $x^2 + y^2 = 1$, which is fine. But how do we model a half circle? We must add constraints such as $x \geq 0$, which cannot be contained within the implicit equation. Furthermore, if two implicitly defined curve segments are joined together, it may be difficult to determine whether their tangent directions agree at their join point. Tangent continuity is critical in many applications.

These two mathematical forms do permit rapid determination of whether a point lies on the curve or on which side of the curve the point lies, as was done in Chapter 3. Normals to the curve are also easily computed. Hence, we shall briefly discuss the implicit form in Section 11.4.

The *parametric representation* for curves, $x = x(t)$, $y = y(t)$, $z = z(t)$ overcomes the problems caused by functional or implicit forms and offers a variety of other attractions that will become clear in the remainder of this chapter. Parametric curves replace the use of geometric slopes (which may be infinite) with parametric tangent vectors (which, we shall see, are never infinite). Here a curve is approximated by a *piecewise polynomial* curve instead of the piecewise linear curve used in the preceding section. Each segment Q of the overall curve is given by three functions, x, y, and z, which are cubic polynomials in the parameter t.

Cubic polynomials are most often used because lower-degree polynomials give too little flexibility in controlling the shape of the curve, and higher-degree polynomials can introduce unwanted wiggles and also require more computation. No lower-degree representation allows a curve segment to interpolate (pass through) two specified endpoints with specified derivatives at each endpoint. Given a cubic polynomial with its four coefficients, four knowns are used to solve for the unknown coefficients. The four knowns might be the two endpoints and the derivatives at the endpoints. Similarly, the two coefficients of a first-order (straight-line) polynomial are determined by the two endpoints. For a straight line, the derivatives at each end are determined by the line itself and cannot be controlled independently. With quadratic (second-degree) polynomials, and hence three coefficients, two endpoints and one other condition, such as a slope or additional point, can be specified.

Also, parametric cubics are the lowest-degree curves that are nonplanar in 3D. You can see this by recognizing that a second-order polynomial's three coefficients can be completely specified by three points and that three points define a plane in which the polynomial lies.

Higher-degree curves require more conditions to determine the coefficients and can "wiggle" back and forth in ways that are difficult to control. Despite this, higher-degree curves are used in applications—such as the design of cars and planes—in which higher-degree derivatives must be controlled to create surfaces that are aerodynamically efficient. In fact, the mathematical development for parametric curves and surfaces is often given in terms of an arbitrary degree n. In this chapter, we fix n at 3.

The cubic polynomials that define a curve segment $Q(t) = [x(t)\ y(t)\ z(t)]$ are of the form

$$x(t) = a_x t^3 + b_x t^2 + c_x t + d_x,$$
$$y(t) = a_y t^3 + b_y t^2 + c_y t + d_y,$$
$$z(t) = a_z t^3 + b_z t^2 + c_z t + d_z, \qquad 0 \le t \le 1. \tag{11.5}$$

To deal with finite segments of the curve, without loss of generality, we restrict the parameter t to the [0, 1] interval.

With $T = [t^3\ t^2\ t\ 1]$, and defining the matrix of coefficients of the three polynomials as

$$C = \begin{bmatrix} a_x & a_y & a_z \\ b_x & b_y & b_z \\ c_x & c_y & c_z \\ d_x & d_y & d_z \end{bmatrix}, \tag{11.6}$$

we can rewrite Eq. (11.5) as

$$Q(t) = [x(t)\quad y(t)\quad z(t)] = T \cdot C. \tag{11.7}$$

This provides a compact way to express the Eq. (11.5).

Figure 11.7 shows two joined parametric cubic curve segments and their polynomials; it also illustrates the ability of parametrics to represent easily multiple values of y for a single value of x with polynomials that are themselves single valued. (This figure of a curve, like all others in this section, shows 2D curves represented by $[x(t)\quad y(t)]$.)

The derivative of $Q(t)$ is the parametric *tangent vector* of the curve. Applying this definition to Eq. (11.7), we have

$$\frac{d}{dt}Q(t) = Q'(t) = \left[\frac{d}{dt}x(t)\quad \frac{d}{dt}y(t)\quad \frac{d}{dt}z(t)\right] = \frac{d}{dt}T \cdot C = [3t^2\quad 2t\quad 1\quad 0] \cdot C$$

$$= [3a_x t^2 + 2b_x t + c_x \quad 3a_y t^2 + 2b_y t + c_y \quad 3a_z t^2 + 2b_z t + c_z]. \tag{11.8}$$

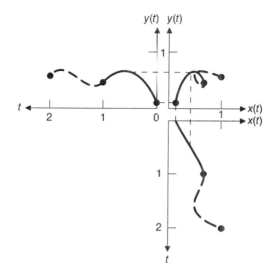

Fig. 11.7 Two joined 2D parametric curve segments and their defining polynomials. The dashed lines between the (x, y) plot and the $x(t)$ and $y(t)$ plots show the correspondence between the points on the (x, y) curve and the defining cubic polynomials. The $x(t)$ and $y(t)$ plots for the second segment have been translated to begin at $t = 1$, rather than at $t = 0$, to show the continuity of the curves at their join point.

If two curve segments join together, the curve has G^0 *geometric continuity*. If the directions (but not necessarily the magnitudes) of the two segments' tangent vectors are equal at a join point, the curve has G^1 geometric continuity. In computer-aided design of objects, G^1 continuity between curve segments is often required. G^1 continuity means that the geometric slopes of the segments are equal at the join point. For two tangent vectors TV_1 and TV_2 to have the same direction, it is necessary that one be a scalar multiple of the other: $TV_1 = k \cdot TV_2$, with $k > 0$ [BARS88].

If the tangent vectors of two cubic curve segments are equal (i. e., their directions *and* magnitudes are equal) at the segments' join point, the curve has first-degree continuity in the parameter t, or *parametric continuity*, and is said to be C^1 continuous. If the direction and magnitude of $d^n/dt^n[Q(t)]$ through the nth derivative are equal at the join point, the curve is called C^n *continuous*. Figure 11.8 shows curves with three different degrees of continuity. Note that a parametric curve segment is itself everywhere continuous; the continuity of concern here is at the join points.

The tangent vector $Q'(t)$ is the velocity of a point on the curve with respect to the parameter t. Similarly, the second derivative of $Q(t)$ is the acceleration. If a camera is moving along a parametric cubic curve in equal time steps and records a picture after each step, the tangent vector gives the velocity of the camera along the curve. The camera velocity and acceleration at join points should be continuous, to avoid jerky movements in the resulting animation sequence. It is this continuity of acceleration across the join point in Fig. 11.8 that makes the C^2 curve continue farther to the right than the C^1 curve, before bending around to the endpoint.

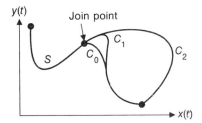

Fig. 11.8 Curve segment S joined to segments C_0, C_1, and C_2 with the 0, 1, and 2 degrees of parametric continuity, respectively. The visual distinction between C_1 and C_2 is slight at the join, but obvious away from the join.

In general, C^1 continuity implies G^1, but the converse is generally not true. That is, G^1 continuity is generally less restrictive than is C^1, so curves can be G^1 but not necessarily C^1. However, join points with G^1 continuity will appear just as smooth as those with C^1 continuity, as seen in Fig. 11.9.

There is a special case in which C^1 continuity does *not* imply G^1 continuity: When both segments' tangent vectors are [0 0 0] at the join point. In this case, the tangent vectors are indeed equal, but their directions can be different (Fig. 11.10). Figure 11.11 shows this concept in another way. Think again of a camera moving along the curve; the camera velocity slows down to zero at the join point, the camera changes direction while its velocity is zero, and the camera accelerates in the new direction.

The plot of a parametric curve is distinctly different from the plot of an ordinary function, in which the independent variable is plotted on the x axis and the dependent variable is plotted on the y axis. In parametric curve plots, the independent variable t is

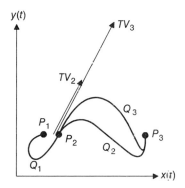

Fig. 11.9 Curve segments Q_1, Q_2, and Q_3 join at the point P_2 and are identical except for their tangent vectors at P_2. Q_1 and Q_2 have equal tangent vectors, and hence are both G^1 and C^1 continuous at P_2. Q_1 and Q_3 have tangent vectors in the same direction, but Q_3 has twice the magnitude, so they are only G^1 continuous at P_2. The larger tangent vector of Q_3 means that the curve is pulled more in the tangent-vector direction before heading toward P_3. Vector TV_2 is the tangent vector for Q_2, TV_3 is that for Q_3.

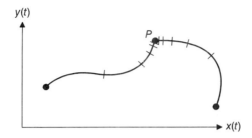

Fig. 11.10 The one case for which C^1 continuity does not imply G^1 continuity: the tangent vector (i.e., the parametric velocity along the curve) is zero at the join joint P. Each tick mark shows the distance moved along the curve in equal time intervals. As the curve approaches P, the velocity goes to zero, then increases past P.

never plotted at all. This means that we cannot determine, just by looking at a parametric curve plot, the tangent vector to the curve. It is possible to determine the direction of the vector, but not its magnitude. This can be seen as follows: if $\gamma(t)$, $0 \leq t \leq 1$ is a parametric curve, its tangent vector at time 0 is $\gamma'(0)$. If we let $\eta(t) = \gamma(2t)$, $0 \leq t \leq \frac{1}{2}$, then the parametric plots of γ and η are identical. On the other hand, $\eta'(0) = 2\ \gamma'(0)$. Thus, two curves that have identical plots can have different tangent vectors. This is the motivation for the definition of geometric continuity: For two curves to join smoothly, we require only that their tangent-vector directions match, not that their magnitudes match.

A curve segment $Q(t)$ is defined by constraints on endpoints, tangent vectors, and continuity between curve segments. Each cubic polynomial of Eq. (11.5) has four coefficients, so four constraints will be needed, allowing us to formulate four equations in the four unknowns, then solving for the unknowns. The three major types of curves discussed in this section are *Hermite*, defined by two endpoints and two endpoint tangent vectors; *Bézier*, defined by two endpoints and two other points that control the endpoint tangent vectors; and several kinds of *splines*, each defined by four control points. The

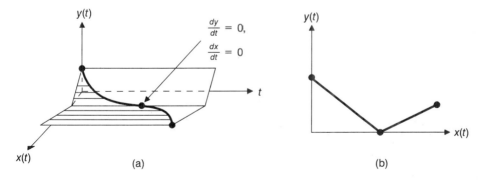

(a)   (b)

Fig. 11.11 (a) View of a 2D parametric cubic curve in 3D (x, y, t) space, and (b) the curve in 2D. At the join, the velocity of both parametrics is zero; that is, $dy/dt = 0$ and $dx/dt = 0$. You can see this by noting that, at the join, the curve is parallel to the t axis, so there is no change in either x or y. Yet at the join point, the parametrics are C^1 continuous, but are not G^1 continuous.

splines have C^1 and C^2 continuity at the join points and come close to their control points, but generally do not interpolate the points. The types of splines are uniform B-splines, nonuniform B-splines, and β-splines.

To see how the coefficients of Eq. (11.5) can depend on four constraints, we recall that a parametric cubic curve is defined by $Q(t) = T \cdot C$. We rewrite the coefficient matrix as $C = M \cdot G$, where M is a 4×4 *basis matrix*, and G is a four-element column vector of geometric constraints, called the *geometry vector*. The geometric constraints are just the conditions, such as endpoints or tangent vectors, that define the curve. We use G_x to refer to the column vector of just the x components of the geometry vector. G_y and G_z have similar definitions. M or G, or both M and G, differ for each type of curve.

The elements of M and G are constants, so the product $T \cdot M \cdot G$ is just three cubic polynomials in t. Expanding the product $Q(t) = T \cdot M \cdot G$ gives

$$Q(t) = [x(t) \quad y(t) \quad z(t)] = [t^3 \quad t^2 \quad t \quad 1] \begin{bmatrix} m_{11} & m_{12} & m_{13} & m_{14} \\ m_{21} & m_{22} & m_{23} & m_{24} \\ m_{31} & m_{32} & m_{33} & m_{34} \\ m_{41} & m_{42} & m_{43} & m_{44} \end{bmatrix} \begin{bmatrix} G_1 \\ G_2 \\ G_3 \\ G_4 \end{bmatrix}. \quad (11.9)$$

Multiplying out just $x(t) = T \cdot M \cdot G_x$ gives

$$x(t) = (t^3 m_{11} + t^2 m_{21} + t\, m_{31} + m_{41})g_{1x} + (t^3 m_{12} + t^2 m_{22} - t\, m_{32} + m_{42})g_{2x}$$
$$+ (t^3 m_{13} + t^2 m_{23} + t\, m_{33} + m_{43})g_{3x} + (t^3 m_{14} + t^2 m_{24} + t\, m_{34} + m_{44})g_{4x}. \quad (11.10)$$

Equation (11.10) emphasizes that the curve is a weighted sum of the elements of the geometry matrix. The weights are each cubic polynomials of t, and are called *blending functions*. The blending functions B are given by $B = T \cdot M$. Notice the similarity to a piecewise linear approximation, for which only two geometric constraints (the endpoints of the line) are needed, so each curve segment is a straight line defined by the endpoints G_1 and G_2:

$$x(t) = g_{1x} (1 - t) + g_{2x} (t),$$
$$y(t) = g_{1y} (1 - t) + g_{2y} (t), \quad\quad\quad (11.11)$$
$$z(t) = g_{1z} (1 - t) + g_{2z} (t).$$

Parametric cubics are really just a generalization of straight-line approximations.

To see how to calculate the basis matrix M, we turn now to specific forms of parametric cubic curves.

11.2.1 Hermite Curves

The Hermite form (named for the mathematician) of the cubic polynomial curve segment is determined by constraints on the endpoints P_1 and P_4 and tangent vectors at the endpoints R_1 and R_4. (The indices 1 and 4 are used, rather than 1 and 2, for consistency with later sections, where intermediate points P_2 and P_3 will be used instead of tangent vectors to define the curve.)

To find the *Hermite basis matrix* M_H, which relates the *Hermite geometry vector* G_H to the polynomial coefficients, we write four equations, one for each of the constraints, in the four unknown polynomial coefficients, and then solve for the unknowns.

Defining G_{H_x}, the x component of the Hermite geometry matrix, as

$$G_{H_x} = \begin{bmatrix} P_1 \\ P_4 \\ R_1 \\ R_4 \end{bmatrix}_x , \qquad (11.12)$$

and rewriting $x(t)$ from Eqs. (11.5) and (11.9) as

$$x(t) = a_x t^3 + b_x t^2 + c_x t + d_x = T \cdot C_x = T \cdot M_H \cdot G_{H_x} \cdot = [t^3 \ t^2 \ t \ 1] M_H \cdot G_{H_x}, \qquad (11.13)$$

the constraints on $x(0)$ and $x(1)$ are found by direct substitution into Eq. (11.13) as

$$x(0) = P_{1_x} = [0 \ 0 \ 0 \ 1] M_H \cdot G_{H_x}, \qquad (11.14)$$
$$x(1) = P_{4_x} = [1 \ 1 \ 1 \ 1] M_H \cdot G_{H_x}. \qquad (11.15)$$

Just as in the general case we differentiated Eq. (11.7) to find Eq. (11.8), we now differentiate Eq. (11.13) to get $x'(t) = [3t^2 \ 2t \ 1 \ 0] M_H \cdot G_{H_x}$. Hence, the tangent-vector–constraint equations can be written as

$$x'(0) = R_{1_x} = [0 \ 0 \ 1 \ 0] M_H \cdot G_{H_x}, \qquad (11.16)$$
$$x'(1) = R_{4_x} = [3 \ 2 \ 1 \ 0] M_H \cdot G_{H_x}. \qquad (11.17)$$

The four constraints of Eqs. (11.14), (11.15), (11.16), and (11.17) can be rewritten in matrix form as

$$\begin{bmatrix} P_1 \\ P_4 \\ R_1 \\ R_4 \end{bmatrix}_x = G_{H_x} = \begin{bmatrix} 0 & 0 & 0 & 1 \\ 1 & 1 & 1 & 1 \\ 0 & 0 & 1 & 1 \\ 3 & 2 & 1 & 0 \end{bmatrix} M_H \cdot G_{H_x}. \qquad (11.18)$$

For this equation (and the corresponding expressions for y and z) to be satisfied, M_H must be the inverse of the 4×4 matrix in Eq. (11.18)

$$M_H = \begin{bmatrix} 0 & 0 & 0 & 1 \\ 1 & 1 & 1 & 1 \\ 0 & 0 & 1 & 0 \\ 3 & 2 & 1 & 0 \end{bmatrix}^{-1} = \begin{bmatrix} 2 & -2 & 1 & 1 \\ -3 & 3 & -2 & -1 \\ 0 & 0 & 1 & 0 \\ 1 & 0 & 0 & 0 \end{bmatrix}. \qquad (11.19)$$

M_H, which is of course unique, can now be used in $x(t) = T \cdot M_H \cdot G_{H_x}$ to find $x(t)$ based on the geometry vector G_{H_x}. Similarly, $y(t) = T \cdot M_H \cdot G_{H_y}$ and $z(t) = T \cdot M_H \cdot G_{H_z}$, so we can write

$$Q(t) = [x(t) \ y(t) \ z(t)] = T \cdot M_H \cdot G_H, \qquad (11.20)$$

where G_H is the column vector

$$\begin{bmatrix} P_1 \\ P_4 \\ R_1 \\ R_4 \end{bmatrix}.$$

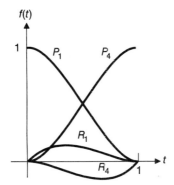

Fig. 11.12 The Hermite blending functions, labeled by the elements of the geometry vector that they weight.

Expanding the product $T \cdot M_H$ in $Q(t) = T \cdot M_H \cdot G_H$ gives the *Hermite blending functions* B_H as the polynomials weighting each element of the geometry vector:

$$Q(t) = T \cdot M_H \cdot G_H = B_H \cdot G_H$$
$$= (2t^3 - 3t^2 + 1)P_1 + (-2t^3 + 3t^2)P_4 + (t^3 - 2t^2 + t)R_1 + (t^3 - t^2)R_4. \quad (11.21)$$

Figure 11.12 shows the four blending functions. Notice that, at $t = 0$, only the function labeled P_1 is nonzero: only P_1 affects the curve at $t = 0$. As soon as t becomes greater than zero, R_1, P_4, and R_4 begin to have an influence. Figure 11.13 shows the four functions weighted by the y components of a geometry vector, their sum $y(t)$, and the curve $Q(t)$.

Figure 11.14 shows a series of Hermite curves. The only difference among them is the length of the tangent vector R_1: the directions of the tangent vectors are fixed. The longer the vectors, the greater their effect on the curve. Figure 11.15 is another series of Hermite curves, with constant tangent-vector lengths but with different directions. In an interactive

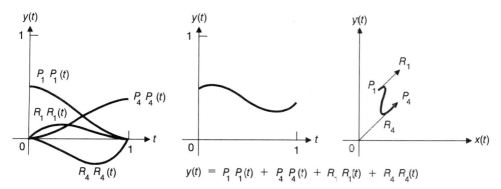

Fig. 11.13 A Hermite curve showing the four elements of the geometry vector weighted by the blending functions (leftmost four curves), their sum $y(t)$, and the 2D curve itself (far right). $x(t)$ is defined by a similar weighted sum.

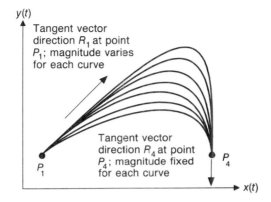

Fig. 11.14 Family of Hermite parametric cubic curves. Only R_1, the tangent vector at P_1, varies for each curve, increasing in magnitude for the higher curves.

graphics system, the endpoints and tangent vectors of a curve are manipulated interactively by the user to shape the curve. Figure 11.16 shows one way of doing this.

For two Hermite cubics to share a common endpoint with G^1 (geometrical) continuity, as in Fig. 11.17, the geometry vectors must have the form

$$\begin{bmatrix} P_1 \\ P_4 \\ R_1 \\ R_4 \end{bmatrix} \text{ and } \begin{bmatrix} P_4 \\ P_7 \\ kR_4 \\ R_7 \end{bmatrix}, \text{ with } k > 0. \tag{11.22}$$

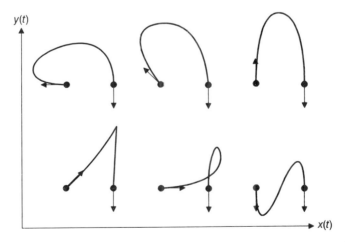

Fig. 11.15 Family of Hermite parametric cubic curves. Only the direction of the tangent vector at the left starting point varies; all tangent vectors have the same magnitude. A smaller magnitude would eliminate the loop in the one curve.

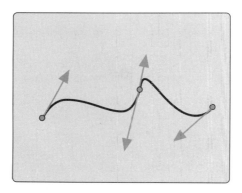

Fig. 11.16 Two Hermite cubic curve segments displayed with controls to facilitate interactive manipulation. The endpoints can be repositioned by dragging the dots, and the tangent vectors can be changed by dragging the arrowheads. The tangent vectors at the join point are constrained to be collinear (to provide C^1 continuity). The user is usually given a command to enforce C^0, C^1, G^1, or no continuity. The tangent vectors at the $t = 1$ end of each curve are drawn in the reverse of the direction used in the mathematical formulation of the Hermite curve, for clarity and more convenient user interaction.

That is, there must be a shared endpoint (P_4) and tangent vectors with at least equal directions. The more restrictive condition of C^1 (parametric) continuity requires that $k = 1$, so the tangent vector direction and magnitude must be equal.

Hermite and other similar parametric cubic curves are simple to display: We evaluate Eq. (11.5) at n successive values of t separated by a step size δ. Figure 11.18 gives the code. The evaluation within the **begin . . . end** takes 11 multiplies and 10 additions per 3D point. Use of Horner's rule for factoring polynomials,

$$f(t) = at^3 + bt^2 + ct + d = ((at + b)t + c)t + d, \qquad (11.23)$$

reduces the effort slightly to nine multiplies and 10 additions per 3D point. In Section 11.2.9, we shall examine much more efficient ways to display these curves.

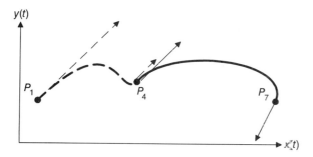

Fig. 11.17 Two Hermite curves joined at P_4. The tangent vectors at P_4 have the same direction but different magnitudes, yielding G^1 but not C^1 continuity.

```
typedef double CoefficientArray[4];
void DrawCurve (
        CoefficientArray cx,          /* Coefficients for x(t): Cₓ = M • Gₓ */
        CoefficientArray cy,          /* Coefficients for y(t): Cᵧ = M • Gᵧ */
        CoefficientArray cz,          /* Coefficients for z(t): C_z = M • G_z */
        int n)                        /* Number of steps */
{
    int i;
    double δ = 1.0 / n;
    double t = 0;

    MoveAbs3 (cx[3], cy[3], cz[3]);   /* t = 0: start at x(0), y(0), z(0) */
    for (i = 0; i < n; i++) {
        double t2, t3, x, y, z;

        t += δ;
        t2 = t * t;
        t3 = t2 * t;
        x = cx[0] * t3 + cx[1] * t2 + cx[2] * t + cx[3];
        y = cy[0] * t3 + cy[1] * t2 + cy[2] * t + cy[3];
        z = cz[0] * t3 + cz[1] * t2 + cz[2] * t + cz[3];
        DrawAbs3 (x, y, z);

    }
}   /* DrawCurve */
```

Fig. 11.18 Program to display a cubic parametric curve.

Because the cubic curves are linear combinations (weighted sums) of the four elements of the geometry vector, as seen in Eq. (11.10), we can transform the curves by transforming the geometry vector and then using it to generate the transformed curve, which is equivalent to saying that the curves are invariant under rotation, scaling, and translation. This strategy is more efficient than is generating the curve as a series of short line segments and then transforming each individual line. The curves are *not* invariant under perspective projection, as will be discussed in Section 11.2.5.

11.2.2   Bézier Curves

The Bézier [BEZI70; BEZI74] form of the cubic polynomial curve segment, named after Pierre Bézier, indirectly specifies the endpoint tangent vector by specifying two intermediate points that are not on the curve; see Fig. 11.19. The starting and ending tangent vectors

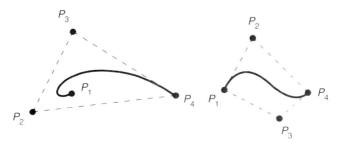

Fig. 11.19 Two Bézier curves and their control points. Notice that the convex hulls of the control points, shown as dashed lines, do not need to touch all four control points.

are determined by the vectors P_1P_2 and P_3P_4 and are related to R_1 and R_4 by

$$R_1 = Q'(0) = 3(P_2 - P_1), R_4 = Q'(1) = 3(P_4 - P_3). \tag{11.24}$$

The Bézier curve interpolates the two end control points and approximates the other two. See Exercise 11.12 to understand why the constant 3 is used in Eq. (11.24).

The *Bézier geometry vector* G_B, consisting of four points, is

$$G_B = \begin{bmatrix} P_1 \\ P_2 \\ P_3 \\ P_4 \end{bmatrix}. \tag{11.25}$$

Then the matrix M_{HB} that defines the relation $G_H = M_{HB} \cdot G_B$ between the Hermite geometry vector G_H and the Bézier geometry vector G_B is just the 4×4 matrix in the following equation, which rewrites Eq. (11.24) in matrix form:

$$G_H = \begin{bmatrix} P_1 \\ P_4 \\ R_1 \\ R_4 \end{bmatrix} = \begin{bmatrix} 1 & 0 & 0 & 0 \\ 0 & 0 & 0 & 1 \\ -3 & 3 & 0 & 0 \\ 0 & 0 & -3 & 3 \end{bmatrix} \begin{bmatrix} P_1 \\ P_2 \\ P_3 \\ P_4 \end{bmatrix} = M_{HB} \cdot G_B. \tag{11.26}$$

To find the *Bézier basis matrix* M_B, we use Eq. (11.20) for the Hermite form, substitute $G_H = M_{HB} \cdot G_B$, and define $M_B = M_H \cdot M_{HB}$:

$$Q(t) = T \cdot M_H \cdot G_H = T \cdot M_H \cdot (M_{HB} \cdot G_B) = T \cdot (M_H \cdot M_{HB}) \cdot G_B = T \cdot M_B \cdot G_B. \tag{11.27}$$

Carrying out the multiplication $M_B = M_H \cdot M_{HB}$ gives

$$M_B = M_H \cdot M_{HB} = \begin{bmatrix} -1 & 3 & -3 & 1 \\ 3 & -6 & 3 & 0 \\ -3 & 3 & 0 & 0 \\ 1 & 0 & 0 & 0 \end{bmatrix}, \tag{11.28}$$

and the product $Q(t) = T \cdot M_B \cdot G_B$ is

$$Q(t) = (1 - t)^3 P_1 + 3t(1 - t)^2 P_2 + 3t^2(1 - t)P_3 + t^3 P_4. \tag{11.29}$$

The four polynomials $B_B = T \cdot M_B$, which are the weights in Eq. (11.29), are called the *Bernstein polynomials*, and are shown in Fig. 11.20.

Figure 11.21 shows two Bézier curve segments with a common endpoint. G^1 continuity is provided at the endpoint when $P_3 - P_4 = k(P_4 - P_5), k > 0$. That is, the three points P_3, P_4, and P_5 must be distinct and collinear. In the more restrictive case when $k = 1$, there is C^1 continuity in addition to G^1 continuity.

If we refer to the polynomials of two curve segments as x^l (for the left segment) and x^r (for the right segment), we can find the conditions for C^0 and C^1 continuity at their join point:

$$x^l(1) = x^r(0), \quad \frac{d}{dt}x^l(1) = \frac{d}{dt}x^r(0). \tag{11.30}$$

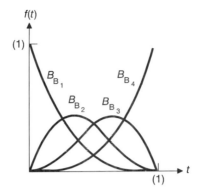

Fig. 11.20 The Bernstein polynomials, which are the weighting functions for Bézier curves. At $t = 0$, only B_{B_1} is nonzero, so the curve interpolates P_1; similarly, at $t = 1$, only B_{B_4} is nonzero, and the curve interpolates P_4.

Working with the x component of Eq. (11.29), we have

$$x^l(1) = x^r(0) = P_{4_x}, \quad \frac{d}{dt}x^l(1) = 3(P_{4_x} - P_{3_x}), \quad \frac{d}{dt}x^r(0) = 3(P_{5_x} - P_{4_x}). \quad (11.31)$$

As always, the same conditions are true of y and z. Thus, we have C^0 and C^1 continuity when $P_4 - P_3 = P_5 - P_4$, as expected.

Examining the four B_B polynomials in Eq. (11.29), we note that their sum is everywhere unity and that each polynomial is everywhere nonnegative for $0 \le t < 1$. Thus, $Q(t)$ is just a weighted average of the four control points. This condition means that each curve segment, which is just the sum of four control points weighted by the polynomials, is completely contained in the *convex hull* of the four control points. The convex hull for 2D curves is the convex polygon formed by the four control points: Think of it as the polygon formed by putting a rubberband around the points (Fig. 11.19). For 3D curves, the convex hull is the convex polyhedron formed by the control points: Think of it as the polyhedron formed by stretching a rubber sheet around the four points.

This convex-hull property holds for all cubics defined by weighted sums of control points if the blending functions are nonnegative and sum to one. In general, the weighted average of n points falls within the convex hull of the n points; this can be seen intuitively

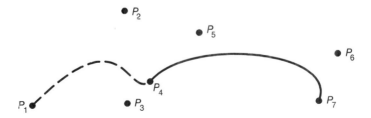

Fig. 11.21 Two Bézier curves joined at P_4 Points P_3, P_4, and P_5 are collinear. Curves are the same as those used in Fig. 11.17.

for $n = 2$ and $n = 3$, and the generalization follows. Another consequence of the fact that the four polynomials sum to unity is that the value of the fourth polynomial for any value of t can be found by subtracting the first three from unity.

The convex-hull property is also useful for clipping curve segments: Rather than clip each short line piece of a curve segment to determine its visibility, we first apply a polygonal clip algorithm to clip the convex hull or its extent against the clip region. If the convex hull (extent) is completely within the clip region, so is the entire curve segment. If the convex hull (extent) is completely outside the clip region, so is the curve segment. Only if the convex hull (extent) intersects the clip region does the curve segment itself need to be examined.

11.2.3   Uniform Nonrational B-Splines

The term *spline* goes back to the long flexible strips of metal used by draftspersons to lay out the surfaces of airplanes, cars, and ships. "Ducks," weights attached to the splines, were used to pull the spline in various directions. The metal splines, unless severely stressed, had second-order continuity. The mathematical equivalent of these strips, the *natural cubic spline*, is a C^0, C^1, and C^2 continuous cubic polynomial that interpolates (passes through) the control points. This is 1 more degree of continuity than is inherent in the Hermite and Bézier forms. Thus, splines are inherently smoother than are the previous forms.

The polynomial coefficients for natural cubic splines, however, are dependent on all n control points; their calculation involves inverting an $n + 1$ by $n + 1$ matrix [BART87]. This has two disadvantages: moving any one control point affects the entire curve, and the computation time needed to invert the matrix can interfere with rapid interactive reshaping of a curve.

B-splines, discussed in this section, consist of curve segments whose polynomial coefficients depend on just a few control points. This is called *local control*. Thus, moving a control point affects only a small part of a curve. In addition, the time needed to compute the coefficients is greatly reduced. B-splines have the same continuity as natural splines, but do not interpolate their control points.

In the following discussion we change our notation slightly, since we must discuss an entire curve consisting of several curve segments, rather than its individual segments. A curve segment need not pass through its control points, and the two continuity conditions on a segment come from the adjacent segments. This is achieved by sharing control points between segments, so it is best to describe the process in terms of all the segments at once.

Cubic B-splines approximate a series of $m + 1$ control points $P_0, P_1, \ldots P_m, m \geq 3$, with a curve consisting of $m - 2$ cubic polynomial curve segments $Q_3, Q_4, \ldots Q_m$. Although such cubic curves might be defined each on its own domain $0 \leq t < 1$, we can adjust the parameter (making a substitution of the form $t = t + k$) so that the parameter domains for the various curve segments are sequential. Thus, we say that the parameter range on which Q_i is defined is $t_i \leq t < t_{i+1}$, for $3 \leq i \leq m$. In the particular case of $m = 3$, there is a single curve segment Q_3 that is defined on the interval $t_3 \leq t < t_4$ by four control points, P_0 to P_3.

For each $i \geq 4$, there is a join point or *knot* between Q_{i-1} and Q_i at the parameter value t_i; the parameter value at such a point is called a *knot value*. The initial and final points at t_3

and t_{m+1} are also called knots, so that there is a total of $m - 1$ knots. Figure 11.22 shows a 2D B-spline curve with its knots marked. A closed B-spline curve is easy to create: The control points P_0, P_1, P_2 are repeated at the end of the sequence—P_0, P_1, ... P_m, P_0, P_1, P_2.

The term *uniform* means that the knots are spaced at equal intervals of the parameter t. Without loss of generality, we can assume that $t_3 = 0$ and the interval $t_{i+1} - t_i = 1$. Nonuniform nonrational B-splines, which permit unequal spacing between the knots, are discussed in Section 11.2.4. (In fact, the concept of knots is introduced in this section to set the stage for nonuniform splines.) The term *nonrational* is used to distinguish these splines from rational cubic polynomial curves, discussed in Section 11.2.5, where $x(t)$, $y(t)$, and $z(t)$ are each defined as the ratio of two cubic polynomials. The "B" stands for basis, since the splines can be represented as weighted sums of polynomial basis functions, in contrast to the natural splines, for which this is not true.

Each of the $m - 2$ curve segments of a B-spline curve is defined by four of the $m + 1$ control points. In particular, curve segment Q_i is defined by points P_{i-3}, P_{i-2}, P_{i-1}, and P_i. Thus, the *B-spline geometry vector* G_{Bs_i} for segment Q_i is

$$G_{Bs_i} = \begin{bmatrix} P_{i-3} \\ P_{i-2} \\ P_{i-1} \\ P_i \end{bmatrix}, \ 3 \le i \le m. \tag{11.32}$$

The first curve segment, Q_3, is defined by the points P_0 through P_3 over the parameter range $t_3 = 0$ to $t_4 = 1$, Q_4 is defined by the points P_1 through P_4 over the parameter range $t_4 = 1$ to $t_5 = 2$, and the last curve segment, Q_m, is defined by the points P_{m-3}, P_{m-2}, P_{m-1}, and P_m over the parameter range $t_m = m - 3$ to $t_{m-1} = m - 2$. In general, curve segment Q_i begins somewhere near point P_{i-2} and ends somewhere near point P_{i-1}. We shall see that the B-spline blending functions are everywhere nonnegative and sum to unity, so the curve segment Q_i is constrained to the convex hull of its four control points.

Just as each curve segment is defined by four control points, each control point (except for those at the beginning and end of the sequence P_0, P_1, ... P_m) influences four curve

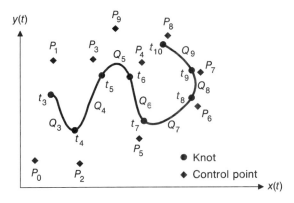

Fig. 11.22   A B-spline with curve segments Q_3 through Q_9. This and many other figures in this chapter were created with a program written by Carles Castellsaquè.

segments. Moving a control point in a given direction moves the four curve segments it affects in the same direction; the other curve segments are totally unaffected (see Fig. 11.23). This is the local control property of B-splines and of all the other splines discussed in this chapter.

If we define T_i as the row vector $[(t - t_i)^3 \quad (t - t_i)^2 \quad (t - t_i) \quad 1]$, then the B-spline formulation for curve segment i is

$$Q_i(t) = T_i \cdot M_{Bs} \cdot G_{Bs_i}, \quad t_i \leq t < t_{i+1}. \tag{11.33}$$

The entire curve is generated by applying Eq. (11.33) for $3 \leq i \leq m$.

The *B-spline basis matrix*, M_{Bs}, relates the geometrical constraints G_{Bs} to the blending functions and the polynomial coefficients:

$$M_{Bs} = \frac{1}{6}\begin{bmatrix} -1 & 3 & -3 & 1 \\ 3 & -6 & 3 & 0 \\ -3 & 0 & 3 & 0 \\ 1 & 4 & 1 & 0 \end{bmatrix}. \tag{11.34}$$

This matrix is derived in [BART87].

The B-spline blending functions B_{Bs} are given by the product $T_i \cdot M_{Bs}$, analogously to the previous Bézier and Hermite formulations. Note that the blending functions for each curve segment are exactly the same, because for each segment i the values of $t - t_i$ range from 0 at $t = t_i$ to 1 at $t = t_{i+1}$. If we replace $t - t_i$ by t, and replace the interval $[t_i, t_{i+1}]$ by [0, 1], we have

$$B_{Bs} = T \cdot M_{Bs} = [B_{Bs-3} \quad B_{Bs-2} \quad B_{Bs-1} \quad B_{Bs0}]$$

$$= \frac{1}{6}[-t^3 + 3t^2 - 3t + 1 \quad 3t^3 - 6t^2 + 4 \quad -3t^3 + 3t^2 + 3t + 1 \quad t^3]$$

$$= \frac{1}{6}[(1 - t)^3 \quad 3t^3 - 6t^2 + 4 \quad -3t^3 + 3t^2 + 3t + 1 \quad t^3], \quad 0 \leq t < 1. \tag{11.35}$$

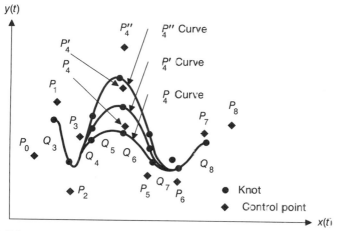

Fig. 11.23 A B-spline with control point P_4 in several different locations.

Figure 11.24 shows the B-spline blending functions B_{Bs}. Because the four functions sum to 1 and are nonnegative, the convex-hull property holds for each curve segment of a B-spline. See [BART87] to understand the relation between these blending functions and the Bernstein polynomial basis functions.

Expanding Eq. (11.33), again replacing $t - t_i$ with t at the second equals sign, we have

$$Q_i(t - t_i) = T_i \cdot M_{Bs} \cdot G_{Bs_i} = T \cdot M_{Bs} \cdot G_{Bs_i}$$

$$= B_{Bs} \cdot G_{Bs_i} = B_{Bs_{-3}} \cdot P_{i-3} + B_{Bs_{-2}} \cdot P_{i-2} + B_{Bs_{-1}} \cdot P_{i-1} + B_{Bs_0} \cdot P_i$$

$$= \frac{(1-t)^3}{6}P_{i-3} + \frac{3t^3 - 6t^2 + 4}{6}P_{i-2} + \frac{-3t^3 + 3t^2 + 3t + 1}{6}P_{i-1}$$

$$+ \frac{t^3}{6}P_i, \ 0 \le t < 1. \tag{11.36}$$

It is easy to show that Q_i and Q_{i+1} are C^0, C^-, and C^2 continuous where they join. When we consider the x components of the adjacent segments, which are $x_i(t - t_i)$ and $x_{i+1}(t - t_{i+1})$ (y and z, as always, are analogous), it is necessary to show only that, at the knot t_{i+1} where they join,

$$x_i(t_{i+1}) = x_{i-1}(t_{i+1}), \quad \frac{d}{dt}x_i(t_{i+1}) = \frac{d}{dt}x_{i+1}(t_{i+1}), \quad \text{and} \quad \frac{d^2}{dt^2}x_i(t_{i+1}) = \frac{d^2}{dt^2}x_{i+1}(t_{i+1}). \tag{11.37}$$

Recalling the substitution of t for $t - t_i$, Eq. (11.37) is equivalent to showing that

$$x_i|_{t-t_i=1} = x_{i+1}|_{t-t_{i+1}=0},$$

$$\frac{d}{dt}x_i|_{t-t_i=1} = 1 \frac{d}{dt}x_{i+1}|_{t-t_{i+1}=0},$$

$$\frac{d^2}{dt^2}x_i|_{t-t_i=1} = \frac{d^2}{dt^2}x_{i+1}|_{t-t_{i+1}=0}. \tag{11.38}$$

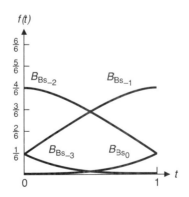

Fig. 11.24 The four B-spline blending functions from Eq. (11.35). At $t = 0$ and $t = 1$, just three of the functions are nonzero.

We demonstrate the equivalence by working with the x component of Eq. (11.36), and its first and second derivatives, to yield

$$x_i|_{t-t_i=1} = x_{i+1}|_{t-t_i=1} = \frac{P_{i-2_x} + 4P_{i-1_x} + P_{i_x}}{6}, \qquad (11.39)$$

$$\frac{d}{dt}x_i|_{t-t_i=1} = \frac{d}{dt}x_{i+1}|_{t-t_{i+1}=0} = \frac{-P_{i-2_x} + P_{i_x}}{2} \qquad (11.40)$$

$$\frac{d^2}{dt^2}x_i|_{t-t_i=1} = \frac{d^2}{dt^2}x_{i+1}|_{t-t_{i+1}=0} = P_{i-2_x} - 2P_{i-1_x} + P_{i_x}. \qquad (11.41)$$

The additional continuity afforded by B-splines is attractive, but it comes at the cost of less control of where the curve goes. The curve can be forced to interpolate specific points by replicating control points; this is useful both at endpoints and at intermediate points on the curve. For instance, if $P_{i-2} = P_{i-1}$, the curve is pulled closer to this point because curve segment Q_i is defined by just three different points, and the point $P_{i-2} = P_{i-1}$ is weighted twice in Eq. (11.36)—once by B_{Bs-2} and once by B_{Bs-1}.

If a control point is used three times—for instance, if $P_{i-2} = P_{i-} = P_i$—then Eq. (11.36) becomes

$$Q_i(t) = B_{Bs-3} \cdot P_{i-3} + (B_{Bs-2} + B_{Bs-1} + B_{Bs0}) \cdot P_i. \qquad (11.42)$$

Q_i is clearly a straight line. Furthermore, the point P_{i-2} is interpolated by the line at $t = 1$, where the three weights applied to P_i sum to 1, but P_{i-3} is not in general interpolated at $t = 0$. Another way to think of this is that the convex hull for Q_i is now defined by just two distinct points, so Q_i has to be a line. Figure 11.25 shows the effect of multiple control points at the interior of a B-spline. The price of interpolating the points in part (c) is loss of G^1 continuity, even though Eq. (11.40) shows that C^1 continuity is preserved (but with a value of zero). This is a case where C^1 continuity does not imply G^1 continuity, as discussed in Section 11.2.

Another technique for interpolating endpoints, *phantom vertices*, is discussed in [BARS83; BART87]. We shall see that, with nonuniform B-splines, discussed in the next section, endpoints and internal points can be interpolated in a more natural way than they can with the uniform B-splines.

11.2.4 Nonuniform, Nonrational B-Splines

Nonuniform, nonrational B-splines differ from the uniform, nonrational B-splines discussed in the previous section in that the parameter interval between successive knot values need not be uniform. The nonuniform knot-value sequence means that the blending functions are no longer the same for each interval, but rather vary from curve segment to curve segment.

These curves have several advantages over uniform B-splines. First, continuity at selected join points can be reduced from C^2 to C^1 to C^0 to none. If the continuity is reduced to C^0, then the curve interpolates a control point, but without the undesirable effect of uniform B-splines, where the curve segments on either side of the interpolated control point are straight lines. Also, starting and ending points can be easily interpolated exactly,

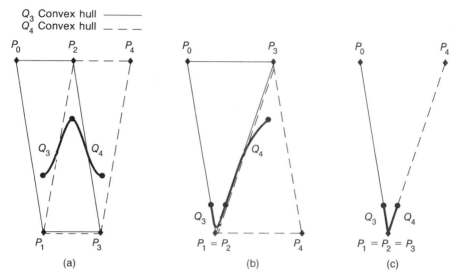

Fig. 11.25 The effect of multiple control points on a uniform B-spline curve. In (a), there are no multiple control points. The convex hulls of the two curves overlap; the join point between Q_3 and Q_4 is in the region shared by both convex hulls. In (b), there is a double control point, so the two convex hulls share edge P_2P_3; the join point is therefore constrained to lie on this edge. In (c), there is a triple control point, and the two convex hulls are straight lines that share the triple point; hence, the join point is also at the triple point. Because the convex hulls are straight lines, the two curve segments must also be straight lines. There is C^2 but only G^0 continuity at the join.

without at the same time introducing linear segments. As is further discussed in Section 11.2.7, it is possible to add an additional knot and control point to nonuniform B-splines, so the resulting curve can be easily reshaped, whereas this cannot be done with uniform B-splines.

The increased generality of nonuniform B-splines requires a slightly different notation than that used for uniform B-splines. As before, the spline is a piecewise continuous curve made up of cubic polynomials, approximating the control points P_0 through P_m. The *knot-value sequence* is a nondecreasing sequence of knot values t_0 through t_{m+4} (that is, there are four more knots than there are control points). Because the smallest number of control points is four, the smallest knot sequence has eight knot values and the curve is defined over the parameter interval from t_3 to t_4.

The only restriction on the knot sequence is that it be nondecreasing, which allows successive knot values to be equal. When this occurs, the parameter value is called a *multiple knot* and the number of identical parameter values is called the *multiplicity* of the knot (a single unique knot has multiplicity of 1). For instance, in the knot sequence (0, 0, 0, 0, 1, 1, 2, 3, 4, 4, 5, 5, 5, 5), the knot value 0 has multiplicity four; value 1 has multiplicity 2; values 2 and 3 have multiplicity 1; value 4 has multiplicity 2; and value 5 has multiplicity 4.

Curve segment Q_i is defined by control points P_{i-3}, P_{i-2}, P_{i-1}, P_i and by blending functions $B_{i-3,4}(t)$, $B_{i-2,4}(t)$, $B_{i-1,4}(t)$, $B_{i,4}(t)$, as the weighted sum

$$Q_i(t) = P_{i-3} \cdot B_{i-3,4}(t) + P_{i-2} \cdot B_{i-2,4}(t) + P_{i-1} \cdot B_{i-1,4}(t) + P_i \cdot B_{i,4}(t)$$

$$3 \le i \le m, \quad t_i \le t < t_{i+1}. \tag{11.43}$$

The curve is not defined outside the interval t_3 through t_{m+1}. When $t_i = t_{i+1}$ (a multiple knot), curve segment Q_i is a single point. It is this notion of a curve segment reducing to a point that provides the extra flexibility of nonuniform B-splines.

There is no single set of blending functions, as there was for other types of splines. The functions depend on the intervals between knot values and are defined recursively in terms of lower-order blending functions. $B_{i,j}(t)$ is the jth-order blending function for weighting control point P_i. Because we are working with fourth-order (that is, third-degree, or cubic) B-splines, the recursive definition ends with $B_{i,4}(t)$ and can be easily presented in its "unwound" form. The recurrence for cubic B-splines is

$$B_{i,1}(t) = \begin{cases} 1, & t_i \le t < t_{i+1} \\ 0, & \text{otherwise,} \end{cases}$$

$$B_{i,2}(t) = \frac{t - t_i}{t_{i+1} - t_i} B_{i,1}(t) + \frac{t_{i+2} - t}{t_{i+2} - t_{i-1}} B_{i+1,1}(t),$$

$$B_{i,3}(t) = \frac{t - t_i}{t_{i+2} - t_i} B_{i,2}(t) + \frac{t_{i+3} - t}{t_{i+3} - t_{i+1}} B_{i+1,2}(t),$$

$$B_{i,4}(t) = \frac{t - t_i}{t_{i+3} - t_i} B_{i,3}(t) + \frac{t_{i+4} - t}{t_{i+4} - t_{i+1}} B_{i+1,3}(t). \tag{11.44}$$

Figure 11.26 shows how Eq. (11.44) can be used to find the blending functions, using the knot vector $(0, 0, 0, 0, 1, 1, 1, 1)$ as an example. The figure also makes clear why eight knot vectors are needed to compute four blending functions. $B_{2,1}(t)$ is unity on the interval $0 \le t < 1$. All other $B_{i,1}(t)$ are zero. $B_{2,2}(t)$ and $B_{3,2}(t)$ are linear ramps, and are the blending functions for linear interpolation between two points. Similarly, $B_{1,3}(t)$, $B_{2,3}(t)$, and $B_{3,3}(t)$ are quadratics, and are the blending functions for quadratic interpolation. For this particular knot vector, the $B_{i,4}(t)$ are the Bernstein polynomials, that is, the Bezier blending functions; compare them to those in Fig. 11.20. Also, for this knot vector, the curve interpolates the control points P_0 and P_3, and is in fact a Bézier curve, with the tangent vector at the endpoints determined by the vectors P_0P_1 and P_2P_3.

Computing the blending functions takes time. By restricting B-spline knot sequences to have intervals that are either 0 or 1, it is possible to store just a small number of matrices corresponding to Eq. (11.44), which covers all such possible knot configurations. This eliminates the need to reevaluate Eq. (11.44) for each curve segment.

It can be shown that the blending functions are nonnegative and sum to one, so nonuniform B-spline curve segments lie within the convex hulls of their four control points. For knots of multiplicity greater than one, the denominators can be zero because successive knot values can be equal: division by zero is defined to yield zero.

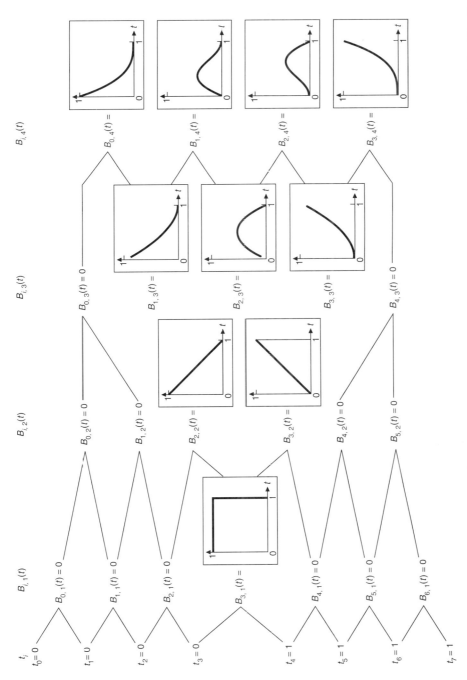

Fig. 11.26 The relationships defined by Eq. (11.44) between the knot vector (0, 0, 0, 0, 1, 1, 1, 1) and the blending functions $B_{i,1}(t)$, $B_{i,2}(t)$, $B_{i,3}(t)$, and $B_{i,4}(t)$.

Increasing knot multiplicity has two effects. First, each knot value t_i will automatically lie within the convex hull of the points P_{i-3}, P_{i-2}, and P_{i-1}. If t_i and t_{i+1} are equal, they must lie in the convex hull of P_{i-3}, P_{i-2}, and P_{i-1}, *and* in the convex hull of P_{i-2}, P_{i-1}, and P_i. This means they must actually lie on the line segment between P_{i-2} and P_{i-1}. In the same way, if $t_i = t_{i+1} = t_{i+2}$, then this knot must lie *at* P_{i-1}. If $t_i = t_{i+1} = t_{i+2} = t_{i+3}$, then the knot must lie both at P_{i-1} and at P_i—the curve becomes broken. Second, the multiple knots will reduce parametric continuity: from C^2 to C^1 continuity for one extra knot (multiplicity 2); from C^1 to C^0 continuity for two extra knots (multiplicity 3); from C^0 to no continuity for three extra knots (multiplicity 4).

Figure 11.27 provides further insight for a specific case. Part (a) shows the case when all knots have multiplicity 1. Each curve segment is defined by four control points and four blending functions, and adjacent curve segments each share three control points. For instance, curve segment Q_3 is defined by points P_0, P_1, P_2, and P_3; curve segment Q_4 is defined by points P_1, P_2, P_3 and P_4; and curve segment Q_5 is defined by points P_2, P_3, P_4, and P_5. Part (b) shows a double knot, $t_4 = t_5$, for which the curve segment Q_4 has zero length. Segments Q_3 and Q_5 are thus adjacent but share only two control points, P_2 and P_3; the two curve segments hence have less "in common," as implied by the loss of 1 degree of continuity. For the triple knot in part (c), only control point P_3 is shared in common: the one that the two curve segments now interpolate. Because only one control point is shared, we can expect only one constraint, C^0 continuity, to be satisfied at the join. The knot of multiplicity 4, shown in part (d), causes a discontinuity, or break, in the curve. Hence, several disjoint splines can be represented by a single knot sequence and set of control points. Figure 11.28 provides additional understanding of the relations among knots, curve segments, and control points. Table 11.1 summarizes the effects of multiple control points and multiple knots.

TABLE 11.1 COMPARISON OF THE EFFECTS OF MULTIPLE CONTROL POINTS AND OF MULTIPLE KNOTS

Multiplicity	Multiple control points	Multiple knots
1	$C^2 G^{2*}$	$C^2 G^{2*}$
2	$C^2 G^1$ Knots constrained to a smaller convex hull.	$C^1 G^1$ Knots constrained to a smaller convex hull of fewer control points.
3	$C^2 G^0$ Curve interpolates the triple control point. Curve segments on either side of the join are linear.	$C^0 G^0$ Curve interpolates control point. Can control shape of curve segments on either side of the join.
4	$C^2 G^0$ Curve interpolates the quadruple control points. Curve segments on either side of the join are linear and interpolate the control points on either side of the join.	 There is a discontinuity in the curve. Curve stops on one control point, resumes at next. Can control shape of curve segments on either side of the discontinuity.

*Except for special case discussed in Section 11.2.

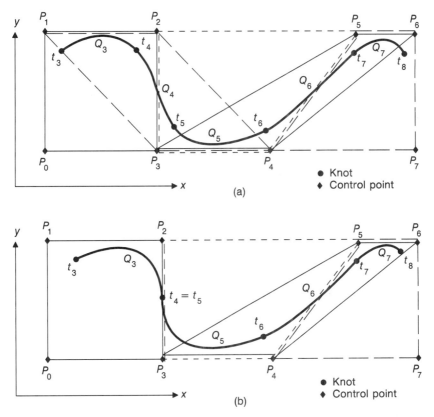

Fig. 11.27 The effect of multiple knots. In (a), with knot sequence (0, 1, 2, 3, 4, 5), there are no multiple knots; all the curve segments join with C^2 and G^2 continuity. The convex hulls containing each curve segment are also shown. In (b), with knot sequence (0, 1, 1, 2, 3, 4), there is a double knot, so curve segment Q_4 degenerates to a point. The convex hulls containing Q_3 and Q_5 meet along the edge P_2P_3, on which the join point is forced to lie. The join has C^1 and G^2 continuity. In (c), with knot sequence (0, 1, 1, 1,

Figure 11.29 illustrates the complexity of shapes that can be represented with this technique. Notice part (a) of the figure, with knot sequence (0, 0, 0, 0, 1, 1, 1, 1): The curve interpolates the endpoints but not the two intermediate points, and is a Bézier curve. The other two curves also start and stop with triple knots. This causes the tangent vectors at the endpoints to be determined by the vectors P_0P_1 and $P_{m-1}P_m$, giving Bézier-like control to the curves at the start and stop points.

Interactive creation of nonuniform splines typically involves pointing at control points, with multiple control points indicated simply by successive selection of the same point. Figure 11.30 shows a way of specifying knot values interactively. Another way is to point directly at the curve with a multibutton mouse: A double click on one button can indicate a double control point; a double click on another button, a double knot.

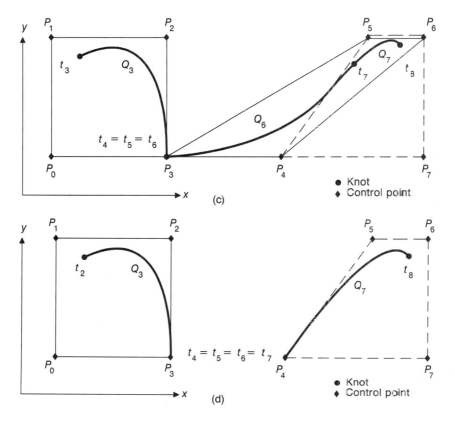

(c)

(d)

2, 3), there is a triple knot, so curve segments Q_4 and Q_5 degenerate to points. The convex hulls containing Q_3 and Q_6 meet only at P_3, where the join point is forced to be located. The two curve segments share only control point P_3, with C_0 continuity. In (d), with knot sequence (0, 1, 1, 1, 1, 2), there is a quadruple knot, which causes a discontinuity in the curve because curve segments Q_3 and Q_7 have no control points in common.

11.2.5   Nonuniform, Rational Cubic Polynomial Curve Segments

General rational cubic curve segments are ratios of polynomials:

$$x(t) = \frac{X(t)}{W(t)}, \quad y(t) = \frac{Y(t)}{W(t)}, \quad z(t) = \frac{Z(t)}{W(t)}, \tag{11.45}$$

where $X(t)$, $Y(t)$, $Z(t)$, and $W(t)$ are all cubic polynomial curves whose control points are defined in homogeneous coordinates. We can also think of the curve as existing in homogeneous space as $Q(t) = [X(t) \quad Y(t) \quad Z(t) \quad W(t)]$. As always, moving from homogeneous space to 3-space involves dividing by $W(t)$. Any nonrational curve can be transformed to a rational curve by adding $W(t) = 1$ as a fourth element. In general, the

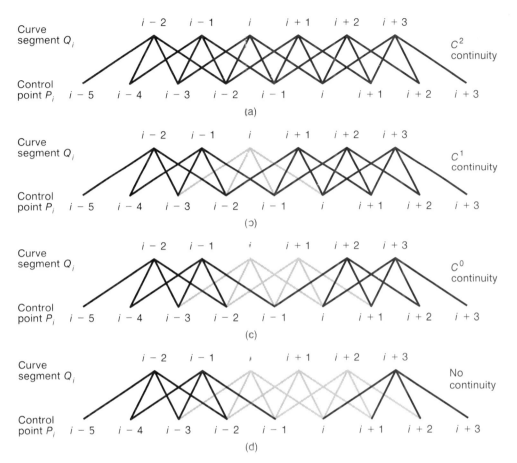

Fig. 11.28 The relationship among curve segments, control points, and multiple knots for nonuniform B-splines. Lines connect curve segments to their control points; gray lines are used for curve segments that do not appear because their knot interval is zero (i.e., the knot multiplicity is greater than one), causing them to have zero length. In (a), all knots are single. In (b), there is a double knot, so segment i is not drawn. In (c), there is a triple knot, so two segments are not drawn; thus, the single point, $i - 1$, is held in common between adjacent segments $i - 1$ and $i + 2$. In (d), with a quadruple knot, segments $i - 1$ and $i + 3$ have no points in common, causing the curve to be disconnected between points $i - 1$ and i.

polynomials in a rational curve can be Bézier, Hermite, or any other type. When they are B-splines, we have nonuniform rational B-splines, sometimes called *NURBS* [FORR80].

Rational curves are useful for two reasons. The first and most important reason is that they are invariant under rotation, scaling, translation and perspective transformations of the control points (nonrational curves are invariant under only rotation, scaling, and translation). This means that the perspective transformation needs to be applied to only the control

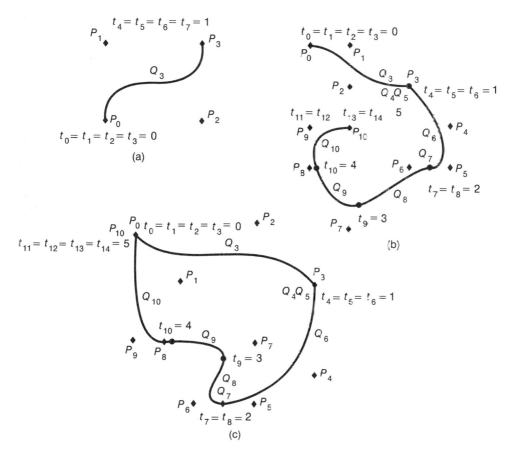

Fig. 11.29 Examples of shapes defined using nonrational B-splines and multiple knots. Part (a) is just a Bézier curve segment, with knot sequence (0, 0, 0, 0, 1, 1, 1, 1), and hence just one curve segment, Q_3. Parts (b) and (c) have the same knot sequence, (0, 0, 0, 0, 1, 1, 1, 2, 2, 3, 4, 5, 5, 5, 5) but different control points. Each curve has curve segments Q_3 to Q_{10}. Segments Q_4, Q_5, and Q_7 are located at multiple knots and have zero length.

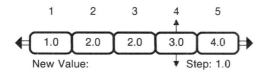

Fig. 11.30 An interaction technique developed by Carles Castellsaguè for specifying knot values. The partial knot sequence is shown, and can be scrolled left and right with the horizontal arrows. One knot value, selected with the cursor, can be incremented up and down using the vertical arrows, in increments specified by value Step. The selected knot value can also be replaced with a new typed-in value.

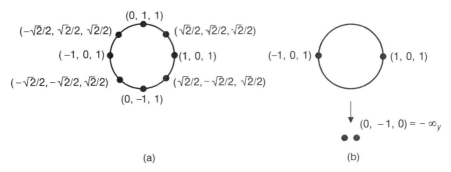

Fig. 11.31 The control points for defining a circle as a rational spline in 2D. Coordinates are (X, Y, W). The knot vector is (0, 0, 0, 1, 1, 2, 2, 3, 3, 4, 4), with the first and last control points repeated. The choice of P_0 is arbitrary.

points, which can then be used to generate the perspective transformation of the original curve. The alternative to converting a nonrational curve to a rational curve prior to a perspective transformation is first to generate points on the curve itself and then to apply the perspective transformation to *each* point, a far less efficient process. This is analogous to the observation that the perspective transformation of a sphere is not the same as a sphere whose center and radius are the transformed center and radius of the original sphere.

A second advantage of rational splines is that, unlike nonrationals, they can define precisely any of the conic sections. A conic can be only approximated with nonrationals, by using many control points close to the conic. This second property is useful in those applications, particularly CAD, where general curves and surfaces as well as conics are needed. Both types of entities can be defined with NURBS.

Defining conics requires only quadratic, not cubic, polynomials. Thus, the $B_{i,3}(t)$ blending functions from the recurrence Eq. (11.44) are used in the curve of the form

$$Q_i(t) = P_{i-2}B_{i-2,3}(t) + P_{i-1}B_{i-1,3}(t) + P_iB_{i,3}(t)$$

$$2 \leq i \leq m, \quad t_i \leq t < t_{i+1}. \tag{11.46}$$

Two ways of creating a unit circle centered at the origin are shown in Fig. 11.31. Note that, with quadratic B-splines, a double knot causes a control point to be interpolated, and triple knots fix the starting and ending points of the curve on control points.

For further discussion of conics and NURBS, see [FAUX79; BÖHM84; TILL83].

11.2.6   Other Spline Forms

Very often, we have a series of positions and want a curve smoothly to interpolate (pass through) them. This might arise with a series of points read from a data tablet or mouse, or a series of 3D points through which a curve or camera path is to pass. The Catmull–Rom family of interpolating or approximating splines [CATM74a], also called *Overhauser splines* [BREW77], are useful for this situation. One member of this spline family is able to interpolate the points P_1 to P_{m-1} from the sequence of points P_0 to P_m. In addition, the tangent vector at point P_i is parallel to the line connecting points P_{i-1} and P_{i+1}, as shown in Fig. 11.32. However, these splines do not posess the convex-hull property. The natural (interpolating) splines also interpolate points, but without the local control afforded by the Catmull–Rom splines.

Designating M_{CR} as the Catmull-Rom basis matrix and using the same geometry matrix G_{Bsi} of Eq. (11.32) as was used for B-splines, the representation is

$$Q^i(t) = T \cdot M_{CR} \cdot G_{Bsi} = \frac{1}{2} \cdot T \cdot \begin{bmatrix} -1 & 3 & -3 & 1 \\ 2 & -5 & 4 & -1 \\ -1 & 0 & 1 & 0 \\ 0 & 2 & 0 & 0 \end{bmatrix} \begin{bmatrix} P_{i-3} \\ P_{i-2} \\ P_{i-1} \\ P_i \end{bmatrix}. \qquad (11.47)$$

A method for rapidly displaying Catmull–Rom curves is given in [BARR88b].

Another spline is the *uniformly shaped β-spline* [BARS88; BAFT87], which has two additional parameters, β_1 and β_2, to provide further control over shape. It uses the same geometry matrix G_{Bsi} as the B-spline, and has the convex hull property. The *β-spline basis matrix M_β* is

$$M_\beta = \frac{1}{\delta} \begin{bmatrix} -2\beta_1^3 & 2(\beta_2 + \beta_1^3 + \beta_1^2 + \beta_1) & -2(\beta_2 + \beta_1^2 + \beta_1 + 1) & 2 \\ 6\beta_1^3 & -3(\beta_2 + 2\beta_1^3 + 2\beta_1^2) & 3(\beta_2 + 2\beta_1^2) & 0 \\ -6\beta_1^3 & 6(\beta_1^3 - \beta_1) & 6\beta_1 & 0 \\ 2\beta_1^3 & \beta_2 + 4(\beta_1^2 + \beta_1) & 2 & 0 \end{bmatrix},$$

$$\delta = \beta_2 + 2\beta_1^3 + 4\beta_1^2 + 4\beta_1 + 2. \qquad (11.48)$$

The first parameter, β_1, is called the *bias* parameter; the second parameter, β_2, is called the *tension* parameter. If $\beta_1 = 1$ and $\beta_2 = 0$, M_β reduces to M_{Bs} (Eq. (11.34)) for B-splines. As β_1 is increased beyond 1, the spline is "biased," or influenced more, by the tangent vector on the parameter-increasing side of the points, as shown in Fig. 11.33. For values of β_1 less than 1, the bias is in the other direction. As the tension parameter β_2 increases, the spline is pulled closer to the lines connecting the control points, as seen in Fig. 11.34.

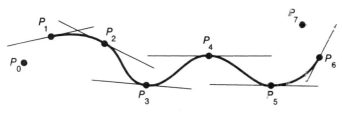

Fig. 11.32 A Catmull–Rom spline. The points are interpolated by the spline, which passes through each point in a direction parallel to the line between the adjacent points. The straight line segments indicate these directions.

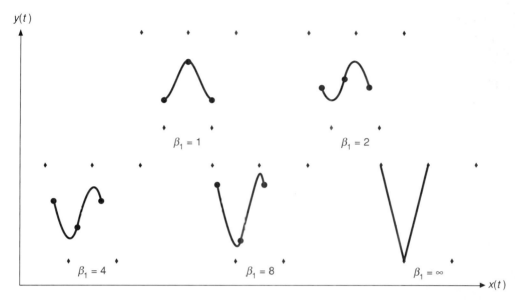

Fig. 11.33 Effect on a uniformly shaped β-spline of increasing the bias parameter β_1 from 1 to infinity.

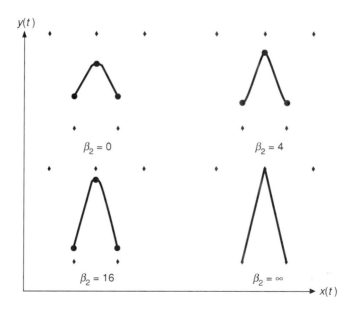

Fig. 11.34 Effect on a uniformly shaped β-spline of increasing the tension parameter β_2 from 0 to infinity.

These β-splines are called *uniformly shaped* because β_1 and β_2 apply uniformly, over all curve segments. This global effect of β_1 and β_2 violates the spirit of local control. *Continuously shaped β-splines* and *discretely shaped β splines* associate distinct values of β_1 and β_2 with each control point, providing a local, rather than a global, effect [BARS83; BART87].

Although β-splines provide more shape generality than do B-splines, they are G^2 but only C^0 continuous at the join points. This is not a drawback in geometric modeling, but can introduce a velocity discontinuity into an animation's motion path. In the special case $\beta_1 = 1$, the β-splines are C^1 continuous.

A variation on the Hermite form useful for controlling motion paths in animation was developed by Kochanek and Bartels [KOCH84]. The tangent vector R_i at point P_i is

$$R_i = \frac{(1 - a_i)(1 + b_i)(1 + c_i)}{2}(P_i - P_{i-1}) + \frac{(1 - a_i)(1 - b_i)(1 - c_i)}{2}(P_{i+1} - P_i),$$
$$(11.49)$$

and the tangent vector R_{i+1} at point P_{i+1} is

$$R_{i+1} + \frac{(1 - a_{i+1})(1 + b_{i-1})(1 - c_{i+1})}{2}(P_i - P_{i-1})$$

$$+ \frac{(1 - a_{i+1})(1 - b_{i+1})(1 + c_{i+1})}{2}(P_{i+1} - P_i).$$
$$(11.50)$$

See Exercise 11.16 for how to find the basis matrix M_{KB}.

The parameters a_i, b_i, and c_i control different aspects of the path in the vicinity of point P_i: a_i controls how sharply the curve bends, b_i is comparable to β_1, the bias of β-splines, and c_i controls continuity at P_i. This last parameter is used to model the rapid change in direction of an object that bounces off another object.

11.2.7 Subdividing Curves

Suppose you have just created a connected series of curve segments to approximate a shape you are designing. You manipulate the control points, but you cannot quite get the shape you want. Probably, there are not enough control points to achieve the desired effect. There are two ways to increase the number of control points. One is the process of *degree elevation*: The degree of the splines is increased from 3 to 4 or more. This adjustment is sometimes necessary, especially if higher orders of continuity are needed, but is generally undesirable because of the additional inflection points allowed in a single curve and the additional computational time needed to evaluate the curve. In any case, the topic is beyond the scope of our discussion; for more details, see [FARI86].

The second, more useful way to increase the number of control points is to *subdivide* one or more of the curve segments into two segments. For instance, a Bézier curve segment with its four control points can be subdivided into two segments with a total of seven control points (the two new segments share a common point). The two new segments exactly match the one original segment until any of the control points are actually moved, then, one or both of the new segments no longer matches the original. For nonuniform B-splines, a more general process know as *refinement* can be used to add an arbitrary number of control points to a curve. Another reason for subdividing is to display a curve or surface. We elaborate on this in Section 11.2.9, where we discuss tests for stopping the subdivision.

Given a Bézier curve $Q(t)$ defined by points P_1, P_2, P_3, and P_4, we want to find a left curve defined by points L_1, L_2, L_3, and L_4, and a right curve defined by points R_1, R_2, R_3, and R_4, such that the left curve is coincident with Q on the interval $0 \le t < \frac{1}{2}$ and the right curve is coincident with Q on the interval $\frac{1}{2} \le t < 1$. The subdivision can be accomplished using a geometric construction technique developed by de Casteljau [DECA59] to evaluate a Bézier curve for any value of t. The point on the curve for a parameter value of t is found by drawing the construction line L_2H so that it divides P_1P_2 and P_2P_3 in the ratio of $t:(1 - t)$, HR_3 so that it similarly divides P_2P_3 and P_3P_4, and L_3R_2 to likewise divide L_2H and HR_3. The point L_4 (which is also R_1) divides L_3R_2 by the same ratio and gives the point $Q(t)$. Figure 11.35 shows the construction for $t = \frac{1}{2}$, the case of interest.

All the points are easy to compute with an add and shift to divide by 2:

$$L_2 = (P_1 + P_2)/2, \; H = (P_2 + P_3)/2, \; L_3 = (L_2 + H)/2, \; R_3 = (P_3 + P_4)/2,$$

$$R_2 = (H + R_3)/2, \; L_4 = R_1 = (L_3 + R_2)/2. \tag{11.51}$$

These results can be reorganized into matrix form, so as to give the left Bézier division matrix D_B^L and the right Bézier division matrix D_B^R These matrices can be used to find the geometry matrices G_B^L of points for the left Bézier curve and G_B^R for the right Bézier curve:

$$G_B^L = D_B^L \cdot G_B = \frac{1}{8}\begin{bmatrix} 8 & 0 & 0 & 0 \\ 4 & 4 & 0 & 0 \\ 2 & 4 & 2 & 0 \\ 1 & 3 & 3 & 1 \end{bmatrix}\begin{bmatrix} P_1 \\ P_2 \\ P_3 \\ P_4 \end{bmatrix},$$

$$G_B^R = D_B^R \cdot G_B = \frac{1}{8}\begin{bmatrix} 1 & 3 & 3 & 1 \\ 0 & 2 & 4 & 2 \\ 0 & 0 & 4 & 4 \\ 0 & 0 & 0 & 8 \end{bmatrix}\begin{bmatrix} P_1 \\ P_2 \\ P_3 \\ P_4 \end{bmatrix}. \tag{11.52}$$

Notice that each of the new control points L_i and R_i is a weighted sum of the points P_i, with the weights positive and summing to 1. Thus, each of the new control points is in the convex hull of the set of original control points. Therefore, the new control points are no farther from the curve $Q(t)$ than are the original control points, and in general are closer

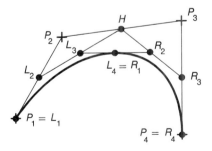

Fig. 11.35 The Bézier curve defined by the points P_i is divided at $t = \frac{1}{2}$ into a left curve defined by the points L_i and a right curve defined by the points R_i.

than the original points. This *variation-diminishing* property is true of all splines that have the convex-hull property. Also notice the symmetry between D_3^L and D_B^R, a consequence of the symmetry in the geometrical construction.

Dividing the Bézier curve at $t = \frac{1}{2}$ often gives the interactive user the control needed, but it might be better to allow the user to indicate a point on the curve at which a split is to occur. Given such a point, it is easy to find the approximate corresponding value of t. The splitting then proceeds as described previously, except that the construction lines are divided in the $t{:}(1 - t)$ ratio (see Exercise 11.22).

The corresponding matrixes D_{Bs}^L and D_{Bs}^R for B-spline subdivision are

$$G_{\mathrm{Bs}_i}^L = D_{\mathrm{Bs}}^L \cdot G_{\mathrm{Bs}_i} = \frac{1}{8} \begin{bmatrix} 4 & 4 & 0 & 0 \\ 1 & 6 & 1 & 0 \\ 0 & 4 & 4 & 0 \\ 0 & 1 & 6 & 1 \end{bmatrix} \begin{bmatrix} P_{i-3} \\ P_{i-2} \\ P_{i-1} \\ P_i \end{bmatrix},$$

$$G_{\mathrm{Bs}_i}^R = D_{\mathrm{Bs}}^R \cdot G_{\mathrm{Bs}_i} = \frac{1}{8} \begin{bmatrix} 1 & 6 & 1 & 0 \\ 0 & 4 & 4 & 0 \\ 0 & 1 & 6 & 1 \\ 0 & 0 & 4 & 4 \end{bmatrix} \begin{bmatrix} P_{i-3} \\ P_{i-2} \\ P_{i-1} \\ P_i \end{bmatrix}. \qquad (11.53)$$

Careful examination of these two equations shows that the four control points of G_{Bs_i} are replaced by a total of five new control points, shared between $G_{\mathrm{Bs}_i}^L$ and $G_{\mathrm{Bs}_i}^R$. However, the spline segments on either side of the one being divided are still defined by some of the control points of G_{Bs_i}. Thus, changes to any of the five new control points or four old control points cause the B-spline to be no longer connected. This problem is avoided with nonuniform B-splines.

Subdividing nonuniform B-splines is not as is simple as specifying two splitting matrices, because there is no explicit basis matrix: The basis is defined recursively. The basic approach is to add knots to the knot sequence. Given a nonuniform B-spline defined by the control points $P_0, \ldots, P_n$ and a value of $t = t'$ at which to add a knot (and hence to add a control point), we want to find the new control points $Q_0, \ldots, Q_{n+1}$ that define the same curve. (The value t' might be determined via user interaction—see Exercise 11.21.) The value t' satisfies $t_j < t' \leq t_{j+1}$. Böhm [BÖHM80] has shown that the new control points are given by

$$\begin{aligned} Q_0 &= P_0 \\ Q_i &= (1 - a_i)P_{i-1} + a_i P_i, \quad 1 \leq i \leq n \\ Q_{n+1} &= P_n \end{aligned} \qquad (11.54)$$

where a_i is given by:

$$\begin{aligned} a_i &= 1, & 1 \leq i \leq j - 3 \\ a_i &= \frac{t' - t_i}{t_{i+3} - t_i}, & j - 2 \leq i \leq j \quad \text{(division by zero is zero)} & \qquad (11.55) \\ a_i &= 0, & j + 1 \leq i \leq n. \end{aligned}$$

This algorithm is a special case of the more general Oslo algorithm [COHE80], which inserts any number of knots into a B-spline in a single set of computations. If more than a few knots are being inserted at once, the Oslo algorithm is more efficient than is the Böhm algorithm.

As an example of Böhm subdivision, consider the knot sequence $(0, 0, 0, 0, 1, 1, 1, 1)$, the four x coordinates of the control point vector $(5.0, 8.0, 9.0, 6.0)$, and a new knot at $t = 0.5$ (i.e., $n = 3, j = 3$). The a_i values defined by Eq. (11.55) are $(0.5, 0.5, 0.5)$. Applying Eq. (11.54) we find that the x coordinates of the new Q_i control points are $(5.0, 6.5, 8.5, 7.5, 6.0)$.

Notice that adding a knot causes two old control points to be replaced by three new control points. Furthermore, segments adjacent to the subdivided segment are defined only in terms of the new control points. Contrast this to the less attractive case of uniform–B-spline subdivision, in which four old control points are replaced by five new ones and adjacent segments are defined with the old control points, which are no longer used for the two new segments.

Hierarchical B-spline refinement is another way to gain finer control over the shape of a curve [FORS89]. Additional control points are added to local regions of a curve, and a hierarchical data structure is built relating the new control points to the original points. Use of a hierarchy allows further additional refinement. Storing the hierarchy rather than replacing the old control points with the larger number of new control points means that the original control points can continue to be used for coarse overall shaping of the curve, while at the same time the new control points can be used for control of details.

11.2.8   Conversion Between Representations

It is often necessary to convert from one representation to another. That is, given a curve represented by geometry vector G_1 and basis matrix M_1, we want to find the equivalent geometry matrix G_2 for basis matrix M_2 such that the two curves are identical: $T \cdot M_2 \cdot G_2 = T \cdot M_1 \cdot G_1$. This equality can be rewritten as $M_2 \cdot G_2 = M_1 \cdot G_1$. Solving for G_2, the unknown geometry matrix, we find

$$M_2^{-1} \cdot M_2 \cdot G_2 = M_2^{-1} \cdot M_1 \cdot G_1, \text{ or } G_2 = M_2^{-1} \cdot M_1 \cdot G_1 = M_{1,2} \cdot G_1. \quad (11.56)$$

That is, the matrix that converts a known geometry vector for representation 1 into the geometry vector for representation 2 is just $M_{1,2} = M_2^{-1} \cdot M_1$.

As an example, in converting from B-spline to Bézier form, the matrix $M_{Bs,B}$ is

$$M_{Bs,B} = M_B^{-1} \cdot M_{Bs} = \frac{1}{6}\begin{bmatrix} 1 & 4 & 1 & 0 \\ 0 & 4 & 2 & 0 \\ 0 & 2 & 4 & 0 \\ 0 & 1 & 4 & 1 \end{bmatrix}. \quad (11.57)$$

The inverse is

$$M_{B,Bs} = M_{Bs}^{-1} \cdot M_B = \begin{bmatrix} 6 & -7 & 2 & 0 \\ 0 & 2 & -1 & 0 \\ 0 & -1 & 2 & 0 \\ 0 & 2 & -7 & 6 \end{bmatrix}. \quad (11.58)$$

Nonuniform B-splines have no explicit basis matrix; recall that a nonuniform B-spline over four points with a knot sequence of $(0, 0, 0, 0, 1, 1, 1, 1)$ is just a Bézier curve. Thus, a way to convert a nonuniform B-spline to any of the other forms is first to convert to Bézier form by adding multiple knots using either the Böhm or Oslo algorithms mentioned in Section 11.2.7, to make all knots have multiplicity 4. Then the Bézier form can be converted to any of the other forms that have basis matrices.

11.2.9 Drawing Curves

There are two basic ways to draw a parametric cubic. The first is by iterative evaluation of $x(t)$, $y(t)$, and $z(t)$ for incrementally spaced values of t, plotting lines between successive points. The second is by recursive subdivision that stops when the control points get sufficiently close to the curve itself.

In the introduction to Section 11.2, simple brute-force iterative evaluation display was described, where the polynomials were evaluated at successive values of t using Horner's rule. The cost was nine multiplies and 10 additions per 3D point. A much more efficient way repeatedly to evaluate a cubic polynomial is with *forward differences*. The forward difference $\Delta f(t)$ of a function $f(t)$ is

$$\Delta f(t) = f(t + \delta) - f(t), \; \delta > 0, \tag{11.59}$$

which can be rewritten as

$$f(t + \delta) = f(t) + \Delta f(t). \tag{11.60}$$

Rewriting Eq. (11.60) in iterative terms, we have

$$f_{n+1} = f_n + \Delta f_n, \tag{11.61}$$

where f is evaluated at equal intervals of size δ, so that $t_n = n\delta$ and $f_n = f(t_n)$.

For a third-degree polynomial,

$$f(t) = at^3 + bt^2 + ct + d = T \cdot C, \tag{11.62}$$

so the forward difference is

$$\Delta f(t) = a(t + \delta)^3 + b(t + \delta)^2 + c(t + \delta) + d - (at^3 + bt^2 + ct + d) \tag{11.63}$$

$$= 3at^2\delta + t(3a\delta^2 + 2b\delta) + a\delta^3 + b\delta^2 + c\delta.$$

Thus, $\Delta f(t)$ is a second-degree polynomial. This is unfortunate, because evaluating Eq. (11.61) still involves evaluating $\Delta f(t)$, plus an addition. But forward differences can be applied to $\Delta f(t)$ to simplify its evaluation. From Eq. (11.61), we write

$$\Delta^2 f(t) = \Delta(\Delta f(t)) = \Delta f(t + \delta) - \Delta f(t). \tag{11.64}$$

Applying this to Eq. (11.63) gives

$$\Delta^2 f(t) = 6a\delta^2 t + 6a\delta^3 - 2b\delta^2. \tag{11.65}$$

This is now a first-degree equation in t. Rewriting (11.64) and using the index n, we obtain

$$\Delta^2 f_n = \Delta f_{n+1} - \Delta f_n. \tag{11.66}$$

Reorganizing and replacing n by $n - 1$ yields

$$\Delta f_n = \Delta f_{n-1} + \Delta^2 f_{n-1}. \tag{11.67}$$

Now, to evaluate Δf_n for use in Eq. (11.61), we evaluate $\Delta^2 f_{n-1}$ and add it to Δf_{n-1}. Because $\Delta^2 f_{n-1}$ is linear in t, this is less work than is evaluating Δf_n directly from the second-degree polynomial Eq. (11.63).

The process is repeated once more to avoid direct evaluation of Eq. (11.65) to find $\Delta^2 f(t)$:

$$\Delta^3 f(t) = \Delta(\Delta^2 f(t)) = \Delta^2 f(t + \delta) - \Delta^2 f(t) = 6a\delta^3. \tag{11.68}$$

The third forward difference is a constant, so further forward differences are not needed. Rewriting Eq. (11.68) with n, and with $\Delta^3 f_n$ as a constant yields

$$\Delta^2 f_{n+1} = \Delta^2 f_n + \Delta^3 f_n = \Delta^2 f_n + 6a\delta^3. \tag{11.69}$$

One further rewrite, replacing n with $n - 2$, completes the development:

$$\Delta^2 f_{n-1} = \Delta^2 f_{n-2} + 6a\delta^3. \tag{11.70}$$

This result can be used in Eq. (11.67) to calculate Δf_n, which is then used in Eq. (11.61) to find f_{n+1}.

To use the forward differences in an algorithm that iterates from $n = 0$ to $n\delta = 1$, we compute the initial conditions with Eqs. (11.62), (11.63), (11.65), and (11.68) for $t = 0$. They are

$$f_0 = d, \; \Delta f_0 = a\delta^3 + b\delta^2 + c\delta, \; \Delta^2 f_0 = 6a\delta^3 + 2b\delta^2, \; \Delta^3 f_0 = 6a\delta^3. \tag{11.71}$$

These initial condition calculations can be done by direct evaluation of the four equations. Note that, however, if we define the vector of initial differences as D, then

$$D = \begin{bmatrix} f_0 \\ \Delta f_0 \\ \Delta^2 f_0 \\ \Delta^3 f_0 \end{bmatrix} = \begin{bmatrix} 0 & 0 & 0 & 1 \\ \delta^3 & \delta^2 & \delta & 0 \\ 6\delta^3 & 2\delta^2 & 0 & 0 \\ 6\delta^3 & 0 & 0 & 0 \end{bmatrix} \begin{bmatrix} a \\ b \\ c \\ d \end{bmatrix}. \tag{11.72}$$

Rewriting, with the 4×4 matrix represented as $E(\delta)$, yields $D = E(\delta)C$. Because we are dealing with three functions, $x(t)$, $y(t)$, and $z(t)$, there are three corresponding sets of initial conditions, $D_x = E(\delta)C_x$, $D_y = E(\delta)C_y$, and $D_z = E(\delta)C_z$.

Based on this derivation, the algorithm for displaying a parametric cubic curve is given in Fig. 11.36. This procedure needs just nine additions and no multiplies per 3D point, and just a few adds and multiplies are used for initialization! This is considerably better than the 10 additions *and* nine multiplies needed for the simple brute-force iterative evaluation using Horner's rule. Notice, however, that error accumulation can be an issue with this algorithm, and sufficient fractional precision must be carried to avoid it. For instance, if $n = 64$ and integer arithmetic is used, then 16 bits of fractional precision are needed; if $n = 256$, 22 bits are needed [BART87].

Recursive subdivision is the second way to display a curve. Subdivision stops adaptively, when the curve segment in question is flat enough to be approximated by a line.

```
void DrawCurveFwdDif (
        int n,                          /* number of steps used to draw a curve */
        double x, double Δx, double Δ²x, double Δ³x,
        /* initial values for x(t) polynomial at t = 0, computed as Dₓ = E(δ)Cₓ. */
        double y, double Δy, double Δ²y, double Δ³y,
        /* initial values for y(t) polynomial at t = 0, computed as Dᵧ = E(δ)Cᵧ. */
        double z, double Δz, double Δ²z, double Δ³z
        /* initial values for z(t) polynomial at t = 0, computed as D_z = E(δ)C_z. */
        /* The step size δ used to calculate Dₓ, Dᵧ, and D_z is 1/n . */
)

{
    int i;

    MoveAbs3 (x, y, z);          /* Go to start of curve */
    for (i = 0; i < n; i++) {
        x += Δx;    Δx += Δ²x;   Δ²x += Δ³x;
        y += Δy;    Δy += Δ²y;   Δ²y += Δ³y;
        z += Δz;    Δz += Δ²z;   Δ²z += Δ³z;
        LineAbs3 (x, y, z);      /* Draw a short line segment */
    }
} /* DrawCurveFwdDif */
```

Fig. 11.36 Procedure to display a parametric curve using forward differences.

Details vary for each type of curve, because the subdivision process is slightly different for each curve, as is the flatness test. The general algorithm is given in Fig. 11.37.

The Bézier representation is particularly appropriate for recursive subdivision display. Subdivision is fast, requiring only six shifts and six adds in Eq. (11.51). The test for "straightness" of a Bézier curve segment is also simple, being based on the convex hull formed by the four control points; see Fig. 11.38. If the larger of distances d_2 and d_3 is less than some threshold ε, then the curve is approximated by a straight line drawn between the endpoints of the curve segment. For the Bézier form, the endpoints are P_1 and P_4, the first and last control points. Were some other form used, the flatness test would be more complicated and the endpoints might have to be calculated. Thus, conversion to Bézier form is appropriate for display by recursive subdivision.

More detail on recursive-subdivision display can be found in [BARS85; BARS87; LANE80]. If the subdivision is done with integer arithmetic, less fractional precision is

```
void DrawCurveRecSub (curve, ε)
{
    if (Straight (curve, ε))      /* Test control points to be within ε of a line */
        DrawLine (curve);
    else {
        SubdivideCurve (curve, leftCurve, rightCurve);
        DrawCurveRecSub (leftCurve, ε);
        DrawCurveRecSub (rightCurve, ε);
    }
} /* DrawCurveRecSub */
```

Fig. 11.37 Procedure to display a curve by recursive subdivision. Straight is a procedure that returns **true** if the curve is sufficiently flat.

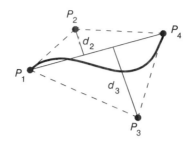

Fig. 11.38 Flatness test for a curve segment. If d_2 and d_3 are both less than some ε, the segment is declared to be flat and is approximated by the line segment P_1P_4.

needed than in the forward difference method. If at most eight levels of recursion are needed (a reasonable expectation), only 3 bits of fractional precision are necessary; if 16, 4 bits.

Recursive subdivision is attractive because it avoids unnecessary computation, whereas forward differencing uses a fixed subdivision. The forward-difference step size δ must be small enough that the portion of the curve with the smallest radius of curvature is approximated satisfactorily. For nearly straight portions of the curve, a much larger step size would be acceptable. [LANE80a] gives a method for calculating the step size δ to obtain a given maximum deviation from the true curve. On the other hand, recursive subdivision takes time to test for flatness. An alternative is to do recursive subdivision down to a fixed depth, avoiding the flatness test at the cost of some extra subdivision (see Exercise 11.30).

A hybrid approach, adaptive forward differencing [LIEN87; SHAN87; SHAN89], uses the best features of both the forward differencing and subdivision methods. The basic strategy is forward differencing, but an adaptive step size is used. Computationally efficient methods to double or halve the step size are used to keep it close to 1 pixel. This means that essentially no straight-line approximations are used between computed points.

11.2.10 Comparison of the Cubic Curves

The different types of parametric cubic curves can be compared by several different criteria, such as ease of interactive manipulation, degree of continuity at join points, generality, and speed of various computations using the representations. Of course, it is not necessary to choose a single representation, since it is possible to convert between all representations, as discussed in Section 11.2.8. For instance, nonuniform rational B-splines can be used as an internal representation, while the user might interactively manipulate Bézier control points or Hermite control points and tangent vectors. Some interactive graphics editors provide the user with Hermite curves while representing them internally in the Bézier form supported by PostScript [ADOB85a]. In general, the user of an interactive CAD system may be given several choices, such as Hermite, Bézier, uniform B-splines, and nonuniform B-splines. The nonuniform rational B-spline representation is likely to be used interally, because it is the most general.

Table 11.2 compares most of the curve forms mentioned in this section. Ease of interactive manipulation is not included explicitly in the table, because the latter is quite

TABLE 11.2 COMPARISON OF SEVEN DIFFERENT FORMS OF PARAMETRIC CUBIC CURVES

	Hermite	Bézier	Uniform B-spline	Uniformly shaped β-spline	Nonuniform B-spline	Catmull–Rom	Kochanek–Bartels
Convex hull defined by control points	N/A	Yes	Yes	Yes	Yes	No	No
Interpolates some control points	Yes	Yes	No	No	No	Yes	Yes
Interpolates all control points	Yes	No	No	No	No	Yes	Yes
Ease of subdivision	Good	Best	Avg	Avg	High	Avg	Avg
Continuities inherent in representation	C^0 G^0	C^0 G^0	C^2 G^2	C^0 G^2	C^2 G^2	C^1 G^1	C^1 G^1
Continuities easily achieved	C^1 G^1	C^1 G^1	C^2 G^{2*}	C^1 G^{2*}	C^2 G^{2*}	C^1 G^1	C^1 G^1
Number of parameters controlling a curve segment	4	4	4	6†	5	4	7

*Except for special case discussed in Section 11.2.
†Four of the parameters are local to each segment, two are global to the entire curve.

application specific. "Number of parameters controlling a curve segment" is the four geometrical constraints plus other parameters, such as knot spacing for nonuniform splines, β_1 and β_2 for β-splines, or a, b, or c for the Kochanek–Bartels case. "Continuity easily achieved" refers to constraints such as forcing control points to be collinear to allow G^1 continuity. Because C^n continuity is more restrictive than G^n, any form that can attain C^n can by definition also attain at least G^n.

When only geometric continuity is required, as is often the case for CAD, the choice is narrowed to the various types of splines, all of which can achieve both G^1 and G^2 continuity. Of the three types of splines in the table, uniform B-splines are the most limiting. The possibility of multiple knots afforded by nonuniform B-splines gives more shape control to the user, as does the use of the β_1 and β_2 shape parameters of the β-splines. Of course, a good user interface that allows the user to exploit this power easily is important.

To interpolate the digitized points of a camera path or shape contour, Catmull–Rom or Kochanek–Bartels splines are preferable. When a combination of interpolation and tangent vector control is desired, the Bézier or Hermite form is best.

It is customary to provide the user with the ability to drag control points or tangent vectors interactively, continually displaying the updated spline. Figure 11.23 shows such a sequence for B-splines. One of the disadvantages of B-splines in some applications is that the control points are not on the spline itself. It is possible, however, not to display the control points, allowing the user instead to interact with the knots (which must be marked so they can be selected). When the user selects a knot and moves it by some (Δx, Δy), the control point weighted most heavily in determining the position of the join point is also moved by (Δx, Δy). The join does not move the full (Δx, Δy), because it is a weighted sum of several control points, only one of which was moved. Therefore, the cursor is repositioned on the join. This process is repeated in a loop until the user stops dragging.

11.3 PARAMETRIC BICUBIC SURFACES

Parametric bicubic surfaces are a generalization of parametric cubic curves. Recall the general form of the parametric cubic curve $Q(t) = T \cdot M \cdot G$, where G, the geometry vector, is a constant. First, for notational convenience, we replace t with s, giving $Q(s) = S \cdot M \cdot G$. If we now allow the points in G to vary in 3D along some path that is parameterized on t, we have

$$ Q(s,\, t) = S \cdot M \cdot G(t) = S \cdot M \cdot \begin{bmatrix} G_1(t) \\ G_2(t) \\ G_3(t) \\ G_4(t) \end{bmatrix}. \tag{11.73} $$

Now, for a fixed t_1, $Q(s, t_1)$ is a curve because $G(t_1)$ is constant. Allowing t to take on some new value—say, t_2—where $t_2 - t_1$ is very small, $Q(s, t)$ is a slightly different curve. Repeating this for arbitrarily many other values of t_2 between 0 and 1, an entire family of curves is defined, each arbitrarily close to another curve. The set of all such curves defines a surface. If the $G_i(t)$ are themselves cubics, the surface is said to be a *parametric bicubic surface*.

Continuing with the case that the $G_i(t)$ are cubics, each can be represented as $G_i(t) = T \cdot M \cdot G_i$, where $G_i = [g_{i1} \quad g_{i2} \quad g_{i3} \quad g_{i4}]^T$ (the G and g are used to distinguish from the G used for the curve). Hence, g_{i1} is the first element of the geometry vector for curve $G_i(t)$, and so on.

Now let us transpose the equation $G_i(t) = T \cdot M \cdot G_i$, using the identity $(A \cdot B \cdot C)^T = C^T \cdot B^T \cdot A^T$. The result is $G_i(t) = G_i^T \cdot M^T \cdot T^T = [g_{i1} \quad g_{i2} \quad g_{i3} \quad g_{i4}] \cdot M^T \cdot T^T$. If we now substitute this result in Eq. (11.73) for each of the four points, we have

$$Q(s, t) = S \cdot M \cdot \begin{bmatrix} g_{11} & g_{12} & g_{13} & g_{14} \\ g_{21} & g_{22} & g_{23} & g_{24} \\ g_{31} & g_{32} & g_{33} & g_{34} \\ g_{41} & g_{42} & g_{43} & g_{44} \end{bmatrix} \cdot M^T \cdot T^T \tag{11.74}$$

or

$$Q(s, t) = S \cdot M \cdot G \cdot M^T \cdot T^T, \quad 0 \le s, t \le 1. \tag{11.75}$$

Written separately for each of x, y, and z, the form is

$$x(s, t) = S \cdot M \cdot G_x \cdot M^T \cdot T^T,$$
$$y(s, t) = S \cdot M \cdot G_y \cdot M^T \cdot T^T,$$
$$z(s, t) = S \cdot M \cdot G_z \cdot M^T \cdot T^T. \tag{11.76}$$

Given this general form, we now move on to examine specific ways to specify surfaces using different geometry matrixes.

11.3.1 Hermite Surfaces

Hermite surfaces are completely defined by a 4×4 geometry matrix G_H. Derivation of G_H follows the same approach used to find Eq. (11.75). We further elaborate the derivation here, applying it just to $x(s, t)$. First, we replace t by s in Eq. (11.13), to get $x(s) = S \cdot M_H \cdot G_{H_x}$. Rewriting this further so that the Hermite geometry vector G_{H_x} is not constant, but is rather a function of t, we obtain

$$x(s, t) = S \cdot M_H \cdot G_{H_x}(t) = S \cdot M_H \begin{bmatrix} P_1(t) \\ P_4(t) \\ R_1(t) \\ R_4(t) \end{bmatrix}_x. \tag{11.77}$$

The functions $P_{1_x}(t)$ and $P_{4_x}(t)$ define the x components of the starting and ending points for the curve in parameter s. Similarly, $R_{1_x}(t)$ and $R_{4_x}(t)$ are the tangent vectors at these points. For any specific value of t, there are two specific endpoints and tangent vectors. Figure 11.39 shows $P_1(t)$, $P_4(t)$, and the cubic in s that is defined when $t = 0.0, 0.2, 0.4, 0.6, 0.8$, and 1.0. The surface patch is essentially a cubic interpolation between $P_1(t) = Q(0, t)$ and $P_4(t) = Q(1, t)$ or, alternatively, between $Q(s, 0)$ and $Q(s, 1)$.

In the special case that the four interpolants $Q(0, t)$, $Q(1, t)$, $Q(s, 0)$, and $Q(s, 1)$ are straight lines, the result is a *ruled surface*. If the interpolants are also coplanar, then the surface is a four-sided planar polygon.

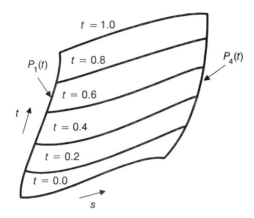

Fig. 11.39 Lines of constant parameter values on a bicubic surface: $P_1(t)$ is at $s = 0$, $P_4(t)$ is at $s = 1$.

Continuing with the derivation, let each of $P_1(t)$, $P_4(t)$, $R_1(t)$, and $R_4(t)$ be represented in Hermite form as

$$P_{1_x}(t) = T \cdot M_H \begin{bmatrix} g_{11} \\ g_{12} \\ g_{13} \\ g_{14} \end{bmatrix}_x, \qquad P_{4_x}(t) = T \cdot M_H \begin{bmatrix} g_{21} \\ g_{22} \\ g_{23} \\ g_{24} \end{bmatrix}_x, \qquad (11.78)$$

$$R_{1_x}(t) = T \cdot M_H \begin{bmatrix} g_{31} \\ g_{32} \\ g_{33} \\ g_{34} \end{bmatrix}_x, \qquad R_{4_x}(t) = T \cdot M_H \begin{bmatrix} g_{41} \\ g_{42} \\ g_{43} \\ g_{44} \end{bmatrix}_x.$$

These four cubics can be rewritten together as a single equation:

$$[P_1(t) \quad P_4(t) \quad R_1(t) \quad R_4(t)]_x = T \cdot M_H \cdot G_{H_x}^T, \qquad (11.79)$$

where

$$G_{H_x} = \begin{bmatrix} g_{11} & g_{12} & g_{13} & g_{14} \\ g_{21} & g_{22} & g_{23} & g_{24} \\ g_{31} & g_{32} & g_{33} & g_{34} \\ g_{41} & g_{42} & g_{43} & g_{44} \end{bmatrix}_x. \qquad (11.80)$$

Transposing both sides of Eq. (11.79) results in

$$\begin{bmatrix} P_1(t) \\ P_4(t) \\ R_1(t) \\ R_4(t) \end{bmatrix}_x = \begin{bmatrix} g_{11} & g_{12} & g_{13} & g_{14} \\ g_{21} & g_{22} & g_{23} & g_{24} \\ g_{31} & g_{32} & g_{33} & g_{34} \\ g_{41} & g_{42} & g_{43} & g_{44} \end{bmatrix}_x M_H^T \cdot T^T = G_{H_x} \cdot M_H^T \cdot T^T. \qquad (11.81)$$

Substituting Eq. (11.81) into Eq. (11.77) yields

$$x(s, t) = S \cdot M_H \cdot G_{H_x} \cdot M_H^T \cdot T^T; \qquad (11.82)$$

similarly,

$$y(s, t) = S \cdot M_H \cdot G_{H_y} \cdot M_H^T \cdot T^T, \quad z(s, t) = S \cdot M_H \cdot G_{H_z} \cdot M_H^T \cdot T^T. \qquad (11.83)$$

The three 4×4 matrixes G_{H_x}, G_{H_y}, and G_{H_z} play the same role for Hermite surfaces as did the single matrix G_H for curves. The meanings of the 16 elements of G_H can be understood by relating them back to Eqs. (11.77) and (11.78). The element g_{11_x} is $x(0, 0)$ because it is the starting point for $P_{1_x}(t)$, which is in turn the starting point for $x(s, 0)$. Similarly, g_{12_x} is $x(0, 1)$ because it is the ending point of $P_{1_x}(t)$, which is in turn the starting point for $x(s, 1)$. Furthermore, g_{13_x} is $\partial x/\partial t(0, 0)$ because it is the starting tangent vector for $P_{1_x}(t)$, and g_{33_x} is $\partial^2 x/\partial s \partial t(0, 0)$ because it is the starting tangent vector of $R_{1_x}(t)$, which in turn is the starting slope of $x(s, 0)$.

Using these interpretations, we can write G_{H_x} as

$$G_{H_x} = \begin{bmatrix} x(0, 0) & x(0, 1) & \dfrac{\partial}{\partial t}x(0, 0) & \dfrac{\partial}{\partial t}x(0, 1) \\[2mm] x(1, 0) & x(1, 1) & \dfrac{\partial}{\partial t}x(1, 0) & \dfrac{\partial}{\partial t}x(1, 1) \\[2mm] \dfrac{\partial}{\partial s}x(0, 0) & \dfrac{\partial}{\partial s}x(0, 1) & \dfrac{\partial^2}{\partial s \partial t}x(0, 0) & \dfrac{\partial^2}{\partial s \partial t}x(0, 1) \\[2mm] \dfrac{\partial}{\partial s}x(1, 0) & \dfrac{\partial}{\partial s}x(1, 1) & \dfrac{\partial^2}{\partial s \partial t}x(1, 0) & \dfrac{\partial^2}{\partial s \partial t}x(1, 1) \end{bmatrix}. \qquad (11.84)$$

The upper-left 2×2 portion of G_{H_x} contains the x coordinates of the four corners of the patch. The upper-right and lower-left 2×2 areas give the x coordinates of the tangent vectors along each parametric direction of the patch. The lower-right 2×2 portion has at its corners the partial derivatives with respect to both s and t. These partials are often called the *twists*, because the greater they are, the greater the corkscrewlike twist at the corners. Figure 11.40 shows a patch whose corners are labeled to indicate these parameters.

This Hermite form of bicubic patches is an alternative way to express a restricted form of the *Coons patch* [COON67]. These more general patches permit boundary curves and slopes to be any curves. (The Coons patch was developed by the late Steven A. Coons [HERZ80], an early pioneer in CAD and computer graphics after whom SIGGRAPH's prestigious *Steven A. Coons Award for Outstanding Contributions to Computer Graphics* is named.) When the four twist vectors in the Hermite form are all zero, the patches are also called Ferguson surfaces after another early developer of surface representations [FERG64; FAUX79].

Just as the Hermite cubic permits C^1 and G^1 continuity from one curve segment to the next, so too the Hermite bicubic permits C^1 and G^1 continuity from one patch to the next. First, to have C^0 continuity at an edge, the matching curves of the two patches must be identical, which means the control points for the two surfaces must be identical along the edge. The necessary conditions for C^1 continuity are that the control points along the edge and the tangent and twist vectors across the edge be equal. For G^1 continuity, the tangent

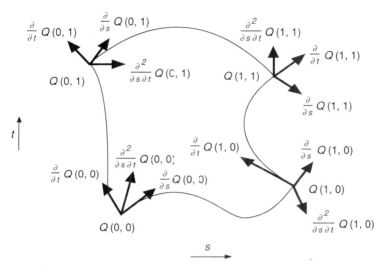

Fig. 11.40 Components of the geometry matrix for a Hermite surface. Each vector is a 3-tuple, the x component of which is given by Eq. (11.84).

vector requirement is relaxed so that the vectors must be in the same direction, but do not need to have the same magnitude. If the common edge for patch 1 is at $s = 1$ and that for patch 2 is at $s = 0$, as in Fig. 11.41, then the values in some rows of the geometry matrices for the two patches must reflect the G^1 conditions, as indicated here:

$$
\begin{array}{cc}
\text{Patch 1} & \text{Patch 2}
\end{array}
$$

$$
\begin{bmatrix}
- & - & - & - \\
g_{21} & g_{22} & g_{23} & g_{24} \\
- & - & - & - \\
g_{41} & g_{42} & g_{43} & g_{44}
\end{bmatrix}
\quad
\begin{bmatrix}
g_{21} & g_{22} & g_{23} & g_{24} \\
- & - & - & - \\
kg_{41} & kg_{42} & kg_{43} & kg_{44} \\
- & - & - & -
\end{bmatrix}
\quad k > 0. \qquad (11.85)
$$

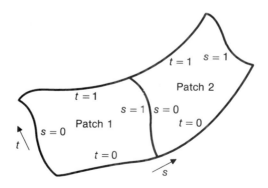

Fig. 11.41 Two joined surface patches.

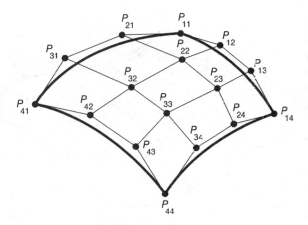

Fig. 11.42 Sixteen control points for a Bézier bicubic patch.

Entries marked with a dash can have any value. If four patches joined at a common corner and along the edges emanating from that corner are to have G^1 continuity, then the relationships are more complex; see Exercise 11.25.

11.3.2   Bézier Surfaces

The Bézier bicubic formulation can be derived in exactly the same way as the Hermite cubic. The results are

$$x(s, t) = S \cdot M_B \cdot G_{B_x} \cdot M_B^T \cdot T^T,$$
$$y(s, t) = S \cdot M_B \cdot G_{B_y} \cdot M_B^T \cdot T^T, \qquad (11.86)$$
$$z(s, t) = S \cdot M_B \cdot G_{B_z} \cdot M_B^T \cdot T^T.$$

The Bézier geometry matrix G consists of 16 control points, as shown in Fig. 11.42. Bézier surfaces are attractive in interactive design for the same reason as Bézier curves are: Some of the control points interpolate the surface, giving convenient precise control, whereas tangent vectors also can be controlled explicitly. When Bézier surfaces are used as an internal representation, their convex-hull property and easy subdivision are attractive.

C^0 and G^0 continuity across patch edges is created by making the four common control points equal. G^1 continuity occurs when the two sets of four control points on either side of the edge are collinear with the points on the edge. In Fig. 11.43, the following sets of control points are collinear and define four line segments whose lengths all have the same ratio k: (P_{13}, P_{14}, P_{15}), (P_{23}, P_{24}, P_{25}), (P_{33}, P_{34}, P_{35}), and (P_{43}, P_{44}, P_{45}).

An alternative way to maintain interpatch continuity, described in more detail in [FAUX79; BEZI70], requires that, at each corner of an edge across which continuity is desired, the corner control points and the control points immediately adjacent to the corner be coplanar.

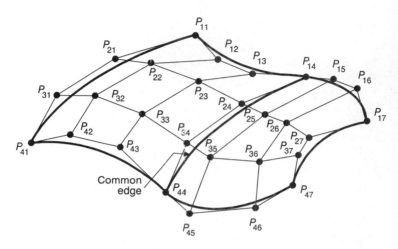

Fig. 11.43 Two Bézier patches joined along the edge P_{14}, P_{24}, P_{34}, and P_{44}.

11.3.3 B-Spline Surfaces

B-spline patches are represented as

$$x(s,\ t) = S \cdot M_{Bs} \cdot G_{Bs_x} \cdot M_{Bs}{}^{T} \cdot T^{T},$$

$$y(s,\ t) = S \cdot M_{Bs} \cdot G_{Bs_y} \cdot M_{Bs}{}^{T} \cdot T^{T}, \tag{11.87}$$

$$z(s,\ t) = S \cdot M_{Bs} \cdot G_{Bs_z} \cdot M_{Bs}{}^{T} \cdot T^{T}.$$

C^2 continuity across boundaries is automatic with B-splines; no special arrangements of control points are needed except to avoid duplicate control points, which create discontinuities.

Bicubic nonuniform and rational B-spline surfaces and other rational surfaces are similarly analogous to their cubic counterparts. All the techniques for subdivision and display carry over directly to the bicubic case.

11.3.4 Normals to Surfaces

The normal to a bicubic surface, needed for shading (Chapter 16), for performing interference detection in robotics, for calculating offsets for numerically controlled machining, and for doing other calculations, is easy to find. From Eq. (11.75), the s tangent vector of the surface $Q(s,\ t)$ is

$$\frac{\partial}{\partial s} Q(s,\ t) = \frac{\partial}{\partial s} (S \cdot M \cdot G \cdot M^{T} \cdot T^{T}) = \frac{\partial}{\partial s} (S) \cdot M \cdot G \cdot M^{T} \cdot T^{T}$$

$$= [3s^{2} \quad 2s \quad 1 \quad 0] \cdot M \cdot G \cdot M^{T} \cdot T^{T}, \tag{11.88}$$

and the t tangent vector is

$$\frac{\partial}{\partial t}Q(s,\,t) = \frac{\partial}{\partial t}(S \cdot M \cdot G \cdot M^{\mathrm{T}} \cdot T^{\mathrm{T}}) = S \cdot M \cdot G \cdot M^{\mathrm{T}} \cdot \frac{\partial}{\partial t}(T^{\mathrm{T}})$$

$$= S \cdot M \cdot G \cdot M^{\mathrm{T}} \cdot [3t^2 \quad 2t \quad 1 \quad 0]^{\mathrm{T}}. \tag{11.89}$$

Both tangent vectors are parallel to the surface at the point $(s,\,t)$ and, therefore, their cross-product is perpendicular to the surface. Notice that, if both tangent vectors are zero, the cross-product is zero, and there is no meaningful surface normal. Recall that a tangent vector can go to zero at join points that have C^1 but not G^1 continuity.

Each of the tangent vectors is of course a 3-tuple, because Eq. (11.75) represents the x, y, and z components of the bicubic. With the notation x_s for the x component of the s tangent vector, y_s for the y component, and z_s for the z component, the normal is

$$\frac{\partial}{\partial s}Q(s,\,t) \times \frac{\partial}{\partial t}Q(s,\,t) = [y_s z_t - y_t z_s \quad z_s x_t - z_t x_s \quad x_s y_t - x_t y_s]. \tag{11.90}$$

The surface normal is a biquintic (two-variable, fifth-degree) polynomial and hence is fairly expensive to compute. [SCHW82] gives a bicubic approximation that is satisfactory as long as the patch itself is relatively smooth.

11.3.5 Displaying Bicubic Surfaces

Like curves, surfaces can be displayed either by iterative evaluation of the bicubic polynomials or by subdivision, which is essentially an adaptive evaluation of the bicubic polynomials. We consider first iterative evaluation, and then subdivision.

Iterative evaluation is best suited for displaying bicubic patches in the style of Fig. 11.44. Each of the curves of constant s and constant t on the surface is itself a cubic, so display of each of the curves is straightforward, as in Fig. 11.45.

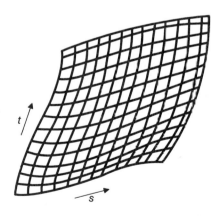

Fig. 11.44 A single surface patch displayed as curves of constant s and constant t.

```
typedef double Coeffs[4][4][3];
void DrawSurface (
        Coeffs coefficients,          /* Coefficients for Q(s,t) */
        int nₛ,                       /* No. of curves of constant s to draw, typically 5–10 */
        int nₜ,                       /* No. of curves of constant t to draw, typically 5–10 */
        int n)                        /* No. of steps used to draw each curve, typically 20–100 */
{
    double δ = 1.0 / n;               /* Step size to use in drawing each curve */
    double δₛ = 1.0 / (nₛ−1);         /* Step size in s to increment to next curve of constant t */
    double δₜ = 1.0 / (nₜ−1);         /* Step size in t to increment to next curve of constant s */
    int i, j; double s, t;
    /* Draw nₛ curves of constant s, for s = 0, δₛ, 2δₛ, ... 1 */
    for (i = 0, s = 0.0; i < nₛ; i++, s += δₛ) {
        /* Draw a curve of constant s, varying t from 0 to 1. */
        /* X, Y, and Z are functions to evaluate the bicubics. */
        MoveAbs3 (X (s, 0.0), Y (s, 0.0), Z (s, 0.0));
        for (j = 1, t = δ; j < n; j++, t += δ) {
            /* n−1 steps are used as t varies from δ to 1 for each curve. */
            LineAbs3 (X (s, t), Y (s, t), Z (s, t));
        }
    }
    /* Draw nₜ curves of constant t, for t = 0, δₜ, 2δₜ, ... 1 */
    for (i = 0, t = 0.0; i < nₜ; i++, t += δₜ) {
        /* Draw a curve of constant t, varying s from 0 to 1. */
        MoveAbs3 (X (0.0, t), Y (0.0, t), Z (0.0, t));
        for (j = 1, s = δ; j < n; j++, s += δ) {
            /* n−1 steps are used as s varies from δ to 1 for each curve. */
            LineAbs3 (X (s, t), Y (s, t), Z (s, t));
        }
    }
} /* DrawSurface */
```

Fig. 11.45 Procedure to display bicubic patch as a grid. Procedures X(s, t), Y(s, t), and Z(s, t) evaluate the surface using the coefficient matrix *coefficients*.

Brute-force iterative evaluation for surfaces is even more expensive than for curves, because the surface equations must be evaluated about $2/\delta^2$ times. For $\delta = 0.1$, this value is 200; for $\delta = 0.01$, it is 20,000. These numbers make the alternative, forward differencing even more attractive than it is for curves. The basic forward-differencing method was developed in Section 11.2.9. The step remaining is to understand how to calculate the initial forward differences for curve $i + 1$ from the forward differences for curve i.

The derivation in Section 11.2.9 used to find $D = E(\delta) \cdot C$ for curves can be used to find

$$DD_x = E(\delta_s) \cdot A_x \cdot E(\delta_t)^{\mathrm{T}} \qquad (11.91)$$

where δ_s is the step size in s, δ_t is the step size in t, and A_x is the 4×4 matrix of coefficients for $x(s, t)$. The 4×4 matrix DD_x has as its first row the values $x(0, 0)$, $\Delta_t x(0, 0)$, $\Delta_t^2 x(0, 0)$, and $\Delta_t^3 x(0, 0)$ (the notation Δ_t means forward difference on t, as opposed to s). Thus, the first row can be used to calculate $x(0, t)$ in increments of δ_t.

After $x(0, t)$ has been computed, how can $x(\delta_s, t)$ be computed, to draw another curve of constant s? (This is the step of calculating the initial forward differences for curve $i + 1$ from the forward differences for curve i.) The other rows of DD_x are the first, second, and third forward differences on s of the first row's forward differences. Therefore, applying the following equations to the rows of DD_x

$$\text{row } 1 := \text{row } 1 + \text{row } 2 \tag{11.92}$$
$$\text{row } 2 := \text{row } 2 + \text{row } 3$$
$$\text{row } 3 := \text{row } 3 + \text{row } 4$$

```
typedef double Coeffs[4][4][3];

void DrawSurfaceFwdDif (
        Coeffs A,    /* Coefficients for Q(s, t) */
        int n_s,     /* Number of curves of constant s to be drawn, typically 5 to 10. */
        int n_t,     /* Number of curves of constant t to be drawn, typically 5 to 10. */
        int n)       /* Number of steps to use in drawing each curve, typically 20 to 100. */
{
    /* Initialize */
    double δ_s = 1.0 / (n_s − 1.0); double δ_t = 1.0 / (n_t − 1.0);
    /* "*" indicates matrix multiplication */
    DD_x = E(δ_s) * A_x * E(δ_t)^T;
    DD_y = E(δ_s) * A_y * E(δ_t)^T;
    DD_z = E(δ_s) * A_z * E(δ_t)^T;

    /* Draw n_s curves of constant s, for s = 0, δ_s, 2δ_s, ... 1 */
    for (i = 0; i < n_s; i++) {
        /* Procedure from Section 11.2.9 to draw a curve */
        DrawCurveFwdDif (n, First row of DD_x, First row of DD_y, First row of DD_z);
        /* Prepare for next iteration */
        Apply equation 11.92 to DD_x, DD_y, and DD_z;
    }
    /* Transpose DD_x, DD_y, DD_z so can continue working with rows */
    DD_x = DD_x^T; DD_y = DD_y^T; DD_z = DD_z^T;
    /* Draw n_t curves of constant t, for t = 0, δ_t, 2δ_t, 3δ_t, ... 1 */
    for (i = 0; i < n_t; i++) {
        DrawCurveFwdDif (n, First row of DD_x, First row of DD_y, First row of DD_z);
        /* Prepare for next iteration */
        Apply equation 11.92 to DD_x, DD_y, and DD_z;
    }
}   /* DrawSurfaceFwdDif */
```

Fig. 11.46 Procedure to display a parametric surface as lines of constant s and t.

```
void DrawSurfaceRecSub (surface, ε)
{
        /* Test whether control points are within ε of a plane */
        if (Flat (surface, ε))
                DrawQuadrilateral (surface);    /* If within ε, draw the surface as a quadrilateral */

        else {                                  /* If not flat enough, subdivide into four patches */
                SubdivideSurface (surface, &surfaceLL, &surfaceLR, &surfaceRL, &surfaceRR);
                DrawSurfaceRecSub (surfaceLL, ε);
                DrawSurfaceRecSub (surfaceLR, ε);
                DrawSurfaceRecSub (surfaceRL, ε);
                DrawSurfaceRecSub (surfaceRR, ε);
        }
}    /* DrawSurfaceRecSub */
```

Fig. 11.47 Procedure to display a parametric surface as a shaded surface. DrawQuadrilateral renders individual, nearly flat quadrilaterals. Flat returns **true** if the surface is
within ε of being flat.

yields in the first row of DD_x the terms $x(\delta_s, 0)$, $\Delta_t x(\delta_s, 0)$, $\Delta_t^2 x(\delta_s, 0)$, and $\Delta_t^3 x(\delta_s, 0)$. These
quantities are now used to compute $x(\delta_s, t)$, using forward differences, as before. Then the
steps of Eq. (11.92) are again repeated, and the first row of D is used to compute $x(2\delta_s, t)$,
and so on.

Drawing the curves of constant t is done similarly. To calculate $x(s, 0)$, we apply Eq.
(11.92) to DD_x but substitute *column* for *row*. Alternatively, DD_x^T can be used in place of
DD_x, so that rows are still used to calculate $x(s, 0)$, $x(s, \delta_t)$, $x(s, 2\delta_t)$, and so on.

The algorithm for displaying a surface as lines of constant s and t using forward
differences is shown in Fig. 11.46.

Surface display using recursive subdivision is also a simple extension from the procedure DrawCurveRecSub of Section 11.2.9, and is presented in Fig. 11.47. Nearly planar
quadrilaterals are created, then are displayed by procedure DrawQuadrilateral as shaded flat
quadrilaterals using the methods described in Chapters 15 and 16. The process is again
simplest if the Bézier form is used.

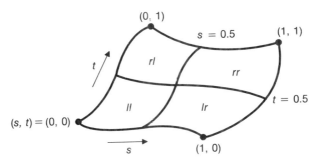

Fig. 11.48 A surface subdivided into four surfaces, *ll*, *lr*, *rl*, and *rr*, each of which is
'flatter' than the original surface.

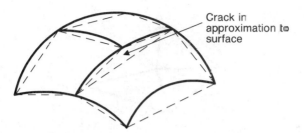

Fig. 11.49 A subdivided surface whose three approximating quadrilaterals introduce a crack into the approximation.

Flatness is tested by computing the plane passing through three of the four corner control points and finding the distance from each of the other 13 control points to the plane; the maximum distance must be less than ε. This is just a generalization of the flatness test used for curves. [LANE79] discusses a different way to perform a more efficient flatness test. Of course, the recursion can again be done to a constant depth, eliminating the flatness test at the price of needless subdivisions.

Surface subdivision is done by splitting the surface along one parameter, say s, and then splitting each of the two resulting surfaces along t. The curve-splitting methods discussed in Section 11.2.7 are applied to each set of four control points running in the direction of the parameter along which the split is being made. Figure 11.48 shows the idea, with the resulting four surfaces labeled ll, lr, rl, and rr as an extension of the notation used in Fig. 11.35. Alternatively, the patch can be split along only one parameter, if the patch is locally flat along the other parameter. [LANE80a] gives a thorough theoretical account of the subdivision process and also describes how it can be used to find curve–curve and surface–surface intersections.

One critical problem with adaptive subdivision is the possibility of cracks between approximating quadrilaterals, as seen in Fig. 11.49. The cracks occur because of the different levels of subdivision applied to adjoining patches. They can be avoided by subdividing to a fixed depth or by making the flatness threshold ε very small. Both solutions, however, cause needless subdivisions. Another way to avoid cracks is to modify adjoining approximating quadrilaterals, as suggested in Fig. 11.50. This basic strategy is

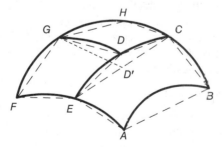

Fig. 11.50 Crack elimination in recursive subdivision. A naive algorithm displays quadrilaterals *ABCE*, *EFGD*, and *GDCH*. A more sophisticated algorithm displays quadrilaterals *ABCE*, *EFGD'*, *and GD'CH*. Vertex *D'* is used instead of *D*.

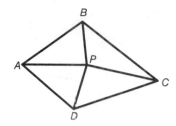

Fig. 11.51 A quadrilateral *ABCD* to be displayed is first subdivided into four triangles. The new point *P* is the average of points *A*, *B*, *C*, and *D*.

used by Clark [CLAR79] and by Barsky, DeRose, and Dippé [BARS87].

Procedure DrawQuadrilateral is given a nearly flat quadrilateral to display. The best way to display the quadrilateral as a shaded surface is to subdivide it further into four triangles, as shown in Fig. 11.51. This strategy avoids visual artifacts.

It is sometimes desirable to display only a portion of a bicubic surface. For instance, there may be a hole in a patch caused by a pipe going through the surface. Displaying only a portion can be done with *trimming curves*, which are just spline curves defined in (s, t) parameter space instead of in (x, y, z) space on the bicubic surface. When displaying a surface that is constrained by a trim curve using DrawSurfaceFwdDif (see Fig. 11.46), the (s, t) values of the trim curve are used to start and stop the iteration.

Other useful ways to display bicubic surfaces are presented in [FORR79].

11.4 QUADRIC SURFACES

The implicit surface equation of the form

$$f(x, y, z) = ax^2 + by^2 + cz^2 + 2dxy + 2eyz + 2fxz + 2gx + 2hy + 2jz + k = 0$$
$$(11.93)$$

defines the family of quadric surfaces. For example, if $a = b = c = -k = 1$ and the remaining coefficients are zero, a unit sphere is defined at the origin. If a through f are zero, a plane is defined. Quadric surfaces are particularly useful in specialized applications such as molecular modeling [PORT79; MAX79], and have also been integrated into solid-modeling systems. Recall, too, that rational cubic curves can represent conic sections; similarly, rational bicubic surfaces can represent quadrics. Hence, the implicit quadratic equation is an alternative to rational surfaces, *if* only quadric surfaces are being represented. Other reasons for using quadrics include ease of

- Computing the surface normal

- Testing whether a point is on the surface (just substitute the point into Eq. (11.93), evaluate, and test for a result within some ε of zero)

- Computing z given x and y (important in hidden-surface algorithms—see Chapter 15) and

- Calculating intersections of one surface with another.

An alternative representation of Eq. (11.93) is:

$$P^T \cdot Q \cdot P = 0, \qquad (11.94)$$

$$\text{with} \quad Q = \begin{bmatrix} a & d & f & g \\ d & b & e & h \\ f & e & c & j \\ g & h & j & k \end{bmatrix} \quad \text{and} \quad P = \begin{bmatrix} x \\ y \\ z \\ 1 \end{bmatrix}. \qquad (11.95)$$

The surface represented by Q can be easily translated and scaled. Given a 4×4 transformation matrix M of the form developed in Chapter 5, the transformed quadric surface Q' is given by

$$Q' = (M^{-1})^T \cdot Q \cdot M^{-1}. \qquad (11.96)$$

The normal to the implicit surface defined by $f(x, y, z) = 0$ is the vector $[df/dx \quad df/dy \quad df/dz]$. This surface normal is much easier to evaluate than is the surface normal to a bicubic surface discussed in Section 11.3.4.

11.5 SUMMARY

This chapter has only touched on some of the important ideas concerning curve and surface representation, but it has given sufficient information so that you can implement interactive systems using these representations. Theoretical treatments of the material can be found in texts such as [BART87; DEBO78; FARI88; FAUX79; MORT85].

Polygon meshes, which are piecewise linear, are well suited for representing flat-faced objects but are seldom satisfactory for curve-faced objects. Piecewise continuous parametric cubic curves and bicubic surfaces are widely used in computer graphics and CAD to represent curve-faced objects because they

- Permit multiple values for a single value of x or y
- Represent infinite slopes
- Provide local control, such that changing a control point affects only a local piece of the curve
- Can be made either to interpolate or to approximate control points, depending on application requirements
- Are computationally efficient
- Permit refinement by subdivision and knot addition, facilitating display and interactive manipulation
- Are easily transformed by transformation of control points.

Although we have discussed only cubics, higher- and lower-order surfaces can also be used. The texts mentioned previously generally develop parametric curves and surfaces for the general case of order n.

EXERCISES

11.1 Develop the equations, similar to Eq. (11.2), for the coefficients A and B of the plane equation. Assume that the polygon vertices are enumerated counterclockwise as viewed toward the plane from the positive side of the plane. The surface normal—given by A, B, and C—points toward the positive side of the plane (which accounts for the need to negate the area computed for B, as discussed in Section 11.1.3).

11.2 Write a program to calculate the plane equation coefficients, given n vertices of a polygon that is approximately planar. The vertices are enumerated in a counterclockwise direction, as defined in Exercise 11.1. Test the program with $n = 3$ for several known planes; then test it for larger n.

11.3 Find the geometry matrix and basis matrix for the parametric representation of a straight line given in Eq. (11.11).

11.4 Implement the procedure DrawCurve given in Fig 11.18. Display a number of curves, varying the coefficients cx, cy, and cz. Try to make the curve correspond to some of the curve segments shown in figures in this chapter. Why it this difficult to do?

11.5 Show that, for a 2D curve $[x(t) \quad y(t)]$, G^1 continuity means that the geometric slope dy/dx is equal at the join points between segments.

11.6 Let $\gamma(t) = (t, t^2)$ for $0 \le t \le 1$, and let $\eta(t) = (2t + 1, t^3 + 4t + 1)$ for $0 \le t \le 1$. Notice that $\gamma(1) = (1, 1) = \eta(0)$, so γ and η join with C^0 continuity.

    a. Plot $\eta(t)$ and $\gamma(t)$ for $0 \le t \le 1$.

    b. Do $\eta(t)$ and $\gamma(t)$ meet with C^1 continuity at the join point? (You will need to compute the vectors $\dfrac{d\gamma}{dt}(1)$ and $\dfrac{d\eta}{dt}(0)$ to check this.)

    c. Do $\eta(t)$ and $\gamma(t)$ meet with G^1 continuity at the join point? (You will need to check ratios from part (b) to determine this).

11.7 Consider the paths

$$\gamma(t) = (t^2 - 2t + 1, t^3 - 2t^2 + t) \quad \text{and} \quad \eta(t) = (t^2 + 1, t^3),$$

both defined on the interval $0 \le t \le 1$. The curves join, since $\gamma(1) = (1, 0) = \eta(0)$. Show that they meet with C^1 continuity, but not with G^1 continuity. Plot both curves as functions of t to demonstrate exactly why this happens.

11.8 Show that the two curves $\gamma(t) = (t^2 - 2t, t)$ and $\eta(t) = (t^2 + 1, t + 1)$ are both C^1 and G^1 continuous where they join at $\gamma(1) = \eta(0)$.

11.9 Analyze the effect on a B-spline of having in sequence four collinear control points.

11.10 Write a program to accept an arbitrary geometry matrix, basis matrix, and list of control points, and to draw the corresponding curve.

11.11 Find the conditions under which two joined Hermite curves have C^1 continuity.

11.12 Suppose the equations relating the Hermite geometry to the Bézier geometry were of the form $R_1 = \beta(P_2 - P_1)$, $R_4 = \beta(P_4 - P_3)$. Consider the four equally spaced Bézier control points $P_1 = (0, 0)$, $P_2 = (1, 0)$, $P_3 = (2, 0)$, $P_4 = (3, 0)$. Show that, for the parametric curve $Q(t)$ to have constant velocity from P_1 to P_4, the coefficient β must be equal to 3.

11.13 Write an interactive program that allows the user to create and refine piecewise continuous cubic curves. Represent the curves internally as B-splines. Allow the user to specify how the curve is to be interactively manipulated—as Hermite, Bézier, or B-splines.

11.14 Show that duplicate interior control points on a B-spline do not affect the C^2 continuity at the join point. Do this by writing out the equations for the two curve segments formed by the control points P_{i-1}, P_i, P_{i+1}, $P_{i+2} = P_{i+1}$, P_{i+3}. Evaluate the second derivative of the first segment at $t = 1$, and that of the second segment at $t = 0$. They should be the same.

11.15 Find the blending functions for the Catmull–Rom splines of Eq. (11.47). Do they sum to 1, and are they everyone nonzero? If not, the spline is not contained in the convex hull of the points.

11.16 Using Eqs. (11.49), (11.50), and (11.19), find the basis matrix M_{KB} for the Kochanek-Bartels spline, using the geometry matrix G_{Bs_i} of Eq. (11.32).

11.17 Write an interactive program that allows the user to create, to manipulate interactively, and to refine piecewise continuous β-spline curves. Experiment with the effect of varying β_1 and β_2.

11.18 Write an interactive program that allows the user to create, to manipulate interactively, and re-fine piecewise continuous Kochanek–Bartels curves. Experiment with the effect of varying a, b, and c.

11.19 Implement both the forward-difference and recursive-subdivision curve-display procedures. Compare execution times for displaying various curves such that the curves are equally smooth to the eye.

11.20 Why is Eq. (11.36) for uniform B-splines written as $Q_i(t - t_i)$, whereas Eq. (11.43) for nonuniform B-splines is written as $Q_i(t)$?

11.21 Given a 2D nonuniform B-spline and an (x, y) value on the curve, write a program to find the corresponding value of t. Be sure to consider the possibility that, for a given value of x (or y), there may be multiple values of y (or x).

11.22 Given a value t at which a Bézier curve is to be split, use the de Casteljau construction shown in Fig. 11.35 to find the division matrices $D_B^L(t)$ and $D_B^R(t)$.

11.23 Apply the methodology used to derive Eq. (11.82) for Hermite surfaces to derive Eq. (11.86) for Bézier surfaces.

11.24 Write programs to display parametric cubic curves and surfaces using forward differences and recursive subdivision. Vary the step size δ and error measure ε to determine the effects of these parameters on the appearance of the curve.

11.25 Given four Hermite patches joined at a common corner and along the edges emanating from that corner, show the four geometry matrices and the relations that must hold between elements of the matrices.

11.26 Let $t_0 = 0$, $t_1 = 1$, $t_2 = 3$, $t_3 = 4$, $t_4 = 5$. Using these values, compute $B_{0,4}$ and each of the functions used in its definition. Then plot these functions on the interval $-3 \le t \le 8$.

11.27 Expand the recurrence relation of Eq. (11.44) into an explicit expression for $B_{i,4}(t)$. Use Fig. 11.26 as a guide.

11.28 Write a program that displays a nonuniform, non-rational B-spline, given as input a knot sequence and control points. Provide a user-controllable option to calculate the $B_{i,4}(t)$ in two ways: (a) using the recurrence relations of Eq. (11.44), and (b) using the explicit expression found in Exercise 11.27. Measure how much time is taken by each method. Is the faster method necessarily the better one?

11.29 Expand the program from Exercise 11.28 to allow interactive input and modification of the B-splines.

11.30 Write procedures to subdivide a curve recursively in two ways: adaptively, with a flatness test, and fixed, with a uniform level of subdivision. Draw a curve first with the adaptive subdivision, noting the deepest level of subdivision needed. Now draw the same curve with fixed subdivision as deep as that needed for the adaptive case. Compare the execution time of the two procedures for a variety of curves.

12
Solid
Modeling

The representations discussed in Chapter 11 allow us to describe curves and surfaces in 2D and 3D. Just as a set of 2D lines and curves does not need to describe the boundary of a closed area, a collection of 3D planes and surfaces does not necessarily bound a closed volume. In many applications, however, it is important to distinguish between the inside, outside, and surface of a 3D object and to be able to compute properties of the object that depend on this distinction. In CAD/CAM, for example, if a solid object can be modeled in a way that adequately captures its geometry, then a variety of useful operations can be performed before the object is manufactured. We may wish to determine whether two objects interfere with each other; for example, whether a robot arm will bump into objects in its environment, or whether a cutting tool will cut only the material it is intended to remove. In simulating physical mechanisms, such as a gear train, it may be important to compute properties such as volume and center of mass. Finite-element analysis is applied to solid models to determine response to factors such as stress and temperature through finite-element modeling. A satisfactory representation for a solid object may even make it possible to generate instructions automatically for computer-controlled machine tools to create that object. In addition, some graphical techniques, such as modeling refractive transparency, depend on being able to determine where a beam of light enters and exits a solid object. These applications are all examples of *solid modeling*. The need to model objects as solids has resulted in the development of a variety of specialized ways to represent them. This chapter provides a brief introduction to these representations.

12.1 REPRESENTING SOLIDS

A representation's ability to encode things that *look* like solids does not by itself mean that the representation is adequate for representing solids. Consider how we have represented objects so far, as collections of straight lines, curves, polygons, and surfaces. Do the lines of Fig. 12.1(a) define a solid cube? If each set of four lines on each side of the object is assumed to bound a square face, then the figure is a cube. However, there is nothing in the representation given that requires the lines to be interpreted this way. For example, the same set of lines would be used to draw the figure if any or all of the faces were missing. What if we decide that each planar loop of connected lines in the drawing by definition determines a polygonal face? Then, Fig. 12.1(b) would consist of all of the faces of Fig. 12.1(a), plus an extra "dangling" face, producing an object that does not bound a volume. As we shall see in Section 12.5, some extra constraints are needed if we want to ensure that a representation of this sort models only solids.

Requicha [REQU80] provides a list of the properties desirable in a solid representation scheme. The *domain* of representation should be large enough to allow a useful set of physical objects to be represented. The representation should ideally be *unambiguous*: There should be no question as to what is being represented, and a given representation should correspond to one and only one solid, unlike the one in Fig. 12.1(a). An unambiguous representation is also said to be *complete*. A representation is *unique* if it can be used to encode any given solid in only one way. If a representation can ensure uniqueness, then operations such as testing two objects for equality are easy. An *accurate* representation allows an object to be represented without approximation. Much as a graphics system that can draw only straight lines forces us to create approximations of smooth curves, some solid modeling representations represent many objects as approximations. Ideally, a representation scheme should make it *impossible to create an invalid representation* (i.e., one that does not correspond to a solid), such as Fig. 12.1(b). On the other hand, it should be *easy to create a valid representation*, typically with the aid of an interactive solid modeling system. We would like objects to maintain *closure* under

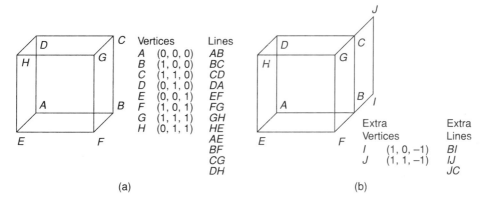

(a)   (b)

Fig. 12.1 (a) A wireframe cube composed of 12 straight lines. (b) A wireframe cube with an extra face.

rotation, translation, and other operations. This means that performing these operations on valid solids should yield only valid solids. A representation should be *compact* to save space, which in turn may save communication time in a distributed system. Finally, a representation should allow the use of *efficient* algorithms for computing desired physical properties, and, most important for us, for creating pictures.

Designing a representation with all these properties is difficult indeed, and compromises are often necessary. As we discuss the major representations in use today, our emphasis will be on providing enough detail to be able to understand how these representations can be interfaced to graphics software. More detail, with an emphasis on the solid modeling aspects, can be found in [REQU80; MORT85; MANT88].

12.2 REGULARIZED BOOLEAN SET OPERATIONS

No matter how we represent objects, we would like to be able to combine them in order to make new ones. One of the most intuitive and popular methods for combining objects is by *Boolean set operations,* such as union, difference, and intersection, as shown in Fig. 12.2. These are the 3D equivalents of the familiar 2D Boolean operations. Applying an ordinary Boolean set operation to two solid objects, however, does not necessarily yield a solid object. For example, the ordinary Boolean intersections of the cubes in Fig. 12.3(a) through (e) are a solid, a plane, a line, a point, and the null object, respectively.

Rather than using the ordinary Boolean set operators, we will instead use the *regularized Boolean set operators* [REQU77], denoted $\cup^*$, $\cap^*$, and $-^*$, and defined such that operations on solids always yield solids. For example, the regularized Boolean intersection of the objects shown in Fig. 12.3 is the same as their ordinary Boolean intersection in cases (a) and (e), but is empty in (b) through (d).

To explore the difference between ordinary and regularized operators, we can consider any object to be defined by a set of points, partitioned into interior points and boundary points, as shown in Fig. 12.4(a). *Boundary* points are those points whose distance from the object and the object's complement is zero. Boundary points need not be part of the object. A *closed* set contains all its boundary points, whereas an *open* set contains none. The union of a set with the set of its boundary points is known as the set's *closure,* as shown in Fig. 12.4(b), which is itself a closed set. The *boundary* of a closed set is the set of its boundary points, whereas the *interior,* shown in Fig. 12.4(c), consists of all of the set's other points, and thus is the complement of the boundary with respect to the object. The *regularization* of

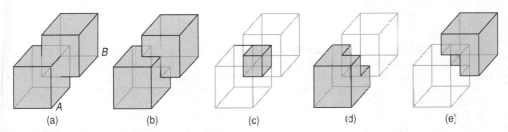

Fig. 12.2 Boolean operations. (a) Objects *A* and *B*, (b) *A* ∪ *B*, (c) *A* ∩ *B*, (d) *A* − *B*, and (e) *B* − *A*.

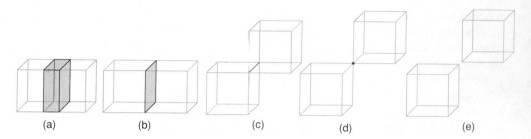

Fig. 12.3 The ordinary Boolean intersection of two cubes may produce (a) a solid, (b) a plane, (c) a line, (d) a point, or (e) the null set.

a set is defined as the closure of the set's interior points. Figure 12.4(d) shows the closure of the object in Fig. 12.4(c) and, therefore, the regularization of the object in Fig. 12.4(a). A set that is equal to its own regularization is known as a *regular set*. Note that a regular set can contain no boundary point that is not adjacent to some interior point; thus, it can have no "dangling" boundary points, lines, or surfaces. We can define each regularized Boolean set operator in terms of the corresponding ordinary Boolean set operator as

$$A \ op^* \ B = \text{closure(interior}(A \ op \ B)), \tag{12.1}$$

where *op* is one of $\cup$, $\cap$, or $-$. The regularized Boolean set operators produce only regular sets when applied to regular sets.

We now compare the ordinary and regularized Boolean set operations as performed on regular sets. Consider the two objects of Fig. 12.5(a), positioned as shown in Fig. 12.5(b). The ordinary Boolean intersection of two objects contains the intersection of the interior and boundary of each object with the interior and boundary of the other, as shown in Fig. 12.5(c). In contrast, the regularized Boolean intersection of two objects, shown in Fig. 12.5(d), contains the intersection of their interiors and the intersection of the interior of each with the boundary of the other, but only a subset of the intersection of their boundaries. The criterion used to define this subset determines how regularized Boolean

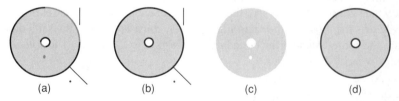

Fig. 12.4 Regularizing an object. (a) The object is defined by interior points, shown in light gray, and boundary points. Boundary points that are part of the object are shown in black; the rest of the boundary points are shown in dark gray. The object has dangling and unattached points and lines, and there is a boundary point in the interior that is not part of the object. (b) Closure of the object. All boundary points are part of the object. The boundary point embedded in the interior of (a) is now part of the interior. (c) Interior of the object. Dangling and unattached points and lines have been eliminated. (d) Regularization of the object is the closure of its interior.

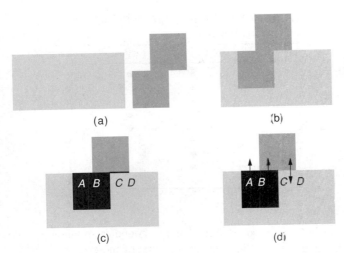

Fig. 12.5 Boolean intersection. (a) Two objects, shown in cross-section. (b) Positions of object prior to intersection. (c) Ordinary Boolean intersection results in a dangling face, shown as line CD in cross-section. (d) Regularized Boolean intersection includes a piece of shared boundary in the resulting boundary if both objects lie on the same side of it (AB), and excludes it if the objects lie on opposite sides (CD). Boundary–interior intersections are always included (BC).

intersection differs from ordinary Boolean intersection, in which all parts of the intersection of the boundaries are included.

Intuitively, a piece of the boundary–boundary intersection is included in the regularized Boolean intersection if and only if the interiors of both objects lie on the same side of this piece of shared boundary. Since the interior points of both objects that are directly adjacent to that piece of boundary are in the intersection, the boundary piece must also be included to maintain closure. Consider the case of a piece of shared boundary that lies in coplanar faces of two polyhedra. Determining whether the interiors lie on the same side of a shared boundary is simple if both objects are defined such that their surface normals point outward (or inward). The interiors are on the same side if the normals point in the same direction. Thus, segment AB in Fig. 12.5(d) is included. Remember that those parts of one object's boundary that intersect with the other object's interior, such as segment BC, are always included.

Consider what happens when the interiors of the objects lie on opposite sides of the shared boundary, as is the case with segment CD. In such cases, none of the interior points adjacent to the boundary are included in the intersection. Thus, the piece of shared boundary is not adjacent to any interior points of the resulting object and therefore is not included in the regularized intersection. This additional restriction on which pieces of shared boundary are included ensures that the resulting object is a regular set. The surface normal of each face of the resulting object's boundary is the surface normal of whichever surface(s) contributed that part of the boundary. (As we shall see in Chapter 16, surface normals are important in shading objects.) Having determined which faces lie in the

TABLE 12.1 REGULARIZED BOOLEAN
SET OPERATIONS

Set	$A \cup^* B$	$A \cap^* B$	$A -^* B$
$A_i \cap B_i$	●	●	
$A_i - B$	●		●
$B_i - A$	●		
$A_b \cap B_i$		●	
$B_b \cap A_i$		●	●
$A_b - B$	●		●
$B_b - A$	●		
$A_b \cap B_b$ same	●	●	
$A_b \cap B_b$ diff			●

boundary, we include an edge or vertex of the boundary–boundary intersection in the boundary of the intersection if it is adjacent to one of these faces.

The results of each regularized operator may be defined in terms of the ordinary operators applied to the boundaries and interiors of the objects. Table 12.1 shows how the regularized operators are defined for any objects A and B; Fig. 12.6 shows the results of performing the operations. A_b and A_i are A's boundary and interior, respectively. $A_b \cap B_b$ *same* is that part of the boundary shared by A and B for which A_i and B_i lie on the same side. This is the case for some point b on the shared boundary if at least one point i adjacent to it is a member of both A_i and B_i. $A_b \cap B_b$ *diff* is that part of the boundary shared by A and B for which A_i and B_i lie on opposite sides. This is true for b if it is adjacent to no such point i. Each regularized operator is defined by the union of the sets associated with those rows that have a ● in the operator's column.

Note that, in all cases, each piece of the resulting object's boundary is on the boundary of one or both of the original objects. When computing $A \cup^* B$ or $A \cap^* B$, the surface normal of a face of the result is inherited from the surface normal of the corresponding face of one or both original objects. In the case cf $A -^* B$, however, the surface normal of each

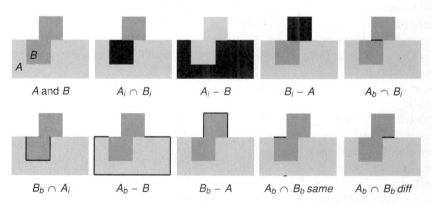

Fig. 12.6 Ordinary Boolean operations on subsets of two objects.

face of the result at which B has been used to excavate A must point in the *opposite* direction from B's surface normal at that face. This corresponds to the boundary pieces $A_t \cap B_b$ *diff* and $B_b \cap A_i$. Alternatively, $A -^* B$ may be rewritten as $A \cap^* \overline{B}$. We can obtain $\overline{B}$ (the complement of B) by complementing B's interior and reversing the normals of its boundary.

The regularized Boolean set operators have been used as a user–interface technique to build complex objects from simple ones in most of the representation schemes we shall discuss. They are also included explicitly in one of the schemes, constructive solid geometry. In the following sections, we shall describe a variety of ways to represent solid objects unambiguously.

12.3 PRIMITIVE INSTANCING

In *primitive instancing*, the modeling system defines a set of primitive 3D solid shapes that are relevant to the application area. These primitives are typically parameterized not just in terms of the transformations of Chapter 7, but on other properties as well. For example, one primitive object may be a regular pyramid with a user-defined number of faces meeting at the apex. Primitive instances are similar to parameterized objects, such as the menus of Chapter 2, except that the objects are solids. A parameterized primitive may be thought of as defining a family of parts whose members vary in a few parameters, an important CAD concept known as *group technology*. Primitive instancing is often used for relatively complex objects, such as gears or bolts, that are tedious to define in terms of Boolean combinations of simpler objects, yet are readily characterized by a few high-level parameters. For example, a gear may be parameterized by its diameter or number of teeth, as shown in Fig. 12.7.

Although we can build up a hierarchy of primitive instances, each leaf-node instance is still a separately defined object. In primitive instancing, no provisions are made for combining objects to form a new higher-level object, using, for example, the regularized Boolean set operations. Thus, the only way to create a new kind of object is to write the code that defines it. Similarly, the routines that draw the objects or determine their mass properties must be written individually for each primitive.

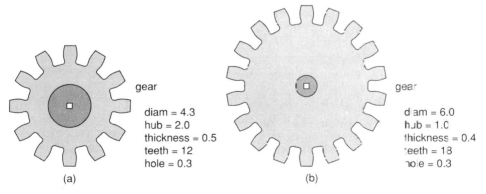

gear

diam = 4.3
hub = 2.0
thickness = 0.5
teeth = 12
hole = 0.3

(a)

gear

diam = 6.0
hub = 1.0
thickness = 0.4
teeth = 13
hole = 0.3

(b)

Fig. 12.7 Two gears defined by primitive instancing.

12.4 SWEEP REPRESENTATIONS

Sweeping an object along a trajectory through space defines a new object, called a *sweep*. The simplest kind of sweep is defined by a 2D area swept along a linear path normal to the plane of the area to create a volume. This is known as a *translational sweep* or *extrusion* and is a natural way to represent objects made by extruding metal or plastic through a die with the desired cross-section. In these simple cases, each sweep's volume is simply the swept object's area times the length of the sweep. Simple extensions involve scaling the cross-section as it is swept to produce a tapered object or sweeping the cross-section along a linear path that is not normal to it. *Rotational sweeps* are defined by rotating an area about an axis. Figure 12.8 shows two objects and simple translational and rotational sweeps generated using them.

The object being swept does not need to be 2D. Sweeps of solids are useful in modeling the region swept out by a machine-tool cutting head or robot following a path, as shown in Fig. 12.9. Sweeps whose generating area or volume changes in size, shape, or orientation as they are swept and that follow an arbitrary curved trajectory are called *general sweeps*. General sweeps of 2D cross-sections are known as *generalized cylinders* in computer vision [BINF71] and are usually modeled as parameterized 2D cross-sections swept at right angles along an arbitrary curve. General sweeps are particularly difficult to model efficiently. For example, the trajectory and object shape may make the swept object intersect itself, making volume calculations complicated. As well, general sweeps do not always generate solids. For example, sweeping a 2D area in its own plane generates another 2D area.

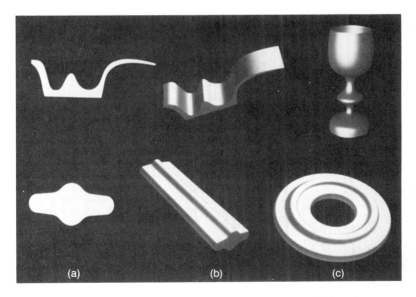

Fig. 12.8 Sweeps. (a) 2D areas are used to define (b) translational sweeps and (c) rotational sweeps. (Created using the Alpha_1 modeling system. Courtesy of the University of Utah.)

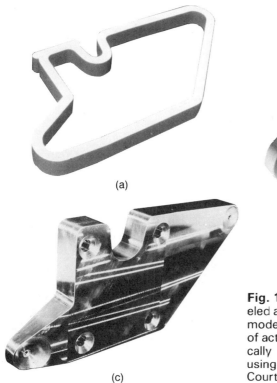

(a)

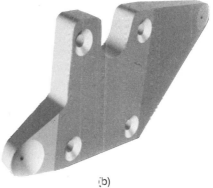

(b)

(c)

Fig. 12.9 (a) Path of a cutting tool, modeled as a solid sweep, is used to define (b) model of an aircraft part. (c) Photograph of actual part that is milled from automatically generated instructions. (Created using the Alpha_1 modeling system. Courtesy of the University of Utah.)

In general, it is difficult to apply regularized Boolean set operations to sweeps without first converting to some other representation. Even simple sweeps are not closed under regularized Boolean set operations. For example, the union of two simple sweeps is in general not a simple sweep, as shown in Fig. 12.10. Despite problems of closure and calculation, however, sweeps are a natural and intuitive way to construct a variety of objects. For this reason, many solid modeling systems allow users to construct objects as sweeps, but store the objects in one of the other representations that we shall discuss.

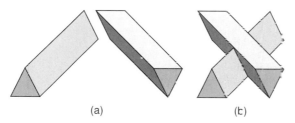

(a)   (b)

Fig. 12.10 (a) Two simple sweeps of 2D objects (triangles). (b) The union of the sweeps shown in (a) is not itself a simple sweep of a 2D object.

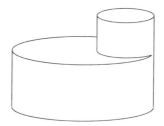

Fig. 12.11 How many faces does this object have?

12.5 BOUNDARY REPRESENTATIONS

Boundary representations (also known as *b-reps*) resemble the naive representations that we discussed in Section 12.1 in that they describe an object in terms of its surface boundaries: vertices, edges, and faces. Some b-reps are restricted to planar, polygonal boundaries, and may even require faces to be convex polygons or triangles. Determining what constitutes a face can be particularly difficult if curved surfaces are allowed, as shown in Fig. 12.11. Curved faces are often approximated with polygons. Alternatively, they can also be represented as surface patches if the algorithms that process the representation can treat the resulting intersection curves, which will, in general, be of higher order than the original surfaces. B-reps grew out of the simple vector representations used in earlier chapters and are used in many current modeling systems. Because of their prevalence in graphics, a number of efficient techniques have been developed to create smooth shaded pictures of polygonal objects; many of these are discussed in Chapter 16.

Many b-rep systems support only solids whose boundaries are *2-manifolds*. By definition, every point on a 2-manifold has some arbitrarily small neighborhood of points around it that can be considered topologically the same as a disk in the plane. This means that there is a continuous one-to-one correspondence between the neighborhood of points and the disk, as shown in Fig. 12.12(a) and (b). For example, if more than two faces share an edge, as in Fig. 12.12(c), any neighborhood of a point on that edge contains points from each of those faces. It is intuitively obvious that there is no continuous one-to-one

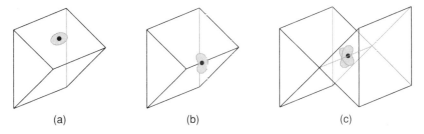

(a)	(b)	(c)

Fig. 12.12 On a 2-manifold, each point, shown as a black dot, has a neighborhood of surrounding points that is a topological disk, shown in gray in (a) and (b). (c) If an object is not a 2-manifold, then it has points that do not have a neighborhood that is a topological disk.

correspondence between this neighborhood and a disk in the plane, although the mathematical proof is by no means trivial. Thus, the surface in Fig. 12.12(c) is not a 2-manifold. Although some current systems do not have this restriction, we limit our discussion of b-reps to 2-manifolds, except where we state otherwise.

12.5.1 Polyhedra and Euler's Formula

A *polyhedron* is a solid that is bounded by a set of polygons whose edges are each a member of an even number of polygons (exactly two polygons in the case of 2-manifolds) and that satisfies some additional constraints (discussed later). A *simple polyhedron* is one that can be deformed into a sphere; that is, a polyhedron that, unlike a torus, has no holes. The b-rep of a simple polyhedron satisfies Euler's formula, which expresses an invariant relationship among the number of vertices, edges, and faces of a simple polyhedron:

$$V - E + F = 2, \tag{12.2}$$

where V is the number of vertices, E is the number of edges, and F is the number of faces. Figure 12.13 shows some simple polyhedra and their numbers of vertices, edges, and faces. Note that the formula still applies if curved edges and nonplanar faces are allowed. Euler's formula by itself states necessary but not sufficient conditions for an object to be a simple polyhedron. One can construct objects that satisfy the formula but do not bound a volume, by attaching one or more dangling faces or edges to an otherwise valid solid, as in Fig. 12.1(b). Additional constraints are needed to guarantee that the object is a solid: each edge must connect two vertices and be shared by exactly two faces, at least three edges must meet at each vertex, and faces must not interpenetrate.

A generalization of Euler's formula applies to 2-manifolds that have faces with holes:

$$V - E + F - H = 2(C - G), \tag{12.3}$$

where H is the number of holes in the faces, G is the number of holes that pass through the object, and C is the number of separate components (parts) of the object, as shown in Fig. 12.14. If an object has a single component, its G is known as its *genus*; if it has multiple components, then its G is the sum of the genera of its components. As before, additional constraints are also needed to guarantee that the objects are solids.

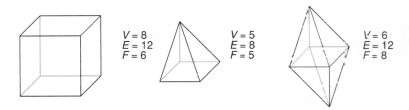

$$
\begin{array}{cccc}
V = 8 & V = 5 & & V = 6 \\
E = 12 & E = 8 & & E = 12 \\
F = 6 & F = 5 & & F = 8
\end{array}
$$

Fig. 12.13 Some simple polyhedra with their V, E, and F values. In each case $V - E + F$ = 2.

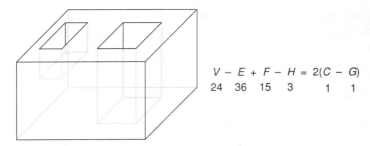

$$V - E + F - H = 2(C - G)$$
$$24 \quad 36 \quad 15 \quad 3 \quad\quad 1 \quad\; 1$$

Fig. 12.14 A polyhedron classified according to Eq. (12.3), with two holes in its top face and one hole in its bottom face.

Baumgart introduced the notion of a set of *Euler operators* that operate on objects satisfying Euler's formula to transform the objects into new objects that obey the formula as well, by adding and removing vertices, edges, and faces [BAUM74]. Braid, Hillyard, and Stroud [BRAI78] show how a small number of Euler operators can be composed to transform objects, provided that intermediate objects are not required to be valid solids, whereas Mäntylä [MANT88] proves that all valid b-reps can be constructed by a finite sequence of Euler operators. Other operators that do not affect the number of vertices, edges, or faces may be defined that *tweak* an object by moving the existing vertices, edges, or faces, as shown in Fig. 12.15.

Perhaps the simplest possible b-rep is a list of polygonal faces, each represented by a list of vertex coordinates. To represent the direction in which each polygon faces, we list a polygon's vertices in clockwise order, as seen from the exterior of the solid. To avoid replicating coordinates shared by faces, we may instead represent each vertex of a face by an index into a list of coordinates. In this representation, edges are represented implicitly by

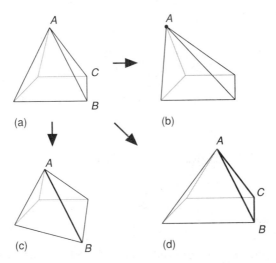

Fig. 12.15 (a) An object on which tweaking operations are performed to move (b) vertex *A*, (c) edge *AB*, and (d) face *ABC*.

the pairs of adjacent vertices in the polygon vertex lists. Edges may instead be represented explicitly as pairs of vertices, with each face now defined as a list of indices into the list of edges. These representations were discussed in more detail in Section 11.1.1.

12.5.2 The Winged-Edge Representation

Simple representations make certain computations quite expensive. For example, discovering the two faces shared by an edge (e.g., to help prove that a representation encodes a valid solid) requires searching the edge lists of all the faces. More complex b-reps have been designed to decrease the cost of these computations. One of the most popular is the *winged-edge* data structure developed by Baumgart [BAUM72; BAUM75]. As shown in Fig. 12.16, each edge in the winged-edge data structure is represented by pointers to its two vertices, to the two faces sharing the edge, and to four of the additional edges emanating from its vertices. Each vertex has a backward pointer to one of the edges emanating from it, whereas each face points to one of its edges. Note that we traverse the vertices of an edge in opposite directions when following the vertices of each of its two faces in clockwise order. Labeling the edge's vertices n and p, we refer to the face to its right when traversing the edge from n to p as its p face, and the face to its right when traversing the edge from p to n as its n face. For edge $E1$ in Fig. 12.16, if n is $V1$ and p is $V2$, then $F1$ is $E1$'s p face, and $F2$ is its n face. The four edges to which each edge points can be classified as follows. The two edges that share the edge's n vertex are the next (clockwise) edge of the n face, and the previous (counterclockwise) edge of the p face, $E3$ and $E2$, respectively. The two edges that share the edge's p vertex are the next (clockwise) edge of the p face, and the previous (counterclockwise) edge of the n face, $E4$ and $E5$, respectively. These four edges are the "wings" from which the winged-edge data structure gets its name.

Note that the data structure described here handles only faces that have no holes. This limitation can be removed by representing each face as a set of edge loops—a clockwise outer loop and zero or more counterclockwise inner loops for its holes—as described in

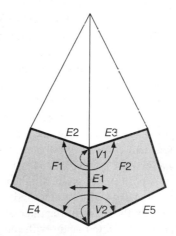

Fig. 12.16 Winged-edge data structure for $E1$. Each of $V1$, $V2$, $F1$, and $F2$ also have a backward pointer to one of their edges (not shown).

Section 19.1. Alternatively, a special auxiliary edge can be used to join each hole's boundary to the outer boundary. Each auxiliary edge is traversed twice, once in each direction, when a circuit of its face's edges is completed. Since an auxiliary edge has the same face on both of its sides, it can be easily identified because its two face pointers point to the same face.

A b-rep allows us to query which faces, edges, or vertices are adjacent to each face, edge, or vertex. These queries correspond to nine kinds of *adjacency relationships*. The winged-edge data structure makes it possible to determine in constant time which vertices or faces are associated with an edge. It takes longer to compute other adjacency relationships. One attractive property of the winged edge is that the data structures for the edges, faces, and vertices are each of a small, constant size. Only the number of instances of each data structure varies among objects. Weiler [WEIL85] and Woo [WOO85] discuss the space–time efficiency of the winged edge and a variety of alternative b-rep data structures.

12.5.3   Boolean Set Operations

B-reps may be combined, using the regularized Boolean set operators, to create new b-reps [REQU85]. Sarraga [SARR83] and Miller [MILL87] discuss algorithms that determine the intersections between quadric surfaces. Algorithms for combining polyhedral objects are presented in [TURN84; REQU85; PUTN86; LAID86], and Thibault and Naylor [THIB87] describe a method based on the binary space-partitioning tree representation of solids discussed in Section 12.6.4.

One approach [LAID86] is to inspect the polygons of both objects, splitting them if necessary to ensure that the intersection of a vertex, edge, or face of one object with any vertex, edge, or face of another, is a vertex, edge, or face of both. The polygons of each object are then classified relative to the other object to determine whether they lie inside, outside, or on its boundary. Referring back to Table 12.1, we note that since this is a b-rep, we are concerned with only the last six rows, each of which represents some part of one or both of the original object boundaries, A_b and B_b. After splitting, each polygon of one object is either wholly inside the other object ($A_b \cap B_i$ or $B_b \cap A_i$), wholly outside the other object ($A_b - B$ or $B_b - A$), or part of the shared boundary ($A_b \cap B_b$ *same* or $A_b \cap B_b$ *diff*).

A polygon may be classified by the ray-casting technique discussed in Section 15.10.1. Here, we construct a vector in the direction of the polygon's surface normal from a point in the polygon's interior, and then find the closest polygon that intersects the vector in the other object. If no polygon is intersected, the original polygon is outside the other object. If the closest intersecting polygon is coplanar with the original polygon, then this is a boundary–boundary intersection, and comparing polygon normals indicates what kind of intersection it is ($A_b \cap B_b$ *same* or $A_b \cap B_b$ *diff*). Otherwise, the dot product of the two polygons' normals is inspected. A positive dot product indicates that the original polygon is inside the other object, whereas a negative dot product indicates that it is outside. A zero dot product occurs if the vector is in the plane of the intersected polygon; in this case, the vector is perturbed slightly and is intersected again with the other object's polygons.

Vertex-adjacency information can be used to avoid the overhead of classifying each polygon in this way. If a polygon is adjacent to (i.e., shares vertices with) a classified polygon and does not meet the surface of the other object, then it is assigned the same classification. All vertices on the common boundary between objects can be marked during the initial polygon-splitting phase. Whether or not a polygon meets the other object's surface can be determined by checking whether or not it has boundary vertices.

Each polygon's classification determines whether it is retained or discarded in the operation creating the composite object, as described in Section 12.2. For example, in forming the union, any polygon belonging to one object that is inside the other object is discarded. Any polygon from either object that is not inside the other is retained, except in the case of coplanar polygons. Coplanar polygons are discarded if they have opposite surface normals, and only one of a pair is retained if the directions of the surface normals are the same. Deciding which polygon to retain is important if the objects are made of different materials. Although $A \cup^* B$ has the same geometric meaning as $B \cup^* A$, the two may have visibly different results in this case, so the operation may be defined to favor one of its operands in the case of coplanar polygons.

12.5.4 Nonpolyhedral b-Reps

Unfortunately, polyhedral representations can only approximate objects that are not themselves polyhedral, and can require large amounts of data to approximate objects with curved surfaces acceptably. Consider the problem of representing a cylindrical object in a cylindrical hole with polyhedral b-reps, as shown in Fig. 12.17. If the boundaries of the actual objects touch, then even if the boundaries of the two polyhedral approximations are initially coincident as well, the approximations will intersect if one is slowly rotated, no matter how many polygons are used in the approximation.

One promising approach to exact b-reps allows sculpted surfaces defined by curves. The Alpha_1 [COHE83] and Geomod [TILL83] modeling systems model such free-form surfaces as tensor products of NURBS (see Section 11.2.5). Since each individual surface may not itself be closed, Thomas [THOM84] has developed an algorithm for Alpha_1 that performs regularized Boolean set operations on objects whose boundaries are only partially specified, as shown in Fig. 12.18. The objects in Color Plate I.31 were modeled with Alpha_1.

Because b-reps tile an object's surface, they do not provide a unique representation of a solid. In addition, as mentioned previously, many b-rep–based systems handle only objects whose surfaces are 2-manifolds. Note that 2-manifolds are not closed under regularized

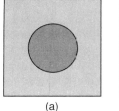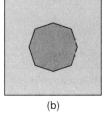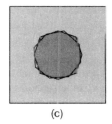

| (a) | (b) | (c) |

Fig. 12.17 (a) Cross-section of a cylinder in a round hole. (b) Polygonal approximation of hole and cylinder. (c) Interference occurs if approximated cylinder is turned relative to hole.

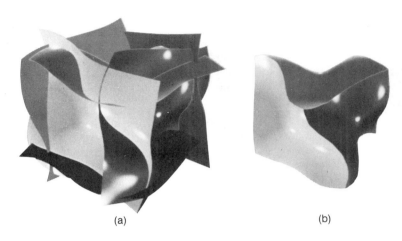

Fig. 12.18 Boolean set operations on partially bounded objects. (a) Six partially bounded sets. (b) Intersection of sets defines a wavy cube. (Courtesy of Spencer W. Thomas, University of Utah.)

Boolean set operations. The regularized union of two b-rep cubes positioned such that they share exactly one common edge, for example, should produce four faces sharing that common edge. This configuration is not allowed in some systems, however, such as those based on the winged-edge representation. Weiler [WEIL88] describes a nonmanifold, boundary-based modeling system that can handle wireframe objects, in addition to surfaces and solids, as illustrated in Color Plate I.32.

12.6 SPATIAL-PARTITIONING REPRESENTATIONS

In *spatial-partitioning* representations, a solid is decomposed into a collection of adjoining, nonintersecting solids that are more primitive than, although not necessarily of the same type as, the original solid. Primitives may vary in type, size, position, parameterization, and orientation, much like the different-shaped blocks in a child's block set. How far we decompose objects depends on how primitive the solids must be in order to perform readily the operations of interest.

12.6.1 Cell Decomposition

One of the most general forms of spatial partitioning is called *cell decomposition*. Each cell-decomposition system defines a set of primitive cells that are typically parameterized and are often curved. Cell decomposition differs from primitive instancing in that we can compose more complex objects from simple, primitive ones in a bottom-up fashion by "gluing" them together. The *glue* operation can be thought of as a restricted form of union in which the objects must not intersect. Further restrictions on gluing cells often require that two cells share a single point, edge, or face. Although cell-decomposition representation of an object is unambiguous, it is not necessarily unique, as shown in Fig. 12.19. Cell

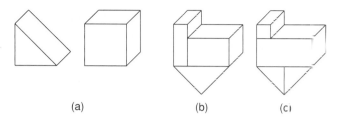

(a)   (b)   (c)

Fig. 12.19 The cells shown in (a) may be transformed to construct the same object shown in (b) and (c) in different ways. Even a single cell type is enough to cause ambiguity.

decompositions are also difficult to validate, since each pair of cells must potentially be tested for intersection. Nevertheless, cell decomposition is an important representation for use in finite element analysis.

12.6.2   Spatial-Occupancy Enumeration

Spatial-occupancy enumeration is a special case of cell decomposition in which the solid is decomposed into identical cells arranged in a fixed, regular grid. These cells are often called *voxels* (volume elements), in analogy to pixels. Figure 12.20 shows an object represented by spatial-occupancy enumeration. The most common cell type is the cube, and the representation of space as a regular array of cubes is called a *cuberille*. When representing an object using spatial-occupancy enumeration, we control only the presence or absence of a single cell at each position in the grid. To represent an object, we need only to decide which cells are occupied and which are not. The object can thus be encoded by a unique and unambiguous list of occupied cells. It is easy to find out whether a cell is inside or outside of the solid, and determining whether two objects are adjacent is simple as well. Spatial-

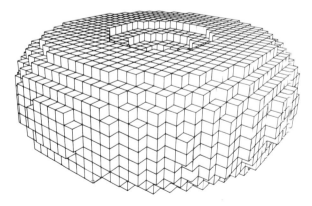

Fig. 12.20 Torus represented by spatial-occupancy enumeration (By AHJ Christensen, SIGGRAPH '80 Conference Proceedings, *Computer Graphics* (14)3, July 1980. Courtesy of Association for Computing Machinery, Inc.)

occupancy enumeration is often used in biomedical applications to represent volumetric data obtained from sources such as computerized axial tomography (CAT) scans.

For all of its advantages, however, spatial-occupancy enumeration has a number of obvious failings that parallel those of representing a 2D shape by a 1-bit-deep bitmap. There is no concept of "partial" occupancy. Thus, many solids can be only approximated; the torus of Fig. 12.20 is an example. If the cells are cubes, then the only objects that can be represented exactly are those whose faces are parallel to the cube sides and whose vertices fall exactly on the grid. Like pixels in a bitmap, cells may in principle be made as small as desired to increase the accuracy of the representation. Space becomes an important issue, however, since up to n^3 occupied cells are needed to represent an object at a resolution of n voxels in each of three dimensions.

12.6.3 Octrees

Octrees are a hierarchical variant of spatial-occupancy enumeration, designed to address that approach's demanding storage requirements. Octrees are in turn derived from *quadtrees,* a 2D representation format used to encode images (see Section 17.7). As detailed in Samet's comprehensive survey [SAME84], both representations appear to have been discovered independently by a number of researchers, quadtrees in the late 1960s to early 1970s [e.g., WARN69; KLIN71] and octrees in the late 1970s to early 1980s [e.g., HUNT78; REDD78; JACK80; MEAG80. MEAG82a].

The fundamental idea behind both the quadtree and octree is the divide-and-conquer power of binary subdivision. A quadtree is derived by successively subdividing a 2D plane in both dimensions to form quadrants, as shown in Fig. 12.21. When a quadtree is used to represent an area in the plane, each quadrant may be full, partially full, or empty (also called black, gray, and white, respectively), depending on how much of the quadrant intersects the area. A partially full quadrant is recursively subdivided into subquadrants. Subdivision continues until all quadrants are homogeneous (either full or empty) or until a predetermined cutoff depth is reached. Whenever four sibling quadrants are uniformly full or empty, they are deleted and their partially full parent is replaced with a full or empty node. (A bottom-up approach can be used instead to avoid this deletion and merging process [SAME90b].) In Fig. 12.21, any partially full node at the cutoff depth is classified as full. The successive subdivisions can be represented as a tree with partially full quadrants at the internal nodes and full and empty quadrants at the leaves, as shown in Fig. 12.22.

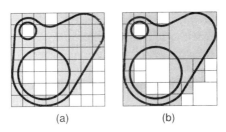

(a)   (b)

Fig. 12.21 An object represented using (a) spatial-occupancy enumeration (b) a quadtree.

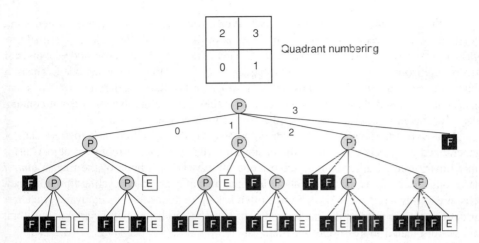

Fig. 12.22 Quadtree data structure for the object in Fig. 12.21. F = full, P = partially full, E = empty.

This idea can be compared to the Warnock area-subdivision algorithm discussed in Section 15.7.1. If the criteria for classifying a node as homogeneous are relaxed, allowing nodes that are above or below some threshold to be classified as full or empty, then the representation becomes more compact, but less accurate. The octree is similar to the quadtree, except that its three dimensions are recursively subdivided into octants, as shown in Fig. 12.23.

Quadrants are often referred to by the numbers 0 to 3, and octants by numbers from 0 to 7. Since no standard numbering scheme has been devised, mnemonic names are also used. Quadrants are named according to their compass direction relative to the center of their parent: NW, NE, SW, and SE. Octants are named similarly, distinguishing between left (L) and right (R), up (U) and down (D), and front (F) and back (B): LUF, LUB, LDF, LDB, RUF, RUB, RDF, and RDB.

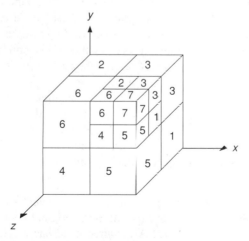

Fig. 12.23 Octree enumeration. Octant 0 is not visible.

With the exception of a few worst cases, it can be shown that the number of nodes in a quadtree or octree representation of an object is proportional to the object's perimeter or surface, respectively [HUNT78; MEAG80]. This relation holds because node subdivision arises only from the need to represent the boundary of the object being encoded. The only internal nodes that are split are those through which part of the boundary passes. Thus, any operation on one of these data structures that is linear in the number of nodes it contains also executes in time proportional to the size of its perimeter or area.

Although the divide-and-conquer approach of the quadtree and octree can be generalized to objects of arbitrary dimension, it is also possible to represent objects using only binary trees. Rather than dividing along all axes at each node of the tree, a *bintree* partitions space into equal halves about a single axis at each node, cycling through a new axis at each level [TAMM84]. A bintree often has more nodes than its equivalent quadtree or octree, but has at most the same number of leaves; as well, many processing algorithms can be formulated more simply for bintrees.

Boolean set operations and transformations.   Much work has been done on developing efficient algorithms for storing and processing quadtrees and octrees [SAME84; SAME90a; SAME90b]. For example, Boolean set operations are straightforward for both quadtrees and octrees [HUNT79]. To compute the union or intersection U of two trees, S and T, we traverse both trees top-down in parallel. Figure 12.24 shows the operations for quadtrees; the generalization to octrees is straightforward. Each matching pair of nodes is examined. Consider the case of union. If either of the nodes in the pair is black, then a corresponding black node is added to U. If one of the pair's nodes is white, then the corresponding node is created in U with the value of the other node in the pair. If both nodes of the pair are gray, then a gray node is added to U, and the algorithm is applied recursively to the pair's children. In this last case, the children of the new node in U must be inspected after the algorithm has been applied to them. If they are all black, they are deleted and their parent in U is changed from gray to black. The algorithm for performing intersection is similar, except the roles of black and white are interchanged. If either of the nodes in a pair is white, then a corresponding white node is added to U. If one of the pair's nodes is black, then the corresponding node is created in U with the value of the other node in the pair. If both nodes of the pair are gray, then a gray node is added to U, and the algorithm is applied recursively to the pair's children. As in the union algorithm, if both nodes are gray, then after the algorithm has been applied to the children of the new node in U, the children must be inspected. In this case, if they are all white, they are deleted and their parent in U must be changed from gray to white.

It is easy to perform simple transformations on quadtrees and octrees. For example, rotation about an axis by multiples of $90°$ is accomplished by recursively rotating the children at each level. Scaling by powers of 2 and reflections are also straightforward. Translations are somewhat more complex, as are general transformations. In addition, as in spatial-occupancy enumeration in general, the problem of aliasing under general transformations is severe.

Neighbor finding.   One important operation in quadtrees and octrees is finding a node's *neighbor*; that is, finding a node that is adjacent to the original node (sharing a face, edge, or vertex) and of equal or greater size. A quadtree node has neighbors in eight possible

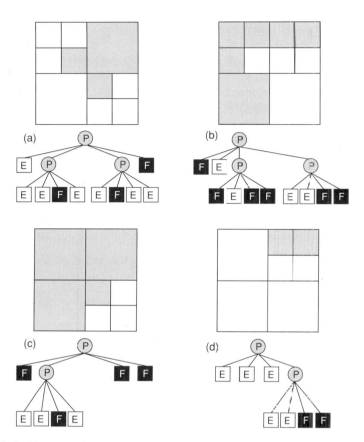

F g. 12.24 Performing Boolean set operations on quadtrees. (a) Object *S* and its quadtree. (b) Object *T* and its quadtree. (c) *S* ∪ *T*. (d) *S* ∩ *T*.

directions. Its N, S, E, W neighbors are neighbors along a common edge, whereas its NW, NE, SW, and SE neighbors are neighbors along a common vertex. An octree node has neighbors in 26 possible directions: 6 neighbors along a face, 12 neighbors along an edge, and 8 neighbors along a vertex.

Samet [SAME89a] describes a way to find a node's neighbor in a specified direction. The method starts at the original node and ascends the quadtree or octree until the first common ancestor of the original node and neighbor is found. The tree is then traversed downward to find the desired neighbor. Two problems must be solved efficiently here: finding the common ancestor and determining which of its descendants is the neighbor. The simplest case is finding an octree node's neighbor in the direction *d* of one of its faces: L, R, U, D, F, or B. As we ascend the tree starting at the original node, the common ancestor will be the first node that is not reached from a child on the node's *d* side. For example, if the search is for an L neighbor, then the first common ancestor is the first node that is not reached from an LUF, LUB, LDF, or LDB child. This is true because a node that has been reached from one of these children cannot have any child that is left of (is an L neighbor of) the original node. When the common ancestor is found, its subtree is descended in a mirror image of the path from the original node to the ancestor, reflected about the common border. Only part of the reflected path is followed if the neighbor is larger than the original node.

A similar method can be used to find a quadtree node's neighbor in the direction of one of its edges. For example, to find the N neighbor of node A of Fig. 12.25, we begin at A, which is a NW child, and follow the path depicted by the thick line in the figure. We ascend from the NW to its parent, from the NW again to its grandparent, and finally from the SW to its great grandparent, the root, stopping because we have approached it from an S node, rather than from an N node. We then follow the mirror-image path downward (reflected about the N–S border), to the root's NW child, and finally to this node's SW child, which is a leaf. Samet [SAME89a] describes the more elaborate algorithms for finding edge and vertex neighbors in octrees, and provides an elegant recursive implementation that uses table lookup to perform such operations as computing the reflected path.

Linear notations. Although a tree data structure with pointers might at first seem necessary to represent a quadtree or octree, pointerless notations are possible. In the *linear quadtree* or *linear octree* notation [GARG82], each full node is represented as a sequence of digits that represents its fully qualified address. There are as many digits as there are levels. Only black leaf nodes need to be stored to represent the object. Nodes that are not at the lowest level include an additional padding character (e.g., "X") in each of their trailing

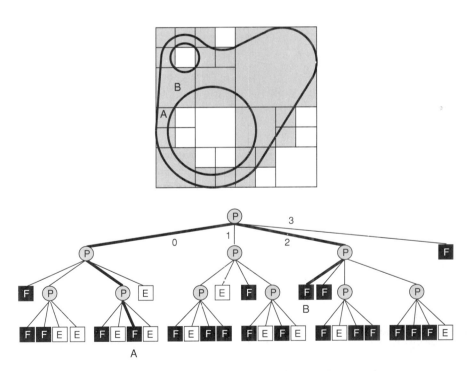

Fig. 12.25 Finding the neighbor of a quadtree node.

digits. For example, a linear octree can be encoded compactly using base-9 numbers (conveniently represented with 4 bits per digit), with 0 through 7 specifying octants and 8 indicating padding. The nodes in the linear octree are stored in sorted order, which represents a postorder traversal of the octree. For example, the linear quadtree representation of the object in Fig. 12.21 is 00X, 010, 011, 020, 022, 100, 102, 10?, 12X, 130, 132, 20X, 21X, 220, 222, 223, 230, 231, 232, 3XX.

A number of operations can be performed efficiently with the linear-quadtree or linear-octree representation. For example, Atkinson, Gargantini, and Ramanath [ATKI84] present an algorithm for determining the voxels that form an octree's border by making successive passes over a list of the octree's nodes. Full nodes of the largest size are considered first. Each such node that abuts full nodes of the same size on all six sides is internal to the object and is therefore not part of the border; it is eliminated from the list. (Each neighbor's code may be derived by simple arithmetic manipulation of the node's code.) Any other node of this size may contain voxels that are part of the border; each of these nodes is broken into its eight constituent nodes, which replace it in the list. The algorithm is repeated for successively smaller node sizes, stopping after voxel-sized nodes are considered. Those nodes remaining are all the voxels on the object's border.

PM octrees. A number of researchers have developed hybrid representations that combine octrees and b-reps to maintain the precise geometry of the original b-rep from which the object is derived [HUNT81; QUIN82; AYAL85; CARL85; FUJI85]. These *PM octrees* (*PM* stands for Polygonal Map) expand on a similar quadtree variant [SAME90a]. The octree is recursively divided into nodes until the node is one of five different leaf types. In addition to full and empty, three new leaf nodes are introduced that are actually special kinds of partially full nodes: vertex nodes, which contain a single vertex and its connected faces and edges; edge nodes, which contain part of a single edge and its faces; and surface nodes, which are cut by a piece of a single face. Restricting the new leaf types to a set of simple geometries, each of which divides the node into exactly two parts, simplifies the algorithms that manipulate the representation, such as Boolean set operations [CARL87; NAVA89].

Section 18.11.4 discusses a number of architectures based on voxel and octree models. Section 15.8 discusses visible-surface algorithms for octrees.

12.6.4 Binary Space-Partitioning Trees

Octrees recursively divide space by planes that are always mutually perpendicular and that bisect all three dimensions at each level of the tree. In contrast, *binary space-partitioning* (BSP) *trees* recursively divide space into pairs of subspaces, each separated by a plane of arbitrary orientation and position. The binary-tree data structure created was originally used in determining visible surfaces in graphics, as described in Section 15.5.2. Thibault and Naylor [THIB87] later introduced the use of BSP trees to represent arbitrary polyhedra. Each internal node of the BSP tree is associated with a plane and has two child pointers, one for each side of the plane. Assuming that normals point out of an object, the left child is behind or inside the plane, whereas the right child is in front of or outside the plane. If the half-space on a side of the plane is subdivided further, then its child is the root of a subtree; if the half-space is homogeneous, then its child is a leaf, representing a region either entirely inside or entirely outside the polyhedron. These homogeneous regions are called "in" cells and "out" cells. To account for the limited numerical precision with which operations are performed, each node also has a "thickness" associated with its plane. Any point lying within this tolerance of the plane is considered to be "on" the plane.

The subdivision concept behind BSP trees, like that underlying octrees and quadtrees, is dimension-independent. Thus, Fig. 12.26(a) shows a concave polygon in 2D, bordered by black lines. "In" cells are shaded light gray, and the lines defining the half-spaces are shown in dark gray, with normals pointing to the outside. The corresponding BSP tree is shown in Fig. 12.26(b). In 2D, the "in" and "out" regions form a convex polygonal tessellation of the plane; in 3D, the "in" and "out" regions form a convex polyhedral tessellation of 3-space. Thus, a BSP tree can represent an arbitrary concave solid with holes as a union of convex "in" regions. Unlike octrees, but like b-reps, an arbitrary BSP tree does not necessarily represent a bounded solid. For example, the 3D BSP tree consisting of a single internal node, with "in" and "out" nodes as children, defines an object that is a half-space bounded by only one plane.

Consider the task of determining whether a point lies inside, outside, or on a solid, a problem known as *point classification* [TILO80]. A BSP tree may be used to classify a point by filtering that point down the tree, beginning at the root. At each node, the point is substituted into the node's plane equation and is passed recursively to the left child if it lies behind (inside) the plane, or to the right child if it lies in front of (outside) the plane. If the node is a leaf, then the point is given the leaf's value, either "out" or "in." If the point lies on a node's plane, then it is passed to both children, and the classifications are compared. If they are the same, then the point receives that value; if they are different, then the point lies on the boundary between "out" and "in" regions and is classified as "on." This approach can be extended to classify lines and polygons. Unlike a point, however, a line or polygon may lie partially on both sides of a plane. Therefore, at each node whose plane intersects the line or polygon, the line or polygon must be divided (clipped) into those parts that are in front of, in back of, or on the plane, and the parts classified separately.

Thibault and Naylor describe algorithms for building a BSP tree from a b-rep, for performing Boolean set operations to combine a BSP tree with a b-rep, and for determining those polygonal pieces that lie on a BSP tree's boundary [THIB87]. These algorithms operate on BSP trees whose nodes are each associated with a list of polygons embedded in

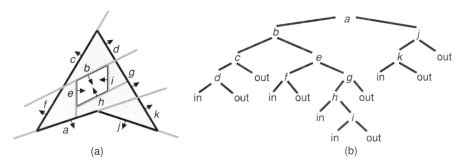

(a)   (b)

Fig. 12.26 A BSP tree representation in 2D. (a) A concave polygon bounded by black lines. Lines defining the half-spaces are dark gray, and "in" cells are light gray. (b) The BSP tree.

the node's plane. Polygons are inserted into the tree using a variant of the BSP tree building algorithm presented in Section 15.5.2.

Although BSP trees provide an elegant and simple representation, polygons are subdivided as the tree is constructed and as Boolean set operations are performed, making the notation potentially less compact than other representations. By taking advantage of the BSP tree's inherent dimension-independence, however, we can develop a closed Boolean algebra for 3D BSP trees that recursively relies on representing polygons as 2D trees, edges as 1D trees, and points as 0D trees [NAYL90].

12.7 CONSTRUCTIVE SOLID GEOMETRY

In *constructive solid geometry* (CSG), simple primitives are combined by means of regularized Boolean set operators that are included directly in the representation. An object is stored as a tree with operators at the internal nodes and simple primitives at the leaves (Fig. 12.27). Some nodes represent Boolean operators, whereas others perform translation, rotation, and scaling, much like the hierarchies of Chapter 7. Since Boolean operations are not, in general, commutative, the edges of the tree are ordered.

To determine physical properties or to make pictures, we must be able to combine the properties of the leaves to obtain the properties of the root. The general processing strategy is a depth-first tree walk, as in Chapter 7, to combine nodes from the leaves on up the tree. The complexity of this task depends on the representation in which the leaf objects are stored and on whether a full representation of the composite object at the tree's root must actually be produced. For example, the regularized Boolean set operation algorithms for b-reps, discussed in Section 12.5, combine the b-reps of two nodes to create a third b-rep and are difficult to implement. The much simpler CSG algorithm discussed in Section 15.10.3, on the other hand, produces a picture by processing the representations of the leaves without explicitly combining them. Other algorithms for creating pictures of CSG representations include [ATHE83; OKIN84; JANS85]; architectures that support CSG are discussed in Sections 18.9.2, 18.10.2 and 18.11.4.

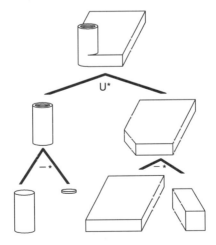

Fig. 12.27 An object defined by CSG and its tree.

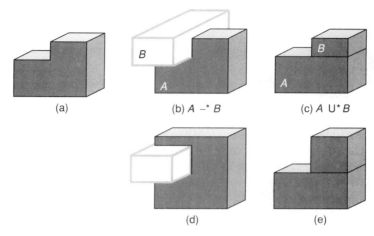

Fig. 12.28 The object shown in (a) may be defined by different CSG operations, as shown in (b) and (c). Tweaking the top face of (b) and (c) upward yields different objects, shown in (d) and (e).

In some implementations, the primitives are simple solids, such as cubes or spheres, ensuring that all regularized combinations are valid solids as well. In other systems, primitives include half-spaces, which themselves are not bounded solids. For example, a cube can be defined as the intersection of six half-spaces, or a finite cylinder as an infinite cylinder that is capped off at the top and bottom by planar half-spaces. Using half-spaces introduces a validity problem, since not all combinations produce solids. Half-spaces are useful, however, for operations such as slicing an object by a plane, which might otherwise be performed by using the face of another solid object. Without half-spaces, extra overhead is introduced, since the regularized Boolean set operations must be performed with the full object doing the slicing, even if only a single slicing face is of interest.

We can think of the cell-decomposition and spatial-occupancy enumeration techniques as special cases of CSG in which the only operator is the implicit glue operator: the union of two objects that may touch, but must have disjoint interiors (i.e., the objects must have a null regularized Boolean intersection).

CSG does not provide a unique representation. This can be particularly confusing in a system that lets the user manipulate the leaf objects with tweaking operators. Applying the same operation to two objects that are initially the same can yield two different results, as shown in Fig. 12.28. Nevertheless, the ability to edit models by deleting, adding, replacing, and modifying subtrees, coupled with the relatively compact form in which models are stored, have made CSG one of the dominant solid modeling representations.

12.8   COMPARISON OF REPRESENTATIONS

We have discussed five main kinds of representations: primitive instancing, sweeps, b-reps, spatial partitioning (including cell decomposition, spatial-occupancy enumeration, octrees, and BSP trees), and CSG. Let us compare them on the basis of the criteria introduced in Section 12.1.

- *Accuracy.* Spatial-partitioning and polygonal b-rep methods produce only approximations for many objects. In some applications, such as finding a path for a robot, this is not a drawback, as long as the approximation is computed to an adequate (often relatively coarse) resolution. The resolution needed to produce visually pleasing graphics or to calculate object interactions with sufficient accuracy, however, may be too high to be practical. The smooth shading techniques discussed in Chapter 16 do not fix the visual artifacts caused by the all-too-obvious polygonal edges. Therefore, systems that support high-quality graphics often use CSG with nonpolyhedral primitives and b-reps that allow curved surfaces. Primitive instancing also can produce high-quality pictures, but does not allow two simpler objects to be combined with Boolean set operators.

- *Domain.* The domain of objects that can be represented by both primitive instancing and sweeps is limited. In comparison, spatial-partitioning approaches can represent any solid, although often only as an approximation. By providing other kinds of faces and edges in addition to polygons bounded by straight lines, b-reps can be used to represent a very wide class of objects. Many b-rep systems, however, are restricted to simple surface types and topologies. For example, they may be able to encode only combinations of quadrics that are 2-manifolds.

- *Uniqueness.* Only octree and spatial-occupancy–enumeration approaches guarantee the uniqueness of a representation: There is only one way to represent an object with a specified size and position. In the case of octrees, some processing must be done to ensure that the representation is fully reduced (i.e., that no gray node has all black children or all white children). Primitive instancing does not guarantee uniqueness in general: for example, a sphere may be represented by both a spherical and an elliptical primitive. If the set of primitives is chosen carefully, however, uniqueness can be ensured.

- *Validity.* Among all the representations, b-reps stand out as being the most difficult to validate. Not only may vertex, edge, and face data structures be inconsistent, but also faces or edges may intersect. In contrast, any BSP tree represents a valid spatial set, but not necessarily a bounded solid. Only simple local syntactic checking needs to be done to validate a CSG tree (which is always bounded, if its primitives are bounded) or an octree, and no checking is needed for spatial-occupancy enumeration.

- *Closure.* Primitives created using primitive instancing cannot be combined at all, and simple sweeps are not closed under Boolean operations. Therefore, neither is typically used as an internal representation in modeling systems. Although particular b-reps may suffer from closure problems under Boolean operations (e.g., the inability to represent other than 2-manifolds), these problem cases can often be avoided.

- *Compactness and efficiency.* Representation schemes are often classified by whether they produce "evaluated" or "unevaluated" models. *Unevaluated* models contain information that must be further processed (or evaluated) in order to perform basic operations, such as determining an object's boundary. With regard to the use of Boolean operations, CSG creates unevaluated models, in that each time computations are performed, we must walk the tree, evaluating the expressions. Consequently, the advantages of CSG are its compactness and the ability to record Boolean operations and changes of transformations quickly, and to undo all of these quickly since they involve only tree-node building. Octrees and BSP trees can also be considered unevaluated models, as can a sequence of Euler operators that creates a b-rep. B-reps and spatial-occupancy enumeration, on the other hand, are often considered *evaluated* models insofar as any Boolean operations used to create an object have already been performed. Note that the use of these terms is relative; if the operation to be performed is determining whether a point is inside an object, for example, more work may be done evaluating a b-rep than evaluating the equivalent CSG tree.

As discussed in Chapter 15, a number of efficient algorithms exist for generating pictures of objects encoded using b-reps and CSG. Although spatial-occupancy enumeration and octrees can provide only coarse approximations for most objects, the algorithms used to manipulate them are in general simpler than the equivalents for other representations. They have thus been used in hardware-based solid modeling systems intended for applications in which the increased speed with which Boolean set operations can be performed on them outweighs the coarseness of the resulting images.

Some systems use multiple representations because some operations are more efficient with one representation than with another. For example, GMSOLID [BOYS82] uses CSG for compactness and a b-rep for quick retrieval of useful data not explicitly specified in CSG, such as connectivity. Although GMSOLID's CSG representation always reflects the current state of the object being modeled, its b-rep is updated only when the operations that require it are executed. Updating may be done by a background process, so that the user can perform other operations while waiting for the result. In addition to systems that maintain two completely separate representations, deriving one from the other when needed, there are also hybrid systems that go down to some level of detail in one scheme, then switch to another, but never duplicate information. The PM octrees discussed in Section 12.6.3 that combine octrees with b-reps provide examples. Some of the issues raised by the use of multiple representations and hybrid representations are addressed in [MILL89].

It is relatively easy to convert all the representations we have discussed to spatial-occupancy–enumeration or octree representations, but only as approximations. Such conversions are not invertible, because they lose information. In addition, it is easy to convert all representations exactly to b-reps and PM octrees. An algorithm for performing Boolean operations on b-reps, such as the one described in Section 12.5, can be used to convert CSG to b-rep by successive application to each level of the CSG tree, beginning with the polyhedral descriptions of the leaf primitives. Rossignac and Voelcker [ROSS89] have implemented an efficient CSG–to–b-rep conversion algorithm that identifies what they call the *active zone* of a CSG node—that part of the node that, if changed, will affect the final solid; only the parts of a solid within a node's active zone need be considered when Boolean operations are performed. On the other hand, conversion from b-rep into CSG is difficult, especially if an encoding into a minimal number of CSG operations is desired. Vossler [VOSS85b] describes a method for converting sweeps to CSG by automatically recognizing patterns of simpler sweeps that can be combined with Boolean operations to form the more complex sweep being converted.

As pointed out in Section 12.1, wireframe representations containing only vertex and edge information, with no reference to faces, are inherently ambiguous. Markowsky and Wesley, however, have developed an algorithm for deriving all polyhedra that could be represented by a given wireframe [MARK80] and a companion algorithm that generates all polyhedra that could produce a given 2D projection [WESL81].

12.9   USER INTERFACES FOR SOLID MODELING

Developing the user interface for a solid modeling system provides an excellent opportunity to put into practice the interface design techniques discussed in Chapter 9. A variety of techniques lend themselves well to graphical interfaces, including the direct application of regularized Boolean set operators, tweaking, and Euler operators. In CSG systems the user may be allowed to edit the object by modifying or replacing one of the leaf solids or subtrees. Blending and chamfering operations may be defined to smooth the transition from one surface to another. The user interfaces of successful systems are largely independent of the internal representation chosen. Primitive instancing is an exception, however, since it encourages user to think of objects in terms of special-purpose parameters.

In Chapter 11, we noted that there are many equivalent ways to describe the same curve. For example, the user interface to a curve-drawing system can let the user enter curves by controlling Hermite tangent vectors or by specifying Bezier control points, while storing curves only as Bezier control points. Similarly, a solid modeling system may let the user create objects in terms of several different representations, while storing them in yet another. As with curve representations, each different input representation may have some expressive advantage that makes it a natural choice for creating the object. For example, a b-rep system may allow an object to be defined as a translational or rotational sweep. The user interface may also provide different ways to define the same object within a single representation. For example, two of the many ways to define a sphere are to specify its center and a point on its surface, or to specify the two endpoints of a diameter. The first may be more useful for centering a sphere at a point, whereas the second may be better for positioning the sphere between two supports.

The precision with which objects must be specified often dictates that some means be provided to determine measurements accurately; for example, through a locator device or through numeric entry. Because the position of one object often depends on those of others, interfaces often provide the ability to constrain one object by another. A related technique is to give the user the ability to define grid lines to constrain object positions, as discussed in Section 8.2.1.

Some of the most fundamental problems of designing a solid modeling interface are those caused by the need to manipulate and display 3D objects with what are typically 2D interaction devices and displays. These general issues were discussed in more detail in Chapters 8 and 9. Many systems address some of these problems by providing multiple display windows that allow the user to view the object simultaneously from different positions.

12.10   SUMMARY

As we have seen, solid modeling is important in both CAD/CAM and graphics. Although useful algorithms and systems exist that handle the objects described so far, many difficult problems remain unsolved. One of the most important is the issue of robustness. Solid modeling systems are typically plagued by numerical instabilities. Commonly used algorithms require more precision to hold intermediate floating-point results than is available in hardware. For example, Boolean set operation algorithms may fail when presented with two objects, one of which is a very slightly transformed copy of the first.

Representations are needed for nonrigid, flexible, jointed objects. Work on transformations that bend and twist objects is described in Chapter 20. Many objects cannot be specified with total accuracy; rather, their shapes are defined by parameters constrained to lie within a range of values. These are known as "toleranced" objects, and correspond to real objects turned out by machines such as lathes and stampers [REQU84]. New representations are being developed to encode toleranced objects [GOSS88].

Common to all designed objects is the concept of "features," such as holes and chamfers, that are designed for specific purposes. One current area of research is exploring the possibility of recognizing features automatically and inferring the designer's intent for what each feature should accomplish [PRAT84]. This will allow the design to be checked to ensure that the features perform as intended. For example, if certain features are designed to give a part strength under pressure, then their ability to perform this function could be validated automatically. Future operations on the object could also be checked to ensure that the features' functionality was not compromised.

EXERCISES

12.1 Define the results of performing $\cup^*$ and $-^*$ for two polyhedral objects in the same way as the result of performing $\cap^*$ was defined in Section 12.2. Explain how the resulting object is constrained to be a regular set, and specify how the normal is determined for each of the object's faces.

12.2 Consider the task of determining whether or not a legal solid is the null object (which has no volume). How difficult is it to perform this test in each of the representations discussed?

12.3 Consider a system whose objects are represented as sweeps and can be operated on using the regularized Boolean set operators. What restrictions must be placed on the objects to ensure closure?

12.4 Implement the algorithms for performing Boolean set operations on quadtrees or on octrees.

12.5 Explain why an implementation of Boolean set operations on quadtrees or octrees does not need to address the distinction between the ordinary and regularized operations described in Section 12.2.

12.6 Although the geometric implications of applying the regularized Boolean set operators are unambiguous, it is less clear how object properties should be treated. For example, what properties should be assigned to the intersection of two objects made of different materials? In modeling actual objects, this question is of little importance, but in the artificial world of graphics, it is possible to intersect any two materials. What solutions do you think would be useful?

12.7 Explain how a quadtree or octree could be used to speed up 2D or 3D picking in a graphics package.

12.8 Describe how to perform point classification in primitive instancing, b-rep, spatial occupancy enumeration, and CSG.

13

Achromatic
and
Colored Light

The growth of raster graphics has made color and gray scale an integral part of contemporary computer graphics. Color is an immensely complex subject, one that draws on concepts and results from physics, physiology, psychology, art, and graphic design. Many researchers' careers have been fruitfully devoted to developing theories, measurement techniques, and standards for color. In this chapter, we introduce some of the areas of color that are most relevant to computer graphics.

The color of an object depends not only on the object itself, but also on the light source illuminating it, on the color of the surrounding area, and on the human visual system. Furthermore, some objects reflect light (wall, desk, paper), whereas others also transmit light (cellophane, glass). When a surface that reflects only pure blue light is illuminated with pure red light, it appears black. Similarly, a pure green light viewed through glass that transmits only pure red will also appear black. We postpone some of these issues by starting our discussion with achromatic sensations—that is, those described as black, gray, and white.

13.1 ACHROMATIC LIGHT

Achromatic light is what we see on a black-and-white television set or display monitor. An observer of achromatic light normally experiences none of the sensations we associate with red, blue, yellow, and so on. Quantity of light is the only attribute of achromatic light. Quantity of light can be discussed in the physics sense of energy, in which case the terms *intensity* and *luminance* are used, or in the psychological sense of perceived intensity, in which case the term *brightness* is used. As we shall discuss shortly, these two concepts are related but are not the same. It is useful to associate a scalar with different intensity levels, defining 0 as black and 1 as white; intensity levels between 0 and 1 represent different grays.

A black-and-white television can produce many different intensities at a single pixel position. Line printers, pen plotters, and electrostatic plotters produce only two levels: the white (or light gray) of the paper and the black (or dark gray) of the ink or toner deposited on the paper. Certain techniques, discussed in later sections, allow such inherently *bilevel* devices to produce additional intensity levels.

13.1.1 Selecting Intensities—Gamma Correction

Suppose we want to display 256 different intensities. Which 256 intensity levels should we use? We surely do not want 128 in the range of 0 to 0.1 and 128 more in the range of 0.9 to 1.0, since the transition from 0.1 to 0.9 would certainly appear discontinuous. We might initially distribute the levels evenly over the range 0 to 1, but this choice ignores an important characteristic of the eye: that it is sensitive to ratios of intensity levels rather than to absolute values of intensity. That is, we perceive the intensities 0.10 and 0.11 as differing just as much as the intensities 0.50 and 0.55. (This nonlinearity is easy to observe: Cycle through the settings on a three-way 50–100–150-watt lightbulb; you will see that the step from 50 to 100 seems much greater than the step from 100 to 150.) On a brightness (that is, perceived intensity) scale, the differences between intensities of 0.10 and 0.11 and between intensities of 0.50 and 0.55 are equal. Therefore, the intensity levels should be spaced logarithmically rather than linearly, to achieve equal steps in brightness.

To find 256 intensities starting with the lowest attainable intensity I_0 and going to a maximum intensity of 1.0, with each intensity r times higher than the preceding intensity, we use the following relations:

$$I_0 = I_0, \; I_1 = rI_0, \; I_2 = rI_1 = r^2 I_0, \; I_3 = rI_2 = r^3 I_0, \; \ldots, \; I_{255} = r^{255} I_0 = 1. \quad (13.1)$$

Therefore,

$$r = (1/I_0)^{1/255}, \; I_j = r^j I_0 = (1/I_0)^{j/255} I_0 = I_0^{(255-j)/255} \qquad \text{for } 0 \le j \le 255, \quad (13.2)$$

and in general for $n + 1$ intensities,

$$r = (1/I_0)^{1/n}, \; I_j = I_0^{(n-j)/n} \qquad \text{for } 0 \le j \le n. \qquad (13.3)$$

With just four intensities ($n = 3$) and an I_0 of $\frac{1}{8}$ (an unrealistically large value chosen for illustration only), Eq. (13.3) tells us that $r = 2$, yielding intensity values of $\frac{1}{8}, \frac{1}{4}, \frac{1}{2}$, and 1.

The minimum attainable intensity I_0 for a CRT is anywhere from about $\frac{1}{200}$ up to $\frac{1}{40}$ of the maximum intensity of 1.0. Therefore, typical values of I_0 are between 0.005 and 0.025. The minimum is not 0, because of light reflection from the phosphor within the CRT. The ratio between the maximum and minimum intensities is called the *dynamic range*. The exact value for a specific CRT can be found by displaying a square of white on a field of black and measuring the two intensities with a photometer. This measurement is taken in a completely darkened room, so that reflected ambient light does not affect the intensities. With an I_0 of 0.02, corresponding to a dynamic range of 50, Eq. (13.2) yields $r = 1.0154595 \ldots$, and the first few and last two intensities of the 256 intensities from Eq. (13.1) are 0.0200, 0.0203, 0.0206, 0.0209, 0.0213, 0.0216, . . ., 0.9848, 1.0000.

Displaying the intensities defined by Eq. (13.1) on a CRT is a tricky process, and recording them on film is even more difficult, because of the nonlinearities in the CRT and film. For instance, the intensity of light output by a phosphor is related to the number of electrons N in the beam by

$$I = kN^\gamma \tag{13.4}$$

for constants k and γ. The value of γ is in the range 2.2 to 2.5 for most CRTs. The number of electrons N is proportional to the control-grid voltage, which is in turn proportional to the value V specified for the pixel. Therefore, for some other constant K,

$$I = KV^\gamma, \text{ or } V = (I/K)^{1/\gamma}. \tag{13.5}$$

Now, given a desired intensity I, we first determine the nearest I_j by searching through a table of the available intensities as calculated from Eq. (13.1) or from its equivalent:

$$j = ROUND(log_r(I/I_0)). \tag{13.6}$$

After j is found, we calculate

$$I_j = r^j I_0. \tag{13.7}$$

The next step is to determine the pixel value V_j needed to create the intensity I_j, by using Eq. (13.5):

$$V_j = ROUND \left((I_j/K)^{1/\gamma} \right). \tag{13.8}$$

If the raster display has no look-up table, then V_j is placed in the appropriate pixels. If there is a look-up table, then j is placed in the pixel and V_j is placed in entry j of the table.

The values of K, γ, and I_0 depend on the CRT in use, so in practice the look-up table is loaded by a method based on actual measurement of intensities [CATM79; COWA83; HALL89]. Use of the look-up table in this general manner is called *gamma correction*, so named for the exponent in Eq. (13.4). If the display has hardware gamma correction, then I_j rather than V_j is placed in either the refresh buffer or look-up table.

Without the use of ratio-based intensity values and gamma correction, quantization errors (from approximating a true intensity value with a displayable intensity value) will be more conspicuous near black than near white. For instance, with 4 bits and hence 16 intensities, a quantization round-off error of as much as $\frac{1}{32} = 0.031$ is possible. This is 50 percent of intensity value $\frac{1}{16}$, and only 3 percent of intensity value 1.0. Using the ratio-based intensities and gamma correction, the maximum quantization error as a percentage of brightness (perceived intensity) is constant.

A natural question is, "How many intensities are enough?" By "enough," we mean the number needed to reproduce a continuous-tone black-and-white image such that the reproduction appears to be continuous. This appearance is achieved when the ratio r is 1.01 or less (below this ratio, the eye cannot distinguish between intensities I_j and I_{j+1}) [WYSZ82, p. 569]. Thus, the appropriate value for n, the number of intensity levels, is found by equating r to 1.01 in Eq. (13.3):

$$r = (1/I_0)^{1/n} \quad \text{or} \quad 1.01 = (1/I_0)^{1/n}. \tag{13.9}$$

TABLE 13.1 DYNAMIC RANGE ($1//_0$) AND NUMBER OF REQUIRED INTENSITIES $n = \log_{1.01}(1//_0)$ FOR SEVERAL DISPLAY MEDIA

Display media	Typical dynamic range	Number of intensities, n
CRT	50–200	400–530
Photographic prints	100	465
Photographic slides	1000	700
Coated paper printed in B/W*	100	465
Coated paper printed in color	50	400
Newsprint printed in B/W	10	234

*B/W = black and white.

Solving for n gives

$$n = \log_{1.01}(1//_0), \tag{13.10}$$

where $1/I_0$ is the dynamic range of the device.

The dynamic range $1/I_0$ for several display media, and the corresponding n, which is the number of intensity levels needed to maintain $r = 1.01$ and at the same time to use the full dynamic range, are shown in Table 13.1. These are theoretical values, assuming perfect reproduction processes. In practice, slight blurring due to ink bleeding and small amounts of random noise in the reproduction decreases n considerably for print media. For instance, Fig. 13.1 shows a continuous-tone photograph; and the succeeding five Figs. 13.2 to 13.6 reproduce the same photograph at 4, 8, 16, 32, and 64 intensity levels. With four and eight levels, the transitions or contours between one intensity level and the next are quite conspicuous, because the ratio r between successive intensities is considerably greater that the ideal 1.01. Contouring is barely detectable with 32 levels, and for these particular

Fig. 13.1 A continuous-tone photo-graph.

Fig. 13.2 A continuous-tone photo-graph reproduced with four intensity levels. (Courtesy of Alan Paeth, University of Waterloo Computer Graphics Lab.)

Fig. 13.3 A continuous-tone photograph reproduced with eight intensity levels. (Courtesy of Alan Paeth, University of Waterloo Computer Graphics Lab.)

Fig. 13.4 A continuous-tone photograph reproduced with 16 intensity levels. (Courtesy of Alan Paeth, University of Waterloo Computer Graphics Lab.)

Fig. 13.5 A continuous-tone photograph reproduced with 32 intensity levels. (Courtesy of Alan Paeth, University of Waterloo Computer Graphics Lab.)

Fig. 13.6 A continuous-tone photograph reproduced with 64 intensity levels. Differences from the picture in Fig. 13.5 are quite subtle. (Courtesy of Alan Paeth, University of Waterloo Computer Graphics Lab.)

images disappears with 64. This suggests that 64 intensity levels is the absolute minimum needed for contour-free printing of continuous-tone black-and-white images on paper such as is used in this book. For a well-adjusted CRT in a perfectly black room, however, the higher dynamic range means that many more levels are demanded.

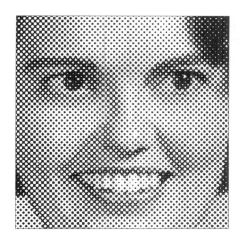

Fig. 13.7 Enlarged halftone pattern. Dot sizes vary inversely with intensity of original photograph. (Courtesy of Alan Paeth, University of Waterloo Computer Graphics Lab.)

13.1.2 Halftone Approximation

Many displays and hardcopy devices are bilevel—they produce just two intensity levels—and even 2- or 3-bit-per-pixel raster displays produce fewer intensity levels than we might desire. How can we expand the range of available intensities? The answer lies in the *spatial integration* that our eyes perform. If we view a very small area from a sufficiently large viewing distance, our eyes average fine detail within the small area and record only the overall intensity of the area.

This phenomenon is exploited in printing black-and-white photographs in newspapers, magazines, and books, in a technique called *halftoning* (also called *clustered-dot ordered dither*[1] in computer graphics). Each small resolution unit is imprinted with a circle of black ink whose area is proportional to the blackness $1 - I$ (where I = intensity) of the area in the original photograph. Figure 13.7 shows part of a halftone pattern, greatly enlarged. Note that the pattern makes a 45° angle with the horizontal, called the *screen angle*. Newspaper halftones use 60 to 80 variable-sized and variable-shaped areas [ULIC87] per inch, whereas halftones in magazines and books use 110 to 200 per inch.

Graphics output devices can approximate the variable-area circles of halftone reproduction. For example, a 2 × 2 pixel area of a bilevel display can be used to produce five different intensity levels at the cost of halving the spatial resolution along each axis. The patterns shown in Fig. 13.8 can be used to fill the 2 × 2 areas with the number of "on" pixels that is proportional to the desired intensity. Figure 13.9 shows a face digitized as a 351 × 351 image array and displayed with 2 × 2 patterns.

An $n \times n$ group of bilevel pixels can provide $n^2 + 1$ intensity levels. In general, there is a tradeoff between spatial resolution and intensity resolution. The use of a 3 × 3 pattern

---

[1]The "ordered dither" contrasts with "random dither," an infrequently used technique.

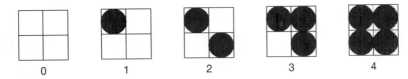

Fig. 13.8 Five intensity levels approximated with four 2 × 2 dither patterns.

cuts spatial resolution by one-third on each axis, but provides 10 intensity levels. Of course, the tradeoff choices are limited by our visual acuity (about 1 minute of arc in normal lighting), the distance from which the image is viewed, and the dots-per-inch resolution of the graphics device.

One possible set of patterns for the 3 × 3 case is shown in Fig. 13.10. Note that these patterns can be represented by the *dither matrix*

$$\begin{bmatrix} 6 & 8 & 4 \\ 1 & 0 & 3 \\ 5 & 2 & 7 \end{bmatrix}. \tag{13.11}$$

To display an intensity I, we turn on all pixels whose values are less than I.

The $n \times n$ pixel patterns used to approximate the halftones must be designed not to introduce visual artifacts in an area of identical intensity values. For instance, if the pattern in Fig. 13.11 were used, rather than the one in Fig. 13.10, horizontal lines would appear in any large area of the image of intensity 3. Second, the patterns must form a *growth sequence* so that any pixel intensified for intensity level j is also intensified for all levels $k > j$. This minimizes the differences in the patterns for successive intensity levels, thereby minimizing the contouring effects. Third, the patterns must grow outward from the center, to create the effect of increasing dot size. Fourth, for hardcopy devices such as laser printers and film recorders that are poor at reproducing isolated ''on'' pixels, all pixels that are ''on'' for a

Fig. 13.9 A continuous-tone photograph, digitized to a resolution of 351 × 351 and displayed using the 2 × 2 patterns of Fig. 13.8. (Courtesy of Alan Paeth, University of Waterloo Computer Graphics Lab.)

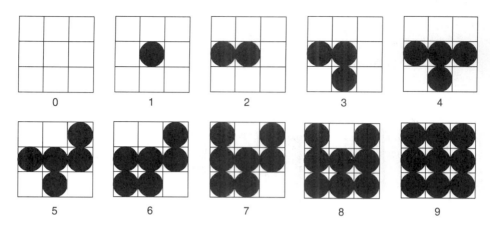

Fig. 13.10 Ten intensity levels approximated with 3 × 3 dither patterns.

particular intensity must be adjacent to other "on" pixels; a pattern such as that in Fig. 13.12 is not acceptable. This is the meaning of the term *clustered-dot* in "clustered-dot ordered dither." Holladay [HOLL80] has developed a widely used method for defining dither matrices for clustered-dot ordered dither. For high-quality reproduction of images, n must be 8 to 10, theoretically allowing 65 to 101 intensity levels. To achieve an effect equivalent to the 150-circle-per-inch printing screen, we thus require a resolution of from $150 \times 8 = 1200$ up to $150 \times 10 = 1500$ pixels per inch. High-quality film recorders can attain this resolution, but cannot actually show all the intensity levels because patterns made up of single black or white pixels may disappear.

Halftone approximation is not limited to bilevel displays. Consider a display with 2 bits per pixel and hence four intensity levels. The halftone technique can be used to increase the number of intensity levels. If we use a 2×2 pattern, we have a total of 4 pixels at our disposal, each of which can take on three values besides black; this allows us to display $4 \times 3 + 1 = 13$ intensities. One possible set of growth sequence patterns in this situation is shown in Fig. 13.13.

Unlike a laser printer, a CRT display is quite able to display individual dots. Hence, the clustering requirement on the patterns discussed previously can be relaxed and *dispersed-dot ordered dither* can be used. There are many possible dither matrices: Bayer [BAYE73] has developed dither matrices that minimize the texture introduced into the displayed images. For the 2×2 case, the dither matrix, called $D^{(2)}$, is

$$D^{(2)} = \begin{bmatrix} 0 & 2 \\ 3 & 1 \end{bmatrix}. \tag{13.12}$$

Fig. 13.11 A 3 × 3 dither pattern inappropriate for halftoning.

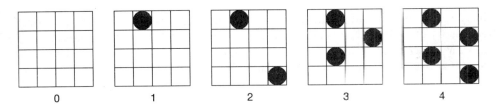

Fig. 13.12 Part of a 4 × 4 ordered dither dot pattern in which several of the patterns have single, nonadjacent dots. Such disconnected patterns are unacceptable for halftoning on laser printers and for printing presses.

This represents the set of patterns of Figure 13.8.

Larger dither matrices can be found using a recurrence relation [JUDI74] to compute $D^{(2n)}$ from $D^{(n)}$. With $U^{(n)}$ defined as an $n \times n$ matrix of 1s, that is,

$$U^{(n)} = \begin{bmatrix} 1 & 1 & 1 & \dots & 1 \\ 1 & 1 & 1 & \dots & 1 \\ 1 & 1 & 1 & \dots & 1 \\ . & . & . & . & . \\ 1 & 1 & 1 & \dots & 1 \end{bmatrix}, \tag{13.13}$$

the recurrence relation is

$$D^{(n)} = \begin{bmatrix} 4D^{(n/2)} + D_{00}^{(2)}U^{(n/2)} & 4D^{(n/2)} + D_{01}^{(2)}U^{(n/2)} \\ 4D^{(n/2)} + D_{10}^{(2)}U^{(n/2)} & 4D^{(n/2)} + D_{11}^{(2)}U^{(n/2)} \end{bmatrix}. \tag{13.14}$$

Applying this relation to $D^{(2)}$ produces

$$D^{(4)} = \begin{bmatrix} 0 & 8 & 2 & 10 \\ 12 & 4 & 14 & 6 \\ 3 & 11 & 1 & 9 \\ 15 & 7 & 13 & 5 \end{bmatrix}. \tag{13.15}$$

The techniques presented thus far have assumed that the image array being shown is smaller than the display device's pixel array, so that multiple display pixels can be used for one

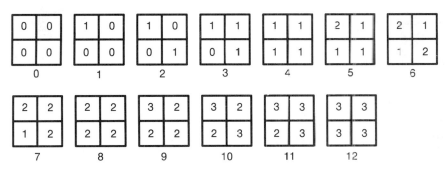

Fig. 13.13 Dither patterns for intensity levels 0 to 13 approximated using 2 × 2 patterns of pixels, with 2 bits (four intensity levels) per pixel. The intensities of the individual pixels sum to the intensity level for each pattern.

image pixel. What if the image and display device arrays are the same size? A simple adaptation of the ordered-dither (either clustered-dot or dispersed-dot) approach can be used. Whether or not to intensify the pixel at point (x, y) depends on the desired intensity $S(x, y)$ at that point and on the dither matrix. To display the point at (x, y), we compute

$$i = x \text{ modulo } n,$$
$$j = y \text{ modulo } n. \tag{13.16}$$

Then, if

$$S(x, y) > D_{ij}^{(n)}, \tag{13.17}$$

the point at (x, y) is intensified; otherwise, it is not. That is, 1 pixel in the image array controls 1 pixel in the display array. Notice that large areas of fixed image intensity are displayed exactly as when the image-array size is less than the display-array size, so the effect of equal image and display arrays is apparent only in areas where intensity varies.

Figure 13.14(a) is a face digitized at 512×512 and shown on a 512×512 bilevel display using $D^{(8)}$. Compare this bilevel result to the multilevel pictures shown earlier in this section. Further pictures displayed by means of ordered dither appear in [JARV76a; JARV76b; ULIC87], where more ways to display continuous-tone images on bilevel displays are described.

Error diffusion, another way to handle the case when the image and display array sizes are equal, was developed by Floyd and Steinberg [FLOY75]; its visual results are often satisfactory. The error (i.e., the difference between the exact pixel value and the approximated value actually displayed) is added to the values of the four image-array pixels to the right of and below the pixel in question: $\frac{7}{16}$ of the error to the pixel to the right, $\frac{3}{16}$ to the pixel below and to the left, $\frac{5}{16}$ to the pixel immediately below, and $\frac{1}{16}$ to the pixel below

(a)   (b)

Fig. 13.14 A continuous-tone photograph reproduced with (a) $D^{(8)}$ ordered dither, and (b) Floyd-Steinberg error diffusion. (Courtesy of Alan Paeth, University of Waterloo Computer Graphics Lab.)

and to the right. This has the effect of spreading, or diffusing, the error over several pixels in the image array. Figure 13.14(b) was created using this method.

Given a picture S to be displayed in the intensity matrix I, the modified values in S and the displayed values in I are computed for pixels in scan-line order, working downward from the topmost scanline.

double *error*;
$K = $ Approximate $(S[x][y])$;   /* Approximate S to nearest displayable intensity */
$I[x][y] = K$;   /* Draw the pixel at (x, y). */
error $= S[x][y] - K$;   /* Error term */

/* Step 1: spread $\frac{7}{16}$ of error into the pixel to the right, at $(x + 1, y)$. */
$S[x + 1][y] \mathrel{+}= 7 * error/16$;

/* Step 2: spread $\frac{3}{16}$ of error into pixel below and to the left. */
$S[x - 1][y - 1] \mathrel{+}= 3 * error/16$;

/* Step 3: spread $\frac{5}{16}$ of error into pixel below. */
$S[x][y - 1] \mathrel{+}= 5 * error/16$;

/* Step 4: spread $\frac{1}{16}$ of error below and to the right. */
$S[x + 1][y - 1] \mathrel{+}= error/16$;

To avoid introducing visual artifacts into the displayed image, we must ensure that the four errors sum exactly to *error*; no roundoff errors can be allowed. This can be done by calculating the step 4 error term as *error* minus the error terms from the first three steps. The function *Approximate* returns the displayable intensity value closest to the actual pixel value. For a bilevel display, the value of S is simply rounded to 0 or 1.

Even better results can be obtained by alternately scanning left to right and right to left; on a right-to-left scan, the left–right directions for errors in steps 1, 2, and 4 are reversed. For a detailed discussion of this and other error-diffusion methods, see [ULIC87]. Other approaches are discussed in [KNUT87].

Suppose the size of the image array is less than the size of the display array, the number of intensities in the image and display are equal, and we wish to display the image at the size of the display array. A simple case of this is an 8-bit-per-pixel, 512×512 image and an 8-bit-per-pixel, 1024×1024 display. If we simply replicate image pixels horizontally and vertically in the display array, the replicated pixels on the display will form squares that are quite obvious to the eye. To avoid this problem, we can interpolate intensities to calculate the pixel values. For instance, if an image S is to be displayed at double resolution, then the intensities I to display (with $x = 2x'$ and $y = 2y'$) are

$I[x][y]$ $= S[x'][y']$;

$I[x + 1][y]$ $= \frac{1}{2}(S[x'][y'] + S[x' + 1][y'])$;

$I[x][y + 1]$ $= \frac{1}{2}(S[x'][y'] + S[x'][y' + 1])$;

$I[x + 1][y + 1] = \frac{1}{4}(S[x'][y'] + S[x' + 1][y'] + S[x'][y' + 1] + S[x' + 1][y' + 1])$;

See Section 17.4 for a discussion of two-pass scaling transformations of images, and Section 3.17 for a description of the filtering and image-reconstruction techniques that are applicable to this problem.

13.2   CHROMATIC COLOR

The visual sensations caused by colored light are much richer than those caused by achromatic light. Discussions of color perception usually involve three quantities, known as hue, saturation, and lightness. *Hue* distinguishes among colors such as red, green, purple, and yellow. *Saturation* refers to how far color is from a gray of equal intensity. Red is highly saturated; pink is relatively unsaturated; royal blue is highly saturated; sky blue is relatively unsaturated. Pastel colors are relatively unsaturated; unsaturated colors include more white light than do the vivid, saturated colors. *Lightness* embodies the achromatic notion of perceived intensity of a reflecting object. *Brightness*, a fourth term, is used instead of lightness to refer to the perceived intensity of a self-luminous (i.e., emitting rather than reflecting light) object, such as a light bulb, the sun, or a CRT.

It is necessary to specify and measure colors if we are to use them precisely in computer graphics. For reflected light, we can do this by visually comparing a sample of unknown color against a set of ''standard'' samples. The unknown and sample colors must be viewed under a standard light source, since the perceived color of a surface depends both on the surface and on the light under which the surface is viewed. The widely used Munsell color-order system includes sets of published standard colors [MUNS76] organized in a 3D space of hue, value (what we have defined as lightness), and chroma (saturation). Each color is named, and is ordered so as to have an equal perceived ''distance'' in color space (as judged by many observers) from its neighbors. [KELL76] gives an extensive discussion of standard samples, charts depicting the Munsell space, and tables of color names.

In the printing industry and graphic design profession, colors are typically specified by matching to printed color samples. Color Plate I.33 is taken from a widely used color-matching system.

Artists often specify color as different tints, shades, and tones of strongly saturated, or pure, pigments. A *tint* results from adding white pigment to a pure pigment, thereby decreasing saturation. A *shade* comes from adding a black pigment to a pure pigment, thereby decreasing lightness. A *tone* is the consequence of adding both black and white pigments to a pure pigment. All these steps produce different colors of the same hue, with varying saturation and lightness. Mixing just black and white pigments creates grays. Figure 13.15 shows the relationship of tints, shades, and tones. The percentage of pigments that must be mixed to match a color can be used as a color specification. The Ostwald [OSTW31] color-order system is similar to the artist's model.

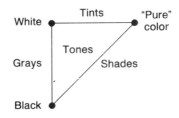

Fig. 13.15 Tints, tones, and shades.

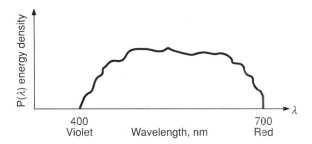

Fig. 13.16 Typical spectral energy distribution $P(\lambda)$ of a light.

13.2.1 Psychophysics

The Munsell and artists' pigment-mixing methods are subjective: They depend on human observers' judgments, the lighting, the size of the sample, the surrounding color, and the overall lightness of the environment. An objective, quantitative way of specifying colors is needed, and for this we turn to the branch of physics known as *colorimetry*. Important terms in colorimetry are dominant wavelength, excitation purity, and luminance.

Dominant wavelength is the wavelength of the color we "see" when viewing the light, and corresponds to the perceptual notion of hue[2]; *excitation purity* corresponds to the saturation of the color; *luminance* is the amount or intensity of light. The excitation purity of a colored light is the proportion of pure light of the dominant wavelength and of white light needed to define the color. A completely pure color is 100 percent saturated and thus contains no white light, whereas mixtures of a pure color and white light have saturations somewhere between 0 and 100 percent. White light and hence grays are 0 percent saturated, containing no color of any dominant wavelength. The correspondences between these perceptual and colorimetry terms are as follows:

Perceptual term	Colorimetry
Hue	Dominant wavelength
Saturation	Excitation purity
Lightness (reflecting objects)	Luminance
Brightness (self-luminous objects)	Luminance

Fundamentally, light is electromagnetic energy in the 400- to 700-nm wavelength part of the spectrum, which is perceived as the colors from violet through indigo, blue, green, yellow, and orange to red. Color Plate I.34 shows the colors of the spectrum. The amount of energy present at each wavelength is represented by a spectral energy distribution $P(\lambda)$, such as shown in Fig. 13.16 and Color Plate I.34. The distribution represents an infinity of numbers, one for each wavelength in the visible spectrum (in practice, the distribution is represented by a large number of sample points on the spectrum, as measured by a

---

[2]Some colors, such as purple, have no true dominant wavelength, as we shall see later.

spectroradiometer). Fortunately, we can describe the visual effect of any spectral distribution much more concisely by the triple (dominant wavelength, excitation purity, luminance). This implies that many different spectral energy distributions produce the same color: They "look" the same. Hence the relationship between spectral distributions and colors is many-to-one. Two spectral energy distributions that look the same are called *metamers*.

Figure 13.17 shows one of the infinitely many spectral distributions $P(\lambda)$, or metamers, that produces a certain color sensation. At the dominant wavelength, there is a spike of energy of level e_2. White light, the uniform distribution of energy at level e_1, is also present. The excitation purity depends on the relation between e_1 and e_2: when $e_1 = e_2$, excitation purity is 0 percent; when $e_1 = 0$, excitation purity is 100 percent. Brightness, which is proportional to the integral of the product of the curve and the luminous efficiency function (defined later), depends on both e_1 and e_2. In general, spectral distributions may be more complex than the one shown, and it is not possible to determine the dominant wavelength merely by looking at the spectral distributions. In particular, the dominant wavelength may *not* be the one whose component in the spectral distribution is largest.

How does this discussion relate to the red, green, and blue phosphor dots on a color CRT? And how does it relate to the *tristimulus theory* of color perception, which is based on the hypothesis that the retina has three kinds of color sensors (called cones), with peak sensitivity to red, green, or blue lights? Experiments based on this hypothesis produce the spectral-response functions of Fig. 13.18. The peak blue response is around 440 nm; that for green is about 545 nm; that for red is about 580 nm. (The terms "red" and "green" are somewhat misleading here, as the 545 nm and 580 nm peaks are actually in the yellow range.) The curves suggest that the eye's response to blue light is much less strong than is its response to red or green.

Figure 13.19 shows the *luminous-efficiency function*, the eye's response to light of constant luminance, as the dominant wavelength is varied: our peak sensitivity is to yellow-green light of wavelength around 550 nm. There is experimental evidence that this curve is just the sum of the three curves shown in Fig. 13.18.

The tristimulus theory is intuitively attractive because it corresponds loosely to the notion that colors can be specified by positively weighted sums of red, green, and blue (the so-called primary colors). This notion is almost true: The three color-matching functions in

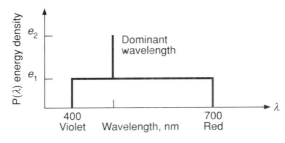

Fig. 13.17 Spectral energy distribution, $P(\lambda)$, illustrating dominant wavelength, excitation purity, and luminance.

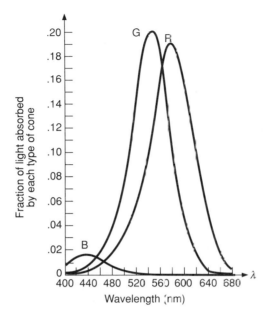

Fig. 13.18 Spectral-response functions of each of the three types of cones on the human retina.

Fig. 13.20 show the amounts of red, green, and blue light needed by an average observer to match a color of constant luminance, for all values of dominant wavelength in the visible spectrum.

A negative value in Fig. 13.20 means that we cannot match the color by adding together the primaries. However, if one of the primaries is added to the color sample, the sample can then be matched by a mixture of the other two primaries. Hence, negative values in Fig. 13.20 indicate that the primary was added to the color being matched. The need for negative values does not mean that the notion of mixing red, green, and blue to obtain other

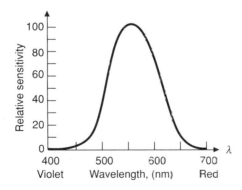

Fig. 13.19 Luminous-efficiency function for the human eye.

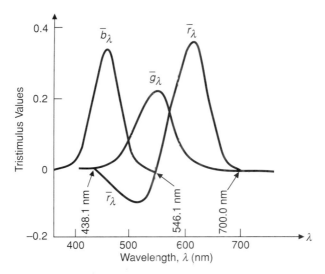

Fig. 13.20 Color-matching functions, showing the amounts of three primaries needed to match all the wavelengths of the visible spectrum.

colors is invalid; on the contrary, a huge range of colors can be matched by positive amounts of red, green, and blue. Otherwise, the color CRT would not work! It does mean, however, that certain colors cannot be produced by RGB mixes, and hence cannot be shown on an ordinary CRT.

The human eye can distinguish hundreds of thousands of different colors in color space, when different colors are judged side by side by different viewers who state whether the colors are the same or different. As shown in Fig. 13.21, when colors differ only in hue, the wavelength between just noticably different colors varies from more than 10 nm at the extremes of the spectrum to less than 2 nm around 480 nm (blue) and 580 nm (yellow).

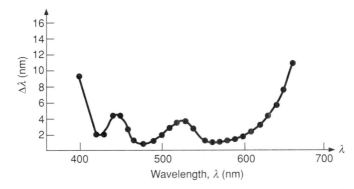

Fig. 13.21 Just-noticable color differences as a function of wavelength λ. The ordinate indicates the minimum detectable difference in wavelength between adjacent color samples. (Source: Data are from [BEDF58].)

Except at the spectrum extremes, however, most distinguished hues are within 4 nm. Altogether about 128 fully saturated hues can be distinguished.

The eye is less sensitive to hue changes in less saturated light. This is not surprising: As saturation tends to 0 percent, all hues tend to white. Sensitivity to changes in saturation for a fixed hue and lightness is greater at the extremes of the visible spectrum, where about 23 distinguishable steps exist. Around 575 nm, only 16 saturation steps can be distinguished [JONE26].

13.2.2   The CIE Chromaticity Diagram

Matching and therefore defining a colored light with a mixture of three fixed primaries is a desirable approach to specifying color, but the need for negative weights suggested by Fig. 13.20 is awkward. In 1931, the *Commission Internationale de l'Éclairage* (CIE) defined three standard primaries, called **X**, **Y**, and **Z**, to replace red, green, and blue in this matching process. The three corresponding color-matching functions, $\bar{x}_\lambda$, $\bar{y}_\lambda$, and $\bar{z}_\lambda$, are shown in Fig. 13.22. The primaries can be used to match, with only positive weights, all the colors we can see. The **Y** primary was intentionally defined to have a color-matching function $\bar{y}_\lambda$ that exactly matches the luminous-efficiency function of Fig. 13.19. Note that $\bar{x}_\lambda$, $\bar{y}_\lambda$, and $\bar{z}_\lambda$ are not the spectral distributions of the **X**, **Y**, and **Z** colors, just as the curves in Fig. 13.20 are not the spectral distributions of red, green, and blue. They are merely auxilliary functions used to compute how much of **X**, **Y**, and **Z** should be mixed together to generate a metamer of any visible color.

The color-matching functions are defined tabularly at 1-nm intervals, and are found in texts such as [WYSZ82; BILL81]. The distributions were defined for color samples that

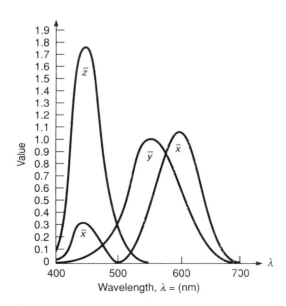

Fig. 13.22 The color-matching functions $\bar{x}_\lambda$, $\bar{y}_\lambda$, and $\bar{z}_\lambda$, for the 1931 CIE **X, Y, Z** primaries.

subtend a 2° field of view on the retina. The original 1931 tabulation is normally used in work relevant to computer graphics. A later 1964 tabulation for a 10° field of view is not generally useful, because it emphasizes larger areas of constant color than are normally found in graphics.

The three CIE color-matching functions are linear combinations of the color-matching functions from Fig. 13.20. This means that the definition of a color with red, green, and blue lights can be converted via a linear transformation into its definition with the CIE primaries, and vice versa.

The amounts of $\mathbf{X}$, $\mathbf{Y}$, and $\mathbf{Z}$ primaries needed to match a color with a spectral energy distribution $P(\lambda)$, are:

$$X = k \int P(\lambda)\, \bar{x}_\lambda\, d\lambda, \quad Y = k \int P(\lambda)\, \bar{y}_\lambda\, d\lambda, \quad Z = k \int P(\lambda)\, \bar{z}_\lambda\, d\lambda. \quad (13.18)$$

For self-luminous objects like a CRT, k is 680 lumens/watt. For reflecting objects, k is usually selected such that bright white has a Y value of 100; then other Y values will be in the range of 0 to 100. Thus,

$$k = \frac{100}{\int P_w(\lambda)\bar{y}_\lambda\, d\lambda} \quad (13.19)$$

where $P_w(\lambda)$ is the spectral energy distribution for whatever light source is chosen as the standard for white. In practice, these integrations are performed by summation, as none of the energy distributions are expressed analytically.

Figure 13.23 shows the cone-shaped volume of XYZ space that contains visible colors. The volume extends out from the origin into the postive octant, and is capped at the smooth curved line terminating the cone.

Let (X, Y, Z) be the weights applied to the CIE primaries to match a color $\mathbf{C}$, as found using Eq. (13.18). Then $\mathbf{C} = X\,\mathbf{X} + Y\,\mathbf{Y} + Z\,\mathbf{Z}$. We define *chromaticity* values (which depend only on dominant wavelength and saturation and are independent of the amount of

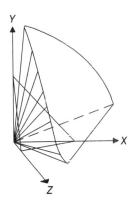

Fig. 13.23 The cone of visible colors in CIE color space is shown by the lines radiating from the origin. The $X + Y + Z = 1$ plane is shown. (Courtesy of Gary Meyer, Program of Computer Graphics, Cornell University, 1978.)

luminous energy) by normalizing against $X + Y + Z$, which can be thought of as the total amount of light energy:

$$x = \frac{X}{(X + Y + Z)}, \; y = \frac{Y}{(X + Y + Z)}, \; z = \frac{Z}{(X + Y - Z)}. \quad (13.20)$$

Notice that $x + y + z = 1$. That is, x, y, and z are on the $(X + Y + Z = 1)$ plane of Fig. 13.23. Color plate II.1 shows the $X + Y + Z = 1$ plane as part of CIE space, and also shows an orthographic view of the plane along with the projection of the plane onto the (X, Y) plane. This latter projection is just the CIE chromaticity diagram.

If we specify x and y, then z is determined by $z = 1 - x - y$. We cannot recover X, Y, and Z from x and y, however. To recover them, we need one more piece of information, typically Y, which carries luminance information. Given (x, y, Y), the transformation to the corresponding (X, Y, Z) is

$$X = \frac{x}{y}Y, \quad Y = Y, Z = \frac{1 - x - y}{y}Y. \quad (13.21)$$

Chromaticity values depend only on dominant wavelength and saturation and are independent of the amount of luminous energy. By plotting x and y for all visible colors, we obtain the CIE chromaticity diagram shown in Fig. 13.24, which is the projection onto the (X, Y) plane of the $(X + Y + Z = 1)$ plane of Fig. 13.23. The interior and boundary of the horseshoe-shaped region represent all visible chromaticity values. (All perceivable colors with the same chromaticity but different luminances map into the same point within this region.) The 100 percent spectrally pure colors of the spectrum are on the curved part of the boundary. A standard white light, meant to approximate sunlight, is formally defined by a

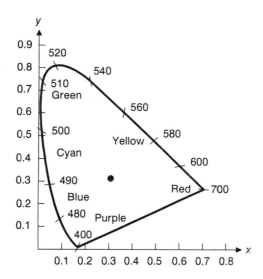

Fig. 13.24 The CIE chromaticity diagram. Wavelengths around the periphery are in nanometers. The dot marks the position of illuminant C.

light source *illuminant C*, marked by the center dot. It is near but not at the point where $x = y = z = \frac{1}{3}$. Illuminant C was defined by specifying a spectral power distribution that is close to daylight at a correlated color temperature of 6774° Kelvin.

The CIE chromaticity diagram is useful in many ways. For one, it allows us to measure the dominant wavelength and excitation purity of any color by matching the color with a mixture of the three CIE primaries. (Instruments called *colorimeters* measure tristimulus X, Y, and Z values, from which chromaticity coordinates are computed using Eq. (13.20). *Spectroradiometers* measure both the spectral energy distribution and the tristimulus values.) Now suppose the matched color is at point A in Fig. 13.25. When two colors are added together, the new color lies somewhere on the straight line in the chromaticity diagram connecting the two colors being added. Therefore, color A can be thought of as a mixture of "standard" white light (illuminant C) and the pure spectral light at point B. Thus, B defines the dominant wavelength. The ratio of length AC to length BC, expressed as a percentage, is the excitation purity of A. The closer A is to C, the more white light A includes and the less pure it is.

The chromaticity diagram factors out luminance, so color sensations that are luminance-related are excluded. For instance; brown, which is an orange-red chromaticity at very low luminance relative to its surrounding area, does not appear. It is thus important to remember that the chromaticity diagram is not a full color palette. There is an infinity of planes in (X, Y, Z) space, each of which projects onto the chromaticity diagram and each of which loses luminance information in the process. The colors found on each such plane are all different.

Complementary colors are those that can be mixed to produce white light (such as D and E in Fig. 13.25). Some colors (such as F in Fig. 13.25) cannot be defined by a

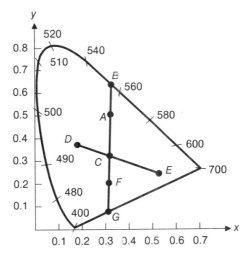

Fig. 13.25 Colors on the chromaticity diagram. The dominant wavelength of color A is that of color B. Colors D and E are complementary colors. The dominant wavelength of color F is defined as the complement of the dominant wavelength of color A.

dominant wavelength and are thus called *nonspectral*. In this case, the dominant wavelength is said to be the complement of the wavelength at which the line through F and C intersects the horseshoe part of the curve at point B, and is designated by a "c" (here about 555 nm c). The excitation purity is still defined by the ratio of lengths (here CF to CG). The colors that must be expressed by using a complementary dominant wavelength are the purples and magentas; they occur in the lower part of the CIE diagram. Complementary colors still can be made to fit the dominant wavelength model of Fig. 13.17, in the sense that if we take a flat spectral distribution and delete some of the light at frequency B, the resulting color will be perceived as F.

Another use of the CIE chromaticity diagram is to define *color gamuts*, or color ranges, that show the effect of adding colors together. Any two colors, say I and J in Fig. 13.26, can be added to produce any color along their connecting line by varying the relative amounts of the two colors being added. A third color K (see Fig. 13.26) can be used with various mixtures of I and J to produce the gamut of all colors in triangle IJK, again by varying relative amounts. The shape of the diagram shows why visible red, green, and blue cannot be additively mixed to match all colors: No triangle whose vertices are within the visible area can completely cover the visible area.

The chromaticity diagram is also used to compare the gamuts available on various color display and hardcopy devices. Color Plate II.2 shows the gamuts for a color television monitor, film, and print. The chromaticity coordinates for the phosphors in two typical monitors are these:

	Short-persistence phosphors			Long-persistence phosphors		
	Red	Green	Blue	Red	Green	Blue
x	0.61	0.29	0.15	0.62	0.21	0.15
y	0.35	0.59	0.063	0.33	0.685	0.063

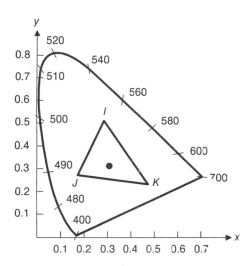

Fig. 13.26 Mixing colors. All colors on the line IJ can be created by mixing colors I and J; all colors in the triangle IJK can be created by mixing colors I, J, and K.

The smallness of the print gamut with respect to the color-monitor gamut suggests that, if images originally seen on a monitor must be faithfully reproduced by printing, a reduced gamut of colors should be used with the monitor. Otherwise, accurate reproduction will not be possible. If, however, the goal is to make a pleasing rather than an exact reproduction, small differences in color gamuts are less important. A discussion of color-gamut compression can be found in [HALL89].

There is a problem with the CIE system. Consider the distance from color $C_1 = (X_1, Y_1, Z_1)$ to color $C_1 + \Delta C$, and the distance from color $C_2 = (X_2, Y_2, Z_2)$ to color $C_2 + \Delta C$, where $\Delta C = (\Delta X, \Delta Y, \Delta Z)$. Both distances are equal to ΔC, yet in general they will not be perceived as being equal. This is because of the variation, throughout the spectrum, of the just noticeable differences discussed in Section 13.2.1. A *perceptually uniform* color space is needed, in which two colors that are equally distant are *perceived* as equally distant by viewers.

The 1976 CIE LUV uniform color space was developed in response to this need. With (X_n, Y_n, Z_n) as the coordinates of the color that is to be defined as white, the space is defined by

$$L^* = 116 \, (Y/Y_n)^{1/3} - 16, \quad Y/Y_n > 0.01$$

$$u^* = 13 \, L^* \, (u' - u'_n),$$

$$v^* = 13 \, L^* \, (v' - v'_n),$$

$$u' = \frac{4X}{X + 15Y + 3Z}, \quad v' = \frac{9Y}{X + 15Y + 3Z}, \tag{13.22}$$

$$u'_n = \frac{4X_n}{X_n + 15Y_n + 3Z_n}, \quad v'_n = \frac{9Y_n}{X_n + 15Y_n + 3Z_n}.$$

The shape of the 3D volume of visible colors defined by these equations is of course different from that for CIE (X, Y, Z) space itself (Fig. 13.23).

With this background on color, we now turn our attention to color in computer graphics.

13.3   COLOR MODELS FOR RASTER GRAPHICS

A color model is a specification of a 3D color coordinate system and a visible subset in the coordinate system within which all colors in a particular color gamut lie. For instance, the RGB color model is the unit cube subset of the 3D Cartesian coordinate system.

The purpose of a color model is to allow convenient specification of colors within some color gamut. Our primary interest is the gamut for color CRT monitors, as defined by the RGB (red, green, blue) primaries in Color Plate II.2. As we see in this color plate, a color gamut is a subset of all visible chromaticities. Hence, a color model cannot be used to specify all visible colors. This is emphasized in Fig. 13.27, which shows that the gamut of a CRT monitor is a subset of (X, Y, Z) space.

Three hardware-oriented color models are RGB, used with color CRT monitors, YIQ, the broadcast TV color system, and CMY (cyan, magenta, yellow) for some color-printing devices. Unfortunately, none of these models are particularly easy to use, because they do not relate directly to intuitive color notions of hue, saturation, and brightness. Therefore,

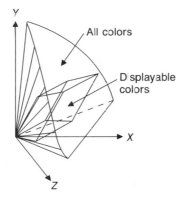

Fig. 13.27 The color gamut for a typical color monitor within the CIE color space. The range of colors that can be displayed on the monitor is clearly smaller than that of all colors visible in CIE space. (Courtesy of Gary Meyer, Program of Computer Graphics, Cornell University, 1978.)

another class of models has been developed with ease of use as a goal. Several such models are described in [GSPC79; JOBL78; MEYE80; SMIT78]. We discuss three, the HSV (sometimes called HSB), HLS, and HVC models.

With each model is given a means of converting to some other specification. For RGB, this conversion is to CIE's (X, Y, Z) space. This conversion is important, because CIE is the worldwide standard. For all of the other models, the conversion is to RGB; hence, we can convert from, say, HSV to RGB to the CIE standard.

13.3.1 The RGB Color Model

The red, green, and blue (RGB) color model used in color CRT monitors and color raster graphics employs a Cartesian coordinate system. The RGB primaries are *additive* primaries; that is, the individual contributions of each primary are added together to yield the result, as suggested in Color Plate II.3. The subset of interest is the unit cube shown in Fig. 13.28. The main diagonal of the cube, with equal amounts of each primary, represents the gray levels: black is $(0, 0, 0)$; white is $(1, 1, 1)$. Color Plates II.4 and II.5 show several views of the RGB color model.

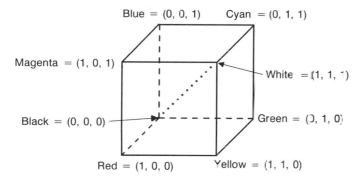

Fig. 13.28 The RGB cube. Grays are on the dotted main diagonal.

The color gamut covered by the RGB model is defined by the chromaticities of a CRT's phosphors. Two CRTs with different phosphors will cover different gamuts. To convert colors specified in the gamut of one CRT to the gamut of another CRT, we can use the transformations M_1 and M_2 from the RGB color space of each monitor to the (X, Y, Z) color space. The form of each transformation is:

$$\begin{bmatrix} X \\ Y \\ Z \end{bmatrix} = \begin{bmatrix} X_r & X_g & X_b \\ Y_r & Y_g & Y_b \\ Z_r & Z_g & Z_b \end{bmatrix} \begin{bmatrix} R \\ G \\ B \end{bmatrix}, \tag{13.23}$$

where X_r, X_g, and X_b are the weights applied to the monitor's RGB colors to find X, and so on.

Defining M as the 3×3 matrix of color-matching coefficients, we write Eq. (13.23) as

$$\begin{bmatrix} X \\ Y \\ Z \end{bmatrix} = M \begin{bmatrix} R \\ G \\ B \end{bmatrix}. \tag{13.24}$$

With M_1 and M_2 the matricies that convert from each of the two monitor's gamuts to CIE, $M_2^{-1}M_1$ converts from the RGB of monitor 1 to the RGB of monitor 2. This matrix product is all that is needed if the color in question lies in the gamuts of both monitors. What if a color C_1 is in the gamut of monitor 1 but is not in the gamut of monitor 2? The corresponding color $C_2 = M_2^{-1}M_1C_1$ will be outside the unit cube and hence will not be displayable. A simple but not very satisfactory solution is to clamp the color values—that is, to replace values of R, G, or B that are less than 0 with 0, and values that are greater than 1 with 1. More satisfactory but also more complex approaches are described in [HALL89].

The chromaticity coordinates for the RGB phosphors are usually available from CRT manufacturers' specifications. If not, a colorimeter can also be used to measure the chromaticity coordinates directly, or a spectroradiometer can be used to measure $P(\lambda)$, which can then be converted to chromaticity coordinates using Eqs. (13.18), (13.19), and (13.20). Denoting the coordinates by (x_r, y_r) for red, (x_g, y_g) for green, and (x_b, y_b) for blue, and defining C_r as

$$C_r = X_r + Y_r + Z_r, \tag{13.25}$$

we can write, for the red primary;

$$x_r = \frac{X_r}{X_r + Y_r + Z_r} = \frac{X_r}{C_r}, \; X_r = x_r \, C_r,$$

$$y_r = \frac{Y_r}{X_r + Y_r + Z_r} = \frac{Y_r}{C_r}, \; Y_r = y_r \, C_r,$$

$$z_r = (1 - x_r - y_r) = \frac{Z_r}{X_r + Y_r + Z_r} = \frac{Z_r}{C_r}, \; Z_r = z_r \, C_r. \tag{13.26}$$

With similar definitions for C_g and C_b, Eq. (13.23) can be rewritten as:

$$\begin{bmatrix} X \\ Y \\ Z \end{bmatrix} = \begin{bmatrix} x_r C_r & x_g C_g & x_b C_b \\ y_r C_r & y_g C_g & y_b C_b \\ (1 - x_r - y_r)C_r & (1 - x_g - y_g)C_g & (1 - x_b - y_b)C_b \end{bmatrix} \begin{bmatrix} R \\ G \\ B \end{bmatrix}. \quad (13.27)$$

The unknowns C_r, C_g, and C_b can be found in one of two ways [MEYE83]. First, the luminances Y_r, Y_g, and Y_b of maximum-brightness red, green, and blue may be known or can be measured with a high-quality photometer (inexpensive meters can be off by factors of 2 to 10 on the blue reading). These measured luminances can be combined with the known y_r, y_g, and y_b to yield

$$C_r = Y_r/y_r, \; C_g = Y_g/y_g, \; C_b = Y_b/y_b. \quad (13.28)$$

These values are then substituted into Eq. (13.27), and the conversion matrix M is thus expressed in terms of the known quantities (x_r, y_r), (x_g, y_g), (x_b, y_b), Y_r, Y_g, and Y_b.

We can also remove the unknown variables from Eq. (13.27) if we know or can measure the X_w, Y_w, and Z_w for the white color produced when $R = G = B = 1$. For this case, Eq. (13.27) can be rewritten as

$$\begin{bmatrix} X_w \\ Y_w \\ Z_w \end{bmatrix} = \begin{bmatrix} x_r & x_g & x_b \\ y_r & y_g & y_b \\ (1 - x_r - y_r) & (1 - x_g - y_g) & (1 - x_b - y_b) \end{bmatrix} \begin{bmatrix} C_r \\ C_g \\ C_b \end{bmatrix}, \quad (13.29)$$

solved for C_r, C_g, and C_b (the only unknowns), and the resulting values substituted into Eq. (13.27). Alternatively, it may be that the white color is given by x_w, y_w, and Y_w; in this case, before solving Eq. (13.29), we first find

$$X_w = x_w \frac{Y_w}{y_w}, \; Z_w = z_w \frac{Y_w}{y_w}. \quad (13.30)$$

13.3.2 The CMY Color Model

Cyan, magenta, and yellow are the complements of red, green, and blue, respectively. When used as filters to subtract color from white light, they are called *subtractive primaries*. The subset of the Cartesian coordinate system for the CMY model is the same as that for RGB except that white (full light) instead of black (no light) is at the origin. Colors are specified by what is removed or subtracted from white light, rather than by what is added to blackness.

A knowledge of CMY is important when dealing with hardcopy devices that deposit colored pigments onto paper, such as electrostatic and ink-jet plotters. When a surface is coated with cyan ink, no red light is reflected from the surface. Cyan subtracts red from the reflected white light, which is itself the sum of red, green, and blue. Hence, in terms of the additive primaries, cyan is white minus red, that is, blue plus green. Similarly, magenta absorbs green, so it is red plus blue; yellow absorbs blue, so it is red plus green. A surface coated with cyan and yellow absorbs red and blue, leaving only green to be reflected from illuminating white light. A cyan, yellow, and magenta surface absorbs red, green, and blue, and therefore is black. These relations, diagrammed in Fig. 13.29, can be seen in Color Plate II.6 and are represented by the following equation:

$$\begin{bmatrix} C \\ M \\ Y \end{bmatrix} = \begin{bmatrix} 1 \\ 1 \\ 1 \end{bmatrix} - \begin{bmatrix} R \\ G \\ B \end{bmatrix}. \tag{13.31}$$

The unit column vector is the RGB representation for white and the CMY representation for black.

The conversion from RGB to CMY is then

$$\begin{bmatrix} R \\ G \\ B \end{bmatrix} = \begin{bmatrix} 1 \\ 1 \\ 1 \end{bmatrix} - \begin{bmatrix} C \\ M \\ Y \end{bmatrix}. \tag{13.32}$$

These straightforward transformations can be used for converting the eight colors that can be achieved with binary combinations of red, green, and blue into the eight colors achievable with binary combinations of cyan, magenta, and yellow. This conversion is relevant for use on ink-jet and xerographic color printers.

Another color model, CMYK, uses black (abbreviated as K) as a fourth color. CMYK is used in the four-color printing process of printing presses and some hard-copy devices.

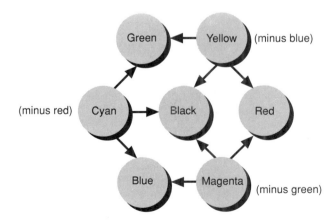

Fig. 13.29 Subtractive primaries (cyan, magenta, yellow) and their mixtures. For instance, cyan and yellow combine to green.

Given a CMY specification, black is used in place of equal amounts of C, M, and Y, according to the relations:

$$K = \min (C, M, Y);$$
$$C = C - K;$$
$$M = M - K;$$
$$Y = Y - K; \tag{13.34}$$

This is discussed further in Section 13.4 and in [STON88].

13.3.3   The YIQ Color Model

The YIQ model is used in U.S. commercial color television broadcasting and is therefore closely related to color raster graphics. YIQ is a recoding of RGB for transmission efficiency and for downward compatibility with black-and-white television. The recoded signal is transmitted using the National Television System Committee (NTSC) [PRIT77] system.

The Y component of YIQ is not yellow but luminance, and is defined to be the same as the CIE **Y** primary. Only the Y component of a color TV signal is shown on black-and-white televisions: the chromaticity is encoded in I and Q. The YIQ model uses a 3D Cartesian coordinate system, with the visible subset being a convex polyhedron that maps into the RGB cube.

The RGB-to-YIQ mapping is defined as follows:

$$\begin{bmatrix} Y \\ I \\ Q \end{bmatrix} = \begin{bmatrix} 0.299 & 0.587 & 0.114 \\ 0.596 & -0.275 & -0.321 \\ 0.212 & -0.523 & 0.311 \end{bmatrix} \begin{bmatrix} R \\ G \\ B \end{bmatrix}. \tag{13.33}$$

The quantities in the first row reflect the relative importance of green and red and the relative unimportance of blue in brightness. The inverse of the RGB-to-YIQ matrix is used for the YIQ-to-RGB conversion.

Equation (13.33) assumes that the RGB color specification is based on the standard NTSC RGB phosphor, whose CIE coordinates are

	Red	Green	Blue
x	0.67	0.21	0.14
y	0.33	0.71	0.08

and for which the white point, illuminant C, is $x_w = 0.31$, $y_w = 0.316$, and $Y_w = 100.0$.

Specifying colors with the YIQ model solves a potential problem with material being prepared for broadcast television: Two different colors shown side by side on a color monitor will appear to be different, but, when converted to YIQ and viewed on a monochrome monitor, they may appear to be the same. This problem can be avoided by specifying the two colors with different Y values in the YIQ color model space (i.e., by adjusting only the Y value to disambiguate them).

The YIQ model exploits two useful properties of our visual system. First, the system is more sensitive to changes in luminance than to changes in hue or saturation; that is, our ability to discriminate spatially color information is weaker than our ability to discriminate spatially monochrome information. This suggests that more bits of bandwidth should be used to represent Y than are used to represent I and Q, so as to provide higher resolution in Y. Second, objects that cover a very small part of our field of view produce a limited color sensation, which can be specified adequately with one rather than two color dimensions. This suggests that either I or Q can have a lower bandwidth than the other. The NTSC encoding of YIQ into a broadcast signal uses these properties to maximize the amount of information transmitted in a fixed bandwidth: 4 MHz is assigned to Y, 1.5 to I, and 0.6 to Q. Further discussion of YIQ can be found in [SMIT78; PRIT77].

13.3.4 The HSV Color Model

The RGB, CMY, and YIQ models are hardware-oriented. By contrast, Smith's HSV (hue, saturation, value) model [SMIT78] (also called the HSB model, with B for brightness) is user-oriented, being based on the intuitive appeal of the artist's tint, shade, and tone. The coordinate system is cylindrical, and the subset of the space within which the model is defined is a hexcone, or six-sided pyramid, as in Fig. 13.30. The top of the hexcone corresponds to $V = 1$, which contains the relatively bright colors. The colors of the $V = 1$ plane are *not* all of the same perceived brightness, however. Color Plates II.7 and II.8 show the color model.

Hue, or H, is measured by the angle around the vertical axis, with red at $0°$, green at $120°$, and so on (see Fig. 13.30). Complementary colors in the HSV hexcone are $180°$

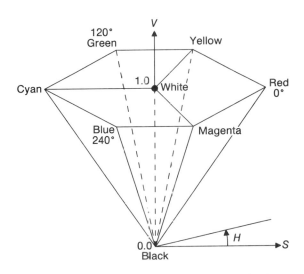

Fig. 13.30 Single-hexcone HSV color model. The $V = 1$ plane contains the RGB model's $R = 1$, $G = 1$, and $B = 1$ planes in the regions shown.

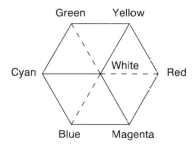

Fig. 13.31 RGB color cube viewed along the principal diagonal. Visible edges of the cube are solid; invisible edges are dashed.

opposite one another. The value of S is a ratio ranging from 0 on the center line (V axis) to 1 on the triangular sides of the hexcone. Saturation is measured relative to the color gamut represented by the model, which is, of course, a subset of the entire CIE chromaticity diagram. Therefore, saturation of 100 percent in the model is less than 100 percent excitation purity.

The hexcone is one unit high in V, with the apex at the origin. The point at the apex is black and has a V coordinate of 0. At this point, the values of H and S are irrelevant. The point $S = 0$, $V = 1$ is white. Intermediate values of V for $S = 0$ (on the center line) are the grays. When $S = 0$, the value of H is irrelevant (called by convention UNDEFINED). When S is not zero, H is relevant. For example, pure red is at $H = 0$, $S = 1$, $V = 1$. Indeed, any color with $V = 1$, $S = 1$ is akin to an artist's pure pigment used as the starting point in mixing colors. Adding white pigment corresponds to decreasing S (without changing V). Shades are created by keeping $S = 1$ and decreasing V. Tones are created by decreasing both S and V. Of course, changing H corresponds to selecting the pure pigment with which to start. Thus, H, S, and V correspond to concepts from the artists' color system, and are not exactly the same as the similar terms introduced in Section 13.2.

The top of the HSV hexcone corresponds to the projection seen by looking along the principal diagonal of the RGB color cube from white toward black, as shown in Fig. 13.31. The RGB cube has subcubes, as illustrated in Fig. 13.32. Each subcube, when viewed along

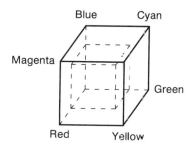

Fig. 13.32 RGB cube and a subcube.

```
void RGB_To_HSV (double r, double g, double b, double *h, double *s, double *v)
/* Given: r, g, b, each in [0,1]. */
/* Desired: h in [0,360), s and v in [0,1] except if s = 0, then h = UNDEFINED, */
/* which is some constant defined with a value outside the interval [0,360]. */
{
    double max = Maximum (r, g, b);
    double min = Minimum (r, g, b);
    *v = max;                             /* This is the value v. */
    /* Next calculate saturation, s. Saturation is 0 if red, green and blue are all 0 */
    *s = (max != 0.0) ? ((max − min) / max) : 0.0;
    if (*s == 0.0)
        *h = UNDEFINED;
    else {                                /* Chromatic case: Saturation is not 0, */
        double delta = max − min;         /* so determine hue. */
        if (r == max)
            *h = (g − b) /delta;          /* Resulting color is between yellow and magenta */
        else if (g == max)
            *h = 2.0 + (b − r) / delta;   /* Resulting color is between cyan and yellow */
        else if (b == max)
            *h = 4.0 + (r − g) / delta;   /* Resulting color is between magenta and cyan */
        *h *= 60.0;                       /* Convert hue to degrees */
        if (*h < 0.0)
            *h += 360.0;                  /* Make sure hue is nonnegative */
    } /* Chromatic case */
}
```

or converting from RGB to HSV color space.

its main diagonal, is like the hexagon in Fig. 13.31, except smaller. Each plane of constant V in HSV space corresponds to such a view of a subcube in RGB space. The main diagonal of RGB space becomes the V axis of HSV space. Thus, we can see intuitively the correspondence between RGB and HSV. The algorithms of Figs. 13.33 and 13.34 define the correspondence precisely by providing conversions from one model to the other.

13.3.5   The HLS Color Model

The HLS (hue, lightness, saturation) color model is defined in the double-hexcone subset of a cylindrical space, as seen in Fig. 13.35. Hue is the angle around the vertical axis of the double hexcone, with red at $0°$ (some discussions of HLS have blue at $0°$; we place red at $0°$ for consistency with the HSV model). The colors occur around the perimeter in the same order as in the CIE diagram when its boundary is traversed counterclockwise: red, yellow, green, cyan, blue, and magenta. This is also the same order as in the HSV single-hexcone model. In fact, we can think of HLS as a deformation of HSV, in which white is pulled

```
void HSV_To_RGB (double *r, double *g, double *b, double h, double s, double v)
/* Given: h in [0,360] or UNDEFINED, s and v in [0,1]. */
/* Desired: r, g, b, each in [0,1]. */
{
    if (s == 0.0) {          /* The color is on the black-and-white center line. */
        /* Achromatic color: There is no hue. */
        if (h == UNDEFINED) {
            *r = v;          /* This is the achromatic case. */
            *g = v;
            *b = v;
        } else
            Error();         /* By our convention, error if s = 0 and h has a value. */
    } else {
        double f,p,q,t;      /* Chromatic color: s != 0, so there is a hue. */
        int i;

        if (h == 360.0)      /* 360 degrees is equivalent to 0 degrees. */
            h = 0.0;
        h /= 60.0;           /* h is now in [0,6). */
        i = floor (h);       /* Floor returns the largest integer <= h */
        f = h - i;           /* f is the fractional part of h. */
        p = v * (1.0 - s);
        q = v * (1.0 - (s * f));
        t = v * (1.0 - (s * (1.0 - f)));
        switch(i) {
            case 0: *r = v;  *g = t;  *b = p; break;
            case 1: *r = q;  *g = v;  *b = p; break;
            case 2: *r = p;  *g = v;  *b = t; break;
            case 3: *r = p;  *g = q;  *b = v; break;
            case 4: *r = t;  *g = p;  *b = v; break;
            case 5: *r = v;  *g = p;  *b = q; break;
        }
    }   /* Chromatic case */
}   /* HSV_To_RGB */
```

Fig. 13.34 Algorithm for converting from HSV to RGB color space.

upward to form the upper hexcone from the $V = 1$ plane. As with the single-hexcone model, the complement of any hue is located 180° farther around the double hexcone, and saturation is measured radially from the vertical axis, from 0 on the axis to 1 on the surface. Lightness is 0 for black (at the lower tip of the double hexcone) to 1 for white (at the upper tip). Color Plate II.9 shows a view of the HLS model. Again, the terms hue, lightness, and saturation in this model are similar to, but are not exactly identical to, the same terms as they were introduced in an earlier section. Color Plate II.10 shows a different view of the space.

The procedures of Figs. 13.36 and 13.37 perform the conversions between HLS and RGB. They are modified from those given by Metrick [GSPC79] to leave H UNDEFINED when $S = 0$, and to have $H = 0$ for red rather than for blue.

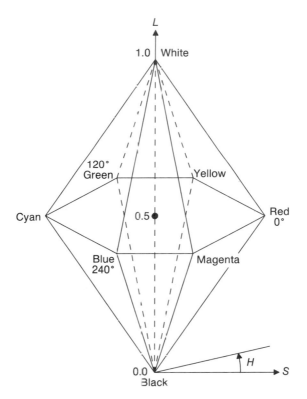

Fig. 13.35 Double-hexcone HLS color model.

The HLS model, like the HSV model, is easy to use. The grays all have $S = 0$, but the maximally saturated hues are at $S = 1$, $L = 0.5$. If potentiometers are used to specify the color-model parameters, the fact that L must be 0.5 to get the strongest possible colors is a disadvantage over the HSV model, in which $S = 1$ and $V = 1$ achieve the same effect. However, analogously to HSV, the colors of the $L = 0.5$ plane are *not* all of the same perceived brightness. Hence two different colors of equal perceived brightness will generally have different values of L. Furthermore, neither HLS nor any of the other models discussed thus far in this section are perceptually uniform, in the sense discussed in Section 13.2.

The recently developed Tektronix TekHVC (hue, value, chroma) color system, a modification of the CIE LUV perceptually uniform color space discussed in Section 13.2, does provide a color space in which measured and perceived distances between colors are approximately equal. This is an important advantage of both the CIE LUV and TekHVC models. Figure 13.38 shows one view of the HVC color model, and Color Plate II.11 shows another view. Details of the transformations from CIE to TekHVC have not been released. However, we see from Eq. (13.22) that the transformation from CIE XYZ to CIE LUV is computationally straightforward, with the cube root being the most computationally intense element. Thus, we expect that perceptually uniform color spaces will come to be more widely used in the future.

```
void RGB_To_HLS (double r, double g, double b, double *h, double *l, double *s)
/* Given: r, g, b each in [0,1]. */
/* Desired: h in [0,360), l and s in [0,1], except if s = 0, then h = UNDEFINED. */
{
    double max = Maximum (r, g, b);
    double min = Minimum (r, g, b);
    *l = (max + min) / 2.0;                    /* This is the lightness. */
    /* Next calculate saturation */
    if (max == min) {                          /* Achromatic case, because r = g = b */
        *s = 0;
        *h = UNDEFINED;
    } else {                                   /* Chromatic case */
        double delta = max - min;

        /* First calculate the saturation. */
        *s = (*l <= 0.5) ? (delta / (max + min)) : (delta / (2.0 - (max + min)));
        /* Next calculate the hue. */
        if (r == max)
            *h = (g - b) / delta;              /* Resulting color is between yellow and magenta */
        else if (g == max)
            *h = 2.0 + (b - r) / delta;        /* Resulting color is between cyan and yellow */
        else if (b == max)
            *h = 4.0 + (r - g) / delta;        /* Resulting color is between magenta and cyan */
        *h *= 60.0;                            /* Convert to degrees */
        if (h < 0.0)
            *h += 360.0;                       /* Make degrees be nonnegative */
    }   /* Chromatic case */
}   /* RGB_To_HLS */
```

Fig. 13.36 Algorithm for converting from RGB to HLS color space.

13.3.6 Interactive Specification of Color

Many application programs allow the user to specify colors of areas, lines, text, and so on. If only a small set of colors is provided, menu selection from samples of the available colors is appropriate. But what if the set of colors is larger than can reasonably be displayed in a menu?

The basic choices are to use English-language names, to specify the numeric coordinates of the color in a color space (either by typing or with slider dials), or to interact directly with a visual representation of the color space. Naming is in general unsatisfactory because it is ambiguous and subjective ("a light navy blue with a touch of green"), and it is also the antithesis of graphic interaction. On the other hand, [BERK82] describes CNS, a fairly well-defined color-naming scheme that uses terms such as "greenish-yellow," "green-yellow," and "yellowish-green" to distinguish three hues between green and

```
void HLS_To_RGB (double *r, double *g, double *b, double h, double l, double s)
/* Given: h in [0,360] or UNDEFINED, l and s in [0,1]. */
/* Desired: r, g, b each in [0,1] */
{
    double m1, m2;

    m2 = (l <= 0.5) ? (l * (l + s)) : (l + s − l * s);
    m1 = 2.0 * l − m2;
    if (s == 0.0) {                    /* Achromatic: There is no hue. */
        if (h == UNDEFINED)
            *r = *g = *b = l;          /* This is the achromatic case. */
        else Error ();                 /* Error if s = 0 and h has a value */
    } else {          /* Chromatic case, so there is a hue */
        *r = Value (m1, m2, h + 120.0);
        *g = Value (m1, m2, h);
        *b = Value (m1, m2, h − 120.0);

    }
}   /* HLS_To_RGB */

static double Value (double n1, double n2, double hue)
{
    if (hue > 360.0)
        hue −= 360.0;
    else if (hue < 0.0)
        hue += 360.0;
    if (hue < 60.0)
        return n1 + (n2 − n1) * hue / 60.0;
    else if (hue < 180.0)
        return n2;
    else if (hue < 240.0)
        return n1 + (n2 − n1) * (240.0 − hue) / 60.0;
    else
        return n1;
}   /* Value */
```

Fig. 13.37 Algorithm for converting from HLS to RGB color space.

yellow. In an experiment, users of CNS were able to specify colors more precisely than were users who entered numeric coordinates in either RGB or HSV space.

Coordinate specification can be done with slider dials, as in Fig. 13.39, using any of the color models. If the user understands how each dimension affects the color, this technique works well. Probably the best interactive specification method is to let the user interact directly with a representation of the color space, as shown in Fig. 13.40. The line on the circle (representing the $V = 1$ plane) can be dragged around to determine which slice of the HSV volume is displayed in the triangle. The cursor on the triangle can be moved around to specify saturation and value. As the line or the cursor is moved, the numeric readouts change value. When the user types new values directly into the numeric readouts, the line and cursor are repositioned. The color sample box shows the currently selected

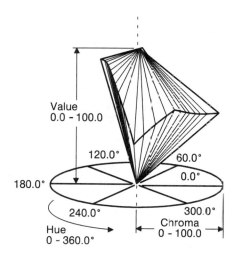

Fig. 13.38 The TekHVC color model. (Courtesy of Tektronix, Inc.)

color. Color Plate II.12 shows a similar method used for the HSV model.

[SCHW87] describes color-matching experiments in which subjects used a data tablet to specify colors in several models including RGB, YIQ, LAB [WYSZ82], and HSV. HSV was found to be slow but accurate, whereas RGB was faster but less accurate. There is a widespread belief that the HSV model is especially tractable, usually making it the model of choice.

Many interactive systems that permit user specification of color show the user the current color settings as a series of adjacent patches of color, as in part (a) of Fig. 13.39, or as the color of the single pixel value currently being set, as in part (b). As the user

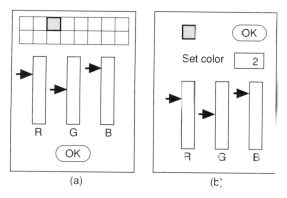

Fig. 13.39 Two common ways of setting colors. In (a), the user selects one of 16 colors to set; the selected color is designated with the thick border. The RGB slider dials control the color; OK is selected to dismiss the color control panel. In (b), the number of the color to be set is typed, and the current color is displayed in the gray-toned box. In both cases, the user must simultaneously see the actual display in order to understand the effects of the color change.

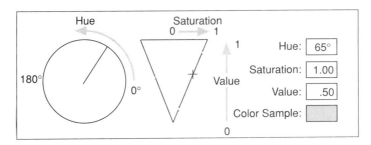

Fig. 13.40   A convenient way to specify colors in HSV space. Saturation and value are shown by the cursor in the triangular area, and hue by the line in the circular area. The user can move the line and cursor indicators on the diagrams, causing the numeric readouts to be updated. Alternatively, the user can type new values, causing the indicators to change. Slider dials for *H*, *S*, and *V* could also be added, giving the user accurate control over a single dimension at a time, without the need to type values.

manipulates the slider dials, the color sample changes. However, a person's perception of color is affected by surrounding colors and the sizes of colored areas, as shown in Color Plate II.13; hence, the color as perceived in the feedback area will probably differ from the color as perceived in the actual display. It is thus important that the user also see the actual display while the colors are being set.

13.3.7   Interpolating in Color Space

Color interpolation is necessary in at least three situations: for Gouraud shading (Section 16.2.4), for antialiasing (Section 3.17), and in blending two images together as for a fade-in, fade-out sequence. The results of the interpolation depend on the color model in which the colors are interpolated; thus, care must be taken to select an appropriate model.

   If the conversion from one color model to another transforms a straight line (representing the interpolation path) in one color model into a straight line in the other color model, then the results of linear interpolation in both models will be the same. This is the case for the RGB, CMY, YIQ, and CIE color models, all of which are related by simple affine transformations. However, a straight line in the RGB model does *not* in general transform into a straight line in either the HSV or HLS models. Color Plate II.14 shows the results of linearly interpolating between the same two colors in the HSV, HSL, RGB, and YIQ color spaces. Consider the interpolation between red and green. In RGB, red = (1, 0, 0) and green = (0, 1, 0). Their interpolation (with both weights equal to 0.5 for convenience) is (0.5, 0.5, 0). Applying algorithm RGB_To_HSV (Fig. 13.33) to this result, we have (60°, 1, 0.5). Now, representing red and green in HSV, we have (0°, 1, 1) and (120°, 1, 1). But interpolating with equal weights in HSV, we have (60°, 1, 1); thus, the value differs by 0.5 from the same interpolation in RGB.

   As a second example, consider interpolating red and cyan in the RGB and HSV models. In RGB, we start with (1, 0, 0) and (0, 1, 1), respectively, and interpolate to (0.5, 0.5, 0.5), which in HSV is represented as (UNDEFINED, 0, 0.5). In HSV, red and cyan are (0°, 1, 1) and (180°, 1, 1). Interpolating, we have (90°, 1, 1); a new hue at maximum value and saturation has been introduced, whereas the "right" result of combining equal amounts of complementary colors is a gray value. Here, again, interpolating and then transforming gives different results from transforming and then interpolating.

For Gouraud shading, any of the models can be used, because the two interpolants are generally so close together that the interpolation paths between the colors are close together as well. When two images are blended—as in a fade-in, fade-out sequence or for antialiasing—the colors may be quite distant, and an additive model, such as RGB, is appropriate. If, on the other hand, the objective is to interpolate between two colors of fixed hue (or saturation) and to maintain the fixed hue (or saturation) for all interpolated colors, then HSV or HLS is preferable. But note that a fixed-saturation interpolation in HSV or HLS is *not* seen as having exactly fixed saturation by the viewer [WARE87].

13.4 REPRODUCING COLOR

Color images are reproduced in print in a way similar to that used for monochrome images, but four sets of halftone dots are printed, one for each of the subtractive primaries, and another for black. In a process called *undercolor removal*, black replaces equal amounts of cyan, magenta, and yellow. This creates a darker black than is possible by mixing the three primaries, and hastens drying by decreasing the amounts of cyan, magenta, and yellow ink needed. The orientation of each of the grids of dots is different, so that interference patterns are not created. Color Plate II.15 shows an enlarged halftone color pattern. Our eyes spatially integrate the light reflected from adjacent dots, so that we see the color defined by the proportions of primaries in adjacent dots. This spatial integration of different colors is the same phenomenon we experience when viewing the triads of red, green, and blue dots on a color monitor.

We infer, then, that color reproduction in print and on CRTs depends on the same spatial integration used in monochrome reproduction. The monochrome dithering techniques discussed in Section 13.1.2 can also be used with color to extend the number of available colors, again at the expense of resolution. Consider a color display with 3 bits per pixel, one each for red, green, and blue. We can use a 2×2 pixel pattern area to obtain 125 different colors: each pattern can display five intensities for each of red, green, and blue, by using the halftone patterns in Fig. 13.8. This results in $5 \times 5 \times 5 = 125$ color combinations.

Not all color reproduction depends exclusively on spatial integration. For instance, xerographic color copiers, ink-jet plotters, and thermal color printers actually mix subtractive pigments on the paper's surface to obtain a small set of different colors. In xerography, the colored pigments are first deposited in three successive steps, then are heated and melted together. The inks sprayed by the plotter mix before drying. Spatial integration may be used to expand the color range further.

A related quantization problem occurs when a color image with n bits per pixel is to be displayed on a display of $m < n$ bits per pixel with no loss of spatial resolution. Here, color resolution *must* be sacrificed. In this situation, there are two key questions: Which 2^m colors should be displayed? What is the mapping from the set of 2^n colors in the image to the smaller set of 2^m colors being displayed?

The simple answers are to use a predefined set of display colors and a fixed mapping from image colors to display colors. For instance, with $m = 8$, a typical assignment is 3 bits to red and green and 2 to blue (because of the eye's lower sensitivity to blue). Thus, the 256 displayable colors are all the combinations of eight reds, eight greens, and four blues. The specific values for the red, green, and blue colors would be spaced across the range of 0.0 to 1.0 range on a ratio scale, as discussed in Section 13.1.1. For an image with 6 bits per color and hence 64 levels for each color, the 64 red colors are mapped into one of the eight displayable reds, and similarly for the greens. The 64 blue colors are mapped into just four blues.

With this solution, however, if all the blue image colors are clustered together in color space, they might all be displayed as the same blue, whereas the other three displayable blues might go unused. An adaptive scheme would take this possibility into account and would divide up the blue-value range on the basis of the distribution of values in the range. Heckbert [HECK82] describes two approaches of this type: the popularity algorithm and the median-cut algorithm.

The *popularity algorithm* creates a histogram of the image's colors, and uses the 2^m most frequent colors in the mapping. The *median-cut algorithm* recursively fits a box around the colors used in the image, splitting the box along its longer dimension at the median in that dimension. The recursion ends when 2^m boxes have been created; the centroid of each box is used as the display color for all image colors in the box. The median-cut algorithm is slower than is the popularity algorithm, but produces better results. Another way of splitting the boxes is described in [WAN88].

Creating an *accurate* color reproduction is much more difficult than is approximating colors. Two display monitors can be calibrated to create the same tristimulus values; the multistep process is described in detail in [COWA83; MEYE83]. The steps are to measure the chromaticity coordinates of the monitor phosphors, then to adjust the brightness and contrast controls of each of the monitor guns so that the same white chromaticity is produced whenever $R = G = B$, and to determine the appropriate gamma correction for each gun.

Making slides or movie film that look exactly like the image on a display is difficult, because many variables are involved. They include the gamma correction of the display and of the CRT used in the film recorder; the color of light emitted by the CRT in the film recorder; the filters used in the film recorder; the type of film used; the quality and temperature of the developing chemicals, the length of time the film is in the chemicals, and the color of light emitted by the bulb in the slide or film projector. Fortunately, all these variables can be quantified and controlled, albeit with considerable difficulty.

Controlling the color match on printed materials is also difficult; the printing process, with its cyan, magenta, yellow, and black primaries, requires careful quality control to maintain registration and ink flow. The paper texture, absorbancy, and gloss also affect the result. Complicating matters further, the simple subtractive CMY color model discussed in Section 13.3.2 cannot be used directly, because it does not take into account these complications of the printing process. More detail can be found in [STON88].

Even if extreme care is taken in color reproduction, the results may not seem to match the original. Lighting conditions and reflections from the display can cause colors with the same measured chromaticity coordinates to appear to be different. Fortunately, the purpose of the reproduction is usually (although not always) to maintain color relationships between different parts of the image, rather than to make an exact copy.

13.5   USING COLOR IN COMPUTER GRAPHICS

We use color for aesthetics, to establish a tone or mood, for realism, as a highlight, to identify associated areas as being associated, and for coding. With care, color can be used effectively for these purposes. In addition, users tend to like color, even when there is no quantitative evidence that it helps their performance. Although cost-conscious buyers may scoff at color monitors, we believe that anything that encourages people to use computers is important!

Careless use of color can make the display less useful or less attractive than a corresponding monochrome presentation. In one experiment, introduction of meaningless color reduced user performance to about one-third of what it was without color [KREB79]. Color should be employed conservatively. Any decorative use of color should be subservient to the functional use, so that the color cannot be misinterpreted as having some underlying meaning. Thus, the use of color, like all other aspects of a user–computer interface, must be tested with real users to identify and remedy problems. Of course, some individuals may have other preferences, so it is common practice to provide defaults chosen on the basis of color usage rules, with some means for the user to change the defaults. A conservative approach to color selection is to design first for a monochrome display, to ensure that color use is purely redundant. This avoids creating problems for color-deficient users and also means that the application can be used on a monochrome display. Additional information on color deficiencies is given in [MEYE88]. The color choices used in the window managers shown in Color Plates I.26 through I.29 are quite conservative. Color is not used as a unique code for button status, selected menu item, and so forth.

Many books have been written on the use of color for aesthetic purposes, including [BIRR61]; we state here just a few of the simpler rules that help to produce color harmony. The most fundamental rule of color aesthetics is to select colors according to some method, typically by traversing a smooth path in a color model or by restricting the colors to planes or hexcones in a color space. This might mean using colors of constant lightness or value. Furthermore, colors are best spaced at equal *perceptual* distances (this is not the same as being at equally spaced increments of a coordinate, and can be difficult to implement). Recall too that linear interpolation (as in Gouraud shading) between two colors produces different results in different color spaces (see Exercise 13.10 and Color Plate II.14).

A random selection of different hues and saturations is usually quite garish. Alvy Ray Smith performed an informal experiment in which a 16×16 grid was filled with randomly generated colors. Not unexpectedly, the grid was unattractive. Sorting the 256 colors according to their H, S, and V values and redisplaying them on the grid in their new order improved the appearance of the grid remarkably.

More specific instances of these rules suggest that, if a chart contains just a few colors, the complement of one of the colors should be used as the background. A neutral (gray) background should be used for an image containing many different colors, since it is both harmonious and inconspicuous. If two adjoining colors are not particularly harmonious, a thin black border can be used to set them apart. This use of borders is also more effective for the achromatic (black/white) visual channel, since shape detection is facilitated by the black outline. Some of these rules are encoded in ACE (A Color Expert), an expert system for selecting user-interface colors [MEIE88]. In general, it is good to minimize the number of different colors being used (except for shading of realistic images).

Color can be used for coding, as discussed in Chapter 9 and illustrated by Color Plate II.16. However, several cautions are in order. First, color codes can easily carry unintended meanings. Displaying the earnings of company A as red and those of company B as green might well suggest that company A is in financial trouble, because of our learned associations of colors with meanings. Bright, saturated colors stand out more strongly than do dimmer, paler colors, and may give unintended emphasis. Two elements of a display that have the same color may be seen as related by the same color code, even if they are not.

This problem often arises when color is used both to group menu items and to distinguish display elements, such as different layers of a printed circuit board or VLSI chip; for example, green display elements tend to be associated with menu items of the same color. This is one of the reasons that use of color in user-interface elements, such as menus, dialogue boxes, and window borders, should be restrained. (Another reason is to leave as many colors as possible free for the application program itself.)

A number of color usage rules are based on physiological rather than aesthetic considerations. For example, because the eye is more sensitive to spatial variation in intensity than it is to variation in chromaticity, lines, text, and other fine detail should vary from the background not just in chromaticity, but in brightness (perceived intensity) as well—especially for colors containing blue, since relatively few cones are sensitive to blue. Thus, the edge between two equal-brightness colored areas that differ only in the amount of blue will be fuzzy. On the other hand, blue-sensitive cones spread out farther on the retina than do red- and green-sensitive ones, so our peripheral color vision is better for blue (this is why many police-car flashers are now blue instead of red).

Blue and black differ very little in brightness, and are thus a particularly bad combination. Similarly, yellow on white is relatively hard to distinguish, because both colors are quite bright (see Exercise 13.11). Color plates I.28 and I.29 show a very effective use of yellow to highlight black text on a white background. The yellow contrasts very well with the black text and also stands out. In addition, the yellow highlight is not as overpowering as a black highlight with reversed text (that is, with the highlighted text in white on a black highlight), as is common on monochrome displays.

White text on a blue background provides a good contrast that is less harsh than white on black. It is good to avoid reds and greens with low saturation and luminance, as these are the colors confused by those of us who are red−green color blind, the most common form of color-perception deficiency. Meyer and Greenberg describe effective ways to choose colors for color-blind viewers [MEYE88].

The eye cannot distinguish the color of very small objects, as already remarked in connection with the YIQ NTSC color model, so color coding should not be applied to small objects. In particular, judging the color of objects subtending less than 20 to 40 minutes of arc is error-prone [BISH60, HAEU76]. An object 0.1 inches high, viewed from 24 inches (a typical viewing distance) subtends this much arc, which corresponds to about 7 pixels of height on a 1024-line display with a vertical height of 15 inches. It is clear that the color of a single pixel is quite difficult to discern (see Exercise 13.18).

The perceived color of a colored area is affected by the color of the surrounding area, as is very evident in Color Plate II.13; this effect is particularly problematic if colors are used to encode information. The effect is minimized when the surrounding areas are some shade of gray or are relatively unsaturated colors.

The color of an area can actually affect its perceived size. Cleveland and McGill discovered that a red square is perceived as larger than is a green square of equal size [CLEV83]. This effect could well cause the viewer to attach more importance to the red square than to the green ones.

If a user stares at a large area of highly saturated color for several seconds and then looks elsewhere, an afterimage of the large area will appear. This effect is disconcerting, and causes eye strain. Use of large areas of saturated colors is hence unwise. Also, large areas of different colors can appear to be at different distances from the viewer, because the index of refraction of light depends on wavelength. The eye changes its focus as the viewer's gaze moves from one colored area to another, and this change in focus gives the impression of differing depths. Red and blue, which are at opposite ends of the spectrum, have the strongest depth-disparity effect, with red appearing closer and blue more distant. Hence, simultaneously using blue for foreground objects and red for the background is unwise; the converse is fine.

With all these perils and pitfalls of color usage, is it surprising that one of our first-stated rules was to apply color conservatively?

13.6 SUMMARY

The importance of color in computer graphics will continue to increase as color monitors and color hardcopy devices become the norm in many applications. In this chapter, we have introduced those color concepts most relevant to computer graphics; for more information, see the vast literature on color, such as [BILL81; BOYN79; GREG66; HUNT87; JUDD75; WYSZ82]. More background on artistic and aesthetic issues in the use of color in computer graphics can be found in [FROM84; MARC82; MEIE88; MURC85]. The difficult problems of precisely calibrating monitors and matching the colors appearing on monitors with printed colors are discussed in [COWA83; STON88].

EXERCISES

13.1 Derive an equation for the number of intensities that can be represented by $m \times m$ pixel patterns, where each pixel has w bits.

13.2 Write the programs needed to gamma-correct a black-and-white display through a look-up table. Input parameters are γ, I_0, m, the number of intensities desired, and K, the constant in Eq. (13.5).

13.3 Write an algorithm to display a pixel array on a bilevel output device. The inputs to the algorithm are an $m \times m$ array of pixel intensities, with w bits per pixel, and an $n \times n$ growth sequence matrix. Assume that the output device has resolution of $m \cdot n \times m \cdot n$

13.4 Repeat Exercise 13.3 by using ordered dither. Now the output device has resolution $m \times m$, the same as the input array of pixel intensities.

13.5 Write an algorithm to display a filled polygon on a bilevel device by using an $n \times n$ filling pattern.

13.6 When certain patterns are used to fill a polygon being displayed on an interlaced raster display, all of the "on" bits fall on either the odd or the even scan lines, introducing a slight amount of flicker. Revise the algorithm from Exercise 13.5 to permute rows of the $n \times n$ pattern so that alternate

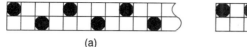   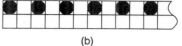

(a)   (b)

Fig. 13.41 Results obtained by using intensity level 1 from Fig. 13.8 in two ways: (a) with alternation (intensified pixels are on both scan lines), and (b) without alternation (all intensified pixels are on the same scan line).

replications of the pattern will alternate use of the odd and even scan lines. Figure 13.41 shows the results obtained by using intensity level 1 from Fig. 13.8, with and without this alternation.

13.7 Given a spectral energy distribution, how would you find the dominant wavelength, excitation purity, and luminance of the color it represents?

13.8 Plot the locus of points of the constant luminance values 0.25, 0.50, and 0.75, defined by $Y = 0.30R + 0.59G + 0.11B$, on the RGB cube, the HLS double hexcone, and the HSV hexcone.

13.9 Why are the opposite ends of the spectrum in the CIE diagram connected by a *straight* line?

13.10 Express, in terms of R, G, and B: the I of YIQ, the V of HSV, and the L of HSL. Note that I, V, and L are not the same.

13.11 Calculate in YIQ color space the luminances of the additive and subtractive primaries. Rank the primaries by luminance. This ranking gives their relative intensities, both as displayed on a black-and-white television and as perceived by our eyes.

13.12 Discuss the design of a raster display that uses HSV or HLS, instead of RGB, as its color specification.

13.13 In which color models are the rules of color harmony most easily applied?

13.14 Verify that Eq. (13.27) can be rewritten as Eq. (13.29) when $R = G = B = 1$.

13.15 If the white color used to calculate C_r, C_g, and C_b in Eq. (13.29) is given by x_w, y_w, and Y_w rather than by X_w, Y_w, and Z_w, what are the algebraic expressions for C_r, C_g, and C_b?

13.16 Rewrite the HSV-to-RGB conversion algorithm to make it more efficient. Replace the assignment statements for p, q, and t with: $vs = v * s$; $vsf = vs * f$; $p = v - vs$; $q = v - vsf$; $t = p + vsf$. Also assume that R, G, and B are in the interval $[0, 255]$, and see how many of the computations can be converted to integer.

13.17 Write a program that displays, side by side, two 16 × 16 grids. Fill each grid with colors. The left grid will have 256 colors randomly selected from HSV color space (created by using a random-number generator to choose one out of 10 equally spaced values for each of H, S, and V). The right grid contains the same 256 colors, sorted on H, S, and V. Experiment with the results obtained by varying which of H, S, and V is used as the primary sort key.

13.18 Write a program to display on a gray background small squares colored orange, red, green, blue, cyan, magenta, and yellow. Each square is separated from the others and is of size $n \times n$ pixels, where n is an input variable. How large must n be so that the colors of each square can be unambiguously judged from distances of 24 and of 48 inches? What should be the relation between the two values of n? What effect, if any, do different background colors have on this result?

13.19 Calculate the number of bits of look-up–table accuracy needed to store 256 different intensity levels given dynamic intensity ranges of 50, 100, and 200.

13.20 Write a program to interpolate linearly between two colors in RGB, HSV, and HSL. Accept the two colors as input, allowing them to be specified in any of these three models.

14

The Quest for
Visual Realism

In previous chapters, we discussed graphics techniques involving simple 2D and 3D primitives. The pictures that we produced, such as the wireframe houses of Chapter 6, represent objects that in real life are significantly more complex in both structure and appearance. In this chapter, we introduce an increasingly important application of computer graphics: creating realistic images of 3D scenes.

What is a *realistic* image? In what sense a picture, whether painted, photographed, or computer-generated, can be said to be "realistic" is a subject of much scholarly debate [HAGE86]. We use the term rather broadly to refer to a picture that captures many of the effects of light interacting with real physical objects. Thus, we treat realistic images as a continuum and speak freely of pictures, and of the techniques used to create them, as being "more" or "less" realistic. At one end of the continuum are examples of what is often called *photographic realism* (or *photorealism*). These pictures attempt to synthesize the field of light intensities that would be focused on the film plane of a camera aimed at the objects depicted. As we approach the other end of the continuum, we find images that provide successively fewer of the visual cues we shall discuss.

You should bear in mind that a more realistic picture is not necessarily a more desirable or useful one. If the ultimate goal of a picture is to convey information, then a picture that is free of the complications of shadows and reflections may well be more successful than a *tour de force* of photographic realism. In addition, in many applications of the techniques outlined in the following chapters, reality is intentionally altered for aesthetic effect or to fulfill a naive viewer's expectations. This is done for the same reasons that science-fiction films feature the sounds of weapon blasts in outer space—an impossibility in a vacuum. For example, in depicting Uranus in Color Plate II.20, Blinn shined an extra light on the

605

night side of the planet and stretched the contrast to make all features visible simultaneously—the night side of the planet would have been black otherwise. Taking liberties with physics can result in attractive, memorable, and useful pictures!

Creating realistic pictures involves a number of stages that are treated in detail in the following chapters. Although these stages are often thought of as forming a conceptual pipeline, the order in which they are performed can vary, as we shall see, depending on the algorithms used. First, models of the objects are generated using methods discussed in Chapters 11, 12, and 20. Next, a viewing specification (as developed in Chapter 6) and lighting conditions are selected. Those surfaces visible to the viewer are then determined by algorithms discussed in Chapter 15. The color assigned to each pixel in a visible surface's projection is a function of the light reflected and transmitted by the objects and is determined by methods treated in Chapter 16. The resulting picture can then be combined with previously generated ones (e.g., to reuse a complex background) by using the compositing techniques of Chapter 17. Finally, if we are producing an animated sequence, time-varying changes in the models, lighting, and viewing specifications must be defined, as discussed in Chapter 21. The process of creating images from models is often called *rendering*. The term *rasterization* is also used to refer specifically to those steps that involve determining pixel values from input geometric primitives.

This chapter presents realistic rendering from a variety of perspectives. First, we look at some of the applications in which realistic images have been used. Then, we examine, in roughly historical progression, a series of techniques that make it possible to create successively more realistic pictures. Each technique is illustrated by a picture of a standard scene with the new technique applied to it. Next, we examine the problems caused by aliasing, which must be dealt with when images are represented as discrete arrays of pixels. Finally, we conclude with suggestions about how to approach the following chapters.

14.1 WHY REALISM?

The creation of realistic pictures is an important goal in fields such as simulation, design, entertainment and advertising, research and education, and command and control.

Simulation systems present images that not only are realistic, but also change dynamically. For example, a flight simulator shows the view that would be seen from the cockpit of a moving plane. To produce the effect of motion, the system generates and displays a new, slightly different view many times per second. Simulators such as those shown in Color Plate I.5 have been used to train the pilots of spacecraft, airplanes, and boats—and, more recently, drivers of cars.

Designers of 3D objects such as automobiles, airplanes, and buildings want to see how their preliminary designs look. Creating realistic computer-generated images is often an easier, less expensive, and more effective way to see preliminary results than is building models and prototypes, and also allows more alternative designs to be considered. If the design work itself is also computer-based, a digital description of the object may already be available to use in creating the images. Ideally, the designer can also interact with the displayed image to modify the design. Color Plate II.17 shows an image produced by an automotive-design system to determine what a car will look like under a variety of lighting conditions. Realistic graphics is often coupled with programs that analyze other aspects of the object being designed, such as its mass properties or its response to stress.

Computer-generated imagery is used extensively in the entertainment world, both in traditional animated cartoons and in realistic and surrealistic images for logos, advertisements, and science-fiction movies (see Color Plates D, F, I.11, I.12, and II.18). Computer-generated cartoons can mimic traditional animation, but can also transcend manual techniques by introducing more complicated motion and richer or more realistic imagery. Some complex realistic images can be produced at less cost than filming them from physical models of the objects. Other images have been generated that would have been extremely difficult or impossible to stage with real models. Special-purpose hardware and software created for use in entertainment include sophisticated paint systems and real-time systems for generating special effects and for combining images. As technology improves, home and arcade video games generate increasingly realistic images.

Realistic images are becoming an essential tool in research and education. A particularly important example is the use of graphics in molecular modeling, as shown in Color Plate II.19. It is interesting how the concept of realism is stretched here: The realistic depictions are not of "real" atoms, but rather of stylized ball-and-stick and volumetric models that allow larger structures to be built than are feasible with physical models, and that permit special effects, such as animated vibrating bonds and color changes representing reactions. On a macroscopic scale, movies made at JPL show NASA space-probe missions, depicted in Color Plate II.20.

Another application for realistic imagery is in command and control, in which the user needs to be informed about and to control the complex process represented by the picture. Unlike simulations, which attempt to mimic what a user would actually see and feel in the simulated situation, command and control applications often create symbolic displays that emphasize certain data and suppress others to aid in decision making

14.2 FUNDAMENTAL DIFFICULTIES

A fundamental difficulty in achieving total visual realism is the complexity of the real world. Observe the richness of your environment. There are many surface textures, subtle color gradations, shadows, reflections, and slight irregularities in the surrounding objects. Think of patterns on wrinkled cloth, the texture of skin, tousled hair, scuff marks on the floor, and chipped paint on the wall. These all combine to create a "real" visual experience. The computational costs of simulating these effects can be high: Creating pictures such as those of Color Plates A–H can take many minutes or even hours on powerful computers.

A more easily met subgoal in the quest for realism is to provide sufficient information to let the viewer understand the 3D spatial relationships among several objects. This subgoal can be achieved at a significantly lower cost and is a common requirement in CAD and in many other application areas. Although highly realistic images convey 3D spatial relationships, they usually convey much more as well. For example, Fig 14.1, a simple line drawing, suffices to persuade us that one building is partially behind the other. There is no need to show building surfaces filled with shingles and bricks, or shadows cast by the buildings. In fact, in some contexts, such extra detail may only distract the viewer's attention from more important information being depicted.

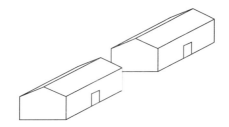

Fig. 14.1 Line drawing of two houses.

One long-standing difficulty in depicting spatial relationships is that most display devices are 2D. Therefore, 3D objects must be projected into 2D, with considerable attendant loss of information—which can sometimes create ambiguities in the image. Some of the techniques introduced in this chapter can be used to add back information of the type normally found in our visual environment, so that human depth-perception mechanisms resolve the remaining ambiguities properly.

Consider the Necker cube illusion of Fig. 14.2(a), a 2D projection of a cube; we do not know whether it represents the cube in part (b) or that in part (c) of this figure. Indeed, the viewer can easily "flip-flop" between the alternatives, because Fig. 14.2(a) does not contain enough visual information for an unambiguous interpretation.

The more the viewers know about the object being displayed, the more readily they can form what Gregory calls an *object hypothesis* [GREG70]. Figure 14.3 shows the Schröder stairway illusion—are we looking down a stairway, or looking up from underneath it? We are likely to choose the former interpretation, probably because we see stairways under our feet more frequently than over our heads and therefore "know" more about stairways viewed from above. With a small stretch of the imagination, however, we can visualize the alternative interpretation of the figure. Nevertheless, with a blink of the eye, a reversal occurs for most viewers and the stairway again appears to be viewed from above. Of course, additional context, such as a person standing on the steps, will resolve the ambiguity.

In the following sections, we list some of the steps along the path toward realistic images. The path has actually been a set of intertwined trails, rather than a single straight road, but we have linearized it for the sake of simplicity, providing a purely descriptive introduction to the detailed treatment in subsequent chapters. We mention first techniques applicable to static line drawings. These methods concentrate on ways to present the 3D spatial relationships among several objects on a 2D display. Next come techniques for

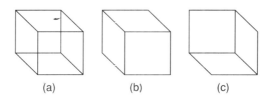

(a) (b) (c)

Fig. 14.2 The Necker cube illusion. Is the cube in (a) oriented like the cube in (b) or like that in (c)?

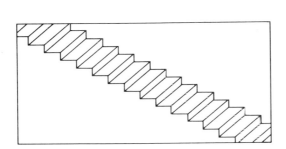

Fig. 14.3 The Schröder stairway illusion. Is the stairway being viewed from above or from below?

shaded images, made possible by raster graphics hardware, that concentrate on the interaction of objects with light. These are followed by the issues of increased model complexity and dynamics, applicable to both line and shaded pictures. Finally, we discuss the possibilities of true 3D images, advances in display hardware, and the future place of picture generation in the context of full, interactive environmental synthesis.

14.3 RENDERING TECHNIQUES FOR LINE DRAWINGS

In this section, we focus on a subgoal of realism: showing 3D depth relationships on a 2D surface. This goal is served by the planar geometric projections defined in Chapter 6.

14.3.1 Multiple Orthographic Views

The easiest projections to create are parallel orthographics, such as plan and elevation views, in which the projection plane is perpendicular to a principal axis. Since depth information is discarded, plan and elevations are typically shown together, as with the top, front, and side views of a block letter ''L'' in Fig. 14.4. This particular drawing is not difficult to understand; however, understanding drawings of complicated manufactured parts from a set of such views may require many hours of study. Training and experience sharpen one's interpretive powers, of course, and familiarity with the types of objects being represented hastens the formulation of a correct object hypothesis. Still, scenes as complicated as that of our ''standard scene'' shown in Color Plate II.21 are often confusing when shown in only three such projections. Although a single point may be unambiguously located from three mutually perpendicular orthographics, multiple points and lines may conceal one another when so projected.

Fig. 14.4 Front, top, and side orthographic projections of the block letter ''L.''

14.3.2   Axonometric and Oblique Projections

In axonometric and oblique projections, a point's z coordinate influences its x and y coordinates in the projection, as exemplified by Color Plate II.22. These projections provide constant foreshortening, and therefore lack the convergence of parallel lines and the decreasing size of objects with increasing distance that perspective projection provides.

14.3.3   Perspective Projections

In perspective projections, an object's size is scaled in inverse proportion to its distance from the viewer. The perspective projection of a cube shown in Fig. 14.5 reflects this scaling. There is still ambiguity, however; the projection could just as well be a picture frame, or the parallel projection of a truncated pyramid, or the perspective projection of a rectangular parallelepiped with two equal faces. If one's object hypothesis is a truncated pyramid, then the smaller square represents the face closer to the viewer; if the object hypothesis is a cube or rectangular parallelepiped, then the smaller square represents the face farther from the viewer.

   Our interpretation of perspective projections is often based on the assumption that a smaller object is farther away. In Fig. 14.6, we would probably assume that the larger house is nearer to the viewer. However, the house that appears larger (a mansion, perhaps) may actually be more distant than the one that appears smaller (a cottage, for example), at least as long as there are no other cues, such as trees and windows. When the viewer knows that the projected objects have many parallel lines, perspective further helps to convey depth, because the parallel lines seem to converge at their vanishing points. This convergence may actually be a stronger depth cue than the effect of decreasing size. Color Plate II.23 shows a perspective projection of our standard scene.

14.3.4   Depth Cueing

The depth (distance) of an object can be represented by the intensity of the image: Parts of objects that are intended to appear farther from the viewer are displayed at lower intensity (see Color Plate II.24). This effect is known as *depth cueing*. Depth cueing exploits the fact that distant objects appear dimmer than closer objects, especially if seen through haze. Such effects can be sufficiently convincing that artists refer to the use of changes in intensity (as well as in texture, sharpness, and color) to depict distance as *aerial perspective*. Thus, depth cueing may be seen as a simplified version of the effects of atmospheric attenuation.

 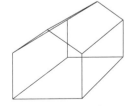

Fig. 14.5 Perspective projection of a cube.

Fig. 14.6 Perspective projection of two houses.

In vector displays, depth cueing is implemented by interpolating the intensity of the beam along a vector as a function of its starting and ending z coordinates. Color graphics systems usually generalize the technique to support interpolating between the color of a primitive and a user-specified depth-cue color, which is typically the color of the background. To restrict the effect to a limited range of depths, PHIGS+ allows the user to specify front and back depth-cueing planes between which depth cueing is to occur. A separate scale factor associated with each plane indicates the proportions of the original color and the depth-cue color to be used in front of the front plane and behind the back plane. The color of points between the planes is linearly interpolated between these two values. The eye's intensity resolution is lower than its spatial resolution, so depth cueing is not useful for accurately depicting small differences in distance. It is quite effective, however, in depicting large differences, or as an exaggerated cue in depicting small ones.

14.3.5   Depth Clipping

Further depth information can be provided by *depth clipping*. The back clipping plane is placed so as to cut through the objects being displayed, as shown in Color Plate II.25. Partially clipped objects are then known by the viewer to be cut by the clipping plane. A front clipping plane may also be used. By allowing the position of one or both planes to be varied dynamically, the system can convey more depth information to the viewer. Back-plane depth clipping can be thought of as a special case of depth cueing: In ordinary depth cueing, intensity is a smooth function of z; in depth clipping, it is a step function. Color Plate II.25 combines both techniques. A technique related to depth clipping is highlighting all points on the object intersected by some plane. This technique is especially effective when the slicing plane is shown moving through the object dynamically, and has even been used to help illustrate depth along a fourth dimension [BANC77].

14.3.6   Texture

Simple vector textures, such as cross-hatching, may be applied to an object. These textures follow the shape of an object and delineate it more clearly. Texturing one of a set of otherwise identical faces can clarify a potentially ambiguous projection. Texturing is especially useful in perspective projections, as it adds yet more lines whose convergence and foreshortening may provide useful depth cues.

14.3.7   Color

Color may be used symbolically to distinguish one object from another, as in Color Plate II.26, in which each object has been assigned a different color. Color can also be used in line drawings to provide other information. For example, the color of each vector of an object may be determined by interpolating colors that encode the temperatures at the vector's endpoints.

14.3.8   Visible-Line Determination

The last line-drawing technique we mention is *visible-line determination* or *hidden-line removal*, which results in the display of only visible (i.e., unobscured) lines or parts of lines. Only surfaces, bounded by edges (lines), can obscure other lines. Thus, objects that are to block others must be modeled either as collections of surfaces or as solids.

Color Plate II.27 shows the usefulness of hidden-line removal. Because hidden-line–removed views conceal *all* the internal structure of opaque objects, they are not necessarily the most effective way to show depth relations. Hidden-line–removed views convey less depth information than do exploded and cutaway views. Showing hidden lines as dashed lines can be a useful compromise.

14.4   RENDERING TECHNIQUES FOR SHADED IMAGES

The techniques mentioned in Section 14.3 can be used to create line drawings on both vector and raster displays. The techniques introduced in this section exploit the ability of raster devices to display shaded areas. When pictures are rendered for raster displays, problems are introduced by the relatively coarse grid of pixels on which smooth contours and shading must be reproduced. The simplest ways to render shaded pictures fall prey to the problem of aliasing, first encountered in Section 3.17. In Section 14.10, we introduce the theory behind aliasing, and explain how to combat aliasing through antialiasing. Because of the fundamental role that antialiasing plays in producing high-quality pictures, all the pictures in this section have been created with antialiasing.

14.4.1   Visible-Surface Determination

By analogy to visible-line determination, *visible-surface determination* or *hidden-surface removal,* entails displaying only those parts of surfaces that are visible to the viewer. As we have seen, simple line drawings can often be understood without visible-line determination. When there are few lines, those in front may not seriously obstruct our view of those behind them. In raster graphics, on the other hand, if surfaces are rendered as opaque areas, then visible-surface determination is essential for the picture to make sense. Color Plate II.28 shows an example in which all faces of an object are painted the same color.

14.4.2   Illumination and Shading

A problem with Color Plate II.28 is that each object appears as a flat silhouette. Our next step toward achieving realism is to shade the visible surfaces. Ultimately, each surface's appearance should depend on the types of light sources illuminating it, its properties (color, texture, reflectance), and its position and orientation with respect to the light sources, viewer, and other surfaces.

In many real visual environments, a considerable amount of *ambient light* impinges from all directions. Ambient light is the easiest kind of light source to model, because in a simple lighting model it is assumed to produce constant illumination on all surfaces, regardless of their position or orientation. Using ambient light by itself produces very unrealistic images, however, since few real environments are illuminated solely by uniform ambient light. Color Plate II.28 is an example of a picture shaded this way.

A *point source,* whose rays emanate from a single point, can approximate a small incandescent bulb. A *directional source,* whose rays all come from the same direction, can be used to represent the distant sun by approximating it as an infinitely distant point source.

Modeling these sources requires additional work because their effect depends on the surface's orientation. If the surface is *normal* (perpendicular) to the incident light rays, it is brightly illuminated; the more oblique the surface is to the light rays, the less its illumination. This variation in illumination is, of course, a powerful cue to the 3D structure of an object. Finally, a *distributed* or *extended source,* whose surface area emits light, such as a bank of fluorescent lights, is even more complex to model, since its light comes from neither a single direction nor a single point. Color Plate II.29 shows the effect of illuminating our scene with ambient and point light sources, and shading each polygon separately.

14.4.3   Interpolated Shading

Interpolated shading is a technique in which shading information is computed for each polygon vertex and interpolated across the polygons to determine the shading at each pixel. This method is especially effective when a polygonal object description is intended to approximate a curved surface. In this case, the shading information computed at each vertex can be based on the surface's actual orientation at that point and is used for all of the polygons that share that vertex. Interpolating among these values across a polygon approximates the smooth changes in shade that occur across a curved, rather than planar, surface.

Even objects that are supposed to be polyhedral, rather than curved, can benefit from interpolated shading, since the shading information computed for each vertex of a polygon may differ, although typically much less dramatically than for a curved object. When shading information is computed for a true polyhedral object, the value determined for a polygon's vertex is used only for that polygon and not for others that share the vertex. Color Plate II.30 shows Gouraud shading, a kind of interpolated shading discussed in Section 16.2.

14.4.4   Material Properties

Realism is further enhanced if the *material properties* of each object are taken into account when its shading is determined. Some materials are dull and disperse reflected light about equally in all directions, like a piece of chalk; others are shiny and reflect light only in certain directions relative to the viewer and light source, like a mirror. Color Plate II.31 shows what our scene looks like when some objects are modeled as shiny. Color Plate II.32 uses Phong shading, a more accurate interpolated shading method (Section 16.2).

14.4.5   Modeling Curved Surfaces

Although interpolated shading vastly improves the appearance of an image, the object geometry is still polygonal. Color Plate II.33 uses object models that include curved surfaces. Full shading information is computed at each pixel in the image.

14.4.6   Improved Illumination and Shading

One of the most important reasons for the "unreal" appearance of most computer graphics images is the failure to model accurately the many ways that light interacts with objects.

Color Plate II.34 uses better illumination models. Sections 16.7–13 discuss progress toward the design of efficient, physically correct illumination models, resulting in pictures such as Color Plates III.19–III.29 and the jacket of this book (Color Plate I.9).

14.4.7 Texture

Object texture not only provides additional depth cues, as discussed in Section 14.3.6, but also can mimic the surface detail of real objects. Color Plates II.35 and II.36 show a variety of ways in which texture may be simulated, ranging from varying the surface's color (as was done with the patterned ball), to actually deforming the surface geometry (as was done with the striated torus and crumpled cone in Color Plate II.36).

14.4.8 Shadows

We can introduce further realism by reproducing shadows cast by objects on one another. Note that this technique is the first we have met in which the appearance of an object's visible surfaces is affected by other objects. Color Plate II.36 shows the shadows cast by the lamp at the rear of the scene. Shadows enhance realism and provide additional depth cues: If object A casts a shadow on surface B, then we know that A is between B and a direct or reflected light source. A point light source casts sharp shadows, because from any point it is either totally visible or invisible. An extended light source casts "soft" shadows, since there is a smooth transition from those points that see all of the light source, through those that see only part of it, to those that see none of it.

14.4.9 Transparency and Reflection

Thus far, we have dealt with opaque surfaces only. Transparent surfaces can also be useful in picture making. Simple models of transparency do not include the refraction (bending) of light through a transparent solid. Lack of refraction can be a decided advantage, however, if transparency is being used not so much to simulate reality as to reveal an object's inner geometry. More complex models include refraction, diffuse translucency, and the attenuation of light with distance. Similarly, a model of light reflection may simulate the sharp reflections of a perfect mirror reflecting another object or the diffuse reflections of a less highly polished surface. Color Plate II.37 shows the effect of reflection from the floor and teapot; Color Plates III.7 and III.10 show transparency.

Like modeling shadows, modeling transparency or reflection requires knowledge of other surfaces besides the surface being shaded. Furthermore, refractive transparency is the first effect we have mentioned that requires objects actually to be modeled as solids rather than just as surfaces! We must know something about the materials through which a light ray passes and the distance it travels to model its refraction properly.

14.4.10 Improved Camera Models

All the pictures shown so far are based on a camera model with a pinhole lens and an infinitely fast shutter: All objects are in sharp focus and represent the world at one instant in time. It is possible to model more accurately the way that we (and cameras) see the world.

For example, by modeling the focal properties of lenses, we can produce pictures, such as Color Plates II.38 and II.39, that show *depth of field*: Some parts of objects are in focus, whereas closer and farther parts are out of focus. Other techniques allow the use of special effects, such as fish-eye lenses. The lack of depth-of-field effects is responsible in part for the surreal appearance of many early computer-generated pictures.

Moving objects look different from stationary objects in a picture taken with a regular still or movie camera. Because the shutter is open for a finite period of time, visible parts of moving objects are blurred across the film plane. This effect, called *motion blur*, is simulated in Color Plates III.16 and IV.14. Motion blur not only captures the effects of motion in stills, but is of crucial importance in producing high-quality animation, as described in Chapter 21.

14.5 IMPROVED OBJECT MODELS

Independent of the rendering technology used, the search for realism has concentrated in part on ways of building more convincing models, both static and dynamic. Some researchers have developed models of special kinds of objects such as gases, waves, mountains, and trees; see, for example, Color Plates IV.11–IV.21. Other investigators have concentrated on automating the positioning of large numbers of objects, such as trees in a forest, which would be too tedious to do by hand (Color Plate IV.25). These techniques are covered in Chapter 20.

14.6 DYNAMICS

By *dynamics,* we mean changes that spread across a sequence of pictures, including changes in position, size, material properties, lighting, and viewing specification—indeed, changes in any parts of the scene or the techniques applied to it. The benefits of dynamics can be examined independently of the progression toward more realistic static images.

Perhaps the most popular kind of dynamics is motion dynamics, ranging from simple transformations performed under user control to complex animation as described in Chapter 21. Motion has been an important part of computer graphics since the field's inception. In the early days of slow raster graphics hardware, motion capability was one of the strong competitive selling points of vector graphics systems. If a series of projections of the same object, each from a slightly different viewpoint around the object, is displayed in rapid succession, then the object appears to rotate. By integrating the information across the views, the viewer creates an object hypothesis.

A perspective projection of a rotating cube, for instance, provides several types of information. There is the series of different projections, which are themselves useful. This is supplemented by the motion effect, in which the maximum linear velocity of points near the center of rotation is lower than that of points distant from the center of rotation. This difference can help to clarify the relative distance of a point from the center of rotation. Also, the changing sizes of different parts of the cube as they change distance under perspective projection provide additional cues about the depth relationships. Motion becomes even more powerful when it is under the interactive control of the viewer. By selectively transforming an object, viewers may be able to form an object hypothesis more quickly.

In contrast to the use of simple transformations to clarify complex models, surprisingly simple models look extremely convincing if they move in a realistic fashion. For example, just a few points positioned at key parts of a human model, when moved naturally, can provide a convincing illusion of a person in motion. The points themselves do not "look like" a person, but they do inform the viewer that a person is present. It is also well known that objects in motion can be rendered with less detail than is needed to represent static objects, because the viewer has more difficulty picking out details when an object is moving. Television viewers, for example, are often surprised to discover how poor and grainy an individual television frame appears.

14.7 STEREOPSIS

All the techniques we have discussed thus far present the same image to both eyes of the viewer. Now conduct an experiment: Look at your desk or table top first with one eye, then with the other. The two views differ slightly because our eyes are separated from each other by a few inches, as shown in Fig. 14.7. The *binocular disparity* caused by this separation provides a powerful depth cue called *stereopsis* or *stereo vision*. Our brain fuses the two separate images into one that is interpreted as being in 3D. The two images are called a *stereo pair*; stereo pairs were used in the stereo viewers popular around the turn of the century, and are used today in the common toy, the View-Master. Color Plate II.19 shows a stereo pair of a molecule. You can fuse the two images into one 3D image by viewing them such that each eye sees only one image; you can do this, for example, by placing a stiff piece of paper between the two images perpendicular to the page. Some people can see the effect without any need for the piece of paper, and a small number of people cannot see it at all.

A variety of other techniques exists for providing different images to each eye, including glasses with polarizing filters and holography. Some of these techniques make possible true 3D images that occupy space, rather than being projected on a single plane. These displays can provide an additional 3D depth cue: Closer objects actually are closer,

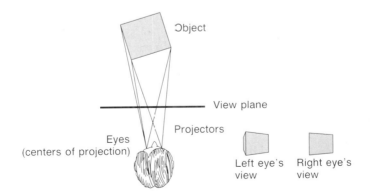

Fig. 14.7 Binocular disparity.

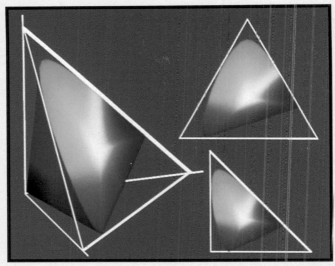

Plate II.1 Several views of the $X + Y + Z = 1$ plane of CIE space. Left: the plane embedded in CIE space. Top right: a view perpendicular to the plane. Bottom right: the projection onto the (X, Y) plane (that is, the $Z = 0$ plane), which is the chromaticity diagram. (Courtesy of Barbara Meier, Brown University.)

Plate II.2 The CIE chromaticity diagram, showing typical color gamuts for an offset printing press, a color monitor, and for slide film. The print colors represent the Graphics Arts Technical Foundation S.W.O.P. standard colors measured under a graphic arts light with a color temperature of 5000° K. The color monitor is a Barco CTVM 3/51 with a white point set to 6500° K and the slide film is Kodak Ektachrome 5017 ISO 64 as characterized under CIE source A: a 2653° K black body that closely approximates a Tungsten lamp. The ×, circle, and square indicate the white points for the print, color monitor, and film gamuts, respectively. (Courtesy of M. Stone, Xerox Palo Alto Research Center. Film gamut measured by A. Paeth, Computer Graphics Lab, University of Waterloo: see also the first appendix of [PAET89].)

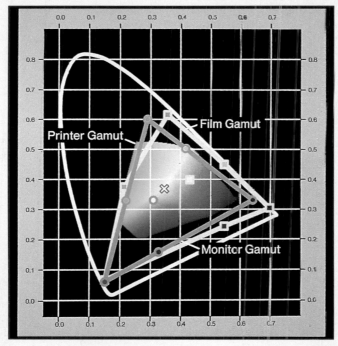

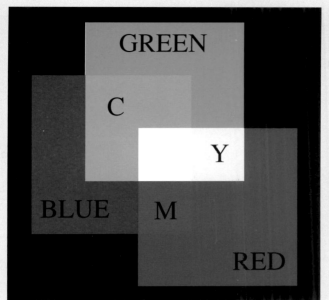

Plate II.3 Additive colors. Red plus green form yellow, red plus blue form magenta, green plus blue form cyan, red plus green plus blue form white.

Plate II.4 The RGB color space, viewed looking along the main diagonal from white to black. Only the black vertex is invisible. (Courtesy of David Small, Visible Language Workshop, MIT Media Lab, Cambridge, MA 02139. © MIT, 1989.)

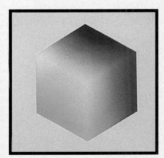

Plate II.5 An interior subcube of the RGB color space. The gray vertex is at (0.5, 0.5, 0.5) Hence the subcube is half the height, width, and depth of the entire space shown in Color Plate II.4. (Courtesy of David Small, Visible Language Workshop, MIT Media Lab, Cambridge, MA 02139. © MIT, 1989.)

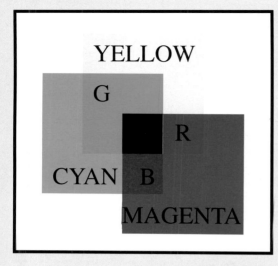

Plate II.6 Subtractive colors. Yellow and magenta subtracted from white form red, yellow and cyan subtracted from white form green, cyan and magenta subtracted from white form blue.

Plate II.7 The HSV color space. (Courtesy of David Small, Visible Language Workshop, MIT Media Lab, Cambridge, MA 02139. © MIT, 1989.)

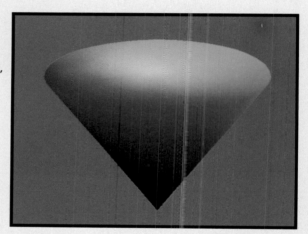

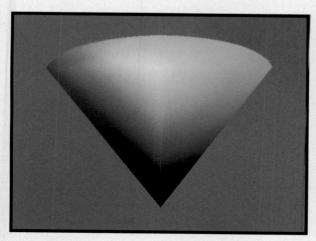

Plate II.8 A vertical cross-section slice of HSV space along the V axis. (Courtesy of David Small, Visible Language Workshop, MIT Media Lab, Cambridge, MA 02139. © MIT, 1989.)

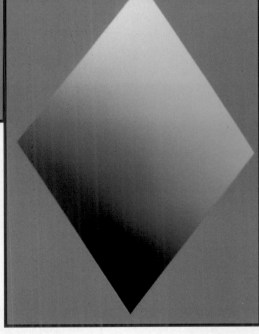

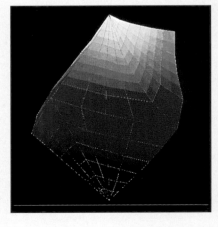

Plate II.9 The HLS color space. (Courtesy of David Small, Visible Language Workshop, MIT Media Lab, Cambridge, MA 02139. © MIT, 1989.)

Plate II.10 A vertical cross-section slice of HLS space along the L axis. (Courtesy of David Small, Visible Language Workshop, MIT Media Lab, Cambridge, MA 02139. © MIT, 1989.)

Plate II.11 The HVC color space. (Courtesy of Tektronix, Inc.)

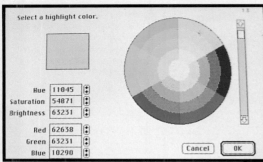

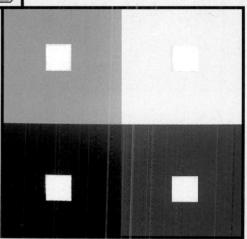

Plate II.13 The same yellow surrounded by different background colors appears to be different shades of yellow.

▼

▲

Plate II.12 An interaction technique used on the Macintosh to specify colors in HSV space. Hue and saturation are shown in the circular area, and value by the slider dial. The user can move the mark in the circular area and change the slider dial, or can type in new HSV or RGB values. The square color area (upper left) shows the current color and the new color. In this picture, taken from a color monitor driven by a 4-bit-per-pixel bit map, many of the colors are created by dithering (see Section 13.4). (Courtesy of Apple Computer, Inc., © 1984.)

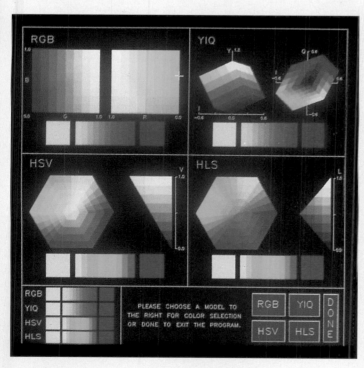

Plate II.14 An interactive program that allows the user to specify and interpolate colors in four different color spaces: RGB, YIQ, HSV, and HLS. The starting and ending colors for a linear interpolation are specified by pointing at the various projections of the color spaces. The interpolation is shown below each color space, and together for comparison in the lower left. (Courtesy of Paul Charlton, The George Washington University.)

Plate II.15 An enlarged halftone color picture. Individual dots of cyan, magenta, yellow, and black combine to create a broad gamut of colors.

Plate II.16 A pseudo-color image showing the topography of Venus. The color scale on the left indicates altitudes from –2 km to + 2 km above or below an average radius for Venus of 6052 km. Data were calculated by the Lunar and Planetary Institute from radar altimetry observations by NASA's Pioneer Venus Orbiter spacecraft. The image was created with the National Space Science Data Center Graphics System. (Courtesy of Lloyd Treinish, NASA Goddard Space Flight Center.)

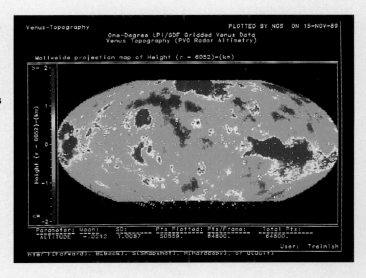

Plate II.17 Chevrolet Camaro lit by five lights with Warn's lighting controls. (Courtesy of David R. Warn, General Motors Research Laboratories.)

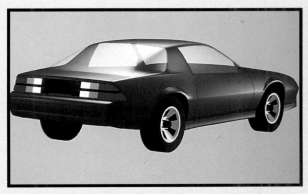

Plate II.18 *'87–'88 NBC Network Package.* By James Dixon (animator) and Glenn Entis (producer), Pacific Data Images, Sunnyvale, CA, for Marks Communications.

Plate II.19 Stereo pair of Polio virus capsid, imaged by placing a sphere of 0.5 nm radius at each alpha carbon position. One pentamer is removed to reveal the interior. Coordinates courtesy of J. Hogle. (Courtesy of David Goodsell and Arthur J. Olson. Copyright © 1989, Research Institute of Scripps Clinic.)

Plate II.20 Simulated flyby of Uranus with rings and orbit. (Courtesy of Jim Blinn, Computer Graphics Lab, Jet Propulsion Lab, California Institute of Technology.)

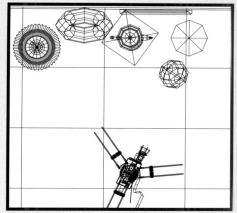

Plate II.21 *Shutterbug.* Living room scene with movie camera. Orthographic projections (Sections 6.1.2 and 14.3.1). (a) Plan view. (b) Front view. (c) Side view. Polygonal models generated from spline patches. Note the "patch cracks" (Section 11.3.5) visible along the entire right front side of the teapot, and how they cause shading discontinuities in the polygon-mesh interpolated-shading models used in Color Plates II.30–II.32. (Copyright © 1990, Pixar. Rendered by Thomas Williams and H.B. Siegel using Pixar's PhotoRealistic RenderMan™ software.)

(a)

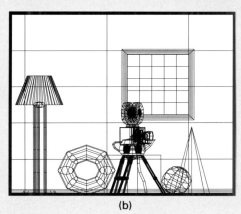

(b)

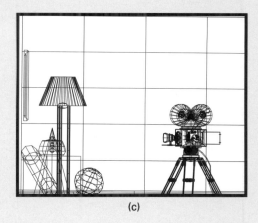

(c)

Plate II.22 *Shutterbug.* Axonometric projection (Sections 6.1.2 and 14.3.2). (Copyright © 1990, Pixar. Rendered by Thomas Williams and H.B. Siegel using Pixar's PhotoRealistic RenderMan™ software.)

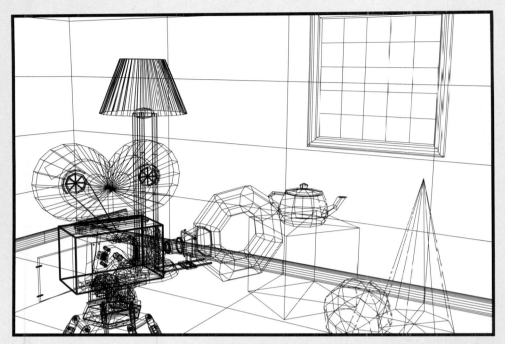

Plate II.23 *Shutterbug.* Perspective projection (Sections 6.1.1 and 14.3.3). (Copyright © 1990, Pixar. Rendered by Thomas Williams and H.B. Siegel using Pixar's PhotoRealistic RenderMan™ software.)

Plate II.24 *Shutterbug.* Depth cueing (Sections 14.3.4 and 16.1.3). (Copyright © 1990, Pixar. Rendered by Thomas Williams and H.B. Siegel using Pixar's PhotoRealistic RenderMan™ software.)

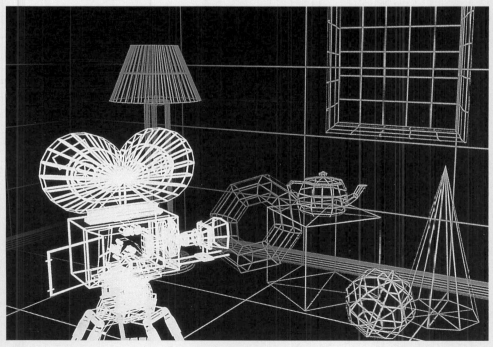

Plate II.25 *Shutterbug.* Depth clipping (Section 14.3.5). (Copyright © 1990, Pixar. Rendered by Thomas Williams and H.B. Siegel using Pixar's PhotoRealistic RenderMan™ software.)

Plate II.26 *Shutterbug.* Colored vectors (Section 14.3.7). (Copyright © 1990, Pixar. Rendered by Thomas Williams and H.B. Siegel using Pixar's PhotoRealistic RenderMan™ software.)

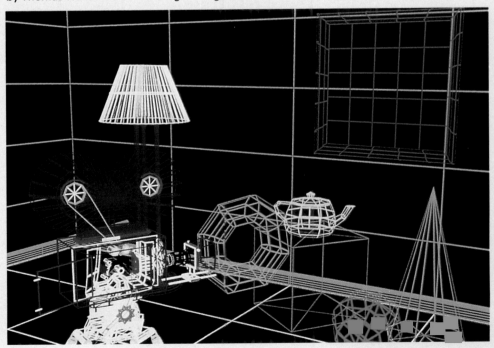

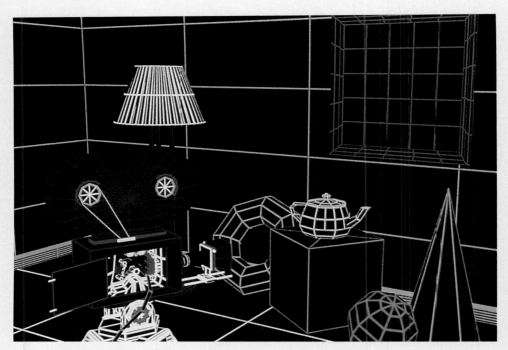

Plate II.27 *Shutterbug.* Visible-line determination (Section 14.3.8). (Copyright © 1990, Pixar. Rendered by Thomas Williams and H.B. Siegel using Pixar's PhotoRealistic RenderMan™ software.)

Plate II.28 *Shutterbug.* Visible-surface determination with ambient illumination only (Sections 14.4.1 and 16.1.1). (Copyright © 1990, Pixar. Rendered by Thomas Williams and H.B. Siegel using Pixar's PhotoRealistic RenderMan™ software.)

Plate II.29 *Shutterbug.* Individually shaded polygons with diffuse reflection (Sections 14.4.2 and 16.2.3). (Copyright © 1990, Pixar. Rendered by Thomas Williams and H.B. Siegel using Pixar's PhotoRealistic RenderMan™ software.)

Plate II.30 *Shutterbug.* Gouraud shaded polygons with diffuse reflection (Sections 14.4.3 and 16.2.4). (Copyright © 1990, Pixar. Rendered by Thomas Williams and H.B. Siegel using Pixar's PhotoRealistic RenderMan™ software.)

Plate II.31 *Shutterbug.* Gouraud shaded polygons with specular reflection (Sections 14.4.4 and 16.2.5). (Copyright © 1990, Pixar. Rendered by Thomas Williams and H.B. Siegel using Pixar's PhotoRealistic RenderMan™ software.)

Plate II.32 *Shutterbug.* Phong shaded polygons with specular reflection (Sections 14.4.4 and 16.2.5). (Copyright © 1990, Pixar. Rendered by Thomas Williams and H.B. Siegel using Pixar's PhotoRealistic RenderMan™ software.)

Plate II.33 *Shutterbug.* Curved surfaces with specular reflection (Section 14.4.5). (Copyright © 1990, Pixar. Rendered by Thomas Williams and H.B. Siegel using Pixar's PhotoRealistic RenderMan™ software.)

Plate II.34 *Shutterbug.* Improved illumination model and multiple lights (Sections 14.4.6 and 16.1). (Copyright © 1990, Pixar. Rendered by Thomas Williams and H.B. Siegel using Pixar's PhotoRealistic RenderMan™ software.)

Plate II.35 *Shutterbug.* Texture mapping (Sections 14.4.7, 16.3.2, 17.4.2, and 17.4.3). (Copyright © 1990, Pixar. Rendered by Thomas Williams and H.B. Siegel using Pixar's PhotoRealistic RenderMan™ software.)

Plate II.36 *Shutterbug.* Displacement mapping (Sections 14.4.7 and 16.3.4) and shadows (Sections 14.4.8 and 16.4). (Copyright © 1990, Pixar. Rendered by Thomas Williams and H.B. Siegel using Pixar's PhotoRealistic RenderMan™ software.)

Plate II.37 Shutterbug. Reflection mapping (Sections 14.4.9 and 16.6). (Copyright © 1990, Pixar. Rendered by Thomas Williams and H.B. Siegel using Pixar's PhotoRealistic RenderMan™ software.)

(a)

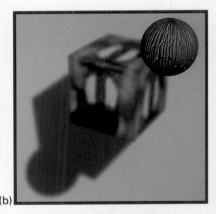

(b)

Plate II.38 Depth of field, implemented by postprocessing (Sections 14.4.10 and 16.10). (a) Focused at cube (550 mm), f/11 aperture. (b) Focused at sphere (290 mm), f/11 aperture. (Courtesy of Michael Potmesil and Indranil Chakravarty, RPI.)

Plate II.39 Depth of field, implemented by distributed ray tracing (Sections 14.4.10 and 16.12.4). (By Robert Cook, Thomas Porter, and Loren Carpenter. Copyright © Pixar 1984. All rights reserved.)

just as in real life, so the viewer's eyes focus differently on different objects, depending on each object's proximity. Methods for producing and viewing stereo images are examined in more detail in Section 18.11.5; the mathematics of stereo projection is described in Exercise 6.27.

14.8 IMPROVED DISPLAYS

In addition to improvements in the software used to design and render objects, improvements in the displays themselves have heightened the illusion of reality. The history of computer graphics is in part that of a steady improvement in the visual quality achieved by display devices. Still, a modern monitor's color gamut and its dynamic intensity range are both a small subset of what we can see. We have a long way to go before the image on our display can equal the crispness and contrast of a well-printed professional photograph! Limited display resolution makes it impossible to reproduce extremely fine detail. Artifacts such as a visible phosphor pattern, glare from the screen, geometric distortion, and the stroboscopic effect of frame-rate flicker are ever-present reminders that we are viewing a display. The display's relatively small size, compared with our field of vision, also helps to remind us that the display is a window on a world, rather than a world itself.

14.9 INTERACTING WITH OUR OTHER SENSES

Perhaps the final step toward realism is the integration of realistic imagery with information presented to our other senses. Computer graphics has a long history of programs that rely on a variety of input devices to allow user interaction. Flight simulators are a current example of the coupling of graphics with realistic engine sounds and motion, all offered in a mocked-up cockpit to create an entire environment. The head-worn simulator of Color Plate I.16 monitors head motion, making possible another important 3D depth cue called *head-motion parallax*: when the user moves her head from side to side, perhaps to try to see more of a partially hidden object, the view changes as it would in real life. Other active work on head-mounted displays centers on the exploration of *virtual worlds*, such as the insides of molecules or of buildings that have not yet been constructed [CHUN89].

Many current arcade games feature a car or plane that the player rides, moving in time to a simulation that includes synthesized or digitized images, sound, and force feedback, as shown in Color Plate I.7. This use of additional output and input modalities points the way to systems of the future that will provide complete immersion of all the senses, including hearing, touch, taste, and smell.

14.10 ALIASING AND ANTIALIASING

In Section 3.17, we introduced the problem of aliasing and discussed some basic techniques for generating antialiased 2D primitives. Here we examine aliasing in more detail so that we can understand when and why it occurs, laying the groundwork for incorporating antialiasing into the visible-surface and shading algorithms covered in the following chapters. Additional material may be found in [CROW77b; CROW81]; an excellent set of examples is included in [BLIN89a; BLIN89b].

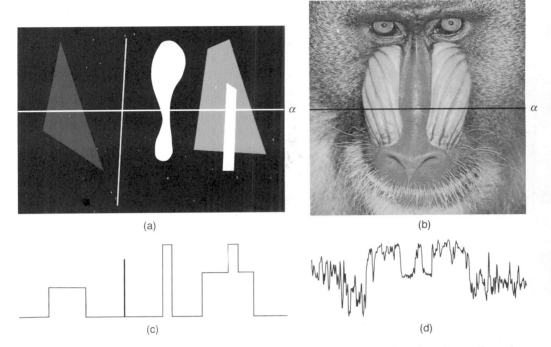

Fig. 14.8 Image. (a) Graphical primitives. (b) Mandrill. (c) Intensity plot of scan line α in (a). (d) Intensity plot of scan line α in (b). (Part d is courtesy of George Wolberg, Columbia University.)

To understand aliasing, we have to introduce some basic concepts from the field of signal processing. We start with the concept of a *signal*, which is a function that conveys information. Signals are often thought of as functions of time, but can equally well be functions of other variables. Since we can think of images as intensity variations over space, we will refer to signals in the *spatial domain* (as functions of spatial coordinates), rather than in the *temporal domain* (as functions of time). Although images are 2D functions of two independent spatial variables (x and y), for convenience our examples will often use the 1D case of a single spatial variable x. This case can be thought of as an infinitesimally thin slice through the image, representing intensity along a single horizontal line. Figure 14.8(a) and (b) show 2D signals, and parts (c) and (d) of the figure show plots of the intensity along the horizontal line α.

Signals can be classified by whether or not they have values at all points in the spatial domain. A *continuous signal*[1] is defined at a continuum of positions in space; a *discrete signal* is defined at a set of discrete points in space. Before scan conversion, the projection of our 3D objects onto the view plane may be treated as a continuous 2D signal whose value

---

[1]Not to be confused with the definition of continuity in calculus.

at each infinitesimal point in the plane indicates the intensity at that point. In contrast, the array of pixel values in the graphics system's frame buffer is a discrete 2D signal whose value is defined only at the positions in the array. Our rendering algorithms must determine the intensities of the finite number of pixels in the array so that they best represent the continuous 2D signal defined by the projection. The precise meaning of ''best represent'' is not at all obvious, however. We shall discuss this problem further.

A continuous signal may contain arbitrarily fine detail in the form of very rapid (high-frequency) variations in its value as its continuous parameter is changed. Since a discrete signal can change value only at discrete points, it clearly has a maximum rate of variation. Therefore, it should be clear that converting a continuous signal to a finite array of values may result in a loss of information. Our goal is to ensure that as little information as possible is lost, so that the resulting pixel array can be used to display a picture that looks as much as possible like the original signal would look if we were able to display it directly. The process of selecting a finite set of values from a signal is known as *sampling,* and the selected values are called *samples.* Once we have selected these samples, we must then display them using a process, known as *reconstruction,* that attempts to recreate the original continuous signal from the samples. The array of pixels in the frame buffer is reconstructed by the graphics system's display hardware, which converts these discrete intensity values to continuous, analog voltages that are applied to the CRT's electron gun (see Chapter 4). An idealized version of this pipeline is shown in Fig. 14.9. Signal-processing theory [GONZ87] establishes the minimum frequency at which samples must be selected from a given signal to reconstruct an exact copy of the signal, and specifies how to perform the reconstruction process. As we show later, however, this minimum sampling frequency will be infinite for many kinds of signals in which we are interested, so perfect reconstruction will often be impossible. Furthermore, as described in Section 14.10.5, the reconstruction method typically used by the display hardware differs from the approach prescribed by theory. Therefore, even properly sampled signals will not be reconstructed perfectly.

14.10.1 Point Sampling

The most straightforward way to select each pixel's value is known as *point sampling.* In point sampling, we select one point for each pixel, evaluate the original signal at this point, and assign its value to the pixel. The points that we select are typically arranged in a regular grid, as shown in Fig. 14.10. Unlike the scan-conversion algorithms of Chapter 3, projected vertices are not constrained to lie on integer grid points. Because the signal's values at a finite set of points are sampled, however, important features of the signal may be missed. For example, objects A and C in Fig. 14.10 are represented by the samples, whereas objects B and D are not. To make matters worse, if the viewing specification changes slightly or if the objects move, objects may pop in or out of visibility. What if we sample at a higher rate? The more samples we collect from the signal, the more we know about it. For example, we can see easily that, by increasing sufficiently the number of samples taken horizontally and vertically in Fig. 14.10, we can make sure that no object is missed in that particular picture. This is a necessary, but *not* a sufficient condition for adequate sampling. Nevertheless, sampling at a higher rate, we can generate images with more pixels representing each portion of the picture. We can also generate an image with

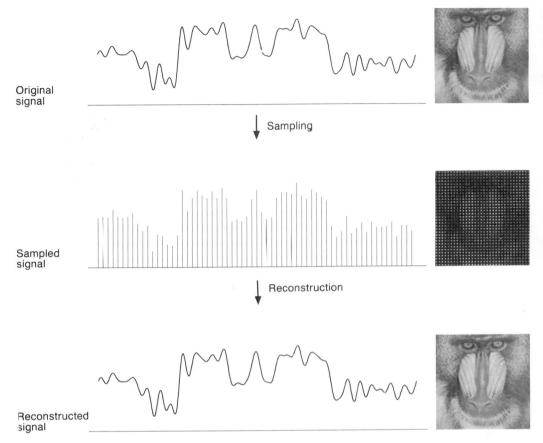

Original
signal

Sampling

Sampled
signal

Reconstruction

Reconstructed
signal

Fig. 14.9 The original signal is sampled, and the samples are used to reconstruct the signal. (Sampled 2D image is an approximation, since point samples have no area.) (Courtesy of George Wolberg, Columbia University.)

fewer pixels, by combining several adjacent samples (e.g., by averaging) to determine the value of each pixel of the smaller image. This means that all the features that would be present in the larger image at least contribute to the smaller one.

The approach of taking more than one sample for each pixel and combining them is known as *supersampling*. It actually corresponds to reconstructing the signal and resampling the reconstructed signal. For reasons described later, sampling the reconstructed signal is often better than sampling the original signal. This technique is popular in computer graphics precisely because it is so easy and often achieves good results, despite the obvious increase in computation. But, how many samples are enough? How do we know that there are no features that our samples are missing? Merely testing whether every object's projection is sampled is not sufficient. The projection may have a complex shape or variations in shading intensity that the samples do not reflect. We would like some way to guarantee that the samples we take are spaced close enough to reconstruct the original

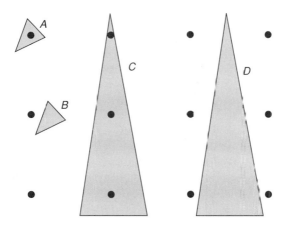

Fig. 14.10 Point-sampling problems. Samples are shown as black dots (●). Objects A and C are sampled, but corresponding objects B and D are not.

signal. As we shall see, sampling theory tells us that, on the basis of a particular signal's properties, we can compute a minimum sampling rate that will be adequate. Unfortunately, the rate turns out to be infinite for certain kinds of signals, including the signal shown in Fig. 14.10! We shall explain the reason for this in more detail later; for now, we can see that taking a finite number of samples cannot guarantee to capture the exact x coordinate at which the intensity jumps from one value to another in the figure. Furthermore, even if we find a finite sampling rate at which all of the current objects are sampled, we can always imagine adding just one more object positioned between samples that will be missed entirely.

14.10.2 Area Sampling

The problem of objects "falling between" samples and being missed suggests another approach: integrating the signal over a square centered about each grid point, dividing by the square's area, and using this average intensity as that of the pixel. This technique, called *unweighted area sampling*, was introduced in Chapter 3. The array of nonoverlapping squares is typically thought of as representing the pixels. Each object's projection, no matter how small, contributes to those pixels that contain it, in strict proportion to the amount of each pixel's area it covers, and without regard to the location of that area in the pixel, as shown by the equal weighting function of Fig. 14.11(a). No objects are missed, as may happen with point sampling. The definition of the definite integral requires evaluating a function at many points of an interval, and then taking the limit as the number of points increases. Thus, integrating amounts to a kind of infinite sampling process.

Unweighted area sampling has drawbacks caused by this evenhandedness with which objects are treated. Consider a small black object wholly contained inside of one of the pixels and surrounded by a white background, as in Fig. 14.11(b). This small object may move freely inside the pixel, and for each position the value computed for the pixel (shown as the pixel's shade) remains the same. As soon as the object crosses over into an adjoining pixel, however, the values of the original pixel and the adjoining pixel are both affected.

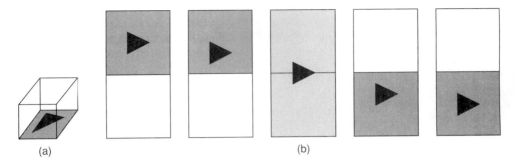

Fig. 14.11 Unweighted area sampling. (a) All points in the pixel are weighted equally. (b) Changes in computed intensities as an object moves between pixels.

Thus, the object causes the image to change only when it crosses pixel boundaries. As the object moves farther from the center of one pixel and closer to the center of another, however, we would like this change to be represented in the image. In other words, we would like the object's contribution to the pixel's intensity to be *weighted* by its distance from the pixel's center: the farther away it is, the less it should contribute.

In Chapter 3, we noted that *weighted area sampling* allows us to assign different weights to different parts of the pixel, and we suggested that the weighting functions of adjacent pixels should overlap. To see why the overlap is needed, we consider a weighting function consisting of an upright pyramid erected over a single pixel, as shown in Fig. 14.12(a). Under this weighting, as desired, an object contributes less to a pixel as it moves away from the pixel's center. But a drawback of unweighted area sampling still remains: An object contributes to only the single pixel that contains it. Consider a subpixel-sized black object moving over a white background from the center of one pixel to the center of an adjacent pixel, as shown in Fig. 14.12(b). As the object moves away from the center of the first pixel, its contribution to the first pixel decreases as it nears its edge. It begins to contribute to the pixel it enters only after it has crossed its border, and reaches its maximum contribution when it reaches the center of the new pixel. Thus, even though the black object has constant intensity, the first pixel increases in intensity before the second pixel decreases in intensity.

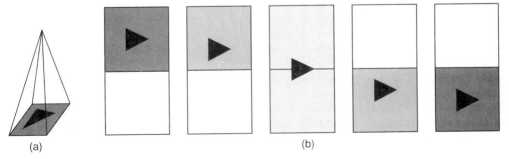

Fig. 14.12 Weighted area sampling. (a) Points in the pixel are weighted differently. (b) Changes in computed intensities as an object moves between pixels.

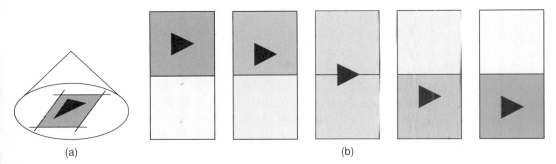

Fig. 14.13 Weighted area sampling with overlap. (a) Typical weighting function. (b) Changes in computed intensities as an object moves between pixels.

The net effect is that the display changes in intensity depending on the object's position, a change that gives rise to flickering as the object moves across the screen. It is clear that, to correct this problem, we must allow our weighting functions to overlap, so that a point on an object can simultaneously influence more than one pixel, as shown in Fig. 14.13. This figure also uses a radially symmetric weighting function. Here, it is appropriate to turn to sampling theory to discover the underlying reasons for increasing the weighting function's size, and to find out exactly what we need to do to sample and reconstruct a signal.

14.10.3   Sampling Theory

Sampling theory provides an elegant mathematical framework to describe the relationship between a continuous signal and its samples. So far, we have considered signals in the *spatial domain*; that is, we have represented each of them as a plot of amplitude against spatial position. A signal may also be considered in the *frequency domain*; that is, we may represent it as a sum of sine waves, possibly offset from each other (the offset is called *phase shift*), and having different frequencies and amplitudes. Each sine wave represents a component of the signal's *frequency spectrum*. We sum these components in the spatial domain by summing their values at each point in space.

Periodic signals, such as those shown in Fig. 14.14, can each be represented as the sum of phase-shifted sine waves whose frequencies are integral multiples (*harmonics*) of the signal's *fundamental* frequency. But what of nonperiodic signals such as images? Since an image is of finite size, we can define its signal to have a value of zero outside the area of the image. Such a signal, which is nonzero over a finite domain, and, more generally, any signal $f(x)$ that tapers off sufficiently fast (faster than $1/x$ for large values of x) can also be represented as a sum of phase-shifted sine waves. Its frequency spectrum, however, will not consist of integer multiples of some fundamental frequency, but may contain any frequency at all. The original signal cannot be represented as a sum of countably many sine waves, but instead must be represented by an integral over a continuum of frequencies. It is often the case, however, that an image (perhaps padded with surrounding zeros) is treated as one cycle of a periodic signal. This was done in Fig. 14.14(b), which shows the first ten components of Fig. 14.8(d). Each signal in the spatial domain has one representation in the frequency domain, and vice versa. As we shall see later, using two representations for a

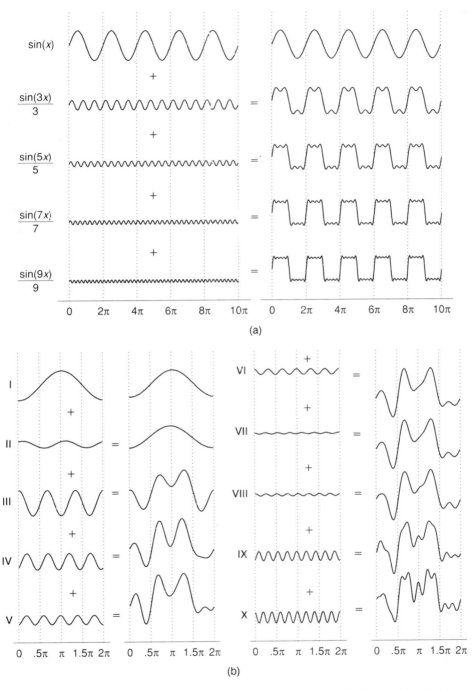

Fig. 14.14 A signal in the spatial domain is the sum of phase-shifted sines. Each component is shown with its effect on the signal shown at its right. (a) Approximation of a square wave. (b) Approximation of Fig. 14.8(d). (Courtesy of George Wolberg, Columbia University.)

signal is advantageous, because some useful operations that are difficult to carry out in one domain are relatively easy to do in the other.

Determining which sine waves must be used to represent a particular signal is the central topic of *Fourier analysis* [GONZ87]. Starting from an original signal, $f(x)$, we can generate a different function, the *Fourier transform* of f, called $F(u)$, whose argument u represents frequency. The value $F(u)$, for each frequency u, tells how much (i.e., the amplitude) of the frequency u appears in the original signal $f(x)$. The function $F(u)$ is therefore also called the *representation of f* (or of *the signal*) *in the frequency domain;* $f(x)$ itself is called the representation of the signal in the spatial domain. The Fourier transform of a continuous, integrable signal $f(x)$ from the spatial domain to the frequency domain is defined by

$$F(u) = \int_{-\infty}^{+\infty} f(x)[\cos 2\pi ux - i\sin 2\pi ux]dx, \qquad (14.1)$$

where $i = \sqrt{-1}$ and u represents the frequency of a sine and cosine pair. (Note that this applies only to functions that taper off sufficiently fast.) Recall that the cosine is just the sine, phase shifted by $\pi/2$. Together they can be used to determine the amplitude and phase shift of their frequency's component. For each u, the value of $F(u)$ is therefore a complex number. This is a clever way of encoding the phase shift and amplitude of the frequency u component of the signal: The value $F(u)$ may be written as $R(u) + iI(u)$, where $R(u)$ and $I(u)$ are the real and imaginary parts, respectively. The amplitude (or magnitude) of $F(u)$ is defined by

$$|F(u)| = \sqrt{R^2(u) + I^2(u)}, \qquad (14.2)$$

and the phase shift (also known as the *phase angle*) is given by

$$\phi(u) = \tan^{-1}\left[\frac{I(u)}{R(u)}\right]. \qquad (14.3)$$

In turn, an integrable signal $F(u)$ may be transformed from the frequency domain to the spatial domain by the *inverse Fourier transform*

$$f(x) = \int_{-\infty}^{+\infty} F(u)[\cos 2\pi ux + i\sin 2\pi ux]du. \qquad (14.4)$$

The Fourier transform of a signal is often plotted as magnitude against frequency, ignoring phase angle. Figure 14.15 shows representations of several signals in both domains. In the spatial domain, we label the abscissa with numbered pixel centers; in the frequency domain, we label the abscissa with cycles per pixel (or more precisely, cycles per interval between pixel centers). In each case, the spike at $u = 0$ represents the DC (direct current) component of the spectrum. Substituting $\cos 0 = 1$ and $\sin 0 = 0$ in Eq. (14.1) reveals that this corresponds to integrating $f(x)$. If .5 were subtracted from each value of $f(x)$ in Fig. 14.15 (a) or (b), the magnitude of the signal's DC component would be 0.

Most of the figures in this chapter that show signals and their Fourier transforms were actually computed using discrete versions of Eqs. (14.1) and (14.4) that operate on signals represented by N regularly spaced samples. The *discrete Fourier transform* is

$$F(u) = \sum_{0 \le x \le N-1} f(x)[\cos (2\pi ux/N) - i\sin (2\pi ux/N)], \quad 0 \le u \le N - 1, \quad (14.5)$$

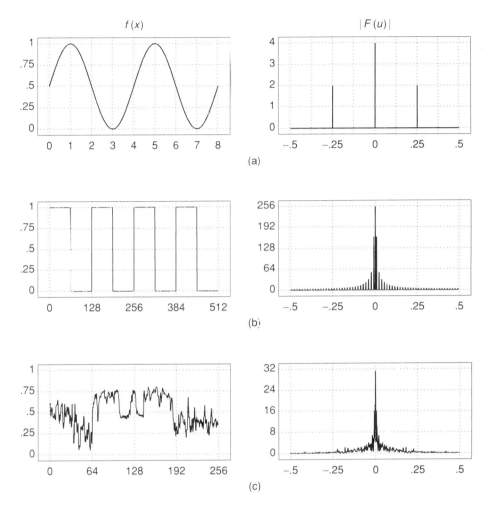

Fig. 14.15 Signals in the spatial and frequency domains. (a) Sine. (b) Square Wave. (c) Mandrill. The DC value in the frequency domain is truncated to make the other values legible and should be 129. (Courtesy of George Wolberg, Columbia Univeristy.)

and the *inverse discrete Fourier transform* is

$$f(x) = \frac{1}{N} \sum_{0 \le u \le N-1} F(u)[\cos (2\pi ux/N) + i\sin (2\pi ux/N)], \quad 0 \le x \le N - 1. \quad (14.6)$$

By choosing a sufficiently high sampling rate, a good approximation to the behavior of the continuous Fourier transform is obtained for most signals. (The discrete Fourier transform may also be computed more efficiently than Eqs. (14.5) and (14.6) would imply, by using a clever reformulation known as the *fast Fourier transform* [BRIG74].) The discrete Fourier transform always yields a finite spectrum. Note that, if a signal is symmetric about the origin, then $I(u) = 0$. This is true because the contribution of each sine term on one side of the origin is canceled by its equal and opposite contribution on the other side. In this case, following [BLIN89a], we will plot the signed function $R(u)$, instead of the magnitude $|F(u)|$.

Sampling theory tells us that a signal can be properly reconstructed from its samples if the original signal is sampled at a frequency that is greater than twice f_h, the highest-frequency component in its spectrum. This lower bound on the sampling rate is known as the *Nyquist rate*. Although we do not give the formal proof of the adequacy of sampling above the Nyquist rate, we can provide an informal justification. Consider one cycle of a signal whose highest-frequency component is at frequency f_h. This component is a sine wave with f_h maxima and f_h minima, as shown in Fig. 14.16. Therefore, at least $2f_h$ samples are required to capture the overall shape of the signal's highest-frequency component. Note that exactly $2f_h$ samples is, in fact, a special case that succeeds only if the samples are taken precisely at the maxima and minima (Fig. 14.16a). If they are taken anywhere else, then the amplitude will not be represented correctly (Fig. 14.16b) and may even be determined to be zero if the samples are taken at the zero crossings (Fig. 14.16c). If we sample below the Nyquist rate, the samples we obtain may be identical to what would have been obtained from sampling a lower-frequency signal, as demonstrated in Fig. 14.17. This phenomenon of high frequencies masquerading as low frequencies in the reconstructed signal is known as *aliasing*: The high-frequency components appear as though they were actually lower-frequency components. Another example of aliasing is demonstrated in Fig. 14.18. Figure 14.18(a) shows an image and a plot of its intensity across a horizontal line, representing a set of intensity fluctuations that increase in spatial frequency from left to right. The image in Fig. 14.18(b) was created by selecting every 8th pixel from each line of Fig. 14.18(a) and replicating it eight times. It shows aliasing as the bands increase in spatial frequency.

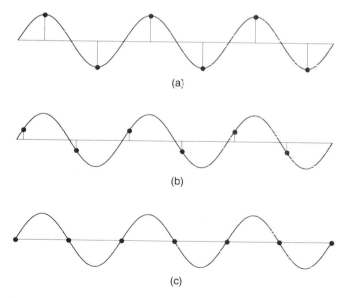

(a)

(b)

(c)

Fig. 14.16 Sampling at the Nyquist rate (a) at peaks, (b) between peaks, (c) at zero crossings.   (Courtesy of George Wolberg, Columbia University.)

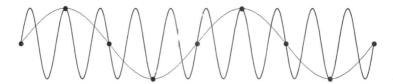

Fig. 14.17 Sampling below the Nyquist rate.   (Courtesy of George Wolberg, Columbia University.)

A signal's shape is determined by its frequency spectrum. The sharper and more angular a waveform is, the richer it is in high-frequency components; signals with discontinuities have an infinite frequency spectrum. Figure 14.10 reveals the sharp edges of the objects' projections that our algorithms attempt to represent. This signal has an infinite frequency spectrum, since the image intensity changes discontinuously at object boundaries. Therefore, the signal cannot be represented properly with a finite number of samples. Computer graphics images thus exhibit two major kinds of aliasing. First, "jaggies" along edges are caused by discontinuities at the projected edges of objects: a point sample either does or does not lie in an object's projection. Even the presence of a single such edge in an environment's projection means that the projection has an infinite frequency spectrum. The frequency spectrum tapers off quite rapidly, however, like those of Fig. 14.15(b) and (c). Second, textures and objects seen in perspective may cause arbitrarily many discontinuities and fluctuations in the environment's projection, making it possible for objects whose projections are too small and too close together to be alternately missed and sampled, as in the right hand side of Fig. 14.18(b). The high frequency components representing the frequency at which these projections cross a scan line may have high amplitude (e.g., alternating black and white checkerboard squares). This often affects picture quality more seriously than jaggies do.

14.10.4 Filtering

There is a partial solution to the problems discussed in the previous section. If we could create a new signal by removing the offending high frequencies from the original signal,

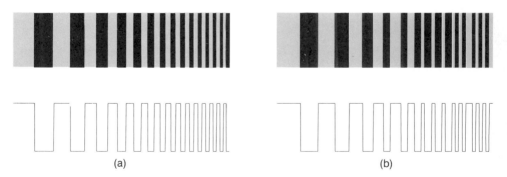

(a)   (b)

Fig. 14.18 Aliasing. (a) Image and intensity plot of a scan line. (b) Sampled image and intensity plot of a scan line.   (Courtesy of George Wolberg, Columbia University.)

then the new signal could be reconstructed properly from a finite number of samples. The more high frequencies we remove, the lower the sampling frequency needed, but the less the signal resembles the original. This process is known as *bandwidth limiting* or *band limiting* the signal. It is also known as *low-pass filtering,* since filtering a signal changes its frequency spectrum; in this case, high frequencies are filtered out and only low frequencies are allowed to pass. Low-pass filtering causes blurring in the spatial domain, since fine visual detail is captured in the high frequencies that are attenuated by low-pass filtering, as shown in Fig. 14.19. We shall revise the pipeline of Fig. 14.9 to include an optional filter, as shown in Fig. 14.20.

A perfect low-pass filter completely suppresses all frequency components above some specified cut-off point, and lets those below the cut-off point pass untouched. We can easily do this filtering in the frequency domain by multiplying the signal's spectrum by a *pulse function,* as shown in Fig. 14.21. We can multiply two signals by taking their product at each point along the paired signals. The pulse function

$$S(u) = \begin{cases} 1, & \text{when } -k \le u \le k, \\ 0, & \text{elsewhere.} \end{cases} \tag{14.7}$$

cuts off all components of frequency higher than k. Therefore, if we were to low-pass filter the signal so as to remove all variation, we would be left with only its DC value.

So far, it would seem that a recipe for low-pass filtering a signal in the spatial domain would involve transforming the signal into the frequency domain, multiplying it by an appropriate pulse function, and then transforming the product back into the spatial domain. Some important relationships between signals in the two domains, however, make this procedure unnecessary. It can be shown that multiplying two Fourier transforms in the frequency domain corresponds exactly to performing an operation called *convolution* on their inverse Fourier transforms in the spatial domain. The *convolution* of two signals $f(x)$

Fig. 14.19 Figure 14.8(b) after low-pass filtering. (Courtesy of George Wolberg, Columbia University.)

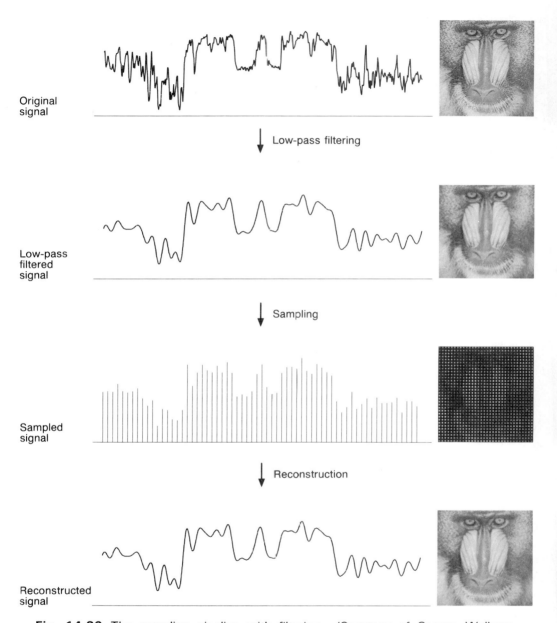

Original signal

Low-pass filtering

Low-pass filtered signal

Sampling

Sampled signal

Reconstruction

Reconstructed signal

Fig. 14.20 The sampling pipeline with filtering. (Courtesy of George Wolberg, Columbia University.)

and $g(x)$, written as $f(x) * g(x)$, is a new signal $h(x)$ defined as follows. The value of $h(x)$ at each point is the integral of the product of $f(x)$ with the filter function $g(x)$ flipped about its vertical axis and shifted such that its origin is at that point. This corresponds to taking a weighted average of the neighborhood around each point of the signal $f(x)$—weighted by a flipped copy of filter $g(x)$ positioned at the point—and using it for the value of $h(x)$ at the point. The size of the neighborhood is determined by the size of the domain over which the filter is nonzero. This is known as the filter's *support*, and a filter that is nonzero over a finite domain is said to have *finite support*. We use τ as a dummy variable of integration when defining the convolution. Thus,

$$h(x) = f(x) * g(x) \overset{\Delta}{=} \int_{-\infty}^{+\infty} f(\tau)g(x - \tau)d\tau. \tag{14.8}$$

Conversely, convolving two Fourier transforms in the frequency domain corresponds exactly to multiplying their inverse Fourier transforms in the spatial domain. The filter function is often called the *convolution kernel* or *filter kernel*.

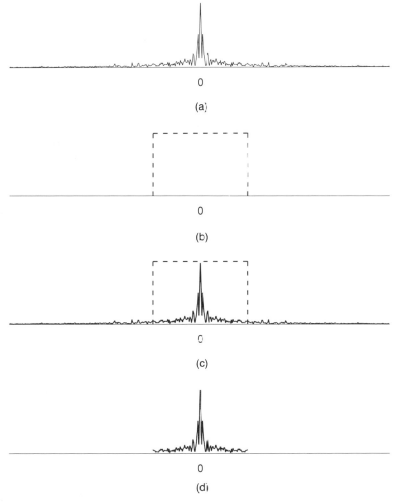

Fig. 14.21 Low-pass filtering in the frequency domain. (a) Original spectrum. (b) Low-pass filter. (c) Spectrum with filter. (d) Filtered spectrum. (Courtesy of George Wolberg, Columbia University.)

Convolution can be illustrated graphically. We will convolve the function $f(x) = 1, 0 \leq x \leq 1$, with the filter kernel $g(x) = c, 0 \leq x \leq 1$, shown in Figs. 14.22(a) and (b). By using functions of τ, we can vary x to move the filter relative to the signal being filtered. To create the function $g(x - \tau)$, we first flip $g(\tau)$ about the origin to yield $g(-\tau)$, and then offset it by x to form $g(x - \tau)$, as depicted in Figs. 14.22(c) and (d). The integral, with respect to τ, of the product $f(\tau)g(x - \tau)$, which is the area of the shaded portions of the figures, is 0 for $-\infty \leq x < 0$, xc for $0 \leq x \leq 1$ (Fig. 14.22e), $(2 - x)c$ for $1 \leq x \leq 2$ (Fig. 14.22f), and 0 for $2 < x \leq \infty$. The convolution $f(x) * g(x)$ is illustrated in Fig. 14.22(g). Note how convolution with this kernel smooths the discontinuities of $f(x)$ while it widens the area over which $f(x)$ is nonzero.

Multiplying by a pulse function in the frequency domain has the same effect as convolving with the signal that corresponds to the pulse in the spatial domain. This signal is known as the *sinc* function, which is defined as $\sin(\pi x)/\pi x$. Figure 14.23 shows the sinc function and an example of the result of convolving it with another signal. Convolving with a sinc function therefore low-pass filters the signal. How do we choose the height and width of the sinc used in Fig. 14.23(c)? As shown in Fig. 14.24, there is a relationship (that we do not prove) between the height and width of the perfect low-pass filter in the spatial and frequency domains. In Fig. 14.24(a), if W is the cutoff frequency and A is the amplitude, then it must be the case that $A/2W = 1$ for all frequencies up to the cutoff frequency to be passed unattenuated. Therefore, $A = 2W$. Both the amplitude and width of the sinc in Fig. 14.24(a) vary with W. When $W = .5$ cycles per pixel (the highest frequency that can be represented when sampling once per pixel), $A = 1$ and the sinc has zero crossings at pixel centers. As the cutoff frequency W is made lower or higher, the sinc becomes shorter and broader, or taller and narrower, respectively. This makes sense because we would like the integral of a filter in the spatial domain to be 1, a necessary restriction if the filter is to maintain the gray level (DC value) of the image, neither brightening nor dimming it. (We

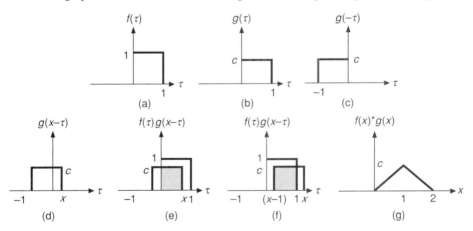

Fig. 14.22 Graphical convolution. (a) Function $f(\tau) = 1, 0 \leq \tau \leq 1$. (b) Filter kernel $g(\tau) = c, 0 \leq \tau \leq 1$. (c) $g(-\tau)$. (d) $g(x - \tau)$. (e) $\int_{-\infty}^{+\infty} f(\tau)g(x - \tau)d\tau = xc, 0 \leq x \leq 1$. (f) $\int_{-\infty}^{+\infty} f(\tau)g(x - \tau)d\tau = (2 - x)c, 1 \leq x \leq 2$. (g) $f(x) * g(x)$.

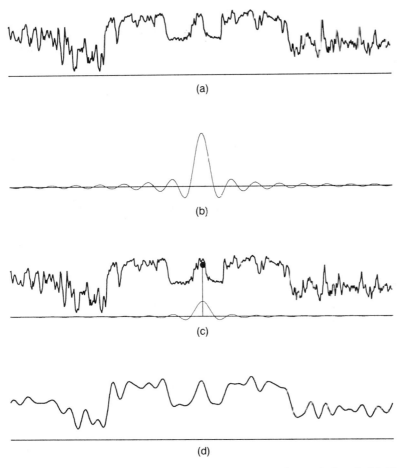

Fig. 14.23 Low-pass filtering in the spatial domain. (a) Original signal. (b) Sinc filter. (c) Signal with filter, with value of filtered signal shown as a black dot (•) at filter's origin. (d) Filtered signal.   (Courtesy of George Wolberg, Columbia University.)

can see that this is true by considering the convolution of a filter with a signal that has the same value c at each point.)

   The sinc function has the unfortunate property that it is nonzero on points arbitrarily far from the origin (i.e., it has *infinite support* since it is infinitely wide) If we truncate the sinc function, by multiplying it by a pulse function, we can restrict the support, as shown in Fig. 14.24(b). This is a special case of a *windowed* sinc function that has been restricted to a finite window. We might reason that we are throwing away only those parts of the filter where the value is very small anyhow, so it should not influence the result too much. Unfortunately, the truncated version of the filter has a Fourier transform that suffers from *ringing* (also called the *Gibbs phenomenon*): A truncated sinc in the spatial domain no longer corresponds to a pure pulse function in the frequency domain, but instead corresponds to a pulse function with ripples near the cutoff frequency, as shown in Fig. 14.24(b). This causes some frequency components to pass that should be suppressed, and both attenuates and amplifies others around the cutoff point; the domain over which this effect occurs decreases in size as a greater portion of the sinc signal is used, but the amplitude of the ringing does not decrease as long as the sinc is truncated. The approximation to a square wave in Fig.14.14(a) exhibits ringing in the spatial domain, which appears as little intensity "ripples" at discontinuities. A truncated sinc is obtained by multiplying the sinc by a pulse function. An alternative is to use a windowed sinc function that has been multiplied by a shape that, unlike the pulse, is not discontinuous, which allows the sinc to fall off smoothly. Blinn [BLIN89b] describes the derivation of one such filter.

One final problem is that the sinc, along with windowed filters derived from it, has parts that dip below zero, known as *negative lobes*. When a signal is convolved with a filter that has negative lobes, the resulting signal may itself dip below zero. If the signal represents intensity values, these values correspond to unrealizable negative intensities, and must therefore ultimately be clamped to zero.

Although windowed sinc functions are useful, they are relatively expensive because the window must be fairly wide; thus, a variety of other functions is often used instead. Filters

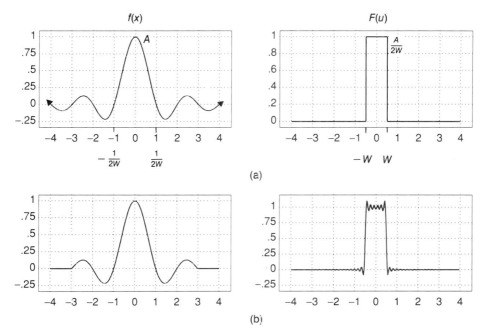

Fig. 14.24 (a) Sinc in spatial domain corresponds to pulse in frequency domain. (b) Truncated sinc in spatial domain corresponds to ringing pulse in frequency domain. (Courtesy of George Wolberg, Columbia University.)

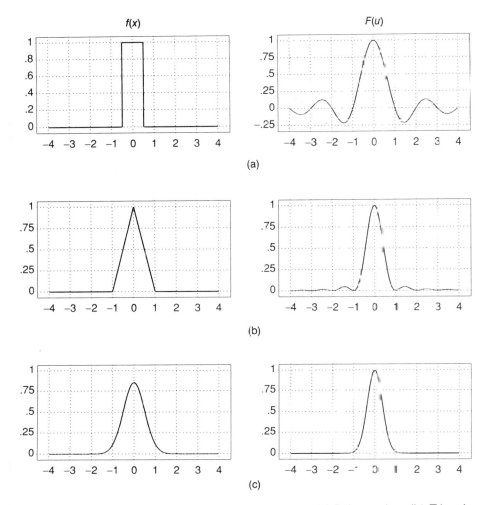

Fig. 14.25 Filters in spatial and frequency domains. (a) Pulse—sinc. (b) Triangle—sinc^2. (c) Gaussian—Gaussian. (Courtesy of George Wolberg, Columbia University.)

with finite support are known as finite impulse-response (FIR) filters, in contrast to the untruncated sinc filter, which is an infinite impulse-response (IIR) filter. Figure 14.25 shows several popular filters in both spatial and frequency domains.

We have now reduced the sampling problem to one of convolving the signal with a suitable filter and then sampling the filtered signal. Notice, however, that if our only use of the filtered signal is to sample it, then the work done filtering the signal anywhere but at the sample points is wasted. If we know in advance exactly where the samples will be taken, we need only to evaluate the convolution integral (Eq. 14.8) at each sample point to determine the sample's value. This is precisely how we perform the weighting operation in using area sampling to determine the intensity of each pixel. The weighting distribution constructed over each pixel's center is a filter. The pulse function with which we convolve the signal in performing unweighted area sampling is often called a *box filter*, because of its appearance. Just as the pulse function in the frequency domain corresponds to the sinc function in the spatial domain, the pulse function in the spatial domain (the box filter's 1D equivalent) corresponds to the sinc function in the frequency domain (Fig. 14.25a). This correspondence underscores how badly a box filter or pulse filter approximates a perfect low-pass filter. Multiplying with a sinc in the frequency domain not only fails to cut off sharply, but passes infinitely high frequencies. Furthermore, the pulse filter attenuates frequencies that are within the desired range, since its Fourier transform—the sinc function—begins to trail off before the ideal low-pass filter. Therefore, it also blurs the image excessively.

14.10.5   Reconstruction

At this point, let us assume that we have sampled the signal $f(x)$ at a frequency f_s to obtain the sampled signal, which we call $\hat{f}(x)$. Sampling theory shows that the frequency spectrum of $\hat{f}(x)$ looks like that of $f(x)$, replicated at multiples of f_s. To see that this relationship holds, we note that sampling a signal corresponds to multiplying it in the spatial domain by a *comb* function, so named because of its appearance, as shown in Fig. 14.26(a). The comb

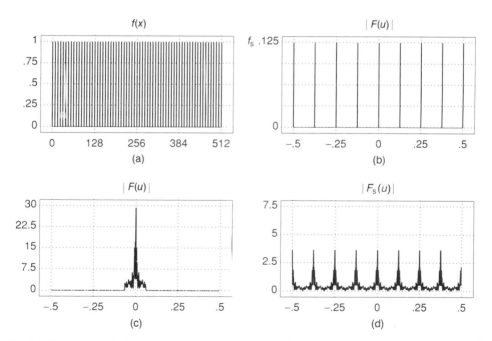

Fig. 14.26 (a) Comb function and (b) its Fourier transform. Convolving the comb's Fourier transform with (c) a signal's Fourier transform in the frequency domain yields (d) the replicated spectrum of the sampled signal. (Courtesy of George Wolberg, Columbia University.)

function has a value of 0 everywhere, except at regular intervals, corresponding to the sample points, where its value is 1. The (discrete) Fourier transform of a comb turns out to be just another comb with teeth at multiples of f_s (Fig. 14.26b). The height of the teeth in the comb's Fourier transform is f_s in cycles/pixel. Since multiplication in the spatial domain corresponds to convolution in the frequency domain, we obtain the Fourier transform of the sampled signal by convolving the Fourier transforms of the comb function and the original signal (Fig. 14.26c). By inspection, the result is the replicated spectrum (Fig. 14.26d). Try performing graphical convolution with the comb to verify this, but note that $F(u)$, not $|F(u)|$ must actually be used. A sufficiently high f_s yields spectra that are replicated far apart from each other. In the limiting case, as f_s approaches infinity, a single spectrum results.

Recall that *reconstruction* is recreation of the original signal from its samples. The result of sampling a signal (Fig. 14.27a) at a finite sampling frequency is a signal with an infinite frequency spectrum (Fig. 14.27b). If once again we deal with the signal in the frequency domain, the familiar operation of multiplying a signal by a pulse function can be used to eliminate these replicated spectra (Fig. 14.27c), leaving only a single copy of the original spectrum (Fig. 14.27d). Thus, we can reconstruct the signal from its samples by multiplying the Fourier transform of the samples by a pulse function in the frequency domain or by convolving the samples with a sinc with $A = 1$ in the spatial domain.

To make the Fourier transforms of signals and filters easier to see in Figs. 14.27–29, we have taken several liberties:

- The DC value of the Fourier transform in part (a) of each figure has been truncated. This corresponds to a signal in the spatial domain with the same shape as shown, but with a negative DC offset. (Such a signal cannot be displayed as an image without further processing, because it contains negative intensity values.)

- Filters in the frequency domain have not been drawn with the correct magnitude. Their heights should be 1 in Fig. 14.27 and 2 in Figs. 14.28–29 to restore the single copy of the spectrum to its original magnitude.

Figure 14.27(e) and (f) show the result of reconstructing the samples with a triangle filter (also known as a Bartlett filter). Convolving with this filter is equivalent to linearly interpolating the samples.

If the sampling frequency is too low, the replicated copies of the frequency spectra overlap, as in Fig. 14.28. In this case, the reconstruction process will fail to remove those parts of the replicated spectra that overlapped the original signal's spectrum. High-frequency components from the replicated spectra are mixed in with low-frequency components from the original spectrum, and therefore are treated like low frequencies during the reconstruction process. Note how an inadequate sampling rate causes aliasing by making a higher frequency appear identical to a lower one before and after reconstruction. There are two ways to resolve this problem. We may choose to sample at a high enough frequency, an approach that is sufficient only if the signal does not have an infinite spectrum. Alternatively, we may filter the signal before sampling to remove all components above $f_s/2$, as shown in Fig. 14.29.

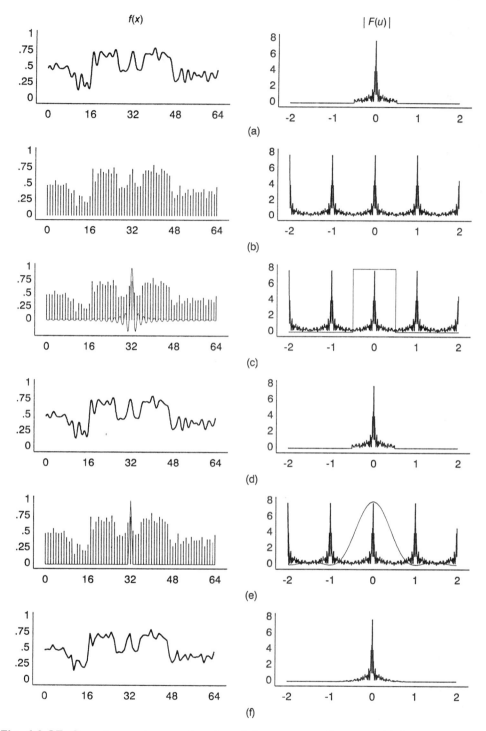

Fig. 14.27 Sampling and reconstruction: Adequate sampling rate. (a) Original signal. (b) Sampled signal. (c) Sampled signal ready to be reconstructed with sinc. (d) Signal reconstructed with sinc. (e) Sampled signal ready to be reconstructed with triangle. (f) Signal reconstructed with triangle. (Courtesy of George Wolberg, Columbia University.)

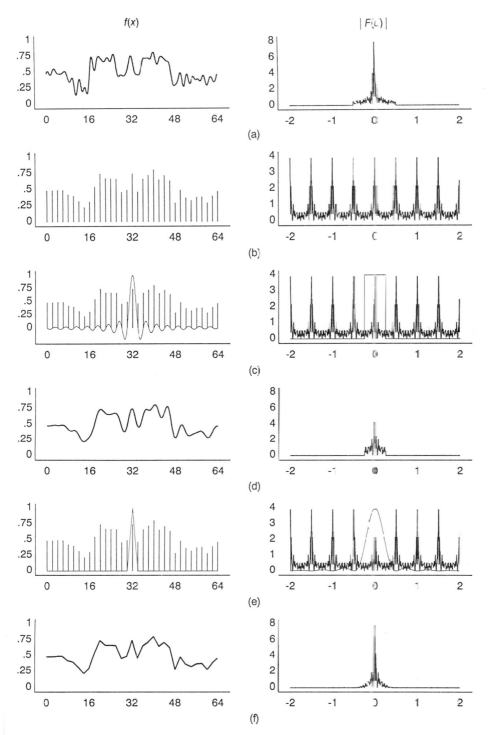

Fig. 14.28 Sampling and reconstruction: Inadequate sampling rate. (a) Original signal. (b) Sampled signal. (c) Sampled signal ready to be reconstructed with sinc. (d) Signal reconstructed with sinc. (e) Sampled signal ready to be reconstructed with triangle. (f) Signal reconstructed with triangle. (Courtesy of George Wolberg, Columbia University.)

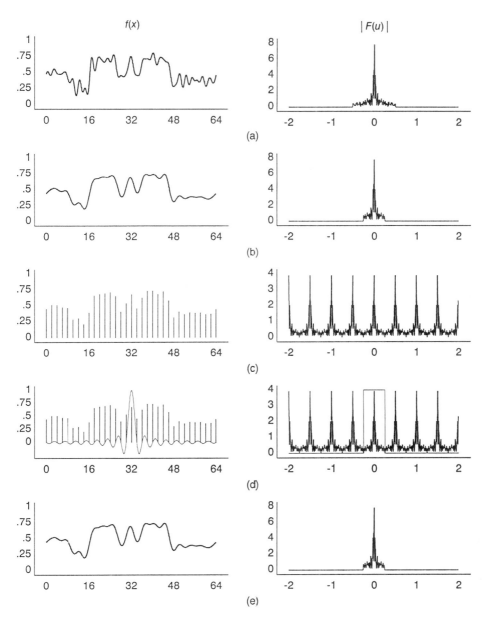

Fig. 14.29 Filtering, sampling, and reconstruction: Sampling rate is adequate after filtering. (a) Original signal. (b) Low-pass filtered signal. (c) Sampled signal. (d) Sampled signal ready to be reconstructed with sinc. (e) Signal reconstructed with sinc.   (Courtesy of George Wolberg, Columbia University.)

What happens if reconstruction is done by convolving with some signal cther than a sinc? Samples in the frame buffer are translated into a continuous video signal, by a process known as *sample and hold*: for the signal to be reconstructed, the value of each successive sample is simply held for the duration of a pixel. This process corresponds to convolving the samples with a 1-pixel-wide box filter, as shown in Fig. 14.30, and gives rise to our common conception of a pixel as one of a set of square boxes tiling the display. The resulting signal has sharp transitions between pixels, corresponding tc high-frequency components that are not represented by the samples. This effect is often known as *rastering*. Although the video hardware nominally samples and holds each pixel's intensity, the circuitry that generates the analog voltages applied to the CRT and the CRT itself are generally not fast enough to produce discontinuous jumps in intensity between pixels. The Gaussian distribution of the CRT spot also reduces this problem. Thus, the sampled signal is reconstructed by the equivalent of convolution with a box filter, followed by convolution with a Gaussian. Rastering is especially easy to see, however, when pixel-replicating zoom is used in raster CRT displays, increasing the amount of screen space allocated to an individual pixel. Rastering is also more evident in printer, digital film recorder, and LCD

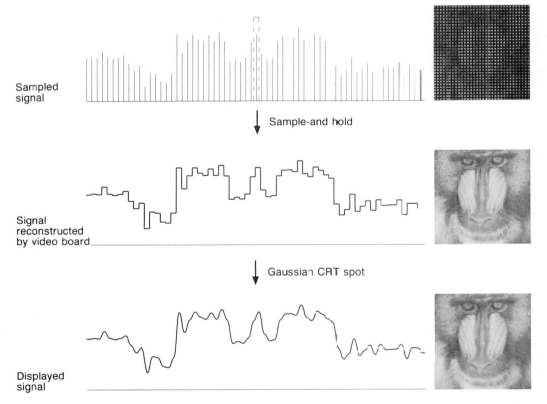

Fig. 14.30 Reconstruction by sample and hold and Gaussian CRT spot. (Courtesy of George Wolberg, Columbia University.)

Fig. 14.31 A signal sampled at slightly over the Nyquist rate.   (Courtesy of George Wolberg, Columbia University.)

technologies, in which pixel-to-pixel transitions are much sharper and produce relatively hard-edged square pixels of constant intensity.

We noted earlier that a signal must be sampled at a frequency greater than $2f_h$ to make perfect reconstruction possible. If the filter used to reconstruct the samples is not an untruncated sinc, as is always the case when displaying an image, then the sampling frequency must be even higher! Consider, for example, a sampling frequency slightly greater than $2f_h$. The resulting samples trace out the original signal modulated by (multiplied by) a low-frequency sine wave, as shown in Fig. 14.31. The low-frequency amplitude modulation remains, compounded by rastering, if the signal is reconstructed with a 1-pixel-wide box filter. If convolution is performed with an untruncated sinc, however, the original signal is recovered. The inevitable use of nonideal filters before and after sampling therefore mandates higher sampling rates. Mitchell and Netravali [MITC88] discuss some of the problems involved in doing a good job of reconstruction.

14.10.6   Antialiasing in Practice

We have seen that image synthesis involves sampling and reconstruction, noting that there is little that we can do (in software) about the reconstruction approach employed in hardware. Rendering algorithms that perform antialiasing use either point sampling or an analytic approach, such as area sampling. In either case, a single value must ultimately be determined for each pixel. Catmull's algorithm, discussed in Section 15.7.3, is an example of an analytic (and expensive) approach using unweighted area sampling. It corresponds to filtering at object precision before calculating the value of each pixel's sample. Filtering before sampling is often called *prefiltering*. When supersampling is used, the samples are combined according to a filter weighting in a discrete version of the continuous convolution and sampling that we discussed earlier. The filter is represented by an array of values. As shown in Fig. 14.32, the filter array is positioned over the array of supersampled values and the sum of the products of values in corresponding positions determines a single sample taken at the center of the filter. The filter array is then moved to the position at which the next sample will be taken, with the number of samples corresponding to the pixel resolution of the filtered image being created. This approach is often called *postfiltering*, since filtering is performed after point sampling. It actually corresponds to reconstructing the signal from its samples only at selected points in space. These reconstructed values are then used as new samples. Supersampling thus performs a discrete approximation to weighted area sampling.

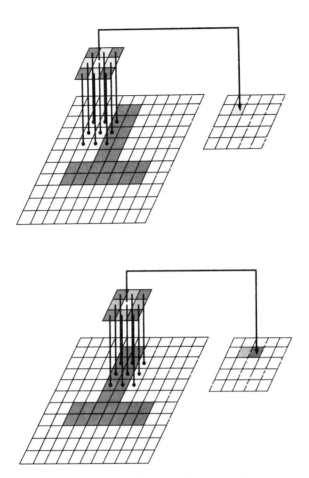

Fig. 14.32 Digital filtering. Filter is used to combine samples to create a new sample.

Although it is computationally attractive to use a 1-pixel-wide box filter that averages all subpixel samples, better filters can produce better results, as demonstrated in Fig. 14.33. Note that, no matter what filter is used to postfilter the samples, damage caused by an inadequate initial sampling rate will not be repaired. A rule of thumb is that supersampling four times in each of x and y often will be satisfactory [WHIT85]. This works because the high frequencies in most graphics images are caused by discontinuities at edges, which have a Fourier transform that tapers off rapidly (like the Fourier transform of a pulse—the sinc). In contrast, images with textures and distant objects viewed in perspective have a Fourier transform that is richer in high frequencies and that may be arbitrarily difficult to filter.

Although it is easy to increase the sampling rate, this approach is limited in its usefulness by corresponding increases in both processing time and storage. A number of variations on point sampling have been implemented to address these issues without sacrificing the conceptually simple mechanism of point sampling itself. In *adaptive*

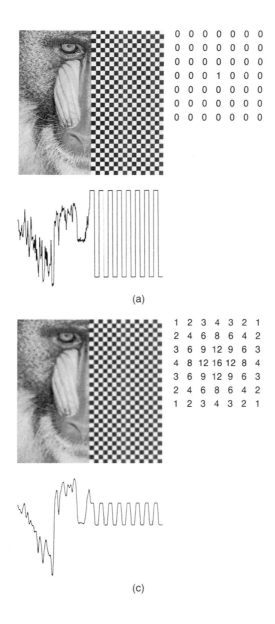

Fig. 14.33 *(Cont'd.)*

supersampling, an example of which is discussed in Section 15.10.4, the sampling rate is varied across the image, with additional samples taken when the system determines that they are needed. *Stochastic supersampling,* discussed in Section 16.12.4, places samples at stochastically determined positions, rather than in a regular grid. This approach produces

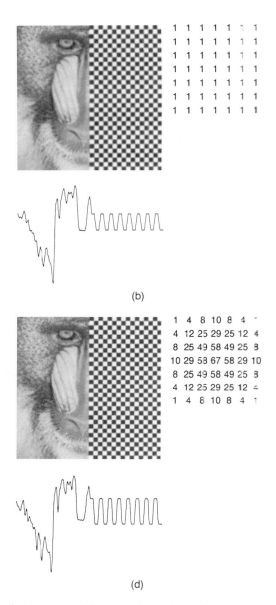

(b)

(d)

Fig. 14.33 Filtered images with intensity plot of middle scan line and filter kernel. (a) Original image. (b) Box filter. (c) Bartlett filter. (d) Gaussian filter. Images are 512 × 512, and filters are 7 × 7. Middle scan line is at bottom of a checkerboard row. Because 2D filter covers light and dark squares above and below scan line, amplitude of filtered checkerboard signal along middle scan line is greatly diminished. (Courtesy of George Wolberg, Columbia University.)

aliasing in the form of noise, which our visual system finds less irritating than the clearly defined frequency components of regular aliasing. These two approaches can be combined, allowing the determination of where to place new samples to be based on the statistical properties of those that have already been obtained.

When the original source signal is itself a sampled image, postfiltering followed by resampling may be used to create a new image that has been scaled, rotated, or distorted in a variety of ways. These *image transformations* are discussed in Chapter 17.

14.11 SUMMARY

In this chapter, we provided a high-level introduction to the techniques used to produce realistic images. We then examined the causes of and cures for aliasing. In the following chapters, we discuss in detail how these techniques can be implemented. There are five key questions that you should bear in mind when you read about the algorithms presented in later chapters:

1. *Is the algorithm general or special purpose?* Some techniques work best only in specific circumstances; others are designed to be more general. For example, some algorithms assume that all objects are convex polyhedra and derive part of their speed and relative simplicity from this assumption.

2. *Can antialiasing be incorporated?* Some algorithms may not accommodate antialiasing as easily as others do.

3. *What is the algorithm's space–time performance?* How is the algorithm affected by factors such as the size or complexity of the database, or the resolution at which the picture is rendered?

4. *How convincing are the effects generated?* For example, is refraction modeled correctly, does it look right only in certain special cases, or is it not modeled at all? Can additional effects, such as shadows or specular reflection, be added? How convincing will they be? Sacrificing the accuracy with which an effect is rendered may make possible significant improvements in a program's space or time requirements.

5. *Is the algorithm appropriate, given the purpose for which the picture is created?* The philosophy behind many of the pictures in the following chapters can be summed up by the credo, "If it looks good, do it!" This directive can be interpreted two ways. A simple or fast algorithm may be used if it produces attractive effects, even if no justification can be found in the laws of physics. On the other hand, a shockingly expensive algorithm may be used if it is the only known way to render certain effects.

EXERCISES

14.1 Suppose you had a graphics system that could draw any of the color plates referenced in this chapter in real time. Consider several application areas with which you are (or would like to be) familiar. For each area, list those effects that would be most useful, and those that would be least useful.

14.2 Show that you cannot infer the direction of rotation from orthographic projections of a monochrome, rotating, wireframe cube. Explain how additional techniques can help to make the direction of rotation clear without changing the projection.

14.3 Consider the pulse function $f(x) = 1$ for $-1 \leq x \leq 1$, and $f(x) = 0$ elsewhere. Show that the Fourier transform of $f(x)$ is a multiple of the sinc function. Hint: The Fourier transform of $f(x)$ can be computed as

$$F(u) = \int_{-1}^{+1} f(x)[\cos 2\pi ux - i\sin 2\pi ux]dx,$$

because the regions where $f(x) = 0$ contribute nothing to the integral, and $f(x) = 1$ in the remaining region. (Apply the inverse Fourier transform to your answer. You should get the original function.)

14.4 Prove that reconstructing a signal with a triangle filter of width 2 corresponds to linearly interpolating its samples. What happens if the filter is wider?

14.5 Write a program that allows you to convolve an image with a filter kernel. Use different filter kernels to create images of the same size from original images with 2, 4, and 8 times the number of pixels in x or y as the new images. You can obtain original images by saving the frame buffer generated by the graphics packages that you have been using. Do your filtered images look better than original images of the same resolution? Does your experience corroborate the rule of thumb mentioned in Section 14.10.6?

15

Visible-Surface Determination

Given a set of 3D objects and a viewing specification, we wish to determine which lines or surfaces of the objects are visible, either from the center of projection (for perspective projections) or along the direction of projection (for parallel projections), so that we can display only the visible lines or surfaces. This process is known as *visible-line* or *visible-surface determination*, or *hidden-line* or *hidden-surface elimination*. In visible-line determination, lines are assumed to be the edges of opaque surfaces that may obscure the edges of other surfaces farther from the viewer. Therefore, we shall refer to the general process as *visible-surface determination*.

Although the statement of this fundamental idea is simple, its implementation requires significant processing power, and consequently involves large amounts of computer time on conventional machines. These requirements have encouraged the development of numerous carefully structured visible-surface algorithms, many of which are described in this chapter. In addition, many special-purpose architectures have been designed to address the problem, some of which are discussed in Chapter 18. The need for this attention can be seen from an analysis of two fundamental approaches to the problem. In both cases, we can think of each object as comprising one or more polygons (or more complex surfaces).

The first approach determines which of *n* objects is visible at each pixel in the image. The pseudocode for this approach looks like this:

```
for (each pixel in the image) {
    determine the object closest to the viewer that is pierced by
        the projector through the pixel;
    draw the pixel in the appropriate color;
}
```

A straightforward, brute-force way of doing this for 1 pixel requires examining all n objects to determine which is closest to the viewer along the projector passing through the pixel. For p pixels, the effort is proportional to np, where p is over 1 million for a high-resolution display.

The second approach is to compare objects directly with each other, eliminating entire objects or portions of them that are not visible. Expressed in pseudocode, this becomes

```
for (each object in the world) {
      determine those parts of the object whose view is unobstructed
            by other parts of it or any other object;
      draw those parts in the appropriate color;
}
```

We can do this naively by comparing each of the n objects to itself and to the other objects, and discarding invisible portions. The computational effort here is proportional to n^2. Although this second approach might seem superior for $n < p$, its individual steps are typically more complex and time consuming, as we shall see, so it is often slower and more difficult to implement.

We shall refer to these prototypical approaches as *image-precision* and *object-precision* algorithms, respectively. Image-precision algorithms are typically performed at the resolution of the display device, and determine the visibility at each pixel. Object-precision algorithms are performed at the precision with which each object is defined, and determine the visibility of each object.[1] Since object-precision calculations are done without regard to a particular display resolution, they must be followed by a step in which the objects are actually displayed at the desired resolution. Only this final display step needs to be repeated if the size of the finished image is changed; for example, to cover a different number of pixels on a raster display. This is because the geometry of each visible object's projection is represented at the full object database resolution. In contrast, consider enlarging an image created by an image-precision algorithm. Since visible-surface calculations were performed at the original lower resolution, they must be done again if we wish to reveal further detail. Recalling our discussion of sampling in Chapter 14, we can think of object-precision algorithms as operating on the original continuous object data, and image-precision algorithms as operating on sampled data; thus, image-precision algorithms fall prey to aliasing in computing visibility, whereas object-precision algorithms do not.

Object-precision algorithms were first developed for vector graphics systems. On these devices, hidden-line removal was most naturally accomplished by turning the initial list of

---

[1]The terms *image space* and *object space*, popularized by Sutherland, Sproull, and Schumacker [SUTH74a]. are often used to draw the same distinction. Unfortunately, these terms have also been used quite differently in computer graphics. For example, *image-space* has been used to refer to objects after perspective transformation [CATM75] or after projection onto the view plane [GILO78], but still at their original precision. To avoid confusion, we have opted for our slightly modified terms. We refer explicitly to an object's perspective transformation or projection, when appropriate, and reserve the terms *image precision* and *object precision* to indicate the precision with which computations are performed. For example, intersecting two objects' projections on the view plane is an object-precision operation if the precision of the original object definitions is maintained.

lines into one in which lines totally hidden by other surfaces were removed, and partially hidden lines were clipped to one or more visible line segments. All processing was performed at the precision of the original list and resulted in a list in the same format. In contrast, image-precision algorithms were first written for raster devices to take advantage of the relatively small number of pixels for which the visibility calculations had to be performed. This was an understandable partitioning. Vector displays had a large address space (4096 by 4096 even in early systems) and severe limits on the number of lines and objects that could be displayed. Raster displays, on the other hand, had a limited address space (256 by 256 in early systems) and the ability to display a potentially unbounded number of objects. Later algorithms often combine both object- and image-precision calculations, with object-precision calculations chosen for accuracy, and image-precision ones chosen for speed.

In this chapter, we first introduce a subset of the visible-surface problem, displaying single-valued functions of two variables. Next, we discuss a variety of ways to increase the efficiency of general visible-surface algorithms. Then, we present the major approaches to determining visible surfaces.

15.1 FUNCTIONS OF TWO VARIABLES

One of the most common uses of computer graphics has been to plot single-valued continuous functions of two variables, such as $y = f(x, z)$. These functions define surfaces like that shown in Fig. 15.1(a). They present an interesting special case of the hidden-surface problem, for which especially fast solutions are possible.

A function of x and z may be approximated by an m by n array Y of values. Each array element may be thought of as representing a height at one point in a regular grid of samples. We assume that each column of the array corresponds to a single x coordinate, and that each row of the array corresponds to a single z coordinate. In other words, the rectangular array is aligned with the x and z axes. The indices of an array element and the element's value together specify the coordinates of a 3D point. A wireframe drawing of the surface may be constructed as a piecewise linear approximation by drawing one set of polylines through the points defined by each row of the array Y (polylines of constant z) and an orthogonal set of polylines through the points defined by each column (polylines of constant x). A

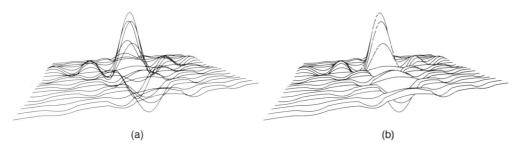

(a)   (b)

Fig. 15.1 A single-valued function of two variables: (a) without and (b) with hidden lines removed. (By Michael Hatzitheodorou, Columbia University.)

hidden-line algorithm must suppress all parts of the lines that would be obscured from the viewpoint by other parts of the surface, as shown in Fig. 15.1(b).

To see how we might accomplish this, we first consider the problem of plotting only polylines of constant z, assuming that the closest polyline to the viewpoint is an edge of the surface. An efficient class of solutions to this problem is based on the recognition that each polyline of constant z lies in a separate, parallel plane of constant z [WILL72; WRIG73; BUTL79]. Since none of these planes (and hence none of the polylines) can intersect any of the others, each polyline cannot be obscured by any polyline of constant z farther from the viewpoint. Therefore, we will draw polylines of constant z in order of increasing distance from the viewpoint. This establishes a *front-to-back* order. Drawing each polyline of constant z correctly requires only that we not draw those parts of the polyline that are obscured by parts of the surface already drawn.

Consider the "silhouette boundary" of the polylines drawn thus far on the view plane, shown as thick lines in Fig. 15.2. When a new polyline is drawn, it should be visible only where its projection rises above the top or dips below the bottom of the old silhouette. Since each new polyline has a constant z that is farther than that of any of the preceding polylines, it cannot pierce any part of the surface already drawn. Therefore, to determine what parts are to be drawn, we need only to compare the current polyline's projected y values with those of the corresponding part of the surface's silhouette computed thus far. When only enough information is encoded to represent a minimum and maximum silhouette y for each x, the algorithm is known as an *horizon line algorithm*.

One way to represent this silhouette, implemented by Wright [WRIG73], uses two 1D arrays, *YMIN* and *YMAX*, to hold the minimum and maximum projected y values for a finite set of projected x values. These are image-precision data structures because they have a finite number of entries. *YMIN* and *YMAX* are initialized with y values that are, respectively, above and below all the projected y values of the surface. When a new polyline is drawn, the projected y values of each pair of adjacent vertices are compared with the values at the corresponding locations in the silhouette arrays. As shown in Fig. 15.3, a vertex whose value is above that in the corresponding position in *YMAX* (A, B, G) or below that in *YMIN* (E, F) is visible; otherwise, it is invisible (C, D). If both vertices are invisible, then the line segment is wholly invisible (CD) and the silhouette arrays remain unchanged.

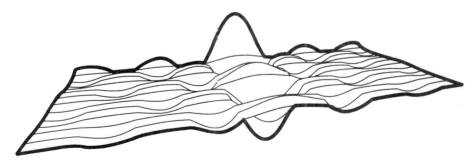

Fig. 15.2 Silhouette of lines drawn. (By Michael Hatzitheodorou, Columbia University.)

If both vertices are visible with regard to the same silhouette array (AB, EF), then the line segment is wholly visible and should be drawn in its entirety, and that silhouette array should be updated. The x coordinates of two adjacent vertices in a polyline of constant z usually map to nonadjacent locations in the silhouette arrays. In this situation, values of y to insert in the intervening silhouette array locations can be obtained by linearly interpolating between the projected y values of the two adjacent elements of Y.

Finally, we must consider the case of a partially visible line, in which both vertices are not visible with regard to the same silhouette array. Although this typically means that one of the vertices is visible and the other is invisible (BC, DE), it may be the case that both vertices are visible, one above $YMAX$ and the other below $YMIN$ (FG). Interpolated y values can be compared with those at the intervening locations in the silhouette arrays to determine the point(s) of intersection. The line should not be visible at those places where an interpolated y value falls inside the silhouette. Only the visible parts of the line segment outside the silhouette should be drawn, and the silhouette array should be updated, as shown in Fig. 15.3. When the two adjacent silhouette elements are found between which the line changes visibility, the line can be intersected with the line defined by the x and y values of those elements to determine an endpoint for a line-drawing algorithm.

Unfortunately, the image-precision $YMIN$ and $YMAX$ silhouette arrays make this algorithm prone to aliasing problems. If the line-drawing primitive used has higher resolution than do the silhouette arrays, aliasing can manifest itself as hidden segments that are drawn or as visible segments that are not. For example, Fig. 15.4 shows three polylines being drawn in front-to-back order. The two polylines of parts (a) and (b) form a gap when

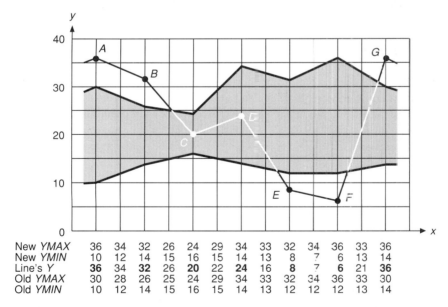

New *YMAX*	36	34	32	26	24	29	34	33	32	34	36	33	36
New *YMIN*	10	12	14	15	16	15	14	13	8	7	6	13	14
Line's *Y*	**36**	34	**32**	26	**20**	22	**24**	16	**8**	7	6	21	**36**
Old *YMAX*	30	28	26	25	24	29	34	33	32	34	36	33	30
Old *YMIN*	10	12	14	15	16	15	14	13	12	12	12	13	14

Fig. 15.3 The y values for positions on the line between the endpoints must be interpolated and compared with those in the silhouette arrays. Endpoint values are shown in boldface type.

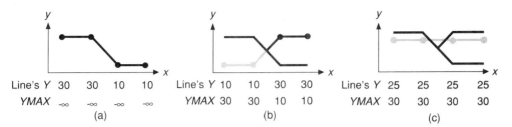

Fig. 15.4 Aliasing problem arising from the use of image-precision silhouette arrays.

they cross. The second line can be correctly hidden by the first by interpolating the values in *YMAX* to determine the intersection of the two lines. After the second line has been drawn, however, both values in *YMAX* are the same, so the third line, drawn in part (c), incorrectly remains hidden when it passes over their intersection. Using higher-resolution silhouette arrays can reduce such problems at the expense of increased processing time.

An alternative to image-precision *YMIN* and *YMAX* arrays is to use object-precision data structures [WILL72]. The *YMIN* and *YMAX* arrays can be replaced by two object-precision polylines representing the silhouette boundaries. As each segment of a polyline of constant *z* is inspected, only those parts projecting above the *YMAX* polyline or below the *YMIN* polyline are drawn. The projected lines representing these visible parts are linked into the silhouette polyline beginning at the point at which they intersect it, replacing the subsequent parts of the silhouette polyline until the next intersection. The accuracy gained by this approach must be weighed against the extra run-time overhead incurred by searching and maintaining the silhouette polylines and the added difficulties of coding a more complex algorithm.

Suppose we wish to draw polylines of constant *x*, instead of polylines of constant *z*, to produce the view shown in Fig. 15.5. In this case, the polyline of constant *x* closest to the observer does not form an edge of the surface. It is the seventh (the most nearly vertical) polyline from the left. To render the surface correctly, we must render polylines to the right

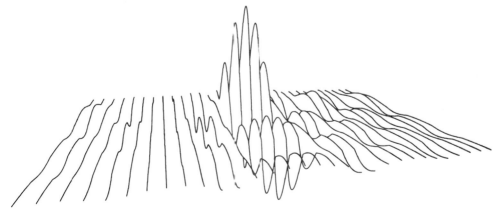

Fig. 15.5 Surface drawn using polylines of constant *x*, instead of polylines of constant *z*. (By Michael Hatzitheodorou, Columbia University.)

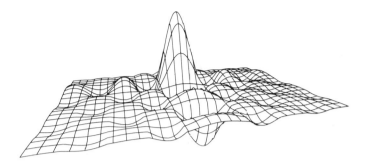

Fig. 15.6 Surface of Fig. 15.5 with lines of constant x and z. (By Michael Hatzithecdo-rou, Columbia University.)

of the closest one from left to right, and those to the left of the closest one from right to left. In both cases, polylines are rendered in front-to-back order relative to the observer.

The image-precision algorithm can be easily extended to plot lines of constant x as well as of constant z, as shown in Fig. 15.6. Although it is tempting to assume that superimposing the correctly plotted polylines of constant x and polylines of constant z would work, this does not allow lines from each set to hide those in the other, as shown in Fig. 15.7. Wright [WRIG73] points out that the correct solution can be obtained by interleaving the processing of the two sets of polylines. The set of those polylines that are most nearly parallel to the view plane (e.g., those of constant z) is processed in the same order as before. After each polyline of constant z is processed, the segments of each polyline of constant x between the just-processed polyline of z and the next polyline of z are drawn. The line segments of x must be drawn using the same copy of the silhouette data structure as was used for drawing the polylines of constant z. In addition, they too must be processed in front-to-back order. Figure 15.8(a) shows lines of constant x as processed in the correct order, from left to right in this case. The lines of constant x in Fig. 15.8(b) have been processed in the opposite, incorrect order, from right to left. The incorrect drawing order causes problems, because each successive line is shadowed in the $YMAX$ array by the lines drawn previously.

Although the algorithms described in this section are both useful and efficient, they fail for any viewing specification for which the silhouette of the object is not a function of x when projected on the view plane. An example of such a viewing specification is shown in Fig. 15.9, which was rendered with an algorithm developed by Anderson [ANDE82] that uses more complex data structures to handle arbitrary viewing specifications.

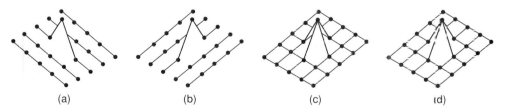

| (a) | (b) | (c) | (d) |

Fig. 15.7 (a) Lines of constant z. (b) Lines of constant x. (c) Superposition of parts (a) and (b). (d) The correct solution. (Based on [WRIG73].)

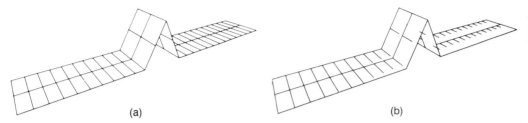

Fig. 15.8 Polylines of constant x, like those of constant z, must be processed in the correct order. (a) Correctly processed lines. (b) Incorrectly processed lines. (By Michael Hatzitheodorou, Columbia University.)

15.2 TECHNIQUES FOR EFFICIENT VISIBLE-SURFACE ALGORITHMS

As we have just seen, a restricted version of the visible-line problem for functions of two variables can be solved efficiently by using clever data structures. What can be done for the general problem of visible-surface determination? The simple formulations of prototypical image-precision and object-precision algorithms given at the beginning of this chapter require a number of potentially costly operations. These include determining for a projector and an object, or for two objects' projections, whether or not they intersect and where they intersect. Then, for each set of intersections, it is necessary to compute the object that is closest to the viewer and therefore visible. To minimize the time that it takes to create a picture, we must organize visible-surface algorithms so that costly operations are performed

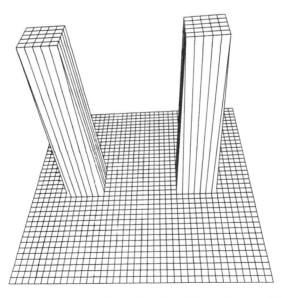

Fig. 15.9 A projection not handled by the algorithm discussed here. (Courtesy of David P. Anderson, University of California, Berkeley.)

as efficiently and as infrequently as possible. The following sections describe some general ways to do this.

15.2.1 Coherence

Sutherland, Sproull, and Schumacker [SUTH74a] point out how visible-surface algorithms can take advantage of *coherence*—the degree to which parts of an environment or its projection exhibit local similarities. Environments typically contain objects whose properties vary smoothly from one part to another. In fact, it is the less frequent discontinuities in properties (such as depth, color, and texture) and the effects that they produce in pictures, that let us distinguish between objects. We exploit coherence when we reuse calculations made for one part of the environment or picture for other nearby parts, either without changes or with incremental changes that are more efficient to make than recalculating the information from scratch. Many different kinds of coherence have been identified [SUTH74a], which we list here and refer to later:

- *Object coherence.* If one object is entirely separate from another, comparisons may need to be done only between the two objects, and not between their component faces or edges. For example, if all parts of object *A* are farther from the viewer than are all parts of object *B*, none of *A*'s faces need be compared with *B*'s faces to determine whether they obscure *B*'s faces.

- *Face coherence.* Surface properties typically vary smoothly across a face, allowing computations for one part of a face to be modified incrementally to apply to adjacent parts. In some models, faces can be guaranteed not to interpenetrate.

- *Edge coherence.* An edge may change visibility only where it crosses behind a visible edge or penetrates a visible face.

- *Implied edge coherence.* If one planar face penetrates another, their line of intersection (the implied edge) can be determined from two points of intersection.

- *Scan-line coherence.* The set of visible object spans determined for one scan line of an image typically differs little from the set on the previous line.

- *Area coherence.* A group of adjacent pixels is often covered by the same visible face. A special case of area coherence is *span coherence,* which refers to a face's visibility over a span of adjacent pixels on a scan line.

- *Depth coherence.* Adjacent parts of the same surface are typically close in depth, whereas different surfaces at the same screen location are typically separated farther in depth. Once the depth at one point of the surface is calculated, the depth of points on the rest of the surface can often be determined by a simple difference equation.

- *Frame coherence.* Pictures of the same environment at two successive points in time are likely to be quite similar, despite small changes in objects and viewpoint. Calculations made for one picture can be reused for the next in a sequence.

15.2.2 The Perspective Transformation

Visible-surface determination clearly must be done in a 3D space prior to the projection into 2D that destroys the depth information needed for depth comparisons. Regardless of the kind of projection chosen, the basic depth comparison at a point can be typically reduced to the following question: Given points $P_1 = (x_1, y_1, z_1)$ and $P_2 = (x_2, y_2, z_2)$, does either point obscure the other? This question is the same: Are P_1 and P_2 on the same projector (see Fig. 15.10)? If the answer is yes, z_1 and z_2 are compared to determine which point is closer to the viewer. If the answer is no, then neither point can obscure the other.

Depth comparisons are typically done after the normalizing transformation (Chapter 6) has been applied, so that projectors are parallel to the z axis in parallel projections or emanate from the origin in perspective projections. For a parallel projection, the points are on the same projector if $x_1 = x_2$ and $y_1 = y_2$. For a perspective projection, we must unfortunately perform four divisions to determine whether $x_1 / z_1 = x_2 / z_2$ and $y_1 / z_1 = y_2 / z_2$, in which case the points are on the same projector, as shown in Fig. 15.10. Moreover, if P_1 is later compared against some P_3, two more divisions are required.

Unnecessary divisions can be avoided by first transforming a 3D object into the 3D screen-coordinate system, so that the parallel projection of the transformed object is the same as the perspective projection of the untransformed object. Then the test for one point obscuring another is the same as for parallel projections. This perspective transformation distorts the objects and moves the center of projection to infinity on the positive z axis, making the projectors parallel (see Fig. 6.56). Figure 15.11 shows the effect of this transformation on the perspective view volume; Fig. 15.12 shows how a cube is distorted by the transformation.

The essence of such a transformation is that it preserves relative depth, straight lines, and planes, and at the same time performs the perspective foreshortening. As discussed in Chapter 6, the division that accomplishes the foreshortening is done just once per point, rather than each time two points are compared. The matrix from Eq. (6.48)

$$M = \begin{bmatrix} 1 & 0 & 0 & 0 \\ 0 & 1 & 0 & 0 \\ 0 & 0 & \dfrac{1}{1 + z_{min}} & \dfrac{-z_{min}}{1 + z_{min}} \\ 0 & 0 & -1 & 0 \end{bmatrix}, \; z_{min} \neq -1 \tag{15.1}$$

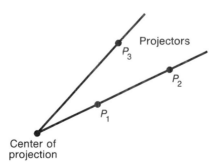

Fig. 15.10 If two points P_1 and P_2 are on the same projector, then the closer one obscures the other; otherwise, it does not (e.g., P_1 does not obscure P_3).

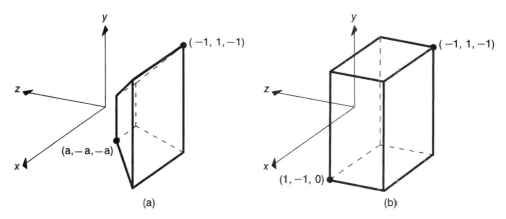

Fig. 15.11 The normalized perspective view volume (a) before and (b) after perspective transformation.

transforms the normalized perspective view volume into the rectangular parallelepiped bounded by

$$-1 \le x \le 1, \quad -1 \le y \le 1, \quad -1 \le z \le 0. \tag{15.2}$$

Clipping can be done against the normalized truncated-pyramid view volume before M is applied, but then the clipped results must be multiplied by M. A more attractive alternative is to incorporate M into the perspective normalizing transformation N_{per} from Chapter 6, so that just a single matrix multiplication is needed, and then to clip in homogeneous coordinates prior to the division. If we call the results of that multiplication (X, Y, Z, W), then, for $W > 0$, the clipping limits become

$$-W \le X \le W, \quad -W \le Y \le W, \quad -W \le Z \le 0. \tag{15.3}$$

These limits are derived from Eq. (15.2) by replacing x, y, and z by X/W, Y/W, and Z/W, respectively, to reflect the fact that x, y, and z in Eq. (15.2) result from division by W. After clipping, we divide by W to obtain (x_p, y_p, z_p). (See Section 6.5.4. for what to do when

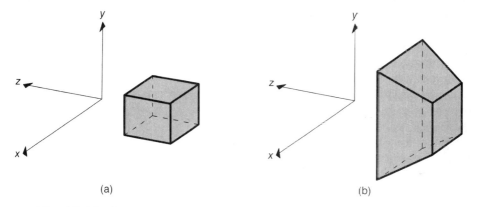

Fig. 15.12 A cube (a) before and (b) after perspective transformation.

$W < 0$.) Note that M assumes the view volume is in the negative z half-space. For notational convenience, however, our examples will often use decreasing positive z values, rather than decreasing negative z values, to indicate increasing distance from the viewer. In contrast, many graphics systems transform their right-handed world into a left-handed viewing coordinate system, in which increasing positive z values correspond to increasing distance from the viewer.

We can now proceed with visible-surface determination unfettered by the complications suggested by Fig. 15.10. Of course, when a parallel projection is specified, the perspective transformation M is unnecessary, because the normalizing transformation N_{par} for parallel projections makes the projectors parallel to the z axis.

15.2.3   Extents and Bounding Volumes

Screen extents, introduced in Chapter 3 as a way to avoid unnecessary clipping, are also commonly used to avoid unnecessary comparisons between objects or their projections. Figure 15.13 shows two objects (3D polygons, in this case), their projections, and the upright rectangular screen extents surrounding the projections. The objects are assumed to have been transformed by the perspective transformation matrix M of Section 15.2.2. Therefore, for polygons, orthographic projection onto the (x, y) plane is done trivially by ignoring each vertex's z coordinate. In Fig. 15.13, the extents do not overlap, so the projections do not need to be tested for overlap with one another. If the extents overlap, one of two cases occurs, as shown in Fig. 15.14: either the projections also overlap, as in part (a), or they do not, as in part (b). In both cases, more comparisons must be performed to determine whether the projections overlap. In part (b), the comparisons will establish that the two projections really do not intersect; in a sense, the overlap of the extents was a false alarm. Extent testing thus provides a service similar to that of trivial reject testing in clipping.

Rectangular-extent testing is also known as *bounding-box* testing. Extents can be used as in Chapter 7 to surround the objects themselves rather than their projections: in this case, the extents become solids and are also known as *bounding volumes*. Alternatively, extents can be used to bound a single dimension, in order to determine, say, whether or not two objects overlap in z. Figure 15.15 shows the use of extents in such a case; here, an extent is the infinite volume bounded by the minimum and maximum z values for each object. There

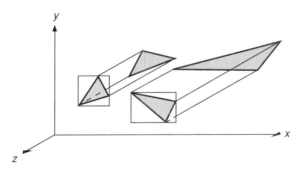

Fig. 15.13 Two objects, their projections onto the (x, y) plane, and the extents surrounding the projections.

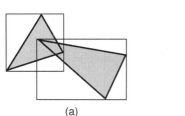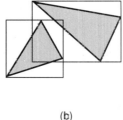

(a)   (b)

Fig. 15.14 Extents bounding object projections. (a) Extents and projections overlap. (b) Extents overlap, but projections do not.

is no overlap in z if

$$z_{max2} < z_{min1} \quad or \quad z_{max1} < z_{min2}. \tag{15.4}$$

Comparing against minimum and maximum bounds in one or more dimensions is also known as *minmax* testing. When comparing minmax extents, the most complicated part of the job is finding the extent itself. For polygons (or for other objects that are wholly contained within the convex hull of a set of defining points), an extent may be computed by iterating through the list of point coordinates and recording the largest and smallest values for each coordinate.

Extents and bounding volumes are used not only to compare two objects or their projections with each other, but also to determine whether or not a projector intersects an object. This involves computing the intersection of a point with a 2D projection or a vector with a 3D object, as described in Section 15.10.

Although we have discussed only minmax extents so far, other bounding volumes are possible. What is the best bounding volume to use? Not surprisingly, the answer depends on both the expense of performing tests on the bounding volume itself and on how well the volume protects the enclosed object from tests that do not yield an intersection. Weghorst, Hooper, and Greenberg [WEGH84] treat bounding-volume selection as a matter of minimizing the total cost function T of the intersection test for an object. This may be expressed as

$$T = bB + oO, \tag{15.5}$$

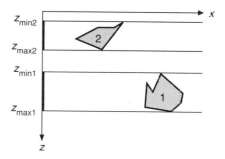

Fig. 15.15 Using 1D extents to determine whether objects overlap.

where b is the number of times the bounding volume is tested for intersection, B is the cost of performing an intersection test on the bounding volume, o is the number of times the object is tested for intersection (the number of times the bounding volume is actually intersected), and O is the cost of performing an intersection test on the object.

Since the object intersection test is performed only when the bounding volume is actually intersected, $o \le b$. Although O and b are constant for a particular object and set of tests to be performed, B and o vary as a function of the bounding volume's shape and size. A "tighter" bounding volume, which minimizes o, is typically associated with a greater B. A bounding volume's effectiveness may also depend on an object's orientation or the kind of objects with which that object will be intersected. Compare the two bounding volumes for the wagon wheel shown in Fig. 15.16. If the object is to be intersected with projectors perpendicular to the (x, y) plane, then the tighter bounding volume is the sphere. If

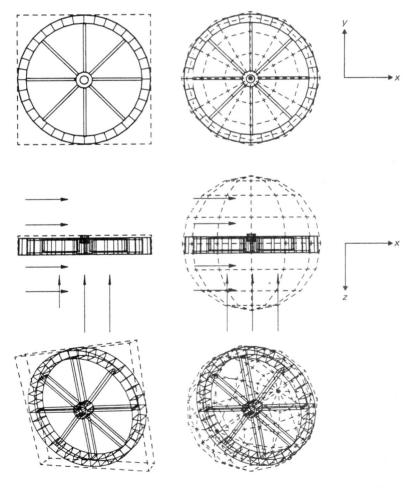

Fig. 15.16 Bounding volume selection. (Courtesy of Hank Weghorst, Gary Hooper, Donald P. Greenberg, Program of Computer Graphics, Cornell University, 1984.)

projectors are perpendicular to the (x, z) or (y, z) planes, then the rectangular extent is the tighter bounding volume. Therefore, multiple bounding volumes may be associated with an object and an appropriate one selected depending on the circumstances.

15.2.4 Back-Face Culling

If an object is approximated by a solid polyhedron, then its polygonal faces completely enclose its volume. Assume that all the polygons have been defined such that their surface normals point out of their polyhedron. If none of the polyhedron's interior is exposed by the front clipping plane, then those polygons whose surface normals point away from the observer lie on a part of the polyhedron whose visibility is completely blocked by other closer polygons, as shown in Fig. 15.17. Such invisible *back-facing* polygons can be eliminated from further processing, a technique known as *back-face culling*. By analogy, those polygons that are not back-facing are often called *front-facing*.

In eye coordinates, a back-facing polygon may be identified by the nonnegative dot product that its surface normal forms with the vector from the center of projection to any point on the polygon. (Strictly speaking, the dot product is positive for a back-facing polygon; a zero dot product indicates a polygon being viewed on edge.) Assuming that the perspective transformation has been performed or that an orthographic projection onto the (x, y) plane is desired, then the direction of projection is $(0, 0, -1)$. In this case, the dot-product test reduces to selecting a polygon as back-facing only if its surface normal has a negative z coordinate. If the environment consists of a single convex polyhedron, back-face culling is the only visible-surface calculation that needs to be performed. Otherwise, there may be front-facing polygons, such as C and E in Fig. 15.17, that are partially or totally obscured.

If the polyhedra have missing or clipped front faces, or if the polygons are not part of polyhedra at all, then back-facing polygons may still be given special treatment. If culling is not desired, the simplest approach is to treat a back-facing polygon as though it were front-facing, flipping its normal in the opposite direction. In PHIGS+, the user can specify a completely separate set of properties for each side of a surface.

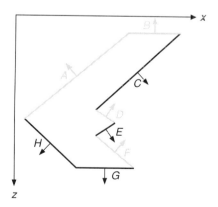

Fig. 15.17 Back-face culling. Back-facing polygons (A,B,D,F) shown in gray are eliminated, whereas front-facing polygons (C,E,G,H) are retained.

Extrapolating from Section 7.12.2's parity-check algorithm for determining whether a point is contained in a polygon, note that a projector passing through a polyhedron intersects the same number of back-facing polygons as of front-facing ones. Thus, a point in a polyhedron's projection lies in the projections of as many back-facing polygons as front-facing ones. Back-face culling therefore halves the number of polygons to be considered for each pixel in an image-precision visible-surface algorithm. On average, approximately one-half of a polyhedron's polygons are back-facing. Thus, back-face culling also typically halves the number of polygons to be considered by the remainder of an object-precision visible-surface algorithm. (Note, however, that this is true only on average. For example, a pyramid's base may be that object's only back- or front-facing polygon.)

As described so far, back-face culling is an object-precision technique that requires time linear in the number of polygons. Sublinear performance can be obtained by preprocessing the objects to be displayed. For example, consider a cube centered about the origin of its own object coordinate system, with its faces perpendicular to the coordinate system's axes. From any viewpoint outside the cube, at most three of its faces are visible. Furthermore, each octant of the cube's coordinate system is associated with a specific set of three potentially visible faces. Therefore, the position of the viewpoint relative to the cube's coordinate system can be used to select one of the eight sets of three potentially visible faces. For objects with a relatively small number of faces, a table may be made up in advance to allow visible-surface determination without processing all the object's faces for each change of viewpoint.

A table of visible faces indexed by viewpoint equivalence class may be quite large, however, for an object with many faces. Tanimoto [TANI77] suggests as an alternative a graph-theoretic approach that takes advantage of frame coherence. A graph is constructed with a node for each face of a convex polyhedron, and a graph edge connecting each pair of nodes whose faces share a polygon edge. The list of edges separating visible faces from invisible ones is then computed for an initial viewpoint. This list contains all edges on the object's silhouette. Tanimoto shows that, as the viewpoint changes between frames, only the visibilities of faces lying between the old and new silhouettes need to be recomputed.

15.2.5 Spatial Partitioning

Spatial partitioning (also known as *spatial subdivision*) allows us to break down a large problem into a number of smaller ones. The basic approach is to assign objects or their projections to spatially coherent groups as a preprocessing step. For example, we can divide the projection plane with a coarse, regular 2D rectangular grid and determine in which grid spaces each object's projection lies. Projections need to be compared for overlap with only those other projections that fall within their grid boxes. This technique is used by [ENCA72; MAHN73; FRAN80; HEDG82]. Spatial partitioning can be used to impose a regular 3D grid on the objects in the environment. The process of determining which objects intersect with a projector can then be sped up by first determining which partitions the projector intersects, and then testing only the objects lying within those partitions (Section 15.10).

If the objects being depicted are unequally distributed in space, it may be more efficient to use *adaptive partitioning*, in which the size of each partition varies. One approach to adaptive partitioning is to subdivide space recursively until some termination criterion is

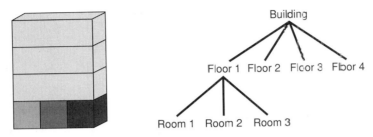

Fig. 15.18 Hierarchy can be used to restrict the number of object comparisons needed. Only if a projector intersects the building and floor 1 does it need to be tested for intersection with rooms 1 through 3.

fulfilled for each partition. For example, subdivision may stop when there are fewer than some maximum number of objects in a partition [TAMM82]. The quadtree, octree, and BSP-tree data structures of Section 12.6 are particularly attractive for this purpose.

15.2.6 Hierarchy

As we saw in Chapter 7, hierarchies can be useful for relating the structure and motion of different objects. A nested hierarchical model, in which each child is considered part of its parent, can also be used to restrict the number of object comparisons needed by a visible-surface algorithm [CLAR76; RUBI80; WEGH84]. An object on one level of the hierarchy can serve as an extent for its children if they are entirely contained within it, as shown in Fig. 15.18. In this case, if two objects in the hierarchy fail to intersect, the lower-level objects of one do not need to be tested for intersection with those of the other. Similarly, only if a projector is found to penetrate an object in the hierarchy must it be tested against the object's children. This use of hierarchy is an important instance of object coherence. A way to automate the construction of hierarchies is discussed in Section 15.10.2.

15.3 ALGORITHMS FOR VISIBLE-LINE DETERMINATION

Now that we have discussed a number of general techniques, we introduce some visible-line and visible-surface algorithms to see how these techniques are used. We begin with visible-line algorithms. The algorithms presented here all operate in object precision and produce as output a list of visible line segments suitable for vector display. The visible-surface algorithms discussed later can also be used for visible-line determination by rendering each surface as a background-colored interior surrounded by a border of the desired line color; most visible-surface algorithms produce an image-precision array of pixels, however, rather than an object-precision list of edges.

15.3.1 Roberts's Algorithm

The earliest visible-line algorithm was developed by Roberts [ROBE63]. It requires that each edge be part of the face of a convex polyhedron. First, back-face culling is used to remove all edges shared by a pair of a polyhedron's back-facing polygons. Next, each remaining edge is compared with each polyhedron that might obscure it. Many polyhedra can be trivially eliminated from the comparison through extent testing: the extents of their projections may fail to overlap in *x* or *y*, or one object's extent may be farther back in *z* than is the other. Those polyhedra that are tested are compared in sequence with the edge. Because the polyhedra are convex, there is at most one contiguous group of points on any line that is blocked from the observer by any polyhedron. Thus, each polyhedron either obscures the edge totally or causes one or two pieces to remain. Any remaining pieces of the edge are compared with the next polyhedron.

Roberts's visibility test is performed with a parametric version of the projector from the eye to a point on the edge being tested. He uses a linear-programming approach to solve for those values of the line equation that cause the projector to pass through a polyhedron, resulting in the invisibility of the endpoint. The projector passes through a polyhedron if it contains some point that is inside all the polyhedron's front faces. Rogers [ROGE85] provides a detailed explanation of Roberts's algorithm and discusses ways in which that algorithm can be further improved.

15.3.2 Appel's Algorithm

Several more general visible-line algorithms [APPE67; GALI69; LOUT70] require only that lines be the edges of polygons, not polyhedra. These algorithms also consider only lines that bound front-facing polygons, and take advantage of edge-coherence in a fashion typified by Appel's algorithm. Appel [APPE67] defines the *quantitative invisibility* of a point on a line as the number of front-facing polygons that obscure that point. When a line passes behind a front-facing polygon, its quantitative invisibility is incremented by 1; when it passes out from behind that polygon, its quantitative invisibility is decremented by 1. A line is visible only when its quantitative invisibility is 0. Line *AB* in Fig. 15.19 is annotated with the quantitative invisibility of each of its segments. If interpenetrating polygons are not allowed, a line's quantitative invisibility changes only when it passes behind what Appel

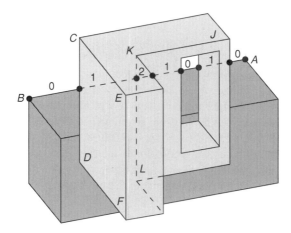

Fig. 15.19 Quantitative invisibility of a line. Dashed lines are hidden. Intersections of *AB*'s projection with projections of contour lines are shown as large dots (●), and each segment of *AB* is marked with its quantitative invisibility.

calls a *contour line*. A contour line is either an edge shared by a front-facing and a back-facing polygon, or the unshared edge of a front-facing polygon that is not part of a closed polyhedron. An edge shared by two front-facing polygons causes no change in visibility and therefore is not a contour line. In Fig. 15.19, edges *AB, CD, DF*, and *KL* are contour lines, whereas edges *CE, EF*, and *JK* are not.

A contour line passes in front of the edge under consideration if it pierces the triangle formed by the eyepoint and the edge's two endpoints. Whether it does so can be determined by a point-in-polygon containment test, such as that discussed in Section 7.12.2. The projection of such a contour line on the edge can be found by clipping the edge against the plane determined by the eyepoint and the contour line. Appel's algorithm requires that all polygon edges be drawn in a consistent direction about the polygon, so that the sign of the change in quantitative invisibility is determined by the sign of the cross-product of the edge with the contour line.

The algorithm first computes the quantitative invisibility of a "seed" vertex of an object by determining the number of front-facing polygons that hide it. This can be done by a brute-force computation of all front-facing polygons whose intersection with the projector to the seed vertex is closer than is the seed vertex itself. The algorithm then takes advantage of edge coherence by propagating this value along the edges emanating from the point, incrementing or decrementing the value at each point at which an edge passes behind a contour line. Only sections of edges whose quantitative invisibility is zero are drawn. When each line's other endpoint is reached, the quantitative invisibility associated with that endpoint becomes the initial quantitative invisibility of all lines emanating in turn from it.

At vertices through which a contour line passes, there is a complication that requires us to make a correction when propagating the quantitative invisibility. One or more lines emanating from the vertex may be hidden by one or more front-facing polygons sharing the vertex. For example, in Fig. 15.19, edge *JK* has a quantitative invisibility of 0, while edge *KL* has a quantitative invisibility of 1 because it is hidden by the object's top face. This change in quantitative invisibility at a vertex can be taken into account by testing the edge against the front-facing polygons that share the vertex.

For an algorithm such as Appel's to handle intersecting polygons, it is necessary to compute the intersections of edges with front-facing polygons and to use each such intersection to increment or decrement the quantitative invisibility. Since visible-line algorithms typically compare whole edges with other edges or objects, they can benefit greatly from spatial-partitioning approaches. Each edge then needs to be compared with only the other edges or objects in the grid boxes containing its projection.

15.3.3   Haloed Lines

Any visible-line algorithm can be easily adapted to show hidden lines as dotted, as dashed, of lower intensity, or with some other rendering style supported by the display device. The program then outputs the hidden line segments in the line style selected, instead of suppressing them. In contrast, Appel, Rohlf, and Stein [APPE79] describe an algorithm for rendering haloed lines, as shown in Fig. 15.20. Each line is surrounded on both sides by a halo that obscures those parts of lines passing behind it. This algorithm, unlike those

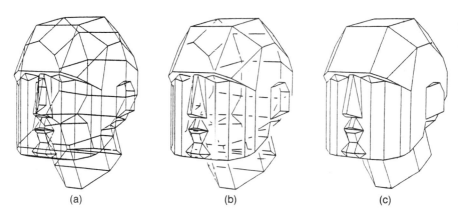

(a)   (b)   (c)

Fig. 15.20 Three heads rendered (a) without hidden lines eliminated, (b) with hidden lines haloed, and (c) with hidden lines eliminated. (Courtesy of Arthur Appel, IBM T.J. Watson Research Center.)

discussed previously, does not require each line to be part of an opaque polygonal face. Lines that pass behind others are obscured only around their intersection on the view plane. The algorithm intersects each line with those passing in front of it, keeps track of those sections that are obscured by halos, and draws the visible sections of each line after the intersections have been calculated. If the halos are wider than the spacing between lines, then an effect similar to conventional hidden-line elimination is achieved, except that a line's halo extends outside a polygon of which it may be an edge.

In the rest of this chapter, we discuss the rich variety of algorithms developed for visible-surface determination. We concentrate here on computing which parts of an object's surfaces are visible, leaving the determination of surface color to Chapter 16. In describing each algorithm, we emphasize its application to polygons, but point out when it can be generalized to handle other objects.

15.4   THE z-BUFFER ALGORITHM

The z-buffer or depth-buffer image-precision algorithm, developed by Catmull [CATM74b], is one of the simplest visible-surface algorithms to implement in either software or hardware. It requires that we have available not only a frame buffer F in which color values are stored, but also a z-buffer Z, with the same number of entries, in which a z-value is stored for each pixel. The z-buffer is initialized to zero, representing the z-value at the back clipping plane, and the frame buffer is initialized to the background color. The largest value that can be stored in the z-buffer represents the z of the front clipping plane. Polygons are scan-converted into the frame buffer in arbitrary order. During the scan-conversion process, if the polygon point being scan-converted at (x, y) is no farther from the viewer than is the point whose color and depth are currently in the buffers, then the new point's color and depth replace the old values. The pseudocode for the z-buffer algorithm is shown in Fig. 15.21. The WritePixel and ReadPixel procedures introduced in Chapter 3 are supplemented here by WriteZ and ReadZ procedures that write and read the z-buffer.

```
void zBuffer(void)
{
    int x, y;

    for (y = 0; y < YMAX; y++) {        /* Clear frame buffer and z-buffer */
        for (x = 0; x < XMAX; x++) {
            WritePixel (x, y, BACKGROUND_VALUE);
            WriteZ (x, y, 0);
        }
    }

    for (each polygon) {                 /* Draw polygons */
        for (each pixel in polygon's projection) {
            double pz = polygon's z-value at pixel coords (x, y);
            if (pz >= ReadZ (x, y)) {    /* New point is not farther */
                WriteZ (x, y, pz);
                WritePixel (x, y, polygon's color at pixel coords (x, y));
            }
        }
    }
}   /* zBuffer */
```

Fig. 15.21 Pseudocode for the z-buffer algorithm.

No presorting is necessary and no object–object comparisons are required. The entire process is no more than a search over each set of pairs $\{Z_i(x, y), F_i(x, y)\}$ for fixed x and y, to find the largest Z_i. The z-buffer and the frame buffer record the information associated with the largest z encountered thus far for each (x, y). Thus, polygons appear on the screen in the order in which they are processed. Each polygon may be scan-converted one scan line at a time into the buffers, as described in Section 3.6. Figure 15.22 shows the addition of two polygons to an image. Each pixel's shade is shown by its color; its z is shown as a number.

Remembering our discussion of depth coherence, we can simplify the calculation of z for each point on a scan line by exploiting the fact that a polygon is planar. Normally, to calculate z, we would solve the plane equation $Ax + By + Cz + D = 0$ for the variable z:

$$z = \frac{-D - Ax - By}{C}. \tag{15.6}$$

Now, if at (x, y) Eq. (15.6) evaluates to z_1, then at $(x + \Delta x, y)$ the value of z is

$$z_1 - \frac{A}{C}(\Delta x). \tag{15.7}$$

Only one subtraction is needed to calculate $z(x + 1, y)$ given $z(x, y)$, since the quotient A/C is constant and $\Delta x = 1$. A similar incremental calculation can be performed to determine the first value of z on the next scan line, decrementing by B/C for each Δy. Alternatively, if

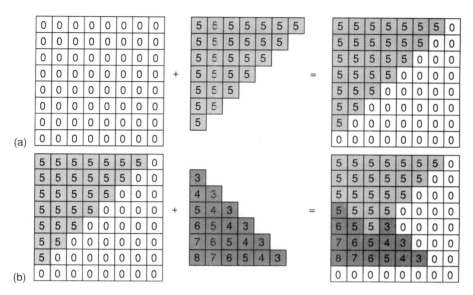

Fig. 15.22 The z-buffer. A pixel's shade is shown by its color, its z value is shown as a number. (a) Adding a polygon of constant z to the empty z-buffer. (b) Adding another polygon that intersects the first.

the surface has not been determined or if the polygon is not planar (see Section 11.1.3), $z(x, y)$ can be determined by interpolating the z coordinates of the polygon's vertices along pairs of edges, and then across each scan line, as shown in Fig. 15.23. Incremental calculations can be used here as well. Note that the color at a pixel does not need to be computed if the conditional determining the pixel's visibility is not satisfied. Therefore, if the shading computation is time consuming, additional efficiency can be gained by performing a rough front-to-back depth sort of the objects to display the closest objects first.

The z-buffer algorithm does not require that objects be polygons. Indeed, one of its most powerful attractions is that it can be used to render any object if a shade and a z-value

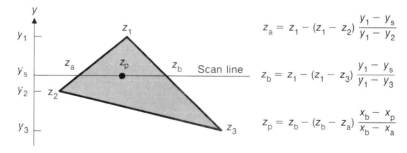

$$z_a = z_1 - (z_1 - z_2) \frac{y_1 - y_s}{y_1 - y_2}$$

$$z_b = z_1 - (z_1 - z_3) \frac{y_1 - y_s}{y_1 - y_3}$$

$$z_p = z_b - (z_b - z_a) \frac{x_b - x_p}{x_b - x_a}$$

Fig. 15.23 Interpolation of z values along polygon edges and scan lines. z_a is interpolated between z_1 and z_2; z_b between z_1 and z_3; z_p between z_a and z_b.

can be determined for each point in its projection; no explicit intersection algorithms need to be written.

The z-buffer algorithm performs radix sorts in x and y, requiring no comparisons, and its z sort takes only one comparison per pixel for each polygon containing that pixel. The time taken by the visible-surface calculations tends to be independent of the number of polygons in the objects because, on the average, the number of pixels covered by each polygon decreases as the number of polygons in the view volume increases. Therefore, the average size of each set of pairs being searched tends to remain fixed. Of course, it is also necessary to take into account the scan-conversion overhead imposed by the additional polygons.

Although the z-buffer algorithm requires a large amount of space for the z-buffer, it is easy to implement. If memory is at a premium, the image can be scan-converted in strips, so that only enough z-buffer for the strip being processed is required, at the expense of performing multiple passes through the objects. Because of the z-buffer's simplicity and the lack of additional data structures, decreasing memory costs have inspired a number of hardware and firmware implementations of the z-buffer, examples of which are discussed in Chapter 18. Because the z-buffer algorithm operates in image precision, however, it is subject to aliasing. The A-buffer algorithm [CARP84], described in Section 15.7, addresses this problem by using a discrete approximation to unweighted area sampling.

The z-buffer is often implemented with 16- through 32-bit integer values in hardware, but software (and some hardware) implementations may use floating-point values. Although a 16-bit z-buffer offers an adequate range for many CAD/CAM applications, 16 bits do not have enough precision to represent environments in which objects defined with millimeter detail are positioned a kilometer apart. To make matters worse, if a perspective projection is used, the compression of distant z values resulting from the perspective divide has a serious effect on the depth ordering and intersections of distant objects. Two points that would transform to different integer z values if close to the view plane may transform to the same z value if they are farther back (see Exercise 15.13 and [HUGH89]).

The z-buffer's finite precision is responsible for another aliasing problem. Scan-conversion algorithms typically render two different sets of pixels when drawing the common part of two collinear edges that start at different endpoints. Some of those pixels shared by the rendered edges may also be assigned slightly different z values because of numerical inaccuracies in performing the z interpolation. This effect is most noticeable at the shared edges of a polyhedron's faces. Some of the visible pixels along an edge may be part of one polygon, while the rest come from the polygon's neighbor. The problem can be fixed by inserting extra vertices to ensure that vertices occur at the same points along the common part of two collinear edges.

Even after the image has been rendered, the z-buffer can still be used to advantage. Since it is the only data structure used by the visible-surface algorithm proper, it can be saved along with the image and used later to merge in other objects whose z can be computed. The algorithm can also be coded so as to leave the z-buffer contents unmodified when rendering selected objects. If the z-buffer is masked off this way, then a single object can be written into a separate set of overlay planes with hidden surfaces properly removed (if the object is a single-valued function of x and y) and then erased without affecting the contents of the z-buffer. Thus, a simple object, such as a ruled grid, can be moved about the image in x, y, and z, to serve as a "3D cursor" that obscures and is obscured by the objects in the environment. Cutaway views can be created by making the z-buffer and frame-buffer writes contingent on whether the z value is behind a cutting plane. If the objects being displayed have a single z value for each (x, y), then the z-buffer contents can also be used to compute area and volume. Exercise 15.25 explains how to use the z-buffer for picking.

Rossignac and Requicha [ROSS86] discuss how to adapt the z-buffer algorithm to handle objects defined by CSG. Each pixel in a surface's projection is written only if it is both closer in z and on a CSG object constructed from the surface. Instead of storing only the point with closest z at each pixel, Atherton suggests saving a list of all points, ordered by z and accompanied by each surface's identity, to form an *object buffer* [ATHE81]. A postprocessing stage determines how the image is displayed. A variety of effects, such as transparency, clipping, and Boolean set operations, can be achieved by processing each pixel's list, without any need to re–scan convert the objects.

15.5   LIST-PRIORITY ALGORITHMS

List-priority algorithms determine a visibility ordering for objects ensuring that a correct picture results if the objects are rendered in that order. For example, if no object overlaps another in z, then we need only to sort the objects by increasing z, and to render them in that order. Farther objects are obscured by closer ones as pixels from the closer polygons overwrite those of the more distant ones. If objects overlap in z, we may still be able to determine a correct order, as in Fig. 15.24(a). If objects cyclically overlap each other, as Fig. 15.24(b) and (c), or penetrate each other, then there is no correct order. In these cases, it will be necessary to split one or more objects to make a linear order possible.

List-priority algorithms are hybrids that combine both object-precision and image-precision operations. Depth comparisons and object splitting are done with object precision. Only scan conversion, which relies on the ability of the graphics device to overwrite the pixels of previously drawn objects, is done with image precision. Because the list of sorted objects is created with object precision, however, it can be redisplayed correctly at any resolution. As we shall see, list-priority algorithms differ in how they determine the sorted order, as well as in which objects get split, and when the splitting occurs. The sort need not be on z, some objects may be split that neither cyclically overlap nor penetrate others, and the splitting may even be done independent of the viewer's position.

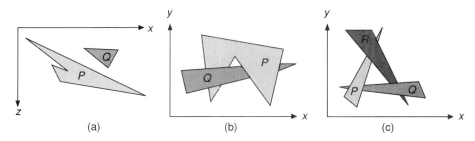

Fig. 15.24 Some cases in which z extents of polygons overlap.

15.5.1 The Depth-Sort Algorithm

The basic idea of the *depth-sort algorithm,* developed by Newell, Newell, and Sancha [NEWE72], is to paint the polygons into the frame buffer in order of decreasing distance from the viewpoint. Three conceptual steps are performed:

1. Sort all polygons according to the smallest (farthest) z coordinate of each

2. Resolve any ambiguities this may cause when the polygons' z extents overlap, splitting polygons if necessary

3. Scan convert each polygon in ascending order of smallest z coordinate (i.e., back to front).

Consider the use of explicit priority, such as that associated with views in SPHIGS. The explicit priority takes the place of the minimum z value, and there can be no depth ambiguities because each priority is thought of as corresponding to a different plane of constant z. This simplified version of the depth-sort algorithm is often known as the *painter's algorithm,* in reference to how a painter might paint closer objects over more distant ones. Environments whose objects each exist in a plane of constant z, such as those of VLSI layout, cartography, and window management, are said to be $2\frac{1}{2}$D and can be correctly handled with the painter's algorithm. The painter's algorithm may be applied to a scene in which each polygon is not embedded in a plane of constant z by sorting the polygons by their minimum z coordinate or by the z coordinate of their centroid, ignoring step 2. Although scenes can be constructed for which this approach works, it does not in general produce a correct ordering.

Figure 15.24 shows some of the types of ambiguities that must be resolved as part of step 2. How is this done? Let the polygon currently at the far end of the sorted list of polygons be called P. Before this polygon is scan-converted into the frame buffer, it must be tested against each polygon Q whose z extent overlaps the z extent of P, to prove that P cannot obscure Q and that P can therefore be written before Q. Up to five tests are performed, in order of increasing complexity. As soon as one succeeds, P has been shown not to obscure Q and the next polygon Q overlapping P in z is tested. If all such polygons pass, then P is scan-converted and the next polygon on the list becomes the new P. The five tests are

1. Do the polygons' x extents not overlap?

2. Do the polygons' y extents not overlap?

3. Is P entirely on the opposite side of Q's plane from the viewpoint? (This is not the case in Fig. 15.24(a), but is true for Fig. 15.25.)

4. Is Q entirely on the same side of P's plane as the viewpoint? (This is not the case in Fig. 15.24(a), but is true for Fig. 15.26.)

5. Do the projections of the polygons onto the (x, y) plane not overlap? (This can be determined by comparing the edges of one polygon to the edges of the other.)

Exercise 15.6 suggests a way to implement tests 3 and 4.

If all five tests fail, we assume for the moment that P actually obscures Q, and therefore test whether Q can be scan-converted before P. Tests 1, 2, and 5 do not need to be repeated,

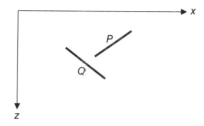

Fig. 15.25 Test 3 is true.

but new versions of tests 3 and 4 are used, with the polygons reversed:

3'. Is Q entirely on the opposite side of P's plane from the viewpoint?

4'. Is P entirely on the same side of Q's plane as the viewpoint?

In the case of Fig. 15.24(a), test 3' succeeds. Therefore, we move Q to the end of the list and it becomes the new P. In the case of Fig 15.24(b), however, the tests are still inconclusive; in fact, there is no order in which P and Q can be scan-converted correctly. Instead, either P or Q must be split by the plane of the other (see Section 3.14 on polygon clipping, treating the clip edge as a clip plane). The original unsplit polygon is discarded, its pieces are inserted in the list in proper z order, and the algorithm proceeds as before.

Figure 15.24(c) shows a more subtle case. It is possible for P, Q, and R to be oriented such that each polygon can always be moved to the end of the list to place it in the correct order relative to one, but not both, of the other polygons. This would result in an infinite loop. To avoid looping, we must modify our approach by marking each polygon that is moved to the end of the list. Then, whenever the first five tests fail and the current polygon Q is marked, we do not try tests 3' and 4'. Instead, we split either P or Q (as if tests 3' and 4' had both failed) and reinsert the pieces.

Can two polygons fail all the tests even when they are already ordered correctly? Consider P and Q in Fig. 15.27(a). Only the z coordinate of each vertex is shown. With P and Q in their current position, both the simple painter's algorithm and the full depth-sort algorithm scan convert P first. Now, rotate Q clockwise in its plane until it begins to obscure P, but do not allow P and Q themselves to intersect, as shown in Fig. 15.27(b). (You can do this nicely using your hands as P and Q, with your palms facing you.) P and Q

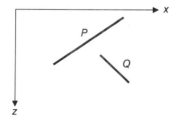

Fig. 15.26 Test 3 is false, but test 4 is true.

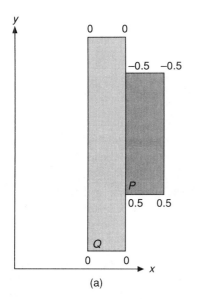
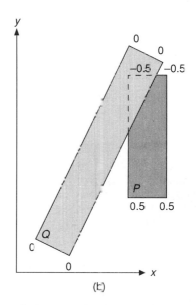

(a)   (b)

Fig. 15.27 Correctly ordered polygons may be split by the depth-sort algorithm. Polygon vertices are labeled with their z values. (a) Polygons P and Q are scan-converted without splitting. (b) Polygons P and Q fail all five tests even though they are correctly ordered.

have overlapping z extents, so they must be compared. Note that tests 1 and 2 (x and y extent) fail, tests 3 and 4 fail because neither is wholly in one half-space of the other, and test 5 fails because the projections overlap. Since tests 3' and 4' also fail, a polygon will be split, even though P can be scan-converted before Q. Although the simple painter's algorithm would correctly draw P first because P has the smallest minimum z coordinate, try the example again with $z = -0.5$ at P's bottom and $z = 0.5$ at P's top.

15.5.2 Binary Space-Partitioning Trees

The binary space-partitioning (BSP) tree algorithm, developed by Fuchs, Kedem, and Naylor [FUCH80; FUCH83], is an extremely efficient method for calculating the visibility relationships among a static group of 3D polygons as seen from an arbitrary viewpoint. It trades off an initial time- and space-intensive preprocessing step against a linear display algorithm that is executed whenever a new viewing specification is desired. Thus, the algorithm is well suited for applications in which the viewpoint changes, but the objects do not.

The BSP tree algorithm is based on the work of Schumacker [SCHU69], who noted that environments can be viewed as being composed of *clusters* (collections of faces), as shown in Fig. 15.28(a). If a plane can be found that wholly separates one set of clusters from another, then clusters that are on the same side of the plane as the eyepoint can obscure, but cannot be obscured by, clusters on the other side. Each of these sets of clusters can be recursively subdivided if suitable separating planes can be found. As shown in Fig. 15.28(b), this partitioning of the environment can be represented by a binary tree rooted at

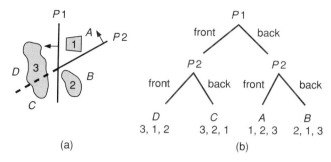

(a)   (b)

Fig. 15.28 Cluster priority. (a) Clusters 1 through 3 are divided by partitioning planes P1 and P2, determining regions A through D in which the eyepoint may be located. Each region has a unique cluster priority. (b) The binary-tree representation of (a). (Based on [SUTH74a].)

the first partitioning plane chosen. The tree's internal nodes are the partitioning planes; its leaves are regions in space. Each region is associated with a unique order in which clusters can obscure one another if the viewpoint is located in that region. Determining the region in which the eyepoint lies involves descending the tree from the root and choosing the left or right child of an internal node by comparing the viewpoint with the plane at that node.

Schumacker selects the faces in a cluster so that a priority ordering can be assigned to each face independent of the viewpoint, as shown in Fig. 15.29. After back-face culling has been performed relative to the viewpoint, a face with a lower priority number obscures a face with a higher number wherever the faces' projections intersect. For any pixel, the correct face to display is the highest-priority (lowest-numbered) face in the highest-priority cluster whose projection covers the pixel. Schumacker used special hardware to determine the frontmost face at each pixel. Alternatively, clusters can be displayed in order of increasing cluster priority (based on the viewpoint), with each cluster's faces displayed in order of their increasing face priority. Rather than take this two-part approach to computing an order in which faces should be scan-converted, the BSP tree algorithm uses a generalization of Schumacker's approach to calculating cluster priority. It is based on the observation that a polygon will be scan-converted correctly (i.e., will not incorrectly overlap or be incorrectly

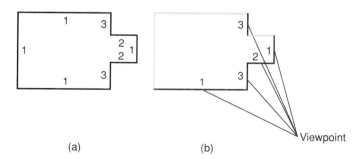

(a)   (b)

Fig. 15.29 Face priority. (a) Faces in a cluster and their priorities. A lower number indicates a higher priority. (b) Priorities of visible faces. (Based on [SUTH74a].)

overlapped by other polygons) if all polygons on the other side of it from the viewer are scan-converted first, then it, and then all polygons on the same side of it as the viewer. We need to ensure that this is so for each polygon.

The algorithm makes it easy to determine a correct order for scan conversion by building a binary tree of polygons, the *BSP tree*. The BSP tree's root is a polygon selected from those to be displayed; the algorithm works correctly no matter which is picked. The root polygon is used to partition the environment into two half-spaces. One half-space contains all remaining polygons in front of the root polygon, relative to its surface normal; the other contains all polygons behind the root polygon. Any polygon lying on both sides of the root polygon's plane is split by the plane and its front and back pieces are assigned to the appropriate half-space. One polygon each from the root polygon's front and back half-space become its front and back children, and each child is recursively used to divide the remaining polygons in its half-space in the same fashion. The algorithm terminates when each node contains only a single polygon. Pseudocode for the tree-building phase is shown in Fig. 15.30; Fig. 15.31 shows a tree being built.

Remarkably, the BSP tree may be traversed in a modified in-order tree walk to yield a correct priority-ordered polygon list for an arbitrary viewpoint. Consider the root polygon. It divides the remaining polygons into two sets, each of which lies entirely on one side of the root's plane. Thus, the algorithm needs to only guarantee that the sets are displayed in the correct relative order to ensure both that one set's polygons do not interfere with the other's and that the root polygon is displayed properly and in the correct order relative to the others. If the viewer is in the root polygon's front half-space, then the algorithm must first display all polygons in the root's rear half-space (those that could be obscured by the root), then the root, and finally all polygons in its front half-space (those that could obscure the root). Alternatively, if the viewer is in the root polygon's rear half-space, then the algorithm must first display all polygons in the root's front half-space, then the root, and finally all polygons in its rear half-space. If the polygon is seen on edge, either display order suffices. Back-face culling may be accomplished by not displaying a polygon if the eye is in its rear half-space. Each of the root's children is recursively processed by this algorithm. Pseudocode for displaying a BSP tree is shown in Fig. 15.32; Fig. 15.33 shows how the tree of Fig.15.31 (c) is traversed for two different projections.

Each polygon's plane equation can be transformed as it is considered, and the polygon's vertices can be transformed by the displayPolygon routine. The BSP tree can also assist in 3D clipping. Any polygon whose plane does not intersect the view volume has one subtree lying entirely outside of the view volume that does not need to be considered further.

Which polygon is selected to serve as the root of each subtree can have a significant effect on the algorithm's performance. Ideally, the polygon selected should cause the fewest splits among all its descendants. A heuristic that is easier to satisfy is to select the polygon that splits the fewest of its children. Experience shows that testing just a few (five or six) polygons and picking the best provides a good approximation to the best case [FUCH83].

Like the depth-sort algorithm, the BSP tree algorithm performs intersection and sorting entirely at object precision, and relies on the image-precision overwrite capabilities of a raster device. Unlike depth sort, it performs all polygon splitting during a pre-processing step that must be repeated only when the environment changes. Note that more

```
typedef struct {
    polygon root;
    BSP_tree *backChild, *frontChild;
} BSP_tree;

BSP_tree *BSP_makeTree (polygon *polyList)
{
    polygon root;
    polygon *backList, *frontList;
    polygon p, backPart, frontPart;        /* We assume each polygon is convex. */

    if (polyList == NULL)
        return NULL;
    else {
        root = BSP_selectAndRemovePoly (&polyList);
        backList = NULL;
        frontList = NULL;
        for (each remaining polygon p in polyList) {
            if (polygon p in front of root)
                BSP_addToList (p, &frontList);
            else if (polygon p in back of root)
                BSP_addToList (p, &backList);
            else {                          /* Polygon p must be split. */
                BSP_splitPoly (p, root, &frontPart, &backPart);
                BSP_addToList (frontPart, &frontList);
                BSP_addToList (backPart, &backList);
            }
        }
        return BSP_combineTree (BSP_makeTree (frontList),
                                root,
                                BSP_makeTree (backList));
    }
}   /* BSP_makeTree */
```

Fig. 15.30 Pseudocode for building a BSP tree.

polygon splitting may occur than in the depth-sort algorithm.

List-priority algorithms allow the use of hardware polygon scan converters that are typically much faster than are those that check the z at each pixel. The depth-sort and BSP tree algorithms display polygons in a back-to-front order, possibly obscuring more distant ones later. Thus, like the z-buffer algorithm, shading calculations may be computed more than once for each pixel. Alternatively, polygons can instead be displayed in a front-to-back order, and each pixel in a polygon can be written only if it has not yet been.

If a list-priority algorithm is used for hidden-line removal, special attention must be paid to the new edges introduced by the subdivision process. If these edges are

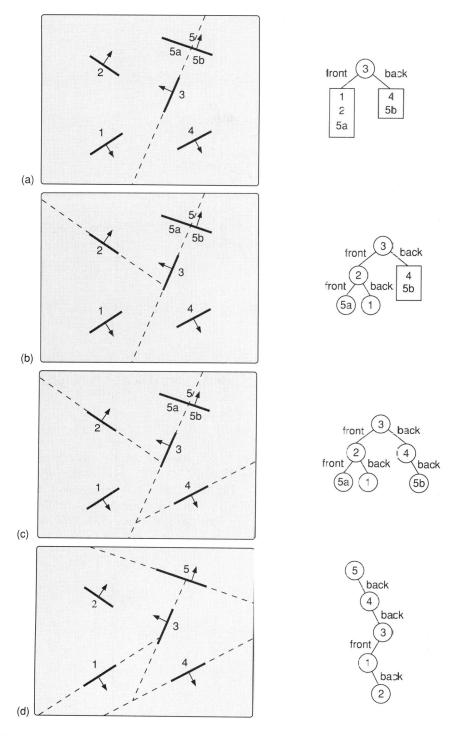

Fig. 15.31 BSP trees. (a) Top view of scene with BSP tree before recursion with polygon 3 as root. (b) After building left subtree. (c) Complete tree. (d) Alternate tree with polygon 5 as root. (Based on [FUCH83].)

```
void BSP_displayTree (BSP_tree *tree)
{
    if (tree != NULL) {
        if (viewer is in front of tree−>root) {
            /* Display back child, root, and front child. */
            BSP_displayTree (tree−>backChild);
            displayPolygon (tree−>root);
            BSP_displayTree (tree−>frontChild);
        } else {
            /* Display front child, roct, and back child. */
            BSP_displayTree (tree−>frontChild);
            displayPolygon (tree−>root);      /* Only if back-face culling not desired */
            BSP_displayTree (tree−>backChild);
        }
    }
}   /* BSP_displayTree */
```

Fig. 15.32 Pseudocode for displaying a BSP tree.

scan-converted like the original polygon edges, they will appear in the picture as unwelcome artifacts, and they thus should be flagged so that they will not be scan-converted.

15.6   SCAN-LINE ALGORITHMS

Scan-line algorithms, first developed by Wylie, Romney, Evans, and Erdahl [WYLI67], Bouknight [BOUK70a; BOUK70b], and Watkins [WATK70], operate at image precision to create an image one scan line at a time. The basic approach is an extension of the polygon scan-conversion algorithm described in Section 3.6, and thus uses a variety of forms of coherence, including scan-line coherence and edge coherence. The difference is that we

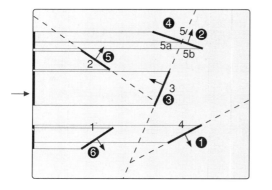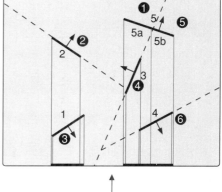

Fig. 15.33 Two traversals of the BSP tree corresponding to two different projections. Projectors are shown as thin lines. White numbers indicate drawing order.

deal not with just one polygon, but rather with a set of polygons. The first step is to create an *edge table* (ET) for all nonhorizontal edges of all polygons projected on the view plane. As before, horizontal edges are ignored. Entries in the ET are sorted into buckets based on each edge's smaller *y* coordinate, and within buckets are ordered by increasing *x* coordinate of their lower endpoint. Each entry contains

1. The *x* coordinate of the end with the smaller *y* coordinate
2. The *y* coordinate of the edge's other end
3. The *x* increment, Δx, used in stepping from one scan line to the next (Δx is the inverse slope of the edge)
4. The polygon identification number, indicating the polygon to which the edge belongs.

Also required is a *polygon table* (PT) that contains at least the following information for each polygon, in addition to its ID:

1. The coefficients of the plane equation
2. Shading or color information for the polygon
3. An in–out Boolean flag, initialized to *false* and used during scan-line processing.

Figure 15.34 shows the projection of two triangles onto the (*x*, *y*) plane; hidden edges are shown as dashed lines. The sorted ET for this figure contains entries for *AB, AC, FD, FE, CB,* and *DE*. The PT has entries for *ABC* and *DEF*.

The *active-edge table* (AET) used in Section 3.6 is needed here also. It is always kept in order of increasing *x*. Figure 15.35 shows ET, PT, and AET entries. By the time the algorithm has progressed upward to the scan line $y = \alpha$, the AET contains *AB* and *AC*, in that order. The edges are processed from left to right. To process *AB*, we first invert the in–out flag of polygon *ABC*. In this case, the flag becomes *true*; thus, the scan is now "in" the polygon, so the polygon must be considered. Now, because the scan is "in" only one polygon (*ABC*), it must be visible, so the shading for *ABC* is applied to the *span* from edge *AB* to the next edge in the AET, edge *AC*. This is an instance of span coherence. At this

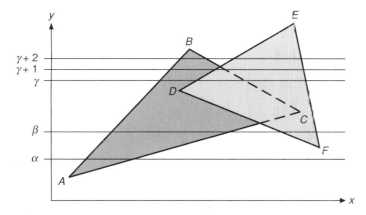

Fig. 15.34 Two polygons being processed by a scan-line algorithm.

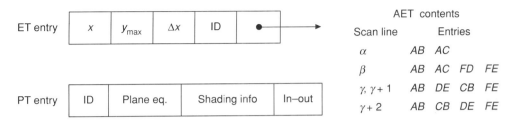

Fig. 15.35 ET, PT, AET for the scan-line algorithm.

edge the flag for *ABC* is inverted to false, so that the scan is no longer "in" any polygons. Furthermore, because *AC* is the last edge in the AET, the scan-line processing is completed. The AET is updated from the ET and is again ordered on *x* because some of its edges may have crossed, and the next scan line is processed.

When the scan line $y = \beta$ is encountered, the ordered AET is *AB*, *AC*, *FD*, and *FE*. Processing proceeds much as before. There are two polygons on the scan line, but the scan is "in" only one polygon at a time.

For scan line $y = \gamma$, things are more interesting. Entering *ABC* causes its flag to become *true*. *ABC*'s shade is used for the span up to the next edge, *DE*. At this point, the flag for *DEF* also becomes *true*, so the scan is "in" two polygons. (It is useful to keep an explicit list of polygons whose in–out flag is *true*, and also to keep a count of how many polygons are on the list.) We must now decide whether *ABC* or *DEF* is closer to the viewer, which we determine by evaluating the plane equations of both polygons for z at $y = \gamma$ and with *x* equal to the intersection of $y = \gamma$ with edge *DE*. This value of *x* is in the AET entry for *DE*. In our example, *DEF* has a larger z and thus is visible. Therefore, assuming nonpenetrating polygons, the shading for *DEF* is used for the span to edge *CB*, at which point *ABC*'s flag becomes *false* and the scan is again "in" only one polygon *DEF* whose shade continues to be used up to edge *FE*. Figure 15.36 shows the relationship of the two polygons and the $y = \gamma$ plane; the two thick lines are the intersections of the polygons with the plane.

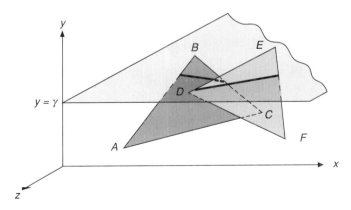

Fig. 15.36 Intersections of polygons *ABC* and *DEF* with the plane $y = \gamma$.

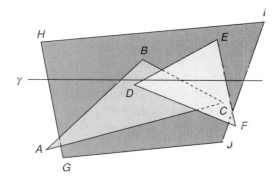

Fig. 15.37 Three nonpenetrating polygons. Depth calculations do not need to be made when scan line γ leaves the obscured polygon *ABC,* since nonpenetrating polygons maintain their relative *z* order.

Suppose there is a large polygon *GHIJ* behind both *ABC* and *DEF,* as in Fig. 15.37. Then, when the y = γ scan line comes to edge *CB,* the scan is still "in" polygons *DEF* and *GHIJ,* so depth calculations are performed again. These calculations can be avoided, however, if we assume that none of the polygons penetrate another. This assumption means that, when the scan leaves *ABC,* the depth relationship between *DEF* and *GHIJ* cannot change, and *DEF* continues to be in front. Therefore, depth computations are unnecessary when the scan leaves an obscured polygon, and are required only when it leaves an obscuring polygon.

To use this algorithm properly for penetrating polygons, as shown in Fig. 15.38, we break up *KLM* into *KLL'M'* and *L'MM'*, introducing the *false edge M'L'*. Alternatively, the algorithm can be modified to find the point of penetration on a scan line as the scan line is processed.

Another modification to this algorithm uses *depth coherence*. Assuming that polygons do not penetrate each other, Romney noted that, if the same edges are in the AET on one scan line as are on the immediately preceding scan line, and if they are in the same order, then no changes in depth relationships have occurred on any part of the scan line and no new depth computations are needed [ROMN68]. The record of visible spans on the previous scan line then defines the spans on the current scan line. Such is the case for scan lines y = γ

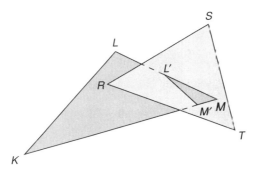

Fig. 15.38 Polygon *KLM* pierces polygon *RST* at the line *L'M'*.

and $y = \gamma + 1$ in Fig.15.34, for both of which the spans from AB to DE and from DE to FE are visible. The depth coherence in this figure is lost, however, as we go from $y = \gamma + 1$ to $y = \gamma + 2$, because edges DE and CB change order in the AET (a situation that the algorithm must accommodate). The visible spans therefore change and, in this case, become AB to CB and DE to FE. Hamlin and Gear [HAML77] show how depth coherence can sometimes be maintained even when edges do change order in the AET.

We have not yet discussed how to treat the background. The simplest way is to initialize the frame buffer to the background color, so the algorithm needs to process only scan lines that intersect edges. Another way is to include in the scene definition a large enough polygon that is farther back than any others are, is parallel to the projection plane, and has the desired shading. A final alternative is to modify the algorithm to place the background color explicitly into the frame buffer whenever the scan is not "in" any polygon.

Although the algorithms presented so far deal with polygons, the scan-line approach has been used extensively for more general surfaces, as described in Section 15.9. To accomplish this, the ET and AET are replaced by a *surface table* and *active-surface table*, sorted by the surfaces' (x, y) extents. When a surface is moved from the surface table to the active-surface table, additional processing may be performed. For example, the surface may be decomposed into a set of approximating polygons, which would then be discarded when the scan leaves the surface's y extent; this eliminates the need to maintain all surface data throughout the rendering process. Pseudocode for this general scan-line algorithm is shown in Fig. 15.39. Atherton [ATHE83] discusses a scan-line algorithm that renders polygonal objects combined using the regularized Boolean set operations of constructive solid geometry.

A scan-line approach that is appealing in its simplicity uses a z-buffer to resolve the visible-surface problem [MYER75]. A single-scan-line frame buffer and z-buffer are cleared for each new scan line and are used to accumulate the spans. Because only one scan line of storage is needed for the buffers, extremely high-resolution images are readily accommodated.

```
add surfaces to surface table;
initialize active-surface table;

for (each scan line) {

    update active-surface table;

    for (each pixel on scan line) {
        determine surfaces in active-surface table that project to pixel;
        find closest such surface;
        determine closest surface's shade at pixel;
    }
}
```

Fig. 15.39 Pseudocode for a general scan-line algorithm.

Crocker [CROC84] uses a scan-line z-buffer to exploit what he calls *invisibility coherence*, the tendency for surfaces that are invisible on one scan line to be invisible on the next. When the active-surface table is made up for a given scan line, a separate *invisible-surface table* is also built. A surface is added to the invisible-surface table if its maximum z value for the current scan line is less than the z values in the previous line's z buffer at the surface's minimum and maximum x values. For example, given the cube and contained triangle shown in Fig 15.40(a), the triangle and the contents of the previous scan line's z-buffer projected onto the (x, z) plane are shown in Fig. 15.40(b). The triangle's z_{max} is less than the previous scan line's z-buffer values at the triangle's x_{min} and x_{max}, so the triangle is added to the invisible-surface table. Placing a surface in the invisible-surface table eliminates it from much of the visible-surface processing. Some surfaces in the invisible-surface table may not belong there. To remedy this, as each pixel on the current scan line is processed, surfaces are removed from the invisible-surface table and are added to the active-surface table if their maximum z value is greater than the z value of what is currently determined to be the visible surface at the pixel. For example, even though the triangle shown in Fig. 15.40(c) was placed in the invisible-surface table, it is actually visible because the cube has been clipped, and it will be removed and added to the active-surface table.

Sechrest and Greenberg [SECH82] have developed an object-precision algorithm for nonintersecting polygons that is somewhat in the spirit of a scan-line algorithm. Their algorithm relies on the fact that the visibility of edges can change only at vertices and edge crossings. It sorts vertices and edge crossings by y, effectively dividing up the scene into horizontal bands inside of which the visibility relationships are constant (see Fig. 15.41). Object-precision coordinates of the edge segments visible in each strip are output as the strip is processed and are supplemented with information from which the contours of visible polygons can be reconstructed for scan conversion. Initially, only vertices that are local minima are inspected in sorted order. An AET is kept, and is modified whenever a vertex is encountered in the scan. Edge crossings are determined on the fly by testing only the active edges for intersections.

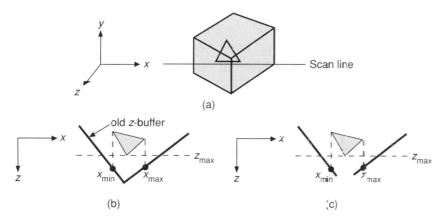

Fig. 15.40 Invisibility coherence. (a) Triangle in a box. (b) Triangle is correctly placed in invisible table. (c) Triangle is incorrectly placed in invisible-surface table. (Based on [CROC84].)

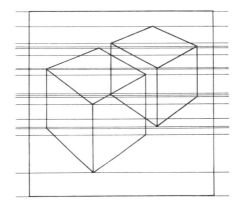

Fig. 15.41 The Sechrest and Greenberg object-precision algorithm divides the picture plane into horizontal strips at vertices and edge crossings. (Courtesy of Stuart Sechrest and Donald P. Greenberg, Program of Computer Graphics, Cornell Univeristy, 1982.)

15.7   AREA-SUBDIVISION ALGORITHMS

Area-subdivision algorithms all follow the divide-and-conquer strategy of spatial partitioning in the projection plane. An area of the projected image is examined. If it is easy to decide which polygons are visible in the area, they are displayed. Otherwise, the area is subdivided into smaller areas to which the decision logic is applied recursively. As the areas become smaller, fewer polygons overlap each area, and ultimately a decision becomes possible. This approach exploits *area coherence,* since sufficiently small areas of an image will be contained in at most a single visible polygon.

15.7.1   Warnock's Algorithm

The area-subdivision algorithm developed by Warnock [WARN69] subdivides each area into four equal squares. At each stage in the recursive-subdivision process, the projection of each polygon has one of four relationships to the area of interest (see Fig. 15.42):

1. *Surrounding polygons* completely contain the (shaded) area of interest (Fig. 15.42a)
2. *Intersecting polygons* intersect the area (Fig. 15.42b)
3. *Contained polygons* are completely inside the area (Fig. 15.42c)
4. *Disjoint polygons* are completely outside the area (Fig. 15.42d).

Disjoint polygons clearly have no influence on the area of interest. The part of an intersecting polygon that is outside the area is also irrelevant, whereas the part of an intersecting polygon that is interior to the area is the same as a contained polygon and can be treated as such.

In four cases, a decision about an area can be made easily, so the area does not need to be divided further to be conquered:

1. All the polygons are disjoint from the area. The background color can be displayed in the area.

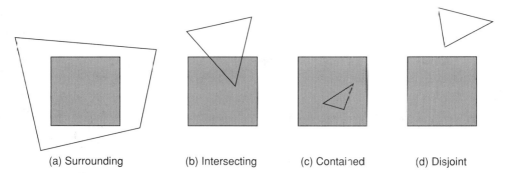

(a) Surrounding   (b) Intersecting   (c) Contained   (d) Disjoint

Fig. 15.42 Four relations of polygon projections to an area element: (a) surrounding, (b) intersecting, (c) contained, and (d) disjoint.

2.   There is only one intersecting or only one contained polygon. The area is first filled with the background color, and then the part of the polygon contained in the area is scan-converted.

3.   There is a single surrounding polygon, but no intersecting or contained polygons. The area is filled with the color of the surrounding polygon.

4.   More than one polygon is intersecting, contained in, or surrounding the area, but one is a surrounding polygon that is in front of all the other polygons. Determining whether a surrounding polygon is in front is done by computing the z coordinates of the planes of all surrounding, intersecting, and contained polygons at the four corners of the area; if there is a surrounding polygon whose four corner z coordinates are larger (closer to the viewpoint) than are those of any of the other polygons, then the entire area can be filled with the color of this surrounding polygon.

Cases 1, 2, and 3 are simple to understand. Case 4 is further illustrated in Fig. 15.43.

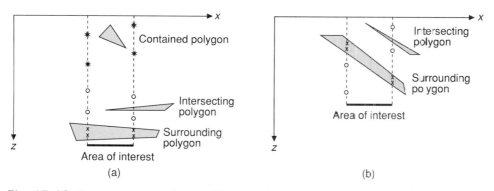

(a)   (b)

Fig. 15.43 Two examples of case 4 in recursive subdivision. (a) Surrounding polygon is closest at all corners of area of interest. (b) Intersecting polygon plane is closest at left side of area of interest. × marks the intersection of surrounding polygon plane; ○ marks the intersection of intersecting polygon plane; * marks the intersection of contained polygon plane.

In part (a), the four intersections of the surrounding polygon are all closer to the viewpoint (which is at infinity on the $+z$ axis) than are any of the other intersections. Consequently, the entire area is filled with the surrounding polygon's color. In part (b), no decision can be made, even though the surrounding polygon seems to be in front of the intersecting polygon, because on the left the plane of the intersecting polygon is in front of the plane of the surrounding polygon. Note that the depth-sort algorithm accepts this case without further subdivision if the intersecting polygon is wholly on the side of the surrounding polygon that is farther from the viewpoint. Warnock's algorithm, however, always subdivides the area to simplify the problem. After subdivision, only contained and intersecting polygons need to be reexamined: Surrounding and disjoint polygons of the original area are surrounding and disjoint polygons of each subdivided area.

Up to this point, the algorithm has operated at object precision, with the exception of the actual scan conversion of the background and clipped polygons in the four cases. These image-precision scan-conversion operations, however, can be replaced by object-precision operations that output a precise representation of the visible surfaces: either a square of the area's size (cases 1, 3, and 4) or a single polygon clipped to the area, along with its Boolean complement relative to the area, representing the visible part of the background (case 2). What about the cases that are not one of these four? One approach is to stop subdividing when the resolution of the display device is reached. Thus, on a 1024 by 1024 raster display, at most 10 levels of subdivision are needed. If, after this maximum number of subdivisions, none of cases 1 to 4 have occurred, then the depth of all relevant polygons is computed at the center of this pixel-sized, indivisible area. The polygon with the closest z coordinate defines the shading of the area. Alternatively, for antialiasing, several further levels of subdivision can be used to determine a pixel's color by weighting the color of each

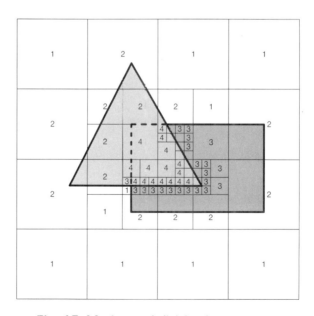

Fig. 15.44 Area subdivision into squares.

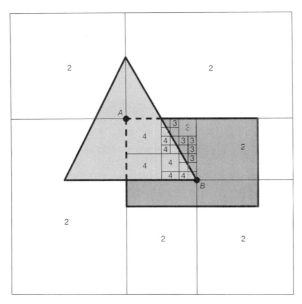

Fig. 15.45 Area subdivision about circled polygon vertices. The first subdivision is at vertex A; the second is at vertex B.

of its subpixel-sized areas by its size. It is these image-precision operations, performed when an area is not one of the simple cases, that makes this an image-precision approach.

Figure 15.44 shows a simple scene and the subdivisions necessary for that scene's display. The number in each subdivided area corresponds to one of the four cases; in unnumbered areas, none of the four cases are true. Compare this approach to the 2D spatial partitioning performed by quadtrees (Section 12.6.3). An alternative to equal-area subdivision, shown in Fig. 15.45, is to divide about the vertex of a polygon (if there is a vertex in the area) in an attempt to avoid unnecessary subdivisions. Here subdivision is limited to a depth of five for purposes of illustration.

15.7.2 The Weiler–Atherton Algorithm

Warnock's algorithm was forced to use image-precision operations to terminate because it could clip a polygon only against a rectangular area. Another strategy, developed later by Weiler and Atherton [WEIL77], subdivides the screen area along polygon boundaries rather than along rectangle boundaries. This approach requires a powerful clipping algorithm, such as that described in Section 19.1.4, that can clip one concave polygon with holes against another. The first step, not mandatory but useful to improve efficiency, is to sort polygons on some value of z, such as on their nearest z coordinate. The polygon closest to the viewer by this criterion is then used to clip all the polygons, including the clip polygon, into two lists containing the pieces inside and outside the clip polygon. All polygons on the inside list that are behind the clip polygon are then deleted, since they are invisible. If any polygon on the inside list is closer than is the clip polygon, the initial sort did not give a correct priority order (in fact, such a priority order does not exist in the case of cyclic overlap discussed in Section 15.5). Each such offending polygon is processed recursively to clip the pieces on the inside list against it. When this recursive subdivision is over, the inside list is displayed. The algorithm then continues to process the polygons on the outside list. Clipping is always performed with a copy of one of the original polygons as the clip polygon, never a fragment, since clipping to the original polygon is assumed to be less expensive than clipping to one or more fragmented pieces of the original polygon. Thus,

```
void WA_visibleSurface (void)
{
    polygon *polyList = list of copies of all polygons;
    sort polyList by decreasing value of maximum z;
    clear stack;

    /* Process each remaining polygonal region. */
    while (polyList != NULL)
        WA_subdivide (first polygon on polyList, &polyList);
}   /* WA_visibleSurface */

void WA_subdivide (polygon clipPolygon, polygon **polyList)
{
    polygon *inList;        /* Fragments inside clipPolygon */
    polygon *outList;       /* Fragments outside clipPolygon */

    inList = NULL;
    outList = NULL;

    for (each polygon in *polyList)
        clip polygon to ancestor of clipPolygon, placing inside pieces on
            inList, outside pieces on outList;

    remove polygons behind clipPolygon from inList;

    /* Process incorrectly ordered fragments recursively. */
    for (each polygon in inList that is not on stack and not a part of clipPolygon) {
        push clipPolygon onto stack;
        WA_subdivide (polygon, &inList);
        pop stack;
    }

    /* Display remaining polygons inside clipPolygon. */
    for (each polygon in inList)
        display polygon;

    *polyList = outList;    /* Subtract inList from *polyList. */
}   /* WA_subdivide */
```

Fig. 15.46 Pseudocode for the Weler–Atherton visible surface algorithm.

when a polygon is clipped, each piece must point back to the original input polygon from which it is derived. As a further efficiency consideration, the clipping algorithm can treat any polygon derived from the clip polygon as a special case and place it on the inside list with no additional testing.

The algorithm uses a stack to handle those cases of cyclic overlap in which one polygon is both in front of and behind another, as in Fig. 15.24(b). The stack contains a list of polygons that are currently in use as clipping polygons, but whose use has been interrupted because of recursive subdivision. If a polygon is found to be in front of the current clip polygon, it is searched for in the stack. If it is on the stack, then no more recursion is necessary since all polygon pieces inside and behind that polygon have already been removed. Pseudocode for the algorithm is shown in Fig. 15.46.

For the simple example of Fig. 15.47, triangle A is used as the first clip polygon because its nearest z coordinate is the largest. A is placed on its own inside list; next, rectangle B is subdivided into two polygons: $B_{in}A$, which is added to the inside list, and $B_{out}A$, which is placed on the outside list. $B_{in}A$ is then removed from the inside list, since it is behind A. Now, since no member of the inside list is closer than A, A is output. $B_{out}A$ is processed next, and is trivially output since it is the only polygon remaining.

Figure 15.48 shows a more complex case in which the original sorted order (or any other order) is incorrect. Part (a) depicts four polygons whose vertices are each marked with their z value. Rectangle A is considered to be closest to the viewer because its maximum z coordinate is greatest. Therefore, in the first call to WA_subdivide, A is used to clip all the polygons, as shown in part (b). The inside list is A, $B_{in}A$, $C_{in}A$, and $D_{in}A$; the outside list is $B_{out}A$, $C_{out}A$, and $D_{out}A$. $B_{in}A$ and $D_{in}A$ are discarded because they are farther back than A is, leaving only A and $C_{in}A$ on the inside list. Since $C_{in}A$ is found to be on the near side of A's plane, however, it is apparent that the polygons were ordered incorrectly. Therefore, recursive subdivision is accomplished by calling WA_subdivide to clip the current inside list against C, the ancestor of the offending polygon, as shown in part (c). The new inside list for this level of recursion is $A_{in}C$ and $C_{in}A$; the new outside list is $A_{out}C$. $A_{in}C$ is removed from the inside list because it is behind C. Only $C_{in}A$ is left on the inside list; since it is a part of the clip polygon, it is displayed. Before returning from the recursive call to WA_subdivide, *polyList* is set to the new outside list containing only $A_{out}C$. Since *polyList* is the caller's *inList*, $A_{out}C$ is displayed next, as shown in part (d), in which displayed

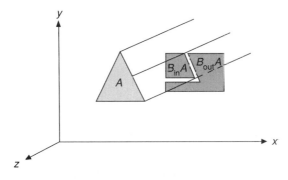

Fig. 15.47 Subdivision of a simple scene using the Weiler–Atherton algorithm.

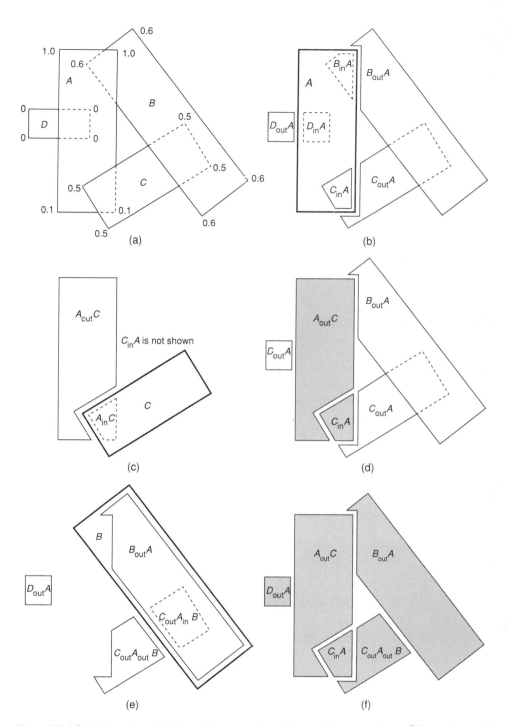

Fig. 15.48 Using the Weiler–Atherton algorithm with recursion. Clip polygon is shown with heavy outline. Displayed polygons are shaded. Numbers are vertex z values. (a) Original scene. (b) Polygons clipped to A. (c) A's inside list clipped to C during recursive subdivision. (d) Visible fragments inside A displayed. (e) Polygons clipped to B. (f) All visible fragments displayed at completion.

fragments are shaded. The initial invocation of WA_subdivide then sets *polyList* to its outside list ($B_{out}A$, $C_{out}A$, and $D_{out}A$) and returns.

Next, WA_subdivide is used to process $B_{out}A$ with the new *polyList* containing only $B_{out}A$, $C_{out}A$ and $D_{out}A$. $B_{out}A$'s ancestor B is used to clip these polygons, producing an inside list of $B_{out}A$ and $C_{out}A_{in}B$ and an outside list of $C_{out}A_{out}B$ and $D_{out}A$, as shown in part (e). $C_{out}A_{in}B$ is discarded because it is behind B, leaving only $B_{out}A$ on the inside list, which is then displayed. The polygon list is then set to the new outside list before WA_subdivide returns. Next, WA_subdivide is called once each to process and display $C_{out}A_{out}B$ and $D_{out}A$. The complete set of displayed fragments is shown in part (f).

15.7.3   Subpixel Area-Subdivision Algorithms

As is true of any object-precision algorithm, the Weiler–Atherton algorithm potentially requires comparing every polygon with every other. Spatial subdivision, discussed in Section 15.2.5, can reduce the number of comparisons by breaking up the screen into areas (or the environment into volumes) whose objects are processed separately [WEIL77]. Even so, the polygons produced must ultimately be rendered, raising the issue of antialiasing. If spatial subdivision is performed at the subpixel level, however, it can also be used to accomplish antialiasing.

Catmull's object-precision antialiasing algorithm.   Catmull [CATM78] has developed an accurate but expensive scan-line algorithm that does antialiasing by performing object-precision unweighted area sampling at each pixel, using an algorithm similar to the Weiler–Atherton algorithm. In essence, the idea is to perform a full visible-surface algorithm at every pixel, comparing only the polygon fragments that project to each pixel. Catmull first uses the Sutherland–Hodgman algorithm of Section 3.14.1 to clip each polygon intersecting the scan line to the pixels on the line it overlaps, as shown in Fig. 15.49(a). This determines the polygon fragments that project to each pixel, spatially partitioning them by the pixel grid. Then an algorithm similar to the Weiler–Atherton algorithm, but designed for simpler polygon geometry, is executed at each pixel to determine the amount of the pixel covered by the visible part of each fragment, as shown in Fig. 15.49(b). This allows a weighted sum of the visible parts' colors to be computed, and to be used to shade the pixel. Thus, each pixel's shade is determined by box filtering the polygon fragments that project to it.

The A-buffer.   Using a full object-precision visible-surface algorithm at each pixel is expensive! Carpenter's A-buffer algorithm [CARP84] addresses this problem by approximating Catmull's per-pixel object-precision area sampling with per-pixel image-precision operations performed on a subpixel grid. It thus provides a discrete approximation to area sampling with a box filter. Polygons are first processed in scan-line order by clipping them to each square pixel they cover. This creates a list of clipped polygon fragments for each pixel. Each fragment is associated with a 4 by 8 bit mask of those parts of the pixel it covers, as shown in Fig. 15.49(c). The bit mask for a fragment is computed by **xor**ing together masks representing each of the fragment's edges. An edge mask has 1s on the edge and to the right of the edge in those rows through which the edge passes, as shown in Fig. 15.49(d). When all polygons intersecting a pixel have been processed, the area-weighted

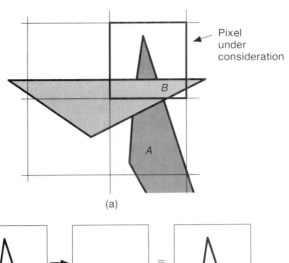

Pixel
under
consideration

A

B

(a)

List of subpixel fragments

(b)

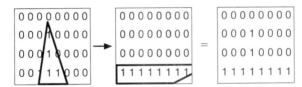

List of subpixel fragments

(c)

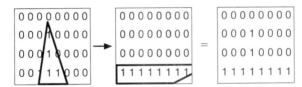

(d)

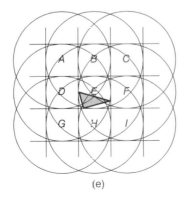

(e)

694

average of the colors of the pixel's visible surfaces is obtained by selecting fragments in depth-sorted order and using their bit masks to clip those of farther fragments. The bit masks can be manipulated efficiently with Boolean operations. For example, two fragment bit masks can be **and**ed together to determine the overlap between them. The A-buffer algorithm saves only a small amount of additional information with each fragment. For example, it includes the fragment's z extent, but no information about which part of the fragment is associated with these z values. Thus, the algorithm must make assumptions about the subpixel geometry in cases in which fragment bit masks overlap in z. This causes inaccuracies, especially where multiple surfaces intersect in a pixel.

Using precomputed convolution tables for better filtering. Both subpixel area-subdivision algorithms described so far use unweighted area sampling; thus, they restrict a fragment's influence to the single pixel to which it is clipped. If we would like to use filters with wider support, however, we must take into account that each fragment lies within the support of a number of filters positioned over nearby pixels, as shown in Fig. 15.49(e). Abram, Westover, and Whitted [ABRA85] describe how to incorporate better filters in these algorithms by classifying each visible fragment into one of a number of classes, based on the fragment's geometry. For each pixel within whose filter the fragment lies (pixels A through I in Fig 15.49e), the fragment's class and its position relative to the pixel are used to index into a look-up table. The look-up table contains the precomputed convolution of the desired filter kernel with prototype fragments at a set of different positions. The selected entry is multiplied by the fragment's intensity value and is added to an accumulator at that pixel. Those fragments that do not fit into one of the classes are approximated either as sums and differences of simpler fragments or by using bit masks.

15.8 ALGORITHMS FOR OCTREES

Algorithms for displaying octree-encoded objects (see Section 12.6.3) take advantage of the octree's regular structure of nonintersecting cubes. Since the octree is spatially presorted, list-priority algorithms have been developed that yield a correct display order for parallel projections [DOCT81; MEAG82a; GARG86]. In a back-to-front enumeration, nodes are listed in an order in which any node is guaranteed not to obscure any node listed after it. For an orthographic projection, a correct back-to-front enumeration can be determined from the VPN alone. One approach is to display the farthest octant first, then those three neighbors that share a face with the farthest octant in any order, then those three neighbors of the closest octant in any order, then the closest octant. In Fig. 15.50, one such enumeration for a VPN from 0 to V is 0, 1, 2, 4, 3, 5, 6, 7. No node in this enumeration can obscure any node enumerated after it. As each octant is displayed, its descendants are displayed recursively in this order. Furthermore, because each leaf node is a cube, at most three of its faces are visible, the identities of which may also be determined from the VPN.

Fig. 15.49 Subpixel area-subdivision algorithms. (a) Sample pixel contents. (b) Catmull algorithm subpixel geometry. (c) A-buffer algorithm subpixel geometry. (d) A-buffer algorithm subpixel mask for a fragment is computed by xoring together masks for its edges. (e) Abram, Westover, and Whitted algorithm adds polygon's contribution to all pixels it affects. (Part e is based on [ABRA85].)

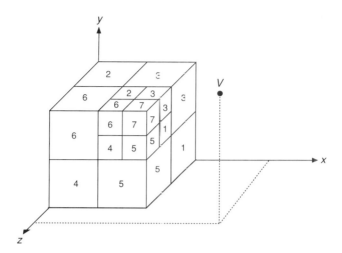

Fig. 15.50 Octree enumeration for back-to-front display. (Node 0 is at the lower-left back corner.) For a VPN from the origin to *V*, nodes may be recursively displayed using several different ordering systems.

Table 15.1 shows eight different back-to-front orders as determined by the signs of the three coordinates of the VPN and the visible octant faces associated with each. (Note that only the first and last octants in each order are fixed.) A positive or negative VPN *x* coordinate means the right (R) or left (L) face is visible, respectively. Similarly, the *y* coordinate determines the visibility of the up (U) and down (D) faces, and the *z* coordinate controls the front (F) and back (B) faces. If any VPN coordinate is zero, then neither of the faces associated with it is visible. Only the VPN's nonzero coordinates are significant in determining an order. Since all octree nodes are identically oriented, the visible faces and their relative polygonal projections for all nodes need to be determined only once. Arbitrary parallel projections can be accommodated by considering the DOP instead of the VPN.

Another approach to back-to-front enumeration for orthographic projections iterates through the octants in slices perpendicular to one of the axes, and in either rows or columns

TABLE 15.1   BACK-TO-FRONT ENUMERATION AND VISIBLE FACES

VPN			Back-to-front order	Visible faces*
z	*y*	*x*		
−	−	−	7,6,5,3,4,2,1,0	B,D,L
−	−	+	6,7,4,2,5,3,0,1	B,D,R
−	+	−	5,4,7,1,6,0,3,2	B,U,L
−	+	+	4,5,6,0,7,1,2,3	B,U,R
+	−	−	3,2, ,7,0,6,5,4	F,D,L
+	−	+	2,3,0,6,1,7,4,5	F,D,R
+	+	−	1,0,3,5,2,4,7,6	F,U,L
+	+	+	0,1,2,4,3,5,6,7	F,U,R

*R = right, L = left; U = up; D = down; F = front; B = back.

within each slice. The sign of each component of the VPN determines the direction of iteration along the corresponding octree axis. A positive component indicates increasing order along its axis, whereas a negative component indicates decreasing order. The order in which the axes are used does not matter. For example, in Fig. 15.50, one such enumeration for a VPN with all positive coordinates is 0, 4, 2, 6, 1, 5, 3, 7. varying first z, then y, and then x. This approach is easily generalized to operate on voxel arrays [FRIE85].

It is not necessary to display all an object's voxels, since those that are surrounded entirely by others will ultimately be invisible; more efficient scan conversion can be accomplished by rendering only the voxels on the octree's border [GARG86]. The set of border voxels can be determined using the algorithm presented in Section 12.6.3. Further improvement may be obtained by noting that, even when only border voxels are displayed, some faces may be drawn and then overwritten. Gargantini [GARG86] uses the information obtained during border extraction to identify for each voxel those faces that abut another voxel. These faces need not be drawn, since they will always be obscured. Rather than scan convert each voxel as a small cube, it is also possible to approximate each voxel with a single upright rectangle (a pixel in the limiting case).

Meagher [MEAG82b] describes a front-to-back algorithm that uses the reverse of the back-to-front order described previously. It represents the image being rendered as a quadtree that is initially empty. Each full or partially full octree node is considered in front-to-back order and is compared with the quadtree nodes that its projection intersects. Those octree nodes whose projections intersect only full quadtree nodes are invisible; they and their descendants are not considered further. If a partially full octree node's projection intersects one or more partially full quadtree nodes, then the octree node's children are compared with the children of these quadtree nodes. If a full octree node's projection intersects partially full quadtree nodes, then only these partially full quadtree nodes are further subdivided to determine the previously empty nodes that are covered by the projection. Any empty quadtree node enclosed by a full octree node's projection is shaded with the octree node's value.

As shown in Fig. 15.51, Meagher bounds each octree-node projection with an upright rectangular extent. Any extent needs to be compared with only four of the lowest-level quadtree nodes whose edge size is at least as great as the extent's largest dimension. These

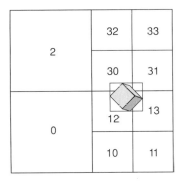

Fig. 15.51 Front-to-back octree scan conversion. Each octree node's projection and its rectangular extent are compared with four quadtree nodes, here 12, 13, 30, and 31.

are the quadtree node containing the extent's lower-left corner and the three adjacent quadtree nodes in the N, E, and NE directions. In Fig. 15.51, for example, these are quadtree nodes 12, 13, 30, and 31. If the rectangular extent intersects a rectangular quadtree node, then whether the octree node's projection (a convex polygon) also intersects the quadtree node can be determined efficiently [MEAG82b]. In contrast to the list-priority back-to-front algorithms, this front-to-back algorithm operates at image precision because it relies on an image-precision, quadtree representation of the projections on the image plane.

15.9   ALGORITHMS FOR CURVED SURFACES

All the algorithms presented thus far, with the exception of the z-buffer, have been described only for objects defined by polygonal faces. Objects such as the curved surfaces of Chapter 11 must first be approximated by many small facets before polygonal versions of any of the algorithms can be used. Although this approximation can be done, it is often preferable to scan convert curved surfaces directly, eliminating polygonal artifacts and avoiding the extra storage required by polygonal approximation.

Quadric surfaces, discussed in Section 11.4, are a popular choice in computer graphics. Visible-surface algorithms for quadrics have been developed by Weiss [WEIS66], Woon [WOON71], Mahl [MAHL72], Levin [LEVI76], and Sarraga [SARR83]. They all find the intersections of two quadrics, yielding a fourth-order equation in x, y, and z whose roots must be found numerically. Levin reduces this to a second-order problem by parameterizing the intersection curves. Spheres, a special case of quadrics, are easier to work with, and are of particular interest because molecules are often displayed as collections of colored spheres (see Color Plate II.19). A number of molecular display algorithms have been developed [KNOW77; STAU78; MAX79; PORT79; FRAN81; MAX84]. Section 15.10 discusses how to render spheres using ray tracing.

Even more flexibility can be achieved with the parametric spline surfaces introduced in Chapter 11, because they are more general and allow tangent continuity at patch boundaries. Catmull [CATM74b; CATM75] developed the first display algorithm for bicubics. In the spirit of Warnock's algorithm, a patch is recursively subdivided in s and t into four patches until its projection covers no more than one pixel. A z-buffer algorithm determines whether the patch is visible at this pixel. If it is, a shade is calculated for it and is placed in the frame buffer. The pseudocode for this algorithm is shown in Fig. 15.52. Since checking the size of the curved patch itself is time consuming, a quadrilateral defined by the patch's corner vertices may be used instead. Extra efficiency may be gained by comparing each patch (or its extent) with the clip window. If it is wholly inside the window, then no patch generated from it needs to be checked for clipping. If it is wholly outside the window, then it may be discarded. Finally, if it may be partially visible, then each patch generated from it must be checked.

Since then, Blinn and Whitted [LANE80b] have each developed scan-line algorithms for bicubics that track the visible edges of the surface from one scan line to the next. Edges may be defined by actual patch boundaries or by *silhouette edges,* as shown in Fig. 15.53. At a silhouette edge, the z component of the surface normal in the 3D screen coordinate system is zero as it passes between positive and negative values.

```
for (each patch) {
    push patch onto stack;

    while (stack not empty) {
        pop patch from stack;

        if (patch covers ≤ 1 pixel) {
            if (patch's pixel closer in z)
                determine shade and draw
        } else {
            subdivide patch into 4 subpatches;
            push subpatches onto stack;
        }
    }
}
```

Fig. 15.52 Pseudocode for the Catmull recursive-subdivision algorithm.

Blinn deals directly with the parametric representation of the patch. For the scan line $y = \alpha$, he finds all s and t values that satisfy the equation

$$y(s, t) - \alpha = 0. \tag{15.8}$$

These values of s and t are then used to evaluate $x(s, t)$ and $z(s, t)$. Unfortunately, Eq. (15.8) does not have a closed-form solution and its roots are therefore found numerically using Newton–Raphson iteration (see Appendix). Since the root-finding algorithm requires an initial value, coherence can be exploited by beginning with the previous scan line's solution for the current scan line. There are also special cases in which the roots cannot be found, causing the algorithm to fail. Similarly, Whitted uses numerical methods plus some approximations to the curve in the (x, z) plane defined by the intersection of the $y = \alpha$ plane

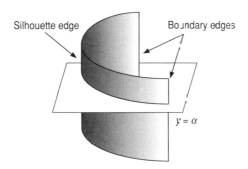

Fig. 15.53 The visible edges of a patch are defined by its boundary edges and silhouette edges.

with the bicubic surface patch. Whitted's algorithm fails to handle certain silhouette edges properly, however; an algorithm that does a more robust job of silhouette-edge detection is described in [SCHW82].

One highly successful approach is based on the adaptive subdivision of each bicubic patch until each subdivided patch is within some given tolerance of being flat. This tolerance depends on the resolution of the display device and on the orientation of the area being subdivided with respect to the projection plane, so unnecessary subdivisions are eliminated. The patch needs to be subdivided in only one direction if it is already flat enough in the other. Once subdivided sufficiently, a patch can be treated like a quadrilateral. The small polygonal areas defined by the four corners of each patch are processed by a scan-line algorithm, allowing polygonal and bicubic surfaces to be readily intermixed.

Algorithms that use this basic idea have been developed by Lane and Carpenter [LANE80b], and by Clark [CLAR79]. They differ in the choice of basis functions used to derive the subdivision difference equations for the surface patches and in the test for flatness. The Lane–Carpenter algorithm does the subdivision only as required when the scan line being processed begins to intersect a patch, rather than in a preprocessing step as does Clark's algorithm. The Lane–Carpenter patch subdivision algorithm is described in Section 11.3.5. Pseudocode for the Lane–Carpenter algorithm is shown in Fig. 15.54.

```
add patches to patch table;
initialize active-patch table;

for (each scan line) {

    update active-patch table;

    for (each patch in active-patch table) {
        if (patch can be approximately by planar quadrilateral)
            add patch to polygon table;
        else {
            split patch into subpatches;
            for (each new subpatch) {
                if (subpatch intersects scan line)
                    add to active-patch table;
                else
                    add to patch table;
            }
        }
    }

    process polygon table for current scan line;
}
```

Fig. 15.54 Pseudocode for the Lane–Carpenter algorithm.

Since a patch's control points define its convex hull, the patch is added to the active-patch table for processing at the scan line whose y value is that of the minimum y value of its control points. This saves large amounts of memory. The test for flatness must determine whether the patch is sufficiently planar and whether the boundary curves are sufficiently linear. Unfortunately, subdivision can introduce cracks in the patch if the same patch generates one patch that is determined to be flat and an adjacent patch that must be subdivided further. What should be a common shared edge between the patches may, instead, be a single line for the first patch and a piecewise linear approximation to a curve for the subpatches derived from the second patch. This can be avoided by changing the tolerance in the flatness test such that patches are subdivided more finely than necessary. An alternative solution uses Clark's method of subdividing an edge as though it were a straight line, once it has been determined to be sufficiently flat.

15.10 VISIBLE-SURFACE RAY TRACING

Ray tracing, also known as *ray casting,* determines the visibility of surfaces by tracing imaginary rays of light from the viewer's eye to the objects in the scene.[2] This is exactly the prototypical image-precision algorithm discussed at the beginning of this chapter. A center of projection (the viewer's eye) and a window on an arbitrary view plane are selected. The window may be thought of as being divided into a regular grid, whose elements correspond to pixels at the desired resolution. Then, for each pixel in the window, an *eye ray* is fired from the center of projection through the pixel's center into the scene, as shown in Fig. 15.55. The pixel's color is set to that of the object at the closest point of intersection. The pseudocode for this simple ray tracer is shown in Fig. 15.56.

Ray tracing was first developed by Appel [APPE68] and by Goldstein and Nagel [MAGI68; GOLD71]. Appel used a sparse grid of rays used to determine shading, including whether a point was in shadow. Goldstein and Nagel originally used their algorithm to simulate the trajectories of ballistic projectiles and nuclear particles; only later

---

[2]Although *ray casting* and *ray tracing* are often used synonymously, sometimes *ray casting* is used to refer to only this section's visible-surface algorithm, and *ray tracing* is reserved for the recursive algorithm of Section 16.12.

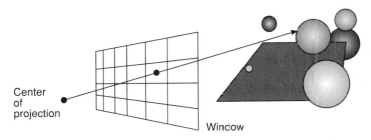

Center of projection

Window

Fig. 15.55 A ray is fired from the center of projection through each pixel to which the window maps, to determine the closest object intersected.

```
select center of projection and window on viewplane;
for (each scan line in image) {
    for (each pixel in scan line) {
        determine ray from center of projection through pixel;
        for (each object in scene) {
            if (object is intersected and is closest considered thus far)
                record intersection and object name;
        }
        set pixel's color to that at closest object intersection;
    }
}
```

Fig. 15.56 Pseudocode for a simple ray tracer.

did they apply it to graphics. Appel was the first to ray trace shadows, whereas Goldstein and Nagel pioneered the use of ray tracing to evaluate Boolean set operations. Whitted [WHIT80] and Kay [KAY79a] extended ray tracing to handle specular reflection and refraction. We discuss shadows, reflection, and refraction—the effects for which ray tracing is best known—in Section 16.12, where we describe a full recursive ray-tracing algorithm that integrates both visible-surface determination and shading. Here, we treat ray tracing only as a visible-surface algorithm.

15.10.1 Computing Intersections

At the heart of any ray tracer is the task of determining the intersection of a ray with an object. To do this task, we use the same parametric representation of a vector introduced in Chapter 3. Each point (x, y, z) along the ray from (x_0, y_0, z_0) to (x_1, y_1, z_1) is defined by some value t such that

$$x = x_0 + t\,(x_1 - x_0), \qquad y = y_0 + t\,(y_1 - y_0), \qquad z = z_0 + t\,(z_1 - z_0). \quad (15.9)$$

For convenience, we define Δx, Δy, and Δz such that

$$\Delta x = x_1 - x_0, \qquad \Delta y = y_1 - y_0, \qquad \Delta z = z_1 - z_0. \quad (15.10)$$

Thus,

$$x = x_0 + t\,\Delta x, \qquad y = y_0 + t\,\Delta y, \qquad z = z_0 + t\,\Delta z. \quad (15.11)$$

If (x_0, y_0, z_0) is the center of projection and (x_1, y_1, z_1) is the center of a pixel on the window, then t ranges from 0 to 1 between these points. Negative values of t represent points behind the center of projection, whereas values of t greater than 1 correspond to points on the side of the window farther from the center of projection. We need to find a representation for each kind of object that enables us to determine t at the object's intersection with the ray. One of the easiest objects for which to do this is the sphere, which accounts for the plethora of spheres observed in typical ray-traced images! The sphere with center (a, b, c) and radius r may be represented by the equation

$$(x - a)^2 + (y - b)^2 + (z - c)^2 = r^2. \quad (15.12)$$

The intersection is found by expanding Eq. (15.12), and substituting the values of x, y, and z from Eq. (15.11) to yield

$$x^2 - 2ax + a^2 + y^2 - 2by + b^2 + z^2 - 2cz + c^2 = r^2, \tag{15.13}$$

$$(x_0 + t\Delta x)^2 - 2a(x_0 + t\Delta x) + a^2 + (y_0 + t\Delta y)^2 - 2b(y_0 + t\Delta y) + b^2 \tag{15.14}$$
$$+ (z_0 + t\Delta z)^2 - 2c(z_0 + t\Delta z) + c^2 = r^2,$$

$$x_0^2 + 2x_0\Delta xt + \Delta x^2 t^2 - 2ax_0 - 2a\Delta xt + a^2 \tag{15.15}$$
$$+ y_0^2 + 2y_0\Delta yt + \Delta y^2 t^2 - 2by_0 - 2b\Delta yt + b^2$$
$$+ z_0^2 + 2z_0\Delta zt + \Delta z^2 t^2 - 2cz_0 - 2c\Delta zt + c^2 = r^2.$$

Collecting terms gives

$$(\Delta x^2 + \Delta y^2 + \Delta z^2)t^2 + 2t[\Delta x(x_0 - a) + \Delta y(y_0 - b) + \Delta z(z_0 - c)] \tag{15.16}$$
$$+ (x_0^2 - 2ax_0 + a^2 + y_0^2 - 2by_0 + b^2 + z_0^2 - 2cz_0 + c^2) - r^2 = 0,$$

$$(\Delta x^2 + \Delta y^2 + \Delta z^2)t^2 + 2t[\Delta x (x_0 - a) + \Delta y(y_0 - b) + \Delta z(z_0 - c)] \tag{15.17}$$
$$+ (x_0 - a)^2 + (y_0 - b)^2 + (z_0 - c)^2 - r^2 = 0.$$

Equation (15.17) is a quadratic in t, with coefficients expressed entirely in constants derived from the sphere and ray equations, so it can be solved using the quadratic formula. If there are no real roots, then the ray and sphere do not intersect; if there is one real root, then the ray grazes the sphere. Otherwise, the two roots are the points of intersection with the sphere; the one that yields the smallest positive t is the closest. It is also useful to normalize the ray so that the distance from (x_0, y_0, z_0) to (x_1, y_1, z_1) is 1. This gives a value of t that measures distance in WC units, and simplifies the intersection calculation, since the coefficient of t^2 in Eq. (15.17) becomes 1. We can obtain the intersection of a ray with the general quadric surfaces introduced in Chapter 11 in a similar fashion.

As we shall see in Chapter 16, we must determine the surface normal at the point of intersection in order to shade the surface. This is particularly easy in the case of the sphere, since the (unnormalized) normal is the vector from the center to the point of intersection: The sphere with center (a, b, c) has a surface normal $((x - a)/r, (y - b)/r, (z - c)/r)$ at the point of intersection (x, y, z).

Finding the intersection of a ray with a polygon is somewhat more difficult. We can determine where a ray intersects a polygon by first determining whether the ray intersects the polygon's plane and then whether the point of intersection lies within the polygon. Since the equation of a plane is

$$Ax + By + Cz + D = 0, \tag{15.18}$$

substitution from Eq. (15.11) yields

$$A(x_0 + t\Delta x) + B(y_0 + t\Delta y) + C(z_0 + t\Delta z) - D = 0, \tag{15.19}$$

$$t(A\Delta x + B\Delta y + C\Delta z) + (Ax_0 + By_0 + Cz_0 - D) = 0, \tag{15.20}$$

$$t = -\frac{(Ax_0 + By_0 + Cz_0 + D)}{(A\Delta x + B\Delta y + C\Delta z)}. \tag{15.21}$$

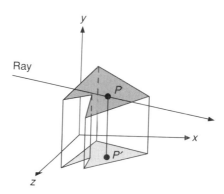

Fig. 15.57 Determining whether a ray intersects a polygon. The polygon and the ray's point of intersection p with the polygon's plane are projected onto one of the three planes defining the coordinate system. Projected point p' is tested for containment within the projected polygon.

If the denominator of Eq. (15.21) is 0, then the ray and plane are parallel and do not intersect. An easy way to determine whether the point of intersection lies within the polygon is to project the polygon and point orthographically onto one of the three planes defining the coordinate system, as shown in Fig. 15.57. To obtain the most accurate results, we should select the axis along which to project that yields the largest projection. This corresponds to the coordinate whose coefficient in the polygon's plane equation has the largest absolute value. The orthographic projection is accomplished by dropping this coordinate from the polygon's vertices and from the point. The polygon-containment test for the point can then be performed entirely in 2D, using the point-in-polygon algorithm of Section 7.12.2.

Like the z-buffer algorithm, ray tracing has the attraction that the only intersection operation performed is that of a projector with an object. There is no need to determine the intersection of two objects in the scene directly. The z-buffer algorithm approximates an object as a set of z values along the projectors that intersect the object. Ray tracing approximates objects as the set of intersections along each projector that intersects the scene. We can extend a z-buffer algorithm to handle a new kind of object by writing a scan-conversion and z-calculation routine for it. Similarly, we can extend a visible-surface ray tracer to handle a new kind of object by writing a ray-intersection routine for it. In both cases, we must also write a routine to calculate surface normals for shading. Intersection and surface-normal algorithms have been developed for algebraic surfaces [HANR83], for parametric surfaces [KAJI82; SEDE84; TOTH85; JOY86], and for many of the objects discussed in Chapter 20. Surveys of these algorithms are provided in [HAIN89; HANR89].

15.10.2 Efficiency Considerations for Visible-Surface Ray Tracing

At each pixel, the z-buffer algorithm computes information only for those objects that project to that pixel, taking advantage of coherence. In contrast, the simple but expensive version of the visible-surface ray tracing algorithm that we have discussed, intersects each of the rays from the eye with each of the objects in the scene. A 1024 by 1024 image of 100 objects would therefore require 100M intersection calculations. It is not surprising that Whitted found that 75 to over 95 percent of his system's time was spent in the intersection routine for typical scenes [WHIT80]. Consequently, the approaches to improving the efficiency of visible-surface ray tracing we discuss here attempt to speed up individual intersection calculations, or to avoid them entirely. As we shall see in Section 16.12, recursive ray tracers trace additional rays from the points of intersection to determine a pixel's shade. Therefore, several of the techniques developed in Section 15.2, such as the perspective transformation and back-face culling, are not in general useful, since all rays do not emanate from the same center of projection. In Section 16.12, we shall augment the techniques mentioned here with ones designed specifically to handle these recursive rays.

Optimizing intersection calculations.   Many of the terms in the equations for object–ray intersection contain expressions that are constant either throughout an image or for a particular ray. These can be computed in advance, as can, for example, the orthographic projection of a polygon onto a plane. With care and mathematical insight, fast intersection methods can be developed; even the simple intersection formula for a sphere given in Section 15.10.1 can be improved [HAIN89]. If rays are transformed to lie along the z axis, then the same transformation can be applied to each candidate object, so that any intersection occurs at $x = y = 0$. This simplifies the intersection calculation and allows the closest object to be determined by a z sort. The intersection point can then be transformed back for use in shading calculations via the inverse transformation.

Bounding volumes provide a particularly attractive way to decrease the amount of time spent on intersection calculations. An object that is relatively expensive to test for intersection may be enclosed in a bounding volume whose intersection test is less expensive, such as a sphere [WHIT80], ellipsoid [BOUV85], or rectangular solid [RUBI80; TOTH85]. The object does not need to be tested if the ray fails to intersect with its bounding volume.

Kay and Kajiya [KAY86] suggest the use of a bounding volume that is a convex polyhedron formed by the intersection of a set of infinite *slabs*, each of which is defined by a pair of parallel planes that bound the object. Figure 15.58(a) shows in 2D an object bounded by four slabs (defined by pairs of parallel lines), and by their intersection. Thus, each slab is represented by Eq. (15.18), where A, B, and C are constant, and D is either D_{min} or D_{max}. If the same set of parameterized slabs is used to bound all objects, each bound can be described compactly by the D_{min} and D_{max} of each of its slabs. A ray is intersected with a bound by considering one slab at a time. The intersection of a ray with a slab can be computed using Eq. (15.21) for each of the slab's planes, producing near and far values of t. Using the same set of parameterized slabs for all bounds, however, allows us to simplify Eq.(15.21), yielding

$$t = (S + D)T, \tag{15.22}$$

where $S = Ax_0 + By_0 + Cz_0$ and $T = -1/(A\Delta x + B\Delta y + C\Delta z)$. Both S and T can be calculated once for a given ray and parameterized slab.

Since each bound is an intersection of slabs, the intersection of the ray with an entire bound is just the intersection of the ray's intersections with each of the bound's slabs. This can be computed by taking the maximum of the near values of t and the minimum of the far values of t. In order to detect null intersections quickly, the maximum near and minimum

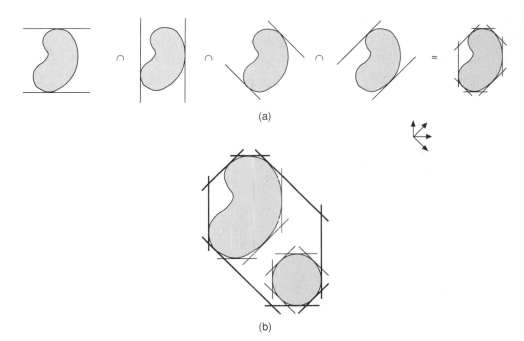

(a)

(b)

Fig. 15.58 Bounds formed intersection of slabs. (a) Object bounded by a fixed set of parameterized slabs. (b) The bounding volume of two bounding volumes.

far values of t for a bound can be updated as each of its slabs is processed, and the processing of the bound terminated if the former ever exceeds the latter.

Avoiding intersection calculations. Ideally, each ray should be tested for intersection only with objects that it actually intersects. Furthermore, in many cases we would like each ray to be tested against only that object whose intersection with the ray is closest to the ray's origin. There is a variety of techniques that attempt to approximate this goal by preprocessing the environment to partition rays and objects into equivalence classes to help limit the number of intersections that need to be performed. These techniques include two complementary approaches introduced in Section 15.2: hierarchies and spatial partitioning.

Hierarchies. Although bounding volumes do not by themselves determine the order or frequency of intersection tests, bounding volumes may be organized in nested hierarchies with objects at the leaves and internal nodes that bound their children [RUBI80; WEGH84; KAY86]. For example, a bounding volume for a set of Kay–Kajiya bounding volumes can be computed by taking for each pair of planes the minimum D_{min} and the maximum D_{max} of the values for each child volume, as shown in Fig. 15.58(b).

A child volume is guaranteed not to intersect with a ray if its parent does not. Thus, if intersection tests begin with the root, many branches of the hierarchy (and hence many objects) may be trivially rejected. A simple method to traverse the hierarchy is

```
void HIER_traverse (ray r, node n)
{
    if (r intersects n's bounding volume)
        if (n is a leaf)
            intersect r with n's object;
        else
            for (each child c of n)
                HIER_traverse (r, c);
}  /* HIER_traverse */
```

Efficient hierarchy traversal. HIER_traverse explores a hierarchy depth first. In contrast, Kay and Kajiya [KAY86] have developed an efficient method for traversing hierarchies of bounding volumes that takes into account the goal of finding the closest intersection. Note that the intersection of a ray with a Kay–Kajiya bound yields two values of t, the lower of which is a good estimate of the distance to the object. Therefore, the best order in which to select objects for intersection tests is that of increasing estimated distance from the ray's origin. To find the closest object intersected by a ray, we maintain the list of nodes to be tested in a priority queue, implemented as a heap. Initially the heap is empty. If the root's bound is intersected by the ray, then the root is inserted in the heap. As long as the heap is not empty and its top node's estimated distance is closer than the closest object tested so far, nodes are extracted from the heap. If the node is a leaf, then its object's ray intersection is calculated. Otherwise, it is a bound, in which case each of its children's bounds is tested and is inserted in the heap if it is intersected, keyed by the estimated distance computed in the bound-intersection calculation. The selection process terminates when the heap is empty or when an object has been intersected that is closer than the estimated distance of any node remaining in the heap. Pseudocode for the algorithm is shown in Fig. 15.59.

Automated hierarchy generation. One problem with hierarchies of bounding volumes, such as those used by the Kay–Kajiya algorithm, is that generating good hierarchies is difficult. Hierarchies created during the modeling process tend to be fairly shallow, with structure designed for controlling objects rather than for minimizing the intersections of objects with rays. In addition, modeler hierarchies are typically insensitive to the actual position of objects. For example, the fingers on two robot hands remain in widely separated parts of the hierarchy, even when the hands are touching. Goldsmith and Salmon [GOLD87] have developed a method for generating good hierarchies for ray tracing automatically. Their method relies on a way of determining the quality of a hierarchy by estimating the cost of intersecting a ray with it.

Consider how we might estimate the cost of an individual bounding volume. Assume that each bounding volume has the same cost for computing whether a ray intersects it. Therefore, the cost is directly proportional to the number of times a bounding volume will be hit. The probability that a bounding volume is hit by an eye ray is the percentage of rays from the eye that will hit it. This is proportional to the bounding volume's area projected on the view plane. On the average, for convex bounding volumes, this value is roughly

```
void KayKajiya (void)
{
    object *p = NULL;        /* Pointer to nearest object hit */
    double t = ∞;            /* Distance to nearest object hit */

    precompute ray intersection;
    if (ray hits root's bound) {
        insert root into heap;
    }
    while (heap is not empty and distance to top node < t) {
        node *c = top node removed from heap;

        if (c is a leaf) {
            intersect ray with c's object;
            if (ray hits it and distance < t) {
                t = distance;
                p = object;
            }
        } else {         /* c is a bound */
            for (each child of c) {
                intersect ray with child's bound;
                if (ray hits child's bound)
                    insert child into heap;
            }
        }
    }
}   /* KayKajiya */
```

Fig. 15.59 Pseudocode for using Kay–Kajiya bounds to find the closest object intersected by a ray.

proportional to the bounding volume's surface area. Since each bounding volume is contained within the root's bounding volume, the conditional probability that a ray will intersect the ith bounding volume if it intersects the root can be approximated by A_i / A_r, where A_i is the surface area of the ith bounding volume and A_r is the surface area of the root.

If a ray intersects a bounding volume, we assume that we must perform an intersection calculation for each of the bounding volume's k children. Thus, the bounding volume's total estimated cost in number of intersections is kA_i / A_r. The root's estimated cost is just its number of children (since $A_i / A_r = 1$), and the cost of a leaf node is zero (since $k = 0$). To compute the estimated cost of a hierarchy, we sum the estimated costs of each of its bounding volumes. Consider, for example, the hierarchy shown in Fig. 15.60 in which each node is marked with its surface area. Assuming the root A is hit at the cost of one intersection, the root's estimated cost is 4 (its number of children). Two of its children (C

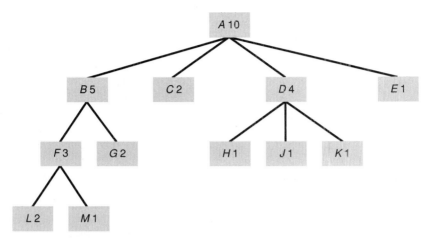

Fig. 15.60 Estimating the cost of a hierarchy. Letter is node name; number is node surface area.

and E) are leaves, and therefore have zero cost. B has two children and a surface area of 5. Thus, its estimated cost is $2(5/10) = 1.0$. D has three children and a surface area of 4, so its estimated cost is $3(4/10) = 1.2$. The only other nonleaf node is F, which has two children and a surface area of 3, giving an estimated cost of $2(3/10) = .6$. The total estimated cost is 1 (to hit the root) $+ 4 + 1.0 + 1.2 + .6 = 7.8$ expected intersections.

Since we are interested in only relative values, there is no need to divide by the root's surface area. Furthermore, we do not need the actual surface area of the bounding volume—we need only a value proportional to it. For example, rather than use $2lw + 2lh + 2wh$ for a rectangular prism, we can factor out the 2 and rearrange terms to yield $(w + h)l + wh$.

Goldsmith and Salmon create the hierarchy incrementally, adding one new node at a time. The order in which nodes are added affects the algorithm. The modeler's order can be used, but for many scenes better results can be obtained by randomizing the order by shuffling nodes. Each node may be added by making it a child of an existing node or by replacing an existing node with a new bounding volume node that contains both the original node and the new node. In each case, instead of evaluating the cost of the new tree from scratch, the incremental cost of adding the node can be determined. If the node is being added as a child of an existing node, it may increase the parent's surface area, and it also increases the parent's number of children by 1. Thus, the difference in estimated cost of the parent is $k (A_{\text{new}} - A_{\text{old}}) + A_{\text{new}}$, where A_{new} and A_{old} are the parent's new and old surface areas, and k is the original number of children. If the node is added by creating a new parent with both the original and new nodes as children, the incremental cost of the newly created parent is $2A_{\text{new}}$. In both cases, the incremental cost to the new child's grandparent and older ancestors must also be computed as $k(A_{\text{new}} - A_{\text{old}})$, where k, A_{new}, and A_{old} are the values for the ancestor node. This approach assumes that the position at which the node is placed has no effect on the size of the root bounding volume.

A brute-force approach would be to evaluate the increased cost of adding the new node at every possible position in the tree and to then pick the position that incurred the least increase in cost. Instead, Goldsmith and Salmon use a heuristic search that begins at the root by evaluating the cost of adding the node to it as a child. They then prune the tree by selecting the subtree that would experience the smallest increase in its bounding volume's surface area if the new node were added as a child. The search then continues with this subtree, the cost of adding the node to it as a child is evaluated, and a subtree of it is selected to follow based on the minimum surface area increase criterion. When a leaf node is reached, the cost is evaluated of creating a new bounding volume node containing the original leaf and the new node. When the search terminates, the node is inserted at the point with the smallest evaluated increase. Since determining the insertion point for a single node requires an $O(\log n)$ search, the entire hierarchy can be built in $O(n \log n)$ time. The search and evaluation processes are based on heuristics, and consequently the generated hierarchies are not optimal. Nevertheless, these techniques can create hierarchies that provide significant savings in intersection costs.

Spatial partitioning. Bounding-volume hierarchies organize objects bottom-up; in contrast, spatial partitioning subdivides space top-down. The bounding box of the scene is calculated first. In one approach, the bounding box is then divided into a regular grid of equal-sized extents, as shown in Fig. 15.61. Each partition is associated with a list of objects it contains either wholly or in part. The lists are filled by assigning each object to the one or more partitions that contain it. Now, as shown in 2D in Fig. 15.62, a ray needs to be intersected with only those objects that are contained within the partitions through which it passes. In addition, the partitions can be examined in the order in which the ray passes through them; thus, as soon as a partition is found in which there is an intersection, no more partitions need to be inspected. Note that we must consider all the remaining objects in the partition, to determine the one whose intersection is closest. Since the partitions follow a regular grid, each successive partition lying along a ray may be calculated using a 3D version of the line-drawing algorithm discussed in Section 3.2.2, modified to list every partition through which the ray passes [FUJI85; AMAN87].

If a ray intersects an object in a partition, it is also necessary to check whether the intersection itself lies in the partition; it is possible that the intersection that was found may be further along the ray in another partition and that another object may have a closer intersection. For example, in Fig. 15.63, object B is intersected in partition 3 although it is encountered in partition 2. We must continue traversing the partitions until an intersection is found in the partition currently being traversed, in this case with A in partition 3. To avoid

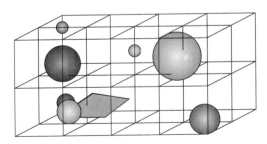

Fig. 15.61 The scene is partitioned into a regular grid of equal-sized volumes.

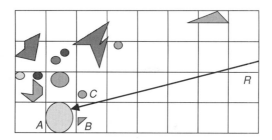

Fig. 15.62 Spatial partitioning. Ray *R* needs to be intersected with only objects *A*, *B*, and *C*, since the other partitions through which it passes are empty.

recalculating the intersection of a ray with an object that is found in multiple partitions, the point of intersection and the ray's ID can be cached with the object when the object is first encountered.

Dippé and Swensen [DIPP84] discuss an adaptive subdivision algorithm that produces unequal-sized partitions. An alternative adaptive spatial-subdivision method divides the scene using an octree [GLAS84]. In this case, the octree neighbor-finding algorithm sketched in Section 12.6.3 may be used to determine the successive partitions lying along a ray [SAME89b]. Octrees, and other hierarchical spatial partitionings, can be thought of as a special case of hierarchy in which a node's children are guaranteed not to intersect each other. Because these approaches allow adaptive subdivision, the decision to subdivide a partition further can be sensitive to the number of objects in the subdivision or the cost of intersecting the objects. This is advantageous in heterogeneous, unevenly distributed environments.

Spatial partitioning and hierarchy can be used together to combine their advantages. Snyder and Barr [SNYD87] describe an approach that uses hand-assembled hierarchies whose internal nodes are either lists or regular 3D grids. This allows the person designing an environment to choose lists for small numbers of sparsely arranged objects and grids for

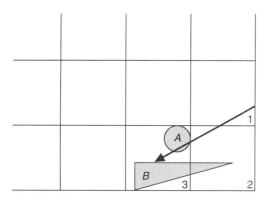

Fig. 15.63 An object may be intersected in a different voxel than the current one.

large numbers of regularly distributed objects. Color Plate III.1 shows a scene with 2×10^9 primitives that was ray-traced with Snyder's and Barr's system.

15.10.3 Computing Boolean Set Operations

Goldstein and Nagel [GOLD71] were the first researchers to ray trace combinations of simple objects produced using Boolean set operations. Determining the 3D union, difference, or intersection of two solids is difficult when it must be done by direct comparison of one solid with another using the methods in Chapter 12. In contrast, ray tracing allows the 3D problem to be reduced to a set of simple 1D calculations. The intersections of each ray and primitive object yield a set of t values, each of which specifies a point at which the ray enters or exits the object. Each t value thus defines the beginning of a span in which the ray is either in or out of the object. (Of course, care must be taken if the ray grazes the object, intersecting it only once.) Boolean set operations are calculated one ray at a time by determining the 1D union, difference, or intersection of spans from the two objects along the same ray. Figure 15.64 shows the spans defined by a ray passing through two objects, and the combinations of the spans that result when the set operations are

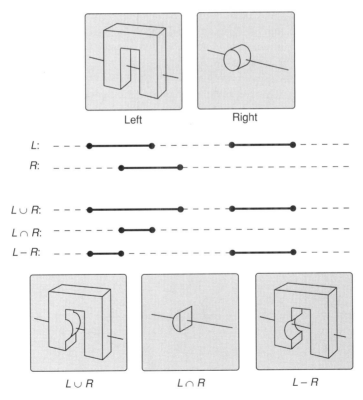

Fig. 15.64 Combining ray–object intersection span lists. (Adapted from [ROTH82] with permission.)

```
span *CSG_intersect (Ray *ray, CSG_node *node)
{
    span *leftIntersect, *rightIntersect;      /* lists of spans */

    if (node is composite) {
        leftIntersect = CSG_intersect (ray, node−>leftChild);
        if (leftIntersect == NULL && node−>op != UNION)
            return NULL;
        else {
            rightIntersect = CSG_intersect (ray, node−>rightChild);
            return CSG_combine (node−>op, leftIntersect, rightIntersect);
        }
    } else      /* node is primitive */
        return intersections of object with ray;
}    /* CSG_intersect */
```

Fig. 15.65 Pseudocode for evaluating the intersection of a ray with a CSG hierarchy.

performed. The CSG hierarchy is traversed for each ray by evaluating the left and right intersection lists at each node, as shown in the pseudocode of Fig. 15.65 Color Plate III.2 is a ray-traced bowl defined by a CSG hierarchy.

Roth points out that, if there is no intersection with the left side of the tree, then there is no reason to intersect with the right side of the tree if the operation is a difference or intersection [ROTH82]. Only if the operation is a union can the result be nonempty. In fact, if we need to determine only whether or not the compound object is intersected (rather than the actual set of intersections), then the right-hand side need not be evaluated if the left-hand side intersects and the operation is a union.

The CSG_combine function takes two lists of intersection records, each ordered by increasing t, and combines them according to the operation being performed. The lists are merged by removing the intersection record that has the next largest value of t. Whether the ray is "in" the left list or the right list is noted by setting a flag associated with the list from which the record is removed. Whether the span starting at that intersection point is in the combined object is determined by table lookup based on the operator and the two "in" flags, using Table 15.2. A record is then placed on the combined list only if it begins or

TABLE 15.2 POINT CLASSIFICATION FOR OBJECTS COMBINED BY BOOLEAN SET OPERATIONS

Left	Right	∪	∩	−
in	in	in	in	out
in	out	in	out	in
out	in	in	out	out
out	out	out	out	out

ends a span of the combined object, not if it is internal to one of the combined object's spans. If a ray can begin inside an object, the flags must be initialized correctly.

15.10.4 Antialiased Ray Tracing

The simple ray tracer described so far uses point sampling on a regular grid, and thus produces aliased images. Whitted [WHIT80] developed an adaptive method for firing more rays into those parts of the image that would otherwise produce the most severe aliasing. These additional samples are used to compute a better value for the pixel. His *adaptive supersampling* associates rays with the corners, rather than with the centers, of each pixel, as shown in Fig. 15.66(a) and (b). Thus, at first, only an extra row and an extra column of rays are needed for the image. After rays have been fired through all four corners of a pixel, the shades they determine are averaged; the average is then used for the pixel if the shades differ from it by only a small amount. If they differ by too much, then the pixel is subdivided further by firing rays through the midpoints of its sides and through its center, forming four subpixels (Fig. 15.66c). The rays at the four corners of each subpixel are then compared using the same criterion. Subdivision proceeds recursively until a predefined maximum subdivision depth is reached, as in the Warnock algorithm, or until the ray shades are determined to be sufficiently similar. The pixel's shade is the area-weighted average of its subpixels' shades. Adaptive supersampling thus provides an improved approximation to unweighted area sampling, without the overhead of a uniformly higher sampling rate.

Consider, for example, Fig. 15.66(a), which shows the rays fired through the corners of two adjacent pixels, with a maximum subdivision depth of two. If no further subdivision is needed for the pixel bordered by rays A, B, D, and E in part (b), then, representing a ray's shade by its name, the pixel's shade is $(A + B + D + E)/4$. The adjacent pixel requires further subdivision, so rays G, H, I, J, and K are traced, defining the vertices of four subpixels in part (c). Each subpixel is recursively inspected. In this case, only the lower-right subpixel is subdivided again by tracing rays L, M, N, O, and P, as shown in part (d). At this point, the maximum subdivision depth is reached. This pixel's shade is

$$\frac{1}{4}\left[\frac{B + G + H + I}{4} + \frac{1}{4}\left[\frac{G + L + M + N}{4} + \frac{L + C + N + O}{4} + \frac{M + N + I + P}{4} + \right.\right.$$

$$\left.\left.\frac{N + O + P + J}{4}\right] + \frac{H + I + E + K}{4} + \frac{I + J + K + F}{4}\right].$$

Aliasing problems can also arise when the rays through a pixel miss a small object. This produces visible effects if the objects are arranged in a regular pattern and some are not visible, or if a series of pictures of a moving object show that object popping in and out of view as it is alternately hit and missed by the nearest ray. Whitted avoids these effects by surrounding each object with a spherical bounding volume that is sufficiently large always to be intersected by at least one ray from the eye. Since the rays converge at the eye, the size of the bounding volume is a function of the distance from the eye. If a ray intersects the

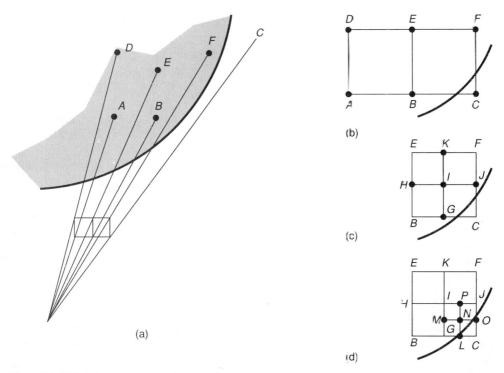

Fig. 15.66 Adaptive supersampling. (a) Two pixels and the rays fired through their corners. (b) The left pixel is not subdivided. (c) The right pixel is subdivided. (d) The lower-right subpixel is subdivided.

bounding volume but does not intersect the object, then all pixels sharing that ray are further subdivided until the object is intersected. Several more recent approaches to antialiased ray tracing are discussed in Section 16.12.

15.11 SUMMARY

Sutherland, Sproull, and Schumacker [SUTH74a] stress that the heart of visible-surface determination is sorting. Indeed, we have seen many instances of sorting and searching in the algorithms, and efficient sorting is vital to efficient visible-surface determination. Equally important is avoiding any more sorting than is absolutely necessary, a goal typically achieved by exploiting coherence. For example, the scan-line algorithms use scan-line coherence to eliminate the need for a complete sort on x for each scan line. Hubschman and Zucker use frame coherence to avoid unnecessary comparisons in animation sequences [HUBS82].

Algorithms can be classified by the order in which they sort. The depth-sort algorithm sorts on z and then on x and y (by use of extents in tests 1 and 2); it is thus called a zxy algorithm. Scan-line algorithms sort on y (with a bucket sort), then sort on x (initially with an insertion sort, then with a bubble sort as each scan line is processed), and finally search in z for the polygon nearest the viewpoint; therefore, they are yxz algorithms. Warnock's algorithm does a parallel sort on x and y, and then searches in z, and hence is an $(xy)z$ algorithm (sorting on a combination of dimensions is indicated by parentheses). The z-buffer algorithm does no explicit sorting and searches only in z; it is called an (xyz) algorithm.

Sancha has argued that the order of sorting is unimportant: There is no intrinsic benefit in sorting along any particular axis first as opposed to another because, at least in principle, the *average* object is equally complex in all three dimensions [SUTH74a]. On the other hand, a graphics scene, like a Hollywood set, may be constructed to look best from a particular viewpoint, and this may entail building in greater complexity along one axis than along another. Even if we assume roughly symmetric object complexity, however, all algorithms are still not equally efficient: They differ in how effectively coherence is used to avoid sorting and other computation and in the use of space–time tradeoffs. The results reported in [SUTH74a, Table VII], which compare the estimated performance of four of the basic algorithms we have presented, are summarized in Table 15.3. The authors suggest that, because these are only estimates, small differences should be ignored, but that "we feel free to make order of magnitude comparisons between the various algorithms to learn something about the effectiveness of the various methods" [SUTH74a, p. 52].

The depth-sort algorithm is efficient for small numbers of polygons because the simple overlap tests almost always suffice to decide whether a polygon can be scan-converted. With more polygons, the more complex tests are needed more frequently and polygon subdivision is more likely to be required. The z-buffer algorithm has constant performance because, as the number of polygons in a scene increases, the number of pixels covered by a single polygon decreases. On the other hand, its memory needs are high. The individual tests and calculations involved in the Warnock area-subdivision algorithm are relatively complex, so it is generally slower than are the other methods.

In addition to these informal estimates, there has been some work on formalizing the visible-surface problem and analyzing its computational complexity [GILO78; FOUR88; FIUM89]. For example, Fiume [FIUM89] proves that object-precision visible-surface algorithms have a lower bound that is worse than that of sorting: Even the simple task of

TABLE 15.3 RELATIVE ESTIMATED PERFORMANCE OF FOUR ALGORITHMS FOR VISIBLE-SURFACE DETERMINATION

	Number of polygonal faces in scene		
Algorithm	100	2500	60,000
Depth sort	1*	10	507
z-buffer	54	54	54
Scan line	5	21	100
Warnock area subdivision	11	64	307

*Entries are normalized such that this case is unity.

computing the visible surfaces of a set of n convex polygons can result in the creation of $\Omega(n^2)$ polygons, requiring $\Omega(n^2)$ time to output, as shown in Fig. 15.67.

In general, comparing visible-surface algorithms is difficult because not all algorithms compute the same information with the same accuracy. For example, we have discussed algorithms that restrict the kinds of objects, relationships among objects, and even the kinds of projections that are allowed. As we shall see in the following chapter, the choice of a visible-surface algorithm is also influenced by the kind of shading desired. If an expensive shading procedure is being used, it is better to choose a visible-surface algorithm that shades only parts of objects that are visible, such as a scan-line algorithm. Depth sort would be a particularly bad choice in this case, since it draws all objects in their entirety. When interactive performance is important, hardware z-buffer approaches are popular. The BSP-tree algorithm, on the other hand, can generate new views of a static environment quickly, but requires additional processing whenever the environment changes. Scan-line algorithms allow extremely high resolution because data structures need to represent fully elaborated versions only of primitives that affect the line being processed. As with any algorithm, the time spent implementing the algorithm and the ease with which it can be modified (e.g., to accommodate new primitives) is also a major factor.

One important consideration in implementing a visible-surface algorithm is the kind of hardware support available. If a parallel machine is available, we must recognize that, at each place where an algorithm takes advantage of coherence, it depends on the results of previous calculations. Exploiting parallelism may entail ignoring some otherwise useful form of coherence. Ray tracing has been a particularly popular candidate for parallel implementation because, in its simplest form, each pixel is computed independently. As we shall see in Chapter 18, there are many architectures that have been designed to execute specific visible-surface algorithms. For example, plummeting memory costs have made hardware z-buffer systems ubiquitous.

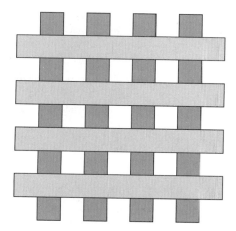

Fig. 15.67 $n/2$ rectangles laid across $n/2$ more distant rectangles can yield $n/2$ visible whole rectangles + $(n/2)$ $(n/2 + 1)$ visible fragments. This is $\Omega(n^2)$ visible polygons. (After [FIUM89].)

EXERCISES

15.1 Prove that the transformation M in Section 15.2.2 preserves (a) straight lines, (b) planes, and (c) depth relationships.

15.2 Given a plane $Ax + By + Cz + D = 0$, apply M from Section 15.2.2 and find the new coefficients of the plane equation.

15.3 How can a scan-line algorithm be extended to deal with polygons with shared edges? Should a shared edge be represented once, as a shared edge, or twice, once for each polygon it borders, with no record kept that it is a shared edge? When the depth of two polygons is evaluated at their common shared edge, the depths will, of course, be equal. Which polygon should be declared visible, given that the scan is entering both?

15.4 Warnock's algorithm generates a quadtree. Show the quadtree corresponding to Fig. 15.44. Label all nodes to indicate how the triangle (T) and the rectangle (R) relate to the node, as (a) surrounding, (b) intersecting, (c) contained, and (d) disjoint.

15.5 For each of the visible-surface algorithms discussed, explain how piercing polygons would be handled. Are they a special case that must be treated explicitly, or are they accommodated by the basic algorithm?

15.6 Consider tests 3 and 4 of the depth-sort algorithm. How might they be implemented efficiently? Consider examining the sign of the equation of the plane of polygon P for each vertex of polygon Q, and vice versa. How do you know to which side of the plane a positive value of the equation corresponds?

15.7 How can the algorithms discussed be adapted to work with polygons containing holes?

15.8 Describe how the visible-line algorithms for functions of two variables, described in Section 15.1, can be modified to work as visible-surface algorithms using the approach taken in the painter's algorithm.

15.9 Why does the Roberts visible-line algorithm not eliminate *all* lines that are edges of a back-facing polygon?

15.10 One of the advantages of the z-buffer algorithm is that primitives may be presented to it in any order. Does this mean that two images created by sending primitives in different orders will have identical values in their z-buffers and in their frame buffers? Explain your answer.

15.11 Consider merging two images of identical size, represented by their frame-buffer and z-buffer contents. If you know the z_{min} and z_{max} of each image and the values of z to which they originally corresponded, can you merge the images properly? Is any additional information needed?

15.12 Section 15.4 mentions the z-compression problems caused by rendering a perspective projection using an integer z-buffer. Choose a perspective viewing specification and a small number of object points. Show how, in the perspective transformation, two points near the center of projection are mapped to different z values, whereas two points separated from each other by the same distance, but farther from the center of projection, are mapped to a single z value.

15.13 a. Suppose view volume V has a front clipping plane at distance F and a back clipping plane at distance B, and that view volume V' has clipping planes at F' and B'. After transformation of each view volume to the canonical-perspective view volume, the back clipping plane of V will be at $z = -1$, and the front clipping plane at $z = A$. For V', the front clipping plane will be at $z = A'$. Show that, if $B / F = B' / F'$, then $A = A'$.

b. Part (a) shows that, in considering the effect of perspective, we need to consider only the ratio of back-plane to front-plane distance. We can therefore simply study the canonical view volume with various values of the front-plane distance. Suppose, then, that we have a canonical-perspective view volume, with front clipping plane $z = A$ and back clipping plane $z = -1$, and we transform it, through the perspective transformation, to the parallel view volume between $z = 0$ and $z = -1$. Write down the formula for the transformed z coordinate in terms of the original z coordinate. (Your answer will depend on A, of course.) Suppose that the transformed z values in the parallel view volume are multiplied by 2^n, and then are rounded to integers (i.e., they are mapped to an integer z-buffer). Find two values of z that are as far apart as possible, but that map, under this transformation, to the same integer. (Your answer will depend on n and A.)

c. Suppose you want to make an image in which the backplane-to-frontplane ratio is R, and objects that are more than distance Q apart (in z) must map to different values in the z-buffer. Using your work in part (b), write a formula for the number of bits of z-buffer needed.

15.14 Show that the back-to-front display order determined by traversing a BSP tree is not necessarily the same as the back-to-front order determined by the depth-sort algorithm, even when no polygons are split. (Hint: Only two polygons are needed.)

15.15 How might you modify the BSP-tree algorithm to accept objects other than polygons?

15.16 How might you modify the BSP-tree algorithm to allow limited motion?

15.17 Suppose that you are designing a ray tracer that supports CSG. How would you handle a polygon that is not part of a polyhedron?

15.18 Some graphics systems implement hardware transformations and homogeneous-coordinate clipping in X, Y, and Z using the same mathematics, so that clipping limits are

$$-W \leq X \leq W, \qquad -W \leq Y \leq W, \qquad -W \leq Z \leq W,$$

instead of

$$-W \leq X \leq W, \qquad -W \leq Y \leq W, \qquad -W \leq Z \leq 0.$$

How would you change the viewing matrix calculation to take this into account?

15.19 When ray tracing is performed, it is typically necessary to compute only whether or not a ray intersects an extent, not what the actual points of intersection are. Complete the ray–sphere intersection equation (Eq. 15.17) using the quadratic formula, and show how it can be simplified to determine only whether or not the ray and sphere intersect.

15.20 Ray tracing can also be used to determine the mass properties of objects through numerical integration. The full set of intersections of a ray with an object gives the total portion of the ray that is inside the object. Show how you can estimate an object's volume by firing a regular array of parallel rays through that object.

15.21 Derive the intersection of a ray with a quadric surface. Modify the method used to derive the intersection of a ray with a sphere in Eqs. (15.13) through (15.16) to handle the definition of a quadric given in Section 11.4.

15.22 In Eq. (15.5), O, the cost of performing an object intersection test, may be partially underwritten by B, the cost of performing a bounding-volume intersection test, if the results of the bounding-volume intersection test can be reused to simplify the object intersection test. Describe an object and bounding volume for which this is possible.

15.23 Implement one of the polygon visible surface algorithms in this chapter, such as a z-buffer algorithm, scan-line algorithm, or BSP tree algorithm.

15.24 Implement a simple ray tracer for spheres and polygons, including adaptive supersampling. (Choose one of the illumination models from Section 16.1.) Improve your program's performance through the use of spatial partitioning or hierarchies of bounding volumes.

15.25 If you have implemented the z-buffer algorithm, then add hit detection to it by extending the pick-window approach described in Section 7.12.2 to take visible-surface determination into account. You will need a SetPickMode procedure that is passed a mode flag, indicating whether objects are to be drawn (drawing mode) or instead tested for hits (pick mode). A SetPick Window procedure will let the user set a rectangular pick window. The z-buffer must already have been filled (by drawing all objects) for pick mode to work. When in pick mode, neither the frame-buffer nor the z-buffer is updated, but the z-value of each of the primitive's pixels that falls inside the pick window is compared with the corresponding value in the z-buffer. If the new value would have caused the object to be drawn in drawing mode, then a flag is set. The flag can be inquired by calling InquirePick, which then resets the flag. If InquirePick is called after each primitive's routine is called in pick mode, picking can be done on a per-primitive basis. Show how you can use InquirePick to determine which object is actually visible at a pixel.

16

Illumination
and Shading

In this chapter, we discuss how to shade surfaces based on the position, orientation, and characteristics of the surfaces and the light sources illuminating them. We develop a number of different *illumination models* that express the factors determining a surface's color at a given point. Illumination models are also frequently called *lighting models* or *shading models*. Here, however, we reserve the term *shading model* for the broader framework in which an illumination model fits. The shading model determines when the illumination model is applied and what arguments it will receive. For example, some shading models invoke an illumination model for every pixel in the image, whereas others invoke an illumination model for only some pixels, and shade the remaining pixels by interpolation.

When we compared the accuracy with which the visible-surface calculations of the previous chapter are performed, we distinguished between algorithms that use the actual object geometry and those that use polyhedral approximations, between object-precision and image-precision algorithms, and between image-precision algorithms that take one point sample per pixel and those that use better filters. In all cases, however, the single criterion for determining the direct visibility of an object at a pixel is whether something lies between the object and the observer along the projector through the pixel. In contrast, the interaction between lights and surfaces is a good deal more complex. Graphics researchers have often approximated the underlying rules of optics and thermal radiation, either to simplify computation or because more accurate models were not known in the graphics community. Consequently, many of the illumination and shading models traditionally used in computer graphics include a multitude of kludges, "hacks," and simplifications that have no firm grounding in theory, but that work well in practice. The first part of this chapter covers these simple models, which are still in common use because they can produce attractive and useful results with minimal computation.

We begin, in Section 16.1, with a discussion of simple illumination models that take into account an individual point on a surface and the light sources directly illuminating it. We first develop illumination models for monochromatic surfaces and lights, and then show how the computations can be generalized to handle the color systems discussed in Chapter 13. Section 16.2 describes the most common shading models that are used with these illumination models. In Section 16.3, we expand these models to simulate textured surfaces.

Modeling refraction, reflection, and shadows requires additional computation that is very similar to, and often is integrated with, hidden-surface elimination. Indeed, these effects occur because some of the "hidden surfaces" are not really hidden at all—they are seen through, reflected from, or cast shadows on the surface being shaded! Sections 16.4 through 16.6 discuss how to model these effects. We next introduce, in Section 16.7, illumination models that more accurately characterize how an individual surface interacts with the light sources directly illuminating it. This is followed by coverage of additional ways to generate more realistic images, in Section 16.8 through 16.10.

Sections 16.11 through 16.13 describe *global illumination models* that attempt to take into account the interchange of light between all surfaces: recursive ray tracing and radiosity methods. Recursive ray tracing extends the visible-surface ray-tracing algorithm introduced in the previous chapter to interleave the determination of visibility, illumination, and shading at each pixel. Radiosity methods model the energy equilibrium in a system of surfaces; they determine the illumination of a set of sample points in the environment in a view-independent fashion before visible-surface determination is performed from the desired viewpoint. More detailed treatments of many of the illumination and shading models covered here may be found in [GLAS89; HALL89].

Finally, in Section 16.14, we look at several different graphics pipelines that integrate the rasterization techniques discussed in this and the previous chapters. We examine some ways to implement these capabilities to produce systems that are both efficient and extensible.

16.1 ILLUMINATION MODELS

16.1.1 Ambient Light

Perhaps the simplest illumination model possible is that used implicitly in this book's earliest chapters: Each object is displayed using an intensity intrinsic to it. We can think of this model, which has no external light source, as describing a rather unrealistic world of nonreflective, self-luminous objects. Each object appears as a monochromatic silhouette, unless its individual parts, such as the polygons of a polyhedron, are given different shades when the object is created. Color Plate II.28 demonstrates this effect.

An illumination model can be expressed by an *illumination equation* in variables associated with the point on the object being shaded. The illumination equation that expresses this simple model is

$$I = k_i. \tag{16.1}$$

where I is the resulting intensity and the coefficient k_i is the object's intrinsic intensity. Since this illumination equation contains no terms that depend on the position of the point being shaded, we can evaluate it once for each object. The process of evaluating the illumination equation at one or more points on an object is often referred to as *lighting* the object.

Now imagine, instead of self-luminosity, that there is a diffuse, nondirectional source of light, the product of multiple reflections of light from the many surfaces present in the environment. This is known as *ambient* light. If we assume that ambient light impinges equally on all surfaces from all directions, then our illumination equation becomes

$$I = I_a k_a. \tag{16.2}$$

I_a is the intensity of the ambient light, assumed to be constant for all objects. The amount of ambient light reflected from an object's surface is determined by k_a, the *ambient-reflection coefficient,* which ranges from 0 to 1. The ambient-reflection coefficient is a *material property.* Along with the other material properties that we will discuss, it may be thought of as characterizing the material from which the surface is made. Like some of the other properties, the ambient-reflection coefficient is an empirical convenience and does not correspond directly to any physical property of real materials. Furthermore, ambient light by itself is not of much interest. As we see later, it is used to account for all the complex ways in which light can reach an object that are not otherwise addressed by the illumination equation. Color Plate II.28 also demonstrates illumination by ambient light.

16.1.2   Diffuse Reflection

Although objects illuminated by ambient light are more or less brightly lit in direct proportion to the ambient intensity, they are still uniformly illuminated across their surfaces. Now consider illuminating an object by a *point light source*, whose rays emanate uniformly in all directions from a single point. The object's brightness varies from one part to another, depending on the direction of and distance to the light source.

Lambertian reflection.   Dull, matte surfaces, such as chalk, exhibit *diffuse reflection,* also known as *Lambertian reflection.* These surfaces appear equally bright from all viewing angles because they reflect light with equal intensity in all directions. For a given surface, the brightness depends only on the angle θ between the direction $\overline{L}$ to the light source and the surface normal $\overline{N}$ of Fig. 16.1. Let us examine why this occurs. There are two factors at work here. First, Fig. 16.2 shows that a beam that intercepts a surface covers an area whose size is inversely proportional to the cosine of the angle θ that the beam makes with $\overline{N}$. If the

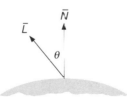

Fig. 16.1 Diffuse reflection.

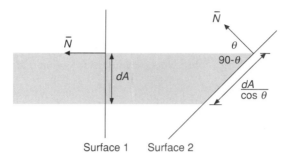

Fig. 16.2 Beam (shown in 2D cross-section) of infinitesimal cross-sectional area dA at angle of incidence θ intercepts area of dA / cos θ.

beam has an infinitesimally small cross-sectional differential area dA, then the beam intercepts an area dA / cos θ on the surface. Thus, for an incident light beam, the amount of light energy that falls on dA is proportional to cos θ. This is true for any surface, independent of its material.

Second, we must consider the amount of light seen by the viewer. Lambertian surfaces have the property, often known as Lambert's law, that the amount of light reflected from a unit differential area dA toward the viewer is directly proportional to the cosine of the angle between the direction to the viewer and $\overline{N}$. Since the amount of surface area seen is inversely proportional to the cosine of this angle, these two factors cancel out. For example, as the viewing angle increases, the viewer sees more surface area, but the amount of light reflected at that angle per unit area of surface is proportionally less. Thus, for Lambertian surfaces, the amount of light seen by the viewer is independent of the viewer's direction and is proportional only to cos θ, the angle of incidence of the light.

The diffuse illumination equation is

$$I = I_p k_d \cos \theta. \tag{16.3}$$

I_p is the point light source's intensity; the material's *diffuse-reflection coefficient* k_d is a constant between 0 and 1 and varies from one material to another. The angle θ must be between 0° and 90° if the light source is to have any direct effect on the point being shaded. This means that we are treating the surface as *self-occluding,* so that light cast from behind a point on the surface does not illuminate it. Rather than include a max(cos θ, 0) term explicitly here and in the following equations, we assume that θ lies within the legal range. When we want to light self-occluding surfaces, we can use abs(cos θ) to invert their surface normals. This causes both sides of the surface to be treated alike, as if the surface were lit by two opposing lights.

Assuming that the vectors $\overline{N}$ and $\overline{L}$ have been normalized (see Appendix), we can rewrite Eq. (16.3) by using the dot product:

$$I = I_p k_d (\overline{N} \cdot \overline{L}). \tag{16.4}$$

The surface normal $\overline{N}$ can be calculated using the methods discussed in Chapter 11. If polygon normals are precomputed and transformed with the same matrix used for the polygon vertices, it is important that nonrigid modeling transformations, such as shears or

Fig. 16.3 Spheres shaded using a diffuse-reflection model (Eq. 16.4). For all spheres, $I_p = 1.0$. From left to right, $k_d = 0.4, 0.55, 0.7, 0.85, 1.0$. (By David Kurlander, Columbia University.)

differential scaling, not be performed; these transformations do not preserve angles and may cause some normals to be no longer perpendicular to their polygons. The proper method to transform normals when objects undergo arbitrary transformations is described in Section 5.6. In any case, the illumination equation must be evaluated in the WC system (or in any coordinate system isometric to it), since both the normalizing and perspective transformations will modify θ.

If a point light source is sufficiently distant from the objects being shaded, it makes essentially the same angle with all surfaces sharing the same surface normal. In this case, the light is called a *directional light source,* and $\overline{L}$ is a constant for the light source.

Figure 16.3 shows a series of pictures of a sphere illuminated by a single point source. The shading model calculated the intensity at each pixel at which the sphere was visible using the illumination model of Eq. (16.4). Objects illuminated in this way look harsh, as when a flashlight illuminates an object in an otherwise dark room. Therefore, an ambient term is commonly added to yield a more realistic illumination equation:

$$I = I_a k_a + I_p k_d (\overline{N} \cdot \overline{L}).$$ (16.5)

Equation (16.5) was used to produce Fig. 16.4.

Light-source attenuation. If the projections of two parallel surfaces of identical material, lit from the eye, overlap in an image, Eq. (16.5) will not distinguish where one surface leaves off and the other begins, no matter how different are their distances from the light source. To do this, we introduce a light-source attenuation factor, f_{att}, yielding

$$I = I_a k_a + f_{att} I_p k_d (\overline{N} \cdot \overline{L}).$$ (16.6)

Fig. 16.4 Spheres shaded using ambient and diffuse reflection (Eq. 16.5). For all spheres, $I_a = I_p = 1.0$, $k_d = 0.4$. From left to right, $k_a = 0.0, 0.15, 0.30, 0.45, 0.60$. (By David Kurlander, Columbia University.)

An obvious choice for f_{att} takes into account the fact that the energy from a point light source that reaches a given part of a surface falls off as the inverse square of d_L, the distance the light travels from the point source to the surface. In this case,

$$f_{att} = \frac{1}{d_L^2}. \tag{16.7}$$

In practice, however, this often does not work well. If the light is far away, $1 / d_L^2$ does not vary much; if it is very close, it varies widely, giving considerably different shades to surfaces with the same angle θ between $\overline{N}$ and $\overline{L}$. Although this behavior is correct for a point light source, the objects we see in real life typically are not illuminated by point sources and are not shaded using the simplified illumination models of computer graphics. To complicate matters, early graphics researchers often used a single point light source positioned right at the viewpoint. They expected f_{att} to approximate some of the effects of atmospheric attenuation between the viewer and the object (see Section 16.1.3), as well as the energy density falloff from the light to the object. A useful compromise, which allows a richer range of effects than simple square-law attenuation, is

$$f_{att} = \min\left(\frac{1}{c_1 + c_2 d_L + c_3 d_L^2}, 1\right). \tag{16.8}$$

Here c_1, c_2, and c_3 are user-defined constants associated with the light source. The constant c_1 keeps the denominator from becoming too small when the light is close, and the expression is clamped to a maximum of 1 to ensure that it always attenuates. Figure 16.5 uses this illumination model with different constants to show a range of effects.

Colored lights and surfaces. So far, we have described monochromatic lights and surfaces. Colored lights and surfaces are commonly treated by writing separate equations for each component of the color model. We represent an object's *diffuse color* by one value of O_d for each component. For example, the triple (O_{dR}, O_{dG}, O_{dB}) defines an object's diffuse red, green, and blue components in the RGB color system. In this case, the illuminating light's three primary components, I_{pR}, I_{pG}, and I_{pB}, are reflected in proportion to $k_d O_{dR}$, $k_d O_{dG}$, and $k_d O_{dB}$, respectively. Therefore, for the red component,

$$I_R = I_{aR} k_a O_{dR} + f_{att} I_{pR} k_d O_{dR} (\overline{N} \cdot \overline{L}). \tag{16.9}$$

Similar equations are used for I_G and I_B, the green and blue components. The use of a single coefficient to scale an expression in each of the equations allows the user to control the amount of ambient or diffuse reflection, without altering the proportions of its components. An alternative formulation that is more compact, but less convenient to control, uses a separate coefficient for each component; for example, substituting k_{aR} for $k_a O_{dR}$ and k_{dR} for $k_d O_{dR}$.

A simplifying assumption is made here that a three-component color model can completely model the interaction of light with objects. This assumption is wrong, as we discuss in Section 16.9, but it is easy to implement and often yields acceptable pictures. In theory, the illumination equation should be evaluated continuously over the spectral range being modeled; in practice, it is evaluated for some number of discrete spectral samples.

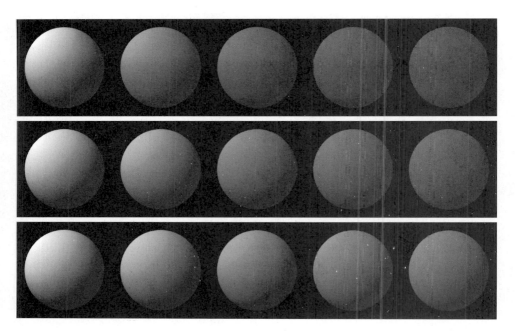

Fig. 16.5 Spheres shaded using ambient and diffuse reflection with a light-source-attenuation term (Eqs. 16.6 and 16.8). For all spheres, $I_a = I_p = 1.0$, $k_a = C.1$, $k_d = 0.9$. From left to right, sphere's distance from light source is 1.0, 1.375, 1.75, 2.125, 2.5. Top row: $c_1 = c_2 = 0.0$, $c_3 = 1.0$ ($1/d_L^2$). Middle row: $c_1 = c_2 = 0.25$, $c_3 = 0.5$. Bottom row: $c_1 = 0.0$, $c_2 = 1.0$, $c_3 = 0.0$ ($1/d_L$). (By David Kurlander, Columbia University.)

Rather than restrict ourselves to a particular color model, we explicitly indicate those terms in an illumination equation that are wavelength-dependent by subscripting them with a λ. Thus, Eq. (16.9) becomes

$$I_\lambda = I_{a\lambda} k_a O_{d\lambda} + f_{att} I_{p\lambda} k_c O_{d\lambda} (\overline{N} \cdot \overline{L}). \tag{16.10}$$

16.1.3 Atmospheric Attenuation

To simulate the atmospheric attenuation from the object to the viewer, many systems provide *depth cueing*. In this technique, which originated with vector-graphics hardware, more distant objects are rendered with lower intensity than are closer cnes. The PHIGS+ standard recommends a depth-cueing approach that also makes it possible to approximate the shift in colors caused by the intervening atmosphere. Front and back depth-cue reference planes are defined in NPC; each of these planes is associated with a scale factor, s_f and s_b, respectively, that ranges between 0 and 1. The scale factors determine the blending of the original intensity with that of a depth-cue color, $I_{dc\lambda}$. The goal is to modify a previously computed I_λ to yield the depth-cued value I'_λ that is displayed. Given z_o, the object's z coordinate, a scale factor s_o is derived that will be used to interpolate between I_λ and $I_{dc\lambda}$, to determine

$$I'_\lambda = s_o I_\lambda + (1 - s_o) I_{dc\lambda}. \tag{16.11}$$

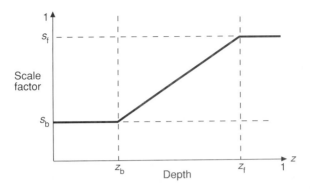

Fig. 16.6 Computing the scale factor for atmospheric attenuation.

If z_o is in front of the front depth-cue reference plane's z coordinate z_f, then $s_o = s_f$. If z_o is behind the back depth-cue reference plane's z coordinate z_b, then $s_o = s_b$. Finally, if z_o is between the two planes, then

$$s_o = s_b + \frac{(z_o - z_b)(s_f - s_b)}{z_f - z_b}. \tag{16.12}$$

The relationship between s_o and z_o is shown in Fig. 16.6. Figure 16.7 shows spheres shaded with depth cueing. To avoid complicating the equations, we ignore depth cueing as we develop the illumination model further. More realistic ways to model atmospheric effects are discussed in Section 20.8.2.

16.1.4 Specular Reflection

Specular reflection can be observed on any shiny surface. Illuminate an apple with a bright white light: The highlight is caused by specular reflection, whereas the light reflected from the rest of the apple is the result of diffuse reflection. Also note that, at the highlight, the apple appears to be not red, but white, the color of the incident light. Objects such as waxed apples or shiny plastics have a transparent surface; plastics, for example, are typically composed of pigment particles embedded in a transparent material. Light specularly reflected from the colorless surface has much the same color as that of the light source.

Fig. 16.7 Spheres shaded using depth cueing (Eqs. 16.5, 16.11, and 16.12). Distance from light is constant. For all spheres, $I_a = I_p = 1.0$, $k_a = 0.1$, $k_d = 0.9$, $z_f = 1.0$, $z_b = 0.0$, $s_f = 1.0$, $s_b = 0.1$, radius = 0.09. From left to right, z at front of sphere is 1.0, 0.77, 0.55, 0.32, 0.09. (By David Kurlander, Columbia University.)

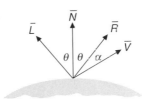

Fig. 16.8 Specular reflection.

Now move your head and notice how the highlight also moves. It does so because shiny surfaces reflect light unequally in different directions; on a perfectly shiny surface, such as a perfect mirror, light is reflected *only* in the direction of reflection $\bar{R}$, which is $\bar{L}$ mirrored about $\bar{N}$. Thus the viewer can see specularly reflected light from a mirror only when the angle α in Fig. 16.8 is zero; α is the angle between $\bar{R}$ and the direction to the viewpoint $\bar{V}$.

The Phong illumination model. Phong Bui-Tuong [BUIT75] developed a popular illumination model for nonperfect reflectors, such as the apple. It assumes that maximum specular reflectance occurs when α is zero and falls off sharply as α increases. This rapid falloff is approximated by $\cos^n \alpha$, where n is the material's *specular-reflection exponent*. Values of n typically vary from 1 to several hundred, depending on the surface material being simulated. A value of 1 provides a broad, gentle falloff, whereas higher values simulate a sharp, focused highlight (Fig. 16.9). For a perfect reflector, n would be infinite. As before, we treat a negative value of $\cos \alpha$ as zero. Phong's illumination model is based on earlier work by researchers such as Warnock [WARN69], who used a $\cos^n \theta$ term to model specular reflection with the light at the viewpoint. Phong, however, was the first to account for viewers and lights at arbitrary positions.

The amount of incident light specularly reflected depends on the angle of incidence θ. If $W(\theta)$ is the fraction of specularly reflected light, then Phong's model is

$$I_\lambda = I_{a\lambda}k_aO_{d\lambda} + f_{att}I_{p\lambda} [k_dO_{d\lambda} \cos \theta + W(\theta) \cos^n \alpha]. \tag{16.13}$$

If the direction of reflection $\bar{R}$, and the viewpoint direction $\bar{V}$ are normalized, then $\cos \alpha = \bar{R} \cdot \bar{V}$. In addition, $W(\theta)$ is typically set to a constant k_s, the material's *specular-reflection coefficient*, which ranges between 0 and 1. The value of k_s is selected experimentally to

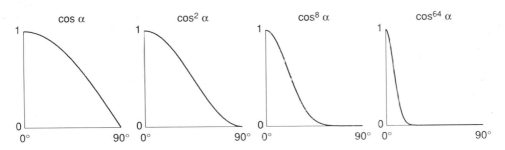

Fig. 16.9 Different values of $\cos^n \alpha$ used in the Phong illumination model.

produce aesthetically pleasing results. Then, Eq. (16.13) can be rewritten as

$$I_\lambda = I_{a\lambda}k_aO_{d\lambda} + f_{att}I_{p\lambda}[k_dO_{d\lambda}(\bar{N} \cdot \bar{L}) + k_s (\bar{R} \cdot \bar{V})^n]. \tag{16.14}$$

Note that the color of the specular component in Phong's illumination model is *not* dependent on any material property; thus, this model does a good job of modeling specular reflections from plastic surfaces. As we discuss in Section 16.7, specular reflection is affected by the properties of the surface itself, and, in general, may have a different color than diffuse reflection when the surface is a composite of several materials. We can accommodate this effect to a first approximation by modifying Eq. (16.14) to yield

$$I_\lambda = I_{a\lambda}k_aO_{d\lambda} + f_{att}I_{p\lambda}[k_dO_{d\lambda}(\bar{N} \cdot \bar{L}) + k_sO_{s\lambda} (\bar{R} \cdot \bar{V})^n], \tag{16.15}$$

where $O_{s\lambda}$ is the object's *specular color*. Figure 16.10 shows a sphere illuminated using Eq. (16.14) with different values of k_s and n.

Calculating the reflection vector. Calculating $\bar{R}$ requires mirroring $\bar{L}$ about $\bar{N}$. As shown in Fig. 16.11, this can be accomplished with some simple geometry. Since $\bar{N}$ and $\bar{L}$ are normalized, the projection of $\bar{L}$ onto $\bar{N}$ is $\bar{N} \cos \theta$. Note that $\bar{R} = \bar{N} \cos \theta + \bar{S}$, where $|\bar{S}|$ is $\sin \theta$. But, by vector subtraction and congruént triangles, $\bar{S}$ is just $\bar{N} \cos \theta - \bar{L}$. Therefore, $\bar{R} = 2 \bar{N} \cos \theta - \bar{L}$. Substituting $\bar{N} \cdot \bar{L}$ for $\cos \theta$ and $\bar{R} \cdot \bar{V}$ for $\cos \alpha$ yields

$$\bar{R} = 2\bar{N} (\bar{N} \cdot \bar{L}) - \bar{L}, \tag{16.16}$$

$$\bar{R} \cdot \bar{V} = (2\bar{N} (\bar{N} \cdot \bar{L}) - \bar{L}) \cdot \bar{V}. \tag{16.17}$$

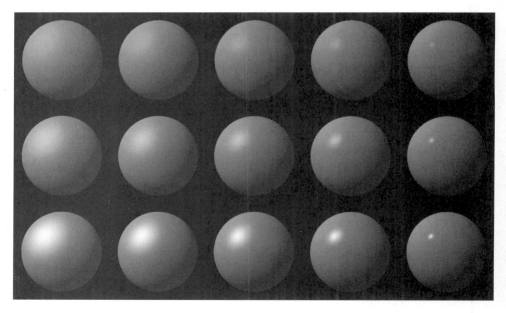

Fig. 16.10 Spheres shaded using Phong's illumination model (Eq. 16.14) and different values of k_s and n. For all spheres, $I_a = I_p = 1.0$, $k_a = 0.1$, $k_d = 0.45$. From left to right, $n = 3.0, 5.0, 10.0, 27.0, 200.0$. From top to bottom, $k_s = 0.1, 0.25, 0.5$. (By David Kurlander, Columbia University.)

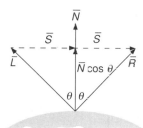

Fig. 16.11 Calculating the reflection vector.

If the light source is at infinity, $\overline{N} \cdot \overline{L}$ is constant for a given polygon, whereas $\overline{R} \cdot \overline{V}$ varies across the polygon. For curved surfaces or for a light source not at infinity, both $\overline{N} \cdot \overline{L}$ and $\overline{R} \cdot \overline{V}$ vary across the surface.

The halfway vector. An alternative formulation of Phong's illumination model uses the *halfway vector* $\overline{H}$, so called because its direction is halfway between the directions of the light source and the viewer, as shown in Fig. 16.12. $\overline{H}$ is also known as the direction of maximum highlights. If the surface were oriented so that its normal were in the same direction as $\overline{H}$, the viewer would see the brightest specular highlight, since $\overline{R}$ and $\overline{V}$ would also point in the same direction. The new specular-reflection term can be expressed as $(\overline{N} \cdot \overline{H})^n$, where $\overline{H} = (\overline{L} + \overline{V}) / |\overline{L} + \overline{V}|$. When the light source and the viewer are both at infinity, then the use of $\overline{N} \cdot \overline{H}$ offers a computational advantage, since $\overline{H}$ is constant. Note that β, the angle between $\overline{N}$ and $\overline{H}$, is not equal to α, the angle between $\overline{R}$ and $\overline{V}$, so the same specular exponent n produces different results in the two formulations (see Exercise 16.1). Although using a $\cos^n$ term allows the generation of recognizably glossy surfaces, you should remember that it is based on empirical observation, not on a theoretical model of the specular-reflection process.

16.1.5   Improving the Point-Light-Source Model

Real light sources do not radiate equally in all directions. Warn [WARN83] has developed easily implemented lighting controls that can be added to any illumination equation to model some of the directionality of the lights used by photographers. In Phong's model, a point light source has only an intensity and a position. In Warn's model, a light L is modeled by a point on a hypothetical specular reflecting surface, as shown in Fig. 16.13. This surface is illuminated by a point light source L' in the direction $\overline{L}'$. Assume that $\overline{L}'$ is normal to the hypothetical reflecting surface. Then, we can use the Phong illumination

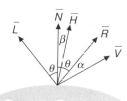

Fig. 16.12 $\overline{H}$, the halfway vector, is halfway between the direction of the light source and the viewer.

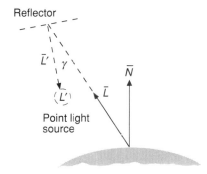

Fig. 16.13 Warn's lighting model. A light is modeled as the specular reflection from a single point illuminated by a point light source.

equation to determine the intensity of L at a point on the object in terms of the angle γ between $\bar{L}$ and $\bar{L}'$. If we further assume that the reflector reflects only specular light and has a specular coefficient of 1, then the light's intensity at a point on the object is

$$I_{L'\lambda} \cos^p \gamma, \qquad (16.18)$$

where $I_{L'\lambda}$ is the intensity of the hypothetical point light source, p is the reflector's specular exponent, and γ is the angle between $-\bar{L}$ and the hypothetical surface's normal, $\bar{L}'$, which is the direction to L'. Equation (16.18) models a symmetric directed light source whose axis of symmetry is $\bar{L}'$, the direction in which the light may be thought of as pointing. Using dot products, we can write Eq.(16.18) as

$$I_{L'\lambda} (-\bar{L} \cdot \bar{L}')^p. \qquad (16.19)$$

Once again, we treat a negative dot product as zero. Equation (16.19) can thus be substituted for the light-source intensity $I_{p\lambda}$ in the formulation of Eq. (16.15) or any other illumination equation. Contrast the intensity distribution of the uniformly radiating point source with the $\cos^p$ distribution of the Warn light source in Fig. 16.14. Each distribution is plotted in cross-section, showing intensity as a function of angular direction around the light's axis in polar coordinates. $\bar{L}'$ is shown as an arrow. These plots are called *goniometric diagrams*. The larger the value of p, the more the light is concentrated along $\bar{L}'$. Thus, a

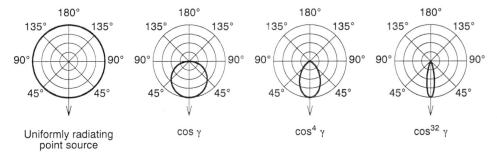

Fig. 16.14 Intensity distributions for uniformly radiating point source and Warn light source with different values of p.

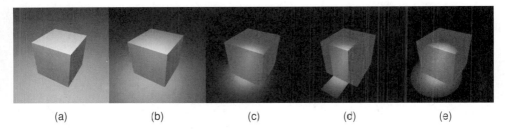

(a)   (b)   (c)   (d)   (e)

Fig. 16.15 Cube and plane illuminated using Warn lighting controls. (a) Uniformly radiating point source (or $p = 0$). (b) $p = 4$. (c) $p = 32$. (d) Flaps. (e) Cone with $\delta = 18°$. (By David Kurlander, Columbia University.)

large value of p can simulate a highly directional spotlight, whereas a small value of p can simulate a more diffuse floodlight. If p is 0, then the light acts like a uniformly radiating point source. Figure 16.15(a–c) shows the effects of different values of p. Verbeck [VERB84] and Nishita et al. [NISH85b] have modeled point light sources with more complex irregular intensity and spectral distributions. In general, however, once we determine a point light source's intensity as seen from a particular direction, this value can be used in any illumination equation.

To restrict a light's effects to a limited area of the scene, Warn implemented *flaps* and *cones*. Flaps, modeled loosely after the "barn doors" found on professional photographic lights, confine the effects of the light to a designated range in x, y, and z world coordinates. Each light has six flaps, corresponding to user-specified minimum and maximum values in each coordinate. Each flap also has a flag indicating whether it is on or off. When a point's shade is determined, the illumination model is evaluated for a light only if the point's coordinates are within the range specified by the minimum and maximum coordinates of those flaps that are on. For example, if $\bar{L}'$ is parallel to the y axis, then the x and z flaps can sharply restrict the light's effects, much like the photographic light's barn doors. Figure 16.16(a) shows the use of the x flaps in this situation. The y flaps can also be used here to

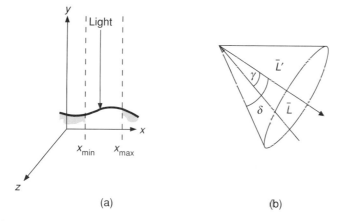

(a)   (b)

Fig. 16.16 The Warn intensity distribution may be restricted with (a) flaps and (b) cones.

restrict the light in a way that has no physical counterpart, allowing only objects within a specified range of distances from the light to be illuminated. In Fig. 16.15(d) the cube is aligned with the coordinate system, so two pairs of flaps can produce the effects shown.

Warn makes it possible to create a sharply delineated spotlight through the use of a cone whose apex is at the light source and whose axis lies along $\bar{L}'$. As shown in Fig. 16.16(b), a cone with a generating angle of δ may be used to restrict the light source's effects by evaluating the illumination model only when $\gamma < \delta$ (or when $\cos \gamma > \cos \delta$, since $\cos \gamma$ has already been calculated). The PHIGS+ illumination model includes the Warn $\cos^p \gamma$ term and cone angle δ. Figure 16.15(e) demonstrates the use of a cone to restrict the light of Fig. 16.15(c). Color Plate II.17 shows a car rendered with Warn's lighting controls.

16.1.6 Multiple Light Sources

If there are m light sources, then the terms for each light source are summed:

$$I_\lambda = I_{a\lambda}k_aO_{d\lambda} + \sum_{1 \le i \le m} f_{atti}I_{p\lambda i} [k_dO_{d\lambda}(\bar{N} \cdot \bar{L}_i) + k_sO_{s\lambda} (\bar{R}_i \cdot \bar{V})^n]. \qquad (16.20)$$

The summation harbors a new possibility for error in that I_λ can now exceed the maximum displayable pixel value. (Although this can also happen for a single light, we can easily avoid it by an appropriate choice of f_{att} and the material coefficients.) Several approaches can be used to avoid overflow. The simplest is to clamp each I_λ individually to its maximum value. Another approach considers all of a pixel's I_λ values together. If at least one is too big, each is divided by the largest to maintain the hue and saturation at the expense of the value. If all the pixel values can be computed before display, image-processing transformations can be applied to the entire picture to bring the values within the desired range. Hall [HALL89] discusses the tradeoffs of these and other techniques.

16.2 SHADING MODELS FOR POLYGONS

It should be clear that we can shade any surface by calculating the surface normal at each visible point and applying the desired illumination model at that point. Unfortunately, this brute-force shading model is expensive. In this section, we describe more efficient shading models for surfaces defined by polygons and polygon meshes.

16.2.1 Constant Shading

The simplest shading model for a polygon is *constant shading*, also known as *faceted shading* or *flat shading*. This approach applies an illumination model once to determine a single intensity value that is then used to shade an entire polygon. In essence, we are sampling the value of the illumination equation once for each polygon, and holding the value across the polygon to reconstruct the polygon's shade. This approach is valid if several assumptions are true:

1. The light source is at infinity, so $\bar{N} \cdot \bar{L}$ is constant across the polygon face
2. The viewer is at infinity, so $\bar{N} \cdot \bar{V}$ is constant across the polygon face
3. The polygon represents the actual surface being modeled, and is not an approximation to a curved surface.

If a visible-surface algorithm is used that outputs a list of polygons, such as one of the list-priority algorithms, constant shading can take advantage of the ubiquitous single-color 2D polygon primitive.

If either of the first two assumptions is wrong, then, if we are to use constant shading, we need some method to determine a single value for each of $\overline{L}$ and $\overline{V}$. For example, values may be calculated for the center of the polygon, or for the polygon's first vertex. Of course, constant shading does not produce the variations in shade across the polygon that should occur in this situation.

16.2.2 Interpolated Shading

As an alternative to evaluating the illumination equation at each point on the polygon, Wylie, Romney, Evans, and Erdahl [WYLI67] pioneered the use of *interpolated shading*, in which shading information is linearly interpolated across a triangle from values determined for its vertices. Gouraud [GOUR71] generalized this technique to arbitrary polygons. This is particularly easy for a scan-line algorithm that already interpolates the z value across a span from interpolated z values computed for the span's endpoints. For increased efficiency, a difference equation may be used, like that developed in Section 15.4 to determine the z value at each pixel. Although z interpolation is physically correct (assuming that the polygon is planar), note that interpolated shading is not, since it only approximates evaluating the illumination model at each point on the polygon.

Our final assumption, that the polygon accurately represents the surface being modeled, is most often the one that is incorrect, which has a much more substantial effect on the resulting image than does the failure of the other two assumptions. Many objects are curved, rather than polyhedral, yet representing them as a polygon mesh allows the use of efficient polygon visible-surface algorithms. We discuss next how to render a polygon mesh so that it looks as much as possible like a curved surface.

16.2.3 Polygon Mesh Shading

Suppose that we wish to approximate a curved surface by a polygonal mesh. If each polygonal facet in the mesh is shaded individually, it is easily distinguished from neighbors whose orientation is different, producing a "faceted" appearance, as shown in Color Plate II.29. This is true if the polygons are rendered using constant shading, interpolated shading, or even per-pixel illumination calculations, because two adjacent polygons of different orientation have different intensities along their borders. The simple solution of using a finer mesh turns out to be surprisingly ineffective, because the perceived difference in shading between adjacent facets is accentuated by the Mach band effect (discovered by Mach in 1865 and described in detail in [RATL72]), which exaggerates the intensity change at any edge where there is a discontinuity in magnitude or slope of intensity. At the border between two facets, the dark facet looks darker and the light facet looks lighter. Figure 16.17 shows, for two separate cases, the actual and perceived changes in intensity along a surface.

Mach banding is caused by *lateral inhibition* of the receptors in the eye. The more light a receptor receives, the more that receptor inhibits the response of the receptors adjacent to

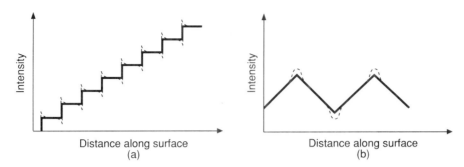

Fig. 16.17 Actual and perceived intensities in the Mach band effect. Dashed lines are perceived intensity; solid lines are actual intensity.

it. The response of a receptor to light is inhibited by its adjacent receptors in inverse relation to the distance to the adjacent receptor. Receptors directly on the brighter side of an intensity change have a stronger response than do those on the brighter side that are farther from the edge, because they receive less inhibition from their neighbors on the darker side. Similarly, receptors immediately to the darker side of an intensity change have a weaker response than do those farther into the darker area, because they receive more inhibition from their neighbors on the brighter side. The Mach band effect is quite evident in Color Plate II.29, especially between adjacent polygons that are close in color.

The polygon-shading models we have described determine the shade of each polygon individually. Two basic shading models for polygon meshes take advantage of the information provided by adjacent polygons to simulate a smooth surface. In order of increasing complexity (and realistic effect), they are known as Gouraud shading and Phong shading, after the researchers who developed them. Current 3D graphics workstations typically support one or both of these approaches through a combination of hardware and firmware.

16.2.4 Gouraud Shading

Gouraud shading [GOUR71], also called *intensity interpolation shading* or *color interpolation shading*, eliminates intensity discontinuities. Color Plate II.30 uses Gouraud shading. Although most of the Mach banding of Color Plate II.29 is no longer visible in Color Plate II.30, the bright ridges on objects such as the torus and cone are Mach bands caused by a rapid, although not discontinuous, change in the slope of the intensity curve; Gouraud shading does not completely eliminate such intensity changes.

Gouraud shading extends the concept of interpolated shading applied to individual polygons by interpolating polygon vertex illumination values that take into account the surface being approximated. The Gouraud shading process requires that the normal be known for each vertex of the polygonal mesh. Gouraud was able to compute these *vertex normals* directly from an analytical description of the surface. Alternatively, if the vertex normals are not stored with the mesh and cannot be determined directly from the actual surface, then, Gouraud suggested, we can approximate them by averaging the surface

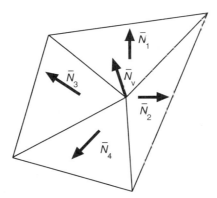

Fig. 16.18 Normalized polygon surface normals may be averaged to obtain vertex normals. Averaged normal $\overline{N}_v$ is $\sum_{1 \leq i \leq n} \overline{N}_i \, / \, | \sum_{1 \leq i \leq n} \overline{N}_i |$.

normals of all polygonal facets sharing each vertex (Fig. 16.18). If an edge is meant to be visible (as at the joint between a plane's wing and body), then we find two vertex normals, one for each side of the edge, by averaging the normals of polygons on each side of the edge separately. Normals were not averaged across the teapot's patch cracks in Color Plate II.30. (See caption to Color Plate II.21.)

The next step in Gouraud shading is to find *vertex intensities* by using the vertex normals with any desired illumination model. Finally, each polygon is shaded by linear interpolation of vertex intensities along each edge and then between edges along each scan line (Fig. 16.19) in the same way that we described interpolating z values in Section 15.4. The term *Gouraud shading* is often generalized to refer to intensity interpolation shading of even a single polygon in isolation, or to the interpolation of arbitrary colors associated with polygon vertices.

The interpolation along edges can easily be integrated with the scan-line visible-surface algorithm of Section 15.6. With each edge, we store for each color component the starting intensity and the change of intensity for each unit change in y. A visible span on a scan line is filled in by interpolating the intensity values of the two edges bounding the span. As in all linear-interpolation algorithms, a difference equation may be used for increased efficiency.

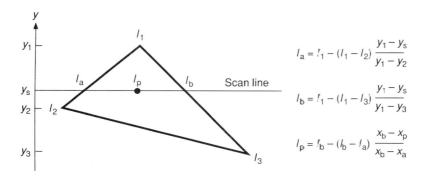

$$I_a = I_1 - (I_1 - I_2) \frac{y_1 - y_s}{y_1 - y_2}$$

$$I_b = I_1 - (I_1 - I_3) \frac{y_1 - y_s}{y_1 - y_3}$$

$$I_p = I_b - (I_b - I_a) \frac{x_b - x_p}{x_b - x_a}$$

Fig. 16.19 Intensity interpolation along polygon edges and scan lines.

16.2.5   Phong Shading

Phong shading [BUIT75], also known as *normal-vector interpolation shading,* interpolates
the surface normal vector $\overline{N}$, rather than the intensity. Interpolation occurs across a polygon
span on a scan line, between starting and ending normals for the span. These normals are
themselves interpolated along polygon edges from vertex normals that are computed, if
necessary, just as in Gouraud shading. The interpolation along edges can again be done by
means of incremental calculations, with all three components of the normal vector being
incremented from scan line to scan line. At each pixel along a scan line, the interpolated
normal is normalized, and is backmapped into the WC system or one isometric to it, and a
new intensity calculation is performed using any illumination model. Figure 16.20 shows
two edge normals and the normals interpolated from them, before and after normalization.

Color Plates II.31 and II.32 were generated using Gouraud shading and Phong shading
respectively, and an illumination equation with a specular-reflectance term. Phong shading
yields substantial improvements over Gouraud shading when such illumination models are
used, because highlights are reproduced more faithfully, as shown in Fig. 16.21. Consider
what happens if n in the Phong $\cos^n \alpha$ illumination term is large and one vertex has a very
small α, but each of its adjacent vertices has a large α. The intensity associated with the
vertex that has a small α will be appropriate for a highlight, whereas the other vertices will
have nonhighlight intensities. If Gouraud shading is used, then the intensity across the
polygon is linearly interpolated between the highlight intensity and the lower intensities of
the adjacent vertices, spreading the highlight over the polygon (Fig. 16.21a). Contrast this
with the sharp drop from the highlight intensity that is computed if linearly interpolated
normals are used to compute the $\cos^n \alpha$ term at each pixel (Fig. 16.21b). Furthermore, if a
highlight fails to fall at a vertex, then Gouraud shading may miss it entirely (Fig. 16.21c),
since no interior point can be brighter than the brightest vertex from which it is interpolated.
In contrast, Phong shading allows highlights to be located in a polygon's interior (Fig.
16.21d). Compare the highlights on the ball in Color Plates II.31 and II.32.

Even with an illumination model that does not take into account specular reflectance,
the results of normal-vector interpolation are in general superior to intensity interpolation,
because an approximation to the normal is used at each point. This reduces Mach-band
problems in most cases, but greatly increases the cost of shading in a straightforward
implementation, since the interpolated normal must be normalized every time it is used in
an illumination model. Duff [DUFF79] has developed a combination of difference

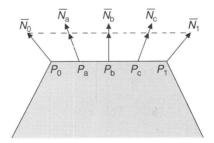

Fig. 16.20 Normal vector interpolation. (After [BUIT75].)

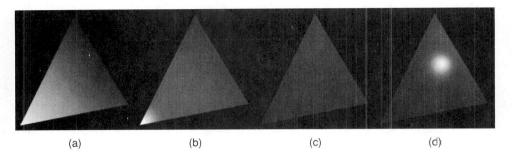

(a)   (b)   (c)   (d)

Fig. 16.21 A specular-reflection illumination model used with Gouraud shading and Phong shading. Highlight falls at left vertex: (a) Gouraud shading, (b) Phong shading. Highlight falls in polygon interior: (c) Gouraud shading, (d) Phong shading. (By David Kurlander, Columbia University.)

equations and table lookup to speed up the calculation. Bishop and Weimer [BISH86] provide an excellent approximation of Phong shading by using a Taylor series expansion that offers even greater increases in shading speed.

Another shading model, intermediate in complexity between Gouraud and Phong shading, involves the linear interpolation of the dot products used in the illumination models. As in Phong shading, the illumination model is evaluated at each pixel, but the interpolated dot products are used to avoid the expense of computing and normalizing any of the direction vectors. This model can produce more satisfactory effects than Gouraud shading when used with specular-reflection illumination models, since the specular term is calculated separately and has power-law, rather than linear, falloff. As in Gouraud shading, however, highlights are missed if they do not fall at a vertex, since no intensity value computed for a set of interpolated dot products can exceed those computed for the set of dot products at either end of the span.

16.2.6 Problems with Interpolated Shading

There are many problems common to all these interpolated-shading models, several of which we list here.

Polygonal silhouette. No matter how good an approximation an interpolated shading model offers to the actual shading of a curved surface, the silhouette edge of the mesh is still clearly polygonal. We can improve this situation by breaking the surface into a greater number of smaller polygons, but at a corresponding increase in expense.

Perspective distortion. Anomalies are introduced because interpolation is performed after perspective transformation in the 3D screen-coordinate system, rather than in the WC system. For example, linear interpolation causes the shading information in Fig. 16.19 to be incremented by a constant amount from one scan line to another along each edge. Consider what happens when vertex 1 is more distant than vertex 2. Perspective foreshortening means that the difference from one scan line to another in the untransformed z value along an edge increases in the direction of the farther coordinate. Thus, if $y_s = (y_1 + y_2) / 2$, then $I_s = (I_1 + I_2) / 2$, but z_s will not equal $(z_1 + z_2) / 2$. This problem can also be

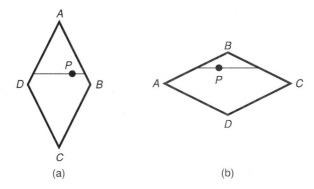

Fig. 16.22 Interpolated values derived for point *P* on the same polygon at different orientations differ from (a) to (b). *P* interpolates *A, B, D* in (a) and *A, B, C* in (b).

reduced by using a larger number of smaller polygons. Decreasing the size of the polygons increases the number of points at which the information to be interpolated is sampled, and therefore increases the accuracy of the shading.

Orientation dependence. The results of interpolated-shading models are not independent of the projected polygon's orientation. Since values are interpolated between vertices and across horizontal scan lines, the results may differ when the polygon is rotated (see Fig. 16.22). This effect is particularly obvious when the orientation changes slowly between successive frames of an animation. A similar problem can also occur in visible-surface determination when the *z* value at each point is interpolated from the *z* values assigned to each vertex. Both problems can be solved by decomposing polygons into triangles (see Exercise 16.2). Alternatively, Duff [DUFF79] suggests rotation-independent, but expensive, interpolation methods that solve this problem without the need for decomposition.

Problems at shared vertices. Shading discontinuities can occur when two adjacent polygons fail to share a vertex that lies along their common edge. Consider the three polygons of Fig. 16.23, in which vertex *C* is shared by the two polygons on the right, but not by the large polygon on the left. The shading information determined directly at *C* for the polygons at the right will typically not be the same as the information interpolated at that point from the values at *A* and *B* for the polygon at the left. As a result, there will be a discontinuity in the shading. The discontinuity can be eliminated by inserting in the

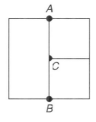

Fig. 16.23 Vertex *C* is shared by the two polygons on the right, but not by the larger rectangular polygon on the left.

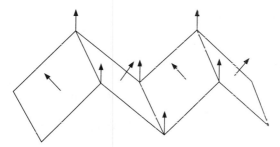

Fig. 16.24 Problems with computing vertex normals. Vertex normals are all parallel.

polygon on the left an extra vertex that shares C's shading information. We can preprocess a static polygonal database in order to eliminate this problem; alternatively, if polygons will be split on the fly (e.g., using the BSP-tree visible-surface algorithm), then extra bookkeeping can be done to introduce a new vertex in an edge that shares an edge that is split.

Unrepresentative vertex normals. Computed vertex normals may not adequately represent the surface's geometry. For example, if we compute vertex normals by averaging the normals of the surfaces sharing a vertex, all of the vertex normals of Fig. 16.24 will be parallel to one another, resulting in little or no variation in shade if the light source is distant. Subdividing the polygons further before vertex normal computation will solve this problem.

Although these problems have prompted much work on rendering algorithms that handle curved surfaces directly, polygons are sufficiently faster (and easier) to process that they still form the core of most rendering systems.

16.3 SURFACE DETAIL

Applying any of the shading models we have described so far to planar or bicubic surfaces produces smooth, uniform surfaces—in marked contrast to most of the surfaces we see and feel. We discuss next a variety of methods developed to simulate this missing surface detail.

16.3.1 Surface-Detail Polygons

The simplest approach adds gross detail through the use of *surface-detail polygons* to show features (such as doors, windows, and lettering) on a base polygon (such as the side of a building). Each surface-detail polygon is coplanar with its base polygon, and is flagged so that it does not need to be compared with other polygons during visible-surface determination. When the base polygon is shaded, its surface-detail polygons and their material properties take precedence for those parts of the base polygon that they cover.

16.3.2 Texture Mapping

As detail becomes finer and more intricate, explicit modeling with polygons or other geometric primitives becomes less practical. An alternative is to map an image, either digitized or synthesized, onto a surface, a technique pioneered by Catmull [CATM74b] and refined by Blinn and Newell [BLIN76]. This approach is known as *texture mapping* or *pattern mapping*; the image is called a *texture map,* and its individual elements are often called *texels.* The rectangular texture map resides in its own (u, v) texture coordinate space. Alternatively, the texture may be defined by a procedure. Color Plate II.35 shows several examples of texture mapping, using the textures shown in Fig. 16.25. At each rendered pixel, selected texels are used either to substitute for or to scale one or more of the surface's material properties, such as its diffuse color components. One pixel is often covered by a number of texels. To avoid aliasing problems, we must consider all relevant texels.

As shown in Fig. 16.26, texture mapping can be accomplished in two steps. A simple approach starts by mapping the four corners of the pixel onto the surface. For a bicubic patch, this mapping naturally defines a set of points in the surface's (s, t) coordinate space. Next, the pixel's corner points in the surface's (s, t) coordinate space are mapped into the texture's (u, v) coordinate space. The four (u, v) points in the texture map define a quadrilateral that approximates the more complex shape into which the pixel may actually map due to surface curvature. We compute a value for the pixel by summing all texels that lie within the quadrilateral, weighting each by the fraction of the texel that lies within the quadrilateral. If a transformed point in (u, v) space falls outside of the texture map, the texture map may be thought of as being replicated, like the patterns of Section 2.1.3.

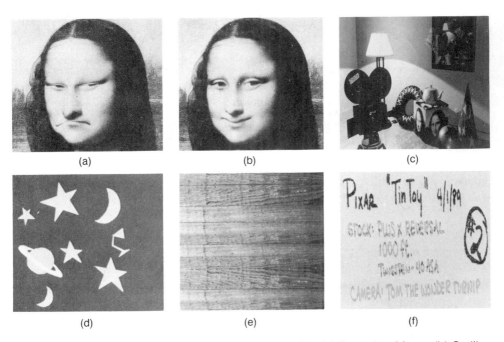

(a)   (b)   (c)

(d)   (e)   (f)

Fig. 16.25 Textures used to create Color Plate II.35. (a) Frowning Mona. (b) Smiling Mona. (c) Painting. (d) Wizard's cap. (e) Floor. (f) Film label. (Copyright © 1990, Pixar. Images rendered by Thomas Williams and H. B. Siegel using Pixar's PhotoRealistic RenderMan™ software.)

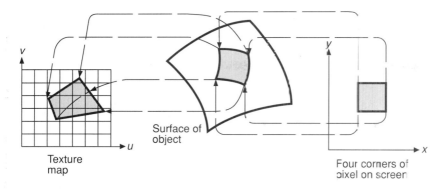

Fig. 16.26 Texture mapping from pixel to the surface to the texture map.

Rather than always use the identity mapping between (s, t) and (u, v), we can define a correspondence between the four corners of the 0-to-1 (s, t) rectangle and a quadrilateral in (u, v). When the surface is a polygon, it is common to assign texture map coordinates directly to its vertices. Since, as we have seen, linearly interpolating values across arbitrary polygons is orientation-dependent, polygons may be decomposed into triangles first. Even after triangulation, however, linear interpolation will cause distortion in the case of perspective projection. This distortion will be more noticeable than that caused when interpolating other shading information, since texture features will not be correctly foreshortened. We can obtain an approximate solution to this problem by decomposing polygons into smaller ones, or an exact solution, at greater cost, by performing the perspective division while interpolating.

The approach just described assumes square pixel geometry and simple box filtering. It also fails to take into account pixels that map to only part of a surface. Feibush, Levoy, and Cook [FEIB80] address these problems for texture-mapping polygons. Think of the square pixel in Fig. 16.26 as the bounding rectangle of the support of an arbitrary filter centered at a pixel. Pixels and texels can then be treated as points. In effect, all texels that lie within the mapped intersection of the transformed bounding rectangle and polygon are selected, and these texels' coordinates are transformed into the coordinate system of the bounding rectangle. Each texel's transformed coordinates are used to index into a filter table to determine the texel's weighting, and the weighted average of the texel intensities is computed. This weighted average must in turn be weighted by the percentage contribution that the polygon makes to the pixel's intensity. The process is repeated for each polygon whose projection intersects the pixel, and the values are summed. Section 17.4.2 discusses this algorithm in more detail.

The Feibush, Levoy, and Cook algorithm can be quite inefficient. Consider mapping a checkerboard pattern onto an infinite ground plane. An extremely large number of texels may have to be weighted and summed just to texture a single distant ground-plane pixel. One solution to this problem is to prefilter the texture and to store the results in a way that is space-efficient and that allows quick determination of the weighted average of texels mapping to a pixel. Algorithms by Williams [WILL83], Crow [CROW84], Glassner [GLAS86], and Heckbert [HECK86a] that take this approach are discussed in Section

17.4.3. Catmull and Smith's efficient technique [CATM80] for mapping an entire texture map directly to a surface is discussed in Exercise 17.10. Heckbert [HECK86] provides a thorough survey of texture-mapping methods.

16.3.3   Bump Mapping

Texture mapping affects a surface's shading, but the surface continues to appear geometrically smooth. If the texture map is a photograph of a rough surface, the surface being shaded will not look quite right, because the direction to the light source used to create the texture map is typically different from the direction to the light source illuminating the surface. Blinn [BLIN78b] developed a way to provide the appearance of modified surface geometry that avoids explicit geometrical modeling. His approach involves perturbing the surface normal before it is used in the illumination model, just as slight roughness in a surface would perturb the surface normal. This method is known as *bump mapping,* and is based on texture mapping.

A *bump map* is an array of displacements, each of which can be used to simulate displacing a point on a surface a little above or below that point's actual position. Let us represent a point on a surface by a vector $\overline{P}$, where $\overline{P} = [x(s, t), y(s, t), z(s, t)]$. We call the partial derivatives of the surface at $\overline{P}$ with respect to the surface's s and t parameterization axes, $\overline{P}_s$ and $\overline{P}_t$. Since each is tangent to the surface, their cross-product forms the (unnormalized) surface normal at $\overline{P}$. Thus,

$$\overline{N} = \overline{P}_s \times \overline{P}_t. \tag{16.21}$$

We can displace point $\overline{P}$ by adding to it the normalized normal scaled by a selected bump-map value B. The new point is

$$\overline{P}' = \overline{P} + \frac{B\overline{N}}{|\overline{N}|}. \tag{16.22}$$

Blinn shows that a good approximation to the new (unnormalized) normal $\overline{N}'$ is

$$\overline{N}' = \overline{N} + \frac{B_u(\overline{N} \times \overline{P}_t) - B_v (\overline{N} \times \overline{P}_s)}{|\overline{N}|}, \tag{16.23}$$

where B_u and B_v are the partial derivatives of the selected bump-map entry B with respect to the bump-map parameterization axes, u and v. $\overline{N}'$ is then normalized and substituted for the surface normal in the illumination equation. Note that only the partial derivatives of the bump map are used in Eq. (16.23), not its values. Bilinear interpolation can be used to derive bump-map values for specified (u, v) positions, and finite differences can be used to compute B_u and B_v.

The results of bump mapping can be quite convincing. Viewers often fail to notice that an object's texture does not affect its silhouette edges. Color Plates III.3 and III.4 show two examples of bump mapping. Unlike texture mapping, aliasing cannot be dealt with by filtering values from the bump map, since these values do not correspond linearly to intensities; filtering the bump map just smooths out the bumps. Instead, subpixel intensities may be computed and filtered for each pixel, or some prefiltering may be performed on the bump map to improve gross aliasing.

16.3.4 Other Approaches

Although 2D mapping can be effective in many situations, it often fails to produce convincing results. Textures frequently betray their 2D origins when mapped onto curved surfaces, and problems are encountered at texture "seams." For example, when a wood-grain texture is mapped onto the surface of a curved object, the object will look as if it were painted with the texture. Peachey [PEAC85] and Perlin [PERL85] have investigated the use of solid textures for proper rendering of objects "carved" of wood or marble, as exemplified by Color Plate IV.21. In this approach, described in Section 20.8.3, the texture is a 3D function of its position in the object.

Other surface properties can be mapped as well. For example, Gardner [GARD84] has used transparency mapping to make impressionistic trees and clouds from otherwise simple shapes, as described in Section 20.8.2. Color Plate IV.24 shows the application of a complex functional transparency texture to objects formed from groups of quadric surfaces. Cook has implemented *displacement mapping,* in which the actual surface is displaced, instead of only the surface normals [COOK84a]; this process, which must be carried out before visible-surface determination, was used to modify the surfaces of the cone and torus in Color Plate II.36. Using fractals to create richly detailed geometry from an initial simple geometric description is discussed in Section 20.3.

So far, we have made the tacit assumption that the process of shading a point on an object is unaffected by the rest of that object or by any other object. But an object might in fact be shadowed by another object between it and a light source; might transmit light, allowing another object to be seen through it; or might reflect other objects, allowing another object to be seen because of it. In the following sections, we describe how to model these effects.

16.4 SHADOWS

Visible-surface algorithms determine which surfaces can be seen from the viewpoint; shadow algorithms determine which surfaces can be "seen" from the light source. Thus, visible-surface algorithms and shadow algorithms are essentially the same. The surfaces that are visible from the light source are not in shadow; those that are not visible from the light source are in shadow. When there are multiple light sources, a surface must be classified relative to each of them.

Here, we consider shadow algorithms for point light sources; extended light sources are discussed in Sections 16.8, 16.12, and 16.13. Visibility from a point light source is, like visibility from the viewpoint, all or nothing. When a point on a surface cannot be seen from a light source, then the illumination calculation must be adjusted to take it into account. The addition of shadows to the illumination equation yields

$$I_\lambda = I_{a\lambda}k_aO_{d\lambda} + \sum_{1 \le i \le m} S_i f_{\text{att}i} I_{p\lambda i} [k_dO_{d\lambda}(\overline{N} \cdot \overline{L}_i) + k_sO_{s\lambda} (\overline{R}_i \cdot \overline{V})^n], \qquad (16.24)$$

where

$$S_i = \begin{cases} 0, \text{ if light } i \text{ is blocked at this point;} \\ 1, \text{ if light } i \text{ is not blocked at this point.} \end{cases}$$

Note that areas in the shadow of all point light sources are still illuminated by the ambient light.

Although computing shadows requires computing visibility from the light source, as we have pointed out, it is also possible to generate "fake" shadows without performing any visibility tests. These can be created efficiently by transforming each object into its polygonal projection from a point light source onto a designated ground plane, without clipping the transformed polygon to the surface that it shadows or checking for whether it is blocked by intervening surfaces [BLIN88]. These shadows are then treated as surface-detail polygons. For the general case, in which these fake shadows are not adequate, various approaches to shadow generation are possible. We could perform all shadow processing first, interleave it with visible-surface processing in a variety of ways, or even do it after visible-surface processing has been performed. Here we examine algorithms that follow each of these approaches, building on the classification of shadow algorithms presented in [CROW77a]. To simplify the explanations, we shall assume that all objects are polygons unless otherwise specified.

16.4.1 Scan-Line Generation of Shadows

One of the oldest methods for generating shadows is to augment a scan-line algorithm to interleave shadow and visible-surface processing [APPEL68; BOUK70b]. Using the light source as a center of projection, the edges of polygons that might potentially cast shadows are projected onto the polygons intersecting the current scan line. When the scan crosses one of these shadow edges, the colors of the image pixels are modified accordingly.

A brute-force implementation of this algorithm must compute all $n(n-1)$ projections of every polygon on every other polygon. Bouknight and Kelley [BOUK70b] instead use a clever preprocessing step in which all polygons are projected onto a sphere surrounding the light source, with the light source as center of projection. Pairs of projections whose extents do not overlap can be eliminated, and a number of other special cases can be identified to limit the number of polygon pairs that need be considered by the rest of the algorithm. The authors then compute the projection from the light source of each polygon onto the plane of each of those polygons that they have determined it could shadow, as shown in Fig. 16.27. Each of these shadowing polygon projections has associated information about the polygons casting and potentially receiving the shadow. While the scan-line algorithm's regular scan keeps track of which regular polygon edges are being crossed, a separate, parallel shadow scan keeps track of which shadowing polygon projection edges are crossed, and thus which shadowing polygon projections the shadow scan is currently "in." When the shade for a span is computed, it is in shadow if the shadow scan is "in" one of the shadow projections cast on the polygon's plane. Thus span bc in Fig. 16.27(a) is in shadow, while spans ab and cd are not. Note that the algorithm does not need to clip the shadowing polygon projections analytically to the polygons being shadowed.

16.4.2 A Two-Pass Object-Precision Shadow Algorithm

Atherton, Weiler, and Greenberg have developed an algorithm that performs shadow determination before visible-surface determination [ATHE78]. They process the object description by using the same algorithm twice, once for the viewpoint, and once for the

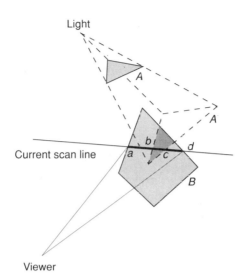

Fig. 16.27 A scan-line shadow algorithm using the Bouknight and Kelley approach. Polygon *A* casts shadow *A'* on plane of *B*.

light source. The results are then combined to determine the pieces of each visible part of a polygon that are lit by the light source, and the scene is scan-converted. Thus, since the shadows are not dependent on the viewpoint, all the shadow calculations may be performed just once for a series of images of the same objects seen from many different viewpoints, as long as the light source and objects are fixed.

The algorithm, shown in overview in Fig. 16.28, first determines those surfaces that are visible from the light source's viewpoint, using the Weiler–Atherton visible-surface algorithm discussed in Section 15.7.2. The output of this pass is a list of lit polygons, each of which is tagged with the identity of its parent polygon. All the objects must fit into the light source's view volume, since parts of the objects that do not fit are not recognized as lit. If a light source's view volume cannot encompass all the objects, multiple nonoverlapping view volumes can be constructed that radiate out from the light source, a technique called *sectoring*.

Next, the lit polygons are transformed back into the modeling coordinates and are merged with a copy of the original database as surface-detail polygons (Section 16.3), creating a viewpoint-independent merged database, shown in Fig. 16 29. Note that the implementation illustrated in Fig. 16.28 performs the same transformations on both databases before merging them. Hidden-surface removal is then performed on a copy of this merged database from the viewpoint of an arbitrary observer, again using the Weiler–Atherton algorithm. All processing so far is performed with object precision and results in a list of polygons. A polygon scan-conversion algorithm is then used to render the image. Visible surfaces covered by surface-detail polygons are rendered as lit, whereas uncovered visible surfaces are rendered in shadow. Color Plate III.5 was generated using this approach. Multiple light sources can be handled by processing the merged database from the viewpoint of each new light source, merging the results of each pass.

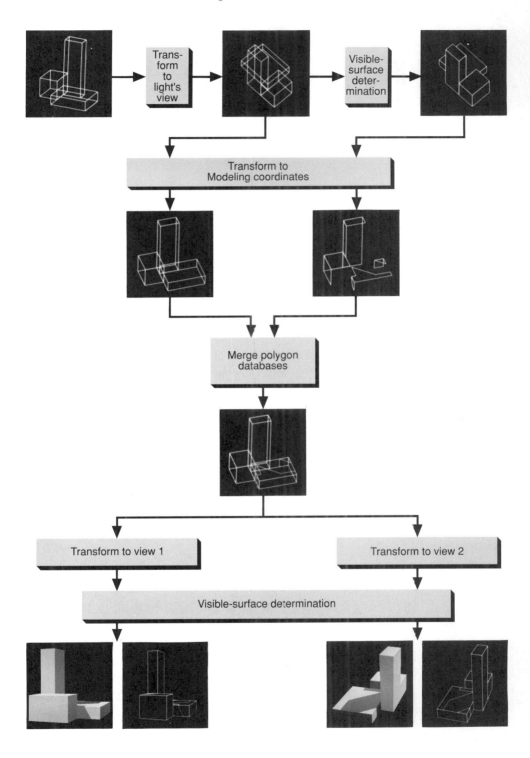

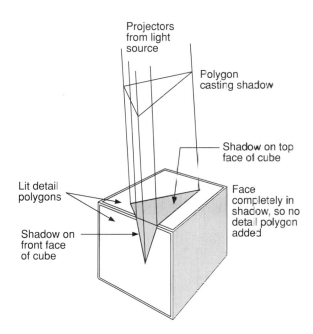

Projectors
from light
source

Polygon
casting shadow

Shadow on top
face of cube

Lit detail
polygons

Face
completely in
shadow, so no
detail polygon
added

Shadow on
front face
of cube

Fig. 16.29 Lit surface-detail polygons.

16.4.3 Shadow Volumes

Crow [CROW77a] describes how to generate shadows by creating for each object a *shadow volume* that the object blocks from the light source. A shadow volume is defined by the light source and an object and is bounded by a set of invisible *shadow polygons*. As shown in Fig. 16.30, there is one quadrilateral shadow polygon for each silhouette edge of the object relative to the light source. Three sides of a shadow polygon are defined by a silhouette edge of the object and the two lines emanating from the light source and passing through that edge's endpoints. Each shadow polygon has a normal that points out of the shadow volume. Shadow volumes are generated only for polygons facing the light. In the implementation described by Bergeron [BERG86a], the shadow volume—and hence each of its shadow polygons—is capped on one end by the original object polygon and on the other end by a scaled copy of the object polygon whose normal has been inverted. This scaled copy is located at a distance from the light beyond which its attenuated energy density is assumed to be negligible. We can think of this distance as the light's *sphere of influence*. Any point outside of the sphere of influence is effectively in shadow and does not require any additional shadow processing. In fact, there is no need to generate a shadow volume for any object wholly outside the sphere of influence. We can generalize this approach to apply to nonuniformly radiating sources by considering a *region of influence*, for example by culling

Fig. 16.28 Shadow creation and display in the Atherton, Weiler and Greenberg algorithm. (Images by Peter Atherton, Kevin Weiler, Donald P. Greenberg, Program of Computer Graphics, Cornell University, 1978.)

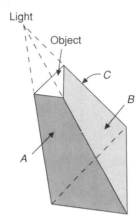

Fig. 16.30 A shadow volume is defined by a light source and an object.

objects outside of a light's flaps and cone. The shadow volume may also be further clipped to the view volume if the view volume is known in advance. The cap polygons are also treated as shadow polygons by the algorithm.

Shadow polygons are not rendered themselves, but are used to determine whether the other objects are in shadow. Relative to the observer, a front-facing shadow polygon (polygon A or B in Fig. 16.30) causes those objects behind it to be shadowed; a back-facing shadow polygon (polygon C) cancels the effect of a front-facing one. Consider a vector from the viewpoint V to a point on an object. The point is in shadow if the vector intersects more front-facing than back-facing shadow polygons. Thus, points A and C in Fig. 16.31(a) are in shadow. This is the only case in which a point is shadowed when V is not shadowed; therefore, point B is lit. If V is in shadow, there is one additional case in which a point is shadowed: when all the back-facing shadow polygons for the object polygons shadowing the eye have not yet been encountered. Thus, points A, B, and C in Fig. 16.31(b) are in shadow,

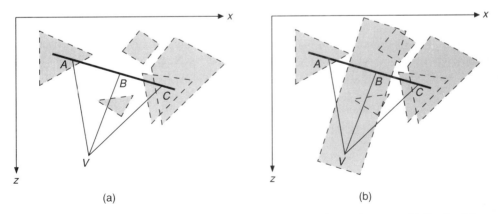

Fig. 16.31 Determining whether a point is in shadow for a viewer at V. Dashed lines define shadow volumes (shaded in gray). (a) V is not in shadow. Points A and C are shadowed; point B is lit. (b) V is in shadow. Points A, B, and C are shadowed.

even though the vector from V to B intersects the same number of front-facing and back-facing shadow polygons as it does in part (a).

We can compute whether a point is in shadow by assigning to each front-facing (relative to the viewer) shadow polygon a value of $+1$ and to each back-facing shadow polygon a value of -1. A counter is initially set to the number of shadow volumes that contain the eye and is incremented by the values associated with all shadow polygons between the eye and the point on the object. The point is in shadow if the counter is positive at the point. The number of shadow volumes containing the eye is computed only once for each viewpoint, by taking the negative of the sum of the values of all shadow polygons intercepted by an arbitrary projector from the eye to infinity.

Although is is possible to compute a shadow volume for each polygon, we can take advantage of object coherence by computing a single shadow volume for each connected polyhedron. This can be accomplished by generating shadow polygons from only those edges that are silhouette edges relative to the light source; these are the contour edges relative to the light source (as defined in Section 15.3.2).

Multiple light sources can be handled by building a separate set of shadow volumes for each light source, marking the volume's shadow polygons with their light source identifier, and keeping a separate counter for each light source. Brotman and Badler [BROT84] have implemented a z-buffer version of the shadow-volume algorithm, and Bergeron [BERG86a] discusses a scan-line implementation that efficiently handles arbitrary polyhedral objects containing nonplanar polygons.

Chin and Feiner [CHIN89] describe an object-precision algorithm that builds a single shadow volume for a polygonal environment, using the BSP-tree solid modeling representation discussed in Section 12.6.4. Polygons are processed in front-to-back order relative to the light source. Each polygon facing the light source is filtered down the tree, dividing the polygon into lit and shadowed fragments. Only lit fragments cast shadows, so the semi-infinite pyramid defined by the light source and each lit fragment is added to the volume. Because of the front-to-back order, every polygon is guaranteed not to lie between the light source and the polygons processed previously. Therefore, since no polygon needs to be compared with the plane of a previously processed polygon, the polygons themselves do not need to be added to the shadow volume. As with the Atherton–Weiler–Greenberg algorithm, the lit fragments may be added to the environment as surface-detail polygons or the lit and shadowed fragments may be displayed together instead. Multiple light sources are accommodated by filtering the polygon fragments of one shadow-volume BSP tree down the shadow-volume BSP tree of the next light source. Each fragment is tagged to indicate the light sources that illuminate it, allowing the resulting fragmented environment to be displayed with any polygon visible-surface algorithm. Because of the shadow volume representation, lights may be positioned anywhere relative to the objects; thus, sectoring is not necessary. Several optimizations and a parallel version of the algorithm are discussed in [CHIN90]. Color Plate III.6(a) is rendered with the algorithm; Color Plate III.6(b) shows the fragments created in filtering the polygons down the shadow-volume BSP tree.

16.4.4 A Two-Pass z-Buffer Shadow Algorithm

Williams [WILL78] developed a shadow-generation method based on two passes through a z-buffer algorithm, one for the viewer and one for the light source. His algorithm, unlike the two-pass algorithm of Section 16.4.2, determines whether a surface is shadowed by using image-precision calculations. Figure 16.32(a) shows an overview of an environment lit by a light at L; a shadowless image from viewpoint V is shown in Fig. 16.32(d). The algorithm begins by calculating and storing just the z-buffer for the image from the viewpoint of the light (Fig. 16.32b). In Fig. 16.32(b), increasing intensities represent increasing distance. Next, the z-buffer (Fig. 16.32c) and the image (Fig. 16.32e) are calculated from the viewpoint of the observer using a z-buffer algorithm with the following modification. Whenever a pixel is determined to be visible, its object-precision coordinates in the observer's view (x_o, y_o, z_o) are transformed into coordinates in the light source's view (x'_o, y'_o, z'_o). The transformed coordinates x'_o and y'_o are used to select the value z_L in the light source's z-buffer to be compared with the transformed value z'_o. If z_L is closer to the light than is z'_o, then there is something blocking the light from the point, and the pixel is shaded as being in shadow; otherwise the point is visible from the light and it is shaded as lit. In analogy to texture mapping, we can think of the light's z-buffer as a *shadow map*. Multiple light sources can be accommodated by use of a separate shadow map for each light source.

Like the regular z-buffer visible-surface algorithm, this algorithm requires that each rendered pixel be shaded. Here, this means that shadow calculations must be performed for the pixel, even if it is ultimately painted over by closer objects. Williams has suggested a variation on his algorithm that exploits the ease with which the z-buffer algorithm can interleave visible-surface determination with illumination and shading, and eliminates shadow calculations for obscured objects. Rather than computing just the shadow map first, the modified algorithm also computes the regular shaded image from the observer's point of view (Fig. 16.32d), along with its z-buffer (all these computations can use conventional z-buffer–based hardware). Shadows are then added using a postprocess that is linear in the

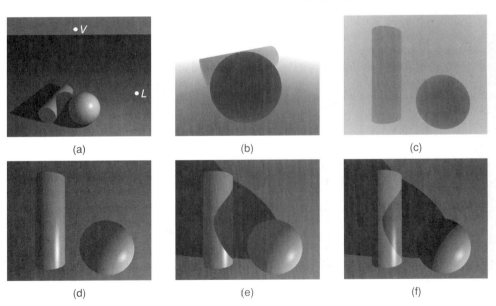

(a)   (b)   (c)

(d)   (e)   (f)

Fig. 16.32 *z*-buffer shadow-generation method. (a) Overview. (b) Light's *z*-buffer. (c) Observer's *z*-buffer. (d) Observer's image. (e) Observer's image with shadows. (f) Observer's image with post-processed shadows. (By David Kurlander, Columbia University.)

Fig. 16.33 Shadow map used to create Color Plate II.36. (Copyright © 1990, Pixar. Shadow map rendered by Thomas Williams and H. B. Siegel using Pixar's PhotoRealistic RenderMan™ software.)

number of pixels in the image to produce Fig. 16.32(f). The same transformation and comparison operation as before are performed for each pixel in the observer's image. If z_L is closer to the light than is z_0', then the pixel's previously computed shade in the observer's image is darkened. Although this approach is significantly more efficient than is the original algorithm, it results in artifacts; most noticeably, shadowed objects will have (darkened) specular highlights, even though there should be no specular highlights on an object that is shielded from the light source. In addition, the z_0 to be transformed is at object precision in the first version, but at the typically lower z-buffer precision here. (See Exercise 16.15.)

Unlike the other shadow algorithms discussed so far, Williams's algorithm makes it especially easy to generate shadows for any object that can be scan-converted, including curved surfaces. Because all operations are performed in image precision, however, allowance must be made for the limited numerical precision. For example, the transformation from z_0 to z_0' should also move z_0' a little closer to the light source, to avoid having a visible point cast a shadow on itself. Like the z-buffer visible-surface algorithm from which it is constructed, this shadow algorithm is prone to aliasing. Williams describes how filtering and dithering can reduce the effects of aliasing. Reeves, Salesin, and Cook [REEV87] demonstrate improvements using *percentage closer filtering*. Each z_0' is compared with values in a region of the shadow map, and the percentage of closer values determines the amount of shadowing. This improved algorithm was used to render Color Plates D, F, and II.36. Figure 16.33 shows the shadow map used to create Color Plate II.36.

16.4.5   Global Illumination Shadow Algorithms

Ray-tracing and radiosity algorithms have been used to generate some of the most impressive pictures of shadows in complex environments. Simple ray tracing has been used to model shadows from point light sources, whereas more advanced versions allow extended light sources. Both are discussed in Section 16.12. Radiosity methods, discussed in Section 16.13, model light sources as light-emitting surfaces that may have the same geometry as any other surface; thus, they implicitly support extended light sources.

16.5 TRANSPARENCY

Much as surfaces can have specular and diffuse reflection, those that transmit light can be transparent or translucent. We can usually see clearly through *transparent* materials, such as glass, although in general the rays are refracted (bent). Diffuse transmission occurs through *translucent* materials, such as frosted glass. Rays passing through translucent materials are jumbled by surface or internal irregularities, and thus objects seen through translucent materials are blurred.

16.5.1 Nonrefractive Transparency

The simplest approach to modeling transparency ignores refraction, so light rays are not bent as they pass through the surface. Thus, whatever is visible on the line of sight through a transparent surface is also geometrically located on that line of sight. Although refraction-less transparency is not realistic, it can often be a more useful effect than refraction. For example, it can provide a distortionless view through a surface, as depicted in Color Plate III.7. As we have noted before, total photographic realism is not always the objective in making pictures.

Two different methods have been commonly used to approximate the way in which the colors of two objects are combined when one object is seen through the other. We shall refer to these as *interpolated* and *filtered* transparency.

Interpolated transparency. Consider what happens when transparent polygon 1 is between the viewer and opaque polygon 2, as shown in Fig. 16.34. *Interpolated transparency* determines the shade of a pixel in the intersection of two polygons' projections by linearly interpolating the individual shades calculated for the two polygons:

$$I_\lambda = (1 - k_{t1})I_{\lambda 1} + k_{t1}I_{\lambda 2}. \tag{16.25}$$

The *transmission coefficient* k_{t1} measures the *transparency* of polygon 1, and ranges between 0 and 1. When k_{t1} is 0, the polygon is opaque and transmits no light; when k_{t1} is 1, the polygon is perfectly transparent and contributes nothing to the intensity I_λ; The value $1 - k_{t1}$ is called the polygon's *opacity*. Interpolated transparency may be thought of as modeling a polygon that consists of a fine mesh of opaque material through which other objects may be seen; k_{t1} is the fraction of the mesh's surface that can be seen through. A totally transparent

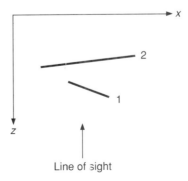

Fig. **16.34** Cross-section of two polygons.

polygon that is processed this way will not have any specular reflection. For a more realistic effect, we can interpolate only the ambient and diffuse components of polygon 1 with the full shade of polygon 2, and then add in polygon 1's specular component [KAY79b].

Another approach, often called *screen-door transparency,* literally implements a mesh by rendering only some of the pixels associated with a transparent object's projection. The low-order bits of a pixel's (x, y) address are used to index into a transparency bit mask. If the indexed bit is 1, then the pixel is written; otherwise, it is suppressed, and the next closest polygon at that pixel is visible. The fewer 1 bits in the mask, the more transparent the object's appearance. This approach relies on having our eyes perform spatial integration to produce interpolated transparency. Note, however, that an object fully obscures any other object drawn with the same transparency mask and that other undesirable interactions between masks are difficult to avoid.

Filtered transparency.   *Filtered transparency* treats a polygon as a transparent filter that selectively passes different wavelengths; it can be modeled by

$$I_\lambda = I_{\lambda_1} - k_{t_1} O_{t\lambda} I_{\lambda_2}, \tag{16.26}$$

where $O_{t\lambda}$ is polygon 1's *transparency color.* A colored filter may be modeled by choosing a different value of $O_{t\lambda}$ for each λ (but see Section 16.9). In either interpolated or filtered transparency, if additional transparent polygons are in front of these polygons, then the calculation is invoked recursively for polygons in back-to-front order, each time using the previously computed I_λ as I_{λ_2}.

Implementing transparency.   Several visible-surface algorithms can be readily adapted to incorporate transparency, including scan-line and list-priority algorithms. In list-priority algorithms, the color of a pixel about to be covered by a transparent polygon is read back and used in the illumination model while the polygon is being scan-converted.

Most z-buffer–based systems support screen-door transparency because it allows transparent objects to be intermingled with opaque objects and to be drawn in any order. Adding transparency effects that use Eqs. (16.25) or (16.26) to the z-buffer algorithm is more difficult, because polygons are rendered in the order in which they are encountered. Imagine rendering several overlapping transparent polygons, followed by an opaque one. We would like to slip the opaque polygon behind the appropriate transparent ones. Unfortunately, the z-buffer does not store the information needed to determine which transparent polygons are in front of the opaque polygon, or even the polygons' relative order. One simple, although incorrect, approach is to render transparent polygons last, combining their colors with those already in the frame buffer, but not modifying the z-buffer; when two transparent polygons overlap, however, their relative depth is not taken into account.

Mammen [MAMM89] describes how to render transparent objects properly in back-to-front order in a z-buffer-based system through the use of multiple rendering passes and additional memory. First, all the opaque objects are rendered using a conventional z-buffer. Then, transparent objects are processed into a separate set of buffers that contain, for each pixel, a transparency value and a flag bit, in addition to the pixel's color and z value. Each flag bit is initialized to off and each z value is set to the closest possible value. If a transparent object's z value at a pixel is closer than the value in the opaque z-buffer, but is more distant than that in the transparent z-buffer, then the color, z value, and transparency are saved in the transparent buffers, and the flag bit is set. After all objects have been processed, the transparent object buffers contain information for the most distant transparent object at each pixel whose flag bit is set. Information for flagged pixels is then blended with that in the original frame buffer and z-buffer. A flagged pixel's transparency z-value replaces that in the opaque z-buffer and the flag bit is reset. This process is repeated to render successively closer objects at each pixel. Color Plate III.7 was made using this algorithm.

Kay and Greenberg [KAY79b] have implemented a useful approximation to the increased attenuation that occurs near the silhouette edges of thin curved surfaces, where light passes through more material. They define k_t in terms of a nonlinear function of the z component of the surface normal after perspective transformation,

$$k_t = k_{t_{min}} + (k_{t_{max}} - k_{t_{min}})(1 - (1 - z_N)^m), \qquad (16.27)$$

where $k_{t_{min}}$ and $k_{t_{max}}$ are the object's minimum and maximum transparencies, z_N is the z component of the normalized surface normal at the point for which k_t is being computed, and m is a power factor (typically 2 or 3). A higher m models a thinner surface. This new value of k_t may be used as k_{t_1} in either Eq. (16.25) or (16.26).

16.5.2 Refractive Transparency

Refractive transparency is significantly more difficult to model than is nonrefractive transparency, because the geometrical and optical lines of sight are different. If refraction is considered in Fig. 16.35, object A is visible through the transparent object along the line of sight shown; if refraction is ignored, object B is visible. The relationship between the angle of incidence θ_i and the angle of refraction θ_t is given by Snell's law

$$\frac{\sin \theta_i}{\sin \theta_t} = \frac{\eta_{t\lambda}}{\eta_{i\lambda}}, \qquad (16.28)$$

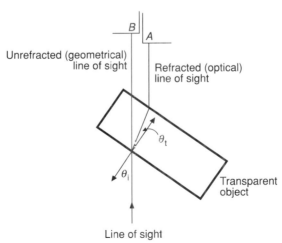

Fig. 16.35 Refraction.

where $\eta_{i\lambda}$ and $\eta_{t\lambda}$ are the *indices of refraction* of the materials through which the light passes. A material's index of refraction is the ratio of the speed of light in a vacuum to the speed of light in the material. It varies with the wavelength of the light and even with temperature. A vacuum has an index of refraction of 1.0, as does the atmosphere to close approximation; all materials have higher values. The index of refraction's wavelength-dependence is evident in many instances of refraction as *dispersion*—the familiar, but difficult to model, phenomenon of refracted light being spread into its spectrum [THOM86; MUSG89].

Calculating the refraction vector. The unit vector in the direction of refraction, $\overline{T}$, can be calculated as

$$\overline{T} = \sin \theta_t \, \overline{M} - \cos \theta_t \, \overline{N}, \tag{16.29}$$

where $\overline{M}$ is a unit vector perpendicular to $\overline{N}$ in the plane of the incident ray $\overline{I}$ and $\overline{N}$ [HECK84] (Fig. 16.36). Recalling the use of $\overline{S}$ in calculating the reflection vector $\overline{R}$ in Section 16.1.4, we see that $\overline{M} = (\overline{N} \cos \theta_i - \overline{I}) / \sin \theta_i$. By substitution,

$$\overline{T} = \frac{\sin \theta_t}{\sin \theta_i} (\overline{N} \cos \theta_i - \overline{I}) - \cos \theta_t \, \overline{N}. \tag{16.30}$$

If we let $\eta_{r\lambda} = \eta_{i\lambda} / \eta_{t\lambda} = \sin \theta_t / \sin \theta_i$, then after rearranging terms

$$\overline{T} = (\eta_{r\lambda} \cos \theta_i - \cos \theta_t) \, \overline{N} - \eta_{r\lambda} \, \overline{I}. \tag{16.31}$$

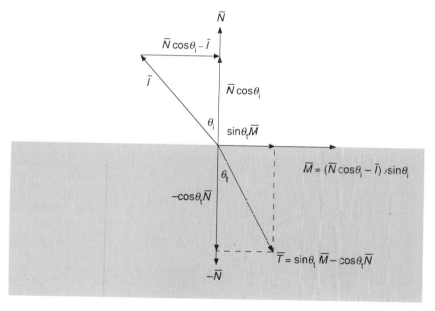

Fig. 16.36 Calculating the refraction vector.

Note that $\cos \theta_i$ is $\overline{N} \cdot \overline{I}$, and $\cos \theta_t$ can be computed as

$$\cos \theta_t = \sqrt{1 - \sin^2\theta_t} = \sqrt{1 - \eta_{r\lambda}^2\sin^2\theta_i} = \sqrt{1 - \eta_{r\lambda}^2(1 - (\overline{N} \cdot \overline{I})^2)}. \quad (16.32)$$

Thus,

$$\overline{T} = \left(\eta_{r\lambda}(\overline{N} \cdot \overline{I}) - \sqrt{1 - \eta_{r\lambda}^2(1 - (\overline{N} \cdot \overline{I})^2)} \right)\overline{N} - \eta_{r\lambda}\overline{I}. \quad (16.33)$$

Total internal reflection.   When light passes from one medium into another whose index of refraction is lower, the angle θ_t of the transmitted ray is greater than the angle θ_i. If θ_i becomes sufficiently large, then θ_t exceeds 90° and the ray is reflected from the interface between the media, rather than being transmitted. This phenomenon is known as *total internal reflection,* and the smallest θ_i at which it occurs is called the *critical angle.* You can observe total internal reflection easily by looking through the front of a filled fish tank and trying to see your hand through a side wall. When the viewing angle is greater than the critical angle, the only visible parts of your hand are those pressed firmly against the tank, with no intervening layer of air (which has a lower index of refraction than glass or water). The critical angle is the value of θ_i at which sin θ_t is 1. If sin θ_t is set to 1 in Eq. (16.28), we can see that the critical angle is $\sin^{-1}(\eta_{t\lambda} / \eta_{i\lambda})$. Total internal reflection occurs when the square root in Eq. (16.33) is imaginary.

Section 16.12 discusses the use of Snell's law in modeling refractive transparency with ray tracing; translucency is treated in Sections 16.12.4 and 16.13. An approximation of refraction can also be incorporated into renderers that proceed in back-to-front order [KAY79b].

16.6   INTEROBJECT REFLECTIONS

Interobject reflections occur when a surface reflects other surfaces in its environment. These effects range from more or less sharp specular reflections that change with the viewer's position (like specular highlights), to diffuse reflections that are insensitive to the viewer's position. Ray tracing (Section 16.12) and radiosity methods (Section 16.13) have produced some of the most visually impressive pictures exhibiting specular and diffuse interobject reflections; earlier techniques, however, can also produce attractive results.

Blinn and Newell [BLIN76] developed *reflection mapping* (also known as *environment mapping*) to model specular interobject reflection. A center of projection is chosen from which to map the environment to be reflected onto the surface of a sphere surrounding the objects to be rendered. The mapped environment can then be treated as a 2D texture map. At each point on an object to be displayed, the reflection map is indexed by the polar coordinates of the vector obtained by reflecting $\overline{V}$ about $\overline{N}$. The reflection map's x and y axes represent longitude (from 0° to 360°) and latitude (from −90° to 90°), respectively, as shown in Fig. 16.37(a). Hall [HALL86] suggests a variant in which the y axis is sin (latitude), so that equal areas on the sphere map to equal areas on the reflection map (Fig.

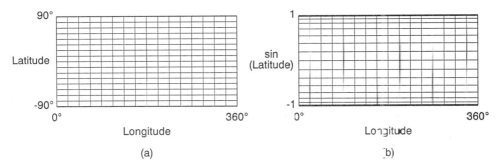

Fig. 16.37 Reflection map coordinate systems. (a) Latitude–longitude. (b) Sin (latitude)–longitude.

16.37b). Alternatively, six projections onto the sides of a surrounding cube may be used. The cube is aligned with the WC axes, so that the largest coordinate of the normalized reflection vector indicates the appropriate side to index. Figure 16.38(a) shows the correspondence between the unfolded sides and the cube; Fig. 16.38(b) is the reflection map used for the teapot in Color Plate II.37. As in texture mapping, antialiasing is accomplished by filtering some number of reflection-map values surrounding the indexed value to determine the reflected light at the given point on the object. In Fig. 16.38(b) an angle slightly wider than 90° was used to provide a margin about each side's borders that helps avoid the need to consider more than one side at a time when filtering.

Although reflection mapping can be used to produce a number of useful effects [GREE86], it provides only an approximation to the correct reflection information. By taking into account just the surface's reflection direction and not its position in the sphere, it models an infinitely large environment sphere. This problem can be partly remedied by using the surface's position to help determine the part of the reflection map to index, modeling a sphere of finite size. In either case, however, the farther a surface is from the center of projection used to create the map, the more distorted a view of the world it shows, since the reflection map takes into account visibility relationships at only a single point. A useful compromise is to create multiple reflection maps, each centered about a key object, and to index into the one closest to an object whose surface is being mapped. Simple but effective reflection effects can be obtained with even a 1D reflection map. For example, the y component of the reflection of $\overline{V}$ may be used to index into an array of intensities representing the range of colors from ground through horizon to sky.

Planar surfaces present difficulties for reflection mapping, because the reflection angle changes so slowly. If reflections from a planar surface are to be viewed from only a single viewpoint, however, another technique can be used. The viewpoint is reflected about the surface's plane and an inverted image of the scene is rendered from the reflected viewpoint, as shown in cross-section in Fig. 16.38(c). This image can then be merged with the original image wherever the surface is visible. Figure 16.38(d) was created with this technique and was used to render the reflections on the floor in Color Plate II.37.

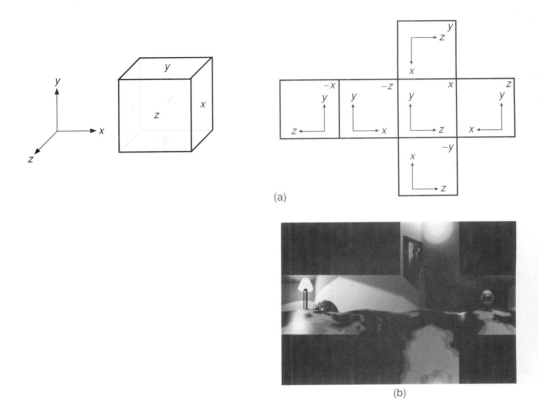

(a)

(b)

16.7 PHYSICALLY BASED ILLUMINATION MODELS

The illumination models discussed in the previous sections are largely the result of a common-sense, practical approach to graphics. Although the equations used approximate some of the ways light interacts with objects, they do not have a physical basis. In this section, we discuss physically based illumination models, relying in part on the work of Cook and Torrance [COOK82].

Thus far, we have used the word *intensity* without defining it, referring informally to the intensity of a light source, of a point on a surface, or of a pixel. It is time now to formalize our terms by introducing the radiometric terminology used in the study of thermal radiation, which is the basis for our understanding of how light interacts with objects [NICO77; SPARR78; SIEG81; IES87]. We begin with *flux*, which is the rate at which light energy is emitted and is measured in watts (W). To refer to the amount of flux emitted in or received from a given direction, we need the concept of a *solid angle*, which is the angle at the apex of a cone. Solid angle is measured in terms of the area on a sphere intercepted by a cone whose apex is at the sphere's center. A *steradian* (sr) is the solid angle of such a cone

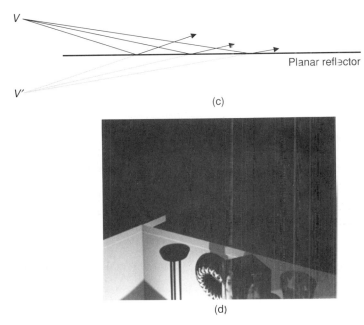

Fig. 16.38 Reflection maps. (a) Cube reflection map layout. (b) Reflection map for teapot in Color Plate II.37. (c) Geometry of planar reflection. (d) Reflected image merged with floor in Color Plate II.37. (Copyright © 1990, Pixar. Images in (b) and (d) rendered by Thomas Williams and H. B. Siegel using Pixar's PhotoRealistic RenderMan™ software.)

that intercepts an area equal to the square of the sphere's radius r. If a point is on a surface, we are concerned with the hemisphere above it. Since the area of a sphere is $4\pi r^2$, there are $4\pi r^2 / 2r^2 = 2\pi$ sr in a hemisphere. Imagine projecting an object's shape onto a hemisphere centered about a point on the surface that serves as the center of projection. The solid angle ω subtended by the object is the area on the hemisphere occupied by the projection, divided by the square of the hemisphere's radius (the division eliminates dependence on the size of the hemisphere). Thus, for convenience, we often speak of solid angle in terms of the area projected on a unit sphere or hemisphere, as shown in Fig. 16.39.

Radiant intensity is the flux radiated into a unit solid angle in a particular direction and is measured in W / sr. When we used the word *intensity* in reference to a point source, we were referring to its radiant intensity.

Radiance is the radiant intensity per unit foreshortened surface area, and is measured in W / (sr · m²). *Foreshortened surface area*, also known as *projected surface area*, refers to the projection of the surface onto the plane perpendicular to the direction of radiation. The foreshortened surface area is found by multiplying the surface area by cos θ_r, where θ_r is the

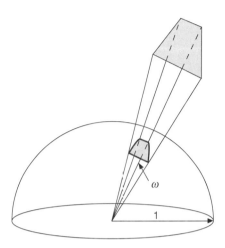

Fig. 16.39 The solid angle subtended by an object from a point on a surface is the area covered by the object's projection onto a unit hemisphere above the point.

angle of the radiated light relative to the surface normal. A small solid angle $d\omega$ may be approximated as the object's foreshortened surface area divided by the square of the distance from the object to the point at which the solid angle is being computed. When we used the word *intensity* in reference to a surface, we were referring to its radiance. Finally, *irradiance,* also known as *flux density,* is the incident flux per (unforeshortened) unit surface area and is measured in W / m^2.

In graphics, we are interested in the relationship between the light incident on a surface and the light reflected from and transmitted through that surface. Consider Fig. 16.40. The irradiance of the incident light is

$$E_i = I_i(\overline{N} \cdot \overline{L}) \, d\omega_i, \tag{16.34}$$

where I_i is the incident light's radiance, and $\overline{N} \cdot \overline{L}$ is $\cos \theta_i$. Since irradiance is expressed per

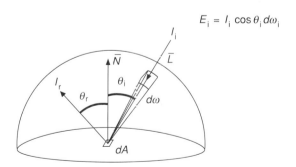

Fig. 16.40 Reflected radiance and incident irradiance.

unit area, whereas radiance is expressed per unit foreshortened area, multiplying by $\overline{N} \cdot \overline{L}$ converts it to the equivalent per unit unforeshortened area.

It is not enough to consider just I_i (the incident radiance) when determining I_r (the reflected radiance); E_i (the incident irradiance) must instead be taken into account. For example, an incident beam that has the same radiant intensity (W / sr) as another beam but a greater solid angle has proportionally greater E_i and causes the surface to appear proportionally brighter. The ratio of the reflected radiance (intensity) in one direction to the incident irradiance (flux density) responsible for it from another direction is known as the *bidirectional reflectivity*, ρ, which is a function of the directions of incidence and reflection,

$$\rho = \frac{I_r}{E_i}. \tag{16.35}$$

Thus, substituting for E_i from Eq. (16.34), we get

$$I_r = \rho I_i (\overline{N} \cdot \overline{L}) d\omega_i. \tag{16.36}$$

The irradiance incident on a pixel in the image (the *image irradiance*) is proportional to the radiance emitted by the scene (the *scene radiance*) that is focused on the pixel [HORN79]. The factor of proportionality is a function of the imaging system being used.

As we have seen, it is conventional in computer graphics to consider bidirectional reflectivity as composed of diffuse and specular components. Therefore,

$$\rho = k_d \rho_d + k_s \rho_s, \tag{16.37}$$

where ρ_d and ρ_s are respectively the diffuse and specular bidirectional reflectivities, and k_d and k_s are respectively the diffuse and specular reflection coefficients introduced earlier in this chapter; $k_d + k_s = 1$. It is important to note that Eq. (16.37) is a useful approximation that is not applicable to all surfaces. For example, the lunar surface has a ρ that peaks in the direction of incidence [SIEG81]. During a full moon, when the sun, earth, and moon are nearly in line, this accounts for why the moon appears as a disk of roughly uniform intensity. If the moon had a Lambertian surface, it would, instead, reflect more light at its center than at its sides.

In addition to the effects of direct light-source illumination, we need to take into account illumination by light reflected from other surfaces. The lighting models discussed so far have assumed that this ambient light is equally incident from all directions, is independent of viewer position, and is not blocked by any nearby objects. Later in this chapter we shall discuss how to lift these restrictions. For now we retain them, modeling the ambient term as $\rho_a I_a$, where ρ_a is the nondirectional ambient reflectivity, and I_a is the incident ambient intensity.

The resulting illumination equation for n light sources is

$$I_r = \rho_a I_a + \sum_{1 \le j \le n} I_{ij} (\overline{N} \cdot \overline{L}_j) \, d\omega_{i_j} (k_d \rho_d - k_s \rho_s). \tag{16.38}$$

To reinterpret the illumination model of Eq. (16.15) in terms of Eq. (16.38), we expressed diffuse reflectivity as the object's diffuse color, and specular reflectivity using the product of the object's specular color and a $\cos^n \alpha$ term. We have already noted some of the inadequacies of that specular reflectivity formulation. Now we shall examine how to replace it.

16.7.1 Improving the Surface Model

The Torrance–Sparrow model [TORR66; TORR67], developed by applied physicists, is a physically based model of a reflecting surface. Blinn was the first to adapt the Torrance–Sparrow model to computer graphics, giving the mathematical details and comparing it to the Phong model in [BLIN77a]; Cook and Torrance [COOK82] were the first to approximate the spectral composition of reflected light in an implementation of the model.

In the Torrance–Sparrow model, the surface is assumed to be an isotropic collection of planar microscopic facets, each a perfectly smooth reflector. The geometry and distribution of these *microfacets* and the direction of the light (assumed to emanate from an infinitely distant source, so that all rays are parallel) determine the intensity and direction of specular reflection as a function of I_p (the point light source intensity), $\overline{N}$, $\overline{L}$, and $\overline{V}$. Experimental measurements show a very good correspondence between the actual reflection and the reflection predicted by this model [TORR67].

For the specular component of the bidirectional reflectivity, Cook and Torrance use

$$\rho_s = \frac{F_\lambda}{\pi} \frac{DG}{(\overline{N} \cdot \overline{V})(\overline{N} \cdot \overline{L})}, \tag{16.39}$$

where D is a distribution function of the microfacet orientations, G is the *geometrical attenuation factor*, which represents the masking and shadowing effects of the microfacets on each other, and F_λ is the Fresnel term computed by Fresnel's equation (described later), which, for specular reflection, relates incident light to reflected light for the smooth surface of each microfacet. The π in the denominator is intended to account for surface roughness (but see [JOY88, pp. 227–230] for an overview of how the equation is derived). The $\overline{N} \cdot \overline{V}$ term makes the equation proportional to the surface area (and hence to the number of microfacets) that the viewer sees in a unit piece of foreshortened surface area, whereas the $\overline{N} \cdot \overline{L}$ term makes the equation proportional to the surface area that the light sees in a unit piece of foreshortened surface area.

16.7.2 The Microfacet Distribution Function

Since the microfacets are considered to be perfect specular reflectors, the model considers only those microfacets whose normals lie along the halfway vector $\overline{H}$, introduced in Section 16.1.4. Only a fraction D of the microfacets have this orientation. Torrance and Sparrow assumed a Gaussian distribution function for D in their original work. Blinn used the Trowbridge and Reitz distribution [TROW75], and Cook and Torrance used the Beckmann distribution function [BECK63]. Cook and Torrance point out the Beckmann distribution has a good theoretical basis and has no arbitrary constants, unlike the distributions used by Torrance and Sparrow, and by Blinn. The Beckmann distribution function for rough surfaces is

$$D = \frac{1}{4m^2 cos^4\beta} e^{-[(\tan \beta)/m]^2}, \tag{16.40}$$

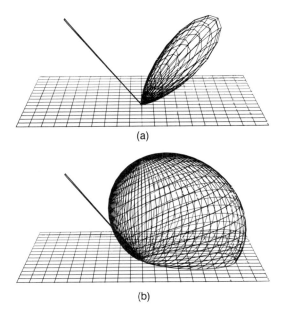

(a)

(b)

Fig. 16.41 Beckmann microfacet distribution function for (a) $m = 0.2$ and (b) $m = 0.6$. (From [COOK82] with permission. By Robert Cook, Program of Computer Graphics, Cornell University.)

where β is the angle between $\overline{N}$ and $\overline{H}$, and m is the root-mean-square slope of the microfacets.[1] When m is small, the microfacet slopes vary only slightly from the surface normal and, as we would expect, the reflection is highly directional (Fig. 16.41a). When m is large, the microfacet slopes are steep and the resulting rough surface spreads out the light it reflects (Fig. 16.41b). To model surfaces that have multiple scales of roughness, Cook and Torrance use a weighted sum of distribution functions,

$$D = \sum_{1 \le j \le n} w_j D(m_j), \tag{16.41}$$

where the sum of the weights w_j is 1.

16.7.3 The Geometrical Attenuation Factor

The model takes into account that some microfacets may shadow others. Torrance and Sparrow and Blinn discuss the calculation of G, considering three different situations. Figure 16.42(a) shows a microfacet whose incident light is totally reflected. Figure 16.42(b) shows a microfacet that is fully exposed to the rays, but has some reflected rays that are shielded by other microfacets. These shielded rays ultimately contribute to the diffuse reflection. Figure 16.42(c) shows a microfacet that is partially shielded from the light. The geometric attenuation factor G ranges from 0 (total shadowing) to 1 (no shadowing).

---

[1]Hall [HALL89] mentions that [COOK82] is missing the 4 in the denominator.

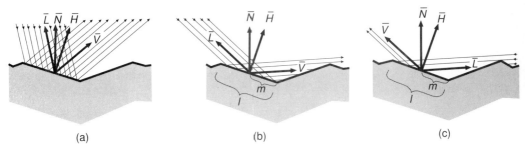

Fig. 16.42 Light rays reflecting from surface microfacets in the Torrance-Sparrow model. (a) No interference. (b) Partial interception of reflected light. (c) Partial interception of incident light. (After [BLIN77a].)

To simplify the analysis, the microfacets are assumed to form V-shaped grooves that are symmetric about the average surface normal $\bar{N}$. In Fig. 16.42(a), all the incident light is reflected to the viewer; thus, G_a is 1. In both other cases, the ratio of intercepted light is given by m/l, where l is the total area of the facet and m is the area whose reflected light is blocked (Fig. 16.42b) or that is itself blocked (Fig 16.42c) from the light. Therefore, $G_b = G_c = 1 - m/l$. Blinn gives a trigonometric derivation of the proportion of reflected light in Fig. 16.42(b) as

$$G_b = \frac{2(\bar{N} \cdot \bar{H})(\bar{N} \cdot \bar{V})}{(\bar{V} \cdot \bar{H})}. \tag{16.42}$$

The ratio for the case in Fig. 16.42(c) follows by noticing that it is the same as the case in part (b), except that $\bar{L}$ and $\bar{V}$ trade places:

$$G_c = \frac{2(\bar{N} \cdot \bar{H})(\bar{N} \cdot \bar{L})}{(\bar{V} \cdot \bar{H})}. \tag{16.43}$$

The denominator does not need to change because $(\bar{V} \cdot \bar{H}) = (\bar{L} \cdot \bar{H})$ by definition of $\bar{H}$ as the halfway vector between $\bar{V}$ and $\bar{L}$.

G is the minimum of the three values:

$$G = \min\left\{1, \frac{2(\bar{N} \cdot \bar{H})(\bar{N} \cdot \bar{V})}{(\bar{V} \cdot \bar{H})}, \frac{2(\bar{N} \cdot \bar{H})(\bar{N} \cdot \bar{L})}{(\bar{V} \cdot \bar{H})}\right\}. \tag{16.44}$$

16.7.4 The Fresnel Term

The Fresnel equation for unpolarized light specifies the ratio of reflected light from a dielectric (nonconducting) surface as

$$F_\lambda = \frac{1}{2}\left(\frac{\tan^2(\theta_i - \theta_t)}{\tan^2(\theta_i + \theta_t)} + \frac{\sin^2(\theta_i - \theta_t)}{\sin^2(\theta_i + \theta_t)}\right) = \frac{1}{2}\frac{\sin^2(\theta_i - \theta_t)}{\sin^2(\theta_i + \theta_t)}\left(1 + \frac{\cos^2(\theta_i + \theta_t)}{\cos^2(\theta_i - \theta_t)}\right), \tag{16.45}$$

where θ_i is the angle of incidence relative to $\overline{H}$ (i.e., $\cos^{-1}(\overline{L}\cdot\overline{H})$), and, as before, θ_t is the angle of refraction; $\sin\theta_t = (\eta_{i\lambda}/\eta_{t\lambda})\sin\theta_i$, where $\eta_{i\lambda}$ and $\eta_{t\lambda}$ are the indices of refraction of the two media. The Fresnel equation can also be expressed as

$$F_\lambda = \frac{1}{2}\frac{(g-c)^2}{(g+c)^2}\left(1 + \frac{[c(g+c)-1]^2}{[c(g-c)+1]^2}\right), \qquad (16.46)$$

where $c = \cos\theta_i = \overline{L}\cdot\overline{H}$, $g^2 = \eta_\lambda^2 + c^2 - 1$, and $\eta_\lambda = \eta_{t\lambda}/\eta_{i\lambda}$.

In a conducting medium, which attenuates light, it is necessary to refer to $\overline{\eta}_\lambda$, the material's *complex index of refraction*, defined as

$$\overline{\eta}_\lambda = \eta_\lambda - i\kappa_\lambda, \qquad (16.47)$$

where κ_λ is the material's *coefficient of extinction*, which measures the amount that the material attenuates intensity per unit path length. To simplify the reflection computations for conductors, κ_λ can be assumed to be zero and a single equivalent real value for η_λ can be determined.

Blinn created Figs. 16.43 and 16.44, comparing the effects of the Phong illumination model and the Torrance–Sparrow model. He made the simplifying assumptions that the specular term depends on only the color of the incident light, and that the viewer and light source are both at infinity. Figures 16.43 and 16.44 show the reflected illumination from a surface for angles of incidence of 30° and 70°, respectively. In each figure, the vertical arrow represents the surface normal, the incoming arrow represents the direction of light rays, and the outgoing arrow represents the direction of reflection for a perfect reflector. The rounded part of each figure is the diffuse reflection, whereas the bump is the specular reflection. For the 30° case in Fig. 16.43, the models produce nearly similar results, but for the 70° case in Fig. 16.44, the Torrance–Sparrow model has much higher specular reflectance and the peak occurs at an angle greater than the angle of incidence. This so-called *off-specular peak* is observed in actual environments. Figure 16.45, also by Blinn, shows a marked difference in the visual effect of the two models as the light source moves away from the viewpoint to the side and then to the rear of a metallic sphere.

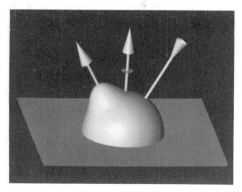

(a) Phong model

(b) Torrance-Sparrow model

Fig. 16.43 Comparison of Phong and Torrance–Sparrow illumination models for light at a 30° angle of incidence. (By J. Blinn [BLIN77a], courtesy of the University of Utah.)

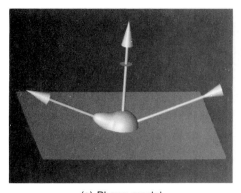 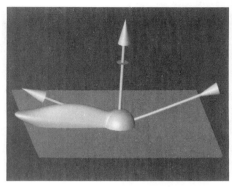

(a) Phong model (b) Torrance-Sparrow model

Fig. 16.44 Comparison of Phong and Torrance–Sparrow illumination models for light at a 70° angle of incidence. (By J. Blinn [BLIN77a], courtesy of the University of Utah.)

The specular-reflection color shift. Like Blinn, Cook and Torrance use the Torrance–Sparrow surface model to determine the specular term. Unlike Blinn, however, they make the color of the specular reflection a function of the interaction between the material and the incident light, depending both on the light's wavelength and on its angle of incidence. This is correct because the Fresnel equation, Eq. (16.45), is responsible for a shift in the specular reflection color based on the angle the incident light makes with the microfacet normal $\overline{H}$, as shown in Fig. 16.46.

When the incident light is in the same direction as $\overline{H}$, then $\theta_i = 0$, so $c = 1$ and $g = \eta_\lambda$. Substituting these values in Eq. (16.46) yields the Fresnel term for $\theta_i = 0$,

$$F_{\lambda 0} = \left(\frac{\eta_\lambda - 1}{\eta_\lambda + 1}\right)^2. \tag{16.48}$$

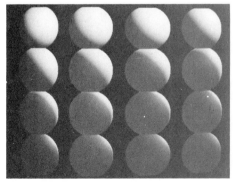 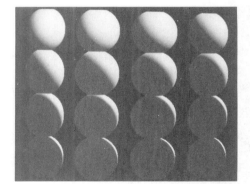

(a) Phong model (b) Torrance-Sparrow model

Fig. 16.45 Comparison of Phong and Torrance–Sparrow illumination models for a metallic sphere illuminated by a light source from different directions. Differences are most apparent for back-lit cases (bottom rows). (By J. Blinn [BLIN77a], courtesy of the University of Utah.)

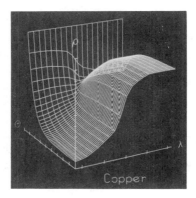

Fig. 16.46 Fresnel term for a copper mirror as a function of wavelength and angle of incidence. (By Robert Cook, Program of Computer Graphics, Cornell University.)

When the incident light grazes the surface of the microfacet, then $\theta_i = \pi / 2$, so $c = 0$. Substituting in Eq. (16.46) yields the Fresnel term for $\theta_i = \pi / 2$,

$$F_{\lambda \pi/2} = 1. \tag{16.49}$$

Thus, if light is normal to the surface, then $F_{\lambda 0}$, and hence the specular reflectance ρ_s, are functions of the surface's index of refraction, which in turn varies with the wavelength. When the light grazes the surface (and when the viewer is looking 180° opposite from the light, since only microfacets with normals of $\overline{H}$ are considered), $F_{\lambda \pi/2}$, and hence the specular reflection, are both 1. Specular reflectance depends on η_λ for all θ_i except $\pi / 2$. For metals, essentially all reflection occurs at the surface and is specular. Only at extreme glancing angles is the specular reflection not influenced by the object's material. Notice how this differs from the Phong specular-reflection term, which was always unaffected by the object color. Cook and Torrance point out that the monochromatic Phong specular term is a good model of plastic, which is colored by pigment particles embedded in a transparent substrate. The presence of these particles causes the diffuse reflection, resulting from light bouncing around in the substrate, to be a function of the pigment and light colors. Specular reflection occurs from the transparent surface, however, and therefore is unaffected by the pigment color. This is why objects rendered with a Phong illumination model look plastic.

If the indices of refraction at different wavelengths are known, they may be used directly in the Fresnel equation. More typically, however, they are not known. Reflectance, however, has been measured for many materials with $\theta_i = 0$ at a variety of wavelengths, as recorded in sources such as [TOUL70; TOUL72a; TOUL72b]. In this case, each η_λ may be determined from Eq. (16.48), as

$$\eta_\lambda = \frac{1 + \sqrt{F_{\lambda 0}}}{1 - \sqrt{F_{\lambda 0}}}. \tag{16.50}$$

A derived value of η_λ may then be used in the Fresnel equation to determine F_λ for an arbitrary θ_i. Rather than perform this calculation for each value of λ, Cook and Torrance simplify the computationally expensive color shift calculation by calculating $F_{avg\theta_i}$ for η_{avg}, the average index of refraction for average normal reflectance. They use the value computed for $F_{avg\theta i}$ to interpolate between the color of the material at $\theta_i = 90°$ and the color of the material at $\theta_i = 0°$ for each component of the color model. Because $F_{\lambda \pi/2}$ is always 1, the color of the material at $\theta_i = 90°$ is the color of the light source. Thus, when the light grazes the surface at a 90° angle of incidence, the color of the reflected light is that of the incident light. Using the RGB system, we call the red component of the material at $\theta_i = 0°$, Red$_0$, and the red component of the light, Red$_{\pi/2}$. Red$_0$ is calculated by integrating the product of F_0, the spectrum of the incident light, and the color-matching curves of Fig. 13.22, and applying the inverse of matrix M of Eq. (13.24) to the result. Red$_{\pi/2}$ is obtained by applying the inverse of M to Eq. (13.18). The approximation computes the color of the material at θ_i as

$$\text{Red}_{\theta i} = \text{Red}_0 + (\text{Red}_{\pi/2} - \text{Red}_0)\frac{\max(0, F_{avg\theta i} - F_{avg0})}{F_{avg\pi/2} - F_{avg0}}. \tag{16.51}$$

Red$_{\theta i}$ is then used in place of F_λ in Eq. (16.39). Because the approximation takes the light's spectrum into account, Eq. (16.38) must be modified to multiply the specular term by a wavelength-independent intensity scale factor, instead of by the light's spectrum. Hall [HALL89] suggests an alternative approximation that interpolates a value for $F_{\lambda\theta i}$, given $F_{\lambda 0}$. Since $F_{\lambda \pi/2}$ is always 1 (as is $F_{avg\pi/2}$ in Eq. 16.51),

$$F_{\lambda\theta i} = F_{\lambda 0} + (1 - F_{\lambda 0})\frac{\max(0, F_{avg\theta i} - F_{avg0})}{1 - F_{avg0}}. \tag{16.52}$$

Color Plate III.8 shows two copper vases rendered with the Cook–Torrance model, both of which use the bidirectional reflectance of copper for the diffuse term. The first models the specular term using the reflectance of a vinyl mirror and represents results similar to those obtained with the original Phong illumination model of Eq. (16.14). The second models the specular term with the reflectance of a copper mirror. Note how accounting for the dependence of the specular highlight color on both angle of incidence and surface material produces a more convincing image of a metallic surface.

In general, the ambient, diffuse, and specular components are the color of the material for both dielectrics and conductors. Composite objects, such as plastics, typically have diffuse and specular components that are different colors. Metals typically show little diffuse reflection and have a specular component color that ranges between that of the metal and that of the light source as θ_i approaches 90°. This observation suggests a rough approximation to the Cook–Torrance model that uses Eq. (16.15) with $O_{s\lambda}$ chosen by interpolating from a look-up table based on θ_i.

Further work. Kajiya [KAJI85] has generalized the Cook–Torrance illumination model to derive *anisotropic illumination models* whose reflective properties are not symmetric about the surface normal. These more accurately model the way that light is reflected by hair or burnished metal—surfaces whose microfeatures are preferentially oriented. To do this, Kajiya extends bump mapping to perturb not just the surface normal, but also the tangent and a binormal formed by the cross-product of the tangent and normal. Together these form a coordinate system that determines the orientation of the surface relative to the anisotropic illumination model. The surface shown in Fig. 16.47 is mapped to an anisotropic texture that represents a cross-weave of threads. Cabral, Max and Springmeyer [CABR87] have developed a method for determining G and ρ for a surface finish specified by an arbitrary bump map by computing the shadowing and masking effects of the bumps.

The Fresnel equation used by Blinn and by Cook and Torrance is correct only for unpolarized light. The polarization state of light changes, however, when light is reflected from a surface, and a surface's ρ is a function of the polarization state of the light incident on it. Wolff and Kurlander [WOLF90] have extended the Cook–Torrance model to take this into account and have generated images that evidence two effects that are most visible after two or more interobject reflections. First, dielectrics have an angle of incidence, known as the *Brewster angle,* at which incident light is completely polarized when reflected, or is not reflected at all if it is inappropriately polarized. If interobject specular reflection of initially unpolarized light occurs between two dielectric surfaces such that the angle of incidence of each reflection is equal to the Brewster angle, and the plane defined by $\overline{N}$ and $\overline{L}$ on one surface is perpendicular to that of the other, then no light at all will be specularly reflected from the second object; we can produce noticeable, but less dramatic, attenuation if the angles and orientations are varied. Second, colored conductors (metals such as copper or gold) tend to polarize light at different wavelengths differently. Therefore, when a colored conductor is reflected from a dielectric surface, the reflection will have a color slightly different from that when polarization is not taken into account.

Fig. 16.47 Anisotropic texture. (By J. Kajiya [KAJI85], California Institute of Technology.)

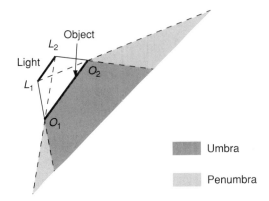

Fig. 16.48 Umbra and penumbra.

16.8   EXTENDED LIGHT SOURCES

The light sources discussed thus far have been point lights. In contrast, *extended* or *distributed* light sources actually have area and consequently cast "soft" shadows containing areas only partially blocked from the source, as shown in Fig. 16.48. The part of a light source's shadow that is totally blocked from the light source is the shadow's *umbra*;

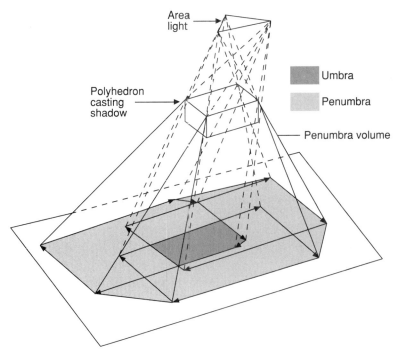

Fig. 16.49 Determining the penumbra and umbra volumes. (After [NISH85a].)

that part of the shadow that is only partially shielded from the source is the shadow's
penumbra. All of a point light source's shadow is umbra. An obvious approach to modeling
an extended light source is to approximate it with closely clustered point light sources
[VERB84; BROT84]. The process is computationally expensive, however, and the results
are less than satisfactory unless there are very many point sources and no specular
reflection.

Nishita and Nakamae [NISH83; NISH85a; NISH85b] have developed an extension of
shadow volumes for modeling linear, convex polygonal, and convex polyhedral light
sources with Lambertian intensity distributions. Their method employs an object-precision
algorithm for determining shadow volumes for convex polyhedral objects. As shown in Fig.
16.49, the shadow volumes defined by each vertex of the source and the polyhedron are
determined. The penumbra volume is then the smallest convex polyhedron containing these
shadow volumes (their convex hull), and the umbra volume is the intersection of the shadow
volumes. The volumes are then intersected with the faces of the objects to determine the
areas in each penumbra or umbra volume. Any point lying within an umbra volume defined
by a light source and any other polyhedron is not affected by the light source. Determining
the color of a point in a penumbra involves computing those parts of the light source visible
from the point on the object. A BSP-tree–based approach is discussed in [CHIN90].

Excellent simulations of extended light sources have been achieved by using variations
on ray-tracing (Section 16.12) and radiosity methods (Section 16.13).

16.9   SPECTRAL SAMPLING

As light is reflected from a surface, the spectral energy distribution P_λ of the incident light is
modified by the spectral reflectance function of the surface, ρ_λ. This curve specifies the
percentage of light of each wavelength λ that is reflected. Therefore, the spectral energy
distribution of the reflected light is $P_\lambda \rho_\lambda$. Similarly, light passing through a material is
modified by the spectral transmittance function of the material, τ_λ. Once a final spectral
energy distribution for light falling on the eye at a particular point (i.e., for a particular
pixel) is determined, then Eq. (13.18) can be used to find the corresponding CIE XYZ
specification for the light, and this result can be converted to RGB using the inverse of M of
Eq. (13.24).

It is tempting to assume that ρ_λ and τ_λ can be replaced by equivalent tristimulus RGB or
XYZ color specifications. If this could be done, then the product $P_\lambda \rho_\lambda$ could be replaced by
a sum of the tristimulus values for each of P_λ and ρ_λ, of the form

$$R\rho_R + G\rho_G + B\rho_B. \tag{16.53}$$

This is clearly incorrect. Consider the P_λ and ρ_λ shown in Fig. 16.50. P_λ is uniform except
for a narrow interval around 600 nanometers, whereas ρ_λ reflects light only at the same
narrow interval. The product $P_\lambda \rho_\lambda$ is thus zero everywhere, and the surface appears black.
On the other hand, the XYZ components of P_λ will be nonzero (this can be seen by applying
the inverse of M to the results of Eq. (13.18). Similarly, substituting ρ_λ for P_λ in Eq.
(13.18) and applying the inverse of M gives nonzero values for ρ_R, ρ_G, ρ_B, so the product
(Eq. 16.53) is also nonzero! This is the wrong answer, and demonstrates that ρ_λ and τ_λ
cannot in general be replaced by an equivalent tristimulus color specification. As Hall

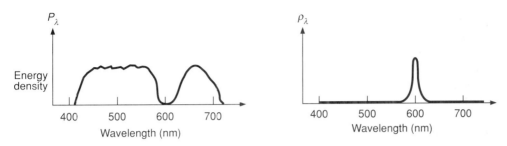

Fig. 16.50 P_λ and ρ_λ whose product is 0 everywhere.

[HALL83] points out, this approach fails because it is actually point sampling in color space and consequently is prone to all the problems that arise from undersampling.

A more accurate representation of a light source's spectral distribution or a surface's reflectivity or transmissivity can be obtained by representing either one as a curve that interpolates a sufficiently large set of samples spaced across the visible spectrum. Color Plate III.9 shows images, generated with different color models, of two overlapping filters lit by a D6500 light source. The filters do not pass a common band of wavelengths, so no transmitted light should be visible where they overlap. Color Plate III.9(a), the control picture, was generated using spectra maintained at 1-nm intervals from 360 to 830 nanometers. Color Plates III.9(b) and III.9(c) were generated with three samples for the primaries of the CIE and RGB color spaces, respectively. Color Plate III.9(d) approximates the spectra of Color Plate III.9(a) with nine spectral values. Note how much more closely Color Plate III.9(d) matches the control picture than do the others.

16.10 IMPROVING THE CAMERA MODEL

Thus far, we have modeled the image produced by a pinhole camera: each object, regardless of its position in the environment, is projected sharply and without distortion in the image. Real cameras (and eyes) have lenses that introduce a variety of distortion and focusing effects.

Depth of field.   Objects appear to be more or less in focus depending on their distance from the lens, an effect known as *depth of field*. A lens has a focal length F corresponding to the distance from the lens at which a perfectly focused image of an object converges. If a point is out of focus, its image converges on a plane that is closer or farther than F. An out-of-focus point projects on a plane at F as a circle known as the *circle of confusion*.

Potmesil and Chakravarty [POTM82] have developed a postprocessing technique for simulating some of the effects of depth of field and other properties of real lenses, demonstrated in Color Plate II.38. Their system first produces images using a conventional pinhole-lens renderer that generates not only the intensity at each point, but also that point's z value. Each sampled point is then turned into a circle of confusion with a size and intensity distribution determined by its z value and the lens and aperture being used. The intensity of each pixel in the output image is calculated as a weighted average of the intensities in the circles of confusion that overlap the pixel. Since the image is initially computed from a single point at the center of projection, the results of this technique are still only an approximation. A real lens's focusing effect causes light rays that would not pass through the pinhole to strike the lens and to converge to form the image. These rays see a slightly different view of the scene, including, for example, parts of surfaces that are not visible to the rays passing through the pinhole. This information is lost in the images created with the Potmesil and Chakravarty model.

Motion blur. *Motion blur* is the streaked or blurred appearance that moving objects have because a camera's shutter is open for a finite amount of time. To achieve this effect, we need to solve the visible-surface problem over time, as well as over space, to determine which objects are visible at a given pixel and when they are visible. Korein and Badler [KORE83] describe two contrasting approaches: an analytic algorithm that uses continuous functions to model the changes that objects undergo over time, and a simple image-precision approach that relies on temporal supersampling. In the temporal-supersampling method, a separate image is rendered for each point in time to be sampled. The motion-blurred image is created by taking a weighted sum of the images, in essence convolving them with a temporal filter. For example, if each of n images is weighted by $1/n$, this corresponds to temporal box filtering. The more closely the samples are spaced, the better the results. Temporal supersampling, like spatial supersampling, suffers from aliasing: Unless samples are spaced sufficiently close together in time, the final image will appear to be a set of discrete multiple exposures. Potmesil and Chakravarty [POTM83] have extended their depth-of-field work to model the ways in which actual camera shutters move. As we shall see in Section 16.12, the stochastic sampling techniques used in distributed ray tracing offer a uniform framework for integrating lens effects, motion blur, and spatial antialiasing demonstrated in Color Plates II.39 and III.16.

16.11 GLOBAL ILLUMINATION ALGORITHMS

An illumination model computes the color at a point in terms of light directly emitted by light sources and of light that reaches the point after reflection from and transmission through its own and other surfaces. This indirectly reflected and transmitted light is often called *global illumination*. In contrast, *local illumination* is light that comes directly from the light sources to the point being shaded. Thus far, we have modeled global illumination by an ambient illumination term that was held constant for all points on all objects. It did not depend on the positions of the object or the viewer, or on the presence or absence of nearby objects that could block the ambient light. In addition, we have seen some limited global illumination effects made possible by shadows, transparency, and reflection maps.

Much of the light in real-world environments does not come from direct light sources. Two different classes of algorithms have been used to generate pictures that emphasize the contributions of global illumination. Section 16.12 discusses extensions to the visible-surface ray-tracing algorithm that interleave visible-surface determination and shading to depict shadows, reflection, and refraction. Thus, global specular reflection and transmission supplement the local specular, diffuse, and ambient illumination computed for a surface. In contrast, the radiosity methods discussed in Section 16.13 completely separate shading and visible-surface determination. They model all an environment's interactions with light sources first in a view-independent stage, and then compute one or more images for the desired viewpoints using conventional visible-surface and interpolative shading algorithms.

The distinction between view-dependent algorithms, such as ray tracing, and view-independent ones, such as radiosity, is an important one. *View-dependent* algorithms discretize the view plane to determine points at which to evaluate the illumination equation, given the viewer's direction. In contrast, *view-independent* algorithms discretize the environment, and process it in order to provide enough information to evaluate the illumination equation at any point and from any viewing direction. View-dependent algorithms are well-suited for handling specular phenomena that are highly dependent on the viewer's position, but may perform extra work when modeling diffuse phenomena that change little over large areas of an image, or between images made from different viewpoints. On the other hand, view-independent algorithms model diffuse phenomena efficiently, but require overwhelming amounts of storage to capture enough information about specular phenomena.

Ultimately, all these approaches attempt to solve what Kajiya [KAJI86] has referred to as the *rendering equation,* which expresses the light being transferred from one point to another in terms of the intensity of the light emitted from the first point to the second and the intensity of light emitted from all other points that reaches the first and is reflected from the first to the second. The light transferred from each of these other points to the first is, in turn, expressed recursively by the rendering equation. Kajiya presents the rendering equation as

$$I(x, x') = g(x, x') \left[\varepsilon(x, x') + \int_S \rho(x, x', x'') I(x', x'') dx'' \right], \qquad (16.54)$$

where x, x', and x'' are points in the environment. $I(x, x')$ is related to the intensity passing from x' to x. $g(x, x')$ is a geometry term that is 0 when x and x' are occluded from each other, and $1 / r^2$ when they are visible to each other, where r is the distance between them. $\varepsilon(x, x')$ is related to the intensity of light that is emitted from x' to x. The initial evaluation of $g(x, x')\varepsilon(x, x')$ for x at the viewpoint accomplishes visible-surface determination in the sphere about x. The integral is over all points on all surfaces S. $\rho(x, x', x'')$ is related to the intensity of the light reflected (including both specular and diffuse reflection) from x'' to x from the surface at x'. Thus, the rendering equation states that the light from x' that reaches x consists of light emitted by x' itself and light scattered by x' to x from all other surfaces, which themselves emit light and recursively scatter light from other surfaces.

As we shall see, how successful an approach is at solving the rendering equation depends in large part on how it handles the remaining terms and the recursion, on what combinations of diffuse and specular reflectivity it supports, and on how well the visibility relationships between surfaces are modeled.

16.12 RECURSIVE RAY TRACING

In this section, we extend the basic ray-tracing algorithm of Section 15.10 to handle shadows, reflection, and refraction. This simple algorithm determined the color of a pixel at the closest intersection of an eye ray with an object, by using any of the illumination models described previously. To calculate shadows, we fire an additional ray from the point of intersection to each of the light sources. This is shown for a single light source in Fig.

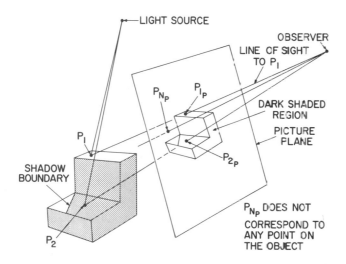

Fig. 16.51 Determining whether a point on an object is in shadow. (Courtesy of Arthur Appel, IBM T.J. Watson Research Center.)

16.51, which is reproduced from a paper by Appel [APPE68]—the first paper published on ray tracing for computer graphics. If one of these *shadow rays* intersects any object along the way, then the object is in shadow at that point and the shading algorithm ignores the contribution of the shadow ray's light source. Figure 16.52 shows two pictures that Appel rendered with this algorithm, using a pen plotter. He simulated a halftone pattern by placing a different size "+" at each pixel in the grid, depending on the pixel's intensity. To compensate for the grid's coarseness, he drew edges of visible surfaces and of shadows using a visible-line algorithm.

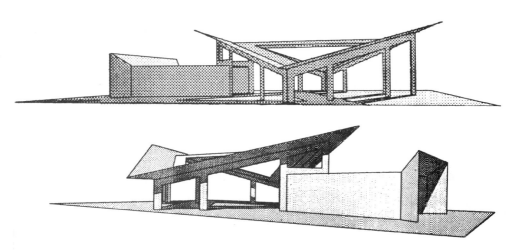

Fig. 16.52 Early pictures rendered with ray tracing. (Courtesy of Arthur Appel, IBM T.J. Watson Research Center.)

The illumination model developed by Whitted [WHIT80] and Kay [KAY79a] fundamentally extended ray tracing to include specular reflection and refractive transparency. Color Plate III.10 is an early picture generated with these effects. In addition to shadow rays, Whitted's recursive ray-tracing algorithm conditionally spawns *reflection rays* and *refraction rays* from the point of intersection, as shown in Fig. 16.53. The shadow, reflection, and refraction rays are often called *secondary rays*, to distinguish them from the *primary rays* from the eye. If the object is specularly reflective, then a reflection ray is reflected about the surface normal in the direction of $\overline{R}$, which may be computed as in Section 16.1.4. If the object is transparent, and if total internal reflection does not occur, then a refraction ray is sent into the object along $\overline{T}$ at an angle determined by Snell's law, as described in Section 16.5.2. (Note that your incident ray may be oppositely oriented to those in these sections.)

Each of these reflection and refraction rays may, in turn, recursively spawn shadow, reflection, and refraction rays, as shown in Fig. 16.54. The rays thus form a *ray tree,* such as that of Fig. 16.55. In Whitted's algorithm, a branch is terminated if the reflected and refracted rays fail to intersect an object, if some user-specified maximum depth is reached or if the system runs out of storage. The tree is evaluated bottom-up, and each node's intensity is computed as a function of its children's intensities. Color Plate III.11(a) and (b) were made with a recursive ray-tracing algorithm.

We can represent Whitted's illumination equation as

$$I_\lambda = I_{a\lambda}k_aO_{d\lambda} + \sum_{1 \le i \le m} S_i f_{atti} I_{p\lambda i}[k_dO_{d\lambda}(\overline{N} \cdot \overline{L}_i) + k_s(\overline{N} \cdot \overline{H}_i)^n] + k_sI_{r\lambda} + k_tI_{t\lambda}, \quad (16.55)$$

where $I_{r\lambda}$ is the intensity of the reflected ray, k_t is the *transmission coefficient* ranging between 0 and 1, and $I_{t\lambda}$ is the intensity of the refracted transmitted ray. Values for $I_{r\lambda}$ and $I_{t\lambda}$ are determined by recursively evaluating Eq. (16.55) at the closest surface that the reflected and transmitted rays intersect. To approximate attenuation with distance, Whitted multiplied the I_λ calculated for each ray by the inverse of the distance traveled by the ray. Rather than treating S_i as a delta function, as in Eq (16.24), he also made it a continuous function

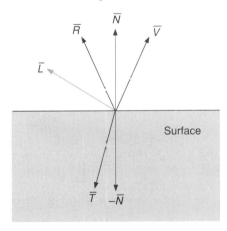

Fig. 16.53 Reflection, refraction, and shadow rays are spawned from a point of intersection.

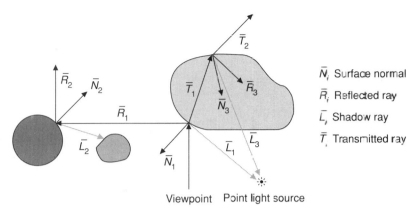

Fig. **16.54** Rays recursively spawn other rays.

of the k_t of the objects intersected by the shadow ray, so that a transparent object obscures
less light than an opaque one at those points it shadows.

Figure 16.56 shows pseudocode for a simple recursive ray tracer. RT_trace determines
the closest intersection the ray makes with an object and calls RT_shade to determine the
shade at that point. First, RT_shade determines the intersection's ambient color. Next, a
shadow ray is spawned to each light on the side of the surface being shaded to determine its
contribution to the color. An opaque object blocks the light totally, whereas a transparent
one scales the light's contribution. If we are not too deep in the ray tree, then recursive calls
are made to RT_trace to handle reflection rays for reflective objects and refraction rays for
transparent objects. Since the indices of refraction of two media are needed to determine
the direction of the refraction ray, the index of refraction of the material in which a ray is
traveling can be included with each ray. RT_trace retains the ray tree only long enough to
determine the current pixel's color. If the ray trees for an entire image can be preserved,
then surface properties can be altered and a new image recomputed relatively quickly, at the

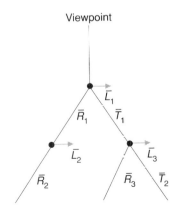

Fig. **16.55** The ray tree for Fig. 16.54.

```
select center of projection and window on view plane;
for (each scan line in image) {
    for (each pixel in scan line) {
        determine ray from center of projection through pixel;
        pixel = RT_trace (ray, 1);
    }
}
```

/* Intersect ray with objects and compute shade at closest intersection. */
/* Depth is current depth in ray tree. */

```
RT_color RT_trace (RT_ray ray, int depth)
{
    determine closest intersection of ray with an object;

    if (object hit) {
        compute normal at intersection;
        return RT_shade (closest object hit, ray, intersection, normal, depth);
    } else
        return BACKGROUND_VALUE;
}   /* RT_trace */
```

/* Compute shade at point on object, tracing rays for shadows, reflection and refraction. */
```
RT_color RT_shade (
    RT_object object,        /* Object intersected */
    RT_ray ray,              /* Incident ray */
    RT_point point,          /* Point of intersection to shade */
    RT_normal normal,        /* Normal at point */
    int depth)               /* Depth in ray tree */
{
    RT_color color;          /* Color of ray */
    RT_ray rRay, tRay, sRay; /* Reflected, refracted, and shadow rays */
    RT_color rColor, tColor; /* Reflected and refracted ray colors */

    color = ambient term;
    for (each light) {
        sRay = ray to light from point;
        if (dot product of normal and direction to light is positive) {
            compute how much light is blocked by opaque and transparent surfaces,
                and use to scale diffuse and specular terms before adding them to color;
        }
    }
```

Fig. 16.56 *(Cont'd.)*

```
    if (depth < maxDepth) {          /* Return if depth is too deep */
        if (object is reflective) {
            rRay = ray in reflection direction from point;
            rColor = RT_trace (rRay, depth + 1);
            scale rColor by specular coefficient and add to color;
        }

        if (object is transparent) {
            tRay = ray in refraction direction from point;
            if (total internal reflection does not occur) {
                tColor = RT_trace (tRay, depth + 1);
                scale tColor by transmission coefficient and add to color;
            }
        }
    }
    return color;                    /* Return color of ray */
}   /* RT_shade */
```

Fig. 16.56 Pseudocode for simple recursive ray tracing without antialiasing.

cost of only reevaluating the trees. Sequin and Smyrl [SEQU89] present techniques that minimize the time and space needed to process and store ray trees.

Figure 16.54 shows a basic problem with how ray tracing models refraction: The shadow ray $\overline{L}_3$ is not refracted on its path to the light. In fact, if we were to simply refract $\overline{L}_3$ from its current direction at the point where it exits the large object, it would not end at the light source. In addition, when the paths of rays that are refracted are determined, a single index of refraction is used for each ray. Later, we discuss some ways to address these failings.

Ray tracing is particularly prone to problems caused by limited numerical precision. These show up when we compute the objects that intersect with the secondary rays. After the x, y, and z coordinates of the intersection point on an object visible to an eye ray have been computed, they are then used to define the starting point of the secondary ray for which we must determine the parameter t (Section 15.10.1). If the object that was just intersected is intersected with the new ray, it will often have a small, nonzero t, because of numerical-precision limitations. If not dealt with, this false intersection can result in visual problems. For example, if the ray were a shadow ray, then the object would be considered as blocking light from itself, resulting in splotchy pieces of incorrectly "self-shadowed" surface. A simple way to solve this problem for shadow rays is to treat as a special case the object from which a secondary ray is spawned, so that intersection tests are not performed on it. Of course, this does not work if objects are supported that really could obscure themselves or if transmitted rays have to pass through the object and be reflected from the inside of the same object. A more general solution is to compute abs(t) for an intersection, to compare it with a small tolerance value, and to ignore it if it is below the tolerance.

The paper Whitted presented at *SIGGRAPH '79* [WHIT80], and the movies he made using the algorithm described there, started a renaissance of interest in ray tracing. Recursive ray tracing makes possible a host of impressive effects—such as shadows, specular reflection, and refractive transparency—that were difficult or impossible to obtain previously. In addition, a simple ray tracer is quite easy to implement. Consequently, much effort has been directed toward improving both the algorithm's efficiency and its image quality. We provide a brief overview of these issues here, and discuss several parallel hardware implementations that take advantage of the algorithm's intrinsic parallelism in Section 18.11.2. For more detail, see [GLAS89].

16.12.1   Efficiency Considerations for Recursive Ray Tracing

Section 15.10.2 discussed how to use extents, hierarchies, and spatial partitioning to limit the number of ray–object intersections to be calculated. These general efficiency techniques are even more important here than in visible-surface ray tracing for several reasons. First, a quick glance at Fig. 16.55 reveals that the number of rays that must be processed can grow exponentially with the depth to which rays are traced. Since each ray may spawn a reflection ray and a refraction ray, in the worst case, the ray tree will be a complete binary tree with $2^n - 1$ rays, where the tree depth is n. In addition, each reflection or refraction ray that intersects with an object spawns one shadow ray for each of the m light sources. Thus, there are potentially $m(2^n - 1)$ shadow rays for each ray tree. To make matters worse, since rays can come from any direction, traditional efficiency ploys, such as clipping objects to the view volume and culling back-facing surfaces relative to the eye, cannot be used in recursive ray tracing. Objects that would otherwise be invisible, including back faces, may be reflected from or refracted through visible surfaces.

Item buffers.   One way of speeding up ray tracing is simply not to use it at all when determining those objects directly visible to the eye. Weghorst, Hooper, and Greenberg [WEGH84] describe how to create an *item buffer* by applying a less costly visible-surface algorithm, such as the z-buffer algorithm, to the scene, using the same viewing specification. Instead of determining the shade at each pixel, however, they record in the item buffer pixel the identity of the closest object. Then, only this object needs to be processed by the ray tracer to determine the eye ray's exact intersection for this pixel, so that further rays may be spawned.

Reflection maps.   Tracing rays can be avoided in other situations, too. Hall [HALL86] shows how to combine ray tracing with the reflection maps discussed in Section 16.6. The basic idea is to do less work for the secondary rays than for primary rays. Those objects that are not directly visible in an image are divided into two groups on the basis of an estimation of their indirect visibility. Ray tracing is used to determine the global lighting contributions of the more visible ones, whereas indexing into a suitably prepared reflection map handles the others. One way to estimate the extent to which an object is indirectly visible is to measure the solid angle subtended by the directly visible objects as seen from the centroid of the indirectly visible object. If the solid angle is greater than some threshold, then the object will be included in the environment to be traced by reflection rays (this environment includes the directly visible objects); otherwise, the object will be represented only in the reflection map. When ray tracing is performed, if a reflection ray does not intersect one of the objects in the reflection-ray environment, then the ray is used to index into the reflection map. Hall also points out that reflected and refracted images are often extremely distorted. Therefore, good results may be achieved by intersecting the reflection and refraction rays with object definitions less detailed than those used for the eye rays.

Adaptive tree-depth control. Although ray tracing is often used to depict highly specular objects, most of an image's area is usually not filled with such objects. Consequently, a high recursion level often results in unnecessary processing for large parts of the picture. Hall [HALL83] introduced the use of *adaptive tree-depth control*, in which a ray is not cast if its contribution to the pixel's intensity is estimated to be below some preset threshold. This is accomplished by approximating a ray's maximum contribution by calculating its intensity with the assumption that the ray's child rays have intensities of 1. This allows the ray's contribution to its parent to be estimated. As the ray tree is built, the maximum contribution of a ray is multiplied by those of its ancestors to derive the ray's maximum contribution to the pixel. For example, suppose that $\overline{R}_1$ and $\overline{R}_2$ in Fig. 16.55 are spawned at surfaces with k_s values of .1 and .05, respectively. At the first intersection, we estimate the maximum contribution to the pixel of $\overline{R}_1$ to be .1. At the second intersection, we estimate the maximum contribution to the pixel of $\overline{R}_2$ to be $.05 \times .1 = .005$. If this is below our threshold, we may decide not to cast $\overline{R}_2$. Although adaptive tree-depth control has been shown to work well for many images, it is easy to design cases in which it will fail. Although one uncast ray may have an imperceptible effect on a pixel's shade, a pixel may receive a significant amount of light from a large number of individually insignificant rays.

Light buffers. We noted that m shadow rays are spawned for each reflection or refraction ray that hits an object. Shadow rays are special, however, in that each is fired toward one of a relatively small set of objects. Haines and Greenberg [HAIN86] have introduced the notion of a *light buffer* to increase the speed with which shadow rays are processed. A light buffer is a cube centered about a light source and aligned with the world-coordinate axes, as shown in Fig. 16.57(a). Each side is tiled with a regular grid of squares, and each square is associated with a depth-sorted list of surfaces that can be seen through it from the light. The

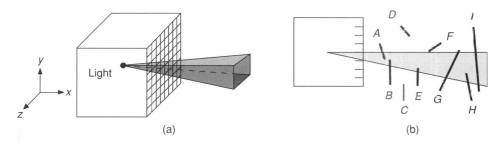

(a)   (b)

Fig. 16.57 Light buffer centered about a light source. (a) Volume defined by one square. (b) Cross-section shows volume of square in 2D with intersected surfaces. Square's depth-sorted list is initially A, B, E, G, H, and I.

lists are filled by scan converting the objects in the scene onto each face of the light buffer with the center of projection at the light. The scan-conversion algorithm places an object on the list of every square covered by that object's projection, no matter how small the overlap. Figure 16.57(b) shows a square's set of intersecting surfaces. A shadow ray is processed by determining the light-buffer square through which it passes. The ray needs to be tested only for intersection against that square's ordered list of surfaces. Thus, a light buffer implements a kind of 3D spatial partitioning of the 3D view of its light.

A number of efficiency speedups are possible. For example, any object whose projection onto the light buffer totally covers a square (e.g., G in Fig. 16.57b) can be associated with a special ''full-occlusion'' record in the square's list; any object more distant from the light than a fully occluding object is purged from the list. In this case, H and I are purged. Whenever the ray from an intersection point is tested against a square's list, the test can be terminated immediately if there is a full-occlusion record closer to the light than the intersection point. In addition, back-face culling may be used to avoid adding any faces to a list that are both part of a closed opaque solid and back facing relative to the light. Color Plate III.12 was made using the light-buffer technique.

Haines and Greenberg also mention an interesting use of object coherence to determine shadows that can be applied even without using light buffers. A pointer is associated with each light and is initialized to null. When an object is found to be shadowed from a light by some opaque surface, the light's pointer is set to the shadowing surface. The next time a shadow ray is cast for the light, it is first intersected with the object pointed at by the light's pointer. If the ray hits it, then intersection testing is finished; otherwise, the pointer is set to null and testing continues.

Ray classification. The spatial-partitioning approaches discussed in Section 15.10.2 make it possible to determine which objects lie in a given region of 3D space. Arvo and Kirk [ARVO87] have extended this concept to partition rays by the objects that they intersect, a technique called *ray classification*. A ray may be specified by its position in 5D *ray space,* determined by the 3D position of its origin in space and its 2D direction in spherical coordinates. A point in ray space defines a single ray, whereas a finite subset of ray space defines a family of rays or *beam*. Ray classification adaptively partitions ray space into subsets, each of which is associated with a list of objects that it contains (i.e,. that one of its rays could intersect). To determine the candidate objects that may be intersected by any ray, we need only to retrieve the list of objects associated with the subset of ray space in which the ray resides.

Instead of using spherical coordinates to specify direction, Arvo and Kirk use the (u, v) coordinate system on each of the six sides of an axis-aligned cube centered about a ray's origin. They subdivide ray space with six copies of a 5D bintree (Section 12.6.3); one copy is needed for each direction along an axis, since a (u, v) pair specifies a position on the cube's side, but not the side itself. As shown in Fig. 16.58(a), in 2D a set of ray origins (a rectangle in (x, y)), combined with a set of ray directions (an interval in u on one of four sides), define a partially bounded polygon that defines the beam. In 3D, shown in Fig. 16.58(b), a set of ray origins (a rectangular parallelepiped in (x, y, z)), combined with a set of ray directions (a rectangle in (u, v)), defines a partially bounded polyhedral volume that defines the beam. Objects (or their extents) may be intersected with this volume (e.g., using

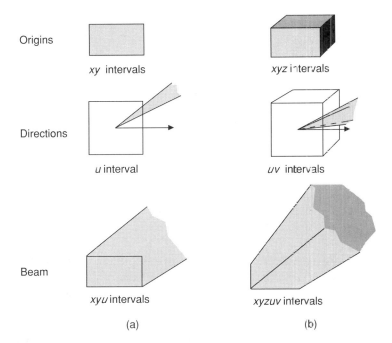

Fig. 16.58 Ray classification: (a) 2-space beams; (b) 3-space beams. (After [ARVO87].)

the BSP-tree-based approach of Section 12.6.4) to determine whether they are contained in it. Initially, each unpartitioned bintree represents positions in all of the environment's 3-space extent, and directions that pass through any part of the bintree's designated side. Each bintree is initially associated with all the objects in the environment.

Arvo and Kirk use *lazy evaluation* to build the trees at the same time that they trace rays. When a ray is traced, its direction selects the root of the bintree whose (u, v) coordinate system it will intersect. If more than some threshold number of objects exist at the node, the bintree is subdivided equally along each of its five axes. With each subdivision, only the child node in which the ray resides is processed; it inherits from its parent those objects that lie within the child. When subdivision stops, only those objects associated with the ray's partition are returned for intersection. Partitioning data structures as the rays are traced minimizes the amount of processing done for objects that are not intersected.

16.12.2   A Better Illumination Model

It is possible to make a number of extensions to Eq. (16.55). Hall [HALL83] has developed a model in which the specular light expressions are scaled by a wavelength-dependent Fresnel reflectivity term. An additional term for transmitted local light is added to take into account the contribution of transmitted light directly emitted by the light sources, and is also scaled by the Fresnel transmissivity term. The global reflected and refracted rays further take into account the transmittance of the medium through which they travel. Hall's model may be expressed as

$$I_\lambda = I_{a\lambda}k_aO_{d\lambda} + \sum_{1 \le i \le m} S_i f_{atti} I_{p\lambda i} [k_dO_{c\lambda}(\overline{N} \cdot \overline{L}_i) + k_s(\overline{N} \cdot \overline{H}_i)^n F_\lambda + k_s(\overline{N} \cdot \overline{H'}_i)^n T_\lambda]$$

$$+ k_s F_\lambda I_{r\lambda} A_r^{d_r} + k_s T_\lambda I_{t\lambda} A_t^{d_t}, \tag{16.56}$$

where d_r is the distance traveled by the reflected ray, d_t is the distance traveled by the transmitted ray, A_r is the transmissivity per unit length of material for the reflected ray, and A_t is the transmissivity per unit length of material for the transmitted ray. $\overline{H}'$ is the normal for those microfacets that are aligned such that they will refract light directly from the light source to the viewer. It may be computed as

$$\overline{H}' = \frac{\overline{V} - (\eta_{avg\theta t} / \eta_{avg\theta i})\overline{L}}{(\eta_{avg\theta t} / \eta_{avg\theta i}) - 1}, \tag{16.57}$$

where $\eta_{avg\theta t}$ is the average coefficient of refraction of the object through which the ray to the light passes. T_λ is the Fresnel transmissivity term for the material. Note that k_t is not used here; instead, k_s is scaled by either F_λ or T_λ. Since all light that is not reflected is transmitted (and possibly) absorbed, $F_\lambda + T_\lambda = 1$.

Color Plate III.13 shows the same scene rendered with Whitted's model and with Hall's model. The color of the glass sphere in part (b) clearly shows the filtering effects resulting from the use of the transmissivity terms.

16.12.3   Area-Sampling Variations

One of conventional ray tracing's biggest drawbacks is that this technique point samples on a regular grid. Whitted [WHIT80] suggested that unweighted area sampling could be accomplished by replacing each linear eye ray with a pyramid defined by the eye and the four corners of a pixel. These pyramids would be intersected with the objects in the environment, and sections of them would be recursively refracted and reflected by the objects that they intersect. A pure implementation of this proposal would be exceedingly complex, however, since it would have to calculate exact intersections with occluding objects, and to determine how the resulting pyramid fragments are modified as they are recursively reflected from and refracted by curved surfaces. Nevertheless, it has inspired several interesting algorithms that accomplish antialiasing, and at the same time decrease rendering time by taking advantage of coherence.

Cone tracing. *Cone tracing*, developed by Amanatides [AMAN84], generalizes the linear rays into cones. One cone is fired from the eye through each pixel, with an angle wide enough to encompass the pixel. The cone is intersected with objects in its path by calculating approximate fractional blockage values for a small set of those objects closest to the cone's origin. Refraction and reflection cones are determined from the optical laws of spherical mirrors and lenses as a function of the surface curvature of the object intersected and the area of intersection. The effects of scattering on reflection and refraction are simulated by further broadening the angles of the new reflection and refraction cones. The soft-edged shadows of extended light sources are reproduced by modeling the sources as spheres. A shadow cone is generated whose base is the cross-section of the light source. The light source's intensity is then scaled by the fraction of the cone that is unblocked by intervening objects. Color Plate III.14 was rendered using cone tracing; the three spheres have successively rougher surfaces, and all cast soft shadows.

Beam tracing. *Beam tracing,* introduced by Heckbert and Hanrahan [HECK84], is an object-precision algorithm for polygonal environments that traces pyramidal beams, rather than linear rays. Instead of tracing beams through each pixel, as Whitted suggested, Heckbert and Hanrahan take advantage of coherence by beginning with a single beam defined by the viewing pyramid. The viewing pyramid's beam is intersected with each polygon in the environment, in front-to-back sorted order, relative to the pyramid's apex. If a polygon is intersected, and therefore visible, it must be subtracted from the pyramid using an algorithm such as that described in Section 19.1.4. For each visible polygon fragment, two polyhedral pyramids are spawned, one each for reflection and refraction. The algorithm proceeds recursively, with termination criteria similar to those used in ray tracing. The environment is transformed into each new beam's coordinate system by means of an appropriate transformation. Although beam tracing models reflection correctly, refraction is not a linear transformation since it bends straight lines, and the refracted beam is thus only approximated. Beam tracing produces an object-precision beam tree of polygons that may be recursively rendered using a polygon scan-conversion algorithm. Each polygon is rendered using a local illumination equation, and then its reflected and refracted child polygons are rendered on top and are averaged with it, taking into account the parent's specular and transmissive properties. Beam tracing takes advantage of coherence to provide impressive speedups over conventional ray tracing at the expense of a more complex algorithm, limited object geometry, and incorrectly modeled refraction. Color Plate III.15 was rendered using this algorithm.

Beam tracing can accommodate shadows by using a variant of the Atherton–Weiler–Greenberg shadow algorithm (Section 16.4.2). Beams are traced from the point of view of each light source to determine all surfaces directly visible from the light sources, and the resulting polygons are added to the data structure as lit detail polygons that affect only the shading. This produces shadows similar to those obtained with conventional ray tracing.

Pencil tracing. Shinya, Takahashi, and Naito [SHIN87] have implemented an approach called *pencil tracing* that solves some of the problems of cone tracing and beam tracing. A *pencil* is a bundle of rays consisting of a central *axial* ray, surrounded by a set of nearby *paraxial* rays. Each paraxial ray is represented by a 4D vector that represents its relationship to the axial ray. Two dimensions express the paraxial ray's intersection with a plane perpendicular to the axial ray; the other two dimensions express the paraxial ray's direction. In many cases, only an axial ray and solid angle suffice to represent a pencil. If pencils of sufficiently small solid angle are used, then reflection and refraction can be approximated well by a linear transformation expressed as a 4×4 matrix. Shinya, Takahashi, and Naito have developed error-estimation techniques for determining an appropriate solid angle for a pencil. Conventional rays must be traced where a pencil would intersect the edge of an object, however, since the paraxial transformations are not valid in these cases.

16.12.4 Distributed Ray Tracing

The approaches we have just discussed avoid the aliasing problems of regular point sampling by casting solid beams rather than infinitesimal rays. In contrast, *distributed ray tracing,* developed by Cook, Porter, and Carpenter [COOK84b], is based on a stochastic approach to supersampling that trades off the objectionable artifacts of aliasing for the less offensive artifacts of noise [COOK86]. As we shall see, the ability to perform antialiased spatial sampling can also be exploited to sample a variety of other aspects of the scene and its objects to produce effects such as motion blur, depth of field, extended light sources, and specular reflection from rough surfaces. The word *distributed* in this technique's name refers to the fact that rays are stochastically distributed to sample the quantities that produce these effects. The basic concepts have also been applied to other algorithms besides ray tracing [COOK87].

Stochastic sampling.   As explained in Section 14.10, aliasing results when a signal is sampled with regularly spaced samples below the Nyquist rate. This is true even if we supersample and filter to compute the value of a pixel. If the samples are not regularly spaced, however, the sharply defined frequency spectrum of the aliases is replaced by noise, an artifact that viewers find much less objectionable than the individually recognizable frequency components of regular aliasing, such as staircasing.

It is not enough, however, merely to replace ray tracing's regular grid of eye rays with an equal number of rays passing through random points on the image plane, since purely random samples cluster together in some areas and leave others unsampled. Cook [COOK86] suggests the desirability of a minimum-distance Poisson distribution in which no pair of random samples is closer than some minimum distance. Calculating such a distribution is expensive, however, and even if one is created in advance, along with filters to determine each sample's contributions to neighboring pixels, a very large look-up table will be required to store the information. Instead, a satisfactory approximation to the minimum-distance Poisson distribution is obtained by displacing by a small random distance the position of each element of a regularly spaced sample grid. This technique is called *jittering*. In sampling the 2D image plane, each sample in a regular grid is jittered by two uncorrelated random quantities, one each for x and y, both generated with a sufficiently small variance that the samples do not overlap (Fig. 16.59). Figure 16.60 shows a minimum-distance Poisson distribution and a jittered regular distribution. In fact, if the

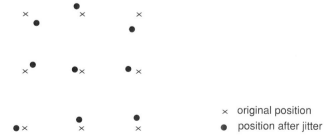

Fig. 16.59 Jittered sampling. Each sample in a regular 2D grid is jittered by two small uncorrelated random quantities. × = original position; ● = position after jitter.

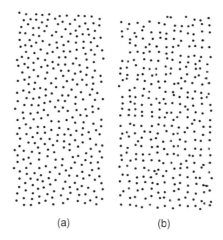

(a)   (b)

Fig. 16.60 (a) A minimum distance Poisson distribution. (b) A jittered regular distribution. (Courtesy of Mark A. Z. Dippé and Earl Wold, University of California, Berkeley.)

amount of jitter is small compared to the filter width, then the filter can be precomputed, taking into account the positions of the unjittered samples. Cook, Porter, and Carpenter found that a 4 × 4 subpixel grid is adequate for most situations. Poisson and jittered sampling are analyzed in [DIPP85], and strategies for performing adaptive stochastic sampling, including the statistical analysis of samples to determine whether to place new ones, are discussed in [DIPP85; LEE85b; KAJI86; MITC87].

Figure 16.61 compares the use of regularly spaced samples with and without added jitter to sample frequencies at rates above and below the Nyquist rate. In Fig. 16.61(a), sampling above the Nyquist rate, the shape of the signal is captured well, but with some added noise. In Fig. 16.61(b), the sampled amplitude is totally random if there is an integral number of cycles in the sampled range. If there is a fractional number of cycles in the range, then some parts of the waveform have a better chance of being sampled than do others, and thus a combination of aliasing and noise will result. The higher the frequency, the greater the proportion of noise to aliasing. Figure 16.62 demonstrates how a comb of regularly spaced triangles, each $(n + 1)/n$ pixels wide, produces an aliased image when it is sampled by regularly spaced sample points, and produces a noisy image when the sample points are jittered.

Sampling other dimensions. As long as the extra rays needed for spatial antialiasing have been cast, this same basic technique of stochastic sampling can also be used to distribute the rays to sample other aspects of the environment. Motion blur is produced by distributing rays in time. Depth of field is modeled by distributing the rays over the area of the camera lens. The blurred specular reflections and translucent refraction of rough surfaces are simulated by distributing the rays according to the specular reflection and transmission functions. Soft shadows are obtained by distributing the shadow rays over the solid angle subtended by an extended light source as seen from the point being shaded. In all cases, distributed ray tracing uses stochastic sampling to perturb the same rays that would be cast to accomplish spatial antialiasing alone.

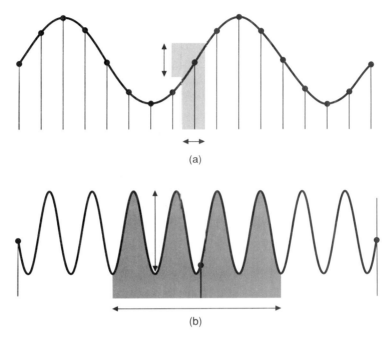

(a)

(b)

Fig. 16.61 Use of regularly spaced samples with added jitter to sample frequencies (a) above and (b) below the Nyquist rate. The nominal position of each sample is shown as a dot (●). Horizontal arrows indicate the range of jittered sample positions. Vertical arrows indicate how much sampled values can vary. (After [COOK86].)

Sampling in a nonspatial dimension is accomplished by associating each of the pixel's subsampled rays with a range of the value being sampled. Jittering is then used to determine the exact sample point. The ranges may be allocated by partitioning the entire interval being sampled into the same number of subintervals as there are subpixels and randomly allocating subintervals to subpixels. Thus, subpixel *ij* of each pixel is always associated with the same range for a particular dimension. It is important to ensure that the method of allocating the ranges for each dimension does not correlate the values of any two dimensions. For example, if temporally earlier samples tended to sample the left side of an extended light source, and later samples tended to sample the right side, then obscuring the right side of the light early in the temporal interval being depicted might have no effect on the shadow cast. In the case of temporal sampling, each object being intersected must first be moved to its position at the point in time associated with the sampling ray. Cook [COOK86] suggests computing a bounding box for the object's entire path of motion, so that the bounding-box test can be performed without the expense of moving the object.

A weighted distribution in some dimension can be simulated by applying unequal weights to evenly distributed samples. Figure 16.63(a) shows such a distribution. A more attractive alternative, however, is to use *importance sampling,* in which proportionately more sample points are located at positions of higher weight. This is accomplished by dividing the weighting filter into regions of equal area and assigning the same number of equally weighted sample points to each, as shown in Fig. 16.63(b). The amount of jitter

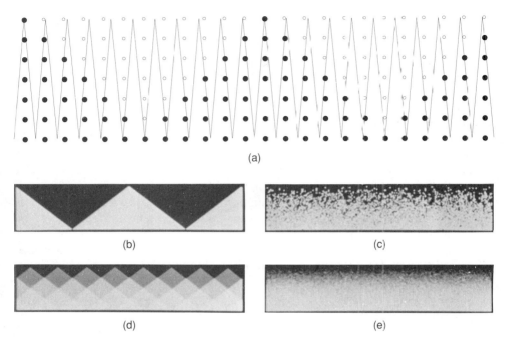

(a)

(b)   (c)

(d)   (e)

Fig. 16.62 Aliasing vs. noise. (a) A comb with regularly spaced triangles, each $(n + 1)/n$ pixels wide, sampled with one sample per pixel. o = samples that fall outside comb; ● = samples that fall inside comb. (b) A comb with 200 triangles, each 1.01 pixels wide and 50 pixels high. 1 sample/pixel, regular grid. (c) 1 sample/pixel, jittered $\pm\frac{1}{2}$ pixel. (d) 16 samples/pixel, regular grid. (e) 16 samples/pixel, jittered $\pm\frac{1}{8}$ pixel. (Images (b)–(e) by Robert Cook, Lucasfilm Ltd.)

associated with a region also varies in proportion to its size. Color Plate III.16 was created using distributed ray tracing. It shows five billiard balls with motion blur and penumbrae cast by extended light sources. Note the blurred shadows and reflections of the four moving billiard balls.

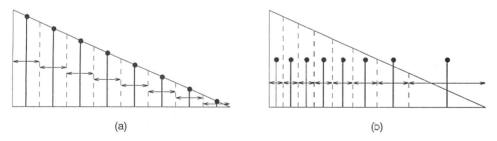

(a)   (b)

Fig. 16.63 Importance sampling is accomplished by partitioning the weighting function into regions of equal area. The horizontal axis is the dimension sampled; the vertical axis is the weighting. Dots show nominal position of samples; arrows show jitter range. (a) Evenly distributed, unequally weighted samples. (b) Importance sampling: unevenly distributed, equally weighted samples.

Path tracing and the integral equation method.   Kajiya [KAJI86] has implemented an efficient variation on distributed ray tracing called *path tracing*. Rather than each ray being grown into a binary tree, exactly one reflection or refraction ray is fired at each intersection to form a linear path, along with one ray to each light source. The decision to shoot either a reflection or a refraction ray is guided by the desired distribution of the different kinds of rays for each pixel. Kajiya has also extended this algorithm to develop a solution to the rendering equation (Eq. 16.54), called the *integral equation method*, that takes into account all ways in which light can reach a point. He uses variance-reduction methods to calculate a random variable based on the specular, diffuse, and transmission coefficients at each intersection. The random variable is used to determine whether the single ray cast from the intersection will be a specular reflection, diffuse reflection, or refraction ray, and the ray's direction is then chosen by sampling. In addition, a shadow ray is cast to a point on a light source, also chosen using variance-reduction methods. Because diffuse rays are traced, this approach models diffuse interobject reflections, an effect that we shall discuss in Section 16.13. Color Plate III.17 was rendered with the integral equation method. All objects shown are gray, except for the floor and green glass balls. The gray objects reflect green light focused by the balls and reddish light diffusely reflected from the floor, phenomena not modeled by conventional ray tracing (or by path tracing).

Kajiya's two approaches evaluate the diffuse reflection separately at each pixel, even though diffuse reflection tends to change relatively little from one pixel to the next. Ward, Rubinstein, and Clear [WARD88] have supplemented a ray tracer with a recursive diffuse reflection stage in which rays are used to trace some number of diffuse bounces from a surface to others illuminating it. Rather than computing the diffuse reflection for each pixel separately, they instead cache all of the values computed. When a pixel is processed, they use an estimate of the illuminance gradient at each cached diffuse reflection value "nearby" the pixel's intersection point to estimate the error associated with using that value. If the error is considered acceptable, then a weighted average of these cached values is used to compute a new value for the pixel; otherwise, a new diffuse calculation is made by tracing rays that sample the hemisphere, and its value is cached. The cached values can then be reused in computing other views of the same scene. Color Plate III.18 shows a series of images rendered using this technique, with different numbers of diffuse bounces. Color Plate III.19 contrasts a photograph of a conference room with a rendered image.

16.12.5   Ray Tracing from the Light Sources

One serious problem with ray tracing is caused by tracing all rays from the eye. Shadow rays are cast only to direct sources of light that are treated separately by the algorithm. Therefore, the effects of indirect reflected and refracted light sources, such as mirrors and lenses, are not reproduced properly: Light rays bouncing off a mirror do not cast shadows, and the shadows of transparent objects do not evidence refraction, since shadow rays are cast in a straight line toward the light source.

It might seem that we would need only to run a conventional ray tracer "backward" from the light sources to the eye to achieve these effects. This concept has been called *backward ray tracing,* to indicate that it runs in the reverse direction from regular ray tracing, but it is also known as *forward ray tracing* to stress that it follows the actual path from the lights to the eye. We call it *ray tracing from the light sources* to avoid confusion!

Done naively, ray tracing from the light sources results in new problems, since an insufficient number of rays ever would strike the image plane, let alone pass through the focusing lens or pinhole. Instead, ray tracing from the light sources can be used to supplement the lighting information obtained by regular ray tracing. Heckbert and Hanrahan [HECK84] suggest an elaboration of their proposed beam-tracing shadow method (Section 16.12.3) to accomplish this. If a light's beam tree is traced recursively, successive levels of the tree below the first level represent indirectly illuminated polygon fragments. Adding these to the database as surface-detail polygons allows indirect specular illumination to be modeled.

Arvo [ARVO86] has implemented a ray tracer that uses a preprocessing step in which rays from each light source are sent into the environment. Each ray is assigned an initial quota of energy, some of which is deposited at each intersection it makes with a diffusely reflecting object. He compensates for the relative sparseness of ray intersections by mapping each surface to a regular rectangular grid of counters that accumulate the deposited energy. Each ray's contribution is bilinearly partitioned among the four counters that bound the grid box in which the ray hits. A conventional ray-tracing pass is then made, in which the first pass's interpolated contributions at each intersection are used, along with the intensities of the visible light sources, to compute the diffuse reflection. Unfortunately, if a light ray strikes an object on the invisible side of a silhouette edge as seen from the eye, the ray can affect the shading on the visible side. Note that both these approaches to ray tracing from the light sources use purely specular reflectivity geometry to propagate rays in both directions.

16.13 RADIOSITY METHODS

Although ray tracing does an excellent job of modeling specular reflection and dispersionless refractive transparency, it still makes use of a directionless ambient-lighting term to account for all other global lighting contributions. Approaches based on thermal-engineering models for the emission and reflection of radiation eliminate the need for the ambient-lighting term by providing a more accurate treatment of interobject reflections. First introduced by Goral, Torrance, Greenberg, and Battaile [GORA84] and by Nishita and Nakamae [NISH85a], these algorithms assume the conservation of light energy in a closed environment. All energy emitted or reflected by every surface is accounted for by its reflection from or absorption by other surfaces. The rate at which energy leaves a surface, called its *radiosity*, is the sum of the rates at which the surface emits energy and reflects or transmits it from that surface or other surfaces. Consequently, approaches that compute the radiosities of the surfaces in an environment have been named *radiosity methods*. Unlike conventional rendering algorithms, radiosity methods first determine all the light interactions in an environment in a view-independent way. Then, one or more views are rendered, with only the overhead of visible-surface determination and interpolative shading.

16.13.1 The Radiosity Equation

In the shading algorithms considered previously, light sources have always been treated separately from the surfaces they illuminate. In contrast, radiosity methods allow any surface to emit light; thus, all light sources are modeled inherently as having area. Imagine breaking up the environment into a finite number n of discrete patches, each of which is assumed to be of finite size, emitting and reflecting light uniformly over its entire area. If we consider each patch to be an opaque Lambertian diffuse emitter and reflector, then, for surface i,

$$B_i = E_i + \rho_i \sum_{1 \le j \le n} B_j F_{j-i} \frac{A_j}{A_i}. \tag{16.58}$$

B_i and B_j are the radiosities of patches i and j, measured in energy/unit time/unit area (i.e., W / m^2). E_i is the rate at which light is emitted from patch i and has the same units as radiosity. ρ_i is patch i's reflectivity and is dimensionless. F_{j-i} is the dimensionless *form factor* or *configuration factor,* which specifies the fraction of energy leaving the entirety of patch j that arrives at the entirety of patch i, taking into account the shape and relative orientation of both patches and the presence of any obstructing patches. A_i and A_j are the areas of patches i and j.

Equation (16.58) states that the energy leaving a unit area of surface is the sum of the light emitted plus the light reflected. The reflected light is computed by scaling the sum of the incident light by the reflectivity. The incident light is in turn the sum of the light leaving the entirety of each patch in the environment scaled by the fraction of that light reaching a unit area of the receiving patch. $B_j F_{j-i}$ is the amount of light leaving a unit area of A_j that reaches all of A_i. Therefore, it is necessary to multiply by the area ratio A_j / A_i to determine the light leaving all of A_j that reaches a unit area of A_i.

Conveniently, a simple reciprocity relationship holds between form factors in diffuse environments,

$$A_i F_{i-j} = A_j F_{j-i}. \tag{16.59}$$

Thus, Eq. (16.58) can be simplified, yielding

$$B_i = E_i + \rho_i \sum_{1 \le j \le n} B_j F_{i-j}. \tag{16.60}$$

Rearranging terms,

$$B_i - \rho_i \sum_{1 \le j \le n} B_j F_{i-j} = E_i. \tag{16.61}$$

Therefore, the interaction of light among the patches in the environment can be stated as a set of simultaneous equations:

$$\begin{bmatrix} 1 - \rho_1 F_{1-1} & -\rho_1 F_{1-2} & \cdots & -\rho_1 F_{1-n} \\ -\rho_2 F_{2-1} & 1 - \rho_2 F_{2-2} & \cdots & -\rho_2 F_{2-n} \\ \cdot & \cdot & \cdots & \cdot \\ \cdot & \cdot & \cdots & \cdot \\ \cdot & \cdot & \cdots & \cdot \\ -\rho_n F_{n-1} & -\rho_n F_{n-2} & \cdots & 1 - \rho_n F_{n-n} \end{bmatrix} \begin{bmatrix} B_1 \\ B_2 \\ \cdot \\ \cdot \\ \cdot \\ B_n \end{bmatrix} = \begin{bmatrix} E_1 \\ E_2 \\ \cdot \\ \cdot \\ \cdot \\ E_n \end{bmatrix}. \tag{16.62}$$

Note that a patch's contribution to its own reflected energy must be taken into account (e.g., it may be concave); so, in the general case, each term along the diagonal is not merely 1. Equation (16.62) must be solved for each band of wavelengths considered in the lighting model, since ρ_i and E_i are wavelength-dependent. The form factors, however, are

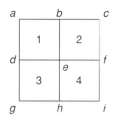

Fig. 16.64 Computing vertex radiosities from patch radiosities.

independent of wavelength and are solely a function of geometry, and thus do not need to be recomputed if the lighting or surface reflectivity changes.

Equation (16.62) may be solved using Gauss–Seidel iteration [PRES88]. yielding a radiosity for each patch. The patches can then be rendered from any desired viewpoint with a conventional visible-surface algorithm; the set of radiosities computed for the wavelength bands of each patch are that patch's intensities. Instead of using faceted shading, we can compute vertex radiosities from the patch radiosities to allow intensity interpolation shading.

Cohen and Greenberg [COHE85] suggest the following approach for determining vertex radiosities. If a vertex is interior to a surface, it is assigned the average of the radiosities of the patches that share it. If it is on the edge, then the nearest interior vertex v is found. The radiosity of the edge vertex when averaged with B_v should be the average of the radiosities of the patches that share the edge vertex. Consider the patches in Fig. 16.64. The radiosity for interior vertex e is $B_e = (B_1 + B_2 + B_3 + B_4) / 4$. The radiosity for edge vertex b is computed by finding its nearest interior vertex, e, and noting that b is shared by patches 1 and 2. Thus, to determine B_b, we use the preceding definition; $(B_b + B_e) / 2 = (B_1 + B_2) / 2$. Solving for B_b, we get $B_b = B_1 + B_2 - B_e$. The interior vertex closest to a is also e, and a is part of patch 1 alone. Thus, since $(B_a + B_e) / 2 = B_1$, we get $B_a = 2B_1 - B_e$. Radiosities for the other vertices are computed similarly.

The first radiosity method was implemented by Goral et al. [GORA84], who used contour integrals to compute exact form factors for convex environments with no occluded surfaces, as shown in Color Plate III.20. Note the correct "color-bleeding" effects due to diffuse reflection between adjacent surfaces, visible in both the model and the rendered image: diffuse surfaces are tinged with the colors of other diffuse surfaces that they reflect. For radiosity methods to become practical, however, ways to compute form factors between occluded surfaces had first to be developed.

16.13.2 Computing Form Factors

Cohen and Greenberg [COHE85] adapted an image-precision visible-surface algorithm to approximate form factors for occluded surfaces efficiently. Consider the two patches shown in Fig. 16.65. The form factor from differential area dA_i to differential area dA_j is

$$dF_{di-dj} = \frac{\cos \theta_i \cos \theta_j}{\pi r^2} H_{ij} \, dA_j. \tag{16.63}$$

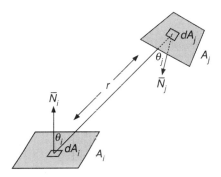

Fig. 16.65 Computing the form factor between a patch and a differential area.

For the ray between differential areas dA_i and dA_j in Fig. 16.65, θ_i is the angle that the ray makes with A_i's normal, θ_j is the angle that it makes with A_j's normal, and r is the ray's length. H_{ij} is either 1 or 0, depending on whether or not dA_j is visible from dA_i. To determine F_{di-j}, the form factor from differential area dA_i to finite area A_j, we need to integrate over the area of patch j. Thus,

$$F_{di-j} = \int_{Aj} \frac{\cos\theta_i \cos\theta_j}{\pi r^2} H_{ij} \, dA_j. \tag{16.64}$$

Finally, the form factor from A_i to A_j is the area average of Eq. (16.64) over patch i:

$$F_{i-j} = \frac{1}{A_i} \int\int_{Ai\,Aj} \frac{\cos\theta_i \cos\theta_j}{\pi r^2} H_{ij} \, dA_j \, dA_i. \tag{16.65}$$

If we assume that the center point on a patch typifies the patch's other points, then F_{i-j} can be approximated by F_{di-j} computed for dA_i at patch i's center.

Nusselt has shown [SIEG81] that computing F_{di-j} is equivalent to projecting those parts of A_j that are visible from dA_i onto a unit hemisphere centered about dA_i, projecting this projected area orthographically down onto the hemisphere's unit circle base, and dividing by the area of the circle (Fig. 16.66). Projecting onto the unit hemisphere accounts for $\cos\theta_j / r^2$ in Eq. (16.64), projecting down onto the base corresponds to a multiplication by $\cos\theta_i$, and dividing by the area of the unit circle accounts for the π in the denominator.

Rather than analytically projecting each A_j onto a hemisphere, Cohen and Greenberg developed an efficient image-precision algorithm that projects onto the upper half of a cube centered about dA_i, with the cube's top parallel to the surface (Fig. 16.67). Each face of this *hemicube* is divided into a number of equal-sized square cells. (Resolutions used in pictures included in this book range from 50 by 50 to several hundred on a face.) All the other patches are clipped to the view-volume frusta defined by the center of the cube and each of its upper five faces, and then each of the clipped patches is projected onto the appropriate face of the hemicube. An item-buffer algorithm (Section 16.12.1) is used that records the

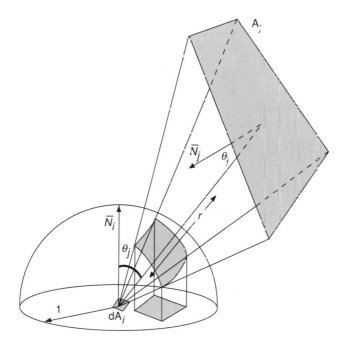

Fig. 16.66 Determining the form factor between a differential area and a patch using Nusselt's method. The ratio of the area projected onto the hemisphere's base to the area of the entire base is the form factor. (After [SIEG81].)

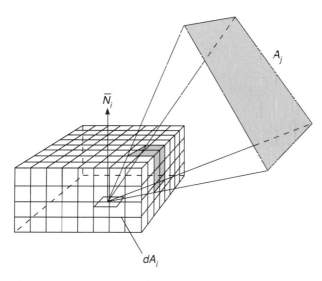

Fig. 16.67 The hemicube is the upper half of a cube centered about the patch. (After [COHE85].)

identity of the closest intersecting patch at each cell. Each hemicube cell p is associated with a precomputed delta form factor value,

$$\Delta F_p = \frac{\cos \theta_i \cos \theta_p}{\pi r^2} \Delta A, \tag{16.66}$$

where θ_p is the angle between the cell p's surface normal and the vector between dA_i and p, r is this vector's length, and ΔA is the area of a cell, as shown in Fig. 16.68. Assume that the hemicube has its own (x, y, z) coordinate system, with the origin at the center of the bottom face. For the top face in Fig. 16.68(a), we have

$$r = \sqrt{x_p^2 + y_p^2 + 1}, \tag{16.67}$$

$$\cos \theta_i = \cos \theta_p = \frac{1}{r},$$

where x_p and y_p are the coordinates of a hemicube cell. Thus, for the top face, Eq. (16.66) simplifies to

$$\Delta F_p = \frac{1}{\pi(x_p^2 + y_p^2 + 1)^2} \Delta A. \tag{16.68}$$

For a side face perpendicular to the hemicube's x axis, as shown in Fig. 16.68(b), we have

$$r = \sqrt{y_p^2 + z_p^2 + 1}, \tag{16.69}$$

$$\cos \theta_i = \frac{z_p}{r}, \qquad \cos \theta_p = \frac{1}{r}.$$

Here, Eq. (16.66) simplifies to

$$\Delta F_p = \frac{z_p}{\pi(y_p^2 + z_p^2 + 1)^2} \Delta A. \tag{16.70}$$

Because of symmetry, the values of ΔF_p need to be computed for only one-eighth of the top face and one-quarter of a single side half face.

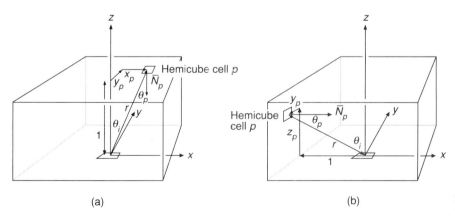

(a)   (b)

Fig. 16.68 Delta form factors. (a) The top face. (b) A side face. (After [COHE85].)

We can approximate F_{di-j} for any patch j by summing the values of ΔF_p associated with each cell p in A_j's hemicube projections. (Note that the values of ΔF_p for all the hemicube's cells sum to 1.) Assuming that the distance between the patches is large relative to the size of the patches, these values for F_{di-j} may be used as the values of F_{i-j} in Eq. (16.62) to compute the patch radiosities. Color Plate III.21(a–b) was made with the hemicube algorithm. Because much of the computation performed using the hemicube involves computing item buffers, it can take advantage of existing z-buffer hardware. On the other hand, because it uses image-precision operations, the hemicube is prone to aliasing.

Nishita and Nakamae [NISH85a] have adopted a different approach to computing form factors in occluded environments by incorporating their shadow algorithm for area light sources (Section 16.8) into a radiosity algorithm that was used to make Color Plate III.22(a–b). Color Plate III.22(c) [NISH86] adds to this a model of sky light, approximated by a large hemispherical source of diffuse light. The hemisphere is divided into bands that are transversely uniform and longitudinally nonuniform. As with other luminous surfaces, the effects of occluding objects are modeled.

16.13.3   Substructuring

The finer the patch parametrization, the better the results, at the expense of increased computation time for n^2 form factors. To prevent this square-law increase in the number of form factors, Cohen, Greenberg, Immel, and Brock [COHE86] adaptively subdivide patches into subpatches at places in the patch mesh at which a high radiosity gradient is found. The subpatches created by this *substructuring* process are not treated like full-fledged patches. Whenever a patch i is subdivided into subpatches, the form factors F_{s-j} from each subpatch s to each patch j are computed using the hemicube technique, but form factors from the patches to the subpatches are not computed. After a patch has been broken into subpatches, however, the previously calculated values of each form factor from the patch to other patches are replaced by the more accurate area-weighted average of the form factors from its m subpatches:

$$F_{i-j} = \frac{1}{A_i} \sum_{1 \leq s \leq m} F_{s-j} A_s. \tag{16.71}$$

After patch radiosities are calculated as described before, the radiosity of each subpatch s of patch i can be computed as

$$B_s = E_i + \rho_i \sum_{1 \leq j \leq n} B_j F_{s-j}. \tag{16.72}$$

The algorithm iterates, adaptively subdividing subpatches at places of high radiosity gradient, until the differences reach an acceptable level. The final subpatch radiosities are then used to determine the vertex radiosities. Color Plate III.21(b), made using a nonadaptive version of the algorithm in which subdivision is specified by the user, shows that the same image takes substantially less time to compute when patches are divided into one level of subpatches, than when an equivalent number of patches are used. The adaptive version of the algorithm is initialized with a "first guess" subdivision specified by the user. Color Plate III.21(c) was created by adaptively subdividing the subpatches of Color Plate III.21(b). Note the improved shadow resolution about the table's legs.

Substructuring allows subpatch radiosities to be determined without changing the size of the matrix to be solved in Eq. (16.62). Note that a subpatch's contribution to other patches is still approximated coarsely by its patch's radiosity, but this is a second-order effect in diffuse environments. In a similar fashion, texture mapping can be implemented by computing a single average reflectivity value for a texture-mapped patch that is used for the radiosity computations [COHE86]. When each pixel in the texture-mapped surface is finally rendered, its shade is scaled by the ratio of the texture-map reflectivity value computed for the pixel and the average reflectivity used for the patch.

16.13.4 Progressive Refinement

Given the high costs of executing the radiosity algorithm described thus far, it makes sense to ask whether it is possible to approximate the algorithm's results incrementally. Can we produce a useful, although perhaps inaccurate, image early on, which can be successively refined to greater accuracy as more time is allocated? The radiosity approach described in the previous sections will not let us do this for two reasons. First, an entire Gauss–Seidel iteration must take place before an estimate of the patch radiosities becomes available. Second, form factors are calculated between all patches at the start and must be stored throughout the computation, requiring $O(n^2)$ time and space. Cohen, Chen, Wallace, and Greenberg [COHE88] have developed a progressive-refinement radiosity algorithm that addresses both of these issues.

Consider the approach described thus far. Evaluating the ith row of Eq. (16.62) provides an estimate of patch i's radiosity, B_i, expressed in Eq. (16.60), based on the estimates of the other patch radiosities. Each term of the summation in Eq. (16.60) represents patch j's effect on the radiosity of patch i:

$$B_i \text{ due to } B_j = \rho_i B_j F_{i-j}, \qquad \text{for all } j. \qquad (16.73)$$

Thus, this approach *gathers* the light from the rest of the environment. In contrast, the progressive-refinement approach *shoots* the radiosity from a patch into the environment. A straightforward way to do this is to modify Eq. (16.73) to yield

$$B_j \text{ due to } B_i = \rho_j B_i F_{j-i}, \qquad \text{for all } j. \qquad (16.74)$$

Given an estimate of B_i, the contribution of patch i to the rest of the environment can be determined by evaluating Eq. (16.74) for each patch j. Unfortunately, this will require knowing F_{j-i} for each j, each value of which is determined with a separate hemicube. This imposes the same overwhelmingly large space–time overhead as does the original approach. By using the reciprocity relationship of Eq. (16.59), however, we can rewrite Eq. (16.74) as

$$B_j \text{ due to } B_i = \rho_j B_i F_{i-j} \frac{A_i}{A_j}, \qquad \text{for all } j. \qquad (16.75)$$

Evaluating this equation for each j requires only the form factors calculated using a single hemicube centered about patch i. If the form factors from patch i can be computed quickly (e.g., by using z-buffer hardware), then they can be discarded as soon as the radiosities shot from patch i have been computed. Thus, only a single hemicube and its form factors need to be computed and stored at a time.

As soon as a patch's radiosity has been shot, another patch is selected. A patch may be selected to shoot again after new light has been shot to it from other patches. Therefore, it is not patch i's total estimated radiosity that is shot, but rather ΔB_i, the amount of radiosity that patch i has received since the last time that it shot. The algorithm iterates until the desired tolerance is reached. Rather than choose patches in random order, it makes sense to select the patch that will make the most difference. This is the patch that has the most energy left to radiate. Since radiosity is measured per unit area, a patch i is picked for which $\Delta B_i A_i$ is the greatest. Initially, $B_i = \Delta B_i = E_i$ for all patches, which is nonzero only for light sources. The pseudocode for a single iteration is shown in Fig. 16.69.

Each execution of the pseudocode in Fig. 16.69 will cause another patch to shoot its unshot radiosity into the environment. Thus, the only surfaces that are illuminated after the first execution are those that are light sources and those that are illuminated directly by the first patch whose radiosity is shot. If a new picture is rendered at the end of each execution, the first picture will be relatively dark, and those following will get progressively brighter. To make the earlier pictures more useful, we can add an ambient term to the radiosities. With each additional pass through the loop, the ambient term will be decreased, until it disappears.

One way to estimate the ambient term uses a weighted sum of the unshot patch radiosities. First, an average diffuse reflectivity for the environment, ρ_{avg} is computed as a weighted sum of the patch diffuse reflectivities,

$$\rho_{avg} = \sum_{1 \le i \le n} \rho_i A_i \Big/ \sum_{1 \le i \le n} A_i. \tag{16.76}$$

This equation is used to compute an overall reflection factor R, intended to take into account the different reflected paths through which energy can travel from one patch to another,

$$R = 1 + \rho_{avg} + \rho_{avg}^2 + \rho_{avg}^3 + \ldots = \frac{1}{1 - \rho_{avg}}. \tag{16.77}$$

select patch i;

calculate F_{i-j} for each patch j;

for (*each patch j*) {
    $\Delta Radiosity = \rho_j \Delta B_i F_{i-j} A_i / A_j;$
    $\Delta B_j \mathrel{+}= \Delta Radiosity;$
    $B_j \mathrel{+}= \Delta Radiosity;$
}

$\Delta B_i = 0;$

Fig. 16.69 Pseudocode for shooting radiosity from a patch.

```
for (each patch i) {
    ΔBᵢ = Eᵢ;
    for (each subpatch s in i)
        Bₛ = Eᵢ;
}
```

$$AreaSum = \sum_{1 \le i \le n} A_i;$$

$$Ambient = R \sum_{1 \le i \le n} (\Delta B_i A_i)/AreaSum;$$

```
while (not converged) {
    select patch i with greatest ΔBᵢAᵢ;
    determine Fᵢ₋ₛ for all subpatches s in all patches;

    /* ΔEnergy is initialized to the total energy shot. */
    ΔEnergy = ΔBᵢAᵢ;

    /* Shoot radiosity from patch i. */
    for (each patch j seen by i) {
        OldΔB = ΔBⱼ;
        for (each subpatch s in j seen by i) {
            ΔRadiosity = ρⱼΔBᵢFᵢ₋ₛAᵢ/Aₛ;
            Bₛ += ΔRadiosity;
            ΔBⱼ += ΔRadiosity Aₛ/Aⱼ;
        }
        /* Decrement ΔEnergy by total energy gained by patch j. */
        ΔEnergy -= (ΔBⱼ − OldΔB) Aⱼ;
    }

    determine vertex radiosities from subpatch radiosities, using
        Bₛ + ρⱼ Ambient as radiosity of subpatch s of patch j;
    if (radiosity gradient between adjacent vertices is too high)
        subdivide offending subpatches and reshoot from patch i to them;
    ΔBᵢ = 0;

    perform view-dependent visible-surface determination and shading;

    /* Use ΔEnergy (energy absorbed by patches hit) to determine new value of Ambient. */
    Ambient -= R ΔEnergy / AreaSum;
}   /* while */
```

Fig. 16.70 Pseudocode for progressive-refinement radiosity method with ambient light and substructuring.

Each patch's unshot radiosity is weighted by the ratio of the patch's area to the environment's area, providing an approximation to the form factor from an arbitrary differential area to that patch. Thus, the estimate of the ambient term accounting for unshot radiosity is

$$Ambient = R \sum_{1 \leq i \leq n} (\Delta B_i A_i) / \sum_{1 \leq i \leq n} A_i. \tag{16.78}$$

This ambient term is used to augment the patch's radiosity for display purposes only, yielding

$$B'_i = B_i + \rho_i Ambient. \tag{16.79}$$

Figure 16.70 shows the pseudocode for the entire algorithm. Substructuring is provided by shooting radiosity from patches to subpatches to determine subpatch radiosities. Thus, hemicubes are created for patches, but not for subpatches. Adaptive subdivision is accomplished by subdividing a patch further when the radiosity gradient between adjacent subpatch vertices is found to be too high. Color Plate III.23, which is rendered using an ambient term, depicts stages in the creation of an image after 1, 2, 24, and 100 iterations.

16.13.5   Computing More Accurate Form Factors

Although the use of fast z-buffer hardware makes the hemicube an efficient algorithm, the technique has a number of failings [BAUM89; WALL89]:

- Recall that the identity of only one patch is stored per hemicube pixel. Therefore, a grid of patches may alias when projected onto a side of the hemicube, just as they would when processed with a z-buffer algorithm. This can show up as a regular pattern of patches that are not represented in the hemicube. Furthermore, a patch that is small when projected on the hemicube may be large when projected on the image plane.

- Use of the hemicube assumes that the center point of a patch is representative of the patch's visibility to other patches. If this assumption is shown to be untrue, the surface can be broken up into subpatches, but there is only a single subdivision granularity for the patch; the same patch cannot be subdivided to different levels for different patches that it views.

- Patches must be far from each other for the hemicube approach to be correct. This is a serious problem if two patches are adjacent; since all calculations are done from the center of the hemicube, the form factor will be underestimated, because the calculations do not take into account the proximity of the adjacent parts of the patches.

A progressive radiosity approach developed by Wallace, Elmquist, and Haines [WALL89] uses ray tracing to evaluate form factors, instead of the hemicube. When a source patch is to shoot its radiosity, rays are fired from each vertex in the scene to the source to compute the form factor from the source to the vertex. This is accomplished by decomposing the source patch into a number of small finite subareas, each of which is the target of a ray shot from a vertex. If the ray is not occluded, then the target is visible, and the form factor between the differential vertex and the finite area target is computed, using an analytic expression, based on some simplifying geometric assumptions. If desired, the ray intersection calculations can be performed with a resolution-independent true curved-surface database, so that the time for an individual ray test does not depend on the number of polygons. The form factor between the vertex and the entire source is computed as an area-weighted average of the form factors between each subarea and the vertex, and the result is used to compute the contribution of the source to the vertex. This approach has a number of advantages. Radiosities are computed at the vertices themselves, where they are ultimately needed for shading. Vertex normals can be used, allowing polygonal meshes that approximate curved surfaces. Nonphysical point light sources can be handled by tracing a single ray to the light source and using its illumination equation to determine the irradiance at each vertex. The number of areas into which a source is decomposed and whether rays are actually fired (i.e., if shadow testing is to be performed) can all be determined individually for each vertex. Color Plates III.24 and III.25 were created using this algorithm.

A contrasting approach to solving inaccuracies caused by the hemicube is taken by Baum, Rushmeier, and Winget [BAUM89]. They recognize that the hemicube form factors often are accurate; therefore, they have developed error-analysis tests to choose, for each patch, when to use the hemicube, when to subdivide the patch further, and when to use a more expensive, but more accurate, analytic technique for computing form factors.

16.13.6 Specular Reflection

The radiosity methods described so far treat only diffuse reflection. Therefore, all of a patch's radiosity may be treated uniformly when it is dispersed to other patches: The radiosity leaving a patch in any direction is influenced by the patch's total radiosity, not by the directions from which its incoming energy was acquired. Immel, Cohen, and Greenberg [IMME86] extended the radiosity method to model specular reflection. Rather than compute a single radiosity value for each patch, they partition the hemisphere over the patch into a finite set of solid angles, each of which establishes a direction for incoming or outgoing energy. Given the patch's bidirectional reflectivity (Section 16.7), they compute the outgoing radiosity in each direction in terms of its emittance in that direction and the incident light from each of the set of directions, weighting each direction's contribution accordingly. Finally, they render a picture from intensities that are determined at each vertex by using the direction from the vertex to the eye to interpolate among the closest directional radiosities. Although the results shown in Color Plate III.26 are promising, the approach has a tremendous overhead in both time and space, which will only increase if highly specular surfaces are modeled. One solution is to combine a radiosity method with ray tracing.

16.13.7 Combining Radiosity and Ray Tracing

Consider the tradeoffs between radiosity methods and ray tracing. Radiosity methods are well suited to diffuse reflection because a diffuse surface's bidirectional reflectivity is constant in all outgoing directions. Thus, all radiosities computed are view-independent. On the other hand, the pure radiosity method for specular surfaces described previously is not practical, because specular reflection from a surface is highly dependent on the angle with which an observer (or another surface) views the surface. Therefore, much extra information must be computed, because no information about the desired view is provided. In addition, this directional information is discretized and must be interpolated to accommodate a specific view. Not only does the interpolation make it impossible to model sharp reflections, but also the sampling performed by the discretization can result in aliasing.

In contrast, ray tracing calculates specular reflections well, since the eyepoint is known in advance. Although conventional ray tracing does not model global diffuse phenomena, some of the approaches discussed in Section 16.12.4 do. Correctly solving for the diffuse reflection from a piece of surface requires that all the surfaces with which a surface exchanges energy be taken into account; in short, it requires a radiosity method.

It makes sense to combine ray tracing and radiosity to take advantage of ray tracing's ability to model specular phenomena and of the radiosity method's ability to model diffuse interactions. Unfortunately, simply summing the pixel values computed by a diffuse radiosity method and a specular ray tracer will not suffice. For example, the diffuse radiosity method will fail to take into account the extra illumination falling on a diffuse surface from a specular surface. It is necessary to account for transfer from diffuse to diffuse, diffuse to specular, specular to diffuse, and specular to specular reflection.

Wallace, Cohen, and Greenberg [WALL87] describe a two-pass approach that combines a view-independent radiosity method, executed in the first pass, with a view-dependent ray-tracing approach, executed in the second pass. As mentioned previously, the first pass must take into account specular, as well as diffuse, reflection. If only perfect, mirrorlike specular reflection is allowed, this can be supported by reflecting each patch about the plane of a specular surface [RUSH86]. Each specular patch is thus treated as a window onto a "mirror world." The form factor from a patch to one of these mirror reflections accounts for the specular reflection from the patch that is doing the mirroring.

In the second view-dependent pass, a *reflection frustum* is erected at each point on a surface that corresponds to a pixel in the image. As shown in Fig. 16.71, the reflection frustum consists of a little z-buffer, positioned perpendicular to the reflection direction and covering the small incoming solid angle that is most significant for the surface's

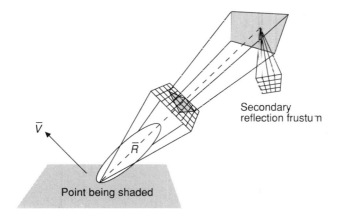

Fig. 16.71 The reflection frustum. (After [WALL87].)

bidirectional reflectivity. The patches are z-buffered onto the frustum, using Gouraud shading to interpolate the patches' first-pass diffuse intensities across their projections. A ray is traced recursively through each pixel on the frustum that sees a specular surface, spawning a new reflection frustum at each intersection. The values computed for each frustum pixel are then weighted to model the surface's ρ_s. The second pass thus uses specular transport to combine radiosities determined during the first pass. Transparency can be accommodated by erecting a transmission frustrum in the direction of refraction. The image on the cover of this book (Color Plate I.9) was created using this algorithm.

The mirror-world approach used in the first pass handles only perfect specular reflection and results in a proliferation of form factors. Shao, Peng, and Liang [SHAO88] have implemented a two-pass approach that allows Phong-like bidirectional reflectance functions in the first pass, without the need to duplicate patches.

Sillion and Puech [SILL89] extend the two-pass technique to calculate *extended form factors* in the first pass that model any number of specular reflections or refractions. Rather than proliferating mirror-reflection form factors, they instead use recursive ray tracing to compute the form factors, as well as in the view-dependent second pass. Color Plate III.27 demonstrates why the diffuse first pass must take specular reflection into account. Color Plate III.27(a) shows the results of a conventional diffuse radiosity approach. (The part of the table near the mirror is lit by light diffusely reflected from the inside of the tall lamp.) The conventional diffuse first pass was augmented with a pure ray-tracing second pass to produce Color Plate III.27(b), which includes a specular reflection from the mirror. In contrast, Color Plate III.27(c) shows the results of Sillion and Puech's two-pass approach. It shares the same ray-tracing second pass as Color Plate III.27(b), but uses extended form factors in the first pass. Each surface acts as a diffuse illuminator in the first pass, but the use of the extended form factors means that the diffusely emitted energy takes specular interreflection into account. Note the light specularly reflected from the mirror onto the table and the back of the vase during the first pass. Color Plate III.28 is a more complex example that includes a reflecting sphere.

16.14   THE RENDERING PIPELINE

Now that we have seen a variety of different ways to perform visible-surface determination, illumination, and shading, we shall review how these processes fit into the standard graphics pipeline introduced in Chapter 7 and depicted in Fig. 7.26. For simplicity, we assume polygonal environments, unless otherwise specified. Chapter 18 provides a more detailed discussion of how some of these pipelines may be implemented in hardware.

16.14.1   Local Illumination Pipelines

z-buffer and Gouraud shading.   Perhaps the most straightforward modification to the pipeline occurs in a system that uses the z-buffer visible-surface algorithm to render Gouraud-shaded polygons, as shown in Fig. 16.72. The z-buffer algorithm has the advantage that primitives may be presented to it in any order. Therefore, as before, primitives are obtained by traversing the database, and are transformed by the modeling transformation into the WC system.

Primitives may have associated surface normals that were specified when the model was built. Since the lighting step will require the use of surface normals, it is important to

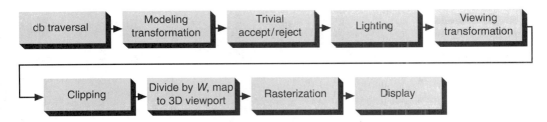

Fig. 16.72 Rendering pipeline for z-buffer and Gouraud shading

remember that normals must be transformed correctly, using the methods discussed in the Appendix. Furthermore, we cannot just ignore stored normals and attempt to recompute new ones later using the correctly transformed vertices. The normals defined with the objects may represent the true surface geometry, or may specify user-defined surface blending effects, rather than just being the averages of the normals of shared faces in the polygonal mesh approximation.

Our next step is to cull primitives that fall entirely outside of the window and to perform back-face culling. This trivial-reject phase is typically performed now because we want to eliminate unneeded processing in the lighting step that follows. Now, because we are using Gouraud shading, the illumination equation is evaluated at each vertex. This operation must be performed in the WC system (or in any coordinate system isometric to it), before the viewing transformation (which may include skew and perspective transformations), to preserve the correct angle and distance from each light to the surface. If vertex normals were not provided with the object, they may be computed immediately before lighting the vertices. Culling and lighting are often performed in a lighting coordinate system that is a rigid body transformation of WC (e.g., VRC when the view orientation matrix is created with the standard PHIGS utilities).

Next objects are transformed to NPC by the viewing transformation and clipped to the view volume. Division by W is performed, and objects are mapped to the viewport. If an object is partially clipped, correct intensity values must be calculated for vertices created during clipping. At this point, the clipped primitive is submitted to the z-buffer algorithm, which performs rasterization, interleaving scan conversion with the interpolation needed to compute the z value and color-intensity values for each pixel. If a pixel is determined to be visible, its color-intensity values may be further modified by depth cueing (Eq. 16.11), not shown here.

Although this pipeline may seem straightforward, there are many new issues that must be dealt with to provide an efficient and correct implementation. For example, consider the problems raised by handling curved surfaces, such as B-spline patches, which must be tessellated. Tessellation should occur after transformation into a coordinate system in which screen size can be determined. This enables tessellation size to be determined adaptively, and limits the amount of data that is transformed. On the other hand, tessellated primitives must be lit in a coordinate system isometric to world coordinates. Abi-Ezzi [ABIE89] addresses these issues, proposing a more efficient, yet more complex, formulation of the pipeline that incorporates feedback loops. This new pipeline uses a lighting coordinate system that is an isometric (i.e., rigid or Euclidean) transformation of WC, yet is computationally close to DC to allow tessellation decisions to be made efficiently.

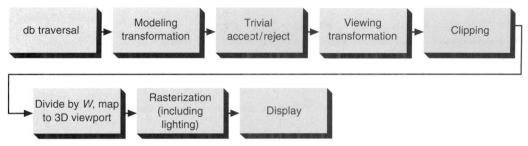

Fig. 16.73 Rendering pipeline for z-buffer and Phong shading.

z-buffer and Phong shading. This simple pipeline must be modified if we wish to accommodate Phong shading, as shown in Fig. 16.73. Because Phong shading interpolates surface normals, rather than intensities, the vertices cannot be lit early in the pipeline. Instead, each object must be clipped (with properly interpolated normals created for each newly created vertex), transformed by the viewing transformation, and passed to the z-buffer algorithm. Finally, lighting is performed with the interpolated surface normals that are derived during scan conversion. Thus, each point and its normal must be backmapped into a coordinate system that is isometric to WC to evaluate the illumination equation.

List-priority algorithm and Phong shading. When a list-priority algorithm is used, primitives obtained from traversal and processed by the modeling transformation are inserted in a separate database, such as a BSP tree, as part of preliminary visible-surface determination. Figure 16.74 presents the pipeline for the BSP tree algorithm, whose preliminary visible-surface determination is view-independent. As we noted in Chapter 7, the application program and the graphics package may each keep separate databases. Here, we see that rendering can require yet another database. Since, in this case, polygons are split, correct shading information must be determined for the newly created vertices. The rendering database can now be traversed to return primitives in a correct, back-to-front order. The overhead of building this database can, of course, be applied toward the creation of multiple pictures. Therefore, we have shown it as a separate pipeline whose output is a new database. Primitives extracted from the rendering database are clipped and normalized, and are presented to the remaining stages of the pipeline. These stages are structured much like those used for the z-buffer pipeline, except that the only visible-surface process they need to perform is to guarantee that each polygon will correctly overwrite any

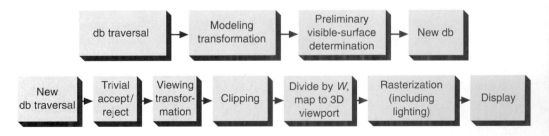

Fig. 16.74 Rendering pipeline for list-priority algorithm and Phong shading.

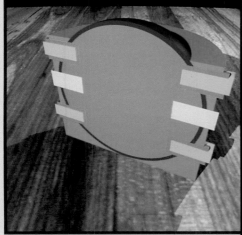

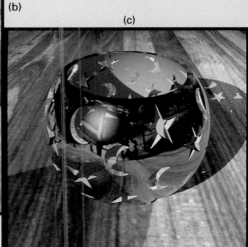

(a)

(b)

(c)

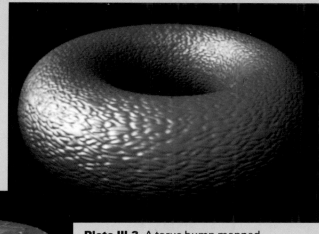

Plate III.3 A torus bump mapped with a hand-generated bump function (Section 16.3.3). (By Jim Blinn. Courtesy of University of Utah.)

Plate III.4 A strawberry bump mapped with a hand-generated bump function (Section 16.3.3). (By Jim Blinn. Courtesy of University of Utah.)

Plate III.5 Objects with shadows generated by two-pass object-precision algorithm of Section 16.4.2. (a) One light source. (b) Two light sources. (Peter Atherton, Kevin Weiler, and Donald P. Greenberg, Program of Computer Graphics, Cornell University, 1978.)

(a)   (b)

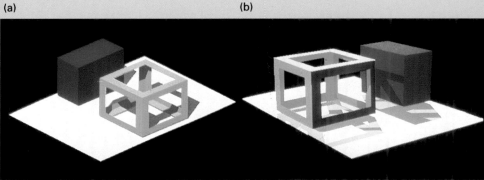

Plate III.6 Room with shadows generated by object-precision shadow-volume BSP tree algorithm of Section 16.4.3. (a) Scene with two point light sources. (b) Same scene with black lines indicating polygon fragmentation. Dark gray fragments are lit by no lights, light gray fragments are lit by one light, and non-gray fragments are lit by both lights. (Courtesy of Norman Chin, Columbia University.)

(a)

(b)

Plate III.7 Nonrefractive transparency using extended z-buffer algorithm of Section 16.5.1. Unterlafette database is courtesy of CAM-I (Computer Aided Manufacturing International, Inc., Arlington, TX). (Rendered on a Stardent 1000 by Abraham Mammen.)

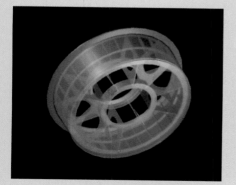

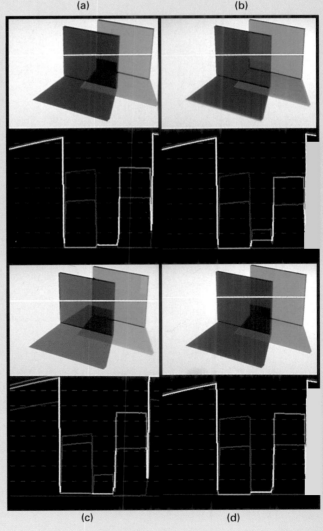

(a)   (b)

Plate III.8 Two vases rendered with the Cook-Torrance illumination model (Section 16.7). Both are lit by two lights with $I_{i_1} = I_{i_2} =$ CIE standard illuminant D6500, $d\omega_{i_1} = 0.0001$, and $d\omega_{i_2} = 0.0002$; $I_a = 0.01 I_{i_1}$; $\rho_d =$ the bidirectional reflectivity of copper for normal incidence; $\rho_a = \pi\rho_d$. (a) Copper-colored plastic: $k_s = 0.1$; $F =$ reflectivity of a vinyl mirror; $D =$ Beckmann function with $m = 0.15$; $k_d = 0.9$. (b) Copper metal: $k_s = 1.0$; $F =$ reflectivity of a copper mirror; $D =$ Beckmann function with $m_1 = 0.4$, $w_1 = 0.4$, $m_2 = 0.2$, $w_2 = 0.6$; $k_d = 0.0$. (By Robert Cook, Program of Computer Graphics, Cornell University.)

Plate III.9 Comparison of spectral sampling techniques for two overlapping filters (Section 16.9). Plots show RGB values for marked scan line with red (R), green (G), and magenta (B) lines. (a) One sample per nm from 360–830 nm. (b) 3 CIE XYZ samples. (c) 3 RGB samples. (d) 9 spectral samples. (Roy A. Hall and Donald P. Greenberg, Program of Computer Graphics, Cornell University, 1983.)

(a)   (b)

(c)   (d)

Plate III.10 Spheres and checkerboard. An early image produced with recursive ray tracing (Section 16.12). (Courtesy of Turner Whitted, Bell Laboratories.)

(a)

Plate III.11 Ray-traced images. (a) Scene from short film *Quest* (1985). (Michael Sciulli, James Arvo, and Melissa White. © Hewlett-Packard.) (b) "Haute Air." Functions were used to modify color, surface normals, and transparency at nearly every pixel. (Courtesy of David Kurlander, Columbia University, 1986.)

(b)

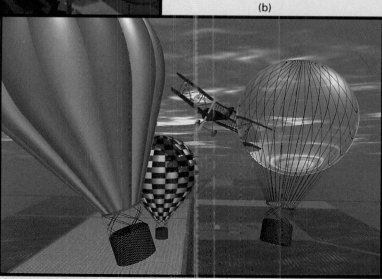

Plate III.12 Images ray-traced with the light-buffer algorithm (Section 16.12.1). Rendered with 50 × 50 light buffers on a VAX 11/780. (a) Glass-leaved tree. 768 objects (6 polygons, 256 spheres, 511 quadrics) and 3 lights. A 512 × 480 resolution version was rendered in 412 minutes with light buffers, 1311 minutes without. (b) Kitchen. 224 objects (1298 polygons, 4 spheres, 76 cylinders, 35 quadrics) and 5 lights. A 436 × 479 resolution version was rendered in 246 minutes with light buffers, 602 minutes without. (Eric Haines and Donald P. Greenberg, Program of Computer Graphics, Cornell University, 1986.)

(a)

(b)

Plate III.13 Comparison of illumination models for ray tracing (Section 16.12.2). Note differences in reflectivity of the base of the dish, and the color of the transparent and reflective spheres. (a) Whitted illumination model. (b) Hall illumination model. (Roy A. Hall and Donald P. Greenberg, Program of Computer Graphics, Cornell University, 1983.)

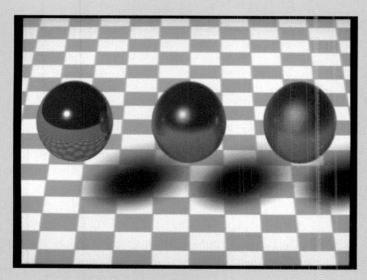

Plate III.14 Cone tracing (Section 16.12.3). Three spheres. Dull reflections are created by increasing the angular spread of reflected rays by 0.0, 0.2, and 0.4 radians, respectively, for spheres from left to right. (Courtesy of John Amanatides, University of Toronto.)

Plate III.15 Beam tracing (Section 16.12.3). A mirrored cube in a texture-mapped room. (Paul Heckbert and Pat Hanrahan, © NYIT 1984.)

Plate III.16 *1984.* Rendered using distributed ray tracing (Section 16.12.4) at 4096 × 3550 pixels with 16 samples per pixel. Note the motion-blurred reflections and shadows with penumbrae cast by extended light sources. (By Thomas Porter. © Pixar 1984. All Rights Reserved.)

Plate III.17 Scene rendered with integral equation method (Section 16.12.4). All opaque objects are Lambertian. Note interobject reflections. Computed at 512 × 512 resolution with 40 paths/pixel in 1221 minutes on an IBM 3081. (J. Kajiya, California Institute of Technology.)

(a)

(b)

Plate III.18 Daylit office rendered by ray tracing with diffuse interreflection (Section 16.12.4). (a) Direct illumination only. (b) 1 diffuse bounce. (c) 7 diffuse bounces. (Courtesy of Greg Ward, Lawrence Berkeley Laboratory.)

(c)

Plate III.19 Conference room. (a) Photograph of actual room. (b) Model rendered by ray tracing, using same software used for Color Plate III.18, but without interreflection calculation. (Courtesy of Greg Ward, Anat Grynberg, and Francis Rubinstein, Lawrence Berkeley Laboratory.)

(a)

(b)

Plate III.20 Radiosity (Section 16.13.1). Cube with six diffuse walls (emissive white front wall is not shown). (a) Photograph of actual cube. (b) Model rendered with 49 patches per side, using constant shading. (c) Model rendered with 49 patches per side, using interpolated shading. (Cindy M. Goral, Kenneth E. Torrance, Donald P. Greenberg, and Bennett Battaile, Program of Computer Graphics, Cornell University, 1984.)

(b)

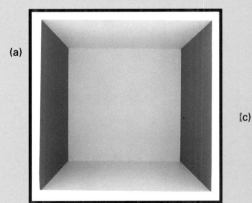

(a)

(c)

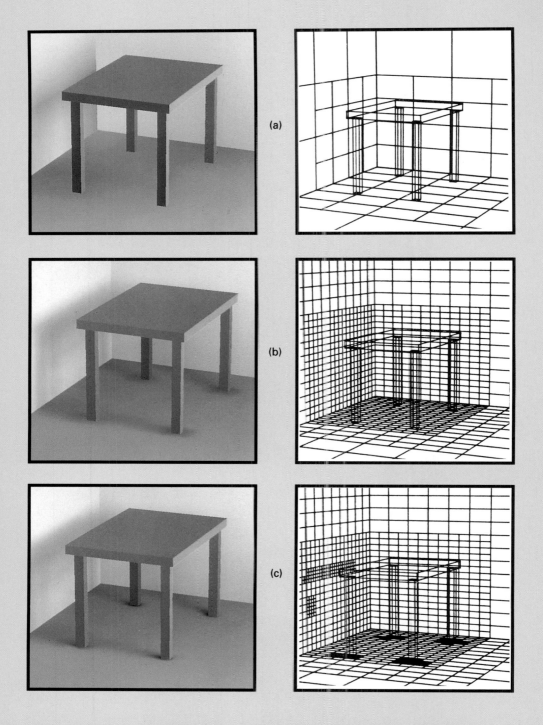

Plate III.21 Radiosity algorithm, using hemicube to compute form factors (Sections 16.13.2–3). (a) Coarse patch solution (145 patches, 10 minutes). (b) Improved solution using either more patches (1021 patches, 175 minutes) or substructuring (1021 subpatches, 62 minutes). (c) Refinement of substructured version of (b) using adaptive subdivision (1306 sub-patches, 24 additional minutes).(Michael F. Cohen, Program of Computer Graphics, Cornell University, 1985.)

Plate III.22 Machine room rendered with different lighting models (Sections 16.13.2 and 20.8.2) and shadow volumes for extended lights (Section 16.8). (a) Lit by area light source window. (b) Lit by overhead panel lights. (c) Lit by model of clear skylight. (d) Lit by model including atmospheric scattering. Parts (a–c) use a radiosity algorithm. (T. Nishita (Fukuyama University) and E. Nakamae (Hiroshima University).)

(a)

(b)

(c)

(d)

Plate III.23 Office rendered with progressive-refinement hemicube radiosity algorithm (Section 16.13.4); 500 patches, 7000 subpatches. Estimated ambient radiosity is added. Computing and displaying each iteration took about 15 seconds on an HP 9000 Model 825 SRX. (a) 1 iteration. (b) 2 iterations. (c) 24 iterations. (d) 100 iterations. (Shenchang Eric Chen, Michael F. Cohen, John R. Wallace, and Donald P. Greenberg, Program of Computer Graphics, Cornell University, 1988.)

(a)

(b)

(c)

(d)

Plate III.24 Nave of Chartres cathedral rendered with progressive-refinement radiosity algorithm, using ray tracing to compute form factors (Section 16.13.5). Two bays, containing 9916 polygons, were processed and copied three more times. Sixty iterations took 59 minutes on HP 9000 Model 835 TurboSRX. (By John Wallace and John Lin, using Hewlett-Packard's Starbase Radiosity and Ray Tracing software. © 1989, Hewlett-Packard Co.)

Plate III.25 Boiler room rendered with progressive-refinement radiosity algorithm, using ray tracing to compute form factors. (By John Wallace, John Lin, and Eric Haines, using Hewlett-Packard's Starbase Radiosity and Ray Tracing software. © 1989, Hewlett-Packard Company.)

Plate III.26 Specular radiosity algorithm (Section 16.13.6); 64 specular patches and 237 diffuse patches. (David S. Immel, Michael F. Cohen, Donald P. Greenberg, Program of Computer Graphics, Cornell University, 1986.)

(a)   (b)

(c)

Plate III.27 Combining radiosity and ray tracing (Section 16.13.7). (a) Diffuse radiosity algorithm. (b) Diffuse first pass and ray-traced second pass. (c) Diffuse first pass with extended form factors and ray-traced second pass. (Courtesy of François Sillion, Liens, Ecole Normale Superieure, Paris, France.)

Plate III.28 Room rendered with combined radiosity and ray tracing. (Courtesy of François Sillion, Liens, Ecole Normale Superieure, Paris, France.)

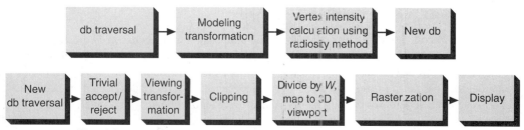

Fig. 16.75 Rendering pipeline for radiosity and Gouraud shading.

previously scan-converted polygon that it intersects. Even this simple overwrite capability is not needed if we instead use an object-precision algorithm that generates a list of fully visible primitives, such as the Weiler–Atherton algorithm.

16.14.2 Global Illumination Pipelines

Thus far, we have ignored global illumination. As we have noted before, incorporating global illumination effects requires information about the geometric relationships between the object being rendered and the other objects in the world. One approach, of which we have seen many examples, is to calculate needed information from a specific viewpoint in advance of scan conversion and to store it in tables (e.g., reflection maps and shadow maps). This eliminates the need to access the full db representation of other objects while processing the current object. In the case of shadows, which depend only on the position of the light source, and not on that of the viewer, preprocessing the environment to add surface-detail polygon shadows is another way to allow the use of an otherwise conventional pipeline.

Radiosity.   The diffuse radiosity algorithms offer an interesting example of how to take advantage of the conventional pipeline to achieve global-illumination effects. These algorithms process objects and assign to them a set of view-independent vertex intensities. These objects may then be presented to a modified version of the pipeline for z-buffer and Gouraud shading, depicted in Fig. 16.75, that eliminates the lighting stage.

Ray tracing.   Finally, we consider ray tracing, whose pipeline, shown in Fig. 16.76, is the simplest because those objects that are visible at each pixel and their illumination are determined entirely in WC. Once objects have been obtained from the database and transformed by the modeling transformation, they are loaded into the ray tracer's WC database, which is typically implemented using the techniques of Sections 15.10.2 and 16.12.1, to support efficient ray intersection calculations.

Fig. 16.76 Rendering pipeline for ray tracing.

16.14.3   Designing Flexible Renderers

As we have seen, a wide variety of illumination and shading models has been created. The choice of which to use may be based on concerns as diverse as increasing efficiency, increasing realism, or obtaining visually interesting effects. Simply put, there is no one model that pleases all users. Therefore, several design approaches have been suggested to increase the ease with which illumination and shading algorithms may be implemented and used.

Modularization.   A straightforward approach is to modularize the illumination and shading model in a part of the rendering system that is often known as its *shader*. Whitted and Weimer [WHIT82] showed that, by establishing a standard mechanism for passing parameters to shaders, different shaders can be used in the same system; the decision about which shader to call can even be made at run time based on some attribute of the object. Their system performs scan conversion using a scan-line algorithm, and accumulates results as a linked list of spans for each line. Each span contains information about a set of values associated with its endpoints, including their x and z values, and additional information such as normal components, and intensities. The shader interpolates specified values across each span. (Since it typically uses the interpolated z values to perform visible-surface determination with a scan-line z-buffer, the term *shader* is being used quite loosely.)

The Doré graphics system [ARDE89] is designed to offer the programmer additional flexibility. It provides a standard way of expressing a scene database in terms of a set of objects that have methods for performing operations such as rendering, picking, or computing a bounding volume. The display list and its traversal functions form a common core that is intended to make it easy to interface to different rendering systems. A programmer can use the standard set of objects, methods, and attributes, or can design her own using the framework.

Special languages.   In contrast to providing extensibility at the level of the programming language in which the system is built, it is possible to design special languages that are better suited to specific graphics tasks. Cook [COOK84a] has designed a special-purpose language in which a shader is built as a tree expression called a *shade tree*. A shade tree is a tree of nodes, each of which takes parameters from its children and produces parameters for its parent. The parameters are the terms of the illumination equation, such as the specular coefficient, or the surface normal. Some nodes, such as *diffuse, specular,* or *square root,* are built into the language with which shade trees are specified. Others can be defined by the user and dynamically loaded when needed. All nodes can access information about the lights. Figure 16.77 shows a shade tree for a description of copper. A shade tree thus describes a particular shading process and is associated with one or more objects through use of a separate modeling language. Different objects may have different shade trees, so that an image can be rendered in which a multiplicity of different special-purpose models are mixed. Similarly, in Cook's system, lights and their parameters are defined by light trees, and atmospheric effects, such as haze, are defined by atmosphere trees.

Perlin [PERL85] has developed the notion of a *pixel-stream editor* that takes as input and produces as output arrays of pixels. A pixel is not rigidly defined and may include

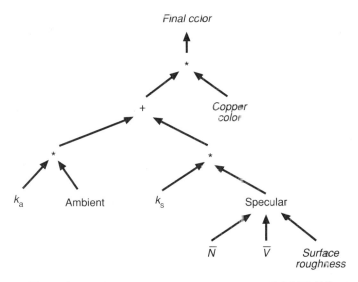

Fig. 16.77 Shade tree for copper. (After [COOK84].)

arbitrary data for a point in the image, such as the material identifier or normal vector at that point. An output pixel need not have the same structure as an input pixel. The pixel-stream editor executes a program written by the user in a high-level language oriented toward pixel manipulation. Thus, the user is encouraged to think of creating images in a series of passes, with intermediate results represented by arrays of pixels that may differ in the kind of information they encode.

The flexibility of shade trees and pixel-stream editors may be combined by designing a rendering system that allows its users to write their own shaders in a special programming language and to associate them with selected objects. This approach is taken in the RenderMan Interface [PIXA88; UPST89], a scene description specification that provides such a shading language. RenderMan defines a set of key places in the rendering process at which user-defined or system-defined shaders can be called. For example, the most common kind of shader, called a *surface shader,* returns the light reflected in a specified direction given a point on the surface, its orientation, and a set of light sources. A user-provided surface shader could implement an illumination equation totally different from those discussed so far. Other shaders include atmosphere shaders that modify the color of light passing between two points, and—in another example of how the word *shader* can be stretched—projection shaders that allow user-defined projections implementing other than parallel or linear perspective projections.

An example. Cook, Carpenter, and Catmull's Reyes Rendering Architecture [COOK87], which was used to produce Color Plates II.24–37, D, and F, provides an interesting example of how to structure a renderer. Reyes chops all objects up into *micropolygons*: small, constant-shaded quadrilaterals that are approximately ½ pixel on a side. This approach, known as *dicing,* occurs along boundaries that are natural for the object. A patch, for example, is diced parallel to its (s,t) coordinate system. Dicing is performed prior to perspective transformation, based on an estimate of the size of the resulting micropolygons after projection. Much like Catmull's patch subdivision algorithm of Section 15.9, which subdivides patches until they are pixel-sized, Reyes subdivides objects until they are sufficiently small. Each kind of object is associated with a procedure that determines whether it should be subdivided further into other primitives or diced. An object is subdivided further if no method has been provided for dicing it directly, if it is determined that it would give rise to too many micropolygons, or if it is estimated that its micropolygons would differ too much in their final projected size. This recursive subdivision must ultimately result in objects that can be diced. To avoid the need to clip objects analytically to the view volume, when Reyes subdivides objects, only those parts that are at least partially within the view volume are kept. Perspective problems that would result from projecting an object that is too close to or behind the eye are avoided by subdividing further any object that spans both the hither plane and another plane that lies slightly in front of the eye.

Dicing an object results in a quadrilateral mesh of micropolygons that is shaded in WC. Because the micropolygons are sufficiently small, each is given a single shade, avoiding all the interpolated shading problems discussed in Section 16.2.6. Since a patch is diced parallel to its (s,t) coordinate system, some of the texture-mapping approaches discussed in Chapter 17 are particularly efficient to use. Dicing and shading can both take advantage of incremental algorithms. Reyes relies on the mapping techniques discussed in this chapter for its global lighting effects.

Visible surface determination is done with a subpixel z-buffer whose subpixel centers are jittered to accomplish stochastic sampling. The closest micropolygon covering a subpixel center is visible at that subpixel. To avoid the need to store micropolygon meshes and subpixel z and intensity values for the entire image, Reyes uses spatial partitioning. The image is divided into rectangular partitions into which each object is sorted by the upper left hand corner of its extent. The partitions are then processed left to right, top to bottom. As objects are subdivided or diced, the resulting subobjects or micropolygons are placed in the partitions that they intersect. Thus, only enough z-buffer memory is needed for a single partition, and other storage needed for a partition can be freed after it is processed.

16.14.4 Progressive Refinement

One interesting modification to the pipelines that we have discussed takes advantage of the fact that the image is viewed for a finite time. Instead of attempting to render a final version of a picture all at once, we can first render the picture coarsely, and then *progressively refine* it, to improve it. For example, a first image might have no antialiasing, simpler object models, and simpler shading. As the user views an image, idle cycles may be spent improving its quality [FORR85]. If there is some metric by which to determine what to do next, then refinement can occur adaptively. Bergman, Fuchs, Grant, and Spach [BERG86b] have developed such a system that uses a variety of heuristics to determine how it should spend its time. For example, a polygon is Gouraud-shaded, rather than constant-shaded, only if the range of its vertex intensities exceeds a threshold. Ray-tracing [PAIN89] and radiosity [COHE88] algorithms are both amenable to progressive refinement.

16.15 SUMMARY

In this chapter, we encountered many different illumination models, some inspired primarily by the need for efficiency, others that attempt to account for the physics of how surfaces actually interact with light. We saw how interpolation could be used in shading models, both to minimize the number of points at which the illumination equation is evaluated, and to allow curved surfaces to be approximated by polygonal meshes. We contrasted local illumination approaches that consider in isolation each surface point and the lights illuminating each point directly, with global approaches that support refraction and reflection of other objects in the environment. In each case, we noted that there are some methods that use the full geometric description of the environment in computing global effects, and others that use simpler descriptions, such as reflection maps.

As we have stressed throughout this chapter, the wide range of illumination and shading algorithms gives rise to a corresponding diversity in the images that can be produced of the same scene with the same viewing specification. The decision about which algorithms should be used depends on many factors, including the purposes for which an image is to be rendered. Although photorealism is often sacrificed in return for efficiency, advances in algorithms and hardware will soon make real-time implementations of physically correct, global illumination models a reality. When efficiency is no longer an issue, however, we may still choose to render some images without texture, shadows, reflections, or refraction, because in some cases this will remain the best way to communicate the desired information to the viewer.

EXERCISES

16.1 (a) Describe the difference in appearance you would expect between a Phong illumination model that used $(\overline{N} \cdot \overline{H})^n$ and one that used $(\overline{R} \cdot \overline{V})^n$. (b) Show that $\alpha = 2\beta$ when all vectors of Fig. 16.12 are coplanar. (c) Show that this relationship is *not* true in general.

16.2 Prove that the results of interpolating vertex information across a polygon's edges and scan lines are independent of orientation in the case of triangles.

16.3 Suppose there are polygons A, B, and C intersecting the same projector in order of increasing distance from the viewer. Show that, in general, if polygons A and B are transparent, the color computed for a pixel in the intersection of their projections will depend on whether Eq. (16.25) is evaluated with polygons A and B treated as polygons 1 and 2 or as polygons 2 and 1.

16.4 Consider the use of texture mapping to modify or replace different material properties. List the effects you can produce by mapping properties singly or in combination. How would you apply antialiasing to them?

16.5 Although using a reflection map may appear to require precomputing the lighting for the environment, a reflection map containing object identities and surface normals could be used instead. What are the disadvantages of using this kind of map?

16.6 Explain how to simulate reflections from surfaces of different roughness using a reflection map.

16.7 What other lighting effects can you think of that would generalize Warn's flaps and cones?

16.8 Suppose that the array of patches shown in Fig. 16.64 is continued for another two rows, adding patches 5 and 6, and that the radiosity values for the patches are $B_1 = B_2 = 2$, $B_3 = B_4 = 4$, $B_5 = B_6 = 6$. Show that B_h and B_e are 5 and 3, respectively. Then show that B_b is 1. Is this a reasonable value?

Notice that it extends the linear trend from h to e. What happens as you add more rows of patches in a similar pattern? Suppose that you added a mirror image of the patches about the line ac and computed the radiosity values. Then B_b would be 2. Does this seem contradictory? Explain your answer.

16.9 Implement a simple recursive ray tracer based on the material in Sections 15.10 and 16.12.

16.10 Make your ray tracer from Exercise 16.9 more efficient by using some of the techniques discussed in Section 16.12.1.

16.11 Extend your ray tracer from Exercise 16.10 to do distributed ray tracing.

16.12 Implement a progressive-refinement radiosity algorithm, based on the pseudocode of Fig. 16.70. Use the hemicube method of computing form factors. Begin by computing only patch to patch exchange (ignoring substructuring). Leave out the ambient computation to make coding and visual debugging easier. Check your hemicube code by verifying that the delta form factors sum to (approximately) 1.

To display your images, you will need to implement a polygon visible-surface algorithm (perhaps the one used by your hemicube) or have access to an existing graphics system. Using constant-shaded polygons will improve interactivity if shaded graphics hardware is not available (and will make programming and debugging easier).

16.13 Explain why lighting must be done before clipping in the pipeline of Fig. 16.72.

16.14 Implement a testbed for experimenting with local illumination models. Store an image that contains for each pixel its visible surface's index into a table of material properties, the surface normal, the distance from the viewer, and the distance from and normalized vector to one or more light sources. Allow the user to modify the illumination equation, the intensity and color of the lights, and the surface properties. Each time a change is made, render the surface. Use Eq. (16.20) with light-source attenuation (Eq. 16.8) and depth-cueing (Eq. 15.11).

16.15 Add a shadow algorithm to a visible-surface algorithm that you have already implemented. For example, if you have built a z-buffer system, you might want to add the two-pass z-buffer shadow algorithm discussed in Section 16.4.4. (The postprocessing variant may be particularly easy to add if you have access to a graphics system that uses a hardware z-buffer. Explain how extra storage at each pixel, as described in Exercise 16.14, could be used to design a shadow postprocess that produced correct shading and proper highlights.)

16.16 Add interobject reflections to a visible-surface algorithm. Use reflection mapping for curved surfaces and the mirror approach for planar surfaces, as described in Section 16.6.

17

Image
Manipulation
and Storage

In this chapter, we explore methods for manipulating and storing images efficiently. We begin by considering the kinds of operations we would like to perform on images. Bear in mind that the images we are manipulating may be used either as images in their own right, or in the manufacture of some subsequent image, as in the environment mapping described in Chapter 16.

Several sorts of operations on images immediately come to mind. One is combining two images by overlaying or blending them, known as *compositing*. One application of compositing is in animation, when we wish to show a character moving around in front of a complicated background that remains unchanged. Rather than rerendering the background for each frame, we can instead render the background once and then generate many frames of the character moving about on a black background. We can then composite these individual frames as overlays to the background frame, thus producing images of a character moving about on the background. In compositing operations like this, antialiasing becomes extremely important to ensure that the outline of the character is not jagged against the background. It is also necessary to distinguish the background of an image from the content; in our example, the black background against which the character is drawn is the *background*, and the character itself is the *content*.

Often, the images to be composited are of different sizes, so we may wish to translate, scale, or rotate them before the composition. We may even wish to distort an image, so that it appears in perspective or appears to have be drawn on a rubber sheet and then stretched. Although we could make these changes by rerendering the image with an appropriate geometric transformation, this is often so difficult or time consuming as to be impractical. Indeed, it can be impossible if, say, the image has been obtained from an optical scan of a photograph, or if the original program or parameters used to create it have been lost.

We might also wish to apply various filters to an image so as to produce false colors, to blur the image, or to accentuate color or intensity discontinuities. This sort of filtering is applied to satellite photographs and to computed-tomography (CT) data, where the intensity of a point in the image reflects the density of material in the body. For example, very slight changes in intensity may indicate the boundaries between normal and cancerous cells, and we may wish to highlight these boundaries.

Images tend to be very large collections of data. A 1024 by 1024 image in which the color of each pixel is represented by a n-bit number takes $n/8$ MB of memory (in an 8-bit-per-byte machine). As described in Chapter 4, many graphics systems dedicate a great deal of memory to image storage (the frame buffer). If the image memory is accessible by other programs, then it may be used for output by one program, and then for input by another, or even for output by two different programs. This happens, for example, when we use a pixel-painting program to adjust individual pixels of a rendered image. This use of image memory (and the rigid structure of the memory, which constitutes a database format for diverse programs) has been called "frame-buffer synergy" by Blinn [BLIN85].

When an image is being stored in secondary memory, it is often convenient to compress the stored data (but not the image). Several schemes have been developed. The look-up tables (LUTs) described in Chapter 4, for example, significantly reduce the storage needed for an image, provided the image contains substantial color repetition. Of course, storing LUTs is typically done only when the frame buffers used for displaying the image support LUTs. We discuss several more sophisticated methods in Section 17.7.

Here we begin by reexamining our notion of an image. Then we describe some elementary operations on images: filtering and geometric transformations. We then discuss techniques for storing additional data with each pixel of an image, and using these data in compositing. Following this, we discuss various image storage formats; finally, we describe a few special effects that can be performed at the image level rather than in modeling or rendering.

17.1   WHAT IS AN IMAGE?

Images, as described in Chapter 14, are (at the most basic level) arrays of *values*, where a value is a collection of numbers describing the attributes of a pixel in the image (in bitmaps, e.g., the values are single binary digits). Often these numbers are fixed-point representations of a range of real numbers; for example, the integers 0 through 255 often are used to represent the numbers from 0.0 to 1.0. Often, too, these numbers represent the intensity at a point in the image (*gray scale*) or the intensity of one color component at that point. The dimensions of the array are called the *width* and *height* of the image, and the number of bits associated with each pixel in the array is called the *depth*.

We often consider an image as more than a mere array of values, however. An image is usually intended to represent an *abstract* image, which is a function of a continuous variable; each position in the abstract image has some value.[1] The images we work with

---

[1] What we are really talking about is a function whose domain is a rectangle in the Euclidean plane, rather than a discrete lattice of points in the plane.

(sometimes called *digital images* or *discrete images*) are functions of a discrete variable; for each $[i, j]$ pair, a value is associated with the pixel labeled $[i, j]$. As described in Chapters 3 and 14, choosing the best discrete image to represent an abstract image is difficult. In this chapter, we sometimes discuss reconstructing the abstract image in order to take new samples from it. Of course, we do not actually perform this reconstruction, since to do so we would need to generate values at infinitely many points. But we can reconstruct any individual value in the abstract image—in particular, we can reconstruct the finitely many values we want to sample.

If we create a discrete image from an abstract image by sampling (see Chapter 14), then reconstruct an abstract image from the digital image, the reconstructed abstract image and the original abstract image may or may not be the same. If the original abstract image had no high-frequency components, then the reconstructed image would be the same as the original, and the reconstruction would be said to be *faithful*. On the other hand, if the original image had components whose frequencies were too high, then the sampled image could not represent it accurately, and the reconstructed image would differ from the original.

One other aspect of images is important. Although filtering theory tells us a great deal about selecting a discrete image to represent an abstract image most accurately, much of the theory assumes that the abstract-image values at each point are real numbers and that the discrete-image values at each pixel will also be real numbers. In the case of bitmaps, however, nothing could be further from the truth: The values are binary. In more complex pixmaps, the values may be small binary numbers (e.g., 4 bits per pixel), or may range over so large a collection of numbers as to be effectively continuous. This *value discretization* leads to significant questions in image manipulation, such as how best to compress a bitmap. If 4 pixels—2 white and 2 black—are to be compressed into 1, should the compressed pixel be black or white? We discuss the consequences of value discretization when they are known and significant, but note that there is much that we do not yet understand.

17.2 FILTERING

Suppose we have an image produced without any antialiasing—for example, a drawing of a graph that was read into memory with an optical scanner that sampled the drawing at an array of points. How can we improve its appearance? The image certainly has jaggies that we would like to remove. But *every* image we can create is correct for *some* source image (where by *correct* we mean that it accurately represents a sample of the source image after low-pass filtering). If applying some mechanism alters and improves one image, applying the same mechanism to another image may damage that image. Thus, the mechanism we are about to describe should be used only on images that need smoothing. If jagged steps are present in a image that has been generated properly, then they are meant to be there, and postfiltering will only blur the image. (After all, what *should* an image of a staircase look like?)

Suppose we do want to smooth out an image to hide some jaggies. What can we do? An obvious start is to replace each pixel with the average of itself and its neighbors. This process, applied to the discrete image rather than to the abstract image, is called *postfiltering*. With postfiltering, pixels near the stair steps in the jaggies are blended so as to hide the steps; see Fig. 17.1, in which the filtering has been exaggerated. As we saw in Chapter 14, this constitutes filtering with a box filter; other, more sophisticated filters may yield better results. Before we examine other filters, let us consider the drawbacks of even this simple filtering method.

Suppose that we point sample a photograph of a picket fence. The pickets and the gaps between them are of the same width, the pickets are white, and the background is black. The pickets are spaced in the photograph so that the width of nine pickets and nine gaps covers a width of 10 pixels in the image. What will the sampled image look like? If the photograph is positioned so that the first pixel is exactly at the left-hand edge of the first picket, then the first pixel will be white, the next 5 pixels will be black, but the sixth through tenth pixels will be at pickets and hence will be white. The next 5 pixels will be black, and so on (see Fig. 17.2).

Now, what does our postfiltering do in this situation? It smoothes out the boundary between the sixth and seventh pixels, and leaves a large block of black followed by a large block of white. It cannot possibly fix all the problems implicit in the image. Clearly, postfiltering is not a good solution to the aliasing problem. In addition, since postfiltering will also blur any other edges in the image (even those that *should* be there), the resulting image will be unpleasantly fuzzy.

This problem can be partly remedied at the cost of shrinking the image: We can convert a $2n$ by $2n$ image into an n by n image by imagining that the source image is overlaid with a grid, each square of the grid enclosing 4 pixels of the source image. We can then average the 4 pixels in the square to create 1 pixel in the target image for each grid square. This amounts to postfiltering the image, then selecting alternate pixels on alternate scan lines. Note that less filtering computation is involved; we need to apply the filter to compute values for only those pixels included in the final image. That is, for only those pixels to appear in the output image, we compute a weighted average of pixels around the corresponding point in the source image. Of course, the resulting image is one-fourth the size of the original.

We can see how this works by recalling the analysis in Chapter 14. If the source image is produced by sampling at a frequency of 2ω, then any component of the original signal whose frequency is between 0 and ω will be accurately represented. For any frequency above ω, say $\omega + \phi$, the sampled signal will contain an alias at frequency $\omega - \phi$. Box filtering the sampled signal with a filter of width 2 substantially (but not completely) filters out the components of this signal with frequencies greater than $\omega/2$ (because the Fourier transform of the box filter is a sinc function, which tapers off rapidly as the frequency increases). Resampling at alternate pixels yields an effective sampling rate of ω; with this

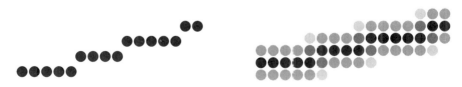

Fig. 17.1 The stair steps are smoothed by box filtering.

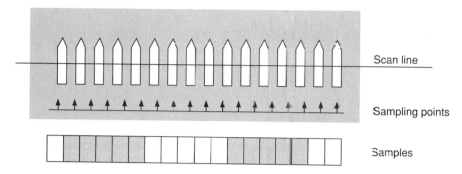

Fig. 17.2 Aliasing in a sampled image.

sampling rate, all frequencies up to $\omega/2$ can be accurately represented. But after applying the filter, these are exactly the frequencies that remain. If the original signal had components $\omega + \phi$ for which ϕ was large (i.e., greater than $\omega/2$), then the aliases of these components occur at frequencies below $\omega/2$, and hence persist in the final image. But for small values of ϕ, the aliases are filtered out, and so supersampling and postfiltering really do help reduce aliases.

Remember that the signals that represent such primitives as lines, rectangles, and any other geometric objects with clearly defined edges have components of arbitrarily high frequencies, so there is no hope of representing these correctly by any such method. At best, we can hope postfiltering will improve a bad image at the cost of fuzziness.

Other filters, such as the sinc filter, the Catmull−Rom filter, and the triangle filter, can produce better postfiltering results than can a pure box filter. The analysis of those filters given in Chapter 14 applies here as well. As a convenient rule of thumb, Whitted has suggested that postfiltering a high-resolution image produces obvious fuzziness, but that a 2048 by 2048 image can usually be postfiltered and sampled down to a 512 by 512 image with good results [WHIT85].

Now consider a temporal analogue of this problem: The spokes on a wagon wheel pass by a pixel on the screen very fast in an animation of a rolling wagon (this is the temporal analog of an object being striped with rapidly changing color; i.e., to closely spaced stripes). The frequency with which the spokes pass a point may be far greater than 30 times per second, the speed of typical video recording. Temporal aliasing is the inevitable result: The spokes appear to stand still or to turn backward. We are used to seeing this effect in movies, of course. In a movie, however, we actually see a *blurred* wagon wheel moving backward, because, in each exposure of a movie frame, the shutter is open for a brief (but not infinitesimal) time period (about one half of the time allocated to the frame; the remaining half is dedicated to moving the film forward). The shutter effectively applies a box filter to the scene in the time dimension. The result is some blurring but aliases are still present. The blurring is due to the box filtering, and the aliases are due to the narrowness of the filter. All the box filters taken together cover only about half of the time sequence of the movie—the remainder is lost while the shutter is closed. The implication for computer graphics is clear: To get movie-quality frames for animation, we need to do (at the very least) box filtering—*prefiltering*—over time. Postfiltering removes some ill effects, but many remain. Notice that, to get really accurate images, we should actually do sinc filtering over the time domain. If movie cameras did this (or even had wider box filters), the wagon wheels would look the way they do in life—they would appear to roll forward and then to blend into a continuous blur.

17.3   IMAGE PROCESSING

Now we briefly turn to a different problem: How can we highlight or suppress certain features in an image? This question is really in the domain of *image processing* rather than computer graphics, but a few basic ideas are worth discussing. By scanning an image for rapid changes in value at adjacent points, we can do *edge detection* and *enhancement*. At places where the values of adjacent points differ sufficiently, we can push the values even further apart. If an image is *noisy*—that is, if random displacements have been added to its pixel values—then it can be *smoothed* by the filtering techniques discussed in the previous section. If the noise is sufficiently random, then filtering, which computes averages of adjacent pixels, should average out the noise, or at least filter its high-frequency components.

Another image-processing technique is *thresholding*, in which the points of an image at or near a particular value are highlighted. In a gray-scale image, this highlighting can be done by converting all pixels below some value to black, and all pixels above that value to white, producing a threshold edge between the black and white regions. The marching-cubes algorithm discussed in Chapter 20 gives a different mechanism for thresholding (in 3D): It explicitly constructs the boundary between the two regions as a surface (or a curve, in the 2D case). The components of this boundary can then be rendered into a new image with appropriate antialiasing to give a smoother indication of the threshold. For further information on this, see [GONZ87; SIG85].

17.4   GEOMETRIC TRANSFORMATIONS OF IMAGES

Suppose we wish to transform an image geometrically. Such transformations include translation, rotation, scaling, and other, nonlinear, operations. How can we do this?

Translating an image makes sense only if the image is thought of as a subimage of some larger image. Suppose we wish to move an n by k array of pixels (the *source*), whose upper-left corner is at (a, b), to a new position, with the upper-left corner at position (c, d) (the *target*). This transformation should be easy; we simply copy pixels from the source position to the target position, and (if we want) replace all source pixels that are not target pixels with the background color (see Fig. 17.3). Provided that care is taken to ensure that the copying is done in an order that prevents overwriting source pixels, when the source and destination overlap, and provided that the four numbers a, b, c, and d are all integers, this approach works fine.

But what if the starting and ending positions are not integers? Then we wish to reconstruct the abstract image for the source image, to translate it, and to sample this translated version. To do this explicitly is not feasible—we certainly do not wish to reconstruct the abstract image at *every* possible location, and then to select just a few of

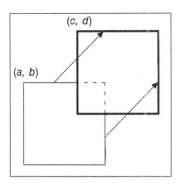

Fig. 17.3 A simple translation of an image.

these (infinitely many) points. Indeed, the same objection holds for scaling and rotation. Algorithms have been developed, however, that perform these operations in ways that are computationally correct (in various senses). Weiman has developed algorithms for performing scaling and shearing of images by rational amounts [WEIM80]. Rotations can be performed by a clever combination of these algorithms (see Exercise 17.1). Finding a similar algorithm for translating by arbitrary rational amounts is posed as Exercise 17.2.

17.4.1 Basic Geometric Transformations

Weiman posits that a gray-scale pixmap represents an abstract image in the following fashion: The abstract image is divided into squares (one square per pixel), and the average intensity of this abstract image in the square is the value assigned to the pixel. He thus assumes that he can perform a faithful reconstruction by drawing a picture consisting of gray squares whose tone is determined by the pixel values. Stretching a pixmap by a factor of p/q takes q columns of the original and stretches them to cover p columns of the target image. Performing area sampling on the result then generates the target image. Filtering theory tells us that this assumption about the nature of a sampled image and the consequent stretching algorithm are wrong in every sense: An abstract image should never be sampled while it has frequency components above the Nyquist frequency, and hence a proper reconstruction of an abstract image from a sampled one never has high-frequency components. An image in which adjacent squares have different (constant) values is a perfect example of an image with lots of high-frequency components, so this is certainly a bad reconstruction. And finally, filtering theory says that when converting such an image to a pixmap, we should use sinc filtering rather than box filtering. Nevertheless, if Weiman's hypotheses are allowed, his algorithm for performing these linear transformations is quite clever. It is also the basis for a very good bitmap-scaling algorithm (see Exercise 17.3).

Suppose we wish to scale an image by a factor p/q (where $p > q$, and p and q are integers with no common factors). The first step is to generate a Rothstein code [ROTH76] for the number p/q. This code is a binary sequence that describes a line whose slope is q/p (any scan-converted line can be used to generate a similar code). Figure 17.4 shows a line of slope $\frac{3}{5}$ with 15 tick marks on it. As the line passes from left to right through the figure, it crosses the horizontal grid lines. If a column contains such a grid-line crossing, it is marked

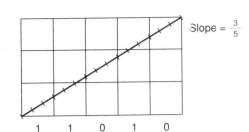

Fig. 17.4 The Rothstein code for a line of slope $\frac{3}{5}$.

with a 1; otherwise, is marked with a 0. Each column contains three tick marks; the bit associated with the column is 0 unless one of the three tick marks is at a multiple of 5, since multiples of 5 are where horizontal-line crossings occur. Thus, the interval between mark 9 and mark 12 is assigned a 1, since mark 10 lies within it. (A tick at the left side of a column is considered to be in the column, whereas ticks on the right are not.)

The Rothstein code may be viewed as a mechanism for distributing q 1s evenly among p binary digits. We can therefore use it to tell us how to distribute each of the q columns of the source image among p columns of the target image. Unfortunately, using the 1s in the Rothstein code as indicators of where to copy the source data leaves some of the target columns blank. The Rothstein code can be cyclically permuted, however, to give different mappings of source to destination.[2] Taking the average of these gives the result.

The pseudocode for this procedure is shown in Fig. 17.5.

To scale by a number smaller than 1, we simply reverse the process. The Rothstein code for q/p tells us which of the source columns should appear in the target (a 1 in the Rothstein code tells us to select that column). Again, we average over all cyclic permutations of the code.

The Rothstein code can also be used to generate a description of shearing. A 1 in the Rothstein code indicates that the corresponding column of the source pixmap should be shifted up 1 pixel. Over the course of q columns, there are p shifts, resulting in a vertical shear of amount q/p. Once again, we should cyclically permute and average the results.

17.4.2 Geometric Transformations with Filtering

Feibush, Levoy, and Cook give a somewhat more sophisticated mechanism for transforming images [FEIB80]. (Their algorithm is developed for use in an algorithm for mapping textures onto surfaces—see Chapter 16.) Before discussing the details, we note the algorithm's good and bad points. The algorithm has the advantage that it computes reasonable values for boundary pixels: If an image is rotated so that some target pixel is only partly covered by a source pixel, the algorithm recognizes that pixel as a special case and processes it accordingly. It computes values by applying a weighted filter to the source image to determine pixel values for the target image, which helps to reduce aliasing in the resulting image. But since this filter is more than 1 pixel wide, if the algorithm is used to

---

[2]A cyclic permutation of a binary sequence is the repeated application of logical shift operations to the sequence.

```
/* Expand the width of an image by p/q. */
void WeimanExpansion(
        const grayscalePixmap source,        /* Source image, size n × k */
        grayscalePixmap target,              /* Target image, width at least k * p/q */
        int n, int k,                        /* Size of source image */
        int p, int q)                        /* Scale factor is p/q */
{
        char roth[MAX];                      /* The array must hold at least p items. */
        int i, j, s;                         /* Loop indices */

        /* Source image is n × k, target image is to be n × ceil (k * p/q).³ */
        int targetWidth = ceil (k * p / (double) q);

        Rothstein (roth, p, q);              /* Store the Rothstein code for p/q in array roth. */
        SetToBlank (target, n, targetWidth); /* Clear the target array. */
        for (i = 0; i < p; i++) {            /* For several passes through the algorithm... */
            int sourceCol = 0;
            Permute (roth);                  /* Apply cyclic permutation to Rothstein code. */
            /* For each column of the target */
            for (j = 0; j < targetWidth; j++) {
                if (roth[j] == 1) {          /* If code says to copy source column */
                    for (s = 0; s < n; s++) {   /* Copy all the pixels. */
                        target[s][j] += source[s][sourceCol];
                    }
                    sourceCol++;             /* Go to next column. */
                }
            }
        }

        /* Divide by q to compensate for adding each source column to target q times. */
        for (i = 0; i < n; i++)
            for (j = 0; j < targetWidth; j++)
                target[i][j] = rint (target[i][j] / (double) q);
}   /* WeimanExpansion */
```

Fig. 17.5 The Weiman algorithm for expanding an image.

perform the identity transformation on an image, it blurs the values. In Section 17.5.3, we discuss this and other drawbacks of transformation algorithms.[4]

At this point, it is worthwhile to separate two aspects of image transformation. The first is computing which point in the source image is mapped to the center of the pixel in the

---

[3] The ceiling of a number is the smallest integer greater than or equal to the number; ceiling(1.6) = 2, ceiling(1.1) = 2, and ceiling(6.0) = 6.

[4] Feibush, Levoy and Cook note that any filter can be used, but describe the algorithm in terms of a filter of diameter 2. The algorithm generally performs better with this filter than it does with a unit-area box filter.

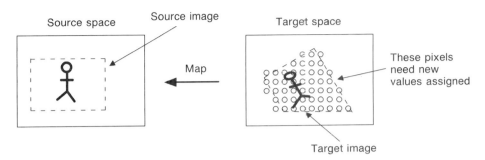

Fig. 17.6 The relationship of the source space, source image, target space, and target image in the Feibush–Levoy–Cook algorithm.

target image. The second is computing the value for the pixel in the target image. The first task is merely algebraic, in that it involves computing values (and inverse values) of a transformation. This may be done efficiently by various incremental methods. The second task also has numerous solutions, all of which involve choosing some filtering function to apply to the original image. The method described in the next few pages assumes a filtering function that is circularly symmetric and has a modest size (i.e., is nonzero only on a small part of the plane).

The algorithm starts with a source image (thought of as lying in one copy of the Euclidean plane, called the *source space*), a projective map[5] from another copy of the Euclidean plane (the *target space*) to the source space, and a polygonal region in the target space. The target image is the collection of pixels in the target space that are near the polygonal region, and it is these pixels whose values need to be assigned (see Fig. 17.6). Note that the projective map here goes from target to source, the reverse of the usual naming convention for mathematical functions.

To start, we choose a symmetric filter function that is nonzero only for (x, y) very close to (0, 0) (perhaps within a 2-pixel distance). The *support* of this filter function is the set of points on which it is nonzero. We take a copy of the bounding rectangle for the support of the filter and translate it to each pixel in the target space. Whenever this rectangle intersects the target polygon, the pixel is considered to be in the target image. This translated rectangle is called the *bounding rectangle for the target pixel*, and the translated support of the filter function is called the pixel's *convolution mask* (see Fig. 17.7).

The vertices of the target polygon are transformed to source space just once, for repeated use. The resulting polygon is called the *source polygon*. The bounding rectangle of each target pixel is transformed to the source space, where it becomes a quadrilateral. A bounding rectangle for this quadrilateral is computed, then is clipped by the source polygon (because clipping a rectangle by the source polygon is much easier than clipping a general quadrilateral). The pixels in the source space that lie in this clipped quadrilateral are transformed to the target space; only those that fall within the target pixel's bounding rectangle are retained.

---

[5]A *projective map* is a map represented by a 3×3 matrix operating on the plane using homogeneous coordinates, in the manner described in Chapter 5.

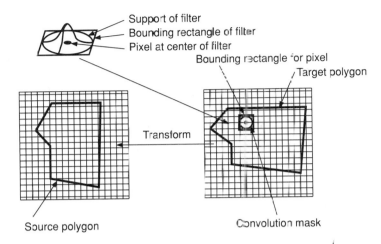

Fig. 17.7 Terms used in the Feibush–Levoy–Cook algorithm.

These transformed pixels are then averaged together by the weights given by the filter to yield a value for the target pixel. This target pixel value is correct only if the entire pixel is within the transformed image boundaries. If the image has been rotated, for example, then the transformed edges of the image may cut across pixels (more precisely, across their convolution masks).

Thus pixels are not entirely determined by the value just computed; that value only contributes to the pixel's value, in proportion to the coverage of the pixels. The contribution can be determined analytically. Figure 17.8 shows the transformed edge of the source image passing through a pixel's bounding rectangle, and within that rectangle passing through the pixel's convolution mask. To find the contribution of the computed value to the pixel's final value, we do the following:

1. Clip the image polygon against the bounding rectangle for the pixel (see Fig. 17.9). The points of intersection with the edges of the bounding rectangle were already computed in determining whether the pixel was in the target image.

2. For each vertex of the clipped polygon (in Fig. 17.9, a single triangle with vertices

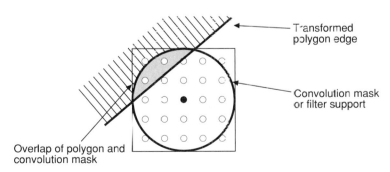

Fig. 17.8 Filtering for a pixel at the edge of the polygon.

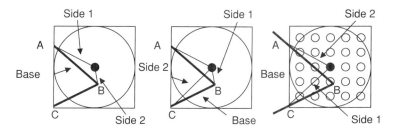

Fig. 17.9 The steps in filtering an edge.

labeled *A*, *B*, and *C*, in clockwise order), construct a triangle with sides *BASE* (the edge from this vertex to the next vertex in clockwise order around the polygon), *SIDE1* (the edge from this vertex to the center of the pixel) and *SIDE2* (the edge from the next vertex to the center of the pixel).

3. Consider the filter function as being plotted in a third dimension above the convolution mask. The weight a region contributes to the total for a pixel is proportional to the volume above that region and under the graph of the filter. So we now compute the volumes above each triangle. As Fig. 17.9 shows, some of these volumes must be added and some subtracted to create the correct total contribution for the region. The rule is that the volume is added if the cross-product of *SIDE1* and *SIDE2* points into the page; otherwise, it is subtracted (see Exercise 17.4).

Computing the volumes in step 3 is easier than it might appear, in that they can be precomputed and then extracted from a look-up table during the actual filtering process. Exercise 17.5 shows how to do this precomputation.

17.4.3   Other Pattern Mapping Techniques

The Feibush-Levoy-Cook algorithm provides excellent results for pattern mapping onto polygons, but requires computing a filtered value at each point, so that for each pixel in the image a filtering computation is performed. In a perspective picture of a plane (receding to a vanishing point) a single pixel in the final image may correspond to thousands of pixels in the source pattern, and thus require an immense filtering computation. Several techniques have been developed to produce more rapid (if sometimes slightly less accurate) filtering.

Williams [WILL83] takes the source image and creates a MIP (*multum in parvo*— many things in a small place) map, which occupies $\frac{4}{3}$ of the memory of the original. If the original image is a 512 by 512 pixel, 24-bit true color image, using 8 bits each for the red, green, and blue information, the MIP map is a 1024 by 1024 by 8 bit image. The red, green, and blue parts of the original image each occupy one quarter of the MIP map, and the remaining quarter is filled with filtered versions of these, as shown in Fig. 17.10. When a target pixel is covered by a collection of source pixels, the MIP map pixels corresponding to this collection most closely are used to give a filtered value. Linear interpolation between levels of filtering is used to further smooth the values.

Crow [CROW84] devised a scheme by which box filtering of an image over any aligned rectangle can be done rapidly. For quick pattern mapping, this suffices in many cases—a rectangular box corresponding closely to the shape of the transformed target pixel is used to

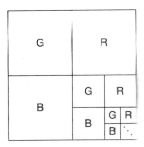

Fig. 17.10 A MIP map. The red, green, and blue channels of the original image fill three quarters of the MIP map. Each is filtered by a factor of 4, and the three resulting images fill up three quarters of the remaining quarter. The process is continued until the MIP map is filled.

compute a filtered pattern value for the pixel. The scheme is based on the algebraic identity $(x + a)(y + b) - (x + a) y - x (y + b) + xy = ab$. Interpreted geometrically, this says that the area of the small white rectangle in Fig. 17.11 can be computed by taking the area of the large rectangle and subtracting the areas of both the vertically and the horizontally shaded rectangles, and then adding back in the crosshatched rectangle (which has been subtracted twice). By taking the source image and creating a new image, whose value at pixel (x, y) is the sum of all the values in the source image in the rectangle with corners $(0, 0)$ and (x, y), we create a *summed area table*, S. We can now compute the sum of the pixels in the rectangle with corners at (x, y) and $(x + a, y + b)$, for example, by taking $S[x + a, y + b] - S[x + a, y] - S[x, y + b] + S[x, y]$.

Glassner [GLAS86] observes that if the transformed pixel is not approximately an aligned rectangle, then summed area tables may blur the result excessively. He therefore develops a system in which the excess area in the aligned bounding box for the pixel is systematically trimmed, in order to provide a more accurate estimate of the filtered source image at the point. This requires detecting the geometry of the inverse-mapped target pixel relative to its bounding box.

Heckbert [HECK86a] proposes a system using both the Feibush-Levoy-Cook method and MIP maps. He maps the target pixel's filter support (which is supposed to be circular,

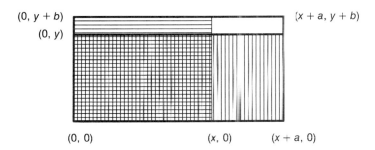

Fig. 17.11 The area of the small white rectangle in the image is computed by subtracting the horizontally and vertically shaded areas from the area of the large rectangle, and then adding back in the area of the crosshatched rectangle.

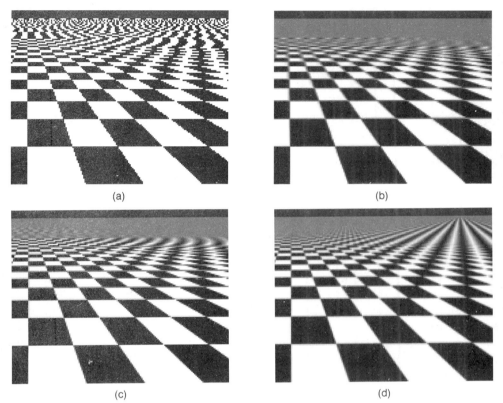

(a)

(b)

(c)

(d)

Fig. 17.12 (a) Point sampling of the source image. (b) MIP map filtering. (c) Summed area table filtering. (d) Elliptical weighted average using MIP maps and a Gaussian filter. (Courtesy of P. Heckbert.)

and is defined by a quadratic function) to an elliptical region in the source image (defined by a different quadratic). Depending on the size of this region in the source image, an appropriate level in a MIP map for the source image is selected, and the pixels within it are collected in a weighted sum over the elliptical region. This weighted sum is the value assigned to the target pixel. This combines the accuracy of the Feibush-Levoy-Cook technique with the efficiency of the MIP map system. A comparison of pattern-mapping results is shown in Fig. 17.12.

17.5 MULTIPASS TRANSFORMATIONS

Suppose that we take the image shown in Fig. 17.13(a) and apply a vertical shearing transformation to it, as shown in part (b), and then we follow this with a horizontal shearing transformation,[6] as shown in part (c). Provided we choose the right transformations, the net effect is to rotate the image as shown [CATM80]. Such a two-pass technique may be much

---

[6]The two shearing transformations are actually shear-and-scale transformations. The first takes a column of pixels and translates and compresses it in the vertical direction. The second does the same for a row of pixels.

(a)

Fig. 17.13 A rotation may be expressed as a composition of a column-preserving and a row-preserving transformation. (a) The original image. (b) A column-preserving transformation has been applied to the image. (c) A row-preserving transformation has been applied to the second image. (Courtesy of George Wolberg, Columbia University.)

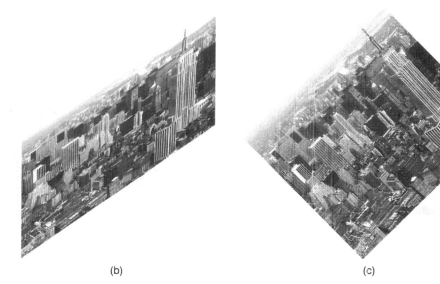

(b)   (c)

faster to compute than a direct application of the rotation transformation, since it operates on one vertical or horizontal line of pixels at a time, and the computations within each such line can be performed incrementally. Also, in many cases, the filtering necessary to avoid aliasing artifacts can be performed line by line as well. More important still is that a wide class of transformations can be implemented as multipass transformations [CATM80, SMIT87]. This multipass technique has been implemented in the Ampex digital optics (ADO) machine [BENN84], which is widely used in video production. A survey of this and other image warping techniques is given in [WOLB90].

Implementing two-pass (or multipass) transformations can be divided into two subtasks: finding the correct transformations for the individual passes, which is a purely algebraic problem, and applying the correct filtering to generate new pixels, which is an antialiasing problem. Since the second part will depend on the solution to the first, we begin by solving the first problem in the case of a rotation.

17.5.1 The Algebra of Multipass Transforms

To simplify the discussion, we will use three different sets of coordinates. The original image will be written in (x, y) coordinates, the vertically sheared image in (u, v) coordinates, and the final image in (r, s) coordinates. The first shearing transformation will be called A, the second B, and their composition, which is the rotation, will be called T. Thus,

$$\begin{pmatrix} u \\ v \end{pmatrix} = A \begin{pmatrix} x \\ y \end{pmatrix},$$

and

$$\begin{pmatrix} r \\ s \end{pmatrix} = B \begin{pmatrix} u \\ v \end{pmatrix} = B \left(A \begin{pmatrix} x \\ y \end{pmatrix} \right) = T \begin{pmatrix} x \\ y \end{pmatrix}.$$

From Chapter 5, we know the formula for T:

$$\begin{pmatrix} r \\ s \end{pmatrix} = T \begin{pmatrix} x \\ y \end{pmatrix} = \begin{pmatrix} x \cos \phi - y \sin \phi \\ x \sin \phi + y \cos \phi \end{pmatrix}.$$

From this, we will determine the formulae for A and B.

The transformation A is supposed to be *column preserving*; that is, it must send each column of the original image into the corresponding column of the transformed image. Thus, if the pixel (x, y) is sent to (u, v) by A, then $u = x$. In other words, A must be written in the form

$$\begin{pmatrix} u \\ v \end{pmatrix} = A \begin{pmatrix} x \\ y \end{pmatrix} = \begin{pmatrix} x \\ f(x, y) \end{pmatrix}$$

for some function f. In the same way, B is supposed to be *row preserving*, so B must be written in the form

$$\begin{pmatrix} r \\ s \end{pmatrix} = B \begin{pmatrix} u \\ v \end{pmatrix} = \begin{pmatrix} g(u, v) \\ v \end{pmatrix}$$

for some function g. To determine the formulae for A and B, we need to find the functions f and g.

Writing out the composite, we have

$$\begin{pmatrix} r \\ s \end{pmatrix} = B \begin{pmatrix} u \\ v \end{pmatrix} = B \left(A \begin{pmatrix} x \\ y \end{pmatrix} \right) = B \begin{pmatrix} x \\ f(x, y) \end{pmatrix} = \begin{pmatrix} g(x, f(x, y)) \\ f(x, y) \end{pmatrix}.$$

From this equation, we see that s and $f(x, y)$ are equal. Thus, the formula for s in terms of x and y gives the formula for $f(x, y)$: $f(x, y) = x \sin \phi + y \cos \phi$. Determining the formula for $g(u, v)$ is more complex. We know that, in terms of x and y, we can write $g(u, v) = x \cos \phi - y \sin \phi$. To write this in terms of u and v, we must solve for x and y in terms of u and v and substitute. Solving for x is easy, since we observed previously that $u = x$. Solving for y is slightly more difficult: $v = f(x, y) = x \sin \phi + y \cos \phi$, so $y = (v - x \sin \phi) / \cos \phi =$

$(v - u \sin \phi) / \cos \phi$. Substituting this result into the formula for $g(u, v)$ in terms of x and y, we get

$$g(u, v) = u \cos \phi - \frac{v - u \sin \phi}{\cos \phi} \sin \phi = u \sec \phi - v \tan \phi.$$

In summary, if we define

$$A\begin{pmatrix} x \\ y \end{pmatrix} = \begin{pmatrix} x \\ x \sin \phi + y \cos \phi \end{pmatrix},$$

and

$$B\begin{pmatrix} u \\ v \end{pmatrix} = \begin{pmatrix} u \sec \phi - v \tan \phi \\ v \end{pmatrix},$$

then computing the composite gives

$$B\left(A\begin{pmatrix} x \\ y \end{pmatrix}\right) = \begin{pmatrix} x \cos \phi - y \sin \phi \\ x \sin \phi + y \cos \phi \end{pmatrix},$$

as desired.

To do this for a general transformation T, we must do exactly the same work. If

$$T\begin{pmatrix} x \\ y \end{pmatrix} = \begin{pmatrix} t_1(x, y) \\ t_2(x, y) \end{pmatrix},$$

then we define $u = x$ and $v = f(x, y) = t_2(x, y)$. To define $g(u, v)$, we need to solve for y in terms of u and v, using these definitions—that is, to find a function h such that $(u, v) = (x, t_2(x, y))$ is equivalent to $(x, y) = (u, h(u, v))$. When we have found h, the formula for $g(u, v)$ is just $g(u, v) = t_2(u, h(u, v))$.

The difficult part of the process is finding h. In fact, in our example, $h(u, v) = (v - u \sin \phi) / \cos \phi$, which is undefined if $\cos \phi = 0$—that is, if $\phi = 90°$ or $270°$—so that finding h may be impossible. Fortunately, rotating by $90°$ is very easy (just map (x, y) to $(-y, x)$), so that this is not a problem. In fact, we shall see that, to rotate nearly $90°$, it is better to rotate the full $90°$ and then to rotate a small amount back; thus, to rotate $87°$, we would rotate $90°$ and then $-3°$. Algebraically, there is no difference between the two maps; at the pixel level, however, where filtering is involved, the difference is significant.

A rotation can also be broken into three transformations so as to avoid this *bottleneck* problem [PAET86; TANA86; WOLB90]. The decomposition for a rotation by ϕ is

$$\begin{bmatrix} \cos \phi & -\sin \phi \\ \sin \phi & \cos \phi \end{bmatrix} = \begin{bmatrix} 1 & -\tan \phi/2 \\ 0 & 1 \end{bmatrix} \begin{bmatrix} 1 & 0 \\ \sin \phi & 1 \end{bmatrix} \begin{bmatrix} 1 & -\tan \phi/2 \\ 0 & 1 \end{bmatrix}.$$

Note that each transformation involves a computation with one multiplication and one addition. Also, when $\phi > 90°$, we can do the rotation by first rotating by $180°$ and then by $180° - \phi$, so that the argument of the tangent function is never greater than $45°$.[7]

---

[7] The tangent function is well behaved for angles near $0°$, but has singularities at $\pm 90°$. Evaluating it for angles near $0°$ is therefore preferable.

To show that the multipass technique is not limited to rotations, let us factor a different map, which distorts a square into a trapezoid. (Such maps arise in the perspective transformations described in Chapter 6.) As an example, we take

$$T\begin{pmatrix} x \\ y \end{pmatrix} = \begin{pmatrix} x/(y + 1) \\ y/(y + 1) \end{pmatrix}.$$

Just as before, we wish to find functions

$$A\begin{pmatrix} x \\ y \end{pmatrix} = \begin{pmatrix} x \\ f(x, y) \end{pmatrix} \quad \text{and} \quad B\begin{pmatrix} u \\ v \end{pmatrix} = \begin{pmatrix} g(u, v) \\ v \end{pmatrix}$$

such that $B(A\begin{pmatrix} x \\ y \end{pmatrix}) = T\begin{pmatrix} x \\ y \end{pmatrix}$. In this case, $v = f(x, y) = t_2(x, y) = y/(y + 1)$. We need to find $g(u, v)$ so that $g(u, v) = x/(y + 1)$. Solving the equation of f for y, we get $y = -v/(v - 1)$. Thus (recalling that $u = x$), we can write $g(u, v) = u/(-v/(v - 1) + 1) = u/(-1/(v - 1)) = u(1 - v)$. Our two passes become

$$\begin{pmatrix} u \\ v \end{pmatrix} = \begin{pmatrix} x \\ y/(y + 1) \end{pmatrix} \quad \text{and} \quad \begin{pmatrix} r \\ s \end{pmatrix} = \begin{pmatrix} u(1 - v) \\ v \end{pmatrix}.$$

You should check that the composition of these transformations is really the original transformation T.

The technique has been generalized to handle other maps by Smith and colleagues [SMIT87]. Translation, rotation, scaling, and shearing all work easily. In addition, Smith considers functions of the form

$$T(x, y) = S(m(x) h_1(y), m(x) h_2(y)),$$

where S is a standard computer graphics transform—that is, a transformation of the plane by translation, scaling, rotation, and perspective transformations—and $m(x)$, $h_1(y)$ and $h_2(y)$ are arbitrary. He also considers maps T whose component functions $t_1(x, y)$ and $t_2(x, y)$ are bicubic functions of x and y, under the special hypothesis that T is injective (i.e., no two (x, y) points map to the same (r, s) point).

17.5.2   Generating Transformed Images with Filtering

When we transform an image by a row-preserving (or column-preserving) transformation, the source pixels are likely not to map exactly to the target pixels. For example, the pixels in a row might all be translated by $3\frac{1}{2}$ pixels to the right. In this case, we must compute values for the target pixels by taking combinations of the source pixels. What we are doing, in effect, is considering the values of the source pixels as samples of a function on a real line (the row); the values at the target pixels will be different samples of this same function. Hence, the process is called *resampling*.

The theoretically ideal resampling process is to take, for a given target pixel, a weighted average of the source pixels whose transformed positions are near it. The weights associated with each source pixel should be sinc(kd), where d is the distance from the transformed source pixel to the target pixel and k is some constant. Unfortunately, this requires that every source pixel in a row contribute to every target pixel. As usual, we can instead work

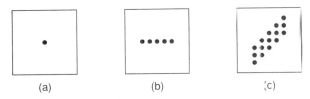

Fig. 17.14 The pixels that contribute to an output pixel in a two-pass rotation form a small area in (x, y) space. (a) A single pixel in (r, s) space; (b) The horizontal span of pixels in (u, v) space that contribute to the value of that pixel; (c) The pixels in (x, y) space that contribute to the values of the pixels in (u, v) space.

with various approximations to the sinc filter. The simplest is a box filter: Each source pixel is assumed to represent an interval in its row, and the endpoints of this interval are transformed. The contribution to the target pixel is the overlap of this transformed interval with the target pixel's interval multiplied by the value of the source pixel.

Using this method, each target pixel has a value that is a weighted average of a short span of source pixels (the length of the span depends on the exact transformation). In a two-pass rotation, a pixel in (r, s)-space has a value that is a weighted average of a horizontal span of (u, v)-pixels. Figure 17.14(a) shows a pixel in (r, s) space, and (b) shows the span of pixels in (u, v) space that contribute to the value of that pixel. Each of these (u, v) pixels, however, has a value that is an average of a vertical span of pixels in (x, y) space. Figure 17.14(c) shows these pixels in (x, y) space. Notice that the vertical spans in (x, y) space form a rhombus rather than a square, since the transformation from (x, y) to (u, v) is a shearing transformation.

We know from Chapter 14 that the pixels contributing to an output pixel really ought to form a circular shape[8] (i.e., the filter should be radially symmetric). If the rhombus is too different from a square, the filtering will begin to degenerate and will produce bad results. The result of such a separation of the filtering process into two component filters is discussed further in [MITC88].

In addition, we want to avoid the bottlenecking problem described previously, where many pixels in the source for a transformation contribute to each output pixel. In the case of a shear-and-scale operation, this occurs when the scale factor is small.

Thus, in doing two-pass rotations (or any other multipass transformation) we want to avoid extreme shearing or bottlenecking in our transformations. This is why rotating by $90°$ and then by $-3°$ is superior to rotating by $87°$. In general, when we are constructing a two-pass transform, we can transform by rows and then columns, or by columns and then rows, or can rotate $90°$ before doing either of these. According to Smith, one of these approaches appears always to resolve the bottlenecking problem, at least for standard operations such as translation, rotation, scaling, and shearing [SMIT87]. Nonetheless, there are more general transformations where this technique may not succeed: If one portion of an image is rotated $90°$ while some other stays fixed (imagine bending a long thin

---

[8]This is particular to the case of a rotation. For a general transformation, the source pixels contributing to an output pixel should consist of those pixels that are transformed into a small disk about the target pixel; these pixels may or may not constitute a disk in the source image.

rectangle into a quarter-circle shape), then there is certain to be bottlenecking at some point, no matter what the order in which the transformations are applied.

Wolberg and Boult [WOLB89] have developed a technique in which two simultaneous versions of a multipass transform are done at once. The original image is first transformed by a row-preserving map and a column-preserving map, and then also is transformed by a 90° rotation and a different pair of maps. For both transformation sequences, the method records the amount of bottlenecking present at each pixel.

Thus, each output pixel can be computed in two different ways. Wolberg and Boult select, for each pixel, the route that has less bottlenecking, so that some portions of the image may be row–column transformed, whereas others are column-row transformed. Since the two sets of transformations can be performed simultaneously in parallel processors, this technique is ideally suited to implementation in hardware.

17.5.3 Evaluating Transformation Methods

There are several criteria for judging image-transformation algorithms. Filtering theory tells us that an image can be reconstructed from its samples, provided the original image had no high-frequency components. Indeed, from *any* set of samples, one can reconstruct *some* image with no high-frequency components. If the original image had no high frequencies, then we get the original back; if it did contain high frequencies, then the sampled image contained aliases, and the reconstructed image is likely to differ from the original (see Exercise 17.6).

So how should we judge a transformation algorithm? Ideally, a transformation algorithm would have the following properties:

- Translation by a zero vector should be the identity

- A sequence of translations should have the same effect as a single, composite translation

- Scaling up by a factor of $\lambda > 1$ and then scaling down by $1/\lambda$ should be the identity transformation

- Rotating by any sequence of angles totaling 360° should be the identity transformation.

Many workable algorithms clearly fail to satisfy any of these criteria. Weiman's algorithm fails on all but the fourth criterion. Feibush, Levoy, and Cook's algorithm fails on the first if a filter more than 1 pixel wide is used. Even Catmull and Smith's two-pass algorithm fails on all four criteria.

None of this is surprising. To resample an image, we ought to reconstruct it faithfully from its samples by convolving with a sinc filter. Thus, each new pixel ought to be a weighted average of *all* the pixels in the original image. Since all the methods are sensible enough to use filters of finite extent (for the sake of computational speed), all of them end up blurring the images.

There are many image-transformation methods not covered here. They each have advantages and disadvantages, mostly in the form of time−space tradeoffs. These are described in detail in an excellent survey by Heckbert [HECK86b].

17.6 IMAGE COMPOSITING

In this section, we discuss compositing of images—that is, combining images to create new images. Porter and Duff [PORT84] suggest that compositing is a good way to produce images in general, since it is fairly easy to do, whereas rendering the individual portions of the image may be difficult. With compositing, if one portion of the image needs alteration, the whole image does not need to be regenerated. Even more important, if some portions of an image are not rendered but have been optically scanned into memory instead, compositing may be the only way to incorporate them in the image.

We describe compositing using the α channel in Section 17.6.1, compositing using frame-buffer hardware in Section 17.6.2, the artificial generation of α values in Section 17.6.3, and an interface for image assembly in Section 17.6.4.

17.6.1 α-Channel Compositing

What sort of operations can be done in compositing? The value of each pixel in the composited image is computed from the component images in some fashion. In an *overlay*, the pixels of the foreground image must be given *transparency values* as well as whatever other values they may have (typically RGB or other color information). A pixel's value in the composited image is taken from the background image unless the foreground image has a nontransparent value at that point, in which case the value is taken from the foreground image. In a *blending* of two images, the resulting pixel value is a linear combination of the values of the two component pixels. In this section, we describe the Porter–Duff mechanism for compositing images using such combinations and transparency values [PORT84].

Suppose we have two images, one of a red polygon and one of a blue polygon, each on a transparent background. If we overlay the two images with the red polygon in front, then, at interior points of the front polygon, only the color red is visible. At points outside the front polygon but inside the back polygon, only blue is visible. But what about a pixel lying on the edge of the front polygon but inside the back polygon (see Fig. 17.15)? Here, the front polygon covers only part of the area of the pixel. If we color it red only, aliasing artifacts will result. On the other hand, if we know that the front polygon covers 70 percent

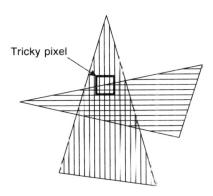

Fig. 17.15 Compositing operations near an edge: How do we color the pixel?

of the pixel, we can make the composited pixel 70 percent red and 30 percent blue and get a much more attractive result.

Suppose that as an image is produced, coverage information is recorded: The color associated with each pixel in the image is given an α *value* representing the coverage of the pixel. For an image that is to become the foreground element of a composited image, many of the pixels are registered as having coverage zero (they are transparent); the remainder, which constitute the important content of the foreground image, have larger coverage values (usually one).

To do compositing in a reasonable fashion, we need this α information at each pixel of the images being composited. We therefore assume that, along with the RGB values of an image, we also have an α value encoding the coverage of each pixel. This collection of α values is often called the α *channel* (see Section 17.7). Some types of renderers generate this coverage information easily, but it may be more difficult to generate for images that have been scanned into memory. We discuss this problem briefly in Section 17.6.3.

How do α values combine? Suppose we have a red polygon covering one-third of the area of a pixel, and a blue polygon that, taken separately, covers one-half of the area of the pixel. How much of the first polygon is covered by the second? As Fig. 17.16 shows, the first polygon can be completely covered, partly covered, or not covered at all. But suppose we know nothing more than the coverage information given. What is a *reasonable* guess for the amount of the first polygon covered by the second? Let us suppose that the area covered by the first is randomly distributed through the pixel area, and that the same is true of the second. Then any tiny spot's chance of being in the red polygon is $\frac{1}{3}$, and its chance of being in the blue polygon is $\frac{1}{2}$, so its chance of being in both is $\frac{1}{6}$. Notice that this value is exactly one-half of $\frac{1}{3}$, so that exactly one-half of the first polygon is covered by the second. This will be our general assumption: The area covered is distributed randomly across the pixel, so that the fraction of the first polygon covered by the second (within a particular pixel) is the same as the fraction of the whole pixel covered by the second polygon. The consequence of this assumption in practice is that compositing images with very fine detail that is parallel in the two images can have bad results. Porter and Duff report, however, that they have had no noticeable problems of this sort [PORT84].

Now, how do we compute the color of the pixel resulting from a 60—40 blend of these 2 pixels? Since the pixel is one-third covered by a color that, if it totally covered the pixel, would generate light of $(1,0,0)$, the color's contribution to the light of the pixel is $(\frac{1}{3})(1,0,0)$. We want to take 60 percent of this and combine it with 40 percent of the other. We thus combine the RGB triple for the red pixel, $(1, 0, 0)$, and the RGB triple for the

No overlap

Total overlap

Proportional overlap

Fig. 17.16 The ways in which polygons can overlap within a pixel. In image composition, the first two cases are considered exceptional; the third is treated as the rule.

TABLE 17.1 AREAS AND POSSIBLE COLORS FOR REGIONS OF OVERLAP IN COMPOSITING

Region	Area	Possible colors
neither	$(1 - \alpha_A)(1 - \alpha_B)$	0
A alone	$\alpha_A(1 - \alpha_B)$	0, A
B alone	$\alpha_B(1 - \alpha_A)$	0, B
both	$\alpha_A\alpha_B$	0, A, B

blue pixel, $(0, 0, 1)$, as follows: We say that

$$0.6 \left(\tfrac{1}{3}\right)(1,0,0) + 0.4 \left(\tfrac{1}{2}\right)(0, 0, 1) = (0.2, 0, 0.2)$$

is the resulting color.

Note that, whenever we combine 2 pixels, we use the product of the α value and the color of each pixel. This suggests that, when we store an image (within a compositing program), we should store not (R, G, B, α), but rather $(\alpha R, \alpha G, \alpha B, \alpha)$ for each pixel, thus saving ourselves the trouble of performing the multiplications each time we use an image. Henceforth, when we refer to an RGBα value for a pixel, we mean exactly this. Thus, it should always be true that the R, G and B components of a pixel are no greater than that pixel's α component.[9] (In rare cases, we may want to consider pixels for which this condition is violated. Such pixels are effectively luminescent.)

Suppose now that two images, A and B, are to be combined, and suppose that we are looking at pixel P. If the α value of P in image A is α_A and the α value of P in image B is α_B, we can ask what fraction of the resulting pixel is covered by A only, what part by B only, what part by both, and what part by neither.

We have already assumed that the amount covered by both is $\alpha_A\alpha_B$. This means that $\alpha_A - \alpha_A\alpha_B$ is covered just by A, and $\alpha_B - \alpha_A\alpha_B$ is covered just by B. The amount left is 1 minus the sum of these three, which reduces algebraically to $(1 - \alpha_A)(1 - \alpha_B)$. In the composited image, the area that was covered by A alone might end up with color A or no color, and similarly for color B. The area that was covered neither by A nor B should end up with no color, and the area covered by both might end up with no color, color A, or color B. Table 17.1 lays out these possibilities.

How many possible ways of coloring this pixel are there? With three choices for the both-colors region, two for each of the single-color regions, and one for the blank region, we have 12 possibilities. Figure 17.17 lists these possibilities.

Of these operations, the ones that make the most intuitive sense (and are most often used) are A **over** B, A **in** B and A **held out by** B, which denote respectively the result of hiding B behind A, showing only the part of A that lies within B (useful if B is a picture of a hole), and showing only the part of A outside of B (if B represents the frame of a window, this is the part that shows through the pane of the window).

---

[9]In a fixed-point scheme for representing the colors, pixels whose α value is small have a more discrete realm of colors than do those whose α value is 1. Porter and Duff say that this lack of resolution in the color spectrum for pixels with small α values has been of no consequence to them.

operation	quadruple	diagram	F_A	F_B
clear	(0, 0, 0, 0)		0	0
A	(0, A, 0, A)		1	0
B	(0, 0, B, B)		0	1
A **over** B	(0, A, B, A)		1	$1-\alpha_A$
B **over** A	(0, A, B, B)		$1-\alpha_B$	1
A **in** B	(0, 0, 0, A)		α_B	0
B **in** A	(0, 0, 0, B)		0	α_A
A held out by B	(0, A, 0, 0)		$1-\alpha_B$	0
B held out by A	(0, 0, B, 0)		0	$1-\alpha_A$
A **atop** B	(0, 0, B, A)		α_B	$1-\alpha_A$
B **atop** A	(0, A, 0, B)		$1-\alpha_B$	α_A
A **xor** B	(0, A, B, 0)		$1-\alpha_B$	$1-\alpha_A$

Fig. 17.17 The possibilities for compositing operations. The quadruple indicates the colors for the "neither," "A," "B," and "both" regions. Adapted from [PORT84]. (Courtesy of Thomas Porter and Tom Duff.)

In each case we can compute, as before, how much of each color should survive in the result. For example, in A **over** B, all the color from image A survives, while only a fraction $(1 - \alpha_A)$ of the color from B survives. The total color in the result is $c_A + (1 - \alpha_A)c_B$, where c_A denotes the color from image A (with α_A already multiplied in).

In general, if F_A denotes the fraction of the pixel from image A that still shows, and similarly for F_B, then the resulting color will be $F_A c_A + F_B c_B$. We must also compute the resulting α value: If fraction F_A of A is showing, and the original contribution of A is α_A, then the new contribution of A to the coverage is $F_A \alpha_A$. The same goes for B; hence, the total coverage for the new pixel is $F_A \alpha_A + F_B \alpha_B$.

A few unary operations can be performed on images. For example, the **darken** operation is defined by

$$\textbf{darken}(A, \rho) := (\rho R_A, \rho G_A, \rho B_A, \alpha_A) \qquad 0 \le \rho \le 1,$$

which effectively darkens a pixel while maintaining the same coverage. In contrast, the **fade** operator acts by

$$\textbf{fade}(A, \delta) := (\delta R_A, \delta G_A, \delta B_A, \delta \alpha_A) \qquad 0 \le \delta \le 1$$

which causes a pixel to become more transparent while maintaining its color (the color components are multiplied by δ because of the requirement that the colors must always be premultiplied by the α value).

A natural third operator (essentially a composite of these two) is the **opaque** operator, which acts on the α channel alone and is defined by

$$\textbf{opaque}(A, \omega) := (R_A, G_A, B_A, \omega \alpha_A).$$

As ω varies between 0 and 1, the coverage of the background by the pixel changes. Of course, if ω is made small, one of the color components may end up larger than the α component. For example, if ω is zero, then we get a pixel with color but a zero α component. Such a pixel cannot obscure anything, but can contribute light to a composited pixel; hence, it is called *luminous*. The possibility that color components can be larger than the α component requires that we clip the colors to the interval [0, 1] when reconstructing the true color (to reconstruct the color, we compute $(R/\alpha, G/\alpha, B/\alpha)$, and then clamp all three numbers to a maximum of 1).

One last binary operator, **plus,** is useful. In this operation, the color components and α components are added. Thus, to fade smoothly from image A to image B, we use

$$\textbf{fade}(A, t) \textbf{ plus } \textbf{fade}(B, 1 - t),$$

and let t vary from 1 to 0. Judicious combinations of these operations let us combine pictures in a great variety of ways.

We should examine the consequences of the assumptions made at the start: If a pixel is covered a fraction F_1 by one polygon and a fraction F_2 by another, then the first polygon (within the pixel) is covered a fraction F_2 by the second. If the two polygons happen to overlap in a reasonable way, this works fine, as in Figure 17.17. But if they happen to cross the pixel as parallel stripes, as in Fig. 17.18, then the assumption is invalid. When geometric entities are being composited, this problem is not particularly likely to occur.

Fig. 17.18 A case where the overlap assumptions fai in compositing.

However, when repeated instances of an image are composited atop one another, it may happen frequently.

To illustrate the use of compositing, we describe the composition of the frame from the Genesis effect described in Chapter 20, and shown in Color Plate IV.14. In this case, there are four images composited: *FFire*, the particle systems in front of the planet; *BFire*, the particle systems in back of the planet; *Planet*, the planet itself; and *Stars*, the background star field. The composite expression for the image is [PORT84, p. 259]:

(*FFire* **plus** (*BFire* **held out by** *Planet*)) **over darken** (*Planet*, 0.8) **over** *Stars*.

The planet is used to mask out the parts of the particle systems behind it, and the results are added to the front particle systems. These are composited over a slightly darkened planet (so that the particles obscure the underlying planet), and the result is placed over the background star field.

17.6.2 Alternate Compositing Methods

Let us consider two other mechanisms for compositing. The first of these is to composite images in compressed form (e.g., bitmaps that are stored with 8 pixels per byte), by doing very simple operations (*A* **over** *B*, *A* **and** *B*, *A* **xor** *B*) on the compressed forms. These operations are simple to implement: For any two possible bytes, we use a bitwise operation in hardware to combine them. In a more sophisticated version, the algorithm can be extended to handle this sort of compositing on run-length−encoded bitmaps.

The other compositing technique uses the frame-buffer hardware to implement compositing. Consider a simple example. We usually think of a 3-bit-per-pixel bitmap as containing a single image with 3 bits per pixel. However, we can also think of it as containing two images, one with 2 bits per pixel and the other with 1 bit per pixel, or as three separate images, each with 1 bit per pixel. In any case, the look-up table is used to select or combine the separate images to form a single composite image displayed on the view surface. For instance, to display only image 2, the image defined by the high-order bit of each pixel value, we load the table as shown in Fig. 17.19. To display image 0, the image

Entry number (decimal)	Entry number (binary)			Contents of look-up table (decimal)
0	0	0	0	0
1	0	0	1	0
2	0	1	0	0
3	0	1	1	0
4	1	0	0	7
5	1	0	1	7
6	1	1	0	7
7	1	1	1	7
	Image 2	Image 1	Image 0	0 = black 7 = white

Fig. 17.19 Look-up table to display an image defined by the high-order bit of each pixel.

Entry number (decimal)	Entry number (binary)			Contents of look-up table (decimal)
0	0	0	0	0
1	0	0	1	2
2	0	1	0	2
3	0	1	1	4
4	1	0	0	2
5	1	0	1	4
6	1	1	0	4
7	1	1	1	6
	Image 2	Image 1	Image 0	

Fig. 17.20 Look-up table to display a sum of three 1-bit images.

defined by the low-order bit of each pixel, we load the table with a 7 in those locations for
which the low-order bit is 1, and with a 0 for the other locations: 0, 7, 0, 7, 0, 7, 0, 7. If the
displayed image is to be the sum of the three images and if each image that is "on" at a
pixel is to contribute two units of intensity, then we load the table as shown in Fig. 17.20. If
1 of the 3 pixel bits is on, a 2 is placed in the table; if 2 of 3 are on, a 4; and if 3 of 3 are on,
a 6.

As another example, think of each image as being defined on parallel planes, as in Fig.
17.21. The plane of image 2 is closest to the viewer; the plane of image 0 is farthest away.
Thus, image 2 obscures both images 0 and 1, whereas image 1 obscures only image 0. This
priority can be reflected in the look-up table, as shown in Fig. 17.22. In this case, image 2
is displayed at intensity 7, image 1 at intensity 5, and image 0 at intensity 3, so that images
"closer" to the viewer appear brighter than those farther away. Where no image is defined,
intensity 0 is displayed.

Yet another possibility is to use the look-up table to store a weighted sum of the
intensities of two images, creating a double-exposure effect. If the weight applied to one
image is decreased over time as the weight applied to the other is increased, we achieve the
fade-out, fade-in effect called a *lap-dissolve*. When colored images are used, the colors
displayed during the fade sequence depend on the color space in which the weighted sum is
calculated (see Chapter 13).

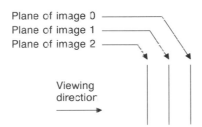

Plane of image 0
Plane of image 1
Plane of image 2

Viewing
direction

Fig. 17.21 Relation of three images to the viewing direction.

Entry number (decimal)	Entry number (binary)			Contents of look-up table (decimal)
0	0	0	0	0 no image present
1	0	0	1	3 image 0 visible
2	0	1	0	5 image 1 visible
3	0	1	1	5 image 1 visible
4	1	0	0	7 image 2 visible
5	1	0	1	7 image 2 visible
6	1	1	0	7 image 2 visible
7	1	1	1	7 image 2 visible
	Image 2	Image 1	Image 0	

Fig. 17.22 Look-up table to assign priorities to three 1-bit images.

Deciding how to load the look-up table to achieve a particular result can be tedious, especially if many images are used and the table has many entries. The Image Composition Language (ICL) [FOLE87c] allows the programmer to declare images (made up of one or more bit planes) as variables. The image to be displayed is described by a composition expression consisting of variables combined by arithmetic, relational, and conditional operations. The lap-dissolve is specified in ICL with the expression

$$newImage * t + oldImage * (1 - t),$$

in which the variables *oldImage* and *newImage* are images in the bit plane and t is a scalar variable varying from 0 to 1. The following composition expression adds red (the triplets in braces are RGB color specifications) to those values of an image c in the range [0.6, 0.8] and green to those values in the range [0.3, 0.5]:

```
if (c < 0.8) and (c > 0.6) then c + {1,0,0}
    else if (c < 0.5) and (c > 0.3) then c + {0,1,0}
    else c
endif endif
```

This short composition expression replaces a code segment that has a considerably larger number of lines.

17.6.3 Generating α Values with Fill Mechanisms

In the preceding section, we described compositing images that come equipped with an α channel. What if an image is produced by scanning of a photograph or is provided by some other source lacking this information? Can it still be composited? If we can generate an α channel for the image, we can use that channel for compositing. Even if we merely assign an α value of zero to black pixels and an α value of 1 to all others, we can use the preceding algorithms, although ragged-edge problems will generally arise.

Recall from Chapters 3 and 4 that there are various ways to *fill* regions of an image with new values. If we use a fill algorithm to alter not the color of a pixel but its α value, we can assign α values to various regions in the image. If the colors in the image represent foreground and background (e.g., a picture of a person standing in front of a white wall), we can choose to fill the background region with its original color but assign it a reduced α value. Fishkin and Barsky give an algorithm for recognizing regions that consist of pixels that are either entirely or partially made up of some color [FISH84]. For the details of this algorithm, see Section 19.5.3.

Of course, applying a seed-fill algorithm (see Section 19.5.2) is bound to fail if the background is not a single connected piece. If we attempt to correct this difficulty by applying the Fishkin–Barsky criterion for similarity to the background to every pixel in the image, items in the foreground whose colors are close to the background color are treated incorrectly. (Imagine the person in our example, standing in front of a white wall. Is the white writing on his green T-shirt part of the background?) If we try to seed fill each separate piece of background, the task may be hopeless. (Imagine our person again and suppose that the background shows through his curly hair. There may be thousands of background regions.) Nonetheless, a soft-seedfill of the background to determine new α values makes a good preliminary step, and for simple images can improve substantially on the approach of assigning α values of 0.0 or 1.0 to every pixel.

17.6.4 An Interface for Image Assembly

How are the tools used for compositing and applying geometric transformations of images used in practice? An image like Color Plate IV.19 is described by a complex collection of operations. The compositing operations such as *A* **over** *B* can be described by a tree structure, where the leaf nodes are images and the internal nodes are operators with operands as child nodes. But before the images can be composited, they must be placed correctly. This requirement suggests an *image-assembly tree* structure, in which each internal node is either an image transformation or a compositing operation, and each leaf node is an image.

Such an image-assembly structure can be implemented in a convenient user interface, in which the user adds nodes or moves pieces of the tree with a mouse, and places a marker at some node to view the image described by that node and its children. This view can be structural, merely showing the relative positions and sizes of the child images within the parent. On a workstation with limited color capabilities, the view can be a dithered version of the true-color image; on a sophisticated workstation, it can be a full-sized version of the image in full color. The structural view can be extremely useful, since the user can edit the geometric transformations in this view by mouse dragging, eliminating the need to type exact coordinates for geometric transformations; of course, the ability to enter precise coordinates is also essential.

An image assembler of this sort has been developed by Kauffman [KAUF88a]. Far more sophisticated image assemblers form the core of the video processors that generate many of the special effects seen on television.

17.7 MECHANISMS FOR IMAGE STORAGE

When we store an image, we are storing a 2D array of *values*, where each value represents the data associated with a pixel in the image. For a bitmap, this value is a binary digit. For a color image, the value may be a collection of three numbers representing the intensities of the red, green, and blue components of the color at that pixel, or three numbers that are indices into tables of red, green, and blue intensities, or a single number that is an index into a table of color triples, or an index into any of a number of other data structures that can represent a color, including CIE or XYZ color systems, or even a collection of four or five spectral samples for each color.

In addition, each pixel may have other information associated with it, such as the z-buffer value of the pixel, a triple of numbers indicating the normal to the surface drawn at that pixel, or the α-channel information. Thus, we may consider an image as consisting of a collection of *channels*, each of which gives some single piece of information about the pixels in the image. Thus, we speak of the *red, green,* and *blue channels* of an image.

Although this idea might seem contrary to good programming practice, in which we learn to collect information associated with a single object into a single data structure, it often helps to separate the channels for convenience in storage. However, some methods of image compression do treat the image as a 2D array, such as the quadtree and fractal encoding schemes described later, so separation into channels is inappropriate.

Before discussing algorithms for storing images as channels or arrays, we describe two important methods for storing pictures: use of the *metafile* and use of *application-dependent data*. Neither of these is, strictly speaking, an image format, but each is a mechanism for conveying the information that is represented in an image.

If an image is produced by a sequence of calls to some collection of routines, a metafile stores this sequence of calls rather than the image that was generated. This sequence of calls may be far more compact than the image itself (an image of the Japanese flag can be produced by one call to a rectangle-drawing routine and one call to a circle-drawing routine, but could take several MB to store as RGB triples). If the routines are sufficiently simple or are implemented in hardware, redisplaying a metafile image may be faster than redisplaying a pixel image. The term *metafile* is also used to refer to a device-independent description of a standardized data structure, such as the PHIGS data structure described in Chapter 7. To store an image in such a metafile, we traverse the current data structure and record the data structure in some device-independent fashion for redisplay later. This description may be not a sequence of function calls, but instead a textual transcription of some hierarchical structure.

The second storage scheme entails application-dependent data. If an application displays a particular class of images, it may be convenient to record the data from which these images were created, or even differences between the data and some standard set of data. If the images are all head-on views of human faces described as polygons, it may be simpler to store just a list of those polygons whose positions are different from their position in some standard facial image (and their new positions, of course). A more extreme version of this sort of condensation of information has been use in the Talking Heads project at the MIT Media Lab, in which only the positions of eyeballs, lips, and other high-level features are stored [BOLT84]. At this point, image description becomes more of a scene description, and properly belongs to the domain of modeling, rather than to that of image storage.

17.7.1 Storing Image Data

Now let us consider how to store the sort of image that consists of several channels of data. If our displays expect to be given information about an image in the form of RGB triples, it may be most convenient to store the image as RGB triples. But if space is at a premium, as is often the case, then it may be worth trying to compress the channels in some way. Approaches to compression must be weighed against the cost of decompression: The more sophisticated the compression technique, the more likely decompression is to be expensive. Although all of these techniques apply equally well to any channel of information, our discussion will be couched in terms of color channels, since these are the ones most often present in images (z-buffer, normal vector, and other information being optional).

If an image has few colors and each color occurs many times (as in an image of a newspaper, in which there may be only black, dark gray, light gray, and white), it may be worthwhile to make a table of colors that occur (here, the table would have only four entries), and then to make a *single* channel that is an index into this color table. In our newspaper example, this single channel would need only 2 bits of information per pixel, rather than perhaps 8 bits per color per pixel; the resulting image is compressed by a factor of 12. In pictures with more colors, the savings are less substantial; in the extreme case where each pixel in the image is a different color, the look-up table is as large as the image would have been if stored as RGB triples, and the indices into the look-up table take even more space. Roughly speaking, indexing into a look-up table begins to be worthwhile if the number of colors is less than one-half the number of pixels. (Of course, if the hardware for displaying the image works by using look-up tables as well, it may be easier and faster to store the image in this fashion than as RGB triples. Typically, such hardware provides a modest space for the look-up table, about 8 to 12 bits per pixel.)

This single-channel approach still requires at least one piece of information per pixel. If the image has a great deal of repetition, it may be possible to compress it further by *run-length encoding* a channel. Run-length encoding consists of giving a count and a value, where the count indicates the number of times the value is to be repeated. The design of the Utah Raster Toolkit [PETE86] includes a number of improvements on this basic idea. For instance, the count, n, is an 8-bit *signed* integer (with values -128 through 127): a negative count indicates that n pixels' worth of unencoded data follow; a nonnegative count indicates that the next piece of information is the value to be used for $n + 1$ pixels. Further improvements might include reserving certain negative values for special meanings: -128 might indicate that the next few bytes of information give a scan line and position to which to jump (in order to skip the recording of large areas of background color), and -127 might be reserved to indicate a jump to the start of a specified scan line. Such a naive run-length–encoding scheme at worst adds 1 byte for every 126 values (a -126 indicating that 126 pixels worth of unencoded data follow), a cost of about 0.25 percent for an image with 8 bits per pixel for each of red, green, and blue. In the best case, an image in which all pixels have the same value, the compression would be by a factor of about 100: 128 pixels' worth of values compress to 1 pixel's worth (24 bits, in this example), but the count byte adds another 8 bits.

There are other clever formats for compressing channels. For example, we could store the value of each pixel from a bitmap in an integer (as a 0 or 1), but most of the bits in the integer would be wasted. Instead, we might store one pixel value in each bit (this is the origin of the term *bitmap*). If the image being represented contains regions filled with patterns whose width is a factor of 8, then we can perform a similar run-length encoding, in which the first byte gives a count, n, and the next byte gives a pattern to be repeated for the next $8n$ pixels of the bitmap. This method is less likely to generate savings than is the ordinary run-length encoding for color images, since a block of 8 values must be repeated for any compression to take place.

Run-length encoding and other standard information-theory approaches such as Huffman encoding treat the image in channels, which can be imagined as linear arrays of values (although multiple channels can be considered a single large channel, so that we can run-length encode sets of RGB triples as well). Other methods treat the image as a 2D array of values, and hence can exploit any inter-row coherence. One of these techniques is based on the use of quadtrees.

The fundamental idea of the quadtree-based image description is that a region of an image may be fairly constant, and hence all pixels in the region can be treated as having the same value. Determining these near-constant regions is the core of the algorithm. This algorithm can be used either on a single component of the image, such as the 2D array of red values, or on the aggregate value associated with each pixel; for simplicity, we shall describe the algorithm for a single numerical component. The algorithm requires a mechanism for determining the mean value of the image in a region, and the extent of the deviations from the mean within a region.

The image is first considered as a whole. If the deviation from the mean in the image is sufficiently small (less than or equal to some nonnegative tolerance), then the image is reported as having a value equal to the mean, repeated over the entire image. (If the tolerance is set to zero, then the image really must be constant for this to occur.) If the deviation from the mean is not smaller than the tolerance, the mean of the image is recorded, the image is divided into quadrants, and the same algorithm is applied to each quadrant. The algorithm terminates because repeated subdivision of quadrants eventually breaks them into single-pixel regions, if necessary; for a single-pixel region, the deviation from the mean must be zero, and hence is less than or equal to any tolerance value.

We can improve the algorithm by recording not the mean of the image, but rather the means of the four quadrants whenever the image is subdivided, and the mean of the image when it is not. The advantage is that, when the image is redisplayed, if the quadtree is parsed breadth-first, the display may be constantly updated to show more and more refined images. The first image is four colored rectangles. Then, each rectangle is subdivided and its color is refined, and so on. In a system designed for scanning through a large number of images, this approach may be extremely convenient: after just a few bytes of information have been transmitted, a general sense of the image may begin to appear, and the user may choose to reject the image and to move on to the next one. This rapid detection of the sense of an image is especially useful if the images are transmitted over a low-bandwidth communications channel. Quadtree compression of images has been exploited by Knowlton, Sloan, and Tanimoto [KNOW80, SLOA79], and the algorithm has been further refined by Hill [HILL83]. Exercise 17.7 discusses other mechanisms for building a quadtree describing an image, some of which may be more efficient than the one described here.

17.7.2 Iterated Function Systems for Image Compression

A second image-compression algorithm is based on the notion of iterated function systems (IFSs). In this case, the compression factor can be extremely high, but the cost of compressing the image tends to be large as well. The algorithm requires, for each image, that the user interactively solve a geometric problem, described later [BARN88a]. Also, like all nondestructive compression schemes, the pigeonhole principle[10] says that, if some images are compressed, others must be expanded by some modest amount (since there can be no one-to-one mapping of all n by k arrays to all p by q arrays where pq is less than nk). The advantage of the IFS technique is that images with substantial geometric regularity are the ones that are compressed, whereas those that look like noise are more likely to be expanded.

An *IFS code* is a finite collection of affine maps $\{w_1, \ldots, w_r\}$ of the plane to itself, together with a probability p_i associated with w_i. The maps must be *contractive*; that is, the distance between points must be reduced by the maps, on the average (the precise requirement is described in [BARN88a]). Recall that an affine map of the plane is given by a formula of the form

$$ w \begin{bmatrix} x \\ y \end{bmatrix} = \begin{bmatrix} a & c \\ b & d \end{bmatrix} \begin{bmatrix} x \\ y \end{bmatrix} + \begin{bmatrix} e \\ f \end{bmatrix} ; \qquad (17.1) $$

so it is entirely determined by six numbers, $a, b, c, d, e,$ and f. Notice that these affine maps are just combinations of rotations, translations and scalings in the plane. The condition that they be contractive says that the scaling factors must be less than 1.

The next several pages give a rough description of how to produce a gray-scale image from an IFS code; the method is easily generalized to producing three gray-scale images from three IFS codes, that can then be used as the RGB components of a color image. ([BARN88a] uses a somewhat different scheme for encoding color.) This production of an image from an IFS code is essentially this decompression part of the IFS algorithm; we discuss it first.

Consider a rectangle, V, in the plane defining our image, and imagine V as divided into a rectangular grid whose subrectangles are $V_{ij}, i = 1, \ldots, n; j = 1, \ldots, k$. Choose a point (x_0, y_0) that remains fixed under one of the maps (say w_1, without loss of generality). We now proceed to apply the maps $w_1, \ldots, w_r$ in fairly random order (determined by the probabilities p_i), and watch where the point (x_0, y_0) is sent. We use the number of times it lands in V_{ij} for each i and j to determine the eventual brightness of pixel $[i, j]$ in the image. The pseudocode for this process is shown in Fig. 17.23

Before the last step of this algorithm, each image$[i, j]$ entry indicates how often the starting point, in the course of being moved randomly by the affine maps, falls into the $[i, j]$th square of the image. For this number accurately to represent the *probability* of falling into the square over an infinite sequence of steps, the number of iterations of the algorithm must be very large: K should be a large multiple of the number of pixels in the image.

The effect of this algorithm is essentially to create a picture of the *attractor* of the IFS. The attractor is a set, A, with the property that, if all the affine maps are applied to A, and the results are combined, the result is A:

$$ A = \bigcup_{i=1}^{r} w_i(A). $$

---

[10] The pigeonhole principle is the observation that, if more than m objects are placed in m boxes, then some box must contain more than one object.

```
void IFS (double image[MAX][MAX])
/* Given a collection of affine maps wᵢ, with associated probabilities pᵢ, */
/* which are global variables, generate a gray-scale image. */
{
    int x, y;                         /* A location in the plane */
    int i, j;                         /* Loop counters */
    int m;

    Initialize x and y to be a fixed point of w₀;
    Initialize image[i][j] to 0 for all i and j;
    for (i = 0; i < K; i++) {
        double r = Random (0, 1);     /* A random number 0 <= r <= 1 */
        double total = p[0];          /* Probability tally */
        int k = 0;
        while (total < r) {
            k++;
            total += p[k];
        }
        apply (k, x, y);              /* Apply wₖ to the point (x, y) */
        for (each i, j pair)
            if (LiesIn (x, y, i, j))  /* TRUE if (x, y) is in Vᵢⱼ */
                image[i][j]++;
    }

    m = maximum of all image[i][j] entries;
    for (each (i, j) pair)
        image[i][j] /= m;
}   /* IFS */
```

Fig. 17.23 The iterated function system rendering algorithm.

The set A consists of the places to which (x_0, y_0) is sent in the course of iterating the maps. Some places are visited more often than others are, and the likelihood of a region being visited defines a probability measure on the set. The measure associated with a small region Q is p if a point, in the course of infinitely many iterations of the maps, spends a fraction p of its time in the region Q. It is this probability measure that we are using to associate values to pixels.

Since K must be so large, the time spent in reconstructing an image from an IFS code is substantial (although the process is highly parallelizable). What about creating an IFS code from an image? To do so, we must find a collection of affine maps of the plane to itself with the property that, after the affine maps have been applied to the original image, the union of the results "looks like" the original image. Figure 17.24 shows how to make a leaf by

Fig. 17.24 A leaf made as a collage. (© Michael Barnsley, *Fractals Everywhere*, Academic Press.)

creating four (slightly overlapping) smaller versions of the leaf and making a collage from them.

The collage theorem [BARN88a] guarantees that any IFS that uses these affine maps has an attractor that looks like the original image. Choosing the probability associated with w_j changes the brightness of the portion of the image coming from w_j. Still, to compress an image into an IFS code, a user must find a way to recreate the original image as a union of repeated subimages, each of which is an affine transform of the original. This is the previously mentioned geometric problem to be solved by the user. Barnsley has announced that this process can be automated [BARN88b]: until a mechanism for doing so is made public, the technique is hardly usable for compressing large numbers of images. It *is* usable for modeling interesting objects, however (see Chapter 20). Color Plate IV.1 shows an entire forest modeled with an IFS.

17.7.3 Image Attributes

When we store an image in the conventional manner as a collection of channels, we certainly must store information about each pixel—namely, the value of each channel at each pixel. Other information may be associated with the image as a whole, such as width and height, and any image-description format must include this kind of information as well. It is insufficient to allocate a few bytes at the start of the image description for width and height; experience has shown that other image attributes will arise. Typical examples are the space required for look-up tables, the depth of the image (the number of bitplanes it occupies), the number of channels that follow, and the name of the creator of the image. For accurate color reproduction of images on other devices, we may also want to record reference spectra for the pure red, green, and blue colors used to make the image, and some indication of what gamma correction, if any, has been applied.

The need to store such properties has prompted the creation of flexible formats such as RIFF [SELF79] and BRIM (derived from RIFF) [MEIE83], which are general attribute-value database systems. In BRIM, for example, an image always has a width, height, and creator, and also a "history" field, which describes the creation of the image and modifications to it. Programs using BRIM can add their own signature and timestamp to the history field so that this information is automatically kept up to date. Figure 17.25 shows a text listing of a typical BRIM header for an image.

```
TYPE (string, 5): BRIM
FORMAT (string, 11): FORMAT_SEQ
TITLE (string, 31): Molecular Modeling Intro Frame
NAME (string, 27): Charles Winston  447 C.I.T.
DATE (string, 25): Sun Oct  9 12:42:16 1988
HISTORY (string, 82): Sun Oct  9 12:42:16 1988 crw RAY/n/
00033: Sun Oct  9 13:13:18 1988 crw brim_convert
DESC (string, 21): A ray-traced picture
IMAGE_WIDTH (int, 1): 640
IMAGE_HEIGHT (int, 1): 512
BRIM_VERSION (int, 1): 1
CHANNEL_DESC (string, 21): RED GREEN BLUE ALPHA
CHANNEL_WIDTH (short, 4): 8 8 8 8
ENCODING (string, 4): RLE
```

Fig. 17.25 A BRIM header for an image.

Many image-handling packages have been developed. One of the most widely used is the Utah Raster Toolkit [PETE86], which was written in fairly portable C so that the same tools can be used on a number of different architectures. Particularly troublesome issues for designing such toolkits are the numbers of bytes per word and the ordering of bytes within a word.

17.8 SPECIAL EFFECTS WITH IMAGES

The image-processing techniques described in Section 17.3 can be applied to an image to generate interesting special effects. If an image is processed with a high-pass filter, only the small details of the image remain, while all slowly varying aspects are deleted. By processing an image with a derivative filter, we can arrange to highlight all points where sharp transitions occur. Filters that reduce all intensity values below a certain level to 0 and increase all other values to 1 can be used to generate high-contrast images, and so on.

A large number of video techniques can be applied to blur images, to fade them, to slide them off a screen in real time, and so on. Many of these effects are created by using the electronic hardware for generating video signals, and modifying the signals as they are being shown. These techniques all lie in the domain of electrical engineering rather than in that of computer graphics, although the combination of effects from both disciplines can be fruitful.

We conclude this chapter by describing a digital technique for simulating neon tubing. If we paint the shape of a neon tube onto a black background, using a constant-width (antialiased) brush of constant color, our image does not look particularly exciting. But suppose we filter the image with an averaging filter—each pixel becomes the average of its immediate neighborhood. If we do this several times, the edges of the band we have drawn become blurred. If we now filter the image with an intensity-mapping filter that brightens those pixels whose intensities are above some threshold and dims those pixels whose intensities are lower than that threshold, the result looks quite a lot like neon tube. (There is another way to produce the same effect; see the discussion of antialiased brushes in Section

19.3.4.) Compositing such an image using an ω value greater than 1 and an α value less than 1 can cause the "neon" to illuminate whatever it is placed over, while the tube remains partially transparent.

17.9 SUMMARY

We have discussed several techniques for storing images, including some that are organized by programming considerations (multiple channels, headers), and some that are motivated by compactness or ease of transmission (quadtrees, IFS encodings). There are many other image storage formats, including a number of commercial formats competing for the privilege of being the "standard." Given the differences of opinion about the amount of color information that should be stored (should it be just RGB or should it consist of multiple spectral samples?), and about what information should be present in an image (should z-buffer values or α values be stored?), we expect no universal image format to evolve for some time.

We have also discussed geometric transformations on images, including multipass algorithms with filtering and the necessity of performing the filtering during such transformations. The number of interesting effects possible with image transformations is quite surprising. Due to the filtering used in such transformations, however, repeated transformations can blur an image. Transforming bitmaps involves other difficulties, since no gray scale is available to soften the aliasing artifacts that arise in the transformations. The simplicity of the data, however, makes it possible to develop very fast algorithms.

We also have discussed image compositing, which has become an extremely popular tool for generating complex images. When the α channel is used, composited images show no seams at the points where the component images overlap, unless the component images have some high geometric correlation. If rendering speed increases to the point where regenerating images is inexpensive, compositing may cease to be as important a tool as it now is. But if progress in computer graphics continues as it has, with each new generation of hardware allowing more complex rendering techniques, we should expect the image quality to increase, but the time-per-image to remain approximately constant. Therefore, we should expect compositing to be in use for some time.

EXERCISES

17.1 Show that the product of the matrices

$$\begin{bmatrix} 1 & \tan(t) \\ 0 & 1 \end{bmatrix} \begin{bmatrix} 1 & 0 \\ -\sin(t)\cos(t) & 1 \end{bmatrix} \begin{bmatrix} 1 & 0 \\ 0 & \cos(t) \end{bmatrix} \begin{bmatrix} 1/\cos(t) & 0 \\ 0 & 1 \end{bmatrix}$$

is exactly

$$\begin{bmatrix} \cos(t) & \sin(t) \\ -\sin(t) & \cos(t) \end{bmatrix}$$

Use this result to show how to create a rotation map from shears and scales. Use this technique to describe a pixmap-rotation algorithm derived from the Weiman algorithm (see Section 17.4.1).

17.2 How would you create a Weiman-style translation algorithm? Suppose a pixmap has alternating columns of black and white pixels. What is the result of translating this pixmap by $\frac{1}{2}$ pixel? What is the result of applying Weiman's scaling algorithm to stretch this image by a factor of 2? What do you think of these results?

17.3 When scaling a bitmap, you cannot perform averaging, as you can in the Weiman algorithm. What is a good selection rule for the value of the target pixel? Is majority rule best? What if you want to preserve features of the image, so that scaling an image with a black line in the middle of a white page should result in a black line still being present? Is the cyclic permutation of the Rothstein code still necessary?

17.4 Show that in the Feibush, Levoy and Cook filtering method (see Section 17.4.2), the correct sign is assigned to volumes associated with triangles in step 3 of the edge-filtering process. (Hint: Evidently *some* sign must be given to each triangle, and this sign is a continuous function of the shape of the triangle—two triangles that look alike will have the same sign. The sign changes only when you modify a triangle by passing it through a degenerate triangle—one where the vertices are collinear. Thus, to do this exercise, you need only to show that the sign is correct for two triangles, one of each orientation.)

17.5 This problem fills in the details of the edge-filtering mechanism in the Feibush, Levoy and Cook image-transformation algorithm (see Section 17.4.2.) Given a triangle within a rectangular region, with one vertex at the center, C, of the rectangle, and a function (drawn as height) on the rectangular region, the volume over the triangle may be computed in the following way:

1. Call the triangle ABC. Draw a perpendicular from C to the base of the triangle, AB, intersecting AB at the point D. Express the triangle as either the sum or the difference of the two triangles ACD and BCD.

2. Find the volume over the triangles ACD and BCD, and use these values to compute the volume over ABC.

3. Observe that, if the filter function is circularly symmetric, then the volume over ACD computed in step (2) is a function of only the length of the base, AD, and the height of the triangle, CD (the same is true for BCD, of course).

    a. Draw a picture of the situation described in step 1. Do this for two cases: angle ACB is less than 90° and angle ACB is greater than 90°.

    b. Find a condition on A, B, and D that determines whether ABD is the sum of the difference of ACD and BCD.

    c. Suggest a method for computing the volume above an arbitrary right triangle as described in step 3. Since the given function may not be integrable in elementary terms, consider Monte Carlo methods.

    d. Describe how you would arrange a table of widths and heights to store all the volumes computed in step 3 in a look-up table.

17.6 Consider the 1 by 3 image that is described as follows. The pixel centers in this image are at the points $(-2,0)$, $(0, 0)$, and $(2, 0)$, and the values at these points are -1, 0, and 1. The Nyquist frequency for the image is 1, and the image can be considered as a sample of a unique image that is a linear combination of sine and cosine functions with frequency 1 or less. All the cosine terms are zero (you can see that they are by noting that the function is odd, in the sense that $f(-x) = -f(x)$ for all x).

    a. Compute the coefficients, a_k, of $\sin(kx)$ (for $0 \leq k < 1$) so that samples of $\Sigma a_k \sin(kx)$ give this image. Hint: $a_r \neq 0$ for only one value of k.

    b. The image might appear to be simply a gray-scale ramp (if we imagine -1 as black and 1 as white). What would happen if we sampled the signal computed in part a at the points $(-1, 0)$, and $(1, 0)$. Would they interpolate the gray-scale ramp as expected?

This exercise shows the difficulty we encounter when we use exact reconstruction without filtering.

17.7 Assume that you are given an 2^k by 2^k gray-scale image with intensity values $0 \ldots 2^n - 1$. You can generate a 2^{k-1} by 2^{k-1} image by condensing 2 by 2 regions of the image into single bits. In Section 17.7.1, we proposed doing the condensation by computing the mean of the region. There are other possibilities, however. Analyze the selection method for condensation, where *selection* means choosing one particular corner of the region as the representative value.

    a. Assume that you want to transmit a 2^k by 2^k gray-scale image that has been completely condensed using selection. How many pixel values do you need to send? (Assume that the receiving hardware knows how to decode the incoming data, and can draw filled rectangles on a display.)

    b. On what class of pictures will the selection method give bad artifacts until the image is nearly completely displayed? Would some other condensation rule work better for these images?

    c. What other condensation rules would be preferable for sending black-and-white documents (such as typical pages from this book, which may contain figures)? Explain your choices.

17.8 (Note: To do this programming problem, you must have access to hardware that supports very rapid *bitBlt* operations on bitmaps.) Write a program that uses a 1-bit-deep α-buffer to composite bitmaps. Add such features as painting in a bitmap with an x-buffer (which determines where the paint "sticks" or shows). This problem is discussed extensively in [SALE85].

17.9 Suppose you were given a corrupted run-length encoded image, from which several bytes were missing. Could you reconstruct most of it? Why or why not? Suggest a run-length encoding enhancement that would make partial recovery of a corrupted image easier.

17.10 We saw in Section 17.5 how various transformations can be implemented in multiple passes.

    a. If a pattern is mapped linearly onto a polygon and then projected onto the viewing plane, show that the composite map from the pattern map (x, y) coordinates to the image (u, v) coordinates has the form

$$(x, y) \rightarrow (u, v),$$

where

$$u = (Ax + By - C)/(Dy + Ey + F)$$
$$v = (Px + Qy + R)/(Sx + Ty + U)$$

    b. Show how to factor this map into two passes as we did for the map

$$u = x/(y + 1), \quad v = y/(y + 1).$$

This idea of using two-pass transforms for texture mapping was introduced by Catmull and Smith in [CATM80]. The names of variables for the coordinates here are chosen to agree with the convention used in Section 17.6 and not with the names of the coordinates used in describing texture mapping elsewhere.

18

Advanced Raster
Graphics
Architecture

**Steven Molnar
and Henry Fuchs**

In this chapter, we discuss in more detail the issues of raster graphics systems architecture introduced in Chapter 4. We examine the major computations performed by raster systems, and the techniques that can be used to accelerate them. Although the range of graphics architectures and algorithms is wide, we concentrate here on architectures for displaying 3D polygonal models, since this is the current focus in high-end systems and is the foundation for most systems that support more complex primitives or rendering methods.

Graphics systems architecture is a specialized branch of computer architecture. It is driven, therefore, by the same advances in semiconductor technology that have driven general-purpose computer architecture over the last several decades. Many of the same speed-up techniques can be used, including pipelining, parallelism, and tradeoffs between memory and computation. The graphics application, however, imposes special demands and makes available new opportunities. For example, since image display generally involves a large number of repetitive calculations, it can more easily exploit massive parallelism than can general-purpose computations. In high-performance graphics systems, the number of computations usually exceeds the capabilities of a single CPU, so parallel systems have become the rule in recent years. The organization of these parallel systems is a major focus of graphics architecture and of this chapter.

We begin by reviewing the simple raster-display architecture described in Chapter 4. We then describe a succession of techniques to add performance to the system, discussing the bottlenecks that arise at each performance level and techniques that can be used to overcome them. We shall see that three major performance bottlenecks consistently resist attempts to increase rendering speed: the number of floating-point operations to perform geometry calculations, the number of integer operations to compute pixel values, and the number of frame-buffer memory accesses to store the image and to determine visible surfaces. These demands have a pervasive influence on graphics architecture and give rise to the diversity of multiprocessor graphics architectures seen today. At the end of the chapter, we briefly discuss several unusual architectures, such as those for ray tracing, for true 3D displays, and for commercial flight simulators.

18.1 SIMPLE RASTER-DISPLAY SYSTEM

As described in Chapter 4, a simple raster-display system contains a CPU, system bus, main memory, frame buffer, video controller, and CRT display (see Fig. 4.18). In such a system, the CPU performs all the modeling, transformation, and display computations, and writes the final image to the frame buffer. The video controller reads pixel data from the frame buffer in raster-scan order, converts digital pixel values to analog, and drives the display.

It is important to remember that, if such a system has sufficient frame-buffer memory, has a suitable CRT display, and is given enough time, it can generate and display scenes of virtually unlimited complexity and realism. None of the architectures or architectural techniques discussed here enhance this fundamental capability (except for a few exotic 3D displays treated in Section 18.11). Rather, most work in graphics architecture concerns the quest for increased rendering speed.

In Chapter 4, we discussed two problems that limit the performance of this simple system: the large number of frame-buffer memory cycles needed for video scanout and the burden that image generation places on the main CPU. We now consider each of these problems in greater detail.

18.1.1 The Frame-Buffer Memory-Access Problem

In Chapter 4, we calculated the time between successive memory accesses when a low-resolution monochrome display is being refreshed. For a system with 16-bit words, the access rate is substantial—one memory access every 864 nanoseconds. Systems with higher-resolution color monitors require much higher memory speeds. For example, refreshing a 1280 by 1024 screen with 32-bit (one-word) pixels at 60 Hz requires that memory accesses occur every $1/(1280 \cdot 1024 \cdot 60) = 12.7$ nanoseconds. Even this is only the average memory access rate, not the peak rate, since pixels are not scanned out during horizontal and vertical retrace times [WHIT84]. A simple *dynamic random-access memory* (DRAM) system, on the other hand, has a cycle time of approximately 200 nanoseconds, a factor of 16 slower than the speed required. Clearly, something must be done to increase the bandwidth to frame-buffer memory.

The following sections discuss solutions that have been used by various system designers. Some of these provide only modest performance increases, but are sufficient for low-resolution systems. Others provide greatly increased memory bandwidth, but incur significant system complexity. We begin by reviewing briefly the fundamentals of DRAM memories, since the characteristics of DRAMs strongly influence the set of solutions available.

18.1.2 Dynamic Memories

DRAMs are the memories of choice for most computer memory systems. *Static random-access memories* (SRAMs), which retain stored data indefinitely, can be made to run faster than DRAMs, which must be accessed every few milliseconds to retain data, but DRAMs are much denser and cheaper per bit. (DRAMs also require more complicated timing for reading and writing data, but these problems are easily solved with supporting circuitry.)

Figure 18.1 is a block diagram of a typical 1-Mbit DRAM chip. As in most DRAMs, single-bit storage elements are arranged in one or more square arrays (in this case, four arrays, each with dimension 512 by 512). Vertical *bit lines* transfer data to and from the storage arrays, one bit line for each column of each array. During read and write operations, one memory cell in each column is connected to its corresponding bit line. A *sense amplifier* attached to each bit line amplifies and restores the tiny signals placed on the bit line during read operations.

In a DRAM chip, read and write operations each require two steps. The first step is to select a row. This is done by asserting the *row address strobe* (RAS) while the desired row address is on the address inputs. The row decoder produces a 512-bit vector, whose bits are

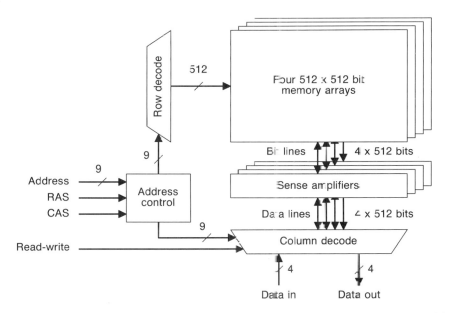

Fig. 18.1 A 1-Mbit (256K × 4) DRAM chip. An entire row is written to or read from each of the four memory arrays at the same time. The column decoder allows a particular element (column) of the selected row to be accessed.

0 everywhere except for a single 1 at the selected row. This bit vector determines which row's storage cells are connected to the bit lines and sense amplifiers.

The second step is to select a column, which is done by asserting the *column address strobe* (CAS) and read–write signal while the desired column address is on the address inputs. The column address selects a single bit from the active row of memory in each array. The selected bits are either buffered for output (during read operations) or set to the value on the data inputs (during write operations). Some DRAMs provide a faster access method called *page mode* for successive reads or writes to memory locations on the same row. In page mode, a row is selected just once, and successive columns are selected using the column address bits and CAS signal. In page mode, consecutive memory accesses require just one address cycle, instead of two. Thus, if adjacent pixels are stored in the same memory row, page mode can nearly double the bandwidth available for updating and displaying from the frame buffer.

Word widths greater than the number of data pins on a single memory chip can be accommodated by connecting multiple memory chips in parallel. With this arrangement, an entire word of data can be read from or written to the memory system in a single memory cycle. For example, eight 4-bit-wide DRAMs can be used to build a 32-bit memory system.

18.1.3   Increasing Frame-Buffer Memory Bandwidth

As we have seen, obtaining sufficient frame-buffer memory bandwidth both for video scanout and for updates by the CPU is a daunting problem. Different solutions have been proposed and used in various systems.

A partial solution, suitable for low-resolution displays, is to place the frame buffer on an isolated bus. This allows video scanout to occur simultaneously with CPU operations that do not affect the frame buffer. Only when the CPU needs to read from or write to the frame buffer must it contend with video scanout for memory cycles.

A second partial solution is to take advantage of DRAMs' page-mode feature. Since video scanout accesses memory locations in order, DRAM page misses are infrequent, so the frame buffer can run at almost twice its normal speed. Note, however, that frame-buffer accesses by the CPU may be less regular and may not be able to take advantage of page mode. We can decrease the number of page misses by the CPU by providing it with a data cache. As in conventional computing, a cache decreases the traffic between the CPU and memory, since a memory location accessed during one cycle is very likely to be accessed again in the near future. Furthermore, since cache entries frequently occupy several words, transferring data between the cache and main memory can exploit page mode. By combining page mode and a data cache, we can reduce the memory-access problem substantially, although further measures, as discussed in Section 18.1.5, are necessary for high-resolution displays.

A third, independent approach is to duplicate the frame-buffer memory, creating a *double-buffered* system in which the image in one buffer is displayed while the image in the other buffer is computed. Figure 18.2 shows one possible implementation, in which multiplexers connect each frame buffer to the system bus and video controller. Double-buffering allows the CPU to have uninterrupted access to one of the buffers while the video

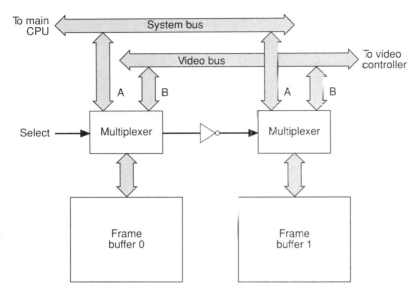

Fig. 18.2 Double-buffered frame buffer.

controller has uninterrupted access to the other. Double-buffering in this manner is expensive, however, since twice as much memory is needed as for a single-buffered display. Also, the multiplexers that provide dual access to the DRAMs require numerous chips, which increase the size of the system. (Actual dual-ported memories, with two fully independent read–write ports, could be used, but their low density and high cost make them impractical in almost all applications.)

18.1.4 The Video RAM

In 1983, Texas Instruments introduced a new type of DRAM, the *video random-access memory* (VRAM), designed specifically to allow video scanout to be independent of other frame-buffer operations [PINK83]. A VRAM chip, as shown in Fig. 18.3, is similar to a conventional DRAM chip, but contains a parallel-in/serial-out data register connected to a second data port. The serial register is as wide as the memory array and can be parallel loaded by asserting the transfer signal while a row of memory is being read. The serial register has its own data clock, enabling it to transfer data out of the chip at high speeds. The serial register and port effectively provide a second, serial port to the memory array. If this port is used for video scanout, scanout can occur in parallel with normal reads from and writes to the chip, virtually eliminating the video-scanout problem.

Since the shift register occupies only a small fraction of a VRAM s chip area and very few pins are needed to control it, VRAMs ideally should be only slightly more expensive than DRAMs. Unfortunately, the economics of scale tend to raise the price of VRAMs relative to DRAMs, since fewer VRAMs are produced (in 1989, VRAMs were roughly twice as expensive as DRAMs of the same density). In spite of this price differential, VRAMs are an excellent choice for many frame-buffer memories.

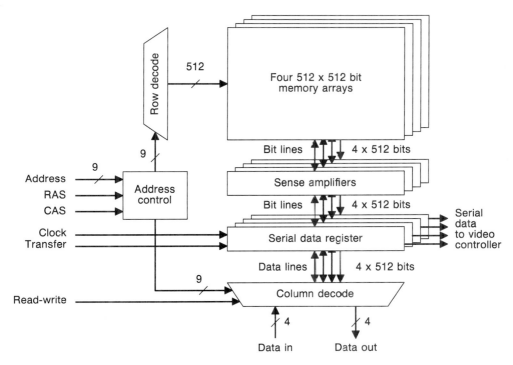

Fig. 18.3 Diagram of a 1-Mbit (256K × 4) VRAM chip. The serial data register provides a second (serial) port to the memory array.

18.1.5 A Frame Buffer for a High-Resolution Display

Figure 18.4 shows a typical frame-buffer design using VRAMs. The CPU has essentially unrestricted access to the frame-buffer memory. Only once every n cycles (where n is the dimension of the memory array) is a memory cycle required to load a new row into the VRAMs' serial registers. With screen resolutions up to 512 by 512 pixels, VRAMs can handle video scanout unassisted. With higher-resolution displays, the pixel rate exceeds the VRAMs' serial-port data rate of 30 MHz or less. A standard solution is to connect multiple banks of VRAMs to a high-speed off-chip shift register, as shown in the figure. Multiple pixels, one from each VRAM bank, can be loaded into the shift register in parallel and then shifted out serially at video rates. (Notice that this 1280- by 1024-pixel system, with five times the resolution of a 512 by 512 system, uses five-way multiplexing.) This shift register frequently is incorporated into a single chip containing look-up tables and digital-to-analog converters, such as Brooktree's Bt458 RAMDAC [BROO88]. In systems with 24 bits per pixel, such as the one shown in Fig. 18.4, three RAMDAC chips are typically used—one for each 8-bit color channel.

VRAMs provide an elegant solution to the frame-buffer memory-access problem. The bottleneck that remains in such systems is CPU processing speed. To generate a raster image (in 2D or 3D), the processor must calculate every pixel of every primitive. Since a typical primitive covers many pixels, and images typically contain thousands of primitives,

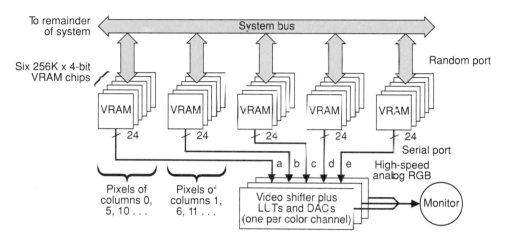

Fig. 18.4 Block diagram of a 1280- by 1024-pixel display using VRAMs. A parallel-in/serial-out shift register provides the high pixel rates required to drive the monitor.

generating a high-resolution image can require many millions of CPU operations. Because of this, even the fastest CPUs have difficulty rendering images quickly enough for interactive use.

18.2 DISPLAY-PROCESSOR SYSTEMS

To build a system with higher performance than the single-CPU system described in the previous section, we must either remove some of the graphics burden from the CPU or increase the CPU's ability to perform these tasks. Here we consider strategies that do not substantially increase the size or cost of the system (we consider larger, multiprocessing solutions in Sections 18.6 through 18.10). These strategies generally fall into three categories: (1) coprocessors that share the system bus with the main CPU, (2) display processors with their own buses and memory systems, and (3) integrated processors containing internal hardware support for graphics operations.

Coprocessors were discussed extensively in Chapter 4 (single-address-space (SAS) architectures). These have been found useful in 2D systems, but have not achieved wide use in 3D systems, largely because 3D systems require a larger set of operations than 2D systems and because bus contention in a SAS architecture severely limits system performance. The latter two approaches have been used successfully for 3D graphics, and we now discuss them further.

18.2.1 Peripheral Display Processors

Figure 4.22 shows a typical peripheral-display-processor system organization. The display processor generally has its own memory system (including the frame buffer) and a fast communication link to the main CPU. The main CPU sends display commands to the display processor, which executes them using resident software or firmware routines, or using specialized hardware.

The display processor may be the same processor type as the main CPU, or it may be a special-purpose processor. Using the same type of processor, as in the Masscomp MC-500 [MASS85], allows simpler and more flexible hardware and software designs. It does not exploit the regularity and specialized nature of most graphics calculations, however, and therefore provides at most a factor of 2 increase in performance, since the overall processing capacity is simply doubled. Most current display-processor systems use peripheral processors specialized for graphics operations.

Single-chip graphics processors.   Single-chip graphics processors are a successful and inexpensive type of peripheral-display processor that developed as functional extensions of single-chip video controllers. Consequently, many current graphics-processor chips combine the functions of the video controller and display processor. (Section 18.2.2 describes one popular graphics processor chip, the TMS34020.)

Graphics-processor chips targeted especially for 3D graphics have been introduced only recently. A pioneering chip of this type is Intel's i860, which can be used either as a stand-alone processor with support for graphics or as a 3D graphics processor. Unlike many 2D graphics-processor chips, the i860 does not provide hardware support for screen refresh or video timing. The i860 will be discussed in depth in Section 18.2.4.

Programming the display processor.   A major point of difference among display processor systems is where they store the model or database from which the image is generated: in the CPU's memory, or in the display processor's memory. Storing the database in the display processor's memory frees the main CPU from database traversal. Consequently, only a low-bandwidth channel is needed between the CPU and the display processor. However, such a system also inherits all the disadvantages of a structure database described in Chapter 7, particularly the inflexibility of a canonical, "hard-wired" database model.

Whether or not the display processor manages the database, it is an extra processor to program. Frequently, this program takes the form of a standard graphics library, such as PHIGS+, which satisfies the needs of many applications. Applications invariably arise, however, that require features not supported by the library. In such cases, users are forced either to program the display processor themselves (which may not even be possible), or to devise cumbersome workarounds using existing display-processor features.

18.2.2   Texas Instruments' TMS34020 — A Single-Chip Peripheral Display Processor[1]

Texas Instruments' TMS34020 [TEXA89] is an example of a single-chip graphics processor designed to accelerate 2D displays on PCs and workstations. It can be paired with a TMS34082 floating-point coprocessor, which rapidly performs 3D geometric transformations and clipping needed for 3D graphics. Unlike graphics-processor chips that perform only graphics-specific operations, the 34020 is a fully programmable 32-bit processor that can be used as a stand-alone processor if desired.

---

[1]Material for this example was contributed by Jerry R. Van Aken of Texas Instruments, Inc.

Figure 18.5 shows a typical system configuration using the 34020 (and optionally the 34082). As indicated in the figure, the graphics processor's local memory may contain VRAMs for the frame buffer and DRAMs for code and data storage. Alternatively, the graphics processor's entire memory may be built from VRAMs. The 34020 contains on-chip timers and registers to control video scanout and DRAM refreshing.

The 34020 supports data types for pixels and pixmaps, allowing pixels to be accessed by their (x, y) coordinates as well as by their addresses in memory. The following instructions implement common 2D graphics operations:

PIXBLT: The PIXBLT (pixel-block transfer) instruction implements a general bitBlt operation. It copies pixels of 1 to 8 bits, automatically aligning, masking, and clipping rows of pixels fetched from the source array before writing them to the destination array. It uses many of the optimizations discussed in Chapter 19, as well as processing several pixels in parallel, so the transfer rate approaches the system's full memory bandwidth—up to 18 million 8-bit pixels per second. A special version of PIXBLT supports text by efficiently expanding packed 1-bit bitmaps into 8-bit pixmaps.

FILL: The FILL instruction fills a rectangular array of pixels with a solid color. Large areas are filled at rates approaching the memory-bus speed. Texas Instruments' 1-Mbit VRAM supports a special block-write mode that allows up to four memory locations to be written at once from the same on-chip color register. Using this block-write mode, the 34020 fills areas at up to 160 million 8-bit pixels per second.

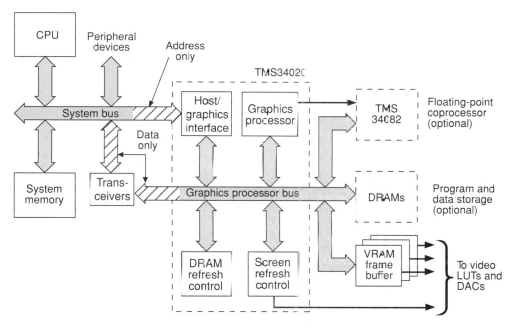

Fig. 18.5 Block diagram of the TMS34020 graphics-processor chip used as a peripheral display processor.

FLINE: The FLINE instruction draws 1-pixel-thick straight lines using a midpoint scan-conversion algorithm (see Section 3.2.2). The FLINE instruction draws up to 5 million pixels per second.

DRAV: The DRAV (draw-and-advance) instruction draws the pixel indicated by a pair of (x, y) coordinates, then increments the x and y coordinates in parallel. It is used in the inner loops of incremental algorithms for drawing circles and ellipses; for example, the inner loop of a midpoint circle routine (see Section 3.3.2) draws 2 million pixels per second.

Software for the 34020 is typically divided into time-critical graphics subroutines, written in assembly language, and other software, written in a high-level language. Software running on the 34020 communicates with the application program running on the main CPU.

The 34020 contains a 512-byte on-chip instruction cache and 30 general-purpose registers—enough memory to store the instructions and data required within the inner loop of many graphics subroutines. Once the instructions and data for the loop have been read from external memory, the memory bus is available exclusively for moving pixels to and from the frame buffer.

The TMS34082 floating-point coprocessor chip interfaces directly to the 34020, providing floating-point instructions and registers that increase the system's capabilities for 3D and other floating-point-intensive applications. The 34082 monitors the 34020's memory bus and receives floating-point instructions and data transmitted over the bus by the 34020. The 34082 can transform a 3D homogeneous point (including the homogeneous divide) every 2.9 microseconds.

18.2.3   Integrated Graphics Processors

Another approach to increasing system performance is to add support for graphics directly to the main CPU. This has become feasible only recently, with the development of very dense VLSI technologies that allow entire systems to be implemented on a single chip. Fully programmable 2D graphics processors, such as TI's 34020, are early examples of this approach, although they dedicate much of their chip area to graphics functions and comparatively little to general-purpose processing.

Intel's i860 is the first microprocessor chip to integrate direct support for 3D graphics. Proponents of this approach argue that the chip area required to support reasonable 3D graphics performance is relatively small and the payoff is high, since 3D graphics has become an integral part of many computing environments. This approach may well produce high-performance, low-cost 3D systems as increasing VLSI densities allow more sophisticated systems and more system components to be built onto a single chip.

18.2.4   Intel's i860—A Single-Chip Microprocessor with Integrated Support for 3D Graphics

Advances in VSLI technology have made it possible to build chips with extremely large numbers of transistors—more than 1 million in 1989. This allows high-performance CPU chips to include other features, such as caches, I/O controllers, and support for specialized instructions. Intel's i860 microprocessor, also known as the 80860, [GRIM89] is an example of such a chip with features supporting 3D graphics. Figure 18.6 is a block diagram of the major data paths in the i860.

According to Intel, the i860 achieves the following benchmarks: 33 million VAX-equivalent instructions per second (on compiled C code), 13 double-precision MFLOPs (using the Linpack benchmark), and 500,000 homogeneous vector transformations [INTE89].

The i860's graphics instructions operate in parallel on as many pixels as can be packed into a 64-bit data word. For applications using 8-bit pixels, this means eight operations can occur simultaneously. For 3D shaded graphics, which generally requires 32-bit pixels, two operations can occur simultaneously. Parallel graphics instructions include:

- Calculating multiple linear interpolations in parallel
- Calculating multiple z-buffer comparisons in parallel
- Conditionally updating multiple pixels in parallel.

For systems using 8-bit pixels (where eight operations can occur in parallel), the i860 can scan convert and shade 50,000 Gouraud-shaded 100-pixel triangles per second.

The i860 may be used either as a peripheral display processor (with an 80486

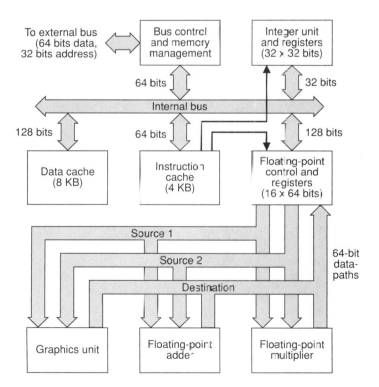

Fig. 18.6 Block diagram of Intel i860 microprocessor datapaths (adapted from [GRIM89]).

microprocessor as the main CPU, for example) or as a stand-alone processor. By combining front-end and back-end capabilities in a single processor, the i860 allows a powerful 3D graphics system to be built with very few parts—essentially the processor, memory, and the video system.

As VLSI densities continue to improve, we can expect to see even higher performance and more complex processors designed for graphics. Features commonly found in 2D graphics-processor chips, such as scanout and video-timing circuitry, may be included in such processors as well.

18.2.5   Three Performance Barriers

Systems can be built with a large range of performances using the techniques described up to this point. Low-end systems using a general-purpose microprocessor for the application processor and a 2D graphics processor are well suited for displays on PCs. Higher-performance systems using a powerful application processor and a high-speed 3D graphics processor, containing display-list memory and transformation hardware, are suitable for engineering and scientific workstations.

But how far can such designs be pushed? Let us imagine a display system made with the fastest available CPU and display processor, and a frame buffer containing the fastest available VRAMs. Such a system will achieve impressive—but still limited—performance. In practice, such *single-stream* architectures have been unable to achieve the speeds necessary to display large 3D databases at interactive rates. Architectures that display more primitives at faster update rates must overcome three barriers:

- *Floating-point geometry processing*: Accelerating the transformation and clipping of primitives beyond the rates possible in a single floating-point processor
- *Integer pixel processing*: Accelerating scan conversion and pixel processing beyond the rates possible in a single display processor and memory system
- *Frame-buffer memory bandwidth*: Providing higher bandwidth into the frame buffer (faster reads and writes) than can be supported by a conventional memory system.

These barriers have analogs in conventional computer design: the familiar processing and memory-bandwidth bottlenecks. In conventional computers, the presence of these bottlenecks has led to the development of concurrent processing. Similarly, the major focus of research in graphics architecture over the last decade has been investigating ways to use concurrency to overcome these performance barriers.

Before we discuss parallel graphics architectures, let us establish some groundwork about the demands of graphics applications and the fundamentals of multiprocessing. Later, we shall discuss various methods for building parallel systems that overcome these three performance barriers.

18.3   STANDARD GRAPHICS PIPELINE

Here we review from a hardware perspective the standard graphics pipeline discussed in Chapter 16. As has been mentioned, the rendering pipeline is a logical model for the computations needed in a raster-display system, but is not necessarily a physical model, since the stages of the pipeline can be implemented in either software or hardware.

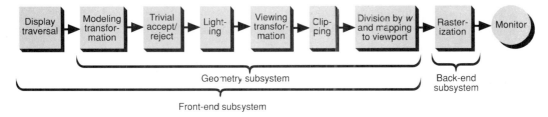

Fig. 18.7 Standard graphics pipeline for Gouraud- or Phong-shaded polygons.

Figure 18.7 shows a version of the rendering pipeline that is typical for systems using conventional primitives (lines and polygons) and conventional shading techniques (constant, Gouraud, or Phong). We shall discuss each stage of the pipeline in turn, paying particular attention to algorithms that have been used successfully in hardware systems and to those that may be useful in the future. At the end of this section, we estimate the number of computations needed at each stage of the graphics pipeline to process a sample database containing 10,000 polygons.

18.3.1 Display Traversal

The first stage of the pipeline is traversal of the display model or database. This is necessary because the image may change by an arbitrary amount between successive frames. All the primitives in the database must be fed into the remainder of the display pipeline, along with context information, such as colors and current-transformation matrices. Chapter 7 described the two types of traversal: immediate mode and retained mode. Both methods have advantages and disadvantages, and the choice between them depends on the characteristics of the application and of the particular hardware architecture used.

Immediate mode offers flexibility, since the display model does not need to conform to any particular display-list structure and the application has the luxury of recreating the model differently for every frame. The main CPU must perform immediate-mode traversal, however, expending cycles it could use in other ways. Retained mode, on the other hand, can be handled by a display processor if the structure database is stored in its local memory. Retained-mode structure traversal can be accelerated by optimizing the database storage and access routines or by using a dedicated hardware traverser. Furthermore, since the main CPU only edits the database each frame, rather than rebuilding it from scratch, a low-bandwidth channel between the main CPU and the display processor is sufficient. Of course, relatively few changes can be made to the structure database between frames, or system performance will suffer.

The choice between traversal modes is a controversial matter for system designers [AKEL89]. Many argue that retained mode offers efficiency and high performance. Others believe that immediate mode supports a wider range of applications and does not necessarily lead to reduced performance if the system has a sufficiently powerful CPU.

Unfortunately, it is difficult to estimate the processing requirements for display traversal, since they depend on the traversal method used and on the characteristics of the particular display model. At the very least, a read operation and a write operation must be performed for each word of data to be displayed. The processing requirements may be much greater if the structure hierarchy is deep or if it contains many modeling transformations (because of the overhead in pointer chasing, state saving, concatenating transformation matrices, etc.).

18.3.2 Modeling Transformation

In this stage of the pipeline, graphics primitives are transformed from the object-coordinate system to the world-coordinate system. This is done by transforming the vertices of each polygon with a single transformation matrix that is the concatenation of the individual modeling transformation matrices. In addition, one or more surface-normal vectors may need to be transformed, depending on the shading method to be applied.

Constant shading requires world-space surface-normal vectors for each polygon. We compute these by multiplying object-space surface normals by the transpose of the inverse modeling transformation matrix. Gouraud and Phong shading require world-space normals for each vertex, rather than for each polygon, so each vertex-normal vector must be multiplied by the transpose inverse transformation matrix.

Let us compute the number of floating-point calculations required to transform a single vertex if Gouraud shading is to be applied. Multiplying a homogeneous point by a 4×4 matrix requires 16 multiplications and 12 additions. Multiplying each vertex normal by the inverse transformation matrix requires 9 multiplications and 6 additions (only the upper-left 3×3 portion of the matrix is needed—see Exercise 18.1). Therefore, transforming a single vertex with surface normal requires $16 + 9 = 25$ multiplications and $12 + 6 = 18$ additions.

18.3.3 Trivial Accept/Reject Classification

In the trivial accept/reject classification stage, primitives (now in world coordinates) are tested to see whether they lie wholly inside or outside the view volume. By identifying primitives that lie outside the view volume early in the rendering pipeline, processing in later stages is minimized. We will clip primitives that cannot be trivially accepted or rejected in the clipping stage.

To trivially accept or reject a primitive, we must test each transformed vertex against the six bounding planes of the view volume. In general, the bounding planes will not be aligned with the coordinate axes. Each test of a vertex against a bounding plane requires 4 multiplications and 3 additions (the dot product of a homogeneous point with a 3D plane equation). A total of $6 \cdot 4 = 24$ multiplications and $6 \cdot 3 = 18$ additions are required per vertex.

18.3.4 Lighting

Depending on the shading algorithm to be applied (constant, Gouraud, or Phong), an illumination model must be evaluated at various locations: once per polygon for constant shading, once per vertex for Gouraud shading, or once per pixel for Phong shading. Ambient, diffuse, and specular illumination models are commonly used in high-performance systems.

In constant shading, a single color is computed for an entire polygon, based on the position of the light source and on the polygon's surface-normal vector and diffuse color (see Eq. 16.9). The first step is to compute the dot product of the surface-normal vector and the light vector (3 multiplications and 2 additions for directional light sources). If an attenuation factor based on the distance to the light source is used, we must calculate it and multiply it by the dot product here. Then, for each of the red, green, and blue color components, we multiply the dot product by the light-source intensity and diffuse-reflection coefficient (2 multiplications), multiply the ambient intensity by the ambient-reflection coefficient (1 multiplication), and add the results (1 addition). If we assume a single directional light source, calculating a single RGB triple requires $3 + 3 \cdot (2 + 1) = 12$ multiplications and $2 + 3 \cdot 1 = 5$ additions. Gouraud-shading a triangle requires three RGB triples—one for each vertex.

Phong shading implies evaluating the illumination model at each pixel, rather than once per polygon or once per polygon vertex. It therefore requires many more computations than does either constant or Gouraud shading. These computations, however, occur during the rasterization stage of the pipeline.

18.3.5   Viewing Transformation

In this stage, primitives in world coordinates are transformed to normalized projection (NPC) coordinates. This transformation can be performed by multiplying vertices in world coordinates by a single 4×4 matrix that combines the perspective transformation (if used) and any skewing or nonuniform scaling transformations needed to convert world coordinates to NPC coordinates. This requires 16 multiplications and 12 additions per vertex. Viewing transformation matrices, however, have certain terms that are always zero. If we take advantage of this, we can reduce the number of computations for this stage by perhaps 25 percent. We will assume that 12 multiplications and 9 additions per vertex are required in the viewing transformation stage.

Note that if a simple lighting model (one that does not require calculating the distance between the light source and primitive vertices) is used, modeling and viewing transformation matrices can be combined into a single matrix. In this case only one transformation stage is required in the display pipeline—a significant savings.

18.3.6   Clipping

In the clipping stage, lit primitives that were not trivially accepted or rejected are clipped to the view volume. As described in Chapter 6, clipping serves two purposes: preventing activity in one screen window from affecting pixels in other windows, and preventing mathematical overflow and underflow from primitives passing behind the eye point or at great distances.

Exact clipping is computationally practical only for simple primitives, such as lines and polygons. These primitives may be clipped using any of the 3D clipping algorithms described in Section 6.5. Complicated primitives, such as spheres and parametrically defined patches, are difficult to clip, since clipping can change the geometric nature of the primitive. Systems designed to display only triangles have a related problem, since a clipped triangle may have more than three vertices.

An alternative to exact clipping is scissoring, described in Section 3.11. Here, primitives that cross a clipping boundary are processed as usual until the rasterization stage, where only pixels inside the viewport window are written to the frame buffer. Scissoring is a source of inefficiency, however, since effort is expended on pixels outside the viewing window. Nevertheless, it is the only practical alternative for clipping many types of complex primitives.

In the pipeline described here, all clipping is performed in homogeneous coordinates. This is really only necessary for z clipping, since the w value is needed to recognize vertices that lie behind the eye. Many systems clip to x and y boundaries after the homogeneous divide for efficiency. This simplifies x and y clipping, but still allows primitives that pass behind the eye to be recognized and clipped before w information is lost.

The number of computations required for clipping depends on how many primitives cross the clipping boundaries, which may change from one frame to the next. A common assumption is that only a small percentage of primitives (10 percent or fewer) need clipping. If this assumption is violated, system performance may decrease dramatically.

18.3.7   Division by w and Mapping to 3D Viewport

Homogeneous points that have had a perspective transformation applied, in general, have w values not equal to 1. To compute true x, y, and z values, we must divide the x, y, and z components of each homogeneous point by w. This requires 3 divisions per vertex. In many systems, vertex x and y coordinates must be mapped from the clipping coordinate system to the coordinate system of the actual 3D viewport. This is a simple scaling and translation operation in x and y that requires 2 multiplications and 2 additions per vertex.

18.3.8   Rasterization

The rasterization stage converts transformed primitives into pixel values, and generally stores them in a frame buffer. As discussed in Section 7.12.1, rasterization consists of three subtasks: *scan conversion, visible-surface determination,* and *shading*. Rasterization, in principle, requires calculating each primitive's contribution to each pixel, an $O(nm)$ operation, where n is the number of primitives and m is the number of pixels.

In a software rendering system, rasterization can be performed in either of two orders: primitive by primitive (object order), or pixel by pixel (image order). The pseudocode in Fig. 18.8 describes each of these two approaches, which correspond to the two main families of image-precision visibility algorithms: z-buffer and scan-line algorithms.

Most systems today rasterize in object order, using the z-buffer algorithm to compute

for (*each primitive P*)	**for** (*each pixel q*)
for (*each pixel q within P*)	**for** (*each primitive P covering q*)
update frame buffer based on color	*compute P's contribution to q,*
and visibility of P at q;	*outputting q when finished;*
(a)	(b)

Fig. 18.8 Pseudocode for (a) object-order and (b) image-order rasterization algorithms.

visibility. The z-buffer algorithm has only recently become practical with the availability of inexpensive DRAM memory. If we assume that visibility is determined using a z-buffer, the number of computations required in the rasterization stage still depends on the scan-conversion and shading methods. Scan-conversion calculations are difficult to categorize, but can be significant in a real system.

Constant shading requires no additional computations in the rasterization stage, since the polygon's uniform color was determined in the lighting stage. Gouraud shading requires red, green, and blue values to be bilinearly interpolated across each polygon. Incremental addition can be used to calculate RGB values for each succeeding pixel. Phong shading requires significantly more computation. The x, y, and z components of the surface normal must be linearly interpolated across polygons based on the normal vectors at each vertex. Since the interpolated vector at each pixel does not, in general, have unit length, it must be normalized. This requires 2 additions, an expensive reciprocal square-root operation, and 3 multiplications for every pixel. Then, the Phong illumination model must be evaluated, requiring a dot product, more multiplications and additions, and, in the general case, the evaluation of an exponential. Bishop and Weimer's approximation to Phong shading, as mentioned in Section 16.2.5, can reduce some of these calculations, albeit at the expense of realism for surfaces with high specularity. Other shading techniques, such as transparency and texturing, may be desired as well. The architectural implications of these techniques are discussed in Section 18.11.

In addition to the shading calculations, updating each pixel requires reading the z-buffer, comparing old and new z values, and, if the primitive is visible, writing new color and z values to the frame buffer.

18.3.9   Performance Requirements of a Sample Application

In Section 18.2, we mentioned the three major performance barriers for raster graphics systems: the number of floating-point operations required in geometry calculations and the number of pixel-oriented computations and frame-buffer accesses required in rasterization. To appreciate the magnitude of these problems, we shall estimate the number of computations needed at each stage of the rendering pipeline to display a sample database at a modest update rate. To make this estimate, we must define a representative database and application.

A sample database.   We use triangles for primitives in our sample database, since they are common and their computation requirements are easy to estimate (complex primitives with shared vertices, such as triangle strips and quadrilateral meshes, are becoming increasingly popular, however. Exercise 18.2 explores the savings that can be achieved using these primitives.) We assume a modest database size of 10,000 triangles, a size that current workstations can display at interactive rates [AKEL88; APGA88; BORD89; MEGA89]. In addition, we assume that each triangle covers an average of 100 pixels.

The number of polygons that fall on clipping boundaries can vary widely from one frame to the next. For simplicity, we assume that no primitives need clipping in our sample application. This means we underestimate the amount of calculations required for clipping, but maximize the work required in succeeding stages. Image *depth complexity*, the average number of polygons mapping to a pixel, depends on the database as well as on the view. We assume arbitrarily that one-half of the pixels of all the triangles are obscured by some other triangle.

We assume that an ambient/diffuse illumination model and Gouraud shading are to be applied to each primitive (this is the lowest common standard for current 3D systems, although Phong illumination combined with Gouraud shading is becoming increasingly popular). We assume a screen size of 1280 by 1024 pixels and an update rate of 10 frames per second, typical of current interactive applications, but far from ideal.

In summary, our sample application has the following characteristics:

- 10,000 triangles (none clipped)
- Each triangle covers an average of 100 pixels, one-half being obscured by other triangles
- Ambient and diffuse illumination models (not Phong)
- Gouraud shading
- 1280 by 1024 display screen, updated at 10 frames per second.

We cannot calculate all the computation and memory-bandwidth requirements in our sample application, since many steps are difficult to categorize. Instead, we concentrate on the three performance barriers: the number of floating-point operations for geometry computations, the number of integer operations for computing pixel values, and the number of frame-buffer accesses for rasterization.

Geometry calculations.   For each frame, we must process $10,000 \cdot 3 = 30,000$ vertices and vertex-normal vectors. In the modeling transformation stage, transforming a vertex (including transforming the normal vector) requires 25 multiplications and 18 additions. The requirements for this stage are thus $30,000 \cdot 25 = 750,000$ multiplications and $30,000 \cdot 18 = 540,000$ additions.

Trivial accept/reject classification requires testing each vertex of each primitive against the six bounding planes of the viewing volume, a total of 24 multiplications and 18 additions per vertex. The requirements for this stage are thus $30,000 \cdot 24 = 720,000$ multiplications and $30,000 \cdot 18 = 540,000$ additions, regardless of how many primitives are trivially accepted or rejected.

Lighting requires 12 multiplications and 5 additions per vertex, a total of $30,000 \cdot 12 = 360,000$ multiplications and $30,000 \cdot 5 = 150,000$ additions.

The viewing transformation requires 8 multiplications and 6 additions per vertex, a total of $30,000 \cdot 8 = 240,000$ multiplications and $30,000 \cdot 6 = 180,000$ additions.

The requirements for clipping are variable; the exact number depends on the number of primitives that cannot be trivially accepted or rejected, which in turn depends on the scene and on the viewing angle. We have assumed the simplest case for our database, that all primitives lie completely within the viewing volume. If a large fraction of the primitives needs clipping, the computational requirements could be substantial (perhaps even more than in the geometric transformation stage).

Division by w requires 3 divisions per vertex, a total of $30,000 \cdot 3 = 90,000$ divisions. Mapping to the 3D viewport requires 2 multiplications and 2 additions per vertex, a total of 60,000 multiplications and 60,000 additions.

Summing the floating-point requirements for all of the geometry stages gives a total of 2,220,000 multiplications/divisions and 1,470,000 additions/subtractions per frame. Since a new frame is calculated every $\frac{1}{10}$ second, a total of 22.2 million multiplications/divisions and 14.7 million additions/subtractions (36.9 million aggregate floating-point operations) as required per second—a very substantial number.

Rasterization calculations and frame-buffer accesses. Let us now estimate the number of pixel calculations and frame-buffer memory accesses required in each frame. We assume that z values and RGB triples each occupy one word (32 bits) of frame-buffer memory (typical in most current high-performance systems). For each pixel that is initially visible (i.e., results in an update to the frame buffer), z, R, G, and B values are calculated (4 additions per pixel if forward differences are used), a z value is read from the frame buffer (1 frame-buffer cycle), the z values are compared (1 subtraction) and new z values and colors are written (2 frame-buffer cycles). For each pixel that is initially not visible, only the z value needs to be calculated (1 addition), and a z value is read from the frame buffer (1 frame-buffer cycle), and the two z values are compared (1 subtraction). Note that initially visible pixels may get covered, but initially invisible pixels can never be exposed.

Since we assume that one-half of the pixels of each triangle are visible in the final scene, a reasonable guess is that three-quarters of the pixels are initially visible and one-quarter of the pixels are initially invisible. Each triangle covers 100 pixels, so $\frac{3}{4} \cdot 100 \cdot 10,000 = 750,000$ pixels are initially visible and $\frac{1}{4} \cdot 100 \cdot 10,000 = 250,000$ pixels are initially invisible. To display an entire frame, therefore, a total of $(750,000 \cdot 5) + (250,000 \cdot 2) = 4.25$ million additions and $(750,000 \cdot 3) + (250,000 \cdot 1) = 2.5$ million frame-buffer accesses is required. To initialize each frame, both color and z-buffers must be cleared, an additional $1280 \cdot 1024 \cdot 2 = 2.6$ million frame-buffer accesses. The total number of frame-buffer accesses per frame, therefore, is 2.5 million + 2.6 million = 5.1 million. If 10 frames are generated per second, 42.5 million additions and 51 million frame-buffer accesses are required per second.

In 1989, the fastest floating-point processors available computed approximately 20 million floating-point operations per second, the fastest integer processors computed approximately 40 million integer operations per second, and DRAM memory systems had cycle times of approximately 100 nanoseconds. The floating-point and integer requirements of our sample application, therefore, are just at the limit of what can be achieved in a single CPU. The number of frame-buffer accesses, however, is much higher than is possible in a conventional memory system. As we mentioned earlier, this database is only modestly sized for systems available in 1989. In the following sections, we show how multiprocessing can be used to achieve the performance necessary to display databases that are this size and larger.

18.4 INTRODUCTION TO MULTIPROCESSING

Displaying large databases at high frame rates clearly requires dramatic system performance, both in terms of computations and of memory of bandwidth. We have seen that the geometry portion of a graphics system can require more processing power than a single CPU can provide. Likewise, rasterization can require more bandwidth into memory than a single memory system can provide. The only way to attain such performance levels is to

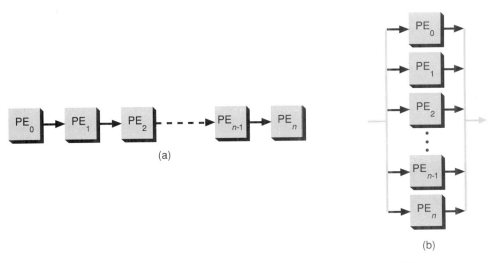

Fig. 18.9 Basic forms of multiprocessing: (a) pipelining, and (b) parallelism.

perform multiple operations concurrently and to perform multiple reads and writes to memory concurrently—we need concurrent processing.

Concurrent processing, or *multiprocessing,* is the basis of virtually all high-performance graphics architectures. Multiprocessing has two basic forms: *pipelining* and *parallelism* (we reserve the term *concurrency* for multiprocessing in general). A *pipeline processor* contains a number of *processing elements* (PEs) arranged such that the output of one becomes the input of the next, in pipeline fashion (Fig. 18.9a). The PEs of a *parallel processor* are arranged side by side and operate simultaneously on different portions of the data (Fig. 18.9b).

18.4.1 Pipelining

To pipeline a computation, we partition it into stages that can be executed sequentially in separate PEs. Obviously, a pipeline can run only as fast as its slowest stage, so the processing load should be distributed evenly over the PEs. If this is not possible, PEs can be sized according to the jobs they must perform.

An important issue in pipeline systems is *throughput* versus *latency.* Throughput is the overall rate at which data are processed; latency is the time required for a single data element to pass from the beginning to the end of the pipeline. Some calculations can be pipelined using a large number of stages to achieve very high throughput. Pipeline latency increases with pipeline length, however, and certain computations can tolerate only a limited amount of latency. For example, real-time graphics systems, such as flight simulators, must respond quickly to changes in flight controls. If more than one or two frames are in the rendering pipeline at once, the system's interactivity may be impaired, regardless of the frame rate.

18.4.2 Parallelism

To parallelize a computation, we partition the data into portions that can be processed independently by different PEs. Frequently, PEs can execute the same program. *Homogeneous* parallel processors contain PEs of the same type; *heterogeneous* parallel processors contain PEs of different types. In any parallel system, the overall computation speed is determined by the time required for the slowest PE to finish its task. It is important, therefore, to balance the processing load among the PEs

A further distinction is useful for homogeneous parallel processors: whether the processors operate in *lock step* or independently. Processors that operate in lock step generally share a single code store and are called *single-instruction multiple-data* (SIMD) processors. Processors that operate independently must have a separate code store for each PE and are called *multiple-instruction multiple-data* (MIMD) processors.

SIMD processors.   Because all the PEs in a SIMD processor share a single code store, SIMD processors are generally less expensive than MIMD processors. However, they do not perform well on algorithms that contain conditional branches or that access data using pointers or indirection. Since the path taken in a conditional branch depends on data specific to a PE, different PEs may follow different branch paths. Because all the PEs in a SIMD processor operate in lock step, they all must follow every possible branch path. To accommodate conditional branches, PEs generally contain an *enable register* to qualify write operations. Only PEs whose enable registers are set write the results of computations. By appropriately setting and clearing the enable register, PEs can execute conditional branches (see Fig. 18.10a).

Algorithms with few conditional branches execute efficiently on SIMD processors. Algorithms with many conditional branches can be extremely inefficient, however, since

<table>
<tr><td>

statement 1;
if not *condition* **then**
   enable = FALSE;
statement 2;
toggle *enable*;
statement 3;
statement 4;
enable = TRUE;
statement 5;
statement 6;

</td><td>

statement 1;
if *condition* **then**
   statement 2;
else
  begin
    statement 3;
    statement 4;
  end
statement 5;
statement 6;

</td></tr>
<tr><td>

Total operations:
10 if condition evaluates TRUE,
10 if condition evaluates FALSE
(a)

</td><td>

Total operations:
5 if condition evaluates TRUE,
6 if condition evaluates FALSE
(b)

</td></tr>
</table>

Fig. 18.10 (a) SIMD and (b) MIMD expressions of the same algorithm. In a SIMD program, conditional branches transform into operations on the enable register. When the enable register of a particular PE is FALSE, the PE executes the current instruction, but does not write the result.

most PEs may be disabled at any given time. Data structures containing pointers (such as linked lists or trees) or indexed arrays cause similar problems. Since a pointer or array index may contain a different value at each PE, all possible values must be enumerated to ensure that each PE can make its required memory reference. For large arrays or pointers, this is an absurd waste of processing resources. A few SIMD processors provide separate address wires for each PE in order to avoid this problem, but this adds size and complexity to the system.

MIMD processors.   MIMD processors are more expensive than SIMD processors, since each PE must have its own code store and controller. PEs in a MIMD processor often execute the same program. Unlike SIMD PEs, however, they are not constrained to operate in lock step. Because of this freedom, MIMD processors suffer no disadvantage when they encounter conditional branches; each PE makes an independent control-flow decision, skipping instructions that do not need to be executed (see Fig. 18.10b). As a result, MIMD processors achieve higher efficiency on general types of computations. However, since processors may start and end at different times and may process data at different rates, synchronization and load balancing are more difficult, frequently requiring FIFO buffers at the input or output of each PE.

18.4.3 Multiprocessor Graphics Systems

Pipeline and parallel processors are the basic building blocks of virtually all current high-performance graphics systems. Both techniques can be used to accelerate front-end and back-end subsystems of a graphics system, as shown in Fig. 18.11.

In the following sections, we examine each of these strategies. Sections 18.5 and 18.6 discuss pipeline and parallel front-end architectures. Sections 18.8 and 18.9 discuss pipeline and parallel back-end architectures. Section 18.10 discusses back-end architectures that use parallel techniques in combination.

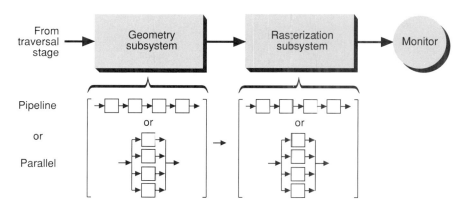

Fig. 18.11 Pipelining and parallelism can be used to accelerate both front-end and back-end portions of a graphics system.

18.5   PIPELINE FRONT-END ARCHITECTURES

Recall from Section 18.3 that the front end of a graphics display system has two major tasks: traversing the display model and transforming primitives into screen space. As we have seen, to achieve the rendering rates required in current applications, we must use concurrency to speed these computations. Both pipelining and parallelism have been used for decades to build front ends of high-performance graphics systems. Since the front end is intrinsically pipelined, its stages can be assigned to separate hardware units. Also, the large numbers of primitives in most graphics databases can be distributed over multiple processors and processed in parallel. In this section, we discuss pipeline front-end systems. We discuss parallel front-end systems in Section 18.6.

In introducing the standard graphics pipeline of Fig. 18.7, we mentioned that it provides a useful conceptual model of the rendering process. Because of its linear nature and fairly even allocation of processing effort, it also maps well onto a physical pipeline of processors. This has been a popular approach to building high-performance graphics systems since the 1960s, as described in [MYER68], a classic paper on the evolution of graphics architectures. Each stage of the pipeline can be implemented in several ways: as an individual general-purpose processor, as a custom hardware unit, or as a pipeline or parallel processor itself. We now discuss implementations for each stage in the front-end pipeline.

18.5.1   Application Program and Display Traversal

Some processor must execute the application program that drives the entire graphics system. In addition to feeding the graphics pipeline, this processor generally handles input devices, file I/O, and all interaction with the user. In systems using immediate-mode traversal, the display model is generally stored in the CPU's main memory. The CPU must therefore traverse the model as well as run the application. In systems using retained mode, the model is generally (but not always) stored in the display processor's memory, with the display processor performing traversal. Because such systems use two processors for these tasks, they are potentially faster, although they are less flexible and have other limitations, as discussed in Section 7.2.2.

Where very high performance is desired, a single processor may not be powerful enough to traverse the entire database with sufficient speed. The only remedy is to partition the database and to traverse it in parallel. This relatively new technique is discussed in Section 18.6.1.

18.5.2   Geometric Transformation

The geometric transformation stages (modeling transformation and viewing transformation) are highly compute-intensive. Fortunately, vector and matrix multiplications are simple calculations that require no branching or looping, and can readily be implemented in hardware.

The most common implementation of these stages is a single processor or functional unit that sequentially transforms a series of vertices. A pioneering processor of this type was the Matrix Multiplier [SUTH68], which could multiply a four-element vector by a homogeneous transformation matrix in 20 microseconds. Other special-purpose geometry processors have been developed since then, most notably Clark's Geometry Engine, which can perform clipping as well (see Section 18.5.5). Recent geometry processors have exploited the power and programmability of commercial floating-point chips.

If pipelining does not provide enough performance, transformation computations can be parallelized in several ways:

- Individual components of a vertex may be calculated in parallel. Four parallel processors, each containing the current transformation matrix, can evaluate the expressions for x, y, z, and w in parallel.

- Multiple vertices can be transformed in parallel. If primitives are all of a uniform type—say, triangles—the three vertices of each triangle can be transformed simultaneously.

- Entire primitives can be transformed in parallel. If n transformation engines are available, each processor can transform every nth primitive. This technique has many of the advantages and disadvantages of parallel front-end systems, which we will discuss in Section 18.6.

18.5.3   Trivial Accept/Reject Classification

Trivial accept and reject tests are straightforward to implement, since they require at worst a dot product and at best a single floating-point comparison (or subtract) to determine on which side of each clipping plane each vertex lies. Because these tests require little computation, they are generally performed by the processor that transforms primitives.

18.5.4   Lighting

Like geometric transformation, lighting calculations are straightforward and are floating-point–intensive. A specialized hardware processor can calculate vertex colors based on a polygon's color and the light vector. More frequently, lighting calculations are performed using a programmable floating-point processor. In lower-performance systems, lighting calculations can be done in the same processor that transforms vertices. Note that if Phong shading is used, lighting calculations are deferred until the rasterization stage.

18.5.5   Clipping

Polygon clipping was once considered cumbersome, since the number of vertices can change during the clipping process and concave polygons can fragment into multiple polygons during clipping. Sutherland and Hodgman [SUTH74] showed that arbitrary convex or concave polygons can be clipped to a convex view volume by passing the polygon's vertices through a single processing unit multiple times. Each pass through the unit clips the polygon to a different plane. In 1980, Clark proposed unwrapping this processing loop into a simple pipeline of identical processors, each of which could be implemented in a single VLSI chip, which he named the *Geometry Engine* [CLAR82]. The Geometry Engine was general enough that it could transform primitives and perform perspective division as well.

Clipping using a Geometry Engine (or similar processor) can be performed either by a single processor that clips each polygon by as many planes as necessary, or by a pipeline of clipping processors, one for each clipping plane. The technique chosen affects the worst-case performance of the graphics system: Systems with only one clipping processor may bog down during frames in which large numbers of primitives need to be clipped, whereas systems with a clipping processor for each clipping plane can run at full speed. However, most of the clipping processors are idle for most databases and views in the latter approach.

General-purpose floating-point units recently have begun to replace custom VLSI transformation and clipping processors. For example, Silicon Graphics, which for many years employed custom front-end processors, in 1989 used the Weitek 3332 floating-point chip for transformations and clipping in their POWER IRIS system (described in detail in Section 18.8.2). The delicate balance between performance and cost now favors commodity processors. This balance may change again in the future if new graphics-specific functionality is needed and cannot be incorporated economically into general-purpose processors.

18.5.6   Division by *w* and Mapping to 3D Viewpoint

Like geometric transformation and lighting, the calculations in this stage are straightforward but require substantial floating-point resources. A floating-point divide is time consuming even for most floating-point processors (many processors use an iterative method to do division). Again, these stages can be implemented in custom functional units or in a commercial floating-point processor. In very high-performance systems, these calculations can be performed in separate, pipelined processors.

18.5.7   Limitations of Front-End Pipelines

Even though pipelining is the predominant technique for building high-performance front-end systems, it has several limitations that are worth considering. First, a different algorithm is needed for each stage of the front-end pipeline. Thus, either a variety of hard-wired functional units must be designed or, if programmable processors are used, different programs must be written and loaded into each processor. In either case, processor or functional-unit capabilities must be carefully matched to their tasks, or bottlenecks will occur.

Second, since the rendering algorithm is committed to hardware (or at least to firmware, since few systems allow users to reprogram pipeline processors), it is difficult to add new features. Even if users have programming support for the pipeline processors, the distribution of hardware resources in the system may not adequately support new features such as complex primitives or collision detection between primitives.

A final shortcoming of pipelined front ends is that the approach breaks down when display traversal can no longer be performed by a single processor, and this inevitably occurs at some performance level. For example, if we assume that traversal is performed by a 20-MHz processor and memory system, that the description of each triangle in the database requires 40 words of data (for vertex coordinates, normal vectors, colors, etc.), and that each word sent to the pipeline requires two memory/processor cycles (one to read it from memory, another to load it into the pipeline), then a maximum of $20,000,000 / (2 \cdot 40) = 250,000$ triangles per second can be displayed by the system, no matter how powerful the processors in the pipeline are. Current systems are rapidly approaching such limits.

What else can be done, then, to achieve higher performance? The alternative to pipelining front-end calculations is to parallelize them. The following section describes this second way to build high-performance front-end systems.

18.6   PARALLEL FRONT-END ARCHITECTURES

Since graphics databases are regular, typically consisting of a large number of primitives that receive nearly identical processing, an alternate way to add concurrency is to partition the data into separate streams and to process them independently. For most stages of the front-end subsystem, such partitioning is readily done; for example, the geometric-transformation stages can use any of the parallel techniques described in Section 18.5.2. However, stages in which data streams diverge (display traversal) or converge (between the front end and back end) are problematic, since they must handle the full data bandwidth.

18.6.1   Display Traversal

Almost all application programs assume a single, contiguous display model or database. In a parallel front-end system, the simplest technique is to traverse the database in a single processor (serial traversal) and then to distribute primitives to the parallel processors. Unfortunately, this serial traversal can become the bottleneck in a parallel front-end system. Several techniques can be used to accelerate serial traversal:

- Traversal routines can be optimized or written in assembly code
- The database can be stored in faster memory (i.e., SRAM instead of DRAM)
- A faster traversal processor (or one optimized for the particular structure format) can be used.

If these optimizations are not enough, the only alternative is to traverse the database in parallel. The database either can be stored in a single memory system that allows parallel access by multiple processors (a shared-memory model), or can be distributed over multiple processors, each with its own memory system (a distributed-memory model).

The advantage of the shared-memory approach is that the database can remain in one place, although traversal must be divided among multiple processors. Presumably, each processor is assigned a certain portion of the database to traverse. Unfortunately, inherited attributes in a hierarchical database model mean that processors must contend for access to the same data. For example, each processor must have access to the current transformation matrix and to other viewing and lighting parameters. Since the data bandwidth to and from a shared-memory system may not be much higher than that of a conventional memory system, the shared-memory approach may not provide enough performance.

In the distributed-memory approach, each processor contains a portion of the database in its local memory. It traverses its portion of the database for each frame and may also perform other front-end computations. Distributing the database presents its own problems, however: Unless the system gives the application programmer the illusion of a contiguous database, it cannot support portable graphics libraries. Also, the load must be balanced over the traversal processors if system resources are to be utilized fully. Hierarchical databases exacerbate both of these problems, since attributes in one level of a hierarchy affect primitives below them, and structures deep in a hierarchy may be referenced by multiple higher-level structure calls.

The following two sections examine two ways to distribute a hierarchical database over multiple processors: by structure, where each traversal processor is given a complete branch of the structure hierarchy; or by primitive, where each traversal processor is given a fraction of the primitives at each block in the hierarchy.

Distributing by structure. Distributing by structure is outwardly appealing, since state-changing elements in the structure apparently need to be stored only once. This can be an illusion, however, since multiple high-level structures may refer to the same lower-level substructure. For example, a database containing several cars, each described by a separate *car* structure, can be distributed by assigning each *car* structure to a separate processor. However, if each *car* structure refers to a number of *wheel* structures, *wheel* structures must also be replicated at every processor.

Load balancing among processors is also difficult. Since primitives in a structure are likely to be spatially coherent, changing the viewpoint or geometry within a scene may cause entire portions of the structure to be clipped or to reappear. Maintaining even loading among the multiple processors would require reassigning portions of the database dynamically.

Distributing by primitive. Distributing by primitive is costly, since the entire hierarchical structure of the database and any state-changing commands must be replicated at each processor. Structure editing is also expensive, since changes must be broadcast to every processor. Load balancing, however, is automatic. Since objects in a hierarchical database typically contain a large number of simple primitives (e.g., polygons forming a tiled surface), these primitives will be scattered over all the processors, and each processor will have a similar processing load.

Parallel display traversal is a relatively new technique. In 1989, the highest-performance architectures were just approaching the point where serial traversal becomes insufficient, and only a few systems had experimented with parallel traversal [FUCH89]. Neither of the distribution techniques for hierarchical databases that we have described is ideal. Compared to geometry processing, which easily partitions into parallel tasks, display traversal is much more difficult. Nevertheless, parallel traversal is likely to become increasingly important as system performance levels increase.

18.6.2   Recombining Parallel Streams

The transition between the front-end and back-end portions of the rendering pipeline is troublesome as well. In a parallel front-end system, the multiple streams of transformed and clipped primitives must be directed to the processor or processors doing rasterization. This can require sorting primitives based on spatial information if different processors are assigned to different screen regions.

A second difficulty in parallel front-end systems is that the ordering of data may change as those data pass through parallel processors. For example, one processor may transform two small primitives before another processor transforms a single, larger one. This does not matter for many graphics primitives and rendering techniques. Certain global commands, however, such as commands to update one window instead of another or to switch between double buffers, require that data be synchronized before and after the command. If a large number of commands such as these occurs, some type of hardware support for synchronization may be necessary. A Raster Technologies system [TORB87] incorporates a special FIFO into each PE that stores tag codes for each command and allows commands to be resynchronized after they have been processed in separate PEs.

18.6.3   Pipelining versus Parallelism

We have seen that both pipelining and parallelism can be used to build high-performance front-end subsystems. Although pipelining has been the predominant technique in systems of the last decade, parallelism offers several advantages, including reconfigurability for different algorithms, since a single processor handles all front-end calculations, and more modularity, since PEs in a parallel system can be made homogeneous more easily than in a pipeline system. Because the performance of a pipeline system is limited by the throughput of its slowest stage, pipelines do not scale up as readily as do parallel systems. Parallel systems, on the other hand, require more complicated synchronization and load balancing and cannot use specialized processors as well as can pipelined systems. Both designs are likely to be useful in the future; indeed, the highest-performance systems are likely to combine the two.

18.7   MULTIPROCESSOR RASTERIZATION ARCHITECTURES

Recall that the output of the front-end subsystem is typically a set of primitives in screen coordinates. The rasterization (back-end) subsystem creates the final image by scan converting each of these primitives, determining which primitives are visible at each pixel, and shading the pixel accordingly. Section 18.2.4 identified two basic reasons why simple display-processor/frame-buffer systems are inadequate for high-performance rasterization subsystems:

1. A single display processor does not have enough processing power for all the pixel calculations.
2. Memory bandwidth into the frame buffer is insufficient to handle the pixel traffic — even if the display processor could compute pixels rapidly enough.

Much of the research in graphics architecture over the past decade has concerned ways to overcome these limitations. A great variety of techniques has been proposed, and many have been implemented in commercial and experimental systems. In this section, we consider low-cost, moderate-performance architectures that cast conventional algorithms into hardware. In Sections 18.8 and 18.9, we consider ways to improve performance by adding large amounts of parallelism to speed the calculation of the algorithm's "inner loop." In Section 18.10, we consider hybrid architectures that combine multiple techniques for improved efficiency or even higher performance. Figure 18.12 summarizes the concurrent approaches we shall discuss here.

Rasterization algorithm	Architectural technique		
	Serial pipeline	Highly parallel	Hybrid
Object order	Pipelined object order	Image parallel	Virtual buffer/ virtual processor
z-buffer, depth-sort, and BSP-tree algorithms	Polygon/edge/span-processor pipeline	Partitioned image memory Logic-enhanced memory	Parallel virtual buffer
Image order	Pipelined image order	Object parallel	
Scanline algorithms	Scan-line pipeline	Processor per primitive pipeline Tree-structured	Image composition

Fig. 18.12 Taxonomy of concurrent rasterization approaches.

18.7.1 Pipelined Object-Order Architectures

A direct way to add concurrency to rasterization calculations is to cast the various steps of a software algorithm into a hardware pipeline. This technique has been used to build a number of inexpensive, moderately high-performance systems. This approach can be used with either of the two main rasterization approaches: object order (z-buffer, depth-sort, and BSP-tree algorithms) and image order (scan-line algorithms). We consider object-order rasterization now and image-order rasterization in Section 18.7.2.

Object-order rasterization methods include the z-buffer, depth-sort, and BSP-tree algorithms (the z-buffer is by far the most common in 3D systems). The outer loop of these algorithms is an enumeration of primitives in the database, and the inner loop is an enumeration of pixels within each primitive. For polygon rendering, the heart of each of these algorithms is rasterizing a single polygon.

Figure 18.13 shows the most common rasterization algorithm for convex polygons. This algorithm is an extension of the 2D polygon scan-conversion algorithm presented in Section 3.6, using fixed-point arithmetic rather than integer arithmetic. Delta values are used to calculate the expressions for x, z, R, G, and B incrementally from scan line to scan line, and from pixel to pixel. We shall describe each step of the algorithm.

Polygon processing. Computations performed only once per polygon are grouped into this stage. The first step is to determine the initial scan line intersected by the polygon (this is determined by the vertex with the smallest y value). In most cases, the polygon intersects this scan line at a single pixel, with two edges projecting upward, the *left* and *right* edges. Delta values are calculated for x, z, R, G, and B for each edge. These delta values are sometimes called *slopes*.

Edge processing. Computations performed once for each scan line are grouped here. Scan lines within each primitive are processed one by one. The delta values computed previously are used to calculate x, z, R, G, and B values at the intersection points of the left and right edges with the current scan line (P_{left} and P_{right} in the figure). A contiguous sequence of pixels on a scan line, such as those between P_{left} and P_{right}, is called a *span*. Delta

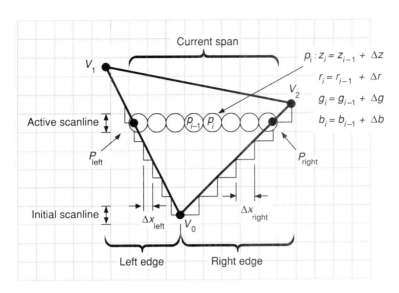

Fig. 18.13 Rasterizing a triangle. Each vertex (V_0, V_1, and V_2), span endpoint (P_{left} and P_{right}), and pixel (p_0, p_1, etc.) has z, R, G, and B components.

values for incrementing z, R, G, and B from pixel to pixel within the span are then calculated from the values at P_{left} and P_{right}.

Span processing. Operations that must be performed for each pixel within each span are performed here. For each pixel within the span, z, R, G, and B values are calculated by adding delta values to the values at the preceding pixel. The z value is compared with the previous z value stored at that location; if it is smaller, the new pixel value replaces the old one.

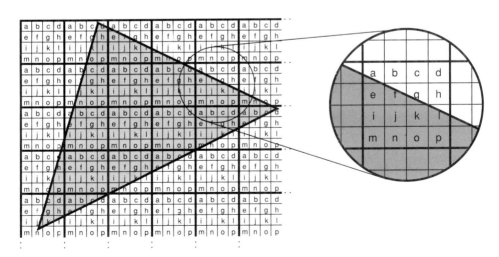

Fig. 18.14 A 4 × 4 interleaved memory organization. Each memory partition (''a'' through ''p'') contains one pixel from each 4 × 4 block of pixels.

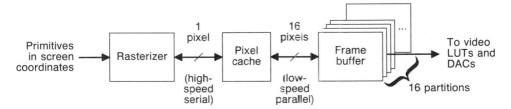

Fig. 18.15 A pixel cache matches bandwidth between a high-speed serial link to the rasterizer and a low-speed parallel link to the frame buffer.

A pipelined system containing one PE for each of the preceding three steps generates images dramatically faster than does a general-purpose display processor. In fact, it may generate pixels faster than a standard frame-buffer memory can handle. The Hewlett-Packard SRX [SWAN86], which uses this approach, generates up to 20 million pixels per second, approximately twice the speed of a typical VRAM memory system. In such systems, the rasterization bottleneck is access to frame-buffer memory.

Pixel cache.   Pixels can be read and written faster if the frame buffer has some degree of parallel access. One way to accomplish this is to divide the memory into multiple—say, 16—partitions, each of which contains every fourth pixel of every fourth scan line, or perhaps every sixteenth pixel in every scan line (see Fig. 18.14). In this way, 16 pixels can be read or written in parallel. This technique, called *memory interleaving*, is also used in general-purpose CPU memory design.

A *pixel register* or *pixel cache* containing 16 pixels can be inserted between the rasterization pipeline and the interleaved image memory [GORI87; APGA88], as in Fig. 18.15. A cache allows the rasterizer to access individual pixels at high speed, assuming that the pixel is already in the cache. Multiple pixel values can be moved in parallel between the cache and the frame buffer at the slower speeds accommodated by the frame buffer.

As in any cache memory unit, performance depends on *locality of reference,* the principle that successive memory accesses are likely to occur in the same portion of memory. Erratic access patterns cause a high percentage of cache misses and degrade performance. For polygon rendering, the access pattern can be predicted precisely, since the extent of the polygon in screen space and the order in which pixels are generated are known before the pixels are accessed. Using this information, a cache controller can begin reading the next block of pixels from the frame buffer while the previous block of pixels is processed [APGA88].

Enhancing a rasterization subsystem with this kind of parallel-access path to frame-buffer memory may well increase the system throughput to the point where the bottleneck now becomes the single-pixel path between the rasterizer and the pixel cache. A logical next step is to enhance the rasterizer so that it can generate multiple pixel values in parallel. We consider such *image-parallel* architectures in Section 18.8.

18.7.2   Pipelined Image-Order Architectures

The alternative to object-order rasterization methods is *image-order* (or *scan-line*) rasterization, introduced in Section 15.4.4. Scan-line algorithms calculate the image pixel by pixel, rather than primitive by primitive. To avoid considering primitives that do not

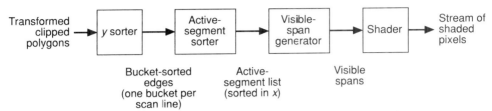

Fig. 18.16 Block diagram of a pipelined scan-line rasterizer.

contribute to the current scan line, most scan-line algorithms require primitives to be transformed into screen space and sorted into *buckets* according to the first scan line in which they each appear.

Scan-line algorithms can be implemented in hardware using the same approach as object-order algorithms: by casting the steps of the software algorithm into a pipelined series of hardware units. Much of the pioneering work on hardware scan-line systems was done at the University of Utah in the late 1960s [WYLI67; ROMN69; WATK70].

Figure 18.16 is a block diagram of a typical scan-line rasterizer. The *y sorter* places each edge of each polygon into the bucket corresponding to the scan line in which it first appears. The *active-segment generator* reads edges from these buckets, maintaining a table of active edges for the current scan line. From this table, it builds a list of active segments (a segment is a span within a single polygon), which is sorted by the *x* value of the left endpoint of each segment. The *visible-span generator* (called the *depth sorter* in the Utah system) traverses the active segment list, comparing *z* values where necessary, and outputs the sequence of visible spans on the current scan line. The *shader* performs Gouraud shading on these spans, producing a pixel stream that is displayed on the video screen.

Notice that no frame buffer is needed in this type of system, provided that the system can generate pixels at video rates. The original Utah scan-line system generated the video signal in real time for a modest number (approximately 1200) of polygons. However, since the rate at which pixels are generated depends on local scene complexity, a small amount of buffering—enough for one scan line, for example—averages the pixel rate within a single scan line. A double-buffered frame buffer allows complete independence of image-generation and image-display rates. This architecture was the basis of several generations of flight-simulator systems built by Evans & Sutherland Computer Corporation in the 1970s [SCHA83].

18.7.3 Limits of Pipeline Rasterization and the Need for Parallelism

Two factors limit the speedup possible in a pipeline approach. First, most rasterization algorithms break down easily into only a small number of sequential steps. Second, some of these steps are performed far more often than are others, particularly the steps in the inner loop of the rasterization algorithm. The processor assigned to these steps, therefore, becomes the bottleneck in the system.

The inner loop in an object-order (*z*-buffer) system is calculating pixels within spans; the inner loop in an image-order (scan-line) system is processing active edges on a scan line. For rasterization to be accelerated beyond the level possible by simple pipelining, these inner-loop calculations must be distributed over a number of processors. In *z*-buffer systems, this produces image parallelism; in scan-line systems, this produces object parallelism. The following two sections discuss each of these approaches. Virtually all of today's high-performance graphics systems use some variation of them.

18.8   IMAGE-PARALLEL RASTERIZATION

Image parallelism has long been an attractive approach for high-speed rasterization architectures, since pixels can be generated in parallel in many ways. Two principal decisions in any such architecture are (1) how should the screen be partitioned? (into rows? into columns? in an interleaved pattern?), and (2) how many partitions are needed? In the following sections, we shall describe the most heavily investigated alternatives, discussing the advantages and disadvantages of each. Also, we shall identify which schemes are approaching fundamental limits in current architectures. Note that, because an image-parallel system rasterizes in object order, a frame buffer is required to store intermediate results.

18.8.1   Partitioned-Memory Architectures

Two obvious partitioning strategies are to divide pixels into contiguous blocks (Fig. 18.17a) [PARK80] and to divide them into an interleaved checkerboard pattern (Fig. 18.17b) [FUCH77a]. In either approach, a processor (or PE) is associated with each frame-buffer partition. Such organizations increase a graphics system's computation power by providing parallel processing, and its memory bandwidth by providing each PE with a separate channel into its portion of frame-buffer memory. During rasterization, polygons are transferred from the front end to the PEs in parallel, and each PE processes primitives in its portion of the frame buffer.

Contiguous partitioning. In the contiguous-region partitioning scheme, primitives need to be processed in only those regions in which they may be visible. These regions can be determined rapidly using geometric extents. If primitives are small compared to the region size, each primitive is likely to fall into a single region. Large primitives may fall into

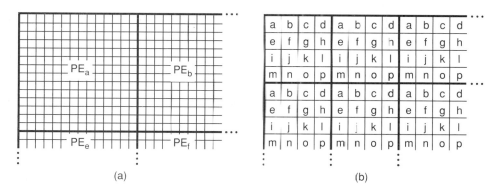

Fig. 18.17 Two schemes for frame-buffer partitioning. In (a), processors are assigned contiguous blocks of pixels; in (b), processors are assigned pixels in an interleaved pattern.

multiple regions. If the region size is chosen appropriately, the number of primitives handled by each processor will be approximately m/p, where m is the number of primitives in the database and p is the number of processors. Note, however, that if the viewpoint is chosen so unfortunately that all of the primitives fall into a single screen region, one processor must rasterize all of the primitives, and system performance decreases dramatically. In a contiguous region system, the frame rate is determined by the number of primitives in the busiest region.

Interleaved partitioning.   Interleaved partitioning, on the other hand, achieves a better balance of workload, since all but the tiniest polygons lie in all partitions of the frame buffer. Since each processor handles every primitive (although only a fraction of its pixels), this scheme is less efficient in the best case than is the contiguous region approach. However, its worst-case performance is much improved, since it depends on the *total* number of primitives, rather than on the number in the busiest region. Because of this intrinsic load balancing, interleaved systems have become the dominant partitioned-memory architecture.

The polygon scan-conversion algorithm described in Section 18.7.1 requires set-up calculations to determine delta values and span endpoints before pixel computations can begin. These calculations need be performed only once per polygon or once per span, and can be shared among a number of PEs. The first proposed interleaved memory architectures [FUCH77a; FUCH79] contained no provision for factoring out these calculations from the PEs (see Fig. 18.18). Since each PE had to perform the entire rasterization algorithm for every polygon, many redundant calculations were performed.

Clark and Hannah [CLAR80] proposed an enhancement of this architecture to take advantage of calculations common to multiple PEs. In their approach, two additional levels of processors are added to perform polygon and edge processing. A single polygon processor receives raw transformed polygon data from the front-end subsystem and determines the polygon's initial scan line, slopes of edges, and so on. Eight edge processors (one per column in an 8×8 grid of pixel processors) calculate x, z, R, G, and B values at span endpoints. The edge processors send span information to the individual PEs (span processors), which interpolate pixel values along the span. The added levels of processing allow the PEs to perform only the calculations that are necessary for each pixel—a large improvement in efficiency. The rasterization portion of Silicon Graphics' recent high-performance systems uses this approach (see Section 18.8.2).

SIMD versus MIMD.   A variation between systems of this type is whether PEs are SIMD or MIMD. Let us consider SIMD processors first Figure 18.14 shows the mapping of processors to pixels in a 4×4 interleaved scheme. With a SIMD processor, the 16 PEs work on a contiguous 4×4 block of pixels at the same time. This arrangement is sometimes called a *footprint processor* because the 4×4 array of processors (the footprint) marches across the polygon, stamping out 16 pixels at a time. Notice that, if any pixel of a 4×4 block needs updating, the footprint must visit that block. For example, in the block of pixels shown in the inset of Fig. 18.14, processors a, b, c, d, g, and h must disable themselves, while processors e, f, i, j, k, l, m, n, o, and p process their respective pixels.

A disadvantage of SIMD processors is that they do not utilize their PEs fully. This occurs for two reasons. First, many of the PEs map to pixels outside the current primitive if

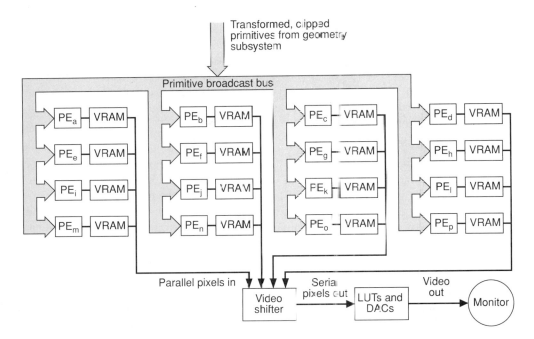

Fig. 18.18 Block diagram of a typical interleaved memory system. Each PE is responsible for one pixel in every 4 × 4 block of pixels.

small primitives are being rendered. For example, PEs in a 4 × 4 footprint processor rasterizing 100-pixel polygons map to pixels within the triangle as little as 45 percent of the time [APGA88]. Second, the choice of rasterization algorithm affects PE utilization. As remarked in Section 18.4.2, algorithms containing few conditional branches (including rasterizing convex polygons with Gouraud shading) can be implemented quite efficiently. Algorithms containing many conditional branches or using complicated data structures (such as rendering curved-surface primitives, texturing, shadowing, or antialiasing with a list of partially covering polygons) can be extremely difficult to make efficient. SIMD processors, however, can be built inexpensively and compactly, since a single code store and controller suffice for all the PEs. This offsets to some degree the poor PE utilization in a SIMD system. Several SIMD interleaved memory systems have been proposed and developed, including Gupta and Sproull's 8 by 8 Display [GUPT81b] and Stellar's GS2000 (see Section 18.11.3).

If we wish to support complex algorithms or to eliminate the idle processor cycles indicated in Fig. 18.14, we can add a control store to each PE, changing it from SIMD to MIMD. In a MIMD system, PEs do not need always to work on the same 4 × 4 pixel block at the same time. If each PE has FIFO input buffering, PEs can even work on different primitives. The separate control stores, FIFO queues, and hardware required to synchronize PEs add size and complexity to the system. Examples of successful MIMD interleaved-memory systems include AT&T's Pixel Machine [MCMI87] and Silicon Graphics' POWER IRIS (Section 18.8.2). Such systems compete well against SIMD systems on more complicated types of primitives or with more complicated rendering algorithms. For example, AT&T's Pixel Machine Model PXM 924 ray traces simple scenes at interactive speeds—a feat unmatched by any SIMD system.

Since interleaved-memory architectures distribute the frame buffer over multiple processors, some provision must be made for scanning out pixels in the uninterrupted stream required by the video controller and display monitor. If the distributed frame buffer is constructed of VRAMs, this can be done in the manner shown in Fig. 18.18. Note that this is very similar to the technique described in Section 18.1.5 for implementing high-speed video scanout in a conventional frame-buffer memory.

Further subdivision.   Suppose we wish to build a system with even higher performance. Since increasing the number of partitions in an interleaved-memory system increases the system's memory bandwidth and processing power, we might consider increasing the number of frame-buffer partitions—say, from 16 to 64, or even more. Unfortunately, the additional processors and datapaths required for each partition make such systems increasingly expensive.

An even more serious difficulty is supporting a larger number of partitions with the same number of frame-buffer memory chips. Each partition requires a minimum number of chips. For example, a partition with a 32-bit datapath between the PE and memory requires 8 4-bit wide chips, or 32 1-bit wide chips. Suppose we wish to build a 16-partition 1024- by 1024-pixel frame buffer with 128 bits per pixel. Using 256K $\times$ 4 VRAM chips, each partition requires 8 256K $\times$ 4 VRAM chips, so $16 \cdot 8 = 128$ chips are needed to support all 16 memory partitions. This is the exact number required to store the pixel data.

Suppose, however, that we increase the number of partitions from 16 to 64 (an 8×8 footprint). Although we still need only 128 memory chips to store the pixel data, we need $64 \cdot 8 = 512$ memory chips to support the PE–memory bandwidth. The extra 384 memory chips are needed only to provide communication bandwidth—not for memory. This is an extra expense that continues to grow as we subdivide the frame buffer further.

Increasing the density of memory parts from 1 Mbit to 4 Mbit exacerbates this problem even further. For example, if 1Mbit $\times$ 4 VRAM memory chips are used in the example mentioned above, 512 chips are still needed, even though each one contains sixteen times the memory actually required. Current systems such as the Silicon Graphics' POWER IRIS GTX (described in the next section), which uses 20 frame-buffer partitions, are already at the bandwidth limit. A way to ameliorate this problem would be for memory manufacturers to provide more data pins on high-density memory parts. Some 4-Mbit DRAM chips have eight data pins, rather than four, which helps somewhat, but only reduces the bandwidth problem by a factor of 2.

18.8.2   Silicon Graphics' POWER IRIS 4D/240GTX—An Interleaved Frame-Buffer Memory Architecture[2,3]

Silicon Graphics' POWER IRIS 4D/240GTX [AKEL88; AKEL89] uses many of the techniques described in this chapter. Like a number of its competitors, including the Ardent

---

[2]Material for this example is adapted from [AKEL88] and [AKEL89].

[3]In 1990, Silicon Graphics announced POWERVISION (similar to the GTX) that renders 1 million Gouraud-shaded triangles/sec and with 268 bits/pixel for antialiasing and texturing.

Titan [BORD89], the Megatek Sigma 70 [MEGA89], and the Stellar GS2000 (Section 18.11.3), the SGI POWER IRIS is a high-end graphics workstation, designed to combine general-purpose processing and high-speed 3D graphics for engineering and scientific applications.

The POWER IRIS has a powerful general-purpose CPU composed of four tightly coupled multiprocessors sharing a single memory bus. Its graphics subsystem can render over 100,000 full-colored, Gouraud-shaded, z-buffered quadrilaterals per second [AKEL89]. The POWER IRIS continues Silicon Graphics' tradition of immediate-mode display traversal, aggressive use of custom VLSI, hardware front-end pipeline, and interleaved-memory frame-buffer architecture. The POWER IRIS's architecture, diagrammed in Fig. 18.19, is composed of five major subsystems:

1. *CPU subsystem*—runs the application and traverses the display model

2. *Geometry subsystem*—transforms and clips graphical data to screen coordinates

3. *Scan-conversion subsystem*—breaks points, lines, and polygons into pixels

4. *Raster subsystem*—computes visibility and writes pixel data to frame buffer

5. *Display subsystem*—displays contents of frame buffer on color monitor.

CPU subsystem. The *CPU subsystem* runs the application and traverses the database. It is composed of four tightly coupled, symmetric, shared-memory multiprocessors. Hardware provides high-speed synchronization between processors, so parallelism can be achieved within a single process (although special programming constructs are required).

Geometry subsystem. The *geometry subsystem* transforms, clips, and lights primitives. It is composed of five floating-point processors arranged in a pipeline. Each of these processors, called a *geometry engine* (GE), contains an input FIFO, a controller, and a floating-point unit capable of 20 MFLOPS. Unlike Silicon Graphics' earlier Geometry Engine (see Section 18.5.4), the POWER IRIS' GEs are based on a commercial floating-point chip, the Weitek 3332.

The first GE transforms vertices and vertex normals. The second GE performs lighting calculations (supporting up to eight point light sources). The third GE performs trivial accept/reject clipping tests. The fourth GE performs exact clipping on primitives that cross clipping boundaries, and also does perspective division for all primitives. The fifth GE clips color components to maximum representable values, calculates depth-cued colors where necessary, and converts all coordinates to screen-space integers.

Scan-conversion subsystem. The *scan-conversion subsystem* rasterizes primitives using the pipeline approach described in Section 18.7.1, except that its spans are vertical columns of pixels, rather than the horizontal rows we have assumed so far (the only effect on the rasterization algorithm is that x and y coordinates are interchanged).

The single *polygon processor* sorts the vertices of each polygon from left to right in screen space. The sorted vertices are then used to decompose the polygon into vertically aligned trapezoids. The upper pair of vertices and the bottom pair of vertices of each trapezoid are used to calculate slopes for use by the edge processors.

The *edge processor* uses vertex and slope information to compute x, y, and z coordinates and color values for each pixel that lies on the top or bottom edges of each

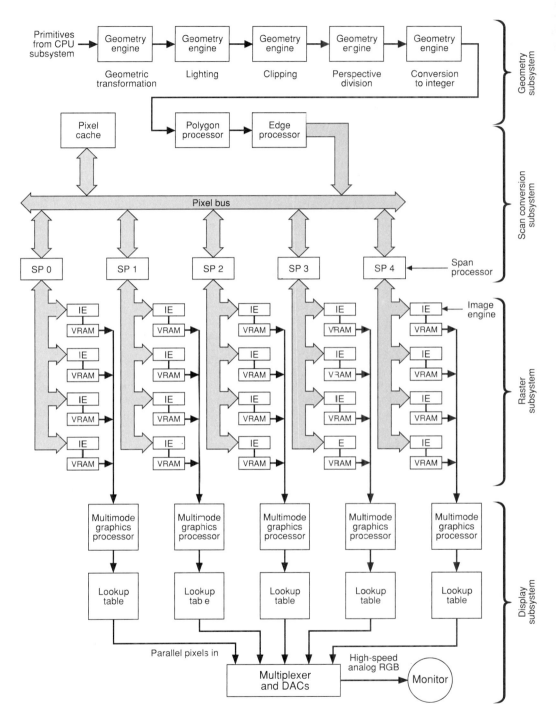

Fig. 18.19 Silicon Graphics' GTX system architecture (based on [AKEL88]).

trapezoid. In a given vertical column, a pair of pixels determines the top and bottom endpoints of a vertical span. These pixel pairs, together with slope information, are passed on to the span processors.

Each of the five parallel *span processors* is responsible for one-fifth of the columns of the display screen. For example, span processor 0 manages scan lines 0, 5, 10, and so on. Span processors calculate z, R, G, B, and α (for transparency and antialiasing) values for each pixel in the span. Because spans generated from a single polygon are adjacent, the processing load over span processors is approximately uniform.

The *pixel cache* buffers blocks of pixels during pixel copy operations so that the full bandwidth of the pixel bus can be used.

Raster subsystem. The *raster subsystem* takes pixel data generated by the span processors and selectively updates the image and z bitplanes of the frame buffer, using the results of a z comparison and α blending. The raster subsystem is composed of 20 *image engines*, each responsible for one-twentieth of the screen's pixels, arranged in a 4- × 5-pixel interleaved fashion. 96 bits are associated with each pixel on the screen: two 32-bit image buffers (r, G, B, and α), a 24-bit z-buffer, four overlay/underlay bitplanes, and four window bitplanes.

The overlay/underlay bitplanes support applications that use pop-up menus or windowing backgrounds. The window bitplanes define the display mode (single- or double-buffered, etc.) and window-masking information.

The 20 image engines work on pixels in parallel. Each can blend values based on the pixel's α value, allowing transparent or semitransparent objects to be displayed, and allowing supersampling antialiasing.

Display subsystem. The display subsystem contains five *multimode graphics processors* (MGPs), each assigned one-fifth of the columns in the display. The MGPs concurrently read image data from the frame buffer (together with window-display-mode bits), process them using the appropriate display mode (RGB or pseudocolor), and send them on to digital-to-analog converters for display.

The GTX's architecture is a good example of many of the techniques we have discussed so far. It provides high performance for polygon rendering at a reasonable cost in hardware. Because the GTX's rendering pipeline is highly specialized for graphics tasks, however, the system has difficulty with the advanced rendering techniques we shall discuss in Section 18.11, and its resources cannot be applied easily to nongraphics tasks. Section 18.11.3 discusses the architecture of Stellar's GS2000, which has complementary advantages and disadvantages.

18.8.3 Logic-Enhanced Memory

Since commercial memories may not support enough frame-buffer partitions, one might consider building custom memories with a large number of concurrently accessible partitions on a single chip. Since each (intrachip) partition must have its own connection to its associated (external) processor, extra pins must be added to each memory package to support these additional I/O requirements. Alternatively, multiple processors could be built onto the chip itself. The first possibility—that of adding pins to memory chips—directly increases the memory bandwidth, but makes the chip package and associated circuit boards larger and more expensive, and also increases the power requirements. These packaging effects become progressively more severe as memory densities increase. (In the past two decades, the number of bits in a typical RAM has increased by a factor of 1000, while the size of the package and the number of pins have changed hardly at all.)

In this section, we shall concentrate on the second option—that of adding processing to multipartition memory chips. In the simplest schemes, only new addressing modes are provided, such as the ability to address an entire rectangle of memory pixels in parallel. At the other extreme, an entire microprocessor (including code store) could be provided for each internal partition of memory.

Before we describe specific logic-enhanced–memory approaches, let us consider the advantages and disadvantages of any logic-enhanced–memory scheme. First, adding logic or processing to memories has the potential to increase vastly the processing power within a system. By increasing the number of internal memory partitions and providing processing for each on the same chip, enormous processor/memory bandwidths can be achieved. Second, in custom VLSI chips, options become available that are impractical in board-level systems, since VLSI technology has an entirely different set of cost constraints for gates, wiring channels, and memory. Third, off-chip I/O bandwidth can potentially be reduced, since the only off-chip communication needed is to control the processor and to scan pixels out of the chip; this translates into fewer pins in the package and thus to a smaller package and less board space.

The principal disadvantages of an enhanced-memory approach are low memory densities and increased cost. With enormous production volumes, commercial DRAM manufacturers can afford to develop specialized, high-density fabrication capabilities and to incur large development costs to fine-tune their designs. Design and fabrication resources for custom memory chips, however, are generally more limited, resulting in densities lower than those of commercial RAMs. The price per chip is also high, since the costs for designing a custom VLSI chip are not offset by such large sales volumes. In spite of these disadvantages, at least one custom memory chip for graphics has become commercially successful—the VRAM. It remains to be seen whether other custom memory designs for graphics have sufficient market appeal to justify large-scale commercial development.

Pixel-Planes.   An early and very general logic-enhanced–memory design is Pixel-Planes [FUCH81]. Pixel-Planes pushes frame-buffer subdivision to its extreme: It provides a separate processor for every pixel in the display. Each SIMD *pixel processor* is a 1-bit processor (ALU) with a small amount of memory. Figure 18.20 shows a block diagram of an enhanced-memory chip in Pixel-Planes 4, a prototype system completed in 1986 [EYLE88]. Its design is similar to that of the VRAM chip of Fig. 18.3, only here the 1-bit ALUs and associated circuitry replace the video shifter. Each enhanced-memory chip contains 128 pixels (columns in the memory array), and each pixel contains 72 bits of local memory (rows within the column).

Pixel-Planes' performance is not based simply on massive parallelism. If it was, each PE would have to perform all the operations for scan conversion independently, resulting in many redundant calculations and a grossly inefficient system. Rather, Pixel-Planes uses a

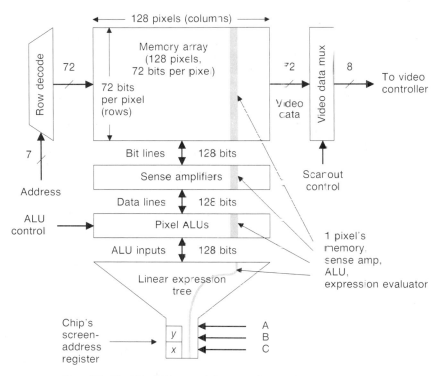

Fig. 18.20   Pixel-Planes 4 logic-enhanced–memory chip.

global computing structure called a *linear expression tree* that evaluates linear expressions of the form $F(x, y) = Ax + By + C$ for every pixel (x, y) of the screen in parallel [FUCH85]. A, B, and C floating-point coefficients are input to the tree; each pixel receives its own value of F in its local memory, 1 bit per clock cycle (approximately 20–30 cycles are required for each linear expression). The linear expression tree is especially effective for accelerating rasterization calculations, since many of these can be cast as linear expressions. For example,

- Each edge of a convex polygon can be described by a linear expression. All points (x, y) on one side of the edge have $F(x, y) \geq 0$; all points on the other side of the edge have $F(x, y) \leq 0$.

- The z value of all points (x, y) within a triangle can be described as a linear expression.

- R, G, and B color components of pixels in a Gouraud-shaded triangle can be described as linear expressions.

Double-buffering is implemented within Pixel-Planes chips by providing a *video-data multiplexer* that reads pixel values from specific bits of pixel memory while the image is computed in the remaining bits. Video data are scanned out of the chip on eight video data pins.

Displaying images on Pixel-Planes requires modifying the algorithms we have assumed so far. In addition to transforming and clipping primitives in the usual manner, the front-end subsystem must compute coefficient sets for the linear equations describing each primitive's edges, z values, and color values. Also, rasterization proceeds in parallel, since large areas of pixels can be affected at once using the linear expression tree. The following section describes a sample algorithm on Pixel-Planes.

Rasterizing a triangle on Pixel-Planes. Here, we briefly describe the algorithm to display Gouraud-shaded triangles on a Pixel-Planes system. Pixel-Planes can display more general polygons, although the algorithms are somewhat more complicated.

Scan conversion. Figure 18.21 shows the steps in scan converting a triangle. The first step is to enable all the pixel processors in the display. Edges are encoded as linear expressions $F(x, y) = Ax + By + C = 0$, as described previously. Each expression is then evaluated in parallel at every pixel in the screen, using the linear expression tree. Each pixel processor tests the sign of F to determine whether it lies on the proper side of the edge. If it lies outside the edge, the pixel processor disables itself by setting its enable bit to 0. After all the edges of a polygon have been tested, the only pixel processors still enabled are those lying within the polygon. These pixel processors alone participate in visibility and shading calculations.

z-buffering. After a polygon has been scan converted, Pixel-Planes evaluates the linear expression for z for all pixels in parallel. Each pixel processor compares this new z value with the one stored in its z-buffer. If the new z value is smaller, the current polygon is visible at the pixel; the pixel processor updates its z-buffer and remains enabled. If the new z value is larger, the pixel disables itself and does not participate in shading calculations.

Gouraud shading. The linear expressions for R, G, and B components of the color are evaluated for each pixel in parallel by the linear expression tree. Pixel processors that are still enabled write the new color components into their pixels' color buffers.

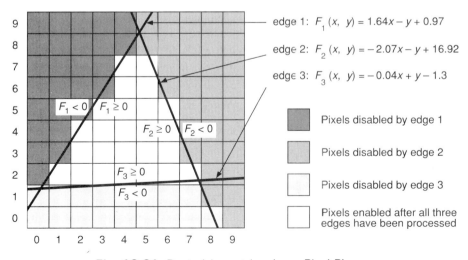

Fig. 18.21 Rasterizing a triangle on Pixel-Planes.

Note that scan conversion in Pixel-Planes is completely independent of a polygon's size, so a large polygon is rasterized as rapidly as a small one. Note, also, that operations that cannot be expressed as linear equations may take much longer to execute on Pixel-Planes than those that can (e.g., a quadratic expression can be calculated in pixel memory by multiplying values 1 bit at a time). Nevertheless, efficient algorithms for drawing spheres, casting shadows, antialiasing, and texture mapping have been developed for Pixel-Planes [FUCH85].

A full-scale system, Pixel-Planes 4, containing 262,144 processors forming a 512- by 512-pixel image, was completed in 1986. Although its performance was impressive for its time (40,000 Gouraud-shaded triangles of arbitrary size per second), it contained 2048 custom memory chips—a prohibitive expense for a commercial graphics system. This highlights the fundamental disadvantage of such a highly parallel SIMD approach: the very low utilization of pixel processors. Since all the PEs work in lock step, they cannot be retargeted to other tasks, even if only a few of them are still calculating useful results. This problem is especially severe when large numbers of small polygons are being drawn, because the first steps of the scan-conversion process disable almost all the screen's pixel processors.

Several logic-enhanced–memory graphics architectures have been developed that are more frugal in their use of silicon, at some sacrifice in either speed or generality. Although neither of the architectures described next directly supports the 3D rendering techniques assumed to this point, both provide very high performance in their respective domains (displaying 2D rectangles and generating 2D halftone images), and both provide insight into the potential of the logic-enhanced–memory approach.

Rectangle area-filling memory chip. Whelan proposed modifying the row and column addressing in the 2D memory-cell grid of a typical RAM to allow an entire rectangular region to be addressed at once [WHEL82]. Minimum and maximum row and column addresses specify the left, right, top, and bottom boundaries of the region. One write operation can store a single data value in every location within the region. This allows upright, constant-shaded rectangles to be rasterized in very few clock cycles—just enough to specify the four address values and the constant data.

Scan Line Access Memory. Demetrescu designed a more complicated chip called a Scan Line Access Memory (SLAM) for rasterizing more general 2D primitives [DEME85]. Like VRAMs and Pixel-Planes, SLAM takes advantage of the fact that, internally, a RAM reads or writes an entire row of its memory array in one cycle. Figure 18.22 shows a block diagram of a single SLAM chip. Each chip contains 255×64 bits of frame-buffer memory. Each row of memory corresponds to 1 bit in a scan line of pixels. In a system with k bits per pixel, a SLAM chip can store up to $64/k$ scan lines of 256 pixels each. In each memory cycle, a SLAM chip can read or write one row of memory from its memory array. By specifying appropriate x_{min} and x_{max} values, one can address any contiguous span of pixels on the current scan line, allowing fast polygon scan conversion. Video scanout is accomplished using a display shifter in exactly the same manner as a VRAM chip.

In a single clock cycle, either a row address, an x_{min} value, an x_{max} value, or a 16-bit repeating data pattern (for specifying halftone patterns) can be specified. Concurrent with

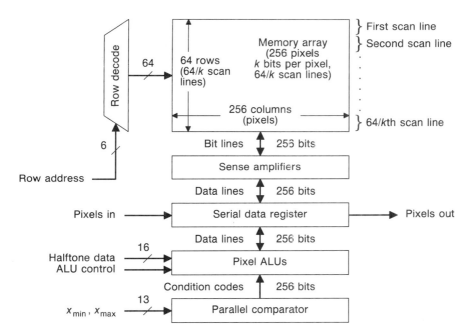

Fig. 18.22 Block diagram of a SLAM chip (for a system configured with k bits per pixel).

any one of these commands, SLAM can write the current scan-line segment into its memory array and can optionally increment the row address. Since, for many primitives, row addresses and halftone patterns need to be specified only once (for the initial scan line), succeeding scan lines can be processed rapidly. SLAM therefore can scan convert a convex polygon covering n scan lines in $2n + 2$ cycles (four cycles to specify the row address, x_{min}, x_{max}, and the halftone pattern for the initial scan line, and two cycles to specify x_{min} and x_{max} for each of the remaining $n - 1$ scan lines).

A SLAM system is composed of a number of SLAM chips (the number depends on the dimensions of the display screen). Figure 18.23 shows a SLAM system for updating a 512 by 512 monochrome display screen. Systems with more bits per pixel require proportionately more SLAM chips. SLAM can also be extended to display Gouraud-shaded polygons by adding a Pixel-Planes–style linear-expression tree. However, this enhanced version of SLAM would require approximately the same amount of hardware as Pixel-Planes and would suffer the same low utilization of PEs, since the pixels in any given (small) primitive would likely be contained in just a few SLAM chips.

Although both Whelan's architecture and the original SLAM architecture use less hardware than does Pixel-Planes, they do not offer the generality necessary to render realistic 3D images. Pixel-Planes and the enhanced version of SLAM do offer this generality, but suffer poor PE utilization. It would be useful to gain the performance of these processor-per-pixel architectures, but with higher PE utilization for small primitives. Section 18.10.1 examines a way to accomplish this using enhanced-memory arrays smaller than the full screen size.

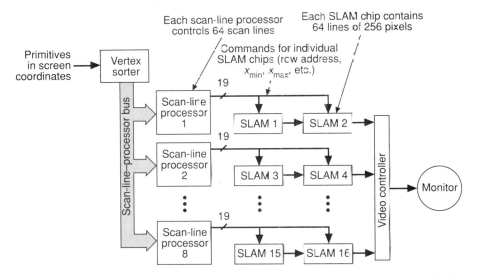

Fig. 18.23 SLAM system for updating a 512- by 512-pixel monochrome display.

18.9   OBJECT-PARALLEL RASTERIZATION

So far, we have focused on image-parallel architectures. The *object-parallel* family of parallel architectures parallelizes the inner loop of image-order (generally scan-line) algorithms. In an object-parallel architecture, multiple primitives (objects) are processed in parallel, so that final pixels may be generated more rapidly.

The usual object-parallel approach is to assign primitives (either statically or dynamically) to a number of homogeneous *object processors,* each of which can generate an entire image containing its primitive(s). During rasterization, each object processor enumerates the pixels of the display in some specific order (generally scan-line), generating color, z, and possibly partial-coverage values for its primitive(s). The pixel streams from each of the object processors are then combined to produce a single pixel stream for the final image. Although any number of primitives may be assigned to each object processor, most designs allocate a single primitive per processor. The advantage is that each processor can perform a well-defined task and thus can be reproduced inexpensively.

General Electric's NASA II.   A pioneering real-time processor-per-primitive system was General Electric's NASA II flight simulator [BUNK89], delivered to NASA in 1967. The NASA II contained a number of hardware units called *face cards,* each of which rasterized a single polygon at video rates. At any given instant, each face card would process the same pixel.

The NASA II used a depth-sort visibility algorithm, rather than a z-buffer. The output of each face card included a bit indicating whether or not the pixel was covered by its polygon, the pixel color, and the polygon priority number. This information was fed into a priority multiplexer so that, at each pixel, the color of the highest-priority visible polygon was output. Since face cards were expensive, they were reassigned to new polygons when their polygons no longer intersected the current scan line. The NASA II system could display a maximum of 60 polygons on any given scan line.

Later processor-per-primitive designs have adopted z-comparison visibility algorithms that allow greater flexibility. Processors are typically arranged in a pipeline or binary tree, so that streams of pixels can be merged to produce the pixel stream of the final image.

18.9.1 Processor-per-Primitive Pipelines

A simple way to combine the multiple pixel color and z streams produced by the multiple object processors is to pipeline the processors so that a stream of color values and z values passes between them (Fig. 18.24). Each processor generates color and z values for its primitive at the current pixel, and compares its z value with the incoming z value. If the incoming z value is smaller, the color and z values are passed on unchanged; if it is greater, the primitive's color and z values are sent out. The output of the last processor in the pipeline is the video stream of the final image.

Cohen and Demetrescu [DEME80] designed what was perhaps the first processor-per-polygon pipeline system. In this design, each polygon is assigned a polygon processor for the duration of the frame-generation time. Weinberg [WEIN81] proposed an enhancement of this architecture to generate antialiased images. Instead of passing pixel color and z values between adjacent processors, Weinberg's design passes, for each pixel, an arbitrarily long packet of polygon-fragment information relating to that pixel. Each polygon processor compares z and edge information for its polygon with the incoming packet describing the pixel. The packet is updated to take the new polygon into account, and is forwarded to the next polygon processor. A set of filtering engines at the end of the pipeline calculates the single color value for each pixel from the (final) packet associated with that pixel.

A team at Schlumberger proposed a design combining aspects of the NASA II, Cohen–Demetrescu, and Weinberg designs [DEER88]. Their Triangle Processor and Normal Vector Shader uses a pipeline of triangle processors that passes along surface-normal and polygon-color data, rather than actual pixel colors. Triangles are assigned to processors only during scan lines in which they are active in the same manner as in the NASA II. A pipeline of Normal Vector Shaders computes the Phong lighting model for pixels emerging from the triangle-processor pipeline. Because lighting and shading calculations are delayed until the end of the pipeline, Phong calculations need to be performed only once for each pixel in the final image, rather than once for each pixel of every polygon—a substantial savings.

18.9.2 Tree-Structured Processor-per-Primitive Architectures

An alternative to pipelining object processors is to arrange them in parallel and to use a binary tree of compositors to merge the color and z streams. This approach allows

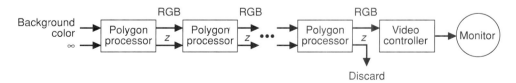

Fig. 18.24 Processor-per-polygon pipeline system.

rasterization within the object processors to be truly synchronous (there is no pipeline delay between the times at which two processors compute the same pixel), and reduces latency incurred by a long pipeline. However, special logic is required to perform the composition operation.

Fussell [FUSS82] proposed the first binary-tree-structured processor-per-primitive design. He observed that, since z comparators are simple, they can be made to run at video rates. Shaw, Green, and Schaeffer [SHAW91] proposed a way to antialias images generated using Fussell's scheme. In their approach, custom VLSI *compositors* combine images at each of the nodes in the image-composition tree. These compositors implement a simplified version of Duff's image-composition algorithm (see Section 17.6), providing proper treatment of many partial-pixel-coverage cases. A disadvantage of this approach is that the antialiasing is not perfect; color bleedthrough between abutting polygons is possible, whereas this does not occur if z values alone are used to determine visibility.

Kedem and Ellis's Ray Casting Machine [KEDE84] directly rasterizes images from a constructive solid geometry (CSG) tree representation (see Chapter 7). The Ray Casting Machine maps a CSG tree to hardware by assigning each CSG primitive to a processor called a *primitive classifier* and each operator to a processor called a *classification combiner*.

The image is traversed pixel by pixel in raster-scan order. For each pixel, primitive classifiers compute the segment of the ray through that pixel that is interior to their respective CSG primitives. These segments are then passed upward to the classification combiners, which perform set operations on them using the techniques described in Section 15.10.3. Segments are split and combined as needed. The updated segments are passed upward in the tree until they reach the root of the tree.

The set of segments emerging from the root of the classification-combiner tree describes the intersection of the current ray with the entire CSG object. The near endpoint of the nearest segment contains the z value of the visible surface at that pixel. This value is used to compute a color value for the pixel using any desired lighting model. If all the segments for a pixel, rather than just the closest one, are considered, the Ray Casting Machine can calculate the volume of the object or other geometric quantities about the CSG object. A prototype Ray Casting Machine completed in 1988 computes the surfaces of CSG objects with 32 primitives in near real time, although shading calculations, which are currently performed by the host computer, take several seconds.

18.9.3 Object Parallelism versus Image Parallelism

Although object-parallel architectures are simple and appealing, they have received much less attention than have the image-parallel techniques discussed previously; a number of experimental object-parallel systems have been proposed, but few have led to commercial products. Several factors may be responsible:

- Object-parallel systems typically require specialized processors. This implies heavy reliance on custom VLSI chips, making system design difficult and expensive. Image-parallel systems, on the other hand, place more reliance on frame-buffer memory, which can be built with commercial parts such as VRAMs.

- The specialized nature of object processors limits the types of primitives that can be displayed and the shading algorithms that can be used.

■   Object-parallel systems have poor overload characteristics. Generally, object-parallel systems perform at full speed as long as there are enough object processors. Special provisions must be made to handle large databases, and performance generally decreases rapidly.

In addition to these factors, system designers have so far been able to increase system performance using image parallelism alone, so the designers of commercial systems by and large have not had to confront the challenges of object-parallel systems. Nevertheless, as discussed in Section 18.8, image parallelism may be reaching a point of diminishing returns, and object parallelism may appeal to the designers of future systems. The following section discusses another promising approach toward increasing system efficiency and performance: building hybrid-parallel systems that combine aspects of the approaches we have discussed so far.

18.10   HYBRID-PARALLEL RASTERIZATION

We have seen that when image parallelism and object parallelism are pushed to the extreme, systems with low utilization result. This poor utilization can be reduced if object-order and image-order rasterization techniques are used in combination. Such hybrid-parallel systems frequently are more complex than are the systems we have discussed so far, but they can be much more efficient. They also provide us with one more layer of parallelism that can be used to build still higher-performance systems.

18.10.1   Virtual Buffers and Virtual Processors

A major drawback of highly parallel architecture designs, both object-parallel and image-parallel, is the low utilization of each PE. As discussed in Section 18.8.2, image-parallel architectures with many partitions can have extremely poor PE utilization. For example, in a fully instantiated processor-per-pixel system such as Pixel-Planes 4, PEs may be doing useful work less than 1 percent of the time. Similarly, in an object-parallel architecture such as Cohen and Demetrescu's processor-per-polygon pipeline, PEs may be actively rasterizing their polygons less than 1 percent of the time.

One way to achieve higher utilization is to build only a fraction of the hardware, but to allocate its resources dynamically around the screen as they are needed. Two variants of this technique exist: *virtual buffers* (for image-parallel systems) and *virtual processors* (for object-parallel systems). Like classic virtual memory, both attempt to increase a system's apparent physical resources by reallocating resources dynamically as needed.

Virtual buffers.   In a virtual-buffer system [GHAR89], the screen is divided (conceptually) into a number of regions of uniform size, and a parallel rasterization buffer the size of a region computes the image one region at a time. Since this buffer is small, it can be built using fast or custom processing/memory at a reasonable price. A full-sized conventional frame buffer is generally provided to store the final image.

A region can be a single scan line, a horizontal or vertical band of pixels, or a rectangular area. Virtual buffers differ from interleaved-memory ''footprint'' processors in one critical respect: A virtual buffer remains in one screen region until *all* the primitives for that region are processed, whereas an interleaved-memory footprint processor moves about the image to rasterize each primitive, typically returning to the same region more than once.

Virtual processors. A virtual-processor system is outwardly similar to a scan-line virtual-buffer system; in both cases, the image is computed one scan line at a time. A virtual-processor system, however, uses object-parallel PEs, rather than image-parallel PEs. Since object processors are needed for only the primitives active on a single scan line, the number of object processors can be a small fraction of the number of primitives. General Electric's NASA II and Deering's Triangle Processor, discussed in Section 18.9, are both virtual-processor systems.

Complete versus incremental bucket sorting. Because virtual-buffer/virtual-processor systems visit a region only once, bucket sorting is required. The shape of the region influences the nature of the bucket sort. In virtual-buffer systems with rectangular regions, primitives can be stored in the buckets of all the regions in which they appear, since most primitives lie entirely within one region. We call this *complete bucket sorting*. In systems with scan-line–sized regions, complete bucket sorting is impractical, since a single primitive typically covers more than one scan line. *Incremental bucket sorting,* in which a primitive is stored only in the bucket associated with its initial scan line, is generally the method of choice.

The virtual-buffer/virtual-processor approach has several advantages and disadvantages. The most important advantage is that it makes possible the rasterization speed of a fully instantiated image-parallel system with a fraction of the hardware. It also decreases traffic to and from the frame buffer, since each region's pixels are written only once. Finally, no full-screen z-buffer is needed.

Virtual-buffer/virtual-processor systems have two major disadvantages, however. First, extra memory is required to buffer the scene during bucket sorting. If transformed primitives require the same amount of storage as do primitives in object coordinates, this approximately doubles the memory requirements in the front end. It also places a hard limit on the number of primitives that can be displayed in a single frame. These disadvantages offset, to some degree, the advantage of not needing a full-screen z-buffer. Another important disadvantage is that latency is added to the display process. Even though bucket sorting can be pipelined with rasterization, bucket sorting for one frame must be completed before rasterization of that frame can begin. This increases the system's latency by one frame time, which can be detrimental in real-time systems.

Systolic Array Graphics Engine (SAGE). We now consider a system that uses the virtual-buffer approach (we discussed several virtual-processor systems in Section 18.9). SAGE is a scan-line virtual-buffer system that uses a 1D array of pixel processors implemented in VLSI [GHAR88]. Like other scan-line systems, it generates the image one scan line at a time. However, SAGE uses an image-parallel z-buffer algorithm to rasterize primitives within a single scan line.

In addition to the array of pixel processors, SAGE contains auxiliary processors to maintain the active-edge list and to break polygons into spans (see Fig. 18.25). A *polygon manager* maintains the list of active polygons as scan lines are processed (at each new scan line, it adds polygons from the next bucket and deletes polygons that are no longer active).

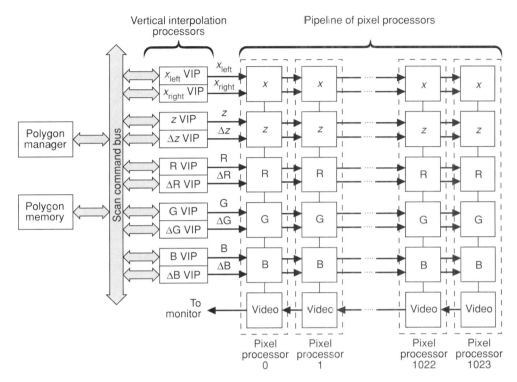

Fig. 18.25 Block diagram of a complete SAGE system.

It also calculates delta values for computing span endpoints on successive scan lines. *Vertical interpolation processors* use these delta values to compute span endpoints for each polygon active on the current scan line. So that many accesses to polygon memory can be avoided, these processors contain internal memory for storing delta values and x, z, R, G, and B values for up to 512 active polygons.

After these set-up operations, the vertical interpolation processors load the endpoints of each active polygon's current span into the pipeline of pixel processors. When a pixel processor receives a span, it compares its local x value against the span's endpoint values. If the pixel lies within the span, the processor calculates z and color values for its pixel (again using the span-endpoint values). If the new z value is smaller than the value stored at the pixel, the z and color values for the pixel are updated. Pixel values are scanned out for display using a serial shifting scheme similar to that used in VRAMs. The video stream flows in the opposite direction from that of the stream of spans.

18.10.2 Parallel Virtual-Buffer Architectures

Another level of parallelism is available in virtual-buffer systems that use rectangular regions and complete bucket sorting. Since complete bucket sorting allows a region to be rasterized without any knowledge of preceding regions (unlike incremental bucket sorting, which requires knowledge of the active-polygon list from the preceding region), a system that uses complete bucket sorting can have multiple rasterization buffers. These rasterization buffers can work in parallel on different screen regions, allowing even faster systems to be built.

In such a system, each buffer is initially assigned to a region. When it has processed all the primitives in the region's bucket, it is assigned to the next region needing processing. This provides an additional coarse-grained level of image parallelism that can be used regardless of the rasterization method used by the individual virtual buffers.

Pixel-Planes 5.   Pixel-Planes 5, which was under construction in 1989 [FUCH89], is one of the first systems to use parallel virtual buffers. Pixel-Planes 5 uses 10 to 16 logic-enhanced memory rasterization buffers that are 128 pixels on a side. Each buffer is a miniature Pixel-Planes 4 array, and is capable of rasterizing all primitives falling into a 128 by 128 region. These rasterizers can be assigned dynamically to any of the 80 regions in a 1280- by 1024-pixel screen.

Rasterization in Pixel-Planes 5 occurs in two phases. First, the front-end processors (16 to 32 floating-point processors) transform and sort primitives into screen regions. Sorting is done by checking a primitive's screen extent against the 128-pixel–aligned region boundaries; primitives that cross region boundaries are placed in the buckets of all regions affected (this occurs approximately 20 percent of the time for 100-pixel triangles). After bucket sorting is complete, the multiple rasterizers process regions in parallel. When a rasterizer finishes a region, it transfers its newly computed image to the appropriate part of a conventional frame buffer and begins processing primitives from an unassigned region (see Fig. 18.26). All communication between system components is performed over a 1.28-gigabyte-per-second token ring.

Pixel-Planes 5 achieves much higher processor utilization than did previous Pixel-Planes systems, since 128 by 128 regions are much closer to the size of most primitives than is a single 512 by 512 region. Since virtual-buffer rasterizers can be assigned to screen regions dynamically, system resources can be concentrated on the regions that need them the most.

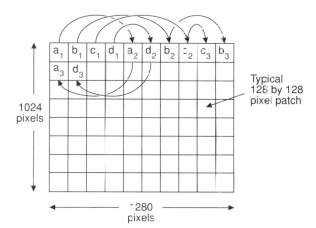

Fig. 18.26 Dynamic assignment of rasterizers to regions in Pixel-Planes 5. (Reprinted with permission from [FUCH89]. © ACM.)

Parallel virtual-buffer systems do present two difficulties. First, transferring buckets to multiple rasterization buffers in parallel requires a high-performance data network between the front-end and rasterization subsystems, as well as sophisticated control and synchronization software [ELLS89]. Second, in some images, most of the primitives in the database can fall into a single region, making the extra layer of parallelism useless. The primitives in the overcrowded region could be allocated to more than one rasterizer, but then the multiple partial images would have to be combined. Although this complicates the rasterization process, it can be done by compositing the multiple images into one buffer at the end of rasterization.

18.10.3   Image-Composition Architectures

The notion of combining images after rasterization can be used to build a second type of multilevel parallel architecture, *image-composition* or *composite* architectures [MOLN88; SHAW88]. The central idea is to distribute primitives over a number of complete rendering systems. The multiple renderers are synchronized so they use identical transformation matrices and compute the same frame at the same time. Each renderer then computes its partial image independently and stores that partial image in its own frame buffer.

Video scanout from each frame buffer occurs in the normal way, except that z-buffer contents are scanned out as well. Scanout processes in each frame buffer are synchronized so that each frame buffer scans out the same pixel at the same time. A tree or pipeline of compositors combines the RGB and z streams from each renderer using the technique

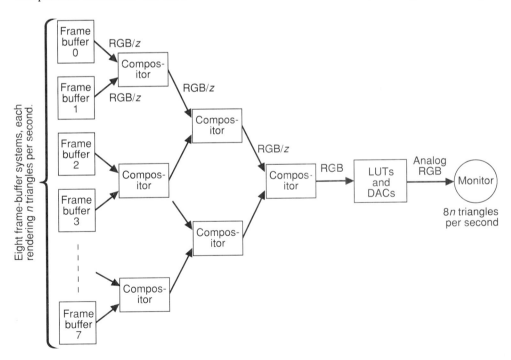

Fig. 18.27 An image-composition system composed of eight individual renderers.

described in Section 18.9.2. Figure 18.27 shows a composite system for displaying $8n$ triangles per second built from eight renderers, each of which can display n triangles per second.

This technique can be exploited to build systems of arbitrarily high performance by using a large number of parallel renderers. The main difficulties with this approach are the need to distribute the database over multiple processors, which incurs all the difficulties of parallel front ends (described in Section 18.6.1); aliasing or erroneous pixels caused by the image-composition operation; and a lack of flexibility, since image composition restricts the class of rasterization algorithms that can be implemented on the machine. Nevertheless, this approach provides an important way to realize systems of extremely high performance.

18.11 ENHANCED DISPLAY CAPABILITIES

This section discusses the architectural implications of a variety of enhancements to the standard Gouraud-shaded polygon-rendering algorithm. Increasing numbers of these features are judged necessary or desirable by suppliers and users. At the end of this section, we discuss a few aspects of flight simulators, the systems that traditionally have included the greatest number of advanced features.

18.11.1 Support for Multiple Windows

As mentioned in Chapter 10, the ability to display multiple overlapping windows controlled by separate applications has become a necessity in current workstations. Without hardware support for this capability, the overall speed of the graphics system may suffer seriously. For example, operations such as pushing one window behind another, popping a window so that all of it becomes visible, and dragging a window around the screen, all require the ability to copy pixels rapidly from one frame-buffer region to another, and, in some cases, to regenerate part or all of an image. Also, if multiple images are to be generated in different windows simultaneously, the rendering pipeline must be able to switch rapidly between applications.

The architectural enhancements needed to provide such support often cut across the design of the entire graphics subsystem: from display traversal, to geometric transformation, to clipping, to rasterization, and to the frame-buffer memory organization. We discuss here some of the main difficulties in building a windowing system that supports multiple interactive applications. For a more complete treatment of these issues, see [RHOD89].

Context switching between applications.   When the graphics system switches from an application running in one window to an application running in another, state information must be saved and restored at many places in the graphics pipeline. For example, in the modeling-transformation stage, the stack of current transformation matrices must be saved for the current application and loaded for the next application; in the video controller, look-up table entries may have to be reassigned. To save and restore state rapidly, local memory is needed at many stages in the rendering pipeline.

Having a fixed amount of local storage, of course, limits the number of applications that can run simultaneously. If fast context switching is not possible, graphics systems generally switch between windows as infrequently as possible (perhaps only a few times per second), causing a noticeable hesitation in the movement of objects in the various windows.

Clipping to nonconvex screen windows. When windows overlap, pixels must be written only to the exposed portions of their respective windows. This requires clipping pixels to window boundaries that may not be convex. Several solutions to this problem are possible.

Writing an entire window to offscreen memory. This allows the rendering pipeline to be largely isolated from windowing issues. A fast pixel copy can transfer exposed portions of the window to the actual frame buffer after each frame update. This requires extra processing for the pixel copy and adds latency to the image-generation process, both of which can seriously hamper interactivity. Alternatively, the video system can assemble the video stream on the fly from disjoint portions of video memory, as is done in Lexidata's Lex 90 system [SUYD86] or Intel's 82786 graphics coprocessor chip [SHIR86]. This approach does not add latency, but may restrict the locations and number of windows, since assembling the video image on the fly from different memory locations places heavy demands on the memory system.

Selectively updating screen pixels. A second alternative is to compute all the pixels for each window, but to update only those pixels in exposed portions of the window. This is analogous to scissoring, described in Chapter 3. To make this operation fast, hardware support is generally needed. A popular approach is to use window ID bits [AKEL88]. Here, a few (generally 4 to 8) additional bits are associated with each pixel. These bits specify a unique ID for each window. When the frame buffer is updated, hardware compares the window ID of the pixel to be written with the window ID stored in the frame buffer. The frame-buffer pixel is updated only if the window IDs agree.

Clipping within the rendering pipeline. The main disadvantage of both of the preceding schemes is that they generate many pixels that may never be displayed. The alternative is to clip within the rendering pipeline, so that the only pixels computed are those that will actually be displayed. The main difficulty with this approach is that the exposed part of a window may not be a simple rectangle: It may have concavities caused by partially overlapping windows of higher priority, or it may even contain a hole consisting of a smaller, higher-priority window. Clipping to arbitrary boundaries such as these is computationally expensive. One solution is to tesselate the exposed region with a series of rectangular windows and to clip primitives to these simple window boundaries. Of course, this too affects system performance, since primitives must be processed multiple times, once for each rectangular region.

It is extremely difficult, in general, to provide full performance for all possible window configurations and desired actions. System designers typically begin with a list of desired windowing capabilities and try to find ways of implementing these without incurring exorbitant system costs. Most systems run at full speed only under certain simple situations, and take a big performance hit otherwise. For example, a system may run at full speed only when the rendering window is fully uncovered (or is mostly uncovered, or when its visible portion is a rectangular region), or its rendering speed may suffer when more than one window is being updated simultaneously.

18.11.2 Support for Increased Realism

Our discussion of graphics architecture thus far has primarily concerned the quest for speed. With the continued increase in speed of affordable systems over the past years, users have desired increasingly realistic images as well. Algorithms for generating realistic images are discussed in Chapters 14, 15, 16, and 20; we discuss here the impact realistic rendering has on graphics system architecture.

Antialiasing. As discussed in Chapter 14, the two main approaches to antialiasing use area sampling and point sampling. In area sampling, we need to know the fractional contribution of each primitive to each pixel (ideally, we would like to weight these contributions using an appropriate filter). Unfortunately, calculating the precise fractional contribution is very difficult for 3D images. Architectures that provide hardware support for antialiasing generally use some sort of supersampling scheme. Depending on the characteristics of the rasterization processors, uniform or adaptive supersampling is used.

Uniform supersampling. Uniform supersampling involves calculating the entire image at high resolution and combining multiple sample points at each pixel to determine the pixel's single color value. This appears to be the only feasible approach in SIMD image-parallel systems. Unfortunately, supersampling with n samples per pixel reduces system performance by a factor of n. For this reason, some systems of this type adopt a successive-refinement approach to antialiasing, in which a crude image is generated at full speed when high update rates are desired; when no changes in the image are pending, the system computes further sample points and uses them to refine the image [FUCH85].

Adaptive supersampling. Adaptive supersampling involves calculating the image at high resolution only where necessary. This can be performed most readily on image-order rasterization systems, where information is available on whether or not pixels are partially covered. A well-known adaptive supersampling technique useful for object-order rasterization is the A-buffer (see Section 15.7.3). The linked lists needed to store partially covering primitives are feasible only in MIMD systems that have an arbitrary amount of memory available for each pixel.

Transparency. As mentioned in Chapter 16, true transparency, including refractions and translucency, is difficult to model in software. Even simple models of transparency that exclude refraction and translucency are difficult to implement on many hardware systems. Image-parallel architectures in particular have difficulty with transparency, since the z-buffer algorithm does not handle multiple surfaces well (an extra z value is potentially needed for every transparent surface). Image-parallel systems with SIMD PEs, or systems with fixed amounts of storage per pixel, can generally display a few transparent objects by rasterizing in multiple passes—one pass for all the opaque primitives, and then a separate pass for each transparent surface [MAMM89]. If more than a few transparent surfaces are required, a screen-door transparency scheme generally must be used. MIMD systems may be able to represent pixels as linked lists of visible surfaces, allowing larger numbers of transparent objects to be displayed.

Object-parallel architectures handle transparency more gracefully, since they do not require intermediate storage for the entire image, and have all the potentially visible polygons in hand when the color for each pixel is computed. The rasterizer, however, must be configured to allow multiple covering polygons and to perform the weighted-sum calculations needed to compute final pixel values.

Textures. Until recently, the only systems that performed texturing at interactive rates were multimillion-dollar flight simulators. Increasingly, however, different forms of texturing are becoming available on graphics workstations and even low-end systems. Textures can be simulated, of course, on any architecture using myriad small triangles with interpolated shading between vertices. This approach, however, places high demands on the display system and is feasible only in high-performance workstations or when simple textures are displayed.

The two traditional methods of texturing are texture maps and procedural textures (see Chapter 16). The drawback of both of these methods is that texturing is applied at the end of the rendering pipeline—after the image has already been converted into pixels. In many architectures, pixel data are not accessible by a general-purpose processor at this point. Flight simulators add an extra hardware stage to perform texture-map lookups. A few graphics workstations, such as the Stellar GS2000 (see Section 18.11.3), store the generated image in main memory, where it is accessible by the system's general-purpose processors.

In architectures in which large-grain MIMD processors have access to the computed image, the texture-map approach is the most appropriate. Texture coordinates, rather than colors, can be stored at each pixel. If each of these MIMD processors is provided with a copy of the texture maps, it can perform the texture-map lookup, replacing the texture coordinates with the appropriate colors. Note that simple texture-map lookup is generally insufficient here—some sort of multiresolution texture map or summed-area table is needed to avoid aliasing.

In architectures in which only fine-grain parallel processors have access to the computed image, procedural textures may be more feasible. Fine-grain processors may not contain enough memory to store the texture maps. If many PEs are available, however, they may be able to compute simple procedural texture models at interactive rates [FUCH89].

Shadows. Computing true shadows, as described in Section 16.4, exacts a high computational price; on many architectures, true shadows cannot be computed at all. For these reasons, few high-performance systems implement true shadows [FUCH85], although a number of techniques can be used to approximate shadows under certain conditions. A common technique used in commercial flight simulators and in a number of workstation systems is to generate shadows for the ground plane only, as described in Section 16.4.

Ray-tracing architectures. Ray tracing, described in Chapters 15 and 16, is a powerful rendering method that can generate extremely realistic images. Unfortunately, it requires a great deal of computation (a typical image can require minutes or hours to compute on a typical workstation). Fortunately, ray-tracing algorithms can be parallelized in several ways, many of which have analogs in conventional rendering:

- *Component parallelism.* Computations for a single ray can be parallelized. For example, reflection, refraction, and intersection calculations all require computing the

x, y, and z components of vectors or points. These three components can be calculated in parallel, resulting in a speedup by a factor of 3.

- *Image parallelism.* Ray–primitive intersections can be calculated in parallel in separate PEs, since the calculations for each ray are independent. To take advantage of this form of parallelism, however, PEs potentially need access to the entire database, since the ray tree for a particular ray may reach any portion of the database.

- *Object parallelism.* Primitives in the database can be distributed spatially over multiple PEs. Each PE, then, is responsible for all rays that pass through its region. It computes ray–object intersections if the ray hits an object, and forwards the ray to the next PE otherwise.

Many architectures for ray tracing have been designed using these techniques alone or in combination. Most use a large number of MIMD PEs, since ray-tracing typically requires a large amount of branching and random addressing.

The simplest type of image-parallel architecture assigns one or more rays to each PE and replicates the entire database at each PE. This technique was used in the LINKS-1 [NISH83a], built at Osaka University in 1983. The LINKS-1 has been used to compute numerous animation sequences. This technique was also used in SIGHT [NARU87], a more recent design done at Nippon Telegraph and Telephone. The SIGHT architecture also takes advantage of component parallelism in its TARAI floating-point unit.

The first proposed object-parallel ray-tracing architectures used uniform spatial subdivision to assign portions of the universe to PEs [CLEA83]. This resulted in poor efficiency for many scenes, since most of the primitives were clustered in a few regions. Other proposed architectures subdivided the scene adaptively to improve the load balance among PEs [DIPP84]. Although this approach improves PE utilization, it makes mapping rays to PEs much more difficult.

Since many ray-tracing architectures closely resemble commercial parallel computers, which offer advantages of lower cost and mature programming environments, research in parallel ray tracing has shifted largely to developing efficient algorithms for commercial multiprocessors, such as hypercubes, Transputer meshes, and the Connection Machine. Two chief concerns are achieving high utilization and balanced load among PEs, particularly when distributed database models are used.

An image-parallel ray-tracing algorithm has been developed for Thinking Machines' SIMD Connection Machine [DELA88], in which the database is repeatedly broadcast to all of the PEs, which perform ray–object intersections in parallel.

Implementations have also been reported on shared-memory multiprocessors, such as the BBN Butterfly [JENK89]. Here, the database does not need to be stored at each PE or broadcast repeatedly; instead, PEs request portions of the database from the memory system as needed. Unfortunately, contention for shared memory resources increases with the number of PEs, so only modest performance increases can be achieved in such systems.

Nemoto and Omachi [NEMO86], Kobayashi and Nakamura [KOBA87], Scherson and Caspary [SCHE88], and others (see [JEVA89]) have proposed various methods for adaptively assigning objects to PEs and for passing rays between those PEs. AT&T's Pixel Machine, a MIMD multiprocessor with PEs based on digital signal-processor chips, ray traces simple images at interactive rates [POTM89]. Such systems offer a dramatic glimpse of the performance possible in parallel ray tracers of the future.

18.11.3   Stellar's GS2000—A Tightly Integrated Architecture that Facilitates Realistic Rendering

Systems such as Silicon Graphics' POWER IRIS (Section 18.8.2) use dedicated hardware to compute images rapidly. Many of these calculations, particularly in the geometric transformation and other front-end stages, are similar to the types of processing needed in many types of scientific computing. The Stellar GS2000 (similar to its predecessor, the Stellar GS1000 [APGA88]) seeks to make its computing resources available both for image generation and for accelerating other compute-intensive jobs that may run on the machine.

Figure 18.28 shows a block diagram of the GS2000 architecture. The Multi-Stream Processor is a single high-performance processor that simultaneously executes instructions from four independent instruction streams; its peak processing rate is 25 million instructions per second. The vector floating-point processor performs scalar and vector floating-point operations; it can process a maximum of 40 million floating-point operations per second. The rendering processor uses a setup processor to perform polygon-processing calculations and a 4×4 SIMD footprint processor to perform pixel operations. The GS2000 renders 150,000 pseudocolored, Gouraud-shaded, z-buffered, 100-pixel triangles per second and 30,000 Phong-shaded polygons per second.

All the GS2000's processing and memory resources are organized around a central 512-bit-wide communication structure called the DataPath. The DataPath has an unusual design in which all of the I/O connections and registers for a single bit of the datapath are built onto a custom gate-array chip (each DataPath chip contains circuitry for 16 bits, so a total of 32 are needed).

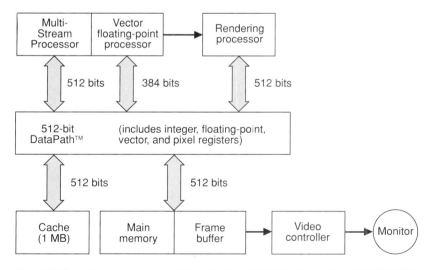

Fig. 18.28 Block diagram of the Stellar GS2000 (based on [APGA88]).

In a typical graphics application, the Multi-Stream Processor traverses a structure database stored in main memory; it then feeds data to the vector processor, which performs geometry calculations. The vector processor sends transformed primitives to the rendering processor, which calculates the pixels of the image. Rather than storing images directly in a frame buffer, the rendering processor stores them in main memory as *virtual pixel maps*, visible portions of which are copied to the appropriate portion of the frame buffer for display.

Because virtual pixel maps are stored in main memory and are accessible to the Multi-Stream Processor and vector processor, a variety of postprocessing operations (as well as image processing and other operations) can be performed. For example, to display textures, the rasterizing unit generates texture indices in pixels, rather than final colors. Later, one of the general-purpose processors passes over the half-generated image and substitutes proper color values for each pixel by table lookup of texture indices. Also, overlapping windows can be implemented easily, since the contents of each screen window are always available in main memory. The main disadvantages of virtual pixel maps are the extra bandwidth and time required to copy image data from main memory to the frame buffer.

18.11.4 Support for Advanced Primitives

We have focused so far on architectures that display polygons rapidly. Increasing demand is being placed on systems to handle other types of primitives. Many complex-surface primitives, such as spline patches and mesh primitives, can be converted into polygons with little time penalty. For other types of primitives, however, such conversions can be either time-consuming or difficult. For example, converting a CSG object to boundary representation is time-consuming, and can result in a large expansion in the amount of data; polygonalizing a volume dataset is slow as well, and tends to obscure data and to produce undesirable artifacts. When more complicated primitives are displayed directly, many of these difficulties can be avoided; in many cases, system performance can be increased as well.

Curved surfaces. As discussed in Chapter 11, polygons are simple, regular primitives that are convenient to display (especially in hardware). Unfortunately, since they are very low-level, they are inconvenient for modeling and lead to inaccuracies, especially for complex, curved surfaces. Other representations for surfaces, such as Bezier patches and NURBS, are more convenient to specify when modeling, but require complicated processing to render directly.

Most hardware systems that display high-order primitives decompose the primitives into polygons for display purposes. For many types of surface primitives (particularly Bezier patches and NURBS), this decomposition can be done rapidly in hardware using forward-difference engines [LIEN87]. In some cases, however, it may be faster to display curved surfaces directly, especially in systems with programmable parallel rasterization processors. When this book was written, few systems provided this capability [MCLE88]. It remains to be seen whether systems of the future will continue to tile such surfaces with polygons, or whether they will render curved surfaces directly.

Volume data.   Volume rendering—the direct rendering of data represented as 3D scalar fields (discussed in Section 20.6)—is becoming an important branch of computer graphics. In many ways, it has an even greater need for hardware acceleration than does polygon rendering, since volume datasets are generally much larger than are polygon datasets (a typical dataset from a CT scanner might be $64 \cdot 256 \cdot 256 = 4.2$ million voxels, whereas few polygon datasets contain more than 1 million polygons). Furthermore, voxel calculations are simpler than polygon calculations.

The first architectures designed to accelerate the display of volume datasets classified voxels as either "occupied" or "empty," and displayed occupied voxels. This approach minimizes the amount of processing but obscures data in the interior of the object and produces a "sugar-cube" effect in the generated image. Phoenix Data Systems' Insight system [MEAG85] uses this approach: It interactively displays volume datasets encoded as octrees. Kaufman's Cube architecture [KAUF88b] provides special hardware for accessing in parallel the entire row of voxels corresponding to a single pixel. In addition, this hardware can determine the nearest visible voxel in the row in logarithmic time. Views from arbitrary angles are implemented by rotating the dataset in Cube's 3D memory.

More recent volume-rendering methods assign partial transparencies (or opacities) to each voxel, rather than using binary classification, and attempt to eliminate sampling artifacts (see Section 20.6). Since more voxels contribute to each pixel than when binary classification is used, these algorithms substantially increase image-generation time.

Volume-rendering architectures based on these algorithms generally use variations of the image- or object-parallel approaches we have seen before. Image-parallel architectures assign PEs to pixels or to groups of pixels [LEVO89]. Object-parallel architectures generally partition the voxels into contiguous 3D regions and assign to each a separate PE [WEST89]. During rendering, PEs compute their voxels' contributions to each pixel in the image as though their voxels were the only ones in the dataset. The contributions from multiple regions are then composited using these aggregate colors and opacities.

The primary advantage of the object-parallel approach is that it divides the database among PEs. The disadvantage is that pixel values calculated in one PE may be obscured by pixels calculated in another PE whose voxels lie nearer to the eyepoint. Image parallelism has complementary advantages and disadvantages: Each PE processes only voxels that are potentially visible, but each PE needs access to the entire (very large) database.

Dynamic Digital Displays' parallel Voxel Processor system is an example of an object-parallel architecture [GOLD88]. A hypercube architecture could also be used in an object-parallel approach by assigning each voxel in each image slice (or even in the entire database) to a separate PE. Levoy proposed a hybrid system using Pixel-Planes 5, in which voxel shading is done in an object-parallel fashion and the image is generated in an image-parallel fashion [LEVO89]. The Pixar Image Computer computes red, green, and blue components of an image in parallel [LEVI84]. Because volume rendering is a relatively new area, it is difficult to predict what architectures (or even algorithms) will be dominant in the future.

Constructive-solid-geometry (CSG) architectures.   As we saw in Chapter 12, CSG is one of the more popular techniques for modeling solid objects. Chapter 15 described ways to display a CSG object directly from that object's binary-tree representation. The two popular approaches for direct CSG rendering are generalizations of the image-order and object-order rasterization techniques described earlier in this chapter.

Image-order CSG rasterization. This approach was described in Section 18.9.2. Kedem and Ellis's Ray Casting Machine is a hardware implementation of this algorithm. Their current system displays small CSG objects at interactive rates.

Object-order CSG rasterization. Chapter 15 also described object-order (or depth-buffer) CSG rasterization algorithms that are generalizations of the z-buffer algorithm. CSG depth-buffer algorithms can be implemented on any architecture that has enough memory for each pixel to store two z-buffers, two color buffers, and three 1-bit flags [GOLD86]. Many current high-performance workstations provide frame buffers with sufficient memory. If enough pixel-level processing is available, depth-buffer CSG display algorithms can display modest objects at interactive speeds [GOLD89]. If more memory per pixel is available, more complicated CSG objects can be displayed even faster [JANS87].

18.11.5   Support for Enhanced 3D Perception

Recall from Chapter 14 that 3D images displayed on a 2D screen contain only a few 3D depth cues: obscuration, kinetic depth effect, lighting, and occasionally shadows. The real 3D world provides such additional powerful cues as stereopsis and head-motion parallax. This section discusses architectures and architectural enhancements that seek to provide these extra cues.

Stereo display.   Stereopsis can be achieved with a 2D display by computing separate images for the left and right eyes and channeling each image to the respective eye. Image pairs can be displayed on separate monitors (or in separate windows on the same monitor), or left and right images can be displayed in alternating frames. In the former case, image pairs can be viewed with a stereo viewer that optically channels the two images to a fixed point in front of the screen where the viewer must be positioned. Disadvantages of this scheme are that only one person at a time can view the scene, and that only one-half of the monitor's resolution is available (unless two monitors are used, in which case the cost of the system increases dramatically).

Multiplexing left and right images in time is a more popular technique. This requires displaying left and right images alternately in rapid succession, and blocking each eye's view while the other eye's image is being displayed. A graphics system displaying stereo images generally must have a frame buffer large enough to store four complete images— enough to double-buffer the image for each eye. Also, some scheme is needed to block each eye's view of the screen at the appropriate time. One approach uses a mechanical shutter synchronized to the frame buffer so that left and right images are displayed at the correct time [LIPS79]. Unfortunately, mechanical shutters can be heavy, noisy, and, in some cases, dangerous (one design used a rapidly spinning cylinder less than 1 inch from the eye).

A more popular mechanism is an electronic shutter that alternately polarizes light in one direction and then another. The electronic shutter may be the same size as and mounted in front of the display screen, or it can be smaller and worn on special goggles. In either case, lenses polarized in opposite directions are placed before each eye. When the polarization of the electronic shutter corresponds to the polarization of one of these lenses, the screen becomes visible; when the polarization is in the opposite direction, the view is blocked. Placing the shutter in front of the display screen allows several users to view the image simultaneously, if each wears a pair of inexpensive, passive glasses. Large electronic shutters are expensive, however. Stereo displays with electronic shutters tend to be darker than mechanical ones as well, since the polarizing film transmits only a fraction of the light from the monitor.

Varifocal mirror. A *varifocal mirror* is an unusual display device that uses an oscillating mirror to display true 3D images. These images provide stereopsis and head-motion parallax without requiring the user to wear special headgear. The basic idea is to use a flexible mirror whose focal length can be changed rapidly, and to position it so that it reflects an image of the display monitor to the viewer (Fig. 18.29) [TRAU67; FUCH82; JOHN82]. When the mirror is vibrated with an ordinary loudspeaker, the mirror's focal length changes sinusoidally. This is generally done at a frequency of approximately 30Hz.

The mirror's periodically changing focal length makes the distance to the monitor appear to increase and decrease by several inches or more during each 30-Hz cycle. Points, lines, and similar data are displayed on a point-plotting (not raster-scan) display monitor. The perceived depth of a point is determined by its position in the display list: "near"

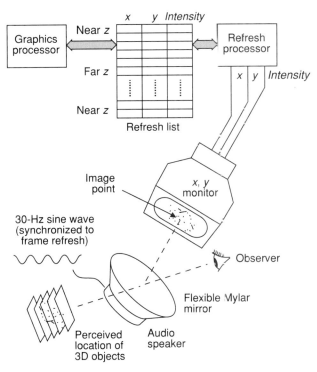

Fig. 18.29 Varifocal-mirror display system.

points are stored in the beginning or end of the refresh list, "far" points are stored in the middle of the refresh list. Note that there are two places in the list at which a point appears at the same depth—when the mirror is moving forward, and when it is moving backward.

Varifocal-mirror displays have several limitations. One drawback is that nearer objects do not obscure more distant ones, and thus only nonobscuring primitives such as points, lines, and transparent volume data can be displayed. A second difficulty is that only a limited amount of data can be displayed at a time—the amount that can be refreshed during a single mirror cycle. In spite of these limitations, the varifocal mirror is one of the very few true 3D display devices to be made into a commercial product, the Genisco SpaceGraph [STOV82].

Head-mounted display. In a seminal address at the 1965 International Federation for Information Processing Congress [SUTH65], Ivan Sutherland proposed that the *ultimate display* would be one that produced images and other sensory input with such fidelity that the observer could not tell the simulated objects from real ones. In 1968, he showed a prototype display that was worn on the head and that demonstrated the most important property of the *ultimate display*—it allowed the user to walk around in a *virtual world*. Specifically, the system comprised the following:

1. Headgear with two small display devices, each optically channeled to one eye
2. A tracking system that allowed the computer system to know the precise location of the user's helmet (and thus head) at all times
3. A hand-held wand, whose position was also tracked by the system, that allowed the user to reach out to grab and move objects in the virtual environment
4. A real-time graphics display system that constantly regenerated the images to the display devices as the user moved, giving the user the illusion of walking around "virtual" objects in the room.

This system, with its rich 3D cues of head-motion parallax and stereopsis and its simple, direct 3D manipulation of objects inside the virtual world, convincingly demonstrated to many people that the conventional way of interacting with 3D scenes using a desktop CRT is an unsatisfying, constrained mechanism that keeps the user outside the CRT's window to the 3D virtual world. Unfortunately several technical problems have prevented the head-mounted display from reaching full effectiveness—indeed, they have kept it to a level discouragingly close to the capabilities of Sutherland's 1968 prototype [FISH86; CHUN89]. These technical problems include

1. Developing headgear with high-resolution displays that allows a wide-screen view of the graphics display screen superimposed on the real world (a difficult optical problem)
2. Developing a tracking system for the helmet and hand that has the range of a room with 1-millimeter resolution and response time of a few milliseconds or less
3. Designing a graphics system that generates at least 60 frames per second with minimal latency (low latency is a particularly important concern here, since latency in a head-mounted display can induce motion sickness [DEYO89]).

The most visible and widespread use of head-mounted displays has been for heads-up displays in cockpits of military aircraft. Heads-up displays, however, give only auxiliary information to the user, rather than creating a virtual world, complete with objects that can be directly manipulated. In 1989, two companies, Autodesk and VPL Research, introduced commercial head-mounted display systems based on off-the-shelf technology. Proponents of such systems predict that these kinds of systems will be the twenty-first century graphics equivalents of Sony Walkman personal stereos, to be used not only for real-time 3D applications but also for general portable interactive computing.

Digital holography.[4]   Holography is another method for displaying true 3D images without using special headgear or tracking the viewer's location. Traditional holograms are produced by exposing photographic film simultaneously to laser light scattered from the object to be recorded and to a reference beam from the same laser. The interference patterns recorded on the film encode the object's appearance from a range of viewpoints. The hologram is viewed by illuminating it with laser light from the opposite direction.

Holograms of imaginary objects can be produced by simulating the laser-interference process on a computer and writing the computed fringes onto high-resolution film. Unfortunately, holograms produced by this technique can require 10^{12} Fourier transforms (each of which requires a large number of multiplications and additions) and need a VLSI-type electron-beam writer to inscribe the results on film [DALL80; TRIC87]. For these reasons, this technique is currently too expensive for almost all applications. Fully computed holograms, however, contain more information than is needed by the human eye. A promising approach is to reduce these calculations to the number actually needed. This is the subject of ongoing research.

Holographic stereograms, which are built up from a sequence of computer-generated perspective views, are attractive in the meantime. In a holographic stereogram, a sequence of approximately 100 views from slightly differing side-to-side viewpoints is projected with laser light onto holographic film, each from the direction from which it was calculated. A second reference beam from the same laser overlaps the projection beam to record the view direction in an interference pattern. After exposure and processing, the film (now the holographic stereogram) is illuminated by a reference beam in the opposite direction. Image beams then diffract back in the directions from which they were projected. An eye moving from one view to the next perceives a smooth progression of perspective information that yields an impression of a solid object or 3D scene floating in the vicinity of the film. Combined with all the conventional monocular depth cues of 3D computer graphics, this holographic image gives a particularly effective sense of shape and space [BENT82].

Although holographic stereograms are much less expensive to produce than are traditional holograms, they still require a large amount of computation (dozens to hundreds of images for a single stereogram). Furthermore, the need to record the stereogram on photographic film adds expense and time to the image-generation process. Consequently, digital holography is unlikely to yield interactive 3D images in the near future, although it

---

[4]Material for this section was contributed by Stephen A. Benton of the MIT Media Laboratory.

may prove useful for recording 3D still images, just as photographic film records 2D still images today.

18.11.6 Real-Time Flight Simulators

The systems that "put it all together" to generate the most realistic simulation of 3D scenes for interactive tasks are the multimillion-dollar flight simulators. Flight simulation is not unique in being able to benefit from truly real-time systems. It is, however, the one application for which customers have consistently been willing to spend millions of dollars for a single system, largely because of the cost and danger of training pilots solely in actual airplanes. Because the community of flight-simulator users is fairly small, and because the systems tend to use proprietary, hardware-specific software provided by the manufacturer, detailed information about flight-simulator architectures has not appeared in the literature.

Early flight simulators include General Electric's NASA II (see Section 18.9) and Evans & Sutherland designs based on the scan-line systems developed at the University of Utah in the late 1960s. Some of these early flight-simulator systems could display 1000 or more polygons in real time, but all used simple shading methods and provided few image enhancements. Later systems have not substantially increased the number of primitives that can be displayed. For example, Evans & Sutherland's current high-end system, the ESIG-1000, displays only 2300 polygons at 60 Hz [EVAN89]. Rather, system developers have increased scene realism and reduced distracting artifacts by incorporating features such as antialiasing, haze and fog, point light sources, clouds, and filtered textures [SCHA83]. The effectiveness of these techniques can be seen in Color Plates I.5(a) and I.5(b).

Flight simulators from major manufacturers such as Evans & Sutherland, General Electric, McDonnell-Douglas, and Singer/Link all share several architectural themes: Since flight simulation involves predictable interactions with very large datasets, these systems tend to use more specialized processing than do other graphics systems. For example, custom processors are frequently built to manage the image database, to transform primitives, to rasterize the image, and to perform image-enhancement operations afterward. A typical simulator system is composed of a long pipeline of proprietary processors [SCHA83].

Certain simplifications can sometimes be made in a flight simulator that are not possible in more general graphics systems. For example, since a typical simulator dataset involves a small number of moving objects and a wide, unchanging backdrop, the generality of the z-buffer visibility algorithm may not be needed and a simpler depth-sort algorithm may suffice.

Flight simulators also must manage complex databases without hesitation. A typical database may represent a region 100 miles square. Detail needed for low-level flight cannot be displayed when the airplane is at 40,000 feet. This requires the system to maintain object descriptions with different levels of detail that can be swapped in and out in real time. The architecture also must handle overloading gracefully, since image complexity may increase drastically at the most crucial times, such as during takeoffs, during landings, and in emergency situations [SCHU80]. Frames must be generated at least 30 times per second—even in these situations.

18.12 SUMMARY

This chapter has provided an overview of the architectural techniques used to build high-performance graphics systems. We have seen that the computational demands of many interactive applications quickly surpass the capabilities of a single processor, and that concurrent processing of various kinds is needed to meet the performance goals of demanding 3D applications, such as computer-aided design, scientific visualization, and flight-simulation.

We have shown how the two basic approaches to concurrency—pipelining and parallelism—can be applied to accelerate each stage of the display process, together with the advantages and limitations of each of these choices. The design of any real graphics . system (indeed, any complex system in general) represents a myriad of compromises and tradeoffs between interrelated factors, such as performance, generality, efficiency, and cost. As a result, many real systems use combinations of architectural techniques we have described.

The current state of hardware technology also plays an important role in deciding what architectural techniques are feasible. For example, the memory-intensive architectures that now dominate the field would have been impractical just ten years ago before inexpensive DRAMs became available. In the future, we can expect rapidly improving technology to continue to improve graphics system performance.

The designs of future systems will be complicated by demands not just for rendering standard primitives such as points, lines, and Gouraud-shaded polygons, but also for rendering with more advanced capabilities—transparency, textures, global illumination, and volume data. These all complicate not only the calculations, but also the basic structure of the display process, making it more difficult to design systems with both high performance for the basic capabilities and sufficient generality to handle the advanced features.

EXERCISES

18.1 Section 5.6 showed that we can transform a plane equation by multiplying it by the transpose of the inverse point-transformation matrix. A surface-normal vector can be considered to be a plane equation in which the D component does not matter. How many multiplications and additions are needed to transform a surface-normal vector if the point-transformation matrix is composed of translations, rotations, and scales? (Hint: Consider the form of transformation matrix.)

18.2 A simple way to reduce the number of front-end calculations when displaying polygonal meshes is to use a mesh primitive, such as a triangle strip. A *triangle strip* is a sequence of three or more vertices, in which every consecutive set of three vertices defines a triangle. A triangle strip of $n + 2$ vertices, therefore, defines a connected strip of n triangles (whereas $3n$ vertices are needed to define n individual triangles). Estimate the number of additions/subtractions and multiplications/divisions required to display the sample database of Section 18.3.9 if the 10,000 triangles are contained in:

  a. 5000 triangle strips, each containing 2 triangles
  b. 1000 triangle strips, each containing 10 triangles
  c. A single triangle strip containing 10,000 triangles.

What is the maximum speedup you could obtain in the front-end subsystem by converting a database of discrete triangles into triangle strips? Are there any disadvantages to using triangle strips?

18.3 Assume that the 10,000-triangle database described in Section 18.3.9 is displayed at 24 Hz on a pipelined graphics system with the following characteristics: 1280 by 1024 color display refreshed at 72 Hz, 32-bit color values, and 32-bit z values.

    a. Estimate the data bandwidth between the following points of the display pipeline: (1) between display-traversal and modeling-transformation stages (assume that 24 32-bit words of data are required for each triangle in the object database); (2) between front-end and back-end subsystems (assume that 15 32-bit words are required for each transformed triangle); (3) between rasterizer and frame buffer; and (4) between frame buffer and video controller.

    b. Repeat the calculations in part (a) for a database with 100,000 polygons with an average area of 10 pixels and the same overlap factor.

    c. Repeat the calculations in part (a) for a database with 100,000 polygons with an average area of 100 pixels, but assume that only 10 percent of the pixels are initially visible.

18.4 Consider the pipelined object-order rasterization architecture described in Section 18.7.1. If separate processors are provided for polygon processing, edge processing, and span processing, all these operations can be overlapped. Assume that we have a sophisticated span processor that can process an entire pixel (i.e. compute its RGB and z values, compare z values, and update the frame buffer) in a single 250-nanosecond clock cycle. Ignoring the time required for clearing the screen between frames, calculate how many triangles per second this system can display under the following conditions:

    a. 100-pixel triangles; negligible time for polygon and edge processing

    b. 100-pixel triangles; 20 microseconds per triangle for polygon processing; negligible time for edge processing

    c. 100-pixel triangles; 20 microseconds per triangle for polygon processing; 2 microseconds per scan line for edge processing (assume that a typical triangle covers 15 scan lines)

    d. 10-pixel triangles; 20 microseconds per triangle for polygon processing; 2 microseconds per scan line for edge processing (assume that a typical triangle covers four scan lines)

    e. 1000-pixel triangles; 20 microseconds per triangle for polygon processing; 2 microseconds per scan line for edge processing (assume that a typical triangle covers 50 scan lines).

18.5 A frame buffer is to be built with 32 bits per pixel, and access to the frame buffer is to be by single pixels (a 32-bit-wide memory system). What frame-buffer sizes with aspect ratios 1:1, 5:4, and 2:1 (up to a maximum dimension of 2048 pixels) are possible if the following commercial memory parts are used and no memory is to be wasted (i.e., all memory in the frame buffer should be used to store visible pixels):

    a. 64K × 4 VRAMs (256 Kbit)

    b. 256K × 4 VRAMs (1 Mbit)

    c. 512K × 8 VRAMs (4 Mbit).

Answer the following questions assuming frame buffers of sizes 512 by 512, 1024 by 1024, and 2048 by 2048 (each refreshed at 60 Hz):

    d. How frequently must the serial port of each memory chip be accessed during video scanout? (Assume that vertical and horizontal retrace times are neglible, and that VRAM outputs are not multiplexed.)

    e. Given that the serial-port cycle time of the fastest VRAMs is about 35 nanoseconds, which of these frame buffers could be built? (Again, assume no multiplexing.)

    f. Which frame buffers could be built if multiple pixels were read simultaneously and multiplexed as described in Section 18.1.5 (again assuming a VRAM cycle time of 35 nanoseconds)? How many pixels would have to be read at once for each of these frame buffers?

18.6 Consider the pipelined, object-order rasterization architecture described in Section 18.7.1.

    a. Determine to what accuracy screen-space (x, y) vertex coordinates must be calculated (i.e., how many bits of precision are needed) if vertices are to be specified to within $\frac{1}{10}$ pixel of their true position in the following displays: a 320 by 200 PC display; a 1280 by 1024 workstation display; and a 1840 by 1035 high-definition TV display.

    b. How many fractional bits are needed in left and right x slopes (calculated during polygon processing) if left and right span endpoints are to lie within $\frac{1}{10}$ pixel of their true position in all polygons displayable in each of the systems in part (a)? (Assume that vertex coordinates have been calculated with infinite precision and that additions are performed with perfect accuracy.)

    c. What are the maximum and minimum possible values for Δx in each of the systems of part (a)? (Assume that horizontal edges have been recognized and removed before delta values are calculated.)

    d. If fixed-point arithmetic is used, how many bits are needed to represent Δx values that can range from the minimum to maximum values calculated in part (c) and the precision calculated in part (b), for the three systems?

18.7 The performance of image-parallel architectures that partition the frame buffer into contiguous blocks of pixels is reduced if many primitives fall into more than one region. Assume that the display screen is divided into a number of regions of width W and height H and that a typical primitive covers a rectangular area of width w ($w \ll W$) and height h ($h \ll H$) on the display screen. Derive an expression in terms of W, H, w, and h for the average number of regions affected by a typical primitive, assuming that the primitive has an equal probability of appearing anywhere on the screen.

19

Advanced
Geometric
and
Raster Algorithms

In Chapter 3, we described a number of methods for clipping and scan converting primitives. In this chapter, we begin by discussing more advanced clipping techniques. These are purely geometric techniques, to be applied to geometric primitives being clipped to geometrically defined regions.

Following these clipping algorithms, we reconsider the description and scan conversion of the primitives discussed in Chapter 3, beginning by analyzing the attributes associated with primitives. This analysis is necessary because attributes such as line style have arisen from diverse demands on raster graphics packages; some line styles, such as dotted lines, are cosmetic, some, such as the dot-dash lines used in mechanical drawings, are geometric. It will be important to understand the differences.

We next consider the criteria for selecting pixels in the scan-conversion process; different criteria sometimes lead to different choices. Then, after doing some analytic geometry, we give algorithms for noninteger lines, noninteger circles, and general ellipses, and discuss the perils of representing arbitrary curves as short line segments in an integer world. We then discuss antialiasing, including its application to rendering thick lines, polylines, and general curves. After this, we analyze the problems associated with drawing text both in bitmap graphics and with gray-scale antialiasing, and we examine some solutions. We also discuss a data structure that can be used to speed the manipulation of scan-converted primitives, especially for bilevel displays, and some techniques for making a fast copyPixel operation for bilevel displays (bitBlt). We conclude the chapter with three further topics: the management of overlapping windows, fill algorithms, and 2D page-description graphics. One example is Interpress [HARR88]; another is POSTSCRIPT

[ADOB85b], which is really more than a page-description model—it also offers the full functionality of a relatively complex programming language, so complex images may be described compactly through the use of notions of iteration and procedural definitions of image elements. Such page-description languages are now being used to provide not merely static image descriptions, but also screen descriptions for interactive graphics.

19.1 CLIPPING

Before giving details of specific clipping algorithms, we first discuss the general process of clipping, and then its specialized application to lines. As described in Chapter 2, *clipping* is the process of determining the portion of a primitive lying within a region called the *clip region*. The clip region is typically either a window on a screen or a view volume. The second case is handled by the Sutherland–Hodgman algorithm described in Chapter 3, so we concentrate on the first here. In the discussion in Chapter 3, the clip region was always a rectangle; because primitives are typically drawn on a rectangular canvas, this is an important special case. In multiple-window environments, such as the Macintosh operating system or the X Windows System, various rectangular windows overlap one another, and the clip region can be an arbitrary set of polygons with only horizontal and vertical edges. In systems such as POSTSCRIPT, a clipping region can be defined by an arbitrary set of outlines in the plane. Furthermore, the primitives being clipped may be 1D (e.g., lines) or 2D (e.g., filled polygons).[1] It is easy to think that once line clipping is solved, so is polygon clipping: Just clip all the edges of the polygon to the window and draw. This assumption fails, however, if the polygon completely encloses the clip window. Clipping 2D primitives is a more difficult problem than is clipping 1D primitives.

One method for drawing clipped primitives deserves discussion, although it is not actually a clipping method per se. It consists of computing the points that would be drawn on an infinite canvas, and then drawing only those points that actually lie within the clip region. This method (called *scissoring* in Chapter 3) has one drawback: the cost of rendering all of a primitive lying substantially outside the clip region. This drawback is offset, however, by scissoring's simplicity and generality, so the technique turns out to be a reasonable approach for many systems. If the time taken to draw a pixel in the frame buffer is long compared to the computation time for each pixel, then, while visible pixels are queued up to be drawn, other invisible ones may be computed. It is also simple to address clipping to multiple windows through this method: An application can maintain a notion of the current window, and the drawing algorithm can simply draw up to the border of this window, then pass control back to the application, which then passes the next window to the drawing algorithm. There are many applications, however, in which clipping to a single clip region is essential. We therefore discuss methods that take into account the geometry of the clip region before scan conversion.

---

[1] References to 1D and 2D primitives refer to the intrinsic geometry of the primitive: Position on a line can be specified with a single number; hence, it is said to be 1D. Position on a surface can be specified by two numbers; it is called 2D. Thus, even a helical curve in 3D is a 1D primitive.

19.1.1 Clipping Lines to Rectangular Regions

Clipping lines to upright rectangular regions is a purely geometric problem, in that it is completely independent of the size or even the existence of the pixels; it involves computing intersections of lines and rectangles in the Euclidean plane. In Chapter 3, we discussed the Cyrus–Beck/Liang–Barsky line-clipping algorithm. Nicholl, Lee, and Nicholl have created a better line clipper for this 2D case [NICH87]. Although the algorithm has a great many cases, the basic idea is simple enough that understanding one case lets us generate all the others.

Before discussing this algorithm, let us restate the problem: Given a collection of (zero-width) line segments and an upright clipping rectangle, find the endpoints of the (possibly empty) intersections of the line segments and the rectangle. Each line segment is given as a pair of endpoints, and the upright clipping rectangle is given by four equations: $x = x_{min}$, $x = x_{max}$, $y = y_{min}$, and $y = y_{max}$ (see Fig. 19.1). For convenience, we assume for the time being that the line segment to be clipped is neither vertical nor horizontal.

The most simple-minded algorithm computes the equation of the line containing the line segment, then computes all intersection points of this line with the clip-rectangle boundary lines. Except for degenerate cases, either zero or two of these points lie within the clip rectangle (see Fig. 19.2); if two, they are compared with the endpoints of the original segment to give the clipped segment. Of course, this comparison requires the computation of four intersections, even if the line segment is entirely within (or entirely outside) the clip region. Recall from Chapter 3 that the parametric algorithm instead computes the parameter values for the intersections of the line with the boundaries of the clip rectangle and compares these with the parameter values 0 and 1 to determine whether the segment lies within the clip rectangle, (the line is parameterized so that parameter values between 0 and 1 correspond to the segment). Only when the parameter values of intersections with the clip rectangle are computed does the algorithm go on to compute the intersection points.

The Nicholl–Lee–Nicholl (NLN) algorithm is based on an improvement of this simple delaying tactic. Consider a segment PQ that is to be clipped. We first determine where P lies. If we divide the plane into the same nine regions used in the parametric clipping algorithm (see Fig. 19.3), then P must lie in one of these regions (each boundary line is assigned to one of the regions it touches). By determining the position of Q relative to the

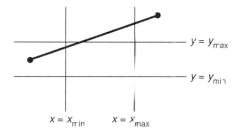

Fig. 19.1 The equations defining the clipping rectangle, and a typical line segment to be clipped.

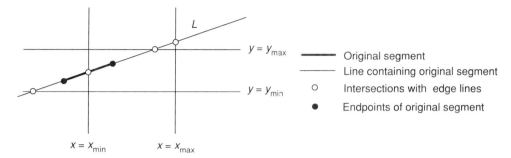

Fig. 19.2 Clipping by finding intersections with all clip-rectangle boundary lines.

lines from P to each of the corners, we can determine which edges of the clip rectangle PQ intersects.

Suppose that P lies in the lower-left–corner region, as in Fig. 19.4. If Q lies below y_{min} or to the left of x_{min}, then PQ cannot intersect the clip region (this amounts to checking the Cohen–Sutherland outcodes). The same is true if Q lies to the left of the line from P to the upper-left corner or if Q lies to the right of the line from P to the lower-right corner. Many cases can be trivially rejected by these checks. We also check the position of Q relative to the ray from P through the lower-left corner. We will discuss the case where Q is above this ray, as shown in Fig. 19.4. If Q is below the top of the clip region, it is either in the clip region or to the right of it; hence the line PQ intersects the clip region either at its left edge or at both the left and right edges. If Q is above the top of the clip region, it may be to the left of the ray from P through the top-left corner. If not, it may be to the right of the right edge of the clip region. This latter case divides into the two cases: Q is to the left of the line from P to the upper-right corner and to the right of it. The regions in Fig. 19.4 are labeled with the edges cut by a segment from P to any point in those regions. The regions are labeled by abbreviations; LT, for example, means "the ray from P to any point in this region intersects both the left and top sides of the clipping rectangle."

Assuming that we have a function LeftSide (*point, line*) for detecting when a point is to the left of a ray, and a function Intersect (*segment, line*) that returns the intersection of a

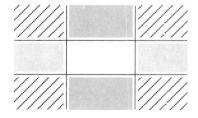

Fig. 19.3 The nine regions of the plane used in the Nicholl–Lee–Nicholl algorithm.

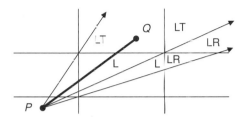

Fig. 19.4 The regions determined by the lines from P to the corners.

segment and a line, the structure of the algorithm for these cases is shown in Fig. 19.5. P and Q are records of type "point" and have x and y fields.

The interesting thing about this computation is the possibility of reusing intermediate results. For example, in computing whether Q is to the left of the ray from P to the upper-right corner (x_{max}, y_{max}), we must check whether

$$(Q.y - P.y)(x_{max} - P.x) - (y_{max} - P.y)(Q.x - P.x)$$

is positive (see Exercise 19.25). Similar computations are used for the other edges, and the numbers $Q.y - P.y$ and $Q.x - P.x$ appear in all of them, so these are kept once computed. The two products in this formula are also reused, so they too are recorded. For example, if Q is to the right of the line, when we compute the intersection of PQ with the right edge, the y coordinate is given by

$$P.y + (Q.y - P.y)(x_{max} - P.x)(1 / (Q.x - P.x)),$$

and the first product can be reused (the formula is just an application of the point-slope formula for a line). Since the reciprocal of $Q.x - P.x$ occurs in computing the intersection with the right edge, it too is stored. We leave it to you to make this particular code fragment as efficient as possible (Exercise 19.1). The remaining cases, where P is in the center region or in one of the side regions, are similar. Thus, it is worthwhile to recognize the symmetries of the various cases and to write a program to transform three general cases (P in the center, in a corner, or in an edge region) into the nine different cases.

Nicholl, Lee, and Nicholl present an analysis of the NLN, Cohen–Sutherland (CS), and Liang–Barsky(LB) algorithms in the plane and find that (1) NLN has the fewest divisions, equal to the number of intersection points for output, and (2) NLN has the fewest comparisons, about one-third of those of the CS algorithm, and one-half of those of the LB algorithm. They also note that—assuming subtraction is slower than addition, division is slower than multiplication, and the first difference is smaller than the second—their algorithm is the most efficient. Of course, unlike the others, NLN works only in 2D.

Clipping lines against more general regions is a special case of clipping generic primitives against such regions. We next discuss clipping polygons against arbitrary polygons. Clipping general primitives to the arbitrary regions defined in POSTSCRIPT and some other imaging models is described later in the chapter, since this is implemented by raster algorithms.

```
/* Clip PQ to a rectangle bounded by xMin, xMax, yMin, and yMax . */
/* This code handles only the case where P is in the lower-left corner of the */
/* region—other cases are similar. */
void PartialNLNclip(point *P, point *Q)
{
    boolean visible;        /* TRUE if clipped segment is nonempty */

    if (Q->y < yMin)
        visible = FALSE;
    else if (Q->x < xMin)
        visible = FALSE;
    else if (LeftSide (Q, ray from P to lower-left corner)) {
        if (Q->y <= yMax) {                                    /* Region L or LR */
            visible = TRUE;
            *P = Intersection (PQ, left edge of clip region);  /* Stores intersection in P */
            if (Q->x > xMax)                                   /* Region LR */
                *Q = Intersection (PQ, right edge of clip region);
        } else {
            /* Above top */
            if (LeftSide (Q, ray from P to upper-left corner))
                visible = FALSE;
            else if (Q->x < xMax) {                            /* First region LT */
                visible = TRUE;
                *P = Intersection (PQ, left edge of clip region);
                *Q = Intersection (PQ, top edge of clip region);
            } else if (LeftSide (Q, ray from P to upper-right corner)) {
                visible = TRUE;                                /* Region LT */
                *P = Intersection (PQ, left edge of clip region);
                *Q = Intersection (PQ, top edge of clip region);
            } else {                                           /* Region LR */
                visible = TRUE;
                *P = Intersection (PQ, left edge of clip region);
                *Q = Intersection (PQ, right edge of clip region);
            }
        }   /* else */
    } else
        /* Cases where Q is to the right of line from P to lower-left corner */
        . . .
}   /* PartialNLNclip */
```

Fig. 19.5 Part of the Nicholl–Lee–Nicholl algorithm.

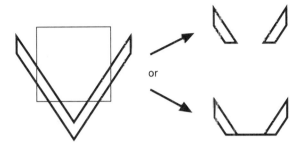

Fig. 19.6 Should the clipped V-shaped polygon contain the degenerate edge?

19.1.2 Clipping Polygons against Rectangles and other Polygons

In drawing a polygon in a rectangular region, we may wish to clip it to the region to save drawing time. For truly general clipping regions (where the interior of the region is specified, for example, by giving a canvas corresponding to a region on the screen, and for which the interior of the clip region consists of those points corresponding to black pixels in the canvas), scissoring is quite practical: We simply compute all the (rasterized) points of the primitive, then draw only those lying within the rasterized clip region. The shape algebra described in Section 19.7 can be used as well, to determine rapidly the regions of overlap between the pixels of the clipping shape and those of the primitive; this is the most efficient technique until the clip regions become extremely complex—for example, a gray-scale bitmap. Since the analytic algorithms for clipping are interesting in their own right, and have other applications beyond windowing systems (e.g., the visible-surface algorithm presented in Chapter 15), we cover two algorithms in detail: the Liang–Barsky (LB) [LIAN83] and Weiler [WEIL80] algorithms.

There is some difference of opinion on what constitutes the clipped version of a polygon. Figure 19.6 shows a polygon being clipped against a rectangular window and the two possible outputs, one connected and one disconnected. The Sutherland–Hodgman [SUTH74b] and Liang–Barsky algorithms both generate connected clipped polygons, although the polygons may have degenerate edges (i.e., edges that overlap other edges of the polygon, or whose length is zero). The Weiler algorithm produces nondegenerate polygons, which are therefore sometimes disconnected. Since the Weiler algorithm is designed to do somewhat more than clipping—it can produce arbitrary Boolean combinations of polygons—it is clear that these combinations may need to be represented by disconnected polygons if they are to be truly disjoint.[2] Figure 19.7 shows two polygons such that A − B and B − A cannot be simultaneously made into connected polygons (by adding just a single degenerate edge pair to each) without an intersection being introduced between them.

In practice, the degenerate edges in the output polygon may be irrelevant. If the polygon is used merely to define a filled area, then the degenerate edges have no area

---

[2]The Weiler algorithm also handles general polygons—that is, polygons with holes in them. These are described by multiple nested contours.

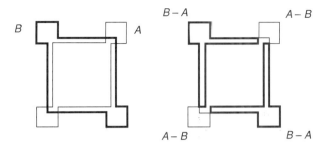

Fig. 19.7 The regions $A - B$ and $B - A$ cannot be made into connected polygons (using edges of the original polygons) without intersecting at least at a point.

between them, and hence cause no problems. If the polygon is used to define a polyline, however, the degenerate edges must be removed; see Exercise 19.2.

19.1.3 Clipping against Rectangles: The Liang–Barsky Polygon Algorithm

Let us begin with the Liang–Barsky (LB) algorithm. To distinguish between the polygon to be clipped and the rectangle against which the polygon is clipped, we call the upright rectangle the *window* and the polygon to be clipped the *input polygon*; the result of clipping is the *output polygon*. Each edge to be clipped is represented parametrically, and the intersections with the window edges are computed only when needed. In contrast to line clipping, however, an edge entirely outside the window can contribute to the output polygon. Consider the case where the input polygon entirely encloses the window: The output polygon is the boundary of the window, as shown in Fig. 19.8.

The mathematically inclined reader may object to the result in the case shown in Fig. 19.9: The interior of the input polygon misses the window entirely, but the LB algorithm produces a polygon that includes all edges of the window (although it includes each one once in each direction, as shown by the dotted lines; these are drawn slightly outside the window so as to be visible). Exercise 19.2 discusses algorithms for removing such excess edges to get a minimal form for a clipped polygon.

We assume the input polygon is given as a sequence of points $P_1, P_2, \ldots, P_n$, where the edges of the polygon are $P_1P_2, P_2P_3, \ldots, P_nP_1$. Each edge can be considered as a vector starting from P_i and going toward P_{i+1}, and this determines the parametric form $P(t) = (1 - t)P_1 + tP_2$. Values of t between 0 and 1 represent points on the edge. (To be more

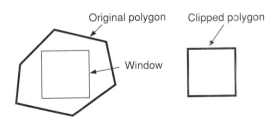

Fig. 19.8 An edge outside the window can contribute to the output (clipped) polygon.

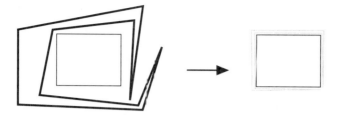

Fig. 19.9 The input polygon lies entirely outside the window, but the Liang–Barsky algorithm produces a nonempty result.

precise, we let values $0 < t \le 1$ represent points on the edge, so that each edge fails to contain its starting point. Each vertex of the polygon is therefore contained in exactly one of the two edges that meet there. The choice to omit the starting point differs from that in Chapter 3, but it makes the explanation of the algorithm slightly simpler.) Other values of t represent points that are on the line containing the edge, but not on the edge itself. In the LB algorithm, we will consider one edge, P_iP_{i+1}, at a time, and let L_i denote the line containing P_iP_{i+1}.

We initially consider only diagonal lines—those that are neither horizontal nor vertical. Such a line must cross each of the lines that determine the boundary of the window. In fact, if we divide the plane into the nine regions determined by the edges of the windows, as in Fig. 19.10, it is clear that every diagonal line passes from one corner region to the opposite one. Each window edge divides the plane in two halfplanes. We call the one containing the window the *inside* halfplane. The nine regions in Fig. 19.10 are labeled by the number of inside halfplanes they lie in. The window is the only region lying in all four, of course. We call the regions at the corners (labeled "inside 2") *corner regions*, and the other outer regions (labeled "inside 3") *edge regions*.

Before we discuss details, we show the use of this algorithm by a few examples. First, if some portion of the edge (not just the line containing it) lies in the window, that portion must be part of the output polygon. The vertices this edge adds to the output polygon may be either the ends of the edge (if it lies entirely within the window) or the intersections of the edge with the window edges (if the endpoints of the edge lie outside the window), or there may be one of each.

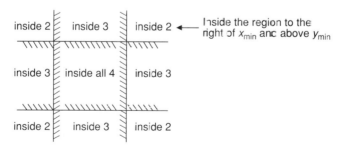

Fig. 19.10 The plane is divided into nine regions by the extended edges of the window. Each region is on the "inside" side of at least two edges.

On the other hand, if the edge lies entirely outside the window, the next edge may intersect the window (see Fig. 19.11). If so, the place where it intersects the window is determined by its starting point: An edge starting in the upper-edge region can begin its intersection with the window only by hitting the top edge of the window; one starting in the upper-left corner region can begin its intersection with the window either along the top boundary or along the left boundary, and so on.

Suppose the last edge to intersect the window generated a vertex at the top of the window, and the next edge to intersect the window will do so on the right edge of the window, as in Fig. 19.12. The output polygon will then have to contain the upper-right corner of the window as a vertex. Since we are processing the polygon one edge at a time, we will have to add this vertex now, in anticipation of the next intersection with the clip window. Of course if the next edge intersected the top edge of the window, this vertex would be redundant; we add it regardless, and handle the removal of redundant vertices as a postprocessing step. The idea is that, after processing of an edge, any intersection point added by the next edge must be able to be reached from the last vertex that we output.

In general, an edge that enters a corner region will add the corresponding corner vertex as an output vertex. Liang and Barsky call such a vertex a *turning vertex*. (The original algorithm operates in a slightly different order: Rather than adding the turning vertex when the edge enters the corner region, it defers adding the vertex until some later edge leaves the corner region. This cannot entirely remove the degenerate-edge problem, and we find that it makes the algorithm more difficult to understand, so we have used our alternative formulation.)

We now examine the various cases carefully, using the analysis of the parametric form of clipping in Chapter 3. The line L_i containing the edge P_iP_{i+1} crosses all four window boundaries. Two crossings are potentially entering and two are potentially leaving. We compute the parametric values of the intersection points and call them t_{in_1}, t_{in_2}, t_{out_1}, and t_{out_2}. Notice that t_{in_1} is the least of these, and t_{out_2} is the greatest, since every nonvertical, nonhorizontal line starts in a corner region and ends in a corner region. The other two values are in between and may be in either order. As noted in Chapter 3, if $t_{in\_2} \leq t_{out\_1}$, the

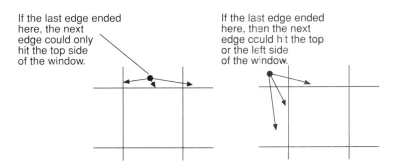

If the last edge ended here, the next edge could only hit the top side of the window.

If the last edge ended here, then the next edge could hit the top or the left side of the window.

Fig. 19.11 If the previous edge terminated in the upper-middle region, and the next edge intersects the window, then it can do so only at the top. If the previous edge terminated in the upper-left region, and the next edge intersects the window, then it can do so only at the top edge or left edge.

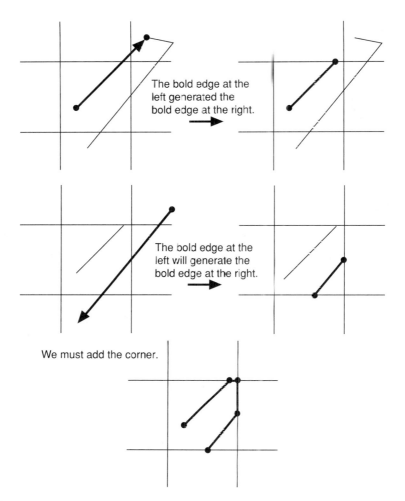

Fig. 19.12 A vertex must be added to the output polygon at the upper-right corner of the window: The next edge (after the one that fails to intersect the window) could intersect either the top or the right side. We must add a vertex that can reach all possible intersection points.

line intersects the window; if $t_{in\_2} > t_{out\_1}$, the line passes through a corner region instead (see Fig. 19.13).

The parameter values $t = 0$ and $t = 1$ define the endpoints of the edge within the line L_i. The relationship between these parameter values and the values of t_{in_1}, t_{in_2}, t_{out_1}, and t_{out_2} characterizes the contribution of the edge to the output polygon. If the edge intersects the window, the visible segment of the edge must be added to the output polygon. In this case, $0 < t_{out\_1}$ and $1 \geq t_{in\_2}$; that is, the edge begins before the containing line leaves the window and also ends after it enters the window—the edge is not entirely outside the window.

If the edge does not intersect the window, the line containing it starts in one corner region, passes through another, and terminates in a third. If the edge enters either of the

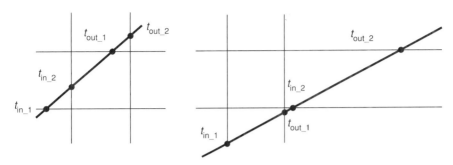

Fig. 19.13 The two possibilities for a line that crosses a window.

latter two corner regions, a turning vertex must be added. Entering the intermediate corner region is characterized by $0 < t_{out\_1} \leq 1$ (since t_{out_1} is the parameter value at which the line enters the corner region). Entering the final corner region is characterized by $0 < t_{out\_2} \leq 1$.

This last statement is true for lines that intersect the window as well—if $0 < t_{out\_2} \leq 1$, then a turning vertex must be added.

Figure 19.14 gives a sketch of the algorithm. Notice that the vertices contributed by each line must be added in order. The complete algorithm is somewhat more complex, since the special cases of vertical and horizontal edges must also be considered. There are

```
for (each edge e) {
        determine direction of edge;
        use this to determine which bounding lines for the clip region the
                containing line hits first;
        find t-values for exit points;
        if (tOut_2 > 0)
                find t-value for second entry point;
        if (tIn_2 > tOut_1) {                    /* No visible segment */
                if (0 < tOut_1 && tOut_1 <= 1)
                        Output_vert (turning_vertex);
        } else {
                if (0 < tOut_1 && 1 >= tIn_2) {      /* There is some visible part. */
                        if (0 <= tIn_2)
                                Output_vert (appropriate side intersection);
                        else
                                Output_vert (starting vertex);
                        if (1 >= tOut_1)
                                Output_vert (appropriate side intersection);
                        else
                                Output_vert (ending vertex);
                }
        }
        if (0 < tOut_2 && tOut_2 <= 1)
                Output_vert (appropriate corner);
}   /* for each edge */
```

Fig. 19.14 A sketch of the Liang–Barsky polygon-clipping algorithm.

two possible approaches. The first is to treat such edges as special cases, and simply to expand the code to detect and process them. Detection is easy: Either *deltaX* or *deltaY* (the two components of the direction vector for the edge) is zero. Processing proceeds on a case-by-case analysis. For example, a vertical edge to the right of the clip window may cross into the upper-right or the lower-right corner, and hence may add a turning vertex. A vertical edge between the left and right window boundaries may cross the window in a visible segment or not at all, and so on. The alternate approach is to force each vertical or horizontal edge to conform to the pattern of the rest of the algorithm by assigning entering and leaving values of $\pm\infty$.

Figure 19.15 gives the entire algorithm for this latter solution. We assume that real variables can be assigned a value, *infinite*, with the property that $x < infinite$ for all x unless $x = infinite$. Exercise 19.3 asks you to generate the details of the algorithm when no such infinite values are available and special casing must be used for vertical and horizontal lines. So that the size of the program can be reduced, the macro AssignTwo, which performs two simultaneous assignments, has been defined. The code also uses several variables (such as *Xin* and *Xout*, which denote the sides of the clip window through which

```
#define MAXPT 50;
#define MAX2 150;

typedef double smallarray[MAXPT];
typedef double bigarray[MAX2];

/* Perform two assignments. */
#define ASSIGNTWO( x, y, a, b) { \
    (x) = (a); \
    (y) = (b); \
}

/* Clip an n-sided input polygon to a window. */
void LiangBarskyPolygonClip(
    int n,
    const smallarray x, const smallarray y,    /* Vertices of input polygon */
    bigarray u, bigarray v,                     /* Vertices of output polygon */
    double xMax, double xMin,                   /* Edges of clip window */
    double yMax, double yMin,
    int *outCount)                              /* Counter for output vertices */
{
    double xIn, xOut, yIn, yOut;                /* Coordinates of entry and exit points */
    double tOut1, tIn2, tOut2;                  /* Parameter values of same */
    double tInX, tOutX, tInY, tOutY;           /* Parameter values for intersections */
    double deltaX, deltaY;                      /* Direction of edge */
    int i;
```

Fig. 19.15 (*Cont.*)

```
x[n] = x[0];
y[n] = y[0];                              /* Make polygon closed */
*outCount = 0;                           /* Initialize output vertex counter */
for (i = 0; i < n; i++) {                /* for each edge */
    deltaX = x[i + 1] − x[i];            /* Determine direction of edge */
    deltaY = y[i + 1] − y[i];
    /* Use this to determine which bounding lines for the clip region the */
    /* containing line hits first. */
    if ((deltaX > 0) || (deltaX == 0 && x[i] > xMax))
        ASSIGNTWO (xIn, xOut, xMin, xMax)
    else
        ASSIGNTWO (xIn, xOut, xMax, xMin)
    if ((deltaY > 0) || (deltaY == 0 && y[i] > yMax))
        ASSIGNTWO (yIn, yOut, yMin, yMax)
    else
        ASSIGNTWO (yIn, yOut, yMax, yMin)
    /* Find the t values for the x and y exit points. */
    if (deltaX != 0)
        tOutX = (xOut − x[i]) / deltaX;
    else if (x[i] <= xMax && xMin <= x[i])
        tOutX = ∞;
    else
        tOutX = −∞;
    if (deltaY != 0)
        tOutY = (yOut − y[i]) / deltaY;
    else if (y[i] <= yMax && yMin <= y[i])
        tOutY = ∞;
    else
        tOutY = −∞;

    /* Order the two exit points. */
    if (tOutX < tOutY)
        ASSIGNTWO (tOut1, tOut2, tOutX, tOutY)
    else
        ASSIGNTWO (tOut1, tOut2, tOutY, tOutX)
    if (tOut2 > 0) {                     /* There could be output—compute tIn2. */
        if (deltaX != 0)
            tInX = (xIn − x[i]) / deltaX;
        else
            tInX = −∞;
        if (deltaY != 0)
            tInY = (yIn − y[i]) / deltaY;
        else
            tInY = −∞;
        if (tInX < tInY)
            tIn2 = tInY;
        else
            tIn2 = tInX;
```

Fig. 19.15 (*Cont.*)

```
    if (tOut1 < tIn2) {                          /* No visible segment */
        if (0 < tOut1 && tOut1 <= 1) {
            /* Line crosses over intermediate corner region */
            if (tInX < tInY)
                OutputVert (u, v, outCount, xOut, yIn);
            else
                OutputVert (u, v, outCount, xIn, yOut);
        }
    } else {
        /* Line crosses through window */
        if (0 < tOut1 && tIn2 <= 1) {
            if (0 < tIn2) {                       /* Visible segment */
                if (tInX > tInY)
                    OutputVert (u, v, outCount, xIn, y[i] + tInX * deltaY);
                else
                    OutputVert (u, v, outCount, x[i] + tInY * deltaX, yIn);

                if (1 > tOut1) {
                    if (tOutX < tOutY)
                        OutputVert (u, v, outCount, xOut, y[i] + tOutX * deltaY);
                        else
                            OutputVert (u, v, outCount, x[i] + tOutY * deltaY, yOut);
                    }
                } else
                    OutputVert (u, v, outCount, x[i + 1], y[i + 1]);
            }
        }
        if (0 < tOut2 && tOut2 <= 1)
            OutputVert (u, v, outCount, xOut, yOut);
    }  /* if tOut2 */
    }  /* for */
}  /* LiangBarskyPolygonClip */
```

Fig. 19.15 The Liang–Barsky polygon-clipping algorithm.

the containing line for the segment enters and leaves) that could be eliminated. But these variables reduce the case structure of the code, and hence make the code more readable. The OutputVert routine (not shown) stores values in u and v and increments a counter.

19.1.4 The Weiler Polygon Algorithm

We now move to the problem of clipping one polygon to another arbitrary polygon, an issue that arose in the visible-surface computations in Section 15.7.2. Figure 19.16 shows several polygons to be clipped and the results of clipping. Notice that the clipped polygon may be disconnected and may be nonconvex even if the original polygon was convex.

The Weiler polygon algorithm [WEIL80] is an improvement on the earlier Weiler–Atherton algorithm [WEIL77], and it is based on the following observation. If we draw the edges of the clipping polygon, A, and the polygon to be clipped, B, in black pencil on a white sheet of paper, then the part of the paper that remains white is divided into disjoint

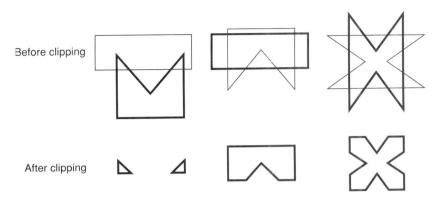

Before clipping

After clipping

Fig. 19.16 Several examples of clipping polygons against polygons.

regions (if the polygon edges are thought of as borders on a map, then these regions are the countries). Each of these regions is entirely in A, entirely in B, entirely contained in both, or contained in neither. The algorithm works by finding a collection of closed polylines in the plane that are the boundaries of these disjoint regions. The clipped input polygon consists of the regions contained in both A and B. In this algorithm, the clipping polygon and the input polygon play identical roles; since we want the regions inside both, we shall refer to them as A and B from now on. (Notice the similarity between this approach to clipping and the polyhedral constructive solid geometry in Chapter 12. In fact, we might use the phrase *constructive planar geometry* to describe this polygon–polygon clipping.)

Before discussing the details of the algorithm, we consider one example that exhibits most of its subtlety. Figure 19.17(a) shows two intersecting polygons, A and B. In part (b), the intersections of the polygons have been added as vertices to each of the polygons; these new vertices are indicated by the dots in the figure. If two edges intersect in a single point (a *transverse* intersection), that point is added as a vertex. If they intersect in a segment, any

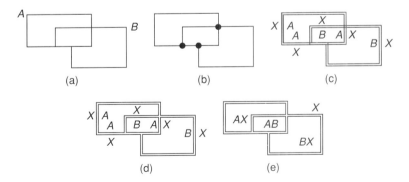

Fig. 19.17 The Weiler polygon algorithm applied to two polygons. (a) The two polygons A and B. (b) Intersections are added as vertices. (c) The polygons are drawn as doubled contours with labels. (d) The contours are reconnected so they do not cross. (e) The labels on the contours are collected into labels for the regions they bound.

vertex of one that lies in the intersection segment is added as a vertex of the other. In part (c), we double the edges of the polygons. Although these doubled polygons are drawn slightly displaced from the original polygon, they should be thought of as infinitely close to the original edge. The resulting curves are called *contours*. Each edge of a polygon contributes to two contours. We shall use the term *segment* for the parts of the contours that it contributes, and reserve the word *edge* for pieces of the original polygons. Once these contours are created, we label each segment of the inner contour of each polygon with the name of the polygon (A or B), those on the outer contour are labeled X. (Only some of the labels are shown; also, the segment where two edges overlap really has four contour segments, but only two are drawn.)

The idea is to rearrange the contours so that they form the borders of the disjoint regions we described, as is done in part (d). In part (e), the labels on each contour are collected to give a label for the region; these labels determine in which of the original polygons the region lies. For the intersection of two polygons, we are interested in only those regions labeled by both A and B (the diagram uses the label AB to indicate this). In reality, the doubled contours are generated when the polygons are first read into the algorithm; in an efficient implementation, the contours can be merged at the same time as the intersections are found.

The algorithm actually works for an arbitrary number of polygons; when more than two are intersected, there may be regions entirely contained in other regions (e.g., a square in a larger square). We will need to determine these containment relationships to complete the algorithm in such cases.

The three steps in the algorithm are setting up, determining the regions, and selecting those regions that are in both A and B. Setting up involves determining all intersections of edges of A with edges of B (since all such intersections will be vertices of the output polygon), then redefining A and B to include these intersection points as vertices. Standard algorithms from computational geometry can be used to determine all edge intersections [PREP85].

To determine the regions, we must rearrange the contours. We want no two contours to intersect. Thus, at each vertex where the two polygons intersect, an adjustment must be made. Suppose we have a transverse intersection of the polygons, as shown in Fig. 19.18(a). The corresponding contours are shown in Fig. 19.18(b). Contours are imple-

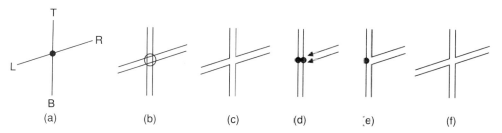

Fig. 19.18 Merging contours when edges cross. (a) The two polygons cross at a vertex. (b) The contours for the edges. (c) The final arrangement of contours. (d) Adding the contour segments contributed by edge R to the vertical contour segments. (e) The result of this addition. (f) The result after a similar merge of the segments from edge L.

mented as doubly linked lists, and we wish to rearrange the links to the pattern shown in Fig. 19.18(c). At a transverse intersection, we do this by taking the contour segments associated with the edges of one polygon and merging in the contour segments associated with the other polygon, a pair at a time. Thus, in Fig. 19.18(d), we start with the vertical contour segments, and we wish to merge the pair of segments associated with edge R. In Fig. 19.18(e), these segments have been merged into the vertical contour segments by rearranging links. The segments associated with the edges T and B have two sides (i.e., there are two vertical contours), and it is important to add the new segments to the proper side. We compare the remote vertex (the one not at the intersection point) of the edge R, to the vertical line (consisting of edges T and B), to determine which side R is on. After this attachment, the segments associated with edge L are left hanging. In Fig. 19.18(f), the segments associated with L have also been merged into the contour, so the resulting contours have no intersections at the vertex. Notice that this process involved only *local* information: we needed to know only the positions of the edges being considered, and did not need to traverse any more of the polygon.

Merging contours is more difficult at a nontransverse intersection, as shown in Fig. 19.19. In part (a), we see a nontransverse intersection of two polygons: They share a short vertical piece. Of course, in the actual data structures, this short vertical piece is an edge in each polygon. We call such edges *coincident*. The remarkable thing about coincident edges is that they are easy to process. Each edge contributes two segments to the contours, one on each side, as shown in Fig. 19.19(b), where one set of contours has been drawn within the other to make them distinct, and where a dotted segment shows the original shared edge. Each segment has an label (we have shown sample labels in Fig. 19.19b). The labels from each pair of segments on one side of the coincident edge are merged together, and the vertical segments corresponding to the coincident edge in one polygon are deleted. The

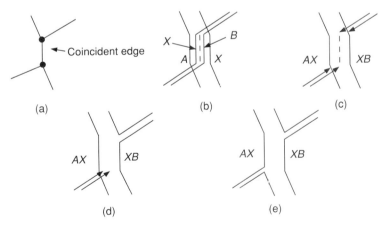

Fig. 19.19 Merging contours along coincident edges. (a) The zig-zag contour and the more vertical contour have short vertical coincident edges. (b) The contours associated with this arrangement of edges; the original vertical edge is shown as a dotted line. (c) The vertical segments from the zig-zag polygon have been deleted, and their labels merged with the labels of the other segments. (d) One adjoining edge's contour segments have been merged. (e) The other adjoining edge's contour segments have been merged as well.

resulting intermediate structure is shown in part (c) of the figure. The merged labels are shown on the remaining segments from the coincident edge. The arrows indicate dangling pointers. In parts (d) and (e), the segments corresponding to the dangling pointers are merged with the other contour just as before. If we process the contours by proceeding in order around one polygon, then we will always have at most one set of dangling pointers. If this set corresponds to a transverse intersection, it can be processed as before; if it corresponds to another coincident edge, it can be processed as this edge was.

There is another class of nontransverse intersections of polygons, as shown in Fig. 19.20(a). Since each of the diagonal edges intersects the vertical edge transversely, the process of merging contours is no more complex than in the original transverse case. The contour structure before and after merging is shown in parts (b) and (c).

Finally, we remark that, in processing intersections, the inside and outside contours associated with the original polygons are split into subcontours; since our output is derived from these subcontours, we must keep track of them. We do this record keeping by maintaining a reference to at least one segment of each contour. If we track all the segments processed at any intersection, this technique is guaranteed to provide such a list of *entry points*, although the list may have several entry points for some contours. In fact, for each intersection, we create a new contour for each segment, and set the startingPoint field of the contour to be the segment. We also set a backpointer (the contourPtr field) from the segment to the contour, which is used later.

These various tasks described lead us to the data structures for the Weiler algorithm: vertices, edges, and contours, shown in Fig. 19.21. An edge has two vertices and two *sides*. These sides are the segments that initially form the inner and outer contours for the polygons, and contribute to the output contours at the end. Thus, an edge side is what we have been calling a segment of a contour. Each edge side points to its clockwise and counterclockwise neighbors, and each edge side also has a list of owners (i.e., labels). Except in the case just described, the contourPtr field of an edge side is NULL.

When the polygons are first read in by the algorithm, they must be processed to establish the data structure given. Doing this efficiently is the task of Exercise 19.4. The second step is to take these data structures for A and B and to create a single data structure consisting of lots of contours, each contour being the boundary of one region. Since all the intersections between edges of A and B appear as vertices of these contours, we first compute these intersection points.

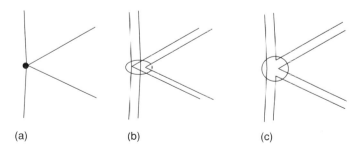

(a)   (b)   (c)

Fig. 19.20 Merging contours at a tangential intersection. (a) The edge configuration. (b) The initial contour configuration. (c) The final contour configuration.

```
#define SIDE 2      /* Each polygon edge has two sides */
#define END  2      /* Each edge has two ends, too */

typedef enum {CW, CCW} direction;
              /* Clockwise, counterclockwise directions for contours */

typedef struct {                    /* Exterior region, A, and B */
     unsigned int X:1;
     unsigned int A:1;
     unsigned int B:1;
} owners;

typedef struct {
     double x, y;
} vertex;

typedef struct contourStruct contour;
typedef struct edgeStruct edge;

struct contourStruct {
     owners belongsTo;              /* Filled in during traversal stage */
     struct {                       /* Where traversal of contour begins */
          edge *entryEdge;
          int entrySide;
     } startingPoint;
};

struct edgeStruct {
     vertex *vertices[END];         /* The ends of the edge */
     edge *edgeLinks[SIDE][2];      /* Double link structure */
     owners edgeOwners[SIDE];       /* Owners of inside and outside */
     contour *contourPtr[SIDE];     /* Points to any contour whose entry point */
                                    /* is this edge side */
};
```

Fig. 19.21 The data structures used in the Weiler algorithm.

We then merge the contours at these intersection points, as described previously, generating new contour data structures as we do so. At this point in the algorithm, we have a collection of contour data structures with startingPoints pointing to various edge sides; by following all the links from such an edge side, we traverse a contour. The owner labels on these edge sides may be different from one another. The owners of the entire contour can be found by taking the union of the owners of the edges sides of the contour.

We must traverse each contour once to collect this information. For each contour, we follow the list of edge sides associated with the startingPoint. If we encounter a vertex pointing back to another contour data structure, that data structure is deleted, so we are left with exactly one contour data structure for each contour in the plane. The pseudocode for this process is given in Fig. 19.22.

We now have a complete collection of contours, each corresponding to a single entry point. If the input polygons are simple closed curves in the plane, we are done: The output polygons are simple closed curves, and no output contour is contained in any other, so we

```
for (each contour c) {
    c.belongsTo = NULL;
    for (each edge-side pair e and s in c, beginning at c.startingPoint) {
        /* if edge side doesn't point to c, delete the contour to which it points */
        if (e.contourPtr[s] != &c)
            delete *e.contourPtr[s];
        c.belongsTo |= e.edgeOwners[s];
    }
}
```

Fig. 19.22 Pseudocode for merging contours.

can simply select those contours whose owner sets contain both A and B. In general, however, the problem is more subtle: The Weiler algorithm can be used to find any Boolean combination of A and B, and some of these combinations may have holes (if A is a square inside another square B, say, then $B - A$ has a hole). Also, A and B may have holes to begin with, and in this case even the intersection may not be nice. Since these cases are important in some applications, such as 3D clipping (see Chapter 15), we continue the analysis. We also note that the algorithm can be applied to polygons defined by such collections of contours, so that unions, differences, and intersections of polygons with holes can all be computed using this algorithm.

The contours we now have are disjoint, and each has an owner set indicating in which, if any, of the original polygons it is located. On the other hand, the regions bounded by these contours may well overlap (as in the case of the two nested squares). To determine the output of the algorithm, we must determine the nesting structure of the contours. We do so by storing the contours in a binary tree structure, in which the left child of a contour is a contour contained within it, and the right child is a contour at the same nesting depth as the parent. (We must first enlarge the data structure for a contour by adding two fields: a containedContour and a coexistingContour, each of which is a cptr—a pointer to a contour.) Figure 19.23 shows a collection of contours and an associated tree structure (this tree structure may not be unique).

Pseudocode for one algorithm for the construction of this tree is shown in Fig. 19.24.

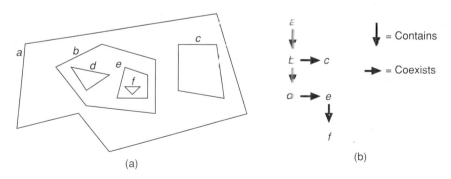

(a)   (b)

Fig. 19.23 (a) A collection of contours in the plane, and (b) an associated tree structure.

```
for (each unassigned contour c) {
    compare this contour with all the others on the unassigned list;
    if (it is inside one and only one, q) {
        remove c from the list;
        if (q.contained == NULL)
            q.contained = &c;
        else
            Insert (&c, &q);      /* Insert c into tree starting at q. */
    } else if (it is contained by more than one)
        skip this contour and go to the next one;
}

void Insert(contour *c, contour *q)
{
    if (q->contained == NULL)
        q->contained = c;
    else if (*c contains *(q->contained)) {
        c->contained = q->contained
        q->contained = c;
    } else if (*(q->contained) contains *c)
        Insert(c, q->contained);
    else if (q->contained->coexist == NULL )
        q->contained->coexist = c;
    else if (*c contains *(q->contained->coexist)) {
        c->contained = q->contained->coexist;
        q->contained->coexist = c;
    } else if (*(q->contained->coexist) contains *c) {
        Insert(c, q->contained->coexist);
    }
}   /* Insert */
```

Fig. 19.24 Pseudocode for building a containment tree structure from a collection of nested contours.

Note that at least one contour is assigned in each pass through the list, so the algorithm will eventually terminate. We encouraged you to find more efficient algorithms for determining the containment tree (see Exercise 19.5).

When the algorithm terminates, we have a tree structure that determines the containment relationships for the contours. We can then select the subtree corresponding to the Boolean operation in which we are interested (for clipping, this subtree consists of all contours whose owner list contains both A and B).

Before we leave the Weiler algorithm, consider what is necessary to make it work for more than two polygons. The owner fields for the edges and for the contours must be enlarged to allow them to contain however many polygons we wish to combine at a time. Aside from this change, the algorithm remains essentially the same. Of course, it may be more efficient to compute the intersection of A, B, and C by computing the intersection of A and B, and then the intersection of this result with C, since the number of intersections of edges of C with edges of the intersection of A and B is likely to be smaller than is the number of intersections of C with all of A and B.

19.2 SCAN-CONVERTING PRIMITIVES

We now return to the topic of scan conversion, discussed in Chapter 3. Each primitive we scan convert has an underlying geometry (i.e., a shape) and certain attributes, such as line style, fill pattern, or line-join style.

The process of determining what pixels should be written for a given object is independent of any clipping, or of the write mode for the pixel-drawing operation. It does depend, however, on attributes that alter the object's shape, and on our criteria for pixel selection. We therefore begin by discussing attributes; then we discuss the geometry of lines and conics and the criteria that can be used for selecting pixels. We complete this section with a scan-conversion algorithm for general ellipses. We delay the consideration of text until after we have discussed antialiasing.

19.2.1 Attributes

Primitives are drawn with various attributes, as discussed in Chapter 3; these include line style, fill style, thickness, line-end style, and line-join style. These may be considered either *cosmetic* or *geometric* attributes. For example, if a line is to be drawn in 4-on, 1-off style, and it is scaled by a factor of 2, should it be drawn 8-on, 2-off? If your answer is yes, then you are treating the line style as a geometric attribute; if no, you are treating it as cosmetic. In this discussion, we assume that all line attributes are cosmetic. Since curves, polylines, circles, and ellipses are also intended to represent infinitely thin shapes, we extend the same assumption to them. What about rectangles, filled circles, and other area-defining primitives? As discussed in Chapter 3, when we apply a fill style to a primitive, we may choose to anchor it either to the primitive, to an arbitrary point, or to the bitmap into which the primitive is drawn. In the first case, the attribute is geometric; in the second, it could be either; in the third, it is cosmetic. The first case is not always entirely geometric, however—in most systems, the fill pattern is not rotated when the primitive is rotated. In some vector systems, on the other hand, cross-hatching (a form of patterning) is applied to primitives in a coordinate system based on the primitive itself, so that rotating a vector–cross-hatched primitive rotates the cross-hatching too; in these systems, the attribute is entirely geometric.

Whether attributes are cosmetic or geometric, whether a pixel lies at the grid center or grid crossing, and whether a window includes its boundary all constitute a *reference model* for a graphics system. A reference model is a collection of rules for determining the semantics of a graphics system, so that all the questions about ambiguities in the specification can be resolved. It should be designed from abstract principles, which are then embodied in the actual algorithms. It will be important to keep a reference model in mind as we construct scan-conversion algorithms; only if we have defined this model clearly can we evaluate the success or correctness of the algorithm.

19.2.2 Criteria for Evaluating Scan-Conversion Algorithms

In drawing a line segment in Chapter 3, we drew the pixels nearest to the segment. For lines of slope greater than 1, we drew 1 pixel in each row, selecting 1 of the 2 pixels the segment passed between; when the segment passed exactly through a pixel, of course, we selected that pixel. The distance from a pixel to a segment can be measured in two ways: as the distance along a grid line, or as the perpendicular distance to the segment. Figure 19.25 shows, by similar triangles, that these distances are proportional, so that our choice of a distance measure is irrelevant.

In deriving the Gupta–Sproull antialiasing algorithm in Section 3.17.4, we found that, if the line equation was $Ax + By + C = 0$, then the perpendicular distance from a point (x, y) to the line was proportional to $F(x, y) = Ax + By + C$. This value, $F(x, y)$, is sometimes called the *residual* at the point (x, y), and the line can therefore be described as the set of all points in the Euclidean plane where the residual is zero. Thus residuals can also be used as a measure of distance to the line; the resulting choices of pixels are the same as with perpendicular distance or grid-line distance.

For circles, also, we can determine pixel choice by grid-line distance, perpendicular distance, or residual value. McIlroy has shown [MCIL83] that, for a circle with integer center and radius (or even one for which the square of the radius is an integer), the three choices agree. On the other hand, for circles whose center or radius fails to satisfy the assumption, the choices disagree in general and we must select among them. (For circles with half-integer centers or radii, the choices are not unique, because the choice made in tie-breaking cases may disagree, but McIlroy shows that there is always only 1 pixel that is a "closest" pixel by all three measures.)

For ellipses, the situation is even worse. Again, there are three ways to measure the amount by which a pixel fails to lie on the ellipse: the grid-line distance, the perpendicular distance, and the residual value. The grid-line distance is well-defined, but may lead to peculiar choices. In the case of the thin slanted ellipse in Fig. 19.26(a), for example, pixels

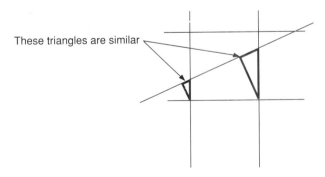

Fig. 19.25 Grid-line distance and perpendicular distance to a line are proportional, as the similar triangles show.

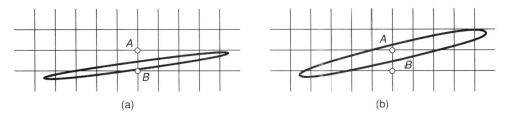

Fig. 19.26 Choosing ellipse points by different criteria. (a) B will be chosen in scan-converting both edges of the ellipse—should it be written twice? (b) In scan converting the bottom of the ellipse, pixel A will be chosen by both the grid-distance method and the residual method, even though B is evidently a better choice.

A and B are at the two ends of a grid line intersected by the upper side of the ellipse. Unfortunately, the bottom side of the ellipse also passes between them. Both sides are closer to B than to A, measured by grid-line distance. If we choose B in scan converting both edges, we will write the same pixel twice. The perpendicular distance to the ellipse is also well defined (it is the minimum of the distances between the point and all points of the ellipse), but a single point may be close to several points on the ellipse. For example, in scan converting the bottom side of the ellipse in Fig. 19.26(b), pixel A is closer to the ellipse than is pixel B, but we would like to draw pixel B regardless, since the *part* of the ellipse to which A is close happens to be unrelated to the part to which B is close. The residuals in this case determine the same (wrong) choice—the residual at A is less than the residual at B. Thus, there is no easy answer in choosing a measure of closeness for an ellipse. For tightly curved ellipses, all measures of closeness fail. We shall discuss ways to circumvent this difficulty later.

Part of the difficulty with using residuals as an error measure is implicit in the nature of residuals. For a circle, for example, it is true that the circle of radius R at the origin consists of all points (x, y) satisfying $x^2 + y^2 - R^2 = 0$, so $x^2 + y^2 - R^2$ is a reasonable measure of the extent to which the point (x, y) fails to lie on the circle. Unfortunately, the circle can also be defined as the set of points satisfying $(x^2 + y^2)^{1/2} - R = 0$, so residuals computed using $(x^2 + y^2)^{1/2} - R$ could be used as well (but they are different from—not even proportional to—the first type of residual), as could residuals computed using $(x^2 + y^2)^a - R^{2a}$ for any positive value of a. Thus, use of residuals is really an arbitrary method of measurement.

Finally, for general curves, there is no clear choice. We still find the midpoint criterion convincing: In a place where the curve is near horizontal, we choose between vertically adjacent pixels by determining on which side of the midpoint the curve passes (this amounts to the grid-distance criterion), and we present an algorithm based on this criterion.

It is important, in designing a scan-conversion algorithm, to choose a way to measure error, and then to design the algorithm to minimize this error. Only if such a measure has been chosen can an algorithm be proved to be correct. It is also important to specify the point at which approximations are incorporated. An algorithm that approximates a curve by line segments, and then scan converts them, may have a very small error if the error is measured as distance to the line segments, but a very large error measured by distance to the curve.

19.2.3   Another Look at Lines

In Chapter 2, we discussed only those line segments that could be easily described in a rasterized world—that is, segments whose endpoints had integer coordinates. For such lines, we developed an incremental algorithm (the midpoint algorithm) for computing which pixels were closest to the line segment. For each integer x value, we chose between two integer y values by examining a decision variable that was then incremented for use at the next x value. Initializing this decision variable was easy, because the coefficients of the line equation ($Ax + By + C = 0$) were all integers, and the starting point of the segment, (x_0, y_0), was guaranteed to satisfy the line equation (i.e., $Ax_0 + By_0 + C = 0$).

Not all line segments have integer endpoints however. How can we draw on a raster device a line segment whose endpoints are real numbers? Suppose we wish to draw a line from $(0, 0)$ to $(10, 0.51)$ on a black-and-white raster device. Clearly, pixels $(0, 0)$ through $(9, 0)$ should be drawn, and pixel $(10, 1)$ should be drawn. If we take the simple approach of rounding the endpoints to integer values, however, we draw pixels $(0, 0)$ to $(5, 0)$ and $(6, 1)$ to $(10, 1)$, which is completely different. Instead, we could compute the equation of the line:

$$1.0y - 0.051x + 0.0 = 0.0,$$

and apply the midpoint algorithm to this line. This approach requires using a floating-point version of the midpoint algorithm, however, which is expensive. Another possibility is to recognize that, if we multiply the line equation by 1000, we get

$$1000y - 51x + 0 = 0,$$

which is an integer line we could draw instead. We can use this approach in general, by converting floating-point numbers into fixed-point numbers and then multiplying by an appropriately large integer to give integer coefficients for the line.[3] In most cases, the multiplier determines the subpixel resolution of the endpoints of the line: If we wish to place endpoints on quarter-integer locations, we must multiply by 4; for tenth-integer locations, we multiply by 10.

Yet another problem arises if the first pixel to be drawn does not lie exactly on the line. Consider the line from $(0, 0.001)$ to $(10, 1.001)$. Its equation is

$$y - 0.1x - 0.001 = 0,$$

or

$$1000y - 100x - 1 = 0,$$

and the first pixel to be drawn is $(0, 0)$, which does not lie exactly on the line. In this case, we need to initialize the decision variable by explicitly computing the value of the residual, $Ax + By + C$, at the starting point; none of the simplification from the original algorithm is possible here. Choosing the starting point in such a case is also a problem. If the actual endpoint is (x_0, y_0), we must choose an integer point near (x_0, y_0). For a line of slope less

---

[3] We must be careful not to multiply by too large an integer; overflow could result.

than one, we can round x_0 to get a starting x value, then compute a y value so that (x, y) lies on the line, and round y (see Exercise 19.6).

Lines with noninteger endpoints do arise naturally, even in an integer world. They are often generated by clipping, as we saw in Chapter 3. Suppose we have a line from $(0, 0)$ to $(10, 5)$, and wish to draw the portion of it that is within the strip between $x = 3$ and $x = 7$. This segment has endpoints $(3, \frac{3}{2})$ and $(7, \frac{7}{2})$, which are not integer values. But note that, when such lines are scan-converted, the equation for the original line should be used, lest roundoff error change the shape of the line (see Exercise 19.7).

In summary, then, we can take an arbitrary line segment, convert its endpoints to rational numbers with some fixed denominator, generate an integer equation for the line, and scan convert with the algorithm from Chapter 3 (after explicitly initializing the decision variable).

19.2.4 Advanced Polyline Algorithms

In creating rasterized polylines (unfilled polygons), there is little more to do than to use the line-drawing algorithm repeatedly. But the issue of a reference model arises here—we must decide what we want before we design the algorithm. Consider a polyline with a very sharp point, as shown in Fig. 19.27. In scan conversion of one edge, the pixels shaded horizontally are drawn. In scan conversion of the other edge, the pixels shaded vertically are drawn. The pixels drawn by both are cross-hatched. If this polyline is drawn in **xor** mode, the pixels drawn by both lines are **xor**ed twice, which is probably not what is wanted. There are two possible solutions: to draw the primitive into an offscreen bitmap in **replace** mode, and then to copy the resulting bitmap to the screen in **xor** mode, or to create a data structure representing the entire primitive and to render this data structure into the bitmap. The shape data structure described in Section 19.7 provides a means for doing this (and can accommodate patterned lines or polylines as well).

19.2.5 Improvements to the Circle Algorithm

We have an algorithm for generating circles rapidly (the midpoint algorithm). In Chapter 3, we discussed using this algorithm to draw thick circles and filled circles. The algorithm presented there, however, handled only circles with integer radii and integer centers. When the center or radius is noninteger, none of the symmetries of the original algorithm apply, and each octant of the circle must be drawn individually, as Fig. 19.28 shows.

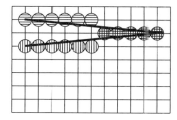

Fig. 19.27 A polyline with a sharp point may cause some pixels to be drawn more than once.

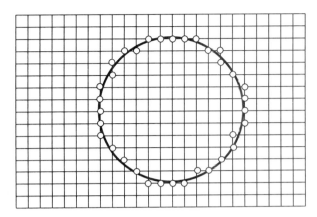

Fig. 19.28 This circle has noninteger center and radius, and each of its octants is different from the others, so no symmetries can be used to speed up scan conversion.

Unfortunately, an arbitrary circle (with real values for center and radius) cannot be converted to an integer conic. If the values of the center and radius are constrained to be rational numbers with a particular denominator,[4] then after computing (in floating point) the coefficients of the equation for the circle, we can multiply through by four times this denominator and round the coefficients. Applying a midpoint algorithm to the resulting equation with integer coefficients yields almost the same points as would result if the algorithm were applied to the original floating-point equation. To see this, suppose the center is $(h/p, k/p)$ and the radius is R. The equation of the circle is

$$S(x, y) = \left(x - \frac{h}{p}\right)^2 + \left(y - \frac{k}{p}\right)^2 - R^2 = 0.$$

Multiplying by $4p$, we get

$$4pS(x, y) = 4px^2 - 8hx + 4py^2 - 8ky + 4\left(\frac{h^2}{p} + \frac{k^2}{p} - pR^2\right) = 0.$$

Recall that, in the midpoint algorithm, we test the sign of the decision variable. Rounding the term in parentheses (the only noninteger) replaces a rational number by an integer, which alters the value of $4pS(x, y)$ by less than 1. Since we are evaluating S at points where one of x or y is an integer and the other is an integer plus $\frac{1}{2}$, the first few terms of the expression for $4pS(x, y)$ are integers; altering an integer by a number less than 1 cannot change its sign, unless the integer is 0.[5] Thus, we can use the rounded version of $4pS$ as our decision variable for a midpoint algorithm; the sole consequence is that, when the circle passes through the midpoint between 2 pixels, the integer and floating-point versions of the algorithm may make opposite choices.

---

[4] We choose to have all numbers have the same denominator, since the algebra is simpler. Since any two fractions can be put over a common denominator, this is not a severe restriction.

[5] We must, in designing a midpoint algorithm, decide whether 0 is positive or negative. Adding a small number to 0 can change this choice of sign.

The partial differences are the same as before, except that they have been multiplied by a constant $4p$. So, rather than incrementing by 2, we increment by $8p$. Initialization is more complex as well. The point resulting from adding $(0, R)$ to the center point is no longer an integer point, so we must choose some nearby point at which to start the circle. To draw the top-right eighth of the circle, we begin with the point at or just to the right of the top of the circle. We get the x coordinate by rounding up h/p to an integer, but then must compute the y coordinate explicitly and initialize the decision variable explicitly. We do these steps only once in the course of the algorithm, so their cost is not particularly significant. The code shown in Fig. 19.29 generates only one-eighth of the circle; seven more similar parts are needed to complete it.

19.2.6 A General Conic Algorithm

Chapter 3 presented an algorithm for scan converting ellipses whose axes are aligned with the axes of the plane. In this section, we describe an algorithm, developed by Van Aken [VANA89], for general conics, including ellipses with tilted axes, hyperbolas, circles, and parabolas. The algorithm is based on Pitteway's curve-tracking algorithm, which was published in 1967 [PITT67], just 2 years after Bresenham introduced his incremental line algorithm. At the time, Pitteway's algorithm received little attention, and much of it has been rediscovered several times.

Algorithms for conics have two separate elements: specifying the conic and performing the scan conversion. Since the general conic can be described as the solution to an equation of the form

$$S(x, y) = Ax^2 + Bxy + Cy^2 + Dx - Ey + F = 0,$$

the conic could be specified by the six coefficients A, B, C, D, E, and F. These are hardly intuitive, however, so we instead consider an alternative. We discuss only ellipses here, but similar techniques can be used for hyperbolas and parabolas (see Exercise 19.9).

A circle in the plane fits nicely into a unit square (see Fig. 19.30a). If an affine transformation (a linear transformation using homogeneous coordinates) is applied to the plane, the square is transformed to a parallelogram and the circle is transformed to an ellipse, as in Fig. 19.30(b). This is a generalization of SRGP's specification of an ellipse, where an aligned rectangle was used as a bounding box for an aligned ellipse. The midpoints of the sides of the parallelogram are points on the ellipse. Specifying these and the center of the parallelogram uniquely determines the parallelogram, and hence the ellipse. So our specification of an ellipse will consist of the center, J, and midpoints of the sides, P and Q, of a parallelogram. Observe that, if we can determine the coefficients in the case where J is the origin, then we can handle the general case: We just apply the simpler case to $P' = P - J$ and $Q' = Q - J$, scan convert, and add the coordinates of J to each output pixel before drawing it. (This works only if J has integer coordinates, of course.) We therefore assume that J is the origin, and that P and Q have been adjusted accordingly. We also assume that the short arc of the ellipse from P to Q goes counterclockwise around the origin; otherwise, we exchange P and Q.

To find the equation of the ellipse, we first find a transformation taking the points $\begin{bmatrix} 1 \\ 0 \end{bmatrix}$ and $\begin{bmatrix} 0 \\ 1 \end{bmatrix}$ to P and Q (it is given by a matrix whose first column is P and whose second column

```
void MidpointEighthGeneralCircle (
    int h, k;                       /* Numerators of x and y coordinates of center */
    int p,                          /* Denominator of both */
    double radius)                  /* Radius of circle */
{
    int x, y,                       /* Last point drawn */
        d,                          /* Decision variable */
        A,D,E,F,                    /* Coefficients for equation */
        A2, A4,                     /* Multiples of A for efficiency */
        deltaE,                     /* d(x + 2,y − 1/2) − d(x + 1, y − 1/2) */
        deltaSE;                    /* d(x + 2,y − 3/2) − d(x + 1, y − 1/2) */
    double temp;

    /* Initialize coefficients x, y and differences */
    A = 4 * p;
    A2 = 2 * A;
    A4 = 4 * A;
    D = −8 * h;
    E = −8 * k;
    temp = 4 * (−p * radius * radius + (h*h + k*k) / (double)p);
    F = round (temp);               /* Introduces error less than 1 */
    x = ceil (h / (double)p);       /* Smallest integer >= h/p */
    y = round (sqrt (radius*radius − (x − h/(double)p) * (x− h/(double)p)) +
        k/(double)p);
    /* The next line must be computed using real arithmetic, not integer; it */
    /* can be rewritten to avoid this requirement. */
    d = round (A * ((x + 1.0) * (x + 1.0) + (y − 0.5) * (y − 0.5)) +
            D * (x + 1.0) + E * (y − 0.5) + F);
    deltaE = A2 * (x + 1) + A + D;
    deltaSE = A2 * (x − y) + 5 * A + D − E;
    DrawPixel (x, y);
    while ((p * y − k) > (p * x − h)) {   /* While within this octant */
        if (d < 0) {                       /* Select E pixel. */
            d += deltaE;
            deltaE += A2;
            deltaSE += A2;
            x++;
        } else {
            d += deltaSE;                  /* Select SE pixel. */
            deltaE += A2;
            deltaSE += A4;
            x++;
            y−−;
        }
        DrawPixel (x, y);
    } /* while */
} /* MidpointEighthGeneralCircle */
```

Fig. 19.29 The general midpoint-circle algorithm.

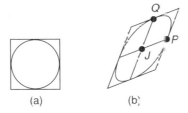

Fig. 19.30 (a) The bounding square for a circle. (b) The transformed square and the ellipse it bounds.

is Q). This transformation takes points on the unit circle, which have the form $\cos(t)\begin{bmatrix}1\\0\end{bmatrix} +$ $\sin(t)\begin{bmatrix}0\\1\end{bmatrix}$, into points on the ellipse, which therefore have the form $\begin{bmatrix}x\\-y\end{bmatrix} = \cos(t)P + \sin(t)Q$. Solving this equation for $\cos(t)$ and $\sin(t)$ gives each as a linear expression in x and y. By substituting these linear expressions into the identity $\cos^2(t) + \sin^2(t) = 1$, we can arrive at a quadratic expression in x and y that describes the ellipse (see Exercise 19.8). If we write P_x, P_y for the coordinates of P, and similarly for Q, the resulting coefficients are

$$A = P_y^2 + Q_y^2, \qquad B = -2(P_xP_y + Q_xQ_y), \qquad C = P_x^2 + Q_x^2,$$

$$D = 0, \qquad\qquad E = 0, \qquad\qquad F = -(P_xQ_y - P_yQ_x)^2.$$

We now translate the resulting ellipse to a new coordinate system centered at the point $-P$; that is, we replace the equation for the ellipse by a new equation:

$$A(x + P_x)^2 + B(x + P_x)(y + P_y) + C(y + P_y)^2 + D(x + P_x) - E(y + P_y) + F = $$
$$A'x^2 + B'xy + C'y^2 + D'x + E'y + F' = 0.$$

The resulting coefficients in this new coordinate system are

$$A' = A, \qquad\qquad B' = B, \qquad\qquad C' = C,$$

$$D' = 2Q_y(P_xQ_y - P_yQ_x) \qquad E' = -2Q_x(P_xQ_y - P_yQ_x) \qquad F' = 0.$$

The origin lies on this new conic, and if we scan convert this conic, but add (P_x, P_y) to each point before drawing it, we get the points of the original conic centered at the origin. Since A, B, and C are unchanged, we use D and E to denote the terms called D' and E' (since the original D and E were both zero).

Now, having derived the coefficients of the ellipse equation, we need to scan convert it. We divide the scan-conversion process into eight *drawing octants* (for the circle algorithm in Chapter 3, these corresponded to octants of the circle; here, they do not). The drawing octant indicates the direction in which the algorithm is tracking. In octant 1, the choice is between moving to the right and moving diagonally up and to the right. The moves to be made are classified as *square moves* or *diagonal moves*, depending on whether one coordinate changes or both do. Figure 19.31 shows the eight octants, a table indicating the directions of motion in each, and the corresponding arcs on a typical ellipse.

Our algorithm has two different loops—one for tracking in odd-numbered octants, terminated by reaching a diagonal octant boundary, and one for even-numbered octants, terminated by reaching a square octant boundary. To determine the starting octant, we observe that, at any point of a conic given by an equation $S(x, y) = 0$, the gradient of S,

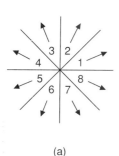

Octant	Square Move		Diagonal Move	
	ΔX	ΔY	ΔX	ΔY
1	1	0	1	1
2	0	1	1	1
3	0	1	−1	1
4	−1	0	−1	1
5	−1	0	−1	−1
6	0	−1	−1	−1
7	0	−1	1	−1
8	1	0	1	−1

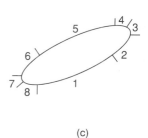

(a)   (b)   (c)

Fig. 19.31 (a) The eight drawing octants. (b) the corresponding directions of motion. (c) a typical ellipse.

which is $(2Ax + By + D, Bx + 2Cy + E)$, points perpendicular to the conic (this was used to determine the ellipse octants in the algorithm in Chapter 3). We use the coordinates of the gradient to determine the direction of motion (by rotating it 90° counterclockwise) and hence the drawing octant. Since our starting point is $(0, 0)$, this gradient is just (D, E). The code fragment in Fig. 19.32 shows how the classification into octants is done.

Now, for each octant we must determine what the value of a decision variable, d, is, what its meaning is, and how to update it. When we move diagonally, we will update d by adding an increment v; for square moves, the increment will be called u. If $S(x, y) = 0$ is the equation of the ellipse, we define d by evaluating S at the midpoint of the segment between the next two possible pixel choices. Since $S(x, y) < 0$ inside the ellipse, and $S(x, y) > 0$ outside the ellipse, a negative value of d will indicate that the ellipse passes outside the midpoint, and we will want to choose the outer pixel. When d is positive, we choose the inner pixel. When d is zero, we must choose between the 2 pixels—Van Aken's choice (in odd-numbered octants) is to make a square step whenever d is negative, and a diagonal step otherwise. In even octants, he makes a diagonal step when d is negative, and a square step otherwise.

In octant 1, if we have just drawn pixel (x_i, y_i), we denote by d_i the value we use to decide between $(x_i + 1, y_i)$ and $(x_i + 1, y_i + 1)$. We write u_{i+1} and v_{i+1} for the quantities to be added to d_i in order to create d_{i+1}. The work to be done at each pixel is therefore (1) drawing the pixel, (2) choosing the next pixel to draw based on the value of d_i, (3) updating u_i and v_i to u_{i+1} and v_{i+1} on the basis of the choice made, (4) updating d_i to d_{i+1} by adding either u_{i+1} or v_{i+1}, and (5) checking for an octant change.

```
int GetOctant (int D, int E)
{
    if (D > 0 && E < 0)
        return (D < −E) ? 1 : 2;
    if ...      /* Handle remaining six cases */
}  /* GetOctant */
```

Fig. 19.32 A function for determining the drawing octant from the components of the gradient.

Recall that d_{i+1} can be computed from d_i by a differencing technique. Suppose we are in the first drawing octant, have just drawn pixel (x_i, y_i), and have decided which pixel to choose next using $d_i = S(x_i + 1, y_i + \frac{1}{2})$. If we make a square move, then $x_{i+1} = x_i + 1$ and $y_{i+1} = y_i$. The new decision variable d_{i+1} is $S(x_i + 2, y_i + \frac{1}{2})$; the difference between this and d_i is

$$
\begin{aligned}
u_{i+1} &= d_{i+1} - d_i \\
&= A(x_i + 2)^2 + B(x_i + 2)(y_i + \tfrac{1}{2}) + C(y_i + \tfrac{1}{2})^2 \\
&\quad + D(x_i + 2) + E(y_i + \tfrac{1}{2}) + F \\
&\quad - [A(x_i + 1)^2 + B(x_i + 1)(y_i + \tfrac{1}{2}) + C(y_i + \tfrac{1}{2})^2 \\
&\quad + D(x_i + 1) + E(y_i + \tfrac{1}{2}) + F] \\
&= A[2(x_i + 1) + 1] + B(y_i + \tfrac{1}{2}) + D \\
&= A(2(x_i) + 1) + B(y_i + \tfrac{1}{2}) + D + 2A.
\end{aligned}
$$

On the other hand, if we make a diagonal move, then d_i is $S(x_i + 2, y_i + \frac{3}{2})$, and the increment is

$$
\begin{aligned}
v_{i+1} &= d_{i+1} - d_i \\
&= (2A + B)x_{i+1} + (B + 2C)y_{i+1} + A + B/2 + D + E \\
&= (2A + B)x_i + (B + 2C)y_i + A + B/2 + D + E + [2A + 2B + 2C].
\end{aligned}
$$

If we let u_i denote $A[2(x_i) + 1] + B(y_i + \frac{1}{2}) + D$, then for the square move we see that $u_{i+1} = u_i + 2A$. Similarly, if v_i denotes $(2A + B)x_i + (B + 2C)y_i + A + B/2 + D + E$, then for a diagonal move, $v_{i+1} = v_i + (2A + 2B + 2C)$. To keep correct values of u_i and v_i for both diagonal and square moves, we must update these values even if they are not used. Thus, for a square move,

$$
\begin{aligned}
v_{i+1} &= (2A + B)x_{i+1} + (B + 2C)y_{i+1} + A + B/2 + D + E \\
&= (2A + B)(x_i + 1) + (B + 2C)y_i + A + B/2 + D + E \\
&= v_i + (2A + B);
\end{aligned}
$$

for a diagonal move, $u_{i+1} = u_i + 2A + B$. We encourage you to work out a table that shows the increments in u_i and v_i for a square move or a diagonal move in each drawing octant (see Exercise 19.10). The algebra is tedious but instructive.

If $k_1 = 2A$, $k_2 = 2A + B$, and $k_3 = 2A + 2B + 2C$, then the update procedure for the us and vs can be described by the following rules.

Square move:

$$u_{i+1} = u_i + k_1, \qquad\qquad v_{i+1} = v_i - k_2.$$

Diagonal move:

$$u_{i+1} = u_i + k_2, \qquad\qquad v_{i+1} = v_i + k_3.$$

Let us now consider how to determine octant changes. We see that we leave drawing octant 1 when the gradient vector points down and to the right—that is, when it is a multiple of $(1, -1)$. In other words, we leave octant 1 when the sum of the two components of the gradient vector goes from being negative to being zero (see Fig. 19.33).

Now observe that the components of the gradient vector,

$$\left(\frac{\partial S}{\partial x}, \frac{\partial S}{\partial y}\right) = (2Ax + By + D, Bx + 2Cy + E),$$

can be expressed in terms of the values of u_i and v_i given previously:

$$\frac{\partial S}{\partial x} = u_i - \frac{k_2}{2}, \qquad\qquad \frac{\partial S}{\partial x} + \frac{\partial S}{\partial y} = v_i - \frac{k_2}{2}.$$

If we therefore check the sign of $v_i - k_2/2$, we can detect when we leave the first drawing octant. The corresponding check for leaving the second drawing octant is the sign of $u_i - k_2/2$.

Before we can write the actual code, however, we need to consider one last issue. When we go from drawing octant 1 to drawing octant 2, the definition of d_i changes, as do those of u_i and v_i; they still correspond to the increments for square moves and diagonal moves, respectively, but the square moves are now vertical rather than horizontal, and the value being updated is no longer $S(x_i + 1, y_i + \frac{1}{2})$ but rather $S(x_i + \frac{1}{2}, y_i + 1)$. Using primes to denote the values in octant 2, and unprimed symbols to denote the values in octant 1, we compute

$$d_i' - d_i = S\left(x_i + \frac{1}{2}, y_i + 1\right) - S\left(x_i + 1, y_i + \frac{1}{2}\right)$$

$$= \frac{v_i}{2} - u_i + \frac{3}{8}k_3 - \frac{1}{2}k_2,$$

$$v_i' - v_i = [(2A + B)x_i + (B + 2C)y_i + \frac{B}{2} + C + D + E]$$

$$- [(2A + B)x_i + (B + 2C)y_i + A + \frac{B}{2} + D + E]$$

$$= -A + C$$

$$u_i' - u_i = v_i - u_i - \frac{k_2}{2} + \frac{k_3}{2}.$$

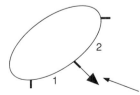

This vector lies on a line of slope -1

Fig. 19.33 While we draw in octant 1, the sum of the components of the gradient is negative. When we enter octant 2, the sum becomes positive.

The computations involved in deriving the first and third equations are straightforward but long. The variables for incrementing u_i and v_i need to be updated as well. Assuming you have worked out the table of increments, it is clear that $k_3' = k_3$, $k_2' = k_2 - k_2$, and $k_1' = k_1 - 2k_2 + k_3$.

We now have all the tools we need to generate the algorithm, at least for two octants. We include the coefficient F (the constant term for the conic) in the code, even though we are assuming it is zero; for a more general conic, whose center is not an integer, the starting point for the algorithm may not lie exactly on the conic, in which case F may be nonzero. We leave it to you to experiment with this case.

The code for the algorithm in Fig. 19.34 is followed by a procedure, Conjugate, which determines the coefficients for an ellipse (at the origin) from the endpoints of conjugate diameters. If the points are P and Q, then the parallelogram whose vertices are $P + Q$, $P - Q$, $-P - Q$, and $-P + Q$ bounds the ellipse; the ellipse is tangent to this parallelogram at the midpoints of the sides as in Fig. 19.30.

The code finishes by entering the ending octant, counting the number of steps in the square-step direction needed to reach the final pixel, then continuing the algorithm until that many steps have been taken. We leave the details of this step to you (see Exercise 19.13). Surprisingly, the code that updates the increments during the first two octant changes actually works for all octant changes.

One last issue remains in drawing ellipses. As shown in Fig. 19.35, sometimes a diagonal step in the algorithm takes the drawing point clear across to the other side of the ellipse—it changes several octants at once. When this occurs, the algorithm breaks down and marches away from the ellipse, as shown. It is remarkable that this is a form of aliasing—the signal $S(x, y)$ that we are sampling contains frequencies too high to be resolved by sampling at integer grid points.

Pratt has proposed a solution to this problem [PRAT85]. While the algorithm is tracking pixels in drawing octant 1, a jump across the ellipse causes the gradient vector to change direction radically. In fact, the gradient vector in drawing octant 1 always has a negative y component and positive x component. In jumping across the ellipse, we arrive at a point in octant 3, 4, 5, or 6. We determine the dividing line between these octants and octants 7, 8, 1, and 2, by setting the x component of the gradient to zero—that is, $2Ax + By + D = 0$. Since $u_i = 2Ax_i + By_i + D + A + B/2$, u_i can be used to detect such crossings. Similar checks can be generated for each octant. Notice that these checks need to be applied during only one type of move for each octant: one type of move steps away from the ellipse, and hence the check is not needed, but one steps toward it, and hence the check is needed. For further information on conic tracking algorithms see Exercise 19.14 and [PITT67; PRAT85; DASI89].

One other type of algorithm for conics has been developed by Wu and Rokne [WU89], but is suited for only gray-scale displays. Instead of scan converting one pixel at a time, it scan converts by blocks of pixels. Suppose we are stepping horizontally, and that the curvature is concave up. If we have just drawn pixel (x, y), and after two more steps we are drawing pixel $(x + 2, y + 2)$, then the intervening pixel must be $(x + 1, y + 1)$. Similarly, if after two more steps we are drawing $(x + 2, y)$, then the intervening pixel must be $(x + 1, y)$. Only if after two steps we draw pixel $(x + 2, y + 1)$ is there any ambiguity: Then, the intervening pixel may have been $(x + 1, y)$ or $(x + 1, y + 1)$. On a gray-scale

```
/* Draw an arc of a conic between the points (xs, ys) and (xe, ye) on the conic; */
/* the conic is given by Ax² + Bxy + Cy² + Dx + Ey + F = 0. If the conic is a */
/* hyperbola, the two points must lie on the same branch  */
void Conic (
        int xs, ys,                     /* Starting point */
        int xe, ye,                     /* Ending point */
        int A, B, C, D, E, F)           /* Coefficients */
{
    int x, y;                           /* Current point */
    int octant;                         /* Current octant */
    int dxsquare, dysquare;             /* Change in (x, y) for square moves */
    int dxdiag, dydiag;                 /* Change in (x, y) for diagonal moves */
    int d,u,v,k1,k2,k3;                 /* Decision variables and increments */
    int dSdx, dSdy;                     /* Components of gradient */
    int octantCount;                    /* Number of octants to be drawn */
    int tmp;                            /* Used to perform a swap */

    octant = GetOctant (D, E);          /* Starting octant number */
    switch (octant) {
        case 1:
            d = round (A + B * 0.5 + C * 0.25 + D + E * 0.5 + F);
            u = round (A + B * 0.5 + D);
            v = round (A + B * 0.5 + D + E);
            k1 = 2 * A;
            k2 = 2 * A + B;
            k3 = k2 + B + 2 * C;
            dxsquare = 1;
            dysquare = 0;
            dxdiag = 1;
            dydiag = 1;
            break;
        case 2:
            d = round (A * 0.25 + B * 0.5 + C + D * 0.5 + E + F);
            u = round (B * 0.5 + C + E);
            v = round (B * 0.5 + C + D + E);
            k1 = 2 * C;
            k2 = B + 2 * C;
            k3 = 2 * A + 2 * B + 2 * C;
            dxsquare = 0;
            dysquare = 1;
```

Fig. 19.34 (*Cont.*)

```
        dxdiag = 1;
        dydiag = 1;
        break;
     . . . six more cases. . .
}   /* switch */


x = xe − xs;                        /* Translate (xs, ys) to origin. */
y = ye − ys;
dSdx = 2 * A * x + B * y + D;       /* Gradient at endpoint */
dSdy = B * x + 2 * C * y + E;
/* This determines the ending octant. */
octantCount = GetOctant (dSdx, dSdy) − octant.
if (octantCount <= 0) octantCount += 8;


/* Now we actually draw the curve. */
x = xs;
y = ys;
while (octantCount > 0) {
    if (octant & 1) {
        while (v <= k2 * 0.5) {
            DrawPixel (x, y);
            if (d < 0) {
                x += dxsquare;
                y += dysquare;
                u += k1;
                v += k2;
                d += u;
            } else {
                x += dxdiag;
                y += dydiag;
                u += k2;
                v += k3;
                d += v;
            }
        }   /* while v <= k2 * 0.5 */
        /* We now cross the diagonal octant boundary. */
        d = round (d − u − v * 0.5 − k2 * 0.5 + 3 * k3 * 0.125);
        u = round (−u + v − k2 * 0.5 + k3 * 0.5);
```

Fig. 19.34 (Cont.)

$$v = \text{round}\ (v - k2 + k3 * 0.5);$$
$$k1 = k1 - 2 * k2 + k3;$$
$$k2 = k3 - k2;$$
$$tmp = dxsquare;$$
$$dxsquare = -dysquare;$$
$$dysquare = tmp;$$
$$\} \textbf{ else } \{\qquad /* \text{ Octant is even } */$$
$$\quad \textbf{while } (u < k2 * 0.5) \ \{$$
$$\qquad \text{DrawPixel } (x, y);$$
$$\qquad \textbf{if } (d < 0) \ \{$$
$$\qquad\quad x\ += dxdiag;$$
$$\qquad\quad y\ += dydiag;$$
$$\qquad\quad u\ += k2;$$
$$\qquad\quad v\ += k3;$$
$$\qquad\quad d\ += v;$$
$$\qquad \} \textbf{ else } \{$$
$$\qquad\quad x\ += dxsquare;$$
$$\qquad\quad y\ += dysquare;$$
$$\qquad\quad u\ += k1;$$
$$\qquad\quad v\ += k2;$$
$$\qquad\quad d\ += u;$$
$$\qquad \}$$
$$\quad \} \quad /* \text{ while } u < k2 * 0.5 \ */$$
$$\quad /* \text{ We now cross over square octant boundary. } */$$
$$\quad d\ += u - v + k1 - k2;\qquad /* \text{ Do } v \text{ first; it depends on } u. */$$
$$\quad v = 2 * u - v + k1 - k2;$$
$$\quad u\ += k1 - k2;$$
$$\quad k3\ += 4 * (k1 - k2);$$
$$\quad k2 = 2 * k1 - k2;$$
$$\quad tmp = dxdiag;$$
$$\quad dxdiag = -\ dydiag;$$
$$\quad dydiag = tmp;$$
$$\} \quad /* \text{ Octant is even } */$$
$$octant++;$$
$$\textbf{if } (octant > 8)\ octant\ -= 8;$$
$$octantCount--;$$
$$\} \quad /* \text{ while } octantCount > 0 \ */$$
Having entered last octant, continue drawing until you reach the last pixel;
$$\} \quad /* \text{ Conic } */$$

Fig. 19.34 (Cont.)

```
/* Specify and draw an ellipse in terms of the endpoints P = (xp, yp) and */
/* Q = (xq, yq) of two conjugate diameters of the ellipse. The endpoints are */
/* specified as offsets relative to the center of the ellipse, assumed to be the */
/* origin in this case. */
void Conjugate (int xp, int yp, int xq, int yq, int mode)
{
    int xprod, tmp, xe, ye, A, B, C, D, E, F;

    xprod = xp * yq − xq * yp;

    if (xprod != 0) {                    /* If it is zero, the points are collinear! */
        if (xprod < 0) {
            tmp = xp; xp = xq; xq = tmp;
            tmp = yp; yp = yq; yq = tmp;
            xprod = −xprod;
        }
        A = yp * yp + yq * yq;
        B = −2 * (xp *yp + xq * yq);
        C = xp * xp + xq * xq;
        D = 2 × yq + xprod;
        E = −2 * xq * xprod;
        F = 0;

        if (mode == FULL_ELLIPSE) {      /* Set starting and ending points equal */
            xe = xp; ye = yp;
        } else {         /* mode == ELLIPSE_ARC; draw only the arc between P and Q */
            xe = xq; ye = yq;
        }
            Conic (xp, yp, xe, ye, A, B, C, D, E, F);
    }  /* if */
}  /* Conjugate */
```

Fig. 19.34 The general ellipse algorithm.

display, however, we can simply draw *both* these pixels at half intensity. Thus, we can step by 2 pixels at a time, reducing the computation substantially. At the junctions of drawing octants, the algorithm must be tuned so that it does not overstep, but this is not too difficult. The algorithm is clearly suited only for gray-scale displays, but illustrates how certain algorithms may be simplified when antialiasing is possible. We shall see this again in our discussion of text.

19.2.7 Thick Primitives

We are now ready to discuss thick primitives: thick lines, thick polylines, and thickened general curves (thick lines, circles, and ellipse arcs were discussed in Chapter 3; here we extend and refine the ideas presented there). The first step in scan converting thick primitives is to decide what is actually in the primitive as a geometric object—that is, to

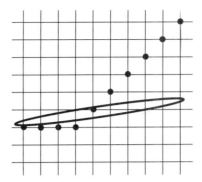

Fig. 19.35 The breakdown of the algorithm for a thin ellipse.

define the reference model for a thick object. For example (see Fig. 19.36), does a thick line look like a rectangle, or like a rectangle with semicircular endcaps, or like something else?

   If we imagine the thick line as being drawn by a broad pen, we are in effect asking whether the pen has a flat or a round tip. More mathematically, we can describe the choice as one between the set of all points whose distance from the center line is less than one-half of the width of the thick line (this includes the rounded ends) and the set of all points whose distance from the center line along a normal (perpendicular) to the center line is less than one-half of the width of the thick line. A third mathematical description that will prove useful later is to consider two parallel copies of the center line, infinitely extended and then pushed off from the center line by the same amount in opposite directions. The thickened line consists of the area between these pushed-off lines, trimmed by two other lines through the endpoints of the original segment. If these trim lines are perpendicular to the original segment, the result is a rectangular thick line; if not, then the ends of the thick line are slanted (see Fig. 19.37). These slanted ends can be joined to make thick polylines; shaping the corners this way is called *mitering*.

   A special case is to consider the line as being drawn with a pen with an aligned tip; that is, the tip is a line segment that is always either vertical or horizontal. A thick line drawn with such a pen looks like a rectangle if it is horizontal or vertical, and like a parallelogram otherwise. You should draw a few such lines, and determine why this is a bad way to draw thick lines. We mention this case only because it can be implemented quickly: We alter the midpoint line-drawing algorithm to place several pixels at once, rather than just a single one. Joints between horizontally and vertically drawn segments can be generated by extending the segments beyond the join points and then, in addition to the original segments, drawing the points lying in both extensions.

Fig. 19.36 A thick line may look like a rectangle or have rounded or slanted ends. Which is the correct version?

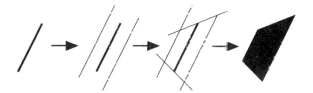

Fig. 19.37 We can define a wide class of thickened lines by pushing off parallel copies of a segment and trimming by arbitrary lines through the endpoints. These slanted ends can then be joined together to make thick polylines in a process called mitering.

Each of these classes of thick lines can be used to make thick polylines, as shown in Fig. 19.38. Butt-ended lines do not join well—they leave a notch at the joints (see Fig. 19.38a). Rounded-end lines join nicely—the exterior of the bend at each joint is a smooth curve, and the interior is a sharp angle (see Fig. 19.38b). Slanted-end lines (of the same thickness) join nicely only if the slant is the same on both sides—otherwise, the slanted edges of the two lines have different lengths. We can achieve the same slant on both sides by choosing the trim line to be midway between the two segments. If we miter-join lines that are nearly parallel, the miter point extends well beyond the actual intersection of the center lines (see Fig. 19.38d). This extension is sometimes undesirable, so trimmed miter joints are sometimes used to join lines. The trim on the miter is a line perpendicular to the miter line at some distance from the center-line intersection (see Fig 19.38e).

These various methods of line joining are available in many drawing packages, including PostScript, QuickDraw, and the X Windows System. Most such graphics packages provide not only a line-join style, but also a line-end style, so that, for example, we can use rounded ends but mitered joins for a polyline that is not closed.

There are several approaches to thickening general curves, including curves produced by freehand drawings or by other nonanalytic methods. To draw a thickened curve, we can use the method in Chapter 3 and simply convert the curve to many short line segments, each of which is then drawn thickened. If the segments are short enough and the resolution of the output device is high enough, the result may be adequate. It is important that the short line segments be constructed without rounding to integer coordinates (although the coefficients for the equations may be converted to integers by the methods discussed for scan converting general lines). If the endpoints of the segments were rounded to grid points, then there would be only a few possible choices for the segment slopes, and the curve would have a highly twisted shape.

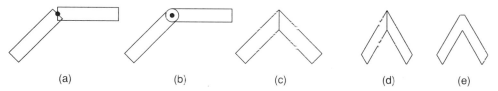

| (a) | (b) | (c) | (d) | (e) |

Fig. 19.38 Joining various classes of lines. (a) Butt-end lines mate poorly at joints. (b) Round-end lines mate nicely, but have curved segments, which may not be desired in some applications. (c) Mitered joints can be made by joining slant-end lines. (d) A miter at a joint where the angle is small may look bad. (e) Such joints can be trimmed.

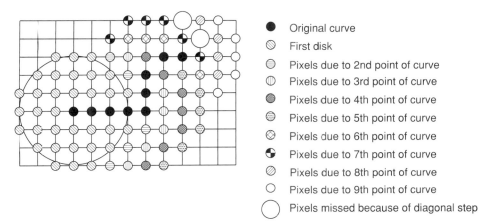

● Original curve
⊘ First disk
⊖ Pixels due to 2nd point of curve
◐ Pixels due to 3rd point of curve
⬤ Pixels due to 4th point of curve
◉ Pixels due to 5th point of curve
⊗ Pixels due to 6th point of curve
◕ Pixels due to 7th point of curve
⊘ Pixels due to 8th point of curve
○ Pixels due to 9th point of curve
◯ Pixels missed because of diagonal step

Fig. 19.39 A disk is drawn around the starting pixel of the thick line. After that, each pixel on the curve generates a semicircle. Notice the 2 pixels that were missed (shown as large circles in the figure).

A different approach is to draw the curve with a circular pen; Posch and Fellner [POSC89] describe a clever way to do this. Their method is of particular interest because it is designed for hardware implementation. The basic notion is first to scan convert the curve into a list of pixels that are adjacent diagonally, vertically, or horizontally (called *eight-way stepping*). This list of pixels is then expanded, so that any 2 pixels are adjacent horizontally or vertically (called *four-way stepping*). At the start of the curve, a filled circle (disk) is drawn. For each subsequent pixel, a half-circle (unfilled) is drawn, centered at the new pixel, and with its diameter perpendicular to the line from the previous pixel to the current one. Since there are only four possible directions of motion, there are only four possible half-circles to be drawn. Figure 19.39 shows the technique being applied to a curve using eight-way stepping instead, to show that, without the four-way stepping, some pixels are missed.

One difficulty with this method is that, for odd-thickness curves, the algorithm must be able to generate the points on a circle of half-integer radius centered on the original curve. These can be generated with a modified midpoint algorithm by multiplying the coefficients of the circle by 4. Another difficulty is that four-way stepping must be used to avoid gaps; unfortunately, this generates rougher curves. The algorithm also generates individual pixels instead of generating spans, so it is difficult to move the pixels to the screen quickly. The shape data structure described in Section 19.7 can be used to assemble the pixels into spans before they are copied to the screen.

19.2.8 Filled Primitives

In Chapter 3, we discussed filled primitives and the interiors of standard geometric primitives such as the circle, rectangle, or ellipse. These were reasonably unambiguous. The definition of interior for self-intersecting primitives is less obvious. We discussed two definitions for closed (possibly self-intersecting) polylines in Chapter 3. One is the even-odd or parity rule, in which a line is drawn from a point to some other point distant

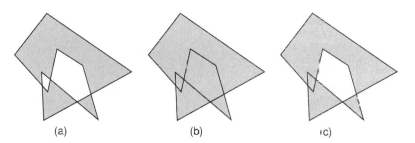

Fig. 19.40 (a) A polygon filled using the even-odd rule. (b) A polygon filled using the nonexterior rule. (c) A polygon filled using the nonzero winding rule.

from the polyline. If this line crosses the polyline an odd number of times, the point is *inside,* if not, it is outside. It is important that the test line pass through no vertices of the polyline, or else the intersection count can be ambiguous. The resulting interior region has a checkerboard appearance, as shown in Fig. 19.40(a). Another rule is the nonexterior rule, in which a point distant from the polyline is used. Any point that can be connected to this seed point by a path that does not intersect the polyline is said to be outside the polyline. The resulting interior region consists of everything one might fill in if asked to fill in whatever is within the curve. Put differently, if we think of the curve as a fence, the interior is the region within which animals can be penned up. See, for example, Fig. 19.40(b).

A third rule is the *nonzero winding rule.* The winding number of a point P with respect to a curve C that does not contain the point is defined as follows. Consider a point Q that travels once around C. The endpoint of a vector from P to Q, after normalization, travels along the unit circle centered at P. If we imagine the track of this endpoint as a rubber band, and let the band contract, it will end up wrapped about the circle some number of times. The winding number is the number of wraps (for clockwise wraps, the winding number is negative).

For closed polylines, this number can be computed much more easily. As before, we take a ray from the point out to a point far away from the polyline. The ray must hit no vertices of the polyline. If the ray is given parametrically as $P + t\mathbf{d}$, and $\mathbf{d} = \begin{bmatrix} x \\ y \end{bmatrix}$, we define $\mathbf{d}' = \begin{bmatrix} -y \\ x \end{bmatrix}$, which is just $\mathbf{d}$ rotated counterclockwise by 90°. Again, we count intersections of the ray with the polyline, but this time each intersection is assigned a value of $+1$ or -1 according to the following rule: If the dot product of the direction vector of the edge of the polyline with $\mathbf{d}'$ is positive, the value is $+1$, if it is negative, the value is -1. The sum of these values is the winding number of C with respect to P. Pixels for which the winding number is nonzero are said to be inside according to the winding-number rule. Figure 19.40(c) shows a region defined by the winding-number rule.

19.3 ANTIALIASING

To antialias a primitive, we want to draw it with fuzzy edges, as discussed in Chapter 3. We must take into account the filtering theory discussed there and in Chapter 14, where we saw that a signal with high-frequency components generates aliases when sampled. This fact indicates that we need to filter the signal before sampling it; the correct filter turned out to be a sinc(x) = sin(x)/x filter. We now consider the consequences of a mathematical analysis of this situation.

If we compute the intensity of two images containing nonoverlapping primitives, we can find the intensity of an image containing both primitives simply by adding the individual intensity values (this *principle of superposition* is a consequence of defining the image by an integral). By this reasoning, if we break down a primitive into many tiny nonoverlapping pieces, we can compute an antialiased picture of it simply by computing the images of each of the little pieces and then adding the results.

Taking this approach to its logical limit, if we can draw an antialiased image of a single point, we can draw any antialiased primitive by representing it as a union of points, and summing (by an integral) the antialiased values for all these points to compute the values that should be drawn in the final image. We propose this not as a workable solution to the antialiasing problem, but as a motivation for various techniques. To avoid the technical difficulties of defining intensities for regions with infinitesimal areas, like points, we will instead speak of very small regions (dots).[6] What is the antialiased picture of such a dot? To compute the intensity at a pixel (x, y), we place a *sinc* filter over the pixel, and convolve it with a function ϕ that is 1 above the dot and 0 elsewhere. Mathematically, assuming the dot is at location (a, b) and the pixel is at (x, y), we get

$$I(x, y) = \int\limits_{-\infty}^{\infty} \int\limits_{-\infty}^{\infty} \phi(t, s) \, \text{sinc}(\sqrt{(t - x)^2 + (s - y)^2}) \, ds \, dt.$$

The integrand will be 0 except at points (t, s) that are close to (a, b); at those points it will be approximately sinc(r), where r is the distance from (x, y) to (a, b)—that is, from the pixel to the dot—and the intensity at (x, y) is approximately proportional to sinc(r). Thus, an antialiased dot (drawn in white on black) has a bright spot near its center and dim concentric rings at larger distances from the center. (These rings are related to the diffraction patterns produced when a light shines through a pinhole—see [BERK68].) Notice that, although sinc(r) is sometimes negative, it is impossible to represent these values accurately, since we cannot draw a color darker than black. In the limit, as the dots get very small, the approximation to sinc(r) becomes exact (although the values must be scaled by the inverse of the areas of the dots to prevent them from becoming 0).

If we now use this relation to antialias a line (which is just a collection of points), the result is a superposition of the individual antialiased patterns for the points[7]; the positive ripples from one point cancel the "negative" ripples from another, and the net result is a bright area near the line that fades gradually to black at greater distances. Furthermore, since a line drawn on a plane has a great deal of symmetry (it is invariant under translation along itself), the sum of the antialiased values is a function of the distance from the line and is independent of position along the line. This invariance suggests that, if we compute the profile of the intensity as we move away from the line along some perpendicular, we might be able to use the profile in a different way. Suppose the line is ever-so-slightly curved. If, at each point of the line, we lay down a copy of the intensity profile along the normal line to

---

[6]The mathematically inclined reader may use delta functions to make this precise.

[7]More precisely, the result is an integral of the contributions from the individual points.

the curve at that point, the sum of these profiles would give a decent filtered image of the curved line. Of course, at some distance from the curve these normal lines overlap, but if the line curvature is small, then the overlap will happen very far out, where the profile value is nearly zero anyway. This idea has been used by Hatfield to generate the general antialiasing scheme described in Section 19.3.3 [HATF89].

To antialias a filled region, we imagine it as a collection of points, or as being built up as a family of the lines described previously. The area solidly within the region has full intensity, and the intensity outside the region falls off with distance. If we compute what an antialiased halfplane looks like, we can antialias other regions by assuming that the edge of the region is (locally) very like a halfplane. In actual practice, however, we first draw antialiased lines or curves for the edges, then fill the region at full intensity.

19.3.1 Antialiasing Lines

In Chapter 3, we discussed the Gupta–Sproull method for generating antialiased lines. For each pixel near a line, the distance to the line is used to determine the brightness of the pixel. In an efficient implementation, this distance is converted to an integer value between 0 and some small number, say 16, and this number is used as an index into a table of gray-scale values. These gray-scale values were computed by determining the overlap between a conical filter and the region represented by the line. For lines of a fixed width, the possible overlaps of the filter and line can be computed a priori, but for general widths (and for rectangles, discussed in Section 19.3.5) it is preferable to compute the weighted overlap of the filter base with a halfplane. The overlap of the filter with a line can then be computed by subtracting its overlap with two slightly offset halfplanes (see Fig. 19.41).

Recall that the distance from the pixel center to the line must be *signed*, since the centers of a three-fourths–covered pixel and one-quarter–covered pixel are at the same distance from the side of the line. A particularly clever trick is available here: In the midpoint-line algorithm, the decision variable d determines whether the pixel center is on one side of the line or on the other. The value of this variable is closely related to the distance from the chosen pixel to the line. If we let $D(x, y) = ax + by + c$, then our decision variable at the point (x_i, y_i) is just $D(x_i, y_i - \frac{1}{2})$, and (x_i, y_i) lies on the line exactly when D is 0. Thus, the amount by which D fails to be 0 measures the signed distance from a (x_i, y_i) to the line. The implementation in Chapter 3 used exactly this fact to determine the distance to the line.

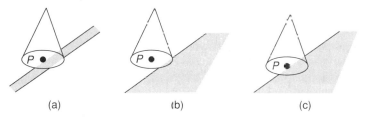

(a)   (b)   (c)

Fig. 19.41 The cone filter centered at P overlaps both sides of the thin line. We can compute the coverage of the filter over two halfplanes (b and c), one bounded by each side of the line, and subtract to obtain the actual line coverage (a).

A more complex indexing scheme is required to handle ends of lines. If the line is butt-ended, we must compute all possible overlaps of a corner of a square with the base of the cone filter, and we must store these in a table. This task is really part of a more general problem of drawing antialiased rectangles, and we postpone further discussion of it to Section 19.3.5 below.

The Gupta–Sproull method works for lines drawn in a foreground color on a background, but does not handle the case where a second line crosses the first. Consider two white lines drawn on a black background. If, during the drawing of the second line, the intensity for each pixel is computed as a mix of white with the background, two results are possible. If the current pixel value is used as the background intensity, then the point at which the lines cross will be overly bright. On the other hand, if the background intensity is taken to be black during the drawing of the second line, then points near the crossing of the two lines will not be bright enough.

The problem is compounded when color is introduced. First, a decision must be made about crossings. Is the color at the crossing point the color of the last line drawn? Or is it a mix of the color already there and the color last drawn? In essence, we must choose one of the compositing operations described in Chapter 17. Unfortunately, the assumption made in the Duff–Porter approach to compositing (that if a primitive covers a fraction α of a pixel, it covers a fraction α of any other primitive in that pixel) is false in the generic case of intersecting lines, so that using an α value compositing approach to choosing a color for the intersection pixel fails us here.

The Texas Instruments TI34020 chip provides a MAX operator that takes two pixel values, *src* and *dest,* and replaces *dest* with the larger of the two values. This use of the larger value to provide a value for pixels at intersections of antialiased colored lines has been a successful compromise.

An early paper by Barros and Fuchs [BARR79] describes a method for producing antialiased lines on a gray-scale device. The method is essentially a scan-line renderer for polygonal regions (which include 1-pixel-wide lines as a special case). All the polygons to be drawn are accumulated, and then the intensity of each pixel is computed by determining the portion of the pixel not covered by lines. A subdivision approach determines disjoint uncovered regions of each pixel, and the areas of such regions are then tallied.

Another approach to antialiasing of lines deserves mention, for the special case where the resolution of the device is very small, perhaps 2 bits (as in the NeXT machine). Here, the choice of pixel value is so coarse that Gupta–Sproull antialiasing is a waste of computation. A strict area-sampling technique works perfectly well instead. (The difference between area sampling and Gupta–Sproull is generally so small that, when area sampling is discretized to one of four levels, the results tend to be the same.) Several authors [PITT87; PITT80] have proposed that the decision variable d for the midpoint algorithm applied to the line $Ax + By + C = 0$ (which can range in value between $-A$ and B, for lines with slope between -1 and 1) be used to compute the antialiased value: We simply compute $(d + A)/(A + B)$, which can range from 0 to 1, for pixels next to the geometric line. If only a few gray-scale values are available (e.g., on a 2-bit-per-pixel machine), this approximation to the weighted overlap proves adequate. Because of its application to displays with few bits per pixel, this approach has been called *2-bit antialiasing*.

Finally, Hatfield's method [HATF89], described in detail in Section 19.3.3, can be applied rapidly to lines; in this case, it degenerates into an extension of a Gupta–Sproull scheme, in which the shape of the filter is defined at will.

19.3.2 Antialiasing Circles

Before we discuss antialiasing of circles, let us establish some terminology. A *disk* is a filled circle. A *circle* is the set of points at a fixed distance from a point in the plane, and hence is infinitely thin. When we refer to a *thick circle*, we mean the set of points whose distance to some center point lies between two values. The difference in the values is the thickness of the thick circle. Thus, a thick circle can be thought of as the (setwise) difference of a large disk and a slightly smaller one.

To antialias a circle drawn with a pen of unit thickness, we can do the following. For each point (x, y) near the circle, let $S(x, y)$ denote the decision variable in the circle algorithm. Then $S(x, y)$ is proportional to the signed distance of the point from the circle. This number, appropriately scaled, can be used as an index into a Gupta-Sproull-style look-up table, just as for lines. Recall that, with lines, we could take the overlap with two offset halfplanes and subtract. For circles, we can do a similar operation: We can compute the weighted overlap of the base of the filter with two concentric disks, and subtract the results to get the overlap with a thickened circle. With circles, however, there is a difference: The overlap of the base of the cone filter and a disk depends not only on the distance from the pixel to the edge of the disk, but also on the radius of the disk (see Fig. 19.42a).

We therefore need different tables for disks of different radii. Observe that, however, if we have a small region (i.e., a region contained in a disk of radius 2) near the edge of a disk whose radius is 10 pixels, as in Fig. 19.42(b), and another at the same distance from a halfplane, the coverage of the regions by the two primitives is similar (the difference is less than 0.004 for most distances). Thus, we can safely approximate all disks of radius 10 or greater as halfplanes, for the purpose of computing the pixel value in antialiasing, and can therefore use the intensity table developed in the straight-line antialiasing algorithm for

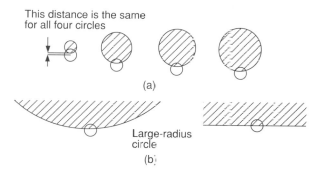

(a)

Large-radius
circle

(b)

Fig. 19.42 (a) The overlap of the base of the cone filter (shown as an open circle) and a disk differs for disks of different radii, even at the same distances from the disks. (b) The overlap of the base of the filter (or any other small region) and a disk of radius 10 is about the same as the overlap of the filter base and a halfplane.

circles of large radii. Smaller circles need individual tables; one table for each integer-sized disk, with linear interpolation to fill in the gaps, gives adequate results.

Pseudocode for an antialised circle algorithm is shown in Fig. 19.43. The algorithm determines the intensity values for pixels near a unit-thickness circle. The method is to determine, for each pixel near the circle of radius r, by how much it overlaps a disk of radius $r + \frac{1}{2}$ and a disk of radius $r - \frac{1}{2}$, and to subtract the two overlap values to find the overlap with a circle of thickness 1 at radius r. Of course, all these overlap computations are *weighted*. The sole difficulty is that, if r is not an integer, the overlaps with the two disks must be linearly interpolated. For example, if $r = 6.25$, we need to know the overlap of the pixel (remember that the pixel represents a *round* area in weighted-area sampling) with the disk of radius 5.75 and with the disk of radius 6.75. We estimate the first number by computing the overlap with the disk of radius 5 and the disk of radius 6, then interpolating three-quarters of the way from the first to the second. The second number is estimated similarly.

Finally, to render a thick circle (say 5 or more pixels), we can draw two concentric circles and invoke a fill algorithm; for thinner circles, we can draw spans, as in Chapter 3.

```
/* Draw an antialiased circle of radius r. */
void AntialiasedCircle (double r)
{
    int r0;                    /* The integer part of (r + 1/2) */
    double f;                  /* The fractional part of (r + 1/2) */
    double i1,                 /* Intensity due to a disk of radius (r0 − 1) */
        i2,                    /* Intensity due to a disk of radius r0 */
        i3;                    /* Intensity due to a disk of radius (r0 + 1) */
    double iInner,             /* Intensity due to a disk of radius (r0 − 0.5) */
        iOuter;                /* Intensity due to a disk of radius (r − 0.5) */

    r0 = greater integer less than or equal to r + .5;
    f = 0.5 + r − r0;
    for (each pixel near the scan-converted circle of radius r) {
        d = distance to circle of radius r;
            /* Proportional to the decision variable, S(x, y) */
        i1 = weighted area coverage of pixel by disk of radius (r0 − 1);
        i2 = weighted area coverage of pixel by disk of radius (r0);
        i3 = weighted area coverage of pixel by disk of radius (r0 + 1);

        iInner = (1 − f) * i1 + f * i2;    /* Interpolations */
        iOuter = (1 − f) * i2 + f * i3;
        intensity = iOuter − iInner;
        WritePixel (current pixel, intensity);
    }
}   /* AntialiasedCircle */
```

Fig. 19.43 Pseudocode for the antialiased circle algorithm.

A somewhat simpler algorithm is based on two observations. The first is that the overlap of the filter with a thickened circle is (for circles with large enough radii) directly related to the distance between the center of the filter and the circle. The second is that this distance is directly related to the value of the residual at the filter center. It is easy to prove that, for a point (x, y) near the circle, the residual $F(x, y) = x^2 + y^2 - R^2$ is approximately $2Rs$, where s is the distance from (x, y) to the circle. Thus, by dividing the residual by twice the radius, we can compute the distance to the circle. This distance can be used as an index into a table of intensity values, and hence can be used to determine the intensities for points near the circle (see Exercise 19.26).

19.3.3   Antialiasing Conics

Considerable effort has been expended on the search for a good way to generate antialiased conics. Pitteway's 2-bit algorithm [PITT87] is fine for machines with a few bits per pixel, but does not extend well to larger numbers of bits per pixel; it makes a linear approximation to the weighted overlap that differs perceptibly from the correct value when displays with several bits per pixel are used. Field's circle and ellipse algorithm [FIEL86] can handle only circles and aligned ellipses with integer centers, and does only unweighted area sampling. If we can keep track of the curvature of the conic at each point, and if the curvature is not too great, then using a collection of Gupta–Sproull–style look-up tables for circles of the same curvature can be made to work, but at considerable cost.

Hagen [HAGE88] gives a general method for antialiasing lines, conics, and cubic curves that is based on using an antialiasing value related to the distance of a point from the curve as usual, but his mechanism for determining nearby pixels is clever. If we want to fuzz out a curve over several pixels, we must determine which pixels are close to the curve. When an incremental algorithm is used to compute the points of the curve, it is either stepping in a principally horizontal direction (choosing between the east and northeast pixels at each stage, for example), or in a principally vertical direction (e.g., choosing between the north and northeast pixels at each stage). When the curve-tracking algorithm is stepping in a vertical direction, we can find points near to the curve by stepping out horizontally, and vice versa. As described in Chapter 3, however, this process leaves "notches" in thick curves at the changes of quadrant. Moreover, if this technique is used to determine which pixels to antialias, it leaves gaps in the antialiasing at the same points. Hagen's solution is to widen horizontally sometimes, vertically other times, and diagonally at other times (see Fig. 19.44).

Of course, this means that some points near the curve are assigned intensity values twice. The two values assigned should be nearly equal, so this reassignment is not a problem (assuming we are drawing in **replace** mode).[8] A difficulty does arise, however, in tightly bent curves (see Exercise 19.18). A pixel can be very near to two different parts of a curve, as in Fig. 19.45, so the value assigned to it should be the *sum* of the values from the

---

[8]All the algorithms we present are best suited for drawing primitives on an empty canvas in **replace** mode. To draw multiple primitives, we can generally draw the primitive on a private canvas, and then copy it to the final canvas using a MAX operator or some compositing operation.

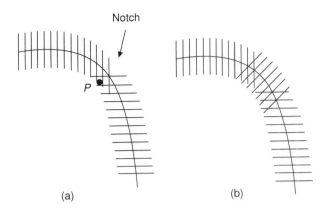

Fig. 19.44 Choosing where to compute antialiased values by determining which pixels are near a curve. If we always move either vertically or horizontally to determine nearby pixels, we get notches, as in (a). If we sometimes move diagonally, these notches can be filled in, as in (b).

two parts. Hagen notes this problem but presents no solution. Note that simply accumulating values in a pixel will not solve the problem: The pixel may be assigned a value twice either because of an overlap between a two different widenings of the curve (e.g., a pixel that is hit by both a horizontal and a diagonal widening, such as pixel P in Fig. 19.44), or because it is close to two different parts of the curve (e.g., pixel Q in Fig. 19.45).

Hagen's paper concludes by proposing a method for antialiasing of such curves using *width scans*: At each point, a line is drawn normal to the curve (using a scan-conversion algorithm for lines), and then an intensity is computed for each (sufficiently close) point along this normal line. This notion, described earlier, has been implemented and improved by Hatfield [HATF89]. He observes that, in scan converting a curve defined by an implicit function (such as $F(x, y) = x^2 + y^2 - R^2$ for the circle), when we compute the residue at each point P of the curve, we are computing various partial derivatives of the function. These in turn give the direction vector for a normal line to the curve.[9]

We can also find a good approximation to the place where a cubic curve crosses between two pixels by comparing the residuals at the pixels and doing a linear interpolation to infer where the residual is zero (see Fig. 19.46). If the residual is not zero at this point, iterating the procedure once will produce a very good estimate of the zero-crossing. (This technique is actually applicable to curves defined by higher-order polynomials as well.)

We can also compute, from the partial differences, a good approximation of the radius of curvature at each point. The formula for this is complex, but involves only the first and second derivatives of the implicit function F. The radius of curvature is the radius of the circle that best approximates the curve at the point; we therefore consider the curve to locally be a circle of that radius.

Thus, for each point on the scan-converted curve, we know the slope of the curve, the direction vector of the normal, the distance to the curve, and the radius of curvature of the

---

[9] Recall that we used the gradient in Chapter 3 to determine the normal vector.

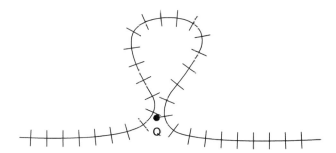

Fig. 19.45 On the inside of a tightly bent curve, points are close to two different pieces of the curve, and so should be brighter.

curve. Instead of horizontal, vertical, or diagonal stepping to widen the curve, we now scan convert the normal line to the curve, and compute the distance to the curve for each pixel. We use this distance as an index into an *intensity profile* describing the falloff of intensity as we move away from a circle whose radius is the current radius of curvature. To do exactly this would require computing (or providing by fine-tuning) an intensity profile for each possible radius of curvature, which is impractical. Fortunately, for radii greater than 10, Hatfield shows that assuming that the curve is straight at the point yields adequate results. For noninteger radii of curvature, indexing into adjacent (integer-radius) tables and interpolating can smooth out the results.

If we start with an intensity profile for an antialiased halfplane, we can compute the appropriate intensity profile for a narrow line or curve by shifting the profile slightly and subtracting. This corresponds to taking a halfplane and subtracting out a slightly shifted halfplane to generate values for a thin line. This technique works well for shifts as small as $\frac{1}{2}$ pixel (see Fig. 19.47). For shifts smaller than this, the lines look faint, but not thin. Of course, the total intensity of the pixels described by this profile curve is proportional to the area under the curve, so, to get comparably intense narrow curves, we must multiply the intensity profile by a number greater than 1. Hatfield reports that choosing the profile so as to maintain the intensity of the line without smearing is still more a matter of art than of science.

We can treat thick lines in a similar fashion, by simply adding up a collection of offset intensity profiles. For very thick curves, it is best to antialias the outside of the curve, and just to area fill the inside.

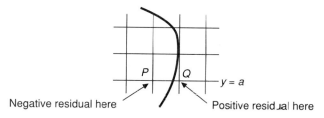

Negative residual here   Positive residual here

Fig. 19.46 The curve passes between the grid points P and Q, and hence the residuals at P and Q have opposite signs. If the residual at P is -10 and the residual at Q is 5, we can estimate that the curve crosses at a point two-thirds of the way from P to Q.

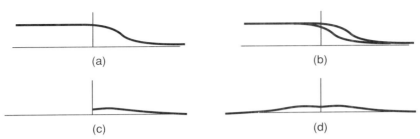

Fig. 19.47 The intensity profile for a halfplane is shown in (a). In (b), a second copy has been slightly displaced from it. In (c), the right half of the difference between them is shown; in (d), we see the full profile for a narrow line.

Note that the various lines along which the antialiasing is done may intersect if the width of the intensity profile is greater than the radius of curvature (see Fig. 19.48). The resulting intensities must be accumulated rather than just stored in the output pixmap.

19.3.4 Antialiasing General Curves

Methods for antialiasing general curves are few. One approach is to consider the curve as a sequence of very short straight lines and to use polygon antialiasing methods [TURK82; CROW78]. Another approach, described by Whitted [WHIT83], actually allows painting with an *antialiased brush*. The brush (a square array of pixels) is created at a very high resolution (it is 16 times as dense in each direction as the canvas into which the paint will be applied), and then is filtered to eliminate high-frequency components (the filter reduces the frequencies to one-sixteenth of the high-resolution sampling frequency; since this high-resolution brush eventually determines the values of pixels in a low-resolution bitmap, this filtering is necessary to avoid aliasing). The path along which the brush is dragged is also stored at high resolution (16 times the resolution in each direction). For each point on the path, those pixels in the high-resolution brush that correspond exactly to pixels in the

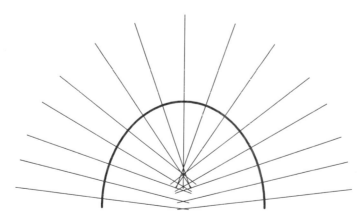

Fig. 19.48 When the radius of curvature is small but the intensity profile is wide, different points of the curve may contribute to the same output pixel.

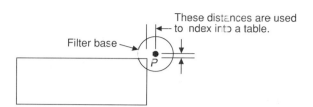

Fig. 19.49 We determine the intensity value for *P* by computing *P*'s distances from each of the edges at the corner. This pair of numbers is then used as an index into a look-up table.

low-resolution output pixmap are copied. Furthermore, each pixel in the brush and the output image is given a *z* value, and a *z*-buffer algorithm is used to control pixel copying. If the brush is given any nonflat (e.g., hemispherical) profile then it does not overwrite itself each time it is moved slightly. Furthermore, α values (coverage values) like those described in Section 17.6.1 are used to enhance the appearance of edges. The results of this technique are impressive (see Color Plate IV.2), but the computations for the image are costly, especially in terms of memory, since each image pixel needs R, G, B, and *z* values, and each brush pixel requires R, G, B, *z*, and α values. On the other hand, the preparation of brushes, although expensive, is done only once per brush and catalogs of brushes can be stored for later use. In particular, brushes that draw lines of various widths can be generated so as to create smooth curves, although this technique becomes impractical for very wide curves.

19.3.5   Antialiasing Rectangles, Polygons, and Line Ends

Gupta and Sproull [GUPT81a] present a method for generating antialiased line ends as well as lines. To begin with, computing antialiasing values for pixels near the corner of a large rectangle can be done explicitly, just as it was for lines. In this case, however, it depends on two numbers—the distances to each of the nearby sides—instead of on just the distance to the line. The overlap of a rectangle and the filter base for a pixel are shown in Fig. 19.49. What if the rectangle is very thin, however, as in Fig. 19.50? The filter base for pixel *Q* hits three sides of the rectangle. We can compute an antialiasing value for *Q* by subtraction: We compute its filter base's weighted overlap with two rectangles whose difference is the small rectangle, and subtract the two numbers to get the weighted overlap with the small rectangle. Thus, instead of having to make a table of values for overlaps for all possible

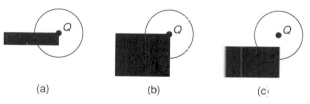

(a)   (b)   (c)

Fig. 19.50 The intensity value for a pixel near the end of a thin rectangle (or a thick line) can be computed by subtraction. Here, intensity for pixel *Q* in (a) is obtained by subtraction of (c) from (b).

distances from the pixel center to the four sides (which would be a table with four indices), we can use a two-index table twice, and perform a subtraction. If the pixel overlaps all four sides, we need to perform another addition and subtraction.

In a similar fashion, we can antialias a rectangle with rounded ends by computing the intensity of a rectangle plus that of a half-disk. Mitered thick lines can be treated by the methods used for a rectangle and, according to Hagen [HAGE88], polygons can be handled similarly. The intensity of a point near a corner of a polygon is computed by lookup into the table for the corner of a rectangle. If the angle is very different from 90°, the results are not particularly good. Hagen uses two additional tables, for 45° and 135° angles, as representative of acute and obtuse angles, and obtains good results with little effort.

19.4 THE SPECIAL PROBLEMS OF TEXT

The algorithms given so far have generated bitmap or antialiased versions of various geometric primitives, but we have not yet dealt with text. Text is a highly specialized entity, and our earlier techniques are usually not sufficient. In Chapter 3, we discussed using a font cache to store characters that could then be copied directly to the bitmap, but we also observed certain limitations of this approach: A different cache may be needed for each size of text, and the intercharacter spacing is fixed. Furthermore, although versions of bold or italic text can be created from this font cache, they are usually unsatisfactory.

Consider the letter "m." How do we create a bitmap version of an "m" from a precise description of it, given as a geometric drawing, by a font designer? Figure 19.51 shows a

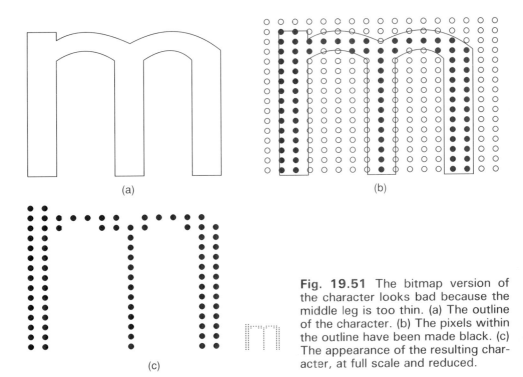

(a)

(b)

(c)

Fig. 19.51 The bitmap version of the character looks bad because the middle leg is too thin. (a) The outline of the character. (b) The pixels within the outline have been made black. (c) The appearance of the resulting character, at full scale and reduced.

drawing and a bitmap representation of an "m." Notice that, even with very careful scan-conversion, the middle leg of the "m" is thinner than are the outer two.

Thus, characters cannot be scan converted on a stroke-by-stroke basis. The geometry of character shape is deeply interrelated—certain elements must have the same width, certain topological characteristics must be preserved, and certain relationships among different characters in the same font must be preserved (in some fonts, for example, a width of a vertical segment of a capital "H" may need to be the same as the width of the hole in a capital "O"). Even if one manages to create characters with the right geometric relationships within and among then, there are artifacts that must be avoided. For example, in generating a capital "O" from a font-designer's plan, we must create two concentric oval arcs. When these are scan-converted to generate pixels representing the letter at some point size, the results can be disastrous. Figure 19.52 shows a letter "O" on a grid and the results of the scan-conversion process. The top of the "O" pokes just above a scan line, so that exactly 1 pixel on that scan line is turned on. The resulting character, which is said to have a *pimple*, is unattractive and difficult to read. Bitmap font-generating software must avoid such artifacts. Various vendors have developed rule-based software for satisfying geometric and typographical considerations such as these, but fonts must still be adjusted by hand, especially at very low resolutions. Such problems as these are only the most obvious. A great many others also arise, and addressing these is the task of the specialized field of *digital typography*; for further information, see [RUBE88].

In many ways, antialiased text is simpler than single-bit-per-pixel text. As long as the character is going to be antialiased, its location is irrelevant (antialiasing happens in the continuous, not in the discrete, world), so subpixel specification of character locations is possible, which is needed for high-quality output. Also, such artifacts as pimples, holes, and uneven-width stems disappear automatically. The problem that does remain is memory. Fonts are typically described by sequences of spline curves giving an outline for each character. Precomputing the appearance of all possible characters in a font (at several different subpixel locations, called *phases*) requires an immense amount of storage. Naiman and Fournier [NAIM87] estimate that, for a typical screen pixel density with a resolution of 8 bits per pixel, storing Roman, bold, italic, and bold-italic versions of two 128-character fonts at five point sizes and eight phases in both the vertical and horizontal directions requires over 50 MB of storage. Having 64 different phases may seem excessive to anyone

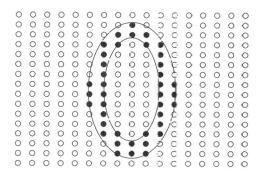

Fig. 19.52 Scan converting a letter "O" can generate a pimple at the top of the letter.

who has not tried to produce high-quality text output. But recall that we are talking about two fonts in only five sizes. Even ignoring phases, if we expand this to 10 fonts in 10 sizes, we soon approach the same 50 MB.

Another way to generate a character from such a family is to scale and translate the spline curves until they represent the character in the correct position,[10] and then to compute the antialiased image of the character at this position. This approach requires recomputing the antialiasing for each character every time it is used, and is computationally impractical unless clever methods for accelerating the process are discovered. Naiman and Fournier have developed just such a method. They decompose each character into subpieces much like the shape data structure described in the next section: each character is represented by a union of rectangles. This decomposition is done by scan converting the character at some very large point size to generate a *master* for it. This master is then broken into rectangles, and all smaller-sized characters are derived from the master by filtering.

At the most basic level, the filtered character is generated by convolving the master character (an $m \times m$ array of 0s and 1s, where m is typically much larger than the largest size character to be produced) with a filter function, which we represent as an $f \times f$ array of numbers whose sum is 1.0. The convolution is done by selecting an array of sample points within the master character array. If the output character is to be a $g \times g$ array (where g is less than m, of course), the sampling grid is also $g \times g$, and the space between samples is m/g. Notice that the sampling grid can be placed in m/g different positions in each of the horizontal and vertical directions (these offsets are the phases of the character). At this point, a copy of the $f \times f$ filter array is placed at each of the points in the sampling grid, and a value for the sample point is computed as follows: For each point in the filter array, the value of the filter is multiplied by the value in the master character bitmap at that point, and these results are summed. The resulting $g \times g$ array of samples is the filtered character (see Fig. 19.53).

Naiman and Fournier observe that computing the filtered value at each pixel is unnecessarily expensive. They represent the filter by a summed area table, as in Section 17.4.3; it is then easy to compute the filtered value of any rectangle. Since the master character is decomposed into rectangular pieces, they simply loop through all the rectangles in the master, compute overlaps with the filter box at the sample point, and determine the contribution to the intensity at the sample point by using summed area-table lookup. These intensities are accumulated over all rectangles in the master; the final result is the intensity of the pixel. Although this calculation must be done for each sample, it is still much faster on the average than is computing the filtered value at each point directly. We can improve the performance of the algorithm considerably by doing extent checking on the rectangle and the filter box before anything else, and by using inter–sample-point coherence in the list of rectangles that are intersected.

Antialiased text looks very good, and is already in use in the YODA display developed at IBM [GUPT86]. This kind of text, at normal size and magnified, is show in Color Plate IV.3.

---

[10]Slightly different curves may be needed to define a font at different sizes—scaling is not always sufficient.

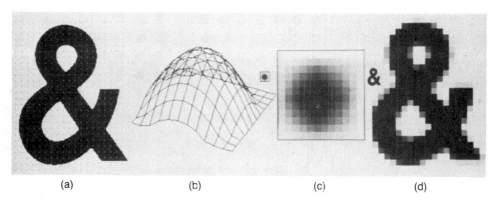

(a)   (b)   (c)   (d)

Fig. 19.53 (a) The master character overlaid with the sample grid. (b) A picture of the continuous filter. (c) A gray-scale representation of the filter, enlarged. (d) The filtered character, also enlarged. Courtesy of Avi Naiman, University of Toronto.

19.5 FILLING ALGORITHMS

Sometimes, after drawing a sequence of primitives, we may wish to color them in, or we may wish to color in a region defined by a freehand drawing. For example, it may be easier to make a mosaic pattern by creating a grid of lines and then filling it in with various colors than it is to lay down the colored squares evenly in the first place. Note that, when the first technique is used, no 2D primitives are drawn: We use only the 2D areas that happen to make up the background after the lines are drawn. Thus, determining how large a region to color amounts to detecting when a border is reached. Algorithms to perform this operation are called *fill algorithms*. Here we discuss *boundary fill*, *flood fill*, and *tint fill*. The last of these is a more subtle algorithm, being a type of *soft fill*. In it, the border of a region is determined not by the point at which another color is detected, but rather by the point at which the original color has faded to zero. Thus, a red region that fades to orange and then yellow (as might occur in the inside of a yellow circle drawn on a red canvas with antialiasing) can be converted to blue using tint fill. The orange areas are partly red, so their red component is replaced by blue; the result is a blue area, fading to green and bounded by yellow.

In all the filling algorithms we discuss, the value to be assigned to the interior pixels is called *newValue*. Following Fishkin and Barsky [FISH84], each algorithm can be logically divided into four components: a *propagation method*, which determines the next point to be considered; a *start procedure*, which initializes the algorithm; an *inside procedure*, which determines whether a pixel is in the region and should be filled; and a *set procedure*, which changes the color of a pixel.

19.5.1 Types of Regions, Connectivity, and Fill

A *region* is a collection of pixels. There are two basic types of regions. A region is *4-connected* if every 2 pixels can be joined by a sequence of pixels using only up, down, left, or right moves. By contrast, a region is *8-connected* if every 2 pixels can be joined by a sequence of pixels using up, down, left, right, up-and-right, up-and-left, down-and-right, or down-and-left moves. Note that every 4-connected region is also 8-connected.

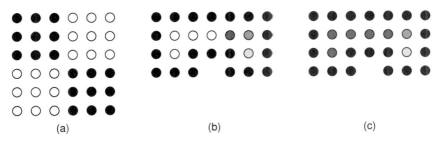

Fig. 19.54 The black pixels in (a) define an 8-connected region that is not 4-connected, since the diagonal between the two squares is not a 4-connection. The white pixels in (b) form the interior of the region if the region is interior-defined. The light- and dark-gray pixels are also in the interior if the region is boundary-defined by black pixels. If we try to fill this region with dark gray, starting at a white pixel, the result may be the one shown in (c), where the pixels on the extreme right were left unfilled because of the dark-gray pixel between them and the starting point.

A region can be defined in two ways. For each, we use a starting pixel, P. The *interior-defined* region is the largest connected region of points whose value is the same as that of the P. A *boundary-defined* region is the largest connected region of pixels whose value is *not* some given *boundary value*. Since most fill algorithms work recursively, and the recursion terminates when the next pixel already has the new color, problems may arise if the new value appears within a boundary-defined region, since some branch of the recursion may return prematurely (see Fig. 19.54).

Algorithms that fill interior-defined regions are called *flood-fill* algorithms; those that fill boundary-defined regions are called *boundary-fill* algorithms. Since both start from a pixel within the region, they are sometimes both called *seed-fill* algorithms.

19.5.2   The Basic Filling Algorithms

The most primitive propagation method is to move from the starting pixel in all four or all eight directions and to apply the algorithm recursively. For the FloodFill and BoundaryFill procedures given here, we have already determined the inside of the region, and the pixel-setting routine is just a call to WritePixel. Figure 19.55 presents the code for the 4-connected versions of the algorithms; the code for the 8-connected version has 8 recursive calls instead of four in each procedure.

These procedures, although simple, are highly recursive, and the many levels of recursion take time and may cause stack overflow when memory space is limited. Much more efficient approaches to region filling have been developed [LIEB78; SMIT79; PAVL81]. They require considerably more logic, but the depth of the stack is no problem except for degenerate cases. The basic algorithm in these approaches works with spans. These spans are bounded at both ends by pixels with value *boundaryValue* and contain no pixels of value *newValue*. Spans are filled in iteratively by a loop. A span is identified by its rightmost pixel; at least one span from each unfilled part of the region is kept on the stack.

The algorithm proceeds as follows. The contiguous horizontal span of pixels containing the starting point is filled. Then the row above the just-filled span is examined from right to left to find the rightmost pixel of each span, and these pixel addresses are

```
void FloodFill4 (
      int x, int y,                    /* Starting point in region */
      color oldValue,                  /* Value that defines interior */
      color newValue)                  /* Replacement value, must differ from oldValue */
{
   if (ReadPixel (x,y) == oldValue) {
      WritePixel (x, y, newValue);
      FloodFill4 (x, y − 1, oldValue, newValue);
      FloodFill4 (x, y + 1, oldValue, newValue);
      FloodFill4 (x − 1, y, oldValue, newValue);
      FloodFill4 (x + 1, y, oldValue, newValue);
   }
}   /* FloodFill4 */

void BoundaryFill4 (
      int x, int y,                    /* Starting point in region */
      color boundaryValue,             /* Value that defines boundary */
      color newValue)                  /* Replacement value */
{
   color c = ReadPixel (x,y);
   if (c != boundaryValue &&          /* Not yet at the boundary... */
       c != newValue) {                /* Nor have we been here before... */
      WritePixel (x, y, newValue);
      BoundaryFill4 (x, y − 1, boundaryValue, newValue);
      three other cases;
   }
}   /* BoundaryFill4 */
```

Fig. 19.55 The flood-fill and boundary-fill algorithms.

stacked. The same is done for the row below the just-filled span. When a span has been processed in this manner, the pixel address at the top of the stack is used as a new starting point; the algorithm terminates when the stack is empty. Figure 19.56 shows how a typical algorithm works. In Fig. 19.56(a), the span containing the starting point has been filled in (the starting point is shown with a hollow center), and the addresses of numbered pixels have been saved on a stack. The numbers indicate order on the stack: 1 is at the bottom and is processed last. The figure shows only part of the region-filling process; we encourage you to complete the process, step by step, for the rest of the region (see Exercises 19.19 and 19.20).

This algorithm can be further improved by avoiding redundant examinations of adjacent scan lines [SMIT79]. If, after a scan line has been filled, the line just above it is scanned for new span, and all the new spans have extents that lie entirely within the extents of the current scan line's spans (called the *shadow* of the current scan line), then during

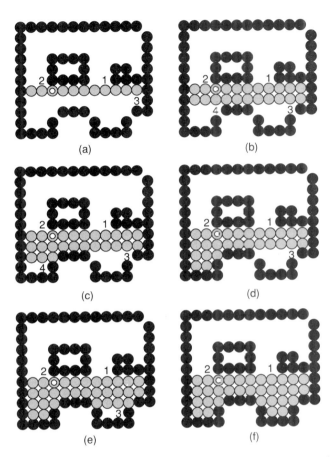

Fig. 19.56 The progress of the recursive fill algorithm. (a) The region with one span of pixels filled. The starting pixel has a hollow center. (b) through (f) Filling of subsequent spans.

processing of the upper scan line, the one beneath it does not need to be scanned for new spans. Also, the process of scanning a line for the spans can be combined with the process of filling the pixels, so multiple reads of each pixel are not necessary.

Better still, the entire process of scanning the lines above and below the current line can be accelerated at the cost of slightly greater memory use. After filling the current span of pixels, the line above is searched for a pixel that is connected to the current span, and this seed pixel is pushed onto the stack, *along with the endpoints of the current span* (henceforth called the *parent span*). The fill procedure is then invoked by starting at the seed pixel. If, after the fill procedure, the span that was filled does not extend past the ends of the parent span, scanning of the shadow of the parent span continues until another seed pixel is found, and this seed is used for starting a fill. In many cases, the span above the current span will be as large or larger than the current span, so that scanning for additional seed points is unnecessary [LEVO82].

19.5.3   Soft-Filling Algorithms

Soft filling is used to fill a region whose edge is blurred for some reason, typically antialiasing. It has been investigated by several authors [LEVO78; SMIT79], and Fishkin and Barsky have greatly extended Smith's techniques [FISH84]. We assume that the region is initially rendered in some foreground color against some other background color. If the region to be filled has an associated α value, as in Section 17.6.1, we can use it to detect the points inside the region and determine how they should be set: The *newValue* is mixed with the background color according to the fraction α, as is discussed in [LEVO78]. But many regions may require recoloring even though an α value is unavailable. Following Fishkin and Barsky, let us make three assumptions:

1. The region is rendered in a foreground color, F, against a background color, C. Each pixel in the image is a convex combination of F and C; that is, $P = tF + (1 - t)C$.

2. We have a region-traversal algorithm that visits each point once. The improved seed-filling algorithm can be tuned to do this; alternatively, we can mark each visited pixel with a flag.

3. The colors F and C are known and are not equal.

The basic algorithm for SoftFill is shown in Fig. 19.57.

Only the second step of this algorithm is difficult. Assuming that the colors are expressed as RGB triples, and writing $F = (F_R, F_G, F_B)$, and similarly for C and P, we know that, for some t, the following equations hold (by assumption 1):

$$P_R = tF_R + (1 - t)C_R, \qquad P_G = tF_G + (1 - t) C_G, \qquad P_B = tF_B + (1 - t) C_B.$$

If $F_R \neq C_R$, we can solve for t using just the first equation. If not, we can use the second, or even the third. Two problems arise. What if all six values on the right-hand sides

```
void LinearSoftFill (
    regionType region,
    color F,        /* Foreground color */
    color C,        /* Background color */
    color N)        /* New foreground color */
{
    for (each pixel in the region) {
        color P = color value for the pixel;
        find t so that P = tF + (1 - t) C.
        replace P with tN - (1 - t) C;
    }
} /* LinearSoftFill */
```

Fig. 19.57 The basic soft-fill algorithm.

are pairwise equal? What if the t values obtained by solving the three equations differ? The first situation occurs only if F and C are identical, which is ruled out by assumption 3. (Note that this assumption is entirely natural: If you were given a picture of a polar bear in a snowstorm and were asked to redraw the polar bear in brown, how would you know where the bear stopped and the snow began?) The second situation is more serious. In the strictest mathematical sense, it cannot happen, because P was formed as a linear combination of F and C. Nonetheless, in an integer world (which is how color values are typically expressed), there is roundoff error. The best inference of the value of t will come from the equation with the greatest difference between the F and C values. Thus, a slightly more robust algorithm is given in Fig. 19.58.

This algorithm has the disadvantage that it allows filling against a single background color only. We would like to be able to fill a picture of a frog sitting on a red-and-black checkerboard. Fishkin and Barsky [FISH84] address this problem by using some linear algebra, as follows. In an n-dimensional linear space, any sufficiently general $n + 1$ points determine a coordinate system. (All that is required is that no $(n - 1)$–dimensional affine subspace contain them all. For example, in 3D, four points are sufficiently general if no plane contains all of them.) If the points are $v_0, v_1, \ldots, v_n$, then any point p in the space

```
void LinearSoftFill (
        regionType region,
        color F,      /* Foreground color */
        color C,      /* Background color */
        color N)      /* New foreground color */
{
    int i;
    int d;

    /* Initialization section */
    find the i that maximizes |Fi−Ci| over i = R, G, B;
    d = |Fi−Ci|;

    /* Inside Test */
    for (each pixel) {
        color P = color value for the pixel;
        int t = (Pi − Ci) / d;
        if (t > some small value) {
            /* Setting pixel value */
            replace P with tN + (1 − t) C;
        }
    }
}   /* LinearSoftFill */
```

Fig. 19.58 The more robust soft-fill algorithm.

can be written uniquely as a combination

$$p = v_0 + t_1(v_1 - v_0) + t_2(v_2 - v_0) + \ldots + t_n(v_n - v_0),$$

where the t_i are real numbers. This is typically done with v_l being the origin of the space and $v_1, \ldots, v_n$ being a basis. By assuming that pictures drawn in several colors have pixels whose values are *linear* combinations of those colors, Fishkin and Barsky observe that each pixel value lies in an affine subspace of the color space. In the case of a foreground color drawn against a background color, this subspace is a line—the line consisting of all color triples between the foreground color and the background color in RGB space. If the foreground color is drawn against two background colors, then the subspace is a plane determined by the locations of the three colors in RGB space (unless the three colors all lie on a line, a degenerate case; this is an example of a set of points being insufficiently general). If the foreground color is drawn against three background colors, then the subspace is the entire RGB space, unless all four lie in a plane (another degeneracy). Notice that the analysis can go no further: *Any* five points in RGB space lie in a 3D affine space, and hence constitute a degenerate case. (If the colors are represented by n spectral samples, where $n > 3$, then more complex cases can be handled by similar methods.)

So let us consider the case of a foreground color, F, drawn against two background colors, C and D. Each pixel in the image is a convex combination of these:

$$P = t * F + s * C + (1 - t - s) * D.$$

The problem is to determine the values of t and s, so we can replace the pixel with the color

$$P = t * N + s * C + (1 - t - s) * D.$$

Writing the first equation in terms of R, G, and B components yields three simultaneous equations in two unknowns. Just as in linear fill, we can use any two of these to determine s and t. If two of the vectors $F - C$, $F - D$ and $C - D$ are close to parallel, however, then using the corresponding two equations produces greater roundoff error. The other problem with linear fill was the possibility that the system of equations had no solution. The analogous problem in this case occurs when the points F, C, and D are colinear in color space. Thus, for the algorithm to be effective, it is important that the colors be in general position in RGB space (i.e., that no three of them lie on a line in that space). This requirement can be seen intuitively as follows. Imagine a background composed of various shades of red, pink, and white, all of which are convex combinations of red and white. Now imagine a foreground image drawn in a salmon color—pink with just a little yellow. It is difficult for us to determine where the salmon ends and the pink begins. The algorithm has troubles making this type of discrimination as well.

We conclude with an extension that does not appear to be in the literature. If a foreground object is rendered in two colors on a background of another two colors, we can recolor the foreground object in a different two colors. Thus, we can change a red-and-green checkerboard lying on a zebra into a yellow-and-orange checkerboard. The mechanism is identical to the four-color extension of the fill algorithm just described. Suppose the two foreground colors are E and F and the background colors are C and D. We can solve the equation

$$P = rE + sF + tC + (1 - r - s - t)D$$

for the values r, s, and t (provided the colors C, D, E, and F are in general position). If we now wish to replace E and F by M and N, we simply set

$$P = rM + sN + tC + (1 - r - s - t)D.$$

An application of this mechanism is the following. A red sphere illuminated by a white light is rendered with careful shading, so the resulting object has smoothly varying colors that are combinations of red and white. This image is composited onto a blue-and-green checkerboard. We now decide that the sphere should have been a bluish-green sphere illuminated by a greenish-blue light. We can perform the preceding operation and generate the new image. Notice that this cannot be done by two applications of the more basic fill algorithm—after one substitution, the general-position condition no longer holds.

19.6   MAKING copyPixel FAST

In all our scan-conversion algorithms, we have tried to maintain scan-line coherence, since copying pixels (or writing pixels in any mode) is fastest when done for many pixels on a scan line at the same time. In the important case of 1-bit graphics, it is also a lot easier to copy a whole word's worth of bits at once. Setting individual bits in a word is almost as expensive as setting all the bits in the word. Thus, in a screen memory organized by words, doing a pixel-by-pixel operation is about n times slower than is doing a word-by-word operation, where there are n bits per word. (Even with 8-bit color, a 32-bit processor can copy 4 pixels at a time.) In discussing this operation in Chapter 3, we simply used SRGP_copyPixel, saying that its implementation was system-dependent. In general, a copyPixel procedure, when applied to 1-bit images, is known as bitBlt (for "bit block-transfer"); in this section, we discuss optimizing the bitBlt procedure, following Pike's description of a fast bitBlt routine for an MC68000 microprocessor [PIKE84].

We want to implement a bitBlt function that supports clipping to a rectangle, arbitrary write modes, and texturing. Texturing is essentially patterning during bitBlt. A window manager can use texturing when a window becomes inactive. By texturing the window with a stipple texture, the window manager can inform the user that the window must be activated before it can be used. Doing this stippling in the course of a bitBlt is much faster than is redrawing all the primitives in the window with a stipple pattern. Thus, we want to define a procedure as shown in Fig. 19.59.

The region to be copied is a rectangle of the same size as *rect* with origin at *pt* in the source bitmap. The target region is the one specified by *rect* in the *destination* bitmap. The texture is a $w \times w$ array of bits, where w is the size of a word on the machine. We assume that w is 32 and that a texture is actually represented by an array of 32 words.

Implementing this procedure is straighgforward, but involves a fair number of cases. If the texture is all 1s, we want to avoid applying it. If either the source rectangle or destination rectangle lies partially or completely outside the corresponding bitmap, we want to avoid accessing those regions. The two bitmaps may be the same, and the source and

```
void bitBlt(
        bitmap source,           /* Source bitmap */
        point pt,                /* Corner of region to be copied */
        texture tex,             /* Texture to apply during copying */
        bitmap destination,      /* Target bitmap */
        rectangle rect,          /* Location of target region */
        writeMode mode);
```

Fig. 19.59 The procedure declaration for bitBlt.

destination rectangles may overlap, so we must do our copying in a nondestructive order. And finally, each write mode may require special handling, since some may be easily implemented by single machine instructions, whereas others may require multiple instructions, especially when they operate on partial words.

It is fortunate that C provides direct access to processor memory, since the bitBlt operation involves operations on individual bits, of course, and doing this as directly as possible can vastly increase the efficiency. The first version of the algorithm that we'll describe uses bit-shifting, bit-masking, pointer arithmetic, and pointer comparison extensively, and by doing so achieves a *reasonable* speed—one which would be impossible in languages that did not provide such direct memory access. Nonetheless, as we'll see, even this is not fast enough for practical use, and the ultimate version of bitBlt must be implemented in assembly language. This represents a standard design trade-off: that for the core of a time-critical system, one must make things as efficient as possible, while operations at the periphery may often be less efficient but more easily maintained or modified.

The basic data structure is the bitmap. To take advantage of word-by-word operations, we must arrange the bitmap as an array of words. We also want to be able to create bitmaps whose size is not a multiple of 32. Our bitmaps are therefore records with three fields: a pointer to an array of words (see Fig. 19.60); a rectangle describing a subset of the bits

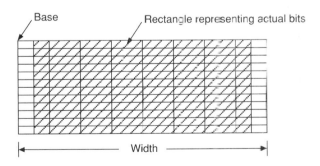

Fig. 19.60 The bitmap is an array of words, containing a rectangle that represents the actual bits of the bitmap.

represented by that array; and an integer, *width*, that says how many bits there are in each group of words storing a row of the rectangle. If the edges of the rectangle are aligned with the word boundaries, this value is just the width of the rectangle in pixels; if not, it is somewhat greater. Figure 19.61 gives the pseudocode for the basic bitBlt algorithm. Unfortunately, the actual code is quite a lot messier. The basic bitBlt code in Pascal is shown in Fig. 19.62.

Pike remarks that a C version of this code takes about 8 minutes to scroll an 800- by 1024-pixel bitmap horizontally, on an 8-MHz MC68000 processor. He also describes several improvements. The first is to eliminate the many calls to MoveBit by constructing a word of bits and moving it all at once, using word-at-a-time logical instructions available in C and assembler. This change gives a speedup of a factor of 16—the same scrolling takes only about 30 seconds.

When we bitBlt a large region on the screen with the basic code, we call the MoveBit routine hundreds of thousands of times. Even if we move only words, we still must do so thousands of times. Executing the smallest possible amount of code in this inner loop is thus extremely desirable. Notice that, when the source and destination bitmaps have the same offsets, much of the bit shifting can be avoided. If regions are to be copied off of and onto some bitmap (typically the screen), keeping the offscreen bitmaps with the same offset as their onscreen correspondents can save a great deal of time.

Since moving large regions on the screen is an extremely common activity, accelerating this process in any way possible is worthwhile. Since all that is really involved is detecting this special case and then calling (repeatedly) the assembler instruction to move a 32-bit word, indirectly, and to increment pointers, we can do nothing more than to hope that the instruction is very fast.

To accelerate bitBlt substantially, we must move to assembler language. The trick here is to look at the regions moved and the mode used, and to determine from these whether to scan left to right or right to left, whether to scan top to bottom or bottom to top, whether any rotation of bits is necessary, and so on. From this information, a fast bitBlt routine can generate optimal assembler code to execute the actual bitBlt, and then can jump to that

> *clip the rectangles to the source and destination bitmaps;*
> *find the width and height of the rectangle in bits;*
> **if** (*either is negative*)
>   *return gracefully from procedure;*
>
> *compute a pointer, p1, to the first bit of the source rectangle;*
> *compute a pointer, p2, to the first bit of the destination rectangle;*
> **if** (*p1 comes before p2 in memory*) {
>   *move p1 to the lower right word in the source rectangle;*
>   *move p2 to the lower right word in the destination rectangle;*
>   *copy rows of the source to rows of the destionation, bottom to top;*
> } **else**
>   *copy rows of the source to rows of the destination, top to bottom;*

Fig. 19.61 Pseudocode for the basic bitBlt algorithm.

```
typedef struct {                          /* This is not the rectangle type of Chapter 2 */
    point topLeft, bottomRight;
} rectangle;

typedef struct {
    char *base;                           /* Pointer to first word of memory for the bitmap */
    int width;
    rectangle rect;
} bitmap;

typedef struct {
    unsigned int bits:32;
} texture;

typedef struct {
    char *wordptr;
    int bit;
} bitPointer;

void bitBlt(
        bitmap map1,                      /* Source bitmap */
        point point1;                     /* Corner of region to be copied */
        texture tex;                      /* Texture to apply during copying */
        bitmap map2;                      /* Target bitmap */
        rectangle rect2;                  /* Location of target region */
        writeMode mode)
{
    int width;
    int height;
    bitPointer p1, p2;

    /* Clip the source and destination rectangles to their bitmaps. */
    clip x-values;                        /* See procedure that follows */
    clip y-values;
    /* width and height of region in bits */
    width = rect2.bottomRight.x − rect2.topLeft.x;
    height = rect2.bottomRight.y − rect2.topLeft.y;
    if (width < 0 || height < 0)
        return;

    p1.wordptr = map1.base;               /* Points at source bitmap */
    p1.bit = map1.rect.topLeft.x % 32;
```

Fig. 19.62 (*Cont.*)

/* And the first bit in the bitmap is a few bits further in */
/* Increment $p1$ until it points to the specified point in the first bitmap */
IncrementPointer $(p1, point1.x - map1.rect.topLeft\_x + map1.width *$
$(point1.y - map1.rect.topLeft.y))$;

/* Same for $p2$—it points to the origin of the destination rectangle */
$p2.worldptr = map2.base$;
$p2.bit = map2.rect.topLeft.x \% 32$;
IncrementPointer $(p2, rect2.topLeft.x - map2.rect.topLeft.x +$
$map2.width * (rect2.topLeft.y - map2.rect.topLeft.y))$;
if $(p1 < p2)$ {
    /* The pointer $p1$ comes before $p2$ in memory; if they are in the same bitmap, */
    /* the origin of the source rectangle is either above the origin for the */
    /* destination or, if at the same level, to the left of it. */
    IncrementPointer $(p1, height * map1.width + width)$;
    /* Now $p1$ points to the lower-right word of the rectangle */
    IncrementPointer $(p2, height * map1.width + width)$;
    /* Same for $p2$, but the destination rectangle */
    $point1.x += width$;
    $point1.y += height$;
    /* This point is now just beyond the lower right in the rectangle */
    while $(height-- > 0)$ {
        /* Copy rows from the source to the target bottom to top, right to left */
        DecrementPointer $(p1, map1.width)$;
        DecrementPointer $(p2, map2.width)$;
        $temp\_y = point1.y \% 32$;   /* Used to index into texture */
        $temp\_x = point1.x \% 32$;
        /* Now do the real bitBlt from bottom right to top left */
        RowBltNegative $(p1, p2, width,$ BitRotate $(tex[temp\_y],temp\_x),mode)$;
    } /* while */
} **else** {   /* if $p1 \geq p2$ */
    while $(height-- > 0)$ {
        /* Copy rows from source to destination, top to bottom, left to right */
        /* Do the real bitBlt, from top left to bottom right */
        RowBltPositive $(same arguments as before)$;

Fig. 19.62 (*Cont.*)

code. The idea is that this assembler code is so brief and efficient that it can be cached and executed very quickly. For example, the screen-scrolling described previously is executed in 0.36 seconds—an impressive speedup! The assembly code generated to scroll the whole screen is a masterpiece of compactness: It consists of only eight instructions (assuming that various registers have been set up beforehand).

```
        increment pointers;
      }  /* while */
   }  /* else */
}  /* bitBlt */

void ClipValues (bitmap *map1, bitmap *map2, point *point1, rectangle *rect2)
{
   if (*point1 not inside *map1) {
      adjust *point1 to be inside *map1;
      adjust origin of *rect2 by the same amount;
   }
   if (origin of *rect2 not inside *map2) {
      adjust origin of *rect2 to be inside *map2;
      adjust *point1 by same amount;
   }
   if (opposite corner of *rect2 not inside *map2)
      adjust opposite corner of *rect2 to be inside;
   if (opposite corner of corresponding rectangle in *map1 not inside *map1)
      adjust opposite corner of rectangle;
}  /* ClipValues */

void RowBltPositive(
      bitPtr p1, bitPtr p2,          /* Source and destination pointers */
      int n,                         /* How many bits to copy */
      char tword,                    /* Texture word */
      writeMode mode)                /* Mode to blt pixels */
{
   /* Copy n bits from position p1 to position p2 according to mode */
   while (n-- > 0) {
      if (BitIsSet (tword, 32))      /* If texture says it is OK to copy... */
         MoveBit (p1, p2, mode);     /* then copy the bit. */
      IncrementPointer (p1);
      IncrementPointer (p2);
      RotateLeft (tword);            /* Rotate bits in tword to the left. */
   }  /* while */
}  /* RowBltPositive */
```

Fig. 19.62 The bitBlt algorithm (with some special cases omitted).

The code for more complex cases is more elaborate but is equally efficient. We *could* design bitBlt by using massive switch statements or case statements to execute all possible combinations of rectangles, textures, modes, and so on. In fact, the entire program could be written as a loop in the form "for each row, for each word, do the following: If the word is a partial word, do . . .; if it needs a texture, do . . .; and so on." The disadvantage with this is that all the cases must be examined, even for the simplest case to be executed. All the assembler code for the massive **if** and **switch** statements would never fit into a tiny instruction cache. Since the loop is executed many times, the cost of loading the code into the instruction cache might far outweigh the cost of actually doing the work of bitBlt. Alternatively, the code might be written as a massive nested **if** statement, in which each possible case is optimally coded and occurs as a branch in the decision tree. Then when this case occurred, that tiny fragment of optimal code could be loaded into the instruction cache and executed very quickly. The problem with this approach is that there are a great many cases; Pike estimates that there are about 2000 different cases, taking about 150 bytes on the average. This makes the code for bitBlt approach 1 MB, which is clearly excessive. So, instead, we have the bitBlt routine collect bits of assembler code, which are then used to execute the loop. Each case in the nested **if** statement contributes its own fragment to the final code to be executed. Of course, since this code must be collected in the data space, instead of in the address space of the processor, the instruction cache must be informed that certain bytes are no longer valid, so that it will be certain to reload the code instead of using the code from the last bitBlt that executed. All this must be combined with a certain amount of knowledgeable juggling to determine whether to separate out a case and to hard code it (e.g., bitBlt for very small rectangles—less than one full word).

Implementors of such systems should look for hardware support as well. The more of bitBlt we implement in microcode, the easier it is to make the rest extremely efficient.

19.7 THE SHAPE DATA STRUCTURE AND SHAPE ALGEBRA

The *shape* data structure has been developed to make raster operations (especially clipping) more efficient [DONA88; GOSL89; STEI89]. It lies somewhere on the boundary between the geometries of the Euclidean plane and the rasterized plane, in that shapes are used to represent raster approximations of regions that are typically defined by geometric constructions, but have been scan-converted into rasterized representations. The advantages of shapes over bit masks in defining regions are twofold: shapes are typically smaller data structures, and Boolean operations on shapes are fast. Furthermore, shapes are organized in a way that takes advantage of scan-line coherence, so that line-by-line processing of shapes can be made fast. Other methods for implementing faster raster operations have been developed as well, including implementations of the shape data structure using run-length encoding [STEIN89], and quadtreelike systems [ATKI86].

Before giving a precise definition of a shape, let's consider an example. The U-shaped region shown in Fig. 19.63(a) can be broken into several rectangular pieces, as shown in part (b).

In fact, any collection of pixels can be broken into a disjoint union of rectangular regions in the plane. In the most extreme case, for example, we can place a small square around each pixel. The shape data structure is designed to describe regions in the rasterized plane as lists of rectangles. More precisely, a shape consists of a list of intervals along the y axis and, for each of these, a list of intervals on the x axis. Each (y interval, x interval) pair represents the rectangle that is the Cartesian product of the two intervals. The region in Fig. 19.63(a), for example, would be decomposed into the rectangles [0, 10] × [0, 2], [0, 3] × [2, 4], and [7, 10] × [2, 4], as shown in Fig. 19.63(b); these would be stored in two groups,

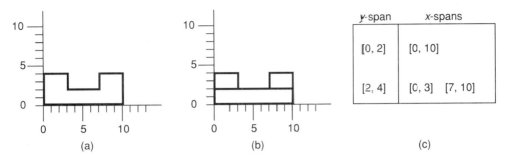

y-span	x-spans	
[0, 2]	[0, 10]	
[2, 4]	[C, 3]	[7, 10]

(a)   (b)   (c)

Fig. 19.63 (a) A region. (b) Its division into rectangles. (c) The shape data structure for the region.

corresponding to the y intervals [0, 2] and [2, 4]. The first group would have one x interval and the second would have two, as shown in Fig. 19.63(c). Note, however, that although this data structure is extremely efficient for rectangular regions and simple regions such as the one in Fig. 19.63(a), for more general regions it becomes less efficient. For a filled circle, for example, there is a rectangle for each horizontal scan line, so the structure becomes just a list of spans.

If we create a shape for a scan-converted primitive, and also have a shape for the region within which we want to draw the primitive (typically a window), we can find the shape of the clipped version of the primitive by taking the intersections of the shapes. Furthermore, creating a shape for the scan-converted primitive may be easy, since many scan-conversion algorithms work in some scan-line order. For example, the polygon scan-conversion algorithm in Chapter 3 used an active-edge table, which it then scanned to generate horizontal spans. These spans are exactly the rectangles needed for the shape structure. A similar technique can be used for a region with curved edges. Since curves can have multiple x values for a single y value, it is important to break them into pieces with the property that for each y value, there is only one x value on the curve segment (see Fig. 19.64), and then to scan convert these with an algorithm like that for the active-edge table, described in Chapter 3.

Shapes can also be used to generate joined lines or polylines without the problems caused by repeated **xor** operations on the same pixel. Here, the entire shape is constructed and then is drawn once in **xor** mode. Figure 19.65 shows how a blunt line join can be represented as a union of shapes (see also Exercise 19.21).

One of the principal virtues of shapes is the ease with which they are combined under Boolean operations (recall from Section 15.10.3 that Boolean operations on intervals in a

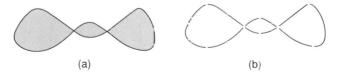

(a)   (b)

Fig. 19.64 The curved outline for the area shown in (a) must be broken into curve segments, as shown in (b), before it can be used to generate a shape structure for the area.

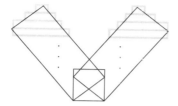

Fig. 19.65 Making a blunt join between two lines using a union of shapes.

line were used in ray tracing to implement constructive solid-geometry operations). Consider the intersection of the two shapes shown in Fig. 19.66(a). The shape structures for both are given in the table, and the intersection and its shape structure are shown in part (b). How can the intersection be computed from the original shapes?

Notice that the intersection of two overlapped rectangles is always a rectangle. Thus, we can compute the intersection of two shapes by searching for overlapping rectangles. We first check to see that the y extents of the shapes overlap (if not, there is no intersection). Then, starting with the first y interval for each shape (i.e., the one with lowest y value), we compare y intervals. If they overlap, we compare x intervals to generate output. If not, we increment the one with the lower y value to the next y interval in its data structure, and repeat. Assuming we have a function, Overlap, that compares two y intervals for overlap, returning a code characterizing the type of overlap, the pseudocode for this operation is as given in Fig. 19.67.

The processing of overlapping x intervals is exactly the same: If two x intervals overlap, the intersection is output and one or both of the two intervals is updated. Thus, the entire algorithm rests on processing the overlaps to determine a result code, then deciding what to do depending on the result code.

The six cases of x-interval overlap are shown in Fig. 19.68. In the first case, shown in part (a), the two segments are disjoint. No output is generated, and the update process consists of taking the next segment in shape2. The second case is the same, as shown in part (b), except that the next segment is taken from shape1. In the third case, in part (c), there is an overlap of the segments given by the minimum end of the segment from shape1 and the maximum end of the segment from shape2. Updating entails taking the next segment from

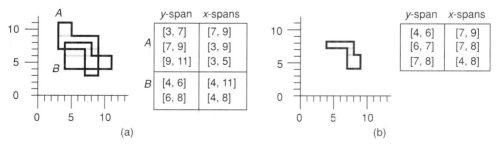

Fig. 19.66 The intersection of two shapes. (a) The two shapes, and their associated data structures. (b) The intersection, and its data structure.

```
void Intersect (shape shape1, shape shape2)
{
        int y11, y12;      /* Endpoints of y interval in shape 1 */
        int y21, y22;      /* Endpoints of y interval in shape 2 */
        int result;

        if (neither shape is empty && bounding boxes overlap) {
            y11 = lowest y-value for shape1;
            y12 = other end of first y-interval in shape1;
            same for y21, y22;

            while (still have y-interval in both shapes {
                result = Overlap (y11, y12, y21, y22)
                if (result says overlap occurred) {
                    output overlap of y-range, determined from code;
                    output overlapping x-ranges if any;
                    if no x-output generated, delete the y-overlap just output
                }
                update one or both y-intervals based on result;
            }
        } else       /* if */
            do nothing;
}     /* Intersect */
```

Fig. 19.67 The algorithm for intersecting two shapes.

shape2. The remaining cases are similar. The algorithms for union and difference are based on the same consideration of the overlap structure (see Exercise 19.22).

The shape algebra can be extended to a combined intersect-and-fill routine to be used in drawing primitives in a clip region. Instead of merely generating the x and y ranges of the shapes, we take each rectangular piece in the output and draw it as a filled rectangle (using a fast copyPixel procedure).

This shape algebra has been used in implementing the NeWS and X11/NeWS window systems. Three optimizations are worth considering. First, in some cases, the shapes representing a primitive are cumbersome (slanted lines are a good example), and, to compute the intersection of the primitive with another shape, we may find it simpler to do

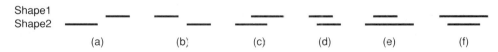

Fig. 19.68 The six ways that two intervals can overlap.

analytic clipping to each rectangle of the shape (Gosling suggests this for lines [GOSL89]). Second, shapes may become fragmented after many operations (taking $(A - B) \cup B$ can do this), and it may be worthwhile to condense a shape after several operations. Third, in window managers, it may be worthwhile to write a special-purpose intersect-and-fill routine that computes the shape intersection between a primitive and a window, optionally applies a pattern to the result, and draws the result all in one operation. Thus, instead of the output shape data structure being generated, the spans generated by the intersection routine are passed directly to a drawing routine.

19.8 MANAGING WINDOWS WITH bitBlt

In a seminal paper, Pike [PIKE83] described using the bitBlt procedure to manage windows (which he called ''layers'') on a bitmapped screen. The critical features were that the overlapping and refreshing of windows were isolated from the application program generating the window contents, that the nonscreen memory used was not too great (about one screen's worth of offscreen memory), and that the windows could be drawn in even when partially or completely obscured. Although overlapping windows had already been introduced in the Smalltalk world [BYTE85], this paper was the first to show how to implement them on an arbitrary machine supporting bitBlt. The ideas of this paper are now seen in the X Windows System, the Lisa operating system, the Macintosh operating system, and many other windowing systems.

Offscreen management of obscured windows is still done in some systems, as we discussed in Chapter 10 (it is called ''backing store'' in the X Windows System), but it has a substantial cost: As the number of windows increases, the amount of backing store required increases as well. The results when the machine runs out of physical memory must be considered. If the writer of applications for the window system knows that the window system provides a ''virtual window'' in which to write, that the application may write to it even when it is obscured, and that the window system takes care of refreshing the screen when the window is moved to the top, then the window system must provide this feature regardless of what else appears on the screen. Since an application's window may be completely covered at some point, the window system must allocate enough memory to provide backing store for the whole window at the time the window is created. Doing this for every one of several applications running simultaneously may become prohibitively expensive.

For this reason, some window systems (e.g., the X Windows System) provide backing store as a option but also allow windows that are not backed up, which must use a different regeneration strategy, as we discussed in Chapter 10. When a window is exposed after being partially or completely hidden, the window manager tells the application which parts of the window need to be refreshed, and the application may regenerate these portions in any manner it chooses. Typically, it redraws any primitive that intersects the newly exposed region. The benefits of such a system are that the application can determine as it runs how much memory it needs (so that the window manager can never tell the application that no more memory is available for storing the offscreen portion of the bitmap), and that the time spent in restoring the offscreen portions can be eliminated in cases where the restoration is unnecessary. The costs are that each application must be aware of the status of the window into which it is drawing, and that application programmers cannot pretend they have completely exposed windows.

Assuming, however, that we wish to have backing store for each window, we still must implement, in an efficient manner, the various window operations described in Chapter 10. These include window creation, deletion, exposure, and hiding, as well as drawing into windows. The remainder of this section is a description of Pike's method for doing these operations.

The data structure representing a window consists of a rectangle and an array of words (i.e., the bitmap record of Section 19.6), together with three additional fields: two window pointers, to the windows in front of and in back of the window; and one pointer to an obscured list, which is a linked list of bitmaps representing obscured portions of a window. The pointers to the windows in front and in back help in making windows visible or hiding them, since the list helps to determine what must be exposed or hidden. The ordering of windows is only partial, so the choices of front and back pointers are not completely determined. In any case where the choice is not obvious, an arbitrary one is made.

Hiding a window entails finding all windows behind it and placing them in front of it, in order. Doing this may require merely clearing space on the screen and calling the application that owns each window to do damage repair or may involve more work if the windows actually maintain information in their obscured list. For example, if the refresh task has been left to the windows' software, then hiding involves bitBlting the obscured portion of the newly exposed window onto the screen, while bitBlting the newly obscured portion of the current window into its obscured list. Fortunately, the amount by which window A can cover window B is exactly the same as the amount by which window B can cover window A, so no new memory needs to be allocated to execute this change of places. Exposing a window is similar, and moving a window involves revealing or hiding new portions and doing bitBlts to move the visible portions of the window. Of course, the assumption that there is a piece of memory that is just the right size to represent the amount by which B covers A or vice versa requires that the obscured lists be very finely divided: Each bounding rectangle for an obscured region must lie entirely within any window that it intersects.

Another task to consider is drawing into a window. In Fig. 19.69, there are two overlapping windows. In drawing an item in the lower window (shown as a shaded region),

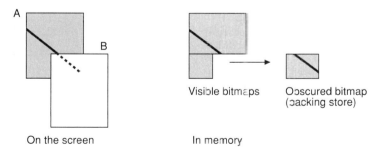

Visible bitmaps   Obscured bitmap
                       (backing store)

On the screen   In memory

Fig. 19.69 Drawing into a partially obscured layer requires drawing in both the visible portion and in some obscured portions. We split the item to be drawn into two pieces, and draw each in the appropriate bitmap.

part of the item is drawn in the visible portion and part is drawn in an obscured rectangle. This is a specific case of a general task: Take some operation and do it in each of the bitmaps representing the target region of the operation. Such an operation might be to clear a rectangle or to draw a line, for example. This operation can be condensed into a single recursive procedure that applies the operation to the intersection of the target region and the window, and then calls itself on each item in the window's obscured list.

Note that the design of the window data structure includes a choice regarding rectangles: each rectangle is defined to contain its left and bottom edges and its lower-left corner, just as it did in Chapter 3. Thus, no two abutting rectangles share any points. This choice vastly simplifies many operations, since it becomes possible to satisfy the rule that each rectangle in any obscured list lies entirely within any window it intersects. If rectangles contained both their edges, satsifying the condition would be impossible.

The original "layers" model for window management has been greatly extended. Several features have been added, including color. When color is added, copying images to and from the screen becomes more complex. Each pixel is represented by a collection of bits, rather than by a single bit, and transferring all the bits for the pixel may take a long time. Suppose, for example, that the display uses 4 bits for each of red, green, and blue. We could imagine this as simply 12 planes' worth of bits needing to be transferred to the screen, and we could apply the bitBlt operation to each. This strategy is called the *plane-serial* approach, since the planes are processed one at a time. The plane-serial approach has the advantage of being easy to implement as an extension of the bitmap version of the window-management software, but has two serious drawbacks: It is (in this case) 12 times as slow, which may be disastrous for performance; and, while the various planes are being transferred, the window may look very peculiar. For example, when all the red planes have been handled but the green and blue have not, the window looks like a blue-green version of the old material with a red overlay of the new material. This effect is extremely distracting if it persists for long enough to be detected. In a color-table system, the results would be even more exotic: During the transfer of planes, the color indices would become permuted wildly, which would result in an extremely distracting appearance. The alternative is the *plane-parallel* approach, in which all the planes of the pixmap are copied at the same time (perhaps by special-purpose hardware). Since the organization of display memory and of main memory can be somewhat different (although the Pike paper assumes they are not), it is essential in doing block transfers to use the most efficient method for the given source and target. This requirement in turn demands that, in any practical implementation of this kind of system, the block transfer operation be implemented at the lowest possible level—in assembler or machine language, or even in hardware.

19.9 PAGE-DESCRIPTION LANGUAGES

A *page-description language* is basically a graphics package developed to insulate the application writer from the machine-dependent details of printers, and to aid in the layout of printed pages in the publishing industry. A page-description language differs from an ordinary graphics package in several ways: it is output-only, it is a 2D package (although 3D extensions to some languages are being developed), it has extensive support for curves and text, and it supports sampled images as first-class primitives. More important, it is a language instead of a subroutine package. Thus, an interpreter for the language can be resident in a printer; as a result, short programs, instead of huge volumes of pixel data, are sent to the printer. Furthermore, page-description languages can be used more readily than can subroutine packages as an interchange format. A sequence of subroutine calls can be made in many different languages; transferring the sequence of calls to another installation may require translation to a new language. A program in a page-description language can be transferred to any installation that supports the language. Thus, a page-description language supersedes the notion of metafiles described in Section 7.11.3.

The best-known page-description language is POSTSCRIPT. The original intent of this language was to describe the appearance of a bitmap page (to be produced typically on a very high-resolution printer). POSTSCRIPT is now being used as a screen-description language as well. Page-description languages are particularly well suited to this task, especially in client–server window managers, where downloading a POSTSCRIPT program to the server can reduce network traffic and overhead on the client. As described in Chapter 10, invoking a dialogue box in a POSTSCRIPT-based window manager can be done by downloading a POSTSCRIPT procedure that displays the dialogue box and then invoking the procedure. Subsequent invocations of the dialogue box are made by simply invoking the procedure again.

There is also interest in generating a national or international standard page-description language derived from POSTSCRIPT and Interpress [ISO]. Such a language might provide a standard format for both the publishing industry and the computing industry.

In this section, we describe aspects of POSTSCRIPT, to give you a sense of how page-description languages work. The *imaging model* of a page-description language is the definition of the abstract behaviour of the language on an ideal 2D plane. In POSTSCRIPT, the imaging model is based on the notion of painting with opaque paint on a plane. The paint is applied by a pen or brush of a user-specified width, and many POSTSCRIPT operators control the position of this pen. This imaging model is actually implemented by having a large raster memory that reflects the contents of a page; the contents of this raster memory are eventually transferred to the output page by a printer.

The POSTSCRIPT language has effectively three components: the syntax, the semantics, and the rendering. The difference between the semantics and the rendering is a subtle one. The POSTSCRIPT program

```
10.5   11.3   moveto
40     53.6   lineto
showpage
```

means "move the pen, without drawing, to position (10.5, 11.3) on the page, draw a line to position (40, 53.6), and display the results." This sentence is an example of the semantics of the language. The *rendering* is the production of actual output on a particular graphics device. On a laser printer, this program might draw 5000 tiny black dots on a piece of paper; on a bitmapped screen, it might draw 87 pixels in black. Thus, what we are calling the rendering of a POSTSCRIPT program is at the level of a device driver for a bitmapped device.

POSTSCRIPT syntax is fairly simple. It is a postfix interpreter in which operands are pushed onto a stack and then are processed by operators that use some number of operands from the stack (popping them off the stack) and place some number of results on the stack. Thus, in the preceding example, the operands 10.5 and 11.3 were pushed on the stack, and the **moveto** operator popped them from the stack and used them. The data types supported include numbers, arrays, strings, and associative tables (also known as dictionaries). (More precisely, there is only one data class—the *object*; each object has a type, some attributes, and a value. The type may be "integer," "real," "operator," etc.) The associative tables are used to store the definitions of various objects, including operator definitions. The flow-of-control constructs include conditionals, looping, and procedures. Thus, a typical application producing POSTSCRIPT output may either (1) produce a long string of standard POSTSCRIPT calls, or (2) define a collection of procedures more closely related to its own needs (called a *prologue*), then produce a collection of calls to these procedures.

POSTSCRIPT also includes the notion of *contexts* that can be saved on a stack, so that the state of the POSTSCRIPT world can be saved before an operation is performed, and restored afterward. Applications that define their own procedures do not need to worry about naming conflicts if they agree to restore the POSTSCRIPT world to its initial state.

The semantics of POSTSCRIPT are more complex. The fundamental entities are graphical entities and operators acting on them. All graphical entities are considered the same, so a line, a circular arc, a cubic curve, a blob, a string of text, and a sampled image can all be translated, rotated, or scaled by identical operators. Various operators are used to support multiple coordinate systems, so objects can be created in one coordinate system and then transformed by arbitrary affine transformations into any other coordinate system. A few operators can detect the environment in which POSTSCRIPT is running, which is important for making device-independent images. Thus, we can write a POSTSCRIPT program to produce a 1- by 1-inch square, regardless of the resolution of the device being used (unless of course its pixels are 1.5 inches wide!), by enquiring the environment to determine the number of pixels per inch on the current device.

POSTSCRIPT operators fall into six categories [ADOB85b]:

1. *Graphics-state operators*. These operators affect a collection of objects defining certain current attributes of the POSTSCRIPT world, such as the current line width, or the current clipping region.

2. *Coordinate-system operators and transformations*. These operators are used to alter the coordinate systems in which further objects are to be defined. In particular, they alter the mapping from coordinates within POSTSCRIPT to the coordinates of the output device.

3. *Path-construction operators*. These operators are used to define and update another graphics-state entity called the *current path*. They can be used to begin a path, to add collections of lines or arcs to the path, or to close the path (i.e., to join its beginning to its end with a straight-line segment). The current path is an abstract entity—it is not rendered on the page unless some painting operator is invoked.

4. *Painting operators*. These "rendering" operators generate data in a raster memory that eventually determine which dots appear on the printed page. All painting operators refer to the current path. If we imagine the path-construction operations as defining a mask, then the painting operators can be thought of as placing paint dots on the raster memory at each place allowed by the mask.

/Helvetica **findfont**	% Find the font object ' Helvetica"
	% previously defined.
188 **scalefont**	% Make it 188 times as big—default font size is
	% one point.
setfont	% Make this the current font (stored as part of
	% the "graphics state").
100 20 **moveto**	% Move to a point on the page.
67 **rotate**	% Rotate coordinates by 67 degrees.
(Hello) **show**	% Place the word "Hello" at the current
	% point (100, 20) and render it on the page.

Fig. 19.70 A PostScript program.

5. *Character and font operators*. This special class of operators is used for specifying, modifying, and selecting fonts. Since fonts are graphical entities like all others, the operators that place text into the current ''path'' are really path-construction operators; they are placed in a special class only because of the specialized nature of fonts.

6. *Device-setup and output operators*. The setup operators establish the correspondence of raster memory with the output device. The output operators control data transfer from memory to the device.

To exhibit the power of the POSTSCRIPT model, we give examples of the use of several of these operators. Each example includes running comments flagged by the ''%'' comment delimiter in POSTSCRIPT.

The first example, shown in Fig. 19.70, generates some text on the page, as shown in Fig. 19.71. The **show** operator is a special one: it both defines the object (a text string) to be shown and renders that object into raster memory. In all examples, a box has been drawn to show the outline of the page, although the instructions that drew the box are not included

Fig. 19.71 The output of the first POSTSCRIPT program.

in the examples. A slash (/) preceding a name pushes that name onto the stack as a literal object.

In Fig. 19.72, we build a rectangle and its label, and draw both with a dotted line, as shown in Fig. 19.73. To do this, we build up the "current path" using path-construction operators. The first of these is the **lineto** operator, which adds a line from the current point to the specified point. The second is the **charpath** operator, which takes two arguments, a text string and a Boolean; if the Boolean is **false,** the outline of the text string in the current font is added to the current path. When the Boolean is **true,** the outline of the text string is converted to a special type of path suitable for use in clipping. (We shall see this outline text in the third example.) The **stroke** operator is used to render the current path and to begin a new current path. (The current path can also be rendered using the **fill** or **eofill** operator. Both of these require that the path be closed. The first fills according to the nonzero winding rule; the second fills by the even–odd fill rule.)

Figure 19.74 shows how text is used for clipping; the result is shown in Fig. 19.75. Clipping to text requires the use of the clip path, which is another part of the POSTSCRIPT graphics state. Initially, the clip path encloses everything. We can create clipped objects by defining a smaller clip path. Here we define a procedure for drawing three horizontal strips, and then display them through two different clipping regions: a cubic curve, which is closed off using the **closepath** operator, and later a large piece of text. Since the **clip** operator always reduces the clipping region to the intersection of the current clipping region and the current path, it is important to save the original clipping region so that we can restore it. To do this, we use the **gsave** and **grestore** operators, which save and restore the entire graphics state.

The procedure definition is somewhat arcane. The **def** operator expects two arguments on the stack: a name and a definition. When used to define a procedure, the name is pushed

/Helvetica **findfont**	% Look for an object named "Helvetica"
	% previously defined.
120 **scalefont**	% Make it 120 times as big—default font size is
	% one point.
setfont	% Make this the current font (stored as part of
	% the "graphics state").
0 0 **moveto**	% Move to a point on the page.
newpath	% Begin the construction of a path.
100 300 **moveto**	% Start at location (100, 300).
500 300 **lineto**	% Add a line to location (500, 300).
500 800 **lineto**	% Continue adding line segments.
100 800 **lineto**	
100 300 **lineto**	% We have constructed a rectangle.
100 50 **moveto**	% Move below the rectangle.
(Rectangle) **false charpath**	
	% Add the text "Rectangle" to the
	% current path.
[9 3] 0 **setdash**	% Set the dash-pattern to 9-on, 3-off, repeating
stroke	% Draw the current path in this dash-pattern.

Fig. 19.72 A more complex POSTSCRIPT program.

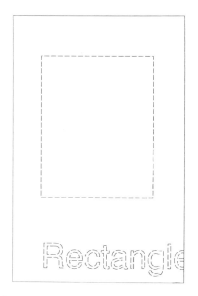

Fig. 19.73 The output of the second POSTSCRIPT program.

on the stack (with a preceding slash to prevent interpretation) and then the body of the procedure (which is a single item—all the material between matched braces). The **def** operator pops these two operands and defines the name to mean the body.

Often, the two operands to **def** are in the opposite order, as in the case where a procedure is called with its operands on the stack. To bind these operands to local variables, we push the variable name on the stack, then invoke the **exch** operator, which exchanges the top two elements on the stack, and then invoke **def.**

These examples give a good sense of the power of the POSTSCRIPT model. POSTSCRIPT is essentially like assembly language—it is powerful, but programming in it is not too pleasant. On the other hand, defining procedures is simple, which makes POSTSCRIPT far easier to use. In fact, the recommended use of POSTSCRIPT is in the form of a prologue, in which various attributes of the graphics state are set and various procedures are defined, followed by the script, which is a sequence of calls to the defined procedures.

The *current path* used in the examples is a very general object. It can be drawn in several ways: the **stroke** operator draws the current path as a sequence of lines and curves whose thickness and patterning are taken from the graphics state; the **fill** operator fills the current path (which must be a closed path for this to make sense) with the current fill pattern; the **eofill** operator fills according to an even–odd rule. As in the examples, the curves defining the outline of a character can be used as part of a path.

POSTSCRIPT also supports the notion of an ''image'' as a primitive, which can be a 1-bit-per-pixel representation or an *n*-bits-per-pixel representation. When an image is rendered into raster memory, it acts just like any other primitive; every pixel in raster memory covered by the image is drawn into with ''paint'' that can be white, black, or (in color implementations) any color. Thus, invoking the **image** operator draws an image on top of whatever is already present (it does no blending or compositing of the form described in Section 17.6). An alternate form, **imagemask,** is suitable for 1-bit images. Such a mask

```
/rect {                        % Define a new operator to
                               % draw a rectangle whose width and height
                               % are on the stack. It is invoked by "w h rect".
   /h exch def                 % Define h as the height, the second argument
                               % which is on the stack.
   /w exch def                 % Define w as the first argument from the
                               % stack.
   w 0 rlineto                 % Draw a line by moving the pen by (w, 0).
   0 h rlineto                 % Then draw a vertical line, moving by (0, h).
   w neg 0 rlineto             % Push w on the stack, negate it, push zero
                               % on the stack and draw a line, moving by
                               % (–w, 0).
   0 h neg rlineto             % Same for h, closing the box.
   gsave                       % Save graphics state, including clip path
   fill                        % Fill the current path, reducing the clip region
                               % to a rectangle.
   grestore                    % Restore the original clip path
   newpath                     % Throw away the current path and start anew.
} def                          % This concludes the definition of rect.

/stripes {                     % Define the "stripes" operator, which
                               % draws three stripes on the page. It
   newpath                     % takes no arguments.
   100 300 moveto              % Go to a point on the screen.
   800 50 rect                 % Draw a rectangle.
   100 200 moveto              % Move down a little and do it again.
   800 50 rect
   100 100 moveto
   800 50 rect                 % Do it yet again.
} def                          % This concludes the definition of stripes.

0 0 moveto                     % Start the current point at the origin.
.95 setgray                    % Set the gray level to very pale.
stripes                        % Show the full stripes.
.4 setgray                     % Set the gray shade a little darker.
gsave                          % Save the current graphics state
                               % (including the clip path).
newpath                        % Start a new path at 50,150.
50 150 moveto
100 250 300 275 250 175
curveto                        % Draw a Bezier curve with control points
                               % at (50, 150), (100, 250), (300, 275),
                               % and (250, 175).
closepath                      % Close off the curve with a straight line.
clip                           % The new clip region is the intersection
                               % of the old clip region (everything) with
                               % the path just constructed.
stripes                        % Draw stripes through the new clipping
                               % region, slightly darker than last time.
grestore                       % Restore the original clipping path.   Fig. 19.74 (Cont.)
```

.2 **setgray**	% Darken the color further
gsave	
/Helvetica **findfont**	
100 **scalefont setfont**	% Create a huge Helvetica font.
newpath	% Start a new path to clip by.
200 80 **moveto**	% Get ready to write a few characters.
(ABC) **true charpath**	% Create a path from the outline of
	% the text.
closepath	% Close the path,
eoclip	% and make this the new clip path, using
	% the even-odd rule.
stripes	% Draw the stripes through this.
grestore	

Fig. 19.74 A complex POSTSCRIPT program.

draws (with the current gray-level) only where there are 1s in the image; in places where there are 0s, the raster memory is untouched. Thus, it effectively transfers the image as a pattern in **transparent** mode, except that this image can be transformed before the operation is performed. In fact, an image can be scaled and rotated, and any other operation (including clipping by the current clip path) can be applied to it.

This last remark brings us to an important question: How are POSTSCRIPT interpreters implemented? How would we draw thickened cubic splines, for example, or rotated images? The exact interpretation is not specified in the POSTSCRIPT *Language Reference Manual* [ADOB85b], because the implementation must necessarily be different for different classes of printers (and for displays). Still, certain aspects of the imaging model are given explicitly. Curves are drawn by being divided into very short line segments. These segments are then thickened to the appropriate width and are drawn, producing a thick curve. Thus, thick lines have small notches in their sides if they are very wide, and the polygonization of

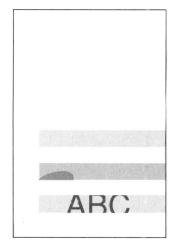

Fig. 19.75 POSTSCRIPT allows general clipping, even using text outlines as a clip path, as shown by this output from the third POSTSCRIPT program.

the curves is coarse (this, too, is user definable). Note that, in POSTSCRIPT, the line width is a geometric rather than cosmetic attribute, in the sense that it is defined in some coordinate system and can later be transformed. If we set the line width and then scale the current transformation by 2, all subsequent lines are drawn twice as thick.

POSTSCRIPT images apparently are transformed by affine maps using a technique similar to the two-pass transform. An image is defined, in the imaging model, as a grid of tiny squares, so a transformed image is drawn by rendering many small qudrilaterals. The method used for clipping by an arbitrary path is not stated so explicitly, but it appears that simple span arithmetic is performed in some implementations: The clipping region is represented by a collection of horizontal spans, each primitive is scan-converted row by row, and then only those pixels lying within the spans are actually painted. Much of the remaining implementation of the language amounts to a massive bookkeeping task; the current clip region, the current path, and the various fill styles must all be maintained, as well as the raster memory and the current transformation matrix.

19.10 SUMMARY

We have discussed some of the geometric and raster algorithms and data structures in use today, as well as their use in implementing various raster packages, including page-description languages. Despite the considerable sophistication of many of these algorithms, work continues to be done on these topics. Geometric clipping (and its extension to 3D, which is used in polyhedral constructive solid geometry) is a subject of active research, and new scan-conversion algorithms, especially with antialiasing, are still appearing frequently in the literature.

One lesson to be drawn from the algorithms is that simplicity may be more important than sophistication in many cases. Scissoring is a widely used clipping technique, the shape data structure makes many operations trivial, and the implementation of bitBlt we described has, as its core, the idea of making short and simple code that can be executed in a cache.

EXERCISES

19.1 Improve the implementation of the Nicholl–Lee–Nicholl line-clipping algorithm by making as much repeated use of intermediate results as possible. Implement all the cases.

19.2 The Liang–Barsky polygon-clipping algorithm described in the text may produce degenerate edges (so may the Sutherland–Hodgman algorithm described in Chapter 3). Develop an algorithm that takes the list of edges generated by the algorithm and ''cancels'' any two successive edges that have opposite directions, and is then applied recursively. The algorithm is made simple by the observation that such edge pairs must be either vertical or horizontal. Explain why this is true. Note that your algorithm should require no arithmetic except comparisons.

Also develop an algorithm to split the polygon into multiple output polygons if necessary, so that no two output polygons intersect. This may be done by applying the first algorithm to the output polygon, and then scanning the result for closed components. To test whether your algorithm works, apply it to several polygons that repeatedly go from one corner region to the adjacent or opposite one.

19.3 Reimplement the Liang–Barsky polygon-clipping algorithm without the use of infinity, by making special cases of horizontal and vertical lines.

19.4 Write an algorithm to convert a polygon in the plane, specified by a list of vertices, into the data structure for a contour described in the Weiler polygon-clipping algorithm. Extend your algorithm to work for polygons with holes, specified by multiple paths.

19.5 Suppose that you are given a set and a partial ordering (called *contained in*) on the set: For any two elements, A and B, A is contained in B, B is contained in A, or neither A nor B is contained in the other. (This partial order has nothing to do with the *element-of* relation in set theory.)

Design an algorithm that constructs a binary tree whose nodes are labeled by the elements of the set, and that has the following two properties: The left child of a node is always contained in the node, whereas the right child of a node (which may be NULL) neither is contained in nor contains the parent. A good algorithm for constructing this tree can be used to improve the postprocessing step in the Weiler polygon algorithm, where the contained/coexists structure of the contours must be determined.

19.6 Show by example that finding an integer starting point for a line with actual endpoint (x_0, y_0) as done in the text can give a different choice from (Round(x_0), Round(y_0)). Which choice is better, and why?

19.7 Suppose we have chosen to allow quarter-pixel resolution for endpoints of line segments, and that we consider the line from $(0, 0)$ to $(40, 1)$. Consider the portion of the line between $x = 15$ and $x = 40$. Show that, if we clip first and then compute the line equation from the clipped endpoints (after rounding to quarter-integers) and scan convert, the result will be different from that obtained by clipping, then using the rounded value of one clipped end as a start point, and scan converting using the equation of the original line.

19.8 Complete the ellipse specification given in Section 19.2.6 as follows. Let

$$\begin{pmatrix} x \\ y \end{pmatrix} = \cos(t) \begin{pmatrix} P_x \\ P_y \end{pmatrix} + \sin(t) \begin{pmatrix} Q_x \\ Q_y \end{pmatrix}.$$

Solve this equation for $\cos(t)$ and for $\sin(t)$ in terms of x, y, P_x, P_y, Q_x, and Q_y. Now use the identity $\cos^2 t + \sin^2 t = 1$ to create a single equation in x, y, P_x, P_y, Q_x and Q_y. Express this equation in the form $Ax^2 + Bxy + Cy^2 + Dx + Ey + F = 0$, and thus derive formulae for the coefficients A, B, C, D, E, and F in terms of P_x, P_y, Q_x, and Q_y. Your answers for D and E should be zero.

19.9 Describe methods for specifying hyperbolas and parabolas, and for computing the coefficients of the conic from the specification. One way to specify a hyperbola is to describe a parallelogram. The long diagonal of the parallelogram is the axis of the hyperbola, the two vertices of the hyperbola lie at the endpoints of this diagonal (the *vertices* are the points on the two branches of the hyperbola that are closest to each other), and the asymptotes are parallel to the sides of the parallelogram. A parabola can be specified by giving a focus (a point), a directrix (a line), and one point on the parabola, but this is not very intuitive. Can you come up with something better?

19.10 Compute the table of increments for the Van Aken conic algorithm. These are the increments in the decision variables for square and diagonal moves in each drawing octant. Show that the code that handles the first and second drawing octants actually will work for every odd or even octant.

19.11 Show that the three different error measures for circles give the same pixel selections when the radius and coordinates of the center of the circle are integers. This is simplest if you assume that the pixel under consideration satisfies $x \geq 0$, and $y \geq x$. (All other cases can be derived from this one by symmetry.) The radial error measure selects between (x, y) and $(x, y - 1)$ by evaluating $F(x, y) = x^2 + y^2 - r^2$ at each of the two points and choosing the one where the absolute value of F is smaller. The axial error measure uses $y' = \sqrt{r^2 - x^2}$; both $y - y'$ and $(y - 1) - y'$ are computed. The one with smaller absolute value is selected. The midpoint error measure selects (x, y) or $(x, y - 1)$, depending on whether the value of $F(x, y - 0.5)$ is negative or positive. What choice do you have to make to ensure that the three ambiguous cases agree (i.e., the cases where $F(x, y) = F(x, y - 1)$, where $y' = y - 0.5$, and where $F(x, y - 0.5) = 0)$? Or is there no consistent choice? At least show that, in the ambiguous cases, there is some pixel that minimizes all three measures of error.

19.12 Study the circle of radius $\sqrt{7}$ centered at the origin by scan converting it with any algorithm you choose. Is the result aesthetically pleasing? What happens if you move the center to $(\frac{1}{2}, 0)$? Are the sharp corners in the scan-converted version irritating? Should circle algorithms try to make curvature constant rather than minimizing distances? This circle, along with a few others whose squared radii are integers, is particularly troublesome. McIlroy [MCIL83] shows that the next case with such sharp corners is $r^2 = 7141$.

19.13 Complete the Van Aken conic algorithm by adding the portion that finishes the conic in the last drawing octant.

19.14 Improve the Van Aken conic algorithm by adding a check for octant jumps. DaSilva [DASI88] recommends using the decision variable to decide which pixel to draw next, but then checking to see whether that pixel has jumped over an octant. If it has, the alternate pixel is chosen instead.

19.15 Write a general line-drawing algorithm. Your algorithm should handle the case where the coordinates of the endpoints are rational numbers with a fixed denominator, p. Be certain that if you draw two lines that share an endpoint, the rasterized lines have the identical endpoints as well. Initializing the decision variable may be the most difficult part of the algorithm.

19.16 By considering the line from $(0, 0)$ to $(4, 2)$ and the line from $(4, 2)$ to $(0, 0)$, show that the midpoint algorithm described in Chapter 3 can draw different pixels, depending on the direction in which the line is specified. Find a way to examine the coordinates of the endpoints of a line and to adjust the comparison (from less than to less than or equal to) in the midpoint algorithm so that the same pixels are always drawn, regardless of the order in which the endpoints of a segment are specified.

19.17 Create a line-drawing algorithm to draw the portion of a line (specified by two endpoints) that lies between two vertical lines. That is, your procedure should look like TrimmedLine (point *start*, point *end*, **int** *xmin*, **int** *xmax*); and should draw the portion of the line segment between *start* and *end* that lies between *xmin* and *xmax*. Implement this algorithm with scissoring, and then with analytic clipping. When doing analytic clipping, be sure to derive the decision variable and increments from the original line, not from the rounded clipped endpoints.

19.18 Explain why a tightly bent curve is difficult to draw with forward-differencing techniques. Explain the problem as a form of aliasing.

19.19 Trace the recursive fill algorithm through a complete example to be sure you understand it. What are the subtle cases in the algorithm?

19.20 Implement the recursive fill algorithm. You can implement it and then execute it on a conventional video terminal, as long as it is cursor-addressable, by using characters to represent different pixel values. Implement both boundary fill and flood fill.

19.21 Show how to construct a mitered joint between two lines using the shape algebra; that is, describe a union, intersection, or difference of shapes that will produce a mitered joint. Do the same for a trimmed mitered joint.

19.22 Develop algorithms for determining the difference between two shapes and the union of two shapes by describing the high-level algorithm in terms of an "'Overlap'' function, and then describing the values returned by the overlap function.

19.23 Implement the improvements to the filling algorithms described in the text. What happens if stack processing is done on a first-in-first-out basis, instead of on a last-in-first-out one? Can you think of frame-buffer architectures in which the first approach is better or worse?

19.24 Consider the two filled circles defined by the equations $(x - 100)^2 + y^2 = 10000.9801$ and $(x + 100)^2 + y^2 = 10000.9801$. Show that, if we scan convert these circles, each generates a pixel at $(0, 2)$; hence, the pixel $(0, 2)$ is contained in the shape data structure for each. Show, on the other hand, that the intersection of these two circles contains only points between $y = -1$ and $y = 1$, and hence should not contain the pixel $(0, 2)$. Is the shape algebra a good way to implement intersections despite this apparent contradiction? Explain the circumstances in which you would accept the shape intersection as a reasonable approximation of the true intersection of geometric primitives.

19.25 In Section 19.1, we talked about determining the side of a ray on which a given point lies. Suppose we have a ray from P to Q, and a point, R.

   a. Show that a ray 90° clockwise from the ray from P to Q is given by $(-Q_y + P_y, Q_x - P_x)$.
   b. Explain why R is to the left of the ray from P to Q only if the vector from P to R lies in the same halfplane as does the vector computed in part a.
   c. Two vectors lie in the same halfplane only if their dot product is positive. Use this fact to show that R lies to the left of the ray from P to Q if and only if

$$(R_x - P_x)(-Q_y + P_y) + (R_y - P_y)(Q_x - P_x)$$

   is positive.

19.26 Implement the simpler antialiasing algorithm for the circle described in Section 19.3.2. You will need some preliminary computations.

   a. Show that, for large enough R and small values of s, a point (x, y) at a distance s outside a circle of radius R has a residual value, $F(x, y) = x^2 + y^2 - R^2$ which is approximately $2Rs$. (Hint: To say that the point is distance s outside the circle is the same as saying its distance to the origin is $R + s$.)
   b. Compute a table of weighted overlap values for a disk of radius 1 and a halfplane; make the table have 32 entries, corresponding to distances between -1 and 1 pixel (a distance of -1 means the pixel center is one unit inside the halfplane).
   c. Now write a scan-conversion algorithm as follows. For each pixel near the circle of radius R (determine these pixels using a midpoint-style algorithm), compute the residual and divide by $2R$ to get the distance. Use this to index into the table of overlap values; use the distance minus 1 to index into the table as well, and subtract to get a coverage value.
   d. Try your algoritnm on both large and small circles, and criticize the performance for small circles.

19.27 Suppose you are given a circle in the plane, with an equation of the form $(x - h)^2 + (y - k)^2 - R^2 = 0$. Describe how to detect whether a point (x, y) lies within the circle. Describe how to determine if a point lies within a distance of one from the circle. Now do the same two problems for an ellipse given by $Ax^2 + 2Bxy + Cy^2 + Dx + Ey + F = 0$. The second problem is much harder in this case, because of the difficult formula for the distance. Suppose that instead you estimate the distance from a point (x, y) to the ellipse as follows: multiply the residual at the point (x, y) by $(AC - B^2) / F^2$, and check whether this value is between 0.99 and 1.01. Explain why this might make a reasonable measure of closeness to the ellipse.

19.28 a. Consider the set of points on the x-axis between $-\frac{1}{2}$ and $\frac{1}{2}$, together with the set of points on the y axis between $-\frac{1}{2}$ and $\frac{1}{2}$. We include only one of the two endpoints in each of these intervals. Since this has the shape of a "+" sign, we will call the shape P. Show that the midpoint algorithms we have discussed will draw the pixel at $(0, 0)$ precisely if the primitive intersects P. (Note that P contains only two of its four possible endpoints. The decision of which two to include amounts to the decision to count an exact midpoint crossing of a horizontal line as contributing the left or the right pixel, and similarly for vertical midpoint crossings. Be sure that your choice of endpoints for P corresponds to the algorithm you are studying.)

    b. Analogously, a pixel Q is drawn by a midpoint algorithm precisely if the primitive intersects a copy of P that has been translated to have its center at Q. Show that a circle of radius 0.49, centered at (0.5, 0.5), therefore causes no pixel to be drawn.

    c. Alternative shapes have been proposed instead of P, including the convex hull of P, and a square box around a pixel. Criticize each of these choices.

19.29 The Posch-Fellner style algorithm for drawing thick curves can be improved somewhat. Instead of considering a circle swept along a curve, consider a *pen polygon* [HOBB89]. A pen polygon is characterized by two properties: opposite sides are parallel, and if the polygon is translated so that one vertex of an edge lies at the origin, then the line containing the opposite edge must pass through a point with integer coordinates. For example, an octagon with vertices $\pm(1, \frac{1}{2})$, $\pm(\frac{1}{2}, 1)$, $\pm(-\frac{1}{2}, 1)$, and $\pm(-1, \frac{1}{2})$ is a pen polygon. Compute the points on a curve through the origin with slope 0.935 using the Posch–Fellner algorithm (with a width of 2) and the pen-polygon algorithm, using the octagonal pen. In general, thick lines drawn with pen polygons have a more uniform appearance.

20
Advanced Modeling Techniques

Earlier chapters have concentrated on geometric models, including transforming and rendering them. In a world made entirely of simple geometric objects, these models would suffice. But many natural phenomena are not efficiently represented by geometric models, at least not on a large scale. Fog, for example, is made up of tiny drops of water, but using a model in which each drop must be individually placed is out of the question. Furthermore, this water-drop model does not accurately represent our perception of fog: We see fog as a blur in the air in front of us, not as millions of drops. Our visual perception of fog is based on how fog alters the light reaching our eyes, not on the shape or placement of the individual drops. Thus, to model the perceptual effect of fog efficiently, we need a different model. In the same way, the shape of a leaf of a tree may be modeled with polygons and its stem may be modeled with a spline tube, but to place explicitly every limb, branch, twig, and leaf of a tree would be impossibly time consuming and cumbersome.

It is not only natural phenomena that resist geometric modeling. Giving an explicit description of the Brooklyn Bridge is also challenging. Much of the detail in the bridge is in rivets, nuts, and bolts. These are not placed in the same location on every strut or cable, so primitive instancing cannot be used; rather, they are placed in ways that can be determined from the locations of the struts or cables (for example, two cables whose ends abut need a coupler between them).

The advanced modeling techniques in this chapter attempt to go beyond geometric modeling, to allow simple modeling of complex phenomena. Typically, this means representing a large class of objects by a single model with easily adjusted and intuitive parameters. Thus, the list of parameters becomes the data from which the model is generated. This technique has been called *database amplification* [SMIT84], a term accurately describing our desire to model elaborate entities that are quite uniform at high levels of detail (e.g., fog, bridges, fire, plants).

Some of the techniques lie somewhere between the extremes of explicit modeling and database amplification, such as the hierarchical splines of [FORS88], and the blobby objects of [BLIN82b] and soft objects of [WYVI86]. *Hierarchical splines* are surface patches having varying densities in their control-point meshes. In regions where the object to be modeled has few features, a coarse mesh is used. In regions with lots of detail, finer meshes subdivide a single rectangle in the coarser mesh. Thus, a modest amount of information (the control points and subdivision hierarchy) describes the shape of the full surface. The *blobby* and *soft objects* are again controlled by locating a few objects and then "blending" them together to form a complex object. The few objects (spheres or blobs of soft material) still required must be placed, but their intersections are smoothed out automatically, freeing the user from having to define fillets explicitly at each object intersection.

Some of the techniques presented here are widely applicable; procedural models, fractals, grammar-based models, and particle systems have all been used to model a wide variety of things. Some of them are special purpose; for example, the ocean-wave models. Nonetheless, many of the models presented here give good pictures without being faithful to the underlying science. The clouds modeled as textured quadrics by Gardner [GARD84] are based not on atmospheric science, but rather on appearances; the water modeled by blobby objects has no basis in the physics of surface tension and the dynamics of water molecules. It is important to recognize the difference between these approaches to modeling and modeling based on the underlying science.

For each modeling technique, new methods of rendering may be required. In discussing a new modeling technique, we therefore introduce any new rendering techniques developed for its use. In one case, volume rendering, the modeling (which consists of the assignment of a value to each point in a 3D region) is not new at all. Scalar fields have been used in physics and mathematics for hundred of years, but only recently have attempts been made to render these fields on 2D images.

Finally, many of the methods presented here have been developed for dynamic models rather than for static ones, and for modeling growth and change as well as form. The individual images produced from these models are of interest, but the full power of the modeling technique comes out when several still images are combined in an animated sequence. Some of the topics covered in this chapter thus concern both *object modeling* and *animation*.

20.1   EXTENSIONS OF PREVIOUS TECHNIQUES

Before starting our survey of new techniques for modeling natural and artificial objects, we discuss two extensions to our previous modeling techniques: hierarchical splines and noise-based pattern mapping. Neither of these handles any shapes or characteristics that we could not model before, but each makes the modeling a great deal simpler. Hierarchical splines make it unnecessary to place many control points in regions with little detail (as would have to be done if a uniformly fine control mesh were used), and noise-based patterns are simply particularly interesting patterns to map onto conventional objects.

20.1.1   Advanced Modeling with Splines

With the tensor-product spline-patch surfaces defined in Chapter 11, more control vertices must be added to gain a higher level of detail. The Oslo algorithm and its descendents [COHE80; BART87] can be applied to the control mesh of such splines to produce new control meshes with more vertices but identical resulting surfaces. This refinement of the control mesh is shown for a line spline in Fig. 20.1. The circled black dots control the shape of the thickened segment in the figure; if one of these is moved, the shape of the thickened segment changes. But how many control vertices do we need to redraw the arc in its changed form? For the portions outside the thickened segment, we can use the (comparatively few) white vertices; for the portion inside the thickened segment, we can use the circled black vertices. This localization of detail is the fundamental notion of hierarchical B-spline modeling developed by Forsey and Bartels [FORS88].

Two problems arise: maintaining a data structure for the hierarchical spline, and altering the large-scale spline without damaging the small-scale one. These two problems can be solved together. We wish to alter the large-scale spline so that the small-scale spline follows the alteration. We do this alteration by describing the locations of the (adjustable) control vertices for the small-scale spline in a coordinate system based on the larger spline. This prescribes the data structure for the splines as well—a tree in which the control vertices of each spline are specified in coordinates based on its parent node in the tree. The initial position of each control vertex defines the origin of its coordinate system, and the displacements along the normal to the large spline and in the directions tangent to the coordinate curves of the large spline determine a basis for this coordinate system. Thus, when the large spline is altered, the origin and basis vectors for the displacement coordinate system are moved as well.

Figure 20.2 shows how this procedure works for a line spline. Color Plate IV.4(a) is an example of the impressive results this technique can yield. Notice that the final object is just a union of portions of various spline patches, so the conventional rendering techniques that can handle splines (including polygonal and ray-tracing renderers) can be adapted to render these objects. About 500 control nodes, each of which contains a parametric position, a level of overlay (i.e., depth in the heirarchy) and an offset, were used to define the dragon's head. By defining the offsets of control vertices relative to particular segments in a skeletal

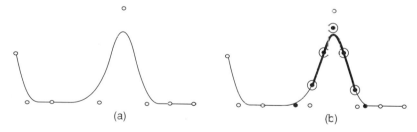

(a)   (b)

Fig. 20.1 The spline curve in (a) is generated from the control vertices shown there. This collection of control vertices can be refined as shown in (b). The black dots in (b) are the new control vertices; the circled black dots are the ones that contribute to the thickened segment.

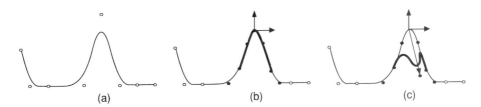

Fig. 20.2 (a) A line spline with its control points. (b) The same spline with subdivided control points in the central segment. Only the middle control point can be moved if continuity is to be maintained. The coordinate system for the displacement of the middle control point is shown as well. (c) The middle control point after it is moved, along with the displacement vector in the new coordinate system.

model (instead of relative to the parent surface), Forsey and Bartels have extended this technique to automate the production of skin, as shown in Color Plate IV.4(b).

Sederberg and Parry describe a different approach to altering spline models [SEDE86] that can be used to alter arbitrary models, although it is based on spline deformations of 3-space. A function from 3-space to 3-space may be thought of as a way to assign new positions to each point in space. Suppose we have such a function and it leaves most points unmoved, but deforms some region of space. (Figure 20.3 shows an analogous deformation in a region of the plane.) If a solid is described by the coordinates of its points in the original space, then applying the function to the coordinates of every point of the solid yields a solid that has been deformed by the function, just as the shaded area was deformed in Fig. 20.3.

Sederberg and Parry use functions from 3-space to 3-space that are based on *Bernstein polynomials*, which have the form[1]

$$Q_{n,i}(t) = \binom{n}{i} t^i (1 - t)^{n-i}, \qquad 0 \le t \le 1.$$

These polynomials have the property that $\sum_{i=0}^{n} Q_{n,i}(t) = 1$ (see Exercise 20.1) and that the individual Qs are always between 0 and 1.

If we establish a coordinate system in 3-space defined by an origin X and three basis vectors S, T, and U, we can form an $(n + 1) \times (m + 1) \times (p + 1)$ lattice of points in 3-space by considering all points

$$P_{ijk} = X + (i/n)\,S + (j/m)T + (k/p)\,U,\ 0 \le i \le n,\ 0 \le j \le m,\ 0 \le k \le p,$$

which is a gridlike arrangement of points in a parallelepiped based at X with sides determined by S, T and U. Any linear combination $\sum c_{ijk} P_{ijk}$ of these points satisfying $0 \le c_{ijk} \le 1$ and $\sum c_{ijk} = 1$ lies within the convex hull of the points P_{ijk}, that is, within the parallelepiped. Furthermore, every point within the parallelepiped can be expressed as a combination $P = X + sS + tT + uU$ for some triple of numbers $0 \le s, t, u \le 1$. Suppose we define a function on the parallelepiped by the formula

---

[1] The notation $\binom{n}{i}$ means $n!/(i!(n-i)!)$.

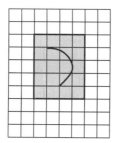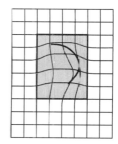

Fig. 20.3 The plane is deformed so that the region inside the rectangle is distorted, but the rest of the plane remains fixed. A figure drawn within the rectangle is also deformed.

$$F(X + sS + tT + uU)$$

$$= \sum_{i=0}^{n} \sum_{j=0}^{m} \sum_{k=0}^{p} \binom{n}{i}\binom{m}{j}\binom{p}{k} t^i (1-t)^{n-i} s^j (1-s)^{m-j} u^k (1-u)^{p-k} P_{ijk}$$

$$= \sum_{i=0}^{n} \sum_{j=0}^{m} \sum_{k=0}^{p} Q_{n,i}(t)\, Q_{m,j}(s)\, Q_{p,k}(u)\, P_{ijk}.$$

Then because of the convexity property of the Bernstein polynomials, the parallelepiped maps to itself, with the boundary going to the boundary. In fact, if the P_{ijk} are left in the positions defined previously, F sends each point in the parallelepiped to itself. If the P_{ijk}s are moved, the map is no longer the identity. As long as only internal P_{ijk}s are moved, however, the map will remain the identity on the boundary of the parallelepiped. Thus, the P_{ijk}s provide shape control over any item within the box. Color Plate IV.5 shows an example of adjusting a free-form shape; Color Plate IV.6 shows a hammer modeled using free-form deformations.

Computing vertices of a polygonal object after transformation by a trivariate Bernstein polynomial is simple (we just express each vertex as a linear combination $X + sS + tT + uU$ and substitute in the formula for F), so the method is suited for use with all polygonal renderers. It is less clear how to ray-trace these deformed objects, although the specialized methods described for another class of deformations by Barr [BARR84] might be applied.

20.1.2 Noise-Based Texture Mapping

Peachey [PEAC85] and Perlin [PERL85] have extended traditional texture mapping by using *solid textures*. Recall that in traditional bump mapping or pattern mapping the texture was extracted from a 2D image that was mapped onto the surface to be rendered (see Chapters 14 and 16). Described differently, for each point of the surface, a point in the 2D texture is computed, the values surrounding this point are averaged by some filter, and the resulting texture value is assigned to the surface point.

This mechanism is altered slightly for solid textures. A texture value is assigned to each point in a 3D *texture space*. To each point of the object to be textured, there is associated some point in the texture space; the value of the texture at that point is also associated with the surface point. We can illustrate this solid texturing by considering an analogous physical example. If we take a block of marble (the texture space), then each point of the marble, both on the surface and in the inside, has some color. Thus, if we carve a sphere from this marble block, the points on the surface of the sphere are also colored. If we carve the sphere from a different section of the marble, the colors are different, of course.

The two tasks associated with this mechanism are the generation of textures and the mapping from objects to the texture space (i.e., the association of points on the object with points in the texture space). The mapping to texture space is easy in systems where the object is modeled in some space, then is transformed into ''world space'' before rendering. In this case, the natural choice for texture space is modeling space. During rendering, a 3D point on the object is transformed by the inverse of the modeling transformation to give a point in modeling space whose coordinates provide the index into the solid texture (this situation corresponds to our carving in marble). When this is done, changing the world-space position of the object does not affect its pattern. Using world-space coordinates as indices into the solid texture can provide interesting special effects. If the marble sphere is translated in the course of an animation, the texture slides through it, and it appears to be continuously recarved from new marble. In other systems, some coordinate system (or else some map from world space to texture space) must be chosen to associate each point on the object with a texture value.

Generating textures is a different matter. Before discussing it, let us reconsider the function of texture mapping. When a texture map is used for environment mapping onto a reflective surface, there is no underlying solid texture. The same is true when a texture map is used, say, to put a label on a box, or when bump mapping is applied to an object to simulate architectural details such as regularly spaced ceiling tiles, or to generate surface characteristics such as the directional reflections on brushed metals. But when we simulate the texture of a material such as concrete, wood, or marble, the internal structure of the underlying material determines the resulting appearance of the object. In such cases, solid textures are most applicable.

One type of intermediate case, too, that is handled nicely by solid textures is surface characteristics, such as the texture of stucco, that should be statistically independent of their surface position. Here ordinary pattern mapping tends to produce an orientation because of the coordinate system in which the pattern map is defined, and because of the transformation from the mapping space onto the object, which tends to compress or expand the pattern in some places (e.g., when mapping onto a sphere with standard coordinates, one tends to compress the pattern near the poles). Solid textures handle this problem by associating values that can be made effectively independent of the shape of the surface (see Color Plate IV.7c).

Generating a solid texture requires associating one or more numbers with each point in some volume. We can specify these numbers by generating them at each point of a 3D lattice (this is sometimes called a *3D image*), and then interpolating to give intermediate values, or simply by giving one or more real-valued functions on a region in 3-space.

Most of the functions used by Perlin are based on noise functions. He defines a function *Noise*(x, y, z) with certain properties: statistical invariance under rigid motions and band limiting in the frequency domain. The first of these means that any statistical property, such as the average value or the variance over a region, is about the same as the value measured over a congruent region in some other location and orientation. The second condition says that the Fourier transform of the signal is zero outside of a narrow range of frequencies (see Section 14.10). In practical terms, this means that the function has no sudden changes, but has no locations where the change is too gradual, either. One way of expressing the band limiting is that, for any unit vector (a, b, c) and any point (x_0, y_0, z_0), the integral

$$\int_0^\infty Noise(x_0 + ta, \ y_0 + tb, \ z_0 + tc)f(mt) \ dt$$

is zero when $f(t) = \sin(t)$ or $\cos(t)$, and m is outside some small range of values. Essentially, this says that the noise along a parameterized line in the (a, b, c) direction has no periodic character with period m.

Such a noise function can be generated in a number of ways, including direct Fourier synthesis, but Perlin has a quick and easily implemented method. For each point in the integer lattice (i.e., for each point (x_0, y_0, z_0) with x_0, y_0, and z_0 all integers) we compute and store four pseudorandom[2] real numbers (a, b, c, d). Compute $d' = d - (ax_0 + by_0 + cz_0)$. Notice that if we substitute the point (x_0, y_0, z_0) into the formula $ax + by - cz + d'$ we get the value d. We now define the *Noise* function at an arbitrary point (x, y, z) by the two rules: If (x, y, z) is a point of the integer lattice, then $Noise(x, y, z) =$ the d value at that lattice point $= ax_0 + by_0 + cz_0 + d'$. For any point not on the lattice, the values of a, b, c, and d' are interpolated from the values at the nearby lattice points (Perlin recommends a cubic interpolation — first in x, then in y, then in z) to give values for a, b, c, and d' at the point (x, y, z). Now $Noise(x, y, z)$ is computed: $Noise(x, y, z) = ax + by + cz + d'$.

Since the coefficients a, b, c, and d' are interpolated by cubics on the integer lattice, it is clear that there are no discontinuities in their values (in fact, they will all be differentiable functions with well-behaved derivatives). Hence, the value of $Noise(x, y, z)$ is also well behaved and has no high-frequency components (i.e., sudden changes).

Noise functions can be used to generate textures by altering colors, normal vectors, and so on [PERL85]. For example, a random gray-scale value can be assigned to a point by setting its color to $(r, g, b) = Noise(x, y, z) * (1.0, 1.0, 1.0)$ (assuming that the *Noise()* function has been scaled so that its values lie between 0 and 1). A random color can be assigned to a point by $(r, g, b) = (NoiseA(x, y, z), NoiseB(x, y, z), NoiseC(x, y, z))$, where *NoiseA()*, *NoiseB()* and *NoiseC()* are all different instances of the *Noise()* function. An alternate way to assign random colors is to use the gradient of the noise function:

$$Dnoise(x, y, z) = (dNoise/dx, dNoise/dy, dNoise/dz),$$

which generates a vector of three values at each point. These values can be mapped to color values.

---

[2] Pseudorandom-number generation is provided by the *Random()* function in many systems. See also [KNUT69].

If an object has sufficiently great extent, it may not be practical to generate a texture for its entire bounding box. Instead, as in Chapter 16, we generate the texture on a finite box (perhaps 256 by 256 by 256) and use the low-order bits of the point's coordinates to index into this array (using modular arithmetic to wrap around from 255 to 0). We can use this finite texture array to generate another type of noise by defining $Noise2(x, y, z) = Noise(2x, 2y, 2z)$. $Noise2$ will have features that are one-half of the size of those generated by $Noise()$. By generating a combination of such multiples of $Noise()$, we can create a number of fascinating textures; see Exercises 20.2 and 20.3. Perlin has extended solid textures to allow the modification of geometry as well [PERL89]. Some examples of the results are shown in Color Plates IV.8 and IV.9.

Peachey [PEAC85] uses somewhat different mechanisms for specifying solid textures. One of the most interesting is what he calls *projection textures*, although the term "extrusion textures" might apply as well. In such textures, the value of the texture function is constant along certain parallel lines in the volume. For example, such a texture might be constant along each line parallel to the z axis, while on any (x, y)-plane cross-section it might look like a conventional 2D texture. The effect is like that of a (nonperspective) slide projector: When someone walks in front of the screen, the image is mapped onto the person instead of onto the screen. These textures are most interesting when several are combined. If the textures are constant along different lines, the results can effectively simulate completely random textures. The textures in Color Plate IV.10 are all based on projection textures.

20.2   PROCEDURAL MODELS

Procedural models describe objects that can interact with external events to modify themselves. Thus, a model of a sphere that generates a polygonal representation of the sphere at a requested fineness of subdivision is procedural: The actual model is determined by the fineness parameter. A model that determines the origin of its coordinate system by requesting information from nearby entities is also procedural. A collection of polygons specified by their vertices is *not* a procedural model.

Procedural models have been in use for a long time. One of their best features is that they save space: It is far easier to say "sphere with 120 polygons" than to list the 120 polygons explicitly. Magnenat-Thalman and Thalman [MAGN85] describe a procedural model for bridges in which a bridge consists of a road, a superstructure, piers, and parapets, and is specified by giving descriptions of these along with an orientation to determine the bridge's position. Each of the pieces (road, piers, etc.) is specified by a number of parameters (length of the road, number of joints in the road, height of the pier, etc.) and the procedure then generates the model from these. This is akin to the primitive instancing of Chapter 12, but differs in that the geometric or topological nature of the object may be influenced by the parameters. Also, the model generated does not need to consist of a collection of solids; it might be a collection of point light sources used to exhibit the bridge in a night scene, for instance. In any case, specifying a few parameters leads to the creation of a very large model. In the case of the bridge, the only things created are various sorts of bridges. In subsequent procedural models, such as particle systems, however, highly variable classes of objects are supported under a single class of procedures.

One important aspect of procedural models is their ability to interact with their environment. Amburn, Grant, and Whitted introduce two extensions to standard procedural models: a communication method through which independent procedures can influence one another's behaviors, and a generalization of the notion of subdivision to include a change of representation [AMBU86].

Interobject communication can be used to control the shapes of objects defined by procedures. Amburn, Grant, and Whitted use as an example a road passing through wooded terrain. The terrain is generated by stochastic subdivision of triangles (see Section 20.3), the trees are generated using grammar-based models (see Section 20.4), and the road is generated by extrusion of a line along a spline path. At the top level, the road must follow the geometry of the terrain. At a finer level of detail, however, the terrain is bulldozed to let the road be smooth. Each of these objects thus must control the other. The bases of the trees must be placed on the terrain, but not too close to the road. To execute this interobject control, each of the subdivision procedures proceeds for a few steps, then checks its progress against that of the others.

This interobject checking can be extremely expensive the road may be modeled with hundreds of rectangles and the terrain with thousands of triangles. Checking for intersections among these and establishing communications between each pair is prohibitively laborious. Instead, during the construction of the road, bounding boxes for the road, for each pair of control points for the road, and for each segment of the road were constructed. Similar bounding boxes were maintained during the subdivision of the triangles. As soon as the bounding box of a child triangle no longer intersected that of the road, communications between the two were severed. Thus, there were only a few overlaps at the finest level of subdivision.

These subdivisions were also subject to changes of representation. At some point in a subdivision process, the current model representation may no longer seem adequate to the modeler; and the modeler (or some other procedure in the model) may request that some procedural object change its representation. Thus, a shape that is initially modeled with Bezier spline patches, recursively subdivided, may at some point be altered to implement further changes using stochastic subdivision to make a "crinkly" material of some specific overall shape. Amburn, Grant, and Whitted store these changes of representation in a script associated either with the individual object or with the class of the object; the script might say, for example, "At the third level of subdivision, change from Bezier to stochastic. At the fifth level, change to a particle system representation." The human modeler is also allowed to interact with the objects as the procedural modifications take place. Our hope is that, in the future, such interactions will no longer be necessary, and that the models will be able to determine for themselves the best possible representation.

Most of the remaining models in this chapter are procedural in some way. Many of them are generated by repeated subdivision or repeated spawning of smaller objects. The subdivision terminates at a level determined by the modeler, the model, or (depending on implementation) the renderer, which can request that no subpixel artifacts be generated, for example. The power of these models is manifested in how they amplify the modeler's effort: Very small changes in specifications can result in drastic changes of form. (Of course, this can be a drawback in some cases, if the modeler cannot direct a tiny change in the result.)

20.3 FRACTAL MODELS

Fractals have recently attracted much attention [VOSS87; MAND82; PEIT86]. The images resulting from them are spectacular, and many different approaches to generating fractals have been developed. The term *fractal* has been generalized by the computer graphics community to include objects outside Mandelbrot's original definition. It has come to mean anything which has a substantial measure of exact or statistical self-similarity, and that is how we use it here, although its precise mathematical definition requires statistical self-similarity at all resolutions. Thus, only fractals generated by infinitely recursive processes are true fractal objects. On the other hand, those generated by finite processes may exhibit no visible change in detail after some stage, so they are adequate approximations of the ideal. What we mean by *self-similarity* is best illustrated by an example, the von Koch snowflake. Starting with a line segment with a bump on it, as shown in Fig. 20.4, we replace each segment of the line by a figure exactly like the original line. This process is repeated: Each segment in part (b) of the figure is replaced by a shape exactly like the entire figure. (It makes no difference whether the replacement is by the shape shown in part (a) or by the shape shown in part (b); if the one in part (a) is used, the result after 2^n steps is the same as the result after n steps if each segment of the current figure is replaced by the entire current figure at each stage.) If this process is repeated infinitely many times, the result is said to be *self-similar:* The entire object is similar (i.e., can be translated, rotated, and scaled) to a subportion of itself.

An object that is not exactly self-similar may still seem fractal; that is, it may be substantially self-similar. The precise definition of statistical self-similarity is not necessary here—we need only to note that objects that "look like" themselves when scaled down are still called fractal.

Associated with this notion of self-similarity is the notion of *fractal dimension*. To define fractal dimension, we shall examine some properties of objects whose dimension we know. A line segment is 1D; if we divide a line into N equal parts, the parts each look like the original line scaled down by a factor of $N = N^{1/1}$. A square is 2D: if we divide it into N parts, each part looks like the original scaled down by a factor of $\sqrt{N} = N^{1/2}$. (For example, a square divides nicely into nine subsquares; each one looks like the original scaled by a factor of $\frac{1}{3}$.) What about the von Koch snowflake? When it is divided into four pieces (the pieces associated with the original four segments in Fig. 20.4a), each resulting piece looks like the original scaled down by a factor of 3. We would like to say it has a dimension d, where $4^{1/d} = 3$. The value of d must be $\log(4)/\log(3) = 1.26$ . . . .. This is the definition of fractal dimension.

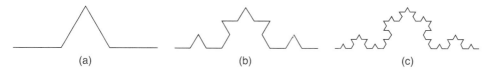

(a)   (b)   (c)

Fig. 20.4 Construction of the von Koch snowflake: each segment in (a) is replaced by an exact copy of the entire figure, shrunk by a factor of 3. The same process is applied to the segments in (b) to generate those in (c).

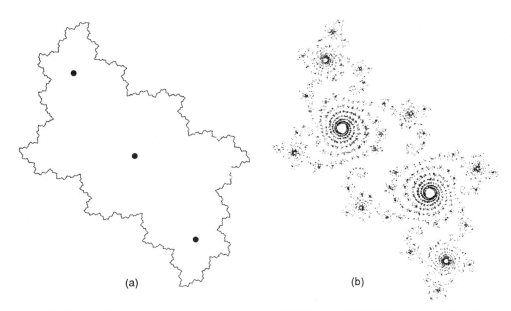

Fig. 20.5 (a) The Julia–Fatou set for $c = -0.12375 + 0.056805i$; (b) the Julia–Fatou set for $c = -0.012 + 0.74i$.

The most famous two fractal objects deserve mention here: the Julia–Fatou set and the Mandelbrot set. These objects are generated from the study of the rule $x \to x^2 + c$ (and many other rules as well—this is the simplest and best known). Here x is a *complex number*,[3] $x = a + bi$. If a complex number has modulus < 1, then squaring it repeatedly makes it go toward zero. If it has a modulus > 1, repeated squaring makes it grow larger and larger. Numbers with modulus 1 still have modulus 1 after repeated squarings. Thus, some complex numbers "fall toward zero" when they are repeatedly squared, some "fall toward infinity," and some do neither—the last group forms the boundary between the numbers attracted to zero and those attracted to infinity.

Suppose we repeatedly apply the mapping $x \to x^2 + c$ to each complex number x for some nonzero value of c, such as $c = -0.12375 + 0.056805i$; some complex numbers will be attracted to infinity, some will be attracted to finite numbers, and some will go toward neither. Drawing the set of points that go toward neither, we get the Julia–Fatou set shown in Fig. 20.5(a).

Notice that the region in Fig. 20.5 (b) is not as well connected as is that in part (a) of the figure. In part (b), some points fall toward each of the three black dots shown, some go

---

[3]If you are unfamiliar with complex numbers, it suffices to treat i as a special symbol and merely to know the definitions of addition and multiplication of complex numbers. If $z = c + di$ is a second complex number, then $x + z$ is defined to be $(a + c) + (b + d)i$, and xz is defined to be $(ac - bd) + (ad + bc)i$. We can represent complex numbers as points in the plane by identifying the point (a, b) with the complex number $(a + bi)$. The *modulus* of the number $a + bi$ is the real number $(a^2 + b^2)^{1/2}$, which gives a measure of the "size" of the complex number.

to infinity, and some do neither. These last points are the ones drawn as the outline of the shape in part (b). The shape of the Julia–Fatou set evidently depends on the value of the number c. If we compute the Julia sets for all possible values of c and color the point c black when the Julia–Fatou set is connected (i.e, is made of one piece, not broken into disjoint "islands") and white when the set is not connected, we get the object shown in Fig. 20.6, which is known as the *Mandelbrot set*. Note that the Mandelbrot set is self-similar in that, around the edge of the large disk in the set, there are several smaller sets, each looking a great deal like the large one scaled down.

Fortunately, there is an easier way to generate approximations of the Mandelbrot set: For each value of c, take the complex number $0 = 0 + 0i$ and apply the process $x \rightarrow x^2 + c$ to it some finite number of times (perhaps 1000). If after this many iterations it is outside the disk defined by modulus < 100, then we color c white; otherwise, we color it black. As the number of iterations and the radius of the disk are increased, the resulting picture becomes a better approximation of the set. Peitgen and Richter [PEIT86] give explicit directions for generating many spectacular images of Mandelbrot and Julia–Fatou sets.

These results are extremely suggestive for modeling natural forms, since many natural objects seem to exhibit striking self-similarity. Mountains have peaks and smaller peaks and rocks and gravel, which all look similar; trees have limbs and branches and twigs, which all look similar; coastlines have bays and inlets and estuaries and rivulets and drainage ditches, which all look similar. Hence, modeling self-similarity at some scale seems to be a way to generate appealing-looking models of natural phenomena. The scale at which the self-similarity breaks down is not particularly important here, since the intent is modeling rather than mathematics. Thus, when an object has been generated recursively through enough steps that all further changes happen at well below pixel resolution, there is no need to continue.

Fournier, Fussell, and Carpenter [FOUR82] developed a mechanism for generating a class of fractal mountains based on recursive subdivision. It is easiest to explain in 1D.

Fig. 20.6 The Mandelbrot set. Each point c in the complex plane is colored black if the Julia set for the process $x \rightarrow x^2 + c$ is connected.

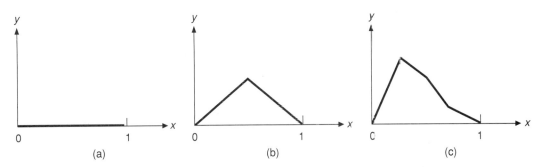

Fig. 20.7 (a) A line segment on the x axis. (b) The midpoint of the line has been translated in the y direction by a random amount. (c) The result of one further iteration.

Suppose we start with a line segment lying on the x axis, as shown in Fig. 20.7(a). If we now subdivide the line into two halves and then move the midpoint some distance in the y direction, we get the shape shown in Fig. 20.7(b). To continue subdividing each segment, we compute a new value for the midpoint of the segment from (x_i, y_i) to (x_{i+1}, y_{i+1}) as follows: $x_{new} = \frac{1}{2}(x_i + x_{i+1})$, $y_{new} = \frac{1}{2}(y_i + y_{i+1}) + P(x_{i+1} - x_i) R(x_{new})$, where $P()$ is a function determining the extent of the perturbation in terms of the size of the line being perturbed, and $R()$ is a random number[4] between 0 and 1 selected on the basis of x_{new} (see Fig. 20.7c). If $P(s) = s$, then the first point cannot be displaced by more than 1, each of the next two points (which are at most at height $\frac{1}{2}$ already) cannot be displaced by more than $\frac{1}{2}$, and so on. Hence, all the resulting points fit in the unit square. For $P(s) = s^a$, the shape of the result depends on the value of a; smaller values of a yield larger perturbations, and vice versa. Of course, other functions, such as $P(s) = 2^{-s}$, can be used as well.

Fournier, Fussell, and Carpenter use this process to modify 2D shapes in the following fashion. They start with a triangle, mark the midpoint of each edge, and connect the three midpoints, as shown in Fig. 20.8 (a). The y coordinate of each midpoint is then modified in the manner we have described, so that the resulting set of four triangles looks like Fig. 20.8 (b). This process, when iterated, produces quite realistic-looking mountains, as shown in Color Plate IV.11 (although, in an overhead view, one perceives a very regular polygonal structure).

Notice that we can start with an arrangement of triangles that have a certain shape, then apply this process to generate the finer detail. This ability is particularly important in some modeling applications, in which the layout of objects in a scene may be stochastic at a low level but ordered at a high level: The foliage in an ornamental garden may be generated by a stochastic mechanism, but its arrangement in the garden must follow strict rules. On the other hand, the fact that the high-level structure of the initial triangle arrangement persists in the iterated subdivisions may be inappropriate in some applications (in particular, the fractal so generated does not have all the statistical self-similarities present in fractals based

---

[4]$R()$ is actually a *random variable*, a function taking real numbers and producing randomly distributed numbers between 0 and 1. If this is implemented by a pseudorandom-number generator, it has the advantage that the fractals are repeatable: We can generate them again by supplying the same seed to the pseudorandom-number generator.

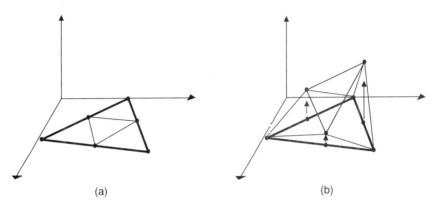

(a)   (b)

Fig. 20.8 (a) The subdivision of a triangle into four smaller triangles. The midpoints of the original triangle are perturbed in the *y* direction to yield the shape in (b).

on Brownian motion [MAND82]). Also, since the position of any vertex is adjusted only once and is stationary thereafter, creases tend to develop in the surface along the edges between the original triangles, and these may appear unnatural.

Voss [VOSS85] describes a modified version of this algorithm in which stage $n + 1$ of a model is created by adding a random displacement to every vertex of the model at stage n, together with the midpoints of the edges at that stage. This method removes many of the artifacts of the original subdivision algorithm but lacks the control provided by that algorithm. Voss also discusses methods that produce models with even greater statistical invariance under scaling and have other mathematical properties more consistent with the original definition of fractals [VOSS85]. In particular, the Weierstrass–Mandelbrot random fractal function gives a computationally tractable mechanism for generating fractal functions of one variable, and can doubtless be extended to two or more.

Mandlebrot has developed another improvement of the midpoint-displacement algorithm [PEIT88]. His first observation is that the displacements in the original midpoint-displacement algorithm are symmetric, so when a fractal mountain of this sort is inverted, it has the same statistical properties as when upright. Real mountains look very different from inverted valleys, and Mandlebrot models this asymmetry by choosing the displacements from a nonsymmetric distribution, such as a binomial distribution. He also relieves some of the ''creasing'' of the midpoint model by choosing a different subdivision method. Rather than starting with an initial mesh of triangles, he starts from an initial mesh of hexagons. Noting that height values need to be associated with only the vertices in a mesh, he changes the topology of the mesh during subdivisions so that the initial edges of the hexagon are no longer edges in the subdivision. Instead, he replaces the hexagon with three smaller hexagons, as shown in Fig. 20.9. The central vertex has its height computed as in the triangle algorithm—as an average of the neighboring vertices in the original hexagon, plus a displacement. The other six new vertices are given heights that are weighted averages of the vertices of the hexagon. Mandlebrot says that different choices of weights give substantially different results. The principle feature of this subdivision is that the edges of

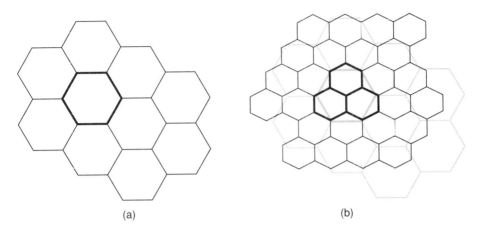

Fig. 20.9 (a) The initial hexagon mesh. One hexagon has been drawn in heavier lines. (b) The subdivided hexagon mesh, with the descendants of the outlined hexagon drawn in heavy lines.

the original hexagons, along which creases might have formed, are now distorted into multiple edges, so that the creases will be far less apparent. The fractals so generated are extremely impressive.

For further fractal algorithms, see [VOSS85; PEIT86].

Other iterative processes can be used to generate a great many interesting images. The grammar-based models and particle systems described in the following sections give some sense of the power of this approach. The changes in those models at deep levels of recursion illustrate a deficiency of the self-similarity model for natural objects. The structure of a tree may be self-similar at certain levels—branches and twigs look a lot alike—but the leaves of a tree do not really look much like a tree.

Rendering fractals can be difficult. If the fractals are rendered into a z-buffer, displaying the entire object takes a long time because of the huge number of polygons involved. In scan-line rendering, it is expensive to sort all the polygons so that only those intersecting the scan line are considered. But ray tracing fractals is extremely difficult, since each ray must be checked for intersection with each of the possibly millions of polygons involved. Kajiya [KAJI83] gave a method for ray tracing fractal objects of the class described in [FOUR82], and Bouville [BOUV85] improves this algorithm by finding a better bounding volume for the objects.

Kajiya points out that, if one starts with a triangle and displaces points within it in the vertical direction, as described in [FOUR82], the resulting object lies within a triangular prism of infinite extent, whose cross-section is the original triangle. If the displacements of the points of the triangle are small enough, then their sum remains finite, and the shape based at the triangle is contained in a truncated triangular prism (''slice of cheesecake''; see Fig. 20.10). We could thus ray trace a fractal mountain by first checking whether a ray hits a cheesecake slice for each of the original triangles; if not, no further checking of that triangle's descendants is necessary. By creating additional slices of cheesecake for further

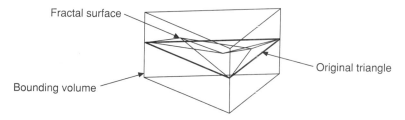

Fractal surface

Original triangle

Bounding volume

Fig. 20.10 A slice of cheesecake that bounds a fractal perturbation of a triangle.

subdivided triangles, we could further reduce intersection testing, although creating a slice for every single facet in the fractal can require prohibitive space.

This method has two disadvantages: detecting whether a ray intersects a cheesecake slice requires computing intersections with several planes (i.e., solving several algebraic equations), and the slice of cheesecake is not a tight bounding volume—lots of rays hit the cheesecake but never hit the fractal. Bouville observed that, when a triangle is subdivided and interior vertices are displaced, the original vertices remain fixed [BOUV85]. He therefore proposed fitting an ellipsoid around the subdivided triangle so that the original three vertices lay on an equator of the ellipsoid, and the displaced internal vertices all lay within the ellipsoid. In fact, as long as the displaced internal vertices lie within the ellipsoid with high probability, the results are attractive (determining this probability requires artistic rather than scientific judgment). If the ellipsoid is made so large as to be certain to contain all possible displaced vertices, it may be a bad bounding region, in the sense that many rays hit the ellipsoid but not the fractal object within. Notice that testing ray–ellipsoid intersection is easy: It amounts to solving one quadratic equation. This makes the Bouville method far faster than is the slice-of-cheescake method. Furthermore, the ellipsoids include much less extraneous volume than do the slices of cheesecake, so fewer levels of recursion are expected.

One other form of fractal modeling deserves mention, and that is the iterated function systems (IFSs) described in Chapter 17. The IFSs described there differ from all the other forms of modeling in this chapter, in that they model the *image* rather than the objects in the image. That is, a specification of a collection of contractive affine maps, associated probabilities, and a coloring algorithm, as described in Section 17.7.2, simply provides a compact description of a pixmap. For example, in the scene shown in Color Plate IV.1, altering a single affine map might distort the image substantially, shearing a limb away from every tree (and a branch away from every limb, and a twig away from every branch). It might also cause a branch to appear where one was not wanted.

IFSs can be used to generate images with great complexity. Since images of this sort are often desirable for pattern mapping, we can expect to see IFSs become a standard part of the modeler's toolkit.

A careful study of IFSs reveals that the technique does not actually depend on the dimension, so IFS models of 3D objects can be made as well. In some sense, the grammar-based models discussed next are quite similar: New parts of a model are generated by transformation of old parts to smaller-sized copies of some or all of the original parts.

20.4 GRAMMAR-BASED MODELS

Smith [SMIT84] presents a method for describing the structure of certain plants, originally developed by Lindenmayer [LIND68], by using parallel graph grammar languages (*L-grammars*), which Smith called *graftals*. These languages are described by a grammar consisting of a collection of productions, all of which are applied at once. Lindenmayer extended the languages to include brackets, so the alphabet contained the two special symbols, "[" and "]." A typical example is the grammar with alphabet {A, B, [,]} and two production rules:

1. A → AA
2. B → A[B]AA[B]

Starting from the axiom A, the first few generations are A, AA, AAAA, and so on; starting from the axiom B, the first few generations are

0. B
1. A[B]AA[B]
2. AA[A[B]AA[B]]AAAA[A[B]AA[B]]

and so on. If we say that a word in the language represents a sequence of segments in a graph structure and that bracketed portions represent portions that branch from the symbol preceding them, then the figures associated with these three levels are as shown in Fig. 20.11.

   This set of pictures has a pleasing branching structure, but a somewhat more balanced tree would be appealing. If we add the parentheses symbols, "(" and ")," to the language and alter the second production to be A[B]AA(B), then the second generation becomes

2. AA[A[B]AA(B)]AAAA(A[B]AA(B))

If we say that square brackets denote a left branch and parentheses denote a right branch, then the associated pictures are as shown in Fig. 20.12. By progressing to later generations in such a language, we get graph structures representing extremely complex patterns. These graph structures have a sort of self-similarity, in that the pattern described by the

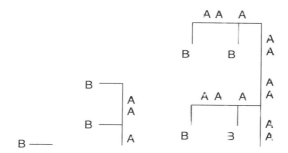

Fig. 20.11 Tree representations of the first three words of the language. All branches are drawn to the left of the current main axis.

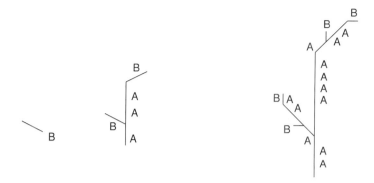

Fig. 20.12 Tree representations of the first three words, but in the language with two-sided branching. We have made each segment of the tree shorter as we progress into further generations.

*n*th-generation word is contained (repeatedly, in this case) in the *(n + 1)*th-generation word.

Generating an object from such a word is a process separate from that of generating the word itself. Here, the segments of the tree have been drawn at successively smaller lengths, the branching angles have all been 45°, and the branches go to the left or to the right. Choosing varying branching angles for different depth branches, and varying thicknesses for the lines (or even cylinders) representing the segments gives different results; drawing a "flower" or "leaf" at each terminal node of the tree further enhances the picture. The grammar itself has no inherent geometric content, so using a grammar-based model requires both a grammar and a geometric interpretation of the language.

This sort of enhancement of the languages and the interpretation of words in the language (i.e., pictures generated from words) has been carried out by several researchers [REFF88; PRUS88]. The grammars have been enriched to allow us to keep track of the "age" of a letter in a word, so that the old and young letters are transformed differently (this recording of ages can be done with rules of the form A → B, B → C, C → D, . . . , Q → QG[Q], so that no interesting transitions occur until the plant has "aged"). Much of the work has been concentrated on making grammars that accurately represent the actual biology of plants during development.

At some point, however, a grammar becomes unwieldy as a descriptor for plants: Too many additional features are added to it or to the interpretation of a word in it. In Reffye's model [REFF88], the simulation of the growth of a plant is controlled by a small collection of parameters that are described in biological terms and that can be cast in an algorithm. The productions of the grammar are applied probabilistically, rather than deterministically.

In this model, we start as before with a single stem. At the tip of this stem is a *bud*, which can undergo one of several transitions: it may die, it may flower and die, it may sleep for some period of time, or it may become an *internode*, a segment of the plant between buds. The process of becoming an internode has three stages: the original bud may generate one or more *axillary buds* (buds on one side of the joint between internodes) a process that is called *ramification*; the internode is added; and the end of the new internode becomes

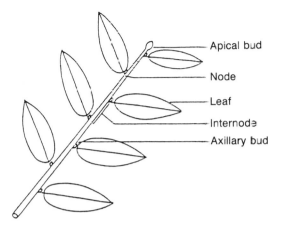

Fig. 20.13 The bud at the tip of a segment of the plant can become an internode; in so doing, it creates a new bud (the *axillary bud*), a new segment (*the internode*), and a new bud at the tip (the *apical bud*).

an *apical bud* (a bud at the very end of a sequence of internodes). Figure 20.13 shows examples of the transition from bud to internode.

Each of the buds in the resulting object can then undergo similar transitions. If we say the initial segment of the tree is of *order 1*, we can define the order of all other internodes inductively: Internodes generated from the apical bud of an order-*i* internode are also of order-*i*; those generated from axillary buds of an order-*i* internode are of order (*i* + 1). Thus, the entire trunk of a tree is order 1, the limbs are order 2, the branches on those limbs are order 3, and so on. Figure 20.14 shows a more complicated plant and the orders of various internodes in the plant.

The discussion so far describes the topology of the plant, but does not describe the shape at all — whether the branches point up, down, or sideways has not been recorded. The

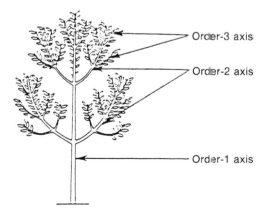

Fig. 20.14 A more complex plant (see Fig. 20.13), with orders attached to the various internodes.

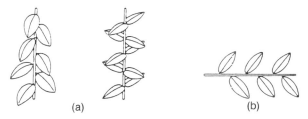

Fig. 20.15 (a) Two different arrangements of leaves: spiraled and distic. (b) The effects of different branching angles.

placement of axillary buds on a sequence of order-i internodes may occur in different ways (see Fig. 20.15a), and the angles at which the order-$(i + 1)$ internodes (if any) branch out from the order-i axillary buds also determine the shape of the plant (see Fig. 20.15b). There are also some anomalies in tree growth, in which the behavior of a collection of order-$(i + 1)$ internodes is not standard, but instead resembles that of some lower order (this is called *reiteration*), and this too must be modeled.

Finally, converting this description into an actual image of a tree requires a model for the shapes of its various components: an order-1 internode may be a large tapered cylinder, and an order-7 internode may be a small green line, for example. The sole requirement is that there must be a leaf at each axillary node (although the leaf may fall at some time).

To simulate the growth of a plant in this model, then, we need the following biological information: the current age of the model, the growth rate of each order of internode, the number of axillary buds at the start of each internode (as a function of the order of the internode), and the probabilities of death, pause, ramification, and reiteration as functions of age, dimension, and order. We also need certain geometric information: the shape of each internode (as a function of order and age), the branching angles for each order and age, and the tropism of each axis (whether each sequence of order-i internodes is a straight line, or curves toward the horizontal or vertical). To draw an image of the plant, we need still more information: the color and texture of each of the entities to be drawn—internodes of various orders, leaves of various ages, and flowers of different ages.

Pseudocode to simulate the growth process is shown in Fig. 20.16.

We can cast this entire discussion in terms of the grammar models that inspired it by assigning different letters in the alphabet to apical and axillary buds of various ages, and associating probabilities with the productions of the language. Since the application of productions amounts to the processing in the pseudocode, however, it is not clear that such a reformulation is particularly valuable.

Varying the values for the probabilities and angles can produce a wide variety of extremely convincing tree models, a few of which are shown in Color Plates IV.12 and IV.13. The correct choices for these parameters depend on knowledge of plant biology or on the modeler's artistic eye; by using the wrong values, we can also generate plants bearing no resemblance at all to anything real.

These plant models are the most spectacular examples of grammar-based modeling. The method has been used in other applications as well, including architecture [STIN78]. In any domain in which the objects being modeled exhibit sufficient regularity, there may be an opportunity to develop a grammar-based model.

```
for (each clock time) {
    for (each bud that is still alive) {
        determine from order, age, etc., what happens to bud;
        if (bud does not die)
            if (bud does not sleep) {
                create an internode (with geometric information
                        about its position, direction. etc.);
                create apical bud;
                for (each possible bud at old bud location)
                    if (ramification)
                        create axillary buds;
            } /* if */
    } /* for */
} /* for */
```

Fig. 20.16 Pseudocode for the plant-growth algorithm. Adapted from [REFF88].

20.5 PARTICLE SYSTEMS

Particle systems are an intriguing approach to modeling objects whose behavior over time cannot easily be described in terms of the surface of the objects (i.e., objects whose topology may change) [REEV83; REEV85]. A *particle system* is defined by a collection of particles that evolves over time. The evolution is determined by applying certain probabilistic rules to the particles: they may generate new particles, they may gain new attributes depending on their age, or they may die (disappear from the object). They also may move according to either deterministic or stochastic laws of motion. Particle systems have been used to model fire, fog, smoke, fireworks, trees. and grass.

Particles have been used for years as elementary entities in graphics modeling, especially in early video games, where they denoted bullets or exploding spaceships. These particles however, were deterministic and had to be placed individually. The *effects* of large collections of particles have also been used before and since to model the transmission and reflection of light in fog and in other diffuse media [BLIN82a; NISH87; RUSH87]. The essence of particle systems is that the positions of the particles are generated automatically, their evolution is controlled automatically, and the individual particles affect the final image directly.

In his first paper on particle systems [REEV83], Reeves describes their use in modeling fire, explosions, and fireworks. Reeves and Blau went on [REEV85] to use them in modeling the grass and trees in a forest. In this context. the particle systems look a great deal like the probabilistic grammar-based models described in the previous section. For example, the trees are modeled as particle systems in which each branch is a particle, each of which is placed randomly along the trunk's length; and each branch may fork or extend according to some probability. The branching angles or the various segments are selected from a distribution, as is the length of the branch (depending on its position in the tree). The particles in this system are like the letters of the alphabet in the grammar-based approach, and the rules for particle birth, death, and transformation correspond to the productions in the grammar.

The modeling of fire in [REEV83] is quite different. Here, the particles have a tree structure (particles have child particles), but the tree structure is not incorporated into the resulting image. Two levels of particle systems were used in modeling the Genesis effect in Color Plate IV.14. The first generated a collection of particles on circles of varying radii centered at a single point on the planet's surface; the particles were distributed about these circles at random positions selected from a probability distribution. Each of these particles was then used as the starting location for a new particle system of a different type (an *explosion* particle system).

In the *Genesis effect*, an explosion particle system is used to model a small burst of sparks from a region on the planet's surface (such systems can also be used to model fireworks and similar phenomena.) The particles of the system are generated in a small disk on the planet's surface with an initial direction of motion that is upward from the surface but may have some horizontal component as well (see Fig. 20.17). The position of each particle at subsequent times is computed by adding its velocity vector to its current position; the velocity vector may be updated by an acceleration vector (which may include gravity) as well. The placement of the particles in the disk, the rate at which they are generated, the initial velocities, and the lifetimes of the particles are all randomly chosen. In each such choice, the value of the property is chosen by a rule of the form

$$property = centralValueForProperty + Random() * VarianceOfProperty,$$

so the central value and variance of the property must be specified as well.

The colors of the particles are initially set to red, with some green and a little blue, and alter over time to fade away, with the red component lasting longer than the green or blue, to simulate the cooling of a white-hot material.

Rendering particle systems is a different matter altogether. Ray tracing a particle system would be impossible, since computing the intersection of each ray with even a bounding box for each of several million particles would be immensely time consuming. To render the fire in the Genesis sequence, Reeves simply took each particle as a small point of light and computed the contribution of this light source to the final image. Since the particles were moving, he actually computed a short line segment representing the path of the particle during the frame being rendered, and then rendered this line segment (antialiased) into the final pixmap.[5] Each pixel value was computed by accumulating the values from each particle, so some pixels that were affected by many particles became clamped to the maximum values of red, green, and blue (especially red, since that was the dominant particle color). Particles that were actually behind other particles still contributed to the image, so no occluding of particles was done at all. Two tricks were used for the numerous fires burning on the planet. First, all the particles on the hidden side of the planet were rendered, then the planet was rendered, and then the front particles were rendered. These were composited together in the order back particles–planet–front particles to prevent the particles on the back from showing through the planet's surface (i.e., no *z* information was stored with the rendered images of the particles). Also, the particle systems contributed light only to the screen image, whereas actual fires would illuminate the nearby portions of

---

[5]This constitutes *motion blur*, which is discussed in Chapters 14 and 21.

Plate IV.1 An image generated with an iterated function system.
The function system contains fewer than 120 affine maps. (Courtesy
of Michael Barnsley, Arnaud Jacquin, François Malassenet,
Laurie Reuter, and Alan Sloan.)

Plate IV.2 Strokes drawn with an antialiased brush.
(Courtesy of Turner Whitted, Bell Laboratories.)

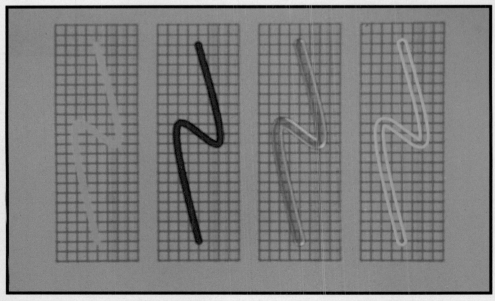

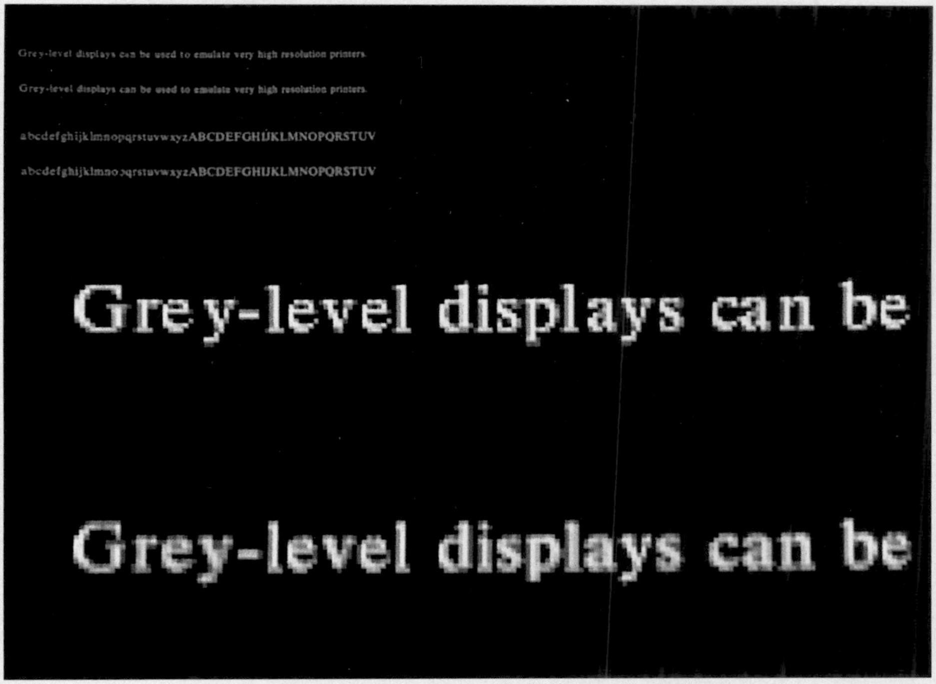

Grey-level displays can be used to emulate very high resolution printers.

Grey-level displays can be used to emulate very high resolution printers.

abcdefghijklmnopqrstuvwxyzABCDEFGHIJKLMNOPQRSTUV

abcdefghijklmno.pqrstuvwxyzABCDEFGHIJKLMNOPQRSTUV

Grey-level displays can be

Grey-level displays can be

Plate IV.3 Antialiased text as displayed by the YODA display.
(Courtesy of Satish Gupta, IBM T. J. Watson Research Center.)

Plate IV.4(a) A dragon modeled with hierarchical splines.
(Plates (a) and (b) courtesy of David Forsey, Computer
Graphics Laboratory, University of Waterloo.)

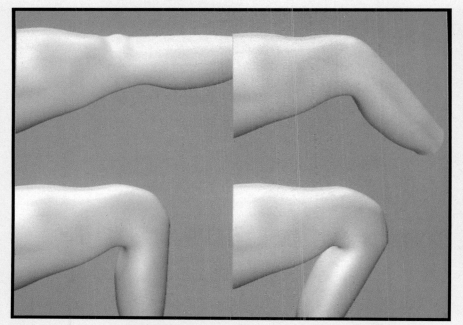

Plate IV.4(b) Skin modeled by defining hierarchical spline offsets relative to a skeletal model.

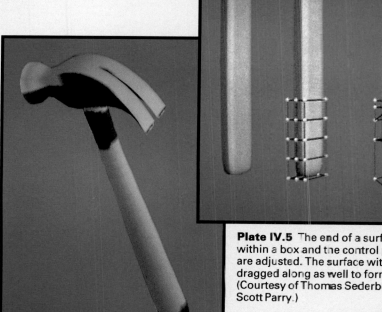

Plate IV.5 The end of a surface is placed within a box and the control points for the box are adjusted. The surface within the box is dragged along as well to form a new shape. (Courtesy of Thomas Sederberg and Scott Parry.)

Plate IV.6 A hammer modeled using free-form deformations (Courtesy of Thomas Sederberg and Alan Zundel.)

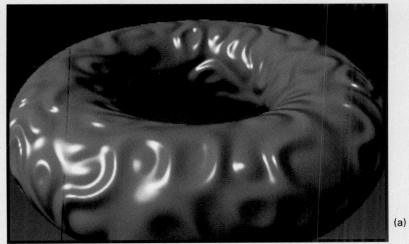

Plate IV.7 Solid textures (a–d). The stucco doughnut is particularly effective. (Courtesy of Ken Perlin.)

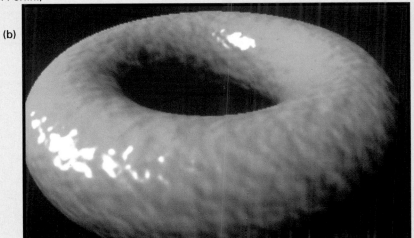

(d)

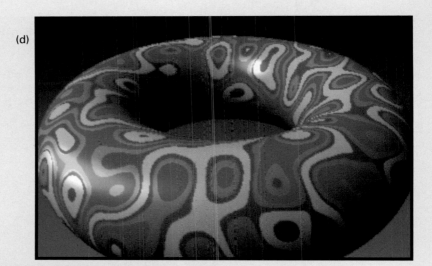

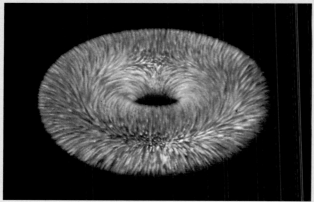

(ə)

(b)

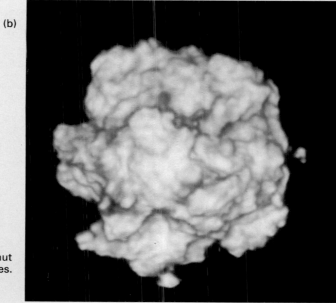

Plate IV.8 (a) A hairy donut
modelled with hypertextures.
(b) A hypertextured blob.
(Courtesy of Ken Perlin.)

Plate IV.9 A hypertextured cube, showing how the texturing affects the geometry as well as the colors and normals of the surface. (Courtesy of Ken Perlin.)

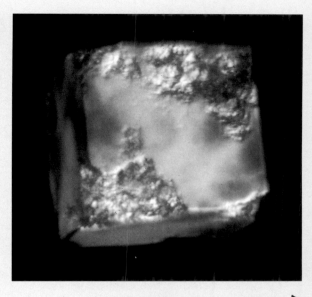

Plate IV.11 "Vol Libre Ridge": ▶ Fractal mountains generated with the Fournier–Fussell–Carpenter algorithm. (Courtesy of Loren Carpenter.)

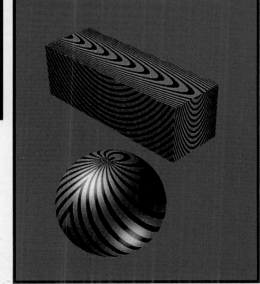

Plate IV.10 Solid textures generated using projection textures. Note that the patterns differ along each of the three principal axes. (Copyright © 1985 by Darwyn Peachey, Univ. of Saskatchewan, reprinted from [PEAC85]).

(a)

(b)

(c)

Plate IV.12 Simple
trees mode ed using
probabilistic grammars:
(a) a palm tree; (b) and
(c) fir trees. [Courtesy of
Atelier de Modilisation et
d'Architecture des
Plantes, © AMAP).

Plate IV.13 More complex trees modeled with the same techniques as in Color Plate IV.12, but with different parameters. (a) A willow tree; (b) a fruit tree in Spring. (Courtesy of Atelier de Modilisation et d'Architecture des Plantes, © AMAP).

(a)

(b)

Plate IV.14 From *Star Trek II: The Wrath of Khan:* One frame from the Genesis effect particle-system animation of an explosion expanding into a wall of fire that engulfs a planet. (Courtesy of Ralph Guggenheim, Pixar. © 1982 Paramount Pictures Corporation, all rights reserved.)

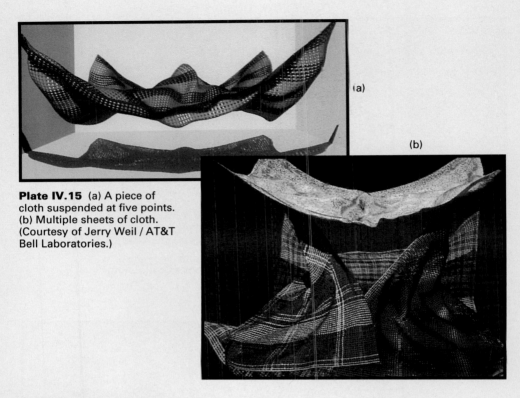

Plate IV.15 (a) A piece of cloth suspended at five points. (b) Multiple sheets of cloth. (Courtesy of Jerry Weil / AT&T Bell Laboratories.)

Plate IV.16 A net falling over a spherical obstacle, with fractures developing. (Courtesy of Demetri Terzopoulos and Kurt Fleischer, Schlumberger.)

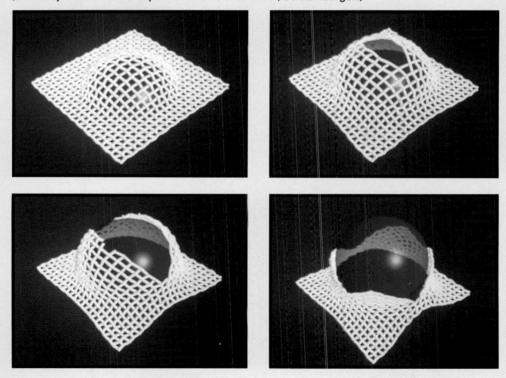

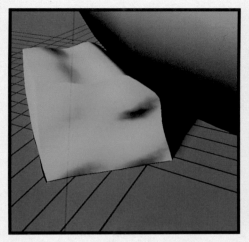
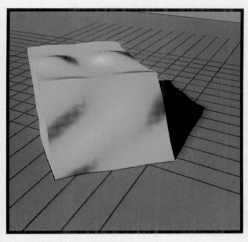

Plate IV.17 An elastic model is squashed by a large sphere and then returns to its rest shape. (Courtesy of Caltech Computer Science Graphics Group, John Platt and Alan Barr.)

Plate IV.18 "Shreve Valley." The terrain is derived from a simple initial terrain consisting of two sloping walls forming a single sloping valley (which becomes the principal stream in the picture). (Courtesy of G. Nielson, Arizona State University.)

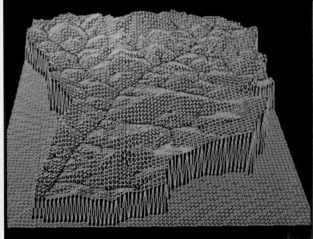

Plate IV.19 A beach at sunset. (Courtesy of Bill Reeves, Pixar, and Alain Fournier, University of Toronto.)

Plate IV.20 A late afternoon scene with a scattering medium in a room. (Holly Rushmeier, Courtesy of Program of Computer Graphics, Cornell University.)

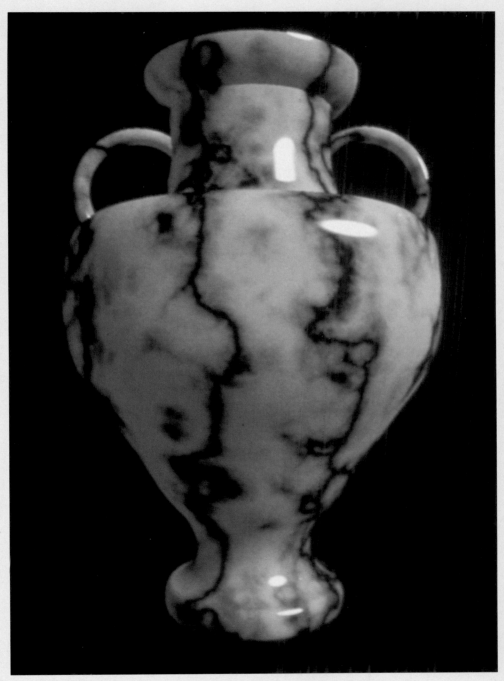

Plate IV.21 A marble vase modeled with solid textures. (Courtesy of Ken Perlin.)

▲

Plate IV.22 A train modeled
with soft objects. ("Entering
Mandrill Space" from *The
Great Train Rubbery* by Brian
Wyvill and Angus Davis,
University of Calgary.)

Plate IV.23 The snake was
produced by Alias Research for
the September 1988 cover of
*IEEE Computer Graphics and
Applications.* The snake was
modeled with the ALIAS
system and rendered with a
color texture map for the skin
markings and a bump map for
the scales. (Produced by Gavin
Miller and Robert LeBlanc of
Alias.)

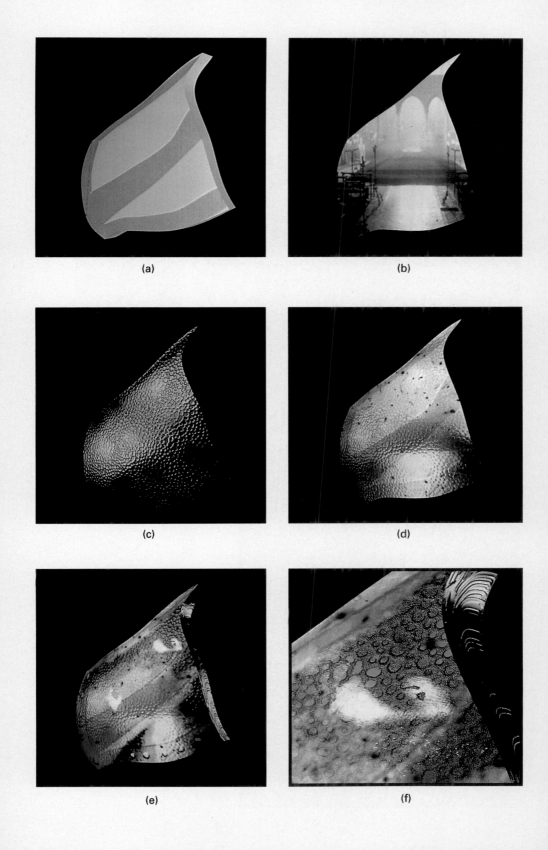

(a)　　　　　　　　　　　　　　　(b)

(c)　　　　　　　　　　　　　　　(d)

(e)　　　　　　　　　　　　　　　(f)

Plate IV.24 The construction of the glass knight for the movie, *Young Sherlock Holmes.* (a) The basic shape of the shoulder guard, with a color map, (b) the piece with an environment map, (c) the environment map modified by a bump map and illumination function, (d) spots of dirt and small bubbles are added, (e) an additional color map is added to provide the stains for the seams and rivets, (f) a detail of the piece, (g) the complete figure; the shoulder piece is in the upper right. (Copyright © 1989 Paramount Pictures. All rights reserved. Courtesy of Industrial Light & Magic.)

(g)

Plate IV.25 The trees in these scenes were positioned with an automatic placement mechanism. The objects are generated using textured quadrics and fractal models. (Courtesy of G.Y. Gardner, Grumman Data Systems.)

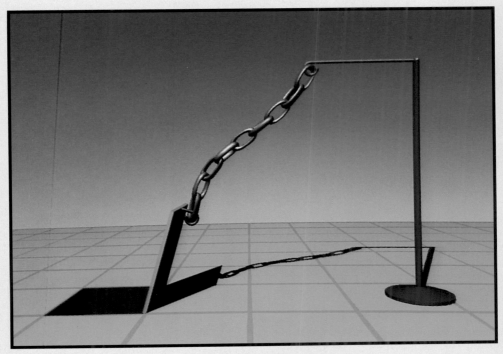

Plate IV.26 A self-assembling system modeled with dynamic constraints. (Courtesy of Caltech Computer Graphics Group, Ronen Barzel and Alan Barr.)

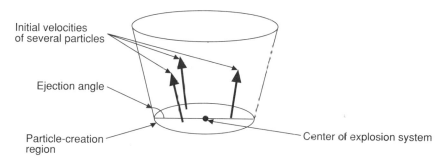

Fig. 20.17 The initial stage of a particle system for modeling an explosion.

the planet. Reeves achieved the nearby lighting by placing a conical light source of high intensity near the surface of the planet, instead of computing the direct illumination from the particles.

In the forest scene for the movie "André and Wally B." [REEV85; LUCA84], a different rendering scheme was required, since the particle systems were no longer light emitters, but instead were trees and grass, which acted as light reflectors. Special-purpose techniques were developed to render the particle systems; some trees obscured others, various portions of the trees were in shadow, the grass was sometimes in shadow from the trees, and so on. The solutions were two-fold: developing probabilistic models for shadowing and using modified z-buffer techniques to compute obscuring. The particles in the tree (leaves and stems) were shaded by computing the depth of the particle into the tree along a ray from the light source to the particle (see Fig. 20.18). This depth was used to compute an exponential drop off in the diffuse component of the light: $D = e^{-kd}$, where D is the diffuse component, k is a constant, and d is the depth of the particle. Particles with small values of d had stochastically computed specular highlights; if d was small and the direction of the light and the direction of the branch were nearly perpendicular, a specular highlight might be added. Finally, the ambient light, which is small inside the tree and larger near its edge, was computed by setting $A = \max(e^{-js}, A_{min})$, where j is a constant, s is the distance from the particle to the edge of the tree (in any direction), and A_{min} is a lower bound for the ambient light (even the deepest parts of the tree are slightly illuminated). If a

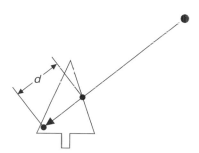

Fig. 20.18 Each point in a tree lies at some depth along the line from the light source to the particle. This distance determines the likelihood of the particle being illuminated.

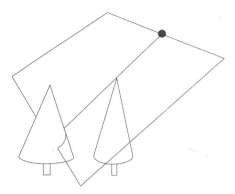

Fig. 20.19 The plane from an adjacent tree, which determines the shadowing of a tree.

tree is in shadow from another tree, the specular and diffuse components should not be added. This was implemented by determining planes from nearby trees to the tree under consideration; the plane contained the top of the nearby tree and the light source, and had the largest possible y component in its normal, as shown in Fig. 20.19. Particles above this plane were lit with all three components, whereas those below were given (probabilistically) less and less diffuse and specular light as the distance from the plane increased.

Even with these simplified lighting computations, visible surfaces still had to be determined. The trees in the scene were sorted back to front, and were rendered in that order. Trees were rendered with a bucket-sort type of z-buffer. Each tree's depth extent was divided into a great many buckets; every particle that was generated was inserted into the bucket for its depth in the tree. When all particles had been generated, they were rendered in back-to-front bucket order. Each particle was drawn as a small circle or short line segment (antialiased). After each tree was rendered, the information about the tree was discarded. The result of this ordering is that a branch of a nearby tree may obscure a branch of one slightly farther away, even though the second branch lies in front of the first, since the first branch is part of a tree that is rendered (entirely) after the second. In scenes with sufficient complexity, this sorting error seems not to be a problem.

Still, this difficulty in rendering the scene does highlight a drawback of particle systems in general: The modeler gets considerable power, but special-purpose rendering techniques may need to be developed for each new application.

20.6 VOLUME RENDERING

Volume rendering is used to show the characteristics of the interior of a solid region in a 2D image. In a typical example, the solid is a machined part that has been heated, and the temperature has been computed at each point of the interior through some physical or mathematical means. It is now of interest to display this temperature visually. This is not, strictly speaking, a modeling issue, as the shape of the part and the characteristics to be displayed are both available a priori. But the conversion of these data to information in a pixel map is a form of modeling; namely, the modeling of the transformation from 3D to

2D. In another example, the density of human or animal tissue may have been computed at each point of a 3D grid through computed tomography (CT). The display of this information should indicate the boundaries of the various types of tissue (as indicated by density changes). The surfaces defining these boundaries must be inferred from the sample data in order to render the solid.

A number associated with each point in a volume is called the *value* at that point. The collection of all these values is called a *scalar field* on the volume. The set of all points in the volume with a given scalar value is called a *level surface* (if the scalar field is sufficiently continuous, this set of points actually does form a surface). *Volume rendering* is the process of displaying scalar fields. It is important to realize that the data being displayed may not be ideal. If the data have been sampled at the points of a regular grid, the scalar field they represent may contain frequencies higher than the Nyquist frequency for the sampling (see Chapter 14). In tomography, for example, the transition from flesh to bone is very abrupt, and hence contains very high frequencies, but the sampling rate is likely to be too low to represent this change accurately. Also, the data that describe the interior of a solid may be clustered in some irregular pattern, as might arise in geographic data taken from core samples, where it may be impossible to sample uniformly.

Several approaches to volume rendering have been developed. They can be divided into two categories: those that compute level surfaces and those that display integrals of density along rays. The two can be combined by assigning density only to certain level surfaces and then ray tracing the result (which amounts to creating a different volume to be displayed). If animation is available, a third category of display is possible: a series of 2D slices of the data is computed and displayed sequentially, using color or brightness to indicate the scalar value at each point of the slices. If interactive control of the slice direction and level is provided, this approach can give an excellent sense of the interior structure of the scalar field.

Nonetheless, it is sometimes useful to view data in the aggregate, rather than by slices. One approach (though by no means the first) is the *marching-cubes* algorithm. In this algorithm, scalar values are assumed to be given at each point of a lattice in 3-space. A particular level surface can be approximated by determining all intersections of the level surface with edges of a lattice.[6] We look for pairs of adjacent lattice points whose field values surround the desired value (i.e., the value of one vertex is greater than the chosen level, the value of the other is less). The location of an intersection of the level surface with the edge is then estimated by linear interpolation.

Each cube in the lattice now has some number of edges marked with intersection points. The arrangement of the intersection points on the edges can be classified into 256 cases (each of eight vertices of each cube in the lattice is either above or below the target value, giving $2^8 = 256$ possible arrangements). For each case, a choice is made of how to fill in the surface within the cube. Figure 20.20 shows two such cases.

---

[6]A *lattice* is an array of points and lines in space, much like a children's jungle gym. The points of the lattice are evenly spaced in the x, y, and z directions, and they are joined by line segments parallel to the coordinate axes. The set of all points with integer coordinates and of all axis-parallel line segments joining them constitutes an example, called the *integer lattice*.

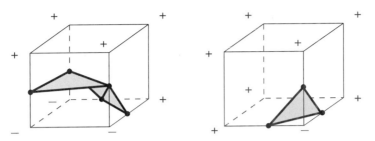

Fig. 20.20 Two possible arrangements of intersections of a level surface with a cube in the integer lattice, with choices of how to fill in a surface for each.

The collection of all the surface pieces just defined constitutes a surface. This surface can be assigned (at each subpolygon) a normal vector to be used for shading in the following manner. At each vertex of the cube, a numerical estimate of the gradient of the scalar field is made. These values are interpolated to estimate the gradient vector at some point of the subsurface. Since the gradient of a scalar field always lies in the direction of the normal vector to the level surface, this interpolated value provides a good estimate for the normal vector. (The special case of zero must be handled separately.)

The resulting level surface can be rendered with conventional techniques. This strategy can be of use in medical imaging to show the shape of the boundary between different types of tissue. Unfortunately, it computes only one shape at a time, and the relative positions of different layers are difficult to see.

Upson and Keeler [UPSO88] also assume that the scalar field varies linearly between sample points, and they present two methods for its display. In both, the user first creates four functions, R, G, B, and O, where O is *opacity*. The arguments of these functions are values of the scalar field; we therefore assume that the scalar field has been normalized to have values between 0 and 1. The choices of the R, G, B, and O functions drastically affect the resulting image. If the functions are chosen to have tight peaks at particular values of the scalar field, the level surfaces for those values are highlighted. If the functions are chosen to vary smoothly over the field values, then color can be used to indicate field value (see Fig. 20.21). Thus, in effect, we obtain sophisticated color-map pseudocoloring.

The interpolation of the scalar field over each cube in the lattice of sample points is a linear equation in each variable, and hence is trilinear in 3-space (i.e., of the form $S(x, y, z) = A + Bx + Cy + Dz + Exy + Fxz + Gyz + Hxyz$). If we parameterize a ray in the form $(x, y, z) = (a, b, c) + t(u, v, w)$ as in ray tracing, then the value of S at points of the ray is a cubic function of t.

The ability to compute this cubic rapidly forms the basis for Upson and Keeler's first rendering method, based on a ray-tracing mechanism for volume data developed in [KAJI84]. For each ray from the eyepoint through an image pixel, the R, G, B, and O values are accumulated for the ray as it passes through the volume data. This accumulation stops when the opacity reaches a value of 1 or the ray exits the volume, whichever happens first. Actually, far more is accumulated: the scalar field, shading function, opacity, and depth cueing are all computed at each of several steps within each pixel volume so as to integrate the cubic interpolant accurately.

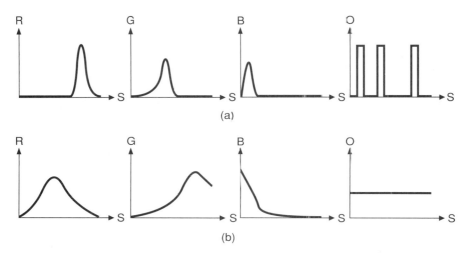

Fig. 20.21 Two different choices for the shapes of the R,G,B, and O functions. In (a), certain level surfaces of the scalar field are highlighted in red, green, and blue. In (b), the color will change gradually as a function of the scalar field.

Upson and Keeler's second rendering method uses the same basic notion of integration along rays, but accumulates values in pixels by processing the cubes in the lattice of values in front-to-back order (which can be easily determined for any particular view orientation). The authors take great pains to ensure the computational efficiency of the process by using adaptive quadrature methods for the integrations and never solving a system of equations more than once at each point (when performing interpolations). It is important to observe, as they do, that this method "is designed as an analytic tool, not as a technique to synthesize realistic images" [UPSO88, p. 64].

Sabella takes a similar approach [SABE88]. He assigns a *density emitter* to each point in the volume to be rendered, to simulate light coming from translucent objects. The simulation models only part of the effects of light in such media; namely, the occlusion of parts deeper in the medium by those nearer the front. Sabella deliberately ignores shadowing and the variation in color due to differences in scattering at different wavelengths, asserting that they may actually detract from the perception of density variation. The density emitters are imagined to be tiny particles that both emit and scatter light. The density of such particles within each small region of space is given by the value of the scalar field there. The light reaching the eye along any ray is computed by summing up the emission from all the emitters along the ray, and then attenuating the light from each emitter by the probability that it is scattered during its travel to the eye. Sabella computes four numbers: M, the peak value of the scalar field along the ray; D, the distance at which that peak is encountered; I, the attenuated intensity just described; and C, the "center of gravity" of the density emitters along the ray. By mapping combinations of these numbers into various color scales (e.g., using hue–saturation–value, he maps M to hue, D to saturation, and I to value), he can highlight various characteristics of the scalar field. He further allows for "lighting" effects by giving a directionality to the particle emissions. Each particle's emissions are attenuated by a Lambert lighting model: Several light sources are positioned around the volume to be rendered, and the emission from a particle at location (x, y, z) is determined by summing the dot products of the gradient of the scalar field and the lighting directions, and multiplying the result by the density at the point. The result is that surfaces of high density look more like reflective surfaces, an effect that helps the eye to disambiguate the information presented.

Even further from the determination of surfaces is the approach taken by Drebin, Carpenter, and Hanrahan at Pixar [DREB88]. These researchers make several important assumptions about the scalar fields being rendered: the volume array of data representing the field is assumed to be sampled at about the Nyquist frequency of the field (or the field has been filtered to ensure this before sampling); the scalar field is modeled by a composition of one or more materials (e.g., bone, fat, and soft tissue) or the volume has several scalar fields attached to it, such as stress and strain in a material. For a multiple-material scalar field, they assume that the materials can be (at least statistically) differentiated by the scalar value at each point, or that information regarding the material composition of each volume element is provided in addition to the scalar field.

Given such information, they create several new scalar fields on the array of sample points: the *material percentage volumes* (they use the term *volume* to mean a scalar field on a volume). The value at a grid point in a material percentage volume is the percentage of one material present in the volume element (or *voxel*) surrounding that point. If multiple fields are specified in the original data, computing these material percentages may be simple. If only a single field is given, the material percentages may have to be estimated by Bayesian analysis.

After computing the material percentage volumes, the authors associate a color and opacity with each material; they then form composite colors and opacities by taking a linear combination of all the colors and opacities for each of the material percentage volumes. (Opacity here is used in the sense of the α channel described in Section 17.6, and the linear combinations are the same as the combinations described there. In particular, the colors are premultiplied by the opacity values before combination.) They further allow compositing with *matte volumes*, which are scalar fields on the volume with values between 0 and 1. By multiplying these matte volumes with the color/opacity volumes, they can obtain slices or portions of the original volumetric data. Making a smooth transition between 0 and 1 preserves the continuity of the data at the matte boundaries.

The lighting model used here is similar to that in the other two algorithms. A certain amount of light enters each voxel (the light from voxels behind the given voxel), and a different amount exits from it. The change in light can be affected by the translucence of the material in the voxel, or by "surfaces" or "particle scatterers" contained in the voxel that may both attenuate the incoming light and reflect light from external light sources. These effects are modeled by (1) requiring that light passing through a colored translucent voxel have the color of that voxel plus the incoming light multiplied by $(1 - \alpha)$ for that voxel (this is the **over** operation of the Feibush–Levoy–Cook compositing model in Section 17.6), and (2) determining surfaces and their reflectance and transmission properties.

The surface determination is not as precise as the ones described previously; each voxel is assigned a density that is a weighted sum of the densities of the component materials for the voxels (weighted by the material percentages). "Surfaces" are simply places where this composite density changes rapidly. The *strength* of a surface is the magnitude of the gradient of the density, and the surface normal used in shading calculations is the direction vector of the gradient. To compute the surface shading, we divide each voxel into regions in front of, on, and behind the surface. The intensity of light leaving the voxel, I', is related to the intensity entering, I, by the rule $I' = (C_{front} \text{ over } (C_{surface} \text{ over } (C_{back} \text{ over } I)))$. The three terms associated with the voxel can be precomputed and mixed because the **over** operator is associative. The surface color is computed by a Cook–Torrance–style model to give both specular and diffuse components; these values are weighted by the strength of the surface so that no reflective lighting appears in homogeneous solids. The colors of the front and back are computed by estimating from which material they came and by using colors from those materials.

The results are excellent. Color Plate I.1 shows the process as applied to data from a CT scan of a child's head. The process is expensive, however. Multiple volumes (i.e. multiple scalar fields) are created in the course of generating the image, and the memory requirements are vast. Also, the assumption that the fields are sampled at or above the Nyquist frequency may not be practical in all cases: sometimes, the data are given, and we wish to see the results even with some aliasing. Finally, the assumption that the data are from a heterogeneous mixture of materials is not always valid, so the applications of the method are limited.

20.7 PHYSICALLY BASED MODELING

The behavior and form of many objects are determined by the objects' gross physical properties (as contrasted with biological systems, whose behavior may be determined by the systems' chemical and microphysical properties). For example, how a cloth drapes over objects is determined by the surface friction, the weave, and the internal stresses and strains generated by forces from the objects. A chain suspended between two poles hangs in an arc determined by the force of gravity and the forces between adjacent links that keep the links from separating. *Physically based modeling* uses such properties to determine the shape of objects (and even their motions in some cases). Current work on this subject is collected in [BARR89].

Most of this modeling uses mathematics well beyond the scope of this book, but we can give the general notions of the techniques. It is in this sort of modeling that the distinction between graphics and other sciences is most blurred. The computations that produce a tear in a model of a thin cloth when it is dropped over an obstruction are purely in the domain of solid mechanics. But such computations would not be done unless the results could be displayed in some fashion, so the motivation for physical research is now being provided by the ability (or desire) to visualize results. At the same time, the wish to generate more realistic graphics models drives research in the physical modeling process. In this section, we discuss a few of the more impressive examples. The next section describes models of natural phenomena that are less directly based on scientific principles and may contain some (or many) compromises in order to produce attractive results. There is a continuous variation between scientific foundations and ad hoc approaches, and the dividing line is not at all clear.

20.7.1 Constraint-Based Modeling

When constructing an object out of primitive objects using Boolean operations, we find it convenient to be able to say "I want to put this sphere on top of this cube so that they touch only at one point." Even with an interactive program that lets the user position objects by eye, it may be difficult to make the two objects touch at a single point.[7] Rules such as this one are called *constraints*. Constraint-based modeling systems allow the user to specify a collection of constraints that the parts of the model are supposed to satisfy. A model may be *underconstrained*, in which case there are additional degrees of freedom that the modeler can adjust (e.g., the location of the point of contact of the sphere and the cube), or *overconstrained*, in which case some of the constraints may not be satisfied (which could happen if both the top and bottom of the sphere were constrained to lie on the top face of the cube). In constraint-based modeling, the constraints must be given a priority, so that the most important constraints can be satisfied first.

The specification of constraints is complex. Certain constraints can be given by sets of mathematical equalities (e.g., two objects that are constrained to touch at specific points), or by sets of inequalities (e.g., when one object is constrained to lie inside another). Other constraints are much more difficult to specify. For example, constraining the motion of an object to be governed by the laws of physics requires the specification of a collection of differential equations. Such constraint systems, however, lie at the heart of physically based modeling.

The earliest constraint-based modeling was done by Sutherland in the Sketchpad system, described in Chapter 21. Many constraint-based modeling systems have been developed since, including constraint-based models for human skeletons [ZELT82; KORE82; BADL87], in which connectivity of bones and limits of angular motion on joints are specified, the *dynamic constraint* system of [BARR88], and the *energy constraints* of [WITK87; WILH87]. These fall into two classes: those in which general constraints can be specified, and those that are tailored for particular classes of constraints. In modeling skeletons, for example, point-to-point constraints, in which corresponding points on two bones are required to touch, are common, as are angular limit constraints, in which the angle between bones at a joint is restricted to lie in a certain range. But constraints that specify that the distance between the centers of mass of two objects be minimized are not so likely to occur. Special-purpose constraint systems may admit analytic solutions of a particular class of constraints, whereas the general-purpose systems are more likely to use numerical methods.

In the energy-constraint system we mentioned, for example, constraints are represented by functions that are everywhere nonnegative, and are zero exactly when the constraints are satisfied (these are functions on the set of all possible states of the objects being modeled). These are summed to give a single function, E. A solution to the constraint problem occurs at a state for which E is zero. Since zero is a minimum for E (its component terms are all nonnegative), we can locate such states by starting at any configuration and altering it so as to reduce the value of E. Finding this minimum is done using numerical methods. In the

---

[7]Typing in numbers is not an adequate compromise, since it may require that the modeler solve a system of equations before typing the numbers.

course of such a process, we may get "stuck" at a local minimum for E, but if we do not, we will eventually reach a global minimum. Such a global minimum is either zero, in which case all constraints are satisfied, or nonzero, in which case some constraints may not be satisfied. By changing the coefficients of the individual constraints in the funtion E, we can stress the importance of some constraints over others. In the case where the system reaches a local minimum, the modeler may start with a different initial configuration, or, in an ideal system, may give a "push" to the configuration to make it move away from the local minimum and toward the global minimum. The sequence of configurations that occurs as the assembly is moving toward a minimum of the function E can be an interesting animation, even though the initial intent was just to model an assembly that satsifies the constraints. In fact, an animation of this sequence of events can be useful in determining characteristics of the function-minimizing algorithm being used.

Further examples of constraint-based modeling are described in Section 20.9 and in Chapter 21.

20.7.2   Modeling Cloth and Flexible Surfaces

Several approaches to modeling cloth and other surfaces have been developed in recent years [WEIL86; WEIL87; TERZ88]. Weil assumes that the cloth is a rectangular weave of threads, each of which is inelastic. The warp and woof positions of a point on the surface provide a coordinate system in which to describe events internal to the cloth, whereas each such point has some 3D location as well. The first assumption in Weil's model is that the cloth is suspended by holding certain points on the cloth at certain positions in 3-space; thus, the "position" of the cloth is initially determined at some finite number of points. The line between any two such points (in the intrinsic coordinate system) is assumed to map onto a catenary curve (which is the shape in which a chain hangs). This determines the positions of several lines in the cloth. Notice that, at a point where two lines cross, the position of the intersection point is overdetermined; Weil simply ignores the lower catenary in any such case. The lines between suspension points on the surface determine regions in the cloth, each of which is filled in with more catenaries. The shape of the cloth has now been determined (at least initially). So far, the structure of the cloth has been ignored: The threads making up the cloth may be stretched, whereas they were supposed to be inelastic. Weil proceeds to a relaxation process that iteratively moves the points in a manner to relieve the "tension" in the threads, by computing the direction vectors between each point and its neighbors. These vectors are multiplied by their own lengths, then are averaged to compute a displacement for the point itself (the multiplication ensures that larger errors have greater effects). This process is iterated until the surface is sufficiently close to satisfying the constraints. A similar method is used to model stiffness of the cloth. Color Plate IV.15 shows the results of this model and the modified model described in [WEIL87].

Terzopoulos and Fleischer [TERZ88] take a more sophisticated approach, and model media more general than cloth as well. They assume that a material is arranged as a grid (possibly 3D, but 2D for cloth), and that adjacent points in the grid are connected by *units* consisting of springs, dashpots (which are like shock absorbers), and plastic slip units. A spring responds to a force by deforming elastically in an amount proportional to the force; when the force goes away, so does the deformation. A dashpot responds to a force by

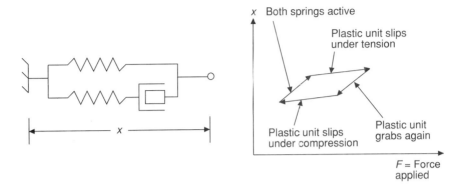

Fig. 20.22 A plastic slip unit connected in series with one spring and in parallel with another creates a unit that responds to a deforming force in a springlike fashion until the force reaches a threshold value. Then the slip unit slips, and retains the deformation until a sufficiently great force restores the unit to its original state.

deforming at a *rate* proportional to the force. Thus, a constant force causes a dashpot to stretch until the force is removed, at which point the dashpot stops deforming. A plastic slip unit responds to a force by doing nothing until the force reaches a certain level, and then slipping freely; these units are best used in combination with other units, such as spring units. Placing a plastic and two spring units in the arrangement shown in Fig. 20.22 creates a unit that stretches gradually (both springs stretching, plastic unit static) until the force on the plastic unit reaches its threshold. At this point, the plastic unit slips and the spring attached to it contracts for a moment, until the other spring takes up some of the load. Thus, at that point, it is as though the system consisted of only the solo spring. Once the applied force is reduced, the lower spring takes up some (compression) load, until the force becomes sufficiently negative to cause the plastic slip unit to slip again.

A grid of such units, subject to laws of physics (modeled globally by rigid-body dynamics but locally by stress and strain rules related to the structure of the units in the material in an internal coordinate system), deforms and stretches. In particular, if threads in the cloth are modeled by plastic slip units, then at some level of tension the units will slip (i.e., the thread will break), and a tear will result. Color Plate IV.16 shows an example of the results.

20.7.3   Modeling Solids

The Terzopoulos and Fleischer model discussed in the previous section can also be used to describe either linear or solid assemblies as collections of points linked by units of varying elasticity or viscosity. Platt and Barr [PLAT88] have done similar work in modeling deformable solids (e.g., putty or gelatin) by combining the solid mechanics underlying such structures with the tools of dynamic constraints. The essence of their work is to set up large collections of differential equations that determine the state of the particle assemblies (or finite-element mesh) at each time, subject to the goals that certain functions (such as energy) be minimized while certain constraints (such as noninterpenetration of objects) are met. Their actual model considers the constraints as objectives to be achieved, along with the minimization of the functions, and thus the constraints are met only approximately. The stronger the effect of each constraint, the more difficult the solution of the differential equations becomes. Despite this numerical difficulty, the results are certainly impressive enough to warrant further research (see Color Plate IV.17).

20.7.4 Modeling Terrain

In another instance of physically based modeling, Kelley and associates [KELL88] extend stream-erosion models from geomorphology. They begin with statistical observations about the distribution of tributaries, the relationships between link length (a *link* is a segment of a system of tributaries between two junctions or between a source and its first junction) and stream gradient, and the mean valley-sidewall slopes. They use these to model the 2D layout of the pattern of streams for a given gross initial terrain, and then to alter the terrain in the vertical dimension so as to compute the finer detail that fits the stream system so constructed. Color Plate IV.18 shows the results for a simple initial drainage system.

20.8 SPECIAL MODELS FOR NATURAL AND SYNTHETIC OBJECTS

A great deal of work has been done on the modeling of natural phenomena by techniques that are not directly related to the underlying causes of the phenomena; modeling of clouds as patterned ellipsoids is a good example. Much work has also gone into the modeling of phenomena that have no specific visual appearance, such as molecules. The examples in this section lie at all points of the range between scientific accuracy and clever manipulations for generating attractive pictures. These models are meant as tools for graphics, rather than as strict scientific visualizations. It is essential that people creating these models understand the underlying phenomena while recognizing the benefits of a good fake.

20.8.1 Waves

Ocean waves were among the earliest natural phenomena modeled in graphics. Ripples resemble sine waves emanating from either a point or a line, and are simple to model as such. If the distance from the eye to the waves is large enough, it may be unnecessary actually to perturb the surface at all, and the entire effect of the ripples can be generated through bump mapping (although one of the first widely shown examples actually raytraced a complete height field [MAX81]). More complex patterns of ripples or waves can be assembled by summing up band-limited noise to make texture maps describing wave trains [PERL85], and then using these to texture map a planar surface. These patterns look best viewed from above, of course, since realistic side views of waves should show the variations in the height of the surface.

Fournier and Reeves [FOUR86], taking a much more sophisticated approach, model the surface of a body of water as a parametric surface rather than as a height field, allowing the possibility of waves curling over. They take into account much of the theory of deep-water waves as well as the effects of underwater topography on surface waves and the refraction and reflection of waves about obstacles (e.g., the way that waves bend around the end of a breakwater). Conversely, in simulating breaking waves, where theoretical knowledge is limited, they provide some clever approximations that generate good results. Their waves are unfortunately somewhat too smooth near the break, and lack a sharp edge between the leading surface and the trailing edge as the wave is about to break. Nonetheless, the results are extremely good (see Color Plate IV.19). Similar work by Peachey [PEAC85] uses a somewhat less complex model; the overall appearance of the waves is not as realistic, but breaking waves are modeled better.

20.8.2 Clouds and Atmosphere

Fog and haze can both be modeled stochastically and then composited onto images. To enhance the realism, we can weight the effect of the fog by the z values of the image onto which it is composited, so that points farther away are more obscured than are those close by. Similarly, fog and haze can be fitted into ray-tracing schemes by attenuating the image by some power of the distance from the eye to the first intersection point (or, even better, for nonuniform fog, by integrating the fog density along the ray to compute an attenuation function). These techniques have some basis in physics, since light is scattered more as it travels farther through fog. Several distinct models of clouds and of atmospheric haze have been developed. Voss [VOSS85] has generated clouds based on fractals, whereas Gardner [GARD84; GARD85] has modeled clouds as textured ellipsoids. Voss's technique is to generate a fractal in 4-space whose fourth coordinate represents a water-vapor density. By allowing local light scattering to vary with the water-vapor density, he generates some realistic clouds (he uses fractal dimensions 3.2 to 3.5).

By contrast, Gardner's method is based completely on the observed shape of clouds—the clouds look like sheets or blobs, and so are modeled as textured planes and ellipsoids. This model consists of a sky plane, in which thin cloud layers reside, ellipsoids (used to model thick clouds, such as cumuli), and a texturing function for each, that handles the varying shading and translucence of the clouds and sky plane.

Gardner creates a particularly simple texture function, akin the ones used by Perlin for solid textures. He defines

$$T(x, y, z) = k\sum_{i=1}^{n}[c_i \sin(f_i x + p_i) + T_0]\sum_{i=1}^{n}[c_i \sin(g_i y + q_i) + T_0],$$

where the c_i are the amplitudes of the texture at various frequencies, the f_i and g_i are frequencies in the x and y directions, respectively, and the p_i and q_i are corresponding phase shifts. This function has different characteristics depending on the values of the various constants. Assigning values with $f_{i+1} = 2f_i$, $g_{i+1} = 2g_i$ and $c_{i+1} = \sqrt{2}/2\ c_i$ produces variations at several different frequencies, with the amplitudes of variations decreasing as the frequencies increase. Notice how similar this is to the fractal models of terrain height: The mountains have large height variations, the boulders on them are smaller, the sharp corners on the boulders are even smaller.

The phase shifts p_i and q_i are used to prevent all the sine waves from being synchronized with one another—that is, to generate randomness (if these are omitted, the texture function has a visible periodicity). For planar texturing, Gardner suggests $p_i = (\pi/2) \sin(g_i y/2)$, and similarly for q_i. For ellipsoidal textures, he defines $p_i = (\pi/2) \sin(g_i y/2) + \pi \sin(f_i z/2)$, which generates phase shifts in all three dimensions, and he finds that using values $0 \le i \le 6$ provides rich textures.

This set of values defines the texture function. The texture function and the sky plane or cloud ellipsoid must now be combined to generate an image. Gardner uses a lighting model of the form

$$I_1 = (1 - s) I_d + sI_s, \; I_2 = (1 - t) I_1 + tI_t, \; I = (1 - a) I_2 + a,$$

where I_d and I_s are the specular and Lambert components of the intensity, computed as in Chapter 16; I_t is $T(x, y, z)$; and $a, t,$ and s determine the fractions of ambient, texture, and specular reflection, respectively. In addition, to get the effect of a cloud rather than of an ellipse with a cloud painted on it, the edges of the cloud must be made translucent. For clouds in the sky plane, regions of the plane must be made translucent. This is done by defining the translucence, V, by the rule

$$V = \begin{cases} 0 & \text{if } I_t \geq V_1 + D, \\ 1 - (I_t - V_1)/D & \text{if } V_1 - D > I_t \geq V_1, \\ 1 & \text{otherwise,} \end{cases}$$

where V_1 and D together determine the range over which the translucence varies from 0 to 1: at $I_t = V_1$ the translucence is 1; at $I_t = V_1 + D$, the translucence has decreased to 0. This is adequate for sky-plane clouds, but for an ellipsoidal cloud, we expect the translucence to be higher at the edges than it is at the center. Gardner determines a function $g()$, which is 1 at the center of the projection of the ellipsoid onto the film plane and 0 on the edge of the projection. With this function, a different translucence function V for ellipsoids can be created, with two different values, V_1 and V_2, determining the translucence threshold at the edge and at the center:

$$V = 1 - (I_t - V_1 - (V_2 - V_1)(1 - g())/D.$$

This value must be clamped between 0 and 1. Combining the lighting and translucence models gives extremely realistic clouds (especially if they are clustered nicely).

Atmospheric effects with less "substance" than clouds—such as haze, dust, and fog—have been generated using scattering models, typically with the assumption that light is scattered only infrequently within any small volume. Blinn's model of the rings of Saturn [BLIN82a] handled the special case of nearly planar scattering layers made of tiny spherical particles by considering four aspects of scattering:

1. *Phase function*—a tiny spherical particle reflects incident light to a viewer in much the same way as the moon reflects the sun's light to us, which depends on the relative positions of the earth, sun, and moon.

2. *Low albedo*—if the reflectivity of each particle is low, then multiple scattering effects (i.e., the light from reflections bouncing off two or more particles) are insignificant.

3. *Shadowing and masking*—particles more distant from a light source are shadowed by particles in front of them, and light emitted from a particle is attenuated by particles between it and the viewer, and both attenuations are exponential functions of depth into the particle layer.

4. *Transparency*—the transparency of a cloud layer can be described as the probability that a ray passing through it hits no particles, and is an inverse exponential function of the length of the ray contained in the layer.

Max [MAX86] extends this model, by incorporating the shadow volumes developed by Crow [CROW77a]. He computes the light reaching the eye from a surface by taking the light reflected from the surface and adding to it all the light reflected by the intervening atmosphere, just as in Blinn's model; however, some portions of the intervening atmosphere (those in the shadow volumes) reflect no additional light. This generates the appearance of columns of shade (or light) in a reflective atmosphere, like the beams one sees coming through a window in a dusty room. Nishita, Miyawaki, and Nakamae [NISH87] developed a similar technique that handles multiple light sources, light sources with varying intensities (discussed later), and scattering media of varying densities. Their technique is based on determining, for each ray in a ray-tracing renderer, through exactly which volumes of illuminated atmosphere the ray passes, and what illumination comes from each such patch. They incorporate a phase function, different from Blinn's, which is based on an approximation to a more complex scattering theory for relatively small particles, such as dust or fog.

Even further along the same direction is Rushmeier and Torrance's extension of the radiosity model to handle scattering [RUSH87], based on similar theories for modeling heat transfer. In their model, each volume in space (which is divided into small cubes) is dealt with as a separate radiosity element, and not only surface-to-surface interactions, but also surface-to-volume and volume-to-volume interactions, are considered. This can generate extremely complicated systems of equations, but the results are extremely realistic—they constitute some of the most impressive images generated by computer graphics so far (see Color Plate IV.20).

Nishita and Nakamae have also studied the effects of scattering on illumination: A light source that might have been purely directional (such as the light of the sun on the moon's surface) can be diffused by an atmosphere (such as the earth's) and become a scattered source of illumination. An object set on the ground outdoors is illuminated not only by direct sunlight, but also by the light from other regions of the sky (by atmospheric scattering). They model the entire sky as a hemispherical light source with varying intensity, then compute the lighting for an object by integrating over this hemisphere. Color Plate III.22(c) shows an interior scene illuminated by this hemisphere.

20.8.3 Turbulence

The accurate mathematical modeling of turbulence has been of interest for many years, and good fluid-mechanics simulators are now available. These can be used to model turbulence directly, as done by Yeager and Upson [YEAG86], or more empirical models can be used to generate good approximations of the effects of turbulence, as done by Perlin [PERL85]. Perlin's model is particularly simple to replicate in the form of a solid texture (see Section 20.1.2). The turbulence at a point $p = (x, y, z)$ is generated by summing up a collection of Noise() functions of various frequencies; pseudocode for this is given in Fig. 20.23.

The resulting Turbulence() function can be used to generate marble textures by defining Marble(x, y, z) = MarbleColor(sin(x + Turbulence(x, y, z))), where MarbleColor maps values between -1 and 1 into color values for the marble. The x within the sin() is used to generate a smoothly varying function, which is then perturbed by the turbulence function. If MarbleColor has sufficiently high derivatives (i.e., sufficiently great intensity changes) at

```
double Turbulence (double x, double y, double z)
{
    double turb = 0.0;      /* Turbulence is a sum of Noise () terms */
    double s = 1.0;         /* s = scale of the noise; 1 = whole image */

    while (s is greater than pixel size) {
        turb += fabs (s * Noise ( x/s, y/s, z/s) );
        s /= 2.0;
    }
    return turb;
} /* Turbulence */
```

Fig. 20.23 Pseudocode for the turbulence function.

a few points, there will be sharp boundaries between the basic marble and the veins that run through it (see Color Plate IV.21).

20.8.4 Blobby Objects

Molecules are typically portrayed by ball-and-stick models. But the actual physics of molecules reveals that the electron clouds around each atom are not spherical, but rather are distorted by one another's presence (and by other effects as well). To get a better image of surfaces of constant electron density, we must consider the effects of neighboring atoms. In the same way, any collection of items, each of which creates a spherically symmetric scalar field and whose fields combine additively, has *isosurfaces* (surfaces along which the field is constant) modeled not by a collection of overlapping spheres, but rather by some more complex shape. Computing the exact isosurfaces may be impractical, but several good approximations have been made. This was first done independently by Blinn [BLIN82b], in whose system the fields created by each item decayed exponentially with distance and by Nishimura et al. for use in the LINKS project [NISH83a]. Wyvill, McPheeters, and Wyvill [WYVI86] modify Blinn's technique nicely. They model "soft objects" by placing a collection of field sources in space and then computing a field value at each point of space. The field value is the sum of the field values contributed by each source, and the value from each source is a function of distance only. They use a function of distance that decays completely in a finite distance, R, unlike Blinn's exponential decay. Their function,

$$C(r) = \begin{cases} -(\tfrac{4}{9})r^6/R^6 + (\tfrac{17}{9})r^4/R^4 - (\tfrac{22}{9})r^2/R^2 + 1 & \text{if } 0 \le r \le R, \\ 0 & \text{if } R < r, \end{cases}$$

has the properties that $C(0) = 1$, $C(R) = 0$, $C'(0) = 0$, $C'(R) = 0$, and $C(R/2) = \tfrac{1}{2}$. Figure 20.24 shows a graph of $C(r)$. These properties ensure that blending together surfaces gives smooth joints, and that the field has a finite extent. They compute a number, m, with the property that the volume of the set where $C(r) \ge m$ is exactly one-half the volume of the set where $2C(r) \ge m$. If two sources are placed at the same location and the level-m isosurface is constructed, it therefore has twice the volume of the isosurface for a single source. Thus,

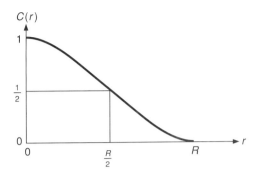

Fig. 20.24 The function $C(r)$.

when soft objects merge, their volumes add. (Notice that, if two sources are far apart, the isosurface may have two separate pieces.)

An isosurface of the field can be computed by an algorithm that resembles the marching-cubes algorithm discussed in Section 20.6, but that is far faster. By evaluating the field at a sequence of grid points along one axis extending from each source, we find a cube with an edge intersected by the isosurface (the edge lies between the last grid point whose value was greater than m and the first whose value is less than m). Because the field value for each source decreases with distance, this collection of cubes (called *seed cubes*) has the property that each piece of the isosurface intersects at least one of them. Thus, by working outward from these seed cubes, we can locate the entire level surface. Additional work can be avoided by flagging each cube that has been processed (these flags, together with various function values, can be stored in a hash table to prevent excessively large data structures). (Another method for computing implicit surfaces is given in [BLOO88].)

The objects modeled with this technique resemble plasticine models [WYVI88] and can be used for molecular modeling, or for modeling droplets of fluid that flow into one another. See Color Plate IV.22 for an example.

20.8.5 Living Things

The plants described in Section 20.4, with their basis in L-grammars, are comparatively simple living things, and the regularity of their form makes them relatively easy to model. Models for shells and coral [KAWA82] and for imaginary living things [KAWA88] have been developed as well. Some biologically simple animals have been modeled recently by physically based techniques, but these models have been adapted to produce good pictures at the cost of some biological realism [MILL88a]. As Miller notes, "One of the great advantages of modeling something like worms is that no one wants to look at them too closely" [MILL88b]. Although the computational costs of biologically and physically realistic models are still prohibitive, the implication of Miller's observation is important—a good eye for appearance may be entirely sufficient to model a peripheral aspect of a scene.

Miller's model of worms and snakes is based on interactions between masses and springs, with muscle contractions modeled as changes in spring tension. The forward motion of the worms and snakes is modeled by adding in directional friction as a force—each segment is allowed to move only forward, and trying to move backward instead draws forward the more tailward segments of the creature. Miller uses bump mapping and pattern mapping to model the appearance of the snakes and worms. He also generates hair for caterpillars by stochastically distributing the bases of the hairs over the body, and distributing the hair ends in a local coordinate system for each hair based on the surface normal and tangent directions to the surface at the base of the hair. He thus can model directional hair. One of his snakes is shown in Color Plate IV.23.

The flight and flocking of birds and schooling of fish have been modeled by Reynolds [REYN87]. The simulation of behavior is so good in this model that the rough appearance of the creatures is only somewhat distracting. As modeling proceeds to the higher genera, the necessity for accuracy increases, since our familiarity with such creatures makes it impossible for us to ignore modeling flaws.

20.8.6 Humans

The modeling of humans is the final frontier. Our ability to recognize and distinguish faces is remarkable; computer graphics images of people must be extremely convincing to satisfy our demands for realism. It is far easier to model a roomful of realistic objects than it is to create one realistic face.

The need for such models has been recognized for some time. Many of the scenes with which we are familiar have people in them, and it would be useful to model these people in a nondistracting way. The eventual goal is to move from this use of people as "extras" in computer-generated movies to their use in "bit parts" and eventually in leading roles. Some progress has been made in this area. Catmull has modeled hands [CATM72] as polygonal objects. The pieces of the hand (fingers, individual joints, etc.) are structured hierarchically, so moving a finger moves all of its joints. Furthermore, each vertex within a joint may be specified either as being a part of the joint itself or in the description of its parent in the hierarchy (the next joint closer to the palm). Thus, when the parent is moved, the shape of the joint may change.

Parke [PARK82], Platt and Badler [PLAT81], and Waters [WATE87] have all developed facial models. Waters models the face as a connected network of polygons whose positions are determined by the actions of several muscles; these muscles are modeled as sheets that can contract. Some of these muscle sheets are anchored to a fixed point in the head, and some are embedded in the skin tissue. The former act by a contraction toward the anchor point, and the latter by contraction within themselves. The facial polygons are modeled by giving their vertices as points on the muscle sheets. Activating a muscle therefore distorts the face into an expression. This arrangement is an improvement on a similar model by Platt and Badler, in which the muscles were modeled as contractable networks of lines, rather than as sheets. Parke also extends this work by allowing control of both the expression and the *conformation* (the characteristics that make one person's face different from another's). In all these models, an essential feature is that the control of the expression is reduced to a few parameters, so that the modeler does not need to place each vertex of each polygon explicitly.

Zeltzer [ZELT82] has done extensive work in modeling the motions of skeletal creatures. The actual structure of the skeletons is comparatively simple (a hierarchical jointed collection of rigid bodies); it is the modeling of the motion that is more complicated. Recent work by Girard [GIRA87] on the motion of legged animals is extremely promising. The modeling of motion is discussed further in Chapter 21.

20.8.7 An Example from the Entertainment Industry

One final example of special-purpose modeling comes from the entertainment industry, in which computer graphics has been widely applied. In the movie *Young Sherlock Holmes,* there is a scene in which a priest hallucinates that he is being attacked by a glass knight that has jumped out from a stained-glass window. The effect would have been quite difficult to produce by conventional animation techniques, as any armatures used to control the knight's motion would have been readily visible through the semi-transparent glass. Computer graphics therefore were used instead.

The series of images in Color Plate IV.24 shows the various techniques involved in modeling the glass. Virtually all of these were implemented by modifying the reflectance function using pattern- and bump-mapping techniques. Part (a) shows a single piece of glass, the shoulder guard, with a color map applied to it, defining its gold stripes. In part (b), an environment map has been applied, showing the church scene behind the piece of glass. In part (c), a bump map has been added, together with an illumination function, and together these modify the environment map of part (b), so that the environment appears refracted through the glass. The shape of the arches is still just barely visible. In part (d), spots of dirt and small bubbles have been added to all the previous effects. In part (e), additional bump maps describe the uneven surfaces on the front of the glass and along the glass's right edge. Part (f) shows a detail of the object. Altogether, three color maps, three bump maps, one transparency map, and one environment map were required to give the glass its realistic appearance. Part (g) shows the complete figure; the shoulder piece is in the upper right.

The pieces of glass were assembled into a hierarchical model and animated using a 3D keyframe animation program. "Spotlights" were strategically placed in the scene so that glints would appear on the knight's sword just as he thrusts it toward the priest. In one shot, the movie camera that photographed the live action was moving, and so the synthetic camera recording the computer-generated action has to move as well, matching the motion of the movie camera exactly. The final effect is most impressive, and in one instance quite startling: When the camera swivels around to show the back side of the knight, we see the same motion, but instead of seeing the back of the knight's head, we see his face again. This gives the motion an uncanny effect, since the limbs seem to bend the wrong way.

20.9 AUTOMATING OBJECT PLACEMENT

Most of this chapter has discussed the creation of objects; some of these objects, such as the terrain molded by erosion, constitute the environment for a scene, but most of them must be *placed* in a scene. Often, a human modeler chooses a location and puts a tree, a flag, or a handkerchief there. When many objects need to be placed in a scene, however, some automation of the process may be necessary. Considering another dimension, we see that the position of a single object at two times may be known, but its position at all intermediate times may need to be determined. This is really the subject of animation, which involves modeling the changes of position and attributes of objects over time, as discussed further in Chapter 21. In situations in which realistic motion of energy-minimizing assemblies is being modeled, we can do the intermediate animation automatically (human motion may be of this form, since humans often try to get from one place to another in the most efficient manner possible). We shall discuss this special case of object placement as well.

Automatic object placement in scenes has not been studied widely. Reeves and Blau [REEV85] discuss a special case in which the trees in a forest are placed automatically by applying a general stochastic rule. The modeler provides a grid size determining spacing between trees and a parameter determining the minimum distance between any two trees, the regions of the horizontal plane to be forested, and the surface contour over these regions, which determines the elevation of the base of the tree. The program then generates at most one tree per grid point, randomly displacing the trees in the x and y directions to avoid giving a gridlike appearance in the final result. If after displacement the new tree would be too close to others, it is eliminated and the algorithm proceeds to the next grid point. This model has some small realism to it: The placement of trees is somewhat random, and forest densities tend to be nearly constant, so that one rarely sees lots of trees all in the same area. Reeves and Blau also let the placement of their trees affect the modeling of the individual trees. The elevation of the tree determines (probabilistically) whether a tree is deciduous (low elevations) or evergreen (higher elevations). This interaction between the terrain and the trees is similar in form to the interacting procedural models of Amburn, Grant, and Whitted [AMBU86], described in Section 20.2, in which characteristics of the terrain influenced the placement of the trees.

Gardner [GARD84] uses a mechanism that encompasses both random displacements and interaction with the terrain, while also forming clusters of objects rather than a regular grid. To determine placements of features in a scene (where to put a tree, for example), he uses a function much like the texture function used in his models for clouds. When this "texture" function is above some critical value, a feature is generated. Using this technique, Gardner generates some exceptionally realistic distributions of features in scenes (Color Plate IV.25).

In all these cases, it is important to avoid both regularity and complete randomness. Much work remains to be done, but it appears that, for such applications, a stochastic control mechanism that can interact with the environment will provide good results.

Another type of automatic object placement is determining the intermediate stages in animations of constrained objects. In some cases, an object's positions in the course of an animation are completely determined by physics; actually computing these position may be very difficult. Witkin and Kass describe a method for determining these intermediate positions [WITK88]. The basic idea is simple: Assuming that an object has been modeled as a physical assembly with various muscles (parts of the assembly that can produce energy) to move other parts, we can describe the states (positions and velocities) of all the parts of the assembly as a function of time (these states include the amount of energy being expended by each muscle at each time, which is related to the muscle tension). This function can be thought of as taking a time value, t, between an initial and a final time, and associating with it a collection of numbers describing the state of the assembly. Thus, the function can be thought of as a path through some high-dimensional space. (The dimension

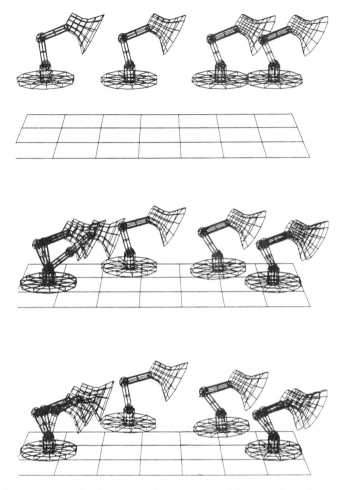

Fig. 20.25 Luxo Jr. is asked to jump from one position on the table to another. An initial path is specified in which Luxo moves above the table. Iterations of a variational technique lead Luxo to find a crouch–stretch–followthrough approach to the motion

of the space is about twice the number of degrees of freedom in the assembly.) Among the collection of all such functions, there are some whose total energy expenditure is lower than that of others. There also are some whose initial position for the parts is the desired initial position and whose ending position is the desired ending position, and we can measure how far a path is from satisfying these conditions. Some functions will represent physically possible sequences of events (e.g., in some paths, the momentum of each part will be, in the absence of external forces, proportional to the derivative of the part's position).

To compute the path of the object over time, we now take an approach called *variational calculus*, which is similar to gradient methods used for finding minima of ordinary real-valued functions. We start with any path and alter it slightly by moving certain points on the path in some direction. We now determine whether the path is closer to a good

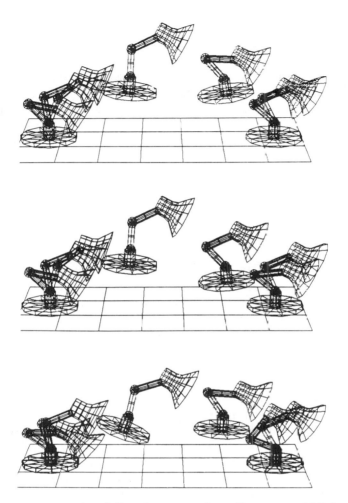

that minimizes energy and satisfies the constraints. (Courtesy of Michael Kass and Andrew Witkin.)

path (where "good" means "low energy expenditure," "laws of physics satisfied," and "starting and ending conditions satisfied") or is farther away. If it is closer, it becomes our new path, and we repeat the operation. If it is farther away, we alter the original path by exactly the opposite perturbations, and let this be our new path. As we iterate this process, we get closer and closer to a low-energy path that satisfies the constraints. Once we reach a path satisfying the constraints, we can continue the process until we reach the lowest-energy path possible. It turns out that the best alteration to the path at any time can be determined, so we approach a minimum-energy path very quickly.

The actual mechanism by which this alteration is effected is extremely complex, but the underlying idea is simple. Figure 20.25 is an example of the method in action; a model of "Luxo Jr." from a Pixar animation [PIXA86], is supposed to jump from one position on the table to another. Luxo is composed of a head, three segments, and a base. Each joint is frictionless and has a muscle to determine the joint angle. The initial path for the computation is the motion of Luxo from one point above the table to a distant point above the table. This path is gradually modified to consist of an initial compression of the body, a stretch and leap, a pulling-up-and-forward of the base and a followthrough to prevent toppling. This motion is remarkable in a number of ways: it is completely synthetic—the crouch and the stretch are not "programmed in"—and at the same time it shows the remarkable intuition of traditional animators, who drew a similar motion for the object and thereby implicitly solved an immensely complex variational problem. Witkin and Kass remark that the solution is general; we can create many constraints to be satisfied and still find the solution using this general technique. Needless to say, however, the method is computationally extremely expensive. One direction for future research is enabling a modeler to suggest directions of modification of the path to accelerate finding the solution.

20.10 SUMMARY

More and more disciplines are contributing to the modeling of complex phenomena in computer graphics, and the richness of the images we now see being generated is due to the variety of techniques used together to produce these phenomena. Successful models still have two forms: those based on replicating the underlying structure or physics of the objects being modeled, and those based on making something that looks good. The second often precedes the first. We anticipate seeing a wider variety of objects modeled in the future. Modeling human form and motion, and animal appearance and behavior, are particularly significant challenges. Even within the realms discussed in this chapter, there is substantial room for further work. The modeling of plants and trees can be extended to modeling of the ecology of a small region, including competition between plant forms for various resources. The modeling of waves can be extended to include more accurately the effects of wind and the appearance of breaking waves. The modeling of interconnected structures such as cloth, clay, and liquids can be extended to include models of fracture, mixed media (how does the movement of a slurry differ from that of a liquid?) and changes of state (e.g., melting ice). We look forward to seeing these new models and their successors, and eagerly await the day when computer-synthesized scenes are routinely mistaken for photographs. Although this ability to fool the eye may not always be the final goal in modeling, it is a good measure of the power available to computer graphics: If we can model reality, we can model anything.

EXERCISES

20.1 Show that the Bernstein polynomials $Q_{n;i}(t)$ used in the Sederberg-Parry deformation technique satisfy $\sum_{i=0}^{n} Q_{n;i}(t) = 1$ by using the binomial theorem, which says that

$$\sum_{i=0}^{n} \binom{n}{i} a^i b^{n-i} = (a + b)^n.$$

20.2 Implement the Perlin texturing model on your computer. Can you fine tune the model to compute textures at only the points of a specific surface (such as a sphere), so that you can generate a real-time texture editor? What are the difficulties in generating multifrequency noise in real time? Try bump mapping the normal vectors by the dNoise() function described in the text—that is, by adjusting the normals by a rule of the form *newNormal* = *oldNormal* + dNoise (*currentPoint*). Let $f(x)$ be a function that is 0 for $x < a$ and is 1 for $x > b$, where a and b are positive numbers with $a < b$. If you assume you do bump mapping with the rule *newNormal* = *oldNormal* + f (Noise (*currentPoint*)) * dNoise (*currentPoint*), what do you expect the result to look like for various values of a and b? Try to replicate the Perlin's stucco texture using this method.

20.3 Perlin uses cubic interpolation to generate values for the coefficients used in computing noise. Can you think of an easy way to speed this process using look-up tables? Can you think of a quicker way to generate band-limited noise?

20.4 Implement a particle system for fireworks, by making the first-stage particle follow a parabolic trajectory, and subsequent particles follow smaller parabolic trajectories. Can you combine this system with the soft-object model to make exploding blobs of water?

20.5 Implement Gardner's cloud model and try to tune the parameters to give good-looking cumulus clouds.

20.6 Think about how you could model a natural 1D, 2D, or 3D phenomenon. By a 1D object, we mean an object on which position can be measured by a single number, such as a curve in the plane (the single number is distance from the starting point of the curve). By a 2D object, we mean an object on which position can be measured by two numbers. For example, the surface of the sphere is a 2D object because position can be measured by longitude and latitude. Notice that 1D phenomena such as hair are difficult to render, since a 1-pixel line is likely to be far wider than is the desired image of the hair. Solving this problem requires an understanding of the filtering theory in Chapters 14 and 17. Some interesting 2D objects are flower petals (can you think of a way to make a movie of a rose unfolding?), ribbed surfaces (such as umbrellas, or skin over a skeleton), and ribbons (can you model the shape of a ribbon by specifying only where a few points lie, and etting mechanics determine the rest?). Some 3D objects you might want to consider are sponge (or is this really fractal?), translucent glass, and mother-of-pearl.

21
Animation

To *animate* is, literally, to bring to life. Although people often think of animation as synonymous with motion, it covers all changes that have a visual effect. It thus includes the time-varying position (*motion dynamics*), shape, color, transparency, structure, and texture of an object (*update dynamics*), and changes in lighting, camera position, orientation, and focus, and even changes of rendering technique.

Animation is used widely in the entertainment industry, and is also being applied in education, in industrial applications such as control systems and heads-up displays and flight simulators for aircraft, and in scientific research. The scientific applications of computer graphics, and especially of animation, have come to be grouped under the heading *scientific visualization*. Visualization is more than the mere application of graphics to science and engineering, however; it can involve other disciplines such as signal processing, computational geometry, and database theory. Often, the animations in scientific visualization are generated from *simulations* of scientific phenomena. The results of the similations may be large datasets representing 2D or 3D data (e.g., in the case of fluid-flow simulations); these data are converted into images that then constitute the animation. At the other extreme, the simulation may generate positions and locations of physical objects, which must then be rendered in some form to generate the animation. This happens, for example, in chemical simulations, where the positions and orientations of the various atoms in a reaction may be generated by simulaton, but the animation may show a ball-and-stick view of each molecule, or may show overlapping smoothly shaded spheres representing each atom. In some cases, the simulation program will contain an embedded animation language, so that the simulation and animation processes are simultaneous.

If some aspect of an animation changes too quickly relative to the number of animated frames displayed per second, *temporal aliasing* occurs. Examples of this are wagon wheels that apparently turn backward and the jerky motion of objects that move through a large field of view in a short time. Videotape is shown at 30 frames per second (fps), and photographic film speed is typically 24 fps, and both of these provide adequate results for many applications. Of course, to take advantage of these rates, we must create a new image for each videotape or film frame. If, instead, the animator records each image on two videotape frames, the result will be an effective 15 fps, and the motion will appear jerkier.[1]

Some of the animation techniques described here have been partially or completely implemented in hardware. Architectures supporting basic animation in real time are essential for building flight simulators and other real-time control systems; some of these architectures were discussed in Chapter 18.

Traditional animation (i.e., noncomputer animation) is a discipline in itself, and we do not discuss all its aspects. Here, we concentrate on the basic concepts of computer-based animation, and also describe some state-of-the-art systems. We begin by discussing conventional animation and the ways in which computers have been used to assist in its creation. We then move on to animation produced principally by computer. Since much of this is 3D animation, many of the techniques from traditional 2D character animation no longer apply directly. Also, controlling the course of an animation is more difficult when the animator is not drawing the animation directly: it is often more difficult to describe *how* to do something than it is to do that action directly. Thus, after describing various animation languages, we examine several animation control techniques. We conclude by discussing a few general rules for animation, and problems peculiar to animation.

21.1 CONVENTIONAL AND COMPUTER-ASSISTED ANIMATION

21.1.1 Conventional Animation

A conventional animation is created in a fairly fixed sequence: The story for the animation is written (or perhaps merely conceived), then a *storyboard* is laid out. A storyboard is an animation in outline form—a high-level sequence of sketches showing the structure and ideas of the animation. Next, the soundtrack (if any) is recorded, a detailed layout is produced (with a drawing for every scene in the animation), and the soundtrack is read—that is, the instants at which significant sounds occur are recorded in order. The detailed layout and the soundtrack are then correlated.[2] Next, certain *key frames* of the animation are drawn—these are the frames in which the entities being animated are at extreme or characteristic positions, from which their intermediate positions can be inferred. The intermediate frames are then filled in (this is called *inbetweening*), and a trial film is made (a *pencil test*). The pencil-test frames are then transferred to *cels* (sheets of acetate

---

[1]This lets the animator generate only half as many frames, however. In some applications, the time savings may be worth the tradeoff in quality.

[2]The order described here is from conventional studio cartoon animation. In fine-arts animation, the soundtrack may be recorded last; in computer-assisted animation, the process may involve many iterations.

film), either by hand copying in ink or by photocopying directly onto the cels. In multiplane animation, multiple layers of cels are used, some for background that remains constant (except perhaps for a translation), and some for foreground characters that change over time. The cels are colored in or painted, and are assembled into the correct sequence; then, they are filmed. The people producing the animation have quite distinct roles: some design the sequence, others draw key frames, others are strictly inbetweeners, and others work only on painting the final cels. Because of the use of key frames and inbetweening, this type of animation is called *key-frame animation*. The name is also applied to computer-based systems that mimic this process.

The organizational process of an animation is described [CATM78a] by its storyboard; by a *route sheet*, which describes each scene and the people responsible for the various aspects of producing the scene; and by the *exposure sheet*, which is an immensely detailed description of the animation. The exposure sheet has one line of information for each frame of the animation, describing the dialogue, the order of all the figures in the frame, the choice of background, and the camera position within the frame. This level of organization detail is essential in producing a coherent animation. For further information on conventional animation, see [LAYB79; HALA68; HALA73].

The entire process of producing an animation is supposed to be sequential, but is often (especially when done with computers) iterative: the available sound effects may cause the storyboard to be modified slightly, the eventual look of the animation may require that some sequences be expanded, in turn requiring new sound-track segments, and so on.

21.1.2 Computer Assistance

Many stages of conventional animation seem ideally suited to computer assistance, especially inbetweening and coloring, which can be done using the seed-fill techniques described in Section 19.5.2. Before the computer can be used, however, the drawings must be digitized. This can be done by using optical scanning, by tracing the drawings with a data tablet, or by producing the original drawings with a drawing program in the first place. The drawings may need to be postprocessed (e.g., filtered) to clean up any glitches arising from the input process (especially optical scanning), and to smooth the contours somewhat. The composition stage, in which foreground and background figures are combined to generate the individual frames for the final animation, can be done with the image-composition techniques described in Section 17.6.

By placing several small low-resolution frames of an animation in a rectangular array, the equivalent of a pencil test can be generated using the pan-zoom feature available in some frame buffers. The frame buffer can take a particular portion of such an image (the portion consiting of one low-resolution frame), move it to the center of the screen (*panning*), and then enlarge it to fill the entire screen (*zooming*).[3] This process can be repeated on the

---

[3]The panning and zooming are actually effected by changing the values in frame-buffer registers. One set of registers determines which pixel in the frame-buffer memory corresponds to the upper-left corner of the screen, and another set of registers determines the pixel-replication factors—how many times each pixel is replicated in the horizontal and vertical direction By adjusting the values in these registers, the user can display each of the frames in sequence, pixel-replicated to fill the entire screen.

several frames of the animation stored in the single image; if done fast enough, it gives the effect of continuity. Since each frame of the animation is reduced to a very small part of the total image (typically one twenty-fifth or one thirty-sixth), and is then expanded to fill the screen, this process effectively lowers the display device's resolution. Nonetheless, these low-resolution sequences can be helpful in giving a sense of an animation, thus acting as a kind of pencil test.

21.1.3   Interpolation

The process of inbetweening is amenable to computer-based methods as well, but many problems arise. Although a human inbetweener can perceive the circumstances of the object being interpolated (is it a falling ball or a rolling ball?), a computer-based system is typically given only the starting and ending positions. The easiest interpolation in such a situation is *linear interpolation*: Given the values, v_s and v_e, of some attribute (position, color, size) in the starting and ending frames, the value v_t at intermediate frames is $v_t = (1 - t)v_s + t\,v_e$; as the value t ranges from 0 to 1, the value of v_t varies smoothly from v_s to v_e. Linear interpolation (sometimes called *lerping*—Linear intERPolation), although adequate in some circumstances, has many limitations. For instance, if lerping is used to compute intermediate positions of a ball that is thrown in the air using the sequence of three key frames shown in Fig. 21.1 (a), the resulting track of the ball shown in Fig. 21.1(b) is entirely unrealistic. Particularly problematic is the sharp corner at the zenith of the trajectory: Although lerping generates continuous motion, it does not generate continuous derivatives, so there may be abrupt changes in velocity when lerping is used to interpolate positions. Even if the positions of the ball in the three key frames all lie in a line, if the distance between the second and third is greater than that between the first and second, then lerping causes a discontinuity in speed at the second key frame. Thus, lerping generates derivative discontinuities in time as well as in space (the time discontinuities are measured by the parametric continuity described in Chapter 11).

Because of these drawbacks of lerping, splines have been used instead to smooth out interpolation between key frames. Splines can be used to vary any parameter smoothly as a function of time. The splines need not be polynomials.[4] For example, to get smooth initiation and termination of changes (called *slow-in* and *slow-out*) and fairly constant rates of change in between, we could use a function such as $f(t)$ in Fig. 21.2. A value can be interpolated by setting $v_t = (1 - f(t))v_s + f(t)v_e$. Since the slope of f is zero at both $t = 0$ and $t = 1$, the change in v begins and ends smoothly. Since the slope of f is constant in the middle of its range, the rate of change of v is constant in the middle time period.

Splines can make individual points (or individual objects) move smoothly in space and time, but this by no means solves the inbetweening problem. Inbetweening also involves interpolating the shapes of objects in the intermediate frames. Of course, we could describe a spline path for the motion of each point of the animation in each frame, but splines give the smoothest motion when they have few control points, in both space and time. Thus, it is preferable to specify the positions of only a few points at only a few times, and somehow to

---

[4]This is an extension of the notion of spline introduced in Chapter 11, where a spline was defined to be a piecewise cubic curve. Here we use the term in the more general sense of any curve used to approximate a set of control points.

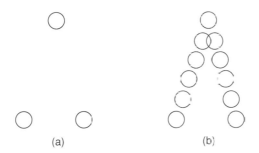

(a)   (b)

Fig. 21.1 Linear interpolation of the motion of a bal generates unrealistic results. (a) Three key-frame positions for the ball. (b) The resulting interpolated positions.

extend the spline interpolation over intermediate points and times. At least one special case deserves mention: A figure drawn as a polyline can be interpolated between key frames by interpolating each vertex of the polyline from its starting to ending position. As long as the key frames do not differ too much, this is adequate (for examples where this fails, see Exercise 21.1).

Several approaches to this have been developed. Burtnyk and Wein [BURT76] made a *skeleton* for a motion by choosing a polygonal arc describing the basic shape of a 2D figure or portion of a figure, and a neighborhood of this arc (see Fig. 21.3). The figure is represented in a coordinate system based on this skeleton. They then specify the thickness of the arc and positions of the vertices at subsequent key frames and redraw the figure in a new coordinate system based on the deformed arc. Inbetweening is done by interpolating the characteristics of the skeleton between the key frames. (A similar technique can be developed for 3D, using the trivariate Bernstein polynomial deformations or the heirarchical B-splines described in Chapter 20.)

Reeves [REEV81] designed a method in which the intermediate trajectories of particular points on the figures in successive key frames are determined by hand-drawn paths (marked by the animator to indicate constant time intervals). A region bounded by two such *moving-points paths* and an arc of the figure in each of the two key frames

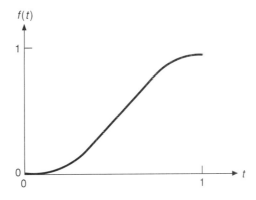

Fig. 21.2 The graph of a function $f(t)$ with zero derivative at its endpoints and constant derivative in its middle section.

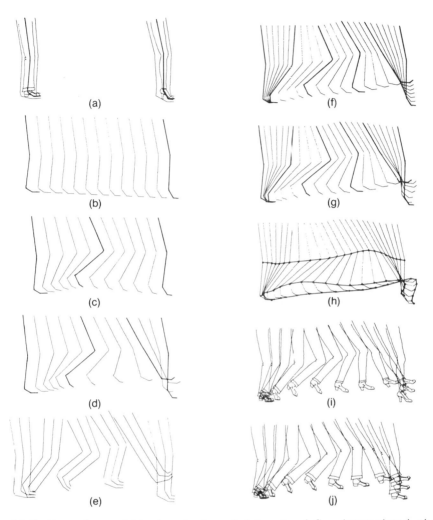

Fig. 21.3 Use of a neighborhood of a skeleton to define interpolated shapes. (Courtesy of M. Wein and N. Burtnyk, National Research Council of Canada.)

determines a *patch* of the animation. The arc of the figure is interpolated by computing its intermediate positions in this patch. The intermediate positions are determined so as to make the motion as smooth as possible.

Both these techniques were devised to interpolate line drawings, but the same problems arise in interpolating 3D objects. The most important difference is that, in most computer-based animation, the 3D objects are likely to be modeled explicitly, rather than drawn in outlines. Thus the modeling and placement information is available for use in interpolation, and the animator does not, in general, need to indicate which points on the objects correspond in different key frames. Nonetheless, interpolation between key frames is a difficult problem.

For the time being, let us consider only the interpolation of the position and orientation of a rigid body. Position can be interpolated by the techniques used in 2D animation: The position of the center of the body is specified at certain key frames, and the intermediate positions are interpolated by some spline path. In addition, the rate at which the spline path is traversed may be specified as well (e.g., by marking equal-time intervals on the trajectory, or by specifying the speed along the interpolating path as a function of time). Many different animation systems implement such mechanisms; some of these are discussed in Section 21.2.3.

Interpolating the orientation of the rigid body is more difficult. In fact, even specifying the orientation is not easy. If we specify orientations by amounts of rotation about the three principal axes (called *Euler angles*), then the order of specification is important. For example, if a book with its spine facing left is rotated $90°$ about the x axis and then $-90°$ about the y axis, its spine will face you, whereas if the rotations are done in the opposite order, its spine will face down. A subtle consequence of this is that interpolating Euler angles leads to unnatural interpolations of rotations: A rotation of $90°$ about the z axis and then $90°$ about the y axis has the effect of a $120°$ rotation about the axis $(1, 1, 1)$. But rotating $30°$ about the z axis and $30°$ about the y axis does not give a rotation of $40°$ about the axis $(1, 1, 1)$—it gives approximately a $42°$ rotation about the axis $(1, 0.3, 1)$!

The set of all possible rotations fits naturally into a coherent algebraic structure, the *quaternions* [HAMI53]. The rotations are exactly the *unit quaternions*, which are symbols of the form $a + b\mathbf{i} + c\mathbf{j} + d\mathbf{k}$, where a, b, c, and d are real numbers satisfying $a^2 + b^2 + c^2 + d^2 = 1$; quaternions are multiplied using the distributive law and the rules $\mathbf{i}^2 = \mathbf{j}^2 = \mathbf{k}^2 = -1$, $\mathbf{ij} = \mathbf{k} = -\mathbf{ji}$, $\mathbf{jk} = \mathbf{i} = -\mathbf{kj}$, and $\mathbf{ki} = \mathbf{j} = -\mathbf{ik}$. Rotation by angle ϕ about the unit vector $[b \quad c \quad d]^t$ corresponds to the quaternion $\cos \phi/2 + b \sin \phi/2\ \mathbf{i} + c \sin \phi/2\ \mathbf{j} + d \sin \phi/2\ \mathbf{k}$. Under this correspondence, performing successive rotations corresponds to multiplying quaternions. The inverse correspondence is described in Exercise 21.7.

Since unit quaternions satisfy the condition $a^2 + b^2 + c^2 + d^2 = 1$, they can be thought of as points on the unit sphere in 4D. To interpolate between two quaternions, we simply follow the shortest path between them on this sphere (a *great arc*). This spherical linear interpolation (called *slerp*) is a natural generalization of linear interpolation. Shoemake [SHOE85] proposed the use of quaternions for interpolation in graphics, and developed generalizations of spline interpolants for quaternions.

The compactness and simplicity of quaternions are great advantages, but difficulties arise with them as well, three of which deserve mention. First, each orientation of an object can actually be represented by two quaternions, since rotation about the axis $\mathbf{v}$ by an angle ϕ is the same as rotation about $-\mathbf{v}$ by the angle $-\phi$; the corresponding quaternions are antipodal points on the sphere in 4D. Thus to go from one orientation to another, we may interpolate from one quaternion to either of two others; ordinarily we choose the shorter of the two great arcs. Second, orientations and rotations are not exactly the same thing: a rotation by $360°$ is very different from a rotation by $0°$ in an animation, but the same quaternion $(1 + 0\mathbf{i} + 0\mathbf{j} + 0\mathbf{k})$ represents both. Thus specifying multiple rotations with quaternions requires many intermediate control points.

The third difficulty is that quaternions provide an *isotropic* method for rotation—the interpolation is independent of everything except the relation between the initial and final rotations. This is ideal for interpolating positions of tumbling bodies, but not for interpolating the orientation of a camera in a scene: Humans strongly prefer cameras to be held upright (i.e., the horizontal axis of the film plane should lie in the (x, z) plane), and are profoundly disturbed by tilted cameras. Quaternions have no such preferences, and therefore should not be used for camera interpolation. The lack of an adequate method for interpolating complex camera motion has led to many computer animations having static cameras or very limited camera motion.

21.1.4 Simple Animation Effects

In this section, we describe a few simple computer-animation tricks that can all be done in real time. These were some of the first techniques developed, and they are therefore hardware-oriented.

In Section 4.4.1, we discussed the use of color look-up tables (luts) in a frame buffer and the process of double-buffering; and in Section 17.6, we described image compositing by color-table manipulations. Recall that lut animation is generated by manipulating the lut. The simplest method is to cycle the colors in the lut (to replace color i with color $i - 1$ mod n, where n is the number of colors in the table), thus changing the colors of the various pieces of the image. Figure 21.4 shows a source, a sink, and a pipe going between them. Each piece of the figure is labeled with its lut index. The lut is shown at the right. By cycling colors 1 through 5, we can generate an animation of material flowing through the pipe.

Using this lut animation is a great deal faster than sending an entire new pixmap to the frame buffer for each frame. Assuming 8 color bits per pixel in a 640 by 512 frame buffer, a single image contains 320 KB of information. Transferring a new image to the frame buffer every thirtieth of a second requires a bandwidth of over 9 MB per second, which is well beyond the capacity of most small computers. On the other hand, new values for the lut can be sent very rapidly, since luts are typically on the order of a few hundred to a few thousand bytes.

Lut animation tends to look jerky, since the colors change suddenly. This effect can be softened somewhat by taking a color to be made visible and changing its lut entry gradually over several frames from the background color to its new color, and then similarly fading it out as the next lut entry is being faded in. Details of this and other tricks are given by Shoup [SHOU79].

Lut animation can be combined with the pan-zoom movie technique described

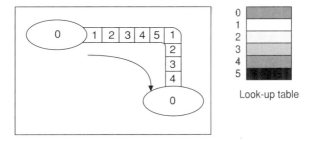

Fig. 21.4 The look-up–table entries can be cycled to give the impression of flow through the pipe.

previously to make longer pan-zoom movies with less color resolution. To make a very long two-color pan-zoom movie on a frame buffer with eight planes of memory, for example, we can generate 200 frames of an animation, each at one-twenty-fifth of full screen resolution. Frames 1 through 25 are arranged in a single image to be used for a pan-zoom movie. The same is done with frames 26 through 50, and so on up to frames 176 through 200, giving a total of eight bitmaps. These are combined, on a pixel-by-pixel basis, into a single 8-bit-deep image, which is then downloaded to the frame buffer. We make all the lut entries black except entry 00000001, which we make white. We then run a 25-frame pan-zoom movie and see the first 25 images of the animation. Then, we set entry 00000001 to black and entry 00000010 to white. Running another 25-frame pan-zoom movie shows us the next 25 images. Continuing in this fashion, we see the full 200-frame animation. By allocating several planes to each image, we can generate shorter pan-zoom movies with additional bits of color.

Finally, let's look at the hardware-based animation technique called *sprites*. A sprite is a small rectangular region of memory that is mixed with the rest of the frame-buffer memory at the video level. The location of the sprite at any time is specified in registers in the frame buffer, so altering the values in these registers causes the sprite to move. The sprites may hide the frame-buffer values at each pixel, or may be blended with them. We can use sprites to implement cursors in frame buffers, and also to generate animations by moving the sprite (or sprites) around on top of a background image. Some frame buffers have been designed to allow several sprites with different priorities. so that some sprites can be "on top of" others.

One of the most popular uses of sprites is in video games, where the animation in the game may consist almost entirely of sprites moving over a fixed background. Since the location and size of each sprite are stored in registers, it is easy to check for collisions between sprites, which further enhances the use of sprites in this application.

21.2 ANIMATION LANGUAGES

There are many different languages for describing animation. and new ones are constantly being developed. They fall into three categories: linear-list notations, general-purpose languages with embedded animation directives, and graphical languages. Here, we briefly describe each type of language and give examples. Many animation languages are mingled with modeling languages, so the descriptions of the objects in an animation and of the animations of these objects are done at the same time.

21.2.1 Linear-List Notations

In linear-list notations for animation such as the one presented in [CATM72], each event in the animation is described by a starting and ending frame number and an action that is to take place (the *event*). The actions typically take parameters, so a statement such as

    42, 53,B ROTATE "PALM", 1, 30

means "between frames 42 and 53, rotate the object called PALM about axis 1 by 30 degrees, determining the amount of rotation at each frame from table B." Thus, the actions are given interpolation methods to use (in this case a table of values) and objects to act on as well. Since the statements describe individual actions and have frame values associated with them, their order is, for the most part, irrelevant. If two actions are applied to the same object at the same time, however, the order may matter: rotating 90° in x and then 90° in y is different from rotating 90° in y and then 90° in x.

Many other linear-list notations have been developed, and many notations are supersets of the basic linear-list idea. Scefo (SCEne FOrmat) [STRA88], for example, has some aspects of linear-list notation, but also includes a notion of groups and object hierarchy and supports abstractions of changes (called *actions*) and some higher-level programming-language constructs (variables, flow of control, and expression evaluation) distinguishing it from a simple linear list. Scefo also supports a model of animation that differs from many animation languages in that it is renderer-independent. A Scefo script describes only an animation; the individual objects in the script can be rendered with any renderer at all, and new renderers can easily be added to the animation system of which Scefo is the core.

21.2.2 General-Purpose Languages

Another way to describe animations is to embed animation capability within a general-purpose programming language [REYN82; SYMB85; MAGN85]. The values of variables in the language can be used as parameters to whatever routines actually generate animations, so the high-level language can actually be used to generate simulations that then generate animations as a side effect. Such languages have great potential (e.g., they can certainly do everything that linear-list notations do), but most of them require considerable programming expertise on the part of the user.

Such systems can use the constructs of the surrounding language to create concise routines that have complex effects. Of course, these can sometimes be cryptic. ASAS [REYN82] is an example of such a language. It is built on top of LISP, and its primitive entities include vectors, colors, polygons, solids (collections of polygons), groups (collections of objects), points of view, subworlds, and lights. A point of view consists of a location and an orientation for an object or a camera (hence, it corresponds to the cumulative transformation matrix of an object in PHIGS). Subworlds are entities associated with a point of view; the point of view can be used to manipulate the entities in the subworld in relation to the rest of the objects in the animation.

ASAS also includes a wide range of geometric transformations that operate on objects; they take an object as an argument and return a value that is a transformed copy of the object. These transformations include *up, down, left, right, zoom-in, zoom-out, forward,* and *backward*. Here is an ASAS program fragment, describing an animated sequence in which an object called my-cube is spun while the camera pans. Anything following a semicolon is a comment. This fragment is evaluated at each frame in order to generate the entire sequence.

```
(grasp my-cube)          ; The cube becomes the current object
(cw 0.05)                ; Spin it clockwise by a small amount
(grasp camera)           ; Make the camera the current object
(right panning-speed)    ; Move it to the right
```

The advantage of ASAS over linear-list notations is the ability to generate procedural objects and animations within the language. This ability comes at the cost of increased skill required of the animator, who must be an able programmer. Scefo lies in the middle ground, providing some flow-of-control constructs, and the ability to bind dynamically with routines written in a high-level language, while being simple enough for nonprogrammers to learn and use readily.

21.2.3   Graphical Languages

One problem with the textual languages we have described is that it is difficult for an animator to see what will take place in an animation just by looking at the script. Of course, this should not be surprising, since the script is a program, and to the extent that the program's language allows high-level constructs, it encodes complex events in compact form. If a real-time previewer for the animation language is available, this is not a problem; unfortunately the production of real-time animations is still beyond the power of most hardware.

Graphical animation languages describe animation in a more visual way. These languages are used for expressing, editing, and comprehending the simultaneous changes taking place in an animation. The principal notion in such languages is substitution of a visual paradigm for a textual one: rather than explicitly writing out descriptions of actions, the animator provides a picture of the action. Some of the earliest work in this area was done by Baecker [BAEC69], who introduced the notion of P-curves in the GENESYS animation system. A P-curve is a parametric representation of the motion (or any other attribute) of an object or assembly of objects within a scene. The animator describes an object path of motion by graphically specifying its coordinates as a function of time (just as splines do, where functions $X(t)$, $Y(t)$, and $Z(t)$ specify the 3D location of a point on a curve as a function of an independent variable). Figure 21.5(a) shows a motion path in the plane; Fig. 21.5(b) of that figure shows the path's x and y components as functions of time. Notice that the curves in part (b)) uniquely determine the curve in part (a), but the opposite is not true: One can traverse the path in part (a) at different speeds. By marking the path in part (a) to indicate constant time steps, we can convey the time dependence of the path, as shown in part (c), which is what Baecker calls a P-curve. Note that part (c) can be constructed as shown in part (d) by graphing the x and y components as functions of t, on coordinate systems that are rotated $90°$ from each other, and then drawing lines to connect corresponding time points. Thus, editing the components of a parametric curve induces changes in the P-curve, and editing the placement of the hash marks on the P-curve induces changes in the components.

The diagrammatic animation language DIAL [FEIN82b] retains some of the features of linear-list notations, but displays the sequence of events in an animation as a series of parallel rows of marks: A vertical bar indicates the initiation of an action, and dashes indicate the time during which the action is to take place. The actions are defined in a DIAL script (by statements of the form "% t1 translate "block" 1.0 7.0 15.3," which defines action t1 as the translation of an object called "block" by the vector (1.0, 7.0, 15.3)), and then the applications of the actions are defined subsequently. The particular instructions that DIAL executes are performed by a user-specified back end given at run time. DIAL

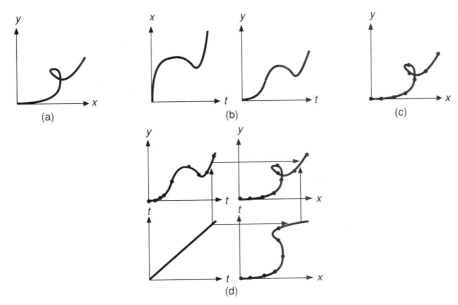

Fig. 21.5 (a) A parametric path in the plane. (b) Its x and y components as functions of time. (c) The original curve marked to indicate equal time steps. (d) The construction of a P-curve from component functions.

itself knows nothing about animation; it merely provides a description of the sequence in which instructions are to be performed. The following is a typical DIAL script (lines beginning with a blank are comments):

```
      Read in an object from a file, and assign it the name "block"
! getsurf "block.d" 5 5 "block"
      Define a window on the xy plane
! window -20 20 -20 20
      Define two actions, (1) a translation,
% t1 translate "block" 10 0 0
      and (2) a rotation in the xy plane by 360 degrees
% r1 rotate "block" 0 1 360
      Now describe a translation, spin, and a further translation:
t1    |---------      |--------
r1                |--------

r1    |-----------------------
```

The line labeled "t1" indicates that action t1 is to take place from frames 1 to 10 (and hence is to translate by one unit per frame, since linear interpolation is the default), and then again from frames 17 to 25. At frame 11, the block stops translating and rotates 40° per frame for six frames (the first line labeled "r1" indicates this), and then rotates and translates for the next three, and then just translates.

For longer animations, each tick mark can indicate multiple frames, so that animations of several seconds' duration can be specified easily without indicating every frame. Long animations can be described by starting a new sequence of tick marks on a new line, following a completely blank line. (The second line labeled "r1" above is an example: it indicates that a 360° turn should take place between frames 26 and 50.) The format is much like that of a conductor's score of a symphony: Each action corresponds to an instrument in the orchestra, and each group of lines corresponds to a staff in the score. DIAL and many linear-list notations have the advantage of being specified entirely in ASCII text, making them portable to different machines (although a back end for the language must be written for each new machine).

The S-Dynamics system [SYMB85] takes this visual paradigm one step further and combines it with parametric descriptions of actions similar to P-curves. To do this, S-Dynamics uses the full power of a bitmapped workstation. Figure 21.6 shows an S-Dynamics window. Just as in DIAL, time runs horizontally across the window. The period during which actions are to take effect is indicated by the width of the region representing the action. Each action (or *sequence* in S-Dynamics terminology) can be shown as a box that indicates the time extent of the action, or the box can be "opened"—that is, made to show more internal detail. A sequence may be a composite of

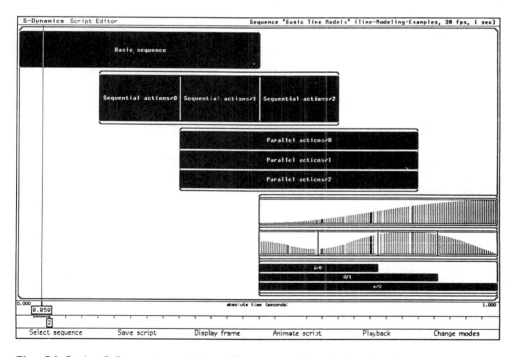

Fig. 21.6 An S-Dynamics window. (Courtesy of Symbolics Graphics Division. The software and the SIGGRAPH paper in which this image first appeared were both written by Craig Reynolds.)

several serial or parallel actions, each of which can be opened to show even more detail, including a graph indicating the time dependence of a parameter of the action.

21.3 METHODS OF CONTROLLING ANIMATION

Controlling an animation is somewhat independent of the language used for describing it—most control mechanisms can be adapted for use with various types of languages. Animation-control mechanisms range from full explicit control, in which the animator explicitly describes the position and attributes of every object in a scene by means of translations, rotations, and other position- and attribute-changing operators, to the highly automated control provided by knowledge-based systems, which take high-level descriptions of an animation ("make the character walk out of the room") and generate the explicit controls that effect the changes necessary to produce the animation. In this section, we examine some of these techniques, giving examples and evaluating the advantages and disadvantages of each.

21.3.1 Full Explicit Control

Explicit control is the simplest sort of animation control. Here, the animator provides a description of everything that occurs in the animation, either by specifying simple changes, such as scaling, translation, and rotation, or by providing key-frame information and interpolation methods to use between key frames. This interpolation may be given explicitly or (in an interactive system) by direct manipulation with a mouse, joystick, data glove, or other input device.

The BBOP system [STER83] provides this interactive sort of control. The underlying object model consists of hierarchical jointed polyhedral objects (i.e., stick figures with pivot points between adjacent sticks), and the animator can control transformation matrices at each of the joints using a joystick or other interactive device. Such interactions specify the transformations at key frames, and interactive programs define the interpolations between key frames. Notice that, in such a system, a sequence of actions defined between key frames may be difficult to modify; extending one action may require shortening the neighboring actions to preserve coherence of the animation. For example, consider an animation in which one ball rolls up and hits another, causing the second ball to roll away. If the first ball is made to move more slowly, the start of the second action (the second ball rolling away) must be delayed.

21.3.2 Procedural Control

In Chapter 20, we discussed procedural models, in which various elements of the model communicate in order to determine their properties. This sort of procedural control is ideally suited to the control of animation. Reeves and Blau [REEV85] modeled both grass and wind in this way, using a particle system modeling technique (see Section 20.5). The wind particles evolved over time in the production of the animation, and the positions of the

Fig. 21.7 The linkage in (a) is moved by rotating the drive wheel. The constraints generate the motions shown in (b), (c), and (d).

grass blades were then determined by the proximity of wind particles. Thus, the particle system describing the grass was affected by aspects of other objects in the scene. This sort of procedural interaction among objects can be used to generate motions that would be difficult to specify through explicit control. Unfortunately, it also requires that the animator be a programmer.

Procedural control is a significant aspect of several other control mechanisms we discuss. In particular, in physically based systems, the position of one object may influence the motion of another (e.g., balls cannot pass through walls); in actor-based systems, the individual actors may pass their positions to other actors in order to affect the other actors' behaviors.

21.3.3 Constraint-Based Systems

Some objects in the physical world move in straight lines, but a great many objects move in a manner determined by the other objects with which they are in contact, and this compound motion may not be linear at all. For example, a ball rolls down an inclined plane. If gravity were the only force acting on the ball, the ball would fall straight down. But the plane is also pushing up and sideways, and so the ball rolls down the plane rather than passing through it. We can model such motion by constraints. The ball is constrained to lie on one side of the plane. If it is dropped from a height, it strikes the plane and bounces off, always remaining on the same side. In a similar way, a pendulum swings from a pivot, which is a point constraint.

Specifying an animated sequence using constraints is often much easier to do than is specifying by using direct control. When physical forces define the constraints, we move into the realm of physically based modeling (see Section 21.3.7), especially when the dynamics[5] of the objects are incorporated into the model. Simple constraint-based modeling, however, can generate interesting results. If constraints on a linkage are used to define its possible positions, as in Fig. 21.7(a), we can view an animation of the linkage by changing it in a simple way. In the figure, for example, the animator can generate an animation of the linkage just by rotating the drive wheel, as shown in parts (b), (c), and (d).

Sutherland's Sketchpad system [SUTH63] was the first to use constraint-based animation of this sort (see Fig. 21.8). It allowed the user to generate parts of an assembly in the same way as 2D drawing programs do today. The parts (lines, circles, etc.) of an assembly could be constrained by point constraints ("this line is free to move, but one end

---

[5] Here we use *dynamics* in the sense of physics, to mean the change in position and motion over time, not merely to mean "change," as in earlier chapters.

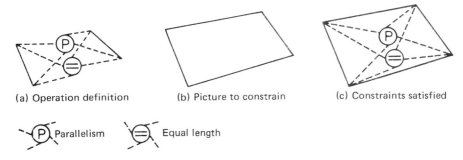

(a) Operation definition   (b) Picture to constrain   (c) Constraints satisfied

Fig. 21.8 Constraint definition and satisfaction in Sketchpad. (Adapted from [SUTH63].)

is held fixed at this point''), linkage constraints (''these lines must always remain joined end to end''), or angular constraints (''these lines must always be parallel'' or ''these lines must meet at a 60° angle''). This allowed the user to draw four lines in a quadrilateral, put linkage constraints on the corners, to put a point constraint at one corner, and to put angular constraints on opposite sides to make them parallel. This generated a parallelogram with one corner held fixed. Constraints were satisfied by a *relaxation technique* in which the assembly was moved so that the constraints came closer to being satisfied. Thus, the user could watch an assembly move so as to satisfy constraints gradually.[6] Of course, it is possible to overconstrain a system, by requiring, for example, that a line have a length of one unit, but that its ends be joined to two points that are three units apart. The constraints in Sketchpad are described by giving an error function—a function whose value is 0 when a constraint is satisfied, and is positive otherwise. Relaxation attempts to make the sum of these functions 0; when it fails, many constraints may be unsatisfied. Similarly, a system may be underconstrained, and have many solutions that satisfy all the constraints. In this case, the relaxation technique finds one solution that is close to the initial configuration.

Borning's similar ThingLab [BORN79] was really a metasystem: It provided a mechanism for defining systems like Sketchpad, but a user could define a system for modeling electrical circuits in the same framework. This system design was later improved to include a graphical interface [BORN86b]. A system, once designed, provided a world in which a user could build experiments. In a world meant to model geometry, for instance, the user could instantiate lines, point constraints, midpoint constraints, and so on, and then could move the assembly under those constraints. Figure 21.9 shows an example; the user has instantiated four MidpointSegments (segments with midpoints), has constrained their ends to be joined, and has also drawn four lines between adjacent midpoints. The user can vary the outer quadrilateral and observe that the inner quadrilateral always remains a parallelogram. For related work, see [BIER86a].

The extension of constraint-based animation systems to constraint systems supporting hierarchy, and to constraints modeled by the dynamics of physical bodies and the structural

---

[6]The animations therefore served two purposes: they generated assemblies satsifying the constraints, and they gave a *visualization* of the relaxation technique.

characteristics of materials (as in the plasticity models described in Section 20.7.3), is a subject of active research.

21.3.4 Tracking Live Action

Trajectories of objects in the course of an animation can also be generated by tracking of live action. There are a number of methods for doing tracking. Traditional animation has used *rotoscoping*: A film is made in which people (or animals) act out the parts of the characters in the animation, then animators draw over the film, enhancing the backgrounds and replacing the human actors with their animation equivalents. This technique provides exceptionally realistic motion. Alternatively, key points on an object may be digitized from a series of filmed frames, and then intermediate points may be interpolated to generate similar motion.

Another live-action technique is to attach some sort of indicator to key points on a person's body. By tracking the positions of the indicators, one can get locations for corresponding key points in an animated model. For example, small lights are attached at key locations on a person, and the positions of these lights are then recorded from several different directions to give a 3D position for each key point at each time. This technique has been used by Ginsberg and Maxwell [GINS83] to form a graphical marionette; the position of a human actor moving about a room is recorded and processed into a real-time video image of the motion. The actor can view this motion to get feedback on the motion that he or she is creating. If the feedback is given through a head-mounted display that can also display prerecorded segments of animation, the actor can interact with other graphical entities as well.

Another sort of interaction mechanism is the data glove described in Chapter 8, which measures the position and orientation of the wearer's hand, as well as the flexion and hyperextension of each finger joint. This device can be used to describe motion sequences in an animation as well, much like a 3D data tablet. Just as 2D motion can be described by drawing P-curves, 3D motion (including orientation) can be described by moving the data glove.

21.3.5 Actors

The use of *actors* is a high-level form of procedural control. An actor in an animation is a small program invoked once per frame to determine the characteristics of some object in the animation. (Thus, an actor corresponds to an "object" in the sense of object-oriented programming, as well as in the sense of animation.) An actor, in the course of its once-per-frame execution, may send messages to other actors to control their behaviors. Thus we could construct a train by letting the engine actor respond to some predetermined set of rules (move along the track at a fixed speed), while also sending the second car in the train the message "place yourself on the track, with your forward end at the back end of the engine." Each car would pass a similar message to the next car, and the cars would all follow the engine.

Such actors were originally derived from a similar notion in Smalltalk [GOLD76] and other languages, and were the center of the ASAS animation system described in Section 21.2.2. The concept has been developed further to include actors with wide ranges of "behaviors" that they can execute depending on their circumstances.

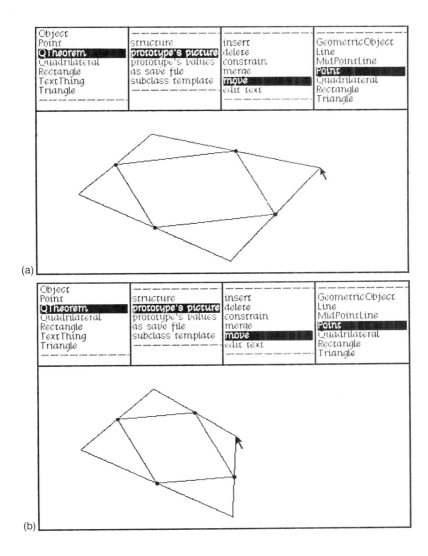

(a)

(b)

21.3.6 Kinematics and Dynamics

Kinematics refers to the positions and velocities of points. A kinematic description of a scene, for example, might say, "The cube is at the origin at time $t = 0$. It moves with a constant acceleration in the direction $(1, 1, 5)$ thereafter." By contrast, *dynamics* takes into account the physical laws that govern kinematics (Newton's laws of motion for large bodies, the Euler–Lagrange equations for fluids, etc.). A particle moves with an acceleration proportional to the forces acting on it, and the proportionality constant is the mass of the particle. Thus, a dynamic description of a scene might be, "At time $t = 0$ seconds the cube is at position (0 meters, 100 meters, 0 meters). The cube has a mass of 100 grams. The

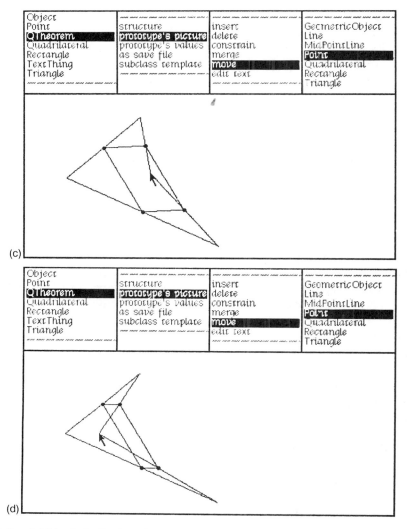

Fig. 21.9 A ThingLab display. (Courtesy of Alan Borning Xerox PARC and University of Washington.)

force of gravity acts on the cube.'' Naturally, the result of a dynamic simulation[7] of such a model is that the cube falls.

Both kinematics and dynamics can be inverted; that is, we can ask the question, ''What must the (constant) velocity of the cube be for it to reach position (12, 12, 42) in 5 seconds?'' or, ''What force must we apply to the cube to make it get to (12, 12, 42) in 5 seconds?'' For simple systems, these sorts of questions may have unique answers; for more complicated ones, however, especially hierarchical models, there may be large families of

---

[7]This simulation could be based on either an explicit analytical solution of the equations of motion or a numerical solution provided by a package for solving differential equations.

solutions. Such approaches to modeling are called *inverse kinematics* and *inverse dynamics*, in contrast to the *forward kinematics* and *dynamics* already described.

For example, if you want to scratch your ear, you move your hand to your ear. But when it gets there, your elbow can be in any of a number of different positions (close to your body or stuck out sideways). Thus, the motions of your upper and lower arm and wrist are not completely determined by the instruction, "move your hand to your ear." Solving inverse kinematic problems can therefore be difficult. In general, however, it is easier to solve equations with unique solutions than it is to solve ones with multiple solutions, so if we add constraints to the problem (e.g., "make the potential energy of your arm as small as possible at each stage of the motion"), then the solution may become unique. Note that you are constrained by the way that your body is constructed and by other objects in the environment—scratching your ear is more difficult when you are wearing a spacesuit than it is when you are wearing a bathing suit.

This type of problem, especially in the animation of articulated human figures, has received wide attention [CGA82; GIRA85; WILH87]. The systems of equations arising from such inverse problems are typically solved by numerical iteration techniques. The starting point for the iteration may influence the results profoundly (e.g., whether a robot's arms reach under a table or above it to grab an object on the other side depends whether they are above or below the table on this side), and the iterative techniques may also take a long time to converge.

Dynamic models using constraints have also been studied [BARR88]. In this case, the dynamics of the model may be much more complex. For example, the force that a floor exerts on the bottom of your foot is proportional to your weight (assuming for the moment that neither you nor the floor is moving). In general, the force of the floor on your foot (even if you are walking or running) is exactly enough to prevent your foot from moving into the floor. That is to say, the force may not be known a priori from the physics of the situation.[8] To simulate the dynamic behavior of such a system, we can use *dynamic constraints*, which are forces that are adjusted to act on an object so as either to achieve or to maintain some condition. When the forces necessary to maintain a constraint have been computed, the dynamics of the model can then be derived by standard numerical techniques. By adding forces that act to satisfy a constraint, we can generate animations showing the course of events while the constraint is being satisfied (much as in Sketchpad). For example, constraining the end of a chain to connect to a post makes it move from where it is toward the post. This example was the subject of an animation by Barr and Barzel, one frame of which is shown in Color Plate IV.26.

21.3.7 Physically Based Animation

The dynamics we have described are examples of physically based animations. So, in animated form, are the physically based models of cloth, plasticity, and rigid-body motion described in Chapter 20. These models are based on simulations of the evolution of physical

---

[8]Of course, the floor actually does move when you step on it, but only a very small amount. We usually want to avoid modeling the floor as a massive object, and instead just model it as a fixed object.

systems. Various formulations of classical mechanical behavior have been developed [GOLD80]; they all represent the evolution of a physical system as a solution to a system of partial differential equations. The solutions to these equations can be found with numerical-analysis packages and can be used to derive animation sequences. In the Kass–Witkin motion modeling described in Chapter 20, the situation is complex. The forces acting on an assembly are not all known beforehand, since the object may be able to supply its own forces (i.e., use its muscles). This allows for physically based animation of a different sort: One seeks the forces that the muscles must apply to generate some action. Of course, there may be many solutions to such a problem, and the Kass–Witkin approach is to choose the path with the minimal work. This sort of animation ties together the work on constraints, dynamics, procedural control, and the actors that we have described. It is also extremely complex; determining the equations governing a mechanical assembly can be very difficult, since these equations may contain hundreds of interrelated variables.

21.4 BASIC RULES OF ANIMATION

Traditional character animation was developed from an art form into an industry at Walt Disney Studio between 1925 and the late 1930s. At the beginning, animation entailed little more than drawing a sequence of cartoon panels—a collection of static images that, taken together, made an animated image. As the techniques of animation developed, certain basic principles evolved that became the fundamental rules for character animation, and are still in use today [LAYB79; LASS87]. Despite their origins in cartoon-character animation, many of them apply equally to realistic 3D animations. These rules, together with their application to 3D character animation, are surveyed in [LASS87]. Here, we merely discuss a few of the most important ones. It is important to recognize, however, that these rules are not absolute. Just as much of modern art has moved away from the traditional rules for drawing, many modern animators have moved away from traditional rules of animation, often with excellent results (see, e.g., [LEAF74; LEAF77]).

The single most important of the traditional rules is *squash and stretch*, which is used to indicate the physical properties of an object by distortions of shape. A rubber ball or a ball of putty both distort (in different ways) when dropped on the floor. A bouncing rubber ball might be shown as elongating as it approachs the floor (a precursor to motion blur), flattening out when it hits, and then elongating again as it rises. By contrast, a metal sphere hitting the floor might distort very little but might wobble after the impact, exhibiting very small, high-frequency distortions. The jump made by Luxo Jr., described in Chapter 20 and simulated by the physically based modeling described in this chapter, is made with a squash and stretch motion: Luxo crouches down, storing potential energy in his muscles; then springs up, stretching out completely and throwing his base forward; and then lands, again crouching to absorb the kinetic energy of the forward motion without toppling over. It is a tribute to the potential of the Kass–Witkin simulation that it generated this motion automatically; it is also a tribute to traditional animators that they are able, in effect, to estimate a solution of a complex partial differential equation.

A second important rule is to use slow-in and slow-out to help smooth interpolations. Sudden, jerky motions are extremely distracting. This is particularly evident in interpolating the *camera position* (the point of view from which the animation is drawn or computed).

An audience viewing an animation identifies with the camera view, so sudden changes in camera position may make the audience feel motion sickness. Thus, camera changes should be as smooth as possible.

A third rule that carries over naturally from the 2D character-animation world to 3D animations, whether they are for the entertainment industry or for scientific visualization, is to *stage* the action properly. This includes choosing a view that conveys the most information about the events taking place in the animation, and (when possible) isolating events so that only one thing at a time occupies the viewer's attention. In the case of animations for scientific visualization, this isolation may not be possible—the events being simulated may be simultaneous—but it may be possible to view the scene from a position in which the different events occupy different portions of the image, and each can be watched individually without visual clutter from the others.

There are many other aspects of the design of animations that are critical. Many of these are matters of "eye" rather than strict rules, although rules of thumb are gradually evolving. The appropriate use of color is too often ignored, and garish animations in which objects are obscured by their colors are the result. The timing of animations is often driven by computing time instead of by final appearance; no time is given to introducing actions, to spacing them adequately, or to terminating them smoothly, and the resulting action seems to fly by. The details of an animation are given too much attention at the cost of the overall feeling, and the result has no aesthetic appeal. When you are planning an animation, consider these difficulties, and allot as much time as possible to aesthetic considerations in the production of the animation.

21.5   PROBLEMS PECULIAR TO ANIMATION

Just as moving from 2D to 3D graphics introduced many new problems and challenges, the change from 3D to 4D (the addition of the time dimension) poses special problems as well. One of these problems is *temporal aliasing*. Just as the aliasing problems in 2D and 3D graphics are partially solved by increasing the screen resolution, the temporal aliasing problems in animation can be partially solved by increasing temporal resolution. Of course, another aspect of the 2D solution is antialiasing; the corresponding solution in 3D is temporal antialiasing.

Another problem in 4D rendering is the requirement that we render many very similar images (the images in an ideal animation do not change much from one frame to the next—if they did, we would get jerky changes from frame to frame). This problem is a lot like that of rendering multiple scan lines in a 2D image: each scan line, on the average, looks a lot like the one above it. Just as scan-line renderers take advantage of this inter–scan-line coherence, it is possible to take advantage of interframe coherence as well. For ray tracing, we do this by thinking of the entire animation as occupying a box in 4D space–time—three spatial directions and one time direction. Each object, as it moves through time, describes a region of 4D space–time. For example, a sphere that does not move at all describes a spherical tube in 4D. The corresponding situation in 3D is shown in Fig. 21.10: If we make the 2D animation of a circle shown in part (a), the corresponding box in 3D space–time is that shown in part (b). The circle sweeps out a circular cylinder in space–time. For the 4D case, each image rendered corresponds to taking a 2D picture of a

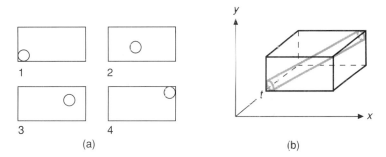

Fig. 21.10 The circle in (a) moves from lower left to upper right. By stacking these pictures along a third axis, we get the space–time animation shown in (b); the set of circles has become a tube in space–time.

3D slice of the 4D space–time. That is to say, we cast rays from a particular space–time point $(x, y, z; t)$ whose direction vectors have a time component of zero, so that all rays hit points whose time coordinate is also t. By applying the usual space-subdivision tricks for ray tracing to this 4D space–time, we can save a lot of time. A single hyperspace subdivision can be used for the entire course of the animation, so the time spent in creating the space subdivision does not need to be repeated once per frame. This idea and other uses of interframe coherence in ray tracing are described in [GLAS88].

High temporal resolution (many frames per second) may seem unnecessary. After all, video motion[9] seems smooth, and it is achieved at only 30 fps. Movies, however, at 24 fps, often have a jerkiness about them, especially when large objects are moving fast close to the viewer, as sometimes happens in a panning action. Also, as noted before, wagon wheels in movies sometimes appear to roll backward because of strobing. Higher temporal resolution helps to solve these problems. Doubling the number of frames per second lets the wagon wheel turn twice as fast before it seems to turn backward, and it certainly helps to smooth out the motion of fast-moving objects on the screen. The new Showscan technology [SHOW89] involves making and showing movies at 60 fps, on 70-millimeter film; this produces a bigger picture, which therefore occupies a larger portion of the visual field, and produces much smoother motion.

Temporal antialiasing can be done by taking multiple samples of a signal and computing their weighted average. In this case, however, the multiple samples must be in the time direction rather than in the spatial direction, so we compute the intensity at a point in the image for several sequential times and weight these to get a value at a particular frame. Many approaches to temporal-aliasing problems have been developed; supersampling, box filtering in the time domain, and all the other tricks (including postfiltering!) from spatial antialiasing have been applied. One of the most successful is the distributed ray tracing described in Chapter 16 [COOK86].

Another trick for reducing temporal aliasing deserves mention: animation on fields. A conventional video image is traced twice; all the even-numbered scan lines are drawn, then

---

[9]We mean video motion filmed by a camera, not synthetically generated.

all the odd-numbered ones, and so on. Each scan line is redrawn every $\frac{1}{30}$ second, but the even-numbered and odd-numbered scan lines are drawn in two different passes. Thus, the electron beam passes over the screen 60 times per second. If the colors of the pixels of the even-numbered scan lines are computed at time t in the animation, and those for the odd-numbered scan lines are computed at time $t + \frac{1}{60}$ second, and these are composed into a single pixmap, and this process is iterated for each frame, then when the animation is displayed the effect is something like a 60-fps animation, even though each scan line is refreshed only every $\frac{1}{30}$ second. This trick has some cost, however: The still frames from an animation do not look as good as they might, since they are composites of images taken at two different times, and they thus seem to flicker if shown on an interlaced display. Also, twice as many frames must be rendered, so twice as many interpolated positions of the objects must be computed, and so on. Despite these drawbacks, the technique is widely employed in the computer-animation industry.

At the other extreme in animation is the process of *animating on twos*, or threes, and so on, in which the animation is produced at a temporal resolution lower than the display's refresh rate. Typically, each frame of the animation is displayed for two frames of video ("on twos"), so the effective refresh rate for video becomes 12 fps rather than 24 fps. This approach necessarily produces jerkier images (if no temporal antialiasing is done) or blurrier images (if it is). Animating on multiple frames and then filling in the intermediate ones can be useful in developing an animation, however, since it allows the animator to get a sense of the animation long before the individual frames have all been created (see Exercise 21.2.)

21.6 SUMMARY

Computer animation is a young field, and high-level animation is a recent development. As the computational power available to animators increases and as animation systems become more sophisticated, generating a high-quality computer animation will become simpler. At present, however, many compromises must be accepted. Simulation software is likely to advance rapidly, and the automated generation of graphical simulations is just a step away. On the other hand, until animation software contains knowledge about the tricks of conventional animation, computer character animation will remain as much an art as a science, and the "eye" of the animator will continue to have an enormous effect on the quality of the animation.

EXERCISES

21.1 Consider a unit square with corners at $(0, 0)$ and $(1, 1)$. Suppose we have a polygonal path defined by the vertices $(0, 1)$, $(1, 1)$, and $(1, 0)$, in that order, and we wish to transform it to the polygonal path defined by the vertices $(1, 0)$, $(0, 0)$, and $(0, 1)$ (i.e., we want to rotate it by 180°). Draw the intermediate stages that result if we linearly interpolate the positions of the vertices. This shows that strict interpolation of vertices is not adequate for key-frame interpolation unless the key frames are not too far apart.

21.2 Suppose that you are creating an animation, and can generate the frames in any order. If the animation is 128 frames long, a first "pencil sketch" can be created by rendering the first frame, and displaying it for a full 128 frames. (This is very low temporal resolution!). A second approximation can be generated by displaying the first frame for 64 frames and the sixty-fourth frame for the next 64. Suppose you have a video recorder that can record a given image at a given video-frame number, for a given number of video frames. Write pseudocode for a sequential-approximation recording scheme based on the idea of rendering frames and recording them such as to show approximations of the entire animation, which successively approach the ideal. You should assume the number of frames in the entire animation is a power of 2. (This exercise was contributed by Michael Natkin and Rashid Ahmad.)

21.3 Using a color-table–based display device, implement the an mation depicted in Fig. 21.4 . Can you think of ways to generate smoother motion?

21.4 Using a frame-buffer that supports *pan* and *zoom* operations, implement the pan-zoom movie technique described in Section 21.1.2.

21.5 Make an animation of fireworks, using the particle systems of Section 20.5. If you do not have a frame buffer capable of displaying the images, you may instead be able to program the particle systems in POSTSCRIPT, and to display them on a printer. Hold the resulting pictures as a book and riffle through them, making a *flip-book* animation.

21.6 Suppose you were trying to make a 2D animation system that started with scanned-in hand drawings. Suggest techniques for cleaning up the hand drawings automatically, including the closing of nearly closed loops, the smoothing of curved lines, but not of sharp corners, etc. The automation of this process is extremely difficult, and trying to imagine how to automate the process suggests the value of interactive drawing programs as a source for 2D animation material

21.7 a. Suppose that q and r are quaternions corresponding to rotations of ϕ and θ about the axis $\mathbf{v}$. Explicitly compute the product qr and use trigonometric identities to show that it corresponds to the rotation about $\mathbf{v}$ by angle $\phi + \theta$.

b. Show that the product of two unit quaternions is a unit quaternion.

c. If q is the unit quaternion $a + b\mathbf{i} + c\mathbf{j} + d\mathbf{k}$, and z is the quaternion $x\mathbf{i} + y\mathbf{j} + z\mathbf{k}$, we can form a new quaternion $s' = qsq^{-1}$, where $q^{-1} = a - b\mathbf{i} - c\mathbf{j} - d\mathbf{k}$. If we write $s' = x'\mathbf{i} + y'\mathbf{j} + z'\mathbf{k}$, then the numbers x', y', and z' depend on the numbers x, y, and z. Find a matrix Q such that $[x' \quad y' \quad z']^t = Q[x \quad y \quad z]^t$. When we generate rotations from quaternions, it is this matrix form that we should use, not an explicit computation of the quaternion product.

d. Show that the vector $[b \quad c \quad d]^t$ is left fixed under multiplication by Q, so that Q represents a rotation about the vector $[b \quad c \quad d]$. It actually represents a rotation by angle $2\cos^{-1}(a)$, so that this describes the correspondence between quaternions and rotations.

Appendix:
Mathematics for
Computer Graphics

This appendix reviews much of the mathematics used in the book. It is by no means intended as a text on linear algebra or geometry or calculus. The approach we take is somewhat unconventional, since most modern books on linear algebra do not mention affine spaces, and we choose to emphasize them. The text is liberally laced with exercises, which you should work through before looking at the solutions provided. The solutions are generally brief, and are intended to let you know whether you did the problem correctly, rather than to tell you how to do it.

The assumption we make in this appendix is that you have had courses in plane geometry, calculus, and linear algebra, but that your familiarity with all three subjects has faded somewhat. Thus, we give definitions for many important terms and state some important results, but the proofs are, for the most part, omitted; we have found that students interested in such proofs can generally construct them, and that those who are not interested in them find them distracting. Readers interested in reviewing this material in more detail should consult [BANC83; HOFF61; MARS85].

The first part of the appendix describes the geometry of affine spaces in some detail. In later sections, in which the material should be more familiar, we give considerably less detail. The final section discusses finding roots of real-valued functions, and is unrelated to the rest of the material.

A.1 VECTOR SPACES AND AFFINE SPACES

A vector space is, loosely, a place where addition and multiplication by a constant make sense. More precisely, a vector space consists of a set, whose elements are called *vectors*

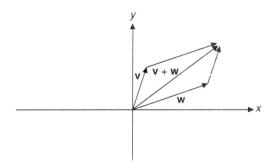

Fig. A.1 Addition of vectors in the plane.

(which we will denote by boldfaced letters, usually **u**, **v**, or **w**), together with two operations: addition of vectors, and multiplication of vectors by real numbers (called *scalar multiplication*).[1] The operations must have certain properties. Addition must be commutative, must be associative, must have an identity element (i.e., there must be a vector, traditionally called **0**, with the property that, for any vector **v**, **0** + **v** = **v**), and must have inverses (i.e., for every vector **v**, there is another vector **w** with the property that **v** + **w** = **0**; **w** is written "−**v**"). Scalar multiplication must satisfy the rules $(\alpha\beta)\mathbf{v} = \alpha(\beta\mathbf{v})$, $1\mathbf{v} = \mathbf{v}$, $(\alpha + \beta)\mathbf{v} = \alpha\mathbf{v} + \beta\mathbf{v}$, and $\alpha(\mathbf{v} + \mathbf{w}) = \alpha\mathbf{v} + \alpha\mathbf{w}$.

This definition of a vector space abstracts the fundamental geometric properties of the plane. We can make the plane into a vector space, in which the set of vectors is precisely the set of points in the plane. This identification of vectors and points is temporary, and is used for this example only. For now, we consider a point in the plane and a vector to be the same thing. To make the plane into a vector space, we must first choose a particular point in the plane, which we call the origin. We define addition of vectors by the well known *parallelogram rule*: To add the vectors **v** and **w**, we take an arrow from the origin to **w**, translate it so that its base is at the point **v**, and define **v** + **w** as the new endpoint of the arrow. If we also draw the arrow from the origin to **v**, and do the corresponding process, we get a parallelogram, as shown in Fig. A.1. Scalar multiplication by a real number α is defined similarly: We draw an arrow from the origin to the point **v**, stretch it by a factor of α, holding the end at the origin fixed, and then $\alpha\mathbf{v}$ is defined to be the endpoint of the resulting arrow. Of course, the same definitions can be made for the real number line or for Euclidean 3-space.

Exercise: Examine the construction of the vector space in the preceding paragraph. Does it depend in any way on assigning coordinates to points in the plane, or is it a purely geometrical construction? Suppose that we assign coordinates to points of the plane in the familiar fashion used in graphing. If we add the vectors whose coordinates are (a, b) and (c, d), what are the coordinates of the resulting vector? Suppose that instead we lay down coordinate lines so that one set of lines runs horizontally, but the other set, instead of

---

[1]Scalars (i.e., real numbers) will be denoted by Greek letters, typically by those near the start of the alphabet.

running vertically, runs at 30° away from vertical. What are the coordinates of the sum now?

Answer: No, it is purely geometrical (where geometry includes distance measure). The vector sum has coordinates $(a + c, b + d)$, in both cases.

The classic example of a vector space is $\mathbf{R}^n$, the set of all ordered n-tuples of real numbers. Addition is defined componentwise, as is scalar multiplication. Elements of $\mathbf{R}^n$ are written vertically, so that a sample element of $\mathbf{R}^3$ is

$$\begin{bmatrix} 1 \\ 3 \\ 1 \end{bmatrix}.$$

We can sum elements;

$$\begin{bmatrix} 1 \\ 3 \\ 1 \end{bmatrix} + \begin{bmatrix} 2 \\ 3 \\ 6 \end{bmatrix} = \begin{bmatrix} 3 \\ 6 \\ 7 \end{bmatrix}.$$

Most of graphics is done in $\mathbf{R}^2$, $\mathbf{R}^3$, or $\mathbf{R}^4$.

Given the two operations available in a vector space, there are some natural things to do with vectors. One of these is forming *linear combinations*. A linear combination of the vectors $\mathbf{v}_1, \ldots, \mathbf{v}_n$ is any vector of the form $\alpha \mathbf{v}_1 + \alpha_2 \mathbf{v}_2 + \ldots + \alpha_n \mathbf{v}_n$. Linear combinations of vectors are used for describing many objects. In the Cartesian plane example, the line through a nonzero point $\mathbf{v}$ and the origin can be described as the set of all vectors of the form $\alpha \mathbf{v}$, where α ranges over the real numbers. The ray from the origin through $\mathbf{v}$ is the same thing, except with α ranging over the nonnegative reals. These are both examples of linear "combinations" of a single vector. We will encounter more complex combinations later.

In general, the collection of all possible linear combinations of a set of vectors is called the *span* of the set. The span of a nonzero vector in the Cartesian plane example was a line through the origin. The span of two vectors that point in different directions is a plane.

Before we go further with vector spaces, we shall discuss affine spaces. An *affine space* is approximately describable as a set in which geometric operations make sense, but in which there is no distinguished point. (In a vector space, the vector $\mathbf{0}$ is special, and this is reflected in the example of the Cartesian plane, in which the origin plays a special role in the definition of addition and scalar multiplication.) A more precise definition of an affine space is that it consists of a set, called the *points* of the affine space; an associated vector space; and two operations. Given two points, P and Q, we can form the *difference* of P and Q, which lies in the vector space; given a point, P, and vector, $\mathbf{v}$, we can add the vector to the point to get a new point, $P + \mathbf{v}$. Again, there are certain properties that these operations must satisfy, such as $(P + \mathbf{v}) + \mathbf{w} = P + (\mathbf{v} + \mathbf{w})$, and $P + \mathbf{v} = P$ if and only if $\mathbf{v} = 0$.

This definition is based on a more classical model of geometry, in which there is no preferred origin. If you think of the surface of a table as an example of a (truncated) plane, there is no *natural* origin—no point of the table is preferred to any other. But if you take a point, P, on the table, and place a set of coordinate axes with their origin at P, every other point of the table can be measured by specifying its displacement from P using that coordinate system. By translating all the points of the coordinate axes by some fixed amount, we get new coordinate axes at another point. In this model, the points of the affine space are the points of the tabletop, and the vectors are arrows between them. Adding a vector $\mathbf{v}$ to a point P amounts to laying down the arrow with its base at P, and seeing where its end is (the endpoint is called $P + \mathbf{v}$). Taking the difference of two points Q and P, $Q - P$, consists of finding an arrow that goes from P to Q.

Affine planes make a natural model for computer graphics. Often, there is no preferred point in graphics. When you are modeling a room, for example, there is no natural point of the room to choose as an origin. Therefore, we shall discuss vector spaces and affine spaces side by side.

Linear combinations of points in an affine space make no sense (there is not even a definition of scalar multiplication), but we can define an *affine combination of the points P and Q by the real number t*. This affine combination is meant to correspond to a point that is a fraction t of the way from P to Q. (If t lies between 0 and 1, this is called a *convex combination*.) We can consider the difference of Q and P, $\mathbf{v} = Q - P$, which we think of as a vector pointing from P to Q. If we multiply this by t, we get a vector that is t times as long. Adding this vector back to P, we get the affine combination of P and Q by t, which is therefore

$$P + t(Q - P).$$

It is often tempting to rewrite this equation by gathering together the terms involving P, to get $(1 - t)P + tQ$; this makes no sense at all, however, since multiplication of points by scalars is undefined. Rather than outlaw this suggestive notation, however, we simply define it: If α and β are scalars that sum to 1, and P and Q are points in an affine space, we define $\alpha P + \beta Q$ to be $P + \beta(Q - P)$.

Affine combinations of more points are defined similarly: Given n points, $P_1, \ldots, P_n$, and n real numbers $t_1, \ldots, t_n$, satisfying $t_1 + \ldots + t_n = 1$, we define the affine combination of the Ps by the ts to be $P_1 + t_2(P_2 - P_1) + \ldots + t_n(P_n - P_1)$, which we also rewrite as $t_1 P_1 + \ldots + t_n P_n$.

Exercise: Every vector space can be made into an affine space. The points of the affine space are the vectors in the vector space. The associated vector space is the original vector space. The difference of points is just defined to be the difference of vectors, and the sum of a point and a vector is the ordinary vector sum. Show that, in this case, the point we have defined as $\alpha P + \beta Q$ (where $\alpha + \beta = 1$) is actually equal, using the operations in the vector space, to the vector $\alpha P + \beta Q$.

Answer: $\alpha P + \beta Q$ is defined to be $P + \beta(Q - P)$. But ordinary vector operations apply, so this is just $P + \beta Q - \beta P = (1 - \beta)P + \beta Q = \alpha P + \beta Q$.

A.1.1   Equation of a Line in an Affine Space

If P and Q are two points in an affine space, the set of points of the form $(1 - t)P + tQ$ forms a line passing though P and Q; this form of a line is sometimes called the *parametric form*, because of the parameter t. The Cartesian plane, whose points are labeled with coordinates (x, y), is an affine space, and the parametric line between the point (a, b) and the point (c, d) is therefore given by

$$L = \{((1 - t)a + tc, (1 - t)b + td) \mid t \text{ is a real number}\}.$$

Exercise: Show that the set of all triples of real numbers of the form $(a, b, 1)$ also forms an affine space, with an associated vector space $\mathbf{R}^2$, provided we define the difference of two points $(a, b, 1)$ and $(c, d, 1)$ to be the vector $(a - c, b - d)$, and define the sum of a point and a vector similarly. Show that, using the definition of a parametric line given previously, the line between the points $(1, 5, 1)$ and $(2, 4, 1)$ consists entirely of points whose last coordinate is 1.

Answer: The definition of the line is the set of points of the form $(1 - t)(1, 5, 1) + t(2, 4, 1)$, which in turn is defined to mean $(1, 5, 1) + t(1, -1)$. These are points of the form $(1 + t, 5 - t, 1)$; hence, their last coordinate is 1.

A.1.2 Equation of a Plane in an Affine Space

If P, Q, and R are three points in an affine space, and they are not colinear (i.e., if R does not lie on the line containing P and Q), then the plane defined by P, Q, and R is the set of points of the form

$$(1 - s)((1 - t)P + tQ) + sR.$$

Exercise: Explain why the preceding expression makes geometric sense.

Answer: The expression is an affine combination of two points. The first point is $(1 - t)P + tQ$; the second is R. The first point is an affine combination of the points P and Q. Hence, all terms make sense.

Once again, this description of the plane is called *parametric,* because of the two parameters s and t.

Exercise: The set $\mathbf{E}^3$, consisting of all triples of real numbers, is an affine space, with an associated vector space $\mathbf{R}^3$, whose elements are also ordered triple of real numbers, but which have componentwise addition and scalar multiplication defined on them. The difference of two points in $\mathbf{E}^3$ is defined componentwise as well, as is the sum of a point and a vector. What points lie in the plane that contains the points $(1, 0, 4)$, $(2, 3, 6)$ and $(0, 0, 7)$?

Answer: The points of the plane are all points of the form $(1 - s)((1 - t)(1, 0, 4) + t(2, 3, 6)) + s(0, 0, 7)$. Because all operations are defined componentwise, we can express this as the set of all points of the form $((1 - s)(1 - t) + 2(1 - s)t, 3(1 - s)t, 4(1 - s)(1 - t) + 6t + 7s)$.

A.1.3 Subspaces

If we have a vector space, V, and a nonempty subset of V called S, then S is a *linear subspace of V* if, whenever $\mathbf{v}$ and $\mathbf{w}$ are in S, so are $\mathbf{v} + \mathbf{w}$ and $\alpha\mathbf{v}$, for every real number α. For example, if $\mathbf{v}$ is a vector, then the set of all vectors of the form $\alpha\mathbf{v}$ constitutes a subspace, because when any two scalar multiples of $\mathbf{v}$ are added, we get a third, and a scalar multiple of a scalar multiple of $\mathbf{v}$ is another scalar multiple of $\mathbf{v}$. In $\mathbf{R}^3$, the subspaces can be listed explicitly. They are (1) the origin, (2) any line through the origin, (3) any plane containing the origin, and (4) $\mathbf{R}^3$ itself.

Exercise: Show that any linear subspace of a vector space must contain the $\mathbf{0}$ vector.

Answer: Let $\mathbf{v}$ be any vector in S. Then $-1\mathbf{v} = -\mathbf{v}$ is also in S, and therefore $\mathbf{v} + (-\mathbf{v})$ is in S. But this is exactly the $\mathbf{0}$ vector. Merely scaling by 0 is not an adequate answer, since there is no a priori reason that $0\mathbf{v} = \mathbf{0}$ in a vector space. As it happens, since $(1 + (-1))\mathbf{v} = \mathbf{v} + (-\mathbf{v}) = 0$, it is actually true that $0\mathbf{v} = \mathbf{v}$; this statement merely happens not to be one of the axioms.

An affine subspace is a more general object. A nonempty subset S of a vector space V is called an *affine subspace* if the set $S' = \{\mathbf{u} - \mathbf{v} \mid \mathbf{u}, \mathbf{v} \text{ in } S\}$ is a linear subspace of V. For example, any line in the Cartesian plane is an affine subspace. If S is such a line, then S' is precisely the line parallel to it through the origin.

If S is an affine subspace of a vector space, then S can be thought of as an affine space in its own right. (Note that it is *not* a vector space. Consider the line $x = 1$ in $\mathbf{R}^2$. Both $\begin{bmatrix} 1 \\ 3 \end{bmatrix}$ and $\begin{bmatrix} 1 \\ 5 \end{bmatrix}$ are in this affine subspace, but their sum, $\begin{bmatrix} 2 \\ 8 \end{bmatrix}$, is not.) The affine-space structure is given as follows: The associated vector space is just S'; the difference of two points in S lies in S' by definition, and the sum of a point in S with a vector in S' is another point in S.

Important Exercise: Show that S, the set of points of the form $(x, y, z, 1)$, forms an affine subspace of $\mathbf{R}^4$. What is the associated vector space? What is the difference of two points in this affine subspace?

Answer: The difference of any two points in S has the form $(a, b, c, 0)$, and the set of all points of this form is a vector space under the usual operations of addition an multiplication (in fact, it is essentially "the same" as $\mathbf{R}^3$). The associated vector space is the set of quadruples of the form $(a, b, c, 0)$. The difference of $(x, y, z, 1)$ and $(x', y', z', 1)$ is just $(x - x', y - y', z - z', 0)$.

The preceding example is important because it is the basis for all the material in Chapter 5. We can see in the example a clear distinction between *points* in the space, which are the things used to specify positions of objects in a graphics world, and *vectors*, which are used to specify displacements or directions from point to point. It is an unfortunate coincidence that a point of the form $(x, y, z, 1)$ can be stored in an array of three **reals** in Pascal, and a vector of the form $(a, b, c, 0)$ can too. Because of this, many people make the error of thinking that points and vectors are interchangeable. Nothing could be further from the truth. Denoting points in both the affine space and the ambient space by columns of numbers,

$$\begin{bmatrix} a \\ b \\ c \\ d \end{bmatrix},$$

further confuses the issue, but it has become standard practice. We refer to the set of points in $\mathbf{R}^4$ whose last coordinate is 1 as the *standard affine 3-space in* $\mathbf{R}^4$. We correspondingly define the standard affine 2-space in $\mathbf{R}^3$ (which we call the standard affine plane), and so on.

Figure A.2 shows the standard affine plane in $\mathbf{R}^3$. This picture is far easier to draw than is the standard affine 3-space in $\mathbf{R}^4$, and we use it to provide intuition into that more complex case. The points in the standard affine plane are triples of the form

$$\begin{bmatrix} x \\ y \\ 1 \end{bmatrix},$$

and the vectors have the form

$$\begin{bmatrix} a \\ b \\ 0 \end{bmatrix}.$$

(We have labeled the horizontal plane with the letters "x" and "y," and the vertical axis with the letter "h." This choice is meant to indicate the special nature of the third coordinate.) The set of points of the affine space forms a plane at height 1 above the (x, y) plane. The endpoints of the vectors (i.e., differences between points in the affine space) all lie in the (x, y) plane, if the starting point is placed at the origin $(0, 0, 0)$, but are drawn as arrows in the affine plane to illustrate their use as differences of points. If we take two points, P and Q, in the affine space as shown, their sum (as vectors in $\mathbf{R}^3$) lies one full unit above the affine space. This shows geometrically the perils of adding points.

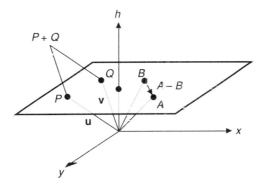

Fig. A.2 The standard affine plane in $\mathbf{R}^3$, embedded as the plane at $h = 1$. P and Q are points in the plane, but their sum lies above the plane. The difference of the points A and B is a horizontal vector.

Figure A.3 shows an important operation on this affine space: homogenization. If we take an arbitrary point

$$\begin{bmatrix} x \\ y \\ h \end{bmatrix}$$

in 3-space, and connect it to the origin by a line, it will intersect the affine plane at a single point.

Exercise: Determine this point of intersection.

Answer: The line from

$$\begin{bmatrix} x \\ y \\ h \end{bmatrix}$$

to the origin consists of all points of the form

$$\begin{bmatrix} \alpha x \\ \alpha y \\ \alpha h \end{bmatrix}.$$

We want to find the point whose third coordinate is 1. This point will be located precisely where $\alpha h = 1$; that is, where $\alpha = 1/h$. The coordinates of this point are therefore

$$\begin{bmatrix} x/h \\ y/h \\ h/h \end{bmatrix} = \begin{bmatrix} x/h \\ y/h \\ 1 \end{bmatrix}.$$

Naturally, this operation fails when $h = 0$, but this is no surprise, geometrically: A point in the (x, y) plane is connected to the origin by a line that never intersects the affine space.

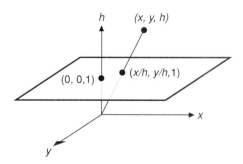

Fig. A.3 The homogenization operation in $\mathbf{R}^3$. The point (x, y, h) is homogenized to the point $(x/h, y/h, 1)$.

A.2 SOME STANDARD CONSTRUCTIONS IN VECTOR SPACES

A.2.1 Linear Dependence and Spans

We have defined the span of a set of vectors as the set of all linear combinations of those vectors. If we consider the special case of $\mathbf{R}^3$, the span of a single vector (except for $\mathbf{0}$) is the line through the origin containing the vector; the span of a pair of vectors (both nonzero, and neither lying in the span of the other) is a plane through the origin containing both; the span of three (sufficiently general) vectors is all of $\mathbf{R}^3$.

When one of the unusual cases (i.e., the cases rules out by the parenthetical conditions) in the preceding paragraph occurs, the vectors involved are said to be *linearly dependent* (or simply *dependent*). Essentially, a set of vectors is linearly dependent if one of them lies in the span of the rest.

Exercise: Show that the three vectors $\mathbf{a} = \left[\begin{smallmatrix}1\\3\end{smallmatrix}\right]$, $\mathbf{b} = \left[\begin{smallmatrix}2\\-6\end{smallmatrix}\right]$, and $\mathbf{c} = \left[\begin{smallmatrix}4\\1\end{smallmatrix}\right]$ are dependent by showing that $\mathbf{b}$ lies in the span of $\mathbf{a}$ and $\mathbf{c}$. Show also that $\mathbf{c}$, however, does not lie in the span of $\mathbf{a}$ and $\mathbf{b}$.

Answer: $\mathbf{b} = 2\mathbf{a} + 0\mathbf{c}$. On the other hand, the span of $\mathbf{a}$ and $\mathbf{b}$ consists of all vectors of the form

$$ t\mathbf{a} + s\mathbf{b} = \begin{bmatrix} t \\ 3t \end{bmatrix} + \begin{bmatrix} 2s \\ 6s \end{bmatrix} = \begin{bmatrix} t + 2s \\ 3t + 6s \end{bmatrix} = (t + 2s) \begin{bmatrix} 1 \\ 3 \end{bmatrix}; $$

hence, any vector in this span must be a scalar multiple of $\left[\begin{smallmatrix}1\\3\end{smallmatrix}\right]$. The vector $\mathbf{c}$ is not.

The more precise definition of linear dependence is that the vectors $\mathbf{v}_1, \ldots, \mathbf{v}_n$ are linearly dependent if there exist scalars $\alpha_1, \ldots, \alpha_n$ such that (1) at least one of the α_is is nonzero, and (2) $\alpha_1\mathbf{v}_1 + \ldots + \alpha_n\mathbf{v}_n = \mathbf{0}$.

Exercise: Show that, if the vectors $\mathbf{v}_1, \ldots, \mathbf{v}_n$ are dependent, then one of them lies in the span of the others.

Answer: There are scalars $\alpha_1, \ldots, \alpha_n$ such that $\alpha_1\mathbf{v}_1 + \ldots + \alpha_n\mathbf{v}_n = \mathbf{0}$ and the scalars are not all zero, since the vectors are dependent. Suppose, by rearranging the order if necessary, that α_1 is nonzero. Then we can solve the preceding equation for $\mathbf{v}_1$ to get $\mathbf{v}_1 = (1/\alpha_1)\alpha_2\mathbf{v}_1 + \ldots + (1/\alpha_1)\alpha_n\mathbf{v}_n$, showing that $\mathbf{v}_1$ is in the span of the remaining vectors.

The vectors $\mathbf{v}_1, \ldots, \mathbf{v}_n$ are said to be *linearly independent* (or just *independent*) if they are not dependent. This definition is troublesome, because it requires verifying a negative statement. Later, we shall see that, at least for vectors in $\mathbf{R}^n$, we can restate it in a positive form: A set of vectors is independent if and only if a certain number (the determinant of a matrix) is nonzero.

We can define dependence and span for affine spaces as well. The span of a set of points $P_1, \ldots, P_n$ in an affine space can be defined in several ways. It is the set of all affine combinations of points in the set. We can also describe it by considering the vectors

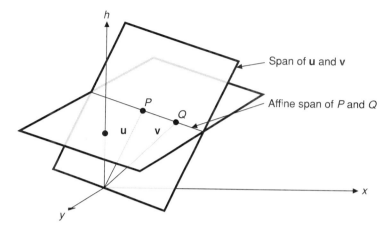

Fig. A.4 The relation between the vector space span of the vectors **u** and **v** in $\mathbf{R}^3$, whose endpoints are the points P and Q in the affine plane, and the affine span of P and Q.

$P_2 - P_1$, $P_3 - P_1$, . . ., $P_n - P_1$ in the associated vector space, taking the span of these vectors, S, and then defining the affine span to be all points of the form $P_1 + \mathbf{v}$, where $\mathbf{v}$ is in S.

Just as for vector spaces, a collection of points in an affine space is said to be dependent if any one of them lies in the (affine) span of the others. It is independent if it is not dependent.

Consider again the special case of the standard affine plane consisting of points of the form

$$\begin{bmatrix} x \\ y \\ 1 \end{bmatrix}$$

in $\mathbf{R}^3$. If we take two points in this affine space, we can form their affine span, which will be the line containing them. We can also form their span in a different way, by considering them as vectors in $\mathbf{R}^3$ and forming the vector-space span. Figure A.4 shows the relationship between these two spans—the affine span is the intersection of the vector-space span (a plane through the origin) with the affine space.

A.2.2   Coordinates, Coordinate Systems, and Bases

We can describe some large sets in a vector space using a compact notation, if we use the notion of spans. For example, we have described lines and planes as the spans of one and two vectors, respectively. We *could* describe a line by choosing two vectors that both lie in it, and saying it is the span of the two vectors, but that would be redundant—each of the two vectors would already be in the span of the other, in general.

A minimal spanning set for a vector subspace (or for an entire space) is called a *basis*. *Minimal* means the following: Any smaller set of vectors has a smaller span. Thus, in our previous example, the two vectors that spanned the line were not minimal, because one could be deleted and the remaining one would still span the line.

Exercise: Show that a basis of a subspace of a vector space is always linearly independent.

Answer: Let $v_1, \ldots, v_n$ be a basis for the subspace S, and suppose that $v_1, \ldots, v_n$ is dependent. Then (by renumbering if necessary), we can find scalars $\alpha_2, \ldots, \alpha_n$ such that $v_1 = \alpha_2 v_2 + \ldots + \alpha_n v_n$. A typical element of the span of $v_1, \ldots, v_n$ is $\beta_1 v_1 + \ldots + \beta_n v_n$. This expression can be rewritten as $\beta_1(\alpha_2 v_2 + \ldots + \alpha_n v_n) + \beta_2 v_2 + \ldots + \beta_n v_n$. This can be rearranged into a linear combination of the vectors $v_2, \ldots, v_n$. Thus, any vector in the span of $v_1, \ldots, v_n$ is also in the span of $v_2, \ldots, v_n$, so $v_1, \ldots, v_n$ is not a minimal spanning set. Hence, the assumption that $v_1, \ldots, v_n$ was dependent must have been false.

Suppose we have a basis for a vector space. Then, every vector v in the space can be written as a linear combination $\alpha_1 v_1 + \ldots + \alpha_n v_n$. Suppose we write v as a *different* linear combination, $v = \beta_1 v_1 + \ldots + \beta_n v_n$. Then, by subtraction, we get $0 = (\beta_1 - \alpha_1)v_1 + \ldots + (\beta_n - \alpha_n)v_n$. Since we assumed that the two linear combinations were different, some α_i must differ from the corresponding β_i. By renumbering, we can assume that $\alpha_1 \neq \beta_1$. But then, just as before, we can solve for v_1 in terms of the remaining vectors, so the set $v_1, \ldots, v_n$ could not have been a minimal spanning set. Thus, every vector in a vector space can be written *uniquely* as a linear combination of the vectors in a basis.

If we have a basis for a vector space, $\mathbf{B} = \{v_1, \ldots, v_n\}$, and a vector v in the vector space, we have just shown that there is a unique set of scalars $\alpha_1, \ldots, \alpha_n$ such that $v = \alpha_1 v_1 + \ldots + \alpha_n v_n$. This set of scalars can be thought of as an element of $\mathbf{R}^n$, and this element of $\mathbf{R}^n$,

$$\begin{bmatrix} \alpha_1 \\ \cdot \\ \cdot \\ \cdot \\ \alpha_n \end{bmatrix},$$

is called the *coordinate vector of v with respect to the basis $v_1, \ldots, v_n$.*

Exercise: In $\mathbf{R}^3$, there is a *standard basis*, $\mathbf{E} = \{e_1, e_2, e_3\}$, where

$$e_1 = \begin{bmatrix} 1 \\ 0 \\ 0 \end{bmatrix}, \qquad e_2 = \begin{bmatrix} 0 \\ 1 \\ 0 \end{bmatrix}, \qquad \text{and } e_3 = \begin{bmatrix} 0 \\ 0 \\ 1 \end{bmatrix}.$$

What are the coordinates of the vector

$$v = \begin{bmatrix} 3 \\ 4 \\ 2 \end{bmatrix}$$

with respect to this basis?

Answer: They are

$$\begin{bmatrix} 3 \\ 4 \\ 2 \end{bmatrix},$$

because $\mathbf{v} = 3\mathbf{e}_1 + 4\mathbf{e}_2 + 2\mathbf{e}_3$.

The corresponding definition in an affine space is quite similar. A set of independent points in an affine space, whose affine span is the entire affine space, is called a *coordinate system*. If $P_1, \ldots, P_n$ is a coordinate system, then every point of the affine space can be written uniquely as an affine combination of $P_1, \ldots, P_n$; the coefficients are called the *affine coordinates of the point with respect to the coordinate system* $P_1, \ldots, P_n$.

Exercise: Show that, if $P_1, \ldots, P_n$ is a coordinate system for an affine space, then $P_2 - P_1, \ldots, P_n - P_1$ is a basis for the associated vector space.

Answer: Let $\mathbf{v}$ be a vector in the associated vector space, and let $Q = P_1 + \mathbf{v}$. Then Q can be written as an affine combination of $P_1, \ldots, P_n$. So there are scalars $\alpha_1, \ldots, \alpha_n$ such that $\alpha_1 + \ldots + \alpha_n = 1$ and $Q = \alpha_1 P_1 + \alpha_2 P_2 + \ldots + \alpha_n P_n = P_1 + \alpha_2(P_2 - P_1) + \ldots + \alpha_n(P_n - P_1)$. But this implies that $\mathbf{v} = \alpha_2(P_2 - P_1) + \ldots + \alpha_n(P_n - P_1)$. Hence, the set $P_2 - P_1, \ldots, P_n - P_1$ spans the associated vector space. If the set were dependent, the corresponding set of points $P_1, \ldots, P_n$ in the affine space would be dependent. Hence, it must both span and be independent, so it is a basis.

A.3   DOT PRODUCTS AND DISTANCES

The vector spaces and affine spaces we have discussed so far are purely algebraic objects. No metric notions—such as distance and angle measure—have been mentioned. But the world we inhabit, and the world in which we do graphics, both do have notions of distance and angle measure. In this section, we discuss the dot (or inner) product on $\mathbf{R}^n$, and examine how it can be used to measure distances and angles. A critical feature of distance measure and angle measure is that they make sense for vectors, not points: To measure the distance between points in an affine space, we take the difference vector and measure its length.

A.3.1   The Dot Product in $\mathbf{R}^n$

Given two vectors

$$\begin{bmatrix} x_1 \\ \cdot \\ \cdot \\ \cdot \\ x_n \end{bmatrix} \quad \text{and} \quad \begin{bmatrix} y_1 \\ \cdot \\ \cdot \\ \cdot \\ y_n \end{bmatrix}$$

in $\mathbf{R}^n$, we define their *inner product* or *dot product* to be $x_1 y_1 + \ldots + x_n y_n$. The dot product of vectors $\mathbf{v}$ and $\mathbf{w}$ is generally denoted by $\mathbf{v} \cdot \mathbf{w}$.

The distance from the point (x, y) in the plane to the origin $(0, 0)$ is $\sqrt{x^2 + y^2}$. In general, the distance from the point $(x_1, \ldots, x_n)$ to the origin in n-space is $\sqrt{x_1^2 + \ldots + x_n^2}$. If we let $\mathbf{v}$ be the vector

$$\begin{bmatrix} x_1 \\ \cdot \\ \cdot \\ \cdot \\ x_n \end{bmatrix},$$

we can see that this is just $\sqrt{\mathbf{v} \cdot \mathbf{v}}$. This is our definition of the *length* of a vector in $\mathbf{R}^n$. We denote this length by $\| \mathbf{v} \|$. The distance between two points in the standard affine n-space is defined similarly: The distance between P and Q is the length of the vector $Q - P$.

Exercise: The points

$$\begin{bmatrix} 1 \\ 3 \\ 1 \end{bmatrix} \qquad \text{and} \qquad \begin{bmatrix} 2 \\ 5 \\ 1 \end{bmatrix}$$

both lie in the standard affine plane, as well as in $\mathbf{R}^3$. What is the distance from each of them to the origin in $\mathbf{R}^3$? What is the distance between them? What is the distance from each to the point

$$\begin{bmatrix} 0 \\ 0 \\ 1 \end{bmatrix}$$

in the standard affine plane? What is the dot product of the two vectors

$$\begin{bmatrix} 1 \\ 3 \\ 1 \end{bmatrix} \qquad \text{and} \qquad \begin{bmatrix} 2 \\ 5 \\ 1 \end{bmatrix} ?$$

Answer: The distances to the origin are $\sqrt{11}$ and $\sqrt{30}$, respectively. The distance between the points is $\sqrt{5}$. The distances to

$$\begin{bmatrix} 0 \\ 0 \\ 1 \end{bmatrix}$$

are $\sqrt{10}$ and $\sqrt{29}$ respectively. The dot product is 18. Note that asking for the dot products of the two *points* in the affine space makes no sense—dot products are defined only for vectors.

A.3.2   Properties of the Dot Product

The dot product has several nice properties. First, it is symmetric: $\mathbf{v} \cdot \mathbf{w} = \mathbf{w} \cdot \mathbf{v}$. Second, it is *nondegenerate*: $\mathbf{v} \cdot \mathbf{v} = 0$ only when $\mathbf{v} = \mathbf{0}$. Third, it is *bilinear*: $\mathbf{v} \cdot (\mathbf{u} + \alpha \mathbf{w}) = \mathbf{v} \cdot \mathbf{u} + \alpha(\mathbf{v} \cdot \mathbf{w})$.

The dot product can be used to generate vectors whose length is 1 (this is called *normalizing a vector*.) To normalize a vector, **v**, we simply compute $\mathbf{v}' = \mathbf{v} / \| \mathbf{v} \|$. The resulting vector has length 1, and is called a *unit vector*.

Exercise: What is the length of the vector

$$\begin{bmatrix} 4 \\ 3 \\ 0 \end{bmatrix}?$$

What do we get if we normalize this vector? Consider the points

$$P = \begin{bmatrix} 1 \\ 1 \\ 1 \end{bmatrix} \quad \text{and} \quad Q = \begin{bmatrix} 2 \\ 3 \\ 1 \end{bmatrix}$$

in the standard affine plane. What is the unit vector pointing in the direction from P to Q?

Answers: The length of the vector is 5. The normalized vector is

$$\begin{bmatrix} 4/5 \\ 3/5 \\ 0 \end{bmatrix}.$$

The unit direction vector from P to Q is

$$\begin{bmatrix} 1/\sqrt{5} \\ 2/\sqrt{5} \\ 0 \end{bmatrix}.$$

Note that the last component is 0.

Dot products can also be used to measure angles (or, from a mathematician's point of view, to *define* angles). The *angle between the vectors* **v** *and* **w** is

$$\cos^{-1}\left(\frac{\mathbf{v} \cdot \mathbf{w}}{\| \mathbf{v} \| \, \| \mathbf{w} \|}\right).$$

Note that, if **v** and **w** are unit vectors, then the division is unnecessary.

If we have a unit vector **v** and another vector **w**, and we project **w** perpendicularly onto **v**, as shown in Fig. A.5, and call the result **u**, then the length of **u** should be the length of **w** multiplied by $\cos(\theta)$, where θ is the angle between **v** and **w**. That is to say,

$$\| \mathbf{u} \| = \| \mathbf{w} \| \cos(\theta)$$

$$= \| \mathbf{w} \| \left(\frac{\mathbf{v} \cdot \mathbf{w}}{\| \mathbf{v} \| \, \| \mathbf{w} \|}\right)$$

$$= \mathbf{v} \cdot \mathbf{w},$$

since the length of **v** is 1. This gives us a new interpretation of the dot product: The dot product of **v** and **w** is the length of the projection of **w** onto **v**, provided **v** is a unit vector.

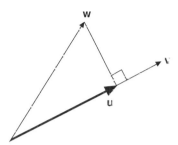

Fig. A.5 The projection of **w** onto the unit vector **v** is a vector **u**, whose length is $\| \mathbf{w} \|$ times the cosine of the angle between **v** and **w**.

Exercise: Show that, if **v** and **w** are unit vectors, then projection of **v** onto **w** and the projection of **w** onto **v** have the same length.

Answer: Both of these are represented by $\mathbf{v} \cdot \mathbf{w}$, so they are the same.

Since $\cos \theta = 0$ precisely when $\theta = 90°, 270°$, and so on, we can use the dot product of vectors to determine when they are perpendicular. Two vectors **v** and **w** are perpendicular exactly when $\mathbf{v} \cdot \mathbf{w} = 0$.

A.3.3   Applications of the Dot Product

Since dot products can be used to measure lengths, we can generate some simple equations using them. For example, if we have a point, P, in an affine plane, the equation for a circle with center P and radius r is easy to write. We simply want all points Q whose distance from P is exactly r. Thus, the equation is

$$\| Q - P \| = r.$$

We can rewrite this as

$$\sqrt{(Q - P) \cdot (Q - P)} = r,$$

or as

$$(Q - P) \cdot (Q - P) = r^2.$$

In the standard affine 3-space, the equation of the plane passing through a point P and perpendicular to a vector **v** is also easy to express. A point Q on this plane is characterized by having the difference $Q - P$ be perpendicular to the vector **v**. Hence, the equation is just

$$(Q - P) \cdot \mathbf{v} = 0.$$

Exercise: Suppose P and Q are points of the standard affine plane; P is the point

$$\begin{bmatrix} a \\ b \\ 1 \end{bmatrix}$$

and Q is the indeterminate

$$\begin{bmatrix} x \\ y \\ 1 \end{bmatrix}.$$

What is the equation, in coordinates, for the circle of radius r about P?

Answer: It is $(x - a)^2 + (y - b)^2 = r^2$, which is the familiar formula from high-school algebra.

Exercise: If P is the point

$$\begin{bmatrix} 1 \\ 2 \\ 3 \\ 1 \end{bmatrix}$$

in the standard affine 3-space, and $\mathbf{v}$ is the vector

$$\begin{bmatrix} 2 \\ 2 \\ 3 \\ 0 \end{bmatrix},$$

what is the equation of the plane perpendicular to $\mathbf{v}$ and passing through P?

Answer: If we let the indeterminate point be

$$\begin{bmatrix} x \\ y \\ z \\ 1 \end{bmatrix},$$

then the equation becomes $2(x - 1) + 2(y - 2) + 3(z - 3) = 0$.

In general, the equation for a plane through the point

$$\begin{bmatrix} x_0 \\ y_0 \\ z_0 \\ 1 \end{bmatrix}$$

and normal to the vector

$$\begin{bmatrix} A \\ B \\ C \\ 0 \end{bmatrix}$$

is $A(x - x_0) + B(y - y_0) + C(z - z_0) = 0$. This can be rewritten as $Ax + By + Cz = Ax_0 +$

$By_0 + Cz_0$. If we are working in $\mathbf{R}^3$ (instead of the standard affine 3-space), this equation just says that the dot product of

$$\begin{bmatrix} A \\ B \\ C \end{bmatrix}$$

with

$$\begin{bmatrix} x \\ y \\ z \end{bmatrix}$$

must be the same as the dot product of

$$\begin{bmatrix} A \\ B \\ C \end{bmatrix}$$

with

$$\begin{bmatrix} x_0 \\ y_0 \\ z_0 \end{bmatrix}.$$

The constant term (on the right side of the equation above) is precisely this second dot product. If

$$\begin{bmatrix} A \\ B \\ C \end{bmatrix}$$

is a unit vector, then this dot product measures the length of the projection of

$$\begin{bmatrix} x_0 \\ y_0 \\ z_0 \end{bmatrix}$$

onto the unit vector, and hence tells us how far the plane is from the origin in $\mathbf{R}^3$.

In the equation for a plane, we are characterizing the plane by specifying its normal vector. This is dangerous in one sense, since normal vectors and ordinary vectors are different in a quite subtle manner, as we shall discuss later.

A.3.4   Distance Formulae

If we define a plane through P, perpendicular to $\mathbf{v}$, by the equation $(Q - P) \cdot \mathbf{v} = 0$, we can ask how far a point R is from the plane. One way to determine this distance is to compute the projection of $R - P$ onto the vector $\mathbf{v}$ (see Fig. A.6). The length of this projected vector is just the distance from R to the plane. But this length is also the dot product of $R - P$ and the vector $\mathbf{v}$, divided by the length of $\mathbf{v}$. Thus, if we consider a plane defined by the equation

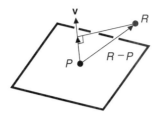

Fig. A.6 We can measure the distance from the point R to the plane by projecting R onto the normal to the plane.

$Ax + By + Cz + D = 0$, the distance from a point (r, s, t) to the plane is exactly $(Ar + Bs + Ct + D) / \sqrt{A^2 + B^2 + C^2}$. Note that the square root in the denominator is just the length of the normal vector to the plane, so if the plane was defined using a *unit* normal vector, no division is necessary.

Exercise: Suppose we are given a line in an affine space in parametric form, as the set of all points $P(t) = P_0 + t\mathbf{v}$, and a point R not on the line. What is the distance from R to the line?

Answer: The distance from a point to a line is defined as the minimum of all distances from the point to points on the line. This minimum will occur when the line from R to the point on the line is perpendicular to the line—that is, when $(R - P(t)) \cdot \mathbf{v} = 0$. Expanding this, we get

$$(R - P_0 - t\mathbf{v}) \cdot \mathbf{v} = 0,$$

$$(R - P_0) \cdot \mathbf{v} = t\mathbf{v} \cdot \mathbf{v},$$

$$t = \frac{(R - P_0) \cdot \mathbf{v}}{\mathbf{v} \cdot \mathbf{v}}.$$

So this is the value of t at which the distance is minimized. Plugging this into the formula for points on the line, we find that the point closest to R is exactly

$$P_0 + \frac{(R - P_0) \cdot \mathbf{v}}{\mathbf{v} \cdot \mathbf{v}} \mathbf{v}.$$

We obtain the distance from R to this point by subtracting the point from R (to get a vector) and then computing its length. The formula fails when $\mathbf{v} = \mathbf{0}$; in this case, however, $P(t) = P_0 + t\mathbf{v}$ does not define a line.

A.3.5   Intersection Formulae

Suppose that, in the standard affine plane, we have a circle, $(X - P) \cdot (X - P) = r^2$, and a line, $S(t) = Q + t\mathbf{v}$. What points lie on the intersection of these two? Well, such a point must be $S(t)$ for some value of t, and it must satisfy the equation of the circle, so we must solve

$$(S(t) - P) \cdot (S(t) - P) = r^2.$$

Algebraic manipulations reduce this expression to

$$t^2 \, (\mathbf{v} \cdot \mathbf{v}) + t \, (2 \, \mathbf{v} \cdot (Q - P)) + ((Q - P) \cdot (Q - P) - r^2) = 0,$$

which is a quadratic equation in t. Solving this with the quadratic formula gives the possible values for t, which can then be used in the formula for $S(t)$ to determine the actual points of intersection. Notice that this in no way depends on the number of coordinates. If we take the set of points in the standard affine 3-space defined by $(X - P) \cdot (X - P) = r^2$, which is a sphere, the same solution gives us the two points of intersection of a line with the sphere.

Exercise: Determine the intersections of the line through the point

$$\begin{bmatrix} 4 \\ 1 \\ 1 \end{bmatrix}$$

(in the standard affine plane) in the direction

$$\begin{bmatrix} 2 \\ 1 \\ 0 \end{bmatrix}$$

with the circle of radius 5 centered at

$$\begin{bmatrix} 3 \\ 1 \\ 1 \end{bmatrix}.$$

Answer: Let t_1 and t_2 be $(-2 \pm 2\sqrt{31})/5$. The intersections occur at

$$\begin{bmatrix} 4 \\ 1 \\ 1 \end{bmatrix} + t_i \begin{bmatrix} 2 \\ 1 \\ 0 \end{bmatrix},$$

for $i = 1, 2$.

Suppose we are given a line and a plane in the standard affine 3-space. How can we determine their intersection? If the plane is given in point-normal form, as $(X - P) \cdot \mathbf{v} = 0$, and the line is given in parametric form, as $Q(t) = Q + t\mathbf{w}$, we can simply replace X by $Q(t)$ and solve:

$$(Q + t\mathbf{w} - P) \cdot \mathbf{v} = 0.$$

Solving this equation for t gives

$$t = \frac{(P - Q) \cdot \mathbf{v}}{\mathbf{w} \cdot \mathbf{v}},$$

and the intersection point is at

$$Q + \frac{(P - Q) \cdot \mathbf{v}}{\mathbf{w} \cdot \mathbf{v}} \mathbf{w}.$$

This technique for finding intersections is quite general. If we have a surface in the standard affine 3-space defined by the equation $F(x, y, z, 1) = 0$, we can substitute the point $P + t\mathbf{v}$ for the argument $(x, y, z, 1)$, which yields an equation in the single variable t. Solving for t gives the parametric value for the point on the ray at the intersection point. Substituting this t value into $P + t\mathbf{v}$ gives the actual point of intersection.

In general, an implicitly defined surface (i.e., a surface defined by an equation of the form $F(x, y, z, 1) = 0$ in the standard affine 3-space) has a surface normal vector at the point $(x, y, z, 1)$; the coordinates of this vector are given by the partial derivatives of F at the point. (The corresponding situation in the plane was discussed in the scan-conversion of ellipses in Chapter 3.) The normal vector is thus

$$
\begin{bmatrix}
\dfrac{\partial F}{\partial x}(x, y, z, 1) \\[2ex]
\dfrac{\partial F}{\partial y}(x, y, z, 1) \\[2ex]
\dfrac{\partial F}{\partial z}(x, y, z, 1) \\[2ex]
0
\end{bmatrix}.
$$

A.3.6 Orthonormal Bases

Two vectors, $\mathbf{u}$ and $\mathbf{v}$, are said to be *orthogonal* if $\mathbf{u} \cdot \mathbf{v} = 0$. If $B = \{\mathbf{b}_1, \ldots, \mathbf{b}_n\}$ is a basis for a vector space, and each $\mathbf{b}_i$ is a unit vector, and every two vectors in the basis are orthogonal, the basis is said to be an *orthonormal basis*. We can express these conditions more simply by saying that B is an orthonormal basis if $\mathbf{b}_i \cdot \mathbf{b}_j = 0$ unless $i = j$, in which case $\mathbf{b}_i \cdot \mathbf{b}_j = 1$.

Orthonormal bases have a number of convenient properties that other bases lack. For example, if **B** is an orthonormal basis, and we wish to write a vector $\mathbf{v}$ as a linear combination of the vectors in B, $\mathbf{v} = \alpha_1\mathbf{b}_1 + \ldots + \alpha_n\mathbf{b}_n$, it is easy to find the value of α_i: It is just $\mathbf{v} \cdot \mathbf{b}_i$.

Exercise: Show that in $\mathbf{R}^n$, the standard basis $E = \{\mathbf{e}_1, \ldots, \mathbf{e}_n\}$, (where $\mathbf{e}_i$ has all entries 0 except the *i*th, which is 1), is an orthonormal basis. Show that the vectors

$$
\begin{bmatrix} 1/\sqrt{5} \\ 2/\sqrt{5} \end{bmatrix} \quad \text{and} \quad \begin{bmatrix} -2/\sqrt{5} \\ 1/\sqrt{5} \end{bmatrix}
$$

form an orthonormal basis for $\mathbf{R}^2$. What are the coordinates of the vector $\begin{bmatrix} 3 \\ 4 \end{bmatrix}$ in this basis?

Answer: The first two parts are direct computations. The coordinates are $11/\sqrt{5}$ and $-2/\sqrt{5}$.

Because of this convenient property, it is often desirable to convert a basis into an orthonormal basis. This is done with the Gram–Schmidt process. The idea of this process is to take each vector in turn, to make it orthogonal to all the vectors considered so far, and then to normalize it. If we start with a basis v_1, v_2, v_3. the process is this:

Let $v_1' = v_1$ (no vectors have been considered so far, so this is trivial).

Let $w_1 = v_1' / \| v_1' \|$.

Let $v_2' = v_2 - (v_2 \cdot w_1)w_1$ (this is orthogonal to w_1).

Let $w_2 = v_2' / \| v_2' \|$.

Let $v_3' = v_3 - (v_3 \cdot w_1)w_1 - (v_3 \cdot w_2)w_2$.

Let $w_3 = v_3' / \| v_3' \|$.

The vectors w_1, w_2, and w_3 are an orthonormal basis. The process for a larger number of vectors is similar. The last step, for the case of three vectors, can be simplified; see Exercise A.7.

A.4 MATRICES

A matrix is a rectangular array of numbers. Its elements are doubly indexed, and by convention the first index indicates the row and the second indicates the column. Mathematical convention dictates that the indices start at 1; certain programming languages use indices that start at 0. We leave it to programmers in those languages to shift all indices by 1. Thus, if A is a matrix, then $a_{3,2}$ refers to the element in the third row, second column. When symbolic indices are used, as in a_{ij}, the comma between them is omitted.

Elements of $\mathbf{R}^n$, which we have been writing in the form

$$\begin{bmatrix} x_1 \\ \cdot \\ \cdot \\ \cdot \\ x_n \end{bmatrix},$$

can be considered to be $n \times 1$ matrices.

A.4.1 Matrix Multiplication

Matrices are multiplied according to the following rule: If A is an $n \times k$ matrix with entries a_{ij}, and B is a $k \times p$ matrix with entries b_{ij}, then AB is defined, and is an $n \times p$ matrix with entries c_{ij}, where $c_{ij} = \sum_{s=0}^{k} a_{is}b_{sj}$. If we think of the columns of B as individual vectors, $B_1, \ldots, B_p$, and the rows of A as vectors $A_1, \ldots, A_k$ as well (but rotated 90° to be horizontal), then we see that c_{ij} is just $A_i \cdot B_j$. The usual properties of multiplication hold, except that matrix multiplication is not commutative: AB is, in general, different from BA. But multiplication distributes over addition: $A(B + C) = AB + AC$, and there is an identity element for multiplication—namely, the *identity matrix*, I, which is a square matrix with all entries 0 except for 1s on the diagonal (i.e., the entries are δ_{ij}, where $\delta_{ij} = 0$ unless $i = j$, and $\delta_{ii} = 1$).

A.4.2 Determinants

The determinant of a square matrix is a single number that tells us a great deal about the matrix. The columns of the matrix are linearly independent if and only if the determinant of the matrix is nonzero. Every $n \times n$ matrix represents a transformation from $\mathbf{R}^n$ to $\mathbf{R}^n$, and the determinant of the matrix tells us the volume change induced by this transformation (i.e., it tells us how much the unit cube is expanded or contracted by the transformation).

Computing the determinant is somewhat complicated, because the definition is recursive. The determinant of the 2×2 matrix $\begin{bmatrix} a & c \\ b & d \end{bmatrix}$ is just $ad - bc$. The determinant of an $n \times n$ matrix is defined in terms of determinants of smaller matrices. If we let A_{1i} denote the determinant of the $(n-1) \times (n-1)$ matrix gotten by deleting the first row and ith column from the $n \times n$ matrix $\mathbf{A}$, then the determinant of $\mathbf{A}$ is defined by

$$\det \mathbf{A} = \sum_{i=1}^{n} (-1)^{i+1}\, a_{1i}\, A_{1i}.$$

An alternate way to compute the determinant is to use *Gaussian elimination*. Gaussian elimination works by sequences of *row operations*. There are three types of row operations on a matrix: (1) exchanging any two rows, (2) multiplying a row by a nonzero scalar, and (3) adding a multiple of row i to row j (row i is left unchanged, and row j is replaced with (row j) $+ \alpha$(row i)). The algorithm for reducing an $n \times n$ matrix $\mathbf{A}$ by Gaussian elimination is simple: Arrange (by exchanging rows and scaling) that $a_{11} = 1$. For each $j \neq 1$, subtract a_{j1} times row 1 from row j, so that a_{j1} then becomes zero. Now, by exchanging the second row with subsequent rows (if necessary) and scaling, arrange that $a_{22} = 1$. For each $j \neq 2$, subtract a_{j2} times row 2 from row j. Continue this process until the matrix becomes the identity matrix.

In the course of this process, it may be impossible to make $a_{ii} = 1$ for some i (this happens when the entire column i is zero, for example); in this case, the determinant is zero. Otherwise, the determinant is computed by taking the multiplicative inverse of the product of all the scalars used in type-2 row operations in Gaussian elimination, and then multiplying the result by $(-1)^k$, where k is the number of row exchanges done during Gaussian elimination.

One special application of the determinant works in $\mathbf{R}^3$: the *cross-product*. The cross-product of two vectors

$$\mathbf{v} = \begin{bmatrix} v_1 \\ v_2 \\ v_3 \end{bmatrix} \qquad \text{and} \qquad \mathbf{w} = \begin{bmatrix} w_1 \\ w_2 \\ w_3 \end{bmatrix}$$

is computed by taking the determinant of the matrix,

$$\begin{bmatrix} \mathbf{i} & \mathbf{j} & \mathbf{k} \\ v_1 & v_2 & v_3 \\ w_1 & w_2 & w_3 \end{bmatrix},$$

where the letters $\mathbf{i}$, $\mathbf{j}$, and $\mathbf{k}$ are treated as symbolic variables. The result is then a linear combination of the variables $\mathbf{i}$, $\mathbf{j}$, and $\mathbf{k}$; at this point, the variables are replaced with the vectors $\mathbf{e}_1$, $\mathbf{e}_2$, and $\mathbf{e}_3$ respectively. The result is the vector

$$\begin{bmatrix} v_2 w_3 - v_3 w_2 \\ v_3 w_1 - v_1 w_3 \\ v_1 w_2 - v_2 w_1 \end{bmatrix},$$

which is denoted by $\mathbf{v} \times \mathbf{w}$. It has the property that it is perpendicular to the plane defined by $\mathbf{v}$ and $\mathbf{w}$, and its length is the product $\|\mathbf{v}\| \, \|\mathbf{w}\| \, |\sin \theta|$, where θ is the angle between $\mathbf{v}$ and $\mathbf{w}$. It also has the property that a matrix whose columns are $\mathbf{v}$, $\mathbf{w}$, and $\mathbf{v} \times \mathbf{w}$ will always have nonnegative determinant.

This last characteristic is an interesting one, and can be used to define *orientation*. Two bases for $\mathbf{R}^n$ are said to have the same orientation if, when the vectors in each basis are used to form the columns of a matrix, the two resulting matrices have determinants of the same sign. A basis is said to be *positively oriented* if it has the same orientation as the standard basis; it is *negatively oriented* otherwise.

> **Exercise:** Show that the basis $\{\mathbf{e}_2, \mathbf{e}_1, \mathbf{e}_3, \mathbf{e}_4\}$ is a negatively oriented basis for $\mathbf{R}^4$.
>
> *Answer:* The determinant of the corresponding matrix is -1.

> **Exercise:** Suppose two planes are defined by the equations $(X - P) \cdot \mathbf{v} = 0$ and $(X - Q) \cdot \mathbf{w} = 0$. What is the direction vector for the line of intersection of the two planes?
>
> *Answer:* Since the line of intersection lies in each plane, its direction vector must be orthogonal to the normal vectors to each plane. One such vector is the cross product $\mathbf{v} \times \mathbf{w}$. If $\mathbf{v}$ and $\mathbf{w}$ are parallel, then the planes either are identical or do not intersect at all; so, in the case where $\mathbf{v} \times \mathbf{w} = 0$, the problem is degenerate anyway.

A.4.3   Matrix Transpose

An $n \times k$ matrix can be flipped along its diagonal (upper left to lower right) to make a $k \times n$ matrix. If the first matrix has entries a_{ij} ($i = 1, \ldots, n; j = 1, \ldots, k$), then the resulting matrix has entries b_{ij} ($i = 1, \ldots, k; j = 1, \ldots, n$), with $b_{ij} = a_{ji}$. This new matrix is called the *transpose* of the original matrix. The transpose of $\mathbf{A}$ is written $\mathbf{A}^t$. If we consider a vector in $\mathbf{R}^n$ as an $n \times 1$ matrix, then its transpose is a $1 \times n$ matrix (sometimes called a row vector). Using the transpose, we can give a new description of the dot product in $\mathbf{R}^n$; namely, $\mathbf{u} \cdot \mathbf{v} = \mathbf{u}^t \mathbf{v}$.

> **Exercise:** Compute one example indicating, and then prove in general, that if $\mathbf{A}$ is $n \times k$ and $\mathbf{B}$ is $k \times p$, then $(\mathbf{AB})^t = \mathbf{B}^t \mathbf{A}^t$.
>
> *Answer:* We leave this problem to you.

A.4.4   Matrix Inverse

Matrix multiplication differs from ordinary multiplication in another way: A matrix may not have a multiplicative inverse. In fact, inverses are defined only for square matrices, and not even all of these have inverses. Exactly those square matrices whose determinants are nonzero have inverses.

If $\mathbf{A}$ and $\mathbf{B}$ are $n \times n$ matrices, and $\mathbf{AB} = \mathbf{BA} = \mathbf{I}$, where $\mathbf{I}$ is the $n \times n$ identity matrix, then $\mathbf{B}$ is said to be the inverse of $\mathbf{A}$, and is written $\mathbf{A}^{-1}$. For $n \times n$ matrices with real number entries, it suffices to show that either $\mathbf{AB} = \mathbf{I}$ or $\mathbf{BA} = \mathbf{I}$—if either is true, the other is as well.

If we are given an $n \times n$ matrix, there are two basic ways to find its inverse: Gaussian elimination and Cramer's rule. Gaussian elimination is the preferred method for anything larger than 3×3.

The inverse of a matrix can be computed using Gaussian elimination by writing down both $\mathbf{A}$ and the identity matrix. As you perform row operations on $\mathbf{A}$ to reduce it to the identity, you perform the same row operations on the identity. When $\mathbf{A}$ has become the identity matrix, the identity matrix will have become $\mathbf{A}^{-1}$. If, during Gaussian elimination, some diagonal entry cannot be made 1, then, as we noted, the determinant is 0, and the inverse does not exist. This technique can be improved in numerous ways. A good reference, including working programs for implementation, is [PRESS88].

A different method for computing inverses is called *Cramer's rule*. It builds the inverse explicitly, but at the cost of computing many determinants. Here is how it works.

To compute the inverse of an $n \times n$ matrix $\mathbf{A}$ with entries a_{ij}, we build a new matrix, $\mathbf{A}'$, with entries A_{ij}. To compute A_{ij}, we delete rows i and j from the matrix $\mathbf{A}$, and then compute the determinant of the resulting $(n - 1) \times (n - 1)$ matrix. Multiplying this determinant by $(-1)^{i+j}$ gives the value for A_{ij}. Once $\mathbf{A}'$ is computed, the inverse of $\mathbf{A}$ is just $(1 \: / \: \det \mathbf{A}) \, (\mathbf{A}')^t$.

Because of the large number of determinants involved, Cramer's rule is impractical for large matrices. For the 2×2 case, however, it is quite useful. It tells us that

$$\begin{bmatrix} a & b \\ c & d \end{bmatrix}^{-1} = \frac{1}{ad - bc} \begin{bmatrix} d & -b \\ -c & a \end{bmatrix}.$$

One last special case for matrix inversion deserves mention. Suppose that $\mathbf{U}$ is a matrix whose columns form an orthonormal basis. This means that $\mathbf{u}_i \cdot \mathbf{u}_j = \delta_{ij}$ for all i and j. Consider what happens when we compute $\mathbf{U}^t\mathbf{U}$. We have noted that the ij entry of the product is the dot product of the ith row of the first factor and the jth column of the second factor. But these are just $\mathbf{u}_i$ and $\mathbf{u}_j$; hence, their dot product is δ_{ij}. This tells us that $\mathbf{U}^t\mathbf{U} = \mathbf{I}$, and hence that $\mathbf{U}^{-1} = \mathbf{U}^t$. Note, by the way, that this means that the columns of $\mathbf{U}^t$ also form an orthonormal basis!

A.5   LINEAR AND AFFINE TRANSFORMATIONS

A *linear transformation* is a map from one vector space to another that preserves linear combinations. More precisely, it is a map $\mathbf{T}$ with the property that $\mathbf{T}(\alpha_1\mathbf{v}_1 + \alpha_2\mathbf{v}_2 + \ldots + \alpha_n\mathbf{v}_n) = \alpha_1\mathbf{T}(\mathbf{v}_1) + \alpha_2\mathbf{T}(\mathbf{v}_2) + \ldots + \alpha_n\mathbf{T}(\mathbf{v}_n)$. Linear transformations are the ones we describe in great detail in Chapter 5.

An *affine transformation* is a map from one affine space to another that preserves affine combinations. More precisely, it is a map $\mathbf{T}$ with the property that $\mathbf{T}(P + \alpha(Q - P)) = \mathbf{T}(P) + \alpha(\mathbf{T}(Q) - \mathbf{T}(P))$. $\mathbf{T}$ extends naturally to a map on the associated vector space. We define $\mathbf{T}(\mathbf{v})$ to be $\mathbf{T}(P) - \mathbf{T}(Q)$, where P and Q are any two points with $Q - P = \mathbf{v}$. Affine transformations include translations, rotations, scales, and shearing transformations. Note that the transformations defined in Chapter 5 are both affine *and* linear transformations. They are linear transformations from $\mathbf{R}^4$ to $\mathbf{R}^4$, but they take the standard affine 3-space (the points of $\mathbf{R}^4$ whose last coordinate is 1) to itself, so that they also describe affine transformations on this affine space.

A.5.1   The Matrix for a Transformation on R^n

Suppose we have n independent vectors, $\mathbf{b}_1, \ldots, \mathbf{b}_n$ in R^n, and we wish to find a linear transformation $\mathbf{T}$ from them to the vectors $\mathbf{a}_1, \ldots, \mathbf{a}_n$. (We have chosen this odd naming convention because the $\mathbf{b}_i$s, being independent, form a basis.) How can we do this? The simplest way to express a linear transformation on R^n is to give a matrix for it. That is to say, we will find an $n \times n$ matrix $\mathbf{A}$ such that $\mathbf{T}(\mathbf{v}) = \mathbf{A}\mathbf{v}$ for all $\mathbf{v}$ in R^n.

We begin by solving a simpler problem. We find a matrix for the transformation that takes the standard basis vectors, $\mathbf{e}_1, \ldots, \mathbf{e}_n$ to an arbitrary set of vectors $\mathbf{v}_1, \ldots, \mathbf{v}_n$.

Suppose we take any $n \times n$ matrix $\mathbf{Q}$ with entries q_{ij} and multiply it by $\mathbf{e}_j$. If we let $\mathbf{r} = \mathbf{Q}\mathbf{e}_j$, then $\mathbf{r}_i = q_{ij}$. That is, multiplying a matrix by the jth standard basis vector extracts the jth column of the matrix. We can reverse this observation to find the matrix that transforms the standard basis vectors into $\mathbf{v}_1, \ldots, \mathbf{v}_n$: We just use the vectors $\mathbf{v}_1, \ldots, \mathbf{v}_n$ as the columns of the matrix.

Exercise: Find a matrix taking the standard basis of R^2 to the vectors $\begin{bmatrix} 1 \\ 2 \end{bmatrix}$ and $\begin{bmatrix} 3 \\ 3 \end{bmatrix}$.

Answer: $\begin{bmatrix} 1 & 3 \\ 2 & 3 \end{bmatrix}$.

To solve the original problem of this section, finding a transformation taking the $\mathbf{b}_i$s to the $\mathbf{a}_i$s, we apply the solution for the simpler problem twice. First, we find a matrix $\mathbf{B}$ (whose columns are the $\mathbf{b}_i$s) that takes the standard basis to the $\mathbf{b}_i$s; then, we find a matrix $\mathbf{A}$ that takes the standard basis to the $\mathbf{a}_i$s. The matrix $\mathbf{B}^{-1}$ will do just the opposite of $\mathbf{B}$, and take the $\mathbf{b}_i$s to the standard basis, so the matrix $\mathbf{A}\mathbf{B}^{-1}$ is the solution to the original problem. It is a matrix taking the $\mathbf{b}_i$s to the $\mathbf{a}_i$s.

Exercise: Find a matrix transformation taking $\begin{bmatrix} 1 \\ 2 \end{bmatrix}$ and $\begin{bmatrix} 2 \\ 5 \end{bmatrix}$ to $\begin{bmatrix} 1 \\ 1 \end{bmatrix}$ and $\begin{bmatrix} 3 \\ 2 \end{bmatrix}$, respectively.

Answer: The matrix taking the standard basis to the first pair of vectors is $\begin{bmatrix} 1 & 2 \\ 2 & 5 \end{bmatrix}$; the matrix taking the standard basis to the second pair is $\begin{bmatrix} 1 & 3 \\ 1 & 2 \end{bmatrix}$. The solution is therefore $\mathbf{T}(\mathbf{v}) = \mathbf{Q}\mathbf{v}$, where

$$\mathbf{Q} = \begin{bmatrix} 1 & 3 \\ 1 & 2 \end{bmatrix} \begin{bmatrix} 1 & 2 \\ 2 & 5 \end{bmatrix}^{-1} = \begin{bmatrix} -1 & 1 \\ 1 & 0 \end{bmatrix}.$$

A.5.2   Transformations of Points and Normal Vectors

When we apply a matrix linear transformation to the points of the standard affine n-space, how do the differences between points (i.e., the vectors of the affine space) transform? Suppose our transformation is defined by $\mathbf{T}(P) = \mathbf{A}P$, and further suppose that this transformation sends the affine plane to itself (i.e., that there is no homogenization required after the transformation—this is equivalent to saying the last row of $\mathbf{A}$ is all 0s, except the bottom-right entry, which is a 1). Then, $\mathbf{T}(Q - P) = \mathbf{A}(Q - P)$. But $Q - P$ has a 0 in its last component (since both P and Q have a 1 there). Hence, the last column of $\mathbf{A}$ has no effect in the result of the transformation. We therefore define $\mathbf{A}'$ to be the same as $\mathbf{A}$, but with its last column replaced by all 0s except the last entry, which we make 1. This matrix, $\mathbf{A}'$, can be used to transform vectors in the affine space.

We mentioned previously that the definition of a plane by its normal vector was dangerous, and here we see why. Suppose we have a plane whose points satisfy $(X - P) \cdot \mathbf{v} = 0$. When we transform this plane by $\mathbf{A}$, we will get a new plane containing $\mathbf{A}P$, so it will have an equation of the form $(Y - \mathbf{A}P) \cdot \mathbf{w} = 0$ for some vector $\mathbf{w}$. We want those points of the form $\mathbf{A}X$, where X is on the original plane, to satisfy this second equation. So we want to find a vector $\mathbf{w}$ with the property that $(\mathbf{A}X - \mathbf{A}P) \cdot \mathbf{w} = 0$ whenever $(X - P) \cdot \mathbf{v} = 0$. Expressed differently, we want

$$(\mathbf{A}X - \mathbf{A}P)^t\, \mathbf{w} = 0 \qquad \text{whenever } (X - P) \cdot \mathbf{v} = 0.$$

By distributing the transpose operator, we see this reduces to

$$(X - P) \cdot \mathbf{A}^t\mathbf{w} = 0 \qquad \text{whenever } (X - P) \cdot \mathbf{v} = 0.$$

This equation will certainly hold if $\mathbf{A}^t\mathbf{w} = \mathbf{v}$—that is, if $\mathbf{w} = (\mathbf{A}^t)^{-1}\mathbf{v}$. Thus, $(\mathbf{A}^t)^{-1}\mathbf{v}$ is the normal vector to the transformed plane. In the event that $\mathbf{A}$ is an orthogonal matrix (as it is, e.g., in the case of rotations), we know that $(\mathbf{A}^t)^{-1} = \mathbf{A}$, so the normal vector transforms in the same way as the point (but with no translation, because the last component of the vector is 0). But this is not true for general matrices. The computation of the inverse transpose of $\mathbf{A}$ can be somewhat simplified by computing instead the inverse transpose of $\mathbf{A}'$, whose effect on vectors is the same as that of $\mathbf{A}$. Since $\mathbf{A}'$ is effectively a smaller matrix (its last row and column are the same as those of the identity matrix), this is often much easier.[2]

Computing the inverse of a matrix may be difficult—and, if you use Cramer's rule, it involves dividing by the determinant. Since the normal vector, after being transformed, will probably no longer be a unit vector and will need to be normalized, leaving out this division does no harm. Thus, people sometimes use the *matrix of cofactors* for transforming normals. Entry ij of this matrix is $(-1)^{i+j}$ times the determinant of the matrix resulting from deleting row i and column j from $\mathbf{A}$.

A.6   EIGENVALUES AND EIGENVECTORS

An *eigenvector* of a transformation $\mathbf{T}$ is a vector $\mathbf{v}$ such that $\mathbf{T}(\mathbf{v})$ is a scalar multiple of $\mathbf{v}$. If $\mathbf{T}(\mathbf{v}) = \lambda\mathbf{v}$, then λ is called the *eigenvalue* associated with $\mathbf{v}$. The theoretical method for finding eigenvalues (at least for a matrix transformation $\mathbf{T}(\mathbf{v}) = \mathbf{A}\,\mathbf{v}$) is to let $\mathbf{B} = \mathbf{A} - x\mathbf{I}$, where $\mathbf{I}$ is the identity matrix, and x is an indeterminate. The determinant of $\mathbf{B}$ is then a polynomial in x, $p(x)$. The roots of p are precisely the eigenvalues. If λ is one such eigenvalue, and λ is a real number, then $\mathbf{T}(\mathbf{v}) = \lambda\mathbf{v}$ must be true for some vector $\mathbf{v}$. By rearranging, we get that $\mathbf{A}\mathbf{v} - \lambda\mathbf{v} = 0$, or $(\mathbf{A} - \lambda\mathbf{I})\mathbf{v} = 0$. Thus, finding all solutions to this last equation gives us all the eigenvectors corresponding to λ.

Although this approach is theoretically feasible, in practice it is not very useful, especially for large matrices. Instead, numerical methods based on iterating the transforma-

---

[2]Differential geometers refer to vectors such as the normal vector as *covectors*, since these vectors are defined by a dot-product relation with ordinary (or *tangent*) vectors. The set of all covectors is sometimes called the *cotangent* space, but this term has no relation to trigonometric functions. More complex objects, called *tensors*, can be made up from mixtures of tangent and cotangent vectors, and the rules for transforming them are correspondingly complex.

tion are used. Chief among these is Gauss–Seidel iteration; for details of this technique, see [PRES88].

We conclude this section with a particularly interesting pair of exercises.

Exercise: Show that eigenvectors of a symmetric matrix (one for which $M^t = M$) corresponding to distinct eigenvalues are always orthogonal. Show that for any square matrix A, the matrix A^tA is symmetric.

Answer: Suppose $Mv = \lambda v$, and $Mu = \mu u$. Let us compute u^tMv in two different ways:

$$u^tMv = u^t\lambda v = \lambda\, u^tv = \lambda\, (u \cdot v).$$

But

$$u^tMv = (u^tM^t)\, v = (Mu)^tv = \mu\, u^tv = \mu\, (u \cdot v).$$

Thus, $\lambda\, (u \cdot v) = \mu\, (u \cdot v)$; hence, $(\lambda - \mu)(u \cdot v) = 0$. Since λ and μ are distinct eigenvalues, we know that $(\lambda - \mu) \neq 0$. Hence, $(u \cdot v) = 0$.

The transpose of (A^tA) is just $A^t(A^t)^t$; but the transpose of the transpose is the original matrix, so result is just A^tA. Hence, A^tA is symmetric.

Exercise: Suppose that $T(x) = Ax$ is a linear transformation on R^2, and that we apply it to all points of the unit circle. The resulting set of points forms an ellipse whose center is the origin. Show that squares of the lengths of the major and minor axes of the ellipse have lengths equal to the maximum and minimum singular values of A, where a *singular value* of A is defined to be an eigenvalue of A^tA.

Answer: The points on the transformed circle are of the form Ax, where $x \cdot x = 1$. The square of the distance from such a transformed point to the origin is just $Ax \cdot Ax$, or, rewriting, $x^t(A^tA)x$. Let u and v be the two unit eigenvectors of A^tA, with corresponding eigenvalues λ and μ. Because they are orthogonal, they form a basis for R^2. We can therefore write x as a linear combination of them: $x = \cos\theta\, u + \sin\theta\, v$. If we now compute $x^t(A^tA)x$, we get

$$x^t(A^tA)x = (\cos\theta\, u^t + \sin\theta\, v^t)\, (\cos\theta\, A^tAu + \sin\theta\, A^tAv)$$

$$= (\cos\theta\, u^t + \sin\theta\, v^t)\, (\cos\theta\, \lambda u + \sin\theta\, \mu v)$$

$$= \lambda \cos^2\theta + \mu \sin^2\theta.$$

This function has its extreme values at $\theta = $ multiples of $90°$—that is, when $x = \pm u$ or $\pm v$. The values at those points are just λ and μ.

A.7 NEWTON–RAPHSON ITERATION FOR ROOT FINDING

If we have a continuous function, f, from the reals to the reals, and we know that $f(a) > 0$ and $f(b) < 0$, then there must be a root of f between a and b. One way to find the root is *bisection*: We evaluate f at $(a + b)/2$; if it is positive, we search for a root in the interval between $(a + b)/2$ and b; if it is negative, we search for a root between a and $(a + b)/2$; if it is zero, we have found a root. Iterating this until the value of f is very near zero will give a good approximation of a root of f.

We can improve this slightly by taking the line between $(a, f(a))$ and $(b, f(b))$, seeing where it crosses the x axis, and using this new point as the subdivision point.

If f happens to be differentiable, we can do somewhat better than this. We can evaluate f at a point, and evaluate its derivative there as well. Using these, we can compute the equation of the tangent line to f at the point. If the graph of f is close enough to the graph of this tangent line, then the place where the tangent line crosses the x axis will be a good approximation of a root of f (see Fig. A.7). If it is not a good enough approximation, we can use it as a starting point and iterate the process (see Fig. A.8).

If the initial guess is x_0, then the equation of the tangent line is

$$y - f(x_0) = f'(x_0)\,(x - x_0).$$

This crosses the x axis when $y = 0$, which happens at the point

$$x_1 = x_0 - \frac{f(x_0)}{f'(x_0)}.$$

In general, we can find the next point, x_{i+1}, from the point x_i by a corresponding formula, and repeat the process until a root is found. This process is called *Newton's method* or *Newton–Raphson iteration*.

Exercise: Apply Newton's method to the function $f(x) = x^2 - 2$, starting at $x = 1$.

Answer: $x_0 = 1$, $x_1 = 1.5$, $x_2 = 1.416\bar{6}$, $x_3 = 1.4142...$, and so on.

The method can fail by *cycling*. For example, it is possible that $x_2 = x_0$, and then the process will repeat itself forever without getting to a better approximation. For example, the function $f(x) = x^3 - 5x$ has a root at $x = 0$, but starting this iterative technique at $x_0 = 1$ will never find that root, because the subsequent choices will be $x_1 = -1$, $x_2 = 1$, and so on.

If the function f is sufficiently nice, the method can be guaranteed to succeed. In particular, if f has everywhere positive derivative and negative second derivative, the method will certainly converge to a root.

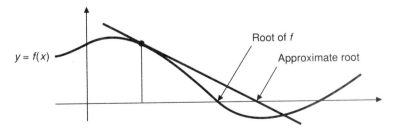

Fig. A.7 If the graph of the tangent line to a function is close enough to the graph of the function, the zero-crossing of the tangent line will be a good approximation to a zero-crossing of the function graph.

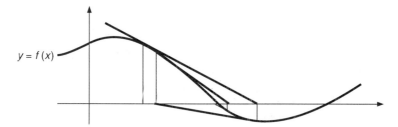

Fig. A.8 Iteration of the process described in Fig. A.7.

EXERCISES

A.1 Light reflects from a plane (in a simple model) according to the rule, "The angle of incidence is equal to the angle of reflection." If the normal to the plane is the vector **n**, and the ray from the light is described by the parametric ray $P + t\mathbf{v}$, what is the direction vector **u** for the reflected ray?

Answer: If we express **v** as a sum of two components—one in the direction of **n** and one perpendicular to **n**—we can easily describe **u**: It is the same as **v**, except with the component in the **n** direction negated. The component of **v** in the **n** direction is just $(\mathbf{v} \cdot \mathbf{n}) \, \mathbf{n} \,/\, \| \, \mathbf{n} \, \|$, so the final result is that $\mathbf{u} = (\mathbf{v} - (\mathbf{v} \cdot \mathbf{n}) \, \mathbf{n} \,/\, \| \, \mathbf{n} \, \|) - (\mathbf{v} \cdot \mathbf{n}) \, \mathbf{n} \,/\, \| \, \mathbf{n} \, \| = \mathbf{v} - 2(\mathbf{v} \cdot \mathbf{n}) \, \mathbf{n} \,/\, \| \, \mathbf{n} \, \|$. If **n** is a unit vector, this is just $\mathbf{v} - 2(\mathbf{v} \cdot \mathbf{n}) \, \mathbf{n}$. (Note that the light ray is the opposite of the ray L in Chapter 16.)

A.2 Find a tranformation from the standard affine plane to itself that leaves h coordinates fixed, but transforms (x, y) coordinates so that, in any constant-h plane, the unit square $[0, 1] \times [0, 1]$ is sent to $[-1, 1] \times [-1, 1]$. What is wrong with the following purported solution to the problem?

"The space in which we are working is 3D, so we will specify the transformation by saying where three basis vectors get sent. Clearly,

$$\begin{bmatrix} 1 \\ 0 \\ 0 \end{bmatrix} \quad \text{goes to} \quad \begin{bmatrix} 1 \\ -1 \\ 0 \end{bmatrix}.$$

and

$$\begin{bmatrix} 0 \\ 1 \\ 0 \end{bmatrix} \quad \text{goes to} \quad \begin{bmatrix} -1 \\ 1 \\ 0 \end{bmatrix}.$$

Also,

$$\begin{bmatrix} 0 \\ 0 \\ 1 \end{bmatrix} \quad \text{goes to} \quad \begin{bmatrix} -1 \\ -1 \\ 1 \end{bmatrix}.$$

So the matrix must be

$$\begin{bmatrix} 1 & -1 & -1 \\ -1 & 1 & -1 \\ 0 & 0 & 1 \end{bmatrix}."$$

Partial Answer: The assumption being made in the purported solution is that the map is a *linear map* on $\mathbf{R}^3$. It is actually an affine map, and includes a translation.

A.3 You are given a list of vertices $v[1], \ldots, v[n]$ as *xyz* triples in $\mathbf{R}^3$, but with each z coordinate equal to zero, defining a closed polygon in the plane (the polygon's edges are v_1v_2, v_2v_3, . . . , $v_{n-1}v_n$, v_nv_1). You wish to define a polyhedron that consists of this object, extruded along the z axis from $z = 0$ to $z = 1$. Assume a right-hand coordinate system.

    a. How would you check that the polygon $v[1]$, . . . , $v[n]$ is counterclockwise (i.e., as you traverse the edges of the polygon, its interior is to your left)?

    b. Describe an algorithm for generating the polygons of the extruded object. For the "sides," you can either use rectangular faces or divide them into triangles. The descriptions of these polygons should be indices into a list of vertices.

    c. Each of the faces given in part (b) consists of a list of vertices. Suppose that you walk around the boundary of a polygon, and the polygon interior is to your right. Did you choose your order for the vertices so that the exterior of the extruded polyhedron is always overhead? If not, modify your answer to part (b).

    d. Each edge of the extruded polyhedron is part of two faces, so during the traversals in part (c), each edge is traversed twice. Are the two traversals always in the same direction? Always in opposite directions? Or is there no particular pattern?

A.4 Given that $P = (x_0, y_0)$ and $Q = (x_1, y_1)$ are points in the plane, show that the equation of the line between them is $(y_1 - y_0) x - (x_1 - x_0) y = y_1x_0 - x_1y_0$. This formulation is especially nice, because it provides a general form for lines in any direction, including vertical lines.

A.5 Given that $v = \begin{bmatrix} x \\ y \end{bmatrix}$ is a vector in the plane, show that $w = \begin{bmatrix} -y \\ x \end{bmatrix}$ is orthogonal to it. This is sometimes called (in analogy with the corresponding case in 3D) the cross-product of a single vector in the plane. The cross-product of $n - 1$ vectors in $\mathbf{R}^n$ can also be defined.

A.6 If P, Q, and R are three points in the standard affine 3-space, then

$$\frac{1}{2} \| (Q - P) \times (R - P) \|$$

is the area of the triangle ΔPQR. If P, Q, and R all lie in the xy plane in the standard affine 3-space, then

$$\frac{1}{2} \begin{bmatrix} 0 \\ 0 \\ 1 \end{bmatrix} \cdot ((Q - P) \times (R - P))$$

gives the *signed area* of the triangle—it is positive if ΔPQR is a counterclockwise loop in the plane and negative otherwise. (Counterclockwise here means "counterclockwise as viewed from a point on the positive z axis, in a right-handed coordinate system.")

    a. Find the signed area of the triangle with vertices $P = (0,0)$, $Q = (x_i, y_i)$, and $R = (x_{i+1}, y_{i+1})$.

    Answer: $\frac{1}{2}(x_i y_{i+1} - x_{i+1} y_i.)$

    b. Suppose we have a polygon in the plane with vertices $v_1, . . . , v_n$, ($v_n = v_1$), and $v_i = (x_i, y_i)$ for each i. Explain why the signed area of the polygon is exactly

$$\frac{1}{2} \sum_{i=1}^{n-1} x_i y_{i+1} - x_{i+1}y_i.$$

Compare this with Eq. 11.2.

A.7 The Gram-Schmidt process described in Section A.3.6 for three vectors can be slightly simplified. After computing w_1 and w_2, we seek a third unit vector, w_3 which is perpendicular to the first two. There are only two choices possible: $w_3 = \pm w_1 \times w_2$. Show that the Gram-Schmidt process chooses the sign in this formula to be the same as the sign of $v_3 \cdot (w_1 \times w_2)$. This implies that if you know that v_1, v_2, v_3 is positively oriented, then you need not even check the sign: $w_3 = w_1 \times w_2$.

Bibliography

What follows is an extensive bibliography in computer graphics. In addition to being a list of references from the various chapters, it is also a fine place to browse. Just looking at the titles of the books and articles can give you a good idea of where research in the field has been and where it is going.

Certain journals are referenced extremely frequently, and we have abbreviated them here. The most important of these are the ACM SIGGRAPH Conference Proceedings, published each year as an issue of *Computer Graphics*, and the *ACM Transactions on Graphics*. These two sources make up more than one-third of the bibliography.

Abbreviations

ACM TOG	*Association for Computing Machinery, Transactions on Graphics*
CACM	*Communications of the ACM*
CG & A	*IEEE Computer Graphics and Applications*
CGIP	*Computer Graphics and Image Processing*
CVGIP	*Computer Vision, Graphics, and Image Processing (formerly CGIP)*
FJCC	*Proceedings of the Fall Joint Computer Conference*
JACM	*Journal of the ACM*
NCC	*Proceedings of the National Computer Conference*
SJCC	*Proceedings of the Spring Joint Computer Conference*
SIGGRAPH 76	*Proceedings of SIGGRAPH '76 (Philadelphia, Pennsylvania, July 14–16, 1976). In Computer Graphics,* 10(2), Summer 1976, ACM SIGGRAPH, New York.
SIGGRAPH 77	*Proceedings of SIGGRAPH '77 (San Jose, California, July 20–22, 1977). In Computer Graphics,* 11(2), Summer 1977, ACM SIGGRAPH, New York.
SIGGRAPH 78	*Proceedings of SIGGRAPH '78 (Atlanta, Georgia, August 23–25, 1978). In Computer Graphics,* 12(3), August 1978, ACM SIGGRAPH, New York.

SIGGRAPH 79	*Proceedings of SIGGRAPH '79 (Chicago, Illinois, August 8–10, 1979). In Computer Graphics,* 13(2), August 1979, ACM SIGGRAPH, New York.
SIGGRAPH 80	*Proceedings of SIGGRAPH '80 (Seattle, Washington, July 14–18, 1980). In Computer Graphics,* 14(3), July 1980, ACM SIGGRAPH, New York.
SIGGRAPH 81	*Proceedings of SIGGRAPH '81 (Dallas, Texas, August 3–7, 1981). In Computer Graphics,* 15(3), August 1981, ACM SIGGRAPH, New York.
SIGGRAPH 82	*Proceedings of SIGGRAPH '82 (Boston, Massachusetts, July 26–30, 1982). In Computer Graphics,* 16(3), July 1982, ACM SIGGRAPH, New York.
SIGGRAPH 83	*Proceedings of SIGGRAPH '83 (Detroit, Michigan, July 25–29, 1983). In Computer Graphics,* 17(3), July 1983, ACM SIGGRAPH, New York.
SIGGRAPH 84	*Proceedings of SIGGRAPH '84 (Minneapolis, Minnesota, July 23–27, 1984). In Computer Graphics,* 18(3), July 1984, ACM SIGGRAPH, New York.
SIGGRAPH 85	*Proceedings of SIGGRAPH '85 (San Francisco, California, July 22–26, 1985). In Computer Graphics,* 19(3), July 1985, ACM SIGGRAPH, New York.
SIGGRAPH 86	*Proceedings of SIGGRAPH '86 (Dallas, Texas, August 18–22, 1986). In Computer Graphics,* 20(4), August 1986, ACM SIGGRAPH, New York.
SIGGRAPH 87	*Proceedings of SIGGRAPH '87 (Anaheim, California, July 27–31, 1987). In Computer Graphics,* 21(4), July 1987, ACM SIGGRAPH, New York.
SIGGRAPH 88	*Proceedings of SIGGRAPH '88 (Atlanta, Georgia, August 1–5, 1988). In Computer Graphics,* 22(4), August 1988, ACM SIGGRAPH, New York.
SIGGRAPH 89	*Proceedings of SIGGRAPH '89 (Boston, Massachusetts, July 31–August 4, 1989). In Computer Graphics,* 23(3), July 1989, ACM SIGGRAPH, New York.

ABIE89   Abi-Ezzi, S.S., *The Graphical Processing of B-Splines in a Highly Dynamic Environment,* Ph.D. Thesis Rensselaer Polytechnic Institute, Troy, NY, May 1989.

ABRA85   Abram, G., L. Westover, and T. Whitted, "Efficient Alias-Free Rendering Using Bit-Masks and Look-Up Tables," *SIGGRAPH 85,* 53–59.

ADOB85a   Adobe Systems, Inc., *PostScript Language Tutorial and Cookbook*, Addison-Wesley, Reading, MA, 1985.

ADOB85b   Adobe Systems, Inc., *PostScript Language Reference Manual*, Addison-Wesley, Reading, MA, 1985.

AKEL88   Akeley, K., and T. Jermoluk, "High-Performance Polygon Rendering," *SIGGRAPH 88,* 239–246.

AKEL89   Akeley, K., "The Silicon Graphics 4D/240GTX Superworkstation," *CG & A,* 9(4), July 1989, 71–83.

ALAV84   Alavi, M., "An Assessment of the Prototyping Approach to Information Systems Development," *CACM,* 27(6), June 1984, 556–563.

AMAN84   Amanatides, J., "Ray Tracing with Cones," *SIGGRAPH 84,* 129–135.

AMAN87   Amanatides, J. and A. Woo, "A Fast Voxel Traversal Algorithm for Ray Tracing," in Maréchal, G., ed., *Eurographics 87: Proceedings of the European Computer Graphics Conference and Exhibition, Amsterdam, August 24–28, 1987,* North Holland, Amsterdam, 1987, 3–10.

AMBU86   Amburn, P., E. Grant, and T. Whitted, "Managing Geometric Complexity with Enhanced Procedural Models," *SIGGRAPH 86,* 189–195.

ANDE82   Anderson, D.P., "Hidden Line Elimination in Projected Grid Surfaces," *ACM TOG,* 1(4), October 1982, 274–288.

ANDE83   Anderson, D., "Techniques for Reducing Pen Plotting Time," *ACM TOG,* 2(3), July 1983, 197–212.

ANSI85a   ANSI (American National Standards Institute), *American National Standard for Human Factors Engineering of Visual Display Terminal Workstations,* ANSI, Washington, DC, 1985.

ANSI85b   ANSI (American National Standards Institute), *American National Standard for Information Processing Systems—Computer Graphics—Graphical Kernel System (GKS) Functional Description,* ANSI X3.124-1985, ANSI, New York, 1985.

ANSI88   ANSI (American National Standards Institute), *American National Standard for Information Processing Systems—Programmer's Hierarchical Interactive Graphics System (PHIGS) Functional Description, Archive File Format, Clear-Text Encoding of Archive File,* ANSI, X3.144-1988, ANSI, New York, 1988

APGA88   Apgar, B., B. Bersack, and A. Mammen, "A Display System for the Stellar Graphics Supercomputer Model GS1000," *SIGGRAPH 88,* 255–262.

APPE67   Appel, A., "The Notion of Quantitative Invisibility and the Machine Rendering of Solids," *Proceedings of the ACM National Conference,* Thompson Books, Washington, DC, 1967, 387–393. Also in FREE80, 214–220.

APPE68   Appel, A., "Some Techniques for Shading Machine Renderings of Solids," *SJCC,* 1968, 37–45.

APPE79   Appel, A., F.J. Rohlf, and A.J. Stein, "The Haloed Line Effect for Hidden Line Elimination," *SIGGRAPH 79,* 151–157.

APPL85   Apple Computer, Inc., *Inside Macintosh,* Addison-Wesley, Reading, MA, 1985.

APPL87   Apple Computer, Inc., *Human Interface Guidelines: The Apple Desktop Interface,* Addison-Wesley, Reading, MA, 1987.

APT85   Apt, C., "Perfecting the Picture," *IEEE Spectrum,* 22(7), July 1985, 60–66.

ARDE89   Ardent Computer Corp. (now Stardent), *Doré Product Literature,* Sunnyvale, CA, 1989.

ARNO88   Arnold, D. B., and P.R. Bono, *CGM and CGI : Metafile and Interface Standards for Computer Graphics,* Springer-Verlag, Berlin, 1988.

ARVO86   Arvo, J., "Backward Ray Tracing," in A.H. Barr, ed., *Developments in Ray Tracing, Course Notes 12 for SIGGRAPH 86,* Dallas, TX, August 18–22, 1986.

ARVO87   Arvo, J., and D. Kirk, "Fast Ray Tracing by Ray Classification," *SIGGRAPH 87,* 55–64.

ATHE78   Atherton, P.R., K. Weiler, and D. Greenberg, "Polygon Shadow Generation," *SIGGRAPH 78,* 275–281.

ATHE81   Atherton, P.R., "A Method of Interactive Visualization of CAD Surface Models on a Color Video Display," *SIGGRAPH 81,* 279–287.

ATHE83   Atherton, P.R., "A Scan-Line Hidden Surface Removal Procedure for Constructive Solid Geometry," *SIGGRAPH 83,* 73–82.

ATKI84   Atkinson, H.H., I. Gargantini, and M.V.S. Ramanath, "Determination of the 3D Border by Repeated Elimination of Internal Surfaces," *Computing*, 32(4), October 1984, 279–295.

ATKI86   Atkinson, W., U.S. Patent 4,622,545, November 1986.

AYAL85   Ayala, D., P. Brunet, R. Juan, and I. Navazo, "Object Representation by Means of Nonminimal Division Quadtrees and Octrees," *ACM TOG*, 4(1), January 1985, 41–59.

BADL87   Badler, N.I., K.H. Manoochehri, and G. Walters, "Articulated Figure Positioning by Multiple Constraints," *CG & A*, 7(6), June 1987, 28–38.

BAEC69   Baecker, R.M., "Picture Driven Animation," *SJCC*, AFIPS Press, Montvale, NJ, 1969, 273–288.

BAEC87   Baecker, R., and B. Buxton, *Readings in Human-Computer Interaction*, Morgan Kaufmann, Los Altos, CA, 1987.

BALD85   Baldauf, D., "The Workhorse CRT: New Life," *IEEE Spectrum*, 22(7), July 1985, 67–73.

BANC77   Banchoff, T.F., and C.M. Strauss, *The Hypercube: Projections and Slicings*, Film, International Film Bureau, 1977.

BANC83   Banchoff, T., and J. Wermer, *Linear Algebra Through Geometry*, Springer-Verlag, New York, 1983.

BARN88a   Barnsley, M., A. Jacquin, F. Malassenet, L. Reuter, and A.D. Sloan, "Harnessing Chaos for Image Synthesis," *SIGGRAPH 88*, 131–140.

BARN88b   Barnsley, M., "Harnessing Chaos for Image Synthesis," Lecture at ACM SIGGRAPH '88 meeting in Atlanta, GA, August 1988.

BARR79   Barros, J., and H. Fuchs, "Generating Smooth 2–D Monocolor Line Drawings on Video Displays," *SIGGRAPH 79*, 260–269.

BARR84   Barr, A., "Global and Local Deformations of Solid Primitives," *SIGGRAPH 84*, 21–30.

BARR88   Barr, A., and R. Barzel, "A Modeling System Based on Dynamic Constraints," *SIGGRAPH 88*, 179–188.

BARR88b   Barry, P. and R. Goldman, "A Recursive Evaluation Algorithm for a Class of Catmull-Rom Splines," *SIGGRAPH 88*, 199–204.

BARR89a   Barr, A.H., ed., *Topics in Physically Based Modeling*, Addison-Wesley, Reading, MA, 1989.

BARS83   Barsky, B., and J. Beatty, "Local Control of Bias and Tension in Beta-Splines," *ACM TOG*, 2(2), April 1983, 109–134.

BARS85   Barsky, B., and T. DeRose, "The Beta2-Spline: A Special Case of the Beta-Spline Curve and Surface Representation," *CG & A*, 5(9), September 1985, 46–58. See also erratum in 7(3), March 1987, 15.

BARS87   Barsky, B., T. DeRose, and M. Dippé, *An Adaptive Subdivision Method with Crack Prevention for Rendering Beta-spline Objects*, Report UCB/CSD 87/348, Department of Computer Science, University of California, Berkeley, CA, 1987.

BARS88   Barsky, B., *Computer Graphics and Geometric Modeling Using Beta-splines*, Springer-Verlag, New York, 1988.

BART87   Bartels, R., J. Beatty, and B. Barsky, *An Introduction to Splines for Use in Computer Graphics and Geometric Modeling*, Morgan Kaufmann, Los Altos, CA, 1987.

BASS88   Bass, L., E. Hardy, K. Hoyt, M. Little, and R. Seacord, *Introduction to the Serpent User Interface Management System*, Software Engineering Institute, Carnegie-Mellon University, Pittsburgh, PA, March 1988.

BAUM72   Baumgart, B.G., *Winged-edge Polyhedron Representation*, Technical Report STAN-CS-320, Computer Science Department, Stanford University, Palo Alto, CA, 1972.

BAUM74   Baumgart, B.G., *Geometric Modeling for Computer Vision*, Ph.D. Thesis, Report AIM-249, STAN-CS-74-463, Computer Science Department, Stanford University, Palo Alto, CA, October 1974.

BAUM75   Baumgart, B.G., "A Polyhedron Representation for Computer Vision," *NCC 75*, 589–596.

BAUM89   Baum, D.R., H.E. Rushmeier, and J.M. Winget, "Improving Radiosity Solutions Through the Use of Analytically Determined Form-Factors," *SIGGRAPH 89*, 325–334.

BAYE73   Bayer, B.E., "An Optimum Method for Two-Level Rendition of Continuous-Tone Pictures," in *Conference Record of the International Conference on Communications*, 1973, 26-11–26-15.

BEAT82   Beatty, J.C., and K.S. Booth, eds., *Tutorial: Computer Graphics*, Second Edition, IEEE Comp. Soc. Press, Silver Spring, MD, 1982.

BECK63   Beckmann, P., and A. Spizzichino, *The Scattering of Electromagnetic Waves from Rough Surfaces*, Macmillan, New York, 1963

BEDF58   Bedford, R. and G. Wyszecki, "Wavelength Discrimination for Point Sources," *Journal of the Optical Society of America*, 48, 1958, 129-ff.

BENN84   Bennet, P.P., and S.A. Gabriel, "System for Spatially Transforming Images," U. S. Patent 4,472,732, September 18, 1984.

BENT82   Benton, S.A., "Survey of Holographic Stereograms," *Proceedings of SPIE*, 367, August 1982, 15–19.

BERG78   Bergeron, R., P. Bono, and J. Foley, "Graphics Programming Using the Core System," *Computing Surveys (Special Issue on Graphics Standards)*, 10(4), December 1978, 389–443.

BERG86a   Bergeron, P., "A General Version of Crow's Shadow Volumes," *CG & A*, 6(9), September 1986, 17–28.

BERG86b   Bergman, L., H. Fuchs, E. Grant, and S. Spach, "Image Rendering by Adaptive Refinement," *SIGGRAPH 86*, 29–37.

BERK68   Berkeley Physics Course, *Waves*, Volume 3, McGraw-Hill, New York, 1968.

BERK82   Berk, T., L. Brownston, and A. Kaufman, "A New Color-Naming System for Graphics Languages," *CG & A*, 2(3), May 1982, 37–44.

BERT81   Bertin, J., *Graphics and Graphics Information Processing*, de Gruyter, New York, 1981. Translated by Berg, W., and F. Scott from *La Graphique et le Traitement Graphique de l'Information*, Flammarion, Paris, 1977.

BERT83   Bertin, J., *Semiology of Graphics*, University of Wisconsin Press, Madison, WI, 1983. Translated by W. Berg from *Sémiologie Graphique*, Editions Gauthier-Villars, Paris; Editions Mouton & Cie, Paris-La Haye; and Ecole Pratique des Hautes Etudes, Paris, 1967.

BEWL83   Bewley, W., T. Roberts, D. Schroit, and W. Verplank, "Human Factors Testing in the Design of Xerox's 8010 'Star' Office Workstation," in *Proceedings CHI '83 Human Factors in Computing Systems Conference*, ACM, New York, 1983, 72–77.

BEZI70   Bézier, P., *Emploi des Machines á Commande Numérique*, Masson et Cie, Paris, 1970. Translated by Forrest, A. R., and A. F. Pankhurst as Bézier, P., *Numerical Control —Mathematics and Applications*, Wiley, London, 1972.

BEZI74   Bézier, P., "Mathematical and Practical Possibilities of UNISURF," in Barnhill, R. E., and R. F. Riesenfeld, eds., *Computer Aided Geometric Design*, Academic Press, New York, 1974.

BIER86a   Bier, E., and M. Stone, "Snap-Dragging," *SIGGRAPH 86*, 233–240.

BIER86b   Bier, E., "Skitters and Jacks: Interactive 3D Positioning Tools," in *Proceedings 1986 Workshop on Interactive 3D Graphics*, ACM, New York, 1987, 183–196.

BILL81   Billmeyer, F., and M. Saltzman, *Principles of Color Technology*, second edition, Wiley, New York, 1981.

BINF71   Binford, T., in *Visual Perception by Computer, Proceedings of the IEEE Conference on Systems and Control*, Miami, FL, December 1971.

BIRR61   Birren, R., *Creative Color*, Van Nostrand Reinhold, New York, 1961.

BISH60   Bishop, A., and M. Crook, *Absolute Identification of Color for Targets Presented Against White and Colored Backgrounds*. Report WADD TR 60-611, Wright Air Development Division, Wright Patterson AFB, Dayton, Ohio, 1960.

BISH86   Bishop, G., and D.M. Weimer, "Fast Phong Shading," *SIGGRAPH 86*, 103–106.

BLES82   Bleser, T., and J. Foley, "Towards Specifying and Evaluating the Human Factors of User-Computer Interfaces," in *Proceedings of the Human Factors in Computer Systems Conference*, ACM, New York, 1982, 309–314.

BLES86   Bleser, B., and J. Ward, "Human Factors Affecting the Problem of Machine Recognition of Hand-Printed Text," in *Computer Graphics '86 Conference Proceedings*, Volume 3, NCGA, Fairfax, VA, 1986, 498–514.

BLES88a   Bleser, T., J. Sibert, and J. P. McGee, "Charcoal Sketching: Returning Control to the Artist," *ACM TOG*, 7(1), January 1988, 76–81

BLES88b   Bleser, T., *TAE Plus Styleguide User Interface Description*. NASA Goddard Space Flight Center, Greenbelt, MD, 1988.

BLIN76   Blinn, J.F., and M.E. Newell, "Texture and Reflection in Computer Generated Images," *CACM*, 19(10), October 1976, 542–547. Also in BEAT82, 456–461.

BLIN77a   Blinn, J.F., "Models of Light Reflection for Computer Synthesized Pictures," *SIGGRAPH 77*, 192–198. Also in FREE80, 316–322.

BLIN77b   Blinn, J.F., "A Homogeneous Formulation for Lines in 3-Space," *SIGGRAPH 77*, 237–241.

BLIN78a   Blinn, J.F., and M.E. Newell, "Clipping Using Homogeneous Coordinates," *SIGGRAPH 78*, 245–251.

BLIN78b   Blinn, J.F., "Simulation of Wrinkled Surfaces," *SIGGRAPH 78*, 286–292.

BLIN78c   Blinn, J.F., *Computer Display of Curved Surfaces*, Ph.D. Thesis, Department of Computer Science, University of Utah, Salt Lake City, UT, December 1978.

BLIN82a   Blinn, J.F., "Light Reflection Functions for the Simulation of Clouds and Dusty Surfaces," *SIGGRAPH 82*, 21–29.

BLIN82b   Blinn, J.F., "A Generalization of Algebraic Surface Drawing," *ACM TOG*, 1(3), July 1982, 235–256.

BLIN85   Blinn, J.F., "Systems Aspects of Computer Image Synthesis and Computer Animation," in *Image Rendering Tricks, Course Notes 12 for SIGGRAPH 85*, New York, July 1985.

BLIN88   Blinn, J.F., "Me and My (Fake) Shadow," *CG & A*, 9(1), January 1988, 82–86.

BLIN89a   Blinn, J.F., "What We Need Around Here is More Aliasing," *CG & A*, 9(1), January 1989, 75–79.

BLIN89b   Blinn, J.F., "Return of the Jaggy," *CG & A*, 9(2), March 1989, 82–89.

BLOO88   Bloomenthal, J., "Polygonisation of Implicit Surfaces," *Computer Aided Geometric Design*, 5, 1988, 341-355.

BOLT80   Bolt, R.A., "'Put-That-There': Voice and Gesture at the Graphics Interface," *SIGGRAPH 80*, 262–270.

BOLT84   Bolt, R.A., *The Human Interface: Where People and Computers Meet*, Lifetime Learning Press, Belmont, CA, 1984.

BORD89   Borden, B.S., "Graphics Processing on a Graphics Supercomputer," *CG & A*, 9(4), July 1989, 56–62.

BORN79   Borning, A., "Thinglab—A Constraint-Oriented Simulation Laboratory," Technical Report SSl-79-3, Xerox Palo Alto Research Center, Palo Alto, CA, July 1979.

BORN86a   Borning, A., and R. Duisberg, "Constraint-Based Tools for Building User Interfaces," *ACM TOG*, 5(4), October 1986, 345–374.

BORN86b   Borning, A., "Defining Constraints Graphically," in *SIGCHI '86 Conference Proceedings*, ACM, New York, 1986, 137–143.

BOUK70a   Bouknight, W.J., "A Procedure for Generation of Three-Dimensional Half-Toned Computer Graphics Presentations," *CACM*, 13(9), September 1970, 527–536. Also in FREE80, 292–301.

BOUK70b   Bouknight, W.J., and K.C. Kelly, "An Algorithm for Producing Half-Tone Computer Graphics Presentations with Shadows and Movable Light Sources," *SJCC*, AFIPS Press, Montvale, NJ, 1970, 1–10.

BOUV85   Bouville, C., "Bounding Ellipsoids for Ray-Fractal Intersection," *SIGGRAPH 85*, 45–52.

BOYN79   Boynton, R. M., *Human Color Vision*. Holt, Rinehart, and Winston, New York, 1979.

BOYS82   Boyse, J.W., and J.E. Gilchrist, "GMSolid: Interactive Modeling for Design and Analysis of Solids," *CG & A*, 2(2), March 1982, 27–40.

BÖHM80   Böhm, W., "Inserting New Knots into B-spline Curves," *Computer Aided Design*, 12(4), July 1980, 199–201.

BÖHM84   Böhm, W., G. Farin, and J. Kahmann, "A Survey of Curve and Surface Methods in CAGD," *Computer Aided Geometric Design*, 1(1), July 1984, 1–60.

BRAI78   Braid, I.C., R.C. Hillyard, and I.A. Stroud, *Stepwise Construction of Polyhedra in Geometric Modelling*, CAD Group Document No. 100, Cambridge University, Cambridge, England, 1978. Also in K.W. Brodlie, ed., *Mathematical Methods in Computer Graphics and Design*. Academic Press, New York, 1980, 123–141.

BRES65   Bresenham, J.E., "Algorithm for Computer Control of a Digital Plotter," *IBM Systems Journal*, 4(1), 1965, 25–30.

BRES77   Bresenham, J.E. "A Linear Algorithm for Incremental Digital Display of Circular Arcs," *Communications of the ACM*, 20(2), February 1977, 100–106.

BRES83   Bresenham, J.E., D.G. Grice, and S.C. Pi, "Bi-Directional Display of Circular Arcs," US Patent 4,371,933, February 1, 1983.

BREW77   Brewer, H., and D. Anderson, "Visual Interaction with Overhauser Curves and Surfaces," *SIGGRAPH 77*, 132–137.

BRIG74   Brigham, E.O., *The Fast Fourier Transform*, Prentice-Hall, Englewood Cliffs, NJ, 1974.

BRIT78   Britton, E., J. Lipscomb, and M. Pique, "Making Nested Rotations Convenient for the User," *SIGGRAPH 78*, 222–227.

BROO88   Brooktree Corporation, *Product Databook 1988*, Brooktree Corporation, San Diego, CA, 1987.

BROT84   Brotman, L.S., and N.I. Badler, "Generating Soft Shadows with a Depth Buffer Algorithm," *CG & A*, 4(10), October 1984, 5–12.

BROW64   Brown, R., "On-Line Computer Recognition of Hand-Printed Characters," *IEEE Trans. Computers*, Vol. EC-13(12), December 1964, 750–752.

BROW82   Brown, C.M., "PADL-2: A Technical Summary," *CG & A*, 2(2), March 1982, 69–84.

BUIT75   Bui-Tuong, Phong, "Illumination for Computer Generated Pictures," *CACM*, 18(6), June 1975, 311–317. Also in BEAT82, 449–455.

BUNK89   Bunker, M., and R. Economy, *Evolution of GE CIG Systems*, SCSD Document, General Electric Company, Daytona Beach, FL, 1989.

BURT74   Burton, R.P., and I. E. Sutherland, "Twinkle Box: A Three-Dimensional Computer Input Device," *NCC 1974*, AFIPS Press, Montvale, NJ, 1974, 513–520.

BURT76   Burtnyk, N., and M. Wein, "Interactive Skeleton Techniques for Enhancing Motion Dynamics in Key Frame Animation," *CACM*, 19(10), October 1976, 564–569

BUTL79   Butland, J., "Surface Drawing Made Simple," *Computer-Aided Design*, 11(1), January 1979, 19–22.

BUXT83   Buxton, W., M.R. Lamb, D. Sherman, and K.C. Smith, "Towards a Comprehensive User Interface Management System," *SIGGRAPH 83*, 35–42.

BUXT85   Buxton, W., R. Hill, and P. Rowley, "Issues and Techniques in Touch-Sensitive Tablet Input," *SIGGRAPH 85*, 215–224.

BUXT86   Buxton, W., "There's More to Interaction Than Meets the Eye: Issues in Manual Input," in Norman, D., and S. Draper, eds., *User-Centered System Design*, Lawrence Erlbaum, Hillsdale, NJ, 1986, 319–337. Also in BAEC 87, 366–375.

BYTE85   *BYTE Magazine*, 10(5), May 1985, 151–167.

CABR87   Cabral, B., N. Max, and R. Springmeyer, "Bidirectional Reflection Functions from Surface Bump Maps," *SIGGRAPH 87*, 273–281.

CACM84   "Computer Graphics Comes of Age: An Interview with Andries van Dam." *CACM*, 27(7), July 1984, 638–648.

CALL88   Callahan, J., D. Hopkins, M. Weiser, and B. Shneiderman, "An Empirical Comparison of Pie vs. Linear Menus," in *Proceedings of CHI 1988*, ACM, New York, 95–100.

CARD78   Card, S., W. English, and B. Burr, "Evaluation of Mouse, Rate-Controlled Isometric Joystick, Step Keys, and Text Keys for Text Selection of a CRT," *Ergonomics*, 21(8), August 1978, 601–613.

CARD80   Card, S., T. Moran, and A. Newell, "The Keystroke-Level Model for User Performance Time with Interactive Systems," *CACM*, 23(7), July 1980, 398–410.

CARD82   Card, S., "User Perceptual Mechanisms in the Search of Computer Command Menus," in *Proceedings of the Human Factors in Computer Systems Conference*, ACM, New York, March 1982, 20–24.

CARD83   Card, S., T. Moran, and A. Newell, *The Psychology of Human-Computer Interaction*, Lawrence Erlbaum Associates, Hillsdale, NJ, 1983.

CARD85   Cardelli, L., and R. Pike, "Squeak: A Language for Communicating with Mice," *SIGGRAPH 85*, 199–204.

CARD88   Cardelli, L., "Building User Interfaces by Direct Manipulation," in *Proceedings of the ACM SIGGRAPH Symposium on User Interface Software*, ACM, New York, 1988, 152–166.

CARL78   Carlbom, I., and J. Paciorek, "Planar Geometric Projections and Viewing Transformations," *Computing Surveys*, 10(4), December 1978, 465–502.

CARL85   Carlbom, I., I. Chakravarty, and D. Vanderschel, "A Hierarchical Data Structure for Representing the Spatial Decomposition of 3-D Objects," *CG & A*, 5(4), April 1985, 24–31.

CARL87   Carlbom, I., "An Algorithm for Geometric Set Operations Using Cellular Subdivision Techniques," *CG & A*, 7(5), May 1987, 44–55.

CARP84   Carpenter, L., "The A-buffer, an Antialiased Hidden Surface Method," *SIGGRAPH 84*, 103–108.

CATM72   Catmull, E., "A System for Computer Generated Movies," in *Proc. ACM Annual Conference*, ACM, New York, NY, August 1972, 422–431.

CATM74a   Catmull, E., and R. Rom, "A Class of Local Interpolating Splines," in Barnhill, R., and R. Riesenfeld, eds., *Computer Aided Geometric Design*, Academic Press, San Francisco, 1974, 317–326.

CATM74b   Catmull, E., *A Subdivision Algorithm for Computer Display of Curved Surfaces*, Ph.D. Thesis, Report UTEC-CSc-74-133, Computer Science Department, University of Utah, Salt Lake City, UT, December 1974

CATM75   Catmull, E., "Computer Display of Curved Surfaces," in *Proc. IEEE Conf. on Computer Graphics, Pattern Recognition and Data Structures*, May 1975. Also in FREE80, 309–315.

CATM78a   Catmull, E., "The Problems of Computer-Assisted Animation," *SIGGRAPH 78*, 348–353.

CATM78b   Catmull, E., "A Hidden-Surface Algorithm with Anti-Aliasing," *SIGGRAPH 78*, 6–11. Also in BEAT82, 462–467.

CATM79   Catmull, E., "A Tutorial on Compensation Tables," *SIGGRAPH 79*, 279–285.

CATM80   Catmull, E., and A.R. Smith, "3-D Transformations of Images in Scanline Order," *SIGGRAPH 80*, 279–285.

CGA82   Special Issue on Modeling the Human Body for Animation, *CG & A*, 2(11) N. Badler, ed., November 1982, 1–81.

CHAP72   Chapanis, A., and R. Kinkade, "Design of Controls," in Van Cott, H., and R. Kinkade, eds., *Human Engineering Guide to Equipment Design*, U.S. Government Printing Office, 1972.

CHAS81   Chasen, S.H., "Historical Highlights of Interactive Computer Graphics," *Mechanical Engineering*, 103, ASME, November 1981 32–41.

CHEN88   Chen, M., J. Mountford, and A. Sellen, "A Study in Interactive 3-D Rotation Using 2-D Control Devices," *SIGGRAPH 88*, 121–129.

CHIN89   Chin, N., and S. Feiner, "Near Real-Time Shadow Generation Using BSP Trees," *SIGGRAPH 89*, 99–106.

CHIN90   Chin, N., *Near Real-Time Object-Precision Shadow Generation Using BSP Trees*, M.S. Thesis, Department of Computer Science, Columbia University, New York, 1990.

CHRI75   Christ, R., "Review and Analysis of Color Coding for Visual Display," *Human Factors*, 17(6), December 1975, 542–570.

CHUN89   Chung, J.C., *et al.*, "Exploring Virtual Worlds with Head-Mounted Displays," *Proc. SPIE Meeting on Non-Holographic True 3-Dimensional Display Technologies*, 1083, Los Angeles, Jan. 15-20, 1989.

CLAR76   Clark, J.H., "Hierarchical Geometric Models for Visible Surface Algorithms," *CACM*, 19(10), October 1976, 547–554. Also in BEAT82, 296–303.

CLAR79   Clark, J., "A Fast Scan-Line Algorithm for Rendering Parametric Surfaces," abstract in *SIGGRAPH 79*, 174. Also in Whitted, T., and R. Cook, eds., *Image Rendering Tricks, Course Notes 16 for SIGGRAPH 86*, Dallas, TX, August 1986. Also in JOY88, 88–93.

CLAR80   Clark, J., and M. Hannah, "Distributed Processing in a High-Performance Smart Image Memory," *Lambda (VLSI Design)*, 1(3), Q4 1980, 40–45.

CLAR82   Clark, J., "The Geometry Engine: A VLSI Geometry System for Graphics," *SIGGRAPH 82*, 127–133.

CLEA83   Cleary, J., B. Wyvill, G. Birtwistle, and R. Vatti, "Design and Analysis of a Parallel Ray Tracing Computer," *Proceedings of Graphics Interface '83*, May 1983, 33–34.

CLEV83   Cleveland, W., and R. McGill, "A Color-Caused Optical Illusion on a Statistical Graph," *The American Statistician*, 37(2), May 1983, 101–105.

CLEV84   Cleveland, W., and R. McGill, "Graphical Perception: Theory, Experimentation and Application to the Development of Graphical Methods," *Journal of the American Statistical Association*, 79(387), September 1984, 531–554.

CLEV85   Cleveland, W., and R. McGill, "Graphical Perception and Graphical Methods for Analyzing Scientific Data," *Science*, 229, August 30, 1985, 828–833.

COHE80   Cohen, E., T. Lyche, and R. Riesenfeld, "Discrete B-Splines and Subdivision Techniques in Computer-Aided Geometric Design and Computer Graphics," *CGIP*, 14(2), October 1980, 87–111.

COHE83   Cohen, E., "Some Mathematical Tools for a Modeler's Workbench," *CG & A*, 3(7), October 1983, 63–66.

COHE85   Cohen, M.F., and D.P. Greenberg, "The Hemi-Cube: A Radiosity Solution for Complex Environments," *SIGGRAPH 85*, 31–40.

COHE86   Cohen, M.F., D.P. Greenberg, D.S. Immel, and P.J. Brock, "An Efficient Radiosity Approach for Realistic Image Synthesis," *CG & A*, 6(3), March 1986, 26–35.

COHE88   Cohen, M.F., S.E. Chen, J.R. Wallace, and D.P. Greenberg, "A Progressive Refinement Approach to Fast Radiosity Image Generation," *SIGGRAPH 88*, 75–84.

CONR85   Conrac Corporation, *Raster Graphics Handbook*, second edition, Van Nostrand Reinhold, New York, 1985.

COOK82   Cook, R., and K. Torrance, "A Reflectance Model for Computer Graphics," *ACM TOG*, 1(1), January 1982, 7–24.

COOK84a   Cook, R.L., "Shade Trees," *SIGGRAPH 84*, 223–231.

COOK84b   Cook, R.L., T. Porter, and L. Carpenter, "Distributed Ray Tracing," *SIGGRAPH 84*, 137–145.

COOK86   Cook, R.L., "Stochastic Sampling in Computer Graphics," *ACM TOG*, 5(1), January 1986, 51–72.

COOK87   Cook, R.L., L. Carpenter, and E. Catmull, "The Reyes Image Rendering Architecture," *SIGGRAPH 87*, 95–102.

COON67   Coons, S. A., *Surfaces for Computer Aided Design of Space Forms*, MIT Project Mac, TR-41, MIT, Cambridge, MA, June 1967.

COSS89   Cossey, G., *Prototyper*, SmethersBarnes, Portland, OR, 1989.

COWA83   Cowan, W., "An Inexpensive Scheme for Calibration of a Colour Monitor in Terms of CIE Standard Coordinates," *SIGGRAPH 83*, 315–321.

CROC84   Crocker, G.A., "Invisibility Coherence for Faster Scan-Line Hidden Surface Algorithms," *SIGGRAPH 84*, 95–102.

CROW77a   Crow, F.C., "Shadow Algorithms for Computer Graphics," *SIGGRAPH 77*, 242–247. Also in BEAT82, 442–448.

CROW77b   Crow, F.C., "The Aliasing Problem in Computer-Generated Shaded Images," *CACM*, 20(11), November 1977, 799–805.

CROW78   Crow, F., "The Use of Grayscale for Improved Raster Display of Vectors and Characters," *SIGGRAPH 78*, 1–5.

CROW81   Crow, F.C., "A Comparison of Antialiasing Techniques," *CG & A*, 1(1), January 1981, 40–48.

CROW84   Crow, F.C., "Summed-Area Tables for Texture Mapping," *SIGGRAPH 84*, 207–212.

CYRU78   Cyrus, M. and J. Beck, "Generalized Two- and Three-Dimensional Clipping," *Computers and Graphics*, 3(1), 1978, 23–28.

DALL80   Dallas, W.J., "Computer Generated Holograms," in *The Computer in Optical Research,* Frieden, B.R., ed., Springer-Verlag, New York, 1980, 291–366.

DASI89   Da Silva, D., *Raster Algorithms for 2D Primitives,* Master's Thesis, Computer Science Department, Brown University, Providence, RI, 1989.

DEBO78   de Boor, C., *A Practical Guide to Splines,* Applied Mathematical Sciences Volume 27, Springer-Verlag, New York, 1978.

DECA59   de Casteljau, F., *Outillage Méthodes Calcul,* André Citroën Automobiles SA, Paris, 1959.

DEER88   Deering, M., S. Winner, B. Schediwy, C. Duffy, and N. Hunt, "The Triangle Processor and Normal Vector Shader: A VLSI System for High Performance Graphics," *SIGGRAPH 88,* 21–30.

DELA88   Delany, H.C., "Ray Tracing on a Connection Machine," in *Proceedings of the 1988 International Conference on Supercomputing,* July 4–8, 1988, St. Malo, France, 659–664.

DEME80   Demetrescu, S., *A VLSI-Based Real-Time Hidden-Surface Elimination Display System,* Master's Thesis, Department of Computer Science, California Institute of Technology, Pasadena, CA, May 1980.

DEME85   Demetrescu, S., "High Speed Image Rasterization Using Scan Line Access Memories," in *Proceedings of the 1985 Chapel Hill Conference on VLSI,* Rockville, MD, Computer Science Press, 221–243.

DEYO89   Deyo, R., and D. Ingebretson, "Notes on Real-Time Vehicle Simulation," in *Implementing and Interacting with Real-Time Microworlds, Course Notes 29 for SIGGRAPH 89,* Boston, MA, August 1989

DIGI89   Digital Equipment Corporation, *DEC XUI Style Guide,* Digital Equipment Corporation, Maynard, MA, 1989.

DIPP84   Dippé, M. and J. Swensen, "An Adaptive Subdivision Algorithm and Parallel Architecture for Realistic Image Synthesis " *SIGGRAPH 84,* 149–158.

DIPP85   Dippé, M., and E.H. Wold, "Antialiasing through Stochastic Sampling," *SIGGRAPH 85,* 69–78.

DOCT81   Doctor, L., and J. Torborg, "Display Techniques for Octree-Encoded Objects," *CG & A,* 1(3), July 1981, 29–38.

DONA88   Donato, N., and R. Rocchetti, "Techniques for Manipulating Arbitrary Regions," in *Course Notes 11 for SIGGRAPH 88,* Atlanta, GA, August, 1988.

DREB88   Drebin, R.A., L. Carpenter, and P. Hanrahan, "Volume Rendering," *SIGGRAPH 88,* 65–74.

DUFF79   Duff, T., "Smoothly Shaded Renderings of Polyhedral Objects on Raster Displays," *SIGGRAPH 79,* 270–275.

DURB88   Durbeck, R., and S. Sherr, eds., *Output Hardcopy Devices,* Academic Press, New York, 1988.

DUVA90   Duvanenko, V., W.E. Robbins, R.S. Gyurcsik, "Improved Line Segment Clipping," *Dr. Dobb's Journal,* July 1990, 36–45, 98–100.

DVOŘ43   Dvořák, A., "There is a Better Typewriter Keyboard," *National Business Education Quarterly,* 12(2), 1943, 51–58.

ELLS89   Ellsworth, D., *Pixel-Planes 5 Rendering Control,* Tech. Rep. TR89-003, Department of Computer Science, University of North Carolina at Chapel Hill, Chapel Hill, NC, 1989.

EMER03   Emerson, R., "Essays: First Series—Self Reliance," in *The Complete Works of Ralph Waldo Emerson,* Houghton Mifflin, Boston, MA, 1903.

ENCA72   Encarnacao, J., and W. Giloi, "PRADIS—An Advanced Programming System for 3-D-Display," *SJCC,* AFIPS Press, Montvale, NJ, 1972, 985–998.

ENDE87   Enderle, G, K. Kansy, and G. Pfaff, *Computer Graphics Programming*, second edition, Springer-Verlag, Berlin, 1987.

ENGE68   Engelbart, D.C., and W.K. English, *A Research Center for Augmenting Human Intellect*, *FJCC* , Thompson Books, Washington, D.C., 395.

ENGL89   England, N., "Evolution of High Performance Graphics Systems," in *Proceedings of Graphics Interface '89,* Canadian Information Processsing Society (Morgan Kauffman in U.S.), 1989.

EVAN81   Evans, K., P. Tanner, and M. Wein, "Tablet-Based Valuators that Provide One, Two or Three Degrees of Freedom," *SIGGRAPH 81,* 91–97.

EVAN89   Evans & Sutherland Computer Corporation, *The Breadth of Visual Simulation Technology,* Evans & Sutherland Computer Corporation, Salt Lake City, UT, 1989.

EYLE88   Eyles, J., J. Austin, H. Fuchs, T. Greer, and J. Poulton, "Pixel-Planes 4: A Summary," in *Advances in Computer Graphics Hardware II* (1987 Eurographics Workshop on Graphics Hardware), Eurographics Seminars, 1988, 183-208.

FARI86   Farin, G., "Triangular Bernstein-Bézier Patches," *Computer Aided Geometric Design*, 3(2), August 1986, 83–127.

FARI88   Farin, G., *Curves and Surfaces for Computer Aided Geometric Design*, Academic Press, New York, 1988.

FAUX79   Faux, I. D., and M. J. Pratt, *Computational Geometry for Design and Manufacture*, Wiley, New York, 1979.

FEIB80   Feibush, E.A., M. Levoy, and R.L. Cook, "Synthetic Texturing Using Digital Filters," *SIGGRAPH 80,* 294–301.

FEIN82a   Feiner, S., S. Nagy, and A. van Dam, "An Experimental System for Creating and Presenting Interactive Graphical Documents," *ACM TOG,* 1(1), January 1982, 59–77.

FEIN82b   Feiner, S., D. Salesin, and T. Banchoff, "DIAL: A Diagrammatic Animation Language," *CG & A,* 2(7), September 1982, 43–54.

FEIN85   Feiner, S., "APEX: An Experiment in the Automated Creation of Pictorial Explanations," *CG & A,* 5(11), November 1985, 29–38.

FEIN88   Feiner, S., "A Grid-Based Approach to Automating Display Layout," in *Proceedings of Graphics Interface '88*, Edmonton, Canada, June 1988, 192–197.

FERG64   Ferguson, J., "Multivariate Curve Interpolation," *JACM*, 11(2), April 1964, 221–228.

FIEL86   Field, D., "Algorithms for Drawing Anti-Aliased Circles and Ellipses," *CGVIP,* 33(1), January 1986, 1–15.

FISH84   Fishkin, K.P., and B.A. Barsky, "A Family of New Algorithms for Soft Filling," *SIGGRAPH 84,* 235–244.

FISH86   Fisher, S.S., M. McGreevy, J. Humphries, and W. Robinett, "Virtual Environment Display System," in *Proceedings of the 1986 Chapel Hill Workshop on Interactive 3D Graphics,* Chapel Hill, NC, 1986, 77–87.

FITT54   Fitts, P., "The Information Capacity of the Human Motor System in Controlling Amplitude of Motion," *Journal of Experimental Psychology*, 47(6), June 1954, 381–391.

FIUM89   Fiume, E.L., *The Mathematical Structure of Raster Graphics,* Academic Press, San Diego, 1989.

FLEC87   Flecchia, M., and R. Bergeron, "Specifying Complex Dialogs in Algae," in *Proceedings of CHI + GI '87*, ACM, New York, 1987, 229–234.

FLOY75   Floyd, R., and Steinberg, L., "An Adaptive Algorithm for Spatial Gray Scale," in *Society for Information Display 1975 Symposium Digest of Technical Papers*, 1975, 36.

FOLE71   Foley, J., "An Approach to the Optimum Design of Computer Graphics Systems," *CACM*, 14 (6), June 1971, 380–390.

FOLE74   Foley, J., and V. Wallace, "The Art of Natural Man–Machine Communication," *Proceedings IEEE*, 62(4), April 1974, 462–470.

FOLE76   Foley, J., "A Tutorial on Satellite Graphics Systems," *IEEE Computer* 9(8), August 1976, 14–21.

FOLE82   Foley, J., and A. van Dam, *Fundamentals of Interactive Computer Graphics*, Addison-Wesley, Reading, MA, 1982.

FOLE84   Foley, J., V. Wallace, and P. Chan, "The Human Factors of Computer Graphics Interaction Techniques," *CG & A*, 4(11), November 1984, 13–48.

FOLE87a   Foley, J., "Interfaces for Advanced Computing," *Scientific American*, 257(4), October 1987, 126–135.

FOLE87b   Foley, J., W. Kim, and C. Gibbs, "Algorithms to Transform the Formal Specification of a User Computer Interface," in *Proceedings INTERACT '87, 2nd IFIP Conference on Human-Computer Interaction*, Elsevier Science Publishers, Amsterdam, 1987, 1001-1006.

FOLE87c   Foley, J., and W. Kim, "ICL—The Image Composition Language," *CG & A*, 7(11), November 1987, 26–35.

FOLE88   Foley, J., W. Kim, and S. Kovacevic, "A Knowledge Base for User Interface Management System," in *Proceedings of CHI '88–1988 SIGCHI Computer-Human Interaction Conference*, ACM, New York, 1988, 67-72.

FOLE89   Foley, J., W. Kim, S. Kovacevic, and K. Murray, "Defining Interfaces at a High Level of Abstraction," *IEEE Software*, 6(1), January 1989, 25–32.

FORR79   Forrest, A. R., "On the Rendering of Surfaces," *SIGGRAPH 79*, 253–259.

FORR80   Forrest, A. R., "The Twisted Cubic Curve: A Computer-Aided Geometric Design Approach," *Computer Aided Design*, 12(4), July 1980, 165–172.

FORR85   Forrest, A. R., "Antialiasing in Practice", in Earnshaw, R. A., ed., *Fundamental Algorithms for Computer Graphics*, NATO ASI Series F: Computer and Systems Sciences, Vol. 17, Springer-Verlag, New York, 1985, 113–134.

FORS88   Forsey, D.R., and R.H. Bartels, "Hierarchical B-spline Refinement," *SIGGRAPH 88*, 205–212.

FOUR82   Fournier, A., D. Fussell, and L. Carpenter, "Computer Rendering of Stochastic Models, " *CACM*, 25(6), June 1982, 371–384.

FOUR86   Fournier, A., and W.T. Reeves, "A Simple Model of Ocean Waves," *SIGGRAPH 86*, 75–84.

FOUR88   Fournier, A. and D. Fussell, "On the Power of the Frame Buffer," *ACM TOG*, 7(2), April 1988, 103–128.

FRAN81   Franklin, W.R., "An Exact Hidden Sphere Algorithm that Operates in Linear Time," *CGIP*, 15(4), April 1981, 364–379.

FREE80   Freeman, H. ed., *Tutorial and Selected Readings in Interactive Computer Graphics*, IEEE Comp. Soc. Press, Silver Spring, MD, 1980.

FRIE85   Frieder, G., D. Gordon, and R. Reynolds, "Back-to-Front Display of Voxel-Based Objects," *CG & A*, 5(1), January 1985, 52–60.

FROM84   Fromme, F., "Improving Color CAD Systems for Users: Some Suggestions from Human Factors Studies," *IEEE Design and Test of Computers*, 1(1), February 1984, 18–27.

FUCH77a   Fuchs, H., J. Duran, and B. Johnson, "A System for Automatic Acquisition of Three-Dimensional Data," in *Proceedings of the 1977 NCC*, AFIPS Press, 1977, 49–53.

FUCH77b   Fuchs, H., "Distributing a Visible Surface Algorithm over Multiple Processors," *Proceedings of the ACM Annual Conference*, Seattle, WA, October 1977, 449–451.

FUCH79   Fuchs, H., and B. Johnson, "An Expandable Multiprocessor Architecture for Video Graphics," *Proceedings of the 6th ACM-IEEE Symposium on Computer Architecture*, Philadelphia, PA, April 1979, 58–67.

FUCH80   Fuchs, H., Z.M. Kedem, and B.F. Naylor, "On Visible Surface Generation by A Priori Tree Structures," *SIGGRAPH 80*, 124–133.

FUCH81   Fuchs, H. and J. Poulton, "Pixel-Planes: A VLSI-Oriented Design for a Raster Graphics Engine," *VLSI Design*, 2(3), Q3 1981, 20–28.

FUCH82   Fuchs, H., S.M. Pizer, E.R. Heinz, S.H. Bloomberg, L. Tsai, and D.C. Strickland, "Design of and Image Editing with a Space-Filling Three-Dimensional Display Based on a Standard Raster Graphics System," *Proceedings of SPIE*, 367, August 1982, 117–127.

FUCH83   Fuchs, H., G.D. Abram, and E.D. Grant, "Near Real-Time Shaded Display of Rigid Objects," *SIGGRAPH 83*, 65–72.

FUCH85   Fuchs, H., J. Goldfeather, J. Hultquist, S. Spach, J. Austin, F. Brooks, J. Eyles, and J. Poulton, "Fast Spheres, Shadows, Textures, Transparencies, and Image Enhancements in Pixel-Planes," *SIGGRAPH 85*, 111–120.

FUCH89   Fuchs, H., J. Poulton, J. Eyles, T. Greer, J. Goldfeather, D. Ellsworth, S. Molnar, G. Turk, B. Tebbs, and L. Israel, "Pixel-Planes 5: A Heterogeneous Multiprocessor Graphics System Using Processor-Enhanced Memories," *SIGGRAPH 89*, 79–88.

FUJI85   Fujimura, K., and Kunii, T. L., "A Hierarchical Space Indexing Method," in Kunii, T. L., ed., *Computer Graphics: Visual Technology and Art*, *Proceedings of Computer Graphics Tokyo '85 Conference*, Springer-Verlag, 1985, 21–34.

FUSS82   Fussell, D., and B. D. Rathi, "A VLSI-Oriented Architecture for Real-Time Raster Display of Shaded Polygons," in *Proceedings of Graphics Interface '82*, Toronto, May 1982, 373–380.

GAIN84   Gaines, B., and M. Shaw, *The Art of Computer Conversation*, Prentice-Hall International, Englewood Cliffs, NJ, 1984.

GALI69   Galimberti, R., and U. Montanari, "An Algorithm for Hidden Line Elimination," *CACM*, 12(4), April 1969, 206–211.

GARD84   Gardner, G.Y., "Simulation of Natural Scenes Using Textured Quadric Surfaces," *SIGGRAPH 84*, 11–20.

GARD85   Gardner, G.Y., "Visual Simulation of Clouds," *SIGGRAPH 85*, 297–303.

GARG82   Gargantini, I., "Linear Octtrees for Fast Processing of Three-Dimensional Objects," *CGIP*, 20(4), December 1982, 365–374.

GARG86   Gargantini, I., T. Walsh, and O. Wu, "Viewing Transformations of Voxel-Based Objects via Linear Octrees," *CG & A*, 6(10), October 1986, 12–21.

GARR80   Garrett, M., *A Unified Non-Procedural Environment for Designing and Implementing Graphical Interfaces to Relational Data Base Management Systems*, Ph.D. dissertation, Technical Report GWU-EE/CS-80-13, Department of Electrical Engineering and Computer Science, The George Washington University, Washington, DC, 1980.

GARR82   Garrett, M., and J. Foley, "Graphics Programming Using a Database System with Dependency Declarations," *ACM TOG*, 1(2), April 1982, 109–128.

GHAR88   Gharachorloo, N., S. Gupta, E. Hokenek, P. Balasubramanian, B. Bogholtz, C. Mathieu, and C. Zoulas, "Subnanosecond Pixel Rendering with Million Transistor Chips," *SIGGRAPH 88*, 41–49.

GHAR89   Gharachorloo, N., S. Gupta, R.F. Sproull, and I.E Sutherland, "A Characterization of Ten Rasterization Techniques," *SIGGRAPH 89*, 355–358.

GILO78   Giloi, W.K., *Interactive Computer Graphics — Data Structures, Algorithms, Languages,* Prentice-Hall, Englewood Cliffs, NJ, 1978.

GINS83   Ginsberg, C.M., and D. Maxwell, "Graphical Marionette," in *Proceedings of the SIGGRAPH/SIGART Interdisciplinary Workshop on Motion: Representation and Perception,* Toronto, April 4–6, 1983, 172–179.

GIRA85   Girard, M., and A.A. Maciejewski, "Computational Modeling for the Computer Animation of Legged Figures," *SIGGRAPH 85,* 253–270.

GIRA87   Girard, M., "Interactive Design of 3D Computer-Animated Legged Animal Motion," *CG & A,* 7(6), June 1987, 39–51.

GLAS84   Glassner, A.S., "Space Subdivision for Fast Ray Tracing," *CG & A,* 4(10), October 1984, 15–22.

GLAS86   Glassner, A.S., "Adaptive Precision in Texture Mapping," *SIGGRAPH 86,* 297–306.

GLAS88   Glassner, A., "Spacetime Raytracing for Animation," *CG & A,* 8(2), March 1988, 60–70.

GLAS89   Glassner, A.S., ed., *An Introduction to Ray Tracing,* Academic Press, London, 1989.

GOLD71   Goldstein, R.A., and R. Nagel, "3-D Visual Simulation," *Simulation,* 16(1), January 1971, 25–31.

GOLD76   Goldberg, A., and Kay, A., *SMALLTALK-72 Instruction Manual,* Learning Research Group, Xerox Palo Alto Research Center, Palo Alto, CA, March 1976.

GOLD80   Goldstein, H., *Classical Mechanics,* Addison-Wesley, Reading, MA, 1980.

GOLD83   Goldberg, A., and D. Robson, *SmallTalk 80: The Language and Its Implementation,* Addison-Wesley, Reading, MA, 1983.

GOLD84   Goldwasser, S.M., "A Generalized Object Display Processor Architecture," in *Proceedings of the 11th Annual International Symposium on Computer Architecture,* Ann Arbor, MI, June 5–7, 1984, *SIGARCH Newsletter,* 12(3), June 1984, 38–47.

GOLD86   Goldfeather, J., J.P.M. Hultquist, and H. Fuchs, "Fast Constructive Solid Geometry Display in the Pixel-Powers Graphics System," *SIGGRAPH 86,* 107–116.

GOLD87   Goldsmith, J., and J. Salmon, "Automatic Creation of Object Hierarchies for Ray Tracing," *CG & A,* 7(5), May 1987, 14–20.

GOLD88   Goldwasser, S.M., R.A. Reynolds, D.A. Taltor, and E.S. Walsh, "Techniques for the Rapid Display and Manipulation of 3-D Biomedical Data," *Comp. Med. Imag. and Graphics,* 12(1), 1988, 1–24.

GOLD89   Goldfeather, J., S. Molnar, G. Turk, and H. Fuchs, "Near Real-Time CSG Rendering Using Tree Normalization and Geometric Pruning," *CG & A,* 9(3), May 1989, 20–28.

GONZ87   Gonzalez, R., and P. Wintz, *Digital Image Processing,* second edition, Addison-Wesley, Reading, MA, 1987.

GORA84   Goral, C.M., K.E. Torrance, D.P. Greenberg, and B. Battaile, "Modeling the Interaction of Light Between Diffuse Surfaces," *SIGGRAPH 84,* 213–222.

GORI87   Goris, A., B. Fredrickson, and H.L. Baeverstad, Jr., "A Configurable Pixel Cache for Fast Image Generation," *CG & A,* 7(3), March 1987, 24–32.

GOSL89   Gosling, J., personal communication, March 1989.

GOSS88   Gossard, D., R. Zuffante, and H. Sakurai, "Representing Dimensions, Tolerances, and Features in MCAE Systems," *CG & A,* 8(2), March 1988, 51–59.

GOUR71   Gouraud, H., "Continuous Shading of Curved Surfaces," *IEEE Trans. on Computers,* C-20(6), June 1971, 623–629. Also in FREE80, 302–308.

GREE85a   Green, M., "The University of Alberta User Interface Management System," *SIGGRAPH 85*, 205–213.

GREE85b   Green, M., *The Design of Graphical User Interfaces*, Technical Report CSRI-170, Department of Computer Science, University of Toronto, Toronto, 1985.

GREE85c   Greene, R., "The Drawing Prism: A Versatile Graphic Input Device," *SIGGRAPH 85*, 103–110.

GREE86   Greene, N., "Environment Mapping and Other Applications of World Projections," *CG & A*, 6(11), November 1986, 21–29.

GREE87a   Green, M., "A Survey of Three Dialog Models," *ACM TOG*, 5(3), July 1987, 244–275.

GREE87b   Greenstein, J. and L. Arnaut, "Human Factors Aspects of Manual Computer Input Devices," in Salvendy, G., ed., *Handbook of Human Factors*, Wiley, New York, 1987, 1450–1489.

GREG66   Gregory, R.L., *Eye and Brain— The Psychology of Seeing*, McGraw-Hill, New York, 1966.

GREG70   Gregory, R.L., *The Intelligent Eye*, McGraw-Hill, London, 1970.

GRIM89   Grimes, J., L. Kohn, and R. Bharadhwaj, "The Intel i860 64-Bit Processor: A General-Purpose CPU with 3D Graphics Capabilities," *CG & A*, 9(4), July 1989, 85–94.

GSPC77   Graphics Standards Planning Committee. "Status Report of the Graphics Standards Planning Committee of ACM/SIGGRAPH." *Computer Graphics*, 11(3), Fall 1977.

GSPC79   Graphics Standards Planning Committee. "Status Report of the Graphics Standards Planning Committee." *Computer Graphics*, 13(3), August 1979.

GTCO82   GTCO Corporation, *DIGI-PAD 5 User's Manual*, GTCO Corporation, Rockville, MD, 1982.

GUPT81a   Gupta, S., and R.E. Sproull, "Filtering Edges for Gray-Scale Displays," *SIGGRAPH 81*, 1–5.

GUPT81b   Gupta, S., R. Sproull, and I. Sutherland, "A VLSI Architecture for Updating Raster-Scan Displays," *SIGGRAPH 81*, 71–78.

GUPT86   Gupta, S., D.F. Bantz, P.N. Sholtz, C.J. Evangelisti, and W.R. DeOrazio, *YODA: An Advanced Display for Personal Computers*, Computer Science Research Report RC11618 (–52213), IBM Thomas J. Watson Research Center, Yorktown Heights, NY, October 1986.

GURW81   Gurwitz, R., R. Fleming and A. van Dam, "MIDAS: A Microprocessor Instructional Display and Animation System," *IEEE Transactions on Education*, February, 1981.

HAEU76   Haeusing, M., "Color Coding of Information on Electronic Displays," in *Proceedings of the Sixth Congress of the International Ergonomics Association*, 1976, 210–217.

HAGE86   Hagen, M., *Varieties of Realism*, Cambridge University Press, Cambridge, England, 1986.

HAGE88   Hagen, R.E., *An Algorithm for Incremental Anti-Aliased Lines and Curves*, Master's Thesis, Department of Electrical Engineering and Computer Science, Massachusetts Institute of Technology, Cambridge, MA, January 1988.

HAIN86   Haines, E.A., and D.P. Greenberg, "The Light Buffer: A Shadow-Testing Accelerator," *CG & A*, 6(9), September 1986, 6–16.

HAIN89   Haines, E., "Essential Ray Tracing Algorithms," in Glassner, A.S., ed., *An Introduction to Ray Tracing*, Academic Press, London, 1989, 33–77.

HALA68   Halas, J., and R. Manvell, *The Technique of Film Animation*, Hastings House, New York, 1968.

HALA73   Halas, J., ed., *Visual Scripting*, Hastings House, New York, 1973.

HALA82   Halasz, F., and T. Moran, "Analogy Considered Harmful," in *Proceedings of the Human Factors in Computer Systems Conference*, ACM, New York, 1982, 383–386.

HALL83   Hall, R.A., and D.P. Greenberg, "A Testbed for Realistic Image Synthesis," *CG & A*, 3(8), November 1983, 10–20.

HALL86   Hall, R., "Hybrid Techniques for Rapid Image Synthesis," in Whitted, T., and R. Cook, eds., *Image Rendering Tricks, Course Notes 16 for SIGGRAPH 86*, Dallas, TX, August 1986.

HALL89   Hall, R., *Illumination and Color in Computer Generated Imagery*, Springer-Verlag, New York, 1989.

HAMI53   Hamilton, W.R., *Lectures on Quaternions: Containing a Systematic Statement of a New Mathematical Method; of Which the Principles Were Communicated in 1843 to the Royal Irish Academy; and Which Has Since Formed the Subject of Successive Courses of Lectures, Delivered in 1848 and Subsequent Years, in the Halls of Trinity College, Dublin: With Numerous Illustrative Examples*, Hodges and Smith, Dublin, 1853.

HAML77   Hamlin, G., Jr., and C.W. Gear, "Raster-Scan Hidden Surface Algorithm Techniques," *SIGGRAPH 77*, 206–213. Also in FREE80, 264–271.

HANA80   Hanau, P., and D. Lenorovitz, "Prototyping and Simulation Tools for User/Computer Dialogue Design," *SIGGRAPH 80*, 271–278.

HANR83   Hanrahan, P., "Ray Tracing Algebraic Surfaces," *SIGGRAPH 83*, 83–90.

HANR89   Hanrahan, P., "A Survey of Ray-Surface Intersection Algorithms," in Glassner, A.S., ed., *An Introduction to Ray Tracing*, Academic Press, London, 1989, 79–119.

HANS71   Hansen, W., "User Engineering Principles for Interactive Systems," in *FJCC 1971*, AFIPS Press, Montvale, NJ, 1971, 523–532.

HARR88   Harrington, S.J., and R.R. Buckley, *Interpress: The Source Book*, Brady, New York, 1988.

HART89   Hartson, R., and D. Hix, "Human–Computer Interface Development: Concepts and Systems," *ACM Computing Surveys*, 21(1), March 1989, 5–92.

HATF89   Hatfield, D., *Anti-Aliased, Transparent, and Diffuse Curves*, IBM Technical Computing Systems Graphics Report 0001, International Business Machines, Cambridge, MA, 1989.

HAYE83   Hayes, P., and Szekely, P., "Graceful Interaction Through the COUSIN Command Interface," *International Journal of Man–Machine Studies*, 19(3), September 1983, 285–305.

HAYE84   Hayes, P., "Executable Interface Definitions Using Form-Based Interface Abstractions," in *Advances in Computer-Human Interaction*, Hartson, H.R., ed., Ablex, Norwood, NJ, 1984.

HAYE85   Hayes, P., P. Szekely, and R. Lerner, "Design Alternatives for User Interface Management Systems Based on Experience with COUSIN," in *CHI '85 Proceedings*, ACM, New York, 1985, 169–175.

HECK82   Heckbert, P., "Color Image Quantization for Frame Buffer Display," *SIGGRAPH 82*, 297–307.

HECK84   Heckbert, P.S., and P. Hanrahan, "Beam Tracing Polygonal Objects," *SIGGRAPH 84*, 119–127.

HECK86a   Heckbert, P.S., "Filtering by Repeated Integration," *SIGGRAPH 86*, 315–321.

HECK86b   Heckbert, P.S., "Survey of Texture Mapping," *CG & A*, 6(11), November 1986, 56–67.

HEDG82   Hedgley, D.R., Jr., *A General Solution to the Hidden-Line Problem*, NASA Reference Publication 1085, NASA Scientific and Technical Information Branch, 1982.

HEME82   Hemenway, K., "Psychological Issues in the Use of Icons in Command Menus," in *Proceedings Human Factors in Computer Systems Conference*, ACM, New York, 1982 20–23.

HERO76   Herot, C., "Graphical Input Through Machine Recognition of Sketches," *SIGGRAPH 76*, 97–102.

HERO78   Herot, C., and G. Weinzapfel, "One-Point Touch Input of Vector Information for Computer Displays," *SIGGRAPH 78*, 210–216.

HERZ80   Herzog, B., "In Memoriam of Steven Anson Coons," *Computer Graphics*, 13(4), February 1980, 228–231.

HILL83   Hill, F.S., Jr., S. Walker, Jr., and F. Gao, "Interactive Image Query System Using Progressive Transmission," *SIGGRAPH 83*, 323–333.

HILL87   Hill, R., "Supporting Concurrency, Communication, and Synchronization in Human-Computer Interaction—The Sassafras UIMS," *ACM TOG*, 5(3), July 1986, 179–210.

HIRS70   Hirsch, R., "Effects of Standard vs. Alphabetical Keyboard Formats on Typing Performance," *Journal of Applied Psychology*, 54, December 1970, 484–490

HOBB89   Hobby, J. D., "Rasterizing Curves of Constant Width," *JACM*, 36(2), April 1989, 209–229.

HODG85   Hodges, L., and D. McAllister, "Stereo and Alternating-Pair Techniques for Display of Computer-Generated Images," *CG & A*, 5(9), September 1985, 38–45.

HOFF61   Hoffman, K., and R. Kunze, *Linear Algebra*, Prentice–Hall, Englewood Cliffs, NJ, 1961.

HOLL80   Holladay, T. M., "An Optimum Algorithm for Halftone Generation for Displays and Hard Copies," *Proceedings of the Society for Information Display*, 21(2), 1980, 185–192.

HOPG86a   Hopgood, F., D. Duce, J. Gallop, and D. Sutcliffe, *Introduction to the Graphical Kernel System (GKS)*, second edition, Academic Press, London, 1986.

HOPG86b   Hopgood, F., D. Duce, E. Fielding, K. Robinson, and A. Williams, eds., *Methodology of Window Management*, Springer-Verlag, New York, 1986.

HORN79   Horn, B.K.P., and R.W. Sjoberg, "Calculating the Reflectance Map," *Applied Optics*, 18(11), June 1979, 1770–1779.

HUBS82   Hubschman, H., and S.W. Zucker, "Frame-to-Frame Coherence and the Hidden Surface Computation: Constraints for a Convex World," *ACM TOG*, 1(2), April 1982, 129–162.

HUDS86   Hudson, S., and R. King, "A Generator of Direct Manipulation Office Systems," *ACM Transactions on Office Information Systems*, 4(2), April 1986, 132–163.

HUDS87   Hudson, S., "UIMS Support for Direct Manipulation Interfaces," *ACM SIGGRAPH Workshop on Software Tools for User Interface Management*, in *Computer Graphics*, 21(2), April 1987, 120–124.

HUDS88   Hudson, S., and R. King, "Semantic Feedback in the Higgens UIMS," *IEEE Transactions on Software Engineering*, 14(8), August 1988, 1188–1206.

HUGH89   Hughes, J., *Integer and Floating-Point Z-Buffer Resolution*, Department of Computer Science Technical Report, Brown University, Providence, RI, 1989.

HULL87   Hull, R., and R. King, "Semantic Database Modeling: Survey, Applications, and Research Issues," *ACM Computing Surveys*, 19(3), September 1987, 201–260.

HUNT78   Hunter, G.M., *Efficient Computation and Data Structures for Graphics*, Ph.D. Thesis, Department of Electrical Engineering and Computer Science, Princeton University, Princeton, NJ, 1978.

HUNT79   Hunter, G.M. and K. Steiglitz, "Operations on Images Using Quad Trees," *IEEE Trans. Pattern Anal. Mach. Intell.*, 1(2), April 1979, 145–153.

HUNT81   Hunter, G.M., *Geometrees for Interactive Visualization of Geology: An Evaluation*, System Science Department, Schlumberger-Doll Research, Ridgefield, CT, 1981.

HUNT87   Hunt, R.W., *The Reproduction of Colour*, fourth edition, Fountain Press, Tolworth, England, 1987.

HURL89   Hurley, D., and J. Sibert, "Modeling User Interface-Application Interactions," *IEEE Software*, 6(1), January 1989, 71–77.

HUTC86   Hutchins, E., J. Hollan, and D. Norman, "Direct Manipulation Interfaces," in Norman, D., and S. Draper, eds., *User Centered System Design*, Erlbaum, Hillsdale, NJ, 1986, 87–124.

IES87   Illuminating Engineering Society, Nomenclature Committee, *ANSI/IES RP-16-1986: American National Standard: Nomenclature and Definitions for Illuminating Engineering*, Illuminating Engineering Society of North America, New York, 1987.

IMME86   Immel, D.S., M.F. Cohen, and D.P. Greenberg, "A Radiosity Method for Non-Diffuse Environments," *SIGGRAPH 86*, 133–142.

INFA85   Infante, C., "On the Resolution of Raster-Scanned CRT Displays," *Proceedings of the Society for Information Display*, 26(1), 1985, 23–36.

INGA81   Ingalls, D., "The SmallTalk Graphics Kernel," *BYTE*, 6(8), August 1981.

INTE85   Interaction Systems, Inc., *TK-1000 Touch System*, Interaction Systems, Inc., Newtonville, MA, 1985.

INTE88   International Standards Organization, *International Standard Information Processing Systems—Computer Graphics—Graphical Kernel System for Three Dimensions (GKS–3D) Functional Description*, ISO Document Number 8805:1988(E), American National Standards Institute, New York, 1988.

INTE89   Intel Corporation, *i860 Microprocessor Family Product Briefs*, Intel Corporation, Santa Clara, CA, 1989.

IRAN71   Irani, K., and V. Wallace, "On Network Linguistics and the Conversational Design of Queueing Networks," *JACM*, 18, October 1971, 616–629.

ISO   International Standards Organization, *Information Processing Text and Office Systems Standard Page Description Language (SPDL)*, ISO Document Number JTC1 SC18/WG8N561, American National Standards Institute, New York.

JACK64   Jacks, E., "A Laboratory for the Study of Man–Machine Communication," in *FJCC 64*, AFIPS, Montvale, NJ, 1964, 343–350.

JACK80   Jackins, C., and S.L. Tanimoto, "Oct-Trees and Their Use in Representing Three-Dimensional Objects," *CGIP*, 14(3), November 1980, 249–270.

JACO83   Jacob, R., "Using Formal Specifications in the Design of the User-Computer Interface," *CACM*, 26(4), April 1983, 259–264.

JACO85   Jacob, R., "A State Transition Diagram Language for Visual Programming," *IEEE Computer*, 18(8), August 1985, 51–59.

JACO86   Jacob, R., "A Specification Language for Direct-Manipulation User Interfaces," *ACM TOG*, 5(4), October 1986, 283–317.

JANS85   Jansen, F.W., "A CSG List Priority Hidden Surface Algorithm," in C. Vandoni, ed., *Proceedings of Eurographics 85*, North-Holland, Amsterdam, 1985, 51–62.

JANS87   Jansen, F.W., *Solid Modelling with Faceted Primitives*, Ph.D. Thesis, Department of Industrial Design, Delft University of Technology, Netherlands, September 1987.

JARV76a   Jarvis, J.F., C.N. Judice, and W.H. Ninke, "A Survey of Techniques for the Image Display of Continuous Tone Pictures on Bilevel Displays," *CGIP*, 5(1), March 1976, 13–40.

JARV76b   Jarvis, J.F., and C.S. Roberts, "A New Technique for Displaying Continuous Tone Images on a Bilevel Display," *IEEE Trans.*, COMM-24(8), August 1976, 891–898.

JENK89   Jenkins, R.A., "New Approaches in Parallel Computing," *Computers in Physics*, 3(1), January–February 1989, 24–32.

JEVA89   Jevans, D.A., "A Review of Multi-Computer Ray Tracing," *Ray Tracing News*, 3(1), May 1989, 8–15.

JOBL78   Joblove, G.H., and D. Greenberg, "Color Spaces for Computer Graphics," *SIGGRAPH 78*, 20–27.

JOHN78   Johnson, S., and M. Lesk, "Language Development Tools," *Bell System Technical Journal*, 57(6,7), July–August 1978, 2155–2176.

JOHN82   Johnson, S.A., "Clinical Varifocal Mirror Display System at the University of Utah," in *Proceedings of SPIE*, 367, August 1982, 145–148.

JONE26   Jones, L., and E. Lowry, "Retinal Sensibility to Saturation Differences," *Journal of the Optical Society of America*, 13(25), 1926.

JOVA86   Jovanović, B., *Visual Programming of Functional Transformations in a Dynamic Process Visualization System*, Report GWU-IIST-86-22, Department of Computer Science, George Washington University, Washington, DC, 1986.

JOY86   Joy, K.I., and M.N. Bhetanabhotla, "Ray Tracing Parametric Surface Patches Utilizing Numerical Techniques and Ray Coherence," *SIGGRAPH 86*, 279–285.

JOY88   Joy, K., C. Grant, N. Max, and L. Hatfield, *Tutorial: Computer Graphics: Image Synthesis*, IEEE Computer Society, Washington, DC, 1988.

JUDD75   Judd, D., and G. Wyszecki, *Color in Business, Science, and Industry*, Wiley, New York, 1975.

JUDI74   Judice, J.N., J.F. Jarvis, and W. Ninke, "Using Ordered Dither to Display Continuous Tone Pictures on an AC Plasma Panel," *Proceedings of the Society for Information Display*, Q4 1974, 161–169.

KAJI82   Kajiya, J.T., "Ray Tracing Parametric Patches," *SIGGRAPH 82*, 245–254.

KAJI83   Kajiya, J., "New Techniques for Ray Tracing Procedurally Defined Objects," *SIGGRAPH 83*, 91–102.

KAJI84   Kajiya, J., and B. Von Herzen, "Ray Tracing Volume Densities," *SIGGRAPH 84*, 165–173.

KAJI85   Kajiya, J.T., "Anisotropic Reflection Models," *SIGGRAPH 85*, 15–21.

KAJI86   Kajiya, J.T., "The Rendering Equation," *SIGGRAPH 86*, 143–150.

KAPL85   Kaplan, G., and E. Lerner, "Realism in Synthetic Speech," *IEEE Spectrum*, 22(4), April 1985, 32–37.

KAPP85   Kappel, M.R., "An Ellipse-Drawing Algorithm for Raster Displays," in Earnshaw, R., ed. *Fundamental Algorithms for Computer Graphics*, NATO ASI Series, Springer-Verlag, Berlin, 1985, 257–280.

KASI82   Kasik, D., "A User Interface Management System," *SIGGRAPH 82*, 99–106.

KAUF88a   Kaufmann, H. E., "User's Guide to the Compositor," Computer Graphics Group Documentation, Brown University, Providence, RI, May 1988.

KAUF88b   Kaufman, A., and R. Bakalash, "Memory and Processing Architecture for 3D Voxel-Based Imagery," *CG & A*, 8(6), November 1988, 10–23.

KAWA82   Kawaguchi, Y., "A Morphological Study of the Form of Nature," *SIGGRAPH 82*, 223–232.

KAWA88   Kawaguchi, Y., film, *ACM SIGGRAPH 88 Electronic Theater and Video Review*, 26, 1988.

KAY79a   Kay, D.S., *Transparency, Refraction and Ray Tracing for Computer Synthesized Images,* M.S. Thesis, Program of Computer Graphics, Cornell University, Ithaca, NY, January 1979.

KAY79b   Kay, D.S., and D. Greenberg, "Transparency for Computer Synthesized Images," *SIGGRAPH 79,* 158–164.

KAY86   Kay, T.L., and J.T. Kajiya, "Ray Tracing Complex Scenes," *SIGGRAPH 86,* 269–278.

KEDE84   Kedem, G., and J. L. Ellis. "The Raycasting Machine," in *Proceedings of the 1984 International Conference on Computer Design,* October 1984, 533–538.

KELL76   Kelly, K., and D. Judd, *COLOR—Universal Language and Dictionary of Names,* National Bureau of Standards Spec. Publ. 440, 003-003-01705-1, U.S. Government Printing Office, Washington, DC, 1976.

KELL88   Kelley, A.D., M.C. Malin, and G.M Nielson, "Terrain Simulation Using a Model of Stream Erosion," *SIGGRAPH 88,* 263–263.

KIER85   Kieras, D., and P. Polson, "An Approach to the Formal Analysis of User Complexity," *International Journal of Man-Machine Studies,* 22(4), April 1985, 365–394.

KLEM71   Klemmer, E., "Keyboard Entry," *Applied Ergonomics,* 2(1), 1971, 2–6.

KLIN71   Klinger, A., "Patterns And Search Statistics," in Rustagi, J., ed., *Optimizing Methods in Statistics,* Academic Press, New York, 1971, 303–337.

KNOW77   Knowlton, K., and L. Cherry, "ATOMS—A Three-D Opaque Molecule System for Color Pictures of Space-Filling or Ball-and-Stick Models," *Computers and Chemistry,* 1, 1977, 161–166.

KNOW80   Knowlton, K., "Progressive Transmission of Gray-Scale and Binary Pictures by Simple, Efficient, and Loss-less Encoding Schemes," *Proc. of IEEE,* 68(7), 1980, 885–896.

KNUT69   Knuth, D.E., *The Art of Computer Programming, Volume 2: Seminumerical Algorithms,* Addison-Wesley, Reading, MA, 1969.

KNUT87   Knuth, D., "Digital Halftones by Dot Diffusion," *ACM TOG,* 6(4), October 1987, 245–273.

KOBA87   Kobayashi, H., T. Nakamura, and Y. Shigei, "Parallel Processing of an Object Synthesis Using Ray Tracing," *Visual Computer,* 3(1), February 1987, 13–22.

KOCA87   Koçak, H., Bisshopp. F., Laidlaw, D.. and T. Banchoff, "Topology and Mechanics with Computer Graphics: Linear Hamiltonian Systems in Four Dimensions," *Advances in Applied Mathematics,* 1986, 282–308.

KOCH84   Kochanek, D., and R. Bartels. "Interpolating Splines with Local Tension, Continuity, and Bias Control," *SIGGRAPH 84,* 33–4..

KOIV88   Koivunen, M., and M. Mäntylä, "HutWindows: An Improved Architecture for a User Interface Management System," *CG & A* 8(1), January 1988, 43–52.

KORE82   Korein, J.U., and N.I. Badler. "Techniques for Generating the Goal-Directed Motion of Articulated Structures," *CG & A,* 2(11), November 1982, 71–81.

KORE83   Korein, J., and N. Badler, "Temporal Anti-Aliasing in Computer Generated Animation," *SIGGRAPH 83,* 377–388.

KREB79   Krebs, M., and J. Wolf, "Design Principles for the Use of Color in Displays," *Proceedings of the Society for Information Display,* 20, 1979, 10–15.

KRUE83   Krueger, M., *Artificial Reality,* Addison-Wesley, Reading, MA, 1983.

KURL88   Kurlander. D., and S. Feiner. "Editable Graphical Histories," in *Proc. 1988 IEEE Workshop on Visual Languages,* October 10–12, 1988, Pittsburgh, PA, 129–132.

KURL90   Kurlander, D., and S. Feiner, "A Visual Language for Browsing, Undoing, and Redoing Graphical Interface Commands," in Chang, S., ed., *Visual Languages and Visual Programming,* Plenum Press, New York, 1990, 257–275.

LAID86   Laidlaw, D.H., W.B. Trumbore, and J.F. Hughes, "Constructive Solid Geometry for Polyhedral Objects," *SIGGRAPH 86,* 161–170.

LAND85   Landauer, T., and D. Nachbar, "Selection from Alphabetic and Numeric Menu Trees Using a Touch-Sensitive Screen: Breadth, Depth, and Width," in *Proceedings CHI '85 Human Factors in Computing Systems Conference,* ACM, New York, 1985, 73–78.

LANE79   Lane, J., and L. Carpenter, "A Generalized Scan Line Algorithm for the Computer Display of Parametrically Defined Surfaces," *CGIP,* 11(3), November 1979, 290–297.

LANE80a   Lane, J., and R. Riesenfeld, "A Theoretical Development for the Computer Generation of Piecewise Polynomial Surfaces," *IEEE Transactions on Pattern Analysis and Machine Intelligence,* PAMI-2(1), January 1980, 35–46.

LANE80b   Lane, J., L. Carpenter, T. Whitted, and J. Blinn, "Scan Line Methods for Displaying Parametrically Defined Surfaces," *CACM,* 23(1), January 1980, 23–34. Also in BEAT82, 468–479.

LANT84   Lantz, K., and W. Nowicki, "Structured Graphics for Distributed Systems," *ACM TOG,* 3(1), January 1984, 23–51.

LANT87   Lantz, K., P. Tanner, C. Binding, K. Huang, and A. Dwelly, "Reference Models, Window Systems, and Concurrency," in Olsen, D., ed., "ACM SIGGRAPH Workshop on Software Tools for User Interface Management," *Computer Graphics,* 21(2), April 1987, 87–97.

LASS87   Lasseter, J., "Principles of Traditional Animation Applied to 3D Computer Animation," *SIGGRAPH 87,* 35–44.

LAYB79   Laybourne, K., *The Animation Book,* Crown, New York, 1979.

LEAF74   Leaf, C., *The Owl Who Married a Goose,* film, National Film Board of Canada, 1974.

LEAF77   Leaf, C., *The Metamorphosis of Mr. Samsa,* film, National Film Board of Canada, 1977.

LEE85a   Lee, S., W. Buxton, and K. Smith, "A Multi-touch Three Dimensional Touch-sensitive Tablet," in *Proceedings of CHI '85 Human Factors in Computing Systems Conference,* ACM, New York, 1985, 21–25.

LEE85b   Lee, M.E., R.A. Redner, and S.P. Uselton, "Statistically Optimized Sampling for Distributed Ray Tracing," *SIGGRAPH 85,* 61–67.

LEVI76   Levin, J., "A Parametric Algorithm for Drawing Pictures of Solid Objects Composed of Quadric Surfaces," *CACM,* 19(10), October 1976, 555–563.

LEVI84   Levinthal, A., and T. Porter, "Chap—a SIMD Graphics Processor," *SIGGRAPH 84,* 77–82.

LEVO78   Levoy, M., *Computer Assisted Cartoon Animation,* Master's Thesis, Department of Architecture, Cornell University, Ithaca, NY, August 1978.

LEVO82   Levoy, M., "Area Flooding Algorithms," in *Two-Dimensional Computer Animation, Course Notes 9 for SIGGRAPH 82,* Boston, MA, July 26–30, 1982.

LEVO89   Levoy, M., "Design for a Real-Time High-Quality Volume Rendering Workstation," in *Proceedings of the Volume Visualization Workshop,* Department of Computer Science, University of North Carolina at Chapel Hill, May 18-19, 1989, 85–90.

LIAN83   Liang, Y-D., and B.A. Barsky, "An Analysis and Algorithm for Polygon Clipping," *CACM,* 26(11), November 1983, 868–877, and Corrigendum, *CACM,* 27(2), February 1984, 151.

LIAN84   Liang, Y-D., and Barsky, B., "A New Concept and Method for Line Clipping," *ACM TOG,* 3(1), January 1984, 1–22.

LIEB78   Lieberman, H., "How to Color in a Coloring Book," *SIGGRAPH 78,* 111–116.

LIEN87   Lien, S.L., M. Shantz, and V. Pratt, "Adaptive Forward Differencing for Rendering Curves and Surfaces," *SIGGRAPH 87,* 111–118.

LIND68   Lindenmayer, A, "Mathematical Models for Cellular Interactions in Development, Parts I and II," *J. Theor. Biol.*, 18, 1968, 280–315.

LINT89   Linton, M., J. Vlissides, and P. Calder, "Composing User Interfaces with Inter-Views," *IEEE Computer*, 22(2), February 1989, 3–22.

LIPS79   Lipscomb, J.S., *Three-Dimensional Cues for a Molecular Computer Graphics System*, Ph.D. Thesis, Department of Computer Science, University of North Carolina at Chapel Hill, 1979.

LOUT70   Loutrel, P.P., "A Solution to the Hidden-Line Problem for Computer-Drawn Polyhedra," *IEEE Trans. on Computers*, EC-19(3), March 1970, 205–213. Also in FREE80, 221–229.

LUCA84   Lucasfilm, Ltd., *The Adventures of André and Wally B.*, film, August 1984.

MACH78   Machover, C., "A Brief Personal History of Computer Graphics," *Computer*, 11(11), November 1978, 38–45.

MACK86   Mackinlay, J., "Automating the Design of Graphical Presentation of Relational Information," *ACM TOG*, 5(2), April 1986, 110–141.

MAGI68   Mathematical Applications Group, Inc., "3-D Simulated Graphics Offered by Service Bureau," *Datamation*, 13(1), February 1968, 69.

MAGN85   Magnenat-Thalmann, N., and Thalmann, D., *Computer Animation: Theory and Practice*, Springer-Verlag, Tokyo, 1985.

MAHL72   Mahl, R., "Visible Surface Algorithms for Quadric Patches," *IEEE Trans. on Computers*, C-21(1), January 1972, 1–4.

MAHN73   Mahnkopf, P., and J.L. Encarnação, *FLAVIS—A Hidden Line Algorithm for Displaying Spatial Constructs Given by Point Sets*, Technischer Bericht Nr. 148, Heinrich Hertz Institut, Berlin, 1973.

MAMM89   Mammen, A., "Transparency and Antialiasing Algorithms Implemented with the Virtual Pixel Maps Technique," *CG & A*, 9(4), July 1989, 43–55.

MAND77   Mandelbrot, B., *Fractals: Form, Chance and Dimension*, W.H. Freeman, San Francisco, CA, 1977.

MAND82   Mandelbrot. B., Technical Correspondence, *CACM*, 25(8), August 1982, 581–583.

MÄNT88   Mäntylä, M. *Introduction to Solid Modeling*, Computer Science Press, Rockville, MD, 1988.

MARC80   Marcus, A., "Computer-Assisted Chart Making from the Graphic Designer's Perspective," *SIGGRAPH 80*, 247–253.

MARC82   Marcus, A., "Color: A Tool for Computer Graphics Communication," in Greenberg, D., A. Marcus, A. Schmidt, and V. Gorter, *The Computer Image*, Addison-Wesley, Reading, MA, 1982, 76–90.

MARC84   Marcus, A., "Corporate Identity for Iconic Interface Design: The Graphic Design Perspective," *CG & A*, 4(12), December 1984, 24–32.

MARK80   Markowsky, G., and M.A. Wesley, "Fleshing Out Wire Frames," *IBM Journal of Research and Development*, 24(5), September 1980, 582–597.

MARS85   Marsden, J., and A. Weinstein, *Calculus I, II, and III*, second edition, Springer Verlag, New York, 1985.

MART89   Martin, G., "The Utility of Speech Input in User–Computer Interfaces," *International Journal of Man–Machine Studies*, 30(4), April 1989, 355–376.

MASS85   Massachusetts Computer Corporation (MASSCOMP), *Graphics Application Programming Manual*, Order No. M-SP40-AP, MASSCOMP, Westford, MA, 1985.

MAUL89   Maulsby, D., and I. Witten, "Inducing Programs in a Direct Manipulation Environment," in *Proceedings CHI 1989*, ACM, New York, 1989, 57–62.

MAX79   Max, N.L., "ATOMLLL: - ATOMS with Shading and Highlights," *SIGGRAPH 79*, 165–173.

MAX81   Max, N., *Carla's Island*, animation, *ACM SIGGRAPH 81 Video Review*, 5, 1981.

MAX82   Max, N., "SIGGRAPH '84 Call for Omnimax Films," Computer Graphics, 16(4), December 1982, 208–214.

MAX84   Max, N.L., "Atoms with Transparency and Shadows," *CVGIP*, 27(1), July 1984, 46–63.

MAX86   Max, N., "Atmospheric Illumination and Shadows," *SIGGRAPH 86*, 117–124.

MAXW46   Maxwell, E. A., *Methods of Plane Projective Geometry Based on the Use of General Homogeneous Coordinates*, Cambridge University Press, Cambridge, England, 1946.

MAXW51   Maxwell, E. A., *General Homogeneous Coordinates in Space of Three Dimensions*, Cambridge University Press, Cambridge, England, 1951.

MAYH90   Mayhew, D., *Principles and Guidelines in User Interface Design*, Prentice-Hall, Englewood Cliffs, NJ, 1990.

MCIL83   McIlroy, M.D., "Best Approximate Circles on Integer Grids," *ACM TOG*, 2(4), October 1983, 237–263.

MCLE88   McLeod, J., "HP Delivers Photo Realism on an Interactive System," *Electronics*, 61(6), March 17, 1988, 95–97.

MCMI87   McMillan, L., "Graphics at 820 MFLOPS," *ESD: The Electronic Systems Design Magazine*, 17(9), September 1987, 87–95.

MEAG80   Meagher, D., *Octree Encoding: A New Technique for the Representation, Manipulation, and Display of Arbitrary 3-D Objects by Computer*, Technical Report IPL-TR-80-111, Image Processing Laboratory, Rensselaer Polytechnic Institute, Troy, NY, October 1980.

MEAG82a Meagher, D., "Geometric Modeling Using Octree Encoding," *CGIP*, 19(2), June 1982, 129–147.

MEAG82b Meagher, D., "Efficient Synthetic Image Generation of Arbitrary 3-D Objects," in *Proceedings of the IEEE Computer Society Conference on Pattern Recognition and Image Processing*, IEEE Computer Socitey Press, Washington, DC, 1982.

MEAG84   Meagher, D., "The Solids Engine: A Processor for Interactive Solid Modeling," in *Proceedings of NICOGRAPH '84*, Tokyo, November 1984.

MEAG85   Meagher, D., "Applying Solids Processing to Medical Planning," in *Proceedings of NCGA '85*, Dallas, 1985, 101–109.

MEGA89   Megatek Corporation, *Sigma 70 Advanced Graphics Workstations*, Megatek Corporation, San Diego, CA, 1989.

MEIE83   Meier, B., *Brim*, Computer Graphics Group Documentation, Computer Science Department, Brown University, Providence, RI, 1983.

MEIE88   Meier, B., "ACE: A Color Expert System for User Interface Design," in *Proceedings of the ACM SIGGRAPH Symposium on User Interface Software*, ACM, New York, 117–128, 1988.

MEYE80   Meyer, G.W., and D.P. Greenberg, "Perceptual Color Spaces for Computer Graphics," *SIGGRAPH 80*, 254–261.

MEYE83   Meyer, G., *Colorimetry and Computer Graphics*, Program of Computer Graphics, Cornell University, Ithaca, NY, 1983.

MEYE88   Meyer, G., and Greenberg, D., "Color-defective Vision and Computer Graphic Displays," *CG & A*, 8(5), September 1988, 28–40.

MICH71   Michaels, S., "QWERTY Versus Alphabetical Keyboards as a Function of Typing Skill," *Human Factors*, 13(5), October 1971, 419–426.

MICR89   Microsoft Corporation, *Presentation Manager*, Microsoft Corporation, Bellevue, WA, 1989.

MILL87   Miller, J.R., "Geometric Approaches to Nonplanar Quadric Surface Intersection Curves," *ACM TOG*, 6(4), October 1987, 274–307

MILL88a   Miller, G.S.P., "The Motion Dynamics of Snakes and Worms," *SIGGRAPH 88*, 169–178.

MILL88b   Miller, G.S.P., "The Motion Dynamics of Snakes and Worms," lecture at ACM SIGGRAPH '88.

MILL88c   Miller, P., and M. Szczur, "Transportable Application Environment (TAE) Plus Experiences in 'Object'ively Modernizing a User Interface Environment," in *Proceedings of OOPSLA '88*, 58–70.

MILL89   Miller, J.R., "Architectural Issues in Solid Modelers," *CG & A*, 9(5), September 1989, 72–87.

MINS84   Minsky, M., "Manipulating Simulated Objects with Real-World Gestures Using a Force and Position Sensitive Screen," *SIGGRAPH 84*, 195–203.

MITC87   Mitchell, D.P., "Generating Antialiased Images at Low Sampling Densities," *SIGGRAPH 87*, 65–72.

MITC88   Mitchell, D.P., and A.N. Netravali, "Reconstruction Filters in Computer Graphics," *SIGGRAPH 88*, 221–228.

MOLN88   Molnar, S., "Combining Z-Buffer Engines for Higher-Speed Rendering," 1988 Eurographics Workshop on Graphics Hardware, Sophia-Antipolis, France, September, 1988. To appear in Kuijk, A.A.M., ed., *Advances in Computer Graphics Hardware III*, Proceedings of 1988 Eurographics Workshop on Graphics Hardware, Eurographics Seminars, Springer-Verlag, Berlin, 1989.

MORR86   Morris, J., M. Satyanarayanan, M.H. Conner, J.H. Howard, D.S.H. Rosenthal, and F.D. Smith, "Andrew: A Distributed Personal Computing Environment," *CACM*, 29(3), March 1986, 184–201.

MORT85   Mortenson, M., *Geometric Modeling*, Wiley, New York, 1985.

MUNS76   Munsell Color Company, *Book of Color*, Munsell Color Company, Baltimore, MD, 1976.

MURC85   Murch, G., "Using Color Effectively: Designing to Human Specifications," *Technical Communications*, Q4 1985, Tektronix Corporation, Beaverton, OR, 14–20.

MUSG89   Musgrave, F.K., "Prisms and Rainbows: A Dispersion Model for Computer Graphics," in *Proceedings of Graphics Interface '89*, London, Ontario, June 19–23, 1989, 227–234.

MYER68   Myer, T., and I. Sutherland, "On the Design of Display Processors," *CACM*, 11(6), June 1968, 410–414.

MYER75   Myers, A.J., *An Efficient Visible Surface Program*, Report to the National Science Foundation, Computer Graphics Research Group, Ohio State University, Columbus, OH, July 1975.

MYER84   Myers, B., "The User Interface for Sapphire," *CG & A*, 4(12), December 1984, 13–23.

MYER85   Myers, B., "The Importance of Percent-Done Progress Indicators for Computer-Human Interfaces," in *Proceedings CHI '85*, ACM, New York, 1985, 11–17.

MYER86   Myers, B., "Creating Highly-Interactive and Graphical User Interfaces by Demonstration," *SIGGRAPH 86*, 249–257.

MYER88   Myers, B., *Creating User Interfaces by Demonstration*, Academic Press, New York, 1988.

MYER89   Myers, B., "User-Interface Tools: Introduction and Survey," *IEEE Software*, 6(1), January 1989, 15–23.

NAIM87   Naiman, A., and A. Fournier, "Rectangular Convolution for Fast Filtering of Characters," *SIGGRAPH 87*, 233–242.

NARU87   Naruse, T., M. Yoshida, T. Takahashi, and S. Naito, "SIGHT—a Dedicated Computer Graphics Machine," *Computer Graphics Forum*, 6(4), December 1987, 327–334.

NAVA89   Navazo, I., "Extended Octree Representation of General Solids with Plane Faces: Model Structure and Algorithms," *Computers and Graphics*, 13(1), January 1989, 5–16.

NAYL90   Naylor, B.F., "Binary Space Partitioning Trees as an Alternative Representation of Polytopes," *CAD*, 22(4), May 1990, 250–253.

NEMO86   Nemoto, K., and T. Omachi, "An Adaptive Subdivision by Sliding Boundary Surfaces for Fast Ray Tracing," in *Proceedings of Graphics Interface '86*, 1986, 43–48.

NEWE72   Newell, M.E., R.G. Newell, and T.L. Sancha, "A Solution to the Hidden Surface Problem," in *Proceedings of the ACM National Conference 1972*, 443–450. Also in FREE80, 236–243.

NEWE74   Newell, M.E., *The Utilization of Procedure Models in Digital Image Synthesis*, Ph.D. Thesis, Technical Report UTEC-CSc-76-218, NTIS AD/A039 008/LL, Computer Science Department, University of Utah, Salt Lake City, UT, 1974.

NEWM68   Newman, W., "A System for Interactive Graphical Programming," *SJCC*, Thompson Books, Washington, DC, 1968, 47–54.

NEWM71   Newman, W. M., "Display Procedures," *CACM*, 14(10), 1971, 651–660.

NEWM73   Newman, W., and R. Sproull, *Principles of Interactive Computer Graphics*, McGraw-Hill, New York, 1973.

NEWM79   Newman, W., and R. Sproull, *Principles of Interactive Computer Graphics*, 2nd ed., McGraw-Hill, New York, 1979.

NICH87   Nicholl, T.M., D.T. Lee, and R.A. Nicholl, "An Efficient New Algorithm for 2-D Line Clipping: Its Development and Analysis," *SIGGRAPH 87*, 253–262.

NICO77   Nicodemus, F.E., J.C. Richmond, J.J. Hsia, I.W. Ginsberg, and T. Limperis, *Geometrical Considerations and Nomenclature for Reflectance*, NBS Monograph 160, U.S. Department of Commerce, Washington DC, October 1977.

NIEL86   Nielson, G., and D. Olsen, Jr., "Direct Manipulation Techniques for 3D Objects Using 2D Locator Devices," in *Proceedings of the 1986 Workshop on Interactive 3D Graphics*, ACM, New York, 1987, 175–182.

NISH83a   Nishimura, H., H. Ohno, T. Kawata, I. Shirakawa, and K. Omura, "LINKS-1: A Parallel Pipelined Multimicrocomputer System for Image Creation," in *Proceedings of the Tenth International Symposium on Computer Architecture, ACM SIGARCH Newsletter*, 11(3), 1983, 387–394.

NISH83b   Nishita, T. and E. Nakamae, "Half-Tone Representation of 3-D Objects Illuminated by Area Sources or Polyhedron Sources," *Proc. IEEE Computer Society International Computer Software and Applications Conference (COMPSAC)*, IEEE Computer Society, Washington, DC, November 1983, 237–241.

NISH85a   Nishita, T., and E. Nakamae, "Continuous Tone Representation of Three-Dimensional Objects Taking Account of Shadows and Interreflection," *SIGGRAPH 85*, 23–30.

NISH85b   Nishita, T., I. Okamura, and E. Nakamae, "Shading Models for Point and Linear Sources," *ACM TOG*, 4(2), April 1985, 124–146.

NISH86   Nishita, T., and E. Nakamae, "Continuous Tone Representation of Three-Dimensional Objects Illuminated by Sky Light," *SIGGRAPH 86*, 125–132.

NISH87   Nishita, T., Y. Miyawaki, and E. Nakamae, "A Shading Model for Atmospheric Scattering Considering Luminous Intensity Distribution of Light Sources," *SIGGRAPH 87*, 303–310.

NOLL67   Noll, M., "A Computer Technique for Displaying N-dimensional Hyperobjects,"
            CACM, 10(8), August 1967, 469–473.

NORM88   Norman, D., *The Psychology of Everyday Things*. Basic Books, New York, 1988.

OKIN84   Okino, N., Y. Kakazu, and M. Morimoto, "Extended Depth-Buffer Algorithms for
            Hidden Surface Visualization," *CG & A*, 4(5), May 1984, 79–88.

OLIV85   Oliver, M., "Display Algorithms for Quadtrees and Octtrees and their Hardware
            Realisation," in Kessener, L., F. Peters, and M. van Lierop, eds., *Data Structures for
            Raster Graphics*, Springer-Verlag, Berlin, 1986, 9–37.

OLSE83   Olsen, D., and E. Dempsey, "SYNGRAPH: A Graphical User Interface Generator,"
            SIGGRAPH 83, 43–50.

OLSE84a   Olsen, D., "Pushdown Automata for User Interface Management," *ACM TOG*, 3(3),
            July 1984, 177–203.

OLSE84b   Olsen, D., W. Buxton, R. Ehrich, D. Kasik, J. Rhyne, and J. Sibert, "A Context for
            User Interface Management," *CG & A*, 4(12), December 1984, 33–42.

OLSE86   Olsen, D., "MIKE: The Menu Interaction Kontrol Environment," *ACM TOG*, 5(4),
            October 1986, 318–344.

OLSE87   Olsen, D., ed., ACM SIGGRAPH Workshop on Software Tools for User Interface
            Management, *Computer Graphics*, 21(2), April 1987, 71–147.

OLSE88   Olsen, D., "Macros by Example in a Graphical UIMS," *CG & A*, 8(1), January 1988,
            68–78.

OLSE89   Olsen, D., "A Programming Language Basis for User Interface Management," in
            Proceedings CHI '89, ACM, New York, 1989, 171–176.

OPEN89a   Open Software Foundation, *OSF/MOTIF™ Manual*, Open Software Foundation,
            Cambridge, MA, 1989.

OPEN89b   Open Software Foundation, *OSF/MOTF™ Style Guide*, Open Software Foundation,
            Cambridge, MA, 1989.

OSTW31   Ostwald, W., *Colour Science*, Winsor & Winsor, London, 1931.

PAET86   Paeth, A.W., "A Fast Algorithm for General Raster Rotation," in *Proceedings
            Graphics Interface '86*, Canadian Information Processing Society, 1986, 77–81.

PAET89   Paeth, A. W., "Fast Algorithms for Color Correction," *Proceedings of the Society for
            Information Display*, 30(3), Q3 1989, 169–175, reprinted as Technical Report
            CS-89-42, Department of Computer Science, University of Waterloo, Waterloo,
            Canada, 1989.

PAIN89   Painter, J., and K. Sloan, "Antialiased Ray Tracing by Adaptive Progressive Refine-
            ment," *SIGGRAPH 89*, 281–288.

PALA88   Palay, A., W. Hansen, M. Kazar M. Sherman, M. Wadlow, T. Neuendorffer, Z.
            Stern, M. Bader, and T. Peters, "The Andrew Toolkit: An Overview," in *Proceedings
            1988 Winter USENIX*, February 1988, 9–21.

PARK80   Parke, F., "Simulation and Expected Performance Analysis of Multiple Processor
            Z-Buffer Systems," *SIGGRAPH 80*, 48–56.

PARK82   Parke, F.I., "Parameterized Models for Facial Animation," *CG & A*, 2(11), November
            1982, 61–68.

PARK88   Parker, R., *Looking Good in Print: A Guide to Basic Design for Desktop Publishing*,
            Ventana Press, Chapel Hill, NC, 1988.

PAVL81   Pavlidis, T. "Contour Filling in Raster Graphics," *CGIP*, 10(2), June 1979, 126–141.

PEAC85   Peachey, D.R., "Solid Texturing of Complex Surfaces," *SIGGRAPH 85*, 279–286.

PEAR86   Pearson, G., and M. Weiser, "Of Moles and Men: The Design of Foot Controls for
            Workstations," in *Proceedings CHI '86*, ACM, New York, 1986, 333–339.

PEAR88   Pearson, G., and M. Weiser, "Exploratory Evaluation of a Planar Foot-operated Cursor Positioning Device," in *Proceedings CHI '88,* ACM, New York, 1988, 13–18.

PEIT86   Peitgen, H.-O., and P.H. Richter, *The Beauty of Fractals: Images of Complex Dynamical Systems,* Springer-Verlag, Berlin, 1986.

PEIT88   Peitgen, H.-O., and D. Saupe, eds., *The Science of Fractal Images*, Springer-Verlag, New York, 1988.

PERL85   Perlin, K., "An Image Synthesizer," *SIGGRAPH 85,* 287–296.

PERL89   Perlin, K., and E. Hoffert, "Hypertexture," *SIGGRAPH 89*, 253–262.

PERR85   Perry, T., and P. Wallach, "Computer Displays: New Choices, New Tradeoffs," *IEEE Spectrum*, 22(7), July 1985, 52–59.

PERR89   Perry, T., and J. Voelcker, "Of Mice and Menus: Designing the User-Friendly Interface," *IEEE Spectrum*, 26(9), September 1989, 46–51.

PERS85   Personics Corporation, *View Control System*, Concord, MA, 1985.

PETE86   Peterson, J.W., R.G. Bogart, and S.W. Thomas, *The Utah Raster Toolkit,* University of Utah, Department of Computer Science, Salt Lake City, UT, 1986.

PHIG88   PHIGS+ Committee, Andries van Dam, chair, "PHIGS+ Functional Description, Revision 3.0," *Computer Graphics*, 22(3), July 1988, 125–218.

PIKE83   Pike, R., "Graphics in Overlapping Bitmap Layers," *ACM TOG*, 17(3), July 83, 331–356.

PIKE84   Pike, R., "Bitmap Graphics," in *Course Notes 4 for SIGGRAPH 84,* Minneapolis, MN, July 23–27,1984.

PINK83   Pinkham, R., M. Novak, and K. Guttag, "Video RAM Excels at Fast Graphics," *Electronic Design*, 31(17), Aug. 18, 1983, 161–182.

PITT67   Pitteway, M.L.V., "Algorithm for Drawing Ellipses or Hyperbolae with a Digital Plotter," *Computer J.,* 10(3), November 1967, 282–289.

PITT80   Pitteway, M.L.V., and D. J. Watkinson, "Bresenham's Algorithm with Grey-Scale," *CACM*, 23(11), November 1980, 625–626.

PITT87   Pitteway, M.L.V., "Soft Edging Fonts," Computer Graphics Technology and Systems, in *Proceedings of the Conference Held at Computer Graphics '87,* London, October 1987, Advanced computing series, 9, Online Publications, London, 1987.

PIXA86   Pixar Corporation, *Luxo, Jr.,* film, Pixar Corporation, San Rafael, CA, 1986.

PIXA88   Pixar Corporation, *The RenderMan Interface,* Version 3.0. Pixar Corporation, San Rafael, CA, May 1988.

PLAT81   Platt, S.M., and N.I. Badler, "Animating Facial Expressions," *SIGGRAPH 81,* 245–252.

PLAT88   Platt, J.C., and A.H. Barr, "Constraint Methods for Flexible Models," *SIGGRAPH 88,* 279–288.

PORT79   Porter, T., "The Shaded Surface Display of Large Molecules," *SIGGRAPH 79,* 234–236.

PORT84   Porter, T., and T. Duff, "Compositing Digital Images," *SIGGRAPH 84,* 253–259.

POSC89   Posch, K.C., and W.D. Fellner, "The Circle-Brush Algorithm," *ACM TOG*, 8(1), January 1989, 1–24.

POTM82   Potmesil, M., and I. Chakravarty, "Synthetic Image Generation with a Lens and Aperture Camera Model," *ACM TOG*, 1(2), April 1982, 85–108.

POTM83   Potmesil, M., and I. Chakravarty, "Modeling Motion Blur in Computer-Generated Images," *SIGGRAPH 83,* 389–399.

POTM89   Potmesil, M., and E. Hoffert, "Pixel Machine: A Parallel Image Computer," *SIGGRAPH 89,* 69–78.

POTT88   Potter, R., L. Weldon, and B. Shneiderman, "Improving the Accuracy of Touch Screens: An Experimental Evaluation of Three Strategies," in *Proceedings CHI '88*, ACM, New York, 27–32.

PRAT84   Pratt, M., "Solid Modeling and the Interface Between Design and Manufacture," *CG & A*, 4(7), July 1984, 52–59.

PRAT85   Pratt, V., "Techniques for Conic Splines," *SIGGRAPH 85*, 151–159.

PREP85   Preparata, F. P., and M.I. Shamos. *Computational Geometry: An Introduction*, Springer-Verlag, New York, 1985.

PRES88   Press, W.H., B.P. Flannery, S.A. Teukolskym, and W.T. Vetterling, *Numerical Recipes in C: The Art of Scientific Computing*, Cambridge University Press, Cambridge, England, 1988.

PRIN71   Prince, D., *Interactive Graphics for Computer Aided Design*, Addison-Wesley, Reading, MA, 1971.

PRIT77   Pritchard, D.H., "U.S. Color Television Fundamentals—A Review," *IEEE Transactions on Consumer Electronics*, CE-23(4), November 1977, 467–478.

PRUS88   Prusinkiewicz, P., A. Lindenmayer, and J. Hanan, "Developmental Models of Herbaceous Plants for Computer Imagery Purposes," *SIGGRAPH 88*, 141–150.

PUTN86   Putnam, L.K., and P.A. Subrahmanyam. "Boolean Operations on n-Dimensional Objects," *CG & A*, 6(6), June 1986, 43–51.

QUIN82   Quinlan, K.M., and J.R. Woodwark, "A Spatially-Segmented Solids Database—Justification and Design," in *Proc. CAD '82 Conf.*, Fifth International Conference and Exhibit on Computers in Design Engineering, Mar. 30–Apr 1, 1982, Butterworth, Guildford, Great Britain, 1982, 126–132.

RATL72   Ratliff, F., "Contour and Contrast," *Scientific American*, 226(6), June 1972, 91–101. Also in BEAT82, 364–375.

REDD78   Reddy, D., and S. Rubin, *Representation of Three-Dimensional Objects*, CMU-CS-78-113, Computer Science Department. Carnegie-Mellon University, Pittsburgh, PA, 1978.

REEV81   Reeves, W.T., "Inbetweening for Computer Animation Utilizing Moving Point Constraints," *SIGGRAPH 81*, 263–269.

REEV83   Reeves, W.T., "Particle Systems—A Technique for Modeling a Class of Fuzzy Objects," *SIGGRAPH 83*, 359–376.

REEV85   Reeves, W.T., and R. Blau, "Approximate and Probabilistic Algorithms for Shading and Rendering Particle Systems," *SIGGRAPH 85*, 313–322.

REEV87   Reeves, W.T., D.H. Salesin, and R.L. Cook, "Rendering Antialiased Shadows with Depth Maps," *SIGGRAPH 87*, 283–291.

REFF88   de Reffye, P., C. Edelin, J. Françcn, M. Jaeger, and C. Puech, "Plant Models Faithful to Botanical Structure and Development," *SIGGRAPH 88*, 151–158.

REIS82   Reisner, P., "Further Developments Toward Using Formal Grammar as a Design Tool," in *Proceedings of the Human Factors in Computer Systems Conference*, ACM, New York, 1982, 304–308.

REQU77   Requicha, A.A.G., *Mathematical Models of Rigid Solids*, Tech. Memo 28, Production Automation Project, University of Rochester, Rochester, NY, 1977.

REQU80   Requicha, A.A.G., "Representations for Rigid Solids: Theory, Methods, and Systems," *ACM Computing Surveys*, 12(4), December 1980, 437–464.

REQU82   Requicha, A.A.G., and H.B. Voelcker, "Solid Modeling: A Historical Summary and Contemporary Assessment," *CG & A*, 2(2), March 1982, 9–24.

REQU83   Requicha, A.A.G., and H.B. Voelcker, "Solid Modeling: Current Status and Research Directions," *CG & A*, 3(7), October 1983, 25–37.

REQU84   Requicha, A.A.G., "Representation of Tolerances in Solid Modeling: Issues and Alternative Approaches," in Pickett, M., and J. Boyse, eds., *Solid Modeling by Computers,* Plenum Press, New York, 1984, 3–22.

REQU85   Requicha, A.A.G., and H.B. Voelcker, "Boolean Operations in Solid Modeling: Boundary Evaluation and Merging Algorithms," *Proc. IEEE,* 73(1), January 1985, 30–44.

REYN82   Reynolds, C.W., "Computer Animation with Scripts and Actors," *SIGGRAPH 82,* 289–296.

REYN87   Reynolds, C.W., "Flocks, Herds and Schools: A Distributed Behavioral Model," *SIGGRAPH 87,* 25–34.

RHOD89   Rhoden, D., and C. Wilcox, "Hardware Acceleration for Window Systems," *SIGGRAPH 89,* 61–67.

RHYN87   Rhyne, J., "Dialogue Management for Gestural Interfaces," *Proceedings ACM SIGGRAPH Workshop on Tools for User Interface Management,* in *Computer Graphics,* 21(2), April 1987, 137–145.

ROBE63   Roberts, L.G., *Machine Perception of Three Dimensional Solids,* Lincoln Laboratory, TR 315, MIT, Cambridge, MA, May 1963. Also in Tippet, J.T., *et al.,* eds., *Optical and Electro-Optical Information Processing,* MIT Press, Cambridge, MA, 1964, 159–197.

ROBE65   Roberts, L.G., *Homogeneous Matrix Representations and Manipulation of N-Dimensional Constructs,* Document MS 1405, Lincoln Laboratory, MIT, Cambridge, MA, 1965.

ROGE85   Rogers, D.F., *Procedural Elements for Computer Graphics,* McGraw-Hill, New York, 1985.

ROGO83   Rogowitz, B., "The Human Visual System: A Guide for the Display Technologist," *Proceedings Society for Information Display,* 24(3), 1983.

ROMN69   Romney, G.W., G.S. Watkins, and D.C. Evans, "Real Time Display of Computer Generated Half-Tone Perspective Pictures," in *Proceedings 1968 IFIP Congress,* North Holland Publishing Co., 1969, 973–978.

ROSE83   Rosenthal, D., "Managing Graphical Resources," *Computer Graphics,* 17(1), January 1983, 38–45.

ROSE85   Rose, C., B. Hacker, R. Anders, K. Wittney, M. Metzler, S. Chernicoff, C. Espinosa, A. Averill, B. Davis, and B. Howard, *Inside Macintosh,* I, Addison-Wesley, Reading, MA, 1985, I-35–I-213.

ROSS86   Rossignac, J.R., and A.A.G. Requicha, "Depth-Buffering Display Techniques for Constructive Solid Geometry," *CG & A,* 6(9), September 1986, 29–39.

ROSS89   Rossignac, J., and H. Voelcker, "Active Zones in CSG for Accelerating Boundary Evaluation, Redundancy Elimination, Interference Detection, and Shading Algorithms," *ACM TOG,* 8(1), January 1989, 51–87.

ROTH76   Rothstein, J., and C.F.R. Weiman, "Parallel and Sequential Specification of a Context Sensitive Language for Straight Lines on Grids," *CGIP,* 5(1), March 1976, 106–124.

ROTH82   Roth, S., "Ray Casting for Modeling Solids," *CGIP,* 18(2), February 1982, 109–144.

RUBE83   Rubel, A., "Graphic Based Applications—Tools to Fill the Software Gap," *Digital Design,* 3(7), July 1983, 17–30.

RUBE84   Rubenstein, R., and H. Hersh, *The Human Factor—Designing Computer Systems for People,* Digital Press, Burlington, MA, 1984.

RUBE88   Rubenstein, R., *Digital Typography,* Addison-Wesley, Reading, MA, 1988.

RUBI80   Rubin, S.M., and T. Whitted, "A 3-Dimensional Representation for Fast Rendering of Complex Scenes," *SIGGRAPH 80,* 110–116.

RUSH86   Rushmeier, H.E., *Extending the Radiosity Method to Transmitting and Specularly Reflecting Surfaces*, M.S. Thesis, Mechanical Engineering Department, Cornell University, Ithaca, NY, 1986.

RUSH87   Rushmeier, H., and K. Torrance, "The Zonal Method for Calculating Light Intensities in the Presence of a Participating Medium," *SIGGRAPH 87*, 293–302.

SABE88   Sabella, P., "A Rendering Algorithm for Visualizing 3D Scalar Fields," *SIGGRAPH 88*, 51–58.

SALE85   Salesin, D., and R. Barzel, *Two-Bit Graphics*, Computer Graphics Project, Computer Division, Lucasfilm, Ltd., San Rafael, CA, 1985; also in CG & A, 6(6), June 1986, 36–42.

SALM96   Salmon, G., *A Treatise on Conic Sections*, Longmans, Green, & Co., 10th edition, London 1896.

SALV87   Salvendy, G., ed., *Handbook of Human Factors*, Wiley, New York, 1987.

SAME84   Samet, H., "The Quadtree and Related Hierarchical Data Structures," *ACM Comp. Surv.*, 16(2), June 1984, 187–260.

SAME88a   Samet, H., and R. Webber, "Hierarchical Data Structures and Algorithms for Computer Graphics, Part I: Fundamentals." *CG & A*, 8(3), May 1988, 48–68.

SAME88b   Samet, H. and R. Webber, "Hierarchical Data Structures and Algorithms for Computer Graphics, Part II: Applications," *CG & A* 8(4), July 1988 59–75.

SAME89a   Samet, H., "Neighbor Finding in Images Represented by Octrees," *CGVIP*, 46(3), June 1989, 367–386.

SAME89b   Samet, H., "Implementing Ray Tracing with Octrees and Neighbor Finding," *Computers and Graphics*, 13(4), 1989, 445–460.

SAME90a   Samet, H., *Design and Analysis of Spatial Data Structures*, Addison-Wesley, Reading, MA, 1990.

SAME90b   Samet, H., *Applications of Spatial Data Structures: Computer Graphics, Image Processing and GIS*, Addison-Wesley, Reading, MA, 1990.

SARR83   Sarraga, R.F., "Algebraic Methods for Intersections of Quadric Surfaces in GMSOLID," *CVGIP* 22(2), May 1983, 222–238.

SCHA83   Schachter, B., *Computer Image Generation*, Wiley, New York, 1983.

SCHE86   Scheifler, R., and J. Gettys, "The X Window System," *ACM TOG*, 5(2), April 1986, 79–109.

SCHE88a   Scheifler, R.W., J. Gettys, and R. Newman, *X Window System*, Digital Press, 1988.

SCHE88b   Scherson, I.D., and E. Caspary, "Multiprocessing for Ray-Tracing: A Hierarchical Self-balancing Approach," *Visual Computer*, 4(4), October 1988, 188–196.

SCHM83   Schmid, C., *Statistical Graphics: Design Principles and Practice*, Wiley, New York, 1983.

SCHM86   Schmucker, K., "MacApp: An Application Framework," *Byte*, 11(8), August 1986, 189–193.

SCHU69   Schumacker, R., B. Brand, M. Gilliland, and W. Sharp, *Study for Applying Computer-Generated Images to Visual Simulation*, Technical Report AFHRL-TR-69-14, NTIS AD700375, U.S. Air Force Human Resources Lab., Air Force Systems Command, Brooks AFB, TX, September 1969.

SCHU80   Schumacker, R., "A New Visual System Architecture," in *Proceedings of the Second Interservice/Industry Training Equipment Conference*, Salt Lake City, UT, 16-20 November 1980.

SCHU85   Schulert, A., G. Rogers, and J. Hamilton. "ADM—A Dialog Manager," in *CHI '85 Proceedings*, San Francisco, CA, Apr 14–18, 1985, 177–183.

SCHW82   Schweitzer, D., and E. Cobb, "Scanline Rendering of Parametric Surfaces," *SIG-GRAPH 82,* 265–271.

SCHW87   Schwarz, M., W. Cowan, and J. Beatty, "An Experimental Comparison of RGB, YIQ, LAB, HSV, and Opponent Color Models," *ACM TOG,* 6(2), April 1987, 123–158.

SECH82   Sechrest, S., and D.P. Greenberg, "A Visible Polygon Reconstruction Algorithm," *ACM TOG,* 1(1), January 1982, 25–42.

SEDE84   Sederberg, T.W., and D.C. Anderson, "Ray Tracing of Steiner Patches," *SIGGRAPH 84,* 159–164.

SEDE86   Sederberg, T.W., and S.R. Parry, "Free-Form Deformation of Solid Geometric Models," *SIGGRAPH 86,* 151–160.

SEDG88   Sedgewick, R., *Algorithms,* second edition, Addison-Wesley, Reading, MA, 1988.

SELF79   Selfridge, P., and K. Sloan, *Raster Image File Format (RIFF): An Approach to Problems in Image Management,* TR61, Department of Computer Science, University of Rochester, Rochester, NY, 1979.

SELI89   Seligmann, D. and S. Feiner, "Specifying Composite Illustrations with Communicative Goals," *Proceedings of ACM UIST '89,* ACM, New York, 1989, 1–9.

SEQU89   Séquin, C.H. and E.K. Smyrl, "Parameterized Ray Tracing," *SIGGRAPH 89,* 307–314.

SHAN87   Shantz, M., and S. Lien, "Shading Bicubic Patches," *SIGGRAPH 87,* 189–196.

SHAN89   Shantz, M. and S. Chang, "Rendering Trimmed NURBS with Adaptive Forward Differencing," *SIGGRAPH 89,* 189–198.

SHAO88   Shao, M.Z., Q.S. Peng, and Y.D. Liang, "A New Radiosity Approach by Procedural Refinements for Realistic Image Synthesis," *SIGGRAPH 88,* 93–101.

SHAW91   Shaw, C.D., M. Green, and J. Schaeffer, "A VLSI Architecture for Image Composition," 1988 Eurographics Workshop on Graphics Hardware, Sophia-Antipolis, France, September, 1988. In Kuijk, A.A.M., ed., *Advances in Computer Graphics Hardware III,* Eurographics Seminars, Springer-Verlag, Berlin, 1991, 183–199.

SHER79   Sherr, S., *Electronic Displays,* Wiley, New York, 1979.

SHIN87   Shinya, M., T. Takahashi, and S. Naito, "Principles and Applications of Pencil Tracing," *SIGGRAPH 87,* 45–54.

SHIR86   Shires, G., "A New VLSI Graphics Coprocessor—The Intel 82786," *CG & A,* 6(10), October 1986, 49–55.

SHNE83   Shneiderman, B., "Direct Manipulation: A Step Beyond Programming Languages," *IEEE Computer,* 16(8), August 1983, 57–69.

SHNE86   Shneiderman, B., *Designing the User Interface: Strategies for Effective Human-Computer Interaction,* Addison-Wesley, Reading, MA, 1986.

SHOE85   Shoemake, K., "Animating Rotation with Quaternion Curves," *SIGGRAPH 85,* 245–254.

SHOU79   Shoup, R.G., "Color Table Animation," *SIGGRAPH 79,* 8–13.

SHOW89   Marketing Department, *Brochure,* Showscan Film Corp., Culver City, CA, 1989.

SIBE86   Sibert, J., W. Hurley, and T. Bleser, "An Object-Oriented User Interface Management System," *SIGGRAPH 86,* 259–268.

SIEG81   Siegel, R., and J. Howell, *Thermal Radiation Heat Transfer,* second edition, Hemisphere, Washington, DC, 1981.

SIG85   *Introduction to Image Processing, Course Notes 26 for SIGGRAPH 85,* San Francisco, California, July 1985.

SILL89   Sillion, F., and C. Puech, "A General Two-Pass Method Integrating Specular and Diffuse Reflection," *SIGGRAPH 89,* 335–344.

SIMP85   Simpson, C., M. McCauley, E. Roland, J. Ruth, and B. Williges, "System Design for Speech Recognition and Generation," *Human Factors*, 27(2), April 1985, 115–142.

SIMP87   Simpson, C., M. McCauley, E. Roland, J. Ruth, and B. Williges, "Speech Control and Displays," in Salvendy, G., ed., *Handbook of Human Factors*, Wiley, New York, 1987, 1490–1525.

SIOC89   Siochi, A., and H. R. Hartson, "Task-Oriented Representation of Asynchronous User Interfaces," in *Proceedings CHI '89*, ACM, New York, 183–188.

SKLA90   Sklar, D., "Implementation Issues for SPHICS (Simple PHIGS)," Technical Report, Computer Science Department, Brown University, Providence, RI, August 1990.

SLOA79   Sloan, K.R., and S.L. Tanimoto, "Progressive Refinement of Raster Images," *IEEE Transactions on Computers*, C-28(11), November 1979, 871–874.

SMIT78   Smith, A.R., "Color Gamut Transform Fairs," *SIGGRAPH 78*, 12–19.

SMIT79   Smith, A.R., "Tint Fill," *SIGGRAPH 79*, 276–283.

SMIT82   Smith, D., R. Kimball, B. Verplank, and E. Harslem, "Designing the Star User Interface," *Byte*, 7(4), April 1982, 242–282.

SMIT84   Smith, A.R., "Plants, Fractals and Formal Languages," *SIGGRAPH 84*, 1–10.

SMIT87   Smith, A.R., "Planar 2-pass Texture Mapping and Warping," *SIGGRAPH 87*, 263–272.

SMIT88   Smith, D.N., "Building Interfaces Interactively," in *Proceedings ACM SIGGRAPH Symposium on User Interface Software*, ACM, New York, 1988, 144–151.

SMIT89   Smith, A.R., "Geometry vs. Imaging," in *Proceedings of NCGA '89*, Philadelphia, PA, April 1989, 359–366.

SNOW83   Snowberry, K., S. Parkinson, and N. Sisson, "Computer Display Menus," *Ergonomics*, 26(7), July 1983, 699–712.

SNYD85   Snyder, H., "Image Quality: Measures and Visual Performance," in TANN85, 70–90.

SNYD87   Snyder, J.M. and A.H. Barr, "Ray Tracing Complex Models Containing Surface Tessellations," *SIGGRAPH 87*, 119–128.

SPAR78   Sparrow, E.M., and R.D. Cess, *Radiation Heat Transfer*, Hemisphere, Washington, DC, 1978.

SPRO82   Sproull, R.F., "Using Program Transformations to Derive Line-Drawing Algorithms," *ACM TOG*, 1(4), October 1982, 259–273.

SRIH81   Srihari, S., "Representation of Three-Dimensional Digital Images," *ACM Computing Surveys*, 13(4), December 1981, 399–424.

STAU78   Staudhammer, J., "On Display of Space Filling Atomic Models in Real Time," *SIGGRAPH 78*, 167–172.

STEI89   Steinhart, J., ed., *Introduction to Window Management*, Course Notes 11 for SIGGRAPH 89, Boston, MA, August 1989.

STER83   Stern, G., "Bbop—A System for 3D Keyframe Figure Animation," in *Introduction to Computer Animation, Course Notes 7 for SIGGRAPH 83*, New York, July 1983, 240–243.

STIN78   Stiny, G., and J. Gips, *Algorithmic Aesthetics: Computer Models for Criticism and Design in the Arts*, University of California Press, Berkeley, 1978.

STON88   Stone, M., W. Cowan, and J. Beatty, "Color Gamut Mapping and the Printing of Digital Color Images," *ACM TOG*, 7(3), October 1988, 249–292.

STOV82   Stover, H., "True Three-Dimensional Display of Computer Data," in *Proceedings of SPIE*, 367, August 1982, 141–144.

STRA88   Strauss, P., *BAGS: The Brown Animation Generation System*, Ph.D. Thesis, Technical Report CS-88-22, Computer Science Department, Brown University, Providence, RI, May 1988.

SUKA88   Sukaviriya, P., "Dynamic Construction of Animated Help from Application Context," in *Proceedings of the ACM SIGGRAPH Symposium on User Interface Software*, ACM, New York, 1988, 190–202.

SUKA90   Sukaviriya, P., and L. Moran, "User Interface for Asia," in Neilsen, J., ed., *Designing User Interfaces for International Use*, Elsevier, Amsterdam, 1990.

SUN86a   Sun Microsystems, *Programmer's Reference Manual for the Sun Window System*, Sun Microsystems, Mountain View, CA, 1986.

SUN86b   Sun Microsystems, *SunView™ Programmer's Guide*, Sun Microsystems, Mountain View, CA, 1986.

SUN87   Sun Microsystems, *NeWS™ Technical Overview*, Sun Microsystems, Mountain View, CA, 1987.

SUN89   Sun Microsystems, *OPEN LOOK Graphical User Interface*, Sun Microsystems, Mountain View, CA, 1989.

SUNF86   Sun Flex Corporation, *Touchpen*, Sun Flex, Novato, CA, 1986.

SUTH63   Sutherland, I.E., "Sketchpad: A Man–Machine Graphical Communication System," in *SJCC*, Spartan Books, Baltimore, MD, 1963.

SUTH65   Sutherland, I.E., "The Ultimate Display," in *Proceedings of the 1965 IFIP Congress*, 2, 1965, 506–508.

SUTH68   Sutherland, I.E., "A Head-Mounted Three Dimensional Display," in *FJCC 1968*, Thompson Books, Washington, DC, 757–764.

SUTH74a   Sutherland, I.E., R.F. Sproull, and R.A. Schumacker, "A Characterization of Ten Hidden-Surface Algorithms," *ACM Computing Surveys*, 6(1), March 1974, 1–55. Also in BEAT82, 387–441.

SUTH74b   Sutherland, I.E., and Hodgman, G.W., "Reentrant Polygon Clipping," *CACM*, 17(1), January 1974, 32–42.

SUTT78   Sutton, J., and R. Sprague, "A Survey of Business Applications," in *Proceedings American Institute for Decision Sciences 10th Annual Conference, Part II*, Atlanta, GA, 1978, 278.

SUYD86   Suydham, B., "Lexidata Does Instant Windows," *Computer Graphics World*, 9(2), February 1986, 57–58.

SWAN86   Swanson, R., and L. Thayer, "A Fast Shaded-Polygon Renderer," *SIGGRAPH 86*, 95–101.

SYMB85   Symbolics, Inc., *S-Dynamics*, Symbolics, Inc., Cambridge, MA, 1985.

TAMM82   Tamminen, M. and R. Sulonen, "The EXCELL Method for Efficient Geometric Access to Data," in *Proc. 19th ACM IEEE Design Automation Conf.*, Las Vegas, June 14–16, 1982, 345–351.

TAMM84   Tamminen, M., and H. Samet, "Efficient Octree Conversion by Connectivity Labeling," *SIGGRAPH 84*, 43–51.

TANA86   Tanaka, A.M., M. Kameyama, S. Kazama, and O. Watanabe, "A Rotation Method for Raster Images Using Skew Transformation," in *Proc. IEEE Conference on Computer Vision and Pattern Recognition*, June 1986, 272–277.

TANI77   Tanimoto, S.L., "A Graph-Theoretic Real-Time Visible Surface Editing Technique," *SIGGRAPH 77*, 223–228.

TANN85   Tannas, L. Jr., ed., *Flat-Panel Displays and CRTs*, Van Nostrand Reinhold, New York, 1985.

TEIT64   Teitelman, W., "Real-Time Recognition of Hand-Drawn Characters," in *FJCC 1964*, *AFIPS Conf. Proc.*, 24, Spartan Books, Baltimore. MD, 559.

TEIT86   Teitelman, W., "Ten Years of Window Systems—A Retrospective View," in Hopgood, F.R.A., *et al.*, eds., *Methodology of Window Management*, Springer-Verlag, New York, 1986, 35–46.

TERZ88   Terzopoulos, D., and K. Fleischer, "Modeling Inelastic Deformation: Viscoelasticity, Plasticity, Fracture," *SIGGRAPH 88*, 269–278.

TESL81   Tesler, L., "The Smalltalk Environment," *Byte*, 6(8), August 1981, 90–147.

TEXA89   Texas Instruments, Inc., *TMS34020 and TMS34082 User's Guide*, Texas Instruments, Dallas, TX, March 1989.

THIB87   Thibault, W.C., and B.F. Naylor, "Set Operations on Polyhedra Using Binary Space Partitioning Trees," *SIGGRAPH 87*, 153–162.

THOM84   Thomas, S.W., *Modeling Volumes Bounded by B-Spline Surfaces*, Ph.D. Thesis, Technical Report UUCS-84-009, Department of Computer Science, University of Utah, Salt Lake City, UT, June 1984.

THOM86   Thomas, S.W., "Dispersive Refraction in Ray Tracing," *The Visual Computer*, 2(1), January 1986, 3–8.

THOR79   Thornton, R.W., "The Number Wheel: A Tablet-Based Valuator for Three-Dimensional Positioning," *SIGGRAPH 79*, 102–107.

TILB76   Tilbrook, D., *A Newspaper Page Layout System*. M.Sc. Thesis, Department of Computer Science, University of Toronto, Toronto, Canada, 1976. Also see *ACM SIGGRAPH Video Tape Review*, 1, May 1980.

TILL83   Tiller, W., "Rational B-Splines for Curve and Surface Representation," *CG & A*, 3(6), September 1983, 61–69.

TILO80   Tilove, R.B., "Set Membership Classification: A Unified Approach to Geometric Intersection Problems," *IEEE Trans. on Computers*, C-29(10), October 1980, 847–883.

TORB87   Torborg, J., "A Parallel Processor Architecture for Graphics Arithmetic Operations," *SIGGRAPH 87*, 197–204.

TORR66   Torrance, K.E., E.M. Sparrow, and R.C. Birkebak, "Polarization, Directional Distribution, and Off-Specular Peak Phenomena in Light Reflected from Roughened Surfaces," *J. Opt. Soc. Am.*, 56(7), July 1966, 916–925.

TORR67   Torrance, K., and E.M. Sparrow, "Theory for Off-Specular Reflection from Roughened Surfaces," *J. Opt. Soc. Am.*, 57(9), September 1967, 1105–1114.

TOTH85   Toth, D.L., "On Ray Tracing Parametric Surfaces," *SIGGRAPH 85*, 171–179.

TOUL70   Touloukian, Y.S., and D.P. DeWitt, eds., *Thermophysical Properties of Matter: The TPRC Data Series, Vol. 7 (Thermal Radiative Properties: Metallic Elements and Alloys)*, Plenum, New York, 1970.

TOUL72a   Touloukian, Y.S., and D.P. DeWitt, eds., *Thermophysical Properties of Matter: The TPRC Data Series, Vol. 8 (Thermal Radiative Properties: Nonmetallic Solids)*, Plenum, New York, 1972.

TOUL72b   Touloukian, Y.S., D.P. DeWitt, and R.S. Hernicz, eds., *Thermophysical Properties of Matter: The TPRC Data Series, Vol. 9 (Thermal Radiative Properties: Coatings)*, Plenum, New York, 1972.

TRAU67   Traub, A.C., "Stereoscopic Display Using Rapid Varifocal Mirror Oscillations," *Applied Optics*, 6(6), June 1967, 1085–1087.

TRIC87   Tricoles, G., "Computer Generated Holograms: an Historical Review," *Applied Optics*, 26(20), October 1987, 4351–4360.

TROW75   Trowbridge, T.S., and K.P. Reitz, "Average Irregularity Representation of a Rough Surface for Ray Reflection," *J. Opt. Soc. Am.*, 65(5), May 1975, 531–536.

TUFT83   Tufte, E., *The Visual Display of Quantitative Information*, Graphics Press, Cheshire, CT, 1983.

TURK82   Turkowski, K., "Anti-Aliasing Through the Use of Coordinate Transformations," *ACM TOG*, 1(3), July 1982, 215–234.

TURN84   Turner, J.A., *A Set-Operation Algorithm for Two and Three-Dimensional Geometric Objects*, Architecture and Planning Research Laboratory, College of Architecture, University of Michigan, Ann Arbor, MI, August 1984.

ULIC87   Ulichney, R., *Digital Halftoning*, MIT Press, Cambridge, MA, 1987.

UPSO88   Upson, C., and M. Keeler, "V-BUFFER: Visible Volume Rendering," *SIGGRAPH 88*, 59–64.

UPST89   Upstill, S., *The RenderMan Companion: A Programmer's Guide to Realistic Computer Graphics*, Addison-Wesley, Reading, MA, 1989.

VANA84   Van Aken, J. R., "An Efficient Ellipse-Drawing Algorithm," *CG&A*, 4(9), September 1984, 24–35.

VANA85   Van Aken, J.R., and M. Novak, "Curve-Drawing Algorithms for Raster Displays," *ACM TOG*, 4(2), April 1985, 147–169.

VANA89   Van Aken, J., personal communication, January 1989.

VANC72   Van Cott, H., and R. Kinkade, *Human Engineering Guide to Equipment Design*, 008-051-00050-0, U.S. Government Printing Office, Washington, DC, 1972.

VAND74   van Dam, A., G.M. Stabler, and R.J. Harrington, "Intelligent Satellites for Interactive Graphics," *Proceedings of the IEEE*, 62(4), April 1974, 483–492.

VERB84   Verbeck, C.P., and D.P. Greenberg, "A Comprehensive Light-Source Description for Computer Graphics," *CG & A*, 4(7), July 1984, 66–75.

VERS84   Versatron Corporation, *Footmouse*, Versatron Corporation, Healdsburg, CA, 1984.

VITT84   Vitter, J., "US&R: A New Framework for Redoing," *IEEE Software*, 1(4), October 1984, 39–52.

VOSS85a   Voss, R., "Random Fractal Forgeries," in Earnshaw, R.A., ed., *Fundamental Algorithms for Computer Graphics*, Springer-Verlag, Berlin, 1985; NATO ASI series F, volume 17, 805–835.

VOSS85b   Vossler, D., "Sweep-to-CSG Conversion Using Pattern Recognition Techniques," *CG & A*, 5(8), August 1985, 61–68.

VOSS87   Voss, R., "Fractals in Nature: Characterization, Measurement, and Simulation," in *Course Notes 15 for SIGGRAPH 87*, Anaheim, CA, July 1987.

WALD64   Wald, G., "The Receptors for Human Color Vision," *Science*, 145, 1964, 1007–1017.

WALL87   Wallace, J.R., M.F. Cohen, and D.P. Greenberg, "A Two-Pass Solution to the Rendering Equation: A Synthesis of Ray Tracing and Radiosity Methods," *SIGGRAPH 87*, 311–320.

WALL89   Wallace, J.R., K.A. Elmquist, and E.A. Haines, "A Ray Tracing Algorithm for Progressive Radiosity," *SIGGRAPH 89*, 315–324.

WAN88   Wan, S., K. Wong, and P. Prusinkiewicz, "An Algorithm for Multidimensional Data Clustering," *ACM Transactions on Mathematical Software*, 14(2), June 1988, 153–162.

WARD85   Ward, J., and B. Blesser, "Interactive Recognition of Handprinted Characters for Computer Input," *CG & A*, 5(9), September 1985, 24–37.

WARD88   Ward, G.J., F.M. Rubinstein, and R.D. Clear, "A Ray Tracing Solution for Diffuse Interreflection," *SIGGRAPH 88*, 85–92.

WARE87   Ware, C., and J. Mikaelian, "An Evaluation of an Eye Tracker as a Device for Computer Input," in *Proceedings of CHI + GI 1987*, ACM, New York, 183–188.

WARE88   Ware, C., and J. Beatty, "Using Color Dimensions to Display Data Dimensions," *Human Factors*, 20(2), April 1988, 127–42.

WARN69   Warnock, J., *A Hidden-Surface Algorithm for Computer Generated Half-Tone Pictures*, Technical Report TR 4-15, NTIS AD-753 671, Computer Science Department, University of Utah, Salt Lake City, UT, June 1969.

WARN83   Warn, D.R., "Lighting Controls for Synthetic Images," *SIGGRAPH 83*, 13–21.

WASS85   Wasserman, A., "Extending Transition Diagrams for the Specification of Human-Computer Interaction," *IEEE Transactions on Software Engineering*, SE-11(8), August 1985, 699–713.

WATE87   Waters, K., "A Muscle Model for Animating Three-Dimensional Facial Expressions," *SIGGRAPH 87*, 17–24.

WATK70   Watkins, G.S., *A Real Time Visible Surface Algorithm*, Ph.D. Thesis, Technical Report UTEC-CSc-70-101, NTIS AD-762 004, Computer Science Department, University of Utah, Salt Lake City, UT, June 1970.

WEGH84   Weghorst, H., G. Hooper, and D.P. Greenberg, "Improved Computational Methods for Ray Tracing," *ACM TOG*, 3(1), January 1984, 52–69.

WEIL77   Weiler, K. and P. Atherton, "Hidden Surface Removal Using Polygon Area Sorting," *SIGGRAPH 77*, 214–222.

WEIL80   Weiler, K., "Polygon Comparison Using a Graph Representation," *SIGGRAPH 80*, 10–18.

WEIL85   Weiler, K., "Edge-Based Data Structures for Solid Modeling in Curved-Surface Environments," *CG & A*, 5(1), January 1985, 21–40.

WEIL86   Weil, J., "The Synthesis of Cloth Objects," *SIGGRAPH 86*, 49–54.

WEIL87   Weil, J., "Animating Cloth Objects," personal communication, 1987.

WEIL88   Weiler, K., "The Radial Edge Structure: A Topological Representation for Non-Manifold Geometric Modeling," in Wozny, M. J., H. McLaughlin, and J. Encarnação, eds., *Geometric Modeling for CAD Applications, IFIP WG5.2 Working Conference, Rensselaerville, NY, 12–14 May 1986*, North-Holland, 1988, 3–36.

WEIM80   Weiman, C.F.R., "Continuous Anti-Aliased Rotation and Zoom of Raster Images," *SIGGRAPH 80*, 286–293.

WEIN81   Weinberg, R., "Parallel Processing Image Synthesis and Anti-Aliasing," *SIGGRAPH 81*, 55–61.

WEIN87   Weingarten, N., personal communication, 1987.

WEIN88   Weinand, A., E. Gamma, and R. Marty, "ET++ —An Object Oriented Application Framework in C++," *OOPSLA 1988 Proceedings*, ACM-SIGPLAN Notices, 23(11), November 1988, 46–57.

WEIS66   Weiss, R.A., "BE VISION, A Package of IBM 7090 FORTRAN Programs to Draw Orthographic Views of Combinations of Plane and Quadric Surfaces," *JACM*, 13(2), April 1966, 194–204. Also in FREE80, 203–213.

WELL76   Weller, D., and R. Williams, "Graphic and Relational Data Base Support for Problem Solving," *SIGGRAPH 76*, 183–189.

WELL89   Wellner, P., "Statemaster: A UIMS Based on Statecharts for Prototyping and Target Implementation," in *Proceedings of CHI '89*, ACM, New York, 177–182.

WERT39   Wertheimer, M., "Laws of Organization in Perceptual Forms," in Ellis, W.D., ed., *A Source Book of Gestalt Psychology*, Harcourt Brace, New York, 1939.

WESL81   Wesley, M.A., and G. Markowsky, "Fleshing Out Projections," *IBM Journal of Research and Development*, 25(6), November 1981, 934–954.

WEST89   Westover, L., "Interactive Volume Rendering," in *Proceedings of Volume Visualization Workshop*, Department of Computer Science, University of North Carolina at Chapel Hill, May 18-19, 1989, 9–16.

WHEL82   Whelan, D., "A Rectangular Area Filling Display System Architecture," *SIGGRAPH 82*, 147–153.

WHIT80   Whitted, T., "An Improved Illumination Model for Shaded Display," *CACM*, 23(6), June 1980, 343–349.

WHIT82   Whitted, T., and S. Weimer, "A Software Testbed for the Development of 3D Raster Graphics Systems," *ACM TOG*, 1(1), January 1982, 43–58.

WHIT83   Whitted, T., "Anti-Aliased Line Drawing Using Brush Extrusion," *SIGGRAPH 83*, 151–156.

WHIT84   Whitton, M., "Memory Design for Raster Graphics Displays," *CG & A*, 4(3), March 1984, 48–65.

WHIT85   Whitted, T., "The Hacker's Guide to Making Pretty Pictures," in *Image Rendering Tricks, Course Notes 12 for SIGGRAPH 85*, New York, July 1985.

WILH87   Wilhelms, J., "Using Dynamic Analysis for Realistic Animation of Articulated Bodies," *CG & A*, 7(6), June 1987, 12–27.

WILL72   Williamson, H., "Algorithm 420 Hidden-Line Plotting Program," *CACM*, 15(2), February 1972, 100–103.

WILL78   Williams, L., "Casting Curved Shadows on Curved Surfaces," *SIGGRAPH 78*, 270–274.

WILL83   Williams, L., "Pyramidal Parametrics," *SIGGRAPH 83*, 1–11.

WITK87   Witkin, A., K. Fleischer, and A. Barr, "Energy Constraints on Parameterized Models," *SIGGRAPH 87*, 225–232.

WITK88   Witkin, A., and M. Kass, "Spacetime Constraints," *SIGGRAPH 88*, 159–168.

WOLB88   Wolberg, G., *Geometric Transformation Techniques for Digital Images: A Survey*, Technical Report CUCS-390-88, Department of Computer Science, Columbia University, New York, December 1988. To appear as Wolberg, G., *Digital Image Warping*, IEEE Computer Society, Washington, DC, 1990.

WOLB89   Wolberg, G., and T.E. Boult, *Separable Image Warping with Spatial Lookup Tables*, SIGGRAPH 89, 369–378.

WOLB90   Wolberg, G., *Digital Image Warping*, IEEE Computer Society Press, Los Alamitos, CA, 1990.

WOLF87   Wolf, C., and P. Morel-Samuels, "The Use of Hand-Drawn Gestures for Text Editing," *International Journal of Man-Machine Studies*, 27(1), July 1987, 91-102.

WOLF90   Wolff, L., and D. Kurlander, "Ray Tracing with Polarization Parameters," *CG&A*, 10(6), November 1990, 44–55.

WOO85   Woo, T., "A Combinatorial Analysis of Boundary Data Structure Schemata," *CG & A*, 5(3), March 1985, 19–27.

WOOD70   Woods, W., "Transition Network Grammars for Natural Language Analysis," *CACM*, 13 (10), October 1970, 591–606.

WOOD76   Woodsford, P. A., "The HRD-1 Laser Display System," *SIGGRAPH 76*, 68–73.

WOON71   Woon, P.Y., and H. Freeman, "A Procedure for Generating Visible-Line Projections of Solids Bounded by Quadric Surfaces," in *IFIP 1971*, North-Holland Pub. Co., Amsterdam, 1971, pp. 1120–1125. Also in FREE80, 230–235.

WRIG73   Wright, T.J., "A Two Space Solution to the Hidden Line Problem for Plotting Functions of Two Variables," *IEEE Trans. on Computers,* 22(1), January 1973, 28–33. Also in FREE80, 284–289.

WU89   Wu, X., and J.G. Rokne, "Double-Step Generation of Ellipses," *CG & A*, 9(3), May 1989, 56–69.

WYLI67   Wylie, C., G.W. Romney, D.C. Evans, and A.C. Erdahl, "Halftone Perspective Drawings by Computer," *FJCC 67*, Thompson Books, Washington, DC, 1967, 49–58.

WYSZ82   Wyszecki, G., and W. Stiles, *Color Science: Concepts and Methods, Quantitative Data and Formulae*, second edition, Wiley, New York, 1982.

WYVI86   Wyvill, G., C. McPheeters, and B. Wyvill, "Data Structures for Soft Objects," *The Visual Computer*, 2(4), April 1986, 227–234.

WYVI88   Wyvill, B., "The Great Train Rubbery," *ACM SIGGRAPH 88 Electronic Theater and Video Review*, 26, 1988.

YEAG86   Yeager, L., and C. Upson, "Combining Physical and Visual Simulation—Creation of the Planet Jupiter for the Film '2010'," *SIGGRAPH 86*, 85–93.

ZDON90   Zdonik, S.B., and D. Maier, *Readings in Object-Oriented Database Systems*, Morgan Kaufmann, San Mateo, CA, 1990.

ZELT82   Zeltzer, D., "Motor Control Techniques for Figure Animation," *CG & A*, 2(11), November 1982, 53–59.

ZIMM87   Zimmerman, T., J. Lanier, C. Blanchard, S. Bryson, and Y. Harvill, "A Hand Gesture Interface Device," in *Proceedings of the CHI + GI 1987 Conference*, ACM, New York, 189–192.

Index

Graphics Software Packages: SRGP and SPHIGS

The SRGP and SPHIGS graphics packages described in this book are archived in multiple formats, and are available on the World Wide Web free for your use.

http//:www.aw.com/cseng/authors/foley/compgrafix/compgrafix.sup.html

These formats allow you to run the packages on many PC, Apple Macintosh, and UNIX platforms. The files are identical across platforms except for the method used in compressing or archiving them. The website indicated above includes specific directions for accessing each format.

PLEASE NOTE BELOW THE SPECIFIC PLATFORMS REQUIRED FOR EACH FORMAT. THE SOFTWARE MAY NOT INSTALL OR RUN PROPERLY ON ANY OTHER PLATFORM—UNDER SOME OTHER C COMPILER, FOR EXAMPLE. WE REGRET THAT WE ARE UNABLE TO OFFER ANY USER SUPPORT IN SUCH CASES.

Requirements:

UNIX Worksations: Requires a workstation running UNIX and the X Window System; X11 release R4 or later; an ANSII C Compiler (gcc is recommended); v4.3 or 4.4 BSD, System V UNIX, or Solaris 2.0.

Apple Macintosh: Requires any model Apple Macintosh with a minimum of 1 megabyte of RAM; 2 megabytes of RAM are required to run the debugger; System Software v7.0 or later; Metrowerks CodeWarrior v.10 or later.

Microsoft Windows for the PC Family: Requires any PC using an 80826 or higher microprocessor with a minimum of 1 megabyte of RAM (combined conventional and extended memory); Hercules monochrome adapter, or EGA color monitor or better; Microsoft Mouse or compatible pointing device; Microsoft Windows v3.1, Windows95, or DOS v5.0 or later; Microsoft Software Development Kit for Windows; Borland Turbo C v2.0 or later.

Instructors Note:

Instructors who adopt this book may obtain a free copy of the Apple Macintosh or Microsoft Windows files on a diskette. Contact your local Addison Wesley Longman representative, send e-mail to aw.cse@aw.com, or (in the U.S.) call 1-800-322-1377. Be sure to specify the format you need.

Plate E Ray-traced radiosity simulation, by K. Howie, B. Trumbore, and D.P. Greenberg, Program of Computer Graphics, Cornell University. (Copyright © 1989 Cornell University, Program of Computer Graphics.)

Plate G "Onlyville," by S. Snibbe, and D. Robbins. (Copyright © 1989 Brown University Computer Graphics Group.)